Creeds and Confessions of Faith in the Christian Tradition

Creeds & Confessions of Faith in the Christian Tradition

Volume III

Part Five: Statements of Faith
in Modern Christianity

edited by Jaroslav Pelikan and Valerie Hotchkiss

YALE UNIVERSITY PRESS   NEW HAVEN & LONDON

Designed by Sonia Shannon
Set in Sabon type by Tseng Information Systems, Inc.
Printed in the United States of America by Sheridan Books.

Library of Congress Cataloging-in-Publication Data
Creeds & confessions of faith in the Christian tradition /
edited by Jaroslav Pelikan and Valerie Hotchkiss.
p.   cm.
Includes bibliographical references and indexes.
Contents: v. 1. Rules of faith in the early church. Eastern Orthodox affirmations
of faith. Medieval Western statements of faith — v. 2. Creeds and confessions of
the Reformation era — v. 3. Statements of faith in modern Christianity —
v. [4]. Credo / Jaroslav Pelikan.
ISBN 0-300-09391-8 (set) (cloth : alk. paper)
ISBN 0-300-09392-6 (v. 3) (cloth : alk. paper)
ISBN 0-300-09916-9 (CD-ROM)
1. Creeds.   2. Creeds—History and criticism.   I. Title: Creeds and confessions
of faith in the Christian tradition.   II. Pelikan, Jaroslav Jan, 1923–
III. Hotchkiss, Valerie R., 1960–   IV. Pelikan, Jaroslav Jan, 1923–   Credo.
BT990.C64 2003
238—dc21
2003043067

A catalogue record for this book is available from the British Library.

The paper in this book meets the guidelines for permanence and durability
of the Committee on Production Guidelines for Book Longevity
of the Council on Library Resources.

10 9 8 7 6 5 4 3 2 1

Contents

Preface

Both for those who profess the name of Christian themselves and for those who are curious, whether in a friendly or in a hostile way, about what these people stand for or about what makes them different (from other people or from one another), creeds and confessions of faith have always been an indispensable resource. Therefore the conclusion of the Gospel of John, about books on the life and teachings of Jesus, "I suppose that the world itself could not contain the books that would be written" (Jn 21.25), though it was not referring explicitly to creeds and confessions of faith, might well have been. For from beginnings in the first century that can no longer be precisely traced to a veritable explosion of new creeds in the twentieth century, when almost every year saw one or more of them appear, the production of creeds and confessions has reached the point that, if not the world, then at any rate even these three stout volumes could not contain them all.

That has obliged the editors to practice a form of scholarly triage and to make difficult choices. Some of the choices were, of course, obvious and unavoidable: above all and in a class by itself, *The Niceno-Constantinopolitan Creed*, but then also, for the West, *The Apostles' Creed*, and, for most Christian churches of most centuries, the doctrinal decrees of the first seven ecumenical councils, as well as the confessional charters of the major groups coming out of the Reformation of the sixteenth century. That was the easy part. After initially casting our net as broadly as possible to assemble what we called a "maximal list" (which was quickly conflated into "maximalist"), and after consulting over a period of several years with scholars, theologians, and church leaders across the ecumenical spectrum and around the world, we gradually formulated, and then refined, additional criteria for deciding the ancient predestinarian question of *cur alii prae aliis*. One such criterion was definitional, although its application proved to be more complicated than it might have seemed to be initially: Does this text qualify as a creed or confession, rather than as a code of behavior or a set of ground rules for church administration, and has it been (or is it still) understood and employed as such a norm by some community that identifies itself as Christian? Once we came up with an affirmative answer to that question, what we dubbed "the Noah's ark principle" came into play: to strive to include (though not always necessarily in pairs) as many species as could fit into our capacious but nevertheless limited number of pages, species here being taken to mean ecclesiastical denominations, geographical regions, historical periods, theological styles, original languages, and literary genres. On that basis, some of these species that have manifested extraordinary fecundity in producing statements of faith (or have been the beneficiaries of unusually busy compilers and editors) have simply had to yield some of their space to assure fair, if not equal, representation for others. As earnestly as historical fairness and ecumenical sensitivity required and as human frailty permitted, each of us has made the effort not to let what we ourselves believe, teach, and confess—or where we pray—tip the scales for or against including any of the formularies, or color what we have said about them.

It would be too cumbersome to list all the editorial guidelines, rules, and exceptions we have worked with to bring some consistency to the presentation of these texts, but a few general comments may aid the reader. As a rule, biblical quotations (and paraphrases) are given as they appear in the creeds and translated accordingly. Biblical quotations in our commentary and notes are generally from the Revised Standard Version (RSV), which is therefore not usually identified. Sometimes they are from the New Revised Standard Version (NRSV). Scriptural citations that have been added by later editors (or by us) are placed in brackets. The citations appear either in the margins or, when numerous, as footnotes keyed to lowercase letters. For the sake of consistency, the spelling of proper names has been conformed to that of the third edition of *The Oxford Dictionary of the Christian Church (ODCC)*, with a few minor exceptions such as the *Council of Basel* (not "Basle"), John Hus (not "Huss"), and *The Smalcald Articles* (not "Schmalkaldic"). For names not found in the *ODCC*, we have followed Library of Congress authority records.

Finally, filial piety requires that we pay a special tribute here to the memory of Philip Schaff (1819–93), the émigré scholar who, in addition to publishing a veritable one-man library of other biblical, historical, patristic, and theological texts that total a hundred volumes or so, managed in 1877 to produce the three volumes of *Bibliotheca Symbolica Ecclesiae Universalis: The Creeds of Christendom*. As his son David said of it in his biography of his father, "Even in Germany such critics as [Isaak August] Dorner declared that it filled an unoccupied place in theological literature and satisfied a real need. 'The very conception of the work was a great thought which presupposed unusual courage and enterprise,' he wrote. . . . The work has been considered by some as his most valuable contribution to theological literature." With all its quirks (for example, *The Confession of Dositheus* in Greek and Latin but not in English, initially even his beloved *Second Helvetic Confession* left in the original Latin untranslated, with only a précis in English) and a Protestant partisanship that does sometimes seem to be excessive, Schaff's set proved to be so useful that for more than 125 years it has remained in print practically without interruption—and, except for a few supplementary texts, has remained fundamentally unrevised through six editions and numerous reprints. Our years of work on the ambitious project of replacing it for the twenty-first century have instilled in us an admiration for Schaff's enduring accomplishment.

Acknowledgments

The scope and duration of this project have required consultation with scholars from diverse fields, correspondence with churches and religious organizations around the world, and the goodwill of the people we work for and the people who work for us. First and foremost, we are indebted to the Lilly Endowment for its generous and continued support through research leaves, project support, and production assistance. We acknowledge with gratitude a special grant from the Virginia H. Farah Foundation that provided for the distribution of these volumes to libraries in Orthodox communities and in the developing world. We are also grateful to Yale University Press for taking on this massive task, and we thank in particular John Ryden, Laura Jones Dooley, Alex Schwartz, Otto Bohlmann, John Rollins, Lauren Shapiro, and Paul Royster. Further, we acknowledge the support of the other institutions that made our work possible: Yale University, Boston College, the Annenberg School for Communication of the University of Pennsylvania, the Library of Congress, and Southern Methodist University, especially the Perkins School of Theology and Bridwell Library. The many presses, denominations, and ecumenical bodies that made texts available for this collection are acknowledged elsewhere in this volume, but we offer here a general and heartfelt word of appreciation for their cooperation.

We express our gratitude to Colin Davey for the translation of *The Confession of Faith of Metrophanes Critopoulos* that he prepared for this project, and to Catharine P. Roth for her translations of *The Encyclical Letter of Photius*, the *Synodical Tomes* of 1341 and 1351, and the confessions of Gregory Palamas and Gennadius I. Through the years, several student researchers have assisted us and deserve thanks for their conscientious work: John Brown, Kirsten Christensen, Drew Cottle, James Ernst, Cinnamon Hearst, Caroline Huey, Brian Matz, Megan McLemore, and Amber Sturgess. We have also been aided by numerous librarians, church officials, and scholars, who helped us overcome various hurdles and whom we list here (in alphabetical order) with gratitude: Gerald H. Anderson, Metropolitan Anthony of Dardanelion/San Francisco, Urs von Arx, C. J. Dyck, Peter C. Erb, Ellen Frost, Brian A. Gerrish, Maria Habito, Ruben Habito, Duane Harbin, Susan Billington Harper, Patrick Henry, Linda Hervey, Sally Hoover, Seth Kasten, Karl Peter Koop, Robin Lovin, James McMillin, E. Ann Matter, Hermann Michaeli, James J. O'Donnell, Father George Papademetriou, Michael Pelikan, Russell Pollard, David Price, Helmut Renders, Charles C. Ryrie, Fred Sand, Lamin O. Sanneh, Barbara von Schlegell, Anthony Scott, Philip Shen, Joe A. Springer, Jane Stranz, Richard A. Taylor, Gayla

Tennison, Page A. Thomas, Bishop Kallistos Ware, Robert L. Wilken, Charles Willard, and Richard Wright.

David Price and Sylvia Pelikan deserve special mention here, though they have already earned a star in their heavenly crowns for their patience. And to son Samuel Price Hotchkiss and grandsons Stefan Daniel Pelikan and Nikolai Ivan Pelikan, who were not born when the project was conceived, we offer thanks for the joy you gave us when we closed our books at the end of the day.

Abbreviations for Creeds and Confessions

All citations of councils and synods — unless accompanied by "act" (= *Acts*), "can" (= *Canons*), "decr" (= *Decrees*), or some other abbreviation — refer specifically to their creedal or doctrinal formulations.

Abbreviation	Title and Date	Location
Abst Prin	*Abstract of Principles for Southern Baptist Seminary,* 1858	3:316–20; McBeth 1990, 304–15
Ad tuendam	*Ad tuendam fidem of Pope John Paul II,* 1998	3:871–76
Adv	*The Fundamental Beliefs of the Seventh-Day Adventist Church,* 1872	3:359–64
Afr Orth	*Doctrine of the African Orthodox Church,* 1921	3:435–36
A-L	*Anglican-Lutheran Pullach Report,* 1972	Gr Agr II 14–34
Alex	*The Creed of Alexander of Alexandria,* c. 321–24	1:79–81; Hahn, 15; NPNF–II 3:39–40
Am Bap	*The Statement of Faith of the American Baptist Association,* 1905	Lumpkin, 378–79
Ang Cat	*The Anglican Catechism,* 1549/1662	2:364–71; Schaff, 3:517–22
Ans	*The Evangelical Counsel of Ansbach [Ansbacher Evangelischer Ratschlag],* 1524	Schmidt-Schornbaum, 183–322
Ant 325	*The First Synod of Antioch,* 325	1:84–86
Ant 341	*The Second [Dedication] Synod of Antioch,* 341	1:87–89; Hahn, 153–56; NPNF–II 4:461
Ap	*The Apostles' Creed*	1:667–69; BLK 21–25; Cochrane, 303–4; Fabbri, 3;

Abbreviation	Title and Date	Location
		Gerrish, 56; Kolb-Wengert, 21–22; Leith, 24–25; Tappert, 18; *Triglotta* 2:30–31; Schaff, 2:45–55
Ap Const	*The Apostolic Constitutions,* c. 350–80	Hahn, 9–10, 129; Schaff, 2:39
Apol Aug	*The Apology of the Augsburg Confession,* 1531	CD-ROM; *BLK* 139–404; Fabbri, 58–328; Kolb-Wengert, 109–294; Tappert, 100–285; *Triglotta* 2:97–451
Ar	*The Creeds of Arius and Euzoius,* c. 320 and 327	1:75–78; Hahn, 186–87; Schaff, 2:28–29
Arist	*The Creed of Aristides of Athens,* 2d c.	1:51–52
Arm Ev	*Armenian Evangelical Churches,* 1846	3:261–63
Arn	*The Arnoldshain Theses,* 1957	3:558–61
Assem	*The Statement of Fundamental Truths of the Assemblies of God,* 1914	3:426–31
Ath	*The Athanasian Creed* [*Quicunque vult*]	1:673–77; *BLK* 28–30; Denzinger, 75–76; Fabbri, 6–8; Gerrish, 62–64; Hahn, 150; Kelly 1964, 17–20; Kolb-Wengert, 23–25; Schaff, 2:66–71; Tappert, 19–21; *Triglotta* 2:30–35
Aub	*The Auburn Declaration,* 1837	3:250–55; Schaff, 3:777–80
Aug	*The Augsburg Confession*	2:49–118; *BLK* 31–137; Fabbri, 11–57; Gerrish, 87–125; Kolb-Wengert, 30–105; Leith, 63–107; Noll, 81–121; Schaff, 3:3–73; Tappert, 23–96; *Triglotta* 2:37–95
Ger	*German,* 1530	
Lat	*Latin,* 1530	
Var	*Variata,* 1540	Reu, 2:398–411

Abbreviation	Title and Date	Location
Balamand	*Uniatism, Method of Union of the Past, and the Present Search for Full Communion:* Joint International Commission for Theological Dialogue Between the Catholic and Orthodox Church. Balamand, Lebanon, 1993	3:848–51; *Gr Agr II* 680–85
Bap Assoc	*The Doctrinal Statement of the North American Baptist Association,* 1950	Lumpkin, 377–81
Bap Aus	*Doctrinal Basis of the Baptist Union of Victoria, Australia,* 1888	Lumpkin, 416–20
Bap Conf	*The Statement of Beliefs of the North American Baptist Conference,* 1982	3:808–12
Bap Gr Br	*The Statement of the Baptist Union of Great Britain and Ireland,* 1888	Lumpkin, 344–46
Bap NZ	*The Doctrinal Basis of the New Zealand Baptist Union,* 1882	Lumpkin, 416
Barm	*The Barmen Declaration* [*Theologische Erklärung zur gegenwärtigen Lage der Deutschen Evangelischen Kirche*], 1934	3:504–8; Cochrane, 332–36; Leith, 517–22; Niesel, 333–37
Bas Bek	*The First Confession of Basel* [*Baseler Bekenntnis*], 1534	2:272–79; Augusti, 103–9; Böckel, 108–14; Cochrane, 89–96; Fabbri, 630–37; Niemeyer, 78–104
Bat	*The Confession of Faith of the Protestant Christian Batak Church (H. K. B. P.),* 1951	3:543–55; Anderson, 213–38; Leith, 555–66
BCP	*The Book of Common Prayer,* 1549, 1552, 1662, 1928, 1979	Blunt

Abbreviation	Title and Date	Location
BEC	*The Profession of Faith of the Salvadoran Basic Ecclesial Communities*, 1984	**3:844-45**
Belg	*The Belgic Confession, 1561/1619*	**2:405-26**; Augusti, 170-98; Bakhuizen van den Brink, 50-141; Böckel, 477-507; Cochrane, 185-219; Fabbri, 701-33; Niemeyer, 360-89; Niesel, 119-36; Schaff, 3:383-436
BEM	*Baptism, Eucharist, and Ministry* ["The Lima Text" of Faith and Order], 1982	**3:813-40**; *Gr Agr* 465-503
Bern	*The Ten Theses of Bern*, 1528	**2:215-17**; Böckel, 35-39; Cochrane, 45-50; Fabbri, 621-22; Leith, 129-30; Niemeyer, 14-15; Schaff, 3:208-10
Boh I	*The [First] Bohemian Confession*, 1535	**1:796-833**; Augusti, 273-326; Böckel, 777-827; Niemeyer, 771-818; Pelikan, 80-149
Boh II	*The [Second] Bohemian Confession*, 1575	CD-ROM; Böckel, 827-49; Niemeyer, 819-51; Reu, 2:424-33
Bonn I	*The Fourteen Theses of the Old Catholic Union Conference at Bonn with Greeks and Anglicans*, 1874	**3:365-67**; Schaff, 2:545-51
Bonn II	*The Old Catholic Agreement at Bonn on the Filioque Controversy*, 1875	Schaff, 2:552-54
Boston	*The Declaration of the Boston National Council*, 1865	Walker, 562-64
Brngr 1059	*The First Confession of Berengar*, 1059	**1:728-29**; Denzinger, 690
Brngr 1079	*The Second Confession of Berengar*, 1079	**1:728-29**; Denzinger, 700

Abbreviation	Title and Date	Location
Br St Luth	*The Brief Statement of the Doctrinal Position of the Evangelical Lutheran Synod of Missouri, Ohio, and Other States*, 1932	3:487–503; Doct Dec 42–57
Camb Dec	*The Cambridge Declaration of the Alliance of Confessing Evangelicals*, 1996	3:861–66
Camb Plat	*The Cambridge Platform*, 1648	3:63–91; Leith, 385–99; Walker, 194–237
Chal	*The Council of Chalcedon*, 451	1:172–81; COD-DEC 75–103; Denzinger, 300–303; Fabbri, 5; Gerrish, 65; Hahn, 146–47; Karmirēs, 1:173–76; Leith, 34–36; Mansi, 7:107–18; Michalcescu, 3–4; NPNF-II 14:243–95; Schaff, 2:62–65
Chile	*The Creed of the Evangelical Presbyterian Church of Chile*, 1983	3:841–43
Chin Man	*The Christian Manifesto of the Three-Self Patriotic Movement: "Directions of Endeavor for Chinese Christianity in the Construction of New China,"* 1950	3:537–39; Anderson, 249–50
Chin Un	*The Bond of Union of the Church of Christ in China*, 1927	3:483–84; Anderson, 249
Chr Dec	*Common Christological Declaration Between the Catholic Church and the Assyrian Church of the East*, 1994	3:852–55; Gr Agr II 711–12
Chr Sci	*Tenets of the Mother Church of Christ, Scientist*, 1879/1892/ 1906	3:370–71

Abbreviation	Title and Date	Location
CNI	*The Church of North India/Pakistan, Plan of Church Union: The Doctrines of the Church,* 1965	3:700–702
Cologne	*The [Mennonite] Concept of Cologne,* 1591	2:749–54
Com Cr	*The "Commission" Creed of the Congregational Church,* 1883/1913	3:372–74; Walker, 577–82
Com Dec	*Common Declaration of Pope John Paul II and [Armenian] Catholicos Karekin I,* 1996	3:867–70; Gr Agr II 707–8
Confut	*The Confutation of the Augsburg Confession,* 1530	Reu, 2:348–83
Cons rep	*The Reaffirmed Consensus of the Truly Lutheran Faith [Consensus repetitus fidei vere lutheranae],* 1655	Henke
Const	*The Council of Constance,* 1414–18	COD-DEC 403–51; Denzinger, 1151–1279
CP I	*The First Council of Constantinople,* 381	1:160–63; COD-DEC 21–35; Denzinger, 151; Karmirēs, 1:130–31; Michalcescu, 2; NPNF-II 14:162–90
CP II	*The Second Council of Constantinople,* 553	1:183–215; COD-DEC 105–22; Denzinger, 421–38; Hahn, 148; Karmirēs, 1:185–97; Leith, 45–50; Mansi, 9:367–90; Michalcescu, 5–7; NPNF-II 14:297–323
CP III	*The Third Council of Constantinople,* 680–81	1:216–29; COD-DEC 123–30; Denzinger, 550–59; Hahn, 149; Karmirēs, 1:221–24; Leith, 50–53; Mansi, 11:631–40; Michalcescu, 7–9; NPNF-II 14:344–46; Schaff, 2:72–73

Abbreviation	Title and Date	Location
CP 360	*The Creed of the Synod of Constantinople of 360*	Hahn, 167
CP 879–80	*The Synod of Constantinople of 879–80*	Karmirēs, 1:268–71
CP 1054	*The Edict of Michael Cerularius and of the Synod of Constantinople of 1054*	1:309–17; Karmirēs, 1:343–48; Mansi, 19:812–21; PG 151:679–82; Will, 155–68
CP 1341	*The Synod of Constantinople of 1341*	1:318–33; Karmirēs, 1:354–66; PG 151:679–82
CP 1347	*The Synod of Constantinople of 1347*	Karmirēs, 1:366–74
CP 1351	*The Synod of Constantinople of 1351*	1:334–74; Karmirēs, 1:374–407; PG 151:717–68
CP 1691	*The Synod of Constantinople of 1691*	Karmirēs, 2:779–83; Mansi, 37:463–72
CP 1838	*The Synod of Constantinople of 1838*	Karmirēs, 2:894–902; Mansi, 40:269–76
Craig	*Craig's Catechism*, 1581	Torrance, 97–165
Crg Sh Cat	*Craig's Short Catechism*, 1592	Torrance, 243–54
CSI 1929	*The Scheme of Union of the Church of South India*, 1929/1942	Schaff, 3:951
CSI 1947	*The Constitution of the Church of South India*, 1947	3:517–24; Anderson, 228–34
Cumb Pres	*The Confession of the Cumberland Presbyterian Church*, 1814/1883	3:223–41; Schaff, 3:771–76
Cum occas	*Cum occasione of Pope Innocent X*, 1653	3:101–3; Denzinger, 2001–7
Cyp	*The Creed of Cyprian of Carthage*, 250	Hahn, 12; Schaff, 2:20
Cyr Jer	*The Baptismal Creed of Jerusalem*, c. 350	1:94–95; Denzinger, 41; Hahn, 124; Schaff, 2:31–32
Czen	*The Hungarian Confession [Confessio Czengerina]*, 1570	Augusti, 241–53; Niemeyer, 539–50
Dec Addr	Thomas Campbell, *Declaration and Address*, 1809: "Propositions"	3:219–22

Abbreviation	Title and Date	Location
Def Plat	*The Definite Platform* (Lutheran), 1855	**3:291-315**
Denck	*Hans Denck's Confession Before the Council of Nuremberg, 1525*	**2:665-72**; Bauman, 51-53
Dêr Bal	*The Dêr Balyzeh Papyrus, c. 200-350*	**1:66-67**; Denzinger, 2; Kelly, 89; Leith, 19
Design	*Christian Church (Disciples of Christ): The Design for the Christian Church, 1968*	**3:726-29**
Dict Pap	*The Dictatus Papae of Pope Gregory VII, 1075*	**1:730-32**
Did	*The Didache, c. 60-150*	**1:41-42**
Dordrecht	*The Mennonite Confession of Faith of Dordrecht, 1632*	**2:768-87**; Fabbri, 922-37; Gerrish, 218-34; Leith, 292-308; Loewen, 63-70; Lumpkin, 66-78
Dort	*The Canons of the Synod of Dort, 1618-19*	**2:569-600**; Augusti, 198-240; Bakhuizen van den Brink, 218-81; Böckel, 508-43; Bray, 455-78; Fabbri, 885-921; Niemeyer, 690-728; Schaff, 3:550-97
Dosith	*The Confession of Dositheus and of the Synod of Jerusalem, 1672*	**1:613-35**; Karmirēs, 2:746-73; Gerrish, 310-41; Kimmel, 1:425-88; Leith, 485-517; Mansi, 34:1723-62; Michalcescu, 123-82; Robertson; Schaff, 2:401-44
Ecth	*The Ecthesis of Emperor Heraclius, 638*	**1:150-54**; BZ 69:21-23; Mansi, 10:991-98
Edict	*The Edict of Emperor Justinian on the True Faith, 551*	**1:122-49**; Schwartz, 73-110; Wesche, 163-98
18 Diss	*Eighteen Dissertations Concerning the Entire Christian Life and of What It Consists, by Balthasar Hubmaier, 1524*	Lumpkin, 19-21

Abbreviation	Title and Date	Location
Eng Dec	*The Declaration of the Congregational Union of England and Wales, 1833*	Schaff, 3:730–34; Walker, 542–52
Ep Apost	*The Epistula Apostolorum, c. 150*	1:53–54; Denzinger, 1; Leith, 17
Eph 431	*The Council of Ephesus, 431*	1:164–71; COD-DEC 37–74; Denzinger, 250–68; Karmirēs, 1:138–56; Michalcescu, 2–3; NPNF-II 14:191–242
Form Un	*The Formula of Union, 433*	1:168–71; COD-DEC 69–70; Denzinger, 271–73
Epiph	*The Creeds of Epiphanius, 373/374*	1:100–101; Denzinger, 42–45; Hahn, 125–26; NPNF-II 14:164–65; Schaff, 2:32–38
Ess	*Friends General Conference, Belief, 1900*	3:399–401
Eun	*The Confession of Eunomius to the Emperor, 383*	1:105–9; Hahn, 190
Eus	*The Creed of Eusebius of Caesarea, 325*	1:82–83; Denzinger, 40; Hahn, 188; Leith, 27–28; NPNF-II 4:74; Schaff, 2:29–30
Ev All	*The Nine Articles of the Evangelical Alliance, 1846*	3:259–60; Schaff, 3:827–28
Fac	*The Creed of Facundus of Hermiane, 6th c.*	Hahn, 51
F&O Ban	*Commission on Faith and Order of the World Council of Churches at Bangalore: A Common Statement of Our Faith, 1978*	3:782–85
F&O Edin	*Faith and Order Conference at Edinburgh: The Grace of Our Lord Jesus Christ; The Affirmation of Union, 1937*	3:511–16; Leith, 569–74
F&O Laus	*Faith and Order Conference at Lausanne: The Call to Unity, 1927*	3:471–82

Abbreviation	Title and Date	Location
Fid cath	On the Catholic Faith [De fide catholica], by Boethius, c. 517–22	1:699–706; LCL 74:52–71
Fid rat	A Reckoning of the Faith [Fidei ratio], by Ulrich Zwingli, 1530	2:249–71; Böckel, 40–61; Niemeyer, 16–35
Flor	The Council of Basel-Ferrara-Florence-Rome	1:751–65; COD-DEC 523–91; Denzinger, 1300–1308
Arm	The Bull of Union with the Armenians, 1439	
Un	The Decree of Union with the East, 1439	
Form Conc	The Formula of Concord	2:166–203; BLK 735–1102;
Epit	The Epitome, 1577	Fabbri, 367–600; Kolb-Wengert, 486–660; Schaff, 3:93–180; Tappert, 464–636; Triglotta 2:774–1103
Sol Dec	The Solid Declaration, 1577	CD-ROM
42 Art	The Forty-Two Articles of the Church of England, 1553	Bray, 284–311; Niemeyer, 592–600
Free Meth	Articles of Religion of the Free Methodist Church, 1866	3:335–40
Free-Will Bap	The Confession of the Free-Will Baptists, 1834/1868/1948	Lumpkin, 367–76; Schaff, 3:749–56
Fréjus	The Synod of Fréjus, 796/797	1:725–27; Denzinger, 616–19
Friends I	A Confession of Faith Containing XXIII Articles, 1673	3:136–48
Friends II	Theses Theologicae of Robert Barclay [The Confession of the Society of Friends, Commonly Called Quakers], 1675	Schaff, 3:789–98
Gall	The French Confession [Confessio Gallica], 1559/1571	2:372–86; Augusti, 110–25; Böckel, 459–74; Cochrane, 137–58; Fabbri, 663–76; Gerrish, 150–63; Niemeyer, 311–39; Niesel, 65–79; Schaff, 3:356–82

Abbreviation	Title and Date	Location
Geloof	*The Doctrine of the True Mennonites or Baptists [De Geloofsleere der Waare Men-noniten of Dopgezinden] by Cornelis Ris, 1766/1895/1902*	3:155–200; Loewen, 85–103
Gen Bap	*General Baptists: The Faith and Practice of Thirty Congregations Gathered According to the Primitive Pattern, 1651*	3:92–100; Lumpkin, 171–88
Gennad	*The Confession of Faith of Gennadius II, 1455–56*	1:385–91; Karmirēs, 1:432–36; Michalcescu, 11–21; *PG* 160:333–52
Genv Cat	*The Geneva Catechism, 1541/1542*	2:320–63; Augusti, 460–531; Böckel, 127–72; Niemeyer, 123–90; Niesel, 1–41; Torrance, 3–65
Genv Con	*The Geneva Confession, 1536*	2:311–19; Cochrane, 117–26; Fabbri, 654–62; Noll, 123–32
Ghana	*Ghana Church Union Committee: The Faith of the Church, 1965*	3:703–8
Greg I	*The Creed of Pope Gregory I, d. 604*	Hahn, 231
Greg Palam	*The Confession of the Orthodox Faith by Gregory Palamas, 1351*	1:375–78; Karmirēs, 1:407–10; Michalcescu, 11–21; *PG* 160:333–52
Greg Thaum	*The Creed of Gregory Thaumaturgus (c. 213–c. 270)*	1:70–71; Hahn, 185; Schaff, 2:24–25
Heid	*The Heidelberg Catechism, 1563*	2:427–57; Augusti, 532–77; Bakhuizen van den Brink, 144–217; Böckel, 395–424; Cochrane, 305–31; Fabbri, 734–69; Niemeyer, 390–461; Niesel, 136–218; Noll, 133–64; Schaff, 3:307–55

Abbreviation	Title and Date	Location
Helv I	*The First Helvetic Confession* [*The Second Basel Confession*], 1536	2:280–91; Augusti, 94–102; Böckel, 115–26; Cochrane, 97–111; Fabbri, 638–51; Niemeyer, 105–23; Schaff, 3:211–31
Helv II	*The Second Helvetic Confession*, 1566	2:458–525; Augusti, 3–93; Böckel, 281–347; Cochrane, 220–301; Fabbri, 770–862; Leith, 131–92; Niemeyer, 462–536; Niesel, 219–75; Schaff, 3:233–306, 831–909
Hipp	*The Creeds of Hippolytus*, c. 170–236	1:60–61; Denzinger, 10; Hahn, 6; Leith, 23
Hond	*The Credo* from *The Mass of the Marginalized People*, Honduras, 1980	3:795–97; Link, 45
Horm	*The Confession of Hormisdas* [*Libellus fidei*], 515	Denzinger, 363–65
Hub Chr Cat	*The Christian Catechism of Balthasar Hubmaier*, 1526	2:673–93
Ign	*The Creeds of Ignatius of Antioch*, c. 107	1:39–40; *ANF* 1:69–70; Hahn, 1; Leith, 16–17; Schaff, 2:11–12
Ild	*The Confession of Ildefonsus of Toledo*, 7th c.	Denzinger, 23; Hahn, 55
Ineff	*Ineffabilis Deus of Pope Pius IX*, 1854	3:289–90; Denzinger, 2800–2804; Leith, 442–46; Schaff, 2:211–12
Iren	*The Creeds of Irenaeus of Lyons*, c. 180–c. 200	1:48–50; *ANF* 1:330–31; Hahn, 5; Leith, 20–21; Schaff, 2:12–16
Irish	*The Irish Articles of Religion*, 1615	2:551–68; Bray, 437–52; Fabbri, 865–84; Schaff, 3:526–44
Jer II 1	*The Reply of Ecumenical Patriarch Jeremias II to the Augsburg Confession*, 1576	1:392–474; Karmirēs, 1:443–503; Mastrantonis, 30–105

Abbreviation	Title and Date	Location
Jer II 2–3	*The Second and Third Replies to the Lutherans of Patriarch Jeremias II of Constantinople,* 1579, 1581	CD-ROM; Karmirēs, 2:435–89; Mastrantonis, 151–214, 288–307
Just	*The Creeds of Justin Martyr,* 155	1:45–47; Hahn, 3; Leith, 18
Korea	*The Theological Declaration by Christian Ministers in the Republic of Korea,* 1973	3:742–43; Anderson, 241–45
Lam	*Lamentabili of Pope Pius X,* 1907	3:402–8; Denzinger, 3401–66
Lamb Art	*The Lambeth Articles,* 1595	2:545–46; Bray, 399–400; Fabbri, 863–64; Schaff, 3:523–25
Lamb Quad	*The Lambeth Quadrilateral* [*The Chicago/Lambeth Quadrilateral*], 1886/1888	3:375–76; Fabbri, 1032–34
Lat 649	*The Lateran Synod of 649*	1:709–14; Denzinger, 500–522
Lat 1215	*The Fourth Lateran Council of 1215: The Lateran Creed*	1:739–42; COD-DEC 227–71; Denzinger, 800–820; Leith, 56–59
Laus Art	*The Lausanne Articles,* 1536	2:292–95; Cochrane, 113–16; Fabbri, 652–53
Laus Cov	*The Lausanne Covenant,* 1974	3:753–60
LDS	*The Articles of Faith of the Church of Jesus Christ of Latter-Day Saints (Mormons),* 1842	3:256–58
Leuen	*The Leuenberg Agreement* [*Konkordie reformatorischer Kirchen in Europa*], 1973	3:744–52; ER 25:355–59; Rusch-Martensen 1989, 144–54
Lit Chrys	*The Divine Liturgy According to Saint John Chrysostom*	1:269–95; Brightman, 353–99; Holy Cross 1–40; Kallis, 44–195; Karmirēs, 1:289–315; Kokkinakis, 86–143; Michalcescu, 277–98; OCA 29–87

Abbreviation	Title and Date	Location
Loll	*The Twelve Conclusions of the Lollards,* 1395	1:784–90
London I	*The [First] London Confession of the Particular Baptists,* 1644	3:47–62; Lumpkin, 144–71
London II	*The Assembly or Second London Confession,* 1677/1678	Lumpkin, 235–95
Lucar	*The Eastern Confession of the Christian Faith by Cyril Lucar,* 1629 (1633)	1:549–58; Bradow 1960, 190–204; Karmirēs, 2:565–70; Kimmel, 1:24–44; Michalcescu, 262–76
LuRC 4	*Lutheran-Roman Catholic Conversation 4: All Under One Christ,* 1980	Gr Agr 241–46
LuRC Just	*Lutheran-Roman Catholic Joint Declaration on the Doctrine of Justification,* 1999	3:877–88
Luth Lg Cat	*The Large Catechism of Martin Luther,* 1529	CD-ROM; *BLK* 543–733; Kolb-Wengert, 379–480; Tappert, 358–461; *Triglotta* 2:565–773
Luth Sm Cat	*The Small Catechism of Martin Luther,* 1529	2:29–48; *BLK* 499–541; Kolb-Wengert, 347–75; Leith, 107–26; Noll, 59–80; Schaff, 3:74–92; Tappert, 338–56; *Triglotta* 2:531–63
Lyons	*The Second Council of Lyons,* 1274	1:743–44; COD-DEC 314; Denzinger, 850–61
Madag	*The Statement of Faith of the Church of Jesus Christ in Madagascar,* 1958/1968	3:562–65
Marburg	*The Marburg Articles,* 1529	2:791–95; Reu, 2:44–47
Mark Eph	*The Confession of Faith of Mark of Ephesus,* 1439	1:379–84; Karmirēs, 1:422–25; *PG* 160:115–204
Masai	*The Masai Creed,* c. 1960	3:568–69; Donovan, 200; Marthaler, 417
Menn Con	*The Mennonite Confession of Faith,* 1963	3:674–85

Abbreviation	Title and Date	Location
Meros	*The Faith in Detail* [*Kata meros pistis*], 6th c.?	Caspari, 18–21
Meth Art	*The Methodist Articles of Religion*, 1784/1804	3:201–7; Leith, 353–60; Schaff, 3:807–13
Meth Braz	*The Social Creed of the Methodist Church of Brazil*, 1971	3:732–35
Meth Kor	*The Doctrinal Statement of the Korean Methodist Church*, 1930	3:485–86; Anderson, 241
Metr Crit	*The Confession of Metrophanes Critopoulos*, 1625	1:475–548; Karmirēs, 2:498–561; Michalcescu, 183–252
Mogila	*The Orthodox Confession of the Catholic and Apostolic Eastern Church by Peter Mogila*, 1638/ 1642	1:559–612; Karmirēs, 2:593–686; Kimmel, 1:56–203; Malvy-Viller, 1–124; Michalcescu, 22–122; Overbeck, 6–162; Schaff, 2:275–400
Morav	*The Easter Litany of the Moravian Church*, 1749	3:149–54; Schaff, 3:799–806
Morav Am	*Moravian Church in America: The Ground of the Unity*, 1995	3:856–60
Munif	*Munificentissimus Deus of Pope Pius XII*, 1950	3:534–36; Denzinger, 3900–3904; Leith, 457–66; Schaff, 2:211–12
N	*The Creed of Nicaea*, 325	1:156–59; *COD-DEC* 5; Denzinger, 125–26; Hahn, 142; Gerrish, 59; Karmirēs, 1:122–23; Leith, 29–31; Mansi, 2:665–68; *NPNF*-II 14:3
Naz	*Articles of Faith of the Church of the Nazarene*, 1908	3:409–14
N-CP	*The Niceno-Constantinopolitan Creed* [*"The Nicene Creed"*], 381	1:160–63; *COD-DEC* 24; Denzinger, 150; Gerrish, 59–60; Hahn, 144; Karmirēs, 1:130–31; Leith, 31–33; Mansi, 3:565–66; *NPNF*-II 14:163; Schaff, 2:57–58

Abbreviation	Title and Date	Location
Occ	*The Western [Occidental] Recension*	**1:670–72**; *BLK* 26–27; Cochrane, 303; Denzinger, 150; Fabbri, 4; Kolb-Wengert, 22–23; Schaff, 2:58–59; Tappert, 18–19; *Triglotta* 2:30–31
New Hamp	*The New Hampshire [Baptist] Confession, 1833/1853*	**3:242–49**; Leith, 334–39; Lumpkin, 360–77; Schaff, 3:742–48
Nic I	*The First Council of Nicaea, 325*	**1:156–59**; *COD-DEC* 1–19; Michalcescu, 1; *NPNF*–II 14:1–56; Schaff, 2:60–61
Nic II	*The Second Council of Nicaea, 787*	**1:230–41**; *COD-DEC* 133–38; Denzinger, 600–615; Karmirēs, 1:238–50; Leith, 53–56; Mansi, 13:373–80; Michalcescu, 10; *NPNF*–II 14:521–87
No Afr	*North African Creeds*	**1:110–12, 683–84**
Novat	*The Creeds of Novatian, c. 240–50*	**1:68–69**; Hahn, 11; Schaff, 2:21
Oberlin	*The Declaration of the Oberlin National Council, 1871*	Walker, 570–76
Orange	*The Synod of Orange, 529*	**1:692–98**; Denzinger, 370–97; Hahn, 174; Leith, 37–45
Origen	*The Creed of Origen, c. 222–30*	**1:62–65**; Hahn, 8; Schaff, 2:21–23
Pasc	*Pascendi dominici gregis of Pope Pius X, 1907*	Denzinger, 3475–3500
Patr	*The Profession of Faith of Patrick, 5th c.*	**1:690–91**
Petr Ab	*The Confession of Faith of Peter Abelard, 1139–42*	**1:735–38**; Gilson 1960, 107–8
Philad	*The Philadelphia Baptist Confession, 1688/1689/1742*	Lumpkin, 348–53; Schaff, 3:738–41

Abbreviation	Title and Date	Location
Philip Ind	*The Declaration of the Faith and Articles of Religion of the Philippine Independent Church,* 1947	3:525–31; Anderson, 255–60
Philip UCC	*The Statement of Faith of the United Church of Christ in the Philippines,* 1986/1992	3:846–47
Phot	*The Encyclical Letter of Photius,* 866	1:296–308; Karmirēs, 1:321–30; PG 102:721–41
Pol Br	*The Catechesis and Confession of Faith of the Polish Brethren,* 1574	2:709–44
Pol Nat Ch	*The Confession of Faith of the Polish National Catholic Church,* 1912/1914	3:423–25
Polyc	*The Creed of Polycarp of Smyrna,* c. 150	1:43–44
Prague	*The Four Articles of Prague,* 1420	1:791–95
Pres So Afr	*The Declaration of Faith of the Presbyterian Church in South Africa,* 1979/1981	3:793–94; Vischer, 27–28
Pres USA	*Confession of the United Presbyterian Church in the United States,* 1967	3:714–25
R	*The Roman Symbol,* 2d c.	1:681–82; Gerrish, 55
Rac	*The Racovian Catechism,* 1605	Rees
RCA	*Reformed Church in America: Our Song of Hope,* 1978	3:786–92
Ref All	*North American Area Council of the World Alliance of Reformed Churches: The Statement of Faith,* 1965	3:712–13
Ref Ep	*The Declaration of Principles of the Reformed Episcopal Church in America,* 1873/1875	Schaff, 3:814–26

Abbreviation	Title and Date	Location
Remon	*The Remonstrance or Arminian Articles, 1610*	**2:547-50**; Bakhuizen van den Brink, 282-87; Böckel, 544-640; Schaff, 3:545-49
Resp Non-Jur	*The Responses of Eastern Orthodox Patriarchs to the Non-Jurors, 1718/1723*	Karmirēs, 2:788-820; Mansi, 37:395-472
Resp Pius IX	*The Response of Eastern Orthodox Patriarchs to Pope Pius IX, 1848*	**3:264-88**; Karmirēs, 2:905-25; Mansi, 40:377-418
Richmond	*The Richmond Declaration of Faith of the Friends Yearly Meeting, 1887*	**3:377-92**
Ries	*The [Mennonite] Short Confession of Faith of Hans de Ries, 1610*	**2:755-67**; Dyck, 11-19
Rom Syn	*The Creed of the Synod of Rome, 680*	**1:722-24**; Denzinger, 546-48
Russ Cat	*The Christian Catechism of the Orthodox Catholic Greco-Russian Church, 1839*	Schaff, 2:445-542
Sacr ant	*Sacrorum antistitum [Anti-Modernist Oath] of Pope Pius X, 1910*	**3:419-22**; Denzinger, 3537-50
Salv Arm	*Religious Doctrines of the Salvation Army, 1878*	**3:368-69**
Sard	*The Western Creed of Sardica, 343*	**1:90-93**; Hahn, 157; *NPNF*-II 3:71-72
Sav	*The Savoy Declaration of Faith and Order, 1658*	**3:104-35**; Schaff, 3:707-29; Walker, 354-408
Sax	*The Saxon Confession, 1551*	Schaff, 3:181-89
Sax Vis	*The Saxon Visitation Articles, 1592*	Fabbri, 611-20; Schaff, 3:181-89
Schleit	*The Schleitheim Confession, 1527*	**2:694-703**; Leith, 281-92; Lumpkin, 22-31; Noll, 47-58
Scot I	*The [First] Scots Confession, 1560*	**2:387-404**; Augusti, 143-69; Böckel, 643-61; Cochrane, 159-84; Fabbri, 677-700;

Abbreviation	Title and Date	Location
		Niemeyer, 340–56; Niesel, 79–117; Schaff, 3:437–79
Scot II	*The King's Confession [The Second Scots Confession]*, 1581	2:541–44; Böckel, 661–63; Niemeyer, 357–59; Schaff, 3:480–85
Send	*The Consensus of Sandomierz [Consensus Sendomiriensis]*, 1570	Augusti, 254–64; Niemeyer, 553–61
Sens	*The Decrees of the Synod of Sens Against Abelard*, 1140/1141	1:733–34; Denzinger, 721–39
17 Art	*The Seventeen Articles for the Use of Visitors in Saxony*, 1527/1528	LW 40:263–320
Shema	*The Shema of* Dt 6.4–9, 11.13–21, Nm 15.37–41	1:29–31
Sheng Kung	*The Sheng Kung Hui Pastoral Letter of the Anglican Bishops of China*, 1950	3:540–42
Shkr	*The Concise Statement of the Principles of the [Shaker] Only True Church*, 1790	3:208–13
Sirm 357	*The Second ["Blasphemy"] Synod of Sirmium*, 357	Hahn, 161; *NPNF*–II 9:6–7
Sirm 359	*The Creed of the Fourth Synod of Sirmium*, 359, and *The Creed of Constantinople*, 360	1:96–99; Hahn, 165; *NPNF*–II 4:454
67 Art	*The Sixty-Seven Articles of Ulrich Zwingli*, 1523	2:207–14; Böckel, 3–9; Cochrane 33–44; Fabbri, 603–10; Niemeyer, 3–13; Noll, 37–46; Schaff, 3:197–207
Smal Art	*The Smalcald Articles* and *The Treatise on the Power and Primacy of the Pope*, 1537	2:119–65; BLK 405–68; Fabbri, 329–66; Kolb-Wengert, 297–328; Tappert, 288–318; *Triglotta* 2:453–529
Smyr	*Confession of the Presbyters of Smyrna Against Noetus*, c. 180–200	1:58–59

Abbreviation	Title and Date	Location
So Bap	*The Faith and Message of the Southern Baptist Convention,* 1925	3:437–44; Lumpkin, 390–400
Soc Ch	*The Social Creed of the Churches,* 1908/1912/1933	3:417–18
Socin	*Confession of Faith of Laelius Socinus [Lelio Sozini],* 1555	2:704–8
Soc Meth	*The Social Creed of Methodism,* 1908	3:415–16; *Meth Doct & Disc,* 479–81
Sri Lanka	*The Scheme of Church Union in Ceylon: Faith and Order,* 1963	3:686–99
Swed Bap	*The Confession of Faith of the Swedish Baptists,* 1861	3:321–23; Lumpkin, 407–10
Syl	*The Syllabus of Errors of Pope Pius IX,* 1864	3:324–34; Denzinger, 2901–80; *Dublin Review* (1865), 513–29; Schaff, 2:213–33
10 Art	*The Ten Articles,* 1536	2:296–310; Bray, 162–74
Tert	*The Creeds of Tertullian,* c. 203–10	1:55–57; *ANF* 3:598; Hahn, 7, 44; Leith, 21–22; Schaff, 2:16–20
Test Dom	*The Testamentum Domini,* 4th–5th c.	Denzinger, 61
Tetrapol	*The Tetrapolitan Confession,* 1530	2:218–48; Augusti, 327–68; Böckel, 363–94; Cochrane, 51–88; Niemeyer, 740–70
Thdr Mops	*The Creed of Theodore of Mopsuestia,* c. 350–428	Denzinger, 51
39 Art	*The Thirty-Nine Articles of the Church of England,* 1571	2:526–40; Augusti, 126–42; Böckel, 664–79; Bray, 285–311; Fabbri, 1017–31; Gerrish, 185–99; Leith, 266–81; Niemeyer, 601–11; Noll, 211–27; Schaff, 3:487–516
Am	*The American Revision,* 1801	
Thorn	*The Colloquy of Thorn [Collegium charitativum],* 1645	Augusti, 411–42; Niemeyer, 669–89

Abbreviation	Title and Date	Location
Tig	The Zurich Consensus [Consensus Tigurinus], 1549	**2:802–15;** Böckel, 173–81; Niemeyer, 191–217
Togo	The Evangelical Church of Togo: Our Faith, 1971	**3:736–37**
Tol I	The First Synod of Toledo, 400/447	**1:685–89;** Denzinger, 188–208; Hahn, 168
Tol III	The Third Synod of Toledo: The Profession of Faith of Recared, 589	**1:707–8;** Denzinger, 470; Hahn, 176
Tol XI	The Eleventh Synod of Toledo, 675	**1:715–21;** Denzinger, 525–41; Hahn, 182
Tome	The Tome of Pope Leo I, 449	**1:113–21;** COD-DEC 77–82; Denzinger, 290–95; NPNF-II 14:254–58
Toraja	Confession of the Church of Toraja, 1981	**3:798–807;** Vischer, 48–58
Trans	The Transylvanian Confession of Faith, 1579	**2:745–48;** Williams, 1131–33
Trent	The Council of Trent, 1545–63	**2:819–71;** COD-DEC 657–799; Denzinger, 1500–1835; Gerrish, 259–92; Leith, 399–439; Noll, 165–205; Schaff, 2:77–206
Trid Prof	The Tridentine Profession of Faith, 1564	**2:872–74;** Denzinger, 1862–70; Leith, 439–42; Noll, 207–10; Schaff, 2:207–10
True Con	A True Confession of the English Separatists (Brownists), 1596	**3:31–46;** Lumpkin, 79–97; Walker, 41–74
UCC	The Statement of Faith of the United Church of Christ, 1959/1981	**3:566–67**
Ulph	The Confession of Ulphilas, 383	**1:102–4;** Hahn, 198
Unam	Unam Sanctam of Pope Boniface VIII, 1302	**1:745–47;** Denzinger, 870–75
Un Ch Can: Crd	New Creed of the United Church of Canada, 1968/1980/1994	**3:730–31**

Abbreviation	Title and Date	Location
Un Ch Can: Union	*The Basis of Union of the United Church of Canada, 1925*	3:445–52; Schaff, 3:935–38
Un Ch Japan	*United Church of Christ in Japan: The Confession of Faith, 1954*	3:556–57; Anderson, 253–54
Un Pres	*The Confessional Statement of the United Presbyterian Church of North America, 1925*	3:453–70
Un Ref Ch	*United Reformed Church (The Reformed Association of the Church of Christ in Britain): The Basis of Union, 1972/ 1981/1997/2000*	3:738–41; Moss, 281–82
Utrecht	*The Old Catholic Declaration of Utrecht, 1889*	3:393–96
Vald	*The Profession of Faith of Valdes, 1180*	1:769–73
Vat I	*The First Vatican Council, 1869–70*	3:341–58; COD-DEC 811–16; Denzinger, 3000–3075; Leith, 447–57; Schaff, 2:234–71
Vat II	*The Second Vatican Council, 1962–65*	3:570–673; COD-DEC 817–1135; Denzinger, 4001–345
Vienne	*The Council of Vienne: Decree on the Foundation of the Catholic Faith, 1311–12*	1:748–50; COD-DEC 360–61; Denzinger, 900–904
Wald	*The Confession of the Waldenses, 1655*	1:774–80; Fabbri, 991–1016; Schaff, 3:757–70
Wash	*The Washington Profession of the Unitarian General Convention, 1935*	3:509–10; Robinson 1970, 160
WCC	*The Doctrinal Basis of the World Council of Churches, 1948/1961*	3:532–33; Leith, 574–77
West	*The Westminster Confession of Faith, 1647*	2:601–49; Bray, 487–520; Fabbri, 938–88; Leith, 192–230; Schaff, 3:600–673

Abbreviation	Title and Date	Location
Am	*The American Revision,* 1729	
West Sh Cat	*The Westminster Shorter Catechism,* 1648	**2:650–62;** Schaff, 3:674–703
Winch	*The Winchester [Universalist] Profession,* 1803	**3:217–18**
Witness	*Statement of Faith of the Jehovah's Witnesses,* 1918	**3:432–34**
Witt Art	*The Wittenberg Articles,* 1536	CD-ROM; Bray, 119–61
Witt Conc	*The Wittenberg Concord,* 1536	**2:796–801**
Wrt	*The Württemberg Confession,* 1552	Reu, 2:418–24
Wyclif	*John Wycliffe: A Confession on the Eucharist,* 1382	**1:781–83**
Zambia	*The Constitution of the United Church of Zambia,* 1965/1984	**3:709–11**

act	acts
anath	anathema
art	article
can	canon
ch	chapter
con	conclusion
decr	decree
def	definition
ecth	ecthesis
ep	epistle
int	introduction
par	paragraph
pr	preface
q	question
st	stanza
ttl	title

Editions, Collections, Journals, and Reference Works

ABD	*The Anchor Bible Dictionary.* Edited by David Noel Freedman. 6 vols. New York: Doubleday, 1992.
ACO	*Acta Conciliorum Oecumenicorum.* Series I edited by E. Schwartz and J. Straub. Strassburg: Wissenschaftliche Gesellschaft in Strassburg, 1914; Berlin: W. de Gruyter, 1922–84. Series II edited sub auspiciis Academiae Scientiarum Bavaricae. Berlin: 1984–.
ACW	*Ancient Christian Writers.* Edited by Johannes Quasten et al. 58 volumes to date. Westminster, Md.: Newman Press, 1946–.
Anderson	Anderson, Gerald H., ed. *Asian Voices in Christian Theology.* Maryknoll, N.Y.: Orbis Books, 1976.
ANF	*The Ante-Nicene Fathers.* Alexander Roberts and James Donaldson, editors. Reprint ed. 10 vols. Grand Rapids, Mich.: William B. Eerdmans, 1950, etc.
ARG	*Archiv für Reformationsgeschichte*
Augusti	Augusti, Johann Christian Wilhelm, ed. *Corpus Librorum Symbolicorum qui in Ecclesia Reformatorum auctoritatem publicam obtinuerunt.* Elberfeld: Bueschler, 1827.
Bakhuizen van den Brink	Bakhuizen van den Brink, J. N. *De Nederlandse Belijdenisgeschriften.* Amsterdam: Bolland, 1976.
Bauer-Arndt-Gingrich	Bauer, Walter. *A Greek-English Lexicon of the New Testament and Other Early Christian Literature.* Translated and adapted by William F. Arndt and F. Wilbur Gingrich. 2d ed. Chicago: University of Chicago Press, 1979.
Bauman	Bauman, Clarence, ed. *The Spiritual Legacy of Hans Denck.* Leiden: E. J. Brill, 1991.
Beck	Beck, Hans-Georg. *Kirche und theologische Literatur im byzantinischen Reich.* Munich: C. H. Beck'sche Verlagsbuchhandlung, 1959.
Blaise-Chirat	Blaise, Albert, and Henri Chirat. *Dictionnaire latin-français des auteurs chrétiens.* Strasbourg: Le Latin Chrétien.

Blass-Debrunner	Blass, Friedrich, and Albert Debrunner. *A Greek Grammar of the New Testament and Other Early Christian Literature.* Edited and translated by Robert W. Funk. Chicago: University of Chicago Press, 1961.
BLK	*Die Bekenntnisschriften der evangelisch-lutherischen Kirche.* 11th ed. Göttingen: Vandenhoeck und Ruprecht, 1992.
Blunt	Blunt, John Henry, ed. *The Annotated Book of Common Prayer, Being an Historical, Ritual, and Theological Commentary on the Devotional System of the Church of England.* Revised ed. New York: E. P. Dutton, 1903.
Böckel	Böckel, Ernst Gottfried Adolf, ed. *Die Bekenntniszschriften der evangelisch-reformirten Kirche.* Leipzig: F. A. Brockaus, 1847.
Bray	Bray, Gerald Lewis, ed. *Documents of the English Reformation.* Minneapolis, Minn.: Fortress Press, 1994.
Brightman	Brightman, Frank Edward, ed. *Liturgies Eastern and Western.* Oxford: Clarendon Press, 1896.
BZ	*Byzantinische Zeitschrift*
Caspari	Caspari, Carl Paul, ed. *Alte und neue Quellen zur Geschichte des Taufsymbols und der Glaubensregel.* Christiania: Mallingische Buchdruckerei, 1879.
CCCM	*Corpus Christianorum, Continuatio Mediaevalis.* 1953–. Turnhout: Brepols.
CCSL	*Corpus Christianorum, Series Latina.* Turnhout: Brepols, 1953–.
Chr Trad	*The Christian Tradition: A History of the Development of Doctrine.* By Jaroslav Pelikan. 5 vols. Chicago: University of Chicago Press, 1971–89.
Cochrane	Cochrane, Arthur C., ed. *Reformed Confessions of the Sixteenth Century.* Philadelphia: Westminster Press, 1966.
COD	*Conciliorum Oecumenicorum Decreta.* Edited by Joseph Alberigo et al. 3d ed. Bologna: Istituto per le scienze religiose, 1973. (Pagination identical with that of *DEC.*)
CR	*Corpus Reformatorum.* Edited by Carl Gottlieb Bretschneider. Berlin: C. A. Schwetschke, 1834–1900.
CSEL	*Corpus Scriptorum Ecclesiasticorum Latinorum.* Vienna: Hoelder-Pichler-Tempsky, 1866–.

CWS	*The Classics of Western Spirituality.* Edited by John Farina. 104 volumes to date. New York: Paulist Press, 1978–.
Day	Day, Peter D., ed. *The Liturgical Dictionary of Eastern Christianity.* Collegeville, Minn.: Liturgical Press, 1993.
DEC	*Decrees of the Ecumenical Councils.* Edited by Norman P. Tanner et al. 2 vols. Washington, D.C.: Georgetown University Press, 1990. (Pagination identical with that of *COD.*)
DECH	*Dictionary of English Church History.* 2d ed. by S. L. Ollard and G. Crosse. London: A. R. Mowbray, [1919].
DEM	*Dictionary of the Ecumenical Movement.* Edited by Nicholas Lossky, José Míguez Bonino, John Pobec, Tom Stransky, Geoffrey Wainwright, and Pauline Webb. Grand Rapids, Mich.: William B. Eerdmans, 1991.
Denzinger	Denzinger, Heinrich, ed. *Enchiridion symbolorum definitionum et declarationum de rebus fidei et morum.* [1854.] 37th ed. Edited by Peter Hünermann. Freiburg: Herder, 1991. (Cited by paragraph numbers.)
DNB	*Dictionary of National Biography*
Doct Dec	*Doctrinal Declarations of the Lutheran Churches.* Saint Louis, Mo.: Concordia, 1957.
Donovan	Donovan, Vincent J. *Christianity Rediscovered.* 2d ed. Maryknoll, N.Y.: Orbis Books, 1982.
Dossetti	Dossetti, Giuseppe Luigi, ed. *Il simbolo di Nicea e di Costantinopoli: Edizione critica.* Rome: Herder, 1967.
DTC	*Dictionnaire de théologie catholique.* Edited by Alfred Vacant, Emile Mangenot, and Emile Amann (15 vols., 1903–50); and "Tables Générales," edited by B. Loth and A. Michel (3 vols., 1951–72). Paris: Libraire Letouzey et Ané.
EC	*The Encyclopedia of Christianity.* Edited by Erwin Fahlbusch, Jan Milič Lochman, John Mbiti, Jaroslav Pelikan, and Lukas Vischer. Translated by Geoffrey W. Bromiley. Foreword by Jaroslav Pelikan. Grand Rapids, Mich.: William B. Eerdmans, 1999–.
EEC	*Encyclopedia of Early Christianity.* 2d ed. Edited by Everett Ferguson. New York: Garland, 1998.
EKL	*Evangelisches Kirchenlexikon: Internationale Theologische Enzyklopädie.* Edited by Erwin Fahlbusch. Göttingen: Vandenhoeck und Ruprecht, 1985–.

ER	*Ecumenical Review*
Fabbri	Fabbri, Romeo, ed. *Confessioni di fede delle chiese cristiane*. Bologna: Edizioni Dehoniane, 1996.
Fabricius	Fabricius, Cajus, ed. *Corpus Confessionum: Die Bekenntnisse der Christenheit*. Berlin: De Gruyter, 1928–43.
FC	*Fontes Christiani: Zweisprachige Neuausgabe christlicher Quellentexte aus Altertum und Mittelalter*. Edited by Norbert Brox, Wilhelm Geerlings, Gisbert Greshake, Rainer Ilgner, and Rudolf Schieffer. Freiburg, Basel, etc.: Herder, 1991–.
FOTC	*Fathers of the Church*. Washington, D.C.: Catholic University of America Press, 1947–.
Gass	Gass, Wilhelm. *Symbolik der griechischen Kirche*. Berlin: Reimer, 1872.
GCS	*Die griechischen christlichen Schriftsteller der ersten Jahrhunderte*. Leipzig and Berlin: Akademie-Verlag, 1897–.
Gerrish	Gerrish, Brian A., ed. *The Faith of Christendom: A Source Book of Creeds and Confessions*. New York: World Publishing, 1963.
GOTR	*Greek Orthodox Theological Review*
Gr Agr	*Growth in Agreement: Reports and Agreed Statements of Ecumenical Conversations on a World Level*. Edited by Harding Meyer and Lukas Vischer. Geneva: World Council of Churches; New York: Paulist Press, 1984.
Gr Agr II	*Growth in Agreement II: Reports and Agreed Statements of Ecumenical Conversations on a World Level, 1982–1988*. Edited by Jeffrey Gros, Harding Meyer, and William G. Rusch. Geneva: World Council of Churches; Grand Rapids, Mich.: William B. Eerdmans, 2000.
Hahn	Hahn, August. *Bibliothek der Symbole und Glaubensregeln der Alten Kirche*. 3d ed. Edited by G. Ludwig Hahn. Foreword by Adolf Harnack. [1897.] Reprint ed. Hildesheim: Georg Olms Verlagsbuchhandlung, 1962. (Cited by document numbers.)
Hefele	Hefele, Karl Joseph. *A History of the Councils of the Church from the Original Documents*. English translation of vols. 1–6 of 2d ed. by William Robinson Clark (vol. 1) and Henry Nutcombe Oxenham (vols. 2–6). Reprint, New York: AMS Press, 1972.

Hefele-Leclercq	Hefele, Charles Joseph, and Henri Leclercq. *Histoire des conciles d'après les documents originaux.* 11 vols. Paris: Letouzey et Ané, 1907–52.
Henke	Henke, Ernst Ludwig Theodor, ed. *Theologorum Saxonicorum consensus repetitus fidei vere Lutheranae.* Marburg: Typis Elwerti Academicis, 1846.
Holy Cross	*Hē Theia Leitourgia: The Divine Liturgy.* Brookline, Mass.: Holy Cross Orthodox Press, 1985.
Horst	Horst, Irvin B., ed. and tr. *Mennonite Confession of Faith Adopted April 21st, 1632, at Dordrecht, The Netherlands.* Lancaster, Pa.: Lancaster Mennonite Historical Society, 1988.
JTS	*Journal of Theological Studies*
Kallis	Kallis, Anastasios, ed. *Liturgie: Die Göttliche Liturgie der Orthodoxen Kirche Deutsch-Griechisch-Kirchenslawisch.* Mainz: Matthias-Grünewald-Verlag, 1989.
Karmirēs	Karmirēs, Ioannēs. *Ta dogmatika kai symbolika mnēmeia tēs orthodoxou katholikēs ekklēsias* [The dogmatic and symbolic monuments of the Orthodox Catholic Church]. 2 vols., 2d ed. Graz: Akademische Druck- und Verlagsanstalt, 1968. (Cited by page numbers of this edition.)
Kelly	Kelly, John Norman Davidson. *Early Christian Creeds.* 3d ed. London: Longman Group, 1972.
Kimmel	Kimmel, Ernst Julius, ed. *Libri symbolici ecclesiae orientalis; Appendix,* ed. H. J. C. Weissenborn. Jena: Apud Carolum Hochhausenium, 1843–50.
Kokkinakis	Kokkinakis, Athenagoras, ed. and tr. *The Liturgy of the Orthodox Church.* London: Mowbrays, 1979.
Kolb-Wengert	Kolb, Robert, and Timothy J. Wengert, eds. *The Book of Concord: The Confessions of the Evangelical Lutheran Church.* Minneapolis, Minn.: Fortress Press, 2000.
Lacoste	Lacoste, Jean-Yves, ed. *Dictionnaire critique de théologie.* Paris: Presses Universitaires de France, 1998.
Lampe	Lampe, Geoffrey W. H., ed. *A Patristic Greek Lexicon.* Oxford: Clarendon Press, 1961.
LCC	*Library of Christian Classics.* 26 vols. Philadelphia: Westminster Press, 1953–66.
LCL	*Loeb Classical Library*

Leith   Leith, John H., ed. *Creeds of the Churches: A Reader in*
                    Christian Doctrine from the Bible to the Present. Garden City,
                    N.Y.: Doubleday, 1963.

Link   Link, Hans-Georg, ed. *Confessing Our Faith Around the*
                    World. 4 vols. Geneva: World Council of Churches, 1980–85.

Loewen   Loewen, Howard John, ed. *One Lord, One Church, One*
                    Hope, and One God: Mennonite Confessions of Faith. Elkhart,
                    Ind.: Institute of Mennonite Studies, 1985.

LTK   *Lexikon für Theologie und Kirche.* Edited by Josef Höfer and
                    Karl Rahner. 2d ed. 10 vols. and index. Freiburg: Herder,
                    1957–67.

Lumpkin   Lumpkin, William L., ed. *Baptist Confessions of Faith.*
                    Revised ed. Valley Forge, Pa.: Judson Press, 1969.

McGlothlin   McGlothlin, William Joseph, ed. *Baptist Confessions of Faith.*
                    Philadelphia: American Baptist Publication Society, 1911.

Malvy-Viller   Malvy, Antoine, and Marcel Viller, eds. *La confession*
                    orthodoxe de Pierre Moghila. Rome: Orientalia Christiana
                    Analecta, 1927.

Mansi   Mansi, Giovanni Domenico, ed. *Sacrorum conciliorum nova*
                    et amplissima collectio. 31 vols. Florence: Antonio Zatta,
                    1759–98.

Marthaler   Marthaler, Berard L. *The Creed.* Mystic, Conn.: Twenty-
                    Third Publications, 1987.

Mastrantonis   Mastrantonis, George, ed. *Augsburg and Constantinople: The*
                    Correspondence Between the Tübingen Theologians and Patri-
                    arch Jeremiah II of Constantinople on the Augsburg Confession.
                    Brookline, Mass.: Holy Cross Orthodox Press, 1982.

ME   *The Mennonite Encyclopedia: A Comprehensive Reference*
                    Work on the Anabaptist-Mennonite Movement. Hillsboro,
                    Kans.: Mennonite Brethren Publishing House, 1955–90.

Meth Doct &   *The Doctrines and Discipline of the Methodist Episcopal*
  Disc   *Church.* New York: Eaton and Mains, 1908.

MGH   *Monumenta Germaniae Historica*

Michalcescu   Michalcescu, Jon, ed. *Thēsauros tēs Orthodoxias: Die*
                    Bekenntnisse und die wichtigsten Glaubenszeugnisse der
                    griechisch-orientalischen Kirche. Introduction by Albert
                    Hauck. Leipzig: J. C. Hinrichs, 1904.

ML   *Mennonitisches Lexikon.* Edited by Christian Hege and
                    Christian Neff. 4 vols. Frankfurt: [n.p.], 1913–67.
MQR   *Mennonite Quarterly Review*
Müller   Müller, E. F. Karl. *Die Bekenntnisschriften der reformierten*
                    Kirche in authentischen Texten mit geschichtlicher Einleitung
                    und Register. Leipzig: A. Deichert, 1903. Reprint, Zurich:
                    Theologische Buchhandlung, 1987.
Nestle/Aland   *Greek-English New Testament.* Edited by Eberhard and Erwin
                    Nestle, revised by Barbara and Kurt Aland. With English
                    translation of the Revised Standard Version. Stuttgart:
                    Deutsche Bibelstiftung, 1994.
Niemeyer   Niemeyer, Hermann Agathon, ed. *Collectio Confessionum in*
                    Ecclesiis Reformatis Publicatarum. Leipzig: Julius Klinkhardt,
                    1840.
Niesel   Niesel, Wilhelm, ed. *Bekenntnisschriften und Kirchenord-*
                    nungen der nach Gottes Wort reformierten Kirche. Munich:
                    Christian Kaiser Verlag, [1938].
Noll   Noll, Mark A., ed. *Confessions and Catechisms of the*
                    Reformation. Grand Rapids, Mich.: Baker Book House, 1991.
NPNF   *A Select Library of the Nicene and Post-Nicene Fathers of*
                    the Christian Church. First and Second Series. Reprint ed.
                    22 vols. Grand Rapids, Mich.: William B. Eerdmans, 1956.
NRSV   *The Holy Bible: Containing the Old and New Testaments with*
                    the Apocryphal/Deuterocanonical Books. Edited by the *NRSV*
                    Bible Translation Committee, Bruce M. Metzger, Chair. New
                    York: Oxford University Press, 1989.
OCA   *The Divine Liturgy According to St. John Chrysostom, with*
                    Appendices. The Orthodox Church in America. 2d ed. South
                    Canaan, Pa.: St. Tikhon's Seminary Press, 1977.
ODCC   *The Oxford Dictionary of the Christian Church.* 3d ed. Edited
                    by F. L. Cross and E. A. Livingstone. Oxford: Oxford
                    University Press, 1997.
OED   *A New [Oxford] English Dictionary on Historical Principles.*
                    Edited by J. A. H. Murray, H. Bradley, W. A. Craigie, and
                    C. T. Onions. 12 vols. and 4 vols. of Supplement. Oxford:
                    Oxford University Press, 1884–1933.

OER   *Oxford Encyclopedia of the Reformation*. Hans Hillerbrand, editor-in-chief. 4 vols. Oxford: Oxford University Press, 1996.

Overbeck   Overbeck, J. J., ed. *The Orthodox Confession of the Catholic and Apostolic Eastern Church from the Version of Peter Mogila*. London: Thomas Baker, 1898.

Pelikan   Pelikan, Jaroslav. "Luther and the *Confessio Bohemica*." Ph.D. diss., University of Chicago, 1946.

PG   *Patrologia Graeca*. Edited by Jacques Paul Migne. 162 vols. Paris: Lutetiae Parisiorum, 1857–66.

PL   *Patrologia Latina*. Edited by Jacques Paul Migne. 221 vols. Paris: Lutetiae Parisiorum, 1844–64.

PO   *Patrologia Orientalis*. Edited by René Graffin and François Nau. Paris: Firmin-Didot, 1907–66.

Prav Slov   *Polnyj pravoslavný bogoslovský enciklopedičeský slovar'* [Complete encyclopedic dictionary of Orthodox theology]. 1913. Reprint ed. London: Variorum Reprints, 1971.

PRE   Johann Jakob Herzog and Albert Hauck, eds., *Realencyklopädie für protestantische Theologie und Kirche*. 3d ed. 21 vols. and index. Leipzig: J. C. Hinrichs'sche Buchhandlung, 1896–1909.

Quasten   Quasten, Johannes, et al. *Patrology*. 4 vols. Westminster, Md.: Newman Press and Christian Classics, 1951–86.

Raby   Raby, F. J. E., ed. *The Oxford Book of Medieval Latin Verse*. Oxford: Clarendon Press, 1959.

Rahner-Vorgrimler   Rahner, Karl, and Herbert Vorgrimler. *Theological Dictionary*. Edited by Cornelius Ernst. Translated by Richard Strachan. New York: Herder and Herder, 1965.

Rees   Rees, Thomas, tr. *The Racovian Catechism, with Notes and Illustrations*. London: Longman, Hurst, Rees, Orme, and Brown, 1818.

Reu   Reu, J. Michael, ed. *The Augsburg Confession: A Collection of Sources with an Historical Introduction*. 2 vols. Chicago: Wartburg Publishing House, 1930.

Robertson   Robertson, J. N. W. B., ed. and tr. *The Acts and Decrees of the Synod of Jerusalem, Sometimes Called the Council of Bethlehem, Holden under Dositheus, Patriarch of Jerusalem in 1672*. London: Thomas Baker, 1899.

SC	*Sources chrétiennes.* Henri de Lubac and Jean Daniélou, founding eds. Paris: Editions du Cerf, 1942–.
Schaff	Schaff, Philip, ed. *Bibliotheca Symbolica Ecclesiae Universalis: The Creeds of Christendom.* 3 vols. New York: Harper and Brothers, 1877. 6th ed., by David S. Schaff. Reprint ed. Grand Rapids, Mich.: Baker Book House, 1990.
Schmidt-Schornbaum	Schmidt, Wilhelm Ferdinand, and Karl Schornbaum, eds. *Die fränkischen Bekenntnisse: Eine Vorstufe der Augsburgischen Konfession.* Munich: Christian Kaiser Verlag, 1930.
Schwartz	Schwartz, Eduard, ed. *Drei dogmatische Schriften Iustinians.* Munich: Bayerische Akademie der Wissenschaften, 1939.
Sophocles	Sophocles, Evangelinus Apostolides, ed. *Greek Lexicon of the Roman and Byzantine Periods (From B.C. 146 to A.D. 1100).* Boston: Little, Brown, 1870.
Tappert	Tappert, Theodore G., Jaroslav Pelikan, Robert H. Fischer, and Arthur Carl Piepkorn, ed. and tr. *The Book of Concord: The Confessions of the Evangelical Lutheran Church.* Philadelphia: Muhlenberg Press, 1959.
Torrance	Torrance, Thomas F., ed. *The School of Faith: The Catechisms of the Reformed Church.* New York: Harper and Brothers, 1959.
TRE	*Theologische Realenzyclopädie.* Edited by G. Krause, G. Müller, et al. Berlin: de Gruyter, 1976–.
Triglotta	*Concordia Triglotta.* Edited by G. Friedrich Bente. 2 vols. in 1. Saint Louis, Mo.: Concordia Publishing House, 1921.
Underhill	Underhill, Edward Bean, ed. *Confessions of Faith and Other Public Documents Illustrative of the History of the Baptist Churches of England in the Seventeenth Century.* London: Hanserd Knollys Society, 1854.
Vischer	Vischer, Lukas, ed. *Reformed Witness Today: A Collection of Confessions and Statements of Faith Issued by Reformed Churches.* Bern: Evangelische Arbeitsstelle Oekumene Schweiz, 1982.
WA	Luther, Martin. *Werke. Kritische Gesamtausgabe.* Weimar: Bohlau, etc., 1883–.
Walker	Walker, Williston, ed. *The Creeds and Platforms of Congregationalism.* [1893.] Reprint ed. Introduction by Douglas Horton. Boston: Pilgrim Press, 1960.

Wesche   Wesche, Kenneth Paul, ed. and tr. *On the Person of Christ: The Christology of Emperor Justinian.* Crestwood, N.Y.: Saint Vladimir's Seminary Press, 1991.

Will   Will, Cornelius, ed. *Acta et scripta quae de controversiis ecclesiae Graecae et Latinae saeculo undecimo composita extant.* [1861.] Reprint ed. Frankfurt: Minerva, 1963.

Williams   Williams, George Huntston. *The Radical Reformation.* 3d ed. Kirksville, Mo.: Sixteenth Century Journal Publishers, 1992.

ZfKT   *Zeitschrift für Katholische Theologie*

ZKG   *Zeitschrift für Kirchengeschichte*

V

Statements of Faith in Modern Christianity

Introduction

The title of this Part Five may well seem to be an oxymoron, above all to anyone who equates modernity with religious skepticism and doctrinal relativism and who therefore feels that even if the time for faith as such may not have passed, the time for teaching Christian faith as authoritative dogma probably has, and the time for confessing it in a normative creedal formulary certainly has.[1] One twentieth-century reference work of Liberal Protestant theology speaks for this modern view of creeds and confessions when, after positing the neutral and unobjectionable definition, "Historically considered, creeds are convenient summaries arising out of definite religious situations, designed to meet urgent contemporary needs, and serving as tests of orthodoxy," it proceeds, by means of a "therefore," to draw from that definition a conclusion diametrically opposed to the traditional one: "Therefore they are inadequate in new crises and unable to secure uniformity of belief."[2] In a time when faith itself has become problematical to so many serious and thoughtful seekers— for whom the confidence of the traditional confessional formula, "We believe, teach, and confess," seems to have been replaced by the poignant cry of the anguished father in the Gospel story, "I believe; help my unbelief!"[3]—the role of the confession of faith cannot avoid being a problematic one. At most, it would seem to be the function of such a confession to acknowledge the reality of the secularization of society and to seek to define (or redefine) the Christian mission in response to it.[4]

Nevertheless, as becomes evident from even a preliminary examination of the dates cited for the texts here in Part Five of *Creeds and Confessions of Faith in the Christian Tradition* (and as a further examination of the many other texts not included here would reinforce), there have been "statements of faith" aplenty in "modern Christianity." They continued to appear in almost every year from the end of the eighteenth century to the end of the twentieth, in many churches, including some that dissented fundamentally from the main body of the Christian tradition, already in the eighteenth century[5] and then in the nineteenth[6] and twentieth,[7] in

1. As described in Baumer 1960.
2. Ferm 1945, 208 (Conrad Henry Moehlman).
3. Mk 9.24.
4. *Camb Dec.*
5. *Shkr* (1790).
6. *Winch* (1803); *LDS* (1842); *Salv Arm* (1878).
7. *Wash* (1935).

almost every part of the globe, and in many languages, some of these languages being quite novel as instruments for the formal confession of Christian doctrine. In fact, during the twentieth century the title "statement of faith" seems to have become preferable (at any rate in English translation) to either "creed" or "confession." To cite only some examples that are widely dispersed both theologically and geographically: _Statement of Faith of the American Baptist Association_ of 1905;[8] _Brief Statement of the Doctrinal Position of the Evangelical Lutheran Synod of Missouri, Ohio, and Other States_ of 1932;[9] _The Statement of Faith of the United Church of Christ_ of 1959;[10] _Statement of Faith of the Church of Jesus Christ in Madagascar,_ 1958/1968;[11] _Statement of Faith of the United Church of Christ in the Philippines,_ 1986 (1982);[12] _Common Statement of Faith_ issued by the Commission on Faith and Order of the World Council of Churches, meeting at Bangalore, India, in 1978[13] — and even such nontraditional confessions as _Bond of Fellowship and Statement of Faith of the Unitarian-Universalist Association_ in 1935[14] and _Statement of Fundamental Truths of the Assemblies of God_ in 1914.[15]

In some ways, moreover, both the new challenges and the new opportunities of Christian faith in the modern era since the opening of the nineteenth century, which has been identified as "the great century" of Christian missions,[16] have been responsible for unprecedented expansion and growth in previously non-Christian areas of Asia and, above all, of Sub-Saharan Africa, where new believers, and eventually new churches, have sought their own ways of responding within their own culture and in their own language to the historic confessional imperative: "If you confess with your lips that Jesus is Lord and believe in your heart that God raised him from the dead, you will be saved. For man believes with his heart and so is justified, and he confesses with his lips and so is saved."[17] New movements dissenting from historic churches, including some very ancient ones, both in the East[18] and in

8. _Am Bap._
9. _Br St Luth._
10. _UCC._
11. _Madag._
12. _Philip UCC._
13. _F&O Ban._
14. _Bnd Fell._
15. _Assem._
16. Latourette 1937–45, 4–6.
17. Rom 10.9–10.
18. _Arm Ev._

the West,[19] have added to the list of confessions. It is these ambiguities as well as these challenges and opportunities that have helped to shape the history of Christian creeds and confessions of faith in the modern era.

The Discomfort with Creed Caused by the Consciousness of Modernity

Hinrich Stoevesandt has used the phrase "the discomfort with creed caused by the consciousness of modernity [*das durch jenes Gegenwartsbewusstsein mitveranlasste Ungehagen am Symbolum*]" as the title for a book that describes the long-standing modern antipathy, outside and even inside the churches, to the very idea of a creed or confession[20]—as well as, of course, the antipathy to specific individual creeds, most vehemently of all to *The Athanasian Creed*.[21] In voicing that antipathy, many modern opponents of creedalism claimed to be carrying out, more consistently than the Protestant Reformers had been in a position to do, the full implications of the Reformation's attack on the authority of church and tradition. On the basis of a "domino theory" of religious authority, the Roman Catholic adversaries of the Reformation had warned already in the sixteenth century that an attack on the papacy would eventually lead to a repudiation of creedal orthodoxy itself. They had seized upon such obiter dicta as Luther's disparaging language about the term *homoousios* or Calvin's comment that it was better to sing *The Nicene Creed* than to speak it as evidence of the beginning of such a repudiation. In reply, the Magisterial Reformers, above all Luther, Calvin, and the spokesmen for Anglicanism, vigorously affirmed their loyalty to the orthodox dogmas of the Trinity and the person of Christ.[22] But during the eighteenth, nineteenth, and twentieth centuries, that Roman Catholic view of the Reformation achieved a vindication of sorts in Liberal Protestantism, for example in Adolf Harnack's description and critique of the vestigial remnants and "the Catholic elements retained by Luther" and the other Reformers.[23] Not only the retention of the Catholic creeds and dogmas by the confessions of the Magisterial Reformation, but the addition of literally hundreds of Protestant creeds and confessions to them, was now seen as an indication that the Reformers themselves had not fully carried out the implications of their own position, which had finally become a possibility only with the modern era. The paradoxes in this situation will

19. *Pol Nat.*
20. Stoevesandt 1970, 12.
21. Compare *39 Art* 8 with *39 Art Am* 8.
22. *Chr Trad* 4:322–23.
23. Harnack [1893] 1961b, 7:230–66.

become evident to present-day readers when they note that it is the Protestant confessions of the Reformation era that repeatedly criticize Roman Catholicism (rather than the other way around, as later polemics might suggest) for allowing too much latitude to the ministry of women: "We teach that baptism should not be administered by women or midwives. For Paul deprived women of ecclesiastical duties, and baptism has to do with these."[24]

Without attempting to present here a capsule history of "the consciousness of modernity," or even of the development of critical theology in the modern period, it is possible to identify several of the movements of modern thought in which such a "discomfort with creed," to the point of antipathy and hostility, has manifested itself, also among Christian theologians standing in various confessional traditions.[25] Claude Welch's comprehensive *Protestant Thought in the Nineteenth Century* may serve as a guide to those movements, although our account must confine itself, even more than his does, to "an interpretation of some central themes,"[26] which, while contradicting each other in many theological particulars, shared this "discomfort with creed."

"The eighteenth and nineteenth centuries" were marked, Welch observes, by "the antidogmatic, antienthusiastic temper of an age tired and disgusted with religious controversies."[27] The rationalism of the Enlightenment was "antidogmatic," and therefore it was anticreedal and anticonfessional. In the celebrated definition by Immanuel Kant, the "Enlightenment is man's exodus from his self-imposed tutelage," a tutelage that had expressed itself "in indecision and lack of courage to use the mind without the guidance of another." Or, in Paul Tillich's definition, the Enlightenment was "the revolution of man's autonomous potentialities over against the heteronomous powers which were no longer convincing." For many disciples of the Enlightenment, including its theological disciples, creeds and confessions were among the most obvious examples of such a "self-imposed tutelage." The rejection of creeds and confessions as "heteronomous powers" and as "no longer convincing," together with a "disgust with religious controversies," was a no less obvious example of such a "revolution." For "it's plain from Church History," the Deist Matthew Tindal wrote in 1730, "that Creeds were the spiritual Arms, with which

24. *Helv II* 20.6, citing 1 Tm 2.11–14, and *Scot I* 22, by contrast with *Lat 1215* 3.
25. *Chr Trad* 5:29–32, 122–28, 269–72; the sources for many of the quotations not identified in footnotes here are given in the marginal notes there.
26. Welch 1972–85, 1:293.
27. Welch 1972–85, 1:31.

contending Parties combated each other; and that those who were the Majority invented such unscriptural Terms, as they thought their adversaries wou'd most scruple, in Order to the stripping them of their Preferments." An Enlightenment thinker like Thomas Jefferson, nominal Anglican though he remained at least officially, strove to go back behind the creeds, and even behind the canonical Gospels as they had been transmitted by an orthodox and creedal Christendom, to find the authentic figure of the human Jesus as the teacher of a rational and universal faith, to set him free from creed and dogma, and to see genuine—and therefore noncreedal and nondogmatic—religion and morality as embodied in him.

Although "the nineteenth century was in many respects a very Christian century," Lionel Trilling observed in 1950, "it is probably true that when the dogmatic principle in religion is slighted, religion goes along for a while on generalized emotion and ethical intention—'morality touched by emotion'—and then loses the force of its impulse, even the essence of its being."[28] For those thinkers who strove to retain some form of the Christian belief in Christ and in the Bible, therefore, the substitute for creeds and confessions in much of the Protestant theology of the eighteenth and nineteenth centuries was one or another configuration of what might be called a new trinity, which Welch identifies as "faith, history, and ethics in balance."[29] All three of these, as well as the relation of each to dogma and creed, had been important components in the tradition of creedal and confessional orthodoxy, too. But now each of them acquired a new significance, and the "balance" of which Welch speaks was at the same time a fundamental and critical reconsideration of that tradition as a whole. There remained great variation in the radicality, as well as in the public acknowledgment, both of the rejection and of the alternatives.

An emphasis on authentic *faith,* which implied a subordination of the objective *fides quae creditur,* "the faith which one believes," of ecclesiastical doctrine, dogma, and creed, to the subjective *fides qua creditur,* "the faith by which one believes," of personal feeling and experience, had already been a pronounced tendency in the distinctive emphasis of Reformed and Lutheran Pietism on the Continent and of Methodism in England. In practice, however, both of these movements employed it to vindicate many traditional beliefs, if not always the formal authority of the creeds and confessions in which those beliefs had been definitively set down, as later confessions would make clear.[30] John Wesley, although he him-

28. Trilling [1950] 2000, 180.
29. Welch 1972–85, 2:1–30.
30. *Morav.*

self strove in his "theology of the heart" to remain orthodox and faithful to Anglicanism's "three creeds,"[31] insisted that "a man may assent to three or three-
and-twenty creeds . . . and yet have no Christian faith at all." But when this
emphasis on experience and feeling was defined by its outstanding expositor, Friedrich Schleiermacher, in his systematic theology, *The Christian Faith,* as "the feeling
of absolute dependence," this eventually superseded not only the traditional proofs
for the existence of God, but dogma, creed, and confession. Therefore, as Welch
summarizes Schleiermacher's view, "every doctrinal form is bound to a particular
time and no claim can be made for its permanent validity."[32] That applied also to
the creeds and confessions of the churches—to all of them. This view of doctrinal
forms brought on what Welch calls "the neglect by theologians (especially Schleiermacher) of the ancient dogmas" and creeds.[33] In Schleiermacher's *Christian Faith,*
moreover, "the confessional writings of the Protestant church [*die evangelischen Bekenntnisschriften*]," Reformed and Lutheran confessions taken together, were to be
cited in support of doctrinal propositions. In the tradition of the Prussian Union,
the differences between the two sets of Reformation confessions on such doctrines
as the eucharist were subordinated to those teachings that they held in common—
and all of these in turn to experiential faith. For although all doctrinal propositions could be interpreted either as "descriptions of conditions of human life" or as
"concepts of divine attributes" or as "statements about the way the world is constituted," it was in fact the first of these three forms of expression that recast and
eventually replaced the conventional language of the creeds and confessions, including the creeds and confessions of the Protestant Reformation, both Reformed and
Lutheran. Toward these creeds and confessions he felt himself bound only according to what he took to be their "meaning and spirit," rather than according to the
letter of the doctrines they professed.[34] Probably the most notorious instance of this
treatment of creedal doctrine was the way Schleiermacher marginalized the dogma
of the Trinity, literally relegating it to an appendix in *The Christian Faith.*

    History, the second member of the triad, likewise led to the undermining
of creedal and confessional authority. The question on all sides was: "Is historical
research . . . a help to faith? And can any security for faith be found in history?"[35]
It was a question that applied with special force to the historic creeds and con-

---

31. *39 Art* 8.
32. Welch 1972–85, 1:72.
33. Welch 1972–85, 1:100.
34. Hirsch 1960, 5:157–58.
35. Welch 1972–85, 2:146.

fessions, which served as the outstanding illustrations of the correctness of Gotthold Ephraim Lessing's axiom that "contingent historical truths can never serve as proof for necessary truths of reason." Matthew Tindal found that "the imposers of creeds, canons, and constitutions" were "the common plagues of mankind." Although there were some efforts to argue "that the New Testament fully supports an Athanasian rather than a Socinian or an Arian Christology, provided we do not allow criticism to become our master,"[36] such efforts were seen as incompatible with the growing historical recognition that the attempt of the Reformation confessions and their later interpreters "to show continuity between the ancient church and the Reformation while distinguishing Protestant from Roman Catholic understandings" was misguided and doomed to fail.[37] Frederick Denison Maurice's *Subscription No Bondage* of 1835 argued "that the requirement at Oxford [of subscription to *The Thirty-Nine Articles of the Church of England*] was not actually a test of one's own religious convictions, but a statement of the basis on which instruction in the university was to be given."[38] But such an argument could be dismissed by both the left and the right as evasion and sophistry; and the accusation of "deviation from the standards of the Westminster Confession"[39] and other Reformation confessions, directed against the historical-critical study of Scripture, was ultimately ineffective. For the method of historical-critical study was applied not only to the Bible (where it was more readily accepted for the Old Testament than for the New) but, in keeping with the Protestant subordination of tradition to Scripture, with still greater freedom to creeds and confessions of faith, even to those that were the most ancient or the most ecumenical and authoritative.

Increasingly, as it was being carried on by such Liberal scholars as Harnack, this historical-critical method was documenting a two-stage historical process: "the recasting of the baptismal confession into a rule of faith," which foliated into many creeds and conciliar confessions of faith in the first several centuries of the history of the church; and then in turn the development by which "the rule of faith was transformed into a compendium of Greek philosophical systems" climaxing in the Eastern and Western forms of scholasticism—two steps that had brought the orthodox creeds of the church a long distance away from the original and true gospel of Jesus.[40] The historical-critical examination of creedal development, above

36. Welch 1972–85, 2:151.
37. Welch 1972–85, 2:15.
38. Welch 1972–85, 1:245.
39. Welch 1972–85, 2:166.
40. Welch 1972–85, 2:179.

all of *The Definition of Faith of the Council of Chalcedon*, led Albert Schweitzer to conclude that "its doctrine of the two natures dissolved the unity of the Person, and thereby cut off the last possibility of a return to the historical Jesus. . . . He was still, like Lazarus of old, bound hand and foot with grave-clothes—the grave-clothes of the dogma of the Dual Nature."[41] In his *Quest of the Historical Jesus*, Schweitzer proceeded to document the historical process by which, beginning with Hermann Samuel Reimarus, an emancipation from that "dogma of the Dual Nature" had led the biblical scholarship of the eighteenth and nineteenth centuries to a series of reconstructions of "the historical Jesus," free of creedal or confessional restraint.

An apt illustration both of the impact and of the problem of such historical-critical study of the creeds and confessions was the "battle over *The Apostles' Creed* [*Apostolikumstreit*]," which Harnack precipitated, almost inadvertently, in 1892. When a Protestant pastor administered baptism to a child without using *The Apostles' Creed*, a storm of controversy broke out, and some of the participants in the controversy appealed to Harnack as an eminent historical authority for his expert opinion. He replied that "the acknowledgment of *The Apostles' Creed* just as it reads is not the criterion of Christian and theological maturity; on the contrary, a mature Christian, who is well informed about the understanding of the gospel and about the history of the church, must take offense at several of the statements in *The Apostles' Creed*." Above all he singled out the article of the creed "conceived by the Holy Spirit, born of the Virgin Mary"[42] as one that many modern Protestants could no longer find acceptable, and that it was therefore dishonest to enforce as a compulsory belief for clergy or laity. But at the same time he affirmed "the high value and great repository of truth" in this creed, though only if it was properly, that is, historically and critically, understood. The reaction in the German Protestant press and in the churches, including the Roman Catholic Church, was partly a continuation of the earlier protests that Harnack had evoked by his historical research into the origins of dogma and by his critique of the place of dogma and creed in the church. But it was also a symptom of the far broader sense of unease over the entire problem of doctrinal and creedal authority within modern Protestantism.[43]

The third member of the triad of "faith, history, and ethics in balance," Christian *ethics*, had long been seen as existing in potential tension with creed and dogma, but that tension, too, acquired new force in the nineteenth century. Sometimes the orthodox Protestant attempt "to relate the classical terms *persona* and *hy-*

41. Schweitzer [1906] 1961, 3.
42. *Ap* 3.
43. Zahn-Harnack 1951, 144–60.

postasis (both in the christological and trinitarian usages) to modern conceptions of personhood centering in self-consciousness"[44] could be used to support the interest in the ethical dimension. But in opposition to any such attempt, the most far-reaching espousal of a new understanding of Christian ethics, which "in the late nineteenth century seemed to be sweeping everything before it," came from an outlook that thought of itself as "freed from dogma considered as unchangeable formulas for belief . . . or the trinitarian dialectic of the Athanasian Creed."[45] The need to discover (or, as they saw it, to recover after centuries of orthodox neglect) the social character of the Christian ethic and to carry it out in political and social action would march under the banner of "the social gospel."[46] This even produced a "social creed" of its own, first for the Methodist Church and then for the Federal Council of Churches in the United States and then for the Methodist Church in Brazil.[47] It evoked from Walter Rauschenbusch, in his *Christianity and the Social Crisis* of 1907, which "became one of the most influential religious books of the century,"[48] the question that formed the title of one of his chapters: "Why Has Christianity Never Undertaken the Work of Social Reconstruction?"[49] In addition to sacramentalism, which promoted a mystical inwardness instead of social reconstruction, and asceticism, which urged a flight from the world and society, a chief culprit in the social apathy of the church, according to Rauschenbusch, was dogma, as it had been formulated by creeds such as *The Athanasian Creed,* with its "subtle definitions on the relation between the persons of the trinity" and "comparatively fruitless speculation."[50]

One direct consequence of this change was—somewhat incongruously, in view of the new emphasis of the social gospel on the corporate dimension of Christianity—the radical individualization of "confession of faith" as a personal religious act, the phenomenon that Welch calls "the Socratic turn to the self."[51] The English poet John Milton had already been its spokesman when, in his posthumously published *Christian Doctrine,* he stated his intention "to puzzle out a creed for myself by my own exertions," because he had "decided not to depend upon the belief or

---

44. Welch 1972–85, 1:279.

45. Welch 1972–85, 2:229.

46. Hopkins 1940; Handy 1966.

47. *Soc Meth; Soc Ch; Meth Braz.*

48. *ODCC* 1368.

49. Rauschenbusch 1907, 143–210.

50. Rauschenbusch 1907, 178–79.

51. Welch 1972–85, 1:126.

judgment of others in religious questions." But the creed that Milton had "puzzled out" by his own exertions turned out to be a "neo-Arian" departure from traditional Nicene and Chalcedonian orthodoxy both on the Trinity and on the person of Christ. It is symptomatic of this new creedal freedom and confessional individualism that in many Protestant divinity schools, even if they are still affiliated with a church body, a course is offered, often for entering seminarians, with the assignment to each class member of producing a "credo," not of what the church has believed, taught, and confessed in its historic creeds and confessions of faith, but of what that particular seminarian *really* believes now—which might possibly correspond to some existing creedal and confessional affirmation, but certainly does not need to.

Old and New Contexts of Christian Confessing

When, as part of its program of *aggiornamento, The Declaration on the Church's Relation to Non-Christian Religions* of the Second Vatican Council of the Roman Catholic Church at its seventh session, on 28 October 1965, opens with the phrase "*Nostra aetate,* In our age,"[52] from which that conciliar decree takes its title, it is expressing the recognition that in the modern era changing times are bringing unique challenges but also unprecedented opportunities to the confessional task of the church. Already its first decree, *The Constitution on the Sacred Liturgy,* entitled *Sacrosanctum concilium,* referring to "those structures which are subject to change" as distinguished from the fixed components of the liturgy and the unchangeable truths of Scripture and tradition, speaks of the obligation "to adapt" them "so as better to meet the needs of our time [*nostrae aetatis necessitates*]."[53] And *Gaudium et spes,* its *Pastoral Constitution on the Church in the World Today,* calls upon the church to discern "the signs of the times," and devotes its introduction to "the condition of humanity in today's world."[54] A century earlier, the confession of the Roman Catholic faith in *The Syllabus of Errors of Pope Pius IX* of 1864 also looks for the signs of its times and locates itself historically in its age, though chiefly in an adversarial posture, when it condemns eighty of "the principal errors *of our time.*"[55] In the period of the Reformation, *The Canons and Decrees of the Council of Trent* speak of the church's right and duty to take account of "changing affairs, times, and

52. *Vat II* 7.1 decr.
53. *Vat II* 3.1 decr.
54. *Vat II* 9. decr.
55. *Syl*; also *Munif* 2.

places" in its practical life,[56] just as *The Augsburg Confession* singles out "the fault of the times" as the culprit in various abuses.[57]

Many other churches have recognized the challenges and opportunities of the modern era, and the imperative to deal with them has been articulated in many other modern statements of faith, including in a special way those that have emanated from Evangelical and "free churches."[58] In 1951, Indonesian Protestants produced their *Confession of Faith of the Protestant Christian Batak Church (H.K.B.P.)*, in which, while according due recognition to the confessions of the past, they nevertheless stated their view that "the church, in opposing heresies which arise, continuously requires *new confessions*. . . . Because of the pressures upon our church, our thinking must be aroused *at the present time* to confront the doctrines and religions around us."[59] As becomes clear from the subtitle, "Directions of Endeavor for Chinese Christianity in the Construction of New China," *The Christian Manifesto* of the "China Christian Patriotic Three-Self Movement" issued in 1950, recognizes the new situation of the church in a "new China" dominated by Marxism-Leninism.[60] Though not a "confessional church" in the usual sense in spite of earlier creedal affirmations in the seventeenth[61] and nineteenth[62] centuries the Society of Friends (Quakers) responded to the twentieth century by issuing *Essential Truths* in 1900 and 1930.[63] And a definition of its time as "the atomic age" raised for European Protestants after the Second World War the question of whether and how "the confession of Christ" could be possible now.[64]

The new contexts of Christian confessing "*nostra aetate,* in our age," were the consequence of forces both inside and outside the life and faith of the institutional churches, forces that were sometimes hostile and sometimes friendly to creeds. One of the most drastic changes, with far-reaching implications for the authority of creeds, was the gradual shift from establishment to disestablishment of the church in relation to the state, as well as in relation to the university, to science, and to culture generally. The implications of disestablishment became visible,

56. *Trent* 21.1.2 decr.
57. *Aug Lat* 22 int 1.
58. *Sav* pr; *Laus Cov* pr; *Camb Dec* pr; Küppers, Hauptmann, and Baser 1964.
59. *Bat* pr; italics added.
60. *Chin Man* 1; see also *PRCC* 3.D-E.
61. *Friends I* (1673).
62. *Richmond* (1887).
63. *Ess.*
64. Wolf 1959.

for example, when the Free Church of Geneva in 1848 issued its elaboration of *The Apostles' Creed* as a confession but in 1883 abolished its authority, replacing it with the original text of *The Apostles' Creed* plus an appendix.[65] For even beyond all of the intellectual, scientific, and religious objections to the traditional functions of creeds and confessions of faith, the political revolutions of the modern era have also made the confessional and creedal tradition, including especially the alliance of that tradition with the political establishment, the object of attack. As part of his attack, Matthew Tindal singled out "this imposing temper of the ecclesiastics." It was, he said, "plain from history that the ambitious, domineering part of the clergy, the imposers of creeds, canons, and constitutions, have proved to be the common plagues of mankind."[66] The role of the emperor Constantine at the First Council of Nicaea in 325, which legislated the dogma of the Trinity, followed a half-century later by the adoption of the Nicene trinitarian creed as part of the law of the Roman empire under Emperor Theodosius I,[67] had made the empire and its successors, in Tindal's phrase, "the imposer of creeds" for more than a millennium. Even the political and religious upheavals of the Protestant Reformation did not, at least initially, shake the hegemony of *The Niceno-Constantinopolitan Creed* as a political force, and in some respects they even strengthened it. Although the criticism of creeds and confessions was already going on while that hegemony was still at least formally being acknowledged, the steady erosion of the religious and intellectual authority of creeds and confessions and the gradual political disestablishment of the churches reinforced each other throughout the eighteenth, nineteenth, and twentieth centuries.

Although the cultural and intellectual disestablishment of Christendom was less directly caught up in the power struggles of the time than was the political disestablishment, its effects on the context of Christian confessing were in some respects even more destructive, at least initially. The same critical-historical method that was used to investigate Homer or the Nordic sagas was applied to biblical, creedal, and confessional texts, showing them to have been fundamentally conditioned by the cosmological presuppositions of their own time, presuppositions, moreover, that the modern age did not and could not share.[68] The undermining, both by this historical-critical study and by the advances of science, of the credibility of biblical miracle stories, from the creation narrative in Genesis to the virgin birth of Christ and the resurrection of Christ in the Gospels to the eschatology

65. *PRE* 6:253–54 (Ch. Correvon).
66. *Chr Trad* 5:31.
67. *Theodosian Code* 16.1.2.
68. Frei 1974.

of the Apocalypse—the same four events of the biblical narrative whose recitation, phrase by phrase, constitutes the core both of *The Niceno-Constantinopolitan Creed* and of *The Apostles' Creed*[69]—put the church of the eighteenth and nineteenth centuries on the defensive against the dominant zeitgeist of the culture.[70] Therefore it called forth reformulations of the Christian confession. Some of these sought compromise, adjustment, or evasion in relation to Darwinian evolution and the new cosmologies.[71] Others strove to affirm the inspiration of the Bible and the truth of the creeds as unequivocally as had the confessional scholasticism of the seventeenth century.

At the same time, political and cultural disestablishment seemed to some to provide a liberating opportunity for the churches to reaffirm their confession without the burden of having to act as apologists for an established order of society that had in various ways, both obvious and subtle, distorted the Christian gospel by adopting it. For confession and creed did not necessarily depend on the state and its laws for enforcement, as the experience of the churches in the United States proved. In spite of all the dire predictions of the eighteenth century, Christian faith and life, and even Christian creedal confession, had managed to thrive under political disestablishment. Therefore it is historically essential to pay equal attention to the continuing tenacity of those whom Welch describes as "traditionalists . . . for whom . . . the gospel portrait was essentially unquestioned as a basis for Christological dogma,"[72] and hence to the continuing context that this tradition went on providing for the formulation of creeds and confessions, also in response to the new contexts that were being forced on the churches by the modern age. The dynamic of this interrelation between the old and the new contexts of Christian confessing makes itself evident in most of the texts in any collection of modern confessions such as this Part Five of *Creeds and Confessions of Faith in the Christian Tradition*, "Statements of Faith in Modern Christianity," under the headings "The Nineteenth Century: Putting Confessionalism and Denominationalism to the Test" and "The Twentieth Century: Globalization of Churches and Confessions."

Among the specific new contexts of confessing within the churches in the nineteenth and twentieth centuries, Geoffrey Wainwright has enumerated the "various 'movements' that had affected wide areas of Christendom over confessional boundaries: the biblical theology movement, the liturgical movement, the ecumeni-

---

69. *N-CP* 1–7; *Ap* 1–7.
70. *Syl* 7; *Bat* 4.
71. *Chr Trad* 5:238–41.
72. Welch 1972–85, 2:146n.

cal movement in its more technical sense, the movement to discover our common patristic roots and even to recover the controversial figures of later history in their originality and authenticity." "These movements," he concludes, "have provided us with a common language and with a greater possibility of substantive understanding and agreement."[73] Each has also provided all the churches with new ways of looking at, and even of formulating, creeds and confessions of faith.

Christian creeds and confessions, as well as Christian theology generally, had, of course, always striven to be *biblical*. In that sense, therefore, it may seem tautological or even presumptuous to use the term "biblical theology" for a twentieth-century development. Nevertheless something new had definitely happened. With some anticipations in the eighteenth and nineteenth centuries, the phenomenon of the new biblical theology in the twentieth century was made possible in part by the revived interest in the vocabulary of the Bible, fostered by the new methods of biblical philology.[74] Biblical theology was an effort to replace the old and supposedly static categories of the creeds and of dogmatics, which were regarded as having been unduly shaped both by Greek philosophical presuppositions and by confessional polemics, with themes that were more dynamic and that corresponded more closely to the biblical "history of salvation [*Heilsgeschichte*]"—which was itself one such theme. The move to biblical theology had a mixed effect on the history of creeds and confessions, whatever it may have meant for the reinterpretation of the tasks both of systematic theology and of biblical exegesis.[75] For on one hand it reinforced the biblical foundations of the traditional doctrines that had been confessed in the creeds and in that sense contributed, at least indirectly, to the vindication of the creeds. But by sometimes exaggerating the contrast between the New Testament and the beginnings of the catholic Christianity that expressed itself in the creeds and eventually in the councils, it did not always lead directly to a rehabilitation of the historic creeds as such. There was, nevertheless, a difference also in newer creeds and confessions as a direct consequence of the new attention to biblical theology. Perhaps nowhere does that change become more evident than in a comparison between the decrees of the First Vatican Council of 1869–70 and those of the Second Vatican Council of 1962–65—in their doctrinal emphasis, but even in their documentation and method of theological argumentation and proof. In the century between those two councils had come not only biblical theology as a whole, which was initially a largely Protestant phenomenon, but specifically the fundamental reappraisal of how the church

---

73. Wainwright 1986, 13.

74. *ABD* 6:483–505 (Henning Graf Reventlow).

75. *ABD* 1:1203–6 (John H. Leith). See, for example, *Leuen* 5.

should interpret Scripture that had been formulated in *Divino afflante Spiritu,* the encyclical issued by Pope Pius XII on 30 September 1943.[76]

Another striking difference of the Second Vatican Council from the First was the prominence of the *liturgy* in its decrees. This applies in a special way, of course, to the *Constitution on the Sacred Liturgy* itself, which, as the first decree of the council, set the tone for all that was to follow.[77] This constitution declares the liturgy, rather than any other dimension of the life and teaching of the church, to be *"the chief means* through which believers are expressing in their lives and demonstrating to others the mystery which is Christ, and the sort of entity the true church really is."[78] That emphasis remained in force when the council, at its fifth session, came to define the nature of the church in *Lumen gentium, The Dogmatic Constitution on the Church.* While reaffirming the "doctrine of the institution, the perpetuity, the force and the nature of the sacred primacy of the Roman pontiff and of his infallible magisterium,"[79] as these were affirmed by the Council of Trent and the First Vatican Council, this constitution concentrates on the church's worship of God and its service to the world rather than on its juridical or even its dogmatic authority. In these and other ways, this Western council was also striving to find a closer affinity with the Christian East, where what the church believes, teaches, and confesses is articulated primarily in the liturgy rather than in the comprehensive confession of the doctrines of the faith, as it is in Reformation Protestantism. There was an analogous development in the Anglican communion, as the historic tension between *The Thirty-Nine Articles of the Church of England* and *The Book of Common Prayer* was increasingly resolved in favor of the latter. But the confessional impact of the liturgical movement extended far beyond these communions, manifesting itself as well in many of the churches that had traditionally eschewed "formalism" and "ritualism" in their worship, and necessitating new attention also to the creeds, notably *The Niceno-Constantinopolitan Creed* for both the Eastern and the Western tradition and *The Apostles' Creed* for the West, as these creeds were imbedded in the liturgies of the churches. But as the Anglican example showed in a heightened form, this change could come at the cost of the specific confessions of the individual churches, in the case of Anglicanism *The Thirty-Nine Articles of the Church of England.*

Beginning as it did within Protestantism (including Anglicanism), *the ecumenical movement,* by bringing together representatives of many confessional tra-

---

76. Denzinger, 3825–3831.
77. *Vat II* 3.
78. *Vat II* 3.2; italics added.
79. *Vat II* 5.1.18.

ditions, also could have the effect of relativizing the authority of their particular confessions. When the Congregationalist *Declaration of the Oberlin National Council* of 1871 declares, "We especially desire, in prosecuting the common work of evangelizing our own land and the world, to observe the common and sacred law, that in the wide field of the world's evangelization, we do our work in friendly cooperation with all those who love and serve our common Lord," that is based on the distressing spectacle of denominational competition in the mission field. Many declarations of fellowship, concordats, mergers, and reunifications across historic confessional divisions took place during the nineteenth and especially the twentieth century.[80] These entailed, sometimes by what they said but perhaps more often by what they left unsaid, the demotion of the traditional confessions of the individual churches to a second-class status or their relegation to history.[81] But when ecumenism began to include not only various Protestant bodies but participants from Eastern Orthodoxy and eventually from Roman Catholicism, the authority of the church and of its traditions and creeds in those communions made the question of confessions more insistent, sometimes therefore reinforcing confessional identity even where it had not been dominant, or had been in decline, previously.[82] For in this ecumenical atmosphere, although it may seem paradoxical to some, members of the several confessional families such as the Reformed also found a new relation within their tradition.[83]

The Flowering of Creedal and Confessional Scholarship in the Modern Era

In its Decree on Ecumenism, the Second Vatican Council urged that "theology. . . *especially of an historical nature* must be taught with a due regard for the ecumenical point of view."[84] But according to an authoritative Roman Catholic theological dictionary, Roman Catholic "theology stagnates during the eighteenth century: development is almost exclusively confined to the historical disciplines (Church history)."[85] Similarly "in the history of Protestant theology," as Karl Barth once commented somewhat ruefully, "the nineteenth century brought with it the none too

80. Ehrenström and Gassmann 1979.

81. *Ev All* con; *Leuen* 37, 27–28.

82. Békés and Meyer 1982.

83. *Un Pres; Ref All.*

84. *Vat II* 5.3.10; italics added.

85. Rahner-Vorgrimler 459.

dignified sight of a general flight, of those heads that were wisest, into the study of history." [86] Although he himself was the leading exception to this pattern of the eighteenth, nineteenth, and twentieth centuries—while at the same time, in his monograph of 1931 on Anselm of Canterbury and above all in the history of Protestant theology during the nineteenth century of 1947 from which that quotation comes, making brilliant contributions to historical theology—he was speaking about some of his most eminent teachers, principally Adolf Harnack. [87] As Page Smith has said, describing a general cultural phenomenon of this era, "tradition had lost its authority," and "history was pressed into service." [88] For just as the decline of belief in the inerrancy of the Bible was, somewhat paradoxically, accompanied by a phenomenal growth in the scholarly study of the Bible, so the nineteenth and twentieth centuries in Protestant theology, for all their antipathy to creeds and confessions— or perhaps even because of it—were at the same time the golden age of a creedal and confessional research that had to be taken no less seriously by those for whom creeds, confessions, and church councils had retained their authority. Therefore *The Fourteen Theses* coming out of the first conference at Bonn between Old Catholic, Eastern Orthodox, and Anglican theologians in 1874 specify that authoritative tradition "is partly to be found in the consensus of the great ecclesiastical bodies standing in historical continuity with the primitive church," an exercise in dogma, but also that it is "partly to be gathered by scientific method from the written documents of all centuries," an exercise in scholarship. [89] As another Roman Catholic reference book acknowledged in 1998, therefore, it was not with Roman Catholic or Eastern Orthodox or confessional Protestant traditionalists but with "Harnack and Kattenbusch that the study of confessions of faith arose at the end of the nineteenth century," [90] in a way and to a degree that had never been true of more "creedal" and "confessional" ages. It was at that time that two massive editions of the Latin and the Greek church fathers—the *Corpus Scriptorum Ecclesiasticorum Latinorum,* begun in 1866, and *Die griechischen christlichen Schriftsteller der ersten drei Jahrhunderte,* begun in 1897—made available, often for the first time, early Christian texts that were critically edited and philologically sound. On that basis it became possible to separate later accretions from original readings, and thus to document, with meticulous attention to detail, the history of the words and phrases that even-

86. Barth 1959, 311.
87. See Zahn-Harnack 1951, 412–18.
88. Smith 1964, 55.
89. *Bonn I* 9.1.
90. Lacoste, 248.

tually came together into creeds. The monumental works on the text and history of *The Apostles' Creed* by Carl Paul Caspari, published between 1866 and 1879, and by Ferdinand Kattenbusch, which came out between 1894 and 1900, laid foundations and provided resources on which every subsequent study of that history, including the present one, has had to rely, and they virtually created a new field of scholarship. In the English-speaking world, such works as James Franklin Bethune-Baker's *Meaning of Homoousios in the "Constantinopolitan" Creed* of 1901 and A. C. McGiffert's *Apostles' Creed: Its Origin, Its Purpose, and Its Historical Interpretation* of 1902, and two generations later J. N. D. Kelly's *Early Christian Creeds* originally published in 1950 and *The Athanasian Creed* of 1964 made major contributions to this new field.

During the same period, partly as an effort to continue this research on early creeds into the Reformation era, and partly as a counterpoise to it, scholarly editions and works on other confessions of faith, including above all the Protestant confessions of the sixteenth and seventeenth centuries, also flourished. A catalog of only some of these will illustrate how many of the critical editions of individual confessions and how many of the collections of confessions on which any scholarship in the field must still draw are the products of the nineteenth and twentieth centuries in many churches and many countries (listed in chronological order of their first editions): J. C. W. Augusti, *Corpus Librorum Symbolicorum qui in Ecclesia Reformatorum auctoritatem publicam obtinuerunt* (1827); H. A. Niemeyer, *Collectio Confessionum in Ecclesiis Reformatis Publicatarum* (1840); E. J. Kimmel, *Libri symbolici ecclesiae orientalis* (1843; *Appendix*, 1850); E. L. T. Henke, *Theologorum Saxonicorum consensus repetitus fidei vere Lutheranae* (1846); E. G. A. Böckel, *Die Bekenntnisschriften der evangelisch-reformirten Kirche* (1847); Heinrich Joseph Denzinger, *Enchiridion Symbolorum et Definitionum* (1854, with dozens of editions since); Edward Bean Underhill, *Confessions of Faith and Other Public Documents Illustrative of the History of the Baptist Churches of England in the Seventeenth Century* (1854); Wilhelm Gass, *Symbolik der griechischen Kirche* (1872); Philip Schaff, *Bibliotheca Symbolica Ecclesiae Universalis: The Creeds of Christendom* (1877); Williston Walker, *The Creeds and Platforms of Congregationalism* (1893); J. J. Overbeck, *The Orthodox Confession of the Catholic and Apostolic Eastern Church of Peter Mogila* (1898).

This development was continued and expanded in the twentieth century: Karl E. F. Müller, *Die Bekenntnisschriften der reformierten Kirche* (1903); Jon Michalcescu, *Thēsauros tēs Orthodoxias: Die Bekenntnisse und die wichtigsten Glaubenszeugnisse der griechisch-orientalischen Kirche* (1904); W. J. McGlothlin, *Baptist Confessions of Faith* (1910); Eduard Schwartz, *Acta Conciliorum Oecumenicorum* (1914); G. Friedrich Bente, *Concordia Triglotta* (1921); Antoine Malvy and Marcel Viller,

La confession orthodoxe de Pierre Moghila (1927); Caius Fabricius, *Corpus Confessionum* (1928–43); *Die Bekenntnisschriften der evangelisch-lutherischen Kirche* (1930); W. F. Schmidt and K. Schornbaum, *Die fränkischen Bekenntnisse: Eine Vorstufe der Augsburgischen Konfession* (1930); J. Michael Reu, *The Augsburg Confession: A Collection of Sources with an Historical Introduction* (1930); Wilhelm Niesel, *Bekenntnisschriften und Kirchenordnungen der nach Gottes Wort reformierten Kirche* (1938); Ioannēs Karmirēs, *Ta dogmatika kai symbolika mnēmeia tēs orthodoxou katholikēs ekklēsias* [The dogmatic and symbolic monuments of the Orthodox Catholic Church] (1952); Thomas F. Torrance, *The School of Faith: The Catechisms of the Reformed Church* (1959); Theodore G. Tappert et al., *The Book of Concord: The Confessions of the Evangelical Lutheran Church* (1959); William L. Lumpkin, *Baptist Confessions of Faith* (1959); Joseph Alberigo, *Conciliorum Oecumenicorum Decreta* (1962); Brian A. Gerrish, *The Faith of Christendom* (1963); John H. Leith, *Creeds of the Churches: A Reader in Christian Doctrine from the Bible to the Present* (1963); Arthur C. Cochrane, *Reformed Confessions of the Sixteenth Century* (1966); George Mastrantonis, *Augsburg and Constantinople: The Correspondence Between the Tübingen Theologians and Patriarch Jeremiah II of Constantinople on the Augsburg Confession* (1982); Howard John Loewen, *One Lord, One Church, One Hope, and One God: Mennonite Confessions of Faith* (1985); Irvin B. Horst, *Mennonite Confession of Faith Adopted April 21st, 1632, at Dordrecht, The Netherlands* (1988); Norman P. Tanner et al., *Decrees of the Ecumenical Councils* (1990); Mark Noll, *Confessions and Catechisms of the Reformation* (1991); Gerald Bray, *Documents of the English Reformation* (1994); Romeo Fabbri, *Confessioni di fede delle chiese cristiane* (1996); and Robert Kolb and Timothy Wengert, *The Book of Concord: The Confessions of the Evangelical Lutheran Church* (2000).

      Creeds and Confessions of Faith in the Christian Tradition seeks to continue that scholarly editorial tradition into the twenty-first century.

In Light of Their History, Do Creeds Have a Future as Well as a Past?

When the review of the history of creeds and confessions of faith is confronted with the unique predicament of creedal Christianity in the modern age, the question becomes urgent: In light of their history, do creeds and confessions of faith have a future as well as a past? This question is, of course, bound up with the broader question of "the future of belief" itself[91] — bound up with it, but not identical to it. There have certainly been many individual Christians, and even some entire Chris-

---

91. Dewart 1966.

tian communities and churches—to cite modern examples, the Church of the Brethren, and the Disciples of Christ or "Christians," in the spirit of Thomas and Alexander Campbell[92]—who did not originally respond to the imperative to "confess
with your lips and believe in your heart"[93] by composing a fixed creed or confession at all, until they were compelled to do something of the sort in the twentieth
century.[94] Instead, they took as literally and permanently true the promise of Christ
in the Gospel: "When they deliver you up, do not be anxious how you are to speak
or what you are to say; for what you are to say will be given to you *in that hour;* for
it is not you who speak, but the Spirit of your Father speaking through you,"[95] a
promise that even so creedal and catholic a theologian as Augustine recommended
as more important than any intellectual and scholarly preparation.[96] Nevertheless,
just as the response to that imperative by the vast majority of churches through the
centuries has taken the form of a confession or creed, so the future of creeds is of
fundamental importance for the future of belief and for the future of the churches
as well, even of churches that might not be thought of as "confessional" in the usual
sense. As Williston Walker summarizes the experience of American Congregationalism in the nineteenth century, leading up to *The "Commission" Creed of 1883:*

> The free system of Congregationalism allows every church to for-
> mulate its own creed; but this confession is coming more and more
> to be employed as a local statement of faith, especially by newly
> formed churches. . . . Though imposed by no authority and ac-
> cepted only in so far as it is its own commendation, it gives the
> Congregational body what no other considerable denomination
> of Christians in America possesses,—a widely recognized creed,
> written in the language and expressing the thought of living men.[97]

Therefore Walker concludes his collection of *Creeds and Platforms of Congregationalism* with this statement of faith.

Without minimizing in any way the likelihood that changes in worldview
during the twenty-first and twenty-second centuries will be even more drastic than

---

92. *Dec Addr.*
93. Rom 10.9.
94. See *Design* of 1968 from the Disciples of Christ.
95. Mt 10.19–20; italics added.
96. Augustine *On Christian Doctrine* 4.15.32 (*NPNF*–I 2:585).
97. Walker, 582.

those of the nineteenth and twentieth have been—in Robert Frost's striking meta-
phor, a hundred-yard dash followed by a pole vault—it is appropriate to be reminded by history that there has in fact been a vast diversity of worldviews, as well
as of creedal forms and confessional genres, during the two millennia of Christian
history. On first glance, the seventeenth-century *Westminster Confession of Faith* and
the twentieth-century *Masai Creed,* when set alongside each other, may not seem
even to belong to the same species, and the cultures in which they arose are poles
apart.[98] And yet the continuity between them is all the more substantial because of
that great diversity. For the history of conflict, compromise, and accommodation of
Christian thought and teaching in relation to shifting worldviews suggests the following paradoxical generalization: there has never been any picture of the world,
whether scientific or philosophical or even "mythological," with which the confession of the Christian faith has been entirely compatible, although undoubtedly it
has found a better fit with some than with others; but there has also never been any
picture of the world within which the confession of the faith has proved to be altogether impossible.[99] It does not appear unwarranted to propose that this paradox
will continue to apply to the confessions and creeds of the future, if any.

Even those who have little or no use for creeds and confessions of faith
are usually prepared to concede, often even with considerable enthusiasm, that the
moral example and the ethical teachings of Jesus have some sort of permanent, even
transcendent, value. In the words of Roden Noël, "What if men take to following
where He leads, Weary of mumbling Athanasian creeds?"[100] The motto of Charles
M. Sheldon's immensely influential novel, *In His Steps,* of 1897, "What would Jesus
do?" is a populist expression of the same elevation of deeds over creeds, which has,
in one form of another, asserted itself repeatedly, especially in the modern period.
It is undeniable that there is an initial attractiveness and a haunting charm to the
eloquent words of Albert Schweitzer as he concluded his account of the process by
which, in the modern period, the orthodox confessional dogma about the person
of Christ had steadily lost its credibility:

> We can find no designation which expresses what He is for us. He
> comes to us as One unknown, without a name, as of old, by the
> lake-side, He came to those men who knew Him not. He speaks
> to us the same word: "Follow thou me!" and sets us to the tasks

98. *West; Masai.*
99. *Laus Cov* 10.
100. Roden Noël, "The Red Flag."

which He has to fulfil for our time. He commands. And to those who obey Him, whether they be wise or simple, He will reveal Himself in the toils, the conflicts, the sufferings which they shall pass through in His fellowship, and, as an ineffable mystery, they shall learn in their own experience Who He is.[101]

Schweitzer himself obeyed this command, "Follow thou me," which is enunciated repeatedly in the Gospel of Matthew,[102] by giving up positions of great academic prestige and devoting himself to a life of service as a medical missionary in French Equatorial Africa. But in twentieth-century Africa, as in first-century Judaea and fourth-century Asia Minor and sixteenth-century Europe, the full measure of obedience to that command could not stop short of facing another challenge, likewise enunciated in the Gospel of Matthew, "Who do you say that I am?" and of dealing with the answer of the apostle Peter to that question, "You are the Christ, the Son of the living God"[103]—which was a confession and a creed, and as such an indispensable component of obedience to the command and imperative of Jesus Christ. In the future, too, the command must lead to the question, and the question must lead to some sort of answer.

In the European Protestant theology that had, during the nineteenth and twentieth centuries, produced Albert Schweitzer and the many other critics of orthodox Christology whose "discomfort with creed" we have been summarizing here, the cultural and political crisis of the first half of the twentieth century answered the question "Do creeds and confessions have a future as well as a past?" in another and an even more dramatic way. The attempt by the ideology of National Socialism to fill the vacuum created by the decline of creedalism seemed, on the face of it, to provide the "German Christians" with the opportunity for a new and "postconfessional" alternative that would be relevant to a new era. But in *The Barmen Declaration* of 1934, which was a confession of faith, the signatories spoke out against "the errors of the 'German Christians' of the present Reich Church government which are devastating the church," and resolved to "confess the following evangelical truths," one of which was: "We reject the false doctrine, as though the church were permitted to abandon the forms of its message and order to its own pleasure or to changes in prevailing ideological and political convictions [*ihrem Belieben oder dem Wechsel der jeweils herrschenden weltanschaulichen und poli-*

101. Schweitzer [1906] 1961, 403.

102. Mt 4.19, 8.29, 9.19, 19.21 (AV).

103. Mt 16.15–16.

tischen Überzeugungen]."[104] It would be foolish to imagine that the Christian faith will never be subjected to such pressures and temptations again, or that when it is, it will not be obliged yet again to "confess evangelical truths" and its "message" in some similar fashion.

At Barmen, this obligation to reject the "false doctrine" of National Socialism and of the German Christians was addressed by German Protestants—Lutheran, Reformed, and United—all of whom stood in one or another confessional tradition and who were therefore accustomed to the use of a creedal statement to combat heresy, even though for some of them the historic confessions had lost some of their authority.[105] But history suggests that such an obligation may also evoke confessional statements from those who had for a long time resisted the idea. Even the Presbyterian critics of extreme confessionalism and defenders of revivalism were obliged, in the Cumberland Presbyterian *Confession of Faith* of 1814/1888 and then in *The Auburn Declaration* of 1837, to employ the formal instrumentality of a confession of faith to make their point. Another instance was the issuance of the new "confessions [*homologiai*]" that were prepared by Eastern Orthodoxy during the sixteenth and seventeenth centuries, which are collected in various editions and in "Affirmations of Faith in Eastern Orthodoxy," Part Two of *Creeds and Confessions of Faith in the Christian Tradition*. The statement of Nikolaj Nikaronovič Glubokovský, "The West incessantly asks us for the symbolical books of Orthodoxy. We have no need of them. The faith of the seven first councils is sufficient for us," expressed the characteristic and historic Eastern view of confessions.[106] But such an answer was in fact rather disingenuous, because Eastern Orthodoxy had indeed found a "need for them" as a response to the direct, and above all the indirect, threat that had come from the Protestant confessionalisms of the Reformation and immediately post-Reformation periods, both Lutheran and Reformed, as well as from the Roman Catholic confessionalism of the Council of Florence and the Council of Trent: the translation of *The Augsburg Confession* into Greek and the confessional texts sent as epistles to the patriarch of Constantinople by Lutheranism;[107] *The Eastern Confession of the Christian Faith by Cyril Lucar* of 1629,[108] which was perceived as Calvinism disguised in Greek Orthodox raiment; and the "Latinism" and scholasticism that dominated much of Eastern Orthodox teaching in the theological acade-

104. *Barm* pr; 3.
105. For an overview of confessional authority in these churches, see Urban 1972.
106. ap. Scott 1928, 351.
107. *Jer II.*
108. *Lucar.*

mies, also in the Russian empire. In a series of confessional documents, therefore, the East was compelled, at least for a while, to adopt the format of the Reformation confessions as an expression for the systematic statement of Orthodox doctrine. In the future, too, the adherents of beliefs that Christians will again find it necessary to condemn will compose creeds and confessions of some kind, requiring a condign rejoinder, if perhaps a reluctant one.

The ecumenical movement of the nineteenth and twentieth centuries produced its own version of that thesis. The unofficial practice by individual Christians and entire church bodies of ignoring denominational borders, to the point of condoning and encouraging eucharistic intercommunion in spite of fundamental doctrinal differences even about the eucharist,[109] has often been seen as synonymous with confessional indifference: indifference not simply to this or that specific confession of the past but to the very notion of a binding and separating confessional definition. Repeatedly, however, when the time has come to make such practices of fellowship official and to justify them both within and beyond the new fellowship, the justification has perforce taken the form of a confessional statement.[110] An ecumenism based on ignoring or forgetting the historic creeds and confessions of faith may well be condemned to repeat the process that had originally produced them. Thus the successive revisions of the formula for reunion and common declaration of the Church of South India in the first half of the twentieth century[111] were made necessary in part by the continuing authority of the mother churches from which the missions had originally come and to which the uniting churches had to give an account. But an even more pressing demand was the need of these uniting churches to give an account to their own membership and to one another of the principles underlying their unification. Whatever new initiatives may arise in the continuing and increasingly urgent quest for Christian unity, it is inherently difficult to imagine their being able to dispense with the confessional statement, even if it is only a statement of why earlier confessional statements are thought no longer to be normative.

The history of creeds and confessions of faith likewise documents the complexity of their relation to personal faith, of the relation between *fides quae creditur,* "the faith which one believes," and *fides qua creditur,* "the faith with which one believes." After affirming concerning *The Niceno-Constantinopolitan Creed,* "This is also my faith, because this is the catholic faith,"[112] Augustine proceeded to show

109. See, for example, *Un Pres* 30.

110. *Leuen.*

111. *CSI 1929; CSI 1947.*

112. Augustine *On the Trinity* 1.4.7 (*NPNF*-II 3:20).

how completely it had become *his* faith by articulating a speculative and yet deeply existential theory of the trinitarian structure of the human soul. Similarly, commenting on the first article of *The Apostles' Creed*, "I believe in God, the Father Almighty, Maker of heaven and earth," which raises all the questions about the doctrine of *creatio ex nihilo* that had dogged theology in the age of medieval scholasticism and the additional questions that would dog theology in the age of modern evolutionism, Luther trumped them all by affirming that the creed was speaking here and now about him, Martin Luther, the offspring of the natural sexual union of his parents: "I believe that God has created me and all that exists."[113] And in his "Legend of the Grand Inquisitor" F. M. Dostoevsky brought a prelate of the church, who turned out to be an atheist with a correct and orthodox creed, into confrontation with the living presence of the One whom that creed confessed.[114]

Perhaps an analogy may be helpful. When compact disks are stacked on the shelves of a music store or a living room, there is nothing so static as CDs. In that form they can be shipped and stored, preserved inert literally for centuries, handed down from parents to children and grandchildren without ever being played or heard. They are a commodity, listed in a catalog to be bought and sold. Yet it is their very "inertness" and static quality, their continuity, that enables them, at a moment's notice, to become suddenly dynamic in the sound of a Beethoven quartet or Mozart's *Magic Flute*—or, for that matter, the *Symbolum Nicaenum* of Johann Sebastian Bach's *Mass in B Minor*. Historically, that is precisely what creeds and confessions of faith have repeatedly done through the centuries.

And they can go on doing it.

113. *Luth Sm Cat* 2.1–2.
114. F. M. Dostoevsky *The Brothers Karamazov*, book 5, ch 5.

The Seventeenth and Eighteenth Centuries: Confessionalizing the Outcome of the Reformation

Many of the confessions of the Reformation, as presented in Part Four above, spoke as though there would be no further need for new confessions; and the reception and authority of some of them during the centuries since the Reformation, notably of *The Book of Concord* of 1580 and *The Westminster Confession of Faith* of 1647, may seem to substantiate that impression of finality.

It is, however, refuted, and massively, by the history of confessions since. For what we are calling here "the outcome of the Reformation" consisted, not only in such codifications as *The Book of Concord* and *The Westminster Confession of Faith*, but in the seemingly fissiparous rise of new churches and movements, schisms and sects—and consequently of new confessions of faith. For a variety of reasons that were often no less political than they were ecclesiastical or doctrinal, a disproportionate number of these new churches and new confessions arose within English-speaking Protestantism during the seventeenth and eighteenth centuries; and they went on arising in the nineteenth and twentieth.

Common to many of them was the concept of "the continuing Reformation," the conviction that the circumstances of the sixteenth century had held back the full force of the reformatory impulse and had led to compromises in doctrine, polity, and morality, which it was now time to rectify. It is that "outcome of the Reformation" that was being confessionalized in many of the confessions from this period that follow here.

English Separatists (Brownists), *A True Confession*, 1596

Technically, this *True Confession* of 1596 belongs, of course, to the sixteenth century. But just as *The Canons of the Synod of Dort* of 1619 and *The Westminster Confession of Faith* of 1647, though composed in the seventeenth century, may properly be seen as a conclusion to Part Four dealing with confessions coming out of the Reformation of the sixteenth century, to which they have been assigned in these volumes, so, conversely, *A True Confession* may fittingly open Part Five on the modern period. For it speaks on behalf of the Puritans, Separatists, and Congregationalists—and, derivatively and eventually, the Baptists—who were to play such a prominent part in the confessional development of English-speaking Protestantism during the seventeenth and eighteenth centuries.

The history of *A True Confession* is bound up with the stormy career of the brilliant but erratic Robert Browne (c. 1550–1633). Although he would eventually accept ordination at the hands of an Anglican bishop, serving as master of St. Olave's School in Southwark, he was, during the most influential years of his life, a principal critic of episcopacy and a leading spokesman for the teaching, as formulated here in *A True Confession* (article 23), that "every Christian congregation hath power and commandment to elect and ordain their own ministry." The teachings underlying this polity are set forth here in a confessional form, effectively for the first time, yet, as Williston Walker notes, "fitted to stand for many years."[1]

But the juxtaposition of this Congregationalist confession and → the English Baptist *London Confession* of 1644 shows the latter to be (as Melanchthon's 1540 revision of *The Augsburg Confession* was called) a *Variata* of the former. Thus, although Browne's own intellectual odyssey led him from radical Separatism to a more or less conventional Anglicanism of a Puritan stripe, it was no less logical to move in the opposite direction, from a Congregationalist view of church and ministry to a Baptist view of church and baptism.

We have reproduced the text of 1596 as it stands, adapting the orthography, capitalization, and spelling much as is done in present-day printings of the Authorized (King James) Version of the English Bible, which was nearly contemporary. In the original edition, the biblical citations were identified in the margin; in his edition, Walker appended them as notes to each article.

1. Walker, 47.

Edition: Walker, 59–74.

Literature: Burrage 1906; *ODCC* 243–44; Walker, 41–48.

English Separatists (Brownists), *A True Confession*, 1596

A True Confession of the faith and humble acknowledgment of the allegiance which we, Her Majesty's subjects, falsely called Brownists, do hold towards God and yield to Her Majesty and all others that are over us in the Lord. Set down in articles or positions, for the better and more easier understanding of those that shall read it, and published for the clearing of ourselves from those unchristian slanders of heresy, schism, pride, obstinacy, disloyalty, sedition, etc., which by our adversaries are in all places given out against us.

We believe with our hearts and confess with our mouths:

1. That there is but[a] one God, one Christ, one Spirit, one church, one truth, one faith,[b] one rule of obedience to all Christians, in all places.

2. That God is a Spirit,[c] whose being is of himself,[d] and giveth being, moving, and preservation to all other things,[e] being himself eternal, most holy, every way infinite, in greatness, wisdom, power, goodness, justice, truth, etc.[f] And that in this Godhead there be three[g] distinct persons,[h] coeternal, coequal, and coessential,[i] being every one of the one and the same God, and therefore not divided, but distinguished one from another by their several and peculiar property: the Father of none,[j] the Son begotten of the Father from everlasting,[k] the Holy Ghost proceeding from the Father and the Son before all beginnings.[l]

3. That God[m] hath decreed in himself from everlasting, touching all things and the very least circumstances of every thing, effectually to work and dispose them according to the counsel of his own will, to the praise and glory of his great name. And touching his chiefest creatures, that God hath[n] in Christ[o] before the foundation

a. [Dt 6.4; Hos 13.4; Mk 12.29, 32; Eph 4.4–6; 1 Cor 12.13]

b. [Rom 16.26; 1 Cor 4.17, 16.1; Gal 1.8–9]

c. [Jn 4.24]

d. [Ex 3.14; Is 43.10–11]

e. [Rom 11.36; Acts 17.28; Gn 1]

f. [1 Tm 1.17; Rv 4.18; Is 6.3, 66.1–2; Ps 145.3, 8–9, 17, 147.5; Rom 1.20]

g. [1 Jn 5.7; Mt 28.19; Hg 2.5–6; Heb 9.14]

h. [Prv 8.22; Jn 1.1; Heb 9.14; Phil 2.6; Jn 5.18; Eph 4.4–6]

i. [Jn 10.30, 38; 1 Cor 2.11–12; Heb 1.3]

j. [Jn 5.26; 1 Cor 8.6]

k. [Jn 1.14, 18, 3.16; Mi 5.2; Ps 2.7]

l. [Jn 14.16, 1.16; Gal 4.16]

m. [Is 46.10; Rom 11.34–36; Acts 15.18, 2.22; Gn 45.5–8; Mt 10.29–30, 20.15; Eph 1.11]

n. [Eph 1.3–4, 11]

o. [Mt 25.34]

of the world,[a] according to the good pleasure of his will,[b] ordered some men and angels to eternal life, to be accomplished through Jesus Christ[c] to the praise of the glory of his grace.[d] And on the other hand hath likewise[e] before of old, according[f] to his just purpose,[g] ordained other both angels and men to eternal condemnation,[h] to be accomplished through their own corruption to the praise of his justice.[i]

4. That in the beginning[j] God made all things, of nothing, very good, and created[k] man after his own image and likeness in righteousness and holiness of truth. That straightway[l] after, by the subtlety of the serpent which Satan used as his instrument,[m] himself with his angels having sinned before and not kept their first estate, but left their own habitation: first Eve,[n] then Adam by her means, did wittingly and willingly fall into disobedience and transgression of the commandment of God. For the which death[o] reigned over all—yes, even[p] over infants also, which have not sinned after the like manner of the transgression of Adam, that is, actually, yet are[q] all since the fall of Adam begotten in his own likeness after his image, being conceived and born in iniquity, and so by nature the children of wrath and servants of sin, and subject to death and all other calamities due unto sin in this world and forever.

5. That all mankind being thus fallen and become altogether dead in sin, and subject to the eternal wrath of God both by original and actual corruption, the elect[r] are redeemed, quickened, raised up, and saved again, not of themselves, neither by works, lest any man should boast himself, but wholly and only by God of his free grace and mercy through faith in Christ Jesus,[s] who of God is made unto

a. [Eph 1.5; Rom 9.11–13; Mal 1.2; 2 Tm 1.9]

b. [Acts 13.48; Eph 1.4–5; 1 Tm 5.21; Mt 25.31, 34]

c. [Eph 1.5, 7, 10; Col 1.14, 17–19, 2.10; Rom 8.19, 30; Rv 19.10]

d. [Eph 1.6–9, 11]

e. [Jude 4]

f. [Rom 9.11–12, 15, 17–18; Mal 1.3; Ex 9.16]

g. [Jude 4, 6; Rom 9.22; Mt 25.41]

h. [2 Pt 2.12; 2 Cor 4.3–4; 1 Pt 2.8; Jn 3.19]

i. [Prv 16.4; Rom 2.5, 9.22]

j. [Gn 1; Col 1.16; Is 45.12; Heb 11.3; Rv 4.11]

k. [Gn 1.26–27; Eph 4.24; Eccl 7.31]

l. [Gn 3.1, 4–5; 2 Cor 11.3; Jn 8.44]

m. [2 Pt 2.4; Jn 8.44; Jude 6]

n. [Gn 3.1–3, 6; 1 Tm 2.14; Eccl 7.31; Gal 3.22]

o. [Rom 5.12, 18–19, 6.23; Gn 2.17]

p. [Rom 5.14, 9.11]

q. [Gn 5.3; Ps 51.5; Eph 2.3]

r. [Gn 3.15; Eph 2.4–5; Gn 15.6; Rom 4.2–5, 3.24–26; Jn 3.16]

s. [1 Cor 1.30–31; Phil 3.8–11; Jer 23.5–6, 9.23–24]

us wisdom and righteousness and sanctification and redemption, that according as it is written, "He that rejoiceth let him rejoice in the Lord."

6. That this therefore only is life[a] eternal, to know the only true God, and whom he hath sent into the world, Jesus Christ. And that on the contrary the[b] Lord will render vengeance in flaming fire unto them that know not God and which obey not the gospel of our Lord Jesus Christ.

7. That the rule of this knowledge, faith, and obedience concerning the[c] worship and service of God and all other Christian duties is not the opinions, devices, laws, or constitutions of men, but the written word of the everlasting God, contained in the canonical books of the Old and New Testament. [Ps 119.105]

8. That in this[d] word Jesus Christ hath revealed whatsoever his Father thought needful for us to know, believe, and obey as touching his[e] person and offices, in whom all the promises of God are Yea and in whom they are Amen, to the praise of God through us. [Heb]

[2 Cor 1.10]

9. That touching his person, the Lord Jesus, of whom[f] Moses and the prophets wrote and whom the apostles preached, is the[g] everlasting Son of God by eternal generation, the brightness of his Father's glory and the engraven form of his person; coessential, coequal, and coeternal, God with him and with the Holy Ghost; by whom he hath made the worlds, by whom he upholdeth and governeth all the works he hath made; who also, when the fullness of time was come, was made man of a woman, of the[h] tribe of Judah, of the[i] seed of David and Abraham, to wit, of Mary that Blessed Virgin, by the Holy Ghost coming upon her and the power of the Most High overshadowing her; and was also[j] in all things like unto us, sin only excepted. [Gal 4.4; Gn 3.15]

10. That touching his office, he[k] only is made the Mediator of the New Testament, even of the everlasting covenant of grace between God and man, to be perfectly and fully the Prophet,[l] Priest, and King of the church of God forevermore.

a. [Jn 17.3, 3.36; Jer 31.33–34]
b. [2 Thes 1.8; Eph 1.6; Jn 3.36]
c. [Ex 10.4–6; Dt 4.2, 5–6; Gn 6.22; Ex 39.42–43; 1 Chr 28.19]
d. [Is 29.13; Mt 15.9; Jn 5.39; 2 Pt 1.16, 19; 2 Tm 3.16–17]
e. [Dt 18.18; Jn 1.18, 15.15, 4.25; Acts 3.22]
f. [Lk 24.44; Jn 5.46; Acts 10.41, 43]
g. [Prv 8.22; Mi 5.2; Jn 1.1–3; Heb 1; Col 1.15–17]
h. [Heb 7.14; Rv 5.5]
i. [Rom 1.3; Gn 22.18; Mt 1.1, etc.; Lk 3.23, etc.; Is 7.14; Lk 1.26–27, etc.; Heb 2.16]
j. [Heb 4.15; Is 53.3–4, 9; Phil 2.7–8]
k. [1 Tm 2.5; Heb 9.15, 13.20; Dn 9.24–25]
l. [Dt 18.15, 18; Ps 110.4; Ps 45; Is 9.6–7; Acts 5.31; Is 55.4; Heb 7.24; Lk 1.32–33]

11. That he[a] was from everlasting, by the just and sufficient authority of the Father and in respect of his manhood from the womb, called and separated hereunto, and anointed also most fully and abundantly with all necessary gifts, as is written: God hath not measured out the Spirit unto him.

[Jn 3.34]

12. That this[b] office, to be Mediator, that is, Prophet, Priest, and King of the church of God, is so proper to him as neither in the whole nor in any part thereof it can be transferred from him to any other.

13. That touching his[c] prophecy, Christ hath perfectly revealed out of the bosom of his Father the whole word and will of God that is needful for his servants, either jointly or severally, to know, believe, and obey: that he hath spoken and doth speak to his church in his own[d] ordinance, by his own ministers and instruments only, and not by any false[e] ministry at any time.

14. That touching his[f] priesthood, being consecrated, he hath appeared once to put away sin by offering and sacrificing of himself, and to this end hath fully performed and suffered all those things by which God through the blood of that, his cross, in an acceptable sacrifice, might be reconciled to his elect. And having[g] broken down the partition wall, and therewith finished and removed all those legal rites, shadows, and ceremonies, is now[h] entered within the veil into the Holy of Holies to the very heaven and presence of God, where he forever liveth and sitteth at the right hand of majesty, appearing before the face of his Father to make intercession for such as come unto the throne of grace by that new and living way; and not that only, but maketh his people a[i] spiritual house, a holy priesthood, to offer up spiritual sacrifices acceptable to God through him. Neither doth the Father accept, or Christ offer, any other sacrifice, worship, or worshipers.

15. That touching his[j] kingdom, being risen, ascended, entered into glory, set at the right hand of God, all power in heaven and earth given to him, which power he[k] now exerciseth over all angels and men, good and bad, to the preserva-

---

a. [Prv 8.23; Is 42.6, 49.1, 5, 11.2–5; Acts 10.38]

b. [1 Tm 2.5; Heb 7.24; Dn 7.14; Acts 4.12; Is 43.11; Lk 1.33]

c. [Dt 18.15, 18; Acts 3.22–24; Mt 3.17; Jn 1.18, 17.8; Eph 1.8–9; 2 Tm 3.15–17]

d. [Prv 9.3; Jn 13.20; Lk 10.16; Mt 10.40–41; Dt 33.8, 10]

e. [Mt 7.15–16, 24.23–24; 2 Pt 2; 2 Tm 4.3–4; Rom 10.14–15; Jer 23.21; 2 Jn 10]

f. [Jn 17.19; Heb 5.7–9, 9.26; Is 53; Rom 5.19; 1 Pt 1.2; Col 1.20; Eph 5.2]

g. [Eph 2.1, 4.15–16; Heb 9–10]

h. [Heb 4.14, 16, 9.24, 10.19–20]

i. [Rom 3.34; 1 Pt 2.5; Rv 1.5–6, 8.3–4; Rom 12.1; Mk 9.49–50; Mal 1.14; Jn 4.23–24; Mt 7.6–8; Is 1.12, etc.]

j. [1 Cor 15.4, etc.; 1 Pt 3.21–22; Mt 28.18, 20]

k. [Jos 5.14; Zec 1.8, etc.; Mk 1.27; Heb 1.14]

tion and salvation of the elect, to the overruling and destruction of the reprobate;[a] communicating and applying the benefits, virtue, and fruits of his prophecy and priesthood unto his elect, namely, to the remission, subduing, and taking away of their sins, to their justification, adoption of sons, regeneration, sanctification, preservation, and strengthening in all their spiritual conflicts against Satan, the world, and the flesh, etc., and continually dwelling in, governing, and keeping their hearts in his true faith and fear by his Holy Spirit. Which, having[b] once given it, he never taketh away from them, but by it still begetteth and nourisheth in them repentance, faith, love, obedience, comfort, peace, joy, hope, and all Christian virtues, unto immortality, notwithstanding that it be sometimes, through sin and temptation, interrupted, smothered, and as it were overwhelmed for the time. Again on the contrary,[c] ruling in the world over his enemies, Satan, and all the vessels of wrath; limiting, using, restraining them by his mighty power, as seemeth good in divine wisdom and justice, to the execution of his determinate counsel, to wit, to their seduction, hardening, and condemnation, delivering them up to a reprobate mind, to be kept in darkness, sin, and sensuality unto judgment.

16. That this kingdom shall be then fully perfected when he shall the[d] second time come in glory with his mighty angels unto judgment, to abolish all rule, authority, and power, to put all his enemies under his feet, to separate and free all his chosen from them forever, to punish the wicked with everlasting perdition from his presence, to gather, join, and carry the godly with himself into endless glory, and then to deliver up the kingdom to God, even the Father, that so the glory of the Father may be full and perfect in the Son, the glory of the Son in all his members, and God be all in all.

17. That in the meantime, besides his absolute rule in the world, Christ hath here on earth a[e] spiritual kingdom and a canonical regimen in his church over his servants. Which church he hath[f] purchased and redeemed to himself, as a peculiar inheritance (notwithstanding[g] many hypocrites do for the time lurk amongst them):

a. [Eph 5.26–27; Rom 5–8, 14.17; Gal 5.22–23; 1 Jn 4.13, etc.]

b. [Ps 51.10–12, 89.30–31, 33–34; Jb 33.29–30; Is 54.8–10; Jn 13.1, 16.31–32; Lk 22.31–32, 40; 2 Cor 12.7–9; Eph 6.10–11, etc.; Rom 11.29; Gal 5.17, 22–23]

c. [Jb 1.6, 2; 1 Kgs 22.19; Is 10.5, 15; Rom 9.17–18, 1.21, 2.4–6; Eph 4.17–19; 2 Pt 3.3; 1 Thes 5.3, 7; Is 57.20–21; 2 Pt 2]

d. [Dn 12.2–3; Jn 5.22, 28–29; Mt 25.31; 1 Cor 15.24; Mt 13.41, 49; 2 Thes 1.9–10; 1 Thes 4.17; Jn 17.22–23; 1 Cor 15.28]

e. [Jn 18.36; Heb 3.6, 10.21; 1 Tm 3.15; Zec 4.17]

f. [Acts 20.28; Ti 2.14]

g. [Mt 13.47, 22.12; Lk 13.25]

calling[a] and winning them by the power of his word unto the faith, separating[b] them from amongst unbelievers, from idolatry, false worship, superstition, vanity, dissolute life, and works of darkness, etc.; making them a royal priesthood, a holy nation, a people set at liberty to show forth the virtues of him that hath called them out of darkness into his marvelous light; gathering[c] and uniting them together as members of one body in his faith, love, and holy order, unto all general and mutual duties, instructing[d] and governing them by such offices and laws as he hath prescribed in his word; by which offices and laws he governeth his church, and by none[e] other.

18. That to this[f] church he hath made the promises, and given the seals of his covenant, presence, love, blessing, and protection.[g] Here are the holy oracles, as in the side of the ark, surely kept and purely taught. Here are[h] all the fountains and springs of his grace, continually replenished and flowing forth. Here is he lifted up to all nations,[i] hither he inviteth all men to his supper, his marriage feast; hither ought[j] all men of all estates and degrees that acknowledge their Prophet, Priest, and King to repair, to be[k] enrolled amongst his household servants, to be under his heavenly conduct and government, to lead their lives in his walled sheepfold and watered orchard, to have communion here with the saints, that they may be made meet to be partakers of their inheritance in the kingdom of God.

19. That as all[l] his servants and subjects are called hither to present their bodies and souls and to bring the gifts God hath given them, so, being come, they are here by himself bestowed in their several order, peculiar place, due use, being fitly compact and knit together by every joint of help, according to the effectual work in the measure of every part, unto the edification of itself in love; whereunto when he[m] ascended up on high, he gave gifts unto men, that he might fill all these things, and

a. [Mk 16.15-16; Col 1.21; 1 Cor 6.11; Ti 3.3-5]

b. [Is 52.11; Ezr 6.21; Acts 2.40; 2 Cor 6.14; Acts 17.3-4, 19.9; 1 Pt 2.4-5, 9, 25]

c. [Is 60.4, 8; Ps 110.3; Acts 2.41; Eph 4.16; Col 2.5-6]

d. [Is 62.6; Jer 3.15; Ez 34; Zec 11.8; Heb 12.29-31; Mt 28.20]

e. [Mt 7.15, 24.23-24; 2 Tm 4.3-4; Jer 7.30-31, 23.21; Dt 12.32; Rv 2.2, 22.18-19]

f. [Lv 26.11-12; Mt 28.19-20; Rom 9.4; Ez 48.35; 2 Cor 6.18]

g. [Is 8.16; 1 Tm 3.15, 4.16, 6.3, 5; 2 Tm 1.15; Ti 1.9; Dt 31.26]

h. [Ps 46.4-5; Ez 47.1, etc.; Jn 7.38-39; Is 11.12; Jn 3.14; Is 49.22]

i. [Is 11.12; Jn 3.14; Is 49.22; Is 55.1; Mt 6.33, 22.2; Prv 9.4-5; Jn 7.37]

j. [Dt 12.5, 11; Is 2.2-3; Zec 14.16-19]

k. [Is 44.5; Ps 87.5-6; Sg 4.12; Gal 6.10; Col 1.12-13; Eph 2.19]

l. [Ex 25.2, 35.5; 1 Cor 12.4-7, 12.18; Rom 12.4-6; 1 Pt 4.10; Eph 4.16; Col 2.5]

m. [Eph 4.8, 10-13; Rom 12.7-8, 16.1; 1 Cor 12.4-8, 11, 14-18, 28; 1 Tm 3, 5.3, 9, 17, 21; Acts 6.2-3, 14.23, 20.27-28; Phil 1.1] hath distributed these gifts unto several functions in his church, having instituted and ratified to[a] continue unto the world's end only this public, ordinary ministry of pastors, teachers, elders, deacons, helpers to the instruction, government, and service of his church.

20. That this ministry is exactly described,[b] distinguished, limited, concerning their office, their calling to their office, their administration of their office, and their maintenance in their office by most perfect and plain[c] laws in God's word; which laws it is not lawful for these ministers, or for the whole church, wittingly to neglect, transgress, or violate in any part, nor yet to receive any other laws brought into the church by any person whatsoever.

21. That[d] none may usurp or execute a ministry but such as are rightly called by the church whereof they stand ministers, and that such, so called, ought to give all diligence[e] to fulfill their ministry, to be found faithful and unblamable in all things.

22. That this ministry is alike given to every Christian congregation, with like power and commission to have and enjoy the same, as God offereth fit men and means, the same rules given to all for the election and execution thereof in all places.[f]

23. That as every Christian congregation[g] hath power and commandment to elect and ordain their own ministry according to the rules prescribed, and[h] whilst they shall faithfully execute their office, to have them in superabundant love for their work's sake, to provide for them, to honor them and reverence them, according to the dignity of the office they execute; so have they also[i] power and commandment when any such default either in their life, doctrine, or administration breaketh out, as by the rule of the word debarreth them from, or depriveth them of, their ministry, by due order to depose them from the ministry they exercised; yes, if the case so require and they remain obstinate and impenitent, to orderly cut them off by excommunication.

a. [Rv 22.18–19; Mt 28.20; 1 Tm 6.13–14]

b. [Prv 8.8–9; Heb 3.2, 6; 1 Tm; Acts 6.3, 5, 6, 14.23, 20.17, etc.; 1 Pt 5.2–3; 1 Cor 5.4–5, 11–13, etc., 9.7, 9, 14]

c. [Heb 2.3, 3.3, 12.25, etc.; 2 Tm 3.14–15; Gal 1.8–9; 1 Tm 6.13–14; Dt 12.32, 4.2; Rv 22.18–19]

d. [Nm 16.5, 40, 18.7; 2 Chr 26.18; Jn 10.1–2, 3.27; Heb 5.4; Acts 6.3, 5–6, 14.23; Ti 1.5]

e. [Acts 2.28; 1 Cor 4.1–2; Col 4.17; 1 Tm 1.18–19, 4.12, 5.21, 6.11–14; 2 Tm 1.13–14, 3.14, 4.5; 1 Pt 5.1–4]

f. [Mt 28.20; 1 Cor 14.33, 36, 12.4–7, 4.17, 16.1; Eph 4.10–13; 1 Cor 3.21–23; Mt 18.17]

g. [Acts 6.3, 5–6, 14.23; 2 Cor 8.19; Acts 15.2–3, 22, 25; 1 Tm 3.10, 4.14, 5.22; Nm 8.9–10]

h. [1 Thes 5.12–13; 1 Tm 5.3, 17; Heb 13.17; 1 Cor 9; Gal 6.6]

i. [1 Tm 3.10, 5.22; Rom 16.17; Phil 3.2, 18–19; 1 Tm 6.3, 5; Ez 44.11, 13; Mt 18.17]

24. That[a] Christ hath given this power to receive or to cut off any member to the whole body together of every Christian congregation, and not to any one member apart or to more members sequestered from the whole, or to any other congregation to do it for them; yet that[b] each congregation ought to use the best help they can hereunto, and the most meet member they have to pronounce the same in their public assembly.

25. That every member of each Christian congregation, how excellent, great, or learned soever, ought to be subject to this censure and judgment of Christ; yet ought not the church without great care and due advice to proceed against such public persons.[c]

26. That for the[d] keeping of this church in holy and orderly communion, as Christ hath placed some special men over the church, who by their office are to govern, oversee, visit, watch, etc. So[e] likewise for the better keeping thereof in all places, by all the members, he hath given authority and laid duty upon them all to watch one over another.

27. That whilst the ministers and people thus remain together in this holy order and Christian communion, each one endeavoring to do the will of God in their calling and thus to walk in the obedience of faith, Christ hath promised to be present with them, to bless and defend them against all adversary power, and that the gates of hell shall not prevail against them.[f]

28. But when and where this holy order and diligent watch was intermitted, neglected, violated, Antichrist, that man of sin, corrupted and altered the holy ordinances, offices, and administrations of the church, brought in and erected a strange new forged ministry, liturgy, and government; and the nations, kingdoms, and inhabitants of the earth were made drunken with this cup of fornications and abominations, and all people enforced to receive the beast's mark and worship his image, and so brought into confusion and Babylonish bondage.[g]

29. That the present ministry retained and used in England, of archbishops, lord bishops, deans, prebendaries, canons, peti-canons, archdeacons, chancellors, commissaries, priests, deacons, parsons, vicars, curates, hireling roving preachers, churchwardens, parish clerks, their doctors, proctors, and whole rabble of those

a. [Ps 122.3; Acts 1.47; Rom 16.2; Lv 20.4–5, 24.14; Nm 5.3; Dt 13.9; Mt 18.17; 1 Cor 5.4; 2 Cor 2.6–8]

b. [1 Cor 3.21–23; Acts 15; 1 Cor 3.4–5, 12.20]

c. [Lv 4; Ps 141.5, 2.10–12, 149.8–9; 1 Chr 26.20; Acts 11.2, 4; 1 Tm 5.19–21]

d. [Sg 3.3; Is 62.6; Ez 33.2; Mt 14.45; Lk 12.42; Acts 20.28; Heb 13.17]

e. [Mk 13.34, 37; Lk 17.3; 1 Thes 5.14; Gal 6.1; Jude 3, 20; Heb 10.24–25, 12.15]

f. [Dt 28.1, etc.; Mt 28.20; Lk 12.35–38; Mt 16.18; Zec 2.5, 12.2–4; Ps 125.2, 132.12–13]

g. [Rv 9, 13, 17–18; 1 Thes 2.3–4, 9–12; Ps 74; Is 14.13–14; Dn 7.25, 8.10–12, 11.31; 1 Tm 4.1–2; 1 Jn 2.18, 22, 4.3]

courts with all from and under them set over these cathedral and parishional assemblies in this confusion, are a strange and anti-Christian ministry and offices, and are not that ministry above named, instituted in Christ's Testament, or allowed in or over his church.[a]

30. That their[b] offices, entrance, administration, and maintenance, with their[c] names, titles, privileges, and prerogatives, the power and rule they usurp over and in these ecclesiastical assemblies over the whole ministry, whole ministration, and affairs thereof, yea over one another by their making priests, citing, suspending, silencing, deposing, absolving, excommunicating, etc., their confounding of ecclesiastical and civil jurisdiction, causes, and proceedings in their persons, courts, commissions, visitations; the rest of less rule, taking their ministry from and exercising it under them, by their[d] prescription and limitation, swearing canonical obedience unto them, administering by their devised, imposed, stinted popish liturgy, etc., are sufficient proofs of the former assertion, the particulars therein being duly examined by and compared to the rules of Christ's Testament.

31. That these ecclesiastical assemblies, remaining in confusion and bondage under this anti-Christian ministry, courts, canons, worship, ordinances, etc., without freedom or power to redress any enormity, have not, in this confusion and subjection, Christ, their Prophet, Priest, and King; neither can be in this estate (whilst we judge them by the rules of God's word) esteemed the true, orderly gathered, or constituted churches of Christ, whereof the faithful ought to become or stand members or to have[e] any spiritual communion with them in their public worship and administration.

32. That[f] by God's commandment all that will be saved must with speed come forth of this anti-Christian estate,[g] leaving the suppression of it unto the magistrate to whom it belongeth.[h] And that both all such as have received or exercised any of these false offices or any pretended function or ministry in or to this false and anti-Christian constitution, are willingly in God's fear to give over and leave those

---

a. [Rv 9.3, etc., 13.15–17, 18.15, 17; Rom 12.7–8; Eph 4.11–12; 1 Tm 3.15, 5.17]

b. [Rv 9.3, etc., 18.15, 17; Jn 10.1; Dn 7.8, 25, 8.10–12; 2 Thes 2.3–4, 8–9; Rv 17.4–5, 16]

c. [Lk 22.25–26; Rv 14.11, 17.3–5, 13.15–17; 1 Pt 5.3; Jn 3.29; Rv 2.1; 1 Kgs 12.27; Zec 11.15–16]

d. [Rv 13.15–17; Is 29.13; Mt 7.7–8; Gal 1.10, etc., 2.4–5; Col 2.20, 22–23; Ez 8.5, 13.9–11, 18–19; Mi 2.11; Mal 1.8, 13–14]

e. [Rv 18.2; 1 Cor 14.33; Jer 15.19; Mal 1.4, 6, 8; Hos 4.14, etc.; Rom 6.16; 2 Pt 2.19; Lv 17; Hos 4.15; 1 Cor 10.18–20; 2 Cor 6.14–16; Rv 18.4; Sg 1.6–7]

f. [Rv 18.4; Is 48.20, 52.11; Jer 50.8, 51.6, 45; Zec 2.6]

g. [2 Chr 15, 27.6; 2 Kgs 23.5, etc.; Rom 13.4; Mt 22.21; Rv 17.16]

h. [Zec 13.2, 4–6; Jer 51.26; Ps 119.59–60, 128; Prv 5.20; Is 8.11–12]

unlawful offices and no longer to minister in this manner to these assemblies in this estate. And that none also, of what sort or condition soever, do give any part of their goods, lands, money, or money-worth to the maintenance of this false ministry and worship upon any commandment or under any color whatsoever.

33. That being come forth of this anti-Christian estate unto the freedom and true profession of Christ, besides the[a] instructing and well guiding of their own families, they are[b] willingly to join together in Christian communion and orderly covenant, and by confession of faith and obedience of Christ to[c] unite themselves into peculiar congregations; wherein, as members of one body whereof Christ is the only head, they are to worship and serve God according to his word, remembering[d] to keep holy the Lord's day.

34. That such as[e] God hath given gifts to interpret the Scriptures, tried in the exercise of prophecy, giving attendance to study and learning, may and ought by the appointment of the congregation to teach publicly the word, until the people be meet for, and God manifest men with able gifts and fitness to such office or offices as Christ hath appointed to the public ministry of his church; but no[f] sacraments to be administered until the pastors or teachers be chosen and ordained into their office.

35. That[g] whereas there shall be a people fit, and men furnished with meet and necessary gifts, they do not only still continue the exercise of prophecy aforesaid, but do also, upon due trial, proceed unto choice and ordination of officers for the ministry and service of the church, according to the rule of God's word; and that so they[h] hold on still to walk forward in the ways of Christ for their mutual edification and comfort, as it shall please God to give knowledge and grace thereunto. And particularly, that[i] such as be of the seed,[1] or under the government of any of the church, be even in their infancy received to baptism and made partakers of the

a. [Gn 18.19; Ex 13.8, 14; Prv 31.26–27; Eph 6.4; Dt 6.7; Ps 78.3–4]

b. [Lk 17.37; Ps 110.3; Mt 6; Is 44.5; Acts 2.41–42; Jer 50.4–5; Neh 9.38; Acts 2.41–42]

c. [1 Cor 1.2, 12.14; Rv 1.20, 2.1, 8, 12, 18, 3.1, 7, 14; Eph 2.19; Col 2.19]

d. [Ex 20.8; Rv 1.10; Acts 20.7; 1 Cor 16.2]

e. [1 Cor 14; Rom 12.6; 1 Cor 12.7; 1 Pt 4.10; Acts 13.15; 1 Thes 5.20]

f. [Nm 16.10, 39–40; Rom 12.7; Heb 5.4; Jn 1.23, 25]

g. [Lv 8; Acts 6.5–6, 14.21–23; Ti 1.5, etc.; 1 Cor 12.7–8, 14–15; 1 Tm 3]

h. [Col 2.5–7; 2 Thes 2.15; Jude 3, etc.; Mt 28.20]

i. [Acts 2.38–39; 1 Cor 7.14; Rom 11.16; Gn 17.7, 12, 27; 1 Cor 10.2; Ps 22.30; Ex 12.48–49; Acts 16.15, 33; 1 Cor 1.16; Mk 10.13–16; Gal 3.29]

1. As article 37 explains, this refers to children who "are the seed of the faithful by one of the parents."

sign of God's covenant made with the faithful and their seed throughout all generations. And that[a] all of the church that are of years and able to examine themselves
do communicate also in the Lord's supper, both men[b] and women, and in[c] both
kinds, bread and wine, in which[d] elements, as also in the water of baptism, even
after they are consecrate, there is neither transubstantiation into, nor consubstantiation with, the body and blood of Jesus Christ, whom the heavens must contain until
the time that all things be restored.[e] But they are in the ordinance of God signs and
seals of God's everlasting covenant, representing and offering to all the receivers,
but exhibiting only to the true believers,[f] the Lord Jesus Christ and all his benefits
unto righteousness, sanctification, and eternal life, through faith in his name, to the
glory and praise of God.

[Acts 3.21, 7.56]

36. That thus[g] being rightly gathered, established, and still proceeding in
Christian communion and obedience of the gospel of Christ, none is to separate for
faults and corruptions which may—and, so long as the church consisteth of mortal
men, will—fall out and arise among them, even in a true constituted church, but by
due[h] order to seek redress thereof.

37. That[i] such as yet see not the truth may hear the public doctrine and
prayers of the church, and with all meekness are to be sought by all means; yet[j] none
who are grown in years to be received into their communion as members, but such
as do make confession of their faith, publicly desiring to be received as members
and promising to walk in the obedience of Christ. Neither any[k] infants, but such
as are the seed of the faithful by one of the parents, or under their education and
government. And further not any[l] from one congregation to be received members
in another, without bringing certificate of their former estate and present purpose.

38. That though congregations be thus distinct and several bodies, every
one as a compact city in itself, yet are they all to walk by one and the same rule, and
by all means convenient to have the counsel and help one of another in all needful

a. [Mt 26.26–27; 1 Cor 11.28, 10.3–4, 16–17; Acts 2.42, 20.7–8]
b. [Gal 3.28; Acts 2.42, 1.14; 1 Cor 12.13]
c. [Mt 26.26–27; 1 Cor 10.3–4, 16, 11.23–29]
d. [1 Cor 10.16–17, 11.23–26, etc.; Mt 26.26–29, 15.17; Jn 12.8]
e. [Gn 17.11; Rom 4.11; Ex 12.13; Heb 13.20]
f. [1 Cor 11.26–29, 10.3–5; Rom 2.28–29; Acts 15.9; Rom ch 5–8]
g. [Lv 4.13, etc.; 2 Chr 15.9, 17, 30.18–19; Rv ch 2–3; 1 Cor 1.10; Phil 2.1–6, 3.15–16; Jude 19]
h. [2 Cor 13.1–2; Rv ch 2–3; 1 Thes 5.14; 2 Thes 3.6, 14; Mt 18.17; 1 Cor. 5.4–5; Acts 15.1–2]
i. [1 Cor 14.24–25; Ps 18.49; Rom 15.9–10; 1 Tm 2.4; 2 Tm 2.25]
j. [2 Cor 6.14–16; Ezr 4.3; Ex 12.43; Lv 22.25; Ex 34.12; Dt 7; Is 44.5; Acts 19.18]
k. [Ex 20.5–6; 1 Cor 7.14; Gn 17.7, 12, 27; Ex 12.48–49; Acts 16.15, 33]
l. [Acts 9.26–27; Rom 16.1–2; 2 Cor 3.23; Col 4.10]

affairs of the church, as members of one body in the common faith, under Christ their head.[a]

39. That it is the office and duty of princes and magistrates, who[b] by the ordinance of God are supreme governors under him over all persons and causes within their realms and dominions, to[c] suppress and root out by their authority all false ministries, voluntary religions, and counterfeit worship of God, to abolish and destroy the idol temples, images, altars, vestments, and all other monuments of idolatry and superstition, and to take and convert to their own civil uses, not only the benefit of all such idolatrous buildings and monuments, but also the revenues, demeans, lordships, possessions, glebes, and maintenance of any false ministries and unlawful ecclesiastical functions whatsoever within their dominions; and on the other hand[d] to establish and maintain by their laws every part of God's word, his pure religion, and true ministry, to cherish and protect all such as are careful to worship God according to his word and to lead a godly life in all peace and loyalty; yea, to enforce all their subjects, whether ecclesiastical or civil, to do their duties to God and men, protecting and maintaining the good, punishing and restraining the evil, according as God hath commanded, whose lieutenants they are here on earth.

40. That therefore the[e] protection and commandments of the princes and magistrates maketh it much more peaceable, though[f] no whit at all more lawful, to walk in the ways and ordinances of Jesus Christ which he hath commanded his church to keep without spot and unrebukable until his appearing in the end of the world.[g] And that in this behalf the brethren, thus minded and proceeding as is beforesaid, do both continually supplicate to God and, as they may, to their princes and governors, that thus and under them they may lead a quiet and peaceable life in all godliness and honesty.

41. That if God incline the magistrates' hearts to the allowance and protection of them therein, they account it a happy blessing of God, who granteth such nourishing fathers and nourishing mothers to his church, and be careful to walk worthy so great a mercy of God in all thankfulness and obedience.[h]

a. [Ps 122.3; Sg 8.8–9; 1 Cor 4.17, 16.1]

b. [Rom 13.3–4; 1 Pt 2.3, 14; 2 Chr 19.4; ch 29, 34; Jgs 17.5–6; Mt 22.21; Ti 3.1]

c. [2 Kgs 10.26–28; 2 Chr 17.6; Prv 16.12, 25.2–5; Acts 19.27; Rv 17.16]

d. [Dt 17.14, 18–20; Jos 1.7–8; 2 Chr 17.4, 7–9, 19.4, etc., ch 29–30; Dn 6.25–26; Ps 2.10–12, 72.1, etc.; Is 49.23; Rv 21.24; Ezr 7.26]

e. [Prv 16.15; Ezr 5–6; Acts 9.31; 1 Tm 2.2; Dn 6.25–26; Rv 21.24]

f. [Acts 4.18–19, 5.28–29; Dn 6.7–10, 22; Lk 21.12–13; Mt 28.20; 1 Tm 5.21, 6.13–14]

g. [Ps 72.1, etc.; 1 Tm 2.2; 2 Chr 15.1–2; Hg 1.4, 14, 2.5]

h. [Ps 126.1, etc.; Is 49.13, 60.16; Ps 72.1, etc.; Rom 13.3; 1 Tm 2.2–4]

42. That if God withhold the magistrates' allowance and furtherance herein, they[a] yet proceed together in Christian covenant and communion thus to walk in the obedience of Christ even through the midst of all trials and afflictions, not accounting their goods, lands, wives, children, fathers, mothers, brethren, sisters, no, nor their own lives dear unto them, so as they may finish their course with joy, remembering always that we ought to obey God rather than man, and grounding[b] upon the commandment, commission, and promise of our Savior Christ, who, as he hath all power in heaven and in earth, so hath also promised if they keep his commandments, which he hath given without limitation of time, place, magistrates' allowance or disallowance, to be with them unto the end of the world, and when they have finished their course and kept the faith, to give them the crown of righteousness, which is laid up for all them that love his appearing.

[Acts 5.29, 17.6–7]

43. That they do all willingly and orderly pay and perform all manner of lawful and accustomed duties unto all men, submitting in the Lord themselves, their bodies, lands, goods, and lives to the magistrates' pleasure. And that every way they acknowledge, reverence, and obey them according to godliness, not because of wrath only but also for conscience's sake.[c]

44. And thus do we, the subjects of God and Her Majesty, falsely called Brownists, labor to give unto God that which is God's and unto Caesar that which is Caesar's, endeavoring ourselves to have always a clear conscience towards God and towards men; and if any take this to be heresy, then do we with the apostle freely confess that after the way which they call heresy we worship God, the Father of our Lord Jesus Christ, believing all things that are written in the law, and in the prophets and apostles, and whatsoever is according to this word of truth published by this state or holden by any Reformed churches abroad in the world.

[Acts 24.14]

45. Finally, whereas we are much slandered, as if we denied or misliked that form of prayer commonly called the Lord's Prayer, we thought it needful here also concerning it to make known that we believe and acknowledge it to be a most absolute and most excellent form of prayer such as no men or angels can set down the like. And that it was taught and appointed by our Lord Jesus Christ, not that we should be tied to the use of those very words, but that we should according to that rule make all our requests and thanksgiving unto God, forasmuch as it is a perfect form and pattern, containing in it plain and sufficient directions of prayer for all

a. [Acts 2.40–42, 4.19, 5.28–29, 41, 16.20, etc., 17.6–7, 20.23–24; 1 Thes 3.3; Phil 1.27–29; Dn 3.16–18, 6.7, 10, 22–24; Lk 14.26–27, 21.12–14; 2 Tm 2.12, 3.12; Heb 10.32, etc.; 1 Pt 4; Rv 2.10, 25–26, 6.9, 12.11]

b. [Mt 28.18–20; 1 Tm 6.13–16; 2 Tm 4.7–8; Rv 2.10, 14.12–13, 22.16–20]

c. [Rom 13.1, 5–7; Mt 22.21; 2 Chr 27; Ezr 7.26; Ti 3.1; 1 Pt 2.13, etc.]

occasions and necessities that have been, are, or shall be to the church of God, or any member thereof to the end of the world.[a]

Now unto him that is able to keep us that we fall not, and to present us faultless before the presence of his glory with joy, that is, to God only wise, our [Jude 24–25] Savior, be glory and majesty and dominion and power, both now and forever. Amen.

a. [Mt 6.9, etc.; Lk 11.2, etc.; Mt 14.30, 26.39, 42; Acts 1.24–25, 4.24, etc.; Rom 8.26–27; Rv 8.3–4; Eph 6.18–19; Phil 4.6; Heb 11.18–21]

Particular Baptists, *[First] London Confession*, 1644

During the half-century following the → *True Confession* of 1596, the ecclesiastical and political situation, but therefore also the confessional position, of English "Separatism" had become vastly more complicated. Among the church groups that had begun to acquire an identity requiring a distinct confessional clarification were the Baptists. Although some English ("General") Baptists stood in the Arminian camp of Reformed Protestantism (see → the Arminian *Remonstrance* of 1610), others shared the Calvinism of the Synod of Dort of 1619 (see → *The Canons of the Synod of Dort*), including the belief in particular election or predestination; hence the label "Particular Baptists." As B. R. White has noted, "The Calvinistic Baptists first appeared as a self-conscious group with the publication of their Confession in London in 1644. This was to provide the basic theological platform for their program of evangelism, church-planting and organization of associations for the years down to the Restoration. . . . Clearly their intentions were to manifest their substantial agreement with the prevailing forms of Calvinistic orthodoxy and to expound the basic elements of their doctrine of the Church."[1]

Both of those intentions become even clearer on the basis of a comparison between this *London Confession* and its predecessor, *A True Confession*. In the words of Stanley A. Nelson, "A True Confession was their confessional model, and post-Dort Calvinism marked their orthodoxy."[2] But in addition, as Glen H. Stassen and then James M. Renihan have shown, there is the possibility of Mennonite influence in its formulations both of the doctrine of the church and of the doctrine of baptism. The question of the compatibility between Calvinistic predestinarianism (articles 3 and 19) and the requirement of a conscious decision of faith for baptism and admission of an individual into the church (article 39) recurs throughout subsequent Baptist confessions.

Edition: Lumpkin, 144–71.

Literature: S. A. Nelson 1994; Renihan 1996, Stassen 1962; B. R. White 1996.

---

1. B. R. White 1996, 59.
2. S. A. Nelson 1994, 42.

Particular Baptists, *[First] London Confession,* 1644

The Confession of Faith, of those churches which are commonly (though falsely) called Anabaptists: presented to the view of all that fear God, to examine by the touchstone of the word of truth: As likewise for the taking off those aspersions which are frequently both in pulpit and print (although unjustly) cast upon them.

Acts 4.20: "We cannot but speak the things which we have seen and heard."

Isaiah 8.20: "To the Law and to the testimony, if they speak not according to this rule, it is because there is no light in them."

2 Corinthians 1.9–10: "But we had the sentence of death in ourselves, that we should not trust in ourselves, but in the living God, which raiseth the dead; who delivered us from so great a death, and doth deliver, in whom we trust that he will yet deliver."

To all that desire the lifting up of the name of the Lord Jesus in sincerity, the poor despised churches of God in London send greeting, with prayers for their further increase in the knowledge of Christ Jesus.

      We question not but that it will seem strange to many men, that such as we are frequently termed to be, lying under that calumny and black brand of heretics, and powers of division as we do, should presume to appear so publicly as now we have done: but yet notwithstanding we may well say, to give answer to such, [1 Sm 29.30] what David said to his brother, when the Lord's battle was a fighting. "Is there not a cause?" Surely, if ever people had cause to speak for the vindication of the truth of Christ in their hands, we have, that being indeed the main wheel at this time that sets us awork; for had anything by men been transacted against our persons only, we could quietly have sat still, and committed our cause to him who is a righteous judge, who will in the great day judge the secrets of all men's hearts by Jesus Christ: But being it is not only us, but the truth professed by us, we cannot, we dare not but speak; it is no strange thing to any observing man, what sad charges are laid, not only by the world, that know not God, but also by those that think themselves much wronged, if they be not looked upon as the chief worthies of the church of God, and watchmen of the city: But it hath fared with us from them, as from the [Sg 5.6, 7] poor spouse seeking her beloved, Cant 5.6, 7. They finding us out of that common roadway themselves walk, have smote us and taken away our veil, that so we may by them be recommended odious in the eyes of all that behold us, and in the hearts of all that think upon us, which they have done both in pulpit and print, charging us with holding free will, falling away from grace, denying original sin, disclaiming of magistracy, denying to assist them either in persons or purse in any of their lawful commands, doing acts unseemly in dispensing the ordinance of baptism, not to be named amongst Christians: All which charges we disclaim as notoriously untrue, though by reason of these calumnies cast upon us, many that fear God are discouraged and forestalled in harboring a good thought, either of us or what we profess; and many that know not God encouraged, if they can find the place of our meeting, to get together in clusters to stone us, as looking upon us as a people holding such things, as that we are not worthy to live: We have therefore for the clearing of the truth we profess, that it may be at liberty, though we be in bonds, briefly published a confession of our faith, as desiring all that fear God, seriously to consider whether (if they compare what we here say and confess in the presence of the Lord Jesus and his saints) men have not with their tongues in pulpit, and pens in print, both spoken and written things that are contrary to truth; but we know our God in his own time will clear our cause, and lift up his Son to make him the chief cornerstone, though he has been (or now should be) rejected of master builders. And because it may be [Ps 118.22] conceived, that what is here published, may be but the judgment of some one particular congregation, more refined than the rest; we do therefore here subscribe it, some of each body in the name, and by the appointment of seven congregations, who though we be distinct in respect of our particular bodies, for convenience sake, being as many as can well meet together in one place, yet are all one in communion, holding Jesus Christ to be our head and Lord; under whose government we desire alone to walk, in following the Lamb wheresoever he goeth; and we believe [Rv 14.4] the Lord will daily cause truth more to appear in the hearts of his saints, and make them ashamed of their folly in the land of their nativity, that so they may with one shoulder, more study to lift up the name of the Lord Jesus, and stand for his appointments and laws; which is the desires and prayers of the condemned churches of Christ in London for all saints. Subscribed in the names of seven churches in London:

William Kiffin
Thomas Patience
John Spilsbery
George Tipping
Samuel Richardson

Thomas Skippard

Thomas Munday

Thomas Gunne

John Mabbatt

John Webb

Thomas Killcop

Paul Hobson

Thomas Goare

Joseph Phelpes

Edward Heath

The Confession of Faith of Those Churches Which Are Commonly (Though Falsely) Called Anabaptists

[1 Tm 6.16]

1. That God as he is in himself, cannot be comprehended of any but himself, dwelling in that inaccessible light, that no eye can attain unto, whom never man saw, nor can see; that there is but one God, one Christ, one Spirit, one faith, one baptism,[a] one rule of holiness and obedience for all saints, at all times,[b] in all places to be observed.

2. That God is of himself, that is, neither from another,[c] nor of another, nor by another, nor for another: but is a Spirit,[d] who as his being is of himself,[e] so he gives being, moving, and preservation to all other things, being in himself eternal, most holy, every way infinite in greatness, wisdom, power, justice, goodness, truth, etc.[f] In this Godhead, there is the Father, the Son, and the Spirit; being every one of them one and the same God; and therefore not divided, but distinguished one from

[1 Cor 8.6]

another by their several properties; the Father being from himself, the Son of the Father from everlasting,[g] the Holy Spirit proceeding from the Father and the Son.[h]

3. That God hath decreed in himself from everlasting touching all things,[i]

a. [1 Tm 2.5; Eph 4.4–6; 1 Cor 12.4–5, 6, 13; Jn 14]

b. [1 Tm 6.3, 13–14; Gal 1.8–9; 1 Tm 3.15]

c. [Is 44.67, 43.11, 46.9]

d. [Jn 4.24]

e. [Ex 3.14]

f. [Rom 11.36; Acts 17.28]

g. [Prv 8.22–23; Heb 1.3; Jn 1.18]

h. [Jn 15.16; Gal 4.6]

i. [Is 46.10; Rom 11.34–36; Mt 10.29–30]

effectually to work and dispose them according to the counsel of his own will, to [Eph 1.11] the glory of his name; in which decree appeareth his wisdom, constancy, truth, and faithfulness; wisdom[a] is that whereby he contrives all things; constancy[b] is whereby the decree of God remains always immutable; truth[c] is that whereby he declares that alone which he hath decreed, and though his sayings may seem to sound sometimes another thing, yet the sense of them doth always agree with the decree; faithfulness [Is 44.10] is that whereby he effects that he hath decreed, as he hath decreed. And touching his creature man, God had in Christ before the foundation of the world,[d] according to the good pleasure of his will, foreordained some men to eternal life through Jesus Christ,[e] to the praise and glory of his grace, leaving the rest in their sin to their just condemnation, to the praise of his justice.

   4. In the beginning God made all things very good,[f] created man after his own image and likeness,[g] filling him with all perfection of all natural excellency and uprightness, free from all sin. But long he abode not in this honor, but by the sub- [Ps 49.20] tlety of the serpent,[h] which Satan used as his instrument, himself with his angels having sinned before, and not kept their first estate,[i] but left their own habitation; first Eve then Adam being seduced[j] did wittingly and willingly fall into disobedience and transgression of the commandment of their great Creator, for the which death came upon all, and reigned over all, so that all since the fall are conceived in sin, and brought forth in iniquities, and so by nature children of wrath, and servants of sin, subjects of death,[k] and all other calamities due to sin in this world and forever, being considered in the state of nature, without relation to Christ.

   5. All mankind being thus fallen, and become altogether dead in sins and trespasses, and subject to the eternal wrath of the great God by transgression; yet [Jer 31.2] the elect, which God hath loved with an everlasting love,[l] are redeemed, quickened, and saved, not by themselves, neither by their own works, lest any man should boast

a. [Col 2.3]

b. [Nm 23.19–20]

c. [Jer 10.10; Rom 3.4]

d. [Eph 1.3–7; 2 Tm 1.9; Acts 13.48; Rom 8.29–30]

e. [Jude 4, 6; Rom 9.11–13; Prv 16.4]

f. [Gn 1; Col 1.16; Heb 11.3; Is 45.12]

g. [Gn 1.26; 1 Cor 15.45–46; Eccl 7.31]

h. [Gn 3.1, 4–5; 2 Cor 11.3]

i. [2 Pt 1.4; Jude 6; Jn 8.44]

j. [Gn 3.1–2, 6; 1 Tm 2.14; Eccl 7.31; Gal 3.22]

k. [Rom 5.12, 18–19, 6.23; Eph 2.3; Rom 5.12]

l. [Gn 3.15; Eph 1.3, 7, 2.4, 9; 1 Thes 5.9; Acts 13.38]

himself, but wholly and only by God of his free grace and mercy through Jesus Christ, who of God is made unto us wisdom, righteousness, sanctification, and redemption, that as it is written, "He that rejoices, let him rejoice in the Lord."[a]

6. This therefore is life eternal, to know the only true God, and whom he hath sent Jesus Christ.[b] And on the contrary, the Lord will render vengeance in flaming fire to them that know not God, and obey not the gospel of our Lord Jesus Christ.

[1 Thes 1.8; Jn 3.36]

7. The rule of this knowledge, faith, and obedience, concerning the worship and service of God, and all other Christian duties, is not man's inventions, opinions, devices, laws, constitutions, or traditions unwritten whatsoever, but only the word of God contained in the canonical Scriptures.[c]

8. In this written word God hath plainly revealed whatsoever he hath thought needful for us to know, believe, and acknowledge, touching the nature and office of Christ, in whom all the promises are Yea and Amen to the praise of God.[d]

9. Touching the Lord Jesus, of whom Moses and the prophets wrote,[e] and whom the apostles preached, is the Son of God the Father, the brightness of his glory, the engraven form of his being,[f] God with him and with his Holy Spirit, by whom he made the world, by whom he upholds and governs all the works he hath made, who also when the fullness of time was come, was made man of a woman, of the tribe of Judah,[g] of the seed of Abraham and David,[h] to wit, of Mary that Blessed Virgin, by the Holy Spirit coming upon her, and the power of the Most High overshadowing her, and was also in all things like unto us, sin only excepted.

[Gal 4.4]

[Is 53.3–5; Phil 2.8]

10. Touching his office, Jesus Christ only is made the Mediator of the new covenant,[i] even the everlasting covenant of grace between God and man to be perfectly and fully the Prophet,[j] Priest, and King of the church of God for evermore.

11. Unto this office he was foreordained from everlasting, by the authority of the Father,[k] and in respect of his manhood, from the womb called and separated,[l]

a. [1 Cor 1.30–31; 2 Cor 5.21; Jer 9.23–24]
b. [Jn 17.3; Heb 5.9; Jer 23.5–6]
c. [Jn 5.39; 2 Tm 3.15–17; Col 2.18, 23; Mt 15.9]
d. [Acts 3.22–23; Heb 1.1–2; 2 Tm 3.15–17; 2 Cor 1.20]
e. [Gn 3.15, 22.18, 49.10; Dn 7.13, 9.14–16]
f. [Prv 8.23; Jn 1.1–3; Col 1.1, 15–17]
g. [Heb 7.14; Rv 5.5; Gn 49.9–10]
h. [Rom 1.3, 9.5; Mt 1.16; Lk 3.23, 26; Heb 2.16]
i. [2 Tm 2.15; Heb 9.15; Jn 14.6]
j. [Heb 1.2, 3.1, 2, 7.24; Is 9.6–7; Acts 5.31]
k. [Prv 8.23; Is 42.6, 49.1, 5]
l. [Is 11.2–5, 61.1–3; Lk 4.17, 22; Jn 1.14, 16, 3.34]

and anointed also most fully and abundantly with all gifts necessary, God having without measure poured the Spirit upon him.

12. In this call the Scripture holds forth two special things considerable; first, the call to the office; secondly, the office itself. First, that none takes this honor but he that is called of God, as was Aaron, so also Christ, it being an action espe- [Heb 5.4-6] cially of God the Father, whereby a special covenant being made, he ordains his Son to this office; which covenant is, that Christ should be made a sacrifice for sin, that [Is 53.10] he shall see his seed, and prolong his days, and the pleasure of the Lord shall prosper in his hand; which calling therefore contains in itself choosing,[a] foreordaining,[b] sending.[c] Choosing respects the end, foreordaining the means, sending the execution itself, all of mere grace, without any condition foreseen either in men, or in [Jn 3.16; Rom 8.32] Christ himself.

13. So that this office to be Mediator, that is, to be Prophet, Priest, and King of the church of God, is so proper to Christ, as neither in the whole,[d] nor in any part thereof, it can be transferred from him to any other.

14. This office itself of which Christ was called is threefold, of a prophet,[e] of priest,[f] and of a king:[g] this number and order of offices is showed; first, by men's necessities grievously laboring under ignorance,[h] by reason whereof they stand in infinite necessity of the prophetical office of Christ to relieve them. Secondly, alien- [Col 1.21; Eph 2.12] ation from God, wherein they stand in need of the priestly office to reconcile them: thirdly, our utter disability to return to him, by which they stand in need of the [Sg 1.3; Jn 6.44] power of Christ in his kingly office to assist and govern them.

15. Touching the prophecy of Christ, it is that whereby he hath perfectly revealed the whole will of God out of the bosom of the Father,[i] that is needful for his servants to know, believe, and obey; and therefore is called not only a prophet [Mt 23.10] and a doctor, and the[j] apostle of our profession, and the angel of the covenant;[k] but also the very wisdom of God,[l] and the treasures of wisdom and understanding.[m]

a. [Is 42.14]
b. [2 Pt 1.20]
c. [Jn 3.17, 9.27, 10.36]
d. [1 Tm 2.5; Heb 7.24; Dn 5.14; Acts 4.12; Lk 1.33; Jn 14.6]
e. [Dt 18.15; Acts 3.22–23]
f. [Ps 110.3; Heb 3.1, 4, 14–15, 5.6]
g. [Ps 2.6]
h. [Acts 26.18; Col 1.3]
i. [Jn 1.18, 12.49–50, 15, 17.8; Dt 18.15]
j. [Heb 3.1]
k. [Mal 3.1]
l. [1 Cor 1.24]
m. [Col 2.3]

16. That he might be such a Prophet as thereby to be every way complete,
it was necessary that he should be God, and withall also that he should be man; for
unless he had been God, he could never have perfectly understood the will of God,
neither had he been able to reveal it throughout all ages; and unless he had been
man, he could not fitly have unfolded it in his own person to man.[a]

17. Touching his priesthood, Christ being consecrated, hath appeared once
to put away sin by the offering and sacrifice of himself,[b] and to this end hath fully
performed and suffered all those things by which God, through the blood of that his
cross in an acceptable sacrifice, might reconcile his elect only;[c] and having broken
down the partition wall, and therewith finished and removed all those rites, shadows, and ceremonies, is now entered within the vail, into the Holy of Holiest, that
is, to the very heavens, and presence of God, where he forever liveth and sitteth at
the right hand of Majesty, appearing before the face of his Father to make intercession for such as come to the throne of grace by that new and living way; and not that
only, but makes his people a spiritual house, a holy priesthood, to offer up spiritual
sacrifice acceptable to God through him;[d] neither doth the Father accept, or Christ
offer to the Father, any other worship or worshipers.

18. This priesthood was not legal, or temporary, but according to the order
of Melchizedek; not by a carnal commandment,[e] but by the power of an endless
life;[f] not by an order that is weak and lame, but stable and perfect, not for a time,
but forever, admitting no successor, but perpetual and proper to Christ, and of him
that ever liveth. Christ himself was the Priest, sacrifice, and altar: he was Priest, according to both natures, he was a sacrifice most properly according to his human
nature: whence in the Scripture it is wont to be attributed to his body, to his blood;[g]
yet the chief force whereby this sacrifice was made effectual, did depend upon his
divine nature,[h] namely, that the Son of God did offer himself for us:[i] he was the
altar properly according to his divine nature, it belonging to the altar to sanctify that
which is offered upon it, and so it ought to be of greater dignity than the sacrifice
itself.

[Jn 1.18, 3.13]

[1 Cor 2.11, 16]

[Heb 7.17]

[Heb 7.24–25]

[Heb 5.6]

a. [Acts 3.22; Dt 18.15; Heb 1.1]

b. [Jn 17.19; Heb 5.7–9, 9.26; Rom 5.19; Eph 5.12; Col 1.20]

c. [Eph 2.14–16; Rom 8.34]

d. [1 Pt 2.5; Jn 4.23–24]

e. [Heb 7.16]

f. [Heb 7.18–21]

g. [Heb 10.10; 1 Pt 1.18–19; Col 1.20, 22; Is 53.10; Mt 20.28]

h. [Acts 20.28; Rom 8.3]

i. [Heb 9.14, 13.10, 12, 15; Mt 23.17; Jn 17.19]

19. Touching his kingdom,[a] Christ being risen from the dead, ascended into heaven, sat on the right hand of God the Father, having all power in heaven and earth, given unto him, he doth spiritually govern his church,[b] exercising his power over all angels and men, good and bad, to the preservation and salvation of the elect, to the overruling and destruction of his enemies, which are reprobates,[c] communicating and applying the benefits, virtue, and fruit of his prophecy and priesthood to his elect, namely, to the subduing and taking away of their sins, to their justification and adoption of sons, regeneration, sanctification, preservation, and strengthening in all their conflicts against Satan, the world, the flesh, and the temptations of them, continually dwelling in, governing, and keeping their hearts in faith and filial fear by his Spirit, which having given it,[d] he never takes away from them, but by it still begets and nourisheth in them faith, repentance, love, joy, hope, and all heavenly light in the soul unto immortality, notwithstanding through our own unbelief, and the temptations of Satan, the sensible sight of this light and love be clouded and overwhelmed for the time.[e] And on the contrary, ruling in the world over his enemies, Satan, and all the vessels of wrath, limiting, using, restraining them by his mighty power, as seems good in his divine wisdom and justice to the execution of his determinate counsel, delivering them up to a reprobate mind, to be kept through their own deserts, in darkness and sensuality unto judgment.

20. The kingdom shall be then fully perfect when he shall the second time come in glory to reign amongst his saints, and to be admired of all them which do believe, when he shall put down[f] all rule and authority under his feet, that the glory of the Father may be full and perfectly manifested in his Son, and the glory of the Father and the Son in all his members.

21. That Christ Jesus by his death did bring forth salvation and reconciliation only for the elect,[g] which were those which God the Father gave him;[h] and that the gospel which is to be preached to all men as the ground of faith is that[i] Jesus is the Christ, the Son of the ever blessed God, filled with the perfection of all heavenly

a. [1 Cor 15.4; 1 Pt 3.21–22; Mt 28.18–20; Lk 24.51; Acts 1.11, 5.30–31; Jn 19.36; Rom 14.17]

b. [Mk 1.27; Heb 1.14; Jn 16.7, 15]

c. [Jn 5.26–27; Rom 5.6–8, 14.17; Gal 5.22–23; Jn 1.4, 13]

d. [Jn 13.1, 10, 28, 29, 14.16–17; Rom 11.29; Ps 51.10–11; Jb 33.29–30; 2 Cor 12.7, 9]

e. [Jb 1–2; Rom 1.21, 2.4–6, 9.17–18; Eph 4.17–18; 2 Pt 2]

f. [1 Cor 15.24, 28; Heb 9.28; 2 Thes 1.9–10; 1 Thes 4.15–17; Jn 17.21, 26]

g. [Jn 15.13; Rom 8.32–34, 5.11, 3.25]

h. [Jn 17.2, 6.37]

i. [Mt 16.16; Lk 2.26; Jn 6.9, 7.3, 20.31; 1 Jn 5.11]

and spiritual excellencies, and that salvation is only and alone to be had through the believing in his name.

22. That faith is the gift of God[a] wrought in the hearts of the elect by the Spirit of God, whereby they come to see, know, and believe the truth of the Scriptures, and not only so,[b] but the excellency of them above all other writings and things in the world as they hold forth the glory of God in his attributes, the excellency of Christ in his nature and offices, and the power of the fullness of the Spirit in its workings and operations; and thereupon are enabled to cast the weight of their souls upon this truth thus believed.

23. Those that have this precious faith wrought in them by the Spirit, can never finally nor totally fall away;[c] and though many storms and floods do arise and beat against them, yet they shall never be able to take them off that foundation and rock which by faith they are fastened upon, but shall be kept by the power of God to salvation, where they shall enjoy their purchased possession, they being formerly engraven upon the palms of God's hands.

24. That faith is ordinarily[d] begot by the preaching of the gospel, or word of Christ, without respect to any power or capacity in the creature, but it is wholly passive,[e] being dead in sin and trespasses, doth believe, and is converted by no less power[f] than that which raised Christ from the dead.

[Rom 9.16]

25. That the tenders of the gospel to the conversion of sinners[g] is absolutely free, no way requiring, as absolutely necessary, any qualifications, preparations, terrors of the law, or preceding ministry of the law, but only and alone the naked soul, as a sinner[h] and ungodly to receive Christ as crucified, dead, and buried, and risen again, being made a Prince[i] and a Savior for such sinners.

26. That the same power that converts to faith in Christ, the same power carries on the soul[j] still through all duties, temptations, conflicts, sufferings, and continually whatever a Christian is, he is by grace, and by a constant renewed opera-

[1 Cor 15.10]

a. [Eph 2.8; Jn 6.29, 4.10; Phil 1.29; Gal 5.22]
b. [Jn 17.17; Heb 4.11–12; Jn 6.63]
c. [Mt 7.24–25; Jn 13.1; 1 Pt 1.4–6; Is 49.13–16]
d. [Rom 10.17; 1 Cor 1.21]
e. [Rom 2.1–2; Ez 16.6; Rom 3.12]
f. [Rom 1.16; Eph 1.19; Col 2.12]
g. [Jn 3.14–15, 1.12; Is 55.1; Jn 7.37]
h. [1 Tm 1.15; Rom 4.5, 5.8]
i. [Acts 5.30–31, 2.36; 1 Cor 1.22–24]
j. [1 Pt 1.5; 2 Cor 12.9]

tion[a] from God, without which he cannot perform any duty to God, or undergo any temptations from Satan, the world, or men.

27. That God the Father and Son and Spirit is one with[b] all believers in their[c] fullness, in[d] relations[e] as head and members,[f] as house and inhabitants,[g] as husband and wife, one with him, as light and love, and one with him in his inheritance, and in all his glory; and that all believers by virtue of this union and oneness with God, are the adopted sons of God and heirs with Christ, co-heirs and joint heirs with him of the inheritance of all the promises of this life, and that which is to come.

[Gal 3.26]

[Jn 17.24]

28. That those which have union with Christ are justified from all their sins, past,[h] present, and to come, by the blood of Christ; which justification we conceive to be a gracious and free[i] acquittance of a guilty, sinful creature, from all sin by God, through the satisfaction that Christ hath made by his death; and this applied in the manifestation of it through faith.

29. That all believers are a holy and sanctified people, and that sanctification is a spiritual grace of the[j] new covenant and effect of the[k] love of God, manifested to the soul, whereby the believer is in truth and reality separated, both in soul and body, from all sin and dead works, through the blood of the everlasting covenant, whereby he also presseth after a heavenly and evangelical perfection in obedience to all the commands which Christ as Head and King in this new covenant has prescribed to him.

[1 Cor 1.1; 1 Pt 2.9]

[Eph 4.24]

[Phil 3.15]

[Mt 28.20]

30. All believers through the knowledge of[l] that justification of life given by the Father and brought forth by the blood of Christ, have this as their privilege of that new covenant, peace with God and reconciliation, whereby they that were afar off were brought nigh by[m] that blood and have (as the Scripture speaks) peace[n]

[Is 54.10, 26.12]

a. [Phil 1.12–13; Jn 15.5; Gal 2.19–20]
b. [1 Thes 1.1; Jn 14.10, 20, 17.21]
c. [Col 2.9–10, 1.19; Jn 1.17]
d. [Jn 20.17; Heb 2.11]
e. [Col 1.18; Eph 5.30]
f. [Eph 2.22; 1 Cor 3.16–17]
g. [Is 16.5; 2 Cor 11.3]
h. [Jn 1.7; Heb 10.14, 9.26; 2 Cor 5.19; Rom 3.23]
i. [Acts 13.38–39; Rom 5.1, 3.25, 30]
j. [Eph 1.4]
k. [1 Jn 4.16]
l. [2 Cor 5.19; Rom 5.9–10]
m. [Eph 2.13–14]
n. [Phil 4.7]

[Rom 5.10-11] passing all understanding, yea, joy in God through our Lord Jesus Christ by whom
we have received the atonement.

31. That all believers in the time of this life are in continual warfare, combat,
and opposition against sin, self, the world, and the devil, and liable to all manner of
afflictions, tribulations, and persecutions,[a] and so shall continue until Christ comes
in his kingdom, being predestinated and appointed thereunto and whatsoever the
saints, any of them do possess or enjoy of God in this life, is only by faith.

[Jn 16.33] 32. That the only strength by which the saints are enabled to encounter with
all opposition and to overcome all afflictions, temptations, persecutions, and trials,
[Heb 2.9-10] is only by Jesus Christ, who is the captain of their salvation, being made perfect
through sufferings, who hath engaged his strength to assist them in all their afflictions and to uphold them under all their temptations, and to preserve them by his
[Jn 15.5] power to his everlasting kingdom.

33. That Christ hath here on earth a spiritual kingdom which is the church,
which he hath purchased and redeemed to himself as a peculiar inheritance: which
church, as it is visible to us, is a company of visible[b] saints,[c] called and separated
[Acts 2.37, 10.37] from the world, by the word and Spirit of God, to the visible profession of the faith
of the gospel, being baptized into that faith and joined to the Lord and each other
by mutual agreement, in the practical enjoyment of the[d] ordinances, commanded
by Christ their Head and King.

34. To this church he hath made his promises[e] and given the signs of his
covenant, presence, love, blessing, and protection: here are the fountains and springs
of his heavenly grace continually flowing forth;[f] thither ought all men to come, of all
estates, that acknowledge him to be their Prophet, Priest, and King, to be enrolled
amongst his household servants, to be under his heavenly conduct and government,
to lead their lives in his walled sheepfold and watered garden, to have communion
here with the saints, that they may be made to be partakers of their inheritance in
the kingdom of God.

35. And all his servants are called thither,[g] to present their bodies and souls,
and to bring their gifts God hath given them; so being come, they are here by himself bestowed in their several order, peculiar place, due use, being fitly compact and

a. [Eph 6.10-13; 2 Cor 10.3; Rv 2.9-10]

b. [1 Cor 1.1; Eph 1.1]

c. [Rom 1.7; Acts 26.18; 1 Thes 1.9; 2 Cor 6.17; Rv 18.18]

d. [Rom 10.10; Acts 20.21; Mt 18.19-20; Acts 2.42; 1 Pt 2.5]

e. [Mt 28.18-20; 2 Cor 6.18]

f. [Is 8.16; 1 Tm 3.15, 4.16, 6.3, 5; Acts 2.41, 47; Sg 4.12; Gal 6.10; Eph 2.19]

g. [1 Cor 2.6-7, 12.18; Rom 12.4-6; 1 Pt 4.10; Eph 4.16; Col 2.5-6, 19; 1 Cor 12.12-31]

knit together, according to the effectual working of every part, to the edification of itself in love.

36. That being thus joined, every church has[a] power given them from Christ for their better well-being, to choose to themselves meet persons into the office of[b] pastors, teachers, elders, deacons, being qualified according to the word, as those which Christ has appointed in his Testament, for the feeding, governing, serving, and building up of his church, and that none other have power to impose them, either these or any other.

37. That the ministers aforesaid, lawfully called by the church, where they are to administer, ought to continue in their calling,[c] according to God's ordinance, and carefully to feed the flock of Christ committed to them, not for filthy lucre, but of a ready mind.

38. That the due maintenance of the officers aforesaid, should be the free and voluntary communication of the church, that according to Christ's ordinance,[d] they that preach the gospel, should live on the gospel and not by constraint to be compelled from the people by a forced law.

39. That baptism is an ordinance of the New Testament,[e] given by Christ, to be dispensed only upon persons professing faith, or that are disciples, or taught,[f] who upon profession of faith, ought to be baptized.

40. The way and manner of the[g] dispensing of this ordinance the Scripture holds out to be dipping or plunging the whole body under water: it being a sign, must answer the thing signified, which are these: first, the[h] washing the whole soul in the blood of Christ. Secondly, that interest the saints have in the death, burial, and resurrection. Thirdly, together with a confirmation of our faith, that as certainly as the body is buried under water, and riseth again, so certainly shall the bodies of the saints be raised by the power of Christ, in the day of the resurrection to reign with Christ. (The word *baptizo,* signifying to dip under water, yet so as with convenient garments both upon the administrator and subject, with all modesty.)

[Rom 6.3–5]

[1 Cor 15.28–29]

41. The persons designed by Christ to dispense this ordinance, the[i] Scrip-

a. [Acts 1.2, 6.3, 15.22, 25; 1 Cor 16.3]

b. [Rom 12.7–8, 16.1; 1 Cor 12.8, 28; 1 Tm 3; Heb 13.7; 1 Pt 5.1–3]

c. [Heb 5.4; Acts 4.23; 1 Tm 4.14; Jn 10.3–4; Acts 20.18; Rom 12.7–8; Heb 13.7, 17]

d. [1 Cor 9.7, 14; Gal 6.6; 1 Thes 5.13; 1 Tm 5.17–18; Phil 4.15–16]

e. [Mt 28.19–20; Mk 16.16]

f. [Acts 2.37–38, 8.36–38, 18.8]

g. [Mt 3.16; Jn 3.23; Acts 8.38]

h. [Rv 1.5, 7.14; Heb 10.22]

i. [Is 8.16; Mt 28.16–19; Jn 4.1–2; Acts 20.7; Mt 26.26]

tures hold forth to be a preaching disciple, it being no where tied to a particular church, officer, or person extraordinarily sent, the commission enjoining the administration, being given to them under no other consideration, but as considered disciples.

42. Christ has likewise given power to his whole church to receive in and cast out, by way of excommunication, any member;[a] and this power is given to every particular congregation, and not one particular person, either member or officer, but the whole.

43. And every particular member of each church,[b] how excellent, great, or learned soever, ought to be subject to this censure and judgment of Christ; and the church ought with great care and tenderness, with due advice to proceed against her members.

44. And as Christ for the keeping of this church in holy and orderly communion,[c] placeth some special men over the church, who by their office are to govern, oversee, visit, watch; so likewise for the better keeping thereof in all places, by the members, he hath given[d] authority, and laid duty upon all, to watch over one another.

45. That also such to whom God hath given gifts, being tied in the church, may and ought by the appointment of the congregation, to prophesy, according to the proportion of faith,[e] and so teach publicly the word of God, for the edification, exhortation, and comfort of the church.

46. Thus being rightly gathered, established, and still proceeding in Christian communion and obedience of the gospel of Christ,[f] none ought to separate for faults and corruptions, which may, and as long as the church consists of men subject to failings, will fall out and arise amongst them, even in true constituted churches, until they have in due order sought redress thereof.

47. And although the particular congregations be distinct and several bodies, every one a compact and knit city in itself;[g] yet are they all to walk by one and the same rule, and by all means convenient to have the counsel and help one of another in all needful affairs of the church, as members of one body in the common faith under Christ their only Head.

a. [Acts 2.47; Rom 16.2; Mt 18.17; 1 Cor 5.4; 2 Cor 2.6–8]

b. [Mt 18.16–18; Acts 11.2–3; 1 Tm 5.19–21]

c. [Acts 20.27–28; Heb 13.17, 24; Mt 24.25; 1 Thes 5.14]

d. [Mk 13.34, 37; Gal 6.1; 1 Thes 5.11; Jude 3, 20; Heb 10.34–35, 12.15]

e. [1 Cor 14; Rom 12.6; 1 Pt 4.10–11; 1 Cor 12.7; 1 Thes 5.17–19]

f. [Rv 2–3; Acts 15.12; 1 Cor 1.10; Eph 2.16, 3.15–16; Heb 10.25; Jude 15; Mt 18.17; 1 Cor 5.4–5]

g. [1 Tm 3.15, 6.13–14; Rv 22.18–19; Col 2.6, 19, 4.16]

48. That a civil magistracy is an ordinance of God set up by God for the punishment of evildoers, and for the praise of them that do well;[a] and that in all lawful things commanded by them, subjection ought to be given by us in the Lord; and that we are to make supplication and prayer for kings, and all that are in authority, that under them we may live a peaceable and quiet life in all godliness and honesty.

49. The supreme magistracy of this kingdom we believe to be the king and Parliament freely chosen by the kingdom, and that in all those civil laws which have been acted by them, or for the present is or shall be ordained, we are bound to yield subjection and obedience unto the Lord, as conceiving ourselves bound to defend both the persons of those thus chosen, and all civil laws made by them, with our persons, liberties, and estates, with all that is called ours, although we should suffer never so much from them in not actively submitting to some ecclesiastical laws, which might be conceived by them to be their duties to establish which we for the present could not see, nor our consciences could submit unto; yet are we bound to yield our persons to their pleasures.

50. And if God should provide such a mercy for us, as to incline the magistrates' hearts so far to tender our consciences, as that we might be protected by them from wrong, injury, oppression, and molestation,[b] which long we formerly have groaned under by the tyranny and oppression of the prelatical hierarchy, which God through mercy hath made this present king and Parliament wonderful, honorable, as an instrument in his hand, to throw down; and we thereby have had some breathing time, we shall, we hope, look at it as a mercy beyond our expectation, and conceive ourselves further engaged forever to bless God for it.

51. But if God withhold the magistrates' allowance and furtherance herein;[c] yet we must notwithstanding proceed together in Christian communion, not daring to give place to suspend our practice, but to walk in obedience to Christ in the profession and holding forth this faith before mentioned, even in the midst of all trials and afflictions, not accounting our goods, lands, wives, children, fathers, mothers, brethren, sisters, yea, and our own lives dear unto us so we may finish our course with joy: remembering always we ought to[d] obey God rather than men, and grounding upon the commandment, commission, and promise of our Lord and Master Jesus Christ, who as he hath all power in heaven and earth, so also hath promised,

a. [Rom 13.1–4; 1 Pt 2.13–14; 1 Tm 2.2]

b. [1 Tm 1.2–4; Ps 126.1; Acts 9.31]

c. [Acts 2.40–41, 4.19, 5.28–29, 41, 20.23; 1 Thes 3.3; Phil 1.27–29; Dn 3.16–17, 6.7, 10, 22–23]

d. [Mt 28.18–20; 1 Tm 6.13–15; Rom 12.1, 8; 1 Cor 14.37; 2 Tm 4.7–8; Rv 2.10; Gal 2.4–5]

if we keep his commandments which he hath given us, to be with us to the end of the world: and when we have finished our course, and kept the faith, to give us the crown of righteousness, which is laid up for all that love his appearing, and to whom we must give an account of all our actions, no man being able to discharge us of the same.

52. And likewise unto all men is to be given whatsoever is their due; tributes, customs, and all such lawful duties, ought willingly to be by us paid and performed, our lands, goods, and bodies, to submit to the magistrate in the Lord, and the magistrate every way to be acknowledged, reverenced, and obeyed, according to godliness;[a] not because of wrath only but for conscience sake. And finally, all men so to be esteemed and regarded, as is due and meet for their place, age, estate, and condition.

53. And thus we desire to give unto God that which is God's, and unto Caesar that which is Caesar's, and unto all men that which belongeth unto them, endeavoring ourselves to have always a clear conscience void of offense towards God and towards man.[b] And if any take this that we have said to be heresy, then do we with the apostle freely confess, that after the way which they call heresy, worship we the God of our fathers, believing all things which are written in the law and in the prophets and apostles, desiring from our souls to disclaim all heresies and opinions which are not after Christ, and to be steadfast, unmovable, always abounding in the work of the Lord, as knowing our labor shall not be in vain in the Lord.

1 Corinthians 1.24:
Not that we have dominion over your faith,
but are helpers of your joy: for by faith we stand.

a. [Rom 13.5–7; Mt 22.21; Ti 3; 1 Pt 2.13; Eph 5.21–22, 6.1, 9; 1 Pt 5.5]
b. [Mt 22.21; Acts 24.14–16; Jn 5.28; 2 Cor 4.17; 1 Tm 6.3–5; 1 Cor 15.58–59]

Congregationalists of New England,
The Cambridge Platform, 1648

The Cambridge Platform holds the distinction of being the first creed or confession to be composed in North America. "Since the time of its promulgation in 1648," as B. R. Burg points out, "the Cambridge Platform has been considered one of seventeenth-century New England's most important documents. . . . The Platform was the recognized standard for Massachusetts Bay's religion until the time of the American Revolution."[1] Its importance comes not only from its detailed consideration, in the final chapter, of the relation between the civil magistrate and the church, and from the possible (though debated) connections between the ecclesiastical "democracy" it advocates (10.3) and political democracy, but from its confessional formulations, especially on the nature of the church and the authority of the ministry.

Coming less than thirty years after the Mayflower Compact of 1620, *The Cambridge Platform* carried the fundamental ecclesiological principles that had been inchoate and implicit there to a new level of systematic clarity and completeness. Indeed, at its three-hundredth anniversary, a celebratory study authorized by the Joint Commission of the Congregational Christian Churches of the United States and the American Unitarian Association could assert: "A new order of Christian churches was announced to the world when the representatives of the churches of four confederated New England colonies, meeting as a synod, at Cambridge, Massachusetts, in 1648, adopted *A Platform of Church Discipline* known historically as the Cambridge Platform."[2]

Scholars have long debated whether it was addressed primarily to the situation of Congregationalists and "Independents" in England or to their new status in New England. In England the principal challenge to Anglicanism was coming from the advocates of a Presbyterian polity; the confessional charter of Presbyterianism was → *The Westminster Confession of Faith* of 1647, which the Westminster Assembly substituted for *The Thirty-Nine Articles of the Church of England*. But that confession did not go far enough for the "Independents," who were moved by their reading of Scripture and their history to a definition of what is called here "a congregational church . . . by the institution of Christ . . . consisting of a company of saints by calling, united into one body by a holy covenant" (2.6).

1. Burg 1974, 470.
2. Fagley and Foote 1948, 3.

The preface to *The Cambridge Platform* declares: "The setting forth of the public confession of the faith of churches hath a double end, and both tending to public edification: first, the maintenance of the faith entire within itself; secondly, the holding forth of unity and harmony, both amongst and with other churches." They went on to affirm that "we profess and believe the same doctrine of the truth of the gospel which generally is received in all the Reformed churches of Christ in Europe," which included especially "the doctrine of faith and truth held forth by the churches of our native country."[3] On the major themes of Reformation teaching, therefore, they accepted the doctrinal stand of *The Westminster Confession*. Where they differed from it was chiefly in their doctrine of the church and its structure, to which the main body of this confession is devoted. *The Cambridge Platform*, like other confessions of the time, presents its biblical references in the margins.

Edition: Walker, 194–237 (spelling and punctuation modernized).

Literature: Burg 1974; Fagley and Foote 1948.

3. Walker, 194.

Congregationalists of New England, *The Cambridge Platform*, 1648

CHAPTER 1. OF THE FORM OF CHURCH GOVERNMENT; AND THAT IT IS ONE, IMMUTABLE, AND PRESCRIBED IN THE WORD OF GOD

1. Ecclesiastical polity or church government or discipline is nothing else but that form and order that is to be observed in the church of Christ upon earth, both for the constitution of it and all the administrations that therein are to be performed.[a]

2. Church government is considered in a double respect, either in regard of the parts of government themselves or necessary circumstances thereof. The parts of government are prescribed in the word, because the Lord Jesus Christ, the King and Lawgiver of his church, is no less faithful in the house of God than was Moses, [Heb 3.5–6] who from the Lord delivered a form and pattern of government to the children of Israel in the Old Testament; and the Holy Scriptures are now also so perfect as they [Ex 25.40] are able to make the man of God perfect and thoroughly furnished unto every good work, and therefore doubtless to the well-ordering of the house of God. [2 Tm 3.16]

3. The parts of church government are all of them exactly described in the word of God,[b] being parts or means of instituted worship according to the second commandment, and therefore to continue one and the same, unto the appearing of [Ex 20.4] our Lord Jesus Christ,[c] as a kingdom that cannot be shaken,[d] until he shall deliver it up unto God, even the Father. So that it is not left in the power of men, officers, [1 Cor 15.22] churches, or any state in the world to add or diminish or alter anything in the least measure therein.[e]

4. The necessary circumstances, as time and place, etc., belonging unto order and decency,[f] are not so left unto men as that under pretense of them they may thrust their own inventions upon the churches, being circumscribed in the word with many general limitations,[g] where they are determined in respect of the matter to be neither worship itself nor circumstances separable from worship.[h] In respect

a. [Ez 43.11; Col 2.5; 1 Tm 3.15]
b. [1 Tm 3.15; 1 Chr 15.13]
c. [1 Tm 6.14, 16]
d. [Heb 12.27–28]
e. [Dt 12.32; Ez 43.8; 1 Kgs 12.31–33]
f. [1 Kgs 12.28–29; Is 29.13]
g. [Col 2.22–23; Acts 15.28]
h. [Mt 15.9; 1 Cor 11.23, 8.34]

of their end, they must be done unto edification; in respect of the manner, decently

[1 Cor 14.26, 40]   and in order, according to the nature of the things themselves, and civil and church

[1 Cor 11.14, 16]   custom. Doth not even nature itself teach you? Yea, they are in some sort determined particularly, namely, that they be done in such a manner as, all circumstances

[1 Cor 14.12, 19]   considered, is most expedient for edification. So, as if there be no error of man concerning their determination, the determining of them is to be accounted as if it were

[Acts 15.28]   divine.

CHAPTER 2. OF THE NATURE OF THE CATHOLIC CHURCH IN
GENERAL, AND IN SPECIAL OF A PARTICULAR VISIBLE CHURCH

1. The catholic church is the whole company of those that are elected, redeemed,
and in time effectually called from the state of sin and death unto a state of grace
and salvation in Jesus Christ.[a]

2. This church is either triumphant or militant: triumphant, the number of
them who are glorified in heaven; militant, the number of them who are conflicting
with their enemies upon earth.[b]

3. This militant church is to be considered as invisible and visible: invisible,
in respect of their relation wherein they stand to Christ, as a body unto the head,
being united unto him by the Spirit of God and faith in their hearts;[c] visible, in respect of the profession of their faith, in their persons, and in particular churches.[d]
And so there may be acknowledged a universal visible church.

4. The members of the militant visible church, considered either as not yet
in church order[e] or as walking according to the church order of the gospel.[f] In order,
and so beside the spiritual union and communion common to all believers, they enjoy moreover a union and communion ecclesiastical-political. So we deny a universal
visible church.

5. The state [of] the members of the militant visible church walking in order

[Gn 18.19]   was either: before the law, economical, that is, in families; or under the law, na-

[Ex 19.6]   tional; or, since the coming of Christ, only congregational (the term Independent
we approve not)—therefore neither national, provincial, nor classical.

6. A congregational church is by the institution of Christ a part of the militant visible church, consisting of a company of saints by calling, united into one

a. [Eph 1.22–23, 5.25–26, 30; Heb 12.23]
b. [Rom 8.17; 2 Tm 2.12, 4.8; Eph 6.12–13]
c. [2 Tm 2.19; Rv 2.17; 1 Cor 6.17; Eph 3.17]
d. [Rom 1.8; 1 Thes 1.8; Is 2.2; 1 Tm 6.12]
e. [Acts 19.1]
f. [Col 2.5; Mt 18.17; 1 Cor 5.12]

body by a holy covenant, for the public worship of God and the mutual edification one of another, in the fellowship of the Lord Jesus.[a]

CHAPTER 3. OF THE MATTER OF THE VISIBLE CHURCH
BOTH IN RESPECT OF QUALITY AND QUANTITY

1. The matter of a visible church are saints by calling.

2. By saints we understand:

(1) such as have not only attained the knowledge of the principles of religion and are free from gross and open scandals, but also do, together with the profession of their faith and repentance, walk in blameless obedience to the word,[b] so as that in charitable discretion they may be accounted saints by calling (though perhaps some or more of them be unsound, and hypocrites inwardly), because the members of such particular churches are commonly by the Holy Ghost called saints and faithful brethren in Christ, and sundry churches have been reproved for receiving and suffering such persons to continue in fellowship amongst them as have been offensive and scandalous.[c] The name of God also by this means is blasphemed,[d] and the holy things of God defiled and profaned,[e] the hearts of godly grieved, and the wicked themselves hardened and helped forward to damnation. The example of such doth endanger the sanctity of others; a little leaven leaveneth the whole lump. [Eph 1.1] [1 Cor 5.6, 7.14]

(2) the children of such, who are also holy. [Jer 2.21]

3. The members of churches, though orderly constituted, may in time degenerate and grow corrupt and scandalous. Which, though they ought not to be tolerated in the church, yet their continuance therein, through the defect of the execution of discipline and just censures, doth not immediately dissolve the being of the church, as appears in the church of Israel and the churches of Galatia and Corinth, Pergamus, and Thyatira.[f] [1 Cor 5.12] [Jer 14]

4. The matter of the church in respect of its quantity ought not to be of greater number than may ordinarily meet together conveniently in one place, nor ordinarily fewer than may conveniently carry on church work. Hence when the Holy Scripture maketh mention of the saints combined into a church estate in a town or city where was but one congregation, it usually calleth those saints [the church] [1 Cor 14.21] [Mt 18.17]

a. [1 Cor 14.23, 36, 1.2, 12.27; Ex 19.5–6; Dt 19.1, 9–15; Acts 2.42; 1 Cor 14.26]

b. [1 Cor 1.2; Eph 1.2; Heb 6.1; 1 Cor 1.5; Rom 15.14; Ps 50.16–17; Acts 8.37; Mt 3.6; Rom 6.17; 1 Cor 1.2; Phil 1.1; Col 1.2]

c. [1 Cor 5.2, 13; Rv 2.14–15, 20; Ez 44.7, 9, 23.38–39; Nm 4.20; Hg 2.13–14]

d. [Rom 2.24]

e. [1 Cor 11.27, 29; Ps 37.21]

f. [Gal 5.4; 2 Cor 12.21; Rv 2.14–15, 24–25]

in the singular number, as the church of the Thessalonians, the church of Smyrna, Philadelphia, and the like.[a] But when it speaketh of the saints in a nation or province, wherein there were sundry congregations, it frequently and usually calleth them by the name of "churches" in the plural number, as the [churches] of Asia, Galatia, Macedonia, and the like.[b] Which is further confirmed by what is written of sundry of those churches in particular, how they were assembled and met together the whole church in one place, as the church at Jerusalem, the church at Antioch, the church at Corinth; and Cenchrea, though it were more near to Corinth, it being the port thereof and answerable to a village; yet being a distinct congregation from Corinth, it had a church of its own as well as Corinth had.[c]

5. Nor can it with reason be thought but that every church appointed and ordained by Christ had a ministry ordained and appointed for the same. And yet plain it is that there were no ordinary officers appointed by Christ for any other than congregational churches. Elders being appointed to feed, not all flocks, but the par-

[Acts 20.28]

ticular flock of God over which the Holy Ghost had made them the overseers, and that flock they must attend, even the whole flock; and one congregation being as much as any ordinary elders can attend—therefore there is no greater church than a congregation which may ordinarily meet in one place.

CHAPTER 4. OF THE FORM OF A VISIBLE CHURCH AND OF CHURCH COVENANT

1. Saints by calling must have a visible political union amongst themselves, or else they are not yet a particular church, as those similitudes hold forth which Scripture makes use of to show the nature of particular churches. As a body, a building or house, hands, eyes, feet, and other members must be united or else, remaining separate, are not a body; stones, timber, though squared, hewn, and polished, are not an house until they are compacted and united—so saints or believers in judgment of charity are not a church unless orderly knit together.[d]

2. Particular churches cannot be distinguished one from another but by their forms. Ephesus is not Smyrna, and Pergamus Thyatira, but each one a distinct

[Rv 1]

society of itself: having officers of their own, which had not the charge of others; virtues of their own, for which others are not praised; corruptions of their own, for which others are not blamed.

a. [Rom 16.2; 1 Thes 1.1; Rv 2.8, 3.7]
b. [1 Cor 16.2, 19; Gal 1.2; 2 Cor 8.1; 1 Thes 2.14]
c. [Acts 2.46, 5.12, 6.2, 14.27, 15.38; 1 Cor 5.4, 14.23; Rom 16.1]
d. [1 Cor 12.27; 1 Tm 3.15; Eph 2.22; 1 Cor 12.15–17]

3. This form is the visible covenant, agreement, or consent whereby they give up themselves unto the Lord, to the observing of the ordinances of Christ together in the same society,[a] which is usually called the church covenant; for we see not otherwise how members can have church power one over another mutually. The comparing of each particular church unto a city, and unto a spouse,[b] seemeth to conclude not only a form, but that that form is by way of a covenant. The covenant, as it was that which made the family of Abraham and children of Israel to be a church and people unto God, so it is that which now makes the several societies of Gentile believers to be churches in these days.[c]

4. This voluntary agreement, consent, or covenant (for all these are here taken for the same): although the more express and plain it is, the more fully it puts us in mind of our mutual duty and stirreth us up to it, and leaveth less room for the questioning of the truth of the church estate of a company of professors and the truth of membership of particular persons, yet we conceive the substance of it is kept where there is a real agreement and consent of a company of faithful persons to meet constantly together in one congregation for the public worship of God and their mutual edification. Which real agreement and consent they do express by their constant practice in coming together for the public worship of God, and by their religious subjection unto the ordinances of God there. The rather, if we do consider how Scripture covenants have been entered into, not only expressly by word of mouth, but by sacrifice, by handwriting, and seal, and also sometimes by silent consent, without any writing or expressions of words at all.[d]

5. This form then being by mutual covenant, it followeth it is not faith in the heart, nor the profession of that faith, nor cohabitation, nor baptism: (1) not faith in the heart, because that is invisible; (2) not a bare profession, because that declareth them no more to be members of one church than of another; (3) not cohabitation, atheists or infidels may dwell together with believers; (4) not baptism, because it presupposeth a church estate, as circumcision in the Old Testament, which gave no being unto the church, the church being before it and in the wilderness without it. Seals presuppose a covenant already in being; one person is a complete subject of baptism, but one person is incapable of being a church.

6. All believers ought, as God giveth them opportunity thereunto, to endeavor to join themselves unto a particular church; and that in respect of the

a. [Ex 19.5, 8; Dt 29.12; Zec 11.14, 9.11]

b. [Eph 2.19; 2 Cor 11.2]

c. [Gn 17.7; Dt 29.12–13; Eph 2.12, 19]

d. [Ex 19.5–8, 24.3, 17; Jos 24.18–24; Ps 50.5; Neh 9.38, 10.1; Gn 17; Dt 29]

honor of Jesus Christ in his example and institution, by the professed acknowledgment of, and subjection unto, the order and ordinances of the gospel, as also in respect of their good of communion, founded upon their visible union and contained in the promises of Christ's special presence in the church. Whence they have fellowship with him and in him, one with another.[a] Also, for the keeping of them in the way of God's commandments, and recovering of them in case of wandering (which all Christ's sheep are subject to in this life), being unable to return of themselves; together with the benefit of their mutual edification and of their posterity,[b] that they may not be cut off from the privileges of the covenant. Otherwise, if a believer offends, he remains destitute of the remedy provided in that behalf. And should all believers neglect this duty of joining to all particular congregations, it might follow thereupon that Christ should have no visible political churches upon earth.

CHAPTER 5. OF THE FIRST SUBJECT OF CHURCH POWER OR TO WHOM CHURCH POWER DOTH FIRST BELONG

1. The first subject of church power is either supreme or subordinate and ministerial: the supreme (by way of gift from the Father) is the Lord Jesus Christ;[c] the ministerial is either extraordinary, as the apostles, prophets, and evangelists,[d] or ordinary, as every particular congregational church.

2. Ordinary church power is either the power of office that is such as is proper to the eldership, or power of privilege such as belongs unto the brotherhood. The latter is in the brethren formally, and immediately from Christ, that is, so as it may according to order be acted or exercised immediately by themselves; the former is not in them formally or immediately, and therefore cannot be acted or exercised immediately by them, but is said to be in them, in that they design the persons unto office who only are to act or to exercise this power.[e]

CHAPTER 6. OF THE OFFICERS OF THE CHURCH, AND ESPECIALLY OF PASTORS AND TEACHERS

1. A church being a company of people combined together by covenant for the worship of God, it appeareth thereby that there may be the essence and being of a church without any officers, seeing there is both the form and matter of a church, [Acts 14.23] which is implied when it is said, the apostles ordained elders in every church.

a. [Acts 2.47, 9.26; Mt 3.13-15, 28.19-20; Ps 133.1-3, 87.7; Mt 18.20; 1 Jn 1.3]
b. [Ps 119.176; 1 Pt 2.25; Eph 4.16; 1 Pt 2.25; Mt 18.15-17]
c. [Mt 28.18; Rv 3.7; Is 9.6; Jn 20.21, 23]
d. [1 Cor 14.32; Ti 1.5; 1 Cor 5.12]
e. [Rom 12.4, 8; Acts 12.3, 6.3-4, 14.23; 1 Cor 12.29-30]

2. Nevertheless, though officers be not absolutely necessary to the simple being of churches when they be called,[a] yet ordinarily to their calling they are, and to their well-being. And therefore the Lord Jesus out of his tender compassion hath appointed and ordained officers, which he would not have done if they had not been useful and needful for the church. Yea, being ascended into heaven, he received gifts for men and gave gifts to men, whereof officers for the church are justly accounted no small parts, they being to continue to the end of the world and for the perfecting of all the saints.[b]

[Eph 4.12-13]

3. The officers were either extraordinary or ordinary: extraordinary, as apostles, prophets, evangelists; ordinary, as elders and deacons. The apostles, prophets, and evangelists, as they were called extraordinarily by Christ, so their office ended with themselves. Whence it is that Paul, directing Timothy how to carry along church administration, giveth no direction about the choice or course of apostles, prophets, or evangelists, but only of elders and deacons.[c] And when Paul was to take his last leave of the church of Ephesus, he committed the care of feeding the church to no other but unto the elders of that church. The like charge doth Peter commit to the elders.

[1 Cor 4.9]

[Acts 20.17, 28]

[1 Pt 5.1-3]

4. Of elders (who are also in Scripture called bishops), some attend chiefly to the ministry of the word, as the pastors and teachers; others attend especially unto rule, who are therefore called ruling elders.[d]

5. The office of pastor and [of] teacher appears to be distinct. The pastor's special work is to attend to exhortation, and therein to administer a word of wisdom. The teacher is to attend to doctrine, and therein to administer a word of knowledge. And either of them to administer the seals of that covenant, unto the dispensation whereof they are alike called, as also to execute the censures, being but a kind of application of the word, the preaching of which, together with the application thereof, they are alike charged withal.

[2 Tm 4.1-2; Ti 1.9]

6. And forasmuch as both pastors and teachers are given by Christ for the perfecting of the saints and edifying of his body, which saints and body of Christ is his church, therefore we account pastors and teachers to be both of them church officers, and not the pastor for the church and the teacher only for the schools.[e] Though this we gladly acknowledge that schools are both lawful, profitable, and

a. [Rom 10.17; Jer 3.15; 1 Cor 12.28; Eph 4.11; Ps 68.18; Eph 4.8, 11]

b. [1 Cor 12.28; Eph 4.11; Gal 1; Acts 8.6, 26.19, 11.28; Rom 11.7-8]

c. [1 Tm 3.1-2, 8-13; Ti 1.5]

d. [Eph 4.11; Rom 12.7-8; 1 Cor 12.8]

e. [1 Sm 10.12, 19-20; 2 Kgs 2.3, 15]

necessary for the training up of such in good literature, or learning, as may after-wards be called forth unto office of pastor or teacher in the church.

CHAPTER 7. OF RULING ELDERS AND DEACONS

1. The ruling elder's office is distinct from the office of pastor and teacher.[a] The ruling elders are not so called to exclude the pastors and teachers from ruling, but because ruling and governing is common to these with the other, whereas attending to teach and preach the word is peculiar unto the former.[b]

[1 Tm 5.17]   2. The ruling elders' work is to join with the pastor and teacher in those acts of spiritual rule which are distinct from the ministry of the word and sacraments committed to them. Of which sort, these be as followeth:[c] (1) to open and shut the doors of God's house, by the admission of members approved by the church, by ordination of officers chosen by the church, and by excommunication of notorious and obstinate offenders renounced by the church, and by restoring of penitents for-
[Acts 21.18, 22–23]   given by the church; (2) to call the church together when there is occasion, and seasonably to dismiss them again; (3) to prepare matters in private, that in public they may be carried [to] an end with less trouble and more speedy dispatch; (4) to moderate the carriage of all matters in the church assembled, as to propound matters to the church, to order the season of speech and silence, and to pronounce sentence according to the mind of Christ, with the consent of the church;[d] (5) to be guides and leaders to the church in all matters whatsoever pertaining to church adminis-trations and actions; (6) to see that none in the church live inordinately out of rank
[Acts 20.28, 32]   and place, without a calling, or idly in their calling; (7) to prevent and heal such of-fenses in life or in doctrine as might corrupt the church; (8) to feed the flock of God
[1 Thes 5.12]   with a word of admonition; (9) and as they shall be sent for, to visit and to pray over their sick brethren;[e] 10) and at other times as opportunity shall serve thereunto.

              3. The office of a deacon is instituted in the church by the Lord Jesus. Some-times they are called "helps."[f] The Scripture telleth us how they should be qualified:
[1 Tm 3.8–9]   "Grave, not double-tongued, not given too much to wine, not given to filthy lucre." They must first be proved and then use the office of a deacon, being found blame-
[Acts 4.35, 6.2–3] less. The office and work of the deacons is to receive the offerings of the church,

a. [Rom 12.7–9; 1 Tm 5.17; 1 Cor 12.28]
b. [Heb 13.17; 1 Tm 5.17]
c. [2 Chr 23.19; Rv 21.12; 1 Tm 4.14; Mt 18.17; 2 Cor 2.7–8; Acts 2.6]
d. [Acts 6.2–3, 13.15; 2 Cor 8.10; Heb 13.7, 17; 2 Thes 2.10–12]
e. [Jas 5.14; Acts 20.20]
f. [Acts 6.3, 6; Phil 1.1; 1 Tm 3.8; 1 Cor 12.28]

gifts given to the church, and to keep the treasury of the church, and therewith to serve the tables which the church is to provide for: as the Lord's table, the table of the ministers, and of such as are in necessity, to whom they are to distribute in simplicity.　　　　　　　　　　　　　　　　　　　　　　　　　　　[Rom 12.8]

4. The office therefore being limited unto the care of the temporal good things of the church, it extends not unto the attendance upon and administration of the spiritual things thereof, as the word and sacraments or the like.　　　[1 Cor 7.17]

5. The ordinance of the apostle and practice of the church commends the Lord's day as a fit time for the contributions of the saints.　　　　　　　[1 Cor 16.1–3]

6. The instituting of all these officers in the church is the work of God himself, of the Lord Jesus Christ, of the Holy Ghost.[a] And therefore such officers as he hath not appointed are altogether unlawful either to be placed in the church or to be retained therein, and are to be looked at as human creatures, mere inventions and appointments of man, to the great dishonor of Christ Jesus, the Lord of his house, the King of his church, whether popes, patriarchs, cardinals, archbishops, lord bishops, archdeacons, officials, commissaries, and the like. These and the rest of that hierarchy and retinue, not being plants of the Lord's planting, shall all certainly be rooted out and cast forth.　　　　　　　　　　　　　　　　　　[Mt 15.13]

7. The Lord hath appointed ancient widows (where they may be had) to minister in the church, in giving attendance to the sick, and to give succor unto them and others in the like necessities.　　　　　　　　　　　　　　　　[1 Tm 5.9-10]

CHAPTER 8. OF THE ELECTION OF CHURCH OFFICERS

1. No man may take the honor of a church officer unto himself, but he that was called of God, as was Aaron.　　　　　　　　　　　　　　　　　[Heb 5.4]

2. Calling unto office is either immediate, by Christ himself—such was the call of the apostles and prophets;[b] this manner of calling ended with them, as hath been said—or mediate, by the church.

3. It is meet that before any be ordained or chosen officers, they should first be tried and proved,[c] because hands are not suddenly to be laid upon any, and both elders and deacons must be of honest and good report.

4. The things in respect of which they are to be tried are those gifts and virtues which the Scripture requireth in men that are to be elected into such places, that is, that elders must be blameless, sober, apt to teach, and endued with such

a. [1 Cor 12.28; Eph 4.8, 11; Acts 20.28]
b. [Gal 1.1; Acts 14.23, 6.3]
c. [1 Tm 5.22; Acts 16.2, 6.3]

other qualifications as are laid down, 1 Tm 3 and 2; Ti 1.6–9. Deacons to be fitted as is directed, Acts 6.3; 1 Tm 3.8–11.

5. Officers are to be called by such churches where they are to minister.[a] Of such moment is the preservation of this power that the churches exercised it in the presence of the apostles.

6. A church, being free, cannot become subject to any but by a free election. Yet when such a people do choose any to be over them in the Lord, then do they become subject and most willingly submit to their ministry in the Lord whom they have so chosen.

[Gal 5.13]

[Heb 13.17]

7. And if the church have power to choose their officers and ministers, then in case of manifest unworthiness and delinquency they have power also to depose them. For to open and shut, to choose and refuse, to constitute in office and remove from office, are acts belonging unto the same power.

[Rom 16.17]

8. We judge it much conducing to the well-being and communion of the churches that where it may conveniently be done, neighbor churches be advised withal and their help made use of in the trial of church officers, in order to their choice.

[Sg 8.8–9]

9. The choice of such church officers belongeth not to the civil magistrates as such, or diocesan bishops, or patrons; for of these or any such like, the Scripture is wholly silent, as having any power therein.

CHAPTER 9. OF ORDINATION, AND IMPOSITION OF HANDS

1. Church officers are not only to be chosen by the church, but also to be ordained by imposition of hands and prayer, with which at ordination of elders fasting also is to be joined.[b]

2. This ordination we account nothing else but the solemn putting of a man into his place[c] and office in the church whereunto he had right before by election, being like the installing of a magistrate in the commonwealth. Ordination, therefore, is not to go before, but to follow election. The essence and substance of the outward calling of an ordinary officer in the church doth not consist in his ordination, but in his voluntary and free election by the church and in his accepting of that election, whereupon is founded the relation between pastor and flock, between such a minister and such a people. Ordination doth not constitute an officer, nor give him the essentials of his office. The apostles were elders without imposition

[Acts 6.5–6, 14.23]

a. [Acts 14.23, 1.23, 6.3–5]
b. [Acts 13.3, 14.23; 1 Tm 5.22]
c. [Nm 8.10; Acts 6.5–6, 13.2–3]

of hands by men; Paul and Barnabas were officers before that imposition of hands, Acts 13.3. The posterity of Levi were priests and Levites before hands were laid on them by the children of Israel.

3. In such churches where there are elders, imposition of hands in ordination is to be performed by those elders.[a]

4. In such churches where there are no elders, imposition of hands may be performed by some of the brethren orderly chosen by the church thereunto. For if the people may elect officers, which is the greater and wherein the substance of the office consists, they may much more (occasion and need so requiring) impose hands in ordination, which is the less and but the accomplishment of the other. [Nm 8.10]

5. Nevertheless, in such churches where there are no elders, and the church so desire, we see not why imposition of hands may not be performed by the elders of other churches. Ordinary officers laid hands upon the officers of many churches: the presbytery of Ephesus laid hands upon Timothy, an evangelist; the presbytery at Antioch laid hands upon Paul and Barnabas. [1 Tm 4.14] [Acts 13.3]

6. Church officers are officers to one church, even that particular over which the Holy Ghost hath made them overseers, insomuch as elders are commanded to feed, not all flocks, but that flock which is committed to their faith and trust and dependeth upon them.[b] Nor can constant residence at one congregation be necessary for a minister—no, nor yet lawful—if he be not a minister to one congregation only, but to the church universal, because he may not attend one part only of the church whereto he is a minister, but he is called to attend unto all the flock. [Acts 20.28]

7. He that is clearly loosed from his office relation unto that church whereof he was a minister cannot be looked at as an officer, nor perform any act of office in any other church unless he be again orderly called unto office. Which when it shall be, we know nothing to hinder, but imposition of hands also in his ordination ought to be used towards him again. For so Paul the apostle received imposition of hands twice at least, from Ananias (Acts 9.17) and Acts 13.3.

CHAPTER 10. OF THE POWER OF THE CHURCH, AND ITS PRESBYTERY

1. Supreme and lordly power over all the churches upon earth doth only belong unto Jesus Christ, who is King of the church and the Head thereof.[c] He hath the gov-

a. [1 Tm 4.14; Acts 13.3; 1 Tm 5.22]
b. [1 Pt 5.2; Acts 20.28]
c. [Ps 2.6; Eph 1.21–22]

ernment upon his shoulders, and hath all power given to him, both in heaven and

[Is 9.6; Mt 28.18]   earth.

2. A company of professed believers ecclesiastically confederate, as they are a church before they have officers, and without them, so even in that estate subordinate church power under Christ, delegated to them by him, doth belong to them,[a] in such a manner as is before expressed in chapter 5, section 2, and as flowing from the very nature and essence of a church, it being natural to all bodies, and so unto a church body, to be furnished with sufficient power for its own preservation and subsistence.

3. The government of the church is a mixed government (and so hath been acknowledged long before the term of Independency was heard of): in respect of Christ, the head and king of the church, and the sovereign power residing in him

[Rv 3.7; 1 Cor 5.12]   and exercised by him, it is a monarchy; in respect of the body or brotherhood of

[1 Tm 5.17]   the church, and power from Christ granted unto them, it resembles a democracy; in respect of the presbytery, and power committed to them, it is an aristocracy.

4. The sovereign power which is peculiar unto Christ is exercised, (1) in

[Gal 1.4; Rv 5.8-9]   calling the church out of the world unto holy fellowship with himself; (2) in instituting the ordinances of his worship and appointing his ministers and officers for the dispensing of them;[b] (3) in giving laws for the ordering of all our ways, and the ways of his house;[c] (4) in giving power and life to all his institutions, and to his people by them; (5) in protecting and delivering his church against and from all the

[Is 32.2; Lk 1.51]   enemies of their peace.

5. The power granted by Christ unto the body of the church and brotherhood is a prerogative or privilege which the church doth exercise: (1) in choosing their own officers, whether elders or deacons; (2) in admission of their own members, and therefore there is great reason they should have power to remove any from their fellowship again.[d] Hence in case of offense any one brother hath power to convince and admonish an offending brother, and in case of not hearing him, to take one or two more to set on the admonition, and in case of not hearing them, to proceed

[Mt 18.15-17]   to tell the church; and as his offense may require, the whole church hath power to proceed to the public censure of him, whether by admonition or excommunication, and upon his repentance to restore him again unto his former communion.[e]

a. [Acts 1.23, 14.23, 6.3-4; Mt 18.17; 1 Cor 5.4-5]
b. [Mt 28.20; Eph 4.8, 12; Jas 4.12; Is 33.22]
c. [1 Tm 3.15; 2 Cor 10.4-5]
d. [Acts 6.3, 5, 14.23, 9.26]
e. [Ti 3.10; Col 4.17; Mt 18.17; 2 Cor 2.7-8]

6. In case an elder offend incorrigibly, the matter so requiring, as the church had power to call him to office, so they have power according to order[a] (the counsel of other churches where it may be had) directing thereto to remove him from his office. And being now but a member, in case he add contumacy to his sin, the church that had power to receive him into their fellowship hath also the same power to cast him out that they have concerning any other member.   [Mt 18.17]

7. Church government or rule is placed by Christ in the officers of the church, who are therefore called rulers while they rule with God;[b] yet in case of maladministration, they are subject to the power of the church, according as hath been said before. The Holy Ghost frequently, yea always, where it mentioneth church rule and church government, ascribeth it to elders, whereas the work and duty of the people is expressed in the phrase of obeying their elders and submitting themselves unto them in the Lord.[c] So as it is manifest that an organic or complete church is a body politic, consisting of some that are governors and some that are governed, in the Lord.

8. The power which Christ hath committed to the elders is to feed and rule the church of God, and accordingly to call the church together upon any weighty   [Acts 20.28]
occasion,[d] when the members so called, without just cause may not refuse to come, nor when they are come depart before they are dismissed, nor speak in the church   [Hos 4.4]
before they have leave from the elders, nor continue so doing when they require silence, nor may they oppose nor contradict the judgment or sentence of the elders without sufficient and weighty cause, because such practices are manifestly contrary unto order and government, and inlets of disturbance, and tend to confusion.

9. It belongs also unto the elders to examine any officers or members before they be received of the church, to receive the accusations brought to the church, and to prepare them for the church's hearing.[e] In handling of offenses and other matters before the church they have power to declare and publish the counsel and will of God touching the same, and to pronounce sentence with the consent of the church. Lastly, they have power, when they dismiss the people, to bless them in the name of the Lord.   [Nm 6.23–26]

10. This power of government in the elders doth not in any wise prejudice the power of privilege in the brotherhood, as neither the power of privilege in the

a. [Col 4.17; Rom 16.17]
b. [1 Tm 5.17; Heb 13.17; 1 Thes 5.12]
c. [Rom 12.8; 1 Tm 5.17; 1 Cor 12.28–29; Heb 13.7, 17]
d. [Acts 6.2; Nm 16.12; Ez 46.10; Acts 13.15]
e. [Rv 2.2; 1 Tm 5.19; Acts 21.18, 22–23; 1 Cor 5.4–5]

brethren doth prejudice the power of government in the elders; but they may sweetly agree together, as we may see in the example of the apostles, furnished with the greatest church power, who took in the concurrence and consent of the brethren in church administration.[a] Also that Scripture, 2 Cor 2.9 and 10.6, do declare that what the churches were to act and do in these matters, they were to do in a way of obedience, and that not only to the direction of the apostles but also of their

[Heb 13.17]   ordinary elders.

       11. From the premises, namely, that the ordinary power of government belonging only to the elders, power of privilege remaineth with the brotherhood (as power of judgment in matters of censure, and power of liberty in matters of liberty), it followeth that in an organic church and right administration all church acts proceed after the manner of a mixed administration, so as no church act can be consummated or perfected without the consent of both.

CHAPTER 11. OF THE MAINTENANCE OF CHURCH OFFICERS

1. The apostle concludes that necessary and sufficient maintenance is due unto the ministers of the word, from the law of nature and nations, from the law of Moses, the equity thereof, as also the rule of common reason.[b] Moreover, the Scripture doth not only call elders laborers and workmen, but also, speaking of them, doth say that the laborer is worthy of his hire, and requires that he which is taught in the word should communicate to him in all good things, and mentions it as an ordinance of the Lord that they which preach the gospel should live of the gospel, and forbiddeth the muzzling of the ox that treadeth out the corn.[c]

       2. The Scriptures alleged requiring this maintenance as a bounden duty and due debt, and not as a matter of alms and free gift. Therefore people are not at liberty to do or not to do what and when they please in this matter, no more than in any other commanded duty and ordinance of the Lord, but ought of duty to minister of their carnal things to them that labor amongst them in the word and doctrine,[d] as well as they ought to pay any other workmen their wages or to discharge and satisfy their other debts or to submit themselves to observe any other ordinance of the Lord.

       3. The apostle, Gal 6.6, enjoining that he which is taught communicate to him that teacheth in all good things, doth not leave it arbitrary what or how much

a. [Acts 14.15, 23, 6.2; 1 Cor 5.4; 2 Cor 2.6–7]
b. [1 Cor 9.9, 15; Mt 9.38, 10.10; 1 Tm 5.18]
c. [Gal 6.6; 1 Cor 9.9, 14; 1 Tm 5.18]
d. [Rom 15.27; 1 Cor 9.14]

a man shall give, or in what proportion, but even the latter as well as the former is
prescribed and appointed by the Lord.   [1 Cor 16.2]

    4. Not only members of churches, but all that are taught in the word, are to
contribute unto him that teacheth, in all good things. In case that congregations are   [Gal 6.6]
defective in their contributions, the deacons are to call upon them to do their duty.
If their call sufficeth not, the church by her power is to require it of their members;   [Acts 6.3–4]
and where church power through the corruption of men doth not or cannot attain
the end, the magistrate is to see [that the] ministry be duly provided for, as appears
from the commended example of Nehemiah. The magistrates are nursing fathers,   [Neh 13.11]
and nursing mothers, and stand charged with the custody of both tables, because   [Is 49.23]
it is better to prevent a scandal that it may not come, and easier also, than to remove it when it is given. It's most suitable to rule that by the church's care each man
should know his proportion, according to rule, what he should do before he do it,   [2 Cor 8.13–14]
that so his judgment and heart may be satisfied in what he doeth, and just offense
prevented in what is done.

CHAPTER 12. OF ADMISSION OF MEMBERS INTO THE CHURCH
1. The doors of the churches of Christ upon earth do not by God's appointment
stand so wide open that all sorts of people, good or bad, may freely enter therein at
their pleasure;[a] but such as are admitted thereto, as members ought to be examined
and tried first whether they be fit and meet to be received into church society or not.
The eunuch of Ethiopia before his admission was examined by Philip whether he
did believe on Jesus Christ with all his heart. The angel of the church at Ephesus is   [Acts 8.37]
commended for trying such as said they were apostles and were not. There is like   [Rv 2.2; Acts 9.26]
reason for trying of them that profess themselves to be believers. The officers are
charged with the keeping of the doors of the church, and therefore are in a special
manner to make trial of the fitness of such who enter. Twelve angels are set at the
gates of the temple, lest such as were ceremonially unclean should enter thereinto.[b]

    2. The things which are requisite to be found in all church members are
repentance from sin and faith in Jesus Christ. And therefore these are the things   [Acts 2.38–42, 8.37]
whereof men are to be examined at their admission into the church, and which then
they must profess and hold forth in such sort as may satisfy rational charity that the
things are there indeed. John Baptist admitted men to baptism, confessing and be-   [Mt 3.6]
wailing their sins; and of others it is said that they came and confessed and showed
their deeds.   [Acts 19.8]

a. [2 Chr 23.19; Mt 13.25, 22.12]
b. [Rv 21.12; 2 Chr 23.19]

3. The weakest measure of faith is to be accepted in those that desire to be admitted into the church, because weak Christians, if sincere, have the substance of that faith, repentance, and holiness which is required in church members; and [Rom 14.1] such have most need of the ordinances for their confirmation and growth in grace. The Lord Jesus would not quench the smoking flax, nor break the bruised reed, [Mt 12.20; Is 40.11] but gather the tender lambs in his arms and carry them gently in his bosom. Such charity and tenderness is to be used as the weakest Christian, if sincere, may not be excluded nor discouraged. Severity of examination is to be avoided.

4. In case any through excessive fear or other infirmity be unable to make their personal relation of their spiritual estate in public, it is sufficient that the elders, having received private satisfaction, make relation thereof in public before the church, they testifying their assents thereunto; this being the way that tendeth most to edification. But whereas persons are of better abilities, there it is most expedient that they make their relations and confessions personally with their own mouth, as [Ps 66.16] David professeth of himself.

5. A personal and public confession and declaring of God's manner of working upon the soul is both lawful, expedient, and useful, in sundry respects and upon sundry grounds. Those three thousands, Acts 2.37, 41, before they were admitted by the apostles, did manifest that they were pricked in their hearts at Peter's sermon, together with earnest desire to be delivered from their sins, which now wounded their consciences, and their ready receiving of the word of promise and exhortation. We are to be ready to render a reason of the hope that is in us to everyone that [1 Pt 3.15] asketh us. Therefore we must be able and ready upon any occasion to declare and show our repentance for sin, faith unfeigned, and effectual calling, because these [Heb 11.1; Eph 1.18] are the reason of a well-grounded hope: "I have not hidden thy righteousness from the great congregation," Ps 40.10.

6. This profession of faith and repentance, as it must be made by such at their admission that were never in church society before, so nothing hindereth but the same may also be performed by such as have formerly been members of some other church, and the church to which they now join themselves as members may lawfully require the same. Those three thousand, Acts 2, which made their confession were members of the church of the Jews before; so were they that were baptized by John. Churches may err in their admission, and persons regularly admitted may fall into offense.[a] Otherwise, if churches might obtrude their members, or if church members might obtrude themselves upon other churches, without due trial, the matter so requiring, both the liberty of churches would hereby be infringed, in that they

a. [Mt 3.5–6; Gal 2.4; 1 Tm 5.24]

might not examine those concerning whose fitness for communion they were unsatisfied; and besides the infringement of their liberty, the churches themselves would [Sg 8.8] unavoidably be corrupted, and the ordinances defiled, whilst they might not refuse but must receive the unworthy. Which is contrary unto the Scripture, teaching that all churches are sisters and therefore equal.

7. The like trial is to be required from such members of the church as were born in the same, or received their membership and were baptized in their infancy or minority by virtue of the covenant of their parents, when being grown up unto years of discretion they shall desire to be made partakers of the Lord's supper. Unto which, because holy things must not be given unto the unworthy,[a] therefore it is requisite that these as well as others should come to their trial and examination, and manifest their faith and repentance, by an open profession thereof before they are received to the Lord's supper, and otherwise not to be admitted thereunto. Yet these church members that were so born, or received in their childhood before they are capable of being made partakers of full communion, have many privileges which others (not church members) have not: they are in covenant with God, have the seal thereof upon them, that is, baptism; and so, if not regenerated, yet are in a more hopeful way of attaining regenerating grace and all the spiritual blessings both of the covenant and seal; they are also under church watch, and consequently subject to the reprehensions, admonitions, and censures thereof for their healing and amendment, as need shall require.

CHAPTER 13. OF CHURCH MEMBERS, THEIR REMOVAL FROM ONE CHURCH TO ANOTHER, AND OF LETTERS OF RECOMMENDATION AND DISMISSION

1. Church members may not remove or depart from the church, and so from one another, as they please, nor without just and weighty cause, but ought to live and dwell together, forasmuch as they are commanded not to forsake the assembling of themselves together. Such departure tends to the dissolution and ruin of the body, [Heb 10.25] as the pulling of stones and pieces of timber from the building, and of members from the natural body, tend to the destruction of the whole.

2. It is therefore the duty of church members, in such times and places when counsel may be had, to consult with the church whereof they are members about their removal, that accordingly they have their approbation, may be encouraged, or otherwise desist. They who are joined with consent should not depart without consent, except forced thereunto. [Prv 11.16]

a. [Mt 7.6; 1 Cor 11.27]

3. If a member's departure be manifestly unsafe and sinful, the church may not consent thereunto; for in so doing they should not act in faith and should partake with him in his sin. If the case be doubtful and the person not to be persuaded, it seemeth best to leave the matter unto God, and not forcibly to detain him.[a]

4. Just reasons for a member's removal of himself from the church are: (1) If [Eph 5.11] a man cannot continue without partaking in sin; (2) In case of personal persecution, so Paul departed from the disciples at Damascus; also in case of general persecution, when all are scattered;[b] (3) In case of real, and not only pretended, want of competent subsistence, a door being opened for a better supply in another place, [Neh 13.20] together with the means of spiritual edification. In these or like cases, a member may lawfully remove, and the church cannot lawfully detain him.

5. To separate from a church either out of contempt of their holy fellow- [2 Tm 4.10] ship or out of covetousness or for greater enlargements with just grief to the church, [Rom 16.17] or out of schism or want of love, and out of a spirit of contention in respect of [Jude 19] some unkindness or some evil only conceived or, indeed, in the church which might [Eph 4.2–3] and should be tolerated and healed with a spirit of meekness, and of which evil the church is not yet convinced (though perhaps himself be) nor admonished[c]—for these or the like reasons to withdraw from public communion, in word or seals or censures, is unlawful and sinful.

6. Such members as have orderly removed their habitation ought to join [Is 56.8; Acts 9.26] themselves unto the church in order where they do inhabit if it may be. Otherwise they can neither perform the duties nor receive the privileges of members. Such an example, tolerated in some, is apt to corrupt others, which if many should follow, [1 Cor 14.33] would threaten the dissolution and confusion of churches, contrary to the Scripture.

7. Order requires that a member thus removing have letters testimonial and of dismission from the church whereof he yet is unto the church whereunto he de- [Acts 18.27] sireth to be joined, lest the church should be deluded, that the church may receive him in faith and not be corrupted by receiving deceivers and false brethren. Until the person dismissed be received into another church, he ceaseth not by his letters of dismission to be a member of the church whereof he was. The church cannot make a member no member but by excommunication.

8. If a member be called to remove only for a time, where a church is, letters [Rom 16.1–2] of recommendation are requisite and sufficient for communion with that church in

a. [Rom 14.23; 1 Tm 5.22; Acts 21.14]
b. [Acts 9.25, 29–30, 8.1]
c. [Col 3.13; Gal 6.1–2]

the ordinances and in their watch; as Phoebe, a servant of the church at Cenchrea, had letters written for her to the church of Rome, that she might be received as becometh saints. [2 Cor 3.1]

9. Such letters of recommendation and dismission were written for Apollos, for Marcus to the Colossians, for Phoebe to the Romans, for sundry others to other churches;[a] and the apostle telleth us that some persons, not sufficiently known otherwise, have special need of such letters, though he for his part had no need thereof. The use of them is to be a benefit and help to the party for whom they are written, and for the furthering of his receiving amongst the saints in the place whereto he goeth, and the due satisfaction of them in their receiving of him. [2 Cor 3.1]

CHAPTER 14. OF EXCOMMUNICATION AND OTHER CENSURES

1. The censures of the church are appointed by Christ for the preventing, removing, and healing of offenses in the church; for the reclaiming and gaining of offending brethren; for the deterring others from the like offenses; for purging out the leaven which may infect the whole lump; for vindicating the honor of Christ and of his church, and the holy profession of the gospel;[b] and for preventing the wrath of God that may justly fall upon the church if they should suffer his covenant and the seals thereof to be profaned by notorious and obstinate offenders. [Rv 2.14-16, 20]

2. If an offense be private (one brother offending another), the offender is to go and acknowledge his repentance for it unto his offended brother, who is then to forgive him.[c] But if the offender neglect or refuse to do it, the brother offended is to go and convince and admonish him of it, between themselves privately. If thereupon the offender be brought to repent of his offense, the admonisher hath won his brother. But if the offender hear not his brother, the brother offended is to take with him one or two more, that in the mouth of two or three witnesses every word may be established (whether the word of admonition if the offender receive it, or the word of complaint if he refuse it). For if he refuse it, the offended brother is by the mouth of the elders to tell the church. And if he hear the church and declare the same by penitent confession, he is recovered and gained. And if the church [Mt 18.15-17] discern him to be willing to hear, yet not fully convinced of his offense, as in the case of heresy, they are to dispense to him a public admonition, which, declaring [Ti 3.10] the offender to lie under the public offense of the church, doth thereby withhold or

a. [Acts 18.27; Col 4.10; Rom 16.1]
b. [1 Tm 5.20; Dt 17.12-13; Jude 23; Dt 13.11; 1 Cor 5.6; Rom 2.24]
c. [Mt 5.23-24; Lk 17.3-4]

suspend him from the holy fellowship of the Lord's supper, till his offense be re-

[Mt 18.17]   moved by penitent confession. If he still continue obstinate, they are to cast him out
by excommunication.

3. But if the offense be more public at first, and of a more heinous and crimi-

[1 Cor 5.4–5]   nal nature, to wit, such as are condemned by the light of nature, then the church,
without such gradual proceeding, is to cast out the offender from their holy communion, for the further mortifying of his sin and the healing of his soul, in the day
of the Lord Jesus.

4. In dealing with an offender, great care is to be taken that we be neither

[Gal 6.1]   overstrict or rigorous nor too indulgent or remiss; our proceeding herein ought to
be with a spirit of meekness, considering ourselves, lest we also be tempted, and that
the best of us have need of much forgiveness from the Lord.[a] Yet the winning and
healing of the offender's soul being the end of these endeavors, we must not daub
with untempered mortar, nor heal the wounds of our brethren slightly: on some
have compassion, others save with fear.

5. While the offender remains excommunicate, the church is to refrain from
all member-like communion with him in spiritual things, and also from all familiar
communion with him in civil things farther than the necessity of natural or domestic or civil relations do require, and are therefore to forbear to eat and drink with
him, that he may be ashamed.[b]

6. Excommunication being a spiritual punishment, it doth not prejudice
the excommunicate in, nor deprive him of, his civil rights, and therefore toucheth
not princes or other magistrates in point of their civil dignity or authority. And, the
excommunicate being but as a publican and a heathen, heathens being lawfully permitted to come to hear the word in church assemblies, we acknowledge therefore the
like liberty of hearing the word may be permitted to persons excommunicate that

[1 Cor 14.24–25]   is permitted unto heathen. And because we are not without hope of his recovery,
[2 Thes 3.14]   we are not to account him as an enemy but to admonish him as a brother.

7. If the Lord sanctify the censure to the offender, so as by the grace of
Christ he doth testify his repentance, with humble confession of his sin and judging
of himself, giving glory unto God, the church is then to forgive him and to comfort him and to restore him to the wonted brotherly communion which formerly he

[2 Cor 2.7–8]   enjoyed with them.

8. The suffering of profane or scandalous livers to continue in fellowship
and partake in the sacraments is doubtless a great sin in those that have power in

a. [Mt 18.34–35, 6.14–15; Ez 13.10; Jer 6.14]
b. [Mt 18.17; 1 Cor 5.11; 2 Thes 3.6, 14]

their hands to redress it and do it not. Nevertheless, inasmuch as Christ and his [Rv 2.14–15, 20] apostles in their times, and the prophets and other godly in theirs, did lawfully [Mt 23.3; Acts 3.1] partake of the Lord's commanded ordinances in the Jewish church, and neither taught nor practiced separation from the same though unworthy ones were permitted therein; and inasmuch as the faithful in the church of Corinth, wherein were many unworthy persons and practices, are never commanded to absent themselves from the sacraments because of the same—therefore the godly in like cases are not [1 Cor 6, 12.15] presently to separate.

9. As separation from such a church wherein profane and scandalous livers are tolerated is not presently necessary, so for the members thereof, otherwise worthy, hereupon to abstain from communicating with such a church in the participation of the sacraments is unlawful.[a] For as it were unreasonable for an innocent person to be punished for the faults of others wherein he hath no hand and whereunto he gave no consent, so it is more unreasonable that a godly man should neglect duty and punish himself in not coming for his portion in the blessing of the seals as he ought, because others are suffered to come that ought not. Especially, considering that himself doth neither consent to their sin nor to their approaching to the ordinance in their sin nor to the neglect of others who should put them away and do not, but on the contrary doth heartily mourn for these things, modestly and seasonably stir up others to do their duty. If the church cannot be reformed, they may use [Ez 9.4] their liberty, as is specified in chapter 13, section 4. But this all the godly are bound unto, even everyone to do his endeavor, according to his power and place, that the unworthy may be duly proceeded against by the church to whom this matter doth appertain.

CHAPTER 15. OF THE COMMUNION OF CHURCHES ONE WITH ANOTHER

1. Although churches be distinct and therefore may not be confounded one with another, and equal and therefore have not dominion one over another,[b] yet all the churches ought to preserve church communion one with another,[c] because they are all united unto Christ, not only as a mystical but as a political head; whence is derived a communion suitable thereunto.

2. The communion of churches is exercised sundry ways:

(1) By way of mutual care in taking thought for one another's welfare; [Sg 8.8]

a. [2 Chr 30.18; Gn 18.25]
b. [Rv 1.4; Sg 8.8; Rom 16.16]
c. [1 Cor 16.19; Acts 15.23; Rv 2.1]

(2) By way of consultation one with another when we have occasion to require the judgment and counsel of other churches, touching any person or cause wherewith they may be better acquainted than ourselves. As the church of Antioch consulted with the apostles and elders of the church at Jerusalem about the question of circumcision of the Gentiles and about the false teachers that broached that doctrine. In which case, when any church wanteth light or peace amongst themselves, it is a way of communion of churches (according to the word) to meet together by their elders and other messengers in a synod, to consider and argue the points in doubt or difference, and having found out the way of truth and peace, to commend the same by their letters and messengers to the churches, whom the same may concern. But if a church be rent with divisions amongst themselves, or lie under any open scandal, and yet refuse to consult with other churches for healing or removing of the same, it is a matter of just offense both to the Lord Jesus and to other churches, as betraying too much want of mercy and faithfulness, not to seek to bind up the breaches and wounds of the church and brethren. And therefore the state of such a church calleth aloud upon other churches to exercise a fuller act of brotherly communion, to wit, by way of admonition.

[Acts 15.2]

[Acts 15.6, 22–23]

[Ez 34.4]

(3) A third way, then, of communion of churches is by way of admonition, to wit, in case any public offense be found in a church, which they either discern not or are slow in proceeding to use the means for the removing and healing of. Paul had no authority over Peter; yet when he saw Peter not walking with a right foot, he publicly rebuked him before the church. Though churches have no more authority over one another than one apostle had over another, yet as one apostle might admonish another, so may one church admonish another, and yet without usurpation. In which case, if the church that lieth under offense do not hearken to the church which doth admonish her, the church is to acquaint other neighbor churches with that offense which the offending church still lieth under, together with their neglect of the brotherly admonition given unto them. Whereupon those other churches are to join in seconding the admonition formerly given. And if still the offending church continue in obstinacy and impenitency, they may forbear communion with them, and are to proceed to make use of the help of a synod or council of neighbor churches walking orderly (if a greater cannot conveniently be had) for their conviction. If they hear not the synod, the synod having declared them to be obstinate, particular churches, approving and accepting of the judgment of the synod, are to declare the sentence of noncommunion respectively concerning them. And thereupon, out of a religious care to keep their own communion pure, they may justly withdraw themselves from participation with them at the Lord's table, and from such other acts of holy communion as the communion of churches doth otherwise allow and require.

[Gal 2.11–14]

[Mt 18.15–17]

Nevertheless, if any members of such a church as lieth under public offense do not consent to the offense of the church, but do in due sort bear witness against it, they are still to be received to wonted communion; for it is not equal that the innocent should suffer with the offensive. Yea furthermore, if such innocent members, after due waiting in the use of all good means for the healing of the offense of their own church, shall at last (with the allowance of the counsel of neighbor churches) withdraw from the fellowship of their own church and offer themselves to the fellowship of another, we judge it lawful for the other church to receive them (being otherwise fit) as if they had been orderly dismissed to them from their own church. [Gn 18.25]

(4) A fourth way of communion of churches is by way of participation: the members of one church occasionally coming unto another, we willingly admit them to partake with us at the Lord's table, it being the seal of our communion not only with Christ, nor only with the members of our own church, but also with all the churches of the saints. In which regard we refuse not to baptize their children presented to us if either their own minister be absent or such a fruit of holy fellowship be desired with us. In like case such churches as are furnished with more ministers than one do willingly afford one of their own ministers to supply the place of an absent or sick minister of another church for a needful season. [1 Cor 12.13]

(5) A fifth way of church communion is by way of recommendation when a member of one church hath occasion to reside in another church: if but for a season, we commend him to their watchful fellowship by letters of recommendation; but if he be called to settle his abode there, we commit him, according to his desire, to the fellowship of their covenant by letters of dismission. [Rom 16.1] [Acts 18.27]

(6) A sixth way of church communion is, in case of need, to minister relief and succor one unto another, either of able members to furnish them with officers, or of outward support to the necessities of poorer churches, as did the churches of the Gentiles contribute liberally to the poor saints at Jerusalem. [Acts 11.22, 29] [Rom 13.26–27]

3. When a company of believers purpose to gather into church fellowship, it is requisite for their safer proceeding and the maintaining of the communion of churches that they signify their intent unto the neighbor churches walking according unto the order of the gospel, and desire their presence and help and right hand of fellowship, which they ought readily to give unto them when there is no just cause of excepting against their proceedings. [Gal 2.1–2, 9]

4. Besides these several ways of communion, there is also a way of propagation of churches. When a church shall grow too numerous, it is a way and fit season to propagate one church out of another, by sending forth such of their members as are willing to remove and to procure some officers to them as may enter with them into church estate amongst themselves. As bees, when the hive is too full, [Is 40.20; Sg 8.8–9]

issue forth by swarms and are gathered into other hives, so the churches of Christ may do the same upon like necessity, and therein hold forth to them the right hand of fellowship, both in their gathering into a church and in the ordination of their officers.

CHAPTER 16. OF SYNODS

1. Synods orderly assembled, and rightly proceeding according to the pattern, Acts 15, we acknowledge as the ordinance of Christ, and, though not absolutely necessary to the being, yet many times, through the iniquity of men and perverseness of times, necessary to the well-being of churches, for the establishment of truth and peace therein.

[Acts 15.2-15]

2. Synods, being spiritual and ecclesiastical assemblies, are therefore made up of spiritual and ecclesiastical causes. The next efficient cause of them, under Christ, is the power of the churches, sending forth their elders [and] other messengers, who, being met together in the name of Christ, are the matter of a synod. And they, in arguing, debating, and determining matters of religion according to the word and publishing the same to the churches whom it concerneth, do put forth the proper and formal acts of a synod, to the conviction of errors and heresies, and the establishment of truth and peace in the churches, which is the end of a synod.

[Acts 15.2-23, 31]

[Acts 16.4, 15]

3. Magistrates have power to call a synod, by calling to the churches to send forth their elders and other messengers to counsel and assist them in matters of religion. But yet the constituting of a synod is a church act, and may be transacted by the churches even when civil magistrates may be enemies to churches and to church assemblies.

[2 Chr 29.4-11]

[Acts 15]

4. It belongeth unto synods and councils: to debate and determine controversies of faith and cases of conscience;[a] to clear from the word holy directions for the holy worship of God and good government of the church; to bear witness against maladministration and corruption in doctrine or manners in any particular church, and to give direction for the reformation thereof;[b] not to exercise church censures in way of discipline, nor any other act of church authority or jurisdiction, which that presidential synod did forbear.

5. The synod's directions and determinations, so far as consonant to the word of God, are to be received with reverence and submission, not only for their agreement therewith (which is the principal ground thereof, and without which they

---

a. [Acts 15.1-2, 6-7; 1 Chr 15.13]

b. [2 Chr 29.6-7; Acts 15.24, 28-29]

bind not at all), but also secondarily, for the power whereby they are made, as being
an ordinance of God appointed thereunto in his word.   [Acts 15]

6. Because it is difficult, if not impossible, for many churches to come all
together in one place in all their members universally, therefore they may assemble
by their delegates or messengers, as the church of Antioch went not all to Jerusalem, but some select men for that purpose. Because none are or should be more fit   [Acts 15.2]
to know the state of the churches, nor to advise of ways for the good thereof, than
elders, therefore it is fit that in the choice of the messengers for such assemblies they
have special respect unto such. Yet inasmuch as not only Paul and Barnabas but certain others also were sent to Jerusalem from Antioch, Acts 15, and when they were   [Acts 15.2, 22–23]
come to Jerusalem, not only the apostles and elders but other brethren also do assemble and meet about the matter, therefore synods are to consist both of elders and
other church members, endowed with gifts and sent by the churches, not excluding
the presence of any brethren in the churches.

CHAPTER 17. OF THE CIVIL MAGISTRATE'S POWER
IN MATTERS ECCLESIASTICAL

1. It is lawful, profitable, and necessary for Christians to gather themselves into
church estate and therein to exercise all the ordinances of Christ according unto
the word, although the consent of the magistrate could not be had thereunto, because the apostles and Christians in their time did frequently thus practice, when
the magistrates, being all of them Jewish or pagan and mostly persecuting enemies,
would give no countenance or consent to such matters.[a]

2. Church government stands in no opposition to civil government of com-
monwealths, nor any entrencheth upon the authority of civil magistrates in their
jurisdictions, nor any whit weakeneth their hands in governing; but rather strength-   [Jn 18.36]
eneth them and furthereth the people in yielding more hearty and conscionable obedience unto them, whatever some ill-affected persons to the ways of Christ have   [Jn 18.36; Acts 25.8]
suggested, to alienate the affections of kings and princes from the ordinances of
Christ. As if the kingdom of Christ in his church could not rise and stand without
the falling and weakening of their government, which is also of Christ. Whereas the   [Is 49.23]
contrary is most true, that they may both stand together and flourish, the one being
helpful unto the other in their distinct and due administrations.

3. The power and authority of magistrates is not for the restraining of
churches or any other good works, but for helping in and furthering thereof.[b] And

a. [Acts 2.41, 47, 4.1–3]
b. [Rom 13.4; 1 Tm 2.2]

therefore the consent and countenance of magistrates, when it may be had, is not to be slighted or lightly esteemed; but on the contrary, it is part of that honor due to Christian magistrates to desire and crave their consent and approbation therein, which being obtained, the churches may then proceed in their way with much more encouragement and comfort.

[Ez 44.7, 9]

4. It is not in the power of magistrates to compel their subjects to become church members and to partake at the Lord's table. For the priests are reproved that brought unworthy ones into the sanctuary; then as it was unlawful for the priests, so it is unlawful to be done by civil magistrates. Those whom the church is to cast

[1 Cor 5.11]

out if they were in, the magistrate ought not to thrust into the church nor to hold them therein.

5. As it is unlawful for church officers to meddle with the sword of the magistrate, so it is unlawful for the magistrate to meddle with the work proper to church

[Mt 20.25–26]

officers. The acts of Moses and David, who were not only princes but prophets, were extraordinary, therefore not imitable. Against such usurpation the Lord witnessed

[2 Chr 26.16–17]

by smiting Uzziah with leprosy for presuming to offer incense.

6. It is the duty of the magistrate to take care of matters of religion, and to improve his civil authority for the observing of the duties commanded in the first, as well as for observing of the duties commanded in the second table. They are called

[Ps 2.2]

"gods." The end of the magistrate's office is not only the quiet and peaceable life of the subject in matters of righteousness and honesty, but also in matters of godliness,

[1 Tm 2.1–2]

yea of all godliness. Moses, Joshua, David, Solomon, Asa, Jehoshaphat, Hezekiah, Josiah are much commended by the Holy Ghost for the putting forth their authority in matters of religion.[a] On the contrary, such kings as have been failing this way are frequently taxed and reproved by the Lord. And not only the kings of Judah, but also Job, Nehemiah, the king of Nineveh, Darius, Artaxerxes, Nebuchadnezzar,[b] whom none looked at as types of Christ (though were it so, there were no place for any just objection) are commended in the book of God for exercising their authority this way.

7. The object of the power of the magistrate are not things merely inward, and so not subject to his cognizance and view, as unbelief, hardness of heart, erro-

[1 Kgs 20.28, 42]

neous opinions not vented, but only such things as are acted by the outward man. Neither is their power to be exercised in commanding such acts of the outward man, and punishing the neglect thereof, as are but mere inventions and devices of men, but about such acts as are commanded and forbidden in the word, yes, such

a. [1 Kgs 15.14, 22.43; 2 Kgs 12.3, 14.4, 15.35]
b. [1 Kgs 20.42; Jb 29.25, 31.26, 28; Neh 13; Jon 3.7; Ezr 7; Dn 3.29]

as the word doth clearly determine, though not always clearly to the judgment of the magistrate or others, yet clearly in itself. In these he of right ought to put forth his authority, though ofttimes actually he doth it not.

8. Idolatry, blasphemy, heresy, venting corrupt and pernicious opinions that destroy the foundation, open contempt of the word preached, profanation of the Lord's day, disturbing the peaceable administration and exercise of the worship and holy things of God, and the like are to be restrained and punished by civil authority.[a]

9. If any church, one or more, shall grow schismatical, rending itself from the communion of other churches, or shall walk incorrigibly or obstinately in any corrupt way of their own, contrary to the rule of the word, in such case the magistrate is to put forth his coercive power as the matter shall require. The tribes on this side Jordan intended to make war against the other tribes for building the altar of witness, whom they suspected to have turned away therein from following of the Lord.   [Jos 22]

a. [Dt 13; 1 Kgs 20.28, 42; Dn 3.29; Zec 13.3; Neh 13.21; 1 Tm 2.2; Rom 13.4]

General Baptists, *The Faith and Practice of Thirty Congregations Gathered According to the Primitive Pattern*, 1651

"Baptists," according to one of their leading twentieth-century historians, W. T. Whitley, "have steadily declined to erect confessions into touch-stones. They are willing at suitable opportunities to say what they do believe at the time, and they are willing to state afresh their current beliefs in unambiguous current phraseology. But though frequent attempts have been made to convert such confessions into standard creeds, by which 'orthodoxy' is to be tested, such attempts have invariably been opposed."[1] And a little later he explains further: "Baptists have never been backward to explain what they believe; they have always been reluctant to erect a confession into a standard, or test of doctrine. . . . The confessions of 1612, 1644, 1656, are interesting landmarks."[2]

Both of those characteristics made their presence felt with the early Baptist confessions, from the → *[First] London Confession* of 1644 to → *The New Hamphire Confession* of 1833/1853 and beyond, as well as here in *The Faith and Practice of Thirty Congregations Gathered According to the Primitive Pattern* of 1651. Even the doctrinal differences between "Particular" (Calvinistic) and "General" (more or less "Arminian") Baptists, while coming to voice in these confessions, did not become enforceable in the way that the doctrines and dogmas of other confessions were — not least because Baptists, although they "do own a magistratical power for the governing of this our English nation, to be determined in a just parliamentary way," as they confess here, were in principle opposed to the use of this "magistratical power" to enforce doctrinal conformity or confessional authority. An earlier version included the acceptance of → *The Apostles' Creed,* → *The Niceno-Constantinopolitan Creed,* and → *The Athanasian Creed;* but this was dropped in later revisions.

Edition: Lumpkin, 174–88.

Literature: Lumpkin, 171–73; Whitley 1923.

1. Whitley 1923, 30.
2. Whitley 1923, 93–94.

General Baptists, *The Faith and Practice of Thirty Congregations Gathered According to the Primitive Pattern*, 1651

Ez 43.11: "And if they be ashamed of all that they have done, show them the form of the house, and the fashion thereof, and the goings out thereof, and the comings in thereof, and all the forms thereof, and all the ordinances thereof, and all the laws thereof; and write it in their sight, that they may keep the whole form thereof, and all the ordinances thereof, and do them."

Mt 5.16: "Let your light so shine before men," etc.

Heb 3.6: "But Christ as a Son, over his own," etc.

1. That that God whom we acknowledge, ought to be worshiped by all, and above all that are called gods, and he is infinite in power and wisdom, universal, invisible, eternal: Ps 96.3–4; Jer 23.24; Col 1.17; Rom 1.20.

2. That God created all creatures visible and invisible, by his own wisdom and power: Col 1.16; Jer 10.12.

3. That God preserveth all creatures which are in being: Neh 9.6; Rom 11.36.

4. That the creation doth plainly declare the power and righteousness of God: Rom 1.20; Is 40.26.

5. That God commandeth men to take a view of his wise, powerful, and righteous works of creation: Is 40.26.

6. That God by his good creatures called or calleth men to a serious consideration, or meditation, that they may further understand his wisdom and power: Rom 1.20.

7. That God doth command men to speak or declare that which they have learned by the teaching of the creatures: Ps 145.5.

8. That the consideration of the Lord's handiworks in creatures, is a means to beget thoughts of God, and of ourselves, suitable to his greatness, and our inferiority: Ps 8.3, 4.

9. That whatsoever good meditations, or serious considerations we have of the glorious works of creation, ought to break forth with admiration unto thankfulness to God: Ps 136.3–9.

10. That those who did refuse to worship or glorify God answerably to the teaching of the creation, the Lord gave them over, or forsook them so far, that they became so desperately wicked, that they did things contrary to nature: Rom 1.26, 27.

11. God created or made Adam a living soul, and in his own likeness in sovereignty or dominion: Gn 1.26-27.

12. That God gave unto Adam laws or commands, that he might know his will: Gn 2.16-17.

13. That God declared unto Adam what penalty or punishment he would cause to befall him, if he disobeyed his will: Gn 2.17.

14. That Adam did sin or disobey the righteous commands of the Lord: Gn 3.6.

15. That God told Adam very plainly what death it should be that he would cause to come on him, and what sorrows should attend him in the meanwhile: Gn 3.17, 19.

16. That all mankind are liable to partake of the same death or punishment which the Lord in his righteous judgment caused to fall on Adam for his transgression: Rom 5.18.

17. That Jesus Christ, through (or by) the grace of God, suffered death for all mankind, or every man: Heb 2.9.

18. That Christ Jesus, the second Adam, will as certainly raise all mankind from that death which fell on them, through or by the first Adam's sin or offense, as surely as they partake of it: Rom 5.18.

19. That Jesus Christ, his lordly or kingly preeminence over all mankind, is vindicated or maintained in the Scripture's account, by virtue of his dying or suffering for them: Rom 14.9.

20. That God's Word, Son, or Spirit, are one: 1 Jn 5.7; Jude 1; Heb 10.29; Rom 15.16. God and his Word are one: Jn 1.1. The Word quickeneth: Ps 119.50. The Son quickeneth: Eph 2.1. And the Spirit quickeneth: Jn 6.63. So they are one. God giveth gifts, and the Son doth the same, also the Holy Ghost, so they are one: Jas 1.71; Eph 4.10, 11; Acts 2.38; 1 Thes 1.5; Jn 6.44, 14.6; Eph 1.18; 1 Cor 12.3; Mt 10.40; Gal 3.2.

21. That the Lord of all mankind, Jesus Christ, hath the power of giving laws for the governing or ruling every man in the world in spiritual worship: Is 9.6, 7; Mt 28.18-20.

22. That this Prince of Peace, Jesus Christ, is the only or principal High Priest, which offered up sacrifice, or made reconciliation for the sins of the people: Heb 2.17.

23. That the High Priest Jesus Christ, is not only king or governor, but also the apostle or prophet of the truth professed, or the true profession of saints: Heb 3.1.

24. That all the riches appertaining to a spiritual and eternal life, were treasured up in Jesus Christ: Col 2.3.

25. That there is not, neither ever was any man endued with any abilities and power to do the revealed will of God, but it was given him from above: Jas 1.17.

26. That the gifts of God spring from the pleasure of his will, or of his free grace; even the Lord Jesus Christ sprung from thence, from whom cometh all spiritual mercies: Rom 8.32; Heb 2.9.

27. That Jesus Christ was faithful in all things whereunto he was appointed: Heb 3.1, 2.

28. That Jesus Christ was not only the lawmaker, but the lawgiver to every man that liveth in the world, in that he giveth every man therein some measure of light: Jn 1.9.

29. That God of his free love giveth several gifts unto men, dividing severally as it pleaseth him, by one and the same Spirit: 1 Cor 12.11; Eph 4.7.

30. That the gifts of God given unto men of his own free grace, though never so richly they may be furnished both with abilities and power, yet those gifts of grace do not demonstrate, or declare them to be faithful servants; but it doth very plainly prove, that they are called upon thereby to be faithful servants: 1 Cor 4.1–2.

31. That those gifts which God of his free grace gives unto men to the enabling or empowering them to obey or believe in his name, are called the grace of God, as they spring from the Spirit of grace: Acts 18.17.

32. That when God of his own bountifulness hath given gifts unto men to be improved by them to the praise of his grace, as to believe or obey, then those so endued are stewards of the grace of God: 1 Pt 4.10.

33. That God requireth or commandeth service of men, answerable to those gifts of grace which he of his good pleasure hath bestowed upon them: Col 2.6; Jn 12.37.

34. That it is the gracious pleasure of God, that Jesus Christ his life, death, and resurrection, should be made known unto men, and by men, as arguments, or motives, to allure or provoke them to live holy and righteous in this present world: Eph 5.1–2; Rom 6.4–14.

35. That God requireth that man should worship him in Spirit and in truth, or with all the heart, before they outwardly make a profession of him: Acts 8.36–37.

36. That all actions performed by man towards God, ought to flow from a principle of love: 1 Cor 13.1, 2, 3.

37. That God loves man first, and declareth, or maketh known his love to men, before any man can act from a principle of love in obedience to him: Jn 15.16.

38. That whosoever obeyeth God with those gifts of his free grace (as abilities and power to do his will), never so faithfully, evangelically, or unfainedly, giving him the glory of those performances; yet thus believing or obeying doth not procure salvation as eternal life, neither are they any cause at all to move God to bestow it: Ez 16.3–10; Eph 2.9; Rom 4.2; Jn 15.15.

39. That the ground or principal end of men's believing or obeying God, ought to be for the advancing of the glory of God, or for the praise of his free grace: 1 Cor 6.19, 20.

40. That those who serve or fear the Lord, honoring or glorifying him with his gifts bestowed on them, to the praise of his free grace, do demonstratively or openly manifest themselves to be his faithful servants, or children: 1 Jn 3.10; Acts 10.35.

41. That those which serve the Lord with integrity of mind and spirit, improving their abilities and power given unto them of God, to his glory and praise, are not only called faithful servants, or the children of the living God, but they have the promises of God to be entrusted with more of the manifestations of himself, which is called the mystery which hath been hid from many ages, and generations, which the disobedient shall not enjoy: Col 1.26, 27.

42. That those which love the Lord Jesus Christ, so as to walk in his appointed ways with that strength of ability and power which God of his own mercy hath given unto them, they shall have peace of conscience, being freed from anguish of spirit, having their hearts comforted by the Holy Ghost: Rom 2.10.

43. That all those that continue steadfastly unto the end of their lives, pressing forward to the mark (Jesus Christ) that is set before them, shall not only have the comfort and joy which is a part of their portion in this life, but they shall also have a crown of eternal glory in the life to come: Rv 22.14; 2 Tm 4.8.

44. That God of his free grace or love, called or calleth sinners to repentance, and afforded or affordeth them time or opportunity to repent or return unto him: Rom 4.2.

45. That all those who refuse to improve the gifts of grace which God hath afforded them, so that they repent not, neither turn to him in obedience to his commands made manifest unto them, they do despise the goodness of God or his free grace, denying the Lord that bought them, and so are liable to destruction: 1 Pt 2.1, 2.

46. That whosoever shall preach, teach, or practice any doctrine in the worship of God, pretending it in the name of Jesus Christ, which is not to be heard or

read of in the record of God, which was given by inspiration of the Holy Ghost; such teachers are liable to the curse of God, howsoever countenanced by men: Gal 1.8, 9.

47. That the baptism which the Lord Jesus commanded his disciples to teach, ought to be known by everyone, before they submit themselves, or obey it: Acts 2.38, 41.

48. That the way and manner of baptizing, both before the death of Christ, and since his resurrection and ascension, was to go into the water, and to be baptized: Mt 3.6; Mt 1.5, 8.9.

49. That when baptism is made known, or any other action of obedience, then for men to refuse it, they are said to reject the counsel of God against themselves: Lk 7.30.

50. That those which received the word of God preached by the ministry of the gospel, and were baptized according to the counsel of God, at the same time or day they were of the visible church of God: Acts 2.41.

51. That the only foundation of the church of God, is the doctrines of the apostles or prophets, as they spring from Jesus Christ the chief cornerstone, whereon this or any other people are to be built together as the house of God: Eph 2.20, 21.

52. That the chief or only ends of a people baptized according to the counsel of God, when they meet together as the congregation or fellowship of Christ, are, or ought to be, for to walk suitably; or to give up themselves unto a holy conformity to all the laws or ordinances of Jesus Christ, answerable to the gifts and graces received, improving them for the glory of God, and the edification of each other in love: Eph 4.15, 16.

53. That Jesus Christ took bread, and the juice of the vine, and broke, and gave to his disciples, to eat and drink with thanksgiving; which practice is left upon record as a memorial of his suffering, to continue in the church until he come again: 1 Cor 11.23–26.

54. That the church ought to call upon God, seeking him by prayer in the name of Jesus Christ, and to be thankful to him for mercies received, sounding forth his praises with understanding: Eph 6.16–18.

55. That if anyone of the fellowship neglect the watching over his own heart, and so break out into an evil life and conversation, and all good means that God hath appointed hath been used toward such a one, and that person hath not performed, then ought not such a one to break bread with obedient walkers, to show forth the death of Christ, seeing he doth deny him in life and conversation: 1 Cor 5.12.

56. That the people of God ought to have a tender respect towards them, as long as there is any hope of being instrumental in the use of that means which God hath appointed for the recovering them out of the snare of sin or wickedness: 2 Thes 3.14, 15.

57. That there be contributions made for the relief of those that cannot help themselves with food and raiment, that are willing to the utmost to put forth their strength and skill in some lawful way or calling, especially those that are of the household of faith; such as through sickness or weakness of body cannot labor: Gal 6.9, 10.

58. That it is the good pleasure of God, which hath given gifts of his grace to the saints or church of God, that some of the gifted men should be appointed or set apart to attend upon the preaching of the word, for the further edifying of the churches, that they may be enabled to stand against all oppositions according as necessity requires, to the glory of God and their comfort: Eph 4.11, 21.

59. That it is the will of God that those saints or members of the fellowship which are appointed so to spend their labors in teaching or exhorting them in the knowledge of God to their edification and consolation, ought to have maintenance of those that receive spiritual food by them: 1 Cor 9.11.

60. That the maintenance of the ministers which labor in the word of God, ought to be the free and charitable benevolence, or the cheerful contribution of those that acknowledge themselves members of the same fellowship: 2 Cor 9.13.

61. That the servants of God, or the ministers of the gospel, ought to be content with necessary food and raiment, and to labor with their hands, that they may not be overchargeable: 1 Cor 4.12, because they are to teach that doctrine to every member: Heb 13.5.

62. That those servants of God which labor in the word much, and well, ought to be had in very good estimation: 1 Tm 5.17.

63. That the church of Jesus Christ ought not to think of any man above what is meet, lest that they give that honor to man which properly and alone belongeth to God: Ps 115.1; 2 Cor 12.6.

64. That the church hath directions of God to set apart some men that are suitably qualified, to oversee, or order the affairs concerning the poor distressed members of Christ, that they may not be neglected, and so perish for want of food and raiment, and to take off that work from lying too heavy upon the care of those which labor in the word and doctrine: Acts 6.3, 4.

65. That if the poor fearing God, cannot conveniently have a competent maintenance, for the supply of their necessities in that society whereunto they must commonly resort, that then those men that have the care laid upon them, send or

give intelligence to the other churches or saints of God, who have engaged themselves by declaring their willingness towards the relief of such a distressed people: Rom 15.26.

66. That those men which the church of God are to make such uses of as the setting them to minister unto the saints in things spiritual or temporal, it is required that the church judge those men found in the faith, that their lives and conversations be unblameable, that those which are without, cannot have any just occasion to speak reproachfully of them, that they be not covetous of filthy lucre, neither self-willed, but loving and patient towards all men, apt to teach, and to do good works answerable to their abilities: Ti 1.7–9; Acts 6.3.

67. That some men amongst the brotherhood who are able to judge in causes of difference that may arise betwixt them in the church, may be approved or appointed to put an end thereto without partiality, that there may be no unnecessary strivings in the law to vex one another: 1 Cor 6.5–7.

68. That whosoever of the society or church of God which shall willfully or carelessly neglect any lawful way or calling, and to fall into hunger and nakedness, ought to be exhorted with love and meekness, to labor with their abilities in some honest way or calling for their relief which being done orderly, and he or they will not reform, so that suitable exhortations take no place, such a one shall be excluded or excommunicated, as one that hath denied the faith: 1 Tm 5.8.

69. That the offended ought to proceed according to rule, not delaying or prolonging time, but out of a tender care, that their hearts may not be hardened by a custom in sin, that thereby the reclaiming of them from sin may be done with less difficulty: Mt 18.15–17.

70. That if any controversy should so fall out, that the case cannot easily be determined by that society or church where it is first presented, that then use be made of some other society which they are in fellowship with, for their assistance therein: Acts 16.1, 2.

71. That there be an orderly improving those gifts that God of his free grace hath bestowed on the saints, that one may not hinder another, but as occasion serveth, one by one, speaking the things that they have learned of God, that the hearers may be profited, and so put in a capacity to judge of things concerning the glory of God, and their own peace: 1 Cor 14.30, 31.

72. That if anyone which hath been of the fellowship of Christ, and hath so far subjected himself to temptations that he denieth to live righteously, or in the fear and love of God and makes shipwreck of faith and a good conscience, for which he hath been excommunicated according to order, that it be recorded, and made known to other the churches, for prevention of evils in them: 1 Tm 1.19, 20.

73. That fasting and prayer ought to be used, and laying on of hands, for the ordaining of servants or officers to attend about the service of God: Acts 13.3.

74. That we ought to behave ourselves towards all men, no otherwise than we would freely and cheerfully they in the like case (if it should fall out) should do toward us, and that we ought to seek a peaceable life with all men, as far as possibly we can, keeping faith and a good conscience: Lk 6.31; Rom 12.18; 1 Tm 1.19.

75. That we ought to clear ourselves, not only from evil thoughts harboring in our hearts, or the evils in life and conversation; but as far as we can, vindicate ourselves from all those scandalous aspersions that daily fall about our ears, setting our good names on fire, to the dishonor of God, whereof many are the instruments by their willful contrivances, or by the misinformations of others, which father upon us such principles and practices as we abhor, through ignorant mistakes cunningly suggested by some evil willers at least: 2 Cor 2.17.

POSTSCRIPT

That we do own a magistratical power for the governing of this our English nation, to be determined in a just parliamentary way; and that we ought to pray for good governors, and good government; that we may live a peaceable and godly life in all honesty; standing ready at all times, as necessity may require, to vindicate such a magistracy or magistrates, not only with arguments of sound reason, but also with our estates and lives; that righteousness may reign, and vice may be overthrown, without respect of persons.

Innocent X, *Cum occasione*, 1653

Having been addressed both to the doctrinal challenges of the Protestant Reformation and to the unfinished business of late medieval theology, the dogmatic formulations of → *The Decrees of the Council of Trent* of 1545–64 left unsettled many issues that were to provide the agenda for further confessional development in the Roman Catholic Church. The most notable of these issues were the immaculate conception of the Virgin Mary, which was not conclusively defined until the bull → *Ineffabilis Deus* of Pope Pius IX in 1854, and the infallibility of the pope, which was promulgated by → the First Vatican Council on 24 April 1870. Like many other confessions both before and since, *The Decrees of the Council of Trent* also became a new context within which schools of thought proposed their reconstructions and on the basis of which the freshly invigorated and centralized authority of the papacy condemned their excesses.

In many respects the most challenging of these developments was Jansenism. The ambivalent position of the teachings of Augustine of Hippo in the confessional controversies of the sixteenth century, as simultaneously the fountainhead of Western Catholic doctrine and the favorite church father of the Protestant Reformers, assured him a prominent place in the subsequent controversies on both sides, in the debates between Calvinism and Arminianism over predestination, but also in the recrudescence of a radical Augustinianism in the thought of Cornelius Jansen (1585–1638). His *Augustinus*, which was begun in 1628 but published posthumously only in 1640, consisted in large part of excerpts from the Augustinian corpus, which he was said to have read ten times and the anti-Pelagian treatises thirty times. The bull *Cum occasione* of Pope Innocent X was a condemnation of "the Five Propostitions" derived from this work, and it became the normative definition of the Jansenist heresy for all the subsequent official condemnations, including the one by Pope Alexander VIII and the Holy Office in 1690.[1]

Like the more famous → *Syllabus of Errors* of Pope Pius IX of 1864, this statement of Roman Catholic doctrine specifies explicitly only the teachings being anathematized, leaving implicit the positive confession being affirmed.

Edition: Denzinger, 2001–7.

---

1. Denzinger, 2290–332.

Translation: Prepared for this edition.

Literature: *Chr Trad* 5:35–48; *DTC* 8:318–529, esp. 474–96 ("Les cinq propositions"); *ODCC* 862–63.

1. Some of God's commandments are impossible for the righteous who wish and try to keep them, according to the present powers that they have; they also lack the grace by which these commandments do become possible.

2. In the state of fallen nature, inner grace is never resisted.

3. For merit or demerit in the state of fallen nature, freedom from necessity is not required in a person, but freedom from coercion is sufficient.

4. The Semipelagians admitted the necessity of prevenient inner grace for individual acts, even for the beginning of faith; and in this they were heretics, because they held this grace to be such as could be either resisted or obeyed by the human will.

5. It is Semipelagian to say that Christ died or shed his blood for all men regardless.

[Censure:] Proposition 1: We declare to be rash, wicked, blasphemous, condemned by anathema, and heretical, and we condemn it as such; proposition 2: heretical; proposition 3: heretical; proposition 4: false and heretical; proposition 5: false, rash, scandalous, and—if it is understood in the sense that Christ died for the salvation only of the predestined—wicked, blasphemous, outrageous, insulting to divine mercy, and heretical. . . .

By this declaration and definition addressed to the five stated propositions we do not by any means intend, however, to approve other opinions that are contained in the book of Cornelius Jansen that has been cited.

British Congregationalists, *The Savoy Declaration of Faith and Order,* 1658

In the history of the "reception" of creeds and confessions, → *The Westminster Confession of Faith* of 1647 has played a special part, going through several significant revisions and recensions across confessional and denominational boundaries during the seventeenth, eighteenth, and nineteenth centuries (listing them chronologically): → *The Savoy Declaration of Faith and Order* of 1658 (Congregationalist); *The Second London Confession* of 1658 (Baptist); *The American Revision of the Westminster Confession* of 1729 (Presbyterian); *The Philadelphia Confession* of 1742 (Baptist); and → *The Confession of Faith of the Cumberland Presbyterian Church* of 1814/1883 (Presbyterian).

Each of these kept substantial portions of the original but also reformulated, added, and subtracted many phrases, sentences, and entire "chapters" (as *The Westminster Confession* calls what other confessions call "articles"). Because of their historical interest and their confessional importance to the present day, they all merit attention in any collection of "Statements of Faith in Modern Christianity" that, like this one, claims to be comprehensive, if not complete. But because of their sheer length, there are good reasons not to reprint in toto all five (including the sections taken over from *Westminster*). *The American Revision,* therefore, appears in footnotes appended to our edition of the 1647 original—also because it retained the name *Westminster Confession. The Confession of Faith of the Cumberland Presbyterian Church* began as a rather light retouching of *Westminster,* but its definitive text of 1883 was sufficiently its own text to warrant inclusion in its entirety.

The Savoy Declaration was produced by the representatives of 120 Congregational churches, meeting in London's Savoy Palace in 1658, who disagreed not with the Reformed dogmatics of *Westminster* but with its Presbyterian polity. Not only because it was the earliest revision of *The Westminster Confession,* but because of its own statement, in the preface by John Owen, that "in drawing up this *Confession of Faith,* we have had before us the *Articles of Religion,* approved and passed by both Houses of Parliament,"[1] referring to *The Westminster Confession* of the preceding decade, the overall differences between *Westminster* and *Savoy* seemed to Philip Schaff to be sufficiently slight to justify his reprinting only chapters 20, 21, 24, and 26, with their *Westminster* counterparts.[2] Militating against that solution, neverthe-

1. Schaff, 3:714.
2. Schaff, 3:718–23.

less, is the intrinsic importance of *The Savoy Declaration,* both in its own time, for New England as well as Great Britain, and since: alone among the revisions listed above (and even among other seventeenth-century confessions of whatever denominational provenance), it was reissued, in a separate book, twice in the twentieth century, in 1959 and again in 1971; and it qualifies for inclusion as a distinct entry in *The Oxford Dictionary of the Christian Church.* In including it here, we have, however, made one concession, accepting and making our own another stipulation in Owen's preface: "There are not Scriptures annexed, as in some Confessions (though in divers others it's otherwise)."[3]

Edition: *Savoy Declaration of Faith and Order* 1971, 9–48.

Literature: Matthews 1959, 9–73; ODCC 1459; *Savoy Declaration of Faith and Order* 1971.

---

3. Schaff, 3:715.

British Congregationalists, *The Savoy Declaration of Faith and Order,* 1658

CHAPTER 1. OF THE HOLY SCRIPTURE

1. Although the light of nature, and the works of creation and providence, do so far manifest the goodness, wisdom, and power of God, as to leave men inexcusable; yet are they not sufficient to give that knowledge of God and of his will, which is necessary unto salvation: therefore it pleased the Lord at sundry times, and in diverse manners, to reveal himself, and to declare that his will unto his church; and afterwards for the better preserving and propagating of the truth, and for the more sure establishment and comfort of the church against the corruption of the flesh, and the malice of Satan and of the world, to commit the same wholly unto writing: which maketh the Holy Scripture to be most necessary; those former ways of God's revealing his will unto his people, being now ceased.

2. Under the name of Holy Scripture, or the word of God written, are now contained all the books of the Old and New Testament; which are these:

Of the Old Testament

Genesis, Exodus, Leviticus, Numbers, Deuteronomy, Joshua, Judges, Ruth, 1 Samuel, 2 Samuel, 1 Kings, 2 Kings, 1 Chronicles, 2 Chronicles, Ezra, Nehemiah, Esther, Job, Psalms, Proverbs, Ecclesiastes, The Song of Songs, Isaiah, Jeremiah, Lamentations, Ezekiel, Daniel, Hosea, Joel, Amos, Obadiah, Jonah, Micah, Nahum, Habakkuk, Zephaniah, Haggai, Zechariah, Malachi.

Of the New Testament

Matthew, Mark, Luke, John, The Acts of the Apostles, Paul's Epistle to the Romans, 1 Corinthians, 2 Corinthians, Galatians, Ephesians, Philippians, Colossians, 1 Thessalonians, 2 Thessalonians, 1 To Timothy, 2 To Timothy, To Titus, To Philemon, The Epistle to the Hebrews, The Epistle of James, The First and Second Epistles of Peter, The First, Second and Third Epistles of John, the Epistle of Jude, the Revelation.

All which are given by the inspiration of God to be the rule of faith and life.

3. The books commonly called Apocrypha, not being of divine inspiration, are no part of the canon of the Scripture; and therefore are of no authority in the

church of God, nor to be any otherwise approved or made use of, than other human writings.

4. The authority of the Holy Scripture, for which it ought to be believed and obeyed, dependeth not upon the testimony of any man or church; but wholly upon God (who is truth itself) the author thereof: and therefore it is to be received, because it is the word of God.

5. We may be moved and induced by the testimony of the church, to a high and reverent esteem of the Holy Scripture; and the heavenliness of the matter, the efficacy of the doctrine, the majesty of the style, the consent of all the parts, the scope of the whole (which is, to give all glory to God), the full discovery it makes of the only way of man's salvation, the many other incomparable excellencies, and the entire perfection thereof, are arguments whereby it doth abundantly evidence itself to be the word of God; yet notwithstanding, our full persuasion and assurance of the infallible truth and divine authority thereof, is from the inward work of the Holy Spirit, bearing witness by and with the word in our hearts.

6. The whole counsel of God concerning all things necessary for his own glory, man's salvation, faith, and life, is either expressly set down in Scripture, or by good and necessary consequence may be deduced from Scripture; unto which nothing at any time is to be added, whether by new revelations of the Spirit, or traditions of men. Nevertheless we acknowledge the inward illumination of the Spirit of God to be necessary for the saving understanding of such things as are revealed in the word: and that there are some circumstances concerning the worship of God and government of the church, common to human actions and societies, which are to be ordered by the light of nature and Christian prudence, according to the general rules of the word, which are always to be observed.

7. All things in Scripture are not alike plain in themselves, nor alike clear unto all: yet those things which are necessary to be known, believed, and observed for salvation, are so clearly propounded and opened in some place of Scripture or other, that not only the learned, but the unlearned, in a due use of the ordinary means, may attain unto a sufficient understanding of them.

8. The Old Testament in Hebrew (which was the native language of the people of God of old) and the New Testament in Greek (which at the time of writing of it was most generally known to the nations) being immediately inspired by God, and by his singular care and providence kept pure in all ages, are therefore authentical; so as in all controversies of religion the church is finally to appeal unto them. But because these original tongues are not known to all the people of God, who have right unto and interest in the Scriptures, and are commanded in the fear of God to read and search them; therefore they are to be translated into the vulgar

language of every nation unto which they come, that the word of God dwelling plentifully in all, they may worship him in an acceptable manner, and through patience and comfort of the Scriptures may have hope.

9. The infallible rule of interpretation of Scripture, is the Scripture itself; and therefore when there is a question about the true and full sense of any Scripture (which is not manifold, but one) it must be searched and known by other places, that speak more clearly.

10. The supreme judge by which all controversies of religion are to be determined, and all decrees of councils, opinions of ancient writers, doctrines of men, and private spirits, are to be examined, and in whose sentence we are to rest, can be no other, but the Holy Scripture delivered by the Spirit; into which Scripture so delivered, our faith is finally resolved.

CHAPTER 2. OF GOD AND OF THE HOLY TRINITY

1. There is but one only living and true God; who is infinite in being and perfection, a most pure Spirit, invisible, without body, parts or passions, immutable, immense, eternal, incomprehensible, almighty, most wise, most holy, most free, most absolute, working all things according to the counsel of his own immutable and most righteous will, for his own glory, most loving, gracious, merciful, long-suffering, abundant in goodness and truth, forgiving iniquity, transgression, and sin, the rewarder of them that diligently seek him; and withal most just and terrible in his judgments, hating all sin, and who will by no means clear the guilty.

2. God hath all life, glory, goodness, blessedness, in, and of himself; and is alone, in, and unto himself, all-sufficient, not standing in need of any creatures, which he hath made, nor deriving any glory from them, but only manifesting his own glory in, by, unto, and upon them: he is the alone fountain of all being, of whom, through whom, and to whom are all things; and hath most sovereign dominion over them, to do by them, for them, or upon them, whatsoever himself pleaseth. In his sight all things are open and manifest, his knowledge is infinite, infallible, and independent upon the creature, so as nothing is to him contingent or uncertain. He is most holy in all his counsels, in all his works, and in all his commands. To him is due from angels and men, and every other creature, whatsoever worship, service, or obedience, as creatures, they owe unto the Creator, and whatever he is further pleased to require of them.

3. In the unity of the Godhead there be three persons, of one substance, power, and eternity, God the Father, God the Son, and God the Holy Ghost. The Father is of none, neither begotten, nor proceeding; the Son is eternally begotten of the Father; the Holy Ghost eternally proceeding from the Father and the Son.

Which doctrine of the Trinity is the foundation of all our communion with God, and comfortable dependence upon him.

CHAPTER 3. OF GOD'S ETERNAL DECREE

1. God from all eternity did by the most wise and holy counsel of his own will, freely and unchangeably ordain whatsoever comes to pass: yet so, as thereby neither is God the author of sin, nor is violence offered to the will of the creatures, nor is the liberty or contingency of second causes taken away, but rather established.

2. Although God knows whatsoever may or can come to pass upon all supposed conditions, yet hath he not decreed anything because he foresaw it as future, or as that which would come to pass upon such conditions.

3. By the decree of God for the manifestation of his glory, some men and angels are predestined unto everlasting life, and others foreordained to everlasting death.

4. These angels and men thus predestinated, and foreordained, are particularly and unchangeably designed, and their number is so certain and definite, that it cannot be either increased or diminished.

5. Those of mankind that are predestinated unto life, God, before the foundation of the world was laid, according to his eternal and immutable purpose, and the secret counsel and good pleasure of his will, hath chosen in Christ unto everlasting glory, out of his mere free grace and love, without any foresight of faith or good works, or perseverance in either of them, or any other thing in the creature, as conditions or causes moving him thereunto, and all to the praise of his glorious grace.

6. As God hath appointed the elect unto glory, so hath he by the eternal and most free purpose of his will foreordained all the means thereunto. Wherefore they who are elected, being fallen in Adam, are redeemed by Christ, are effectually called unto faith in Christ by his Spirit working in due season, are justified, adopted, sanctified, and kept by his power, through faith, unto salvation. Neither are any other redeemed by Christ, or effectually called, justified, adopted, sanctified, and saved, but the elect only.

7. The rest of mankind God was pleased, according to the unsearchable counsel of his own will, whereby he extendeth or withholdeth mercy, as he pleaseth, for the glory of his sovereign power over his creatures, to pass by and to ordain them to dishonor and wrath for their sin, to the praise of his glorious justice.

8. The doctrine of this high mystery of predestination is to be handled with special prudence and care, that men attending the will of God revealed in his word, and yielding obedience thereunto, may from the certainty of their effectual vocation,

be assured of their eternal election. So shall this doctrine afford matter of praise, reverence, and admiration of God, and of humility, diligence, and abundant consolation to all that sincerely obey the gospel.

CHAPTER 4. OF CREATION

1. It pleased God the Father, Son, and Holy Ghost, for the manifestation of the glory of his eternal power, wisdom, and goodness, in the beginning, to create or make out of nothing the world, and all things therein, whether visible or invisible, in the space of six days, and all very good.

2. After God had made all other creatures, he created man, male and female, with reasonable and immortal souls, endued with knowledge, righteousness, and true holiness, after his own image, having the law of God written in their hearts, and power to fulfill it; and yet under a possibility of transgressing, being left to the liberty of their own will, which was subject unto change. Besides this law written in their hearts, they received a command not to eat of the tree of the knowledge of good and evil; which while they kept, they were happy in their communion with God, and had dominion over the creatures.

CHAPTER 5. OF PROVIDENCE

1. God the great Creator of all things, doth uphold, direct, dispose, and govern all creatures, actions, and things from the greatest even to the least by his most wise and holy providence, according to his infallible foreknowledge, and the free and immutable counsel of his own will, to the praise of the glory of his wisdom, power, justice, goodness, and mercy.

2. Although in relation to the foreknowledge and decree of God, the first cause, all things come to pass immutably and infallibly; yet by the same providence he ordereth them to fall out according to the nature of second causes, either necessarily, freely, or contingently.

3. God in his ordinary providence maketh use of means, yet is free to work without, above, and against them at his pleasure.

4. The almighty power, unsearchable wisdom, and infinite goodness of God, so far manifest themselves in his providence, in that his determinate counsel extendeth itself even to the first fall, and all other sins of angels and men (and that not by a bare permission) which also he most wisely and powerfully boundeth, and otherwise ordereth and governeth in a manifold dispensation to his own most holy ends; yet so, as the sinfulness thereof proceedeth only from the creature, and not from God, who being most holy and righteous, neither is, nor can be the author or approver of sin.

5. The most wise, righteous, and gracious God doth oftentimes leave for a season his own children to manifold temptations, and the corruption of their own hearts, to chastise them for their former sins, or to discover unto them the hidden strength of corruption, and deceitfulness of their hearts, that they may be humbled; and to raise them to a more close and constant dependence for their support upon himself, and to make them more watchful against all future occasions of sin, and for sundry other just and holy ends.

6. As for those wicked and ungodly men, whom God as a righteous judge, for former sins, doth blind and harden, from them he not only withholdeth his grace, whereby they might have been enlightened in their understandings, and wrought upon in their hearts; but sometimes also withdraweth the gifts which they had, and exposeth them to such objects, as their corruption makes occasions of sin; and withal gives them over to their own lusts, the temptations of the world, and the power of Satan; whereby it comes to pass that they harden themselves, even under those means which God useth for the softening of others.

7. As the providence of God doth in general reach to all creatures, so after a most special manner it taketh care of his church, and disposeth all things to the good thereof.

CHAPTER 6. OF THE FALL OF MAN, OF SIN, AND OF THE PUNISHMENT THEREOF

1. God having made a covenant of works and life, thereupon, with our first parents and all their posterity in them, they being seduced by the subtlety and temptation of Satan did willfully transgress the law of their creation, and break the covenant in eating the forbidden fruit.

2. By this sin they, and we in them, fell from original righteousness and communion with God, and so became dead in sin, and wholly defiled in all the faculties and parts of soul and body.

3. They being the root, and by God's appointment standing in the room and stead of all mankind, the guilt of this sin was imputed, and corrupted nature conveyed to all their posterity descending from them by ordinary generation.

4. From this original corruption, whereby we are utterly indisposed, disabled, and made opposite to all good, and wholly inclined to all evil, do proceed all actual transgressions.

5. This corruption of nature during this life, doth remain in those that are regenerated; and although it be through Christ pardoned and mortified, yet both itself and all the motions thereof are truly and properly sin.

6. Every sin, both original and actual, being a transgression of the righ-

teous law of God, and contrary thereunto, doth in its own nature bring guilt upon the sinner, whereby he is bound over to the wrath of God, and curse of the law, and so made subject to death, with all miseries, spiritual, temporal, and eternal.

CHAPTER 7. OF GOD'S COVENANT WITH MAN

1. The distance between God and the creature is so great, that although reasonable creatures do owe obedience unto him as their Creator, yet they could never have attained the reward of life, but by some voluntary condescension on God's part, which he hath been pleased to express by way of covenant.

2. The first covenant made with man, was a covenant of works, wherein life was promised to Adam, and in him to his posterity, upon condition of perfect and personal obedience.

3. Man by his fall having made himself incapable of life by that covenant, the Lord was pleased to make a second, commonly called the covenant of grace; wherein he freely offereth unto sinners life and salvation by Jesus Christ, requiring of them faith in him that they may be saved, and promising to give unto all those that are ordained unto life, his Holy Spirit, to make them willing and able to believe.

4. This covenant of grace is frequently set forth in the Scripture by the name of a testament, in reference to the death of Jesus Christ the testator, and to the everlasting inheritance, with all things belonging to it, therein bequeathed.

5. Although this covenant hath been differently and variously administered in respect of ordinances and institutions in the time of the law, and since the coming of Christ in the flesh; yet for the substance and efficacy of it, to all its spiritual and saving ends, it is one and the same; upon the account of which various dispensations, it is called the Old and New Testament.

CHAPTER 8. OF CHRIST THE MEDIATOR

1. It pleased God, in his eternal purpose, to choose and ordain the Lord Jesus his only-begotten Son, according to a covenant made between them both, to be the Mediator between God and man; the Prophet, Priest, and King, the Head and Savior of his church, the Heir of all things and Judge of the world; unto whom he did from all eternity give a people to be his seed, and to be by him in time redeemed, called, justified, sanctified, and glorified.

2. The Son of God, the second person in the Trinity, being very and eternal God, of one substance and equal with the Father, did, when the fullness of time was come, take upon him man's nature, with all the essential properties and common infirmities thereof, yet without sin, being conceived by the power of the Holy Ghost, in the womb of the Virgin Mary, of her substance: so that two whole perfect and

distinct natures, the Godhead and the manhood, were inseparably joined together in one person, without conversion, composition, or confusion; which person is very God and very man, yet one Christ, the only Mediator between God and man.

3. The Lord Jesus in his human nature, thus united to the divine in the person of the Son, was sanctified and anointed with the Holy Spirit above measure, having in him all the treasures of wisdom and knowledge, in whom it pleased the Father that all fullness should dwell; to the end that being holy, harmless, undefiled, and full of grace and truth, he might be thoroughly furnished to execute the office of a mediator and surety; which office he took not unto himself, but was thereunto called by his Father, who also put all power and judgment into his hand, and gave him commandment to execute the same.

4. This office the Lord Jesus did most willingly undertake; which that he might discharge, he was made under the law, and did perfectly fulfill it, and underwent the punishment due to us, which we should have borne and suffered, being made sin and a curse for us, enduring most grievous torments immediately from God in his soul, and most painful sufferings in his body, was crucified, and died; was buried, and remained under the power of death, yet saw no corruption. On the third day he arose from the dead with the same body in which he suffered, with which also he ascended into heaven, and there sitteth at the right hand of his Father, making intercession; and shall return to judge men and angels at the end of the world.

5. The Lord Jesus by his perfect obedience and sacrifice of himself, which he through the eternal Spirit, once offered up unto God, hath fully satisfied the justice of God, and purchased not only reconciliation, but an everlasting inheritance in the kingdom of heaven, for all those whom the Father hath given unto him.

6. Although the work of redemption was not actually wrought by Christ till after his incarnation; yet the virtue, efficacy, and benefits thereof were communicated to the elect in all ages, successively from the beginning of the world, in and by those promises, types, and sacrifices wherein he was revealed and signified to be the seed of the woman, which should bruise the serpent's head, and the Lamb slain from the beginning of the world, being yesterday and today the same, and forever.

7. Christ in the work of mediation acteth according to both natures; by each nature doing that which is proper to itself; yet by reason of the unity of the person, that which is proper to one nature, is sometimes in Scripture attributed to the person denominated by the other nature.

8. To all those for whom Christ hath purchased redemption, he doth certainly and effectually apply and communicate the same; making intercession for them; and revealing unto them in and by the word, the mysteries of salvation; effec-

tually persuading them by his Spirit to believe and obey, and governing their hearts by his word and Spirit; overcoming all their enemies by his almighty power and wisdom, and in such manner and ways as are most consonant to his most wonderful and unsearchable dispensation.

CHAPTER 9. OF FREE WILL

1. God hath endued the will of man with that natural liberty and power of acting upon choice that it is neither forced, nor by any absolute necessity of nature determined to do good or evil.

2. Man in his state of innocency had freedom and power to will and to do that which was good and well-pleasing to God; but yet mutably, so that he might fall from it.

3. Man by his fall into a state of sin, hath wholly lost all ability of will to any spiritual good accompanying salvation; so as a natural man being altogether averse from that good, and dead in sin, is not able by his own strength to convert himself, or to prepare himself thereunto.

4. When God converts a sinner, and translates him into the state of grace, he freeth him from his natural bondage under sin, and by his grace alone enables him freely to will and to do that which is spiritually good; yet so as that, by reason of his remaining corruption, he doth not perfectly nor only will that which is good, but doth also will that which is evil.

5. The will of man is made perfectly and immutably free to do good alone in the state of glory only.

CHAPTER 10. OF EFFECTUAL CALLING

1. All those whom God hath predestinated unto life, and those only, he is pleased in his appointed and accepted time effectually to call by his word and Spirit, out of that state of sin and death in which they are by nature, to grace and salvation by Jesus Christ; enlightening their minds spiritually and savingly to understand the things of God, taking away their heart of stone, and giving unto them an heart of flesh; renewing their wills, and by his almighty power determining them to that which is good; and effectually drawing them to Jesus Christ; yet so, as they come most freely, being made willing by his grace.

2. This effectual call is of God's free and special grace alone, not from any thing at all foreseen in man, who is altogether passive therein, until being quickened and renewed by the Holy Spirit he is thereby enabled to answer this call, and to embrace the grace offered and conveyed in it.

3. Elect infants dying in infancy, are regenerated and saved by Christ, who worketh when, and where, and how he pleaseth: so also are all other elect persons who are incapable of being outwardly called by the ministry of the word.

4. Others not elected, although they may be called by the ministry of the word, and may have some common operations of the Spirit, yet not being effectually drawn by the Father, they neither do nor can come unto Christ, and therefore cannot be saved: much less can men not professing the Christian religion, be saved in any other way whatsoever, be they never so diligent to frame their lives according to the light of nature, and the law of that religion they do profess: and to assert and maintain that they may, is very pernicious, and to be detested.

CHAPTER 11. OF JUSTIFICATION

1. Those whom God effectually calleth, he also freely justifieth; not by infusing righteousness into them, but by pardoning their sins, and by accounting and accepting their persons as righteous; not for anything wrought in them, or done by them, but for Christ's sake alone; nor by imputing faith itself, the act of believing, or any other evangelical obedience to them, as their righteousness; but by imputing Christ's active obedience to the whole law, and passive obedience in his death for their whole and sole righteousness, they receiving and resting on him and his righteousness by faith; which faith they have not of themselves, it is the gift of God.

2. Faith thus receiving and resting on Christ, and his righteousness, is the alone instrument of justification; yet it is not alone in the person justified, but is ever accompanied with all other saving graces, and is no dead faith, but worketh by love.

3. Christ by his obedience and death did fully discharge the debt of all those that are justified, and did by the sacrifice of himself, in the blood of his cross, undergoing in their stead the penalty due unto them make a proper, real, and full satisfaction to God's justice in their behalf. Yet in as much as he was given by the Father for them, and his obedience and satisfaction accepted in their stead, and both freely, not for any thing in them, their justification is only of free grace, that both the exact justice and rich grace of God might be glorified in the justification of sinners.

4. God did from all eternity decree to justify all the elect, and Christ did in the fullness of time die for their sins, and rise again for their justification: nevertheless, they are not justified personally, until the Holy Spirit doth in due time actually apply Christ unto them.

5. God doth continue to forgive the sins of those that are justified; and although they can never fall from the state of justification, yet they may by their sins

fall under God's fatherly displeasure: and in that condition they have not usually the light of his countenance restored unto them, until they humble themselves, confess their sins, beg pardon, and renew their faith and repentance.

6. The justification of believers under the Old Testament, was in all these respects one and the same with the justification of believers under the New Testament.

CHAPTER 12. OF ADOPTION

1. All those that are justified, God vouchsafeth in and for his only Son Jesus Christ to make partakers of the grace of adoption, by which they are taken into the number, and enjoy the liberties and privileges of the children of God, have his name put upon them, receive the Spirit of adoption; have access to the throne of grace with boldness, are enabled to cry, Abba Father; are pitied, protected, provided for, and chastened by him as by a father; yet never cast off, but sealed to the day of redemption, and inherit the promises as heirs of everlasting salvation.

CHAPTER 13. OF SANCTIFICATION

1. They that are united to Christ, effectually called and regenerated, having a new heart and a new spirit created in them, through the virtue of Christ's death and resurrection, are also further sanctified really and personally through the same virtue, by his word and Spirit dwelling in them; the dominion of the whole body of sin is destroyed and the several lusts thereof are more and more weakened, and mortified, and they more and more quickened, and strengthened in all saving graces, to the practice of all true holiness, without which no man shall see the Lord.

2. This sanctification is throughout in the whole man, yet imperfect in this life; there abideth still some remnants of corruption in every part; whence ariseth a continual and irreconcilable war, the flesh lusting against the Spirit, and the Spirit against the flesh.

3. In which war, although the remaining corruption for a time may much prevail, yet through the continual supply of strength from the sanctifying Spirit of Christ, the regenerate part doth overcome, and so the saints grow in grace, perfecting holiness in the fear of God.

CHAPTER 14. OF SAVING FAITH

1. The grace of faith, whereby the elect are enabled to believe to the saving of their souls, is the work of the Spirit of Christ in their hearts, and is ordinarily wrought by the ministry of the word; by which also, and by the administration of the seals, prayer, and other means, it is increased and strengthened.

2. By this faith a Christian believeth to be true whatsoever is revealed in the word, for the authority of God himself speaking therein, and acteth differently upon that which each particular passage thereof containeth; yielding obedience to the commands, trembling at the threatenings, and embracing the promises of God for this life, and that which is to come. But the principal acts of saving faith are, accepting, receiving, and resting upon Christ alone, for justification, sanctification, and eternal life, by virtue of the covenant of grace.

3. This faith, although it be different in degrees, and may be weak or strong, yet it is in the least degree of it different in the kind or nature of it (as is all other saving grace) from the faith and common grace of temporary believers; and therefore, though it may be many times assailed and weakened, yet it gets the victory, growing up in many to the attainment of a full assurance through Christ, who is both the author and finisher of our faith.

CHAPTER 15. OF REPENTANCE UNTO LIFE AND SALVATION

1. Such of the elect as are converted at riper years, having sometime lived in the state of nature, and therein served diverse lusts and pleasures, God in their effectual calling giveth them repentance unto life.

2. Whereas there is none that doth good, and sinneth not, and the best of men may through the power and deceitfulness of their corruptions dwelling in them, with the prevalency of temptation, fall into great sins and provocations; God hath in the covenant of grace mercifully provided, that believers so sinning and falling, be renewed through repentance unto salvation.

3. This saving repentance is an evangelical grace, whereby a person being by the Holy Ghost made sensible of the manifold evils of his sin, doth by faith in Christ humble himself for it with godly sorrow, detestation of it, and self-abhorrence, praying for pardon and strength of grace, with a purpose, and endeavor by supplies of the Spirit, to walk before God unto all well-pleasing in all things.

4. As repentance is to be continued through the whole course of our lives, upon the account of the body of death, and the motions thereof; so it is every man's duty to repent of his particular known sins particularly.

5. Such is the provision which God hath made through Christ in the covenant of grace, for the preservation of believers unto salvation, that although there is no sin so small, but it deserves damnation; yet there is no sin so great, that it shall bring damnation on them who truly repent; which makes the constant preaching of repentance necessary.

CHAPTER 16. OF GOOD WORKS

1. Good works are only such as God hath commanded in his holy word, and not such as without the warrant thereof are devised by men out of blind zeal, or upon pretense of good intentions.

2. These good works done in obedience to God's commandments, are the fruits and evidences of a true and lively faith; and by them believers manifest their thankfulness, strengthen their assurance, edify their brethren, adorn the profession of the gospel, stop the mouths of the adversaries, and glorify God, whose workmanship they are, created in Christ Jesus thereunto; that having their fruit unto holiness, they may have the end, eternal life.

3. Their ability to do good works is not at all of themselves, but wholly from the Spirit of Christ. And that they may be enabled thereunto, besides the graces they have already received, there is required an actual influence of the same Holy Spirit to work in them to will and to do of his good pleasure; yet are they not hereupon to grow negligent, as if they were not bound to perform any duty unless upon a special motion of the Spirit; but they ought to be diligent in stirring up the grace of God that is in them.

4. They who in their obedience attain to the greatest height which is possible in this life, are so far from being able to supererogate, and to do more than God requires, as that they fall short of much which in duty they are bound to do.

5. We cannot by our best works merit pardon of sin, or eternal life at the hand of God, by reason of the great disproportion that is between them and the glory to come; and the infinite distance that is between us and God, whom by them we can neither profit, nor satisfy for the debt of our former sins; but when we have done all we can, we have done but our duty, and are unprofitable servants; and because, as they are good, they proceed from the Spirit, and as they are wrought by us, they are defiled and mixed with so much weakness and imperfection, that they cannot endure the severity of God's judgment.

6. Yet notwithstanding, the persons of believers being accepted through Christ, their good works also are accepted in him; not as though they were in this life wholly unblameable and unreproveable in God's sight; but that he looking upon them in his Son is pleased to accept and reward that which is sincere, although accompanied with many weaknesses and imperfections.

7. Works done by unregenerate men, although for the matter of them they may be things which God commands, and of good use both to themselves and to others: yet because they proceed not from a heart purified by faith; nor are done in a right manner, according to the word; nor to a right end, the glory of God; they are therefore sinful, and cannot please God, nor make a man meet to receive

grace from God; and yet their neglect of them is more sinful, and displeasing unto God.

CHAPTER 17. OF THE PERSEVERANCE OF THE SAINTS

1. They whom God hath accepted in his Beloved, effectually called and sanctified by his Spirit, can neither totally nor finally fall away from the state of grace; but shall certainly persevere therein to the end, and be eternally saved.

2. This perseverance of the saints depends not upon their own free will, but upon the immutability of the decree of election; from the free and unchangeable love of God the Father; upon the efficacy of the merit and intercession of Jesus Christ, and union with him; the oath of God; the abiding of his Spirit; and of the seed of God within them; and the nature of the covenant of grace; from all which ariseth also the certainty and infallibility thereof.

3. And though they may, through the temptation of Satan, and of the world, the prevalency of corruption remaining in them, and the neglect of the means of their preservation, fall into grievous sins; and for a time continue therein, whereby they incur God's displeasure, and grieve his Holy Spirit; come to have their graces and comforts impaired; have their hearts hardened, and their consciences wounded; hurt and scandalize others, and bring temporal judgments upon themselves; yet they are and shall be kept by the power of God through faith unto salvation.

CHAPTER 18. OF THE ASSURANCE OF GRACE AND SALVATION

1. Although temporary believers and other unregenerate men may vainly deceive themselves with false hopes, and carnal presumptions of being in the favor of God, and state of salvation, which hope of theirs shall perish; yet such as truly believe in the Lord Jesus, and love him in sincerity, endeavoring to walk in all good conscience before him, may in this life be certainly assured that they are in the state of grace, and may rejoice in the hope of the glory of God, which hope shall never make them ashamed.

2. This certainty is not a bare conjectural and probable persuasion, grounded upon a fallible hope; but an infallible assurance of faith, founded on the blood and righteousness of Christ, revealed in the gospel, and also upon the inward evidence of those graces unto which promises are made, and on the immediate witness of the Spirit, testifying our adoption, and as a fruit thereof, leaving the heart more humble and holy.

3. This infallible assurance doth not so belong to the essence of faith, but that a true believer may wait long, and conflict with many difficulties before he be partaker of it; yet being enabled by the Spirit to know the things which are freely

given him of God, he may, without extraordinary revelation, in the right use of ordinary means attain thereunto. And therefore it is the duty of every one to give all diligence to make his calling and election sure; that thereby his heart may be enlarged in peace and joy in the Holy Ghost, in love and thankfulness to God, and in strength and cheerfulness in the duties of obedience, the proper fruits of this assurance; so far is it from inclining men to looseness.

4. True believers may have the assurance of their salvation diverse ways shaken, diminished, and intermitted; as by negligence in preserving of it; by falling into some special sin, which woundeth the conscience, and grieveth the Spirit; by some sudden or vehement temptation; by God's withdrawing the light of his countenance; suffering even such as fear him to walk in darkness, and to have no light; yet are they neither utterly destitute of that seed of God, and life of faith, that love of Christ and the brethren, that sincerity of heart and conscience of duty, out of which by the operation of the Spirit this assurance may in due time be revived, and by the which in the meantime they are supported from utter despair.

CHAPTER 19. OF THE LAW OF GOD

1. God gave to Adam a law of universal obedience written in his heart, and a particular precept of not eating the fruit of the tree of knowledge of good and evil, as a covenant of works, by which he bound him and all his posterity to personal, entire, exact and perpetual obedience; promised life upon the fulfilling, and threatened death upon the breach of it; and endued him with power and ability to keep it.

2. This law, so written in the heart, continued to be a perfect rule of righteousness after the fall of man; and was delivered by God upon Mount Sinai in ten commandments, and written in two tables; the four first commandments containing our duty towards God, and the other six our duty to man.

3. Beside this law, commonly called moral, God was pleased to give to the people of Israel ceremonial laws, containing several typical ordinances; partly of worship, prefiguring Christ, his graces, actions, sufferings, and benefits, and partly holding forth diverse instructions of moral duties. All which ceremonial laws being appointed only to the time of reformation, are by Jesus Christ the true Messiah and only lawgiver, who was furnished with power from the Father for that end, abrogated and taken away.

4. To them also he gave sundry judicial laws, which expired together with the state of that people, not obliging any now by virtue of that institution, their general equity only being still of moral use.

5. The moral law doth for ever bind all, as well justified persons as others, to the obedience thereof; and that not only in regard of the matter contained in it,

but also in respect of the authority of God the Creator, who gave it: neither doth Christ in the gospel any way dissolve, but much strengthen this obligation.

6. Although true believers be not under the law, as a covenant of works, to be thereby justified or condemned; yet it is of great use to them as well as to others, in that, as a rule of life, informing them of the will of God, and their duty, it directs and binds them to walk accordingly; discovering also the sinful pollutions of their nature, hearts, and lives; so as examining themselves thereby, they may come to further conviction of, humiliation for, and hatred against sin; together with a clearer sight of the need they have of Christ, and the perfection of his obedience. It is likewise of use to the regenerate, to restrain their corruptions, in that it forbids sin; and the threatenings of it serve to show what even their sins deserve, and what afflictions in this life they may expect for them, although freed from the curse thereof threatened in the law. The promises of it in like manner show them God's approbation of obedience, and what blessings they may expect upon the performance thereof, although not as due to them by the law, as a covenant of works; so as a man's doing good, and refraining from evil, because the law encourageth to the one, and deterreth from the other, is no evidence of his being under the law, and not under grace.

7. Neither are the forementioned uses of the law contrary to the grace of the gospel, but do sweetly comply with it; the Spirit of Christ subduing and enabling the will of man to do that freely and cheerfully, which the will of God revealed in the law required to be done.

CHAPTER 20. OF THE GOSPEL, AND OF THE
EXTENT OF THE GRACE THEREOF

1. The covenant of works being broken by sin, and made unprofitable unto life, God was pleased to give unto the elect the promise of Christ, the seed of the woman, as the means of calling them, and begetting in them faith and repentance: in this promise the gospel, as to the substance of it, was revealed, and was therein effectual for the conversion and salvation of sinners.

2. This promise of Christ, and salvation by him, is revealed only in and by the word of God; neither do the works of creation or providence, with the light of nature, make discovery of Christ, or of grace by him, so much as in a general or obscure way; much less that men destitute of the revelation of him by the promise or gospel, should be enabled thereby to attain saving faith or repentance.

3. The revelation of the gospel unto sinners, made in diverse times, and by sundry parts, with the addition of promises and precepts for the obedience required therein, as to the nations and persons to whom it is granted, is merely of the sover-

eign will and good pleasure of God, not being annexed by virtue of any promise to the due improvement of men's natural abilities, by virtue of common light received without it, which none ever did make or can so do. And therefore in all ages the preaching of the gospel hath been granted unto persons and nations, as to the extent or straitening of it, in great variety, according to the counsel of the will of God.

4. Although the gospel be the only outward means of revealing Christ and saving grace, and is as such abundantly sufficient thereunto; yet that men who are dead in trespasses, may be born again, quickened, or regenerated, there is moreover necessary an effectual, irresistible work of the Holy Ghost upon the whole soul, for the producing in them a new spiritual life, without which no other means are sufficient for their conversion unto God.

CHAPTER 21. OF CHRISTIAN LIBERTY, AND LIBERTY OF CONSCIENCE

1. The liberty which Christ hath purchased for believers under the gospel, consists in their freedom from the guilt of sin, the condemning wrath of God, the rigor and curse of the law; and in their being delivered from this present evil world, bondage to Satan, and dominion of sin, from the evil of afflictions, the fear and sting of death, the victory of the grave, and everlasting damnation; as also in their free access to God, and their yielding obedience unto him, not out of slavish fear, but a childlike love and willing mind. All which were common also to believers under the law, for the substance of them; but under the New Testament the liberty of Christians is further enlarged in their freedom from the yoke of the ceremonial law, the whole legal administration of the covenant of grace, to which the Jewish church was subjected; and in greater boldness of access to the throne of grace, and in fuller communications of the free Spirit of God, than believers under the law did ordinarily partake of.

2. God alone is Lord of the conscience, and hath left it free from the doctrines and commandments of men which are in any thing contrary to his word, or not contained in it; so that to believe such doctrines, or to obey such commands out of conscience, is to betray true liberty of conscience; and the requiring of an implicit faith, and an absolute and blind obedience, is to destroy liberty of conscience, and reason also.

3. They who upon pretense of Christian liberty do practice any sin, or cherish any lust, as they do thereby pervert the main design of the grace of the gospel to their own destruction; so they wholly destroy the end of Christian liberty, which is, that being delivered out of the hands of our enemies, we might serve the Lord without fear, in holiness and righteousness before him all the days of our life.

CHAPTER 22. OF RELIGIOUS WORSHIP, AND THE SABBATH DAY

1. The light of nature showeth that there is a God, who hath lordship and sovereignty over all, is just, good, and doth good unto all, and is therefore to be feared, loved, praised, called upon, trusted in, and served with all the heart, and all the soul, and with all the might. But the acceptable way of worshiping the true God is instituted by himself, and so limited by his own revealed will, that he may not be worshiped according to the imaginations and devices of men, or the suggestions of Satan, under any visible representations, or any other way not prescribed in the Holy Scripture.

2. Religious worship is to be given to God the Father, Son, and Holy Ghost, and to him alone; not to angels, saints, or any other creatures; and since the fall, not without a Mediator, nor in the mediation of any other but of Christ alone.

3. Prayer, with thanksgiving, being one special part of natural worship, is by God required of all men; but that it may be accepted, it is to be made in the name of the Son by the help of his Spirit, according to his will, with understanding, reverence, humility, fervency, faith, love, and perseverance; and when with others in a known tongue.

4. Prayer is to be made for things lawful, and for all sorts of men living, or that shall live hereafter; but not for the dead, nor for those of whom it may be known that they have sinned the sin unto death.

5. The reading of the Scriptures, preaching, and hearing the word of God, singing of psalms; as also the administration of baptism and the Lord's supper, are all parts of religious worship of God, to be performed in obedience unto God with understanding, faith, reverence, and godly fear. Solemn humiliations, with fastings and thanksgivings upon special occasions, are in their several times and seasons to be used in a holy and religious manner.

6. Neither prayer, nor any other part of religious worship, is now under the gospel either tied unto, or made more acceptable by any place in which it is performed, or towards which it is directed; but God is to be worshiped everywhere in spirit and in truth, as in private families daily, and in secret each one by himself, so more solemnly in the public assemblies, which are not carelessly nor willfully to be neglected, or forsaken, when God by his word or providence calleth thereunto.

7. As it is of the law of nature, that in general a proportion of time by God's appointment be set apart for the worship of God; so by his word in a positive, moral, and perpetual commandment, binding all men in all ages, he hath particularly appointed one day in seven for a Sabbath to be kept holy unto him; which from the beginning of the world to the resurrection of Christ, was the last day of the week; and from the resurrection of Christ was changed into the first day of the

week, which in Scripture is called the Lord's day, and is to be continued to the end of the world as the Christian Sabbath, the observation of the last day of the week being abolished.

8. This Sabbath is then kept holy unto the Lord, when men after a due preparing of their hearts, and ordering their common affairs beforehand, do not only observe a holy rest all the day from their own works, words, and thoughts about their worldly employments and recreations; but also are taken up the whole time in the public and private exercises of his worship, and in the duties of necessity and mercy.

CHAPTER 23. OF LAWFUL OATHS AND VOWS

1. A lawful oath is a part of religious worship, wherein the person swearing in truth, righteousness, and judgment, solemnly calleth God to witness what he asserteth or promiseth, and to judge him according to the truth or falsehood of what he sweareth.

2. The name of God only is that by which men ought to swear, and therein it is to be used with all holy fear and reverence. Therefore to swear vainly, or rashly, by that glorious or dreadful name, or to swear at all by any other thing, is sinful and to be abhorred. Yet as in matters of weight and moment an oath is warranted by the word of God under the New Testament, as well as under the Old; so a lawful oath, being imposed by lawful authority in such matters, ought to be taken.

3. Whosoever taketh an oath, warranted by the word of God, ought duly to consider the weightiness of so solemn an act, and therein to avouch nothing but what he is fully persuaded is the truth: neither may any man bind himself by oath to any thing, but what is good and just, and what he believeth so to be, and what he is able and resolved to perform. Yet it is a sin to refuse an oath touching any thing that is good and just, being lawfully imposed by authority.

4. An oath is to be taken in the plain and common sense of the words, without equivocation or mental reservation. It cannot oblige to sin, but in any thing not sinful, being taken it binds to performance, although to a man's own hurt; nor is it to be violated, although made to heretics or infidels.

5. A vow, which is not to be made to any creature, but God alone, is of the like nature with a promissory oath, and ought to be made with the like religious care, and to be performed with the like faithfulness.

6. Popish monastical vows of perpetual single life, professed poverty, and regular obedience, are so far from being degrees of higher perfection, that they are superstitious and sinful snares, in which no Christian may entangle himself.

CHAPTER 24. OF THE CIVIL MAGISTRATE

1. God the supreme Lord and King of all the world, hath ordained civil magistrates to be under him, over the people for his own glory and the public good; and to this end hath armed them with the power of the sword, for the defense and encouragement of them that do good, and for the punishment of evildoers.

2. It is lawful for Christians to accept and execute the office of a magistrate, when called thereunto: in the management whereof, as they ought specially to maintain justice and peace, according to the wholesome laws of each commonwealth; so for that end they may lawfully now under the New Testament wage war upon just and necessary occasion.

3. Although the magistrate is bound to encourage, promote, and protect the professors and profession of the gospel, and to manage and order civil administrations in a due subserviency to the interest of Christ in the world, and to that end to take care that men of corrupt minds and conversations do not licentiously publish and divulge blasphemy and errors, in their own nature subverting the faith and inevitably destroying the souls of them that receive them: yet in such differences about the doctrines of the gospel, or ways of the worship of God, as may befall men exercising a good conscience, manifesting it in their conversation, and holding the foundation, not disturbing others in their ways or worship that differ from them; there is no warrant for the magistrate under the gospel to abridge them of their liberty.

4. It is the duty of people to pray for magistrates, to honor their persons, to pay them tribute and other dues, to obey their lawful commands, and to be subject to their authority for conscience sake. Infidelity, or difference in religion, doth not make void the magistrate's just and legal authority, nor free the people from their obedience to him: from which ecclesiastical persons are not exempted, much less hath the pope any power or jurisdiction over them in their dominions, or over any of their people, and least of all to deprive them of their dominions or lives, if he shall judge them to be heretics, or upon any other pretense whatsoever.

CHAPTER 25. OF MARRIAGE

1. Marriage is to be between one man and one woman: neither is it lawful for any man to have more than one wife, nor for any woman to have more than one husband at the same time.

2. Marriage was ordained for the mutual help of husband and wife; for the increase of mankind with a legitimate issue, and of the church with a holy seed, and for preventing of uncleanness.

3. It is lawful for all sorts of people to marry, who are able with judgment to give their consent. Yet it is the duty of Christians to marry in the Lord; and therefore such as profess the true reformed religion, should not marry with infidels, papists, or other idolaters: neither should such as are godly, be unequally yoked by marrying with such as are wicked in their life, or maintain damnable heresies.

4. Marriage ought not to be within the degrees of consanguity or affinity forbidden in the word; nor can such incestuous marriages ever be made lawful by any law of man, or consent of parties, so as those persons may live together as man and wife.

CHAPTER 26. OF THE CHURCH

1. The catholic or universal church, which is invisible, consists of the whole number of the elect, that have been, are, or shall be gathered into one under Christ, the Head thereof, and is the spouse, the body, the fullness of him that filleth all in all.

2. The whole body of men throughout the world, professing the faith of the gospel and obedience unto God by Christ according to it, not destroying their own profession by any errors everting the foundation, or unholiness of conversation, are, and may be called the visible catholic church of Christ; although as such it is not entrusted with the administration of any ordinances, or have any officers to rule or govern in, or over the whole body.

3. The purest churches under heaven are subject both to mixture and error, and some have so degenerated as to become no churches of Christ, but synagogues of Satan: nevertheless Christ always hath had, and ever shall have, a visible kingdom in this world, to the end thereof, of such as believe in him, and make profession of his name.

4. There is no other head of the church but the Lord Jesus Christ; nor can the pope of Rome in any sense be head thereof; but is that Antichrist, that man of sin, and son of perdition, that exalteth himself in the church against Christ, and all that is called God, whom the Lord shall destroy with the brightness of his coming.

5. As the Lord in his care and love towards his church, hath in his infinite wise providence exercised it with great variety in all ages, for the good of them that love him, and his own glory; so according to his promise, we expect that in the latter days, Antichrist being destroyed, the Jews called, and the adversaries of the kingdom of his dear Son broken, the churches of Christ being enlarged, and edified through a free and plentiful communication of light and grace, shall enjoy in this world a more quiet, peaceable, and glorious condition than they have enjoyed.

CHAPTER 27. OF THE COMMUNION OF SAINTS

1. All saints that are united to Jesus Christ their Head, by his Spirit and faith, although they are not made thereby one person with him, have fellowship in his graces, sufferings, death, resurrection, and glory: and being united to one another in love, they have communion in each other's gifts and graces, and are obliged to the performance of such duties, public and private, as do conduce to their mutual good, both in the inward and outward man.

2. All saints are bound to maintain a holy fellowship and communion in the worship of God, and in performing such other spiritual services as tend to their mutual edification; as also in relieving each other in outward things, according to their several abilities and necessities: which communion, though especially to be exercised by them in the relations wherein they stand, whether in families or churches, yet as God offereth opportunity, is to be extended unto all those who in every place call upon the name of the Lord Jesus.

CHAPTER 28. OF THE SACRAMENTS

1. Sacraments are holy signs and seals of the covenant of grace, immediately instituted by Christ, to represent him and his benefits, and to confirm our interest in him, and solemnly to engage us to the service of God in Christ, according to his word.

2. There is in every sacrament a spiritual relation, or sacramental union, between the sign and the thing signified; whence it comes to pass that the names and effects of the one are attributed to the other.

3. The grace which is exhibited in or by the sacraments rightly used, is not conferred by any power in them; neither doth the efficacy of a sacrament depend upon the piety or intention of him that doth administer it, but upon the work of the Spirit, and the word of institution; which contains, together with a precept authorizing the use thereof, a promise of benefit to worthy receivers.

4. There be only two sacraments ordained by Christ our Lord in the Gospel, that is to say, baptism and the Lord's supper; neither of which may be dispensed by any but a minister of the word lawfully called.

5. The sacraments of the Old Testament, in regard of the spiritual things thereby signified and exhibited, were for substance the same with those of the New.

CHAPTER 29. OF BAPTISM

1. Baptism is a sacrament of the New Testament, ordained by Jesus Christ to be unto the party baptized a sign and seal of the covenant of grace, of his engrafting into Christ, of regeneration, of remission of sins, and of his giving up unto God

through Jesus Christ to walk in newness of life; which ordinance is by Christ's own appointment to be continued in his church until the end of the world.

2. The outward element to be used in this ordinance, is water, wherewith the party is to be baptized in the name of the Father, and of the Son, and of the Holy Ghost, by a minister of the gospel lawfully called.

3. Dipping of the person into the water is not necessary; but baptism is rightly administered by pouring or sprinkling water upon the person.

4. Not only those that do actually profess faith in and obedience unto Christ, but also the infants of one or both believing parents are to be baptized, and those only.

5. Although it be a great sin to condemn or neglect this ordinance, yet grace and salvation are not so inseparably annexed unto it, as that no person can be regenerated or saved without it; or that all that are baptized are undoubtedly regenerated.

6. The efficacy of baptism is not tied to that moment of time wherein it is administered; yet notwithstanding, by the right use of this ordinance, the grace promised is not only offered, but really exhibited and conferred by the Holy Ghost to such (whether of age or infants) as that grace belongeth unto, according to the counsel of God's own will in his appointed time.

7. Baptism is but once to be administered to any person.

CHAPTER 30. OF THE LORD'S SUPPER

1. Our Lord Jesus in the night wherein he was betrayed, instituted the sacrament of his body and blood, called the Lord's supper, to be observed in his churches to the end of the world, for the perpetual remembrance, and showing forth of the sacrifice of himself in his death, the sealing of all benefits thereof unto true believers, their spiritual nourishment, and growth in him, their further engagement in and to all duties which they owe unto him, and to be a bond and pledge of their communion with him, and with each other.

2. In this sacrament Christ is not offered up to his Father, nor any real sacrifice made at all for remission of sin of the quick or dead, but only a memorial of that one offering up of himself upon the cross once for all, and a spiritual oblation of all possible praise unto God for the same; so that the popish sacrifice of the mass (as they call it) is most abominable, injurious to Christ's own only sacrifice, the alone propitiation for all the sins of the elect.

3. The Lord Jesus hath in this ordinance appointed his ministers to pray and bless the elements of bread and wine, and thereby to set them apart from a common to an holy use; and to take and break the bread, to take the cup, and (they commu-

nicating also themselves) to give both to the communicants; but to none who are not then present in the congregation.

4. Private masses, or receiving the sacrament by a priest, or any other, alone; as likewise the denial of the cup to the people; worshiping the elements, the lifting them up, or carrying them about for adoration, and the reserving them for any pretended religious use; are contrary to the nature of this sacrament, and to the institution of Christ.

5. The outward elements in this sacrament duly set apart to the uses ordained by Christ, have such relation to him crucified, as that truly, yet sacramentally only, they are sometimes called by the name of the things they represent, to wit, the body and blood of Christ; albeit, in substance and nature, they still remain truly and only bread and wine as they were before.

6. The doctrine which maintains a change of the substance of bread and wine into the substance of Christ's body and blood (commonly called transubstantiation) by consecration of a priest, or by any other way, is repugnant not to Scripture alone, but even to common sense and reason; overthroweth the nature of the sacrament; and hath been and is the cause of manifold superstitions, yea, of gross idolatries.

7. Worthy receivers outwardly partaking of the visible elements in this sacrament, do then also inwardly by faith, really and indeed, yet not carnally and corporally, but spiritually, receive and feed upon Christ crucified, and all benefits of his death; the body and blood of Christ being then not corporally or carnally in, with, or under the bread or wine; yet as really, but spiritually present to the faith of believers in that ordinance, as the elements themselves are to their outward senses.

8. All ignorant and ungodly persons, as they are unfit to enjoy communion with Christ, so are they unworthy of the Lord's table, and cannot without great sin against him, while they remain such, partake of these holy mysteries, or be admitted thereunto; yea, whosoever shall receive unworthily, are guilty of the body and blood of the Lord, eating and drinking judgment to themselves.

CHAPTER 31. OF THE STATE OF MAN AFTER DEATH, AND OF THE RESURRECTION OF THE DEAD

1. The bodies of men after death return to dust, and see corruption; but their souls (which neither die nor sleep) having an immortal subsistence, immediately return to God who gave them. The souls of the righteous being then made perfect in holiness, are received into the highest heavens, where they behold the face of God in light and glory, waiting for the full redemption of their bodies: and the souls of the

wicked are cast into hell, where they remain in torment and utter darkness, reserved to the judgment of the great day: Besides these two places for souls separated from their bodies, the Scripture acknowledgeth none.

2. At the last day such as are found alive shall not die, but be changed; and all the dead shall be raised up with the selfsame bodies, and none other, although with different qualities, which shall be united again to their souls for ever.

3. The bodies of the unjust shall by the power of Christ be raised to dishonor; the bodies of the just, by his Spirit unto honor, and to be made conformable to his own glorious body.

CHAPTER 32. OF THE LAST JUDGMENT

1. God hath appointed a day wherein he will judge the world in righteousness by Jesus Christ, to whom all power and judgment is given of the Father. In which day, not only the apostate angels shall be judged, but likewise all persons that have lived upon earth shall appear before the tribunal of Christ, to give an account of their thoughts, words, and deeds, and to receive according to what they have done in the body, whether good or evil.

2. The end of God's appointing this day is for the manifestation of the glory of his mercy in the eternal salvation of the elect, and of his justice in the damnation of the reprobate, who are wicked and disobedient. For then shall the righteous go into everlasting life, and receive that fullness of joy and glory, with everlasting reward in the presence of the Lord; but the wicked who know not God, and obey not the gospel of Jesus Christ, shall be cast into eternal torments, and be punished with everlasting destruction from the presence of the Lord, and from the glory of his power.

3. As Christ would have us to be certainly persuaded that there shall be a judgment, both to deter all men from sin, and for the greater consolation of the godly in their adversity; so will he have that day unknown to men, that they may shake off all carnal security, and be always watchful, because they know not at what hour the Lord will come, and may be ever prepared to say, Come Lord Jesus, come quickly, Amen.

The Institution of Churches, and the Order Appointed in Them by Jesus Christ

1. By the appointment of the Father all power for the calling, institution, order, or government of the church, is invested in a supreme and sovereign manner in the Lord Jesus Christ, as King and Head thereof.

2. In the execution of this power wherewith he is so entrusted, the Lord Jesus calleth out of the world unto communion with himself, those that are given unto him by his Father, that they may walk before him in all the ways of obedience, which he prescribeth to them in his word.

3. Those thus called (through the ministry of the word by his Spirit) he commandeth to walk together in particular societies or churches, for their mutual edification, and the due performance of that public worship, which he requireth of them in this world.

4. To each of these churches thus gathered, according to his mind declared in his word, he hath given all that power and authority, which is any way needful for their carrying on that order in worship and discipline, which he hath instituted for them to observe, with commands and rules for the due and right exerting and executing of that power.

5. These particular churches thus appointed by the authority of Christ, and entrusted with power from him for the ends before expressed, are each of them as unto those ends, the seat of that power which he is pleased to communicate to his saints or subjects in this world, so that as such they receive it immediately from himself.

6. Besides these particular churches, there is not instituted by Christ any church more extensive or catholic entrusted with power for the administration of his ordinances, or the execution of any authority in his name.

7. A particular church gathered and completed according to the mind of Christ, consists of officers and members. The Lord Christ having given to his called ones (united according to his appointment in church order) liberty and power to choose persons fitted by the Holy Ghost for that purpose, to be over them, and to minister to them in the Lord.

8. The members of these churches are saints by calling, visibly manifesting and evidencing (in and by their profession and walking) their obedience unto that call of Christ; who, being further known to each other by their confession of the faith wrought in them by the power of God, declared by themselves or otherwise manifested, do willingly consent to walk together according to the appointment of Christ; giving up themselves to the Lord, and to one another by the will of God in professed subjection to the ordinances of the gospel.

9. The officers appointed by Christ, to be chosen and set apart by the church so called, and gathered for the peculiar administration of ordinances, and execution of power and duty which he entrusts them with, or calls them to, to be continued to the end of the world, are pastors, teachers, elders and deacons.

10. Churches thus gathered and assembling for the worship of God, are

thereby visible and public, and their assemblies (in whatever place they are, according as they have liberty or opportunity) are therefore church or public assemblies.

11. The way appointed by Christ for the calling of any person, fitted and gifted by the Holy Ghost, unto the office of pastor, teacher, or elder in a church, is, that he be chosen thereunto by the common suffrage of the church itself, and solemnly set apart by fasting and prayer, with imposition of hands of the eldership of that church, if there be any before constituted therein. And of a deacon, that he be chosen by the like suffrage, and set apart by prayer, and the like imposition of hands.

12. The essence of this call of a pastor, teacher, or elder unto office, consists in the election of the church, together with his acceptation of it, and separation by fasting and prayer. And those who are so chosen, though not set apart by imposition of hands, are rightly constituted ministers of Jesus Christ, in whose name and authority they exercise the ministry to them so committed. The calling of deacons consisteth in the like election and acceptation with separation by prayer.

13. Although it be incumbent on the pastors and teachers of the churches to be instant in preaching the word, by way of office; yet the work of preaching the word is not so peculiarly confined to them, but that others also gifted and fitted by the Holy Ghost for it, and approved (being by lawful ways and means in the providence of God called thereunto) may publicly, ordinarily, and constantly perform it; so that they give themselves up thereunto.

14. However, they who are engaged in the work of public preaching, and enjoy the public maintenance upon that account, are not thereby obliged to dispense the seals to any other than such as (being saints by calling, and gathered according to the order of the gospel) they stand related to, as pastors or teachers. Yet ought they not to neglect others living within their parochial bounds, but besides their constant public preaching to them, they ought to inquire after their profiting by the word, instructing them in, and pressing upon them (whether young or old) the great doctrines of the gospel, even personally and particularly, so far as their strength and time will admit.

15. Ordination alone without the election or precedent consent of the church, by those who formerly have been ordained by virtue of that power they have received by their ordination, doth not constitute any person a church officer, or communicate office power to him.

16. A church furnished with officers (according to the mind of Christ) hath full power to administer all his ordinances; and where there is want of any one or more officers required, that officer, or those which are in the church, may administer all the ordinances proper to their particular duty and offices; but where there are

no teaching officers, none may administer the seals, nor can the church authorize any so to do.

17. In the carrying on of church administrations, no person ought to be added to the church, but by the consent of the church itself; that so love (without dissimulation) may be preserved between all the members thereof.

18. Whereas the Lord Jesus Christ hath appointed and instituted as a means of edification, that those who walk not according to the rules and laws appointed by him (in respect of faith and life, so that just offense doth arise to the church thereby) be censured in his name and authority. Every church hath power in itself to exercise and execute all those censures appointed by him in the way and order prescribed in the gospel.

19. The censures so appointed by Christ, are admonition and excommunication. And whereas some offenses are or may be known only to some, it is appointed by Christ, that those to whom they are so known, do first admonish the offender in private: in public offenses where any sin, before all. Or in case of nonamendment upon private admonition, the offense being related to the church, and the offender not manifesting his repentance, he is to be duly admonished in the name of Christ by the whole church, by the ministry of the elders of the church; and if this censure prevail not for his repentance, then he is to be cast out by excommunication with the consent of the church.

20. As all believers are bound to join themselves to particular churches, when and where they have opportunity so to do, so none are to be admitted unto the privileges of the churches who do not submit themselves to the rule of Christ in the censures for the government of them.

21. This being the way prescribed by Christ in case of offense, no church members upon any offenses taken by them, having performed their duty required of them in this matter, ought to disturb any church order, or absent themselves from the public assemblies, or the administration of any ordinances upon that pretense, but to wait upon Christ in the further proceeding of the church.

22. The power of censures being seated by Christ in a particular church, is to be exercised only towards particular members of each church respectively as such; and there is no power given by him unto any synods or ecclesiastical assemblies to excommunicate, or by their public edicts to threaten excommunication, or other church censures against churches, magistrates, or their people upon any account, no man being obnoxious to that censure, but upon his personal miscarriage, as a member of a particular church.

23. Although the church is a society of men, assembling for the celebration of the ordinances according to the appointment of Christ, yet every society

assembling for that end or purpose, upon the account of cohabitation within any civil precincts and bounds, is not thereby constituted a church, seeing there may be wanting among them, what is essentially required thereunto; and therefore a believer living with others in such a precinct, may join himself with any church for his edification.

24. For the avoiding of differences that may otherwise arise, for the greater solemnity in the celebration of the ordinances of Christ, and the opening a way for the larger usefulness of the gifts and graces of the Holy Ghost; saints living in one city or town, or within such distances as that they may conveniently assemble for divine worship, ought rather to join in one church for their mutual strengthening and edification, than to set up many distinct societies.

25. As all churches and all the members of them are bound to pray continually for the good or prosperity of all the churches of Christ in all places, and upon all occasions to further it (every one within the bounds of their places and callings, in the exercise of their gifts and graces). So the churches themselves (when planted by the providence of God, so as they may have opportunity and advantage for it) ought to hold communion amongst themselves for their peace, increase of love, and mutual edification.

26. In cases of difficulties or differences, either in point of doctrine or in administrations, wherein either the churches in general are concerned, or any one church in their peace, union, and edification, or any member or members of any church are injured in, or by any proceeding in censures, not agreeable to truth and order: it is according to the mind of Christ, that many churches holding communion together, do by their messengers meet in a synod or council, to consider and give their advice in, or about that matter in difference, to be reported to all the churches concerned. Howbeit, these synods so assembled are not entrusted with any church power, properly so called, or with any jurisdiction over the churches themselves, to exercise any censures, either over any churches or persons, or to impose their determinations on the churches or officers.

27. Besides these occasional synods or councils, there are not instituted by Christ any stated synods in a fixed combination of churches, or their officers in lesser or greater assemblies; nor are there any synods appointed by Christ in a way of subordination to one another.

28. Persons that are joined in church fellowship, ought not lightly or without just cause to withdraw themselves from the communion of the church whereunto they are so joined. Nevertheless, where any person cannot continue in any church without his sin, either for want of the administration of any ordinances instituted by Christ, or by his being deprived of his due privileges, or compelled to

anything in practice not warranted by the word, or in case of persecution, or upon the account of conveniency of habitation; he consulting with the church, or the officer or officers thereof, may peaceably depart from the communion of the church, wherewith he hath so walked, to join himself with some other church, where he may enjoy the ordinances in the purity of the same, for his edification and consolation.

29. Such reforming churches as consist of persons sound in the faith and of conversation becoming the gospel, ought not to refuse the communion of each other, so far as may consist with their own principles respectively, though they walk not in all things according to the same rules of church order.

30. Churches gathered and walking according to the mind of Christ, judging other churches (though less pure) to be true churches, may receive unto occasional communion with them, such members of those churches as are credibly testified to be godly, and live without offense.

Society of Friends (Quakers), *A Confession of Faith Containing XXIII Articles,* 1673

The history of the Society of Friends or "Quakers" is an important chapter in the complicated history of Christian spirituality because of their emphasis on the "inner light" of "Christ in us"[1] and their consequent austerity about traditional outward forms, including the liturgy and even the sacraments. It is, if anything, an even more important chapter in the scarcely less complicated history of Christian attitudes toward peace and war because, together with the Mennonites and other "peace churches" coming out of the Radical Reformation, the Quakers articulated in systematic form the case against violence, whether by the individual or by the state, and demonstrated the alternative to it in Christian service.

Rather unexpectedly, however, the Friends from their earliest days have also made significant contributions to the history of confessions. These confessional contributions were doubtless due to the attacks on them from their critics and gainsayers[2] (as were, of course, the confessions of most other groups). The first was the work of the Scottish Quaker, Robert Barclay (1648–90), published in 1673 under the full title *Catechism and Confession of Faith.* His *Theses Theologicae* of two years later are theologically more sophisticated, and Schaff chose to publish them instead, under the title (which apparently Schaff himself supplied) *The Confession of the Society of Friends, Commonly Called Quakers, A.D. 1675.*[3] But the text that Barclay himself entitled *A Confession of Faith Containing XXIII Articles* would seem to fit the definition of a "confession" more accurately. It turns out to be a catena of biblical quotations; but, as always, the selection, order, and arrangement of the quotations are themselves a confession of faith.

Edition: Barclay 1857, 76–92.

Literature: Brinton 1973; Eeg-Olofsson 1954; R. Jones [1927] 2002; Steere 1955.

1. Eeg-Olofsson 1954.
2. Bitterman 1973.
3. Schaff, 3:789–98.

Society of Friends (Quakers), *A Confession of Faith Containing XXIII Articles*, 1673

ARTICLE 1. CONCERNING GOD, AND THE TRUE AND SAVING KNOWLEDGE OF HIM

There is one God.[a] Who is a spirit.[b] And this is the message which the apostles heard of him, and declared unto the saints, that he is light, and in him is no darkness at all. There are three that bear record in heaven, the Father, the Word, and the Holy Ghost, and these three are one. The Father is in the Son, and the Son is in the Father.[c] No man knoweth the Son, but the Father; neither knoweth any man the Father, but the Son, and he to whomsoever the Son will reveal him.[d] The Spirit searcheth all things, yea the deep things of God. For the things of God knoweth no man but the Spirit of God: now the saints have received not the spirit of the world, but the Spirit which is of God, that they might know the things which are freely given them of God. For the Comforter, which is the Holy Ghost, whom the Father sends in Christ's name, he teacheth them all things, and bringeth all things to their remembrance.

[1 Jn 1.5]

[1 Jn 5.7 var]

[1 Cor 2.10]

[1 Cor 2.11–12]

[Jn 14.26]

ARTICLE 2. CONCERNING THE GUIDE AND RULE OF CHRISTIANS

Christ prayed to the Father, and he gave the saints another Comforter, that was to abide with them forever, even the Spirit of truth, whom the world cannot receive, because it seeth him not, nor knoweth him; but the saints know him; for he dwelleth with them, and is to be in them. Now if any man have not the Spirit of Christ, he is none of his: for as many as are led by the Spirit of God, they are the sons of God. For this is the covenant that God hath made with the house of Israel, he hath put his laws in their mind, and writ them in their hearts; and they are all taught of God. And the anointing, which they have received of him, abideth in them; and they need not that any man teach them, but as the same anointing teacheth them of all things, and is truth, and is no lie.

[Jn 14.16–17]

[Rom 8.9, 14]

[Heb 8.10–11]

[1 Jn 2.27]

a. [Eph 4.6; 1 Cor 8.4, 6]
b. [Jn 4.24]
c. [Jn 10.38, 14.10–11, 5.26]
d. [Mt 11.27; Lk 10.22]

ARTICLE 3. CONCERNING THE SCRIPTURES

Whatsoever things were written aforetime, were written for our learning, that we
[Rom 15.4]   through patience and comfort of the Scriptures might have hope. Which are able
to make wise unto salvation, through faith which is in Christ Jesus: all Scripture
being given by inspiration of God, and is profitable for doctrine, for reproof, for
correction, for instruction in righteousness, that the man of God may be perfect,
[2 Tm 3.15–17]   thoroughly furnished unto all good works. No prophecy of the Scripture is of any
private interpretation; for the prophecy came not in old time by the will of man, but
[2 Pt 1.20–21]   holy men of God spake as they were moved by the Holy Ghost.

ARTICLE 4. CONCERNING THE DIVINITY OF CHRIST,
AND HIS BEING FROM THE BEGINNING

In the beginning was the Word, and the Word was with God, and the Word was
God; the same was in the beginning with God; all things were made by him, and
[Jn 1.1–3]   without him was not anything made that was made. Whose goings forth have been
from of old, from everlasting.[a] For God created all things by Jesus Christ.[b] Who
[Phil 2.6]   being in the form of God, thought it not robbery to be equal with God. And his
name is called Wonderful, Counsellor, the Mighty God, the Everlasting Father, the
Prince of Peace.[c] Who is the image of the invisible God, the firstborn of every crea-
[Heb 1.3]   ture,[d] the brightness of the Father's glory, and the express image of his substance.
Who was clothed with a vesture dipped in blood; and his name is called the Word
of God.[e] In him dwelleth all the fullness of the Godhead bodily.[f] And in him are hid
[Col 2.3]   all the treasures of wisdom and knowledge.

ARTICLE 5. CONCERNING HIS APPEARANCE IN THE FLESH

[Jn 1.14]   The Word was made flesh. For he took not on him the nature of angels; but he
[Heb 2.16–17]   took on him the seed of Abraham, being in all things made like unto his brethren.
Touched with a feeling of our infirmities; and in all things tempted, like as we are,
[Heb 4.15]   yet without sin. He died for our sins, according to the Scriptures; and he was buried,
[1 Cor 15.3–4]   and he rose again the third day, according to the Scriptures.

a. [Mi 5.2]
b. [Eph 3.9]
c. [Is 9.6]
d. [Col 1.15]
e. [Rv 19.13]
f. [Col 2.9]

ARTICLE 6. CONCERNING THE END AND
USE OF THAT APPEARANCE

God sent his own Son in the likeness of sinful flesh, and for sin condemned sin in the flesh. For this purpose the Son of God was manifested, that he might destroy [Rom 8.3] the works of the devil.[a] Being manifested to take away our sins.[b] For he gave himself for us, an offering and a sacrifice to God for a sweet smelling savor, having obtained [Eph 5.2] eternal redemption for us, and through the eternal Spirit offered himself without spot unto God to purge our consciences from dead works, to serve the living God. [Heb 9.12, 14] He was the Lamb that was slain from the foundation of the world. Of whom the [Rv 5.8, 12, 13.8] fathers did all drink; for they drank of that spiritual rock that followed them, and that rock was Christ. Christ also suffered for us, leaving us an example, that we [1 Cor 10.1–4] should follow his steps. For we are to bear about in the body, the dying of the Lord [1 Pt 2.21] Jesus, that the life also of Jesus might be made manifest in our body, being always delivered unto death for Jesus' sake, that the life also of Jesus may be made manifest in our flesh. That we may know him, and the power of his resurrection, and the [2 Cor 4.10–11] fellowship of his sufferings, being made conformable to his death. [Phil 3.10]

ARTICLE 7. CONCERNING THE INWARD
MANIFESTATION OF CHRIST

God dwelleth with the contrite and humble in spirit. For he hath said, He will dwell [Is 57.15] in them and walk in them. And Christ standeth at the door, and knocketh; if any [2 Cor 6.16] man hear his voice, and open the door, he will come in to him, and sup with him, and he with him. And therefore ought we to examine ourselves, and prove our own [Rv 3.20] selves, knowing how that Christ is in us except we be reprobates. For this is the [2 Cor 13.5] riches of the glory of the mystery, which God would make known among (or rather IN) the Gentiles, Christ in you, the hope of glory. [Col 1.27]

ARTICLE 8. CONCERNING THE NEW BIRTH

Except a man be born again, he cannot see the kingdom of God. Therefore ought [Jn 3.3] we to put off the old man with his deeds, and put on the new man, which is renewed in knowledge after the image of him that created him, and which after God is created in righteousness and true holiness.[c] For henceforth know we no man after the flesh; yea, though we have known Christ after the flesh, yet now henceforth know

a. [1 Jn 3.8]
b. [1 Jn 3.5]
c. [Eph 4.23–24; Col 3.10]

[2 Cor 5.16]   we him no more. For if any man be in Christ, he is a new creature, old things are
[2 Cor 5.17]   passed away; behold, all things are become new. For such have put on the Lord
                Jesus Christ.ᵃ And are renewed in the spirit of their minds.ᵇ For as many as have
[Gal 3.27]   been baptized into Christ, have put on Christ. Being born again, not of corrupt-
                ible seed, but of incorruptible, by the word of God, which liveth and abideth for
[1 Pt 1.23]   ever. And glory in nothing, save in the cross of the Lord Jesus Christ, by whom the
[Gal 6.14]   world is crucified unto them, and they unto the world. For in Christ Jesus, neither
[Gal 6.15]   circumcision availeth any thing, nor uncircumcision, but a new creature.

ARTICLE 9. CONCERNING THE UNITY OF
THE SAINTS WITH CHRIST

[Heb 2.11]   He that sanctifieth, and they who are sanctified, are all of one. For by the exceed-
                ing great and precious promises that are given them, they are made partakers of
[2 Pt 1.4]   the divine nature. Because for this end prayed Christ, they all might be one, as the
                Father is in him, and he in the Father, that they also might be one in them; and the
                glory which he had gotten from the Father, he gave them, that they might be one,
                even as the Father and he is one; Christ in the saints, and the Father in Christ, that
[Jn 17.21–23]   they might be made perfect in one.

ARTICLE 10. CONCERNING THE UNIVERSAL LOVE
AND GRACE OF GOD TO ALL

                God so loved the world, that he gave his only-begotten Son, that whosoever be-
[Jn 3.16]   lieveth in him should not perish, but have everlasting life. And in this was manifested
                the love of God towards us, because that God sent his only-begotten Son, that we
[1 Jn 4.9]   might live through him. So that if any man sin, we have an advocate with the Father,
                Jesus Christ the righteous; and he is the propitiation for our sins; and not for ours
[1 Jn 2.1–2]   only, but also for the sins of the whole world. For by the grace of God he hath tasted
                death for every man.ᶜ And gave himself a ransom for all, to be testified in due time.ᵈ
[1 Tm 2.4]   Willing all men to be saved, and to come to the knowledge of the truth. Not willing
[2 Pt 3.9]   that any should perish, but that all should come to repentance. For God sent not
                his Son into the world to condemn the world, but that the world through him might
[Jn 3.17]   be saved. And Christ came a light into the world, that whosoever believeth in him,
[Jn 12.46]   should not abide in darkness. Therefore, as by the offense of one, judgment came

a. [Rom 13.14]
b. [Eph 4.23]
c. [Heb 2.9]
d. [1 Tm 2.6]

upon all men to condemnation; even so by the righteousness of one, the free gift
came upon all men to justification of life.   [Rom 5.18]

ARTICLE 11. CONCERNING THE LIGHT THAT ENLIGHTENETH EVERY MAN

The gospel was preached to every creature under heaven. Which gospel is the power   [Col 1.23]
of God unto salvation, to them that believe. And if it be hid, it is hid to them which   [Rom 1.16]
are lost, in whom the god of this world hath blinded the minds of them which believe not, lest the light of the glorious gospel of Christ should shine on them. And   [2 Cor 4.3–4]
this is the condemnation, that light is come into the world, and men love darkness
rather than light, because their deeds are evil. And this was the true light, which   [Jn 3.19]
lighteth every man that cometh into the world. By which all things that are reprov-   [Jn 1.9]
able, are made manifest; for whatsoever maketh manifest is light. Every one that   [Eph 5.11]
doth evil, hateth the light, neither cometh to the light, lest his deeds should be reproved: but he that doeth truth, cometh to the light, that his deeds may be made
manifest, that they are wrought in God. And they that walk in the light, as he is   [Jn 3.20]
in the light, have fellowship one with another, and the blood of Jesus Christ his
Son, cleanseth them from all sin. Therefore ought we to believe in the light, while   [1 Jn 1.7]
we have the light, that we may be the children of the light. Therefore today, if we   [Jn 12.36]
will hear his voice, let us not harden our hearts. For Christ wept over Jerusalem,   [Heb 4.7]
saying, If thou hadst known, even thou, at least in this thy day, the things which
belong unto thy peace, but now they are hid from thine eyes. And he would often   [Lk 19.42]
have gathered her children, as a hen gathereth her chickens; but they would not.   [Mt 23.37]
For the stiff-necked and uncircumcised in heart and ears, do always resist the Holy
Ghost, and are of those that rebel against the light. Therefore God's Spirit will not   [Acts 7.51; Jb 24.13]
always strive with man. For the wrath of God is revealed from heaven against all   [Gn 6.3]
ungodliness and unrighteousness of men, who hold the truth in unrighteousness,   [Rom 1.18–19]
because what is to be known of God is manifest in them; for God hath showed it
unto them. And a manifestation of the Spirit is given to every man to profit withal.   [1 Cor 12.7]
For the grace of God that brings salvation, hath appeared to all men, teaching us,
that denying ungodliness and worldly lusts, we should live soberly, righteously, and
godly in this present world. And this word of his grace is able to build up and give   [Ti 2.11–12]
an inheritance among all those that are sanctified. For the word of God is quick   [Acts 20.32]
and powerful, and sharper than any two-edged sword, piercing even to the dividing
asunder of the soul and spirit, and of the joints and marrow, and is a discerner of the
thoughts and intents of the heart. This is that more sure word of prophecy, where-   [Heb 4.12]
unto we do well that we take heed, as unto a light that shineth in a dark place, until
the day dawn, and the day-star arise in the heart. And this is the word of faith which   [2 Pt 1.19]

[Rom 10.8] the apostles preached, which is nigh in the mouth, and in the heart. For God, who commanded the light to shine out of darkness, hath shined in our hearts, to give the
[2 Cor 4.6] light of the knowledge of the glory of God in the face of Jesus Christ. But we have
[2 Cor 4.7] this treasure in earthen vessels, that the excellency of the power may be of God and
[Lk 17.20–21] not of us; for the kingdom of God cometh not by observation, but is within us.

ARTICLE 12. CONCERNING FAITH AND JUSTIFICATION

Faith is the substance of things hoped for, and the evidence of things not seen, with-
[Heb 11.1, 6] out which it is impossible to please God. Therefore we are justified by faith, which worketh by love.[a] For faith without works being dead, is by works made perfect.[b]
[Rom 3.20] By the deeds of the law there shall no flesh be justified. Nor yet by the works of righteousness which we have done; but according to his mercy we are saved, by the
[Ti 3.5] washing of regeneration, and renewing of the Holy Ghost. For we are both washed,
[1 Cor 6.11] sanctified and justified in the name of the Lord Jesus, and by the Spirit of our God.

ARTICLE 13. CONCERNING GOOD WORKS

If we live after the flesh, we shall die; but if we, through the Spirit, do mortify the
[Rom 8.13] deeds of the body, we shall live. For they which believe in God must be careful to maintain good works.[c] For God will render to every man according to his deeds.[d] According to his righteous judgment, to them who by patient continuance in well-doing, seek for glory, honor and immortality, eternal life: For such are counted
[2 Thes 1.5] worthy of the kingdom of God. And cast not away their confidence, which hath
[Heb 10.35] great recompense of reward. Blessed then are they that do his commandments, that they may have right to the tree of life, and may enter in through the gates into the
[Rv 22.14] city.

ARTICLE 14. CONCERNING PERFECTION

[Rom 6.14] Sin shall not have dominion over such as are not under the law, but under grace. For there is no condemnation to those that are in Christ Jesus, who walk not after the flesh, but after the Spirit; for the law of the Spirit of life maketh free from the law of
[Rom 8.1–2] sin and death. For such are become dead unto sin, and alive unto righteousness; and
[Rom 2.18] being made free from sin, are become servants of righteousness. Therefore ought

a. [Gal 5.6]
b. [Jas 2.22, 26]
c. [Ti 3.8]
d. [Rom 2.6]

we to be perfect, as our heavenly Father is perfect. For the yoke of Christ is easy, [Mt 5.48]
and his burden is light.[a] And his commandments are not grievous.[b] And whosoever will enter into life must keep the commandments. Hereby do we know that we [Mt 19.17]
know God, if we keep his commandments. He that saith, I know him, and keepeth [1 Jn 2.3]
not his commandments, is a liar, and the truth is not in him. Whosoever abideth in [1 Jn 2.4]
him, sinneth not; whosoever sinneth, hath not seen him, neither known him. Let
no man deceive us; he that doth righteousness is righteous, even as he is righteous;
he that committeth sin is of the devil; whosoever is born of God doth not commit
sin; for his seed remaineth in him and he cannot sin, because he is born of God. For [1 Jn 3.6–9]
not everyone that saith Lord, Lord, shall enter into the kingdom of heaven; but he
that doth the will of the Father, which is in heaven. Circumcision is nothing, and [Mt 7.21]
uncircumcision is nothing, but the keeping the commandments of God. [1 Cor 7.19]

ARTICLE 15. CONCERNING PERSEVERANCE
AND FALLING FROM GRACE

We ought to give diligence to make our calling and election sure, which things if we
do, we shall never fall. For even Paul kept under his body, and brought it into subjec- [2 Pt 1.10]
tion, lest by any means, when he preached to others, he himself become a castaway. [1 Cor 9.27]
Let us therefore take heed, lest there be in any of us an evil heart of unbelief, in departing from the living God. Likewise let us labor to enter into that rest, lest any [Heb 3.12]
man fall after the same example of unbelief. For it is impossible for those who were [Heb 4.11]
once enlightened, and have tasted of the heavenly gift, and were made partakers of
the Holy Ghost, and have tasted of the good word of God, and the powers of the
world to come, if they shall fall away, to renew them again unto repentance. For he [Heb 6.4–6]
that abideth not in Christ is cast forth, and is withered. Yet such as overcome, he [Jn 15.16]
will make as pillars in the temple of his God, and they shall go no more out. And [Rv 3.12]
these are persuaded, that nothing shall be able to separate them from the love of
God, which is in Christ Jesus. [Rom 8.38]

ARTICLE 16. CONCERNING THE CHURCH AND MINISTRY

The church of God is the pillar and ground of truth. Whereof the dear Son of God [1 Tm 3.15]
is the head. From which all the body by joints and bands, having nourishment min- [Col 1.18]
istered and knit together, increaseth with the increase of God. Which church of [Col 2.19]
God are they that are sanctified in Christ Jesus. Who when he ascended up on high, [1 Cor 1.2]

a. [Mt 11.30]
b. [1 Jn 5.3]

gave gifts unto men: And he gave some apostles, some prophets, some evangelists, some pastors and teachers, for the perfecting of the saints, for the work of the min-

[Eph 4.8, 11–12] istry.Who ought to be blameless, vigilant, sober, of good behavior, given to hospitality, apt to teach; not given to wine, no strikers, not greedy of filthy lucre, but

[1 Tm 3.2–3] patient; not brawlers, nor covetous. Lovers of good men, sober, just, holy, temperate, holding fast the faithful word, as they have been taught, that they may be able

[Ti 1.8–9] by sound doctrine, both to exhort and to convince gainsayers. Taking heed to themselves and to the flock, over which the Holy Ghost hath made them overseers, to

[Acts 20.28] feed the church of God. Taking the oversight thereof, not by constraint, but willingly; not for filthy lucre, but of a ready mind; neither as being lords over God's

[1 Pt 5.2–3] heritage, but as being ensamples to the flock. And such elders as rule well, are to be counted worthy of double honor, especially they who labor in the word and doctrine.[a] And to be esteemed very highly in love for their works' sake.[b] As every man hath received the gift, so ought the same to be ministered: if any man speak, let him speak as the oracles of God; if any man minister, let him do it as of the ability

[1 Pt 4.10–11] which God giveth. Preaching the gospel, not with the wisdom of words, lest the

[1 Cor 1.17] cross of Christ should be made of none effect. Nor yet with enticing words of man's wisdom, but in demonstration of the Spirit and of power; that the faith may not stand in the wisdom of men, but in the power of God. Howbeit such speak wisdom among them that are perfect; yet not the wisdom of this world, nor of the princes of this world, which cometh to nought; but they speak the wisdom of God in a mystery, even the hidden wisdom, which God ordained before the world to their glory. Which things they also speak not in the words which man's wisdom teacheth, but

[1 Cor 2.4–7, 13] which the Holy Ghost teacheth. For it is not they that speak, but the Holy Ghost, or

[Mt 10.20] Spirit of the Father, that speaketh in them. Who if they sow spiritual things, ought to reap carnal things, for so the Lord hath ordained, that they which preach the gospel, should live of the gospel; for the Scripture saith, Thou shalt not muzzle the

[1 Cor 9.11, 14, 9] mouth of the ox that treadeth out the corn; and the laborer is worthy of his reward. Yet a necessity is laid upon them; yea, woe is unto them if they preach not the gospel; and their reward is, that when they preach the gospel, they make the gospel of

[1 Cor 9.16–18] Christ without charge. Not coveting any man's silver or gold, or apparel; but their hands minister to their necessities, that so laboring, they may support the weak; remembering the words of the Lord Jesus, how he said, It is more blessed to give,

[Acts 20.33–34] than to receive. For they are not of the greedy dogs that can never have enough. Nor of the shepherds that look to their own way, everyone for his gain from his

a. [1 Tm 5.17]
b. [1 Thes 5.12]

quarter.[a] That feed themselves, and not the flock.[b] That make the people err, biting with their teeth, and crying peace, and preparing war against all such as put not into their mouths, teaching for hire, and divining for money. Nor yet of those which [Mi 3.5, 11] teach things which they ought not, for filthy lucre's sake. That run greedily after [Ti 1.11] the error of Balaam for reward, loving the wages of unrighteousness, and through covetousness, with feigned words, making merchandise of souls. Men of corrupt minds, destitute of the truth, supposing that gain is godliness. But they know that [2 Pt 2.15, 3] godliness with contentment is great gain. And having food and raiment, they are therewith content. [1 Tm 6.5-6, 8]

ARTICLE 17. CONCERNING WORSHIP

The hour cometh, and now is, when the true worshipers shall worship the Father in Spirit and in truth; for the Father seeketh such to worship him. God is a Spirit, and [Jn 4.23-24] they which worship him, must worship him in Spirit and in truth. For the Lord is nigh to all them that call upon him, to all that call upon him in truth. He is far from [Ps 145.18] the wicked; but he heareth the prayers of the righteous. And this is the confidence [Prv 15.29] that we have in him, that if we ask anything according to his will, he heareth us. [1 Jn 5.14] What is it then? We must pray with the Spirit, and with the understanding also. [1 Cor 14.15] Likewise the Spirit also helpeth our infirmities; for we know not what we should pray for as we ought; but the Spirit itself maketh intercession for us, with groanings which cannot be uttered: and he that searcheth the heart, knoweth what is the mind of the Spirit, because he maketh intercession for the saints, according to the will of God. [Rom 8.26-27]

ARTICLE 18. CONCERNING BAPTISM

As there is one Lord, one faith, so there is one baptism. Which doth also now save [Eph 4.5] us, not the putting away of the filth of the flesh, but the answer of a good conscience towards God, by the resurrection of Jesus Christ. For John indeed baptized [1 Pt 3.21-22] with water, but Christ with the Holy Ghost and with fire. Therefore as many as are [Mt 3.11] baptized into Jesus Christ, are baptized into his death, and are buried with him by baptism into death, that like as Christ was raised up from the dead by the glory of the Father, even so they also should walk in newness of life.[c] Having put on Christ.[d]

a. [Is 56.11]
b. [Ez 34.8]
c. [Rom 6.3-4]
d. [Gal 3.27]

ARTICLE 19. CONCERNING EATING OF BREAD AND WINE, WASHING OF ONE ANOTHER'S FEET, ABSTAINING FROM THINGS STRANGLED, AND FROM BLOOD, AND ANOINTING OF THE SICK WITH OIL

The Lord Jesus the same night in which he was betrayed, took bread; and when he had given thanks, he broke it, and said, Take, eat, this is my body which is broken for you; this do in remembrance of me: After the same manner also he took the cup, when he had supped, saying, This cup is the new testament in my blood; this do ye, as oft as ye drink it, in remembrance of me; for as oft as ye do eat this bread, and drink this cup, ye do shew forth the Lord's death till he come. Jesus knowing that [1 Cor 11.23–26] the Father had given all things into his hands, and that he was come from God, and went to God, he riseth from supper, and laid aside his garments, and took a towel, and girded himself; after that he poured water into a basin, and began to wash the disciples' feet, and to wipe them with the towel wherewith he was girded: So after he had washed their feet, and had taken his garments, and was set down again, he said unto them, Know ye what I have done unto you? Ye call me Master and Lord, and ye say well; for so I am; if then I, your Lord and Master, have washed your feet, ye also ought to wash one another's feet; for I have given you an example, that ye [Jn 13.2–5, 12–15] should do as I have done unto you. For it seemed good to the Holy Ghost and to us, to lay upon you no greater burden than these necessary things. That ye abstain from meats offered to idols, from blood, and from things strangled, and from for- [Acts 15.28–29] nication; from which if ye keep yourselves ye do well. Is any man sick among you, let him call for the elders of the church, and let them pray over him anointing him [Jas 5.14] with oil.

ARTICLE 20. CONCERNING THE LIBERTY OF SUCH CHRISTIANS AS ARE COME TO KNOW THE SUBSTANCE, AS TO THE USING OR NOT USING OF THESE RITES, AND OF THE OBSERVATION OF DAYS

The kingdom of God is not meat and drink, but righteousness and peace, and joy [Rom 14.17] in the Holy Ghost. Let no man therefore judge us in meat or drink, or in respect of an holy day, or of the new moon, or of the sabbath days. For if we be dead with Christ from the rudiments of the world, why, as though living in the world, are we subject to ordinances? Let us not touch, or taste, or handle, which all are to per- [Col 2.16, 20–22] ish with the using, after the commandments and doctrines of men. For now, after we have known God, or rather are known of him, why should we turn again unto the weak and beggarly elements, or desire again to be in bondage to observe days [Gal 4.9–11] and months, and times and years, lest labor have been bestowed on us in vain? If

one man esteem a day above another, another esteems every day alike; let every man
be fully persuaded in his own mind: He that regardeth a day, regardeth it unto the
Lord: and he that regardeth not the day, to the Lord he doth not regard it.   [Rom 14.5–6]

ARTICLE 21. CONCERNING SWEARING, FIGHTING, AND PERSECUTION

It hath been said by them of old, Thou shalt not forswear thyself, but shalt perform unto the Lord thine oaths: but Christ says unto us, Swear not at all, neither
by heaven, for it is God's throne; nor by the earth, for it is his footstool; neither by
Jerusalem, for it is the city of the great King; neither shalt thou swear by thy head,
because thou canst not make one hair white or black; but let your communication
be yea, yea; nay, nay; for whatsoever is more than these, cometh of evil. And James   [Mt 5.33–37]
chargeth us, Above all things not to swear; neither by heaven, neither by the earth,
neither by any other oath; but let your yea, be yea, and your nay, nay, lest ye fall
into condemnation. Though we walk in the flesh, we are not to war after the flesh;   [Jas 5.12]
for the weapons of our warfare are not to be carnal, but mighty through God to
the pulling down of strongholds, casting down imaginations, and every high thing
that exalts itself against the knowledge of God, and bringing into captivity every
thought to the obedience of Christ. For wars and fightings come of the lusts, that   [2 Cor 10.3–5]
war in the members. Therefore Christ commands not to resist evil; but whosoever   [Jas 4.1–2]
will smite thee on the right cheek, to turn the other also. Because Christians are   [Mt 5.39]
lambs among wolves, therefore are they hated of all men for Christ's sake. And all   [Lk 10.3; Mt 10.22]
that will live godly in Christ Jesus, must suffer persecution. Such are blessed, for   [2 Tm 3.12]
theirs is the kingdom of heaven. For though they have lost their lives, yet shall they   [Mt 5.10]
save them. And because they have confessed Christ before men, he will also confess   [Mt 16.25]
them before the angels of God. We ought not then to fear them which kill the body,   [Lk 12.8–9]
but are not able to kill the soul; but rather fear him which is able to destroy both
soul and body in hell.   [Mt 10.28]

ARTICLE 22. CONCERNING MAGISTRACY

Let every soul be subject to the higher powers; for there is no power but of God; the
powers that be, are ordained of God. Whosoever therefore resists the power, resists
the ordinance of God; and they that resist, shall receive to themselves damnation:
for rulers are not a terror to good works, but to the evil. Wilt thou then not be afraid
of the power? Do that which is good, and thou shalt have praise of the same; for he
is the minister of God to thee for good: but if thou do that which is evil, be afraid;
for he beareth not the sword in vain: For he is the minister of God, a revenger to
execute wrath upon him that doth evil. Wherefore we must needs be subject, not

only for wrath, but also for conscience sake; for, for this cause pay we also tribute; for they are God's ministers, attending continually upon this very thing: Render
therefore to all their dues; tribute to whom tribute is due, custom to whom custom,
[Rom 13.1–7]   fear to whom fear, honor to whom honor. Therefore are we to submit ourselves to
every ordinance of man for the Lord's sake; whether it be to the king, as supreme;
or unto governors, as unto them that are sent by him for the punishment of evildoers, and for the praise of them that do well. For so is the will of God, that with
[1 Pt 2.13–15]   well doing, we may put to silence the ignorance of foolish men. Yet it is right in the
[Acts 4.19]   sight of God, to hearken unto him more than unto them. And though they straitly
[Acts 5.28–29]   command us not to teach in Christ's name, we ought to obey God rather than men.

ARTICLE 23. CONCERNING THE RESURRECTION

[Acts 24.15]   There shall be a resurrection of the dead, both of the just and unjust. They that have
done good, unto the resurrection of life; and they that have done evil unto the resur-
[Jn 5.29]   rection of damnation. Flesh and blood cannot inherit the kingdom of God; neither
[1 Cor 15.50]   doth corruption inherit incorruption. Nor is that body sown that shall be; but God
giveth it a body as it hath pleased him, and to every seed his own body: It is sown in
corruption, it is raised in incorruption: it is sown in dishonor, it is raised in glory:
it is sown in weakness, it is raised in power: it is sown a natural body, it is raised a
spiritual body.[a]

---

a. [1 Cor 15.37–38, 42–44]

Moravian Church (Unitas Fratrum), *Easter Litany,* 1749

The Moravian Church or "Unitas Fratrum" received its name from the Hussite church of that name, which produced → *The [First] Bohemian Confession* of 1535, with a foreword by Martin Luther. But that church was driven into exile in the Thirty Years' War, and its last bishop, Jan Amos Komenský (Comenius), died in the Netherlands in 1670. In 1721 Count Nicholas von Zinzendorf, leader of a German Lutheran Pietist community at Herrnhut, welcomed the remnants of the exiled Unitas Fratrum, and they formed one church, taking that name. Zinzendorf and the Moravians were a significant influence on the development of John Wesley, although they eventually parted ways.

This *Easter Litany* knits together passages from the Bible, chiefly the New Testament, from → *The Apostles' Creed,* and from → Luther's *Small Catechism.* The petition, "Hear us, gracious Lord and God" (5), does mark it as a "litany"; but the declarations of "I believe" and "This I assuredly believe," which are repeated throughout, make it even more explicitly "the principal confession of faith of the Bohemian Brethren."[1]

Edition and translation: Schaff, 3:799–806 (translation by Bishop Edmund de Schweinitz).

Literature: Hamilton 1900; Langton 1956; J. T. Müller 1922–31; Schweinitz 1901.

1. *ODCC* 522.

Moravian Church (Unitas Fratrum), *Easter Litany*, 1749

1. I believe in the one only God, Father, Son, and Holy Ghost, who created all things by Jesus Christ,[a] and was in Christ, reconciling the world unto himself.[b]

[Eph 1.4] I believe in God, the Father of our Lord Jesus Christ, who hath chosen us in him before the foundation of the world;

[Col 1.13] Who hath delivered us from the power of darkness, and hath translated us into the kingdom of his dear Son;

[Eph 1.3] Who hath blessed us with all spiritual blessings in heavenly places in Christ;

Who hath made us meet to be partakers of the inheritance of the saints in [Col 1.12] light: having predestinated us unto the adoption of children by Jesus Christ to himself, according to the good pleasure of his will, to the praise of the glory of his grace, [Eph 1.5–6] wherein he hath made us accepted in the Beloved.

This I verily believe.

2. We thank thee, O Father, Lord of heaven and earth, because thou hast hid these things from the wise and prudent, and hast revealed them unto babes. Even so, [Mt 11.25–26] Father: for so it seemed good in thy sight.

[Jn 12.28] Father, glorify thy name.

Our Father which art in heaven, hallowed be thy name; thy kingdom come; thy will be done in earth, as it is in heaven; give us this day our daily bread; and forgive us our trespasses, as we forgive them that trespass against us; and lead us not into temptation, but deliver us from evil: for thine is the kingdom, and the power, [Mt 6.9–13 (AV)] and the glory, forever and ever: Amen.

I believe in the name of the only-begotten Son of God, by whom are all [1 Cor 8.6] things, and we through him;

[Jn 1.14] I believe that he was made flesh, and dwelt among us; and took on him the [Phil 2.7] form of a servant;

[Lk 1.35] By the overshadowing of the Holy Ghost was conceived of the Virgin Mary; as the children are partakers of flesh and blood, he also himself likewise took part of the same;[c] was born of a woman;[d]

[Phil 2.8] And being found in fashion as a man, was tempted in all points like as we [Heb 4.15] are, yet without sin:

a. [Col 1.16; Heb 1.2]
b. [2 Cor 5.19]
c. [Heb 2.14]
d. [Gal 4.4]

For he is the Lord, the Messenger of the covenant, whom we delight in. [Mal 3.1]
The Lord and his Spirit hath sent him to proclaim the acceptable year of the Lord; [Is 61.2; Lk 4.19]
He spoke that which he did know, and testified that which he had seen: as [Jn 3.11]
many as received him, to them gave he power to become the sons of God. [Jn 1.12]
Behold the Lamb of God, which taketh away the sin of the world; [Jn 1.29]
Suffered under Pontius Pilate, was crucified, dead, and buried;
The third day rose again from the dead,[1] and with him many bodies of the
saints which slept; [Mt 27.52]
Ascended into heaven, and sitteth on the throne of the Father; whence he
will come,[2] in like manner as he was seen going into heaven. [Acts 1.11]
The Spirit and the bride say, Come.
And let him that heareth say, Come. [Rv 22.17]

Amen! come, Lord Jesus! come, we implore thee!
With longing hearts we now are waiting for thee.
Come soon, O come!

The Lord will descend from heaven with a shout, with the voice of the
archangel, and with the trump of God, to judge both the quick and the dead.[3] [1 Thes 4.16]
This is my Lord, who redeemed me, a lost and undone human creature,
purchased and gained me from sin, from death, and from the power of the devil;
Not with gold or silver, but with his holy precious blood, and with his
innocent suffering and dying;
To the end that I should be his own, and in his kingdom live under him and
serve him, in eternal righteousness, innocence, and happiness;
Even as he, being risen from the dead, liveth and reigneth, world without
end.[4]
This I most certainly believe.

3. I believe in the Holy Ghost, who proceedeth from the Father, and whom our Lord
Jesus Christ sent,[a] after he went away, that he should abide with us forever;[b]

a. [Jn 15.26]
b. [Jn 14.16]

1. *Ap* 4-5.
2. *Ap* 6-7.
3. *Ap* 7.
4. *Luth Sm Cat* 2.2.

[Is 66.13]   That he should comfort us, as a mother comforteth her children;

That he should help our infirmities, and make intercession for us with
[Rom 8.26]   groanings which can not be uttered;

That he should bear witness with our spirit, that we are the children of
[Rom 8.15-16]   God, and teach us to cry, Abba, Father;

[Rom 5.5]   That he should shed abroad in our hearts the love of God, and make our
bodies his holy temple;[a]

And that he should work all in all, dividing to every man severally as he
[1 Cor 12.11]   will.

[Eph 3.21]   To him be glory in the church, which is in Christ Jesus, the holy, universal Christian church, in the communion of saints, at all times, and from eternity to
eternity. Amen.

I believe that by my own reason and strength I can not believe in Jesus
Christ my Lord, or come to him;

But that the Holy Ghost calleth me by the gospel, enlighteneth me with his
gifts, sanctifieth and preserveth me in the true faith;

Even as he calleth, gathereth, enlighteneth, and sanctifieth the whole church
on earth, which he keepeth by Jesus Christ in the only true faith;

In which Christian church God forgiveth me and every believer all sin daily
and abundantly.

This I assuredly believe.[5]

4. I believe that by holy baptism I am embodied a member of the church of Christ,
which he hath loved, and for which he gave himself, that he might sanctify and
[Eph 5.26]   cleanse it with the washing of water by the word. Amen.

In this communion of saints my faith is placed upon my Lord and Savior
Jesus Christ, who died for us, and shed his blood on the cross for the remission
of sins, and who hath granted unto me his body and blood in the Lord's supper,
as a pledge of grace; as the Scripture saith: Our Lord Jesus Christ, the same night
in which he was betrayed, took bread: and when he had given thanks, he broke it,
and gave it to his disciples, and said, Take, eat; this is my body which is given for
you; this do in remembrance of me. After the same manner, also, our Lord Jesus
Christ, when he had supped, took the cup, gave thanks, and gave it to them, saying,
Drink ye all of it; this is my blood, the blood of the New Testament, which is shed

a. [1 Cor 6.19; Eph 2.21]

5. *Luth Sm Cat* 2.3.

for you, and for many, for the remission of sins. This do ye, as oft as ye drink it, in
remembrance of me.   [1 Cor 11.23–25]

      Therefore he abideth in me and I in him, and I have eternal life, and he will
raise me up on the last day. Amen.   [Jn 15.4, 6.40]

5. I have a desire to depart, and to be with Christ, which is far better; I shall never   [Phil 1.23]
taste death; yea, I shall attain unto the resurrection of the dead; for the body which   [Phil 3.11]
I shall put off, this grain of corruptibility, shall put on incorruption: my flesh shall [1 Cor 15.53]
rest in hope;   [Ps 16.9; Acts 2.26]

      And the God of peace, that brought again from the dead our Lord Jesus,
that great Shepherd of the sheep, through the blood of the everlasting covenant,   [Heb 13.20]
shall also quicken these our mortal bodies, if so be that the Spirit of God hath dwelt
in them.   [Rom 8.11]

      Amen.

      We poor sinners pray, Hear us, gracious Lord and God;

      6. And keep us in everlasting fellowship with our brethren, and with our
sisters, who have entered into the joy of their Lord;

      Also with the servants and handmaids of our church, whom thou hast called
home in the past year, and with the whole church triumphant; and let us rest together
in thy presence from our labors.   [Rv 14.13]

      Amen.

     They are at rest in lasting bliss,
       Beholding Christ our Savior:
     Our humble expectation is
       To live with him forever.

     Lord, grant me thy protection,
       Remind me of thy death
     And glorious resurrection,
       When I resign my breath:
     Ah! then, though I be dying,
       'Midst sickness, grief, and pain,
     I shall, on thee relying,
       Eternal life obtain.

Glory be to him who is the Resurrection and the Life; he was dead, and behold, he
is alive for evermore;   [Rv 2.8]

[Jn 11.25]   And he that believeth in him, though he were dead, yet shall he live.

[Eph 3.21]   Glory be to him in the church which waiteth for him, and in that which is around him:

Forever and ever.

Amen.

The grace of our Lord Jesus Christ, and the love of God, and the commu-

[2 Cor 13.14]   nion of the Holy Ghost, be with us all.

Amen.

Mennonite Church, *Mennonite Articles of Faith by Cornelis Ris,* 1766/1895/1902

The classic confessional formulations of the Mennonite-Anabaptist alternative both to Roman Catholicism and to Magisterial Protestantism were, above all, → *The Schleitheim Confession* of 1527 and → *The Mennonite Confession of Faith of Dordrecht* of 1632. With due allowance for the steadfast refusal of Mennonites to accord a "normative" status to any human or ecclesiastical statement of faith, it may nevertheless be said that, seen as responses for their own time to external challenge and internal need, confessions such as *Schleitheim* and *Dordrecht* did speak for the Mennonite churches in the Low Countries and Germany during the sixteenth and seventeenth centuries.

But both the continuing persecution and the persistent propensity for schism made it necessary in the eighteenth century and beyond for Mennonites to produce new confessions. Among the several of these that arose, *De geloofsleere der waare Mennoniten if Doopsgezinden,* composed in 1766 by Cornelis Ris (1717-90), acquired special standing as an expression of confessional continuity, also because it was in part a reworking of *Dordrecht.* Translated into German in 1849 and eventually into English in 1902 for use in America, "it became the unofficial confession of the [General Conference Mennonite] Church of North America. It has continued to serve as a symbol of identification with a theological heritage, as an introduction for the devout study of scripture, and as instruction for church members."[1]

Edition: Ris 1766, 1–194.

Translation: Loewen, 85–103 (from Ris 1904).

Literature: Loewen, 26; *ME* 2:339–40.

---

1. Loewen, 28.

Mennonite Church, *Mennonite Articles of Faith* by Cornelis Ris, 1766/1895/1902

1. OF THE KNOWLEDGE OF GOD FROM NATURE

1. We believe that there necessarily must be and actually is a supremely perfect being, exalted above all other beings; a being possessing in himself infinite wisdom, power, and glory, by whom all things were made and are continually sustained and governed;—this we believe not only because of the testimony of the Holy Scriptures, but because we may also clearly gather it from the things created.

2. Leaving our own being out of consideration, we see the heavens (Ps 19.1, 8.3), the earth (Ps 24.1; Jb 26.7), the seas (Ps 89.9; Jer 5.22) and all that in them is (Jb 12.7-9; Ps 107.23, 24; Ps 104) proclaim that such a greatness (Ps 104.24) and glory (Ps 8.9, 19.5, 104.1-3), skill and mastery (Ps 104, 139.1-18), fixed order (Ps 148.6; Is. 40.26; Jer 31.35, 36), innumerable benefits (Acts 14.17; Ps 119.64) and much besides, must of necessity have an author who himself is infinitely great, glorious, wise, powerful, and good, just as the perfectness of a work of art gives evidence of the ability and insight of the artist.

3. Considering ourselves also, we find that this is no less verified when we thoughtfully observe the ingenious mechanism of our body (Jb 10.11, 12), the marvelous qualities and capabilities of the soul, as well as the union and reciprocal relation of both, all of which points to a supreme author or creator and teaches us our exalted duties toward the same. Mal 1.6; Acts 17.27. In this we are also especially confirmed by the consciousness of peace or fear, accordingly as we obey or disobey the voice of the law as it is written in our hearts. Rom 2.15.

4. All this, together with the concurring testimony of all thinking people in all ages, leads us to the conclusion that the thought that all things are eternal and self-existent or have been brought into existence by chance, and work independent of the control of a higher being, is so irrational that only presumptuous fools (Ps 14.1; Is 29.15, 16) or the stubbornly hardened (Jer 5.1-5) can entertain it, and that they do violence to their better convictions in order that, continuing in such unbelief, they may sin the more unhindered.

2. OF THE HOLY SCRIPTURES

1. Although, as has been said, we conceive from the things that are created that there must be a God who in his own being possesses infinite perfections, nevertheless, without a further revelation concerning the nature of his being, his perfection, his

ways and his works, his holy will, and (since we have sinned) especially concerning the way and means of being reconciled with God, we would be much in the dark, as has been generally true of all the heathen.

2. Therefore we conceive it an incalculable boon that God has spoken at sundry times and in diverse manners in times past to the fathers and prophets and in the fullness of time through his only-begotten Son, as also through his holy apostles (Heb 1.1, 2), and that in his gracious pleasure he has had as much of it recorded as is necessary for us as a rule of faith and conduct. Rom 15.4; 2 Tm 3.15-17.

3. Under the term Holy Scriptures we include all those books known as regular or canonical, from the Pentateuch to Revelation. These Scriptures we call holy, because they are inspired by God and written by holy men of God as they were moved by the Holy Spirit. 2 Pt 1.21. We accept them, therefore, not as the word of man, but of God; as the only infallible and sufficient rule of faith and conduct to which we owe supreme reverence and obedience.

4. There are many and weighty arguments upon which this our faith rests. Of these we give the following: (a) The teaching contained in these holy books transcends the laws or the light of nature, but in no wise contradicts them. (b) The contents thereof are altogether worthy of God and invite reverence for him. (c) All that is contained therein serves to the attainment of holy ends; as the glory of God, the good of one's neighbor, and one's own happiness. (d) The holy writers were persons of distinguished piety and uprightness, who neither evidenced credulity nor sought their own glory, justification or temporal advantage in this work, much less could they obtain such; but their sole object was the glory of God and the salvation and peace of their fellowmen. (e) By means of supernatural miracles, fulfillment of prophecies, and many other things, God convinced them, and us through them, of their divine mission. Moreover, everyone who yields himself in honest obedience and submission to the word of God, finds peace of heart and obtains for himself the assurance of the truth.

3. OF GOD'S BEING AND PERFECTIONS

1. In accordance with these Holy Scriptures and as taught by them we believe there is an only God (Dt 6.4; 1 Cor 8.4-6), a being wholly perfect (Mt 5.48), a Spirit (Jn 4.24), self-existent (Ps 90.2), unchangeable (Jas 1.17; Ps 102.28), omnipresent (Jer 23.23, 24; Ps 139.7-10), all-sufficient (Acts 17.25), and altogether perfect in his attributes, that is, holy (1 Pt 1.16; Lv 11.44), righteous (Ps 11.7), omnipotent (Gn 17.1), omniscient (Ps 139.1-18), all-wise (Is 40.28; Ps 104.24), merciful (Jas 5.11), gracious, long-suffering, of great goodness and truth (Ex 34.6; Ps 145.8), in a word, God is love (1 Jn 4.16), the source of life (Ps 36.16; Jer 2.13), and author of all good

(Jas 1.17; Ps 102.28), the creator and preserver of all things, visible and invisible (Col 1.16, 17), worthy to be reverenced, loved, and glorified by all his creatures.

4. OF THE HOLY TRINITY

1. This one God (Dt 6.4) is more definitely revealed in Holy Scripture (Jn 1.18) and distinguished as Father, Son, and Holy Spirit (Jn 14.16, 17; Is 48.16; Mt 3.16, 17; 1 Cor 12.4–6), yet with the added declaration that these three are one.

2. The Father is presented to us as the author (Jn 5.26, 17.5, 6) and source of all things (1 Cor 8.6), of whom, in an inscrutable manner, the Son is begotten (Ps 2.7–8) from eternity (Jn 1.1, 2), before all creatures. Col 1.15, 16.

3. The Son is the Father's eternal Word and wisdom (Jn 1.1; 1 Cor 1.24; Col 2.3), through whom all things are (Col 1.15, 16), the effulgence of the Father's glory and the very image of his being. Heb 1.2, 3.

4. The Holy Spirit belongs, as a divine entity, to the essence of God. He is as well the Spirit of the Father (Mt 10.20) as of the Son (Gal 4.6; Rom 8.9), and proceeds from the Father and from the Son (Jn 15.26) as the mighty worker of all divine and spiritual things. Phil 1.19.

5. We profess that these three are not divided or separated from one another, but united and one (Jn 10.30) in essence as well as in will and operation, since the same names, attributes, and works are predicated of the Father, the Son, and the Holy Spirit, so, too, the same divine regard, as the Savior so explicitly commands to baptize in the name of the Father, the Son, and the Holy Spirit (Mt 28.19), and as also every believer has need of the grace, love, and communion of these three (2 Cor 13.14), for which reasons equal honor and equal service are due them (see of the Son Lk 24.52; Jn 5.23, 14.23, 24; Phil 2.10, 11; Rv 5.12. Of the Holy Spirit Eph 4.30, 1 Cor 3.16).

5. OF THE CREATION AND ALL THINGS AND
OF MAN IN PARTICULAR

1. We believe that this eternal God—Father, Son, and Holy Spirit—is the omnipotent Creator of heaven and earth, who in the beginning (Gn 1.1), in six days (Ex 20.11), made the heavens with all their host (Neh 9.6), the stars, the holy angels, and celestial spirits, as also the earth and the seas with all that is found in and on the same, and lastly, on the sixth day, man who is the masterpiece of all God's works upon earth. Gn 1.26, 27. Man's body is indeed made of the earth (Gn 2.7, 3.19), but his spirit is by the breath, or a direct powerful working, of the Almighty (Jb 33.4) and is therefore immaterial and immortal. Mt 10.28.

2. Man being thus, especially after the spirit, of such exalted and divine origin (Acts 17.28) he is created likewise unto a noble end, that is, to know God, to love him, and to glorify him (Rom 1.19–21), which is the essence of all true godliness. Jn 17.3; Jer 9.23, 24.

3. Further, God gave Adam a wife for his help (Gn 2.18), built of one of his ribs (Gn 2.22) that there should be between them the closest union and the most intimate love. Gn 2.23, 24. Out of her all mankind have sprung. Acts 17.26.

6. OF GOD AS PRESERVER AND RULER

1. We believe that God in his supreme wisdom, power, righteousness, and goodness, provides for (Acts 17.25; Ps 145.15), directs (Jb 37.1–13; Gn 50.20), and governs (Ps 103.19; Ps 104; Ps 147) all things that he has made, so that nothing takes place (Lam 3.37), however insignificant it may seem, without this divine providence and control; as Jesus also plainly taught that no sparrow falls to the earth without the will of our heavenly Father. Lk 12.6, 7; Mt 10.29. Yet we must here carefully distinguish between what God works directly (Jas 1.16, 17; 2 Cor 3.5; Phil 2.13) and what he permits and overrules (Gn 31.7; Is 10.5–15) according to the nature of things and in consonance with his divine perfection. (It is of the highest importance to note this distinction, wherefore James says, "Do not err." God does not bring about the evil of sin, but permits, yet limits and overrules it). Above all do we believe in God's control, protection, and direction exercised with solicitous care (Zec 2.8) and in minute detail (Mt 10.30; 1 Tm 4.10) over them that fear him (Ps 33.18, 34.7, 9, 10, 15, 17), love him (Rom 8.28), and obey him. Jn 15.10.

7. OF THE CONDITION OF MAN BEFORE THE FALL

1. Concerning the condition of man before the fall, we believe that God made man upright (Eccl 7.29) and good (Gn 1.31), in his image and after his likeness (Gn 1.26, 5.1); in which holy and good condition our first parents were glorious and happy creatures, endowed and adorned with exalted wisdom, pure affections and impulses, and with a free will whereby they could (under God's permission) accept without compulsion, or of their own accord reject, what was presented to them, whether it be the counsel and will of God (Gn 2.16, 17) or the counsel and will of the evil one (Gn 3.4, 5) as the issue demonstrated. To prove this, God laid upon them a certain duty (namely, first of all the law of nature written in their hearts [Rom 2.14, 15]; wherefore God could ask Cain, Gn 4.7: "Is it not thus?"—Luther's translation), and made, as it were, a covenant with them. Hos 6.7.

2. As long as this good condition lasted, they doubtless enjoyed a perfect

and intimate converse with God (Gn 3.8) in childlike love and reverence, which, had they continued therein, could have issued only in a pure blessedness for soul and body in all eternity.

8. OF THE FALL OF MAN AND ITS CONSEQUENCES

1. We believe that our first parents, Adam and Eve, remained not in this blessed condition, but allowed themselves to be led astray through the crafty deceit of the serpent, the devil, or Satan (Gn 3.1–5; Rv 20.2; Jn 8.44) who with his angels had before fallen away from God and been cast out. Jude 6; 2 Pt 2.4. Our parents fell in that they, against their conscience, transgressed the plain command of God and ate of the tree (Gn 3.1–8) of which God had bidden them not to eat under pain of death. Gn 2.16, 17.

2. Through this one disobedience sin with all its sad consequences came into the world. We acknowledge the far-reaching effects of this in every relation, first of all, however, for our first parents. Rom 5.12–21. Through it they fell from their innocence and were filled with shame; in the place of their filial reverence and openheartedness came fear and pangs of conscience (Gn 3.1–8); in place of the unrestricted and intimate converse with God, a condition of antipathy and estrangement from him (Jn 3.20), yea, the wrath and severity of the holy and righteous Creator. Eph 2.3. Besides the peace with God they lost also the peace with their created surroundings, they must pass under the sentence of death (Rom 5), were driven from the garden of Eden, the way to the tree of life was closed for them (Gn 3.24), the earth itself was cursed on their account, and they were doomed to much pain and hard work. Gn 3.16–19.

3. All this misery and wretchedness passed as a natural heritage upon all their posterity (1 Cor 15.21, 22), for how could they bring forth seed different from themselves (Jb 14.4; Jn 3.6), or how could they transmit prerogatives which they themselves had lost? Therefore we believe that they and all their posterity in, through, and with them, have become subject to physical (Rom 5.14; 1 Cor 15.21, 22), spiritual (Eph 4.18; Jas 1.15; Rom 7.13), and eternal death (Rom 6.23), and utterly unable to be saved therefrom either by their own efforts (Rom 3.23; Jer 13.23) or through any creature. Ps 49.7, 8. In this miserable condition they would, therefore, have to remain forever, if God had not come to them in his mercy. Ez 16.5, 6.

9. OF THE ELECTION OF GRACE OR
ELECTION AND REJECTION

1. We believe that God from eternity foresaw and knew all things that have been, that are, and that yet shall be, both good and evil (Acts 15.18; Is 41.21–26; Heb 4.13),

therefore also the above-named sad fall of man with its fatal consequences, which is clearly indicated by the foreordaining of Christ as Mediator (Eph 1.4; 1 Pt 1.20; Rv 13.8); nevertheless, that he in no wise caused the fall or made it necessary (Jas 1.13; Ps 145.17) but only permitted it for reasons known only to his infinite wisdom. Rom 11.33. Since he is the eternal, highest good (Mt 19.17) and the fountainhead of all life (Ps 36.9), we understand and confess that he is the author, source, and doer only of those things that are good and pure and holy, and in harmony with his nature (Jas 1.16, 17), but in no wise of sin or impurity, which are damnable. Everywhere he commands (1 Pt 1.15, 16; Eph 5.1) and desires the good, commends it (2 Cor 5.20) and incites to it by means of great promises (Dt 28.1, 2; Mt 5.1–12; 2 Cor 7.1). On the other hand he prohibits the evil (Rom 12.9), warns against it (Gn 4.6, 7), threatens the evildoers (Dt 28.15), punishes them often in this life (1 Sm 15.23; Ps 73.16–19), and finally pronounces upon them an eternal punishment. Mt 25.46, 3.12. He thus declares himself the enemy of sin, and that all unrighteousness is offensive to his nature. Ps 45.8. As it is, therefore, impossible that God should lie (Nm 23.19; Ti 1.2), so it is also impossible that he should work in a manner contrary to his perfectly holy nature. Gn 18.25; Jb 8.3; 2 Tm 2.13.

2. We, therefore, cannot and must not believe that God should in his free pleasure have decreed to leave by far the greater part of fallen humanity in their sins withholding from them altogether the needed grace for conversion and salvation, much less that he should have created them to the end that they should be damned (1 Jn 4.8), and that thus he willed and made necessary their impenitence and hardness of heart in order to bring them into perdition (Ps 51.6); for as the Lord liveth he hath no pleasure in the death of the wicked but in that he turn from his way and live. Ez 33.11; 2 Pt 3.9; 1 Tm 2.4.

3. We do indeed gladly and heartily believe that God in and of himself formed an eternal purpose (Eph 3.11, 1.9; Rom 8.28) concerning all that which he would in time perform (Eph 1.11) especially how and by what means he would redeem fallen man (Acts 4.28); likewise, that he decreed to impart his love, his grace, and his gifts in larger measure to some, in smaller measure to others (Lk 8.10; Mt 25.15; Rom 9.13), and this according to his own will and pleasure (Mt 20.15; 2 Tm 2.20), as experience proves;—but that nevertheless his loving kindness is so great, so far-reaching, and so all-inclusive (2 Cor 5.19; Jn 3.16, 1.7; 1 Jn 2.2) that no one is excluded therefrom without a just cause. Ps 145.9; Acts 17.30; Ti 2.11, 12. This he confirmed by his command that the gospel of this universal grace, love, and goodwill shall be proclaimed and offered to every creature. Mk 16.15, 16; Lk 24.47.

4. Moreover, we confess that in the wisdom and the ways of God, especially in this matter, there are depths which will ever be beyond our ability to fathom in

this life. Therefore we deem it best not to seek to penetrate further into the mysteries of the divine purposes, but in our confession to rest satisfied with a statement of the nature of those persons respectively whom God has decreed to save or to condemn.

5. Everyone, namely, who with a penitent and believing heart (Mk 1.15; Acts 20.21) apprehends, accepts, and abides in the proffered salvation (Jn 1.12, 13; Acts 2.41; Rv 3.20; Mt 24.13; 1 Jn 2.19; Rv 2.10) him has God before the foundation of the world, out of free grace, and for Christ's sake, elected (2 Thes 2.13; Jas 2.5; 1 Pt 2.9) and ordained (Eph 1.5) to make him partaker of his kingdom and his glory (Mt 25.34, 41); him has God foreknown (1 Pt 1.1, 2) and called by his name. 2 Tm 2.19; Rv 3.5.

6. On the other hand, they that despise and reject the proffered grace (Rom 2.4, 5; Heb 10.29), love darkness rather than light (Jn 3.19), and continue in sin and unbelief (Jn 3.18)—these he has ordained to eternal destruction from his face (2 Thes 1.9) by reason of their own willful wickedness (Mt 23.37; Prv 1.24–32) as those that thrust from them the word and judge themselves unworthy of eternal life. Acts 13.46. Seeing they despise the Lord's supper to which they were invited, they shall never taste of it. Lk 14.24.

10. OF MAN'S RESTORATION

1. Since God purposed even from the foundation of the world to redeem fallen man through his Son, Jesus Christ, as above set forth, he in his goodness did not leave him long in his hopeless condition, but revealed unto him, immediately after the fall, his purpose of grace by the promise of a redeemer, who as the seed of the woman should crush the serpent's head, although it should bruise his heel. (This promise, mysterious as it may seem, is the basis of all succeeding promises. Gn 3.15.)

2. This, together with many other evidences of God's goodness, gave our first parents such a great consolation that they could perceive how that by faith in God's promises, in a sincere conversion to him, grace and salvation could be obtained. Heb 11.4. (It seems that Eve already at the birth of Cain drew comfort from this hope. Gn 4.1.) Thus, through the inestimable grace of God in Christ, revealed to them as above stated, there was given to them, in distinction from the fallen angels, the possibility and hope of being restored to blessedness, and with them to all their posterity in so far as these would not cut themselves off by their own guilt and the rejection of God's grace.

3. This revelation of his grace in and through the promise of a redeemer, was renewed and confirmed both to the devout patriarchs (Gn 12.2, 3) and through all the prophets (Lk 1.70, 24.27) as also by means of many symbols and types (Heb 9.8–10), in order that they should exercise faith in this coming Messiah (1 Pt 1.10,

11), wait with confidence for their redemption through him (Rom 4.20), and look forward to the same with desire (Lk 10.24) as many among them did in a remarkable manner. Jn 8.56.

11. OF MAN'S FREEDOM AND ABILITY AFTER THE FALL

1. Regarding man's free agency, we believe, that however great may be the loss and the ruin that have come upon mankind through the fall in sin (as set forth in art. 9), yet through God's grace the light of reason and of conscience has not been wholly quenched, as we are taught by Holy Scripture (Rom 1.19–21, 2.1–15) as well as by experience; further, that man still left in the position of a free agent, can either by and through the power of the grace of restoration accept or else reject the divine instruction and the good offered by God in his Son Jesus Christ—that he can incline in a degree his heart unto them, or turn away and withdraw himself from them. Dt 11.26–28, 30.15–20. This freedom is so essential to the nature of a rational being that without it his actions could not be reasonably judged as good or bad, nor could they, if virtuous, deserve reward, or, if sinful, come under righteous condemnation, which, however, is most certainly the case with man.

2. For this reason we acknowledge, that, although without God's prevenient grace it is entirely impossible for our corrupt nature to seek, choose, and apprehend the good, and even if the universal gift of divine grace alone arouses and assists our nature, these acts still come very hard and are possible only in a rudimentary way—yet they must, nevertheless, not be considered as wholly impossible, but rather as actually possible, in a way since the Lord our God certainly deals with us so that, on the one hand, he holds out to us commands (Ex 20.3–17; Mt 17.5), counsel (Rv 3.18), motives (Is 55.1–7; 2 Cor 5.11, 18–21, 6.1), promises (Is 55; Mt 11.28, 29; 2 Cor 6.17, 18), blessings for good undertakings (Is 45.22; Lk 18.29, 30), and finally an eternal reward (Mt 25), but on the other hand, warning (Gn 4.6, 7; 1 Cor 10.11), threatenings (Dt 27.26), chastisements (Heb 12.5–11; 1 Pt 1.6, 7; Rv 3.19), and terrible judgments (Dt 28.15, 29.19, 20) both temporal (Is 29.13–15) and eternal (Mt 25.46); all of which would otherwise seem strange and inconsistent. Dt 32.3, 4.

3. However, from what has thus far been said in a general way, we must be careful not to draw the conclusion that man is as capable to use his free agency aright in spiritual things as he is in natural things. Lk 12.54–57. Far be it! The contrary is plainly taught not only by the Holy Scripture (1 Cor 2.14), but also by reason and our daily experience. Mt 7.13.

4. For this reason we conclude that ordinary impulses in the direction of good, moving simply on the plane of reason, must be carefully distinguished from

those that are spiritual, far more powerful (Ez 36.25–27), and special (Rom 9.12–18); that the former, nevertheless, are sufficient to awaken in us certain incipient longings (Prv 2.4–7), and that such seeking is the God-ordained way to obtain more (1 Chr 28.9; Prv 8.17; Mt 7.7) yet by grace (Is 55.7); that, accordingly, fallen man, to whom grace has come (Mi 6.8; Rv 3.20), has still the ability left to him to take to heart more or less the general promptings of grace, to prove them, to adapt himself to them, and wait for more grace. Ps 37.24, 27.14; Is 40.31; Lam 3.24, 25. (See further art. 17.)

12. OF THE PERSON OF THE REDEEMER AND HIS APPEARING IN THE FLESH

1. When the time was fulfilled (Gal 4.4) of which the prophets had spoken (Gn 49.10; Dn 9.24), God let his Son proceed forth from himself (Jn 8.42, 16.28) and sent him into the world (Jn 6.38), into the womb of a highly favored virgin named Mary (Lk 1.27, 28), where and by whom he (the seed of the woman, Gn 3.15; of Abraham, Gal 3.16–19; of David, Rom 1.3) was conceived through divine quickening and overshadowing of the Holy Spirit (Lk 1.35); became partaker of flesh and blood, and was made like unto us in all things yet without sin (Heb 2.14–17, 4.15), in that in the natural course of time he was born of her, as it was written, in Bethlehem (Lk 2.11; Mi 5.1), and was called Jesus because he should save his people from their sins. Mt 1.21.

2. This Jesus, born of Mary in Bethlehem and brought up in Nazareth (Mt 2.23), is the one whom we confess to be Christ, the Son of the living God (Mt 16.16) the only-begotten of the Father, full of grace and truth (Jn 1.14), the Word which was with God and was God (Jn 1.1; Gn 1.3; 1 Jn 1.1), and became flesh. Jn 1.14; Gal 4.4; Phil 2.7–11. Not as though the divine essence of the eternal Word had been changed to visible, mortal flesh or a visible man (Heb 1.8–12), and had ceased to be Spirit, Divinity, or God (1 Tm 3.16), but so, that the eternal Son of God (Mi 5.2) continued to be what he was before (Jn 3.13; Col 1.17; Rv 22.13), namely God (Rom 9.5) and Spirit (2 Cor 3.17; 1 Cor 15.45–47), and became what he was not, namely flesh or man.

3. Therefore we confess that Jesus is our Immanuel, true God and man in one person (Col 2.9; 1 Tm 3.16), and thus qualified and fitted to be a Redeemer and the propitiation for the sins of the whole world. 1 Jn 2.1, 2.

13. OF THE WORK OF REDEMPTION IN GENERAL

1. The great purpose for which God the Father out of his infinite love to man thus gave his Son Jesus Christ (Jn 3.16; Rom 5), and to which end the Son of God will-

ingly humbled himself (Eph 5.2; Phil 2.7), was to reconcile unto God the world lost in sin (2 Cor 5.19), to redeem it (Heb 2.15, 17) and to save it. 1 Tm 1.15.

2. To accomplish fully this great work committed to him of the Father (Jn 17.4), for which, according to the divine purpose and preordination he was anointed and set apart even before the foundation of the world, and which out of pure love and obedience he took upon himself (Heb 10.4, 9.10), he must be first put under the law (Gal 4.4, 5) that by a perfect obedience he might fulfill all its demands (Mt 5.17–18); and this he actually did. Jn 17.4.

3. Having lived a holy and spotless life (Heb 7.26; 1 Pt 2.22, 23) to the age of about thirty years (Lk 3.23), fully satisfying in this respect the will and pleasure of the Father, he received a public approval from heaven (Mt 3.16, 17) and was as to his human nature also anointed and endowed in an especial manner with the Holy Ghost from God the Father (Acts 10.38) to carry out the momentous work of salvation (Col 1.19, 20), in which he as our Mediator (1 Tm 2.5; Heb 9.15, 12.24) approved himself in the exalted threefold capacity as a Prophet (Lk 24.19), High Priest (Heb 10.21), and King (Jn 12.15, 18.37), whom God had promised to send into the world, and whom we must hear (Dt 18.15–18), believe (Jn 3.16, 6.40, 47), and obey (Jn 8.12, 10.27–30), as will be more fully shown in the following chapters.

14. OF CHRIST'S OFFICE AS PROPHET

1. After the Son of God had been solemnly anointed and had passed victoriously through sundry hellish temptations (Lk 4.1–13; Mk 1.12–15, 22) he presented himself at once to the world (Mt 4.17) as the great Prophet (Lk 7.16) who had been promised of God (Acts 3.22, 23; Dt 18.15, 18), in that he taught the way of God in truth (Mt 22.16) as one who had authority (Mk 1.22) and with a wisdom (Mt 13.54) which no one could withstand; preached the gospel of the kingdom of God, repentance, and faith (Mk 1.14, 15); testified likewise how one must walk to be pleasing to God (Mt 5.3–12), foretold also things to come (Mt 20.18, 19, 21.2, 24.2); and confirmed it all with many wonderful miracles. Mt 11.5. Moreover, he lived just as he taught (Jn 8.46) and has thus left us both in his teaching and his life an example which we are to follow. 1 Pt 2.21.

2. Further, as the Lord Christ taught and led his people under the old covenant as the angel of God's presence, through Moses and all the prophets, in whom his Spirit was, and as he now did the same in his own person, so he continued his teaching office through his apostles and evangelists (Eph 4.11; Lk 10.1–7), whom he called (Lk 9.1–6), instructed (Acts 1.2, 3), endowed with the Holy Spirit (Acts 1.8, 2.1–4), and sent forth (Jn 20.21) to be his witnesses to the ends of the earth. Acts 1.8. And these were faithful even unto death and kept back nothing that is profitable

(Acts 20.20, 24) but declared the whole counsel of God unto salvation, to which God also bore witness by signs and wonders and by manifold gifts of the Holy Spirit according to his own will. Heb 2.4.

3. The Lord Jesus also continues his work as teacher by means of his holy word, seeing he has given a short yet sufficiently complete account of his holy life and divine teaching as well as of those of his holy apostles to be transmitted in the books of the New Testament, in which, together with the books of the Old Testament, there is included everything needful to a rule of faith and life. (See art 2.) Through the teaching, reading, and hearing of this word he continues to bring about faith, conversion, and sanctification, for it is the power of God unto salvation to every one that believeth. Rom 1.16.

4. Finally the Lord Jesus teaches also through the Spirit according to his promise, both convincing and winning the unbelieving, and leading the believers into all truth. Jn 16.13. In this work the Spirit never contradicts the true meaning of the written word (Jas 3.11, 1.17), but enlightens the believer's mind to a right understanding of the word (Lk 24.45), gives them assurance of its truth, and brings to remembrance the things that the Lord has spoken. Jn 14.26.

5. It is, therefore, necessary to prove the spirits whether they are of God (1 Jn 4.1) and to hold fast to the unerring word of God (2 Tm 3.14-17; 2 Pt 1.19-21) concerning which we have received assurance and know who has taught us the same. Gal 1.6-12.

15. OF CHRIST AS HIGH PRIEST

1. As the true High Priest (Heb 4.14) and only Mediator of the new and eternal covenant (1 Tm 2.5), Christ prayed to his heavenly Father for his apostles and also for them that should believe on him through their word (Jn 17.9, 20), yea even for those who crucified him and would take his life. Lk 23.34.

2. Moreover, he obediently took upon himself the most grievous suffering (Phil 2.8) and offered himself through the eternal Spirit without blemish unto God (Heb 9.14), both in soul and body, to make propitiation for the sins of the people (Heb 2.17, 7.26, 27). We believe that this most bitter suffering of soul as well as of body, begun in Gethsemane and finished on Calvary, is an offering whose efficacy is eternal (Heb 9.12; Is 53) and by which he has perfected forever them that come to God through him, are obedient to him, and are sanctified. Heb 10.14. We take the obedience of the Son of God, his precious suffering, shed blood, and sacrificial death on the cross once for all (1 Pt 2.24) to be the ransom (Mt 20.28; 1 Tm 2.6) or price (Heb 9.13, 14) of our redemption, all-sufficient for the sins of the whole world (1 Jn 2.2); through which, accordingly, all who truly believe on him, are reconciled

with God (2 Cor 5.19–21), are brought into a condition of peace, and attain unto a well-grounded hope and assurance of eternal life. Rom 5.1, 5, 9, 10.

3. Now, when the Lord Jesus Christ had finished his high-priestly work upon earth through his death, he was buried and on the third day arose again from the dead and appeared unto the apostles and many others (1 Cor 15) with many infallible proofs by the space of forty days. Acts 1.3, 9–12. Thereafter he ascended into heaven as a triumphant victor (Eph 4.8; Col 2.15) before the eyes of all his faithful apostles (Lk 24.50–52) and sat down at the right hand of the Father (Mk 16.19) crowned with honor and glory. Heb 2.9; Jn 17.5.

4. There, and thus clothed, he continues his holy office as our High Priest. Heb 8.1. For as he is the servant of the true tabernacle, he has entered not through the blood of goats and calves, but through his own blood once into heaven itself (Heb 9.11, 24), to appear before the face of God in behalf of the believers. Wherefore he is called of God a High Priest for ever after the order of Melchizedek (Heb 5.10; Ps 110.4) to the great comfort of the believers in their infirmities. Heb 4.14–16. And as he has an everlasting priesthood, since he abides forever, he is able to save to the uttermost them that come unto God through him, seeing he ever liveth to make intercession for them. Heb 7.24, 25; 1 Jn 2.1, 2.

5. Lastly, as it was the part of the High Priest, after completing the offering of atonement, to return to the waiting and praying people to bless them, so Christ, the great High Priest, is continually bestowing upon his own the fruit, the power, and the sufficiency of his sacrifice that they may benefit by them. Acts 3.26. Having the power and the right to forgive sins (Mk 2.10; Mt 28.18), he grants this blessing to the penitent (Acts 5.31); through his blood of sprinkling he purges the conscience from dead works (Heb 9.14) and thus gives boldness and confidence to draw nigh unto God. Eph 3.12. He baptizes them with his Spirit (Jn 1.33), holds spiritual and intimate communion with them (Rv 3.20; Jn 14.21–23), yea, and he makes his holy and redeemed people themselves to be a royal priesthood to offer up spiritual sacrifices acceptable to God. 1 Pt 2.5, 9.

6. From all this follows self-evidently that the Levitical priesthood (Heb 10.5–9), and with it the whole ceremonial law, has been fulfilled, has come to an end, and has been abolished. The law had only the shadow of good things to come (Heb 10.1) and it ended in Christ (Rom 10.4) to whom be glory forever. Amen!

16. OF CHRIST AS KING

1. The Lord Jesus Christ as the one promised and heavenly King of the new covenant (Ps 2.6; Jer 23.5; Lk 1.32, 33), having by his glorious resurrection proved himself victor over the devil, over death and the grave (Col 2.15; 2 Tm 1.10; Heb 2.14, 15), at

once began to set up and order his spiritual kingdom when he gave his apostles command and instruction as to how the same should be established (Mt 28.19, 20; Mk 16.15; Lk 24.47); yet more especially when he ascended on high (Eph 4.8), entered into his glory (Lk 24.26), and sat down on the right hand of his Father in heaven (Heb 1.3) of which he gave the strongest proof when on the day of Pentecost he poured forth abundantly the Holy Spirit upon his apostles. Acts 2.33–36.

2. Thenceforth the kingdom of God came with power, so that from that day on, through the instrumentality of the apostles, great numbers of believing and spiritually minded people were gathered (Acts 2.41, 47, 4.32, 33) who confessed Jesus Christ as their Lord, to the glory of God the Father. Phil 2.9–11.

3. The spiritual kingdom, generally called the kingdom of heaven, the Lord Jesus has committed in part to his servants here on earth to administer according to the spiritual laws of his kingdom. Eph 4.11, 12; 1 Pt 5.1–4. Yet above all and in particular he himself administers the same direct from heaven. He rules the hearts of his people through the Holy Spirit (Jn 16.13, 14.26), in accordance with his word, with passionate love; he protects and shelters them as under his wings, equips them with spiritual weapons against his and their enemies (Eph 6.11–18), and is to them a very present help in trouble so that in him they are more than conquerors (Rom 8.37); he prepares for them a place in heaven (Jn 14.2) and will by grace give victory and a crown of righteousness in the life eternal (2 Tm 4.7, 8) to all who continue faithful to him in the spiritual conflict with sin and Satan (Rv 2.10; Mt 24.13); but his enemies he will put under his feet. Mt 22.24.

17. OF THE UNIVERSAL OFFER OF GRACE AND THE CALL OF GOD UNTO FAITH

1. By universal grace as we confess it (Ti 2.11–14) we do not understand that God dispenses gifts and favors alike great to all men and at all times (see art. 9) even not under the preaching of the gospel; much less that through the death of Christ all men without distinction are reconciled with God (Jn 3.36) and received and adopted as children (Jn 1.12), for then would conversion (Mk 1.15), regeneration (Jn 3.3), and a willingness to become reconciled to God (2 Cor 5.20) be no longer necessary, upon which, however, the gospel lays great stress (Acts 2.38–40), ascribing the grace of justification only to them who truly believe. Rom 3.22, 25, 26; Acts 10.43, 13.39.

2. We understand rather, thereby, in the first place, the all-including love of God and of Jesus Christ in the work of salvation (Jn 3.16), seeing that the Lord Jesus died not only for many (Mt 20.28) but for all men (2 Cor 5.15; 1 Tm 2.5, 6; Heb 2.9), not only for the reconciliation of the believers (Jn 10.15; Acts 20.28) but for the sins of the whole world (1 Jn 2.2); that, namely, God so reconciled the world

unto himself (2 Cor 5.10) that he in view of the perfect obedience (Rom 5.18, 19) and death (Is 53.11, 12) of Christ—as the ransom for all—has made his throne of grace accessible (Heb 10.19–22) to all sinners (1 Tm 1.15; Lk 19.10) without distinction (Rom 10.12, 2.11; Is 45.22), and therefore has ordered that universal forgiveness be proclaimed (Acts 17.30) to all the world (Mk 16.15, 16), so that everyone who believes (Jn 3.15) and is converted (Lk 24.47) shall not perish but shall have forgiveness of sins and inherit eternal life (Acts 13.38, 39). Wherefore, then, we have confidence that no one will be eternally damned for Adam's transgression, but indeed for his own obstinacy, his unbelief, his disobedience, etc., and that thus we need not fear condemnation for little children, but rather we may cherish for them the hope of the kingdom of God for Christ's sake. Mk 10.13–16.

3. Again we confess to believe that with whatever power (Gal 2.8; Eph 1.19) and absolute authority (Mt 20.15; 1 Cor 12.11; Eph 1.11) it may please God to work at certain times to bring about conviction and conversion (Is 44.3), and though some nations and persons are preferred before others (Lk 8.10), all of which we heartily believe and reverently adore—it is yet withal sufficiently plain and evident that God's work of grace to incite man to faith and conversion (Acts 3.26) is so far general that he does not altogether pass by any one (Rom 1.20, 2.14, 15) but manifests to all and every one his goodness (Ps 145.9) and justice, and even the common mercies of his providence have this in view (Acts 17.27) and lead to this end. Rom 2.4.

4. Seeing then, as we do, that all grace shown by God to fallen man from the gates of paradise on through all times, is the fruit only and solely of Christ's mediation, and that it has pleased God to reveal the same very differently and by degrees, we regard ourselves as both disqualified (1 Cor 4.5; Rom 14.4) and unable to define with exactness what the Lord our God through his omnipresent Spirit and his unceasing works of providence does and will do (Jb 33.14, 24, 28–30), in the consciences of such nations and persons who hitherto have been deprived of the knowledge of the gospel. For this reason we hold it best to maintain a holy silence on this point, since we know that God's decisions are always in themselves in the proffered hope (Heb 6.18, 10.19–23; Rom 3.24, 25) and also to commend it to all others and invite souls thereto (Rv 22.17) as the experience of all those who are in any measure constrained by the love of Christ proves. 2 Cor 5.13–15.

18. OF FAITH BY WHICH WE PARTAKE OF THE GRACE OF GOD IN CHRIST

1. We hold that it is not enough to have simply a historical knowledge of the truth (Rom 2.17–24), or to assent to it, or even to be able to talk eloquently and beau-

tifully about it (1 Cor 4.20); more particularly that true faith does not consist in a self-assumed favorable position (Jn 8.32, 33; Mt 3.9; Rom 2.28, 29, 9.6–8) and assurance (Mt 7.21, 22, 15.13; Jn 3.27), for this may all be found apart from the heart-renewing and cleansing power (2 Cor 5.17; Gal 6.15; Acts 15.9), apart from true love (2 Thes 2.10) and good works (Mt 7.17) without which true faith unto righteousness (Rom 10.10) cannot exist. Jas 2.17; Gal 5.6.

2. Saving faith therefore includes both a profound conviction (Heb 11.1) and understanding of divine truth, and an appreciation of its sublimity and worth (Mt 13.44–46). It is thus, viewed in its inception, nothing less than a light from God shining in our souls. 2 Cor 4.6. Further, faith may be defined as including a hearty consent (Rom 7.16), approval (Ps 119.128), and appropriation (Ps 119.97) of all God's testimonies (Ps 19.7), promises (Ps 119.49, 50), and blessings (Ps 116.12), especially the gift of his Son, and all this out of love (1 Jn 4.8, 19) combined with a deep reverence and sense of unworthiness (Lk 7.6); frequently also with much anxiety and fear so that the joy in the Holy Spirit (1 Thes 1.6), which should otherwise follow without fail, may for a time remain suppressed through the weakness of the faith.

3. This faith naturally begets a passionate desire to partake by experience of the whole Christ and in consequence of this an humble looking for and to the Lamb of God that taketh away the sin of the world (Jn 1.29, 3.14, 15). In other words, it amounts to fleeing to Christ for refuge (Heb 6.18; Mt 11.28, 29), actually accepting him in all respects (though in varying degrees as to clearness and power according to the measure of faith) with much crying for mercy (Mt 9.27), repentance and forgiveness of sins (Acts 5.31; Mt 8.2; Ps 51.1–17) and a participation in all the blessings he has obtained for us. Jn 1.16; 1 Jn 5.12.

4. To this fleeing for refuge in such a frame of mind there belongs a sincere prayer for acceptance (Lk 15.19), an actual self-surrender and unfeigned submission (Is 44.5; Acts 16.30), henceforth not to live unto one's self but unto him who died for us and rose again (2 Cor 5.15), the soul being constrained thereto by love, with great desire (2 Cor 5.9, 14) and joy. Prv 21.15.

5. In all this, faith acts and is sustained (Heb 11.33–38) by a deeply felt trust in God (Rom 4.3), holding him to be faithful that promised (Rom 10.23) and that having not spared his own Son, he will with him freely give us all things (Rom 8.32; Heb 4.16), which trust is fully answered by his actual dealings in his own time.

6. This true faith we recognize as a gift of God (Phil 1.29; Eph 2.8) wrought in us (Phil 1.6; 1 Cor 12.7–11; 2 Thes 1.11) through his word (Rom 10.17) and by his Spirit (Acts 16.14; Lk 24.45; Jn 16.8, 15) out of free grace, yet so that in order to its proper reception it is necessary that we give an attentive ear to what the Lord

says (Is 55.3-7) and do not harden our hearts against it (Prv 1.23-33, 28.13, 14; Heb 3.7, 8) but give room to the power of conviction and yield to it (Mk 4.23-25); for in them that draw back the Lord has no pleasure. Heb 10.38, 3.13, 19.

7. By this faith one becomes a child of God (Gal 3.36), overcomes the world (1 Jn 5.4), and is fortified against the crafty attacks of the devil (Eph 6.16); but without it, it is impossible to please God. Heb 11.6. As faith is the ordained means of becoming a partaker of the grace of God in Christ, so it is also the means of abiding in Christ, of holding fast to him, of becoming more intimately united with him, and of drawing from him, as the head of the body or as the true vine, all spiritual life power and thus walk worthy of God who has called us unto his kingdom and glory. 1 Thes 2.12.

19. OF CONVERSION AND THE NEW BIRTH

1. Since the heart of man is evil from his youth (Gn 8.21; Jn 3.6) and carnally minded (Rom 8.5) which is enmity against God (Rom 8.7), it is self-evident that such a faith as set forth in the preceding chapter includes and brings about a sincere amending of one's way (Eph 4.25-29; 1 Pt 4.2-4), conversion (Acts 3.19), and a newness of life. Rom 6.4, 11, 8.1, 4. Therefore equally as strong emphasis is laid upon conversion as upon faith (Mt 18.3; Acts 2.38) and the Lord Jesus has declared most solemnly, that no one can see the kingdom of God unless he be born again. Jn 3.3; Lk 13.3-5.

2. This teaches us that all men must be converted if they are to receive remission of sins (Is 45.22; Lk 24.47), be fitted for fellowship with God who is light (1 Jn 1.5-7) and bring forth good fruit (Mt 12.33-35; Jn 15.8); since neither profession (Mt 7.21) nor baptism, nor the Lord's supper, nor any other outward act apart from regeneration can avail anything to please God. Gal 5.6, 6.15; Eph 4.22-24.

3. That this essential experience of conversion may be truly a turning unto the Lord (Hos 14.2; Jer 4.1), it is not sufficient that one be convinced in his conscience that he must leave the evil and do good, for this is found among the heathen (Rom 2.14, 15) and with many of the worst sinners. Acts 24.25. Again, it is not enough to make some good resolutions now and then (Mt 21.28-30), or to do this or that good deed (Mk 6.20) without a sincere turning of the heart to God (Acts 8.21), for in this way one may indeed come near to the kingdom of God (Mt 13.20-22; Mk 12.34) and yet be excluded from it just the same. Mt 25.11, 12; Lk 13.24. But in order to a true conversion there must be such an understanding and conviction of sin (Ps 51; Jn 16.8) that we repent of it not only because of the punishment that it brings, but primarily because through it we have dishonored, offended, and lost God (Is 1.2-4; Dt 32.5, 6; Dn 9.5-19); for it is sorrow for God that worketh

unto salvation a repentance which bringeth no regret. 2 Cor 7.10. They who thus sorrow, shall be comforted. Mt 5.4. Those who are thus exercised abhor themselves (Jb 42.6; Ez 36.31), hate and leave sin (Ps 119.104), and from the heart make the resolve,—I will arise (Lk 15.18), I will confess. Ps 32.5. And this they do in that they penitently plead for forgiveness (Lk 18.13; Ps 51), make a complete surrender of their will (Rom 6.17), and seek to know (Acts 22.10) and to do (Ps 40.8; Eph 6.6) what is well pleasing unto the Lord. Eph 5.10.

4. In view of the inner renewing of the understanding and the will (Rom 12.2; Ti 3.5) as well as of the outward active change and renewing of the life (Mt 18.3; Rom 6.4), this true conversion is also called a new birth, a being born again (Jn 3.7), a new creation (2 Cor 5.17; Eph 2.10–15) and the like, because the change of condition and activity that is brought about is as though a heart of stone had been removed and one of flesh received, upon which the Lord would write his law. Ez 36. The effect is therefore nothing less than a transition from sin to virtue (Rom 6.17–22), from death unto life (1 Jn 3.14), from darkness to light (Eph 5.8), from the power of Satan unto God (Acts 26.18), etc., though weak in its inception and needing growth (Col 1.11–14) and strengthening. Eph 6.10.

5. This true conversion or new birth is therefore a spiritual life, which, like faith, comes from God (Eph 4.18; Rom 6.11; Gal 2.19, 20; Acts 11.18; Ti 3.5; Ps 51.10; a gift of God in Christ for which we must ask and return thanks as for a blessing upon which depends our whole happiness. Ti 3.5; 1 Pt 1.3, 21–23, 2.25). Nevertheless, to obtain it, there is required on our part, accompanying the divine work of grace and through the same, earnest effort (Lk 8.18, 13.24; Jas 1.21) and great diligence as is plainly evident from the many exhortations and promises (Ez 18.30–32; Mk 1.15; Is 55.7; Lk 7.30–34; Mt 11.20) as well as warnings and rebukes pointing this way.

20. OF JUSTIFICATION AND FAITH

1. Through faith, which, as shown above, stands directly connected with conversion and the new birth, a poor, grief-stricken sinner (Mt 5.3; Lk 18.13) obtains true justification from God (Rom 3.24–26, 8.33), not for any merit of his own, but alone out of grace (Ti 3.5) by virtue of the full obedience and sufficient offering of Christ (Rom 5.18, 19; Heb 10.10–14), being made free and absolved from all his sins (Acts 13.38, 39), however great they may be (Is 1.18; Ps 32; Ps 51; Rom 5.6–10) called into fellowship with Christ (1 Cor 1.9), and made a rightful partaker of him (Heb 3.14) and of the blessings of salvation which he obtained for his people (1 Cor 1.30) and which out of his fullness and in his wisdom he gives each in his time. Eph 4.7; Jn 1.14–16.

2. In the counsel of God this boon, great beyond all comprehension (Jn 3.16; Rom 5.6–10), has been accomplished and bestowed once for all (2 Cor 5.17–19) when the Son of God, as the surety of a better covenant (Heb 7.22) and the Redeemer of his people, offered (1 Tm 2.5, 6; Heb 10.4–10), accomplished (Jn 17.4), and suffered (Phil 2.8–10) in their stead, all that the offended majesty of God demanded to be reconciled with the world. Wherefore the Son of God could say on the cross as he gave his soul into death, "It is finished" (Jn 19.30); and to this also bear witness the rending of the veil (Heb 10.14–20), Christ's glorious resurrection and ascension (Rom 1.4, 4.18–25), the giving of the Holy Spirit, and the preaching of the gospel in all the world.

3. But before the tribunal of conscience this comes to pass only then when true faith is exercised, and not before, since faith is distinctly the God-ordained means (Jn 3.16, 6.40) of becoming actually and personally a partaker of Christ and the blessings he obtained for us. For this reason evangelical justification is always associated with faith (Rom 3.22, 28, 30; Jn 3.16–18, 36) and remains thus inseparably associated.

4. Thus it is (as set forth in art. 18) that a really convicted sinner, poor (Is 66.2) and heavy laden (Mt 11.28), flies for refuge to this gracious Christ. Utterly undone in himself, he hungers after Christ with weeping and sighing (Jer 3.21, 22), falls at his feet praying for forgiveness of sins and adoption into the sonship of God (2 Cor 6.16–18; Gal 4.4–6); he tastes and realizes that the Lord is gracious (1 Pt 2.3) in that he covers our nakedness and condescends to dwell in us (Jn 14.23; Eph 3.17) and we are found in him. Rom 8.1; Phil 3.9. We come praying that we may be healed of our infirmities (Mt 9.12), of our spiritual blindness (Is 35.5; Eph 1.18; Rv 3.18), deafness, barrenness (Ps 63.1, 119.81–83), leprosy (Ps 38.3–8; Is 1.6), and every form of spiritual disease (Ps 103.3); that he baptize us with his Holy Spirit (Mt 3.11); that he satisfy our hunger and thirst with heavenly food and drink (Jn 6.48–51, 7.37, 38), and make us partakers of his divine nature (2 Pt 1.2–4) so that his mind may be in us (Phil 2.5; Mt 5.44–48), that by his grace our old man may be crucified with him. (Rom 6.4–6; Gal 5.24) and his life may be manifested in us (2 Cor 4.10, 11) being conformed unto his death and risen again to a newness of life thus to know by personal experience the power of his resurrection (Phil 3.10; Eph 1.19, 20) to the praise and glory of his heavenly Father. Rom 6.17.

5. This is what we call knowing Christ after the Spirit whereby eternal life is received (Jn 10.4, 14, 17.3), and we frankly submit that without this spiritual knowledge, this inward exercise and experience, a knowledge of Christ historically or according to the letter does not suffice unto salvation. Rom 2.14–20, 28, 29; 1 Cor 13.1-3. However, the soul that in truth seeks refuge in Christ (Ps 145.18) with

steadfastness in prayer (Lk 18.7; Rom 12.12) we believe will assuredly find grace (Mt 7.7–11) in God's own time, and be received into the covenant of God (2 Cor 6.18) whereby everyone thus constituted, becomes the property of Jesus Christ. 2 Tm 2.19.

6. The most certain outward proof of this great work of salvation, we hold is to be found in the fruits of righteousness, such as unfeigned love to God (1 Cor 8.3; Lk 7.47) and to the brethren (1 Jn 3.14) yea to all men, active godliness (1 Jn 3.18, 19) and an earnest observance of God's commandments (1 Jn 5.1–4). The inward verification is found in the experience of peace with God (Rom 5.1; Is 32.17), a new spiritual joy (Is 29.19, 61.10), as also a strong assurance (Rom 8.38, 39) and sealing of the Holy Spirit (2 Cor 1.21, 22, 5.5; Rom 8.16; Eph 1.13, 4.7, 30; 1 Jn 4.13); and all this according to the measure of the gift of Christ.

21. OF GOOD WORKS, OR THE PIETY OF TRUE BELIEVERS

1. By good works, for which the believers in Christ Jesus are created that they should walk in them (Eph 2.10), those works must not be meant which are only outward (Lk 11.39) and have simply the appearance of good like the works of the Pharisees (Mt 23.28): nor those that are performed from natural or civil motives (Mt 5.44– 47; Lk 6.32) which, though good and becoming in themselves, are not distinctly characteristic of true Christianity; and not those which spring out of a servile or legal spirit (Jn 15.15; Gal 4.7; Rom 9.31, 32, 10.1–4) more out of fear and compulsion (Rom 8.15; 1 Jn 4.18) than out of love (Gal 5.6; 1 Tm 1.5); for the disciple of Christ is called unto a better righteousness than is found in all these. Mt 5.20.

2. Therefore we hold those only to be good works which are well pleasing to God in Christ (1 Pt 2.5; Rom 12.1, 2; Heb 12.28), being wrought in God (Jn 3.21), proceeding out of faith (Heb 11.6) and love (1 Jn 4.8) and true thankfulness (1 Jn 4.19) out of a changed and renewed mind (Eph 5.8–10; Rom 12.2), a childlike fear (Prv 14.27), in short out of a fellowship with Christ (Jn 15.5) in and through the power of the Holy Spirit. Gal 5.22–24; Eph 5.9–11.

3. In our relation to God this life requires a humble walking with him (Mi 6.8) and before his face (Gn 17.1) in heartfelt love (Mt 22.37–40; Eph 5.1, 2), gratitude (Col 1.12), praise (1 Cor 6.20), childlike fear (1 Pt 1.17), obedience (Eph 6.6), etc.

4. In relation to our fellowmen, good works consist in a practical and unwearying exercise of righteousness (Ti 2.12; 1 Jn 3.18), forbearance (Phil 4.5; Ti 3.2; Jas 3.17), gentleness (1 Pt 3.8; 2 Tm 2.24; Phil 2.3, 4), readiness to serve (Gal 5.3), benevolence (1 Tm 6.17, 18; Heb 3.16), etc., in the endeavor to promote the best interests of our neighbors both in soul and body (Lv 19.17) and this not only of the

brethren (Rom 12.10; Heb 13.1; 1 Jn 3.16) but of all (2 Pt 1.7; 1 Thes 3.12), yea even of our enemies. Rom 12.20.

5. In reference to one's self there is required a holy watchfulness and warfare (Lk 12.1–5, 17.3, 21.34; Eph 6.10–18; Heb 12.1–4, 12–17; 2 Pt 3.17) against all manner of intemperance (Ti 2.4–6; 1 Tm 2.9, 10) and worldly lusts (2 Pt 1.4; 1 Jn 2.16), against all unclean affections and lusts of the flesh (Rom 13.14; 1 Pt 2.12), against pride (Rom 11.20; Ps 19.13) and all its miserable issues (Jas 4.1–6; Mt 15.19) such as hatred, envy, and anger; or thoughtless, frivolous, and harsh words (Gal 5.19–21; Mt 12.36, 5.37; Jas 5.11, 12), corrupt speech (Eph 4.29), and the like. Thus the deeds of the body of sin (Rom 8.13, 7.23, 24) with all its members upon the earth, must be mortified (Col 3.5) and the opposite virtues be put on (Col 3.12–14) in order that we may live unto righteousness (1 Pt 2.24), increase in holiness (Heb 12.14; Rv 22.11) unto perfection in the fear of God. 2 Cor 7.1; 1 Thes 3.13.

22. OF PERSEVERANCE IN HOLINESS

1. The true believer applies himself with all diligence in this new spiritual life to walk worthily of the Lord (Col 1.10, 11; 1 Thes 2.12) and to be fruitful in good works, not only because he is called and in duty bound thereto (Eph 4.1–3; 2 Pt 1.5–10), but because by virtue of his new birth from God (1 Jn 3.9) there is within him an inward impulse (Ps 119.35), an inbred disposition to the same. 2 Cor 5.9. He finds in it a holy delight (Rom 7.22), a great spiritual, yea divine, peace and comfort (Acts 9.31), a growth in the knowledge of God (Col 1.10, 11) and of Jesus Christ (Eph 4.15), in short, the life of the soul. By a contrary course a believer does violence to his own soul (Prv 8.36), pursues death (Rom 6.16, 8.6) and brings upon himself great misery. 1 Tm 6.10.

2. It is therefore contrary to the renewed nature of the believers and in antagonism with it, to sin. 1 Jn 3.6–9. Moreover, they are carefully watched over and kept (Ps 23; Zec 2.8; Jude 1) by the faithful Shepherd (Jn 10.1–16; Ez 34.11–31) and Bishop of their souls (1 Pt 2.25), as also by his heavenly Father who is greater than all (Jn 10.29), so that it is impossible for any power, however great, to pluck them out of such faithful hands in which they are kept unto salvation. 1 Pt 1.5; Jn 10.28, 29.

3. Wherefore also it seems unnecessary that anyone should teach them (1 Jn 2.27) if they will but abide in him constantly as they ought (1 Jn 3.6) and will let that abide in them which they have heard from the beginning. 1 Jn 2.24.

4. But since they have this treasure in earthen vessels (2 Cor 4.7) and in their flesh there dwelleth no good thing (Rom 7.18) but on the contrary a law that wars against the law of their mind (Rom 7.23), since they are, moreover, surrounded by various seductions of the world (1 Jn 2.16) and temptations of the devil (Eph 6.11;

1 Pt 5.8), and since the Lord permits all this that he may prove their faith and their obedience (Dt 8.2, 16–18) and keep them in humility through the experience of their weakness (2 Cor 12.7); there is required of them, notwithstanding what has been said above, or rather by reason of it (1 Pt 1.5–7; Phil 2.13), nothing less than resolute watchfulness and earnest care (1 Cor 6.13) that they may not fall back (1 Tm 1.6, 6.20, 21; Heb 3.12), become slothful (Heb 6.12, 3.13; Rom 12.11), lose again that which they have already obtained (2 Jn 8), fall from their stronghold (2 Pt 3.17), and be overcome of sin (2 Pt 2.20), as is shown to have been the case with many who at first ran well (Gal 5.7) but afterward grew weary (Heb 12.3–5) and were but scarcely brought back to the right path (1 Pt 4.18; Ps 40.1, 2) not without agony of soul (2 Sm 24.14) and grievous chastisement (Ps 38.1–19, 51, 130)—let alone that such escape is not recorded of all.

5. For this reason the Scriptures are everywhere full of admonition to take heed (Heb 3.12–15), to watch (Lk 21.36; Rv 16.15; Mt 26.41), to pray always (Eph 6.18; Lk 18.1; Rom 12.12) that we may be zealous (Ti 2.14), rich (1 Tm 6.18), full (Acts 9.36), yea abounding (1 Cor 15.58; 2 Cor 9.8; 2 Pt 1.8) in good works (Ti 3.8); also that we consider one another (Heb 10.24, 25), exhort one another (1 Thes 5.11) and pray with and for one another (Jas 5.14–18); and it is indicated that even the most sincere hearts may not consider this to be useless or unnecessary. 2 Pt 1.12, 13, 3.1; Phil 3.1; Heb 3.12–14.

23. OF THE CHURCH OF CHRIST

1. All such believing, converted, and from the heart obedient ones (Rom 6.17) together constitute as so many living stones (1 Pt 2.5) a holy temple in the Lord (1 Cor 3.16, 17; Eph 2.20, 21), the true church (Heb 12.23), the people of God (Heb 4.9), the church of Jesus Christ (Mt 16.18) which he has purchased through his own blood. Acts 20.28.

2. This church, according to our confession, is but one (Jn 10.16), its members (1 Cor 12), however many (Rv 7.9), and however varied in their achievements (Rom 12.4–6), constituting but one body (Eph 4.4–6) of which Jesus Christ is the head. Col 1.18, 2.19. It is known by such names as, people of God (Heb 4.9), his saints (Ps 50.4; Rom 8.27), the kingdom of heaven (Mt 13.18, 23, 25.1), the kingdom of God (Mt 12.28), the kingdom of his dear Son (Col 1.13; Eph 5.5), etc.

3. We call this church holy, not saying by this that its members are freed from the condition of sinfulness as long as they live here below (1 Jn 1.8), but because they are sanctified by God the Father (Jude 1) in Christ Jesus (1 Cor 1.2) as well as by his sanctifying himself for them (Jn 17.19; Eph 5.26; Heb 2.11) as also by their actual separation from the world (2 Pt 1.4; 2 Cor 6.17) and their transition

into the kingdom of the Son of God (Col 1.13) to serve the Lord in holiness and righteousness all the days of their life. Lk 1.74, 75.

4. That this church is general we confess, because in it the distinction between different nationalities falls away (Rom 10.12; Eph 2.14) and its members are scattered in all parts of the earth (Mt 24.31) among all nations, and tribes, and peoples, and tongues (Rv 5.9, 7.9); wherefore it is self-evident that this true church must not be sought among any particular nation or a particular class of professors (Acts 10.35; 1 Cor 3.1–5) or limited to such to the exclusion of others. Lk 17.21–23; Mt 24.26; Mk 13.21.

5. We call the church Christian, because we thereby mean only those that believe in Jesus Christ (Jn 1.12), are united with him (Jn 15), belong to him as his sheep, know him, hear and follow him (Jn 10.12, 27) and are therefore most tenderly loved (Jn 13.1), cherished (Eph 5.29, 30), led, protected and kept (Jn 10) by him, the weak as well as the strong. Is 40.11, 25–31.

6. Because of the intimate relation which the members of Christ's spiritual body sustain to each other, it is his expressed will (Mk 10.42–45; Mt 23.11; Mk 9.35) that these his saints shall cultivate fellowship (Jn 13.34, 35, 17.22, 26) and this not in a restricted way (Mt 5.46–48), as for instance only with those, with whom we are especially united, or with those whose association may seem desirable for our own benefit—for this would follow of itself—but with all believers in general (Acts 4.32; 1 Thes 3.12, 5.15; 2 Thes 1.3), even with those who seem to be the weakest (Acts 20.35; Rom 14.1; 1 Thes 5.14) and most insignificant (1 Cor 12.22–24), for such have special need of spiritual help. Gal 6.1. Has not God put together and endowed the members of the body in such a manner that they must have care one for another (1 Cor 12.18–31; Rom 12.3–10), so that those that are strong bear the infirmities of the weak and do not have pleasure in themselves? Rom 15.1–3. For this reason it is not proper, on the one hand, that any among them think of others,—I have no need of thee (1 Cor 12.21, 22), nor on the other hand, that anyone should possess his gifts for himself alone (Rom 12.4–8); but it is the duty of each one to use the same as much as possible for the general good. Mk 4.21; 1 Pt 4.10, 11.

7. From this arises the necessity for the assembling of believers in meetings (1 Cor 11.18; Acts 2.1), of which both the Lord Jesus and his apostles spoke with approval. Mt 18.19, 20; Heb 10.23–25. Therefore, too, our Lord himself was a regular attendant at such meetings (Lk 4.16) and likewise his loving disciples came together even at the risk of their lives (Jn 20.19; Acts 12.12–16) thus to serve God publicly (Acts 13.1–3; Eph 4.11, 12) and to praise him together as with one accord (Rom 15.6; Acts 11.18); to confess Jesus Christ before the whole world (Mt 10.32; Rom 10.10; 1 Tm 6.12), cultivate fellowship among themselves (Acts 2.42) in edification (1 Tm

4.13; 1 Cor 14.26) and continue in the breaking of bread (Acts 20.7) and in prayer. Mt 18.19, 20. Therefore we pray all disciples of Christ Jesus not to withdraw themselves from such meetings out of obstinacy or self-conceit (Heb 10.23–25) seeing that even the weakest and least talented can be useful in the Lord's temple if only their lives show a good example (1 Pt 3.1–5), if they are active in works of love (Rom 16.1–6; Heb 6.10) and by earnest intercession strengthen the hands of the servants of the Lord.

8. And though hypocrites (2 Tm 3.5; Jude 12) and the unconverted (Rom 12.2) should mingle in great numbers with the flock of Jesus who are his own (Jn 10.14, 27), as has at all times been the case, sometimes less and sometimes more, in the outward fold of the church—a condition unavoidable on account of the limitations in our ability to discern the intents of the heart—the true disciples of Jesus (Jn 8.31) must not be soon alarmed or draw back discouraged, but must seek to let their lights shine (Mt 5.13–16) and become pillars in the house of their God (Rv 3.12), remembering that the Son of God represented the economy and outward union of the church as composed partly by foolish virgins. Mt 25.2; Lk 17.34–36. Nevertheless, the firm foundation of God standeth, having this seal, The Lord knoweth them that are his: and, Let everyone that nameth the name of the Lord depart from unrighteousness. 2 Tm 2.19.

24. OF THE MINISTRY OF THE CHURCH

1. In reference to the ministers of the church we reverently consider that God is not a God of disorder (1 Cor 14.33) and that the Lord Jesus Christ in order to promote the above-mentioned unity and edification of his people (Eph 4.12–15) instituted various offices and conditions in his church (1 Pt 4.10), in that he gave some to be apostles and some prophets and some evangelists and some pastors and teachers for the perfecting of the saints unto the work of ministering, unto the building up of his body (Eph 4.11–16), etc.

2. Now, although our Lord did this directly (Mk 3.14; Lk 9.1, 2) and by original authority (Jn 15.16) as long as he was here on earth and as far as the first founders of his church were concerned (1 Cor 3.10–15; Eph 2.20, 21), whom he therefore also endowed with much grace (2 Cor 4.5, 6) and extraordinary gifts of the Holy Spirit (Acts 2.1–4), we yet know full well that he must have willed and commanded (as Acts 1.2, 3 cf. Rom 15.18 suggests) that later on this be done indirectly, in respect to the regular and ordinary ministers of his church who should simply continue to build on the foundation already laid (1 Cor 3.11) and for this reason ever remained subordinate to the first, "the apostles." 1 Cor 14.37. Moreover we hold ourselves assured of this partly because good order requires it (Mt 12.25)

and the promise of Christ's presence is given to the ministers of the gospel even unto the end of the world. (Mt 28.20) and partly because it accords with the constant practice and directions of the apostles. Acts 14.23; Ti 1.5.

3. Therefore we believe it is the duty of all assemblies of saints that they observe this order after the example and direction of the apostles (2 Tm 2.2; 1 Cor 11.2; 2 Thes 2.15), namely, that they pray, as Christ commanded, that the Lord of the harvest send forth laborers into his harvest (Mt 9.38); that they, however, also look about for such men as are of good report, possessing the gift of the Spirit and true faith (Acts 6.2–5) and other essential characteristics (2 Tm 2.24–26; Ti 1.6–9) in the highest measure obtainable; further, that to such men, chosen with prayer (Acts 1.24) and with the greatest possible unanimity (thus not doing violence to the rights common to the whole brotherhood, much less disregarding the same) (Acts 6.5; Jas 2.1–9; 1 Pt 5.1–4), the administering of the affairs of the church shall be committed (Acts 6.3) and they solemnly installed in their office (1 Tm 4.14) provided they accept the call and have first been examined and proved. 1 Tm 3.10; 1 Cor 9.

4. Those who have been thus lawfully chosen to the office of overseer (1 Tm 3.1) and have accepted the same faith as of the Lord (Col 4.17) have in consequence resting on them very weighty obligations toward the church, as the latter also has toward them. It is incumbent upon the shepherds and teachers to pasture the church of God, speaking always as is proper according to sound doctrine (1 Tm 6.3–5; 2 Tm 1.13; Ti 1.9, 2.1; 1 Pt 5.1, 2), to proclaim unto her the whole counsel of God (Acts 20.26–28) and, as much as in them is, as faithful and wise stewards (1 Cor 4.1, 2; 2 Tm 2.2; Lk 12.42) to impart unto each one in particular according to his circumstances and condition (1 Cor 9.22; 1 Tm 5.1; 1 Pt 4.10), to watch over the church (Heb 13.17) and to set before her a good example in a godly life. 1 Pt 5.3; 1 Tm 4.12.

5. The deacons have likewise and in many points similar holy responsibilities. 1 Tm 3.8–13. They must help to rule the church in the fear of God (1 Tm 5.17), collect the useful offerings, exercise faithful stewardship with these, and whatever other gifts there may be, and according to need distribute in the best way, impartially, with kindness and love. 2 Cor 8.19–21, 9.5–14.

6. The church on her part owes it to hold them in honor (Phil 2.29), to obey them (Heb 13.17), to esteem them for their work's sake (1 Thes 5.12, 13), not lightly blame them (1 Tm 5.19), much less to grieve them and quench the Spirit (1 Thes 5.19) but to pray for them (Col 4.3, 4; Phil 1.19, 4.10–19; 2 Thes 3.1, 2; Heb 13.18) and kindly care for them with a proper competence (Gal 6.6; Mt 10.10; 1 Cor 9.7–14; 2 Cor 11.7–9; 1 Tm 5.18); yet in all this is the respect for their office and

administration not to be in any wise binding upon the conscience, except in so far as their words and management are in accord with the word of God (Mt 15.9; Phil 3.17; 1 Jn 4.1; Mt 7.16) as the only rule of faith and life. 1 Tm 6.3–5.

25. OF WATER BAPTISM

1. In the church of Jesus Christ and through its ministers, we believe there is to be maintained not only the ministry of the word but also, as has already been said, the ordinances commanded by the Lord, namely baptism and the Lord's supper. (Mt 28.19, 20 — "Go ye, therefore and make disciples of all nations, baptizing them in the name of the Father, and of the Son, and of the Holy Ghost; teaching them to observe all things whatsoever I commanded you.") The first of these is to be a sign and a means of incorporation (Gal 3.27; 1 Cor 12.13), the second a means of strengthening in the covenant with God (Lk 22.19, 20) and in communion with Christ. 1 Cor 10.16.

2. Concerning the act of holy baptism we understand it to be an immersing of the whole body in water (Rom 6.4; Mt 3.16; Acts 8.37, 38), or a liberal sprinkling with water (which latter mode we in these northern latitudes consider more generally appropriate, since the same blessings are signified by it), and this most solemnly into the name of the Father, and of the Son, and of the Holy Spirit (Mt 28.19), God on his account thus giving most positive assurance of the benefits of his covenant of grace, that everyone truly believing in Jesus Christ (Rom 10.10) and penitently seeking refuge in him to lay hold of the hope set before us (Rom 3.25; Heb 6.18) shall certainly and truly partake of the blessings signified thereby, namely, the washing away of sins through the blood of Christ (Acts 22.16; Rv 1.5) together with all the blessed results that follow. Rom 8.17, 28–39.

3. On the part of the believer to be baptized this ordinance is also exceedingly important and precious in that he, by the act of presenting himself for baptism, most solemnly professes his faith in Jesus Christ and his blood (Rom 3.25), that in him are to be found righteousness and strength (Is 45.24), and that he imploringly prays to be permitted to partake thereof; that as much as in him is, he lays hold on the Savior (Jn 1.12) and most humbly offers and surrenders himself to him (Lk 9.23, 14.26, 27; Mt 10.37) out of gratitude and reciprocating love (1 Jn 4.19; 2 Cor 5.14, 15; Eph 5.2) to live for his honor and glory. Is 44.5; Rom 6.16, 17, 12.1.

4. If Christian water baptism is thus devoutly desired (Acts 8.36), administered (2 Cor 3.6), and received (Acts 2.41; 1 Thes 2.13), we hold it in high esteem as a means of communicating and receiving spiritual blessings (1 Pt 3.20, 21), nothing less than a washing of regeneration and renewing of the Holy Spirit. Ti 3.5; Eph 5.26. This blessed result and work is, however, not obtained through the outward

element of the water (1 Pt 3.21, "even baptism, not the putting away of the filth of the flesh but a prayer addressed to God for a good conscience, through the resurrection of Jesus Christ"), but through the Holy Spirit (Mt 3.11; Ti 3.5), only on the ground of true faith and the searching of a good conscience before God, wherefore in the absence of this condition in the one baptized the blessing is not found. Acts 8.21.

5. Therefore it is, in our estimation, self-evident that children in their infancy are not qualified to receive the Christian rite of water baptism because they can neither understand nor believe these things. Rom 10.14. Further, it does not seem to us right to administer this sacredly important covenant act after the manner of the fleshly law of circumcision and the condition of the church in its infancy (Gal 4.1–3, 5.1–6; Heb 7.18, 19, 8.7–12, 10.19–22; Jn 4.23, 24) on the ground of a superficial assertion (Rom 2.29; Phil 3.3; Col 2.11–15) that baptism has taken the place of circumcision, seeing that in the church of the New Testament everything is founded on grace and truth (Jn 1.17), or on the reality of the things typified (Heb 10.1). Neither can we assent to infant baptism on the strength of the indefinite and uncertain accounts of the baptizing of Jewish proselytes which are founded on the Jewish Talmud, a book known to be spun through with many fabulous tales. Finally, and of more especial weight is the fact that in all the books of the New Testament we do not find a single convincing indication that in the early church any but grown people were baptized. Of the households that were baptized there are everywhere things said that are not applicable to little children (Acts 10.2, 47, 48, 16.15, 34), and in the most detailed reports we find indeed that more and more were added to the church of such as believed in the Lord, both of men and women (Acts 5.14), but of the baptizing of children there is nowhere any mention. Acts 8.12.

6. Since then there is not a single plain evidence concerning infant baptism; since salvation does not depend on any outward sign; since every testimony and narration in the Holy Scriptures points only to the baptism of grown persons, even as the nature of the case demands; since the Son of God himself has led the way otherwise, and it is well known that in the first centuries the most eminent teachers of the church, though born of believing parents, were baptized only when they had come to years, and that it was not without serious complaint and strong opposition that in the second and third centuries infant baptism increased and prevailed: we therefore come to the conclusion that we must wait with baptism until our children attain to years of riper understanding, that we must carefully instruct them from youth up (2 Tm 3.15), pray with them and for them, lay before them the importance of the matter, and the necessity of faith and conversion, and that in this we must keep on and on. As many of them as in the course of time with constancy confess their faith,

their repentance and a decision for the good, and also in their lives do not manifest the contrary, shall be baptized, we believe, and added to the church, calling on the name of the Lord (Acts 22.16) according to the example of the apostolic church.

26. OF THE HOLY SUPPER

1. By the supper of the Lord we understand the sacred and solemn act of the Lord with his disciples in the night in which he was betrayed (1 Cor 11.23–26) when after the eating of the Passover meal (Lk 22.15) he took of the bread which they had, blessed (Lk 22.19, 20) and broke it and gave to the disciples (Mt 26.26–28) with the gracious words, "Take, eat; this is my body which is broken and given for you: this do in remembrance of me."

2. Likewise also he took the cup after the eating of the supper, gave thanks again (Mk 14.22, 23) and gave it to the disciples with the loving words, "Drink ye all of it, for this is my blood, the blood of the new covenant, which is shed for you and for many; this do, as oft as ye drink it, in remembrance of me."

3. That the Lord instituted this sacrament with the intention that it is to be observed by his disciples in his church in all time, is plainly seen, we think, not only from the words already quoted, and repeated by the Lord—"This do in remembrance of me," but also from the renewed command given evidently for this reason, directly to the apostle Paul and through him to the church, in the same words; further, from the careful observance of this sacred act by the first and best Christians (Acts 2.46, 20.7); finally also from the fact that the apostles did not revoke the institution when great disorder and abuse crept in with its observance, but rather insisted on reformation and a return to its right use.

4. When we consider, moreover, the ends for which this sacrament was instituted, ends worthy of God and positively useful to the church, we find our esteem for the same to grow at every turn. On the part of God and Christ it serves as a means to confirm and seal unto us in the most emphatic manner the great blessings comprehended in the gospel. The great love of the Father manifested to us (Jn 3.14–17); Jesus Christ as crucified, the author of eternal salvation (Heb 5.9), the true bread of life (Jn 6.35, 50, 51, 53–58), both all-sufficient (Heb 10.14) as well as ready and willing to give us the life—all this is here, as it were, set before our eyes for the strengthening of our faith and hope (Gal 3.1; Jn 12.32); and this the Holy Spirit confirms unto the souls that are susceptible to it.

5. On the side of the believer the celebration of this holy feast has likewise important ends to serve and is useful in more ways than one. In general to bring to grateful remembrance, with deep reverence, the great work of redemption; to proclaim the Lord's death as well as the occasion (1 Jn 4.9, 10; Rom 5.6–8; 2 Cor 8.9)

and the effects (Is 53.5, 6; Rom 8.1) of the same; to lay stress upon the exalted duties of the believers toward God (1 Cor 6.20; 1 Pt 1.14–19) and Jesus Christ (2 Cor 5.14, 15), as well as toward one another (1 Jn 4.11; Col 3.13); and more of like nature. But especially according to each one's attitude and inclination, may persons who stand in the assurance of a blessed participation in Christ have fellowship and eat with joy, in love and singleness of heart; burdened ones may fall together at Jesus' feet with new confession of guilt, with humiliation and self-surrender seeking in him righteousness and strength and looking for his grace; yea, even the most unworthy and the most timid among the people of the Lord, if they hunger indeed after the truth and his righteousness (Mt 5.6) and desire to be wholly his, may confidently disclose this longing and this desire, and rest in the hope of his grace, remembering that he never cast out those that came to him in humility (Jn 6.37) crying to him for mercy, asking for the crumbs, and counting themselves happy if they could but touch the hem of his garment.

6. If the Lord's holy supper is thus desired, and celebrated with this end in view, we believe that the true blessing as indicated—the communion with Jesus Christ and the knitting together of the believers (Mt 26.26–28; Jn 6.55; 1 Cor 10.16, 17), will be realized in no small measure, and be furthered thereby. But where this essential frame of mind is lacking (Mt 22.11–13) there this fruit can not with reason be expected (2 Chr 16.9); and if the elements are taken unworthily, that is, if one does not with reverence discern the body and blood of the Lord, such a one eateth and drinketh judgment unto himself. 1 Cor 11.27–29.

7. For this reason we may invite none to the Lord's table but such as truly believe in Jesus Christ and honestly desire to live through and for him, those who have openly professed this before God and man, who have been baptized according to the Scriptures (1 Cor 12.13) and have been duly received into the church, who do not by their lives give just cause for offense in the church (Rom 16.17), who live with her in peace (Mt 5.23, 24), and as much as in them is have peace with all men (Rom 12.18), who bear with and forgive one another (Mt 6.14, 15, 18.23–35); in short none but disciples of Christ who have a desire and are determined solemnly to renew and confirm the covenant once entered into. Wherefore we admonish everyone to prove himself (1 Cor 11.28). Moreover we exclude no one except those who by offensive teaching or disgraceful life (2 Thes 3.14; 1 Cor 5.9–13) are subject to discipline.

27. OF BROTHERLY CARE AND CHURCH DISCIPLINE

1. We believe that in a Christian church every brother and every sister must share, according to ability and gifts bestowed, in a mutual care among the members, inciting one another to love and good works. Heb 10.24. True love to one's neighbor

requires this (Lv 19.17, 18), and it is commanded by Christ our Lord (Mt 18.15–20), and also enjoined by his apostles after him. 1 Thes 5.14, 15; Jas 5.16–20. More especially should this be observed by those who are set as overseers (Acts 20.28; Ti 1.7–11), whose work it is by virtue of their office to shepherd the flock (1 Pt 5.1–4) and watch over the spiritual welfare of the church. Heb 13.17; Ez 3.17, 33.2–9.

2. The cases that call for the notice, reproof, and discipline of the church are not those shortcomings and mistakes which to a greater or less degree are common to all believers (Jas 3.2; 1 Jn 1.8; Ps 130.2, 143.2), but errors in teaching (Gal 1.8; 1 Tm 6.3–5; Ti 3.10) or conduct (2 Thes 3.6; Phil 3.18, 19) so far-reaching that those who commit the error are in apparent danger of losing their soul's inheritance (1 Cor 6.5–10) or become a cause of offense and stumbling to the church (Gal 5.10; Rv 2.20; 1 Cor 5.6, 7; Mt 18.7), leading souls astray (Mt 24.10–12; 2 Tm 3.13; Jude 3, 4) and causing the name of God and the church of Christ to be evil spoken of. 2 Pt 2.2; Rom 2.24; 1 Tm 6.1; Ti 2.3–5.

3. In dealing with offenders we distinguish the following four stages to be observed: First, when with a reasonable degree of certainty it becomes known that a brother or sister is guilty of this or that dangerous practice or clearly interdicted sin (1 Cor 5.11–13; 2 Pt 2.20; Gal 5.19–21), but the matter is not as yet generally known, the person is to be called to account in private, examined with all possible discretion, and warned in tender love (Gal 6.1–3; Jas 3.13–18), so that, if possible, such a one may be brought back into the right way (Jas 5.19, 20) before the evil seed spread further. Gal 5.9; Heb 12.15.

4. If, in the second place, some one is guilty of manifest works of the flesh (Gal 5.19–21; Eph 5.3–7) and such fact is surely known, though the sin be committed under circumstances which seem in a degree to palliate the offense, as for instance being taken unawares or having acted hastily, such a one is to be solemnly called to account, the evil of his sin and its consequence set before him with the admonition to humble himself before God (Acts 8.22; Jas 4.7–10; Ps 51) and man (Mt 5.23–26; Lk 17.1–4), according as the transgression may have been, and all possible means applied to bring about true repentance (Rv 3.2, 3; Is 55.6, 7); and if necessary he should be counseled not to come to the Lord's table for a time (Jude 22, 23), until by clear proof of an amended life the offense that was given may be removed, or, in the judgment of his fellow members (2 Cor 2.6–8) it be blotted out.

5. The third stage is reached in the case of one who, regardless of the first and second reproof given in private, continues and grows hardened in his sin (Eph 4.17–19; Acts 19.9; Heb 3.13). He is to be made known to the congregation in order that the whole congregation may decide what is to be done with such a member and take such action that, being reproved in the presence and by the judgment of all, he

may be ashamed and be brought to repentance. 2 Thes 3.14, 15. This properly must be accompanied with earnest prayer that, if possible, the result may be reformation and forgiveness. Jas 5.15; 1 Jn 5.16, 17.

6. If, however, all this is fruitless and the reproved one continues and hardens himself in his evil way, he must finally, by the decision of the whole congregation, be excluded from membership and denied all spiritual church-fellowship (Eph 5.11) till he is truly converted and gives evident proof thereof. However, all must be done with due regard to position and circumstances (1 Tm 5.1, 19–21), yet without respect of person.

7. This ecclesiastical care and discipline we consider most necessary, not only because Jesus Christ and his apostles enjoined it and by neglecting the same we have to fear just condemnation (1 Cor 11.30, 31), but also because it works many a benefit, namely, keeping the church free from open blemish, saving it from harmful contempt, and preventing the estrangement of weak souls or the leading astray of established hearts; yea, much more tending to deter these from evil and on the other hand to move the reproved ones to shame and repentance.

8. In order, however, that this manner of treatment may have its desired effect, there must be far removed from us all inordinate desire for authority and all self-conceit of superior holiness, since in the use of these keys (Mt 16.19) there is a power to which we resort only out of obedience (consider with what holy reserve the apostles went to work: Acts 5.1–13, 13.8–11; 1 Cor 5.3–5; 1 Tm 1.20), and which must be applied in deep humility (2 Cor 2.1–4) because we dare not neglect it (1 Cor 9.16–22; Ez 3.17–21), and in the fear of the Lord. Mt 10.14. There is in it, therefore, also no condemning or absolving power further than as it is in perfect accord with God's judgment and his holy testimony. Prv 17.15; 2 Tm 2.2, 15, 24–26; Ti 1.9, 2.2, 7, 8.

9. For this reason the separation from the persons under discipline must not proceed out of a spirit of Pharisaic holiness (1 Cor 4.7), as though we said, "Depart from me, for I am holier than thou," but out of a holy fear lest we manifest a fellowship with the unfruitful works of darkness (Eph 5.11; 1 Cor 6.17; 1 Tm 5.22; Rv 18.4), in accordance with the apostolic injunction to have nothing in common with such; with which there must, nevertheless, be combined a Christlike compassion (Rom 9.1–3) and continued admonition until one is compelled reluctantly to leave such a person to himself. Between husband and wife this separation cannot in all cases take place unless it be for adultery or fornication. Mt 5.32, 19.9; 1 Cor 7.3–5, 10, 16, 39.

10. In conclusion, we believe in reference to this subject, that as soon as the erring one gives conclusive evidence of sincere sorrow and amendment (Lk 17.3,

4; 2 Cor 7.7, 16) he must be met with added love, encouraged, and after public and humble confession, received back into communion (Ps 130.4; Jer 3.1; Ez 33.11), with cordial love and joy (Lk 15.1–10) and full forgiveness (2 Cor 2.10), even as God also in Christ Jesus has forgiven us. Eph 4.32; Col 3.13; Mt 18.

28. OF THE OFFICE OF TEMPORAL GOVERNMENT

1. We believe that although men have by nature no right to rule over one another with violence, but only in a brotherly spirit to control themselves and come to one another's assistance (Acts 17.26, 27; Mt 7.12), nevertheless, the office of government has become necessary by reason of man's great corruptness (Gn 6.12, 13) and that the Lord our God therefore has not only permitted but determined and ordained it (Rom 13.1–8) first through his divine providence in general but then, too, among his people, Israel, by specific command (Dt 16.18; Ex 18.25; Nm 11.11, 16, 17) and that the same seems still absolutely necessary as well for the observance of right and good order in social life as for the punishment of the evil and the protection of the good, and other like objects.

2. For this reason we hold ourselves in duty bound towards our lawful government to regard the same as God's servant for our good, to honor it with due reverence (1 Pt 2.12–21), to be obedient unto it in all things that are not in violation of God's commandments or of one's good conscience (Acts 4.19, 20), to pay cheerfully and faithfully all proper taxes and assessments, and devoutly to pray for it (1 Tm 2.1–4; Jer 29.7), etc. All this we need to observe the more in all cases since we know that "promotion cometh neither from the east nor from the west nor from the south; but God is the judge: he putteth down one and lifteth up another" (Ps 75.6, 7) according to his will (Prv 8.15, 16), now to bless and now to chastise.

3. Should, however, such an office be conferred upon us, we would hesitate and would not dare to accept it, not knowing the will of Christ as to how such office should be administered. (True, there are other things, too, in civil life concerning which we have no explicit direction, but they are less difficult and can more easily be ordered according to God's word.) No direction whatever concerning it is found among all his commandments respecting the administration of his kingdom, nor among all the instructions of his apostles. (We know nothing as to how the government is to be instituted or how the office should be administered. This gives us reason to be scrupulous.) Moreover when we consider that the Lord Jesus seems everywhere to warn his disciples against bearing rule according to the manner of the world (Mt 20.25, 26; Lk 22.25–30; Jn 18.36), as well as against all vengeance (Mt 5.39, 40; Rom 12.19), the swearing of oaths, and all worldly conformity, we consider it a very difficult matter to administer this office according to faith. We

hold, too, that the power vested for a time in the Jewish government (Dt 17.8–12; 2 Chr 10.5–11) is in Christ fulfilled, brought to an end, and abolished (Mt 5.17; Eph 1.20–23; Col 2.15–23, 3.16–25), and hence can not be applicable to Christ's people (Heb 7.12); on the other hand it seems to us no less calculated to arouse scruples when human laws are to be enforced which are at variance with the principles of civil law which God himself laid down for Israel. Cases occur which often cause judges to hesitate: compare the present laws concerning theft and adultery with Ex 22.1; Lv 20.10.

4. For these various reasons we consider ourselves fortunate to be exempt from this most important and at best dangerous service (we regard it a favor not to be called or impressed into civil office) while at the same time we can live in peace and quiet under the protection of such a benign government, who, though not recognizing for themselves the difficulties mentioned (but rather seeing in their office a divine calling) have yet granted to us such great privileges and exemptions (exemption from oaths and military service) for which we can not thank God enough (1 Tm 2.1–4) and owe our government all reverence and love.

29. OF REVENGE AND WAR

1. We believe we do not err when by nature we judge that avenging or retaliating of every injustice is but just. Nevertheless, it is certain that though the Lord our God permitted his people in the olden times to exercise revenge (Mt 5.38, 43), by reason of their hardness of heart (Mt 19.8), yet it primarily and properly belongs to God himself (Rom 12.17–21; Heb 10.30; Lv 19.17–18; Dt 32.35) who also is alone able correctly and with exactness to judge of the measure of the evil and of the just punishment (Is 28.17; Jer 17.10; Lk 12.47, 48) for which we are often incapacitated by our imperfect knowledge, our unbridled self-love, and excited passions. Jas 1.20; Prv 27.4. For this reason, we believe, our Lord Jesus Christ, when he would establish his spiritual and heavenly kingdom in accord with the will of God as it was from the beginning, forbade his followers not only all practice of revenge (Mt 5.38–44) but even all vindictiveness (1 Jn 3.15), as did likewise his apostles after him. Rom 12.19; 1 Thes 5.15; 1 Pt 3.9. On the contrary, he insisted on their putting in practice the law of love to a degree far in advance of the teaching of nature (Lk 6.32, 33) or of the Jewish rabbis (Mt 5.20), as well as on an exercise of patience that should be perfect (Jas 1.4) after his own example (2 Thes 3.5; 1 Pt 2.21– 23); that is, instead of violently resisting the evil with the object of destroying it, rather to suffer repeated wrong (Mt 5.38–40); rather put up with material loss and injustice than to be quick to quarrel (1 Cor 6.1–8); to render to no one evil for evil (Rom 12.17, 20) not even reviling for reviling (1 Pt 3.9); but always to follow after that which is good toward

one another and toward all; to overcome by doing good (Rom 12.21); to manifest love even to our enemy: if he is hungry, feed him; if he is thirsty, give him drink (Prv 25.21, 22; Rom 12.20); to bless them that curse us; to do good to them that hate us, and to pray for them that do violence to us and persecute us. Only as we do this shall we be children pleasing to our Father in heaven (Mt 5.44–48), and true followers of Jesus Christ (Jn 12.26), who, when he was reviled, reviled not again; when he suffered, threatened not; but committed all to him that judgeth righteously (1 Pt 2.21–23), in all of which he left us an example that we should follow in his steps. Phil 2.5.

2. Hence it is, as we think, self-evident that the use of deadly weapons and the carrying on of warfare to the destruction of our enemies—and even of innocent ones who have not wronged us but upon whom in war often falls the burden of misery and sorrow—is entirely unseemly for a true follower of Jesus and therefore not allowed (Mt 5.39, 40, 43, 44; 2 Cor 10.3, 4). For we are persuaded that war, as we know it, cannot possibly be carried on without manifestly violating the fundamental principles of Christ's kingdom (Jn 18.36; Eph 4.31, 32) and without nurturing vice and practices contrary to those principles (Gal 5.19–21), whereby there is often manifested the likeness of wild beasts and of devils, rather than of followers of the Lamb of God (Is 53.7) and of those that show forth his excellencies. 1 Pt 2.9.

3. We therefore hold that it is our duty carefully to abstain from the use of all warlike weapons and from the above-mentioned hostile resistance; that it is allowed to flee from the evil as much as is in our power (Mt 10.23), to adopt such measures against an enemy that without working to his destruction we may prevent and bring to naught his hostile purposes (Acts 23.6–9), and by means of defensive reasoning and good words (Jn 18.23; Acts 4.8–13, 19, 20) and manifold kindnesses to bring him to reflect and be at peace (Mt 5.25, 26; Lk 12.58; Gn 21.25–27). Moreover, we are of the opinion that all malevolent treatment that we experience must serve to exercise us in the faith and patience of the saints, as we follow the example of Jesus Christ, his holy apostles, and many thousands of Christians in the early and later centuries, who when for conscience sake they had to suffer adversities (Mt 5.10) experienced in this the grace of God making all things work for their good (Rom 8.28; 2 Cor 1.3–6, 4.17, 18, 6.10), not to mention that the merciful God often gives an issue and an escape (2 Cor 11.23–33) beyond all human thought (2 Cor 1.8–11; 2 Tm 3.11, 4.17, 18). Besides all this, it was plainly prophesied that such a peaceful and nonresistant life (Mt 10.16; Lk 10.3) would be found among the subjects of Christ's kingdom (Is 2.4, 11.6–8; Mi 4.1–3; Zec 9.9, 10). Wherefore we pray that this blessed kingdom may come (Mt 6.10) and come soon, Amen!

30. OF OATHS

1. In the question of taking oaths we believe that though it is possible to take an oath with a devout purpose, as did the holy patriarchs at times (Gn 14.22, 23, 21.30, 31) and as it was permitted under the Mosaic dispensation, God himself being often represented as speaking in this human manner (Heb 6.13-17; Ps 89.35, 95.11, 110.4), yet such a practice is nowhere enjoined by a command of God (Ex 20.7; Lv 19.12) but simply defined and restrained. Ex 22.11. Thus it is evident that swearing, like divorce and some other practices, was in reality permitted because of the want of love and of the prevailing mistrust, and the increasing degeneracy among mankind. Wherefore the Lord Jesus, in order to correct also this violation of and deviation from the original purpose of God, entirely prohibited the use of oaths in his spiritual and heavenly kingdom, when he said: "But I say unto you, Swear not at all," etc. Mt 5.34-37.

2. The reason why we cannot regard these words as a prohibition simply of the frivolous and notorious habit of profane swearing, or of swearing in things of minor importance, but consider it far safer to regard them as doing away entirely with all swearing are, besides those already mentioned and others, the following: First, because the Lord Jesus is evidently not speaking against trivial swearing but refers to the legal use of the oath, as it was said to them of old time, "Thou shalt not forswear thyself but shalt perform unto the Lord thine oaths" (obviously the Lord here refers to Ex 20.7 and Lv 19.12). Further because the Lord says, — "But I say unto you, Swear not at all—but let your speech be Yea, yea; Nay, nay, and whatsoever is more than these is of the evil one." Further, because James, repeating the same words, adds: "But above all things, my brethren, swear not—neither by any other oath—that ye fall not under judgment." Jas 5.12. Again, because such a view does not forbid an earnest assertion of the truth of our statements, when the honor of God and the love of the truth calls for it—such as the Lord Jesus often made (Jn 14.12) likewise the apostle Paul, now and then (Rom 1.9, 9.1; 2 Cor 1.23; Gal 1.20; Phil 1.8), since Christ does not mean to say that one shall use no words except Yea and Nay, but that our Yea shall be yea, and since we cannot regard such manner of emphasis as in reality an oath but an intense effort, proceeding from a holy motive, to awaken attention and deepen the impression; and even if in a few instances (like 1 Thes 5.27) this should be found to have taken the form of an oath (which, however, is not conceded) it is well to observe that this was done by persons of unimpeachable truthfulness, and probably in the spirit of forbearance, but not to serve us as a pattern. Again, because it is far more commendable to keep our yea and nay as faithfully as though we had sworn to it; and this confidence in one's given word is in harmony with the kingdom of Jesus. Further, because by reason

of the depravity of human nature it is to be feared that the very practice of making oath is taken by godless men as a cause for attaching no weight to simple assurances and making light of lying. Rv 21.27, 22.15. Further, because the Christians of the first centuries in general seem to have understood these words thus, and we have on record the testimonies of almost all the old teachers of the church against the use of oaths. Finally, because a look at civil life and the requirements of a well-regulated state does not seem to reveal the need of swearing, since godless and faithless men are not to be trusted even though they swear (Jer 5.2) and such persons have often so little fear of an oath that it is known full well beforehand and afterwards established that false oaths are sworn without number, a fact that causes godly rulers as well as true Christians in general to sigh, and which makes it necessary in spite of the use of the oath, to provide civil punishment for the untruthful.

3. As for ourselves, we hold that if under our solemn affirmation of the truth, which is put in place of the oath, we should deal faithlessly or fail to come up to our word, we are just as guilty and subject to just punishment as though we had sworn the heaviest oaths. It behooves us indeed to excel in this respect and thus to confirm our testimony with our acts, and it is therefore not to be feared that through our abstaining from the oath good order and fidelity shall suffer even in the least.

31. OF MARRIAGE

1. We believe that the married state should be held in honor by all (Heb 13.4) and that it is not only permitted but also needful (Gn 1.28), expedient (Gn 2.18–24; Prv 18.22), and well pleasing to God (Mt 19.4–6), if it is entered upon in the true spirit (Gn 24; Prv 19.14, 31.10–30; 1 Cor 7.39) and so continued in. Eph 5.22–33. We are assured of this through the fact of God's own appointment (Gn 2.18–24), and the reaffirming of the same (Mk 10.3–12) and through the action of Jesus, who hallowed a marriage by his presence (Jn 2.1–11), as well as through the example of the most eminent saints who, living in a married state, walked with God (Gn 5.22) and had the testimony that they pleased God (Heb 11.5), including even the priests (Lv 21.7–9), the high priest (Lv 21.13–15), the prophets (e.g., David, Ezekiel, Hosea), and the apostles of the Lord (1 Cor 9.5; Mt 8.14). It appears indeed that the teaching of the Bible holds this state to be expedient for overseers in the church (1 Tm 3.2, 12, 5.9, 10; Ti 1.6) wherefore we are certain that the throwing of suspicion on the married state proceeds from superstition and the prohibiting of it is anti-Christian and an abomination. 1 Tm 4.3.

2. On the general question involved the will of God concerning this state is clearly expressed, namely, that only two persons free from all others and not of too close blood relationship may enter into it, to be united and bound together without

any reserve even unto death. Mt 19.5; Eph 5.28. The separation of such is moreover, altogether prohibited except for the cause of fornication. Mt 5.31, 32, 19.7–10; 1 Cor 7.10, 11.

3. Further, we believe that in cases of marrying as in all things, the Lord our God directs and disposes—yet so as not thereby to annul man's freedom—be it that he in his goodness graciously brings them about (Gn 24.14, 50; Mt 19.6; Jos 23.12, 13) or that he in his righteous displeasure and chastisement permits them (e.g., Jgs 14.3, 4, 14; 1 Kgs 11.1–6; Ezr 9.10–15; Neh 13.23–27). Therefore marriage is not to be regarded as an explicit general command (Mt 19.11, 12; 1 Cor 7.7, 17, 27, 28) or as a universally ordained destiny, but as a thing in which man may act with freedom, so far as this is not limited by God's holy directions, and that it be in the Lord. 1 Cor 7.39. These limitations are clearly to be seen in the prohibition of marriage with unbelieving persons (Gn 24.14, 50; Mt 19.6; Jos 23.12, 13); the transgression of God's repeated command in this respect (Gn 6.1–3, 26.34, 35, 27.46) and God's holy displeasure thereat (1 Kgs 11.1–9); and in the necessity of putting away the strange wives out of Israel in order that the enkindled wrath of the Almighty might be turned from them (Ezr 9.10–15, 10.1–19; Neh 13.23–28) as well as many occurrences showing the evil and hurtful consequences of carnal marriages in which only the natural passions are followed. Lk 17.26–28.

4. For this reason it is exceedingly important that a person purposing either to enter this state or to abstain from it should examine himself, consider well his qualities, in faith seek to know God's will concerning himself (1 Cor 7.12–17), take counsel of God and his word (Prv 3.6; Ps 119.9–11; Phil 4.6, 7), and not decide upon one or the other course until in faith and with a good conscience he is convinced that in that course he will be pleasing unto the Lord Jesus Christ. 1 Cor 10.31; 2 Cor 5.9, 10; Col 3.17. Those who thus marry have good reason to hope that it is in the Lord and that his blessing will accompany it.

5. If matrimony is thus begun in the fear of the Lord and conducted in a Christian manner (Eph 5.22–33) in accordance with the principles of the gospel, as laid down for the direction of both husbands and wives (1 Tm 2.8–13; Ti 2.3–8; 1 Pt 3.1–7), then shall the man, who is the head of the woman, strive to be a worthy copy of Jesus Christ in his relation to his church. The wife shall be saved through the childbearing (1 Tm 2.15), her seed shall be blessed (Gn 18.18, 19; Eph 6.4) and all things shall work together for good to them. Mt 6.33; Rom 8.28.

6. That this married life may be a happy one we consider it essential, as much as possible, to remain within one's own church communion (after the example of the patriarchs, Gn 24.3, 4, 28.1–8; Rom 15.5, 6; Phil 2.1, 2) to avoid disgraceful contentions and many unpleasant consequences which are so apt to arise out of

differences in the bringing up, in the manner of life, and in intellectual views (as exemplified in 1 Cor 3.4) and which crop out when it comes to bringing up their own children as well as in other things, being often discovered too late. It is, therefore not only proper but also to their advantage for young people to counsel—next to God—with their parents and other intimate relatives, listen to their advice and not to grieve them but rather give them cause for joy. Prv 10.1. But everything in the fear of the Lord.

32. OF DEATH

1. Of the state of the soul after this life and the necessity of a godly preparation for a blissful departure.

2. That it is appointed unto man once to die (Heb 9.27; Ps 89.48) is, we believe, a result of the transgression of our first parents (Rom 5.12–14; Gn 2.17, 3.19; 1 Cor 15.21) and is thus in reality a punishment for sin. Rom 6.23. But we also believe that through the obedience and death of Jesus Christ (Rom 5.19; Heb 2.14, 15; Is 25.8) the sting of death has been removed (1 Cor 15.55–57; Hos 13.14) for all them that truly believe on him (Jn 6.40, 50, 51, 58); so that these need not fear death (Heb 2.14, 15; Is 25.8), but can thank God through Jesus Christ that it is theirs sometime to die. For though our body—which, be it remembered, is of the earth (Gn 2.7; Eccl 12.7), polluted through sinful lusts (Rom 7.5, 23, 24; 2 Cor 7.1), and altogether unfitted for heaven without great change (1 Cor 15.36, 50; Phil 3.21)—continues under the necessity of a return to its first element (Rom 8.10), and though such a thought is indeed appalling to them that live after the flesh (Rom 8.6, 13; Lk 12.16–21) and are the servants of sin (Rom 6.16; 2 Cor 5.10; Heb 10.31), yea, also to the godly in a certain degree after the physical nature; yet to the believer the thought of death brings true comfort (1 Thes 4.17, 18) amid the hardships (Jas 5.7, 8; 2 Cor 4.17, 18, 5.1–9) and imperfections (1 Cor 13.8–12; 1 Jn 3.2) of this earthly life, knowing that to be absent from the body and at home with the Lord, to be set free and be with Christ, is by far better (2 Cor 5.6–8; Phil 1.20–23), and finally that the putting of the body in the earth like the grain of wheat (Jn 12.24) is the divinely ordained way to the reaping of better things. 1 Cor 15.35–44.

3. As to the soul, the immortal nature of which has already been spoken of under article 5, we believe that the same immediately upon its release from the body, returns to God—not to the full and final condition of glory or punishment (Mt 25.46; Jude 6) for this will come only after the resurrection of the body and the reunion of the soul with the same, in the day of the final judgment (Mt 25.34–46)— but to a lively anticipation of that state (Lk 16.23, 24; Rv 6.10, 11) though in greater or less measure (Lk 12.47, 48; 2 Pt 2.9, 10) according to the degree of unrighteous-

ness (Mt 10.15, 11.22, 24) and estrangement from God (Mt 25.30; Lk 13.24–30), or of holiness (2 Tm 2.20–22) and intimate union with him (Jn 14.21–23; 15.10, 17.23, 24; 1 Cor 15.58; 2 Pt 1.8), as it evidently follows from the justice of God (Gal 6.7, 8; 2 Cor 9.6) and the nature of the case. With many their conscience bears witness to this even while they seek to deafen it, Rom 1.21–25, how much more when it awakes. Lk 16.23; Is 57.21. The ungodly and unconverted sinners pass at death to a condition of imprisonment (2 Pt 2.4, 9, 17), of regret that is too late, of chagrin and pain. Is 66.24; Mt 18.34; Mk 9.48. Those who die in the Lord (Rv 14.13) pass to a condition of comfort (Lk 16.25), of peace and happiness. Lk 23.43. In this state of being, kept by the hand of Jesus Christ (Rv 1.18; 3.7), they await either in fear (Mt 8.29; Heb 10.27) or with desire (2 Pt 3.12–14) the last sentence or final judgment. For of a purging of the soul after death (as taught by the Roman church) we confess to know nothing, but rather that the judgment is connected with death (Heb 9.27) and that the tree will lie as it falls. Eccl 11.3; Lk 16.22, 23.

4. It is therefore of the utmost importance that we seek to prepare for the hour of death in time (Jn 9.4) while it is yet today (Heb 3.15) not only by a solemn contemplation of these things (Dt 32.29; Ps 39.4, 5; Ps 90) but also by a true conversion (Acts 9.1–18; 1 Pt 2.25) and a striving after faith and holiness (1 Tm 6.11; 2 Tm 2.22; Heb 12.14), to be found in Christ (Phil 3.9–14), to have always a conscience void of offense (Acts 24.16; 1 Jn 3.20, 21), to do gladly and with our might what our hands find to do (Eccl 9.10), and whatever there is more of like import. Phil 4.8. All this because (being repeatedly warned of the Lord, Mk 13.37) we know not at what time or hour he will come (Mt 24.42, 25.13; Lk 12.35–46), that we may always be ready as those that wait for their Lord that we may not be ashamed at his coming (2 Jn 2.28) but may be found of him in peace without spot, and blameless. 2 Pt 3.14.

5. Seeing, moreover, that for this most necessary and most important preparation very much is required, namely, that we look forward to death in faith as to a messenger of peace (Lk 2.29, 30), regard the putting off of our body as a deliverance (2 Tm 4.6) and a redemption (Rom 8.23) and commit our spirit with a well-founded calmness of mind unto the hands of God as our heavenly Father of Jesus Christ as our dear Redeemer (Acts 7.58), we need to this end nothing less than saving faith (Jn 3.14, 15, 6.40), true peace with God (Rom 5.1), a resignation to his will (Mt 6.10, 26.39; Phil 1.20–23), a relinquishing of all earthly things (Phil 3.7–11; Heb 11.13), the experience of his love (Rom 5.5), and the comfort of the Holy Spirit (2 Cor 5.5; Rom 8.15, 16). These all being gifts of grace bestowed on us by reason of the obedience and death of our dear Savior, the Lord Jesus Christ (Rom 5.17, 8.37; 2 Cor 5.15; 2 Tm 1.10), we must seek these gifts in persevering prayer, moved throughout

by a lively realization of our dependence, and then receive and acknowledge them in such measure as the Lord may impart to us, in deep humility, as his undeserved mercy. Ps 103.10–14, 32.6, 7.

33. OF THE RESURRECTION OF THE DEAD

1. That the great mystery (1 Cor 15.51) of the resurrection was revealed and known to the saints in the old dispensation (Dn 12.2), though less clearly than to us (Heb 11.13–16), we know from the words of Christ when he said, to the confusion of the Sadducees: "Ye do err, not knowing the Scriptures nor the power of God." "God is not the God of the dead but of the living." Mt 22.29, 32; Mk 12.24, 26, 27. The same is also evident from the many tokens and testimonies that they lived and died in this faith. This fundamental doctrine (Heb 6.1, 2) has, however, been set forth in a much clearer light through the gospel (2 Tm 1.9, 10), by which we now know definitely that before the final judgment there is to be a resurrection of the dead, both of the just and the unjust (Acts 24.15) so that all men that ever lived and died, whether buried on land or in the sea (Jn 5.28, 29; 1 Cor 15.21, 22; Rv 20.12, 13) shall awake and be made manifest. Jn 6.39; Ez 37.1–14.

2. As to the possibility of such an occurrence, surpassing all human thought, our faith rests not only on the above-mentioned and many other clear testimonies, but on the omnipotence (Mt 19.26; Lk 1.37; Zec 8.6), justice, and faithfulness of him who has promised and will perform it (Heb 10.23; Nm 23.19), namely God the Father (Rom 4.17; Dt 32.39) through his Son Jesus Christ (2 Cor 4.14; Jn 6.40; Phil 3.21) in the all-availing power and working of the Holy Spirit (Rom 8.11), seeing that he to whom nothing is impossible, who calls into being that which is not (Rom 4.17) should much less find it impossible to call them to whom the seed yet remaineth. 1 Cor 15.35–44; Jn 12.14. This faith rests further on the cases of those who in times past were raised from the dead (Jn 11.23, 44), and especially on the resurrection of our Lord himself (1 Cor 15.12–18), for in that he was thus declared the Son of God with power (Rom 1.4), having power to take his life again (Jn 10.18), we can with confidence rely on his word (Jn 6.54, 14.19) knowing that he is our Redeemer (Jb 19.25, 26) and that he as the first fruit (1 Cor 15.20–23; Rom 11.16; Acts 26.23) and the head of the church (Col 1.18) not only can but without fail will fulfill all his promises. Rv 1.18.

3. Concerning the way and manner, how all this shall take place, we see from the word of the Lord, that Christ himself shall descend from heaven with a shout, with the voice of the archangel, and with the trump of God (1 Thes 4.16) accompanied by the angels of his power (2 Thes 1.7; Mt 25.31); that then all that are in the graves shall hear the voice of the Son of God and shall come forth, they that

have done good unto the resurrection of life, and they that have done evil unto the resurrection of judgment (Jn 5.29); that this shall take place with the same bodies in which they have thus lived (Is 26.19; Rom 8.11) yet so changed and made incorruptible (1 Cor 15.53, 54) that they can either live forever in bliss or continue in eternal woe; that these changes shall take place instantly as in the twinkling of an eye, and yet each in this own order (1 Cor 15.23), for they that have died in Christ shall rise first and they that are yet alive and remain shall be changed likewise. 1 Thes 4.16.

 4. Finally, as regards the time of this coming of the Lord (1 Thes 3.13; Jas 5.7, 8; 2 Pt 3.12) it shall be in the last day (Jn 6.39, 44, 54) immediately before the last judgment, when the Lord shall come to hold judgment, the day and hour of which it is not for us to know. Mt 24.36; Mk 13.32; Acts 1.7. For though there are various prophecies and signs of the times given (Mt 24.1–38), which we are to observe with deep reverence and which seem to indicate that the time of the end is near at hand (Dn 12.4–9; 1 Tm 4.1–3; 2 Tm 3.1–5; 2 Pt 3.3–18), yet it must be preceded by the transpiring of great things—there is, nevertheless, nothing more certain than that the Lord will come in an hour when men will not be looking for him (Mt 24.44) and in a time when thoughtlessness and worldly-mindedness shall predominate in the world (Mt 24.37–39; Lk 18.8; 1 Thes 5.2, 3; 2 Tm 3.1–5), wherefore the Lord Jesus so often admonishes always to watch, as has been more fully set forth in the foregoing article.

34. OF THE FINAL JUDGMENT

1. That in immediate connection with the aforenamed resurrection of the dead the final and general judgment will take place, we believe—first because of the idea of God's justice so deeply impressed on the conscience of all men that the consciousness of evil fills us with fear (Rom 2.15; Gn 42.21, 22), and, on the contrary, the consciousness of good inspires a heartfelt confidence (1 Jn 3.20, 21), and this in such a manner that even the most godless can scarcely and at most only for a time deaden the impression (Is 57.20, 21; Rom 6.13–17); secondly, because we do not always see justice carried out in this life (Ps 73) and are thus led to look for it in the hereafter (Eccl 8.11–13; 2 Cor 5.10), since the above-mentioned idea can in no wise be denied or gotten rid of (Rom 1.19, 2.15), for which reasons all intelligent peoples in all ages, even though being without special divine revelation, have believed in a coming judgment. Our belief in this rests still much more on the explicit statements found in the Scriptures of the Old Testament (Eccl 12.14, 11.9; Dn 7.9, 10, 12.1–3; Mal 4.1) and more especially in those of the New.

 2. The one who is to hold this great judgment is God, the Father (Acts 17.31; Rom 3.6), the Judge of all (Heb 12.23); yet it will be through Jesus Christ, his Son

(Acts 10.42), to whom he has committed all judgment (Jn 5.22, 27) because of his willing humiliation and his obedience even unto death (Phil 2.6–11) by which he, as Mediator between God and man (1 Tm 2.5; Heb 12.24), has obtained the right (Ps 2.8–12) to rule over all. Ps 72.8; Jn 5.27. Wherefore he will show his kingly power not only to his friends (Mt 25.34, 28.18–20) but also to his foes (Lk 19.27; Rv 1.7) as it is written,—"That in the name of Jesus every knee should bow, of things in heaven and things on earth, and things under the earth and that every tongue should confess that Jesus Christ is Lord to the glory of God the Father." Phil 2.10, 11.

3. Those who shall be judged are all nations as whole (Mt 25.31, 32) and every individual person in particular, be he great or small (Rv 20.12, 13), rich or poor as well as the humblest beggar, yea also the fallen angels. Mt 25.41; 2 Pt 2.4; Jude 6; Rv 20.10.

4. The manner of the appearing of the great Judge, Jesus Christ, at his coming in judgment will be in the highest degree terrible, and the bringing of all nations before his judgment seat, without any escape (Mt 24.29, 30); for the Lord himself shall descend from heaven (1 Thes 4.16) with the clouds of heaven (Rv 1.7; Dn 7.13, 14), with great power and glory (Lk 9.26, 21.25–27), with ten thousands of his saints (Jude 14, 15), and all the holy angels with him, amid accompanying circumstances so mighty that all nature will be moved and amazed. 2 Pt 3.10. When he shall thus sit upon the throne of his glory before the eyes of all, even of his bitterest enemies, then shall the angels of his power (Mt 13.41–44; 2 Thes 1.7) gather before his judgment seat all nations to give account (Rom 14.12; Mt 25) of the time (Rv 3.3; Lk 19.44), the means (Lk 16.2; Mt 11.20–24; Heb 2.1–4), and the gifts which they have received. Lk 12.47, 48.

5. Moreover, the things concerning which account shall be required are not only a few of the most prominent actions of men, but every one of them in particular, subjective as well as objective (Heb 4.12, 13), not only words (Mt 12.36, 37; Jude 15) and deeds (Rom 2.6; Rv 2.23) but even the hidden thoughts (1 Cor 4.5) and inclinations of the heart. Rom 2.16.

6. The standard of judgment will be perfect righteousness itself (Is 28.17; Ps 9.8, 96.10, 98.9) which belongs to this great Judge as an essential quality (Ps 45.7, 8; Heb 1.8, 9) by which he is always known. Gn 18.25. And his judgment is unerring (Ps 139.1–13; Is 29.15, 16), since he is the omniscient one (Jn 2.25; Heb 4.13), the searcher of all hearts (Acts 1.24), before whom no manner of false plea or any pretense can in the least avail. Mt 7.22, 23. Moreover, he will judge with exactness (Dn 5.27; Prv 24.12) according to that which is written in the books of his omniscience (Mal 3.16), of conscience (Rom 2.15), and of divine revelation (Jn 12.48, 5.45), in each case according to the circumstances under which the person

has lived (Rom 2.12) and after the measure of gifts he received and the means and opportunities he had of obtaining the same (Mt 13.16, 17) as well as the use or abuse or total neglect of them. 1 Cor 3.10–15.

7. All this shall proceed on the basis of the covenant of grace (Jn 3.14–18, 5.24) by virtue of which they who sincerely believe (Rom 8.1), who earnestly strive after that which is good (1 Cor 9.24–27; Phil 3.7–14; Heb 12.14) and do the same (1 Jn 2.4, 29, 3.4–10) even though in weakness (Ps 103.10–14; 1 Jn 1.6–10) and amid much stumbling (Jas 3.2; Ps 37.24), will obtain mercy for Christ's sake (Jude 21; Rom 6.23); those however who continue in unbelief and obey not the truth but obey unrighteousness, unto them shall be wrath and indignation. Rom 2.4–8.

8. As to the award of this righteous judgment we see that Jesus Christ the great Judge shall bring together as his chosen ones those who shall be found to be his sheep (Jn 10.27, 28), who have done good and have been faithful in a very little (Lk 16.10, 19.17), and shall set them on his right hand receiving them with this most gracious greeting: "Come, ye blessed of my Father, inherit the kingdom prepared for you from the foundation of the world." But those who have done evil and not good (whose names are not found in the book of life, Rv 3.5, 20.15, 21.27), set on his left hand as the servants of unrighteousness, he shall banish from his presence with these most terrible words: "Depart from me, ye cursed, into everlasting fire prepared for the devil and his angels."

9. The time when this final judgment shall take place the Father has put in his own power (Mk 13.32–37; Acts 1.7) but upon us he enjoins a life of pious preparation and watchfulness in the fear of God. Lk 21.34–36.

35. OF ETERNAL LIFE

1. The kingdom which the blessed shall inherit in the day of the final judgment (Mt 25.34) we understand (1 Jn 3.2) to be in general a condition of joy (Mt 25.21; Ps 16.11; Is 51.11) and glory (1 Pt 1.4) far exceeding our conceptions in this life of humble limitations. 1 Tm 6.16. For this reason the Holy Spirit, in order to help our infirmity, speaks of it throughout figuratively, in terms of such things as in this life are esteemed the most agreeable and delightful. Mt 8.11, 22.2; Heb 11.10; Rv 19.7, 21, 22.

2. To speak of it more in particular, we believe that it will consist in a life of eternal and heavenly bliss (Lk 15.7; Rv 19.7), imperishable and unfading, which will be enjoyed under conditions of perfect delight and satisfaction in soul and body, spoken of as a fullness of joy in God's presence and pleasures at his right hand forever more.

3. The body will be freed from all its present imperfections and infirmities,

altogether changed (Phil 3.21), spiritual, heavenly (1 Cor 15.40–44, 49, 50), shining glory (Mt 13.43), fashioned like unto the glorified body of Jesus Christ in heaven.

4. In no less degree will the soul be set free from all that is yet painful and grievous (Rv 7.16, 21.4) and on the contrary will be clothed with all the perfection of which it is capable, both in knowledge (1 Cor 13.9–13) and in glory (2 Thes 2.14; 1 Pt 5.10; Rv 21.27), perfectly at one with God, and thus transformed into that image of glory (2 Cor 3.18) toward which the upward progress in this life is but as the beginning, though its consummation be sought with longing desire. 2 Cor 5.1, 2; Rom 8.23.

5. The place of this blissful state is heaven, where God dwells (Is 57.15; Jn 14.2), a city that has foundations whose builder and maker is God, of which the greatest glory on earth is but a shadow.

6. Though there will be degrees of glory (1 Cor 3.8), some shining as the sun (Dn 12.3; Mt 13.43), others as the stars, even as also one star differeth from another in glory, according as they suffered much and contended rightly (2 Tm 2.5–12; 1 Cor 15.58; Rv 3.4, 5) or have excelled in holiness and zeal (2 Jn 8; Rv 2.17, 3.12), yet each one according to his capability will be filled and satisfied.

7. The company of the blessed will be extremely delightful. First there will be the perfectly blessed and all-sufficient God (Mt 5.8; 1 Jn 3.2; Rv 21.3), and Jesus Christ as the Lamb that was slain (Rv 5.6; Jn 12.26, 14.3, 17.19–24), then the holy angels of God (Rv 7.11; Heb 12.22–24) together with all just men made perfect from Eden to the end of the world. Lk 13.28–30. Among all these there will not be found the least contention or disagreement, but on the contrary, the fullest accord (Rv 5.8–14, 7.9–12) and the most passionate love. 1 Jn 4.7–21. In all probability they will know each other (Mt 17.3; Lk 16.19–31) and also communicate to one another their knowledge, their experiences, and their enjoyments, all of which will be the source of unspeakable joy. Ps 79.13.

8. The blessed will be occupied largely in beholding unveiled all the perfections of God (Ps 63.3–6; Ex 34.5–8) and Jesus Christ as the Mediator between God and man, and all the divine providences and works both in nature and in grace, especially the work of redemption (Rv 1.5) as well as that of conversion and sanctification (Col 1.12), etc. Thus beholding all the wonderful things in God, in his saints, and especially in one's own self (Rv 15.34; 2 Thes 1.10; Ti 3.3–7; Eph 2.3–10) under the unbroken influence of the Spirit of glory, the overshadowing of the Almighty, and the guidance of the Lamb in the midst of the throne, both body and soul will be continually refreshed, and be absorbed in the delight of united and responsive praise, worship, and glorifying (Rv 7.10–12) in all eternity.

36. OF ETERNAL PUNISHMENT

1. Respecting the condition of those who in the final judgment will be condemned, we believe that it will be unhappy and terrible beyond all conception (Dn 12.2), because the Holy Spirit represents it throughout in terms of all that is dreadful and insufferable (Heb 12.29; Is 33.14), speaking of it now as hell (Mt 10.28, 18.9; 2 Pt 2.4) or the valley of the children of Hinnom where the idolatrous Israelites formerly cast their children as an offering into the glowing arms of Moloch to be burned with fire; then as a furnace of fire (Mt 13.50), a pit burning with fire and brimstone (Rv 19.20, 20.10, 14, 15, 21.8), an outer darkness (Mt 25.30), the gnawing of a worm that dieth not (Mk 9.43–48), and fire that is not quenched (Mt 3.12), and more of like import (Mt 18.34). From all these dreadful representations we have every reason to assume that that condition will be one of utter perdition from God (2 Thes 1.9; Mt 7.23; Lk 13.27, 28), from all good, all comfort (Lk 16.24, 25), and all salvation, as also a realization of the insufferable wrath of Almighty God (Rv 6.16, 17) and his avenging justice (2 Thes 1.8; Heb 10.30, 31), both as to soul and body, without any hope of escape or relief in all eternity. Mt 25.46.

2. In their bodies, as we can conceive of it, the condemned will be standing without (Lk 13.25) when the blessed have been caught up to meet the Lord in the air (1 Thes 4.17), when all the doors of hope and of escape both on earth and in heaven shall be shut (Mt 25.10), when all the elements, kindled with fire, will be burned up (2 Pt 3.10–12), the bottomless abyss opening to engulf alive these unhappy ones as were in their time Korah, Dathan, and Abiram (Nm 16.32, 33) and the Sodomites, they being thus consumed with the earth and all that is upon it that they loved (2 Tm 3.2–4; Ps 17.14; Lk 17.26–30; 1 Jn 2.15–17; 2 Pt 3.7), yet their changed bodies being indestructible, they are not annihilated (Rv 9.6) but will suffer the fire of eternal punishment.

3. Regarding the soul, they will not only, as said above, be separated by a great gulf from God and the blessed and from every sort of comfort, but will, moreover, be most painfully tormented, by the undying recollection of so many proffered means of grace (Mt 21.20–24), opportunities (Mt 11.28, 23.37; Is 55), and convincing appeals to God's goodness (Acts 14.17; Rom 1.16–25; 2.1–24; Rv 3.20), and the willful neglect and refusal of the same (Mt 22.5; Heb 2.3, 10.29; Acts 13.40–46) as well as all manner of unrighteous deeds. This consciousness with the consequent belated repentance, chagrin, and despair (Gn 4.13, 14; Mt 27.3–5), will cause a torment far exceeding all our present conception.

4. All this will be aggravated by the exceeding terribleness of the company of the devil and his angels (Mt 25.41) together with all wicked sinners (Gal 5.19–21; Eph 5.3–6; Jude 14–16; Rv 22.15) and by the sound of their blasphemies against

God and all that is good. Rv 16.9, 11, 21. Moreover, that which makes this unhappy condition most desperately terrible is the fact that the Holy Scriptures do not give the least ground to expect a release from the same, but on the contrary they call it an eternal punishment, an everlasting fire, an unquenchable fire, a worm that dieth not, etc.

5. However, it is certain that there will be degrees in these punishments (Lk 12.47, 48), so that it will be more tolerable for them of Tyre and Sidon, and of Sodom and Gomorrah in the day of judgment than for such places and persons among whom the Lord has manifested himself with especial means of knowledge and convicting power (Mt 12.41, 42), such distinction being indeed a necessary part of the exercise of the most perfect justice, which will be manifested in this as in all other works of God. Gal 6.7, 8.

6. May he give us grace, that in the right way we may flee from this wrath to come! Amen.

Methodist Episcopal Church,
The Articles of Religion, 1784/1804

As it was originally envisioned by its founder, John Wesley (1703–91), Methodism was to be a movement within the Church of England, not a separate church with its own church order and confessional standard. But in the event that was just what it became, with far-reaching consequences for the history of Christianity during the nineteenth and twentieth centuries, in Great Britain, in the newly founded United States, and throughout the world.

As much as this development meant ecclesiastically, it also had confessional implications. For the official confessional standard of the Anglican Church was, and continued to be, → *The Thirty-Nine Articles* of 1571. But the emergence of a separate Methodist Episcopal Church, especially in the United States with the ordination of Bishop Francis Asbury (1745–1816), coinciding as it did with the American War of Independence, made it imperative for Methodism, in the United States of America at any rate, to have its own confession and articles of faith.

These were provided by John Wesley himself, in *The Articles of Religion* of 1784. They are an abridgment and revision of *The Thirty-Nine Articles,* adapted to the new situation of a new political reality—and a new ecclesiastical one. Scholars and theologians have carefully compared them with their Anglican prototype, and have sought to discern the doctrinal, ethical, and pastoral—or pragmatic—explanation for each omission.[1] The argument from silence has led to its usual inconclusive results, and the hermeneutics of the Methodist *Articles of Religion,* as of the theology of John Wesley as a whole, remains fascinating but tantalizing. Article 23, recognizing the reality of the Revolution and the American Constitution, became an official part of the confession in 1804, twenty years after its original composition.

Edition: Schaff, 3:807–13.

Literature: Blankenship 1964; Harmon and Bardsley 1953; Lawson 1974; *ODCC* 1077–80; Outler 1991.

---

1. Harmon and Bardsley 1953; Lawson 1974.

Methodist Episcopal Church,
The Articles of Religion, 1784/1804

1. OF FAITH IN THE HOLY TRINITY

There is but one living and true God, everlasting, without body or parts, of infinite power, wisdom, and goodness; the Maker and Preserver of all things, visible and invisible. And in unity of this Godhead there are three persons, of one substance, power, and eternity, the Father, the Son, and the Holy Ghost.

2. OF THE WORD, OR SON OF GOD,
WHO WAS MADE VERY MAN

The Son, who is the Word of the Father, the very and eternal God, of one substance with the Father, took man's nature in the womb of the Blessed Virgin; so that two whole and perfect natures—that is to say, the Godhead and manhood—were joined together in one person, never to be divided, whereof is one Christ, very God and very man, who truly suffered, was crucified, dead, and buried, to reconcile his Father to us, and to be a sacrifice, not only for original guilt, but also for the actual sins of men.

3. OF THE RESURRECTION OF CHRIST

Christ did truly rise again from the dead, and took again his body, with all things appertaining to the perfection of man's nature, wherewith he ascended into heaven, and there sitteth until he return to judge all men at the last day.

4. OF THE HOLY GHOST

The Holy Ghost, proceeding from the Father and the Son, is of one substance, majesty, and glory with the Father and the Son, very and eternal God.

5. THE SUFFICIENCY OF THE HOLY
SCRIPTURES FOR SALVATION

The Holy Scriptures contain all things necessary to salvation; so that whatsoever is not read therein, nor may be proved thereby, is not to be required of any man that it should be believed as an article of faith, or be thought requisite or necessary to salvation. In the name of the Holy Scripture we do understand those canonical books of the Old and New Testament of whose authority was never any doubt in the church. The names of the canonical books are—

Genesis, Exodus, Leviticus, Numbers, Deuteronomy, Joshua, Judges, Ruth, The First Book of Samuel, The Second Book of Samuel, The First Book of Kings, The Second Book of Kings, The First Book of Chronicles, The Second Book of Chronicles, The Book of Ezra, The Book of Nehemiah, The Book of Esther, The Book of Job, The Psalms, The Proverbs, Ecclesiastes or the Preacher, Cantica or Songs of Solomon, Four Prophets the greater, Twelve Prophets the less.

All the books of the New Testament, as they are commonly received, we do receive and account canonical.

6. OF THE OLD TESTAMENT

The Old Testament is not contrary to the New; for both in the Old and New Testament everlasting life is offered to mankind by Christ, who is the only Mediator between God and man, being both God and man. Wherefore they are not to be heard who feign that the old fathers did look only for transitory promises. Although the law given from God by Moses, as touching ceremonies and rites, doth not bind Christians, nor ought the civil precepts thereof of necessity be received in any commonwealth, yet, notwithstanding, no Christian whatsoever is free from the obedience of the commandments which are called moral.

7. OF ORIGINAL OR BIRTH SIN

Original sin standeth not in the following of Adam (as the Pelagians do vainly talk), but it is the corruption of the nature of every man, that naturally is engendered of the offspring of Adam, whereby man is very far gone from original righteousness, and of his own nature inclined to evil, and that continually.

8. OF FREE WILL

The condition of man after the fall of Adam is such that he can not turn and prepare himself, by his own natural strength and works, to faith and calling upon God; wherefore we have no power to do good works, pleasant and acceptable to God, without the grace of God by Christ preventing us, that we may have a good will, and working with us, when we have that good will.

9. OF THE JUSTIFICATION OF MAN

We are accounted righteous before God only for the merit of our Lord and Savior Jesus Christ by faith, and not for our own works or deservings. Wherefore, that we are justified by faith only is a most wholesome doctrine, and very full of comfort.

10. OF GOOD WORKS

Although good works, which are the fruits of faith, and follow after justification, can not put away our sins, and endure the severity of God's judgments; yet are they pleasing and acceptable to God in Christ, and spring out of a true and lively faith, insomuch that by them a lively faith may be as evidently known as a tree is discerned by its fruit.

11. OF WORKS OF SUPEREROGATION

Voluntary works—besides, over, and above God's commandments—which are called works of supererogation, can not be taught without arrogancy and impiety. For by them men do declare that they do not only render unto God as much as they are bound to do, but that they do more for his sake than of bounden duty is required: whereas Christ saith plainly, "When ye have done all that is commanded [Lk 17.10] you, say, We are unprofitable servants."

12. OF SIN AFTER JUSTIFICATION

Not every sin willingly committed after justification is the sin against the Holy Ghost, and unpardonable. Wherefore, the grant of repentance is not to be denied to such as fall into sin after justification: after we have received the Holy Ghost, we may depart from grace given, and fall into sin, and, by the grace of God, rise again and amend our lives. And therefore they are to be condemned who say they can no more sin as long as they live here; or deny the place of forgiveness to such as truly repent.

13. OF THE CHURCH

The visible church of Christ is a congregation of faithful men, in which the pure word of God is preached, and the sacraments duly administered, according to Christ's ordinance, in all those things that of necessity are requisite to the same.

14. OF PURGATORY

The Romish doctrine concerning purgatory, pardon, worshiping, and adoration, as well of images as of relics, and also invocation of saints, is a fond thing, vainly invented, and grounded upon no warrant of Scripture, but repugnant to the word of God.

15. OF SPEAKING IN THE CONGREGATION IN SUCH A TONGUE AS THE PEOPLE UNDERSTAND

It is a thing plainly repugnant to the word of God, and the custom of the primitive church, to have public prayer in the church, or to minister the sacraments, in a tongue not understood by the people.

16. OF THE SACRAMENTS

Sacraments ordained of Christ are not only badges or tokens of Christian men's profession, but rather they are certain signs of grace, and God's good will toward us, by the which he doth work invisibly in us, and doth not only quicken, but also strengthen and confirm our faith in him.

There are two sacraments ordained of Christ our Lord in the gospel; that is to say, baptism and the supper of the Lord.

Those five commonly called sacraments, that is to say, confirmation, penance, orders, matrimony, and extreme unction, are not to be counted for sacraments of the gospel, being such as have partly grown out of the *corrupt* following of the apostles; and partly are states of life allowed in the Scriptures, but yet have not the like nature of baptism and the Lord's supper, because they have not any visible sign or ceremony ordained of God.

The sacraments were not ordained of Christ to be gazed upon, or to be carried about, but that we should duly use them. And in such only as worthily receive the same they have a wholesome effect or operation; but they that receive them unworthily purchase to themselves condemnation, as St. Paul saith, 1 Cor 11.29.

17. OF BAPTISM

Baptism is not only a sign of profession, and mark of difference, whereby Christians are distinguished from others that are not baptized; but it is also a sign of regeneration, or the new birth. The baptism of young children is to be retained in the church.

18. OF THE LORD'S SUPPER

The supper of the Lord is not only a sign of the love that Christians ought to have among themselves one to another, but rather is a sacrament of our redemption by Christ's death; insomuch that, to such as rightly, worthily, and with faith receive the same, the bread which we break is a partaking of the body of Christ; and likewise the cup of blessing is a partaking of the blood of Christ.

Transubstantiation, or the change of the substance of bread and wine in the supper of our Lord, can not be proved by holy writ, but is repugnant to the plain words of Scripture, overthroweth the nature of a sacrament, and hath given occasion to many superstitions.

The body of Christ is given, taken, and eaten in the supper only after a heavenly and spiritual manner. And the means whereby the body of Christ is received and eaten in the supper is faith.

The sacrament of the Lord's supper was not by Christ's ordinance reserved, carried about, lifted up, or worshiped.

19. OF BOTH KINDS

The cup of the Lord is not to be denied to the lay people; for both the parts of the Lord's supper, by Christ's ordinance and commandment, ought to be administered to all Christians alike.

20. OF THE ONE OBLATION OF CHRIST, FINISHED UPON THE CROSS

The offering of Christ, once made, is that perfect redemption, propitiation, and satisfaction for all the sins of the whole world, both original and actual; and there is none other satisfaction for sin but that alone. Wherefore the sacrifice of masses, in the which it is commonly said that the priest doth offer Christ for the quick and the dead, to have remission of pain or guilt, is a blasphemous fable and dangerous deceit.

21. OF THE MARRIAGE OF MINISTERS

The ministers of Christ are not commanded by God's law either to vow the estate of single life or to abstain from marriage: therefore it is lawful for them, as for all other Christians, to marry at their own discretion, as they shall judge the same to serve best to godliness.

22. OF THE RITES AND CEREMONIES OF CHURCHES

It is not necessary that rites and ceremonies should in all places be the same, or exactly alike; for they have been always different, and may be changed according to the diversity of countries, times, and men's manners, so that nothing be ordained against God's word. Whosoever, through his private judgment, willingly and purposely doth openly break the rites and ceremonies of the church to which he belongs, which are not repugnant to the word of God, and are ordained and approved by common authority, ought to be rebuked openly, that others may fear to do the like, as one that offendeth against the common order of the church, and woundeth the consciences of weak brethren.

Every particular church may ordain, change, or abolish rites and ceremonies, so that all things may be done to edification.

23. OF THE RULERS OF THE UNITED STATES OF AMERICA

The president, the Congress, the general assemblies, the governors, and the councils of state, *as the delegates of the people,* are the rulers of the United States of America, according to the division of power made to them by the Constitution of the United States, and by the constitutions of their respective states. And the said states are a sovereign and independent nation, and ought not to be subject to any foreign jurisdiction.[1]

24. OF CHRISTIAN MEN'S GOODS

The riches and goods of Christians are not common, as touching the right, title, and possession of the same, as some do falsely boast. Notwithstanding, every man ought, of such things as he possesseth liberally to give alms to the poor, according to his ability.

25. OF A CHRISTIAN MAN'S OATH

As we confess that vain and rash swearing is forbidden Christian men by our Lord Jesus Christ and James his apostle, so we judge that the Christian religion doth not prohibit but that a man may swear when the magistrate requireth, in a cause of faith and charity, so it be done according to the prophet's teaching, in justice, judgment, and truth.

---

1. As far as it respects civil affairs, we believe it the duty of Christians, and especially all Christian ministers, to be subject to the supreme authority of the country where they may reside, and to use all laudable means to enjoin obedience to the powers that be; and therefore it is expected that all our preachers and people who may be under the British or any other government will behave themselves as peaceable and orderly subjects.

Shaker Church, *A Concise Statement of the Principles of the Only True Church*, 1790

This *Concise Statement of Principles* is a dramatic illustration of how the creedal and confessional imperative can assert itself even in a Christian community that has not had a tradition of theological learning, when external attacks and internal pressures make it necessary to render an account.

The Shakers—or, to give them their more official title, "The United Society of Believers in Christ's Second Appearing"—were founded in England by James and Jane Wardley in 1747. Their successor, "Mother Ann" Lee, moved the small community to upstate New York, site of other revivalist and millennial groups. In 1784, Mother Ann was succeeded in turn by Joseph Meacham and Lucy Wright. It is probably to the first of these that we owe this *Concise Statement of Principles of the Only True Church,* written in 1790; as Priscilla Brewer puts it, "numerous Shakers credited Father Joseph with its authorship, especially since there were few other Believers alive at the time who possessed the skill to write such a treatise."[1] Some of the biblical citations are not identified in the text, while others are, though sometimes erroneously; therefore we have employed marginal citations throughout.

Like the Quakers, with whom they may have had some direct historical connection, the "Shakers" seem to have been given that name by their detractors because of the manifestations of religious ecstasy in their worship. As is evident from the *Concise Statement*, the foundation of their belief was a series of divine dispensations and revelations, beginning with the patriarchs and culminating in "the only true church." Even their critics were impressed by the simplicity and austerity of their lifestyle, which included compulsory celibacy.

Edition: Brown [1812] 1977, 33–39.

Literature: Brewer 1986, 24–25; *ODCC* 1492–93; Richmond 1977, 1:145; Whitson 1983.

---

1. Brewer 1986, 24.

Shaker Church, *A Concise Statement of the Principles of the Only True Church*, 1790

A concise statement of the principles of the only true church, according to the gospel of the present appearance of Christ; as held to, and practiced upon, by the true followers of the living Savior, at New Lebanon and a number of other places.

1. We believe that the first light of salvation was given or made known to the patriarchs by promise; and they that believed in the promise of Christ, and were obedient to the command of God made known unto them, were the people of God; and were accepted by him as righteous, or perfect in their generation, according to the measure of light and truth manifested unto them; which were as waters to the ankles; signified by Ezekiel's vision of the holy waters. And although they could not receive [Ex 47.1–12] regeneration, or the fullness of salvation, from the fleshly or fallen nature in this life; because the fullness of time was not yet come that they should receive the baptism [Gal 4.4] of the Holy Ghost and fire, for the destruction of the body of sin, and purification [Mt 3.11] of the soul. But Abraham being called and chosen of God, as the father of the faith- [Rom 6.6] ful, was received into covenant relation with God by promise; that in him, and his [Rom 4.11] seed, all the families of the earth should be blessed. And the earthly blessings, which [Gn 12.3] were promised to Abraham, were a shadow of gospel or spiritual blessings to come. [Col 2.17; Heb 10.1] And circumcision, or outward cutting of the foreskin of the flesh, did not cleanse the man from sin, but was a sign of the spiritual baptism of the Holy Ghost and fire. Which is by the power of God manifested in diverse operations and gifts of the spirit, as in the days of the apostles, which does indeed destroy the body of sin or fleshly nature, and purify the man from all sin, both soul and body. So that Abraham, though in the full faith of the promise, yet as he did not receive the substance of the thing promised, his hopes of eternal salvation was in Christ, by the gospel to be attained in the resurrection from the dead.

2. The second dispensation was the law that was given of God to Israel, by the hand of Moses; which was a farther manifestation of that salvation, which was promised through Christ by the gospel, both in the order and ordinances which was instituted and given to Israel, as the church and people of God, according to that dispensation which was as waters to the knees —by which they were distin- [Ez 47.4] guished from all the families of the earth. For while they were faithful and strictly obedient to all the commands, ordinances, and statutes that God gave; approbated of God according to the promise for life, and blessing promised unto them in the

[Dt 28.2, 15] line of obedience; cursing and death in disobedience. For God, who is ever jealous for the honor and glory of his own great name, always dealt with them according to his word. For while they were obedient to the commands of God, and purged out sin from among them, God was with them, according to his promise. But when they disobeyed the commands of God, and committed sin, and became like other people, the hand of the Lord was turned against them; and those evils came upon them which God had threatened. So we see that they that were wholly obedient to the will of God, made known in that dispensation were accepted as just or righteous. Yet as that dispensation was short, they did not attain that salvation which was promised in the gospel; so that, as it respected the new birth, or real purifica-

[Heb 7.19] tion of the man from all sin, the law made nothing perfect—but was a shadow of

[Col 2.17; Heb 10.1] good things to come. Their only hope of eternal redemption was in the promise of Christ by the gospel, to be attained in the resurrection from the dead.

3. The third dispensation was the gospel of Christ's first appearance in the

[Ez 47.4] flesh, which was as waters to the loins—and that salvation which took place in consequence of his life, death, resurrection, and ascension to the right hand of the

[Rom 8.29] Father, being accepted in his obedience, as the first born among many brethren—he received power and authority to administer the power of the resurrection and eternal judgment to all the children of men. So that he has become the author of eternal

[Heb 5.9] salvation unto all that obey him. And as Christ had this power in himself, he did administer power and authority to his church at the day of Pentecost, as his body, with all the gifts that he had promised them; which was the first gifts of the Holy

[Jn 14.16] Ghost, as an in-dwelling Comforter, to abide with them forever; and by which they

[Rom 6.3] were baptized into Christ's death; death to all sin: and were in the hope of the resurrection from the dead, through the operation of the power of God, which wrought in them. And as they had received the substance of the promise of Christ's coming in the flesh, by the gift and power of the Holy Ghost, they had power to preach the

[Mk 16.15] gospel, in Christ's name, to every creature; and to administer the power of God to as many as believed, and were obedient to the gospel which they preached; and to

[Mt 18.18] remit and retain sins in the power and authority of Christ on earth. So that they that believed in the gospel, and were obedient to that form of doctrine which was taught them,[a] by denying all ungodliness and worldly lust,[b] and became entirely dead to the law, by the body of Christ, or power of the Holy Ghost, were in the travail of

[Rom 8.23] the resurrection from the dead, or the redemption of the body. So that they who took up a full cross against the world, flesh, and devil, and who forsook all for

a. [Rom 6.17]
b. [Ti 2.12]

Christ's sake, and followed him in the regeneration, by persevering in that line of
obedience to the end, found the resurrection from the dead, and eternal salvation
in that dispensation. But as the nature of that dispensation was only as water to
the loins, the mystery of God was not finished, but there was another day prophe-   [Ex 47.4]
sied of, called the second appearance of Christ, or final and last display of God's
grace to a lost world, in which the mystery of God should be finished, as he has   [Rv 10.7]
spoken by his prophets, since the world began: which day could not come, except   [Lk 1.70]
there was a falling away from that faith and power that the church then stood in.ᵃ In
which Antichrist was to have his reign, whom Christ should destroy with the spirit
of his mouth, and brightness of his appearance. Which falling away began soon   [2 Thes 2.8]
after the apostles, and gradually increased in the church, until about 457 years (or
thereabouts); at which time the power of the holy people, or church of Christ was
scattered or lost, by reason of transgression; and Antichrist, or false religion, got   [Dn 12.7, 8.12]
to be established. Since that time, the witnesses of Christ have prophesied in sack-
cloth, or under darkness. And although many have been faithful to testify against   [Rv 11.3]
sin, even to the laying down of their lives for the testimony which they held, so that
God accepted them in their obedience, which they were faithful and just to live, or
walk up to the measure of light and truth of God, revealed or made known unto
them. But as it is written, that all they that will live godly in Christ Jesus, shall suffer persecution; and so it has been: and those faithful witnesses lost their lives by   [2 Tm 3.12]
those falsely called the church of Christ, which is Antichrist. For the true church of
Christ never persecuted any; but were inoffensive, harmless, separate from sin. For   [Mt 16.24]
the true church of Christ, taking up their cross against the world, flesh, and devil,
and all sin; living in obedience to God, they earnestly contend for the same. Therefore, it may be plainly seen and known where the true church is. But as it is written
Antichrist, or false churches, should prevail against the saints, and overcome them,
before Christ's second appearance. "Let no man deceive you by any means, for that
day shall not come, except there come a falling away first, and that man of sin be
revealed, the son of perdition." And it was given unto him to overcome all kindreds,   [2 Thes 2.3]
tongues, and nations. And this is the state Christ prophesied the world of mankind   [Rv 13.7]
should be in, at his second appearance. And as it was in the days of Noah, so shall   [Lk 17.22–37]
it be in the days of the Son of man. Even so shall it be in the days when the Son of   [Lk 17.30]
man is revealed: Plainly referring to his second appearing, to consume and destroy
Antichrist, and make a final end of sin, and establish his kingdom upon earth.ᵇ But
as the revelation of Christ is spiritual, consequently must be in his people, whom

a. [2 Thes 2.3; 2 Tm 4.3; Dn 11.36–38, 12]
b. [Is 65.24; Jer 32.33–34; Dn 2.44, 7.18, 27, 9.24; Ob 21; Rv 11.15]

he had chosen to be his body, to give testimony of him, and to preach his gospel to a lost world.

4. The fourth dispensation is the second appearance of Christ, or final and last display of God's grace to a lost world; in which the mystery of God will be finished, and a decisive work, to the final salvation or damnation of all the children of men: which according to the prophecies, rightly calculated and truly understood, began in the year of our Savior 1747 (see Daniel and the Revelations) in the manner following: To a number, in the manifestation of great light, and mighty trembling, by the invisible power of God, and visions, revelations, miracles, and prophecies. Which has progressively increased with administrations of all those spiritual gifts that were administered to the apostles at the day of Pentecost: which is the Comforter that has led us into all truth; and which was promised to abide with the true church of Christ unto the end of the world. And by which we find baptism into Christ's death, death to all sin, become alive to God, by the power of Christ's resurrection, which worketh in us mightily. By which a dispensation of the gospel is committed unto us, and woe be unto us if we preach not the gospel of Christ; for in sending so great a salvation and deliverance from the law of sin and death, in believing and obeying this gospel, which is the gospel of Christ; in confessing and forsaking all sin, and denying ourselves, and bearing the cross of Christ against the world, flesh, and devil, we have found forgiveness of all our sins, and are made partakers of the grace of God, wherein we now stand. Which all others, in believing and obeying, have acceptance with God, and find salvation from their sins as well as we.[a] God being no respecter of persons,[b] but willing that all men should come to the knowledge of the truth and be saved.

[Jn 16.13]

[Rom 6.3]

[Col 1.29]

[1 Cor 9.16]

[1 Pt 5.12]

Thus we have given a short information of what we believe of the dispensation of God's grace to mankind, both past and present; and in what manner the people of God have found justification, or acceptance with God. Which was, and is still, in believing and obeying the light and truth of God revealed or made known in the day or dispensation in which they live. "For as the wrath of God is revealed from heaven, against all ungodliness, worldly lusts, and unrighteousness of men, who hold the truth in unrighteousness," or live in any known sin against him: so his mercy and grace is towards all them who truly love and fear him, and turn from all their sins by repentance, confessing, and forsaking: which is the way and manner in which all have, and must find forgiveness of their sins, and acceptance with God, through our Lord Jesus Christ, or finally fail of the grace of God, and that salva-

[Rom 1.18]

a. [Acts 10.34]
b. [1 Tm 2.4]

tion brought to light by the gospel. But to conclude, in short; as we believe and do testify that the present gospel of God's grace unto us is the day which in the Scriptures is spoken or prophesied of, as the second appearing of Christ to consume, or destroy Antichrist, or false religion; and to make an end of the reigning power of sin over the children of men; and to establish his kingdom, and that righteousness that will stand forever; and that the present display of the work and power of God, will increase until it is manifested to all, which it must be in due time. For every eye shall see him, and he will reward every man according to his deeds,[a] and none can stand in sin, or unrighteousness, but in that righteousness which is pure and holy, even without fault before the throne of God, which is obtained by grace, through   [Rv 14.5] faith, in obedience to the truth of the everlasting gospel of our Lord Jesus Christ; in denying all ungodliness and worldly lusts, by confessing all sin, and taking up   [Ti 2.12] the cross of Christ against the world, flesh, and devil. We desire, therefore, that the children of men would believe the testimony of truth, and turn from their sins by repentance, that they may obtain the mercy of God, and salvation from sin, before it be too late.

a. [Rv 1.7; Mt 16.27; Rom 2.6]

The Nineteenth Century: Putting Confessionalism and Denominationalism to the Test

"New occasions teach new duties; time makes ancient good uncouth": during the nineteenth century this slogan from *The Present Crisis,* a poem by the American man of letters James Russell Lowell (1819–91) that became a favorite Protestant hymn, applied with special force to the confessions of the Reformation and even to the creeds of the ancient church. → *The Augsburg Confession,* → *The Thirty-Nine Articles,* and → *The Westminster Confession* all underwent revision and modernization, the latter several times; and for many → *The Athanasian Creed* simply disappeared from the roster of "the three ecumenical creeds."

That became evident already in the first two "confessions" on our roster: → *The Winchester Profession* by the Universalist Church (1803) and → Thomas Campbell's *Propositions* (1809). The first of these, especially when seen in the light of the eventual merger of Universalism and Unitarianism, was a rejection of the creedal and confessional consensus of the tradition of Christian orthodoxy, as shared by Roman Catholics, Orthodox, and Protestants; and the second, in the name of the imperative of Christian unity, was a declaration that creeds—not merely this or that creed, but *all* creeds, even the most ancient and the most ecumenical—were no longer binding, if indeed they really ever had been. In another nineteenth-century formula, applied by Friedrich Schleiermacher (1768–1834) to certain confessional doctrines if not overtly to all confessions as such, they "should be returned to history, to which they properly belong."

That mind-set, and the opposition to it in most churches and denominations, made the nineteenth century a time of confessional experimentation and confessional ferment. Challenges from beyond the borders of the churches, above all the challenge of the evolutionary teachings of Charles Darwin (1809–82) to the traditional doctrine of creation but also the challenge of the historical-critical study of the Bible and other Christian sources including creeds, elicited defenses in the form of new confessions. At the same time, the recovery of tradition was giving new attention as well to the received texts of creeds and confessions. New and radically untraditional faiths such as Mormonism and Christian Science also arose during the nineteenth century, and also were obliged to resort to creedal and confessional statements, however minimalist these may have been. And the issue of Christian unity—the reality of division and schism, but increasingly also the demand for realization of the prayer "that they all may be one" (Jn 17.21)—was not only challenging the old denominational confessions but creating new, ecumenical confessions, anticipating the twentieth century.

Universalist Church, *The Winchester Profession*, 1803

Although "liberal religion in the American context," as Peter Williams has put it, "may be defined as the impulse to reject dogma in favor of free inquiry," American Universalists, as he goes on to point out, "were nevertheless moved early on—in part out of the necessity of obtaining legal recognition—to draw up loose creedal statements."[1] The most influential of these was *The Winchester Profession* of 1803. It was drawn up and adopted by a gathering of "eighteen or twenty ministers and twenty-two laymen as 'messengers,' or delegates, representing thirty-eight societies" in New England, New York, and Pennsylvania.[2] It is trine in form but not trinitarian in doctrine; and its most distinctive formulation, by which its proponents came to be identified, was the expression of the hope that God would "finally restore *the whole family of mankind* to holiness and happiness," in opposition to the traditional orthodox belief in the eternity not only of salvation but of damnation.

> **Edition:** *Winchester Centennial* 1903.

> **Literature:** Lippy and Williams 1988, 1:579–93; R. E. Miller 1979–85; *Winchester Centennial* 1903.

---

1. Lippy and Williams 1988, 1:579, 582.
2. *Winchester Centennial* 1903, 9.

We believe that the Holy Scriptures of the Old and New Testaments contain a revelation of the character of God and of the duty, interest, and final destination of mankind.

2. We believe that there is one God,[a] whose nature is love,[b] revealed in one Lord Jesus Christ, by one Holy Spirit of grace, who will finally restore the whole family of mankind to holiness and happiness.

3. We believe that holiness and true happiness are inseparably connected, and that believers ought to be careful to maintain order and practice good works; for these things are good and profitable unto men.

[Ti 3.8]

a. [Dt 6.4]
b. [1 Jn 4.8]

Thomas Campbell, *Propositions* from *Declaration and Address,* 1809

Coming out of Scotch Presbyterianism, Thomas Campbell (1763–1854) and his more prominently known son Alexander (1788–1866) laid the intellectual and theological foundation for the church usually identified as the "Disciples of Christ," which was founded by Alexander Campbell in 1827. The Disciples were part of the movement (now often called the Restoration Movement) to restore original New Testament Christianity and reunite separated Christians. Accordingly, Disciples have, as a matter of principle, eschewed creedal and confessional formulations. In presenting these thirteen *Propositions* in his *Declaration and Address* of 1809, therefore, Thomas Campbell took pains to warn: "Let none imagine that the subjoined propositions are at all intended as an overture towards a new creed, or standard, for the church. . . . They are merely designed for opening up the way, that we may come fairly and firmly to original ground upon clear and certain premises and take up things just as the apostles left them. . . . disentangled from the accruing embarrassment of intervening ages."[1]

But historically they have for that very reason functioned (to employ an almost unavoidable oxymoron) as a "Disciples confession." In 1968 they would issue another, under the title → *Design for the Christian Church.*

Edition: Olbricht and Rollmann 2000, 18–20, part of a critical edition of the entire *Declaration and Address* prepared by Ernest C. Stefanik.

Literature: Norris 1978; Olbricht and Rollmann 2000; Webb 1990.

---

1. In Olbricht and Rollmann 2000, 17–18.

Thomas Campbell, *Propositions* from *Declaration and Address*, 1809

1. That the church of Christ upon earth is essentially, intentionally, and constitutionally one; consisting of all those in every place that profess their faith in Christ and obedience to him in all things according to the Scriptures, and that manifest the same by their tempers and conduct, and of none else as none else can be truly and properly called Christians.

2. That although the church of Christ upon earth must necessarily exist in particular and distinct societies, locally separate one from another; yet there ought to be no schisms, no uncharitable divisions among them. They ought to receive each [Rom 15.7] other as Christ Jesus hath also received them to the glory of God. And for this purpose, they ought all to walk by the same rule, to mind and speak the same thing; [1 Cor 1.10] and to be perfectly joined together in the same mind, and in the same judgment.

3. That in order to this, nothing ought to be inculcated upon Christians as articles of faith; nor required of them as terms of communion; but what is expressly taught, and enjoined upon them, in the word of God. Nor ought any thing be admitted, as of divine obligation, in their church constitution and managements, but what is expressly enjoined by the authority of our Lord Jesus Christ and his apostles upon the New Testament church; either in express terms, or by approven precedent.

4. That although the Scriptures of the Old and New Testament are inseparably connected, making together but one perfect and entire revelation of the divine will, for the edification and salvation of the church; and therefore in that respect cannot be separated; yet as to what directly and properly belongs to their immediate object, the New Testament is as perfect a constitution for the worship, discipline, and government of the New Testament church, and as perfect a rule for the particular duties of its members; as the Old Testament was for the worship, discipline, and government of the Old Testament church, and the particular duties of its members.

5. That with respect to the commands and ordinances of our Lord Jesus Christ, where the Scriptures are silent, as to the express time or manner of performance, if any such there be; no human authority has power to interfere, in order to supply the supposed deficiency, by making laws for the church; nor can anything more be required of Christians in such cases, but only that they so observe these commands and ordinances, as will evidently answer the declared and obvious end of their institution. Much less has any human authority power to impose new commands or ordinances upon the church, which our Lord Jesus Christ has not en-

joined. Nothing ought to be received into the faith or worship of the church; or be made a term of communion amongst Christians, that is not as old as the New Testament.

6. That although inferences and deductions from Scripture premises, when fairly inferred, may be truly called the doctrine of God's holy word: yet are they not formally binding upon the consciences of Christians farther than they perceive the connection, and evidently see that they are so; for their faith must not stand in the wisdom of men; but in the power and veracity of God—therefore no such deductions can be made terms of communion, but do properly belong to the after and progressive edification of the church. Hence it is evident that no such deductions or inferential truths ought to have any place in the church's confession. [1 Cor 2.5]

7. That although doctrinal exhibitions of the great system of divine truths, and defensive testimonies in opposition to prevailing errors, be highly expedient; and the more full and explicit they be, for those purposes, the better; yet, as these must be in a great measure the effect of human reasoning, and of course must contain many inferential truths, they ought not to be made terms of Christian communion: unless we suppose, what is contrary to fact, that none have a right to the communion of the church, but such as possess a very clear and decisive judgment; or are come to a very high degree of doctrinal information; whereas the church from the beginning did, and ever will, consist of little children and young men, as well as fathers.

8. That as it is not necessary that persons should have a particular knowledge or distinct apprehension of all divinely revealed truths in order to entitle them to a place in the church; neither should they, for this purpose, be required to make a profession more extensive than their knowledge: but that, on the contrary, their having a due measure of scriptural self-knowledge respecting their lost and perishing condition by nature and practice; and of the way of salvation through Jesus Christ, accompanied with a profession of their faith in, and obedience to him, in all things according to his word, is all that is absolutely necessary to qualify them for admission into his church.

9. That all that are enabled, through grace, to make such a profession, and to manifest the reality of it in their tempers and conduct, should consider each other as the precious saints of God, should love each other as brethren, children of the same family and father, temples of the same spirit, members of the same body, subjects of the same grace, objects of the same divine love, bought with the same price, and joint heirs of the same inheritance. Whom God hath thus joined together no man should dare to put asunder. [Mt 19.6]

10. That division among Christians is a horrid evil, fraught with many evils.

It is anti-Christian, as it destroys the visible unity of the body of Christ; as if he were divided against himself, excluding and excommunicating a part of himself. It is anti-scriptural, as being strictly prohibited by his sovereign authority; a direct violation of his express command. It is anti-natural, as it excites Christians to contemn, to hate and oppose one another, who are bound by the highest and most endearing obligations to love each other as brethren, even as Christ has loved them. In a word, it is productive of confusion, and of every evil work.

[1 Cor 1.13]

[Jn 15.9]

11. That (in some instances) a partial neglect of the expressly revealed will of God; and (in others) an assumed authority for making the approbation of human opinions, and human inventions, a term of communion, by introducing them into the constitution, faith, or worship, of the church; are, and have been, the immediate, obvious, and universally acknowledged causes, of all the corruptions and divisions that ever have taken place in the church of God.

12. That all that is necessary to the highest state of perfection and purity of the church upon earth is, first, that none be received as members, but such as having that due measure of scriptural self-knowledge described above, do profess their faith in Christ and obedience to him in all things according to the scriptures; nor, secondly, that any be retained in her communion longer than they continue to manifest the reality of their profession by their tempers and conduct. Thirdly, that her ministers, duly and scripturally qualified, inculcate none other things than those very articles of faith and holiness expressly revealed and enjoined in the word of God. Lastly, that in all their administrations they keep close by the observance of all divine ordinances, after the example of the primitive church, exhibited in the New Testament; without any additions whatsoever of human opinions or inventions of men.

13. Lastly. That if any circumstantials indispensably necessary to the observance of divine ordinances be not found upon the page of express revelation, such, and such only, as are absolutely necessary for this purpose, should be adopted, under the title of human expedients, without any pretence to a more sacred origin—so that any subsequent alteration or difference in the observance of these things might produce no contention nor division in the church.

Cumberland Presbyterian Church in the United States, *Confession of Faith*, 1814/1883

Ever since the preaching of Jonathan Edwards and George Whitefield, revivalism in America has existed in an uneasy or even paradoxical relation with Calvinism: the summons to repentance and a personal decision for Christ, even when issued by such predestinarian preachers as Edwards and Whitefield, seemed to presuppose the ability to make such a decision, which in turn seemed to contradict the Calvinist-Presbyterian assertion of → *The Westminster Confession of Faith* of 1647 that by the fall of Adam "we are utterly indisposed, disabled, and made opposite to all good," as well as its teaching that some are "predestinated unto everlasting life, and others foreordained to everlasting death."[1] That paradox became dramatic when the preaching of revival among Presbyterians in Kentucky evoked criticism, on the grounds that many of the revivalists lacked the scholarly and theological credentials for ministry and that they were contravening *The Westminster Confession*. The criticism led to controversy, and eventually to schism, and in 1810 to the creation of the Cumberland Presbyterian Church.[2]

As Hubert W. Morrow has observed, "It soon became clear . . . that their theological position required not simply scruples about certain interpretations of the Westminster Confession, but the more drastic action of a deletion of some sections and a revision of the wording of other sections."[3] These efforts of the Cumberland Presbyterians to come to terms with *The Westminster Confession* passed through several stages.[4] At first, confessional subscription to it was permitted with the qualifying stipulation that this did not include "the idea of fatality" implied in its blanket assertion that "God from all eternity did . . . freely and unchangeably ordain *whatever comes to pass*."[5] After the formation of the Cumberland Presbyterian Church, however, it became clear to many that a more fundamental consideration of the confessional question was called for; and on 14 October 1814 a revised version of *The Westminster Confession* was adopted.[6] Then in 1883 the Cumberland Presbyterian

---

1. *West* 6.4, 3.3.
2. See the chapters in Barrus et al. 1972.
3. Morrow 1970, 205.
4. See the chapter "Creedal Statements" in Stephens 1941, 103–11.
5. *West* 3.1; italics added.
6. These revised chapters of 1814 are placed alongside the original ones of 1647 in Schaff, 3:771–76.

Church adopted the definitive recension of its confession, which we present here; according to the historical introduction to its official promulgation, it "retains the same essential doctrines enunciated in the revision of 1814, though in somewhat briefer form and with a more logical arrangement."[7] That edition prints some of the biblical proof texts in full in its footnotes, but we have indicated all of them by our usual system of marginal citation.

Edition: *Creed and Constitution of the Cumberland Presbyterian Church* 1892, 11–62.

Literature: Barrus et al. 1972; Morrow 1970; Stephens 1941.

---

7. *Creed and Constitution of the Cumberland Presbyterian Church*, 11.

Cumberland Presbyterian Church in the United States, *Confession of Faith*, 1814/1883

HOLY SCRIPTURES

1. The Holy Scriptures comprise all the books of the Old and the New Testament which are received as canonical, and which are given by inspiration of God to be the rule of faith and practice, and are these:

Old Testament

Genesis, Exodus, Leviticus, Numbers, Deuteronomy, Joshua, Judges, Ruth, I. Samuel, II. Samuel, I. Kings, II. Kings, I. Chronicles, II. Chronicles, Ezra, Nehemiah, Esther, Job, Psalms, Proverbs, Ecclesiastes, Song of Solomon, Isaiah, Jeremiah, Lamentations, Ezekiel, Daniel, Hosea, Joel, Amos, Obadiah, Jonah, Micah, Nahum, Habakkuk, Zephaniah, Haggai, Zechariah, Malachi.

New Testament

Matthew, Mark, Luke, John, The Acts, Romans, I. Corinthians, II. Corinthians, Galatians, Ephesians, Philippians, Colossians, I. Thessalonians, II. Thessalonians, I. Timothy, II. Timothy, Titus, Philemon, Hebrews, James, I. Peter, II. Peter, I. John, II. John, III. John, Jude, Revelation.

2. The authority of the Holy Scriptures depends not upon the testimony of any man or church, but upon God alone.[a]

3. The whole counsel of God, concerning all things necessary for his own glory—in creation, providence, and man's salvation—is either expressly stated in the Scriptures, or by necessary consequence may be deduced therefrom; unto which nothing at any time is to be added by man, or from the traditions of men; nevertheless, we acknowledge the inward illumination of the Spirit of God to be necessary for the saving understanding of such things as are revealed in the word.[b]

4. The best rule of interpretation of the Scriptures is the comparison of scripture with scripture.[c]

a. [2 Tm 3.16; 1 Jn 5.9; 1 Thes 2.13]
b. [1 Jn 2.20, 27; Jn 16.13–14; Gal 1.8; 1 Cor 2.10–12; Jn 6.45]
c. [1 Cor 2.2, 13; Acts 15.15; Mt 22.29]

THE HOLY TRINITY

5. There is but one living and true God, a self-existent Spirit, infinite, eternal, and unchangeable in his being, wisdom, power, holiness, justice, goodness, and truth.[a]

6. God has all life, glory, goodness, and blessedness in himself; not standing in need of any creatures which he has made, nor deriving any essential glory from them; and has most sovereign dominion over them to do whatsoever he may please.[b]

7. In the unity of the Godhead there are three persons of one substance, power, and eternity: God the Father, Son, and Holy Spirit.[c]

DECREES OF GOD

8. God, for the manifestation of his glory and goodness, by the most wise and holy counsel of his own will, freely and unchangeably ordained or determined what he himself would do, what he would require his intelligent creatures to do, and what should be the awards, respectively, of the obedient and the disobedient.[d]

9. Though all divine decrees may not be revealed to men, yet it is certain that God has decreed nothing contrary to his revealed will or written word.[e]

CREATION

10. It pleased God, for the manifestation of the glory of his eternal power, wisdom, and goodness, to create the world and all things therein, whether visible or invisible; and all very good.[f]

11. After God had made all other creatures, he created man in his own image; male and female created he them, enduing them with intelligence, sensibility, and will; they having the law of God written in their hearts, and power to fulfill it, being upright and free from all bias to evil.[g]

PROVIDENCE

12. God the Creator upholds and governs all creatures and things by his most wise and holy providence.[h]

a. [Dt 6.4; 1 Cor 8.4, 6; 1 Thes 1.9; Jn 4.24; Ex 3.14; 1 Tm 1.17; Ps 145.3; Gn 17.1; Rom 16.27; Mal 3.6]

b. [Jn 5.26; Acts 7.2; Ps 119.68; 1 Tm 6.15; Rom 9.15; Acts 17.24–25; Jb 22.2–3; Rom 11.36; Rv 4.11]

c. [2 Cor 13.14; Mt 3.16–17, 28.19]

d. [Ps 135.6; Is 46.9–11; Ex 20.3–17; Mt 22.33, 39; Eccl 12.13; 2 Cor 5.10; Rv 22.12; Mt 16.27]

e. [Dt 29.29; Acts 1.7; 1 Thes 5.1; Acts 20.27; Rom 2.12, 16; Rv 20.12]

f. [Gn 1.1; Is 44.24; Rom 1.20; Col 1.16; Heb 11.3; Gn 1.31; Ex 20.11]

g. [Gn 2.7, 1.26; Rom 2.14–15; Eccl 7.29]

h. [Heb 1.3; Mt 10.29–31; Rom 9.17]

13. God, in his providence, ordinarily works through the instrumentality of laws or means, yet is free to work with and above them, at his pleasure.[a]

14. God never leaves nor forsakes his people; yet when they fall into sin he chastises them in various ways, and makes even their own sin the occasion of discovering unto them their weakness and their need of greater watchfulness and dependence upon him for supporting grace.[b]

15. God's providence over the wicked is not designed to lead them to destruction, but to a knowledge of his goodness, and of his sovereign power over them, and thus to become a means of their repentance and reformation, or to be a warning to others; and if the wicked make it an occasion of hardening their hearts, it is because of their perversity, and not from necessity.[c]

16. While the providence of God, in general, embraces all creatures, it does, in a special manner, extend to his church.[d]

FALL OF MAN

17. Our first parents, being seduced by the subtlety and temptation of Satan, sinned in eating the forbidden fruit; whereupon, God was pleased, for his own glory and the good of mankind, to reveal the covenant of grace in Christ, by which a gracious probation was established for all men.[e]

18. By this sin they fell from their original uprightness, lost their communion with God, and so became dead in sin and defiled in all the faculties of their moral being. They being the root of all mankind, sin entered into the world through their act, and death by sin, and so death passed upon all men.[f]

19. From this original corruption also proceeds actual transgression.[g]

20. The remains of this corrupt nature are felt by those who are regenerated, nor will they altogether cease to operate and disturb during the present life.[h]

21. Sin, being a transgression of the law of God, brings guilt upon the transgressor, and subjects him to the wrath of God and to endless torment, unless pardoned through the mediation of Christ.[i]

a. [Mt 5.45; Is 9.10–11; Acts 27.24, 31; Hos 1.7; Rom 4.19–20; 2 Kgs 6.6]
b. [Ps 37.28; 2 Cor 12.7–9; Rom 8.2–3; Ps 119.71, 75; Heb 13.5–11]
c. [Jas 1.13; Mt 9.13; Lk 24.47; Rom 2.4; Prv 1.24–25; Jn 5.40; Ex 8.15, 22; Acts 12.23]
d. [Mt 16.18; Rom 8.28–31; Acts 5.11, 18.21]
e. [Gn 3.13; 2 Cor 11.3; Rom 5.12; Gn 3.15; Is 9.6; Mt 4.16; Jn 3.16–17; Rom 5.2–3; Rom 14]
f. [Gn 3.7–8; Eccl 7.29; Rom 3.23; Eph 2.1; Gn 6.5; Jer 17.9]
g. [Rom 5.12, 15–19; Jb 15.4; Ps 51.5; Jb 14.4; Jn 3.6; Eph 2.3]
h. [Rom 7.14, 17, 18, 23; Prv 20.9; Rom 7.20, 5, 7, 25]
i. [1 Jn 3.4; Rom 3.19; Gal 3.13; Rom 6.23]

GOD'S COVENANT WITH MAN

22. The first covenant made with man was a covenant of works, wherein life was promised to Adam upon condition of perfect and personal obedience.[a]

23. Man, by his fall, having made himself incapable of life by that covenant, the Lord was pleased to make the second, commonly called the covenant of grace, wherein he freely offers unto sinners life and salvation by Jesus Christ, requiring of them faith in him, that they may be saved. This covenant is frequently set forth in the Scriptures by the name of a testament, in reference to the death of Jesus Christ, the testator, and to the everlasting inheritance, with all things belonging to it, therein bequeathed.[b]

24. Under the Old Testament dispensation the covenant of grace was administered by promises, prophecies, sacrifices, circumcision, the paschal lamb, and other types and ordinances delivered to the Jews—all foresignifying Christ to come —which were sufficient, through the operation of the Holy Spirit, to instruct them savingly in the knowledge of God, and build them up in the faith of the Messiah.[c]

25. Under the New Testament dispensation, wherein Christ, the substance, is set forth, the ordinances in which the covenant of grace is dispensed are the preaching of the word and the administration of the sacraments of baptism and the Lord's supper, which are administered with more simplicity, yet in them it is held forth in more fullness and spiritual efficacy to all nations, Jews and Gentiles.[d]

26. As children were included with their parents in the covenant of grace under the Old Testament dispensation, so are they included in it under the New, and should, as under the Old, receive the appropriate sign and seal thereof.[e]

CHRIST THE MEDIATOR

27. Jesus Christ, the only-begotten Son of God, was verily appointed before the foundation of the world to be the Mediator between God and man, the Prophet, Priest, and King, the heir of all things, the propitiation for the sins of all mankind, the Head of his church, the Judge of the world, and the Savior of all true believers.[f]

28. The Son of God, the second person in the Trinity, did, when the full-

---

a. [Jb 9.32–33; Gal 3.12; Gn 2.16–17]

b. [Gal 3.21; Rom 8.3; Is 42.6; Mk 16.15–16; Jn 3.16; Heb 9.15–17, 7.22; Lk 22.20]

c. [2 Cor 3.6–9; Heb 8.9–10; Rom 4.11; Col 2.11, 17; 1 Cor 5.7]

d. [1 Cor 10.1–4; Heb 11.13; Gal 3.7–9, 14; 1 Cor 11.23–25]

e. [Gn 17.7, 11, 13; Acts 2.39; Rom 9.8; Acts 16.15, 33; 1 Cor 1.16]

f. [1 Pt 1.19–20; 1 Tm 2.5; Jn 3.16; Acts 3.22; Heb 5.6; Ps 2.6; Lk 1.33; Heb 1.2; 1 Jn 2.2, 4.10; Eph 2.20–22; Mt 21.42; 2 Tm 4.1, 8; 1 Pt 4.5; Acts 10.42; Rom 14.10; Lk 2.11; Jn 4.42; Acts 5.31; 1 Tm 4.10]

ness of time was come, take upon himself man's nature, yet without sin, being very God and very man, yet one Christ, the only Mediator between God and man.[a]

29. Jesus Christ, in his human nature, thus united to the divine, was sanctified and anointed with the Holy Spirit above measure, having in him all the treasures of wisdom and knowledge, in whom it pleased the Father that all fullness should dwell, to the end that, being holy, harmless, undefiled, and full of grace and truth, he might be thoroughly furnished to execute the office of a mediator and surety.[b]

30. That he might discharge the office of Mediator, Jesus Christ was made under the law, which he perfectly fulfilled, was crucified, died, and was buried, and remained under the power of death for a time, yet saw no corruption. On the third day he arose from the dead, and afterward ascended to heaven, where he sits on the right hand of God, making intercession for transgressors.[c]

31. Jesus Christ, by his perfect obedience and sacrifice of himself, which he, through the eternal Spirit, once offered unto God, became the propitiation for the sins of the whole world, so God can be just in justifying all who believe in Jesus.[d]

32. Although the work of redemption was not actually wrought by Christ until after his incarnation, yet the benefits thereof were communicated unto the believer, in all ages, successively, from the beginning of the world, by the Holy Spirit, and through such instrumentalities as God was pleased to employ.[e]

33. Jesus Christ tasted death for every man, and now makes intercession for transgressors, by virtue of which the Holy Spirit is given to convince of sin and enable man to believe and obey, governing the hearts of believers by his word and Spirit, overcoming all their enemies, by his almighty power and wisdom, in such manner and ways as are most consonant to his wonderful and unsearchable dispensation.[f]

FREE WILL

34. God, in creating man in his own likeness, endued him with intelligence, sensibility, and will, which form the basis of moral character, and render man capable of moral government.[g]

a. [Jn 1.1, 14; 1 Jn 5.20; Phil 2.6; Gal 4.4; Heb 2.17, 4.15; Rom 1.3-4; 1 Tm 2.5]

b. [Ps 14.7; Jn 3.34; Col 2.3, 1.19; Heb 7.22, 26; Acts 10.38]

c. [Gal 4.4; Mt 3.15, 5.17, 27.35, 50; Acts 2.31, 13.30, 37; 1 Cor 15.4; Mk 16.19; Rom 8.34; Heb 7.25; Rom 14.9-10]

d. [Heb 9.14; Rom 3.25-26, 5.6, 8, 10, 11; 2 Cor 5.14-15; Heb 2.9; 1 Jn 2.2]

e. [Gal 4.4-5; Gn 15.6; Rom 4.3, 5-7; Neh 9.20; Ps 143.10; Ps 51.11-12; Heb 1.1; Nm 12.6]

f. [Heb 2.9; 1 Jn 2.1; Rom 8.34; Jn 14.16-18, 16.8-11, 17.6, 8-11; Rom 8.33-39]

g. [Gn 1.26-27; Eph 4.24; Rv 22.17; Jn 5.40]

35. The freedom of the will is a fact of human consciousness, and is the sole ground of human accountability. Man, in his state of innocence, was both free and able to keep the divine law, also to violate it. Without any constraint, from either physical or moral causes, he did violate it.[a]

36. Man, by disobedience, lost his innocence, forfeited the favor of God, became corrupt in heart and inclined to evil. In this state of spiritual death and condemnation, man is still free and responsible; yet, without the illuminating influences of the Holy Spirit, he is unable either to keep the law or lay hold upon the hope set before him in the gospel.[b]

37. When the sinner is born of God, he loves him supremely, and steadfastly purposes to do his will; yet, because of remaining corruption, and of his imperfect knowledge of moral and spiritual things, he often wills what in itself is sinful. This imperfect knowledge and corruption remain, in greater or less force, during the present life; hence the conflict between the flesh and the spirit.[c]

DIVINE INFLUENCE

38. God the Father, having set forth his Son Jesus Christ as a propitiation for the sins of the world, does most graciously vouchsafe a manifestation of the Holy Spirit with the same intent to every man.[d]

39. The Holy Spirit, operating through the written word, and through such other means as God in his wisdom may choose, or directly, without means, so moves upon the hearts of men as to enlighten, reprove, and convince them of sin, of their lost estate, and of their need of salvation; and, by so doing, inclines them to come to Christ.[e]

40. This call of the Holy Spirit is purely of God's free grace alone, and not because of human merit, and is antecedent to all desire, purpose, and intention on the part of the sinner to come to Christ; so that while it is possible for all to be saved with it, none can be saved without it.[f]

41. This call is not irresistible, but is effectual in those only who, in penitence and faith, freely surrender themselves wholly to Christ, the only name whereby men can be saved.[g]

a. [Jos 24.15; Prv 1.29–31; Rom 2.12–15]

b. [Rom 5.12; Ez 18.4; Rom 8.6–8, 1.18–20, 3.19–20; 1 Cor 2.14; Jn 6.44, 1.9; 1 Cor 12.7; Rom 8.26]

c. [Rom 8.14–16; Jn 14.15; Rom 7.14–15, 23–24; Gal 5.17; Eccl 7.20]

d. [Rom 3.25; 1 Jn 2.2, 4.10; Heb 2.9; Jn 1.9; Is 49.6; 1 Cor 12.7]

e. [Heb 4.12; Rv 22.17; Jn 16.8, 12.32; Rom 5.5]

f. [1 Tm 1.9; Ti 3.4–5; 1 Cor 2.14; Rom 8.7; Eph 2.5; Jn 6.37]

g. [Prv 1.24–25; Jn 5.40; Acts 7.51; 1 Thes 5.19; Mt 9.28–29; Lk 13.3, 5]

REPENTANCE UNTO LIFE

42. Repentance unto life is a change of mind and feeling toward God, induced by the agency of the Holy Spirit, wherein the sinner resolutely purposes to forsake all sin, to turn unto God, and to walk in all his commandments.[a]

43. There is no merit in repentance, or in any other human exercise; yet God is pleased to require all men to repent.[b]

44. As all men are required to make full and frank confession of sin to God, so he that gives grounds of offense to the church, or trespasses against his brother, should confess his errors, make amendment and due restitution, so far as is in his power.[c]

SAVING FAITH

45. Saving faith, including assent to the truth of God's holy word, is the act of receiving and resting upon Christ alone for salvation, and is accompanied by contrition for sin and a full purpose of heart to turn from it and to live unto God.[d]

46. While there is no merit in faith, yet it is the condition of salvation. It is not of the nature of good works, from which it must be distinguished.[e]

47. This faith may be tried in many ways, but the believer has the promise of ultimate victory through Christ.[f]

JUSTIFICATION

48. All those who truly repent of their sins, and in faith commit themselves to Christ, God freely justifies, not by infusing righteousness into them, but by pardoning their sins and by counting and accepting their persons as righteous; not for any thing wrought in them or done by them, but for Christ's sake alone; not by imputing faith itself, or any other evangelical obedience, to them as their righteousness, but by imputing the obedience and satisfaction of Christ unto them, they receiving and resting on him and his righteousness by faith.[g]

49. Justification is purely of God's free grace, and is a full pardon for all sins, and exemption from all their penal consequences; but it imparts no moral

a. [Acts 11.18; Jn 3.27, 15.5; Lk 24.47; Acts 20.21; Ez 18.30–31, 36.31; 2 Cor 7.11]

b. [Is 64.6; Ez 16.63; Acts 2.38, 3.19, 17.30]

c. [Ps 32.5–6; Prv 28.13; 1 Jn 1.9; Jas 5.16; Lk 17.3–4, 19.8; 2 Cor 2.8]

d. [Ps 2.12; 1 Pt 2.2, 6; Jn 14.1, 11.26–27, 6.68–69; Mt 19.27–29; 2 Cor 4.13; Rom 10.14, 17; Eph 2.8; Rom 1.16–17; 1 Thes 2.13; 1 Jn 5.10]

e. [Rom 4.16; Jn 3.36; Acts 16.31; Jn 3.14–16, 18]

f. [Lk 22.31–32; Mt 6.30, 8.10; Rom 4.19–20; Heb 5.13–14, 10.22; 1 Jn 5.4–5; Heb 12.2]

g. [Rom 3.24, 4.5, 8; 2 Cor 5.19, 21; Rom 5.17–19]

qualities or merits to the believer, being strictly a legal transaction. Though of free grace alone, it is conditioned upon faith, and is assured to none but penitent and true believers, who, being justified, have peace with God through our Lord Jesus Christ.[a]

50. God continues to forgive the sins of those who are justified, and although he will never permit them to fall from the state of justification, yet they may, by their sins, fall under God's fatherly displeasure, and not have the light of his countenance restored unto them until they humble themselves, confess their sins, and renew their consecration to God.[b]

REGENERATION

51. Those who believe in the Lord Jesus Christ are regenerated, or born from above, renewed in spirit, and made new creatures in Christ.[c]

52. The necessity for this moral purification arises out of the enmity of the human heart against God, its insubordination to his law, and its consequent incapacity to love and glorify God.[d]

53. Regeneration is of God's free grace alone, and is the work of the Holy Spirit, who, by taking of the things which are Christ's and showing them unto the sinner, enables him to lay hold on Christ. This renewal of the heart by the Holy Spirit is not of the nature of a physical but of a moral work—a purification of the heart by faith.[e]

54. All infants dying in infancy, and all persons who have never had the faculty of reason, are regenerated and saved.[f]

ADOPTION

55. All those who are regenerated, and are thus changed into the image of his Son, God the Father is pleased to make partakers of the grace of adoption, by which they are taken into the number, and enjoy the liberties and privileges, of the children of God; have his name put upon them; receive the Spirit of adoption; have access to the throne of grace with boldness; are enabled to cry, Abba, Father; are pitied, protected, provided for, and chastened by him, as by a father, yet never cast off,

a. [Phil 3.9; Rom 3.25–26; Jn 5.24; Rom 8.1]

b. [Mt 6.12; 1 Jn 2.1; Lk 22.32; Jn 10.28; Heb 10.14; Ps 89.31–33; Ps 51]

c. [1 Jn 5.1; Jn 3.5–7; Rom 12.2; Ti 3.5; 2 Cor 5.17; Eph 2.10]

d. [Rom 8.6–7; 2 Cor 6.15; Am 3.3; Rom 1.28–32; Mt 15.18–20]

e. [Eph 2.8; Phil 1.29; Jn 3.5–6, 1.13; Ti 3.5; Jn 16.13–14; 1 Cor 2.10; 1 Jn 2.27; 1 Cor 12.3; Jn 3.5–6; Zec 4.6; Acts 15.9; 1 Pt 1.22–23; Gal 3.7, 26; 1 Jn 5.1; Jn 1.12; 2 Cor 3.13; Ti 3.5]

f. [Lk 18.15–16; Acts 2.38–39; Jn 3.3]

but sealed to the day of redemption, and inherit the promises as heirs of everlasting salvation.[a]

SANCTIFICATION

56. Sanctification is a doctrine of the Holy Scriptures, and it is the duty and privilege of believers to avail themselves of its inestimable benefits, as taught in the word of God. A state of sinless perfection in this life is not authorized by the Scriptures, and is a dogma of dangerous tendency.[b]

GROWTH IN GRACE

57. Growth in grace is secured by personal consecration to the service of God, regular attention to the means of grace, the reading of the Holy Scriptures, prayer, the ministrations of the sanctuary, and all known Christian duties. By such means the believer's faith is much increased, his tendency to sin weakened, the lusts of the flesh mortified, and he more and more strengthened in all saving graces, and in the practice of holiness, without which no man shall see the Lord.[c]

GOOD WORKS

58. Good works are such only as God has commanded in his word, and not such as may be devised by men out of blind zeal, or any pretense of good intention.[d]

59. Those who, in their obedience and love, attain the greatest height in this life, still fall short of that perfection which the divine law requires; yet their good works are accepted of God, who, looking upon them in his Son, is pleased to accept and reward that which is sincere, although accompanied with many weaknesses and imperfections.[e]

PRESERVATION OF BELIEVERS

60. Those whom God has justified, he will also glorify; consequently, the truly regenerated soul will not totally fall away from a state of grace, but will be preserved to everlasting life.[f]

a. [Eph 1.5; Gal 4.4–6; Rom 8.15–17; Ps 103.13; Mal 3.17; Mt 6.30, 32; 1 Pt 5.7; Heb 12.6; Lam 3.31; Eph 4.30, 1.13; Heb 6.12; Gal 3.29; 1 Pt 1.4; Heb 1.14]

b. [2 Thes 2.13; 1 Pt 1.2; Heb 9.13–14; 2 Cor 6.16–18; Ps 4.3; 1 Thes 5.23; Eph 5.26–27; 2 Cor 7.1; Rom 6.22; 1 Cor 6.11; 1 Thes 5.23; Phil 3.12]

c. [2 Pt 3.18; 2 Cor 6.17; Ps 4.3; 2 Cor 7.1; Jn 5.29; 2 Cor 13.7; Phil 3.9–11; Col 1.9; 1 Thes 5.17, 23; Heb 10.26; Acts 2.42, 13.42, 16.13, 18.4; Heb 6.12; 2 Pt 1.5, 10; Col 1.11; Eph 3.16; Mk 4.28, 31–32; 1 Pt 2.2]

d. [Mi 6.8; Rom 12.2; Heb 13.21; Mt 15.9; Jn 16.2]

e. [Lk 17.10; Jb 9.2–3; Gal 5.17; Eph 1.6; 1 Pt 2.5; Heb 11.4; 2 Cor 8.12; Heb 6.10]

f. [Ps 37.28; Rom 8.38–39; Jn 3.16, 5.24, 10.28–29]

61. The preservation of believers depends on the unchangeable love and power of God, the merits, advocacy, and intercession of Jesus Christ, the abiding of the Holy Spirit and seed of God within them, and the nature of the covenant of grace. Nevertheless, true believers, through the temptations of Satan, the world, and the flesh, and the neglect of the means of grace, may fall into sin, incur God's displeasure, and grieve the Holy Spirit, and thus be deprived of some measure of their graces and comforts, and have their consciences wounded; but the Christian will never rest satisfied therein.[a]

CHRISTIAN ASSURANCE

62. Those who truly believe in the Lord Jesus Christ, and love him in sincerity, endeavoring to walk in all good conscience before him, may, in this life, be certainly assured that they are in a state of grace, and may rejoice in the hope of the glory of God, which hope shall never make them ashamed.[b]

63. This assurance is founded upon the divine promises, the consciousness of peace with God, the testimony of the Holy Spirit witnessing with their spirits that they are the children of God, and is the earnest of their inheritance.[c]

64. This comfortable assurance of salvation is not an invariable accompaniment of faith in Christ; hence the believer may have many sore conflicts before he is made a partaker of it; yet he may, by the right use of the means of grace—through the agency of the Holy Spirit—attain thereunto; therefore, it is the duty of everyone to give diligence to make his calling and election sure.[d]

65. As this assurance may be very much strengthened by full consecration to God and fidelity in his service, so it may be weakened by worldly-mindedness and negligence in Christian duty, which result in darkness and in doubt; yet true believers have the promise of God that he will never leave nor forsake them.[e]

THE LAW OF GOD

66. The moral law is the rule of duty growing immediately out of the relations of rational creatures to their Creator and to each other. These relations being the product of the divine purpose, the law has its ultimate source in the will of the Creator.[f]

---

a. [2 Tm 2.19; Jer 31.3; 1 Pt 1.5; 1 Jn 2.1; Rom 5.10; Col 3.3; Heb 7.25, 10.10, 14; Jn 14.16–17; 1 Jn 3.9; Jer 32.40; Jn 17.9, 21–22; 2 Sm 12.13–14; Rv 3.4; Lk 22.31–34]

b. [1 Jn 2.3, 5.13; Rom 5.2, 5; 2 Cor 5.1, 6]

c. [Heb 6.17–18; 2 Pt 1.4–5, 10–11; 1 Jn 3.14, 2.3; 2 Cor 1.12; Rom 8.15–16; Eph 1.13–14]

d. [1 Jn 5.10; 1 Cor 2.12; 1 Jn 4.13; Heb 6.11–12; 2 Pt 1.10; Rom 5.5, 14.17, 15.13; Ps 119.32; 2 Pt 1.10]

e. [Ps 51.8, 12, 14; Eph 4.30; Jn 3.20; Jb 13.15; Mi 7.7–9]

f. [Mt 22.37; Ex 20.1–2; Eph 6.1, 4, 5, 9, 5.22, 26; Ti 3.1; Heb 13.7; Is 46.10; Ps 33.11, 105.3]

67. This law is of universal and perpetual obligation, and is written primarily upon the hearts of all accountable beings. It was sufficiently known to Adam to enable him to know and do the will of God, and thus, by the righteousness of works, secure eternal life.[a]

68. After Adam's fall, and that of his posterity through him, a written form of the law became necessary. This was given in the Decalogue, or Ten Commandments, a summary of which is given in these words: Thou shalt love the Lord thy God with all thy heart, and with all thy soul, and with all thy strength, and with all thy mind, and thy neighbor as thyself.[b]

69. This law is not set aside, but rather established, by the gospel, which is the divine expedient by which sinners are saved, and the end of the law fully met. It accordingly remains in full force as the rule of conduct. It must not, therefore, be confounded with the ceremonial law, which was abolished under the New Testament dispensation.[c]

70. The penalties of this law are the natural and subjective sequences of transgression, and, unless set aside by the provisions of the gospel, must of necessity be eternal; and such are they declared to be by the Holy Scriptures. These moral retributions must be distinguished from judicial punishments, which are arbitrary, objective, and temporary, and are always inflicted, as occasion may require, for administrative purposes.[d]

CHRISTIAN LIBERTY

71. The liberty that Christ has secured to believers under the gospel consists in freedom from the guilt and penal consequences of sin, in their free access to God, and in their yielding obedience to him, not from a slavish fear, but from a cheerful and confiding love.[e]

72. God, who alone is Lord of the conscience, has left it free, in matters of faith and worship, from such opinions and commandments of men as may be contrary to his word.[f]

73. Those who, upon pretense of Christian liberty, practice any sin, or cherish any lust, do thereby destroy the end of Christian liberty, which is, that being

a. [Gn 1.26, 2.17; Rom 1.18–19, 2.14–15, 10.5; Jn 1.9]

b. [Rom 5.12, 19; Ex 20.1–17; Mk 12.30]

c. [Mt 5.17–18; Gal 3.21, 24; Rom 3.24–25, 31, 6.15, 13.8–9]

d. [Gn 2.17; Rom 6.23, 8.6; Jn 3.36; Mt 25.46; Jn 5.29; Rv 14.11; Lk 16.24; 1 Pt 3.19–20; Jude 7; Gn 6.5, 19.24–25; Acts 12.23]

e. [Ti 2.14; Gal 1.4, 3.13; Rom 8.14–15; 1 Jn 4.18; Jn 14.21]

f. [Rom 14.4; Acts 4.19, 5.29]

delivered from the dominion of sin, we may serve the Lord without fear in righteousness all our days.[a]

74. Those who, upon a similar pretense, shall oppose the proper exercise of any lawful authority, whether civil or ecclesiastical, and thereby resist the ordinance of God, may lawfully be called to account, and be subjected to the censures of the church.[b]

RELIGIOUS WORSHIP

75. Religious worship is to be rendered to God the Father, Son, and Holy Spirit, and to him alone; not to angels, saints, or any other creature; and, since the fall, this worship is acceptable only through the mediation of the Lord Jesus Christ.[c]

76. Prayer with thanksgiving, being one special part of religious worship, is required of all men; and, by the help of the Holy Spirit, is made efficacious through Christ, when offered according to his will. Prayer is to be made for things lawful, and for the living, but not for the dead.[d]

77. The reading of the Holy Scriptures, attendance upon the ministrations of the word, the use of psalms and sacred songs, the proper observance of the Christian sacraments, visiting the sick, contributing to the relief of the poor, and the support and spread of the gospel, are all proper acts of religious worship. Religious vows, solemn fastings, and thanksgivings, are also acts of religious worship, and are of much benefit when properly performed.[e]

78. God is to be worshiped in spirit and in truth, in secret, in private families daily, and in the public assembly.[f]

SABBATH DAY

79. God has been pleased to appoint one day in seven to be kept holy unto him, which, from the beginning of the world to the resurrection of Christ, was the last day of the week; and, after the resurrection of Christ, was changed unto the first day of the week, which in the Scriptures is called the Lord's day.[g]

80. The Sabbath is kept holy unto the Lord by resting from employments

a. [Gal 5.13; 1 Pt 2.16; 2 Pt 2.19; Jn 7.34]

b. [1 Pt 2.13–14; Heb 13.17; 1 Cor 5.1, 5, 11, 13; 2 Thes 3.14]

c. [Jn 5.22; Col 2.18; 2 Cor 13.14; Rv 19.10; Rom 1.25; Jn 14.6; 1 Tm 2.5; Eph 2.13]

d. [Phil 4.6; Ps 65.2; Jn 14.13–14; Rom 8.26; 1 Jn 5.14; 1 Tm 2.1–2; 2 Sm 12.21–23]

e. [Jn 5.39; Acts 17.11; Lk 24.27, 32, 45; Col 3.16; Lk 22.19; Mt 28.19; Jos 1.17; Mt 25.22–23; 2 Cor 9.7; Dt 15.10, 25.4; 1 Cor 9.14; Prv 3.9; Acts 18.18; Jl 2.12; Mt 9.15]

f. [Jn 4.23–24; Jb 1.6; 2 Sm 6.18, 20; Mt 6.6, 11; Heb 10.25; Acts 2.42]

g. [Ex 20.3–11; Is 56.2, 4; Gn 2.3; 1 Cor 16.1–2; Acts 20.7; Rv 1.10] and recreations of a secular character, by the public and private worship of God, and by works of necessity and mercy.[a]

LAWFUL OATHS AND VOWS

81. The name of God only is that by which men ought to swear, and therein it is to be used with all reverence; therefore, to swear vainly or rashly by that glorious and dreadful name, or to swear at all by any other thing, is sinful. Yet, an oath is warranted by the word of God, under the New Testament as well as under the Old, when imposed by lawful authority.[b]

82. Whosoever takes an oath ought duly to consider the weightiness of so solemn an act, and therein to avouch nothing but what he is fully persuaded is the truth. Neither may a man bind himself by oath to anything but what is good and just, or what he believes so to be, and what he is able and resolved to perform.[c]

83. An oath is to be taken in the plain and common sense of the words, without equivocation or mental reservation. It cannot oblige to sin; but in anything not sinful, being taken, it binds to performance, although to a man's own hurt.[d]

84. A vow is of a like nature with an oath, and ought to be made with the like religious care, and to be performed with the like faithfulness. No man may vow to do anything forbidden in the word of God, or what would hinder any duty therein commanded, or which is not in his own power, and for the performance whereof he has no promise or ability from God.[e]

CIVIL GOVERNMENT

85. God, the supreme Lord and King of all the world, has ordained civil officers to be under him over one people, for his own glory and the public good; and, to this end, has armed them with power for the defense of the innocent and the punishment of evildoers.[f]

86. It is lawful for Christians to accept civil offices when called thereunto, in the management whereof they ought especially to maintain piety, justice, and peace, according to the wholesome laws of each commonwealth.[g]

87. Civil officers may not assume to themselves the administration of the

a. [Ex 16.29–30, 31.15–16; Mt 12.4–8]

b. [Dt 6.11; Jer 5.7; Jas 5.12; Heb 6.16; 1 Kgs 8.31]

c. [Jer 4.2; Gn 24.2–3; Neh 5.12]

d. [Ps 24.4; Jer 13; Ps 15.4]

e. [Is 19.21; Eccl 5.4–5; Ps 66.13–14; Acts 23.12; Mk 6.26]

f. [Rom 13.1, 3–4; 1 Pt 2.13–14]

g. [Prv 8.15–16; Ps 82.3–4; 2 Sm 23.3; Lk 3.14; Acts 10.1–2; Rom 13.4]

word and the sacraments, or in the least interfere in matters of faith; yet it is their duty to protect the church of our common Lord, without giving preference to any denomination of Christians. And, as Jesus Christ has appointed a government and discipline in his church, no law of any commonwealth should interfere therewith, but should provide that all religious and ecclesiastical assemblies shall be held without molestation or disturbance.[a]

88. It is the duty of the people to pray for magistrates, to obey their lawful commands, and to be subject to their authority for conscience' sake.[b]

MARRIAGE AND DIVORCE

89. Marriage is to be between one man and one woman; neither is it lawful for any man to have more than one wife, nor for any woman to have more than one husband, at the same time.[c]

90. Marriage was ordained for the mutual help of husband and wife, and for the benefit of the human race.[d]

91. Marriages ought not to be within the degrees of consanguinity or affinity forbidden in the word of God, nor can such marriages be justified by any human law.[e]

92. The marriage relation should not be dissolved for any cause not justified by the teachings of the word of God, and any immorality in relation to its dissolution is cognizable by the church courts.[f]

THE CHURCH

93. The universal church, which is invisible, consists of all those who have become children of God by faith, and joint heirs with Christ, who is the head thereof.[g]

94. The visible church consists of those who hold to the fundamental doctrines of Christianity in respect to matters of faith and morals, and have entered into formal covenant with God and some organized body of Christians for the maintenance of religious worship. The children of such are included in the covenant relations of their parents, and are properly under the special care of the church.[h]

a. [2 Chr 26.16; 1 Cor 4.1–2; Jn 18.36; Mal 2.7; Is 59.21; Ps 105.15; 2 Sm 23.3; 1 Tm 2.1]
b. [1 Tm 2.1–2; 1 Pt 2.17; Rom 13.5–7; Ti 3.1]
c. [1 Cor 7.2; Mk 10.6–9]
d. [Gn 2.13; 1 Cor 7.28]
e. [1 Cor 5.1; Mk 6.18]
f. [Mt 1.18–20, 5.31–32, 19.9; Rom 7.2–3; 1 Cor 7.15]
g. [Eph 1.10, 22–23; Col 1.18; Eph 5.23, 27, 32]
h. [1 Cor 1.2, 12.12–13; Ps 2.8; Gn 17.7; Acts 2.39; Rom 11.16; Gal 3.7, 9, 14; Prv 22.6]

95. Unto this visible church Christ has given the ministry, the word, and the ordinances for its edification, and, by his own presence in spirit, makes them effectual thereunto. The Lord Jesus Christ is the only head of his church on earth.[a]

CHRISTIAN COMMUNION

96. All those united to Christ by faith have fellowship with him, and, being united to one another in love, have communion one with another, and are required to bear one another's burdens, and so fulfill the law of Christ.[b]

97. While it is required of all Christians to live in fellowship, it is the especial duty of those belonging to the same denomination; and also to cooperate in sustaining public worship, and whatever measures are adjudged best for the spiritual interests of the church and the glory of God.[c]

THE SACRAMENTS

98. As under the Old Testament dispensation two sacraments were ordained, circumcision and the Passover; so, under the New, there are but two—that is to say, baptism and the Lord's supper.[d]

BAPTISM

99. Water baptism is a sacrament of the New Testament, ordained by Jesus Christ as a sign or symbol of the baptism of the Holy Spirit, and as the seal of the covenant of grace.[e]

100. The outward element to be used in this sacrament is water, wherewith the party is to be baptized into the name of the Father, and of the Son, and of the Holy Spirit, by an ordained minister of the gospel.[f]

101. Baptism is rightly administered by pouring or sprinkling water upon the person, yet the validity of this sacrament does not depend upon any particular mode of administration.[g]

102. The proper subjects of water baptism are believing adults; also infants, one or both of whose parents or guardians are believers.[h]

a. [Eph 4.11–13; Is 59.21; Mt 28.19–20; Col 1.18; Eph 1.22]

b. [1 Jn 1.3; Eph 3.16–17; Jn 1.16; Phil 3.10; Eph 4.15–16; 1 Thes 5.11, 14]

c. [Heb 10.24–25; Acts 2.42, 46; 1 Jn 3.17; Gn 28.22; Nm 18.21; 2 Chr 31.4–5; Neh 13.10–12]

d. [Lk 22.19–20; 1 Cor 11.23–26; Mt 28.19–20]

e. [Mt 3.11; Jn 3.5; Ti 3.5; Rom 4.11; Gn 17.10]

f. [Acts 10.47, 8.36, 38; Mt 28.19]

g. [Acts 2.41, 16.33; Mk 7.4; Lk 11.38; Heb 9.10, 19–21; 1 Pt 3.21]

h. [Acts 10.47–48; Mt 28.19; Gn 17.7, 9; Acts 2.38–39, 16.14–15, 33; 1 Cor 1.16]

103. There is no saving efficacy in water baptism, yet it is a duty of all believers to confess Christ in this solemn ordinance, and it is also the duty of all believing parents to consecrate their children to God in baptism.[a]

THE LORD'S SUPPER

104. The sacrament, commonly called the Lord's supper, was instituted by the Lord Jesus Christ at the close of his last Passover supper, as a perpetual remembrancer of his passion and death on the cross, by which sacrifice of himself he was made the propitiation for the sins of the whole world.[b]

105. In this sacrament no sacrifice of any kind is offered for sin, but the one perfect offering of Christ as a sufficient sacrifice is set forth and commemorated by appropriate symbols. These symbols are bread and wine, which, though figuratively called the body and blood of Christ, nevertheless remain, after consecration, literal bread and wine, and give no countenance to the doctrines of consubstantiation and transubstantiation.[c]

106. As in this sacrament the communicants have visibly set before them symbols of the Savior's passion, they should not approach the holy communion without due self-examination, reverence, humility, and gratitude.[d]

107. All who love the Lord Jesus in sincerity and in truth should, on all suitable occasions, express their devotion to him by the use of the symbols of his death. But none who have not faith to discern the Lord's body should partake of his holy communion.[e]

CHURCH AUTHORITY

108. The Lord Jesus, as King and Head of his church, has therein appointed a government entrusted to church officers, distinct from the civil government.[f]

109. By divine appointment the officers of the visible church have the power to admit members into its communion, to admonish, suspend, or expel the disorderly and to restore those who, in the judgment of charity, have repented of their sins.[g]

---

a. [Acts 8.13, 23; Lk 23.43; Rom 4.10–11, 2.26–29; Gn 17.10, 27]
b. [Lk 22.19–20; 1 Cor 11.23–26; Heb 7.23–24, 27, 10.11–12, 14, 18; Rom 3.25; 1 Jn 2.2, 4, 10]
c. [Heb 10.11–12, 14, 18; Lk 22.19–20; Acts 3.21; Lk 24.6, 39]
d. [1 Cor 5.7–8, 10.16, 11.28]
e. [1 Cor 5.6–8, 13, 10.21, 11.27, 29; 2 Cor 6.14–16; 2 Thes 3.6, 14–15; Ex 12.14]
f. [Is 9.6–7; Jn 18.36; 1 Tm 5.17; 1 Thes 5.12; 1 Cor 12.28; Ps 2.6–9]
g. [Acts 2.41, 5.14; 1 Thes 5.12; 2 Thes 3.6, 14–15; Mt 18.15–17; 1 Tm 5.20]

CHURCH COURTS

110. Church government implies the existence of church courts, invested with legislative, judicial, and executive authority; and the Scriptures recognize such institutions, some of subordinate and some of superior authority, each having its own particular sphere of duties and privileges in reference to matters ministerial and ecclesiastical, yet all subordinate to the same general design.[a]

111. It is the prerogative of these courts, ministerially, to determine controversies of faith and questions of morals, to set down rules and directions for the better ordering of the public worship of God and government of his church, to receive complaints in cases of maladministration, and authoritatively to determine the same, which determinations are to be received with reverence and submission.[b]

DEATH AND THE RESURRECTION

112. The bodies of men, after death, return to dust; but their spirits, being immortal, return to God who gave them. The spirits of the righteous are received into heaven, where they behold the face of God in light and glory, waiting for the full redemption of their bodies; and the spirits of the wicked are cast into hell, where they are reserved to the judgment of the great day. The Scriptures speak of no other place for departed spirits.[c]

113. At the resurrection, those who are alive shall not die, but be changed; and all the dead shall be raised up, spiritual and immortal, and spirits and bodies be reunited forever. There shall be a resurrection both of the just and the unjust: of the unjust to dishonor, and of the just unto honor; the bodies of the latter shall be fashioned like unto Christ's glorious body.[d]

THE JUDGMENT

114. God has appointed a day wherein he will judge the world in righteousness by Jesus Christ—to whom all power and judgment are given by the Father—in which not only the apostate angels shall be judged, but likewise all persons who have lived upon earth shall appear before the tribunal of Christ, and shall receive according to what they have done, whether good or evil.[e]

115. After the judgment, the wicked shall go away into eternal punishment, but the righteous into eternal life.[f]

a. [Acts 15.2, 4, 6, 22–23, 25]

b. [Acts 16.4; 1 Tm 4.14; Acts 14.23, 20.17; 1 Tm 5.17; Ti 1.5; Jas 5.14]

c. [Gn 3.19; Acts 13.36; Lk 23.43; Eccl 12.7; Heb 12.23; Phil 1.23; 2 Cor 5.1; 1 Jn 3.2; Lk 16.22, 24; Mt 25.46; Jude 6–7]

d. [1 Thes 4.17; 1 Cor 15.51–52; Acts 24.15; Jn 5.28–29; Phil 3.21]

e. [Acts 17.31; Jn 5.22, 27; Jude 6; 2 Pt 2.4; 2 Cor 5.10; Eccl 12.14; Rom 2.16, 14.10, 12; Mt 12.36–37]

f. [Mt 25.46; Rv 14.11; Jude 7]

New Hampshire Baptist Convention, *Declaration of Faith (The New Hampshire Confession)*, 1833/1853

Described by the editor of the standard comprehensive collection of Baptist creeds and confessions, William L. Lumpkin, as "the most widely disseminated creedal declaration of American Baptists," which has been adopted by a diverse roster of Baptist church bodies in America who have made it their own,[1] *The New Hampshire Confession*, as its name indicates, came into being as a response to the perceived need of Baptist congregations in New Hampshire, autonomous though each of them of course was, for "such a declaration of faith and practice, together with a covenant, as may be thought agreeable and consistent with the views of all our churches in this state."

Its final draft, submitted on 15 January 1833 and accepted by the New Hampshire Convention, was the work of John Newton Brown, on the basis of earlier committee versions. Twenty years later, in 1853, Brown, who had meanwhile become the editorial secretary of the American Baptist Publication Society, revised the original *Confession* of 1833 in numerous passages and expanded it by the addition of articles 8 and 10, "Of Repentance and Faith" and "Of Sanctification." (Lumpkin uses brackets and footnotes to indicate the variant readings between the versions of 1833 and 1853 but does not supply the proof texts, which Schaff does.) As we have done with other confessions, for example → *The Confession of Faith of the Cumberland Presbyterian Church*, it is the definitive version of 1853 that we present here.

Edition: Lumpkin, 361–67.

Literature: Lumpkin, 360–61; Schaff, 3:742–48.

---

1. Lumpkin, 361.

New Hampshire Baptist Convention, *Declaration of Faith (The New Hampshire Confession)*, 1833/1853

1. OF THE SCRIPTURES

We believe that the Holy Bible was written by men divinely inspired, and is a perfect treasure of heavenly instruction;[a] that it has God for its author, salvation for its end,[b] and truth without any mixture of error for its matter;[c] that it reveals the principles by which God will judge us;[d] and therefore is, and shall remain to the end of the world, the true center of Christian union,[e] and the supreme standard by which all human conduct, creeds, and opinions should be tried.[f]

2. OF THE TRUE GOD

We believe that there is one, and only one, living and true God, an infinite, intelligent Spirit, whose name is Jehovah, the Maker and Supreme Ruler of heaven and earth;[g] inexpressibly glorious in holiness,[h] and worthy of all possible honor, confidence, and love;[i] that in the unity of the Godhead there are three persons, the Father, the Son, and the Holy Ghost;[j] equal in every divine perfection,[k] and executing distinct and harmonious offices in the great work of redemption.[l]

3. OF THE FALL OF MAN

We believe that man was created in holiness, under the law of his Maker;[m] but by voluntary transgression fell from that holy and happy state;[n] in consequence of which all mankind are now sinners,[o] not by constraint, but choice;[p] being by nature

a. [2 Tm 3.16-17; 2 Pt 1.21; 1 Sm 23.2; Acts 1.16, 3.21; Jn 10.35; Lk 16.29-31; Ps 119.111; Rom 3.1-2]

b. [2 Tm 3.15; 1 Pt 1.10-12; Acts 11.14; Rom 1.16; Mk 16.16; Jn 5.38-39]

c. [Prv 30.5-6; Jn 17.17; Rv 22.18-19; Rom 3.4]

d. [Rom 2.12; Jn 12.47-48; 1 Cor 4.3-4; Lk 10.10-16, 12.47-48]

e. [Phil 3.16; Eph 4.3-6; Phil 2.1-2; 1 Cor 1.10; 1 Pt 4.11]

f. [1 Jn 4.1; Is 8.20; 1 Thes 5.21; 2 Cor 13.5; Acts 17.11; 1 Jn 4.6; Jude 3, 5; Eph 6.17; Ps 119.59-60; Phil 1.9-11]

g. [Jn 4.24; Ps 147.5, 83.18; Heb 3.4; Rom 1.20; Jer 10.10]

h. [Ex 15.11; Is 6.3; 1 Pt 1.15-16; Rv 4.6-8]

i. [Mk 12.30; Rv 4.11; Mt 10.37; Jer 2.12-13]

j. [Mt 28.19; Jn 15.26; 1 Cor 12.4-6; 1 Jn 5.7]

k. [Jn 10.30, 5.17, 14.23, 17.5, 10; Acts 5.3-4; 1 Cor 2.10-11; Phil 2.5-6]

l. [Eph 2.18; 2 Cor 13.14; Rv 1.4-5, 2.7]

m. [Gn 1.27, 31; Eccl 7.29; Acts 16.26; Gn 2.16]

n. [Gn 3.6-24; Rom 5.12]

o. [Rom 5.19; Jn 3.6; Ps 51.5; Rom 5.15-19, 8.7]

p. [Is 53.6; Gn 6.12; Rom 3.9-18]

utterly void of that holiness required by the law of God, positively inclined to evil; and therefore under just condemnation to eternal ruin,[a] without defense or excuse.[b]

4. OF THE WAY OF SALVATION

We believe that the salvation of sinners is wholly of grace,[c] through the mediatorial offices of the Son of God;[d] who by the appointment of the Father, freely took upon him our nature, yet without sin;[e] honored the divine law by his personal obedience,[f] and by his death made a full atonement for our sins;[g] that having risen from the dead, he is now enthroned in heaven;[h] and uniting in his wonderful person the tenderest sympathies with divine perfections, he is every way qualified to be a suitable, a compassionate, and an all-sufficient Savior.[i]

5. OF JUSTIFICATION

[Jn 1.16; Eph 3.8] We believe that the great gospel blessing which Christ secures to such as believe in him is justification;[j] that justification includes the pardon of sin,[k] and the promise of eternal life on principles of righteousness;[l] that it is bestowed, not in consideration of any works of righteousness which we have done, but solely through faith in the Redeemer's blood;[m] by virtue of which faith his perfect righteousness is freely imputed to us of God;[n] that it brings us into a state of most blessed peace and favor with God, and secures every other blessing needful for time and eternity.[o]

6. OF THE FREENESS OF SALVATION

We believe that the blessings of salvation are made free to all by the gospel;[p] that it is the immediate duty of all to accept them by a cordial, penitent, and obedient

a. [Eph 2.1–3; Rom 1.18, 32, 2.1–16; Gal 3.10; Mt 20.15]

b. [Ez 18.19–20; Rom 1.20, 3.19; Gal 3.22]

c. [Eph 2.5; Mt 18.11; 1 Jn 4.10; 1 Cor 3.5–7; Acts 15.11]

d. [Jn 3.16, 1.1–14; Heb 4.14, 12.24]

e. [Phil 2.6–7; Heb 2.9, 14; 2 Cor 5.21]

f. [Is 42.21; Phil 2.8; Gal 4.4–5; Rom 3.21]

g. [Is 53.4–5; Mt 20.28; Rom 4.25, 3.21–26; 1 Jn 4.10, 2.2; 1 Cor 15.1–3; Heb 9.13–15]

h. [Heb 1.8, 3, 8.1; Col 3.1–4]

i. [Heb 7.25; Col 2.9; Heb 2.18, 7.26; Ps 89.19; Ps 14]

j. [Acts 13.39; Is 3.11–12; Rom 8.1]

k. [Rom 5.9; Zec 13.1; Mt 9.6; Acts 10.43]

l. [Rom 5.17; Ti 3.5–6; 1 Pt 3.7; 1 Jn 2.25; Rom 5.21]

m. [Rom 4.4–5, 5.21, 6.23; Phil 3.7–9]

n. [Rom 5.19, 3.24–26, 4.23–25; 1 Jn 2.12]

o. [Rom 5.1–3, 11; 1 Cor 1.30–31; Mt 6.33; 1 Tm 4.8]

p. [Is 55.1; Rv 22.17; Lk 14.17]

faith;[a] and that nothing prevents the salvation of the greatest sinner on earth but his own inherent depravity and voluntary rejection of the gospel;[b] which rejection involves him in an aggravated condemnation.[c]

7. OF GRACE IN REGENERATION

We believe that, in order to be saved, sinners must be regenerated, or born again;[d] that regeneration consists in giving a holy disposition to the mind;[e] that it is effected in a manner above our comprehension by the power of the Holy Spirit, in connection with divine truth,[f] so as to secure our voluntary obedience to the gospel;[g] and that its proper evidence appears in the holy fruits of repentance, and faith, and newness of life.[h]

8. OF REPENTANCE AND FAITH

We believe that repentance and faith are sacred duties, and also inseparable graces, wrought in our souls by the regenerating Spirit of God;[i] whereby being deeply convinced of our guilt, danger, and helplessness, and of the way of salvation by Christ,[j] we turn to God with unfeigned contrition, confession, and supplication for mercy;[k] at the same time heartily receiving the Lord Jesus Christ as our Prophet, Priest, and King, and relying on him alone as the only and all-sufficient Savior.[l]

9. OF GOD'S PURPOSE OF GRACE

We believe that election is the eternal purpose of God, according to which he graciously regenerates, sanctifies, and saves sinners;[m] that being perfectly consistent with the free agency of man, it comprehends all the means in connection with the end;[n] that it is a most glorious display of God's sovereign goodness, being infinitely

a. [Rom 16.26; Mk 1.15; Rom 1.15–17]

b. [Jn 5.40; Mt 23.37; Rom 9.32; Prv 1.24; Acts 13.46]

c. [Jn 3.19; Mt 11.20; Lk 19.27; 2 Thes 1.8]

d. [Jn 3.3, 6–7; 1 Cor 1.14; Rv 8.7–9, 21.27]

e. [2 Cor 5.17; Ez 36.26; Dt 30.6; Rom 2.28–29, 5.5; 1 Jn 4.7]

f. [Jn 3.8, 1.13; Jas 1.16–18; 1 Cor 1.30; Phil 2.13]

g. [1 Pt 1.22–25; 1 Jn 5.1; Eph 4.20–24; Col 3.9–11]

h. [Eph 5.9; Rom 8.9; Gal 5.16–23; Eph 3.14–21; Mt 3.8–10, 7.20; 1 Jn 5.4, 18]

i. [Mk 1.15; Acts 11.18; Eph 2.8; 1 Jn 5.1]

j. [Jn 16.8; Acts 2.37–38, 16.30–31]

k. [Lk 18.13, 15.18–21; Jas 4.7–10; 2 Cor 7.11; Rom 10.12–13; Ps 51]

l. [Rom 10.9–11; Acts 3.22–23; Heb 4.14; Ps 2.6; Heb 1.8, 8.25; 2 Tm 1.12]

m. [2 Tm 1.8–9; Eph 1.3–14; 1 Pt 1.1–2; Rom 11.5–6; Jn 15.15; 1 Jn 4.19; Hos 12.9]

n. [2 Thes 2.13–14; Acts 13.48; Jn 10.16; Mt 20.16; Acts 15.14] free, wise, holy, and unchangeable;[a] that it utterly excludes boasting, and promotes humility, love, prayer, praise, trust in God, and active imitation of his free mercy;[b] that it encourages the use of means in the highest degree;[c] that it may be ascertained by its effects in all who truly believe the gospel; that it is the foundation of Christian assurance;[d] and that to ascertain it with regard to ourselves demands and deserves the utmost diligence.[e]

[1 Thes 1.4–10]

10. OF SANCTIFICATION

We believe that sanctification is the process by which, according to the will of God, we are made partakers of his holiness;[f] that it is a progressive work;[g] that it is begun in regeneration;[h] and that it is carried on in the hearts of believers by the presence and power of the Holy Spirit, the Sealer and Comforter, in the continual use of the appointed means—especially the word of God, self-examination, self-denial, watchfulness, and prayer.[i]

11. OF THE PERSEVERANCE OF SAINTS

We believe that such only are real believers as endure unto the end;[j] that their persevering attachment to Christ is the grand mark which distinguishes them from superficial professors;[k] that a special providence watches over their welfare;[l] and they are kept by the power of God through faith unto salvation.[m]

12. OF THE HARMONY OF THE LAW AND THE GOSPEL

We believe that the law of God is the eternal and unchangeable rule of his moral government;[n] that it is holy, just, and good;[o] and that the inability which the Scrip-

a. [Ex 23.18–19; Mt 20.15; Eph 1.11; Rom 9.23–24; Jer 31.3; Rom 11.28–29; Jas 1.17–18; 2 Tm 1.9; Rom 11.32–36]

b. [1 Cor 4.7, 1.26–31; Rom 3.27, 4.16; Col 3.12; 1 Cor 3.5–7, 15.10; 1 Pt 5.10; Acts 1.24; 1 Thes 2.13; 1 Pt 2.9; Lk 18.7; Jn 15.16; Eph 1.16; 1 Thes 2.12]

c. [2 Tm 2.10; 1 Cor 9.22; Rom 8.28–30; Jn 6.37–40; 2 Pt 1.10]

d. [Rom 8.28–30; Is 52.16; Rom 11.29]

e. [2 Pt 1.10–11; Phil 3.12; Heb 6.11]

f. [1 Thes 4.3, 5.23; 2 Cor 7.1, 13.9; Eph 1.4]

g. [Prv 4.18; 2 Cor 3.18; Heb 6.1; 2 Pt 1.5–8; Phil 3.12–16]

h. [Jn 2.29; Rom 8.5; Jn 3.6; Phil 1.9–11; Eph 1.13–14]

i. [Phil 2.12–13; Eph 4.11–12; 1 Pt 2.2; 2 Pt 3.18; 2 Cor 13.5; Lk 11.35, 9.23; Mt 26.41; Eph 6.18, 4.30]

j. [Jn 8.31; 1 Jn 2.27–28, 3.9, 5.18]

k. [1 Jn 2.19; Jn 13.18; Mt 13.20–21; Jn 6.66–69; Jb 17.9]

l. [Rom 8.28; Mt 6.30–33; Jer 32.40; Ps 121.3, 91.11–12]

m. [Phil 1.6, 2.12–13; Jude 24–25; Heb 1.14; 2 Kgs 6.16; Heb 13.5; 1 Jn 4.4]

n. [Rom 3.31; Mt 5.17; Lk 16.17; Rom 3.20, 4.15]

o. [Rom 7.12, 7,14, 22; Gal 3.21; Ps 119]

tures ascribe to fallen men to fulfill its precepts arises entirely from their love of sin;[a] to deliver them from which, and to restore them through a Mediator to unfeigned obedience to the holy law, is one great end of the gospel, and of the means of grace connected with the establishment of the visible church.[b]

13. OF A GOSPEL CHURCH

We believe that a visible church of Christ is a congregation of baptized believers,[c] associated by covenant in the faith and fellowship of the gospel;[d] observing the ordinances of Christ;[e] governed by his laws,[f] and exercising the gifts, rights, and privileges invested in them by his word;[g] that its only scriptural officers are bishops, or pastors, and deacons, whose qualifications, claims, and duties are defined in the Epistles to Timothy and Titus.[h]

14. OF BAPTISM AND THE LORD'S SUPPER

We believe that Christian baptism is the immersion in water of a believer,[i] into the name of the Father, and Son, and Holy Ghost;[j] to show forth, in a solemn and beautiful emblem, our faith in the crucified, buried, and risen Savior, with its effect in our death to sin and resurrection to a new life;[k] that it is prerequisite to the privileges of a church relation; and to the Lord's supper,[l] in which the members of the church, by the sacred use of bread and wine, are to commemorate together the dying love of Christ;[m] preceded always by solemn self-examination.[n]

a. [Rom 8.7–8; Jos 24.19; Jer 13.23; Jn 6.44, 5.44]

b. [Rom 8.2, 4, 10.4; 1 Tm 1.5; Heb 8.10; Jude 20–21; Heb 12.14; Mt 16.17–18; 1 Cor 12.28]

c. [1 Cor 1.1–13; Mt 18.17; Acts 5.11, 8.1, 11.31; 1 Cor 4.17, 14.23; 3 Jn 9; 1 Tm 3.5]

d. [Acts 2.41–42; 2 Cor 8.5; Acts 2.47; 1 Cor 5.12–13]

e. [1 Cor 11.2; 2 Thes 3.6; Rom 16.17–20; 1 Cor 11.23; Mt 18.15–20; 1 Cor 5.6; 2 Cor 2.7; 1 Cor 4.17]

f. [Mt 28.20; Jn 14.15, 15.12; 1 Jn 4.21; Jn 14.21; 1 Thes 4.2; 2 Jn 6; Gal 6.2; all the epistles]

g. [Eph 4.7; 1 Cor 14.12; Phil 1.27; 1 Cor 12.14]

h. [Phil 1.1; Acts 14.23, 15.22; 1 Tm 3; Ti 1]

i. [Acts 8.36–39; Mt 3.5–6; Jn 3.22–23, 4.1–2; Mt 28.19; Mk 16.16; Acts 2.38, 8.12, 16.32–34, 18.8]

j. [Mt 28.19; Acts 10.47–48; Gal 3.27–28]

k. [Rom 6.4; Col 2.12; 1 Pt 3.20–21; Acts 22.16]

l. [Acts 2.41–42; Mt 28.19–20; Acts and epistles]

m. [1 Cor 11.26; Mt 26.26–29; Mk 14.22–25; Lk 22.14–20]

n. [1 Cor 11.28, 5.1, 8, 10.3–32, 11.17–32; Jn 6.26–71]

15. OF THE CHRISTIAN SABBATH

We believe that the first day of the week is the Lord's day, or Christian Sabbath;[a] and is to be kept sacred to religious purposes,[b] by abstaining from all secular labor and sinful recreations,[c] by the devout observance of all the means of grace, both private[d] and public;[e] and by preparation for that rest that remaineth for the people of God.

[Heb 4.3-11]

16. OF CIVIL GOVERNMENT

We believe that civil government is of divine appointment, for the interests and good order of human society;[f] and that magistrates are to be prayed for, conscientiously honored and obeyed;[g] except only in things opposed to the will of our Lord Jesus Christ,[h] who is the only Lord of the conscience, and the prince of the kings of the earth.[i]

17. OF THE RIGHTEOUS AND THE WICKED

We believe that there is a radical and essential difference between the righteous and the wicked;[j] that such only as through faith are justified in the name of the Lord Jesus, and sanctified by the Spirit of our God, are truly righteous in his esteem;[k] while all such as continue in impenitence and unbelief are in his sight wicked, and under the curse;[l] and this distinction holds among men both in and after death.[m]

18. OF THE WORLD TO COME

We believe that the end of the world is approaching;[n] that at the last day Christ will descend from heaven,[o] and raise the dead from the grave to final retribution;[p] that

a. [Acts 20.7; Gn 2.3; Col 2.16-17; Mk 2.27; Jn 20.19; 1 Cor 16.1-2]

b. [Ex 20.8; Rv 1.10; Ps 118.24]

c. [Is 58.13-14, 56.2-8]

d. [Ps 113.15]

e. [Heb 10.24-25; Acts 11.26, 13.44; Lv 19.30; Ex 46.3; Lk 4.16; Acts 17.2-3; Ps 26.8, 87.3]

f. [Rom 13.1-7; Dt 16.18; 1 Sm 23.3; Ex 18.23; Jer 30.21]

g. [Mt 22.21; Ti 3.1; 1 Pt 2.13; 1 Tm 2.1-8]

h. [Acts 5.29; Mt 10.28; Dn 3.15-18, 6.7-10; Acts 4.18-20]

i. [Mt 23.10; Rom 14.4; Rv 19.16; Ps 72.11; Ps 2; Rom 14.9-13]

j. [Mal 3.18; Prv 12.26; Is 5.20; Gn 18.23; Jer 15.19; Acts 10.34-35; Rom 6.16]

k. [Rom 1.17, 7.6; 1 Jn 2.29, 3.7; Rom 6.18, 22; 1 Cor 11.32; Prv 11.31; 1 Pt 4.17-18]

l. [1 Jn 5.19; Gal 3.10; Jn 3.36; Is 57.21; Ps 10.4; Is 55.6-7]

m. [Prv 14.32; Lk 16.25; Jn 8.21-24; Prv 10.24; Lk 12.4-5, 9.23-26; Jn 12.25-26; Eccl 3.17; Mt 7.13-14]

n. [1 Pt 4.7; 1 Cor 7.29-31; Heb 1.10-12; Mt 24.35; 1 Jn 2.17; Mt 28.20, 13.39-40; 2 Pt 3.3-13]

o. [Acts 1.11; Rv 1.7; Heb 9.28; Acts 3.21; 1 Thes 4.13-18, 5.1-11]

p. [Acts 24.15; 1 Cor 15.12-59; Lk 14.14; Dn 12.2; Jn 5.28-29, 6.40, 11.25-26; 2 Tm 1.10; Acts 10.42] a solemn separation will then take place;[a] that the wicked will be adjudged to end-less punishment, and the righteous to endless joy;[b] and that this judgment will fix forever the final state of men in heaven or hell, on principles of righteousness.[c]

a. [Mt 13.49, 37–43, 24.30–31, 25.31–33]

b. [Mt 25.35–41; Rv 22.11; 1 Cor 6.9–10; Mk 9.43–48; 2 Pt 2.9; Jude 7; Phil 3.19; Rom 6.32; 2 Cor 5.10–11; Jn 4.36; 2 Cor 4.18]

c. [Rom 3.5–6; 2 Thes 1.6–12; Heb 6.1–2; 1 Cor 4.5; Acts 17.31; Rom 2.2–16; Rv 20.11–12; 1 Jn 2.28, 4.17]

Presbyterian Church, *The Auburn Declaration*, 1837

The confessional crisis within American Presbyterianism over revivalism did not end with the separation of the Cumberland Presbyterian Church and its revision of → *The Westminster Confession of Faith* into a new confession of 1814 (and, eventually, of 1888). The division between the "Old School" proponents of a strict construction of *The Westminster Confession* and the "New School" advocates of a softening of what they took to be its harsh language about original sin, free will, and predestination led to further charges against the New School before the General Assembly of the Presbyterian Church. Meeting in Auburn, New York, in August 1837, the defenders of the New School itemized those charges and responded to each in turn. Although *The Auburn Declaration* has sometimes been printed without the charges, for example by Schaff,[1] we have included them as the necessary context for understanding the affirmations at Auburn. A third of a century later, in 1869, Old School and New School were reunited.

Edition: Marsden 1970, 252–55, from *Minutes of the Auburn Convention, Held August 17, 1837, to Deliberate upon the Doings of the Last General Assembly* (Auburn, N.Y., 1837), 27–31.

Literature: Armstrong, Loetscher, and Anderson 1956, 146–71; Marsden 1970, 252–55; Schaff, 3:777–81.

1. Schaff, 3:777–81.

Presbyterian Church, *The Auburn Declaration*, 1837

Whereas it is declared in the "Circular letter" of the late General Assembly of the Presbyterian Church "to all the churches of Jesus Christ," that "very serious" and "alarming" errors and disorders have long prevailed in the bounds of the exscinded synods and other portions of the church, and as the late assembly appears to have been influenced in deciding on the case of these synods, by these alleged errors and disorders, therefore

1. *Resolved,* That while we bear in mind that with the excitement of extensive revivals indiscretions are sometimes intermingled—and that in the attempt to avoid a ruinous practical Antinomianism, human obligation is sometimes urged in a manner that favors Arminian errors—yet, we are bound to declare, that such errors and irregularities have never been sanctioned by these synods or presbyteries—that the prejudice has in a great degree arisen from censorious and exaggerated statements, and from the conduct of persons not in connection with the Presbyterian Church—that all such departures from the sound doctrine or order of the Presbyterian Church we solemnly disapprove, and when known, deem it our duty to correct by every constitutional method.

2. *Resolved,* That, as the declaration of the religious sentiments of the synods and presbyteries whom we represent, we cordially embrace the *Confession of Faith* of the Presbyterian Church, "as containing the system of doctrine taught in the Holy Scriptures," as understood by the church ever since the Adopting Act of 1729; namely, "And in case any minister of the synod, or any candidate for the ministry, shall have any scruple with respect to any article or articles of said confession, he shall in time of making said declaration, declare his scruples to the synod or presbytery; who shall, notwithstanding, admit him to the exercise of the ministry within our bounds, and to ministerial communion, if the synod or presbytery shall judge his scruples *not essential* or *necessary* in *doctrine, worship,* or *government.*"

3. *Resolved,* That in accordance with the above declaration, and also to meet the charges contained in the before-mentioned circular and other published documents of the late General Assembly, this convention cordially disapprove and condemn the list of errors condemned by the late General Assembly, and adopt, as the expression of their own sentiments, and as they believe, the prevalent sentiments of the churches of these synods on the points in question, the list of "true doctrines" adopted by the minority of the said assembly in their "Protest" on this subject, as follows, namely:

ERRORS AND TRUE DOCTRINE

First Error. "That God would have prevented the existence of sin in our world, but was not able, without destroying the moral agency of man; or, that for aught that appears in the Bible to the contrary, sin is incidental to any wise moral system."

True Doctrine. God permitted the introduction of sin, not because he was unable to prevent it, consistently with the moral freedom of his creatures, but for wise and benevolent reasons which he has not revealed.

Second Error. "That election to eternal life is founded on a foresight of faith and obedience."

True Doctrine. Election to eternal life is not founded on a foresight of faith and obedience, but is a sovereign act of God's mercy, whereby, according to the counsel of his own will, he has chosen some to salvation; "yet so as thereby neither is violence offered to the will of the creatures, nor is the liberty or contingency of second causes taken away, but rather established;"[1] nor does this gracious purpose ever take effect independently of faith and a holy life.

Third Error. "That we have no more to do with the first sin of Adam than with the sins of any other parent."

True Doctrine. By a divine constitution, Adam was so the head and representative of the race, that, as a consequence of his transgression, all mankind become morally corrupt, and liable to death, temporal and eternal.

Fourth Error. "That infants come into the world as free from moral defilement as was Adam when he was created."

[Gn 1.27]   True Doctrine. Adam was created in the image of God, endowed with knowledge, righteousness, and true holiness. Infants come into the world, not only destitute of these, but with a nature inclined to evil and only evil.

Fifth Error. "That infants sustain the same relation to the moral government of God, in this world, as brute animals, and that their sufferings and death are to be accounted for on the same principles as those of brutes, and not by any means to be considered as penal."

True Doctrine. Brute animals sustain no such relation to the moral government of God as does the human family. Infants are a part of the human family; and their sufferings and death are to be accounted for on the ground of their being involved in the general moral ruin of the race induced by the apostasy.

Sixth Error. "That there is no other original sin than the fact, that all the posterity of Adam, though by nature innocent, will always begin to sin when they begin to exercise moral agency; that original sin does not include a sinful bias of the

1. *West* 3.1.

human mind, and a just exposure to penal suffering; and that there is no evidence in Scripture, that infants, in order to salvation, do need redemption by the blood of Christ, and regeneration by the Holy Ghost."

True Doctrine. Original sin is a natural bias to evil, resulting from the first apostasy, leading invariably and certainly to actual transgression. And all infants, as well as adults, in order to be saved, need redemption by the blood of Christ, and regeneration by the Holy Ghost.

Seventh Error. "That the doctrine of imputation, whether of the guilt of Adam's sin, or of the righteousness of Christ, has no foundation in the word of God, and is both unjust and absurd."

True Doctrine. The sin of Adam is not imputed to his posterity in the sense of a literal transfer of personal qualities, acts, and demerit; but by reason of the sin of Adam, in his peculiar relation, the race are treated as if they had sinned. Nor is the righteousness of Christ imputed to his people in the sense of a literal transfer of personal qualities, acts, and merit; but by reason of his righteousness, in his peculiar relation, they are treated as if they were righteous.

Eighth Error. "That the sufferings and death of Christ were not truly vicarious and penal, but symbolical, governmental, and instructive only."

True Doctrine. The sufferings and death of Christ were not symbolical, governmental, and instructive only, but were truly vicarious, i.e., a substitute for the punishment due to transgressors. And while Christ did not suffer the literal penalty of the law, involving remorse of conscience and the pains of hell, he did offer a sacrifice, which infinite wisdom saw to be a full equivalent. And by virtue of this atonement, overtures of mercy are sincerely made to the race, and salvation secured to all who believe.

Ninth Error. "That the impenitent sinner is by nature, and independently of the renewing influence or almighty energy of the Holy Spirit, in full possession of all the ability necessary to a full compliance with all the commands of God."

True Doctrine. While sinners have all the faculties necessary to a perfect moral agency and a just accountability, such is their love of sin and opposition to God and his law, that, independently of the renewing influence or almighty energy of the Holy Spirit, they never will comply with the commands of God."

Tenth Error. "That Christ does not intercede for the elect until after their regeneration."

True Doctrine. The intercession of Christ for the elect is previous as well as subsequent to their regeneration, as appears from the following Scripture, namely, "I pray not for the world, but for them which thou hast given me, for they are thine.

Neither pray I for these alone, but for them also which shall believe on me through their word."

[Jn 17.9, 20]

Eleventh Error. "That saving faith is not an effect of the operations of the Holy Spirit, but a mere rational belief of the truth or assent to the word of God."

True Doctrine. Saving faith is an intelligent and cordial assent to the testimony of God concerning his Son, implying reliance on Christ alone for pardon and eternal life; and in all cases it is an effect of the special operations of the Holy Spirit.

Twelfth Error. "That regeneration is the act of the sinner himself, and that it consists in change of his governing purpose, which he himself must produce, and which is the result, not of any direct influence of the Holy Spirit on the heart, but chiefly of a persuasive exhibition of the truth, analogous to the influence which one man exerts over the mind of another; or that regeneration is not an instantaneous act, but a progressive work."

True Doctrine. Regeneration is a radical change of heart, produced by the special operations of the Holy Spirit, "determining the sinner to that which is good," and is in all cases instantaneous.

Thirteenth Error. "That God has done all that *he can do* for the salvation of all men, and that man himself must do the rest."

True Doctrine. While repentance for sin and faith in Christ are indispensable to salvation, all who are saved are indebted from first to last to the grace and Spirit of God. And the reason that God does not save all, is not that he wants the *power* to do it, but that in his wisdom he does not see fit to exert that power further than he actually does.

Fourteenth Error. "That God cannot exert such influence on the minds of men, as shall make it certain that they will choose and act in a particular manner, without impairing their moral agency."

True Doctrine. While the liberty of the will is not impaired, nor the established connexion betwixt means and end broken by any action of God on the mind, he can influence it according to his pleasure, and does effectually determine it to good in all cases of true conversion.

Fifteenth Error. "That the righteousness of Christ is not the sole ground of the sinner's acceptance with God; and that in no sense does the righteousness of Christ become ours."

True Doctrine. All believers are justified, not on the ground of personal merit, but solely on the ground of the obedience and death, or, in other words, the righteousness of Christ. And while that righteousness does not become theirs, in the sense of a literal transfer of personal qualities and merit; yet, from respect to it, God can and does treat them as if they were righteous.

Sixteenth Error. "That the reason why some differ from others in regard to their reception of the gospel is, that they make themselves to differ."

True Doctrine. While all such as reject the gospel of Christ do it, not by coercion but freely—and all who embrace it do it, not by coercion but freely—the reason why some differ from others is, that *God* has made them to differ.

In further illustration of the doctrines prevalent in these sections of the church, the convention declare that the authors whose exposition and defense of the articles of our faith are most approved and used in these synods—are President Edwards, Witherspoon, and Dwight—Dr. Smalley, and Andrew Fuller—and the commentators, Henry, Doddridge, and Scott.

Church of Jesus Christ of Latter-Day Saints
(Mormons), *Articles of Faith*, 1842

The Church of Jesus Christ of Latter-Day Saints (Mormons) and the Church of Christ, Scientist both arose in the American Northeast during the nineteenth century, and both espoused a version of Christian teaching that diverged radically from any of the creeds and confessions of faith that had preceded them.

The distinctive beliefs and practices of the Church of Jesus Christ of Latter-Day Saints (Mormons) all stem from the revelations to Joseph Smith (1805–44), which led him to the discovery of *The Book of Mormon*. To the general public, Mormonism was notorious above all for advocating polygamy, which was also supported by a revelation to Smith, but which has since been disavowed by the members the Church of Jesus Christ of Latter-Day Saints. But in these thirteen *Articles of Faith* there are articulated, in the standard form of a creed, other beliefs that manifest both the affinities and the differences (authority of *The Book of Mormon*) between Mormonism and traditional Christian doctrine. They appear in the conclusion of the so-called Wentworth Letter, which was written by Joseph Smith to John Wentworth, editor of the *Chicago Democrat,* and was published in the official newspaper of the church, *Times and Seasons,* on 1 March 1842.

Edition: Millet 1989, 107–8.

Literature: Millet 1989; O'Dea 1957.

Church of Jesus Christ of Latter-Day Saints (Mormons), *Articles of Faith*, 1842

1. We believe in God the Eternal Father, and in his Son Jesus Christ, and in the Holy Ghost.

2. We believe that men will be punished for their own sins and not for Adam's transgression.

3. We believe that through the atonement of Christ all mankind may be saved by obedience to the laws and ordinances of the gospel.

4. We believe that these ordinances are first, faith in the Lord Jesus Christ; second, repentance; third, baptism by immersion for the remission of sins; fourth, laying on of hands for the gift of the Holy Ghost.

5. We believe that a man must be called of God by "prophecy, and by laying on of hands" by those who are in authority to preach the gospel and administer in the ordinances thereof.

6. We believe in the same organization that existed in the primitive church, that is, apostles, prophets, pastors, teachers, evangelists, etc. [Eph 4.11]

7. We believe in the gift of tongues, prophecy, revelation, visions, healing, interpretation of tongues, etc.

8. We believe the Bible to be the word of God as far as it is translated correctly; we also believe the Book of Mormon to be the word of God.

9. We believe all that God has revealed, all that he does now reveal, and we believe that he will yet reveal many great and important things pertaining to the kingdom of God.

10. We believe in the literal gathering of Israel and in the restoration of the Ten Tribes. That Zion will be built upon this continent. That Christ will reign personally upon the earth, and that the earth will be renewed and receive its paradasaic glory.

11. We claim the privilege of worshiping Almighty God according to the dictates of our conscience, and allow all men the same privilege let them worship how, where, and what they may.

12. We believe in being subject to kings, presidents, rulers, and magistrates, in obeying, honoring, and sustaining the law.

13. We believe in being honest, true, chaste, benevolent, virtuous, and in doing good to *all men;* indeed we may say that we follow the admonition of Paul,

[1 Cor 13.7]   "we believe all things, we hope all things," we have endured many things and hope
               to be able to endure all things. If there is any thing virtuous, lovely, or of good report
[Phil 4.8]   or praiseworthy, we seek after these things.

Evangelical Alliance, *General Principles (Basis)*, 1846

Described by *The Oxford Dictionary of the Christian Church* as "the only definitely ecumenical organization which arose out of the evangelical movement of the 19th century," the World's Evangelical Alliance was founded in 1846 in London; an American Branch was founded in 1867. Its stated purpose was to "associate and concentrate the strength of an enlightened Protestantism against the encroachments of Popery and Puseyism, and to promote the interests of a Scriptural Christianity"; by "Puseyism" the Evangelical Alliance was referring to the Tractarian movement in the Church of England, named for E. B. Pusey (1800–1882). While making it clear that they did not intend to establish a new denomination, nor to propound a new confession or creed, the founders of the Evangelical Alliance did feel obliged, on the basis of earlier theses,[1] to formulate a doctrinal basis, which was shared by Evangelicals of the several denominations. Thus they were among the first to adopt the procedure, which was to become widespread in the ecumenical movement of the twentieth century, of propounding an unofficial confession that was said to transcend (but not to abrogate) the official confessions.

Edition: Ewing 1946, 17–18.

Literature: Ewing 1946; Hauzenberger 1985; Kessler 2001; *ODCC* 578–79; Schaff, 3:827–28.

---

1. Parallel tables in Hauzenberger 1985, 455–57.

Evangelical Alliance, *General Principles (Basis)*, 1846

That the parties composing the Alliance shall be such persons only as hold and maintain what are usually understood to be Evangelical views, in regard to the matters of doctrine understated, namely:

1. The divine inspiration, authority, and sufficiency of the Holy Scriptures.

2. The right and duty of private judgment in the interpretation of the Holy Scriptures.

3. The unity of the Godhead, and the Trinity of persons therein.

4. The utter depravity of human nature, in consequence of the fall.

5. The incarnation of the Son of God, his work of atonement for sinners of mankind, and his mediatorial intercession and reign.

6. The justification of the sinner by faith alone.

7. The work of the Holy Spirit in the conversion and sanctification of the sinner.

8. The immortality of the soul, the resurrection of the body, the judgment of the world by our Lord Jesus Christ, with the eternal blessedness of the righteous, and the eternal punishment of the wicked.

9. The divine institution of the Christian ministry, and the obligation and perpetuity of the ordinances of baptism and the Lord's supper.

i. It is, however, distinctly declared that this brief summary is not to be regarded, in any formal or ecclesiastical sense, as a creed or confession, nor the adoption of it as involving an assumption of the right authoritatively to define the limits of Christian brotherhood.

ii. In this Alliance it is also distinctly declared that no compromise of the views of any member, or sanction of those of others on the points wherein they differ, is either required or expected; but that all are held free as before to maintain and advocate their religious convictions with due forbearance and brotherly love.

iii. It is not contemplated that this Alliance should assume or aim at the character of a new ecclesiastical organization, claiming and exercising the functions of a Christian church. Its simple and comprehensive object, it is strongly felt, may be successfully promoted without interfering with, or disturbing the order of, any branch of the Christian church to which its members may respectively belong.

Armenian Evangelical Church, *Confession of Faith,* 1846

By tradition, Armenia regards itself as the first nation to have officially adopted Christianity; this happened in 301. Being Oriental Orthodox, the Apostolic Church of Armenia accepts the decrees and creeds of the Councils of Nicaea (325), Constantinople (381), and Ephesus (431), but not those of the Council of Chalcedon (451) and subsequent councils. In spite of that separation, it has periodically had relations with other churches; historically the most noteworthy of these was → *The Decree for the Armenians of the Council of Florence* in 1438–39, which proved to be more important as a codification of Western sacramental doctrine than as a reunion document.

Armenian Christianity has also produced an Armenian Evangelical Church, growing out of the missionary activity of Evangelical churches from the West as early as 1831 but also expressing indigenous forces that had grown critical of the Armenian Apostolic Church. And so, in Haidostian's words, "on July 1, 1846, what was once a reform movement in the Armenian Apostolic Church, supported by foreign Protestant missionaries, and faced with rejection from the church, became the 'First Armenian Evangelical Church of Constantinople.'"[1]

As part of the process of forming the Armenian Evangelical Church, this *Confession of Faith* was formulated; it reflects the body of shared Evangelical teachings seen in other confessions in the West but reflects as well its special background, as in the rejection of "the use of relics, pictures, crosses, and images of any sort, in any act of worship" (9). An interesting variant is the use of the second person singular, "You believe."

Edition: Armenian text no longer extant; for an earlier version of the text in Armenian (signed 22 January 1846), see Eutudjian 1914, 160–62.

Translation: Tootikian 1982, 244–45 (from Dwight 1854).

Literature: Dwight 1854; Haidostian 1996; Tootikian 1982.

---

1. Haidostian 1996, 57.

Armenian Evangelical Church, *Confession of Faith*, 1846

1. You believe in the existence of one only living and true God, the Creator, Preserver, and Governor of the universe; omnipotent, omniscient, omnipresent; self-existent, independent, immutable; possessed of infinite benevolence, wisdom, holiness, justice, mercy, and truth, and who is the only proper object of worship.

2. You believe that God exists in three persons, the Father, the Son, and the Holy Ghost; and that these three are one God.

3. You believe that the Scriptures of the Old and New Testaments were given by inspiration of God, and are a revelation of his will to man, and the sufficient and only rule of faith and practice.

4. You believe that mankind, in their natural state, are destitute of holiness, and entirely depraved, and justly exposed to the divine wrath.

5. You believe that the Lord Jesus Christ, perfect God and perfect man, is the only Savior of sinners, and the only Mediator and Intercessor between God and man; and that by his perfect obedience, sufferings, and death, he made full atonement for sin, so that all who believe in him will assuredly be saved, and that there is no other sacrifice for sin.

6. You believe that in consequence of the utter wickedness of man, it is necessary that all should be regenerated by the power of the Holy Ghost, in order to be saved.

7. You believe that we are justified by the righteousness of Christ alone, through faith, and not by any fastings, alms, penances, or other deeds of our own; and that while good works are inseparable from true faith, they can never be meritorious ground of salvation before God.

8. You believe that holiness of life, and a conscientious discharge of the various duties we owe to God, to our fellowmen, and to ourselves, are not only constantly binding upon all believers, but essential to the Christian character.

9. You believe that, besides God, no other being is to be worshiped and adored, and that each person in the sacred Trinity is worthy of our worship, which, to be acceptable, must be offered through no other mediation than that of Jesus Christ alone; and that the use of relics, pictures, crosses, and images of any sort, in any act of worship, and of the intercession of saints, is directly contrary to the Scriptures, and highly displeasing to God; and that prayer of the dead is not authorized in the word of God.

10. You believe that there will be a resurrection of the dead, both of the just

and of the unjust, and a day of judgment; and that the happiness of the righteous, and the punishment of the wicked, commence at death, and continue without end.

11. You believe that any number of believers, duly organized, constitute a church of Christ, of which Christ is the only Head; and that the only sacraments of Christ's church are baptism and the Lord's supper; the former being the seal of the covenant, and a sign of the purifying operation of the Holy Spirit, and the token of admission into the visible church, and the latter, in shewing forth by visible symbols the death of Christ, being a perpetual memento of his atoning love, and a pledge of union and communion with him and with all true believers.

12. You believe that the gospel is the chief instrument appointed by Christ for the conversion of men and for the edification of his people, and that it is the duty of his church to carry into effect the Savior's command, "Go ye into all the world, and preach the gospel to every creature."

[Mt 28.19]

Eastern Orthodox Patriarchs,
Response to Pope Pius IX, 1848

Pope Pius IX, who is represented here by his bull → *Ineffabilis Deus* of 1854, defining the dogma of the immaculate conception of the Virgin Mary, by → *The Syllabus of Errors* of 1864 against modern heresies inside and outside Christendom, and by the → *Dogmatic Constitution on the Catholic Faith* of the First Vatican Council of 1869–70, defining the dogma of the infallibility of the pope, began his reign on 16 June 1846. A year and a half later, in the encyclical *Ad Orientales*,[1] dated 6 January 1848 (which was the Feast of the Epiphany on the calendar of the the Western Church, and the Feast of the Nativity according to the Julian calendar observed by Eastern Christendom), he addressed what was intended to be a fraternal and conciliatory invitation to the Eastern Orthodox churches to reunion with Rome "with a minimum of conditions."

In this response of 1848, bearing the signatures of many Eastern patriarchs and prelates, the definition of Orthodox doctrine on church and tradition, formulated at considerable length in the seventeenth-century *Confessions* of → Metrophanes Critopoulos, → Peter Mogila, and → Dositheus of Jerusalem, was restated with a force and clarity that the situation of the nineteenth century seemed to require: in the summary judgment of Karmirēs, the pope had issued an invitation "not to unity but to submission."[2] The Orthodox restatement, of course, was anything but an innovation, and the principal polemic of the *Response* is indeed the rejection of any innovation—above all, the two innovations of the addition of the Filioque to → *The Niceno-Constantinopolitan Creed* and the definition of the authority of Rome as supreme rather than as *primus inter pares,* as the East insisted. Coming as it did before the development of modern ecumenism and therefore before the change in the relation of Eastern Orthodoxy to the rest of Christendom during the second half of the twentieth century that Karmirēs in 1967 could describe as "the theological dialogue commencing between the Orthodox Catholic Church and the heterodox churches: Roman Catholic, Anglican, Old Catholic, the non-Chalcedonian, and those Protestant churches and confessions that take part in the World Council of Churches,"[3] it once more draws the line. Among the numerous other reaffirmations

---

1. *Pii IX Pontificis Maximi Acta* (1854–78), 1:78–91; there does not seem to be an English translation.
2. Karmirēs, 2:982.
3. Karmirēs, 2:vi.

of Orthodox teaching in the modern period, therefore,[4] it carries special force. It is noteworthy also for its articulation of the position that "the protector of religion is the very body of the church, even the people themselves" (17).

Edition: Karmirēs 2:985-1005.

Translation: *Encyclical Epistle . . . 1848* 1867, 5-32, adapted and annotated.

Literature: *Encyclical Epistle . . . 1848* 1867, 33-45; Karmirēs 2:982-84; Popescu 1935.

---

4. Karmirēs, 2:863-1123.

Eastern Orthodox Patriarchs,
Response to Pope Pius IX, 1848

To all the bishops everywhere, beloved in the Holy Ghost, our venerable, most dear brethren; and to their most pious clergy; and to all the genuine Orthodox sons of the one, holy, catholic, and apostolic church: brotherly salutation in the Holy Spirit, and every good from God, and salvation.

The holy, evangelical, and divine gospel of salvation should be set forth by all in its original simplicity, and should evermore be believed in its unadulterated purity, even the same as it was revealed to his holy apostles by our Savior, who for this very cause, descending from the bosom of God the Father, made himself of no [Phil 2.7] reputation and took upon him the form of a servant; even the same, also, as those apostles, who were ear- and eye-witnesses, sounded it forth, like clear-toned trumpets, to all that are under the sun (for their sound is gone out into all lands, and their [Ps 19.4] words into the ends of the world); and, last of all, the very same as the many great and glorious fathers of the catholic church in all parts of the earth, who heard those apostolic voices, both by their synodical and their individual teachings handed it down to all everywhere, and even unto us. But the prince of evil, that spiritual enemy of man's salvation, as formerly in Eden, craftily assuming the pretext of profitable counsel, made man to become a transgressor of the divinely spoken command. So in the spiritual Eden, the church of God, he has from time to time beguiled many; and, mixing the deleterious drugs of heresy with the clear streams of orthodox doctrine, gives of the potion to drink to many of the innocent who live unguardedly, [Heb 2.1] not giving earnest heed to the things they have heard, and to what they have been [Dt 32.7] told by their fathers, in accordance with the gospel and in agreement with the ancient doctors; and who, imagining that the preached and written word of the Lord and the perpetual witness of his church are not sufficient for their souls' salvation, impiously seek out novelties, as we change the fashion of our garments, embracing a counterfeit of the evangelical doctrine.

2. Hence have arisen manifold and monstrous heresies, which the catholic church, even from her infancy, taking unto her the whole armor of God, and [Eph 5.13–17] assuming the sword of the Spirit, which is the word of God, has been compelled to combat. She has triumphed over all unto this day, and she will triumph forever, being manifested as mightier and more illustrious after each struggle.

3. Of these heresies, some already have entirely failed, some are in decay, some have wasted away, some yet flourish in a greater or less degree vigorous until

the time of their return to the faith, while others are reproduced to run their course from their birth to their destruction. For being the miserable cogitations and devices of miserable men, both one and the other, struck with the thunderbolt of the anathema of the seven ecumenical councils, shall vanish away, though they may last a thousand years; for the orthodoxy of the catholic and apostolic church, by the living word of God, alone endures for ever, according to the infallible promise of the Lord: "The gates of hell shall not prevail against it." Certainly, the mouths [Mt 16.18] of ungodly and heretical men, however bold, however plausible and fair-speaking, however smooth they may be, will not prevail against the orthodox doctrine winning its way silently and without noise. But, wherefore doth the way of the wicked prosper?ᵃ Why are the ungodly exalted and lifted up as the cedars of Lebanon,ᵇ to defile the peaceful worship of God? The reason of this is mysterious, and the church, though daily praying that this cross, this messenger of Satan, may depart from her, ever hears from the Lord: "My grace is sufficient for thee, my strength is made perfect in weakness." Wherefore she gladly glories in her infirmities, that the power of [2 Cor 12.9] Christ may rest upon her, and that they which are approved may be made manifest. [1 Cor 11.19]

4. Of these heresies diffused, with what sufferings the Lord hath known, over a great part of the world, was formerly Arianism, and at present is the papacy. This, too, as the former has become extinct, although now flourishing, shall not endure, but pass away and be cast down, and a great voice from heaven shall cry: "It is cast down." [Rv 12.10]

5. The new doctrine, that "the Holy Ghost proceeds from the Father and the Son," is contrary to the memorable declaration of our Lord, emphatically made respecting it, "which proceedeth from the Father," and contrary to the universal [Jn 15.26] confession of the catholic church as witnessed by the seven ecumenical councils, uttering "which proceedeth from the Father."[1]

i. This novel opinion destroys the oneness from the one cause, and the diverse origin of the persons of the Blessed Trinity, both of which are witnessed to in the gospel.

ii. Even into the divine hypostases or persons of the Trinity, of equal power and equally to be adored, it introduces diverse and unequal relations, with a confusion or commingling of them.

iii. It reproaches as imperfect, dark, and difficult to be understood, the previous confession of the one holy, catholic, and apostolic church.

a. [Jer 12.1]
b. [Ps 37.35]

1. *N-CP* 8.

iv. It censures the holy fathers of the First Ecumenical Council of Nicaea and of the Second Ecumenical Council at Constantinople, as imperfectly expressing what relates to the Son and Holy Ghost, as if they had been silent respecting the peculiar property of each person of the Godhead, when it was necessary that all their divine properties should be expressed against the Arians and Macedonians.

v. It reproaches the fathers of the third, fourth, fifth, sixth, and seventh ecumenical councils, which had published over the world a divine creed, perfect and complete, and interdicted under dread anathemas and penalties not removed, all addition, or diminution, or alteration, or variation in the smallest particular of it, by themselves or any whomsoever. Yet this was quickly to be corrected and augmented, and consequently the whole theological doctrine of the catholic fathers was to be subjected to change, as if a new property even in regard to the three persons of the Blessed Trinity had been revealed.

[Mt 7.15] vi. It clandestinely found an entrance at first in the churches of the West, "a wolf in sheep's clothing," that is, under the signification not of procession, according to the Greek meaning in the Gospel and the creed, but under the signification of sending, as Pope Martin explained it to the Confessor Maximus, and as Anastasius Bibliothecarius explained it to John VIII.[2]

vii. It exhibits incomparable boldness, acting without authority, and forcibly puts a false stamp upon the creed, which is the common inheritance of Christianity.

viii. It has introduced huge disturbances into the peaceful church of God, and divided the nations.

ix. It was publicly proscribed, at its first promulgation, by two ever-to-be-remembered popes, Leo III and John VIII, the latter of whom, in his epistle to the blessed Photius, classes with Judas those who first brought the interpolation into the creed.

x. It has been condemned by many holy synods of the four patriarchs of the East.

xi. It was subjected to anathema, as a novelty and augmentation of the creed, by the Eighth Ecumenical Council, congregated at Constantinople for the pacification of the Eastern and Western churches.[3]

2. The letter of Anastasius Bibliothecarius to Pope John VIII (*MGH Ep* 7:415–18) deals with other issues between East and West, including the use of the title "ecumenical patriarch" but not with the Filioque as such.

3. The Fourth Council of Constantinople (869/870) decreed in its first canon: "If we wish to proceed without offense along the true and royal road of divine justice, we must keep the declarations and teachings of the holy fathers" (*DEC* 1:166).

xii. As soon as it was introduced into the churches of the West, it brought forth disgraceful fruits, bringing with it, little by little, other novelties, for the most part contrary to the express commands of our Savior in the Gospel—commands which till its entrance into the churches were closely observed. Among these novelties may be numbered sprinkling instead of baptism, denial of the divine cup to the laity, elevation of one and the same bread broken, the use of wafers, unleavened instead of real bread, the disuse of the benediction in the liturgies, even of the sacred invocation of the Allholy and consecrating Spirit, the abandonment of the old apostolic mysteries of the church, such as not anointing baptized infants, or their not receiving the eucharist, the exclusion of married men from the priesthood, the infallibility of the pope and his claim as vicar of Christ, and the like. Thus it was that the interpolation led to the setting aside of the old apostolic pattern of well nigh all the mysteries and all doctrine, a pattern which the ancient, holy, and orthodox Church of Rome kept when she was the most honored part of the holy, catholic, and apostolic church.

xiii. It drove the theologians of the West, as its defenders, since they had no ground either in Scripture or the fathers to countenance heretical teachings, not only into misrepresentations of the Scriptures, such as are seen in none of the fathers of the holy catholic church, but also into adulterations of the sacred and pure writings of the fathers alike of the East and West.

xiv. It seemed strange, unheard-of, and blasphemous, even to those reputed Christian communions, which, before its origin, had been for other just causes for ages cut off from the catholic fold.[4]

xv. It has not yet been even plausibly defended out of the Scriptures, or with the least reason out of the fathers, from the accusations brought against it, notwithstanding all the zeal and efforts of its supporters. The doctrine bears all the marks of error arising out of its nature and peculiarities. All erroneous doctrine touching the catholic truth of the Blessed Trinity, and the origin of the divine persons, and the subsistence of the Holy Ghost, is and is called heresy, and they who so hold are deemed heretics, according to the sentence of St. Damasus, pope of Rome, who says: "If anyone rightly holds concerning the Father and the Son, yet holds not rightly of the Holy Ghost, he is a heretic."[5] Wherefore the one, holy, catholic, and apostolic

---

4. The Oriental Orthodox ("Monophysite") Churches, such as that of Armenia, and the Assyrian ("Nestorian") Church of the East, were separated from Eastern Orthodoxy and Roman Catholicism by the councils of the fifth century at Ephesus and Chalcedon, but rejected the addition of the Filioque.

5. ap. Theodoret *Ecclesiastical History* 5.11 (*NPNF*–II 3:140).

church, following in the steps of the holy fathers, both Eastern and Western, proclaimed of old to our progenitors and again teaches today synodically, that the said novel doctrine of the Holy Ghost proceeding from the Father and the Son is essentially heresy, and its maintainers, whoever they be, are heretics, according to the sentence of Pope St. Damasus, and that the congregations of such are also heretical, and that all spiritual communion in worship of the orthodox sons of the catholic church with such is unlawful. Such is the force of the seventh canon of the Third Ecumenical Council.[6]

6. This heresy, which has united to itself many innovations, as has been said, appeared about the middle of the seventh century, at first and secretly, and then under various disguises, over the Western provinces of Europe, until by degrees, creeping along for four or five centuries, it obtained precedence over the ancient orthodoxy of those parts, through the heedlessness of pastors and the countenance of princes. Little by little it overspread not only the hitherto orthodox churches of Spain, but also the German, and French, and Italian churches, whose orthodoxy at one time was sounded throughout the world, with whom our divine fathers such as the great Athanasius and heavenly Basil conferred,[7] and whose sympathy and fellowship with us until the Seventh Ecumenical Council preserved unharmed the doctrine of the catholic and apostolic church. But in process of time, by envy of the devil, the novelties respecting the sound and orthodox doctrine of the Holy Ghost, the blasphemy of whom shall not be forgiven unto men either in this world or the next, according to the saying of our Lord, and others that succeeded respecting the divine mysteries, particularly that of the world-saving baptism, and the holy communion, and the priesthood, like prodigious births, overspread even Old Rome; and thus sprung, by assumption of special distinctions in the church as a badge and title, the papacy. Some of the bishops of that city, styled popes, for example Leo III and John VIII, did indeed, as has been said, denounce the innovation, and published the denunciation to the world, the former by those silver plates, the latter by his letter to the holy Photius at the Eighth Ecumenical Council, and another to Sphendopulcrus, by the hands of Methodius, bishop of Moravia. The greater part, however, of their successors, the popes of Rome, enticed by the antisynodical privileges offered them for the oppression of the churches of God, and finding in them much worldly advantage, and "much gain," and conceiving a monarchy in the catholic church and a monopoly of the gifts of the Holy Ghost, changed the ancient worship at will, sepa-

[Mt 12.32]

[Acts 16.6]

---

6. *Eph* (431) can 7 (*NPNF*–II 14:231).

7. Athanasius *Apologia contra Arianos* 29 (*NPNF*–II 4:115); Basil of Caesarea *Epistles* 69–70 (*NPNF*–II 8:165–66).

rating themselves by novelties from the old received Christian polity. Nor did they cease their endeavors, by lawless projects (as veritable history assures us), to entice the other four patriarchates into their apostasy from orthodoxy, and so subject the catholic church to the whims and ordinances of men.

7. Our illustrious predecessors and fathers, with united labor and counsel, seeing the evangelical doctrine received from the fathers to be trodden under foot, and the robe of our Savior woven from above to be torn by wicked hands, and stimu- [Jn 19.23–24] lated by fatherly and brotherly love, wept for the desolation of so many Christians "for whom Christ died." They exercised much zeal and ardor, both synodically and [Rom 14.15] individually, in order that the orthodox doctrine of the holy catholic church being saved, they might knit together as far as they were able that which had been rent; and like approved physicians they consulted together for the safety of the suffering member, enduring many tribulations, and contempts, and persecutions, if haply the body of Christ might not be divided, or the definitions of the divine and august synods be made of none effect. But veracious history has transmitted to us the relentlessness of the Western perseverance in error. These illustrious men proved indeed on this point the truth of the words of our holy father Basil the sublime, when he said, from experience, concerning the bishops of the West, and particularly of the pope: "They neither know the truth nor endure to learn it, striving against those who tell them the truth, and strengthening themselves in their heresy."[8] Thus, after a first and second brotherly admonition, knowing their impenitence, shaking them [Ti 3.10] off and avoiding them, they gave them over to their reprobate mind. "War is better [Rom 1.28] than peace, apart from God," as said our holy father Gregory, concerning the Arians.[9] From that time there has been no spiritual communion between us and them; for they have with their own hands dug deep the chasm between themselves and Orthodoxy.

8. Yet the papacy has not on this account ceased to annoy the peaceful church of God, but sending out everywhere so-called missionaries, men of reprobate minds, it compasses land and sea to make one proselyte, to deceive one of [Mt 23.15] the Orthodox, to corrupt the doctrine of our Lord, to adulterate, by addition, the divine creed of our holy faith, to prove the baptism which God gave us superfluous, the communion of the cup void of sacred efficacy, and a thousand other things which the demon of novelty dictated to the all-daring schoolmen of the Middle Ages and to the bishops of the elder Rome, venturing all things through lust of power.

8. Basil of Caesarea *Epistle* 239.2 (*NPNF*-II 8:281).
9. A frequent theme, for example, Gregory of Nazianzus *Orations* 33.1–2 (*NPNF*-II 7:328–29).

Our blessed predecessors and fathers, in their piety, though tried and persecuted in many ways and means, within and without, directly and indirectly, "yet confident

[Ps 125.1] in the Lord," were able to save and transmit to us this inestimable inheritance of our fathers, which we too, by the help of God, will transmit as a rich treasure to the generations to come, even to the end of the world. But notwithstanding this, the papists do not cease to this day, nor will cease, according to wont, to attack Ortho-

[Wis 2.14] doxy,—a daily living reproach which they have before their eyes, being deserters from the faith of their fathers. Would that they made these aggressions against the heresy which has overspread and mastered the West. For who doubts that had their zeal for the overthrow of Orthodoxy been employed for the overthrow of heresy and novelties, agreeable to the God-loving counsels of Leo III and John VIII, those glorious and last orthodox popes, not a trace of it, long ago, would have been re-membered under the sun, and we should now be saying the same things, according

[1 Cor 1.10] to the apostolic command. But the zeal of those who succeeded them was not for the protection of the orthodox faith, in conformity with the zeal worthy of all re-membrance which was in Leo III, now among the blessed.

9. In a measure the aggressions of the later popes in their own persons had ceased, and were carried on only by means of missionaries. But lately, Pius IX, be-coming bishop of Rome and proclaimed pope in 1846, published on the sixth of January, in this present year, an encyclical letter addressed to the Easterns, consist-ing of twelve pages in the Greek version, which his emissary has disseminated, like a plague coming from without, within our Orthodox fold. In this encyclical, he addresses those who at different times have gone over from different Christian com-munions, and embraced the papacy, and of course are favorable to him, extending his arguments also to the Orthodox, either particularly or without naming them; and, citing our divine and holy fathers, he manifestly calumniates them and us, their successors and descendants: them, as if they admitted readily the papal commands and rescripts without question because issuing from the popes as undoubted arbi-ters of the catholic church; us, as unfaithful to their examples (for thus he trespasses on the fold committed to us by God), as severed from our fathers, as careless of our sacred trusts, and of the soul's salvation of our spiritual children. Usurping as his own possession the catholic church of Christ, by occupancy, as he boasts, of the episcopal throne of St. Peter, he desires to deceive the more simple into apostasy from Orthodoxy, choosing for the basis of all theological instruction these para-doxical words: "Nor is there any reason why you refuse a return to the true church and communion with this my holy throne."

10. Each one of our brethren and sons in Christ who have been piously brought up and instructed, wisely regarding the wisdom given him from God, will

decide that the words of the present bishop of Rome, like those of his schismatical predecessors, are not words of peace, as he affirms, and of benevolence, but words of deceit and guile, tending to self-aggrandizement, agreeably to the practice of his antisynodical predecessors. We are therefore sure, that even as heretofore, so hereafter the Orthodox will not be beguiled. For the word of our Lord is sure: "A stranger will they not follow, but flee from him, for they know not the voice of strangers."

[Jn 10.5]

11. For all this we have esteemed it our paternal and brotherly need, and a sacred duty, by our present admonition to confirm you in the Orthodoxy you hold from your forefathers, and at the same time point out the emptiness of the syllogisms of the bishop of Rome, of which he is manifestly himself aware. For not from his apostolic confession does he glorify his throne, but from his apostolic throne seeks to establish his dignity, and from his dignity, his confession. The truth is the other way. The throne of Rome is esteemed that of St. Peter by a single tradition, but not from Holy Scripture, where the claim is in favor of Antioch, whose church is therefore witnessed by the great Basil to be "the most venerable of all the churches in the world."[10] Still more, the Second Ecumenical Council, writing to a council of the West (to the most honorable and religious brethren and fellow servants, Damasus, Ambrose, Britto, Valerian, and others), witnesses, saying: "The oldest and truly apostolic church of Antioch, in Syria, where first the honored name of Christians was used."[11] We say, then, that the apostolic Church of Antioch had no right of exemption from being judged according to Divine Scripture and synodical declarations, though truly venerated for the throne of St. Peter. But what do we say? The blessed Peter, even in his own person, was judged before all for the truth of the gospel, and, as Scripture declares, was found blamable and not walking uprightly. What opinion is to be formed of those who glory and pride themselves solely in the possession of his throne, so great in their eyes? Nay, the sublime Basil the Great, the ecumenical teacher of orthodoxy in the catholic church, to whom the bishops of Rome are obliged to refer us, has clearly and explicitly above shown us what estimation we ought to have of the judgments of the inaccessible Vatican: "They neither," he says, "know the truth, nor endure to learn it, striving against those who tell them the truth, and strengthening themselves in their heresy." So that these our holy fathers whom His Holiness the Pope, worthily admiring as lights and teachers even of the West, accounts as belonging to us, and advises us to follow, teach

[Gal 2.11–14]

---

10. Basil of Caesarea *Epistle* 66 (to Athanasius) (*NPNF*–II 8:164).

11. *Synodical Epistle of the First Council of Constantinople to Pope Damasus and the Eastern Bishops* (PL 13:1202).

us not to judge orthodoxy from the holy throne, but the throne itself and him that
is on the throne by the sacred Scriptures, by synodical decrees and limitations, and
by the faith which has been preached, even the orthodoxy of continuous teaching.
Thus did our fathers judge and condemn Honorius, pope of Rome, and Dioscorus,
pope of Alexandria, and Macedonius and Nestorius, patriarchs of Constantinople,
and Peter Gnapheus, patriarch of Antioch, with others. For if the abomination of
[Mt 24.15] desolation stood in the holy place, according to the testimony of the Scriptures, why
not innovation and heresy upon a holy throne?

Hence is exhibited in a brief compass the weakness and feebleness of the
efforts in behalf of the despotism of the pope of Rome. For, unless the church of
Christ was founded upon the immovable rock of St. Peter's confession, "Thou art
the Christ, the Son of the living God" (which was the answer of the apostles in com-
[Mt 16.15-16] mon, when the question was put to them, "Whom say ye that I am?" as the fathers,
both Eastern and Western, interpret the passage to us), the church was built upon
a slippery foundation, even on Cephas himself, not to say on the pope, who, after
monopolizing the keys of the kingdom of heaven, has made such an administration
of them as is plain from history. But our divine fathers, with one accord, teach that
the sense of the thrice-repeated command, "Feed my sheep," implied no prerogative in St. Peter over the other apostles, least of all in his successors. It was a simple
restoration to his apostleship, from which he had fallen by his thrice-repeated denial. Saint Peter himself appears to have understood the intention of the thrice-
repeated question of our Lord: "Lovest thou me, and more, than these?" for, calling
to mind the words, "They all shall be offended because of thee, yet will I never be
[Mt 26.33] offended," he was grieved because he said unto him the third time, "Lovest thou
[Jn 21.15-17] me?" But his successors, from self-interest, understand the expression as indicative
of St. Peter's more ready mind.

12. His Holiness the Pope says that our Lord said to Peter, "I have prayed
for thee, that thy faith fail not: and when thou art converted, strengthen thy breth-
[Lk 22.32] ren." Our Lord so prayed because Satan had sought to overthrow the faith of all
the disciples, but the Lord allowed him Peter only, chiefly because he had uttered
words of boasting, and justified himself above the rest: "Though all shall be of-
[Mt 26.33] fended, because of thee, yet will I never be offended." The permission to Satan was
[Mt 26.74] but temporary. "He began to curse and to swear: I know not the man." So weak is
[Mt 26.41] human nature, left to itself. "The spirit is willing, but the flesh is weak." It was but
temporary, that, coming again to himself by his return in tears of repentance, he
might the rather strengthen his brethren who had neither perjured themselves nor
denied. Oh! the wise judgment of the Lord! How divine and mysterious was the last
night of our Savior upon earth! That sacred supper is believed to be consecrated

to this day in every church: "This do in remembrance of me"; and "As often as ye   [Lk 22.19]
eat this bread and drink this cup, ye do show the Lord's death till he come." Of   [1 Cor 11.26]
the brotherly love thus earnestly commended to us by the common Master, saying,
"By this shall all men know that ye are my disciple, if ye have love one to another,"   [Jn 13.35]
have the popes first broken the stamp and seal, supporting and receiving heretical
novelties, contrary to the things delivered to us and canonically confirmed by our
teachers and fathers in common. This love acts at this day with power in the souls
of Christian people, and particularly in their leaders. We boldly avow before God
and men, that the prayer of our Savior to God and his Father for the common love
and unity of Christians in the one holy, catholic, and apostolic church in which we
believe, "that they may be one, ever as we are one," works in us no less than in His   [Jn 17.22]
Holiness. Our brotherly love and zeal meet that of His Holiness, with only this difference, that in us it works for the covenanted preservation of the pure, undefiled,
divine, spotless, and perfect Creed of the Christian faith, in conformity to the voice
of the gospel and the decrees of the seven holy ecumenical councils and the teachings of the ever-existing catholic church: but it works in His Holiness to prop and
strengthen the authority and dignity of them that sit on the apostolic throne, and
their new doctrine. Behold then, the head and front, so to speak, of all the differences and disagreements that have happened between us and them, and the middle
wall of partition— which we hope will be taken away in the time of His Holiness,   [Eph 2.14]
and by the aid of his renowned wisdom—according to the promise of God: "Other
sheep I have which are not of this fold: them also I must bring and they shall hear my
voice (Who proceedeth from the Father)." Let it be said then, in the third place: If   [Jn 10.16]
it be supposed, according to the words of His Holiness, that this prayer of our Lord
for Peter when about to deny and perjure himself, remained attached and united to
the throne of Peter, and is transmitted with power to those who from time to time
sit upon it—although, as has before been said, nothing contributes to confirm the
opinion as we are strikingly assured from the example of the blessed Peter himself,
even after the descent of the Holy Ghost—yet are we convinced from the words of
our Lord, that the time will come when that divine prayer concerning the denial of
Peter, "that his faith might not fail forever" will operate also in some one of the
successors of his throne, who will also weep, as he did, bitterly, and being sometime
converted will strengthen us, his brethren, still more in the orthodox confession,
which we hold from our forefathers. Would that His Holiness might be this true successor of the blessed Peter! To this our humble prayer, what hinders that we should
add our sincere and hearty counsel in the name of the holy catholic church? We dare
not say, as does His Holiness, that it should be done "without any delay"; but without haste, after mature consideration, and also, if need be, after consultation with

the more wise, religious, truth-loving, and prudent of the bishops, theologians, and doctors, to be found at the present day, by God's good providence, in every nation of the West.

13. His Holiness says that the bishop of Lyons, St. Irenaeus, writes in praise of the church of Rome: "That the whole church, namely, the faithful from everywhere, must come together in that church, because of its primacy, in which church the tradition, given by the apostles, has in all respects been observed by the faithful everywhere."[12] Although this saint says by no means what the followers of the Vatican would make out, yet even granting their interpretation, we reply: Who denies that the ancient Roman church was apostolic and orthodox? None of us will question that it was a model of orthodoxy. We will specially add, for its greater praise, from the historian Sozomen, the passage, which His Holiness has overlooked, respecting the mode by which for a time she was enabled to preserve the orthodoxy which we praise:—"For, as everywhere," saith Sozomen, "the church throughout the West, being guided purely by the doctrines of the fathers, was delivered from contention and deception concerning these things."[13] Would any of the fathers or ourselves deny her canonical privilege in the rank of the hierarchy, so long as she was guided purely by the doctrines of the fathers, walking by the plain rule of Scripture and the holy councils? But at present we do not find preserved in her the dogma of the Blessed Trinity according to the creed of the holy fathers assembled first in Nicaea and afterwards in Constantinople, which the other five ecumenical councils confessed and confirmed with such anathemas on those who adulterated it in the smallest particular, as if they had thereby destroyed it. Nor do we find the apostolic pattern of holy baptism, nor the invocation of the consecrating Spirit upon the holy elements; but we see in that church the eucharistic cup, heavenly drink, considered superfluous (what profanity!), and very many other things, unknown not only to our holy fathers, who were always entitled the catholic, clear rule and index of orthodoxy, as His Holiness, revering the truth, himself teaches, but also unknown to the ancient holy fathers of the West. We see that very primacy, for which His Holiness now contends with all his might, as did his predecessors, transformed from a brotherly character and hierarchical privilege into a lordly superiority.

What then is to be thought of his unwritten traditions, if the written have undergone such a change and alteration for the worse? Who is so bold and confident in the dignity of the apostolic throne as to dare to say that if our holy father, St. Irenaeus, were alive again, seeing it was fallen from the ancient and primitive teach-

12. Irenaeus of Lyons *Against Heresies* 3.3.2 (*ANF* 1:415–16).
13. Sozomen *Ecclesiastical History* 3.13 (*NPNF*–II 2:291).

ing in so many most essential and catholic articles of Christianity, he would not be himself the first to oppose the novelties and self-sufficient constitutions of that church which was lauded by him as guided purely by the doctrines of the fathers? For instance, when he saw the Roman Church not only rejecting from her liturgical canon, according to the suggestion of the schoolmen, the very ancient and apostolic invocation of the consecrating Spirit,[14] and miserably mutilating the sacrifice in its most essential part, but also urgently hastening to cut it out from the liturgies of other Christian communions also,—His Holiness slanderously asserting, in a manner so unworthy of the apostolic throne on which he boasts himself, that it "crept in after the division between the East and West"—what would not the holy father say respecting this novelty? Irenaeus assures us: "That bread, from the ground, receiving the evocation of God, is no longer common bread," etc., meaning by "evocation" invocation: for that Irenaeus believed the mystery of the sacrifice to be consecrated by means of this invocation is especially remarked even by François Feuardent, of the order of popish monks called Minorites, who in 1639 edited the writings of that saint with comments, who says that Irenaeus teaches "that the bread and mixed cup become the true body and blood of Christ by the words of invocation."[15] Or, hearing of the vicarial and appellate jurisdiction of the pope, what would not the saint say, who, for a small and almost indifferent question concerning the celebration of Easter, so boldly and victoriously opposed and defeated the violence of Pope Victor in the free church of Christ?[16] Thus he who is cited by His Holiness as a witness of the primacy of the Roman Church, shows that its dignity is not that of a lordship, nor even appellate, to which St. Peter himself was never ordained, but is a brotherly privilege in the catholic church, and an honor assigned the popes on account of the greatness and privilege of the city. Thus, also, the Fourth Ecumenical Council, for the preservation of the gradation in rank of churches canonically established by the Third Ecumenical Council,[17]—following the Second,[18] as that again followed the First,[19] which called the appellate jurisdiction of the pope over the West a custom,—thus uttered its determination: "On account of that city being the imperial city, the fathers have with reason given it prerogatives."[20] Here

14. Epiclesis (*Lit Chrys* II.F.5).

15. François Feuardent (1539–1610); see *ODCC* 607.

16. Eusebius of Caesarea *Ecclesiastical History* 5.24.11–18 (*NPNF*-II 1:243–44).

17. *Eph* (431) can 8 (*NPNF*-II 14:234–35).

18. *CP I* (381) can 3 (*NPNF*-II 14:179).

19. *Nic I* (325) can 6 (*NPNF*-II 14:15).

20. *Chal* (451) can 28 (*NPNF*-II 14:287).

nothing is said of the pope's special monopoly of the apostolicity of St. Peter, still less of a vicarship in Rome's bishops, and a universal pastorate. This deep silence in regard to such great privileges—not only so, but the reason assigned for the primacy, not "Feed my sheep," not "On this rock will I build my church," but simply old custom, and the city being the imperial city; and these things, not from the Lord, but from the fathers—will seem, we are sure, a great paradox to His Holiness entertaining other ideas of his prerogatives. The paradox will be the greater, since, as we shall see, he greatly honors the said Fourth Ecumenical Synod as one to be found a witness for his throne; and St. Gregory, the eloquent, called the Great, was wont to speak of the four ecumenical councils as the four Gospels, and the four-sided stone on which the catholic church is built.[21]

14. His Holiness says that the Corinthians, divided among themselves, referred the matter to Clement, pope of Rome, who wrote to them his decision on the case; and they so prized his decision that they read it in the churches. But this event is a very weak support for the papal authority in the house of God. For Rome being then the center of the imperial province and the chief city, in which the emperors lived, it was proper that any question of importance, as history shows that of the Corinthians to have been, should be decided there, especially if one of the contending parties ran thither for external aid: as is done even to this day. The patriarchs of Alexandria, Antioch, and Jerusalem, when unexpected points of difficulty arise, write to the patriarch of Constantinople, because of its being the seat of empire, as also on account of its synodical privileges; and if this brotherly aid shall rectify that which should be rectified, it is well; but if not, the matter is reported to the province, according to the established system. But this brotherly agreement in Christian faith is not purchased by the servitude of the churches of God. Let this be our answer also to the examples of a fraternal and proper championship of the privileges of Julius and Innocent, bishops of Rome, by St. Athanasius the Great and St. John Chrysostom, referred to by His Holiness, for which their successors now seek to recompense us by adulterating the divine creed. Yet Julius himself was indignant against some for "disturbing the churches by not maintaining the doctrines of Nicaea," and threatening excommunication, "if they ceased not their innovations."[22] In the case of the Corinthians, moreover, it is to be remarked that the patriarchal thrones being then but three, Rome was the nearer and more accessible to the Corinthians, to which, therefore, it was proper to have resort. In all this we

21. Gregory I *Epistles* 1.25 (*NPNF*-II 12:81).
22. Sozomen *Ecclesiastical History* 3.8 (*NPNF*-II 2:287–88).

see nothing extraordinary, nor any proof of the despotic power of the pope in the free church of God.

15. But, finally, His Holiness says that the Fourth Ecumenical Council (which by mistake he quite transfers from Chalcedon to Carthage), when it read the epistle of Pope Leo I, cried out, "Peter has thus spoken by Leo." It was so indeed. But His Holiness ought not to overlook how, and after what examination, our fathers cried out, as they did, in praise of Leo. Since however His Holiness, consulting brevity, appears to have omitted this most necessary point, and the manifest proof that an ecumenical council is not only above the pope but above any council of his, we will explain to the public the matter as it really happened. Of more than six hundred fathers assembled in the Council of Chalcedon, about two hundred of the wisest were appointed by the council to examine both as to language and sense the said epistle of Leo; nor only so, but to give in writing and with their signatures their own judgment upon it, whether it were orthodox or not. These, about two hundred judgments and resolutions on the epistle, as chiefly found in the fourth session of the said holy council in such terms as the following:

"Maximus of Antioch in Syria said: 'The epistle of the holy Leo, archbishop of imperial Rome, agrees with the decisions of the three hundred and eighteen holy fathers at Nicaea, and the hundred and fifty at Constantinople, which is new Rome, and with the faith expounded at Ephesus by the most holy Bishop Cyril: and I have subscribed it.'"

And again: "Theodoret, the most religious Bishop of Cyrus: 'The epistle of the most holy archbishop, the lord Leo, agrees with the faith established at Nicaea by the holy and blessed fathers, and with the symbol of faith expounded at Constantinople by the hundred and fifty, and with the epistles of the blessed Cyril. And accepting it, I have subscribed the said epistle.'"

And thus all in succession: "The epistle corresponds," "the epistle is consonant," "the epistle agrees in sense," and the like. After such great and very severe scrutiny in comparing it with former holy councils, and a full conviction of the correctness of the meaning, and not merely because it was the epistle of the pope, they cried aloud, ungrudgingly, the exclamation on which His Holiness now vaunts himself. But if His Holiness had sent us statements concordant and in unison with the seven holy ecumenical councils, instead of boasting of the piety of his predecessors lauded by our predecessors and fathers in an ecumenical council, he might justly have gloried in his own orthodoxy, declaring his own goodness instead of that of his fathers. Therefore let His Holiness be assured that if, even now, he will write us such things as two hundred fathers on investigation and inquiry shall find consonant and agreeing with the said former councils, then, we say, he shall hear from us sinners today, not only, "Peter has so spoken," or anything of like honor, but this also, "Let the holy hand be kissed which has wiped away the tears of the catholic church."

16. And surely we have a right to expect from the prudent forethought of His Holiness a work so worthy the true successor of St. Peter, of Leo I, and also of Leo III, who for security of the orthodox faith engraved the divine creed unaltered upon imperishable plates—a work which will unite the churches of the West to the holy catholic church, in which the canonical chief seat of His Holiness, and the seats of all the bishops of the West remain empty and ready to be occupied. For the catholic church, awaiting the conversion of the shepherds who have fallen off from her with their flocks, does not separate in name only those who have been privily introduced to the rulership by the action of others, thus making little of the priesthood. But we are expecting the "word of consolation," and hope that he, as St. Basil wrote to St. Ambrose, bishop of Milan, will "tread again the ancient footprints of the fathers."[23] Not without great astonishment have we read the said encyclical letter to the Easterns, in which we see with deep grief of soul His Holiness, famed for prudence, speaking, like his predecessors in schism, words that urge upon us the adulteration of our pure holy creed, on which the ecumenical councils have set their seal; and doing violence to the sacred liturgies, whose heavenly structure alone, and the names of those who framed them, and their tone of reverend antiquity, and the stamp that was placed upon them by the Seventh Ecumenical Council,[24] should have paralyzed him, and made him to turn aside the sacrilegious and all-daring hand that has thus smitten the King of Glory. From these things we estimate into what an unspeakable labyrinth of wrong and incorrigible sin of revolution the papacy has thrown even the wiser and more godly bishops of the Roman Church, so that, in order to preserve the innocent, and therefore valued vicarial dignity, as well as the despotic primacy and the things depending upon it, they know no other means than to insult the most divine and sacred things, daring everything for that one end. Clothing themselves, in words, with pious reverence for "the most venerable antiquity," in reality there remains, within, the innovating temper; and yet His Holiness really bears hard upon himself when he says that we "must cast from us everything that has crept in among us since the separation," (!) while he and his have spread the poison of their innovation even into the supper of our Lord.

His Holiness evidently takes it for granted that in the Orthodox Church

23. Basil of Caesarea to Ambrose of Milan, *Epistle* 197.1 (*NPNF*–II 8:235).
24. *Nic II* decr.

the same thing has happened which he is conscious has happened in the church of Rome since the rise of the papacy: to wit, a sweeping change in all the mysteries, and corruption from scholastic subtleties, a reliance on which must suffice as an equivalent for our sacred liturgies and mysteries and doctrines: yet all the while totally reverencing our "venerable antiquity," and all this by a condescension entirely apostolic!—"without," as he says, "troubling us by any harsh conditions"! From such ignorance of the apostolic and catholic food on which we live emanates another sententious declaration of his: "It is not possible that unity of doctrine and sacred observance should be preserved among you," paradoxically ascribing to us the very misfortune from which he suffers at home; just as Pope Leo IX wrote to the blessed Michael Cerularius, accusing the Greeks of changing the creed of the catholic church, without blushing either for his own honor or for the truth of history. We are persuaded that if His Holiness will call to mind ecclesiastical archaeology and history, the doctrine of the holy fathers and the old liturgies of France and Spain, and the sacramentary of the ancient Roman church, he will be struck with surprise on finding how many other monstrous daughters, now living, the papacy has brought forth in the West: while Orthodoxy, with us, has preserved the catholic church as an incorruptible bride for her bridegroom, although we have no temporal power, nor, as His Holiness says, any "sacred observances," but by the sole tie of love and affection to a common mother are bound together in the unity of a faith sealed with the seven seals of the Spirit, and by the seven ecumenical councils, and [Rv 5.1] in obedience to the truth. He will find, also, how many modern papistic doctrines and mysteries must be rejected as "commandments of men" in order that the church [Mt 15.9] of the West, which has introduced all sorts of novelties, may be changed back again to the immutable catholic orthodox faith of our common fathers. As His Holiness recognizes our common zeal in this faith, when he says, "Let us take heed to the doctrine preserved by our forefathers," so he does well in instructing us to follow the old pontiffs and the faithful of the Eastern metropolitans. What these thought of the doctrinal fidelity of the archbishops of the elder Rome, and what idea we ought to have of them in the Orthodox Church, and in what manner we ought to receive their teachings, they have synodically given us an example, and the sublime Basil has well interpreted it. As to the supremacy, since we are not setting forth a treatise, let the same great Basil present the matter in a few words, "I preferred to address myself to Him who is Head over them."

17. From all this, everyone nourished in sound catholic doctrine, particularly His Holiness, must draw the conclusion, how impious and anticonciliar it is to attempt the alteration of our doctrine and liturgies and other divine offices which are, and are proved to be, coeval with the preaching of Christianity: for which rea-

son reverence was always bestowed on them, and they were confided in as pure even by the old orthodox popes themselves, to whom these things were an inheritance in common with ourselves. How becoming and holy would be the mending of the innovations, the time of whose entrance in the church of Rome we know in each case; for our illustrious fathers have testified from time to time against each novelty. But there are other reasons which should incline His Holiness to this change. First, because those things that are ours were once venerable to the Westerns, as having the same divine offices and confessing the same creed; but the novelties were not known to our fathers, nor could they be shown in the writings of the orthodox Western fathers, nor as having their origin either in antiquity or catholicity. Moreover, neither patriarchs nor councils could then have introduced novelties amongst us, because the protector of religion is the very body of the church, even the people themselves, who desire their religious worship to be ever unchanged and of the same kind as that of their fathers. For as, after the schism, many of the popes and Latinizing patriarchs made attempts that came to nothing even in the Western church, and as, from time to time, either by fair means or foul, the popes have commanded novelties for the sake of expediency (as they have explained to our fathers, although they were thus dismembering the body of Christ), so now again the pope, for the sake of a truly divine and most just expediency indeed (not mending the nets, but himself rending the garment of the Savior)[a] dares to oppose the venerable things of antiquity,—things well fitted to preserve religion, as His Holiness confesses, and which he himself honors, as he says, together with his predecessors; for he repeats that memorable expression of one of those blessed predecessors (Celestine, writing to the Third Ecumenical Council): "Let novelty cease to attack antiquity."[25] And let the catholic church enjoy this benefit from this so far blameless declaration of the popes. It must by all means be confessed, that in such his attempt, even though Pius IX be eminent for wisdom and piety, and, as he says, for zeal after Christian unity in the catholic church, he will meet, within and without, with difficulties and toils. And here we must put His Holiness in mind, if he will excuse our boldness, of that portion of his letter: "That in things which relate to the confession of our divine religion, nothing is to be feared, when we look to the glory of Christ, and the reward which awaits us in eternal life." It is incumbent on His Holiness to show before God and man that, as prime mover of the counsel which pleases God, so is he a willing protector of the ill-treated evangelical and conciliar truth, even to the sac-

a. [Mt 4.21; Jn 19.23–24]

25. Perhaps a reference to Pope Celestine *Epistles* 19.1 (*PL* 50:541).

rifice of his own interests, according to the prophet, "a ruler in peace and a bishop in righteousness." So be it! But until there be this desired returning of the apostate churches to the body of the one, holy, catholic, and apostolic church, of which Christ is the Head and each of us "members in particular," all advice proceeding from them, and every officious exhortation tending to the dissolution of our pure faith handed down from the fathers is condemned, as it ought to be, synodically, not only as suspicious and to be eschewed, but as impious and soul-destroying: and in this category, among the first we place the said *Encyclical to the Easterns* from Pope Pius IX, bishop of the elder Rome; and such we proclaim it to be in the catholic church.

[Is 60.17 (LXX)]

[1 Cor 12.27]

18. Wherefore, beloved brethren and fellow ministers of our humble person, as always, so also now, particularly on this occasion of the publication of the said encyclical, we hold it to be our inexorable duty, in accordance with our patriarchal and synodical responsibility, in order that none may be lost to the divine fold of the catholic orthodox church, the most holy mother of us all, to encourage each other, and to urge you that, reminding one another of the words and exhortations of St. Paul to our holy predecessors when he summoned them to Ephesus, we reiterate to each other: "Take heed, therefore, unto yourselves, and to all the flock, over the which the Holy Ghost hath made you overseers, to feed the church of God, which he hath purchased with his own blood. For know this, that after my departing shall grievous wolves enter in among you not sparing the flock. Also of your own selves shall men arise, speaking perverse things, to draw away disciples after them. Therefore, watch." Then our predecessors and fathers, hearing this divine charge, wept sore, and falling upon his neck, kissed him. Come, then, and let us, brethren, hearing him admonishing us with tears, fall in spirit, lamenting, upon his neck, and, kissing him, comfort him by our own firm assurance that no one shall separate us from the love of Christ, no one mislead us from evangelical doctrine, no one entice us from the safe path of our fathers, as none was able to deceive them, by any degree of zeal which they manifested, who from time to time were raised up for this purpose by the tempter. So as last we shall hear from the Master: "Well done, good and faithful servant,"[a] receiving the end of our faith, even the salvation of our souls,[b] and of the reasonable flock over whom the Holy Ghost has made us shepherds.

[Acts 20.28–31]

[Rom 8.39]

[Acts 20.28]

19. This apostolic charge and exhortation we have quoted for your sake, and address it to all the Orthodox congregation, wherever they be found settled on the earth, to the priests and abbots, to the deacons and monks, in a word, to all the

a. [Mt 25.21]
b. [1 Pt 1.9]

clergy and godly people, the rulers and the ruled, the rich and the poor, to parents and children, to teachers and scholars, to the educated and uneducated, to masters and servants, that we all, supporting and counseling each other, may be able to stand against the wiles of the devil. For thus St. Peter the apostle exhorts us: "Be sober, be vigilant because your adversary the devil, as a roaring lion walketh about, seeking

[1 Pt 5.8–9] whom he may devour. Whom resist, steadfast in the faith."

20. For our faith, brethren, is not of men nor by man, but by revelation of

[Gal 1.1, 12] Jesus Christ, which the divine apostles preached, the holy ecumenical councils confirmed, the greatest and wisest teachers of the world handed down in succession, and the shed blood of the holy martyrs ratified. Let us hold fast to the confession which

[Heb 4.14, 10.23] we have received unadulterated from such men, turning away from every novelty as a suggestion of the devil. He that accepts a novelty reproaches with deficiency the preached orthodox faith. But that faith has long ago been sealed in completeness, not to admit of diminution or increase, or any change whatever; and he who dares to do, or advise, or think of such a thing has already denied the faith of Christ, has already of his own accord been struck with an eternal anathema, for blaspheming the Holy Ghost as not having spoken fully in the Scriptures and through the ecumenical councils. This fearful anathema, brethren and sons beloved in Christ, we do not pronounce today, but our Savior first pronounced it: "Whosoever speaketh against the Holy Ghost, it shall not be forgiven him, neither in this world, neither

[Mt 12.32] in the world to come." Saint Paul pronounced the same anathema: "I marvel that ye are so soon removed from him that called you into the grace of Christ, unto another gospel: which is not another; but there be some that trouble you, and would pervert the gospel of Christ. But though we, or an angel from heaven, preach any other gospel unto you, than that which we have preached unto you, let him be ac-

[Gal 1.6–8] cursed." This same anathema the seven ecumenical councils and the whole choir of God-serving fathers pronounced. All, therefore, who innovate, either by heresy or schism, have voluntarily clothed themselves, according to the Psalm, "with a curse

[Ps 109.18] as with a garment," whether they be popes, or patriarchs, or clergy, or laity; nay, if anyone, though an angel from heaven, preach any other gospel unto you than that you have received, let him be accursed. Thus our wise fathers, obedient to the soul-saving words of St. Paul, were established firm and steadfast in the faith handed down unbrokenly to them, and preserved it unchanged and uncontaminate in the midst of so many heresies, and have delivered it to us pure and undefiled, as it came pure from the mouth of the first servants of the word. Let us, too, being wise, transmit it, pure as we have received it, to coming generations, altering nothing, that they may be, as we are, full of confidence, and with nothing to be ashamed of when speaking of the faith of their forefathers.

21. Therefore, brethren, and sons beloved in the Lord, having purified your souls in obeying the truth, let us give the more earnest heed to the things which we have heard, lest at any time we should let them slip. The faith and confession we have received is not one to be ashamed of, being taught in the Gospel from the mouth of our Lord, witnessed by the holy apostles, by the seven sacred ecumenical councils, preached throughout the world, witnessed to by its very enemies, who, before they apostatized from orthodoxy to heresies, themselves held this same faith, or at least their fathers and fathers' fathers thus held it. It is witnessed to by continuous history, as triumphing over all the heresies which have persecuted or now persecute it, as you see even to this day. The succession of our holy divine fathers and predecessors beginning from the apostles, and those whom the apostles appointed their successors, to this day, forming one unbroken chain, and joining hand to hand, keep fast the sacred enclosure of which the door is Christ, in which all the Orthodox flock is fed in the fertile pastures of the mystical Eden, and not in the pathless and rugged wilderness, as His Holiness supposes. Our church holds the infallible and genuine deposit of the Holy Scriptures, of the Old Testament a true and perfect version, of the New the divine original itself.[26] The rites of the sacred mysteries, and especially those of the Divine Liturgy, are the same glorious and heartquickening rites, handed down from the apostles. No nation, no Christian communion, can boast of such liturgies as those of James, Basil, Chrysostom. The august ecumenical councils, those seven pillars of the house of Wisdom, were organized in it and among us. This, our church, holds the originals of their sacred definitions. The chief pastors in it, and the honorable presbytery, and the monastic order, preserve the primitive and pure dignity of the first ages of Christianity, in opinions, in polity, and even in the simplicity of their vestments. Yes! verily, "grievous wolves" have constantly attacked this holy fold, and are attacking it now, as we see for ourselves, according to the prediction of the apostle, which shows that the true lambs of the great Shepherd are folded in it. But that church has sung and shall sing forever: "They compassed me about; yea, they compassed me about: but in the name of the Lord I will destroy them." Let us add one reflection, a painful one indeed, but useful in order to manifest and confirm the truth of our words: All Christian nations whatsoever that are today seen calling upon the name of Christ (not excepting either the West generally, or Rome herself, as we prove by the catalog of her earliest popes), were taught the true faith in Christ by our holy predecessors and fathers; and yet afterwards deceitful men, many of whom were shepherds, and chief shepherds, too, of those nations,

[1 Pt 1.22]

[Heb 2.1]

[Jn 10.7, 9]

[Prv 9.1]

[Acts 20.29]

[Ps 118.11]

26. That is, the Greek Septuagint version of the Old Testament, and the original Greek of the New.

by wretched sophistries and heretical opinions dared to defile, alas! the orthodoxy of those nations, as veracious history informs us, and as St. Paul predicted.[a]

22. Therefore, brethren, and you our spiritual children, we acknowledge how great the favor and grace which God has bestowed upon our Orthodox faith, and on his one, holy, catholic, and apostolic church, which, like a mother who is unsuspected of her husband, nourishes us as children of whom she is not ashamed, and who are excusable in our high-toned boldness concerning the hope that is in us. But what shall we sinners render to the Lord for all that he hath bestowed upon

[1 Pt 3.15] us? Our bounteous Lord and God,[b] who has redeemed us by his blood,[c] requires nothing else of us but the devotion of our whole soul and heart to the blameless, holy faith of our fathers, and love and affection to the orthodox church, which has regenerated us not with a novel sprinkling, but with the divine washing of apostolic baptism. She it is that nourishes us, according to the eternal covenant of our Savior, with his own precious body, and abundantly, as a true mother, gives us to drink of that precious blood poured out for us and for the salvation of the world. Let us then

[Ps 84.3 (LXX)] encompass her in spirit, as the young their parent bird, wherever on earth we find ourselves, in the north or south, or east, or west. Let us fix our eyes and thoughts upon her divine countenance and her most glorious beauty. Let us take hold with both our hands on her shining robe which the Bridegroom, "altogether lovely," has with his own undefiled hands thrown around her, when he redeemed her from the

[Ps 45.2; Rv 21.2] bondage of error, and adorned her as an eternal bride for himself. Let us feel in our own souls the mutual grief of the children-loving mother and the mother-loving children, when it is seen that men of wolfish minds and making gain of souls are zealous in plotting how they may lead her captive, or tear the lambs from their mothers. Let us, clergy as well as laity, cherish this feeling most intensely now, when the unseen adversary of our salvation, combining his fraudful arts, employs such powerful in-

[1 Pt 5.8] strumentalities, and walketh about everywhere, as St. Peter says, seeking whom he may devour; and when in this way, in which we walk peacefully and innocently, he sets his deceitful snares.

23. "Now, the God of peace, that brought again from the dead that great Shepherd of the sheep," "He that keepeth Israel," who "shall neither slumber nor sleep," "keep your hearts and minds," "and direct your ways to every good work."[d]

a. [1 Tm 4.3–4; Acts 20.29]
b. [Ps 116.12]
c. [Acts 20.28]
d. [Heb 13.20–21; Ps 121.4; Phil 4.7; Lk 1.79]

Peace and joy be with you in the Lord.

May 1848, Indiction 6.

Anthimus, by the mercy of God, archbishop of Constantinople, new Rome, and ecumenical patriarch, a beloved brother in Christ our God, and suppliant.

Hierotheus, by the mercy of God, patriarch of Alexandria and of all Egypt, a beloved brother in Christ our God, and suppliant.

Methodius, by the mercy of God, patriarch of the great city of God, Antioch, and of all Anatolia, a beloved brother in Christ our God, and suppliant.

Cyril, by the mercy of God, patriarch of Jerusalem and of all Palestine, a beloved brother in Christ our God, and suppliant.

The Holy Synod in Constantinople:

Paisius of Caesarea

Anthimus of Ephesus

Dionysius of Heraclea

Joachim of Cyzicus

Dionysius of Nicodemia

Hierotheus of Chalcedon

Neophytus of Derci

Gerasimus of Adrianople

Cyril of Neocaesarea

Theocletus of Berea

Meletius of Pisidia

Athanasius of Smyrna

Dionysius of Melenicus

Paisius of Sophia

Daniel of Lemnos

Panteleimon of Deyinopolis

Joseph of Ersecium

Anthimus of Bodeni

The Holy Synod in Antioch:

Zacharias of Arcadia

Methodios of Emesa

Joannicius of Tripolis

Artemius of Laodicea

The Holy Synod in Jerusalem:
Meletius of Petra
Dionysius of Bethlehem
Philemon of Gaza
Samuel of Neapolis
Thaddeus of Sebaste
Joannicius of Philadelphia
Hierotheus of Tabor

Pius IX, *Ineffabilis Deus*, 1854

The question of whether the Virgin Mary, who, as the New Testament taught, had conceived her Son without a human father, and who, as the Council of Ephesus affirmed in 431, was entitled to the name *Theotokos*, God-bearer or Mother of God, had herself been conceived without the stain of original sin was a matter of controversy for many centuries. When Augustine, in his treatise *Nature and Grace*, was arguing for the universality of original sin, he interrupted himself by asking that question, but he left it unanswered. So stalwart a defender of Catholic orthodoxy as Thomas Aquinas (c. 1225–74) was unwilling to answer it in the affirmative, for fear of diminishing the uniqueness of the sinless person of Christ and the universality of his redemption of the entire human race, including his Mother. The Franciscan theologian Johannes Duns Scotus (c. 1265–1308) constructed a powerful speculative case for the teaching, but it remained only a theologoumenon. In 1439 the Council of Basel affirmed it, but by that time its decrees and actions on the relation between pope and council had vitiated its future standing as an ecumenical council. The Council of Trent made it clear that its reaffirmation of the doctrine of original sin was not intended to refer to the Virgin. Support for the immaculate conception continued to grow. But for many the principal problem was not its correctness as a pious belief or theological position but its definability as a dogma of the church.

In his Apostolic Constitution of 8 December 1854, *Ineffabilis Deus,* Pope Pius IX took the decisive step of proclaiming it as a dogma. Outside the Roman Catholic Church, it was criticized for its doctrinal content as evidence that Mary was being exalted to or near the status of Christ; but inside, it was largely the problem of papal authority that seemed to be at stake. In that sense, therefore, *Ineffabilis Deus* was a prelude to the First Vatican Council and its → *Dogmatic Constitution on the Catholic Faith,* which would define the authority of the pope "on his own [*ex sese*]" to speak infallibly on matters of doctrine and morals.

Edition: Denzinger, 2803–4.

Translation: Palmer 1952, 86–87.

Literature: O'Connor 1958.

Pius IX, *Ineffabilis Deus*, 1854

The Dogmatic Definition of the Immaculate Conception

. . . To the honor of the holy and undivided Trinity, to the glory and adornment of the Virgin Mother of God, to the exaltation of the Catholic faith, and the increase of the Catholic religion, we, by the authority of Jesus Christ our Lord, of the blessed apostles, Peter and Paul, and by our own, declare, pronounce, and define that the doctrine which holds that the Blessed Virgin Mary, at the first instant of her conception, by a singular privilege and grace of the omnipotent God, in consideration of the merits of Jesus Christ, the Savior of mankind, was preserved free from all stain of original sin, has been revealed by God, and therefore is to be firmly and constantly believed by all the faithful.

Therefore, if any shall presume—which God forbid—to think in their hearts anything different from what has been defined by us, let them know and realize that they are condemned by their own judgment, that they have suffered shipwreck of the faith, and have broken with the unity of the church; moreover, if they shall dare to signify, by word or writing or any other external means, what they think in their hearts, by that very fact [*facto ipso*] they subject themselves to the penalties by law established.

Lutheran General Synod, *The Definite Synodical Platform, Doctrinal and Disciplinarian*, 1855

During much of the seventeenth and eighteenth centuries, the confessional experimentation documented here in Part Five had left the Lutheran Church in Germany
and Scandinavia largely untouched—at least officially. The effort of orthodox Lutherans to formulate a *Reaffirmed Consensus of the Truly Lutheran Faith* in 1655 was
not successful; the controversies over Pietism were carried on, theoretically at any
rate, within the political, ecclesiastical, and confessional boundaries of → *The Augsburg Confession* and → *The Book of Concord*; and even the Prussian Union of 1817
did not write a new confession, but strove to bring adherents of the Lutheran and
Reformed confessions together.

In the conditions of the New World, however, such confessional hegemony
faced new challenges, both from the religious freedom guaranteed by the Constitution and from "the dominant theological tradition in the English-speaking colonies
of North America, Calvinism."[1] In practice, the confessional boundaries between
Reformed and Lutheran were often blurred, and an "American Lutheranism" was
given systematic clarification in the thought of S. S. Schmucker (1799–1873). As
Christa Ressmeyer Klein has summarized Schmucker's program, he "had vowed
as a seminarian [at Princeton] to raise Augsburg 'out of the dust,'" but "he made
only selective use of the founding confession of Lutheranism."[2] Yet the arrival of
confessionally oriented Lutherans in the United States during the first half of the
nineteenth century, which was to lead eventually to the strictly confessional → *Brief
Statement of the Doctrinal Position of the Missouri Synod* of 1932, brought vigorous
opposition to such "unionism." The General Synod of the Evangelical Lutheran
Church, founded in 1820, became the institutional expression of "American Lutheranism." Its confessional expression was this *Definite Platform* of 1855, including the
abbreviated articles from *The Book of Concord*.

We have included in the first part, "Doctrinal Basis or Creed," the revised
and abbreviated articles from *The Augsburg Confession*, which sometimes conflate
the Latin and the German versions or even substitute new wording. But because
the "List of Symbolic Errors" making up the second part reproduces passages from

1. Baird Tipson in Lippy and Williams 1988, 1:451.
2. In Lippy and Williams 1988, 1:437.

The Book of Concord, which we have included in Part Four of this set, we have not duplicated them here, but have identified their location in footnotes.

Edition: *Definite Platform* 1856, 2–42.

Literature: Ahlstrom 1972, 515–26; Lippy and Williams 1988, 1:409–50; E. C. Nelson 1980.

Lutheran General Synod, *The Definite Synodical Platform, Doctrinal and Disciplinarian,* 1855

Preface

This Definite Synodical Platform was prepared and published by consultation and cooperation of ministers of different eastern and western synods, connected with the General Synod, at the special request of some western brethren, whose churches desire a more specific expression of the General Synod's doctrinal basis, being surrounded by German churches, which profess the entire mass of former symbols.

As the American Recension, contained in this platform, adds not a single sentence to the Augsburg Confession, nor omits anything that has the least pretension to be considered "a fundamental doctrine of Scripture," it is perfectly consistent with the doctrinal test of the General Synod, as contained in her Formula of Government and Discipline, chapter 18, section 5, and 19, section 2. The Apostles' and Nicene Creeds are also universally received by our churches. Hence any district synod, connected with the General Synod, may, with perfect consistency, adopt this platform, if the majority of her members approve the synodical disclaimer, contained in part 2.

It is, moreover, exceedingly important, for the sake of uniformity, that any synod adopting this platform, should receive it entire, without alteration. In regard to the Formula of Government and Discipline, it need not be reprinted by the district synods, as it is contained in the hymn book. Such alterations or additions as may be desired, might be made by each synod in the form of by-laws, and if deemed necessary, printed for its own use.

Part 2 of this Definite Synodical Platform, is not a part of the pledge or doctrinal basis, to be individually subscribed, but is published by synod, as a disclaimer of the symbolical errors often imputed to her.

N.B.—Some obscurity having resulted, in the first edition, from the selection of the term Platform, as the name of the whole pamphlet, after it had been employed in the work to designate a particular part of it, the nomenclature has been changed in the Preface and captions of the several parts, but not a single word altered in the discussions of the work itself.

Part 1. Preliminary Principles; and the Doctrinal Basis
or Creed to Be Subscribed

Whereas it is the duty of the followers of Christ to profess his religion before the world (Mt 10.32) not only by their holy walk and conversation, but also by "walking in the apostles' doctrines" (1 Cor 14.32), and bearing testimony "to the faith once delivered to the saints" (Jude 3), Christians have, from the earlier ages, avowed some brief summary of their doctrines or a confession of their faith. Such confessions, also called symbols, were the so-called Apostles' Creed, the Nicene Creed, etc., of the first four centuries after Christ.

Thus also did the Lutheran Reformers of the sixteenth century, when cited by the emperor to appear before the Diet at Augsburg, present the confession, bearing the name of that city, as an exposé of their principal doctrines; in which they also professedly reject only the *greater part* of the errors that had crept into the Romish church. (See conclusion of the Abuses Corrected.) Subsequently, Luther and his co-adjutors still further changed their views on some subjects in that confession, such as the mass; and seven years later taught purer views in the Smalcald Articles.

Again, a quarter of a century after Luther's death, these and other writings of Luther and Melanchthon, together with another work which neither of them ever saw, the Form of Concord, were made binding on ministers and churches, not by the church herself, acting of her own free choice, but by the civil authorities of certain kingdoms and principalities. The majority of Lutheran kingdoms, however, rejected one or more of them, and the Augsburg Confession alone has been acknowledged by the entire Lutheran Church.

Whereas the entire Lutheran Church of Germany has rejected the symbolical books as a whole, and also abandoned some of the doctrines of the Augsburg Confession, among others the far greater part of them the doctrine of the bodily presence of the Savior in the eucharist, and our fathers in this country also more than half a century ago, ceased to require a pledge to any of these books, whilst they still believed and in various ways avowed the great fundamental doctrines contained in them:

And whereas the General Synod of the American Lutheran Church, about a quarter of a century ago, again introduced a qualified acknowledgment of the Augsburg Confession, in the constitution of her theological seminary, and in her constitution for district synods, at the ordination and licensure of ministers, without specifying the doctrines to be omitted, except by the designation that they are not fundamental doctrines of Scripture; and whereas a general desire has prevailed amongst our ministers and churches, to have this basis expressed in a more definite manner; and the General Synod has left this matter optional with each district synod:

Therefore we regard it as due to the cause of truth, as well as to ourselves and to the public, to specify more minutely what tenets of the Augsburg Confession, and of the former symbolic system are rejected, some by all, others by the great mass of the ministers and churches of the General Synod, in this country.

Accordingly, the following *American Recension of the Augsburg Confession* has been prepared, by consultation and cooperation of a number of Evangelical Lutheran ministers of eastern and western synods belonging to the General Synod, at the special request of western brethren, whose churches particularly need it, being intermingled with German churches, which avow the whole mass of the former symbols. In this revision, not a single sentence has been added to the Augsburg Confession, whilst those several aspects of doctrine have been omitted, which have long since been regarded by the great mass of our churches as unscriptural, and as remnants of Romish error.

The only errors contained in the confession (which are all omitted in this recension) are—

1. The approval of the ceremonies of the mass.

2. Private confession and absolution.

3. Denial of the divine obligation of the Christian Sabbath.

4. Baptismal regeneration.

5. The real presence of the body and blood of the Savior in the eucharist.

With these few exceptions, we retain the entire Augsburg Confession, with all the great doctrines of the Reformation.

The other errors rejected in the second part of this synodical platform, such as exorcism, etc., are contained not in the Augsburg Confession, but in the other former symbolical books, and are here introduced as among the reasons for our rejection of all the other books except the Augsburg Confession.

At the same time, whilst we will not admit into our synod anyone who believes in *exorcism, private confession and absolution,* or the *ceremonies of the mass,* we grant liberty in regard to the other omitted topics, and are willing, as heretofore, to admit ministers who receive them, provided they regard them as nonessential, and are willing to cooperate in peace with those who reject them, and to subscribe the pledge defined in the following resolutions:—

1. *Therefore, Resolved,* That this synod hereby avows its belief in the following doctrinal basis, namely, the so-called *Apostles' Creed,* the *Nicene Creed,* and the *American Recension of the Augsburg Confession,* as a more definite expression of the doctrinal pledge prescribed by the General Synod's Constitution for District

Synods, and as a correct exhibition of the Scripture doctrines discussed in it: and that we regard agreement among brethren on these subjects as a sufficient basis for harmonious cooperation in the same church.

2. *Resolved,* That we receive the General Synod's Formula of Government and Discipline, contained in her hymn book, as our directory; and that any additions or alterations we may desire, we will embody in by-laws; so that our beloved church may possess and exhibit to the world entire harmony in the reception of one doctrinal and disciplinarian platform.

3. *Resolved,* That we will not receive into our synod any minister who will not adopt the pledge defined in these resolutions, and faithfully labor to maintain its discipline in his charge.

Note. Part 2, containing the Synodical Disclaimer, being not included in the above pledge, is not intended for subscription, but is published by the synod to discourage the views there rejected, and to repel the charge of avowing them.

Doctrinal Basis or Creed

Of the Evangelical Lutheran Synod of ———, *Connected with the General Synod of the Evangelical Lutheran Church in America*

THE OLD AND NEW TESTAMENT THE ONLY INFALLIBLE
RULE OF FAITH AND PRACTICE

1. "We believe, teach, and confess, that the only rule and standard, according to which all doctrines and teachers alike ought to be tried and judged, are the prophetic and apostolic Scriptures of the Old and New Testaments alone, as it is written, Ps 119.105: "Thy word is a lamp unto my feet, and a light unto my path." And St. Paul, Gal 1.8, says: "Though an angel from heaven preach any other gospel unto you than that which we have preached unto you, let him be accursed."

2. "But all human writings and symbols, are not authorities like the Holy Scriptures; but they are only a testimony and explanation of our faith, showing the manner in which at any time the Holy Scriptures were understood and explained by those who then lived, in respect to articles that had been controverted in the church of God, and also the grounds on which doctrines that were opposed to the Holy Scriptures, had been rejected and condemned."[1]

---

1. *Form Conc Epit* pr 1–2.

THE APOSTLES' CREED

I believe in God the Father Almighty, the Maker of heaven and earth:

And in Jesus Christ, his only Son our Lord; who was conceived by the Holy Ghost, born of the Virgin Mary, suffered under Pontius Pilate, was crucified, dead, and buried. — The third day he rose from the dead, he ascended into heaven, and sitteth on the right hand of God the Father Almighty, from whence he shall come to judge the quick and the dead.

I believe in the Holy Ghost, the holy universal church; the communion of saints; the forgiveness of sins; the resurrection of the body, and the life everlasting.

THE NICENO-CONSTANTINOPOLITAN CREED

I believe in one God, the Father Almighty, Maker of heaven and earth and of all things visible and invisible.

And in one Lord Jesus Christ, the only-begotten Son of God, begotten of his Father before all worlds; God of God, Light of light, true God of the true God, begotten not made, being of one substance with the Father, by whom all things were made; who for us men and for our salvation, came down from heaven, and was incarnate by the Holy Ghost of the Virgin Mary, and was made man and was crucified also for us under Pontius Pilate. He suffered and was buried, and the third day he rose again, according to the Scriptures, and ascended into heaven, and sitteth on the right hand of the Father; and he shall come again with glory to judge both the quick and the dead; whose kingdom shall have no end.

And I believe in the Holy Ghost, the Lord and Giver of life, who proceedeth from the Father and the Son, who with the Father and the Son together is worshiped and glorified, who spake by the prophets. And I believe in one holy universal and apostolic church. I acknowledge one baptism for the remission of sins; and I look for the resurrection of the dead and the life of the world to come.

American Recension of the Augsburg Confession

ARTICLE 1. OF GOD

Our churches with one accord teach, that the decree of the Council of Nicaea, concerning the unity of the divine essence, and concerning the three persons, is true, and ought to be confidently believed, namely: that there is one divine essence, which is called and is God, eternal, incorporeal, indivisible, infinite in power, wisdom, and goodness, the Creator and Preserver of all things visible and invisible; and yet, that there are three persons, who are of the same essence and power, and are coeternal, the Father, the Son, and the Holy Spirit. And the term person they use in the same sense in which it is employed by ecclesiastical writers on this subject: to signify, not a part or quality of something else, but that which exists of itself.

ARTICLE 2. OF NATURAL DEPRAVITY

Our churches likewise teach, that since the fall of Adam, all men who are naturally engendered, are born with sin, that is, without the fear of God or confidence towards him, and with sinful propensities: and that this disease, or natural depravity, is really sin, and still causes eternal death to those who are not born again. And they reject the opinion of those, who, in order that they may detract from the glory of the merits and benefits of Christ, allege that man may be justified before God by the powers of his own reason.

ARTICLE 3. OF THE SON OF GOD AND
HIS MEDIATORIAL WORK

They likewise teach, that the Word, that is, the Son of God, assumed human nature, in the womb of the Blessed Virgin Mary, so that the two natures, human and divine, inseparably united in one person, constitute one Christ, who is true God and man, born of the Virgin Mary; who truly suffered, was crucified, died, and was buried, that he might reconcile the Father to us, and be a sacrifice not only for original sin, but also for all the actual sins of men. Likewise that he descended into hell (the place of departed spirits), and truly arose on the third day; then ascended to heaven, that he might sit at the right hand of the Father, might perpetually reign over all creatures, and might sanctify those who believe in him, by sending into their hearts the Holy Spirit, who governs, consoles, quickens, and defends them against the devil and the power of sin. The same Christ will return again openly, that he may judge the living and the dead, etc., according to the Apostolic Creed.

ARTICLE 4. OF JUSTIFICATION

They in like manner teach, that men cannot be justified before God by their own strength, merits, or works; but that they are justified gratuitously for Christ's sake, through faith; when they believe, that they are received into favor, and that their sins are remitted on account of Christ, who made satisfaction for our transgressions by his death. This faith God imputes to us as righteousness. Rom 3.4.

ARTICLE 5. OF THE MINISTERIAL OFFICE

In order that we may obtain this faith, the ministerial office has been instituted, whose members are to teach the gospel, and administer the sacraments. For through the instrumentality of the word and sacraments, as means of grace, the Holy Spirit is given, who, in his own time and place (or more literally, when and where it pleases God), produces faith in those who hear the gospel message, namely, that God, for Christ's sake, and not on account of any merit in us, justifies those who believe that on account of Christ they are received into (the divine) favor.

ARTICLE 6. CONCERNING NEW OBEDIENCE
(OR A CHRISTIAN LIFE)

They likewise teach, that this faith must bring forth good fruits; and that it is our duty to perform those good works which God has commanded, because he has enjoined them, and not in the expectation of thereby meriting justification before him. For, remission of sins and justification are secured by faith; as the declaration of Christ himself implies: "When ye shall have done all those things, say, we are unprofitable servants." [Lk 17.10]

The same thing is taught by the ancient ecclesiastical writers: for Ambrose says, "this has been ordained by God, that he who believes in Christ is saved without works, receiving remission of sins gratuitously through faith alone."[2]

ARTICLE 7. OF THE CHURCH

They likewise teach, that there will always be one holy church. The church is the congregation of the saints, in which the gospel is correctly taught, and the sacraments are properly administered. And for the true unity of the church nothing more is required, than agreement concerning the doctrines of the gospel, and the administration of the sacraments. Nor is it necessary, that the same human traditions, that is, rites and ceremonies instituted by men, should be everywhere observed. As Paul says: "One faith, one baptism, one God and Father of all," etc. [Eph 4.5]

ARTICLE 8. WHAT THE CHURCH IS

Although the church is properly a congregation of saints and true believers; yet in the present life, many hypocrites and wicked men are mingled with them.

ARTICLE 9. CONCERNING BAPTISM

Concerning baptism, our churches teach, that it is "a necessary ordinance," that it is a means of grace, and ought to be administered also to children, who are thereby dedicated to God, and received into his favor.

---

2. *Ambrosiaster (PL* 17:195).

ARTICLE 10. OF THE LORD'S SUPPER

In regard to the Lord's supper they teach that Christ is present with the communicants in the Lord's supper, "under the emblems of bread and wine."

ARTICLE 11. OF CONFESSION

[As private confession and absolution, which are inculcated in this article, though in a modified form, have been universally rejected by the American Lutheran Church, the omission of this article is demanded by the principle on which the American Recension of the Augsburg Confession is constructed; namely, to omit the several portions, which are rejected by the great mass of our churches in this country, and to add nothing in their stead.]

ARTICLE 12. OF REPENTANCE (AFTER BACKSLIDING)

Concerning repentance they teach, that those who have relapsed into sin after baptism, may at any time obtain pardon, when they repent. But repentance properly consists of two parts. The one is contrition, or being struck with terrors of conscience, on account of acknowledged sin. The other is faith, which is produced by the gospel; which believes that pardon for sin is bestowed for Christ's sake; which tranquilizes the conscience, and liberates it from fear. Such repentance must be succeeded by good works as its fruits.

ARTICLE 13. OF THE USE OF THE SACRAMENTS

Concerning the use of the sacraments our churches teach, that they were instituted not only as marks of a Christian profession amongst men; but rather as signs and evidences of the divine disposition towards us, tendered for the purpose of exciting and confirming the faith of those who use them. Hence the sacraments ought to be received with faith in the promises which are exhibited and proposed by them.

They therefore condemn the opinion of those who maintain, that the sacraments produce justification in their recipients as a matter of course, and who do not teach that faith is necessary, in the reception of the sacraments, to the remission of sins.

ARTICLE 14. OF CHURCH ORDERS (OR THE MINISTRY)

Concerning church orders they teach, that no person ought publicly to teach "or preach," in the church, or to administer the sacraments, without a regular call.

ARTICLE 15. OF RELIGIOUS CEREMONIES

Concerning ecclesiastical ceremonies they teach, that those ceremonies ought to be observed, which can be attended to without sin, and which promote peace and good order in the church, such as certain holy days, festivals, etc. Concerning matters of this kind, however, men are cautioned, lest their consciences be burdened, as though such observances were necessary to salvation. They are also admonished that human traditionary observances instituted with a view to appease God, and to merit his favor, and make satisfaction for sins, are contrary to the gospel and the doctrine of faith "in Christ." Wherefore vows and traditionary observances concerning meats, days, etc., instituted to merit grace and make satisfaction for sins, are useless, and contrary to the gospel.

ARTICLE 16. OF POLITICAL AFFAIRS

In regard to political affairs our churches teach that legitimate political enactments are good works of God; that it is lawful for Christians to hold civil offices, to pronounce judgment, and decide cases according to existing laws; to inflict just punishment, wage just wars, and serve in them; to make lawful contracts; hold property; to make oath when required by the magistrate, to marry, and to be married.

Hence Christians ought necessarily to yield obedience to their civil officers and laws; unless they should command something sinful; in which case it is a duty to obey God rather than man. Acts 5.29.

ARTICLE 17. OF CHRIST'S RETURN TO JUDGMENT

Our churches also teach, that at the end of the world, Christ will appear for judgment; that he will raise all the dead; that he will bestow upon the pious and elect eternal life and endless joys but will condemn wicked men and devils to be punished without end.

ARTICLE 18. OF FREE WILL

Concerning free will our churches teach, that the human will possesses some liberty for the performance of civil duties, and for the choice of those things lying within the control of reason. But it does not possess the power, without the influence of the Holy Spirit, of being just before God, or yielding spiritual obedience: for the natural man receiveth not the things which are of the Spirit of God: but this is accomplished [1 Cor 2.14] in the heart, when the Holy Spirit is received through the word.

The same is declared by Augustine in so many words: "We confess that all men have a free will, which possesses the judgment of reason, by which they cannot indeed, without the divine aid, either begin or certainly accomplish what is becoming in things relating to God; but only in 'outward' works of the present life, as well good as evil. In good works, I say, which arise from our natural goodness, such as to choose to labor in the field, to eat and drink, to choose to have a friend, to have clothing, to build a house, to take a wife, to feed cattle, to learn various and useful arts, or to do any good thing relative to this life; all which things, however, do not exist without the divine government; yea, they exist and begin to be from him and through him. And in evil works (men have a free will), such as to choose to worship an idol, to will to commit murder, etc."[3]

It is not possible by the mere powers of nature, without the aid of the Holy Spirit, to love God above all things, and to do his commands according to their intrinsic design. For, although nature may be able, after a certain manner, to perform external actions, such as to abstain from theft, from murder, etc., yet it cannot perform the inner motions, such as the fear of God, faith in God, chastity, patience, etc.

ARTICLE 19. OF THE AUTHOR OF SIN

On this subject they teach, that although God is the Creator and Preserver of nature, the cause of sin must be sought in the depraved will of the devil and of wicked men, which, when destitute of divine aid, turns itself away from God: agreeably to the declaration of Christ, "When he speaketh a lie, he speaketh of his own." Jn 8.44.

ARTICLE 20. OF GOOD WORKS

Our writers are falsely accused of prohibiting good works. Their publications on the ten commandments, and other similar subjects, show, that they gave good instructions concerning all the different stations and duties of life, and explained what course of conduct, in any particular calling, is pleasing to God. Concerning these things, preachers formerly said very little, but urged the necessity of puerile and useless works, such as certain holy days, fasts, brotherhoods, pilgrimages, worship of saints, rosaries, monastic vows, etc. These useless things, our adversaries, having been admonished, now unlearn, and no longer teach as formerly. Moreover, they now begin to make mention of faith, about which they formerly observed a marvelous silence. They now teach, that we are not justified by works alone, but join faith to works, and maintain that we are justified by faith and works. This doctrine is more tolerable than their former belief, and is calculated to impart more consolation to the mind. Inasmuch, then, as the doctrine concerning faith, which should

---

3. Pseudo-Augustine *Hypomnesticon* 3.4–5 (*PL* 45:1623).

be regarded as a principal one by the church, had so long been unknown; for all must confess, that concerning the righteousness of faith, the most profound silence reigned in their sermons, and the doctrine concerning works alone was discussed in the churches; our divines have admonished the churches as follows:—

First, that our works cannot reconcile God, merit the remission of sins, and grace, and justification: but this we can attain only by faith, when we believe that we are received into favor, for Christ's sake, who alone is appointed our Mediator and propitiatory sacrifice, by whom the Father can be reconciled. He, therefore, who expects to merit grace by his works, casts contempt on the merits and grace of Christ, and is seeking the way to God, in his own strength, without the Savior; who nevertheless has told us, "I am the way, the truth, and the life." This doctrine concerning faith, is incessantly inculcated by the apostle Paul (Eph 2), "Ye are saved by grace, through faith, and that not of yourselves, it is the gift of God," not of works, etc. And lest anyone should cavil at our interpretation, and charge it with novelty, we state that this whole matter is supported by the testimony of the fathers. For Augustine devotes many volumes to the defenses of grace, and the righteousness of faith, in opposition to the merit of good works. And Ambrose, on the calling of the Gentiles, etc., inculcates the same doctrine. For thus he says, concerning the calling of the Gentiles: "Redemption by the blood of Christ is of little value, nor is the honor of human works subordinated to the mercy of God, if justification, which is of grace, is supposed to be merited by previous works, so as to be not the gift of him that bestows it, but the reward of him that earned it."[4] But although this doctrine is despised by the inexperienced, the consciences of the pious and timid find it a source of much consolation, for they cannot attain peace of conscience in any works, but in faith alone, when they entertain the confident belief that, for Christ's sake, God is reconciled to them. Thus Paul teaches us (Rom 5), "Being justified by faith, we have peace with God." This whole doctrine must be referred to the conflict in the conscience of the alarmed sinner, nor can it be otherwise understood. Hence the inexperienced and worldly minded are much mistaken, who vainly imagine that the righteousness of the Christian is nothing else than what in common life and in the language of philosophy is termed morality.

Formerly the consciences of men were harassed by the doctrine of works, nor did they hear any consolation from the gospel. Some conscience drove into deserts, and into monasteries, hoping there to merit the divine favor by a monastic life. Others invented different kinds of works, to merit grace, and make satisfaction for their sins. There was therefore the utmost necessity, that this doctrine concern-

[Jn 14.6]

Eph 2[.8–9]

Rom 5[.1]

---

4. Pseudo-Ambrose (Prosper of Aquitaine) *On the Calling of the Gentiles* 1.17 (PL 51:670).

ing faith in Christ should be inculcated anew; in order that timid minds might find consolation, and know that justification and the remission of sins are obtained by faith in the Savior. The people are also now instructed, that faith does not signify a mere historical belief, such as wicked men and devils have; but that in addition to a historical belief, it includes an acquaintance with the consequences of the history, such as remission of sins, by grace through Christ, righteousness, etc., etc.

Now he who knows that the Father is reconciled to him through Christ, possesses a true acquaintance with God, confides in his providence, and calls upon his name: and is therefore not without God as are the Gentiles. For the devil and wicked men cannot believe the article concerning the remission of sins. But they hate God as an enemy, do not call upon his name, nor expect anything good at his hands. Augustine, in speaking of the word faith, admonishes the reader that in Scripture this word does not signify mere knowledge, such as wicked men possess, but that confidence or trust, by which alarmed sinners are comforted and lifted up.[5] We moreover teach, that the performance of good works is necessary, because it is commanded of God, and not because we expect to merit grace by them. Pardon of sins and grace are obtained only by faith. And because the Holy Spirit is received by faith, the heart of man is renovated, and new affections produced, that he may be able to perform good works. Accordingly Ambrose states, faith is the source of holy volitions and an upright life.[6] For the faculties of man, unaided by the Holy Spirit, are replete with sinful propensities, and too feeble to perform works that are good in the sight of God. They are moreover under the influence of Satan, who urges men to various sins, and impious opinions, and open crimes; as may be seen in the examples of the philosophers who, though they endeavored to lead moral lives, failed to accomplish their designs, and were guilty of many notorious crimes. Such is the imbecility of man, when he undertakes to govern himself by his own strength without faith and the Holy Spirit.

From all this it is manifest, that our doctrine, instead of being charged with prohibiting good works, ought much rather to be applauded, for teaching the manner in which truly good works can be performed. For without faith, human nature is incapable of performing the duties either of the first or second table. Without it, man does not call upon God, nor expect anything from him, nor bear the cross: but seeks refuge amongst men, and reposes on human aid. Hence when faith and confidence in God are wanting, all evil desires and human schemes reign in the heart;

---

5. Augustine *Homilies on the First Epistle of John* 10.2 (NPNF–I 7:521).
6. Pseudo-Ambrose (Prosper of Aquitaine) *On the Calling of the Gentiles* 1.25 (PL 51:676).

wherefore Christ also says, "without me ye can do nothing" (Jn 15); and the church   Jn 15[.5]
responds, Without thy favor there is nothing good in man.[7]

ARTICLE 21. OF THE INVOCATION OF SAINTS

Concerning the invocation of saints our churches teach, that the saints ought to be
held in remembrance, in order that we may, each in his own calling, imitate their
faith and good works; that the emperor may imitate the example of David, in carrying on war to expel the Turks from our country; for both are kings. But the sacred
volume does not teach us to invoke saints or to seek aid from them. For it proposes
Christ to us as our only Mediator, Propitiation, High Priest, and Intercessor. On
his name we are to call, and he promises, that he will hear our prayers, and highly
approves of this worship, namely: that he should be called upon in every affliction
(1 Jn 2): "If any one sin, we have an advocate with the Father," etc.   1 Jn 2[.1]

This is about the substance of our doctrines, from which it is evident that
they contain nothing inconsistent with the Scriptures. Under these circumstances,
those certainly judge harshly, who would have us regarded as heretics. But the difference of opinion between us (and the Romanists) relates to certain abuses, which
have crept into the (Romish) churches without any good authority; in regard to
which, if we do differ, the bishops ought to treat us with lenity and tolerate us, on
account of the confession which we have just made.

Part 2. Synodical Disclaimer; List of Symbolic Errors, Rejected by the Great Body of the Churches Belonging to the General Synod

The extraordinary length of the other former symbolic books as a whole, is sufficient reason for their rejection as a prescribed creed, even if all their contents were
believed to be true; because neither the Scriptures nor the practice of the early centuries, affords any warrant for an uninspired and therefore fallible creed, nearly as
large as the entire Old and New Testament together. The exaction of such an extended creed, is subversive of all individual liberty of thought and freedom of scriptural investigation.

On this subject the Lutheran Church in this country, connected with the
General Synod, stands firmly based on the principle, proclaimed by the immortal
Luther, in his *Smalcald Articles,* which, though employed to bind the consciences of
men after his decease, was never written for that purpose, nor, as long as he lived,

---

7. Stephen Langton, "Veni Sancte Spiritus."

perverted to it. "We ought (says he) not to form articles of faith out of the words or works of the fathers; otherwise their diet, their kinds of dress, their houses, etc., would have to be made articles of faith, as men have sported with the relics of saints. But we have another rule, namely, that the word of God forms articles of faith, and no one else, *not even an angel.*" [8]

The following extracts from the former symbolical books we reject, not because they do not contain some sentences of truth; but because the particular doctrine taught in each, is regarded as erroneous by the great mass of the churches in connection with the General Synod.

The extracts themselves are generally taken from the revised edition of the symbolical books published in Newmarket, Va., 1854, which we found it necessary in a few cases to correct by its original, the German. Only the extracts from the *Abuses Corrected* were taken from Schmucker's Lutheran Manual. In these extracts, we have, in each case, given only as much as was necessary to present the doctrine in question.

List of Symbolic Errors Rejected

Or, Extracts from the former Symbolical Books of the Lutheran Church in Europe, which are rejected by the great body of the American Lutheran Church

TOPIC 1. CEREMONIES OF THE MASS

The error taught on this subject in the Augsburg Confession and Apology to it, was rejected by the Reformers themselves a few years after the Confession was first published. Accordingly the Lutheran Church, both in Europe and America, has unanimously repudiated alike the mass and its ceremonies, as a Romish superstition, though inculcated with various qualifications, in the following passages. These passages therefore afford reason enough why we cannot receive the Augsburg Confession without qualification. When all agree in denying the error taught in them, how can any one consistently profess to receive the passages which teach it? We therefore reject the following: [9] . . . .

In refutation of the tolerant views of the mass above expressed, we add the following extract from the Smalcald Articles, written seven years later: [10] . . . .

8. *Smal Art* 2.17.
9. *Aug Ger* 24.1–3; *Apol Aug* 24.1, 11–12.
10. *Smal Art* 2.1–2, 6–7.

TOPIC 2. EXORCISM

This superstitious practice, which consists in a prescribed formula of adjuration, accompanied by various menacing demonstrations, by the use of which the priest professes to expel the evil spirits from an individual, of whom they are supposed to have taken possession, was practiced in the Romish church, principally before the baptism of infants. This rite was retained, with an altered interpretation, in various parts of the Lutheran Church in Europe for several centuries. In the American Lutheran Church it was never received, and is regarded as unscriptural, and highly objectionable, under the most favorable explanation that can be given of it.

We therefore reject the following passages:[11] . . . .

TOPIC 3. PRIVATE CONFESSION AND ABSOLUTION

The necessity of enumerating all our particular sins to the priest at confession, termed *auricular confession,* Luther and his adherents rejected; but *private confession,* at which the individual confessed his sinfulness and penitence in general, together with *absolution,* was long retained in the Lutheran Church of Germany, although rejected from the beginning in Sweden and Denmark, where nothing more than a public confession of the congregation together, before communion, was retained. . . .

As the Sacred Volume contains not a single command, that laymen should confess their sins to ministers, any more than ministers to laymen; and as not a single such example of confession and absolution is contained in the word of God, our American church has universally repudiated the practice. By the old Lutheran Synod of Missouri, consisting entirely of Europeans, this rite is still observed.

We therefore reject the following passages:[12] . . . .

How dangerous the entire doctrine of absolution and sin-forgiving power of the ministry is, to the spirituality of the church, and to the doctrine of justification by grace alone through faith in Jesus Christ, is clearly evident.

The Scriptures, and also the Reformers, teach that pardon or justification can be obtained only through the merits of Christ, which merits must be apprehended by a living faith, which living faith can be found only in the regenerate or converted soul. Hence, as none but a regenerate sinner can exercise living faith, no other can be pardoned, whatever else he may do or possess. Now those who attend confession are either regenerate, or they are not. If they were regenerated or converted before they went to confession, they had faith, and were pardoned before; if they were unregenerate or unconverted, then neither their confession, nor the

11. *Luth Sm Cat* "Baptismal Booklet" 11–12, 15.
12. *Aug* 11.1–2, 25.1–4, 28.5.

priest's absolution, can confer pardon on them, because they have not a living faith, although they may be sincere and exercise some sorrow for their sins. On the other hand, if any amount of seriousness and penitence, short of true conversion or regeneration, could, through the confessional, or any other rite, confer pardon of sin; the line of distinction between converted and unconverted, between mere formalists and true Christians would be obliterated; we should have pardoned saints and pardoned sinners in the church, converted and unconverted heirs of the promise, believing and unbelieving subjects of justification, and the words of the Lord Jesus would prove a lie, "That unless a man be born again, he cannot enter the kingdom of heaven!"

[Jn 3.3]

As to the passage, Mt 18.18, "Whatsoever ye shall bind on earth, shall be bound in heaven; and whatsoever ye shall loose on earth, shall be loosed in heaven;" it evidently refers to acts of church discipline, such as "telling it to the church," etc., which are expressly mentioned in the previous part of the passage. And that in Jn 20.23, "Whosesoever sins ye remit they are remitted unto them, and whosesoever sins ye retain, they are retained," was uttered on a different occasion, after the Savior's resurrection; and either refers to a miraculous power bestowed on the apostles to discern the condition of the heart, and to announce pardon of God to truly penitent individuals; or it confers on the ministry, in all ages, the power to announce *in general,* the conditions on which God will pardon sinners; but it contains no authority for applying these promises to individuals, as is done in private absolution.

TOPIC 4. THE DENIAL OF THE DIVINE INSTITUTION AND OBLIGATION OF THE CHRISTIAN SABBATH

Our American churches believe in the divine institution and obligation of the Christian Sabbath, or Lord's day, convinced that the Old Testament Sabbath was not a mere Jewish institution; but that it was appointed by God at the close of the creative week, when he rested on the seventh day, and blessed it, and sanctified it (Gn 2.2, 3), that is, set it apart for holy purposes, for reasons of universal and perpetual nature, Ex 20.11. Even in the reenactment of it in the Mosaic code, its original appointment is acknowledged, "*Remember* the Sabbath day—because in six days God made heaven and earth—and rested on the *seventh; wherefore* he (*then,* in the beginning), *blessed the Sabbath day, and hallowed it.*" Now this reason has no more reference to the Jews than to any other nation, and if it was sufficient to make the observance of the Sabbath obligatory on them, it must be equally so for all other nations before and after them.

Since therefore the observance and sanctification of a portion of his time, is based on universal reasons in the nature of man, especially as a religious being, and the proportion of time was fixed at a *seventh*, by the example and precepts of the Creator in the beginning; the Sabbath must be universally obligatory, and the abrogation of the Mosaic ritual, can at most only repeal those ceremonial additions which that ritual made, and must leave the original Sabbath as it found it. Now whilst the apostles, and first Christians under the inspired guidance, for a season also attended worship on the Jewish Sabbath, yet they observed the day of the Lord's resurrection, the first day of the week, as their day of special religious convocations; and this inspired example is obligatory on Christians in all ages. Still the essence of the institution consists, not in the particular day of the week, though that is now fixed, but in the religious observance of one day in seven.

We therefore reject the doctrine taught in the former symbolical books, in which the Sabbath is treated as a mere Jewish institution, and supposed to be totally revoked; whilst the propriety of retaining it as a day of religious worship, is supposed to rest only on the agreement of the churches for the convenience of general convocation. Hence we reject the following passages:[13] . . . .

TOPIC 5. BAPTISMAL REGENERATION

By this designation is meant the doctrine that baptism is necessarily and invariably attended by spiritual regeneration; and that such water baptism is unconditionally essential to salvation.

In the case of all adults, the Scriptures represent *faith in Christ* as the necessary prerequisite to baptism, and baptism as a rite by which those who had already consecrated themselves to Christ, or been converted, made a public profession of the fact, received a pledge of the divine favor, or of forgiveness of sins, and were admitted to membership in the visible church. The same inspired records also teach, that if men are destitute of this faith, if they believe not, they shall be damned, notwithstanding their baptism. "He that *believeth* and is baptized shall be saved, and he that *believeth* not, shall be damned," Mt 16.16. And Philip said to the eunuch, "If thou *believest* with all thy heart thou mayest be baptized," Acts 8.37. "*Repent* and be baptized," Acts 2.38, 8.62, 18.8. Hence if baptism required previous faith and repentance or conversion in adults, and if, when they were destitute of this faith or conversion, they were damned notwithstanding their baptism; it follows that baptism was not, and is not, a converting ordinance in adults, and does not necessarily effect or secure their regeneration.

13. *Aug* 28.53–61.

Now that baptism cannot accomplish more in infants than in adults, is self-evident; hence if it is not a converting ordinance in adults, it cannot be in infants.

The effects of baptism on infants, are nowhere specified in Scripture; hence we must suppose them to be the same as in adults, so far as children are naturally capable of them. Of *regeneration,* in the proper sense of the term, infants are incapable; for it consists in a radical change in our religious views of the divine character, law, etc.; a change in our religious feelings, and in our religious purposes and habits of action; of none of which are children capable.

Again, as regeneration does not destroy but merely restrains the natural depravity, or innate, sinful dispositions of the Christian, (for these still remain in him after conversion), it must consist mainly in a change of that *increased* predisposition to sin arising from action, of that preponderance of *sinful habits* formed by voluntary indulgence of our natural depravity, after we have reached years of moral agency. But infants have no such *increased* predisposition, no *habits* of sin prior to moral agency, consequently there can be no change of them, no regeneration in this meaning of the term. Hence if baptism even did effect regeneration in adults, which we have proved it does not, still it could have no such influence on infants, as they are *naturally incapable* of the mental exercises involved in it. The child, on its first attainment of moral agency, has merely natural depravity, until by voluntary indulgence in sin, it contracts personal guilt, and forms habits of sinful action. If the child, by the grace of God and proper religious instruction, continues to resist the solicitations of its depraved nature, its continued obedience will form holy habits, and this preponderance of holy habits, when established, constitutes its regeneration. If the growing child, as its powers of moral agency are developed, for any reason indulges its innate sinful propensities, it becomes a confirmed sinner; and its subsequent regeneration, if it take place, will be the more striking, as its change of habits must be greater.

Baptism in *adults,* is a means of making a public profession of previous faith, or of being received into the visible church, as well as a pledge and condition of obtaining those blessings purchased by Christ, and offered to all who repent, believe in him, and profess his name by baptism.

Baptism in *infants,* is the pledge of the bestowment of those blessings purchased by Christ for all. "As in Adam all die, even so in Christ shall all be made alive." And "The promise is to you and your *children,*" Acts 2.39. These blessings are forgiveness of sins, or exemption from the penal consequences of natural depravity (which would at least be exclusion from heaven on account of moral disqualification for admission), reception into the visible church of Christ, grace to help in every time of need, and special provision for the nurture and admonition in the Lord, to which parents pledge themselves.

The language of the Savior to Nicodemus, Jn 3.6, "*Unless a man be born of water and the spirit,*" doubtless refers also to baptism, which had been known to the Jews, and practiced by John the Baptist, before the ministry of Christ, as a mode of *public reception* of proselytes, who were then said to be new born. Its import is to inform Nicodemus, that he must *publicly* profess the religion of Jesus by baptism, and also be regenerated by the Holy Spirit, if he desired to enter the kingdom of heaven. Thus, also, the words, Acts 22.16, "*Arise and be baptized, and wash away thy sins,*" were addressed to Paul *after* he had surrendered himself to Christ, and signifies: "Arise, and publicly profess Christ by baptism, and thus complete your dedication of yourself to his cause, the condition, on the sincere performance of which, God will for Christ's sake, pardon your sins."

Baptismal regeneration, either in infants or adults, is therefore a doctrine not taught in the word of God, and fraught with much injury to the souls of men, although inculcated in the former symbolical books. At the same time, whilst the doctrine of baptismal regeneration certainly did prevail in our European churches, it is proper to remark, that the greater part of the passages in the former symbols relating to this subject, are (and doubtless may be) explained by many, to signify no more than we above inculcate.

The following passages are therefore rejected:[14] . . . .

TOPIC 6. THE OUTWARD FORM OF BAPTISM

The peculiar views of Luther on the mode of baptism, were never adopted by his coadjutors, nor never insisted on by himself. They were not introduced even in the church at Wittenberg, much less in any other part of the Lutheran Church.

The controversy on this subject has always been regarded by our most enlightened divines, including Luther, Melanchthon, and Chemnitz, as one of comparatively inferior importance. It has no connection with the question of infant baptism, because churches which baptize by immersion may and often do practice infant baptism (the Greek church); and those who baptize by affusion or aspersion, may confine the ordinance to adults. The Augsburg Confession, therefore, whilst it distinctly enjoins the baptism of infants, specifies nothing as to the mode of applying the water. The question in dispute is not whether baptism by immersion is valid; this is admitted; though that mode is thought less suitable to a refined sense of moral

14. *Aug* 2.2; *Apol Aug* 9.1; *Luth Sm Cat* 4.5–6, 9–10; *Luth Lg Cat* 4.41–43, 5.23.

feeling than the other, especially in countries where public bathing is unusual, and familiarity with its accompanying scenes has not divested them of their indelicacy. But the question is whether immersion is enjoined in Scripture, and consequently is *one essential part* of baptism, so that without it no baptism is valid, though it contain every other requisite. On this subject the Lutheran Church, including Luther himself, has always agreed with the great majority of Christian denominations, in maintaining the negative, and in regarding the quantity of water employed in baptism, as well as the mode of exhibiting it, not essential to the validity of the ordinance.

The reason is obvious: *because no circumstances can be necessary to the validity of a divine ordinance, excepting those which God has commanded in his word. And as God has not commanded immersion in his word; therefore, it is not necessary to the validity of the ordinance of baptism.*

The Greek words for baptize and baptism, used in the New Testament (Heb 9.10; Mk 7.4, Lk 11.38) (*baptizo, baptismos*), signify various applications of water practiced by the Jews in their different rites; which certainly included sprinkling, pouring, washing, bathing; but in no case, certainly, immersion. See Nm 19.18, etc. Any mode of applying the water, will therefore meet the New Testament import of baptism; and as various reasons render affusion, or aspersion, more suitable in our age, we, in common with the *entire* Lutheran Church, practice this method, and therefore reject the following passages of the former symbolic books as inconsistent with our views:[15] . . . .

TOPIC 7. ERRORS CONCERNING THE PERSONAL OR HYPOSTATIC UNION OF THE TWO NATURES IN CHRIST

The chief error on this subject, is the supposition that the human and divine natures of Christ, to a certain extent interchange attributes. This, in common with all other Protestant churches, we regard as contrary to the Holy Volume, which speaks of the union of two natures in one person in the Savior, precisely as it does of the union of soul and body into one person in man, without any one supposing them to teach an exchange of properties in the latter case. And yet (matter, or) the body and soul, are not more entirely and unchangeably distinct and different, than the Creator and creature, the human and the divine nature in Christ. To suppose that humanity could, in any case, acquire any of the distinctive attributes of the divinity, tends to destroy the immutable distinction between the Creator and the creature, the Infinite and the finite; which is the ground of the exclusive claim of God to our

15. *Luth Lg Cat* 4.64–65; *Smal Art* 3.5.1.

worship. The supposition that humanity in any case acquired some attributes of divinity, tends to give plausibility to the apotheosis of heroes and the pagan worship of inferior deities in general, as well as to the Romish worship of the Virgin Mary. Has not God himself taught us, "I am the Lord thy God—thou shalt have no other [Ex 20.2–3] gods beside me." The idea, moreover, that the divinity was in any sense or degree conceived and brought forth by the frail mortal, the Virgin Mary, is preposterous in the view of common sense, as well as flatly contradictory to the declaration of Paul, Rom 9.5, "Whose are the fathers, and of whom (through the Virgin Mary), as concerning the *flesh* (not his divinity) Christ came." Hence we reject the following passages:[16] . . . .

TOPIC 8. THE SUPPOSED SPECIAL SIN-FORGIVING POWER OF THE LORD'S SUPPER

The word of God clearly inculcates the doctrine, to which Luther and his coadjutors gave such prominence, that no one can be justified or pardoned except by a living faith in Christ, and such a faith is found only in the regenerate mind. And whenever the sinner exercises this living faith in Christ he is justified, that is, his sins are pardoned. Now, every communicant either possesses this faith, or he does not. If he does, he is justified or pardoned before he communes; if he is destitute of this faith, his communing cannot justify or pardon him; for man is justified by faith alone. Yet are there thousands of church members who afford no satisfactory evidence of regeneration, of that faith which works by love, and justifies the heart, and overcomes the world; who, because they approach the sacramental table with seriousness and sincerity, and perhaps with some sorrow for their sins, believe that they obtain pardon of their transgressions, and yet still continue in their unregenerate state. We reject the following passages, not because they clearly teach the above error, but because they are not sufficiently guarded, and are understood by many as inculcating the doctrine, that a sincere and devout participation of the Lord's supper secures the pardon of sin, even where satisfactory evidences of regeneration are wanting, the persons referred to mistaking a mere historical belief for a living faith. Hence, as the Scripture nowhere connects the forgiveness of sins with the duty of sacramental communion, any more than with the performance of any other prominent Christian duty, it is not proper that we should do so. The design of the holy supper is to show forth the Lord's death, to profess the name of the Redeemer before the world, to confirm the previous faith of the communicant, to bring him into

16. *Form Conc Epit* 8.9–11; *Form Conc Sol Dec* 8.70, 76.

closest communion with his blessed Savior, and to secure his special spiritual blessing: but not to bestow forgiveness for sins upon the unregenerate, however serious they may be. Hence we reject the following passages:[17] . . . .

TOPIC 9. THE REAL PRESENCE OF THE BODY AND BLOOD OF CHRIST IN THE EUCHARIST

The Reformers justly rejected the Romish error, that the bread and wine were transformed and transubstantiated into the body and blood of Christ. But they still adhered to the opinion, that the real body and blood of the Savior are present at the eucharist, in some mysterious way, and are received by the mouth of every communicant, worthy or unworthy.

For this view we find no authority in Scripture. (a) On the contrary, when Christ uttered the words: "This (bread) is my body," his body was *not yet dead,* but was reclining at their side at the table; and therefore was certainly not received by them into their mouths. The language was therefore figurative, such as Jesus was wont often to employ. Thus, "I am the *door,*" Jn 10.9. "I am the *true vine,*" 15.1. "The *field* is the *world,*" "the *seed* is the word," etc.

(b) Christ himself exhorts us, "Do this in *remembrance* of me:" but remembrance is applicable only to that which is past and absent. Paul also represents the design of this ordinance to be, "To show, or publish, the Lord's death," a *past* event and not a present person. Thus we come into the communion with, or are reminded of, the Lord's body and blood through the emblems of bread and wine.

(c) It contradicts the clear and indisputable testimony of our senses, for as the body and blood are to be received by the *mouth* of the communicant, it *must* be a *local* and *material reception,* which, if it did occur, at sacramental celebrations, could be observed by the senses.

(d) It contradicts the observation of all nations and ages, that, every body or material substance, must occupy a definite portion of space, and cannot be at more than one place at the same time, and therefore not at a hundred different places where the communion is received at the same time.

For these and other reasons the great mass of our ministers and churches reject this doctrine, and the annexed passages of the former symbolical books in which it is taught. The disposition to reject this error was manifested by Melanchthon himself, and it prevailed extensively in the latter third of the sixteenth century. But during the first quarter of this century, the conviction that our Reformers did not purge away the whole of the Romish error from this doctrine, gained ground,

17. *Apol Aug Ger* 12.42, 24.90; *Luth Sm Cat* 5.5-6; *Luth Lg Cat* 5.20-22.

universally, until the great mass of the whole Lutheran Church, before the year 1817, had rejected the doctrine of the real presence.

Rejected Passages:[18] . . . .

In addition to the above clear passages, incontestably teaching the real presence, it deserves to be ever remembered, that only fourteen years after the Form of Concord was published, when Duke Frederick William, during the minority of Christian II, published the Visitation Articles of Saxony, in 1594, in order to suppress the Melanchthonian tendencies to reject this and other peculiarities of the symbols, the article on this subject which was framed by men confessedly adhering to the old symbols, and designing to re-enunciate their true import, and which was enforced upon the whole church in Saxony as symbolic, gives the most objectionable view of this doctrine.[19] Now we cannot persuade ourselves, that this is the view of a single minister of the General Synod, or of many out of it; and yet these are the views that those are obligated to receive who avow implicit allegiance to the former symbolical books of our church in Europe. If any adopt the modification received by many of our distinguished divines, such as Remhardt and others, they do not faithfully embrace the symbolical doctrine, and cannot fairly profess to do so.

We therefore reject all these passages, as teaching a doctrine not contained in the good word of God, our only infallible rule of faith and practice.

---

18. *Aug* 10.1; *Apol Aug* 10.1–2; *Smal Art* 3.6.1; *Lu Sm Cat* 5.1–2; *Form Conc Epit* 7.6–7, 16.
19. *Sax Vis* 1.1, 4.

Southern Baptists, *Abstract of Principles for Southern Baptist Seminary,* 1858

Although the widely held impression that, in the words quoted earlier from W. T. Whitley, "Baptists have steadily declined to erect confessions into touch-stones," so that "though frequent attempts have been made to convert such confessions into standard creeds, by which 'orthodoxy' is to be tested, such attempts have invariably been opposed,"[1] is essentially correct, it was itself severely tested by the rise of the historical-critical method of interpreting the Bible. When Baptist churches recognized that the autonomy of the local congregation was not adequate for the enforcement of educational requirements for ordination to the ministry, and that therefore a system of seminary education was called for, some sort of "touch-stone" did seem to be necessary for the professors who were to teach in the seminary. To meet what he identified as "a crisis in Baptist doctrine," James P. Boyce (1827–88), founder of Southern Baptist Seminary, proposed in 1856 the adoption of this *Abstract of Principles,* which was prepared by Basil Manly, Jr., and adopted in 1858. This became, in McBeth's words, "the first confession of faith adopted by any Southern Baptist group."[2] Significantly, it was intended for the seminary rather than for the churches, whether individually or as a denomination.

Edition: Mueller 1959, 238–41.

Literature: Mueller 1959; McBeth 1990, 304–15; Schroeder 1898.

---

1. Whitley 1923, 30.
2. McBeth 1990, 305.

Southern Baptists, *Abstract of Principles for Southern Baptist Seminary,* 1858

The following is an excerpt from the Fundamental Laws of the Seminary written into its charter on April 30, 1858: "9. Every professor of the institution shall be a member of a regular Baptist church; and all persons accepting professorships in this Seminary, shall be considered by such acceptance, as engaging to teach in accordance with, and not contrary to, the Abstract of Principles hereinafter laid down."

1. THE SCRIPTURES

The Scriptures of the Old and New Testaments were given by inspiration of God, and are the only sufficient, certain, and authoritative rule of all saving knowledge, faith, and obedience.

2. GOD

There is but one God, the Maker, Preserver, and Ruler of all things, having in and of himself, all perfections, and being infinite in them all; and to him all creatures owe the highest love, reverence, and obedience.

3. THE TRINITY

God is revealed to us as Father, Son, and Holy Spirit each with distinct personal attributes, but without division of nature, essence, or being.

4. PROVIDENCE

God from eternity, decrees, or permits all things that come to pass, and perpetually upholds, directs, and governs all creatures and all events; yet so as not in any wise to be the author or approver of sin nor to destroy the free will and responsibility of intelligent creatures.

5. ELECTION

Election is God's eternal choice of some persons unto everlasting life—not because of foreseen merit in them, but of his mere mercy in Christ—in consequence of which choice they are called, justified, and glorified.

6. THE FALL OF MAN

God originally created man in his own image, and free from sin; but, through the temptation of Satan, he transgressed the command of God, and fell from his original holiness and righteousness; whereby his posterity inherit a nature corrupt and wholly opposed to God and his law, are under condemnation, and as soon as they are capable of moral action, become actual transgressors.

7. THE MEDIATOR

Jesus Christ, the only-begotten Son of God, is the divinely appointed Mediator between God and man. Having taken upon himself human nature, yet without sin, he perfectly fulfilled the law, suffered and died upon the cross for the salvation of sinners. He was buried, and rose again the third day, and ascended to his Father, at whose right hand he ever liveth to make intercession for his people. He is the only Mediator, the Prophet, Priest, and King of the church, and Sovereign of the universe.

8. REGENERATION

Regeneration is a change of heart, wrought by the Holy Spirit, who quickeneth the dead in trespasses and sins, enlightening their minds spiritually and savingly to understand the word of God, and renewing their whole nature, so that they love and practice holiness. It is a work of God's free and special grace alone.

9. REPENTANCE

Repentance is an evangelical grace, wherein a person being, by the Holy Spirit, made sensible of the manifold evil of his sin, humbleth himself for it, with godly sorrow, detestation of it, and self-abhorrence, with a purpose and endeavor to walk before God so as to please him in all things.

10. FAITH

Saving faith is the belief, on God's authority, of whatsoever is revealed in his word concerning Christ; accepting and resting upon him alone for justification and eternal life. It is wrought in the heart by the Holy Spirit, and is accompanied by all other saving graces, and leads to a life of holiness.

11. JUSTIFICATION

Justification is God's gracious and full acquittal of sinners, who believe in Christ, from all sin, through the satisfaction that Christ has made; not for anything wrought in them or done by them; but on account of the obedience and satisfaction of Christ, they receiving and resting on him and his righteousness by faith.

12. SANCTIFICATION

Those who have been regenerated are also sanctified, by God's word and Spirit dwelling in them. This sanctification is progressive through the supply of divine strength, which all saints seek to obtain, pressing after a heavenly life in cordial obedience to all Christ's commands.

13. PERSEVERANCE OF THE SAINTS

Those whom God hath accepted in the Beloved, and sanctified by his Spirit, will never totally nor finally fall away from the state of grace, but shall certainly persevere to the end; and though they may fall, through neglect and temptation, into sin, whereby they grieve the Spirit, impair their graces and comforts, bring reproach on the church, and temporal judgments on themselves, yet they shall be renewed again unto repentance, and be kept by the power of God through faith unto salvation.

14. THE CHURCH

The Lord Jesus is the Head of the church, which is composed of all his true disciples, and in him is invested supremely all power for its government. According to his commandment, Christians are to associate themselves into particular societies or churches; and to each of these churches he hath given needful authority for administering that order, discipline, and worship which he hath appointed. The regular officers of a church are bishops or elders, and deacons.

15. BAPTISM

Baptism is an ordinance of the Lord Jesus, obligatory upon every believer, wherein he is immersed in water in the name of the Father, and of the Son, and of the Holy Spirit, as a sign of his fellowship with the death and resurrection of Christ, of remission of sins, and of his giving himself up to God, to live and walk in newness of life. It is prerequisite to church fellowship, and to participation in the Lord's supper.

16. THE LORD'S SUPPER

The Lord's supper is an ordinance of Jesus Christ, to be administered with the elements of bread and wine, and to be observed by his churches till the end of the world. It is in no sense a sacrifice, but is designed to commemorate his death, to confirm the faith and other graces of Christians, and to be a bond, pledge, and renewal of their communion with him, and of their church fellowship.

17. THE LORD'S DAY

The Lord's day is a Christian institution for regular observance, and should be employed in exercises of worship and spiritual devotion, both public and private, resting from worldly employments and amusements, works of necessity and mercy only excepted.

18. LIBERTY OF CONSCIENCE

God alone is Lord of the conscience; and he hath left it free from the doctrines and commandments of men, which are in anything contrary to his word, or not contained in it. Civil magistrates being ordained of God, subjection in all lawful things commanded by them ought to be yielded by us in the Lord, not only for wrath, but also for conscience sake.

19. THE RESURRECTION

The bodies of men after death return to dust, but their spirits return immediately to God—the righteous to rest with him; the wicked, to be reserved under darkness to the judgment. At the last day, the bodies of all the dead, both just and unjust, will be raised.

20. THE JUDGMENT

God hath appointed a day, wherein he will judge the world by Jesus Christ, when everyone shall receive according to his deeds: the wicked shall go into everlasting punishment; the righteous, into everlasting life.

Swedish Baptists, *Confession of Faith*, 1861

The German, Swiss, and Dutch Anabaptists of the Reformation period, from whom there came such confessions as → *Schleitheim* and → *Dordrecht,* were not, in spite of the similarities in doctrine and piety, the ancestors of the Baptist movements in Northern Europe during the modern period. These were rather, in the main, indebted to the missionary activity of the Baptist churches of the English-speaking world and to indigenous stirrings of protest within the state churches.

Such stirrings, and the Baptist churches that came out of them, did not automatically produce confessions: authentic personal faith, not creedal precision, was what constituted the true believer and therefore the true church. But in a nation like Sweden, where the established Lutheran folk church had, since the Reformation, defined itself confessionally, above all in → *The Augsburg Confession* of 1530, other churches such as the Baptists, too, were constrained (quoting a favorite text of theirs) "to make a defense to any one who calls you to account."[1]

As Lumpkin summarizes its history, "Shortly before 1861 a Confession was drawn up and adopted by the First Baptist Church of Stockholm. It was presented at the Conference of Swedish Baptist Churches held in Stockholm on June 23–28, 1861, and the Conference adopted it. This Confession is still acknowledged by the Union as 'The Confession of Faith of the Swedish Baptists.'"[2]

Edition: Nordström 1928, 161–63 (reprinted from Handlingar 1861, 56–57).

Translation: Lumpkin, 408–10 (Eric Ruden).

Literature: Erickson 1996, 112–13; Lumpkin, 401–10; Nordström 1928; Schroeder 1898.

1. 1 Pt 3.15.
2. Lumpkin, 408.

Swedish Baptists, *Confession of Faith*, 1861

1. We believe that the Holy Scriptures of both the Old and the New Testament (the commonly so-called Apocryphal Books excepted) are inspired by God and constitute the one perfect rule for our Christian faith and practice.

2. We believe that there is one only living and true God—who is a Spirit infinite in all perfections—; who has revealed himself in three equal persons, the Father, the Son, and the Holy Ghost.

3. We believe that the first man Adam was created holy, in the image of God, but fell by voluntary transgression of the law of God into a state of sin and death; and that in consequence of his fall all his natural posterity have inherited his corruption, are void of all will to turn to God, and without power perfectly to keep his law, and therefore they are guilty before the wrath of God and condemned to eternal punishment.

4. We believe that our Lord Jesus Christ in his one person united true Godhead and true manhood, that he through his perfect obedience before the law of God and through his atoning death has opened for all a way to redemption and salvation from this lost state, and that everyone who from his heart believes in him shall become a partaker of this redemption and salvation without any merit or worthiness of his own.

5. We believe that the gospel—that is, the glad tidings of the salvation which is acquired through Christ—ought to be preached to the whole world; that everyone who hears the gospel is under obligation to repent—that is, with a sincere grief before God to confess and abandon his sins, and at the same time to believe in Christ as his only and all-sufficient Savior, and that whosoever may refuse to do so will incur upon himself a worse condemnation.

6. We believe that saving faith is a gift from God and entirely a fruit of the working of the Holy Spirit through the word; that all who are to be saved have been given by the Father to the Son and were chosen in him for salvation and sonship before the foundation of this world was laid; and that we ought with utmost diligence to seek to obtain assurance of our own election.

7. We believe that the law of God has for its end to be: (1) a restraint for the ungodly to restrain them from performing all the evil purpose of their heart; (2) a schoolmaster to bring sinners to Christ, inasmuch as it sets before them the just claims of God and his wrath over sin, shows them their inability to fulfill these claims, and thus awakens in them the need of grace and forgiveness of sin; (3) a rule

for the walk of believers to be followed in the spirit of the new covenant; and that, therefore, with these ends in view the law ought to be inculcated in all.

8. We believe that baptism ought to be administered only to such as have personally by a trustworthy confession given evidence of possessing a living faith in Christ; that it is properly administered only through the immersion of the whole person in water; and that it should precede admittance into the fellowship of the church and participation in the Lord's supper.

9. We believe that a true Christian church is a union of believing and baptized Christians, who have covenanted to strive to keep all that Christ has commanded, to sustain public worship, under the guidance of the Holy Spirit to choose among themselves shepherds or overseers, and deacons, to administer baptism and the Lord's supper, to practice Christian church discipline, to promote godliness and brotherly love, and to contribute to the general spread of the gospel;—also that every such church is an independent body, free in its relation to other Christian churches and acknowledging Christ only as its Head.

10. We believe that the first day of the week was kept holy by the apostolic churches as the Lord's day, instead of the Jewish Sabbath, and that we specially on this day are together for common worship and to exercise ourselves in godliness.

11. We believe that civil government is ordained by God, and regard it our duty to honor and pray for the king and the magistracy and in all things to obey the laws of the land, unless they plainly are in conflict with the law of Christ.

12. We believe that this world is to come to an end; that our Lord Jesus Christ will again appear on the earth on the last day, wake up the dead from their graves, and execute a general judgment in which all wicked men will be irrevocably condemned to eternal punishment, while all believing and righteous men will be solemnly established in their possession of the kingdom which was prepared for them from the beginning of the world.

Pius IX, *The Syllabus of Errors*, 1864

From the very inception of his pontificate in 1846, Pope Pius IX had confronted modern secular culture in a series of challenges. The most publicized of these challenges were political, when the papacy was caught in the revolutionary crossfire of the Italian Risorgimento and lost control over the traditional "papal states."

But the intellectual challenges were no less threatening and were, in the eyes of many, even more fundamental. By means of what are called here in the title of *The Syllabus of Errors* "consistorial allocutions, encyclicals, and other apostolic letters of our Most Holy Father, Pope Pius IX [*Sanctissimi Domini Nostri Pii Papae IX*]," he spoke out repeatedly against various of these. He was urged by some of his advisers, including the future Pope Leo XIII, Cardinal Vincenzo Gioacchino Pecci, to pull these condemnations together into a comprehensive document and to issue it in conjunction with the promulgation of the dogma of the immaculate conception of the Virgin Mary in → *Ineffabilis Deus* of 1854. For a variety of reasons both inside and outside the Roman Catholic Church, however, it became a separate text. It was issued to accompany the papal encyclical *Quanta cura* and promulgated with it on 8 December 1864.

The cross-references to the pope's earlier statements are handled differently in different editions, itemized in the introduction (Denzinger), footnoted under both the Latin and the English versions (Schaff), footnoted only under the Latin (*Dublin Review*). Although the translation presented by Schaff is the one usually seen and cited, the Roman Catholic version published in Ireland a month after issuance has a special interest and is the one that appears here, even with its questionable renderings. Various scholars—including Clemens Schrader (supportive of the *Syllabus*) and J. B. Bury (critical of it)—have helpfully transposed its theses from condemnation of errors to positive affirmations.

Edition: Denzinger, 2901–80.

Translation: *Dublin Review*, n.s., 4 (January 1865): 513–29; Schaff, 2:213–33.

Literature: *DTC* 14:2877–2912 (L. Brigué); *ODCC* 1565–66; Bury 1964, 1–46; McElrath 1964; Schrader 1865.

Pius IX, *The Syllabus of Errors*, 1864

Syllabus, embracing the principal errors of our time which are censured in consistorial allocutions, encyclicals, and other apostolic letters of our most holy father, Pope Pius IX

1. PANTHEISM, NATURALISM, AND ABSOLUTE RATIONALISM

1. There exists no supreme all-wise and most provident divine Being distinct from this universe, and God is the same as the nature of things, and therefore liable to change; and God is really made both in man and in the world, and all things are God and have the self-same substance of God; and God is one and the same thing with the world, and therefore spirit is the same thing with matter, necessity with liberty, truth with falsehood, good with evil, and just with unjust.[1]

2. All action of God on mankind and on the world is to be denied.[2]

3. Human reason, without any regard whatever being had to God, is the one judge of truth and falsehood, of good and evil; it is a law to itself, and suffices by its natural strength for providing the good of men and peoples.[3]

4. All the truths of religion flow from the natural force of human reason; hence reason is the chief rule whereby man can and should obtain the knowledge of all truths of every kind.[4]

5. Divine revelation is imperfect, and therefore subject to a continuous and indefinite progress corresponding to the advance of human reason.[5]

6. The faith of Christ is opposed to human reason; and divine revelation not only nothing profits, but is even injurious to man's perfection.[6]

7. The prophecies and miracles recorded and narrated in Scripture are poetical fictions, and the mysteries of Christian faith a result of philosophical investigations; and in the books of both testaments are contained mythical inventions; and Jesus Christ himself is a mythical fiction.[7]

---

1. Allocution *Maxima quidem*, 9 June 1862.
2. Allocution *Maxima quidem*, 9 June 1862.
3. Allocution *Maxima quidem*, 9 June 1862.
4. Encyclical *Qui pluribus*, 9 November 1846; Encyclical *Singulari quidem*, 17 March 1856; Allocution *Maxima quidem*, 9 June 1862.
5. Encyclical *Qui pluribus*, 9 November 1846; Allocution *Maxima quidem*, 9 June 1862.
6. Encyclical *Qui pluribus*, 9 November 1846; Allocution *Maxima quidem*, 9 June 1862.
7. Encyclical *Qui pluribus*, 9 November 1846; Allocution *Maxima quidem*, 9 June 1862.

2. MODERATE RATIONALISM

8. Since human reason is on a level with religion itself, therefore theological studies are to be handled in the same manner as philosophical.[8]

9. All the dogmas of the Christian religion are without distinction the object of natural science or philosophy; and human reason, with no other than a historical cultivation, is able from its own natural strength and principles to arrive at true knowledge of even the more abstruse dogmas, so only these dogmas have been proposed to the reason itself as its object.[9]

10. Since the philosopher is one thing, philosophy another, the former has the right and duty of submitting himself to that authority which he may have approved as true; but philosophy neither can nor should submit itself to any authority.[10]

11. The church not only ought never to animadvert on philosophy, but ought to tolerate the errors of philosophy, and leave it in her hands to correct herself.[11]

12. The decrees of the Apostolic See and of Roman congregations interfere with the free progress of science.[12]

13. The method and principles whereby the ancient scholastic doctors cultivated theology are not suited to the necessities of our time and to the progress of the sciences.[13]

14. Philosophy should be treated without regard had to supernatural revelation.[14]

N.B.—To the system of Rationalism belong mostly the errors of Antony Günther, which are condemned in the epistle to the cardinal-archbishop of Cologne, *Eximiam tuam,* June 15, 1857, and in that to the bishop of Breslau, *Dolore haud mediocri,* April 30, 1860.

3. INDIFFERENTISM, LATITUDINARIANISM

15. Every man is free to embrace and profess that religion which, led by the light of reason, he may have thought true.[15]

---

8. Allocution *Singulari quadam perfusi,* 9 December 1854.

9. Epistle *Gravissimas inter,* 11 December 1862; Epistle *Tuas libenter,* 21 December 1863.

10. Epistle *Gravissimas inter,* 11 December 1862; Epistle *Tuas libenter,* 21 December 1863

11. Epistle *Gravissimas inter,* 11 December 1862.

12. Epistle *Tuas libenter,* 21 December 1863.

13. Epistle *Tuas libenter,* 21 December 1863.

14. Epistle *Tuas libenter,* 21 December 1863.

15. Apostolic Letter *Multiplices inter,* 10 June 1851; Allocution *Maxima quidem,* 9 June 1862.

16. Men may in the practice of any religion whatever find the path of eternal salvation, and attain eternal salvation.[16]

17. At least good hopes should be entertained concerning the salvation of all those who in no respect live in the true church of Christ.[17]

18. Protestantism is nothing else than a different form of the same Christian religion, in which it is permitted to please God equally as in the true Catholic Church.[18]

4. SOCIALISM, COMMUNISM, SECRET SOCIETIES, BIBLE SOCIETIES, CLERICO-LIBERAL SOCIETIES

Pests of this kind are often reprobated, and in the most severe terms in the Encyclical *Qui pluribus*, November 9, 1846; the Allocution *Quibus Quantisque*, April 20, 1849; the Encyclical *Noscitis et Nobiscum*, December 8, 1849; the Allocution *Singulari quadam*, December 9, 1854; the Encyclical *Quanto conficiamur*, August 10, 1863.

5. ERRORS CONCERNING THE CHURCH AND HER RIGHTS

19. The church is not a true and perfect society fully free, nor does she enjoy her own proper and permanent rights given to her by her divine Founder, but it is the civil power's business to define what are the church's rights, and the limits within which she may be enabled to exercise them.[19]

20. The ecclesiastical power should not exercise its authority without permission and assent of the civil government.[20]

21. The church has not the power of dogmatically defining that the religion of the Catholic Church is the only true religion.[21]

22. The obligation by which Catholic teachers and writers are absolutely bound is confined to those things alone which are propounded by the church's infallible judgment, as dogmas of faith to be believed by all.[22]

---

16. Encyclical *Qui pluribus*, 9 November 1846; Allocution *Ubi primum*, 17 December 1847; Encyclical *Singulari quidem*, 17 March 1856.

17. Allocution *Singulari quadam perfusi*, 9 December 1854; Encyclical *Quanto conficiamur*, 17 August 1863.

18. Encyclical *Nostis et nobiscum*, 8 December 1849.

19. Allocution *Singulari quadam perfusi*, 9 December 1854; Allocution *Multis gravibusque*, 17 December 1860; Allocution *Maxima quidem*, 9 June 1862.

20. Allocution *Meminit unusquisque*, 30 September 1861.

21. Apostolic Letter *Multiplices inter*, 10 June 1851.

22. Epistle *Tuas libenter*, 21 December 1863.

23. Roman pontiffs and ecumenical councils have exceeded the limits of their power, usurped the rights of princes, and erred even in defining matters of faith and morals.[23]

24. The church has no power of employing force, nor has she any temporal power direct or indirect.[24]

25. Besides the inherent power of the episcopate, another temporal power has been granted expressly or tacitly by the civil government, which may therefore be abrogated by the civil government at its pleasure.[25]

26. The church has no native and legitimate right of acquiring and possessing.[26]

27. The church's sacred ministers and the Roman pontiff should be entirely excluded from all charge and dominion of temporal things.[27]

28. Bishops ought not, without the permission of the government, to publish even letters apostolic.[28]

29. Graces granted by the Roman pontiff should be accounted as void unless they have been sought through the government.[29]

30. The immunity of the church and of ecclesiastical persons had its origin from the civil law.[30]

31. The ecclesiastical forum for the temporal causes of clerics, whether civil causes or criminal, should be altogether abolished, even without consulting, and against the protest of, the Apostolic See.[31]

32. Without any violation of natural right and equity, that personal immunity may be abrogated, whereby clerics are exempted from the burden of undertaking and performing military services; and such abrogation is required by civil progress, especially in a society constituted on the model of a free rule.[32]

---

23. Apostolic Letter *Multiplices inter,* 10 June 1851.

24. Apostolic Letter *Ad apostolicae sedis,* 22 August 1851.

25. Apostolic Letter *Ad apostolicae sedis,* 22 August 1851.

26. Allocution *Numquam fore,* 15 December 1856; Encyclical *Incredibili afflictamur,* 17 September 1863.

27. Allocution *Maxima quidem,* 9 June 1862.

28. Allocution *Numquam fore,* 15 December 1856.

29. Allocution *Numquam fore,* 15 December 1856.

30. Apostolic Letter *Multiplices inter,* 10 June 1851.

31. Allocution *Acerbissimum,* 27 September 1852; Allocution *Numquam fore,* 15 December 1856.

32. Epistle *Singularis nobisque,* 29 September 1864.

33. It does not appertain exclusively to ecclesiastical jurisdiction by its own proper and native right to direct the teaching of theology.[33]

34. The doctrine of those who compare the Roman pontiff to a prince, free and acting in the universal church, is the doctrine which prevailed in the Middle Age.[34]

35. Nothing forbids that by the judgment of some general council, or by the act of all peoples, the supreme pontificate should be transferred from the Roman bishop and city to another bishop and another state.[35]

36. The definition of a national council admits no further dispute, and the civil administration may fix the matter on this footing.[36]

37. National churches separated and totally disjoined from the Roman pontiff's authority may be instituted.[37]

38. The too arbitrary conduct of Roman pontiffs contributed to the church's division into East and West.[38]

6. ERRORS CONCERNING CIVIL SOCIETY, CONSIDERED BOTH IN ITSELF AND IN ITS RELATIONS TO THE CHURCH

39. The state, as being the origin and fountain of all rights, possesses a certain right of its own, circumscribed by no limits.[39]

40. The doctrine of the Catholic Church is opposed to the good and benefit of human society.[40]

41. The civil power, even when exercised by a non-Catholic ruler, has an indirect negative power over things sacred; it has consequently not only the right which they call *exequatur,* but that right also which they call *appel comme d'abus.*[41]

42. In the case of a conflict between laws of the two powers, civil law prevails.[42]

33. Epistle *Tuas libenter,* 21 December 1863.

34. Apostolic Letter *Ad apostolicae sedis,* 22 August 1851.

35. Apostolic Letter *Ad apostolicae sedis,* 22 August 1851.

36. Apostolic Letter *Ad apostolicae sedis,* 22 August 1851.

37. Allocution *Multis gravibusque,* 17 December 1860; Allocution *Iamdudum cernimus,* 18 March 1861.

38. Apostolic Letter *Ad apostolicae sedis,* 22 August 1851.

39. Allocution *Maxima quidem,* 9 June 1862.

40. Encyclical *Qui pluribus,* 9 November 1846; Allocution *Quibus quantisque,* 20 April 1849.

41. Apostolic Letter *Ad apostolicae sedis,* 22 August 1851.

42. Apostolic Letter *Ad apostolicae sedis,* 22 August 1851.

43. The lay power has the authority of rescinding, of declaring null, and of voiding solemn conventions (commonly called concordats), concerning the exercise of rights appertaining to ecclesiastical immunity, which have been entered into with the Apostolic See,—without this see's consent, and even against its protest.[43]

44. The civil authority may mix itself up in matters which appertain to religion, morals, and spiritual rule. Hence it can exercise judgment concerning those instructions which the church's pastors issue according to their office for the guidance of consciences; nay, it may even decree concerning the administration of the holy sacraments, and concerning the dispositions necessary for their reception.[44]

45. The whole governance of public schools wherein the youth of any Christian state is educated, episcopal seminaries only being in some degree excepted, may and should be given to the civil power; and in such sense be given, that no right be recognized in any other authority of mixing itself up in the management of the schools, the direction of studies, the conferring of degrees, the choice or approbation of teachers.[45]

46. Nay, in the very ecclesiastical seminaries, the method of study to be adopted is subject to the civil authority.[46]

47. The best constitution of civil society requires that popular schools which are open to children of every class, and that public institutions generally which are devoted to teaching literature and science and providing for the education of youth, be exempted from all authority of the church, from all her moderating influence and interference, and subjected to the absolute will of the civil and political authority [so as to be conducted] in accordance with the tenets of civil rulers, and the standard of the common opinions of the age.[47]

48. That method of instructing youth can be approved by Catholic men, which is disjoined from the Catholic faith and the church's power, and which regards exclusively, or at least principally, knowledge of the natural order alone, and the ends of social life on earth.[48]

---

43. Allocution *In consistoriali,* 1 November 1850; Allocution *Multis gravibusque,* 17 December 1860.

44. Allocution *In consistoriali,* 1 November 1850; Allocution *Maxima quidem,* 9 June 1862.

45. Allocution *In consistoriali,* 1 November 1850; Allocution *Quibus luctuosissimis,* 5 September 1851.

46. Allocution *Numquam fore,* 15 December 1856.

47. Epistle *Cum non sine,* 14 July 1864.

48. Epistle *Cum non sine,* 14 July 1864.

49. The civil authority may prevent the bishops and faithful from free and mutual communication with the Roman pontiff.[49]

50. The lay authority has of itself the right of presenting bishops, and may require of them that they enter on the management of their dioceses before they receive from the Holy See canonical institution and apostolical letters.[50]

51. Nay, the lay government has the right of deposing bishops from exercise of their pastoral ministry; nor is it bound to obey the Roman pontiff in those things which regard the establishment of bishoprics and the appointment of bishops.[51]

52. The government may, in its own right, change the age prescribed by the church for the religious profession of men and women, and may require religious orders to admit no one to solemn vows without its permission.[52]

53. Those laws should be abrogated which relate to protecting the condition of religious orders and their rights and duties; nay, the civil government may give assistance to all those who may wish to quit the religious life which they have undertaken, and to break their solemn vows; and in like manner it may altogether abolish the said religious orders, and also collegiate churches and simple benefices, even those under the right of a patron, and subject and assign their goods and revenues to the administration and free disposal of the civil power.[53]

54. Kings and princes are not only exempted from the church's jurisdiction, but also are superior to the church in deciding questions of jurisdiction.[54]

55. The church should be separated from the state, and the state from the church.[55]

7. ERRORS CONCERNING NATURAL AND CHRISTIAN ETHICS

56. The laws of morality need no divine sanction, and there is no necessity that human laws be conformed to the law of nature, or receive from God their obligatory force.[56]

---

49. Allocution *Maxima quidem*, 9 June 1862.

50. Allocution *Numquam fore*, 15 December 1856.

51. Apostolic Letter *Multiplices inter*, 10 June 1851; Allocution *Acerbissimum*, 27 September 1852.

52. Allocution *Numquam fore*, 15 December 1856.

53. Allocution *Acerbissimum*, 27 September 1852; Allocution *Probe memineris*, 22 January 1855; Allocution *Cum saepe*, 26 July 1855.

54. Apostolic Letter *Multiplices inter*, 10 June 1851.

55. Allocution *Acerbissimum*, 27 September 1852.

56. Allocution *Maxima quidem*, 9 June 1862.

57. The science of philosophy and morals, and also the laws of a state, may and should withdraw themselves from the jurisdiction of divine and ecclesiastical authority.[57]

58. No other strength is to be recognized except material force; and all moral discipline and virtue should be accounted to consist in accumulating and increasing wealth by every method, and in satiating the desire of pleasure.[58]

59. Right consists in the mere material fact; and all the duties of man are an empty name, and all human facts have the force of right.[59]

60. Authority is nothing else but numerical power and material force.[60]

61. The successful injustice of a fact brings with it no detriment to the sanctity of right.[61]

62. The principle of non-intervention (as it is called) should be proclaimed and observed.[62]

63. It is lawful to refuse obedience to legitimate princes, and even rebel against them.[63]

64. A violation of any most sacred oath, or any wicked and flagitious action whatever repugnant to the eternal law, is not only not to be reprobated, but is even altogether lawful, and to be extolled with the highest praise when it is done for love of country.[64]

8. ERRORS CONCERNING CHRISTIAN MATRIMONY

65. It can in no way be tolerated that Christ raised matrimony to the dignity of a sacrament.[65]

66. The sacrament of marriage is only an accessory to the contract, and separable from it; and the sacrament itself consists in the nuptial benediction alone.[66]

---

57. Allocution *Maxima quidem*, 9 June 1862.

58. Allocution *Maxima quidem*, 9 June 1862; Encyclical *Quanto conficiamur*, 17 August 1863.

59. Allocution *Maxima quidem*, 9 June 1862.

60. Allocution *Maxima quidem*, 9 June 1862.

61. Allocution *Iamdudum cernimus*, 18 March 1861.

62. Allocution *Novos et ante*, 28 September 1860.

63. Encyclical *Qui pluribus*, 9 November 1846; Allocution *Quisque vestrum*, 4 October 1847; Encyclical *Nostis et nobiscum*, 8 December 1849; Apostolic Letter *Cum catholica Ecclesia*, 16 March 1860.

64. Allocution *Quibus quantisque*, 20 April 1849.

65. Apostolic Letter *Ad apostolicae sedis*, 22 August 1851.

66. Apostolic Letter *Ad apostolicae sedis*, 22 August 1851.

67. The bond of matrimony is not indissoluble by the law of nature; and in various cases divorce, properly so called, may be sanctioned by the civil authority.[67]

68. The church has no power of enacting diriment impediments to marriage; but that power is vested in the civil authority, by which the existing impediments may be removed.[68]

69. In later ages the church began to enact diriment impediments not in her own right, but through that right which she had borrowed from the civil power.[69]

70. The canons of Trent, which inflict the censure of anathema on those who dare to deny the church's power of enacting diriment impediments, are either not dogmatical, or are to be understood of this borrowed power.[70]

71. The form ordained by the Council of Trent does not bind on pain of nullity wherever the civil law may prescribe another form, and may will that, by this new form, matrimony shall be made valid.[71]

72. Boniface VIII was the first who asserted that the vow of chastity made at ordination annuls marriage.[72]

73. By virtue of a purely civil contract there may exist among Christians marriage, truly so called; and it is false that either the contract of marriage among Christians is always a sacrament, or that there is no contract if the sacrament be excluded.[73]

74. Matrimonial causes and espousals belong by their own nature to the civil form.[74]

N.B.—To this head may be referred two other errors: on abolishing clerical celibacy, and on preferring the state of marriage to that of virginity. They are condemned, the former in the Encyclical *Qui pluribus*, Nov. 9, 1846; the latter in the Apostolic Letters, *Multiplices inter*, June 10, 1851.

---

67. Apostolic Letter *Ad apostolicae sedis*, 22 August 1851; Allocution *Acerbissimum*, 27 September 1852.

68. Apostolic Letter *Multiplices inter*, 10 June 1851.

69. Apostolic Letter *Ad apostolicae sedis*, 22 August 1851.

70. Apostolic Letter *Ad apostolicae sedis*, 22 August 1851.

71. Apostolic Letter *Ad apostolicae sedis*, 22 August 1851.

72. Apostolic Letter *Ad apostolicae sedis*, 22 August 1851.

73. Apostolic Letter *Ad apostolicae sedis*, 22 August 1851; *Letter to the King of Sardinia*, 9 September 1852; Allocution *Acerbissimum*, 27 September 1852; Allocution *Multis gravibusque*, 17 December 1860.

74. Apostolic Letter *Ad apostolicae sedis*, 22 August 1851; Allocution *Acerbissimum*, 27 September 1852.

9. ERRORS CONCERNING THE ROMAN
PONTIFF'S CIVIL PRINCEDOM

75. Children of the Christian and Catholic Church dispute with each other on the compatibility of the temporal rule with the spiritual.[75]

76. The abrogation of that civil power which the Apostolic See possesses would conduce in the highest degree to the church's liberty and felicity.[76]

N.B.—Besides these errors explicitly branded, many others are implicitly reprobated in the exposition and assertion of that doctrine, which all Catholics ought most firmly to hold concerning the Roman pontiff's civil princedom. This doctrine is clearly delivered in the Allocution, *Quibus quantisque,* April 20, 1849; in the Allocution, *Si semper antea,* May 20, 1850; in the Apostolic Letters *Cum Catholica Ecclesia,* March 26, 1860; in the Allocution *Novos,* Sept. 28, 1861; in the Allocution *Iamdudum,* March 18, 1861; in the Allocution *Maxima quidem,* June 9, 1862.

10. ERRORS WHICH HAVE REFERENCE TO THE
LIBERALISM OF THE DAY

77. In this our age it is no longer expedient that the Catholic religion should be treated as the only religion of the state, all other worships whatsoever being excluded.[77]

78. Hence it has been laudably provided by law in some Catholic countries, that men thither immigrating should be permitted the public exercise of their own several worships.[78]

79. For truly it is false that the civil liberty of all worships, and the full power granted to all of openly and publicly declaring any opinions or thoughts whatever, conduces to more easily corrupting the morals and minds of peoples and propagating the plague of indifferentism.[79]

80. The Roman pontiff can and ought to reconcile and harmonize himself with progress, with liberalism, and with modern civilization.[80]

75. Apostolic Letter *Ad apostolicae sedis,* 22 August 1851.
76. Allocution *Quibus quantisque,* 20 April 1849.
77. Allocution *Nemo vestrum,* 26 July 1855.
78. Allocution *Acerbissimum,* 27 September 1852.
79. Allocution *Numquam fore,* 15 December 1856.
80. Allocution *Iamdudum cernimus,* 18 March 1861.

Free Methodist Church, *The Articles of Religion,* 1866

The answer to the question that forms the title of a standard work on the Free Methodist Church, *Why Another Sect?*[1] is, as *The Oxford Dictionary of the Christian Church* puts it, that "in every case the reason for division was not doctrinal but constitutional."[2]

That becomes evident in these *Articles of Religion* of 1866. They are a mild revision of the Methodist → *Articles of Religion* of 1784/1804—which had been, in turn, a somewhat less mild revision of the Anglican → *Thirty-Nine Articles.* The principal difference in the version of 1866 was the addition of the thirteenth article, on "Entire Sanctification," which, coming after justification and being "wrought instantaneously upon the consecrated," brings deliverance "from all inward sin— from evil thoughts and evil tempers."

Edition:: *The Doctrines and Discipline of the Free Methodist Church* 1866, 17-25. In the original numbering of the articles, which we have retained, "XII" is omitted.

Literature: Lippy and Williams 1988, 2:818; Roberts 1984.

1. Roberts 1984.
2. *ODCC* 1661.

Free Methodist Church, *The Articles of Religion*, 1866

1. OF FAITH IN THE HOLY TRINITY

There is but one living and true God, everlasting, without body or parts, of infinite power, wisdom, and goodness; the Maker and Preserver of all things, visible and invisible. And in unity of this Godhead, there are three persons, of one substance, power, and eternity,—the Father, the Son, and the Holy Ghost.

2. OF THE WORD, OR SON OF GOD, WHO WAS MADE VERY MAN

The Son, who is the Word of the Father, the very and eternal God, of one substance with the Father, took man's nature in the womb of the Blessed Virgin; so that two whole and perfect natures, that is to say, the Godhead and manhood, were joined together in one person, never to be divided, whereof is the Christ, very God and very man, who truly suffered, was crucified, dead and buried, to reconcile his Father to us, and to be a sacrifice, not only for original guilt, but also for actual sins of men.

3. OF THE RESURRECTION OF CHRIST

Christ did truly rise again from the dead, and took again his body, with all things appertaining to the perfection of man's nature, wherewith he ascended into heaven, and there sitteth until he return to judge all men at the last day.

4. OF THE HOLY GHOST

The Holy Ghost, proceeding from the Father and the Son, is of one substance, majesty, and glory with the Father and the Son, very and eternal God.

5. THE SUFFICIENCY OF THE HOLY SCRIPTURES FOR SALVATION

The Holy Scriptures contain all things necessary to salvation: so that whatsoever is not read therein, nor may be proved thereby, is not to be required of any man, that it should be believed as an article of faith, or be thought requisite or necessary to salvation. In the name of the Holy Scripture, we do understand those canonical books of the Old and New Testament, of whose authority was never any doubt in the church.

The names of the canonical books. Genesis, Exodus, Leviticus, Numbers, Deuteronomy, Joshua, Judges, Ruth, The First Book of Samuel, The Second Book of Samuel, The First Book of Kings, The Second Book of Kings, The First Book of Chronicles, The Second Book of Chronicles, The Book of Ezra, The Book of Nehemiah, The Book of Esther, The Book of Job, The Psalms, The Proverbs, Ecclesiastes, or the Preacher, Cantica, or Songs of Solomon, Four Prophets the greater, Twelve Prophets the less; All the books of the New Testament, as they are commonly received, we do receive and account canonical.

6. OF THE OLD TESTAMENT

The Old Testament is not contrary to the New; for both in the Old and New Testaments everlasting life is offered to mankind by Christ, who is the only Mediator between God and man. Wherefore they are not to be heard who feign that the old fathers did look only for transitory promises. Although the law given from God by Moses, as touching ceremonies and rites, doth not bind Christians, nor ought the civil precepts thereof of necessity to be received in any commonwealth; yet, notwithstanding, no Christian whatsoever is free from the obedience of the commandments which are called moral.

7. OF ORIGINAL OR BIRTH SIN

Original sin standeth not in the following of Adam (as the Pelagians do vainly talk), but it is the corruption of the nature of every man that naturally is engendered of the offspring of Adam, whereby man is very far gone from original righteousness, and of his own nature inclined to evil, and that continually.

8. OF FREE WILL

The condition of man after the fall of Adam is such, that he cannot turn and prepare himself, by his own natural strength and works, to faith and calling upon God; wherefore we have no power to do good works, pleasant and acceptable to God, without the grace of God by Christ preventing us, that we may have a good will, and working with us, when we have that good will.

9. OF THE JUSTIFICATION OF MAN

We are accounted righteous before God, only for the merit of our Lord and Savior Jesus Christ by faith, and not for our own works or deservings: wherefore, that we are justified by faith only, is a most wholesome doctrine, and very full of comfort.

10. OF GOOD WORKS

Although good works, which are the fruits of faith, and follow after justification, cannot put away our sins, and endure the severity of God's judgments; yet they are pleasing and acceptable to God in Christ, and spring out of a true and lively faith, insomuch that by them a lively faith may be as evidently known as a tree is discerned by its fruits.

[Mt 7.16–20]

11. OF WORKS OF SUPEREROGATION

Voluntary works—besides, over and above God's commandments—which are called works of supererogation, cannot be taught without arrogancy and impiety. For by them men do declare that they do not only render unto God as much as they are bound to do, but that they do more for his sake than of bounden duty is required: whereas Christ saith plainly, "When ye have done all that is commanded you, say, We are unprofitable servants."

[Lk 17.10]

13. ENTIRE SANCTIFICATION

Merely justified persons, while they do not outwardly commit sin, are nevertheless conscious of sin still remaining in the heart. They feel a natural tendency to evil, a proneness to depart from God, and cleave to the things of earth. Those that are sanctified wholly are saved from all inward sin—from evil thoughts and evil tempers. No wrong temper, none contrary to love remains in the soul. All the thoughts, words and actions are governed by pure love.

Entire sanctification takes place subsequently to justification, and is the work of God wrought instantaneously upon the consecrated, believing soul. After a soul is cleansed from all sin, it is then fully prepared to grow in grace.

14. FUTURE REWARD AND PUNISHMENT

God has appointed a day in which he will judge the world in righteousness by Jesus Christ, according to the gospel. The righteous shall have in heaven an inheritance incorruptible, undefiled, and that fadeth not away. The wicked shall go away into everlasting punishment, where their worm dieth not, and their fire is not quenched.

15. OF SPEAKING IN THE CONGREGATION IN SUCH
A TONGUE AS THE PEOPLE UNDERSTAND

It is a thing plainly repugnant to the word of God, and the custom of the primitive church, to have public prayer in the church, or to minister the sacrament in a tongue not understood by the people.

16. OF THE CHURCH

The visible church of Christ is a congregation of faithful men, in which the pure word of God is preached, and the sacraments duly administered, according to Christ's ordinance, in all those things that of necessity are requisite to the same.

17. OF THE SACRAMENTS

Sacraments ordained of Christ, are not only badges or tokens of Christian men's profession; but rather they are certain signs of grace, and God's goodwill toward us, by the which he doth work invisibly in us, and doth not only quicken, but also strengthen and confirm our faith in him.

18. OF BAPTISM

Baptism is not only a sign of profession, and mark of difference, whereby Christians are distinguished from others that are not baptized; but it is also a sign of regeneration, or the new birth. The baptism of young children is to be retained in the church.

19. OF THE LORD'S SUPPER

The supper of the Lord is not merely a sign of the love that Christians ought to have among themselves, one to another, but rather is a sacrament of our redemption by Christ's death; insomuch that, to such as rightly, worthily, and with faith receive the same, the bread which we break is a partaking of the body of Christ; and likewise the cup of blessing is a partaking of the blood of Christ.

Transubstantiation, or the change of the substance of bread and wine in the supper of our Lord, cannot be proved by Holy Writ, but it is repugnant to the plain words of Scripture, overthroweth the nature of a sacrament, and hath given occasion to many superstitions.

The body of Christ is given, taken, and eaten in the supper, only after a heavenly and spiritual manner. And the means whereby the body of Christ is received and eaten in the supper, is faith.

The sacrament of the Lord's supper was not by Christ's ordinance reserved, carried about, lifted up, or worshiped.

20. OF THE ONE OBLATION OF CHRIST, FINISHED UPON THE CROSS

The offering of Christ, once made, is that perfect redemption, propitiation, and satisfaction for all the sins of the whole world, both original and actual: and there is none other satisfaction for sin but that alone. Wherefore the sacrifice of the masses, in the which it is said that the priest doth offer Christ for the quick and the dead, to have remission of pain or guilt, is a blasphemous fable and dangerous deceit.

21. OF THE RITES AND CEREMONIES OF CHURCHES

It is not necessary that rites and ceremonies should in all places be the same, or exactly alike; for they have been always different, and may be changed according to the diversity of countries, times, and men's manners, so that nothing be ordained against God's word. Whosoever, through his private judgment, willingly and purposely doth openly break the rites and ceremonies of the church to which he belongs, which are not repugnant to the word of God, and are ordained and approved by common authority, ought to be rebuked openly, that others may fear to do the like, as one that offendeth against the common order of the church, and woundeth the consciences of weak brethren.

Every particular church may ordain, change, or abolish rites and ceremonies, so that all things may be done to edification.

22. OF CHRISTIAN MEN'S GOODS

The riches and goods of Christians are not common, as touching the right, title, and possession of the same, as some do falsely boast. Notwithstanding, every man ought, of such things as he possesseth, liberally to give alms to the poor, according to his ability.

23. OF A CHRISTIAN MAN'S OATH

As we confess that vain and rash swearing is forbidden Christian men by our Lord [Mt 5.34; Jas 5.12]   Jesus Christ, and James the apostle; so we hold that the Christian religion doth not prohibit, but that a man may swear when the magistrate requireth, in a cause of faith and charity, so it be done according to the prophet's teaching, in justice, judgment, [Jer 4.2]   and truth.

Roman Catholic Church, First Vatican Council, *The Dogmatic Constitution on the Catholic Faith* and *The Dogmatic Constitution on the Church of Christ*, 1870

From the adjournment of the Council of Trent in 1563 to the gathering of the First Vatican Council in 1869 was an interim of just over three centuries—revolutionary centuries that were momentous, in some respects even calamitous, especially in the relations of the Roman Catholic Church to modern culture and the state but also within the authority structure of the church itself. Pope Pius IX had aggressively addressed the former of these with his → *Syllabus of Errors* of 1864 and had dramatically raised the question of the latter in 1854 by promulgating in → *Inneffabilis Deus* the dogma of the immaculate conception of the Virgin Mary without having to resort to the traditional instrumentrality of a creedal or doctrinal definition by a church council.

There was, therefore, a full agenda of unfinished business, in these doctrinal areas but also in the fields of canon law and liturgy, that had never been dealt with by a council but only by papal actions. Politically, the times were, to say the least, not propitious for a council: with the Franco-Prussian War looming—it would break out the day after the council issued its decree on papal infallibility—a reuniting Germany under Prince Otto von Bismarck (1815–98) was hostile to many of the claims of the Roman Catholic Church and was about to launch the bitter conflicts of the *Kulturkampf,* while a reuniting Italy was challenging the jurisdiction of the Vatican over the Papal States.

The Dogmatic Constitution on the Catholic Faith was accepted at the third session of the council on 24 April 1870, *The Dogmatic Constitution on the Church of Christ* (including the dogma of papal infallibility) at its fourth session on 18 July in spite of opposition by a substantial minority who abstained; study of hitherto unavailable documents from the preparatory commission confirms the weight that was given to the perceived tensions between the claims of papal infallibility and such events from the history of the church as the condemnation of Pope Honorius I by the Sixth Ecumenical Council in 681.[1] In condemning yet again the notion "that it is lawful to appeal from the judgments of the Roman pontiffs to an ecumenical

---

1. Pottmeyer 1968.

council as if this were an authority superior to the Roman pontiff,"[2] the council was responding both to the Orthodox East and to lingering conciliarism in the West. Retroactively, the definition of infallibility was also seen as conferring conciliar authority on the papal definition of the dogma of the immaculate conception sixteen years earlier in *Ineffabilis Deus*.

Edition and translation: *DEC* 2:804–*816.

Literature: *DTC* 15:2536–85 (Joseph Brugerette, Emile Amann); Hasler 1981; Pottmeyer 1968, 1975; Tierney 1988.

2. *Vat I* 4.3.

Roman Catholic Church, First Vatican Council, *The Dogmatic Constitution on the Catholic Faith* and *The Dogmatic Constitution on the Church of Christ*, 1870

Session 3: Dogmatic Constitution on the Catholic Faith

Pius bishop, servant of the servants of God, with the approval of the sacred council, for an everlasting record. The Son of God, Redeemer of the human race, our Lord Jesus Christ, promised, when about to return to his heavenly Father, that he would be with this church militant upon earth all days even to the end of the world. Hence [Mt 28.20] never at any time has he ceased to stand by his beloved bride, assisting her when she teaches, blessing her in her labors and bringing her help when she is in danger. Now this redemptive providence appears very clearly in unnumbered benefits, but most especially is it manifested in the advantages which have been secured for the Christian world by ecumenical councils, among which the Council of Trent requires special mention, celebrated though it was in evil days. Thence came a closer definition and more fruitful exposition of the holy dogmas of religion and the condemnation and repression of errors; thence too, the restoration and vigorous strengthening of ecclesiastical discipline, the advancement of the clergy in zeal for learning and piety; the founding of colleges for the training of the young for the service of religion; and finally the renewal of the moral life of the Christian people by a more accurate instruction of the faithful, and a more frequent reception of the sacraments. What is more, thence also came a closer union of the members with the visible head, and an increased vigor in the whole mystical body of Christ. Thence came the multiplication of religious orders and other organizations of Christian piety; thence too that determined and constant ardor for the spreading of Christ's kingdom abroad in the world, even at the cost of shedding one's blood.

While we recall with grateful hearts, as is only fitting, these and other outstanding gains, which the divine mercy has bestowed on the church especially by means of the last ecumenical synod, we cannot subdue the bitter grief that we feel at most serious evils, which have largely arisen either because the authority of the sacred synod was held in contempt by all too many, or because its wise decrees were neglected. Everybody knows that those heresies, condemned by the fathers of Trent, which rejected the divine magisterium of the church and allowed religious questions to be a matter for the judgment of each individual, have gradually collapsed into

343

a multiplicity of sects, either at variance or in agreement with one another; and by this means a good many people have had all faith in Christ destroyed. Indeed even the Holy Bible itself, which they at one time claimed to be the sole source and judge of the Christian faith, is no longer held to be divine, but they begin to assimilate it to the inventions of myth. Thereupon there came into being and spread far and wide throughout the world that doctrine of rationalism or naturalism, utterly opposed to the Christian religion, since this is of supernatural origin, which spares no effort to bring it about that Christ, who alone is our Lord and Savior, is shut out from the minds of people and the moral life of nations. Thus they would establish what they call the rule of simple reason or nature. The abandonment and rejection of the Christian religion, and the denial of God and his Christ, has plunged the minds of many into the abyss of pantheism, materialism, and atheism, and the consequence is that they strive to destroy rational nature itself, to deny any criterion of what is right and just, and to overthrow the very foundations of human society. With this impiety spreading in every direction, it has come about, alas, that many even among the children of the Catholic Church have strayed from the path of genuine piety, and as the truth was gradually diluted in them, their Catholic sensibility was weakened.

[Heb 13.9] Led away by diverse and strange teachings and confusing nature and grace, human knowledge and divine faith, they are found to distort the genuine sense of the dogmas which holy mother church holds and teaches, and to endanger the integrity and genuineness of the faith.

At the sight of all this, how can the inmost being of the church not suffer anguish? For just as God "wills all people to be saved and come to the knowledge of the truth,"[a] just as Christ "came to save what was lost"[b] and "to gather into one
[Jn 11.52] the children of God who were scattered abroad," so the church, appointed by God to be mother and mistress of nations, recognizes her obligations to all and is always ready and anxious to raise the fallen, to steady those who stumble, to embrace those who return, and to strengthen the good and urge them on to what is better. Thus
[Wis 16.12] she can never cease from witnessing to the truth of God which heals all and from declaring it, for she knows that these words were directed to her: "My spirit which is upon you, and my words which I have put in your mouth, shall not depart out
[Is 59.21] of your mouth from this time forth and for evermore." And so we, following in the footsteps of our predecessors, in accordance with our supreme apostolic office, have never left off teaching and defending Catholic truth and condemning erroneous doctrines. But now it is our purpose to profess and declare from this chair of Peter

a. [1 Tm 2.4]
b. [Lk 19.10]

before all eyes the saving teaching of Christ, and, by the power given us by God, to reject and condemn the contrary errors. This we shall do with the bishops of the whole world as our co-assessors and fellow-judges, gathered here as they are in the Holy Spirit by our authority in this ecumenical council, and relying on the word of God in Scripture and tradition, as we have received it, religiously preserved and authentically expounded by the Catholic Church.

CHAPTER 1. ON GOD THE CREATOR OF ALL THINGS

The holy, catholic, apostolic, and Roman church believes and acknowledges that there is one true and living God, Creator and Lord of heaven and earth, almighty, eternal, immeasurable, incomprehensible, infinite in will, understanding, and every perfection. Since he is one, singular, completely simple, and unchangeable spiritual substance, he must be declared to be in reality and in essence, distinct from the world, supremely happy in himself and from himself, and inexpressibly loftier than anything besides himself which either exists or can be imagined. This one true God, by his goodness and almighty power, not with the intention of increasing his happiness, nor indeed of obtaining happiness, but in order to manifest his perfection by the good things which he bestows on what he creates, by an absolutely free plan, together from the beginning of time brought into being from nothing the twofold created order, that is the spiritual and the bodily, the angelic and the earthly, and thereafter the human which is, in a way, common to both since it is composed of spirit and body.[1] Everything that God has brought into being he protects and governs by his providence, which "reaches from one end of the earth to the other and orders all things well.[a] All things are open and laid bare to his eyes,"[b] even those which will be brought about by the free activity of creatures.

CHAPTER 2. ON REVELATION

The same Holy Mother Church holds and teaches that God, the source and end of all things, can be known with certainty from the consideration of created things, by the natural power of human reason: "ever since the creation of the world, his invisible nature has been clearly perceived in the things that have been made." It was, [Rom 1.20] however, pleasing to his wisdom and goodness to reveal himself and the eternal laws of his will to the human race by another, and that a supernatural, way. This is how

a. [Wis 8.1]
b. [Heb 4.13]

1. *Lat IV* 1.

the apostle puts it: "In many and various ways God spoke of old to our fathers by

[Heb 1.1–2] the prophets; but in these last days he has spoken to us by a Son."

It is indeed thanks to this divine revelation, that those matters concerning God which are not of themselves beyond the scope of human reason, can, even in the present state of the human race, be known by everyone without difficulty, with firm certitude and with no intermingling of error. It is not because of this that one must hold revelation to be absolutely necessary; the reason is that God directed human beings to a supernatural end, that is a sharing in the good things of God that utterly surpasses the understanding of the human mind; "indeed eye has not seen, neither has ear heard, nor has it come into our hearts to conceive what things God

[1 Cor 2.9] has prepared for those who love him." Now this supernatural revelation, according to the belief of the universal church, as declared by the sacred Council of Trent, is contained in written books and unwritten traditions, which were received by the apostles from the lips of Christ himself, or came to the apostles by the dictation of the Holy Spirit, and were passed on as it were from hand to hand until they reached us.[2] The complete books of the Old and the New Testament with all their parts, as they are listed in the decree of the said council and as they are found in the old Latin Vulgate edition, are to be received as sacred and canonical. These books the church holds to be sacred and canonical not because she subsequently approved them by her authority after they had been composed by unaided human skill, nor simply because they contain revelation without error, but because, being written under the inspiration of the Holy Spirit, they have God as their author, and were as such committed to the church. Now since the decree on the interpretation of Holy Scripture, profitably made by the Council of Trent, with the intention of constraining rash speculation, has been wrongly interpreted by some, we renew that decree and declare its meaning to be as follows: that in matters of faith and morals, belonging as they do to the establishing of Christian doctrine, that meaning of Holy Scripture must be held to be the true one, which Holy Mother Church held and holds, since it is her right to judge of the true meaning and interpretation of Holy Scripture. In consequence, it is not permissible for anyone to interpret Holy Scripture in a sense contrary to this, or indeed against the unanimous consent of the fathers.

CHAPTER 3. ON FAITH

Since human beings are totally dependent on God as their Creator and Lord, and created reason is completely subject to uncreated truth, we are obliged to yield to God the revealer full submission of intellect and will by faith. This faith, which is

2. *Trent* 4 decr 1.

the beginning of human salvation, the Catholic Church professes to be a supernatural virtue, by means of which, with the grace of God inspiring and assisting us, we believe to be true what he has revealed, not because we perceive its intrinsic truth by the natural light of reason, but because of the authority of God himself, who makes the revelation and can neither deceive nor be deceived. "Faith," declares the apostle, "is the assurance of things hoped for, the conviction of things not seen." Nevertheless, in order that the submission of our faith should be in accordance with reason, it was God's will that there should be linked to the internal assistance of the Holy Spirit outward indications of his revelation, that is to say divine acts, and first and foremost miracles and prophecies, which clearly demonstrating as they do the omnipotence and infinite knowledge of God, are the most certain signs of revelation and are suited to the understanding of all. Hence Moses and the prophets, and especially Christ our Lord himself, worked many absolutely clear miracles and delivered prophecies; while of the apostles we read: "And they went forth and preached everywhere, while the Lord worked with them and confirmed the message by the signs that attended it." Again it is written: "We have the prophetic word made more sure; you will do well to pay attention to this as to a lamp shining in a dark place." Now, although the assent of faith is by no means a blind movement of the mind, yet no one can accept the gospel preaching in the way that is necessary for achieving salvation without the inspiration and illumination of the Holy Spirit, who gives to all facility in accepting and believing the truth. And so faith in itself, even though it may not work through charity, is a gift of God, and its operation is a work belonging to the order of salvation, in that a person yields true obedience to God himself when he accepts and collaborates with his grace which he could have rejected. Therefore, by divine and Catholic faith all those things are to be believed which are contained in the word of God as found in Scripture and tradition, and which are proposed by the church as matters to be believed as divinely revealed, whether by her solemn judgment or in her ordinary and universal magisterium. Since, then, "without faith it is impossible to please God" and reach the fellowship of his sons and daughters, it follows that no one can ever achieve justification without it, neither can anyone attain eternal life unless he or she perseveres in it to the end.

[Heb 11.1]

[Mk 16.20]

[2 Pt 1.19]

[Heb 11.6]

So that we could fulfill our duty of embracing the true faith and of persevering unwaveringly in it, God, through his only-begotten Son, founded the church, and he endowed his institution with clear notes to the end that she might be recognized by all as the guardian and teacher of the revealed word. To the Catholic Church alone belong all those things, so many and so marvelous, which have been divinely ordained to make for the manifest credibility of the Christian faith. What is more, the church herself by reason of her astonishing propagation, her outstanding holiness and her inexhaustible fertility in every kind of goodness, by her Catholic unity and her unconquerable stability, is a kind of great and perpetual motive of credibility and an incontrovertible evidence of her own divine mission. So it comes

[Is 11.12]

about that, like a standard lifted up for the nations, the church invites to herself those who have not yet believed, and likewise assures her sons and daughters that the faith they profess rests on the firmest of foundations. To this witness is added the effective help of power from on high. For the kind Lord stirs up those who go astray and helps them by his grace so that they may come to the knowledge of the

[1 Tm 2.3]

truth, and also confirms by his grace those whom he has translated into his admi-

[1 Pt 2.9; Col 1.13]

rable light, so that they may persevere in this light, not abandoning them unless he is first abandoned. Consequently, the situation of those, who by the heavenly gift of faith have embraced the Catholic truth, is by no means the same as that of those who, led by human opinions, follow a false religion; for those who have accepted the faith under the guidance of the church can never have any just cause for changing this faith or for calling it into question. This being so, "giving thanks to God

[Col 1.12]

the Father who has made us worthy to share with the saints in light," let us not neglect "so great a salvation,"[a] but looking unto "Jesus the author and finisher of our

[Heb 10.23]

faith"[b] "let us hold the unshakeable confession of our hope."

CHAPTER 4. ON FAITH AND REASON

The perpetual agreement of the Catholic Church has maintained and maintains this: that there is a twofold order of knowledge, distinct not only as regards its source, but also as regards its object. With regard to the source, we know at the one level by natural reason, at the other level by divine faith. With regard to the object, besides those things to which natural reason can attain, there are proposed for our belief mysteries hidden in God which, unless they are divinely revealed, are incapable of being known. Wherefore, when the apostle, who witnesses that God was known to

[Rom 1.20]

the Gentiles from created things, comes to that of the grace and truth which came

[Jn 1.17]

by Jesus Christ he declares: "We impart secret and hidden wisdom of God, which God decreed before the ages for our glorification. None of the rulers of this age understood this. God has revealed it to us through the Spirit. For the Spirit searches

[1 Cor 2.7–8, 10]

everything, even the depths of God." And the Only-begotten himself, in his confession to the Father, acknowledges that the Father has hidden these things from the

[Mt 11.25]

wise and prudent and revealed them to the little ones. Now reason, if it is enlightened by faith, does indeed when it seeks persistently, piously, and soberly, achieve by

a. [Heb 2.3]
b. [Heb 12.2]

God's gift some understanding, and that most profitable, of the mysteries, whether by analogy from what it knows naturally, or from the connection of these mysteries with one another and with the final end of humanity; but reason is never rendered capable of penetrating these mysteries in the way in which it penetrates those truths which form its proper object. For the divine mysteries, by their very nature, so far surpass the created understanding that, even when a revelation has been given and accepted by faith, they remain covered by the veil of that same faith and wrapped, as it were, in a certain obscurity, as long as in this mortal life "we are away from the Lord, for we walk by faith, and not by sight."   [2 Cor 5.6–7]

Even though faith is above reason, there can never be any real disagreement between faith and reason, since it is the same God who reveals the mysteries and infuses faith, and who has endowed the human mind with the light of reason. God cannot deny himself, nor can truth ever be in opposition to truth. The appearance   [2 Tm 2.13] of this kind of specious contradiction is chiefly due to the fact that either the dogmas of faith are not understood and explained in accordance with the mind of the church, or unsound views are mistaken for the conclusions of reason. Therefore we define that every assertion contrary to the truth of enlightened faith is totally false. Furthermore the church which, together with its apostolic office of teaching, has received the charge of preserving the deposit of faith, has by divine appointment the right and duty of condemning what wrongly passes for knowledge, lest anyone be led astray by philosophy and empty deceit. Hence all faithful Christians are for-   [Col 2.8] bidden to defend as the legitimate conclusions of science those opinions which are known to be contrary to the doctrine of faith, particularly if they have been condemned by the church; and furthermore they are absolutely bound to hold them to be errors which wear the deceptive appearance of truth.

Not only can faith and reason never be at odds with one another but they mutually support each other, for on the one hand right reason establishes the foundations of the faith and, illuminated by its light, develops the science of divine things; on the other hand, faith delivers reason from errors and protects it and furnishes it with knowledge of many kinds. Hence, so far is the church from hindering the development of human arts and studies, that in fact she assists and promotes them in many ways. For she is neither ignorant nor contemptuous of the advantages which derive from this source for human life, rather she acknowledges that those things flow from God, the Lord of sciences, and, if they are properly used, lead to God by the help of his grace. Nor does the church forbid these studies to employ, each within its own area, its own proper principles and method; but while she admits this just freedom, she takes particular care that they do not become infected with errors by conflicting with divine teaching, or, by going beyond their proper limits, intrude upon what belongs to faith and engender confusion. For the doctrine of the faith which God has revealed is put forward not as some philosophical discovery capable of being perfected by human intelligence, but as a divine deposit committed to the spouse of Christ to be faithfully protected and infallibly promulgated. Hence, too, that meaning of the sacred dogmas is ever to be maintained which has once been declared by Holy Mother Church, and there must never be any abandonment of this sense under the pretext or in the name of a more profound understanding. May understanding, knowledge, and wisdom increase as ages and centuries roll along, and greatly and vigorously flourish, in each and all, in the individual and the whole church: but this only in its own proper kind, that is to say, in the same doctrine, the same sense, and the same understanding.

Canons
1. ON GOD THE CREATOR OF ALL THINGS

1. If anyone denies the one true God, Creator and Lord of things visible and invisible: let him be anathema.

2. If anyone is so bold as to assert that there exists nothing besides matter: let him be anathema.

3. If anyone says that the substance or essence of God and that of all things are one and the same: let him be anathema.

4. If anyone says that finite things, both corporal and spiritual, or at any rate, spiritual, emanated from the divine substance; or that the divine essence, by the manifestation and evolution of itself, becomes all things; or, finally, that God is a universal or indefinite being which by self-determination establishes the totality of things distinct in genera, species, and individuals: let him be anathema.

5. If anyone does not confess that the world and all things which are contained in it, both spiritual and material, were produced, according to their whole substance out of nothing by God; or holds that God did not create by his will free from all necessity, but as necessarily as he necessarily loves himself; or denies that the world was created for the glory of God: let him be anathema.

2. ON REVELATION

1. If anyone says that the one, true God, our Creator and Lord, cannot be known with certainty from the things that have been made, by the natural light of human reason: let him be anathema.

2. If anyone says that it is impossible, or not expedient, that human beings

should be taught by means of divine revelation about God and the worship that should be shown him: let him be anathema.

3. If anyone says that a human being cannot be divinely elevated to a knowledge and perfection which exceeds the natural, but of himself can and must reach finally the possession of all truth and goodness by continual development: let him be anathema.

4. If anyone does not receive as sacred and canonical the complete books of Sacred Scripture with all their parts, as the holy Council of Trent listed them, or denies that they were divinely inspired: let him be anathema.

3. ON FAITH

1. If anyone says that human reason is so independent that faith cannot be commanded by God: let him be anathema.

2. If anyone says that divine faith is not to be distinguished from natural knowledge about God and moral matters, and consequently that for divine faith it is not required that revealed truth should be believed because of the authority of God who reveals it: let him be anathema.

3. If anyone says that divine revelation cannot be made credible by external signs, and that therefore men and women ought to be moved to faith only by each one's internal experience or private inspiration: let him be anathema.

4. If anyone says that all miracles are impossible, and that therefore all reports of them, even those contained in Sacred Scripture, are to be set aside as fables or myths; or that miracles can never be known with certainty, nor can the divine origin of the Christian religion be proved from them: let him be anathema.

5. If anyone says that the assent to Christian faith is not free, but is necessarily produced by arguments of human reason; or that the grace of God is necessary only for living faith which works by charity: let him be anathema.

6. If anyone says that the condition of the faithful and those who have not yet attained to the only true faith is alike, so that Catholics may have a just cause for calling in doubt, by suspending their assent, the faith which they have already received from the teaching of the church, until they have completed a scientific demonstration of the credibility and truth of their faith: let him be anathema.

4. ON FAITH AND REASON

1. If anyone says that in divine revelation there are contained no true mysteries properly so-called, but that all the dogmas of the faith can be understood and demonstrated by properly trained reason from natural principles: let him be anathema.

2. If anyone says that human studies are to be treated with such a degree of

liberty that their assertions may be maintained as true even when they are opposed to divine revelation, and that they may not be forbidden by the church: let him be anathema.

3. If anyone says that it is possible that at some time, given the advancement of knowledge, a sense may be assigned to the dogmas propounded by the church which is different from that which the church has understood and understands: let him be anathema.

And so in the performance of our supreme pastoral office, we beseech for the love of Jesus Christ and we command, by the authority of him who is also our God and Savior, all faithful Christians, especially those in authority or who have the duty of teaching, that they contribute their zeal and labor to the warding off and elimination of these errors from the church and to the spreading of the light of the pure faith.

But since it is not enough to avoid the contamination of heresy unless those errors are carefully shunned which approach it in greater or less degree, we warn all of their duty to observe the constitutions and decrees in which such wrong opinions, though not expressly mentioned in this document, have been banned and forbidden by this holy see.

Session 4: First Dogmatic Constitution on the Church of Christ

Pius bishop, servant of the servants of God, with the approval of the sacred council,

[1 Pt 2.25] for an everlasting record. The eternal Shepherd and Guardian of our souls, in order to render permanent the saving work of redemption, determined to build a church in which, as in the house of the living God, all the faithful should be linked by the bond of one faith and charity. Therefore, before he was glorified, he besought his Father, not for the apostles only, but also "for those who were to believe in him through their word, that they all might be one as the Son himself and the Father are one."[a] So then, just as he sent apostles, whom he chose out of the world,[b] even as he

[Jn 20.21] had been sent by the Father, in like manner it was his will that in his church there should be shepherds and teachers until the end of time. In order, then, that the episcopal office should be one and undivided and that, by the union of the clergy, the whole multitude of believers should be held together in the unity of faith and communion, he set blessed Peter over the rest of the apostles and instituted in him the

a. [Jn 17.20–21]
b. [Jn 15.19]

permanent principle of both unities and their visible foundation. Upon the strength of this foundation was to be built the eternal temple, and the church whose topmost part reaches heaven was to rise upon the firmness of this foundation. And since the gates of hell trying, if they can, to overthrow the church, make their assault with a hatred that increases day by day against its divinely laid foundation, we judge it necessary, with the approbation of the sacred council, and for the protection, defense and growth of the Catholic flock, to propound the doctrine concerning the institution, permanence, and nature of the sacred and apostolic primacy, upon which the strength and coherence of the whole church depends. This doctrine is to be believed and held by all the faithful in accordance with the ancient and unchanging faith of the whole church. Furthermore, we shall proscribe and condemn the contrary errors which are so harmful to the Lord's flock.

CHAPTER 1. ON THE INSTITUTION OF THE
APOSTOLIC PRIMACY IN BLESSED PETER

We teach and declare that, according to the Gospel evidence, a primacy of jurisdiction over the whole church of God was immediately and directly promised to the blessed apostle Peter and conferred on him by Christ the Lord. It was to Simon alone, to whom he had already said, "You shall be called Cephas," that the Lord, [Jn 1.42] after his confession, "You are the Christ, the Son of the living God," spoke these words: "Blessed are you, Simon Bar-Jona. For flesh and blood has not revealed this to you, but my Father who is in heaven. And I tell you, you are Peter, and on this rock I will build my church, and the gates of the underworld shall not prevail against it. I will give you the keys of the kingdom of heaven, and whatever you bind on earth shall be bound in heaven, and whatever you loose on earth shall be loosed in heaven." And it was to Peter alone that Jesus, after his resurrection, confided the [Mt 16.16–19] jurisdiction of supreme pastor and ruler of his whole fold, saying: "Feed my lambs, feed my sheep." To this absolutely manifest teaching of the Sacred Scriptures, as it [Jn 21.15–17] has always been understood by the Catholic Church, are clearly opposed the distorted opinions of those who misrepresent the form of government which Christ the Lord established in his church, and deny that Peter, in preference to the rest of the apostles, taken singly or collectively, was endowed by Christ with a true and proper primacy of jurisdiction. The same may be said of those who assert that this primacy was not conferred immediately and directly on blessed Peter himself, but rather on the church, and that it was through the church that it was transmitted to him in his capacity as her minister.

Therefore, if anyone says that blessed Peter the apostle was not appointed by Christ the Lord as prince of all the apostles and visible head of the whole church militant, or that it was a primacy of honor only and not one of true and proper jurisdiction that he directly and immediately received from our Lord Jesus Christ himself: let him be anathema.

CHAPTER 2. ON THE PERMANENCE OF THE PRIMACY
OF BLESSED PETER IN THE ROMAN PONTIFFS

That which our Lord Jesus Christ, the Prince of shepherds and great Shepherd of the sheep, established in the blessed apostle Peter, for the continual salvation and permanent benefit of the church, must of necessity remain forever, by Christ's authority, in the church which, founded as it is upon a rock, will stand firm until [Mt 7.25; Lk 6.48] the end of time. For no one can be in doubt, indeed it was known in every age, that the holy and most blessed Peter, prince and head of the apostles, the pillar of faith and the foundation of the Catholic Church, received the keys of the kingdom from our Lord Jesus Christ, the Savior and Redeemer of the human race; and that to this day and for ever he lives and presides and exercises judgment in his successors the bishops of the holy Roman see, which he founded and consecrated with his blood. Therefore whoever succeeds to the chair of Peter obtains, by the institution of Christ himself, the primacy of Peter over the whole church. So what the truth has ordained stands firm, and blessed Peter perseveres in the rocklike strength he was granted, and does not abandon that guidance of the church which he once received. For this reason it has always been necessary for every church—that is to say the faithful throughout the world—to be in agreement with the Roman church because of its more effective leadership.[3] In consequence of being joined, as members to head, with that see, from which the rights of sacred communion flow to all, they will grow together into the structure of a single body.

Therefore, if anyone says that it is not by the institution of Christ the Lord himself (that is to say, by divine law) that blessed Peter should have perpetual successors in the primacy over the whole church; or that the Roman pontiff is not the successor of blessed Peter in this primacy: let him be anathema.

CHAPTER 3. ON THE POWER AND CHARACTER OF
THE PRIMACY OF THE ROMAN PONTIFF

And so, supported by the clear witness of Holy Scripture, and adhering to the manifest and explicit decrees both of our predecessors the Roman pontiffs and of general councils, we promulgate anew the definition of the ecumenical council of Florence,[4]

3. Irenaeus of Lyons *Against Heresies* 3.3.2 (*ANF* 1:415–16).
4. *Flor Un.*

which must be believed by all faithful Christians, namely, that the apostolic see and the Roman pontiff hold a worldwide primacy, and that the Roman pontiff is the successor of blessed Peter, the prince of the apostles, true vicar of Christ, head of the whole church, and father and teacher of all Christian people. To him, in blessed Peter, full power has been given by our Lord Jesus Christ to tend, rule, and govern the universal church. All this is to be found in the acts of the ecumenical councils and the sacred canons.

Wherefore we teach and declare that, by divine ordinance, the Roman church possesses a preeminence of ordinary power over every other church, and that this jurisdictional power of the Roman pontiff is both episcopal and immediate. Both clergy and faithful, of whatever rite and dignity, both singly and collectively, are bound to submit to this power by the duty of hierarchical subordination and true obedience, and this not only in matters concerning faith and morals, but also in those which regard the discipline and government of the church throughout the world. In this way, by unity with the Roman pontiff in communion and in profession of the same faith, the church of Christ becomes one flock under one supreme shepherd. This is the teaching of the Catholic truth, and no one can depart from it [Jn 10.16] without endangering his faith and salvation.

This power of the supreme pontiff by no means detracts from that ordinary and immediate power of episcopal jurisdiction, by which bishops, who have succeeded to the place of the apostles by appointment of the Holy Spirit, tend and govern individually the particular flocks which have been assigned to them. On the contrary, this power of theirs is asserted, supported, and defended by the supreme and universal pastor; for St. Gregory the Great says: "My honor is the honor of the whole church. My honor is the steadfast strength of my brethren. Then do I receive true honor, when it is denied to none of those to whom honor is due."[5]

Furthermore, it follows from that supreme power which the Roman pontiff has in governing the whole church, that he has the right, in the performance of this office of his, to communicate freely with the pastors and flocks of the entire church, so that they may be taught and guided by him in the way of salvation. And therefore we condemn and reject the opinions of those who hold that this communication of the supreme head with pastors and flocks may be lawfully obstructed; or that it should be dependent on the civil power, which leads them to maintain that what is determined by the apostolic see or by its authority concerning the government of the church, has no force or effect unless it is confirmed by the agreement of the civil authority.

5. Gregory I *Epistles* 8.29 (30) to Eulogius of Alexandria.

Since the Roman pontiff, by the divine right of the apostolic primacy, governs the whole church, we likewise teach and declare that he is the supreme judge of the faithful, and that in all cases which fall under ecclesiastical jurisdiction recourse may be had to his judgment. The sentence of the apostolic see (than which there is no higher authority) is not subject to revision by anyone, nor may anyone lawfully pass judgment thereupon. And so they stray from the genuine path of truth who maintain that it is lawful to appeal from the judgments of the Roman pontiffs to an ecumenical council as if this were an authority superior to the Roman pontiff.

So, then, if anyone says that the Roman pontiff has merely an office of supervision and guidance, and not the full and supreme power of jurisdiction over the whole church, and this not only in matters of faith and morals, but also in those which concern the discipline and government of the church dispersed throughout the whole world; or that he has only the principal part, but not the absolute fullness, of this supreme power; or that this power of his is not ordinary and immediate both over all and each of the churches and over all and each of the pastors and faithful: let him be anathema.

CHAPTER 4. ON THE INFALLIBLE TEACHING AUTHORITY OF THE ROMAN PONTIFF

That apostolic primacy which the Roman pontiff possesses as successor of Peter, the prince of the apostles, includes also the supreme power of teaching. This holy see has always maintained this, the constant custom of the church demonstrates it, and the ecumenical councils, particularly those in which East and West met in the union of faith and charity, have declared it. So the fathers of the Fourth Council of Constantinople, following the footsteps of their predecessors, published this solemn profession of faith: "The first condition of salvation is to maintain the rule of the true faith. And since that saying of our Lord Jesus Christ, 'You are Peter, and [Mt 16.18] upon this rock I will build my church,' cannot fail of its effect, the words spoken are confirmed by their consequences. For in the apostolic see the catholic religion has always been preserved unblemished, and sacred doctrine been held in honor. Since it is our earnest desire to be in no way separated from this faith and doctrine, we hope that we may deserve to remain in that one communion which the apostolic see preaches, for in it is the whole and true strength of the Christian religion."[6] What is more, with the approval of the second Council of Lyons, the Greeks made the following profession: "The Holy Roman Church possesses the supreme and full primacy and principality over the whole Catholic Church. She truly and humbly ac-

---

6. Fourth Council of Constantinople (869-70): see *DEC* 1:157-59.

knowledges that she received this from the Lord himself in blessed Peter, the prince and chief of the apostles, whose successor the Roman pontiff is, together with the fullness of power. And since before all others she has the duty of defending the truth of the faith, so if any questions arise concerning the faith, it is by her judgment that they must be tended."[7] Then there is the definition of the Council of Florence: "The Roman pontiff is the true vicar of Christ, the head of the whole church and the father and teacher of all Christians; and to him was committed in blessed Peter, by our Lord Jesus Christ, the full power of tending, ruling, and governing the whole church."[8]

To satisfy this pastoral office, our predecessors strove unwearyingly that the saving teaching of Christ should be spread among all the peoples of the world; and with equal care they made sure that it should be kept pure and uncontaminated wherever it was received. It was for this reason that the bishops of the whole world, sometimes individually, sometimes gathered in synods, according to the long-established custom of the churches and the pattern of ancient usage, referred to this apostolic see those dangers especially which arose in matters concerning the faith. This was to ensure that any damage suffered by the faith should be repaired in that place above all where the faith can know no failing. The Roman pontiffs, too, as the circumstances of the time or the state of affairs suggested, sometimes by summoning ecumenical councils or consulting the opinion of the churches scattered throughout the world, sometimes by special synods, sometimes by taking advantage of other useful means afforded by divine providence, defined as doctrines to be held those things which, by God's help, they knew to be in keeping with Sacred Scripture and the apostolic traditions. For the Holy Spirit was promised to the successors of Peter not so that they might, by his revelation, make known some new doctrine, but that, by his assistance, they might religiously guard and faithfully expound the revelation or deposit of faith transmitted by the apostles. Indeed, their apostolic teaching was embraced by all the venerable fathers and reverenced and followed by all the holy orthodox doctors, for they knew very well that this see of St. Peter always remains unblemished by any error, in accordance with the divine promise of our Lord and Savior to the prince of his disciples: "I have prayed for you that your faith may not fail; and when you have turned again, strengthen your brethren." [Lk 22.32]

This gift of truth and never-failing faith was therefore divinely conferred on Peter and his successors in this see so that they might discharge their exalted office for the salvation of all, and so that the whole flock of Christ might be kept

7. *Lyons.*
8. *Flor Un.*

away by them from the poisonous food of error and be nourished with the suste-
nance of heavenly doctrine. Thus the tendency to schism is removed and the whole
church is preserved in unity, and, resting on its foundation, can stand firm against
[Mt 16.18]   the gates of hell.

But since in this very age when the salutary effectiveness of the apostolic
office is most especially needed, not a few are to be found who disparage its authority, we judge it absolutely necessary to affirm solemnly the prerogative which
the only-begotten Son of God was pleased to attach to the supreme pastoral office.

Therefore, faithfully adhering to the tradition received from the beginning
of the Christian faith, to the glory of God our Savior, for the exaltation of the Catholic religion and for the salvation of the Christian people, with the approval of the
sacred council, we teach and define as a divinely revealed dogma that when the Roman pontiff speaks *ex cathedra,* that is, when, in the exercise of his office as shepherd
and teacher of all Christians, in virtue of his supreme apostolic authority, he defines
a doctrine concerning faith or morals to be held by the whole church, he possesses,
by the divine assistance promised to him in blessed Peter, that infallibility which the
divine Redeemer willed his church to enjoy in defining doctrine concerning faith or
morals. Therefore, such definitions of the Roman pontiff are of themselves, and not
by the consent of the church, irreformable.

So then, should anyone, which God forbid, have the temerity to reject this
definition of ours: let him be anathema.

Seventh-Day Adventist Church,
The Statement of Belief, 1872

The Adventist movement of the nineteenth century was the consequence of the evangelistic preaching of William Miller (1782–1849), who had become convinced that the return of Christ or "second advent," so long delayed, was now finally to come to pass, and more specifically that the prophecies pointed to 1843/44 as the date. He found hearers and followers for this message in many of the churches.

When that hope was not realized, Miller's followers separated into several groups, each of which sought to come to terms with what this *Statement of Belief* explicitly calls "the mistake of Adventists in 1844." It insists, however, that the mistake "pertained to the nature of the event then to transpire, not to the time," which, according to the prophecy of the Book of Daniel, "terminated in that year, and brought us to an event called the cleansing of the sanctuary" (9).

The second distinctive teaching of the Seventh-Day Adventist Church was the continuing force of the Old Testament prescription of the Sabbath as "the seventh day of the week, commonly called Saturday" (12).

But these two doctrines, which are incorporated into the very name of the church body, were to be seen as part of a total context of beliefs, which in 1872 it resolved to affirm in a confessional *Statement of Belief.* But even this is hedged in with the stipulation in the preface: "In presenting to the public this synopsis of our faith, we wish to have it distinctly understood that *we have no articles of faith, creed, or discipline, aside from the Bible.*" That stipulation applied as well to the later statement of faith in 1931 and to the current statement of 1980. In keeping with this version of the doctrine of *sola Scriptura,* this noncreedal confession incorporates references to biblical proof texts as part of its text, which makes redundant our usual system of identifying such references in the margin.

Edition: Land 1998, 191–95.

Literature: Froom 1946–54, esp. vol. 4.

Seventh-Day Adventist Church, *The Statement of Belief,* 1872

In presenting to the public this synopsis of our faith, we wish to have it distinctly understood that we have no articles of faith, creed, or discipline, aside from the Bible. We do not put forth this as having any authority with our people, nor is it designed to secure uniformity among them, as a system of faith, but is a brief statement of what is and has been, with great unanimity, held by them. We often find it necessary to meet inquiries on this subject, and sometimes to correct false statements circulated against us, and to remove erroneous impressions which have obtained with those who have not had an opportunity to become acquainted with our faith and practice. Our only object is to meet this necessity.

As Seventh-Day Adventists, we desire simply that our position shall be understood; and we are the more solicitous for this because there are many who call themselves Adventists, who hold views with which we can have no sympathy, some of which, we think, are subversive of the plainest and most important principles set forth in the word of God.

As compared with other Adventists, Seventh-Day Adventists differ from one class in believing in the unconscious state of the dead, and the final destruction of the unrepentant wicked; from another, in believing in the perpetuity of the law of God, as summarily contained in the Ten Commandments, in the operation of the Holy Spirit in the church, and in setting no times for the advent to occur; from all, in the observance of the seventh day of the week as the Sabbath of the Lord, and in many applications of the prophetic Scriptures.

With these remarks, we ask the attention of the reader to the following propositions which aim to be a concise statement of the more prominent features of our faith.

1. That there is one God, a personal, spiritual being, the Creator of all things, omnipotent, omniscient, and eternal, infinite in wisdom, holiness, justice, goodness, truth, and mercy; unchangeable, and everywhere present by his representative, the Holy Spirit. Ps 139.7.

2. That there is one Lord Jesus Christ, the Son of the Eternal Father, the one by whom God created all things, and by whom they do consist; that he took on him the nature of the seed of Abraham for the redemption of our fallen race; that he dwelt among men, full of grace and truth, lived our example, died our sacrifice, was raised for our justification, ascended on high to be our only Mediator in the

sanctuary in heaven, where, with his own blood he makes atonement for our sins; which atonement, so far from being made on the cross, which was but the offering of the sacrifice, is the very last portion of his work as Priest, according to the example of the Levitical priesthood, which foreshadowed and prefigured the ministry of our Lord in heaven. See Lv 16; Heb 8.4, 5, 9.6, 7; etc.

3. That the Holy Scriptures, of the Old and New Testaments, were given by inspiration of God, contain a full revelation of his will to man, and are the only infallible rule of faith and practice.

4. That baptism is an ordinance of the Christian church, to follow faith and repentance, an ordinance by which we commemorate the resurrection of Christ, as by this act we show our faith in his burial and resurrection, and, through that, of the resurrection of all the saints at the last day; and that no other mode fitly represents these facts than that which the Scriptures prescribe, namely, immersion. Rom 6.3–5; Col 2.12.

5. That the new birth comprises the entire change necessary to fit us for the kingdom of God and consists of two parts: first, a moral change wrought by conversion and a Christian life; second, a physical change at the second coming of Christ, whereby, if dead, we are raised incorruptible, and, if living, are changed to immortality in a moment, in the twinkling of an eye. Jn 3.3, 5; Lk 20.36.

6. We believe that prophecy is a part of God's revelation to man; that it is included in that Scripture which is profitable for instruction; 2 Tm 3.16; that it is designed for us and our children; Dt 29.29; that so far from being enshrouded in impenetrable mystery, it is that which especially constitutes the word of God a lamp to our feet and a light to our path; Ps 119.105; 2 Pt 2.19; that a blessing is pronounced upon those who study it; Rv 1.1–3; and that, consequently, it is to be understood by the people of God, sufficiently to show them their position in the world's history, and the special duties required at their hands.

7. That the world's history from specified dates in the past, the rise and fall of empires, and chronological succession of events down to the setting up of God's everlasting kingdom, are outlined in numerous great chains of prophecy; and that these prophecies are now all fulfilled except the closing scenes.

8. That the doctrine of the world's conversion and temporal millennium is a fable of these last days, calculated to lull men into a state of carnal security, and cause them to be overtaken by the great day of the Lord as by a thief in the night; that the second coming of Christ is to precede, not follow, the millennium; for until the Lord appears, the papal power, with all its abominations, is to continue, the wheat and tares grow together, and evil men and seducers wax worse and worse, as the word of God declares.

9. That the mistake of Adventists in 1844 pertained to the nature of the event then to transpire, not to the time; that no prophetic period is given to reach to the second advent, but that the longest one, the two thousand and three hundred days of Dn 8.14, terminated in that year, and brought us to an event called the cleansing of the sanctuary.

10. That the sanctuary of the new covenant is the tabernacle of God in heaven, of which Paul speaks in Heb 8, and onward, of which our Lord, as great High Priest, is minister; that this sanctuary is the antitype of the Mosaic tabernacle, and that the priestly work of our Lord, connected therewith, is the antitype of the work of the Jewish priests of the former dispensation; Heb 8.1–5, etc.; that this is the sanctuary to be cleansed at the end of the 2,300 days, what is termed its cleansing being in this case, as in the type, simply the entrance of the High Priest into the most holy place, to finish the round of service connected therewith, by blotting out and removing from the sanctuary the sins which had been transferred to it by means of the ministration in the first apartment; Heb 9.22, 23; and that this work, in the antitype, commencing in 1844, occupies a brief but indefinite space, at the conclusion of which the work of mercy for the world is finished.

11. That God's moral requirements are the same upon all men in all dispensations; that these are summarily contained in the commandments spoken by Jehovah from Sinai, engraven on the tables of stone, and deposited in the ark, which was in consequence called the "ark of the covenant," or testament; Nm 10.33; Heb 9.4; etc.; that this law is immutable and perpetual, being a transcript of the tables deposited in the ark in the true sanctuary on high, which is also, for the same reason, called the ark of God's testament; for under the sounding of the seventh trumpet we are told that "the temple of God was opened in heaven, and there was seen in his temple the ark of his testament." Rv 11.19.

12. That the fourth commandment of this law requires that we devote the seventh day of each week, commonly called Saturday, to abstinence from our own labor, and to the performance of sacred and religious duties; that this is the only weekly Sabbath known to the Bible, being the day that was set apart before paradise was lost, Gn 2.2, 3, and which will be observed in paradise restored, Is 66.22, 23; that the facts upon which the Sabbath institution is based confine it to the seventh day, as they are not true of any other day; and that the terms, Jewish Sabbath and Christian Sabbath, as applied to the weekly rest-days are names of human invention, unscriptural in fact, and false in meaning.

13. That, as the man of sin, the papacy, has thought to change times and laws (the laws of God), Dn 7.25, and has misled almost all Christendom in regard to the fourth commandment, we find a prophecy of a reform in this respect to be

wrought among believers just before the coming of Christ. Is 56.1, 2; 1 Pt 1.5; Rv 14.12, etc.

14. That, as the natural or carnal heart is at enmity with God and his law, this enmity can be subdued only by a radical transformation of the affections, the exchange of unholy for holy principles; that this transformation follows repentance and faith, is the special work of the Holy Spirit, and constitutes regeneration or conversion.

15. That, as all have violated the law of God and cannot of themselves render obedience to his just requirements, we are dependent on Christ, first for justification from our past offenses, and secondly, for grace whereby to render acceptable obedience to his holy law in time to come.

16. That the Spirit of God was promised to manifest itself in the church through certain gifts, enumerated especially in 1 Cor 12 and Eph 4, that these gifts are not designed to supersede, or take the place of, the Bible, which is sufficient to make us wise unto salvation, any more than the Bible can take the place of the Holy Spirit; that in specifying the various channels of its operation, that Spirit has simply made provision for its own existence and presence with the people of God to the end of time, to lead to an understanding of that word which it had inspired, to convince of sin, and work a transformation in the heart and life; and that those who deny to the Spirit its place and operation do plainly deny that part of the Bible which assigns to it this work and position.

17. That God, in accordance with his uniform dealings with the race, sends forth a proclamation of the approach of the second advent of Christ, that this work is symbolized by the three messages of Rv 14, the last one bringing to view the work of reform on the law of God, that his people may acquire a complete readiness for that event.

18. That the time of the cleansing of the sanctuary (as proposition 10), synchronizing with the time of the proclamation of the third message, is a time of investigative judgment, first, with reference to the dead, and, at the close of probation, with reference to the living, to determine who of the myriads now sleeping in the dust of the earth are worthy of a part in the first resurrection, and who of its living multitudes are worthy of translation—points which must be determined before the Lord appears.

19. That the grave, whither we all tend, expressed by the Hebrew *sheol* and the Greek *hades,* is a place of darkness in which there is no work, device, wisdom, or knowledge. Eccl 9.10.

20. That the state to which we are reduced by death is one of silence, inactivity, and entire unconsciousness. Ps 146.4; Eccl 9.5, 6; Dn 12.2, etc.

21. That out of this prison house of the grave mankind are to be brought by a bodily resurrection: the righteous having part in the first resurrection, which takes place at the second advent of Christ; the wicked, in the second resurrection, which takes place a thousand years thereafter. Rv 20.4–6.

22. That at the last trump, the living righteous are to be changed in a moment, in the twinkling of an eye, and with the resurrected righteous are to be caught up to meet the Lord in the air, so forever to be with the Lord.

23. That these immortalized ones are then taken to heaven, to the New Jerusalem, the Father's house in which there are many mansions, Jn 14.1–3, where they reign with Christ a thousand years, judging the world and fallen angels, that is, apportioning the punishment to be executed upon them at the close of the one thousand years; Rv 20.4; 1 Cor 6.2, 3; that during this time the earth lies in a desolate and chaotic condition, Jer 4.20–27, described, as in the beginning, by the Greek term *abussos* [. . .] bottomless pit (Septuagint of Gn 1.2); and that here Satan is confined during the thousand years, Rv 20.1, 2, and here finally destroyed; Rv 20.10; Mal 4.1; the theater of the ruin he has wrought in the universe, being appropriately made for a time his gloomy prison house, and then the place of his final execution.

24. That at the end of the thousand years, the Lord descends with his people and the New Jerusalem, Rv 21.2, the wicked dead are raised and come up upon the surface of the yet unrenewed earth, and gather about the city, the camp of the saints, Rv 20.9, and fire comes down from God out of heaven and devours them. They are then consumed root and branch, Mal 4.1, becoming as though they had not been. Ob 15, 16. In this everlasting destruction from the presence of the Lord, 2 Thes 1.9, the wicked meet the everlasting punishment threatened against them. Mt 25.46. This is the perdition of ungodly men, the fire which consumes them being the fire for which "the heavens and the earth which are now" are kept in store, which shall melt even the elements with its intensity, and purge the earth from the deepest stains of the curse of sin. 2 Pt 3.7–12.

25. That a new heavens and earth shall spring by the power of God from the ashes of the old, to be, with the New Jerusalem for its metropolis and capital, the eternal inheritance of the saints, the place where the righteous shall evermore dwell. 2 Pt 3.13; Ps 47.11, 29; Mt 5.5.

Old Catholic Church, *The Fourteen Theses of the First Reunion Conference at Bonn*, 1874

The definition of the dogma of the infallibility of the pope by the First Vatican Council in its → *Dogmatic Constitution on the Catholic Faith* of 14 April 1870 did not silence the contrary voices. Some of these, even more opposed to schism than they were to the promulgation of the new dogma, remained in the church, but during the years after the council a small group of German-speaking Roman Catholics formed the Old Catholic Church (*die altkatholische Kirche*). Their scholarly and theological leadership came from the church historian Johann Joseph Ignaz von Döllinger (1799–1890), who had been excommunicated in 1871 for his opposition to the decree of infallibility but who did not formally affiliate himself with the Old Catholic Church. Like the sixteenth-century Reformers, and with even greater intensity, the Old Catholics sought fellowship with others who claimed to be truly "Catholic" and to preserve the continuity of church and tradition without submission to the authority of Rome. Two of the most prominent such groups were the Eastern Orthodox ("Greeks") and the Anglicans. On 14–16 September 1874, a "Union Conference," chaired by Döllinger, was held at Bonn, leading to these fourteen theses. One unusual note is the assertion that genuine Christian tradition "partly is to be gathered by a scientific [*wissenschaftlich*] method from the written documents of all centuries" (9a), which gives historical scholarship a confessional assignment.

In September 1889 the Old Catholic Church in the Netherlands produced → *The Declaration of Utrecht,* which would become the standard confession of faith for Old Catholics everywhere.

Edition: Schaff, 2:545–51.

Translation: *Resolutions* 1874, 14–16.

Literature: Moss 1964, 257–70; *ODCC* 225, 1179–80.

Old Catholic Church, *The Fourteen Theses of the First Reunion Conference at Bonn*, 1874

Preliminary Declaration

The way in which the word *filioque* was inserted into the Nicene Creed was illegal, and, with a view to future peace and unity, it is much to be desired that the whole church should seriously set itself to consider whether the creed could possibly be restored to its primitive form, without sacrifice of any true doctrine expressed in the present Western form.

Articles Agreed To

1. The apocryphal or deutero-canonical books of the Old Testament are not of the same canonicity as the books contained in the Hebrew canon.

2. No translation of Holy Scripture can claim an authority superior to that of the original text.

3. The reading of Holy Scripture in the vulgar tongue cannot lawfully be forbidden.

4. In general it is more fitting and in accordance with the spirit of the church that the liturgy should be in the tongue understood by the people.

5. Faith working by love, not faith without love, is the means and condition of man's justification before God.

6. Salvation cannot be merited by merit of condignity, because there is no proportion between the infinite worth of the salvation promised by God and the finite worth of man's works.

7. The doctrine of "opera supererogationis" and of a "thesaurus meritorum sanctorum," i.e., that the overflowing merits of the saints can be transferred to others either by the rulers of the church, or by the authors of the good works themselves, is untenable.

8. (*a*) The number of the sacraments was fixed at seven first in the twelfth century, and then was received into the general teaching of the church, not as a tradition coming down from the apostles or from the earliest times, but as the result of theological speculation.

(*b*) Roman Catholic theologians (e.g., Bellarmine) acknowledge and we acknowledge with them that baptism and the holy eucharist are "principalia, praecipua, eximia salutis nostrae sacramenta."

9. (*a*) The Holy Scriptures being recognized as the primary rule of the faith, we agree that genuine tradition, i.e., the unbroken transmission, partly oral, partly by writing, of the doctrine delivered by Jesus Christ and the apostles, is an authoritative source of teaching for all successive generations of Christians.

This tradition is partly to be found in the consensus of the great ecclesiastical bodies, standing in historical continuity with the primitive church, partly is to be gathered by a scientific method from the written documents of all centuries.

(*b*) We acknowledge that the Church of England, and the churches derived through her, have maintained unbroken the episcopal succession.[1]

10. We reject the new Roman doctrine of the immaculate conception of the Blessed Virgin Mary, as being contrary to the tradition of the first thirteen centuries, according to which Christ alone is conceived without sin.

11. The practice of confession of sins before the congregation or the priest, together with the exercise of the power of the keys, has come down to us from the primitive church and, purged from abuses and freed from constraint, it should be preserved in the church.

12. Indulgences can only refer to penalties actually imposed by the church herself.

13. The practice of commemorating the faithful departed, i.e., the calling down of a richer outpouring of Christ's grace upon them, has come down to us from the primitive church, and is to be preserved in the church.

14. The eucharistic celebration in the church is not a continuous repetition or renewal of the propitiatory sacrifice offered once for ever upon the cross, but its sacrificial character consists in this, that it is the permanent memorial of it and a representation [*Darstellung*] and presentation [*Vergegenwärtigung*] on earth of that one oblation of Christ for the salvation of redeemed mankind, which according to the Epistle to the Hebrews (9.11, 12) is continuously presented in heaven by Christ, who now appears in the presence of God for us (9.24).

While this is the character of the eucharist in regard to the sacrifice of Christ, it is also a sacred feast, wherein the faithful receiving the body and blood of our Lord have communion one with another (1 Cor 10.17).

[We acknowledge that the invocation of saints is not commanded as a duty necessary to salvation for every Christian.][2]

---

1. On this point the Orientals reserved their judgement, on the ground that they had not studied the question. Dr. von Döllinger and Bishop Reinkens declared themselves as fully satisfied of the Anglican, as they were of the Roman, succession.
2. Deferred for the consideration of the next Conference, the Orientals not being prepared to come to a final decision upon it.

Salvation Army (The Christian Mission),
Religious Doctrines, 1878

The founder of the Salvation Army, which was originally called "the Christian Mission," was William Booth (1829–1912), who came out of British Methodism. Best known for its charitable work among the poor and suffering, the Salvation Army was and is highly successful as a revivalist church. It holds to doctrines that it shares with Protestant evangelicalism; noteworthy by their omission, in the second half of the nineteenth century, are the doctrines of the church and of the sacraments.

Edition: Sandall [1947–73] 1979, 1:262–63.

Literature: Sandall [1947–73] 1979.

Salvation Army (The Christian Mission),
Religious Doctrines, 1878

1. We believe that the Scriptures of the Old and New Testaments were given by inspiration of God and that they only constitute the divine rule of Christian faith and practice.

2. We believe there is only one God, who is infinitely perfect, the Creator, Preserver, and Governor of all things, and who is the only proper object of religious worship.

3. We believe that there are three persons in the Godhead, the Father, the Son, and the Holy Ghost, undivided in essence and coequal in power and glory.

4. We believe that in the person of Jesus Christ the divine and human natures are united, so that he is truly and properly God, and truly and properly man.

5. We believe that our first parents were created in a state of innocency, but by their disobedience they lost their purity and happiness, and that in consequence of their fall, all men have become sinners totally depraved and as such are justly exposed to the wrath of God.

6. We believe that the Lord Jesus Christ has, by his suffering and death, made an atonement for the whole world, so that whosoever will may be saved.

7. We believe that repentance towards God, faith in our Lord Jesus Christ, and regeneration by the Holy Spirit are necessary to salvation.

8. We believe that we are justified by grace through faith in our Lord Jesus Christ and that he that believeth hath the witness in himself.

9. We believe that continuance in a state of salvation depends upon continued obedient faith in Christ.

10. We believe that it is the privilege of all believers to be "wholly sanctified" and that "their whole spirit and soul and body" may "be preserved blameless unto the coming of our lord Jesus Christ" (1 Thes 23).

11. We believe in the immortality of the soul—in the resurrection of the body—in the general judgment at the end of the world—in the eternal happiness of the righteous—and in the endless punishment of the wicked.

Church of Christ, Scientist, *Tenets of the Mother Church, the First Church of Christ, Scientist,* 1879/1892/1906

Although it is not regarded by the mainstream churches as Christian or as a church, Christian Science does lay claim to the name "Christian" — and it does have something resembling a creed, to which it requires subscription.

The founder of Christian Science was Mary Baker Eddy (1821–1910), who experienced, then practiced and advocated, the healing of disease through prayer, which, in her *Key to the Scriptures,* she affirmed to be the teaching of the New Testament, rightly understood. "In the spring of 1879," the official account says, "a little band of earnest seekers after Truth went into deliberations over forming *a church without creeds,* to be called the 'CHURCH OF CHRIST, SCIENTIST.' . . . Mrs. Eddy was appointed on the committee to draft the Tenets of The Mother Church" (italics added).

These "tenets without a creed," which were adopted by "The First Church of Christ, Scientist" at its founding in 1892, and modified slightly by Eddy before her death in 1910, now regularly appear as part of her *Science and Health, with a Key to the Scriptures,* from which this text is taken.

Edition: Eddy 1906, 497.

Literature: Cather and Milmine 1993; Peel 1958.

Church of Christ, Scientist, *Tenets of the Mother Church, the First Church of Christ, Scientist,* 1879/1892/1906

To be signed by those uniting with the First Church of Christ, Scientist, in Boston, Mass.

1. As adherents of truth, we take the inspired word of the Bible as our sufficient guide to eternal life.

2. We acknowledge and adore one supreme and infinite God. We acknowledge his Son, one Christ; the Holy Ghost or divine Comforter; and man in God's image and likeness.

3. We acknowledge God's forgiveness of sin in the destruction of sin and the spiritual understanding that casts out evil as unreal. But the belief in sin is punished so long as the belief lasts.

4. We acknowledge Jesus' atonement as the evidence of divine, efficacious love, unfolding man's unity with God through Christ Jesus the Way-shower; and we acknowledge that man is saved through Christ, through truth, life, and love as demonstrated by the Galilean prophet in healing the sick and overcoming sin and death.

5. We acknowledge that the crucifixion of Jesus and his resurrection served to uplift faith to understand eternal life, even the allness of soul, spirit, and the nothingness of matter.

6. And we solemnly promise to watch, and pray for that Mind to be in us which was also in Christ Jesus; to do unto others as we would have them do unto [Phil 2.5] us; and to be merciful, just, and pure. [Mt 7.12]

Mary Baker Eddy

Congregational Church in America,
The "Commission" Creed, 1883/1913

The church historian Williston Walker, who edited *The Creeds and Platforms of Congregationalism*, which is still the standard collection, closed his edition with *The "Commission" Creed* of 1883, adding the following estimate: "Probably the creed was agreed upon with as great a degree of unanimity as any statement of faith in modern language, and of a definite character, would be in the present age." He went on to aver: "It gives the Congregational body what no other considerable denomination of Christians in America possesses,—a widely recognized creed, written in the language and expressing the thought of living men."[1]

The "Commission" Creed was composed in response to the growing sense of need for a confession of faith that would improve upon the two earlier nineteenth-century Congregationalist formularies, the so-called *Declaration of the Boston National Council ["Burial Hill"]* of 1865 and *The Declaration of the Oberlin National Council* of 1871, which were deemed partial and inadequate, and that would not be burdened with archaic language, as were → *The Cambridge Platform,* → *The Savoy Declaration,* and similar creeds and confessions from the seventeenth and eighteenth centuries. To that end, a commission of twenty-five was appointed, which included the presidents of Amherst and Oberlin, as well as George Park Fisher, who was Williston Walker's predecessor at Yale, and George Leon Walker, who was his father. The creed was presented by the commission on 19 December 1883, and reaffirmed in 1913.

Edition: Walker, 580–82.

Literature: Walker, 577–82.

1. Walker, 582.

Congregational Church in America,
The "Commission" Creed, 1883/1913

1. We believe in one God, the Father Almighty, Maker of heaven and earth, and of all things visible and invisible;

And in Jesus Christ, his only Son, our Lord, who is of one substance with the Father; by whom all things were made;

And in the Holy Spirit, the Lord and Giver of life, who is sent from the Father and Son, and who together with the Father and Son is worshiped and glorified.

2. We believe that the providence of God, by which he executes his eternal purposes in the government of the world, is in and over all events; yet so that the freedom and responsibility of man are not impaired, and sin is the act of the creature alone.

3. We believe that man was made in the image of God, that he might know, love, and obey God, and enjoy him forever; that our first parents by disobedience fell under the righteous condemnation of God; and that all men are so alienated from God that there is no salvation from the guilt and power of sin except through God's redeeming grace.

4. We believe that God would have all men return to him; that to this end he has made himself known, not only through the works of nature, the course of his providence, and the consciences of men, but also through supernatural revelations made especially to a chosen people, and above all, when the fullness of time was come, through Jesus Christ his Son.

5. We believe that the Scriptures of the Old and New Testaments are the records of God's revelation of himself in the work of redemption; that they were written by men under the special guidance of the Holy Spirit; that they are able to make wise unto salvation; and that they constitute the authoritative standard by which religious teaching and human conduct are to be regulated and judged.

6. We believe that the love of God to sinful men has found its highest expression in the redemptive work of his Son; who became man, uniting his divine nature with our human nature in one person; who was tempted like other men, yet without sin; who by his humiliation, his holy obedience, his sufferings, his death on the cross, and his resurrection, became a perfect Redeemer; whose sacrifice of himself for the sins of the world declares the righteousness of God, and is the sole and sufficient ground of forgiveness and of reconciliation with him.

7. We believe that Jesus Christ, after he had risen from the dead, ascended into heaven, where, as the one Mediator between God and man, he carries forward his work of saving men; that he sends the Holy Spirit to convict them of sin, and to lead them to repentance and faith; and that those who through renewing grace turn to righteousness, and trust in Jesus Christ as their Redeemer, receive for his sake the forgiveness of their sins, and are made the children of God.

8. We believe that those who are thus regenerated and justified, grow in sanctified character through fellowship with Christ, the indwelling of the Holy Spirit, and obedience to the truth; that a holy life is the fruit and evidence of saving faith; and that the believer's hope of continuance in such a life is in the preserving grace of God.

9. We believe that Jesus Christ came to establish among men the kingdom of God, the reign of truth and love, righteousness and peace; that to Jesus Christ, the Head of his kingdom, Christians are directly responsible in faith and conduct; and that to him all have immediate access without mediatorial or priestly intervention.

10. We believe that the church of Christ, invisible and spiritual, comprises all true believers, whose duty it is to associate themselves in churches, for the maintenance of worship, for the promotion of spiritual growth and fellowship, and for the conversion of men; that these churches, under the guidance of the Holy Scriptures and in fellowship with one another, may determine—each for itself—their organization, statements of belief, and forms of worship, may appoint and set apart their own ministers, and should cooperate in the work which Christ has committed to them for the furtherance of the gospel throughout the world.

11. We believe in the observance of the Lord's day, as a day of holy rest and worship; in the ministry of the word; and in the two sacraments, which Christ has appointed for his church: baptism, to be administered to believers and their children, as a sign of cleansing from sin, of union to Christ, and of the impartation of the Holy Spirit; and the Lord's supper, as a symbol of his atoning death, a seal of its efficacy, and a means whereby he confirms and strengthens the spiritual union and communion of believers with himself.

12. We believe in the ultimate prevalence of the kingdom of Christ over all the earth; in the glorious appearing of the great God and our Savior Jesus Christ; in the resurrection of the dead; and in a final judgment, the issues of which are everlasting punishment and everlasting life.

Anglican Bishops, *The Lambeth Quadrilateral* (*The Chicago/Lambeth Quadrilateral*), 1886/1888

William Reed Huntington was rector of the All Saints Episcopal Church in Worcester, Massachusetts, from 1862 to 1883, and was a major contributor to the 1892 American version of the *Book of Common Prayer*. In a sermon entitled "The Church of the Reconciliation" in 1870 he proposed what he called "'the Quadrilateral' of pure Anglicanism" as a charter for the reunion of the churches. In 1886, this original proposal, which has been called "somewhat minimalist and reductionist" as well as "rather anti-confessional,"[1] was taken up and modified by the General Convention of the Protestant Episcopal Church in the United States, meeting in Chicago. Two years later, the 1888 session of the Lambeth Conference of Anglican bishops issued it, with slight revisions, as the Anglican definition of the requisites for Christian unity and reunion. As Günther Gassmann has said, "probably the briefest text in the history of the ecumenical movement, it has become one of the most influential within that movement."[2] It is that final version of *The Lambeth Quadrilateral* of 1888 that we present here.

Edition: Wright 1988, viii–ix.

Literature: Evans and Wright 1991; Gassmann 1988; *ODCC* 946; Wright 1988.

1. Wright 1988, 10.
2. Gassmann 1988, 301.

Anglican Bishops, *The Lambeth Quadrilateral* (*The Chicago/Lambeth Quadrilateral*), 1886/1888

A. The Holy Scriptures of the Old and New Testaments, as "containing all things necessary to salvation,"[1] and as being the rule and ultimate standard of faith.

B. The Apostles' Creed, as the baptismal symbol; and the Nicene Creed, as the sufficient statement of the Christian faith.

C. The two sacraments ordained by Christ himself—baptism and the supper of the Lord—ministered with unfailing use of Christ's words of institution, and of the elements ordained by him.

D. The historic episcopate, locally adapted in the methods of its administration to the varying needs of the nations and peoples called of God into the unity of his church.

1. *39 Art 6.*

Friends Yearly Meeting,
The Richmond Declaration of Faith, 1887

By the very nature of the distinctive interpretation of Christian experience and teaching in the Society of Friends, early formulations of Quaker teaching such as → *A Confession of Faith Containing XXIII Articles* by Robert Barclay of 1673 did not, and were not intended to, function in the same way that creeds and confessions of faith did in other churches. But by the nineteenth century, the rise among Quakers of the tension between Conservative and Liberal that was visible in other churches as well had convinced many Friends, especially on the Conservative side, that some more definitive statement of faith and doctrine was called for. In 1887 the Indiana Yearly Meeting convoked an assembly involving most of the Quaker yearly meetings in the United States. It met in Richmond, Indiana, location of Wabash College.

The outcome of the assembly was this *Richmond Declaration of Faith.* It was an effort to unite the special teachings of the Friends about the inner light and about peace and war with as much as possible of shared Evangelical teaching. "Two things were made very clear. First, the document was drawn together from existing sources. . . . Secondly, if adopted, it was not to supersede the affirmations which individual yearly meetings had already made, nor was it to interfere with the autonomy and independence of judgment of any of the yearly meetings."[1] Although there were some yearly meetings, and of course many individual Friends, who refused to accept it as binding, "in 1912 the Kansas, Western, and California Meetings asked that the Richmond Declaration and the Letter of George Fox to the Governor of Barbadoes be made . . . creeds"; and in 1947 representatives of these and several other yearly meetings "declared the Richmond Declaration and the Barbadoes letter their creeds."[2] The proof texts in footnotes are part of the official text as provided by the Friends United Meeting.

Edition: *Constitution and Discipline* 1925, 76–100.

Literature: R. Jones [1927] 2002; Minear 1987, 130–34; Steere 1955.

---

1. Minear 1987, 131.
2. Melvin B. Endy, Jr., in Lippy and Williams 1988, 1:610.

Friends Yearly Meeting,
The Richmond Declaration of Faith, 1887

It is under a deep sense of what we owe to him who has loved us that we feel called upon to offer a declaration of those fundamental doctrines of Christian truth that have always been professed by our branch of the church of Christ.

1. OF GOD

We believe in one holy,[1] almighty,[2] all-wise,[3] and everlasting[4] God, the Father,[5] the Creator[6] and Preserver[7] of all things; and in Jesus Christ, his only Son, our Lord, by whom all things were made,[8] and by whom all things consist;[9] and in one Holy Spirit, proceeding from the Father and the Son,[10] the Reprover[11] of the world, the Witness for Christ,[12] and the Teacher,[13] Guide,[14] and Sanctifier[15] of the people of God; and that these three are one in the eternal Godhead;[16] to whom be honor, praise, and thanksgiving, now and forever. Amen.

[1] Is 6.3, 57.5; [2] Gn 17.1; [3] Rom 11.33, 16.27; [4] Ps 90.1, 2; [5] Mt 11.25–27; [6] Gn 1.1; [7] Jb 7.20; [8] Jn 1.3; [9] Col 1.17; [10] Jn 15.26, 16.7; [11] Jn 16.8; [12] Jn 15.26; [13] Jn 15.26; [14] Jn 16.13; [15] 2 Thes 2.13; [16] Mt 28.19

2. THE LORD JESUS CHRIST

It is with reverence and thanksgiving that we profess our unwavering allegiance to our Lord and Savior, Jesus Christ. No man hath seen God at any time; the only-begotten Son, who is in the bosom of the Father, he hath declared him.[1] In him was life; and the life was the light of men.[2] He is the true light which lighteth every man that cometh into the world;[3] through whom the light of truth in all ages has proceeded from the Father of lights.[4] He is the eternal Word[5] who was with God and was God, revealing himself in infinite wisdom and love, both as man's Creator and Redeemer; for by him were all things created that are in heaven and that are on earth, visible and invisible.[6] Conceived of the Holy Ghost,[7] born of the Virgin Mary,[8] the Word was made flesh, and dwelt amongst men.[9] He came in the fullness[10] of the appointed time, being verily foreordained before the foundation of the world[11] that he might fulfill[12] the eternal counsel of the righteousness and love of God for the redemption of man.[13] In him dwelleth all the fullness of the Godhead bodily.[14] Though he was rich, yet, for our sakes, he became poor, veiling in the form of a servant,[15] the brightness of his glory, that, through him the kindness and good might appear in a manner every way suited to our wants and finite capacities. He went about doing good;[16] for us he endured[17] sorrow, hunger, thirst, weariness,[18] pain, unutterable anguish[19] of body and of soul, being in all points tempted like as we are, yet without sin.[20] Thus humbling himself that we might be exalted, he emphatically recognized the duties and the sufferings of humanity as among the means whereby, through the obedience of faith, we are to be disciplined for heaven, sanctifying them to us, by himself performing and enduring them, leaving us the one perfect example[21] of all righteousness[22] in self-sacrificing love.

But not only in these blessed relations must the Lord Jesus be ever precious to his people. In him is revealed as true God and perfect man,[23] a Redeemer, at once able to suffer and almighty to save. He became obedient[24] unto death, even the death of the cross, and is the propitiation for our sins, and not for ours only, but also for the sins of the whole world;[25] in whom we have redemption through his blood,[26] the forgiveness of sins according to the riches of his grace. It is our joy to confess that the remission of sins which any partake of is only in and by virtue of his most satisfactory sacrifice and no otherwise.[27] He was buried and rose again the third day[28] according to the Scriptures, becoming the first fruits[29] of them that sleep, and having shown himself alive after his passion, by many infallible proofs,[30] he ascended into heaven, and hath sat down at the right hand of the Majesty on high, now to appear in the presence of God for us.[31] With the apostles who beheld his ascension, we rest in the assurance of the angelic messengers, "This same Jesus, which is taken up from you into heaven shall so come in like manner as ye have seen him go into heaven."[32] With the apostle John, we would desire to unite in the words "Amen; even so, come, Lord Jesus."[33] And now, whilst thus watching and waiting, we rejoice to believe that he is our King and Savior. He is the one Mediator of the new and everlasting covenant,[34] who makes peace and reconciliation between God offended and man offending;[35] the great High Priest whose priesthood is unchangeable.[36] He is able to save them to the uttermost that come unto God by him, seeing he ever liveth to make intercession for them.[37] All power is given unto him in heaven and in earth.[38] By him the world shall be judged in righteousness;[39] for the Father judgeth no man, but hath committed all judgment unto the Son, that all men should honor the Son even as they honor the Father.[40] All that are in the graves hear his voice, and shall come forth, they that have done good unto the resurrection of life, and they that have done evil until the resurrection of judgment.[41]

We reverently confess and believe that divine honor and worship are due to the Son of God, and that he is in true faith to be prayed unto, and his name to be called upon, as the primitive Christians did because of the glorious oneness of the Father and the Son; and that we cannot acceptably offer prayers and praises to

God, nor receive from him a gracious answer or blessing, but in and through his dear Son.[42]

We would, with humble thanksgiving, bear an especial testimony to our Lord's perpetual dominion and power in his church. Through him the redeemed in all generations have derived their light, their forgiveness, and their joy. All are members of this church, by whatsoever name they may be called among men, who have been baptized by the one Spirit into the one body; who are builded as living stones upon Christ, the eternal foundation, and are united in faith and love in that fellowship which is with the Father and with the Son. Of this church the Lord Jesus Christ is the alone Head.[43] All its true members are made one in him. They have washed their robes and made them white in his precious blood,[44] and he has made them priests unto God and his Father.[45] He dwells in their hearts by faith, and gives them of his peace. His will is their law, and in him they enjoy the true liberty, a freedom from the bondage of sin.

[1]Jn 1.18; [2]Jn 1.4; [3]Jn 1.9; [4]Jas 1.17; [5]Jn 1.1; [6]Col 1.13–16; [7]Mt 1.20; [8]Mt 1.23–25, Lk 1.35; [9]Jn 1.14; [10]Gal 4.4; [11]1 Pt 1.20; [12]Is 11.1–5, 52.13–15; [13]Is 53; [14]Col 2.9; [15]Phil 2.7; [16]Acts 10.38; [17]Is 53.4; Lk 12.50, 19.41, 22.44; [18]Jn 4.6; [19]Lk 22.43, 44; [20]Heb 4.15; [21]1 Pt 2.21; [22]Mt 3.15; [23]Eph 4.13; [24]Phil 2.8; [25]Jn 2.2; [26]Eph 1.7; [27]Barclay's *Apology*, Propos.5 and 6 par. 15, p. 141; [28]1 Cor 15.4; [29]1 Cor 15.23; [30]Acts 1.3; [31]Heb 1.3, 9.24; [32]Acts 1.11, and see 5.7; [33]Rv 22.20; [34]1 Tm 2.5; Heb 9.15; [35]George Fox's Epistle to the Governor of Barbadoes; [36]Heb 4.14, 7.24; [37]Heb 7.25; [38]Mt 28.18; [39]Acts 17.31; [40]Jn 5.22, 23; [41]Jn 5.28, 29; [42]Declaration of 1693, in Sewell's Hist., vol. II, 379; [43]Eph 1.22; [44]Rv 7.14; [45]Rv 1.6

3. THE HOLY SPIRIT

We believe that the Holy Spirit is, in the unity of the eternal Godhead, one with the Father and with the Son.[1] He is the comforter "whom," saith Christ, "the Father will send in my name."[2] He convinces the world of sin, of righteousness, and of judgment.[3] He testifies of and glorifies Jesus.[4] It is the Holy Spirit who makes the evil manifest. He quickens them that are dead in trespasses and sins, and opens the inward eye to behold the Lamb of God that taketh away the sin of the world.[5] Coming in the name and with the authority of the risen and ascended Savior, he is the precious pledge of the continued love and care of our exalted King. He takes of the things of Christ and shows them, as a realized possession, to the believing soul.[6] Dwelling in the hearts of believers,[7] he opens their understandings that they may understand the Scriptures, and becomes, to the humbled and surrendered heart, the Guide, Comforter, Support, and Sanctifier.

We believe that the essential qualification for the Lord's service is bestowed upon his children through the reception and baptism of the Holy Ghost. This Holy Spirit is the seal of reconciliation to the believer in Jesus,[8] the witness to his adoption into the family of the redeemed;[9] the earnest and the foretaste of the full communion and perfect joy which are reserved for them that endure into the end.

We own no principle of spiritual light, life, or holiness, inherent by nature in the mind or heart of man. We believe in no principle of spiritual light, life, or holiness, but the influence of the Holy Spirit of God, bestowed on mankind, in various measures and degrees, through Jesus Christ our Lord. It is the capacity to receive this blessed influence, which, in an especial manner, gives man preeminence above the beasts that perish; which distinguishes him, in every nation and in every clime, as an object of the redeeming love of God; as a being not only intelligent but responsible; for whom the message of salvation through our crucified Redeemer is, under all possible circumstances, designed to be a joyful sound. The Holy Spirit must ever be distinguished, both from the conscience which he enlightens, and from the natural faculty of reason, which when unsubjected to his holy influence, is, in the things of God, very foolishness. As the eye is to the body, so is the conscience to our inner being, the organ by which we see; and, as both light and life are essential to the eye, so conscience, as the inward eye, cannot see aright, without the quickening and illumination of the Spirit of God. One with the Father and the Son, the Holy Spirit can never disown or dishonor our once crucified and now risen and glorified Redeemer. We disavow all professed illumination or spirituality that is divorced from faith in Jesus Christ of Nazareth, crucified for us without the gates of Jerusalem.

[1]Mt 28.19; 2 Cor 13.14; [2]Jn 14.26; [3]Jn 16.8; [4]Jn 16.14; [5]Eph 2.1; [6]Jn 16.14; [7]Jn 16.17; [8]Eph 1.13, 14; [9]Rom 13.15, 16

4. THE HOLY SCRIPTURES

It has ever been, and still is, the belief of the Society of Friends that the Holy Scriptures of the Old and New Testament were given by inspiration of God; that, therefore, there can be no appeal from them to any other authority whatsoever; that they are able to make wise unto salvation, through faith which is in Jesus Christ. "These are written that ye might believe that Jesus is the Christ the Son of God; and that believing ye might have life through his name."[1] The Scriptures are the only divinely authorized record of the doctrines which we are bound, as Christians, to accept, and of the moral principles which are to regulate our actions. No one can be required to believe, as an article of faith, any doctrine which is not contained in them; and whatsoever any one says or does, contrary to the Scriptures, though under profession of the immediate guidance of the Holy Spirit, must be reckoned and accounted a mere delusion. To the Christian, the Old Testament comes with the solemn and repeated attestation of his Lord. It is to be read in the light and completeness of the New; thus will its meaning be unveiled, and the humble disciple will be taught to discern the unity and mutual adaptation of the whole, and the many-sidedness and harmony of its testimony to Christ. The great Inspirer of Scripture is ever its true Interpreter. He performs this office in condescending love, not by superseding our understandings, but by renewing and enlightening them. Where Christ presides, idle speculation is hushed; his doctrine is learned in the doing of his will, and all knowledge ripens into a deeper and richer experience of his truth and love.

[1] 2 Tm 3.15–16; Jn 20.31

5. MAN'S CREATION AND FALL

It pleased God, in his wisdom and goodness, to create man out of dust of the earth, and to breathe into his nostrils the breath of life, so that man became a living soul; formed after the image and likeness of God, capable of fulfilling the divine law, and of holding communion with his Maker.[1] Being free to obey, or to disobey, he fell into transgression, through unbelief, under the temptation of Satan,[2] and, thereby, lost that spiritual life of righteousness, in which he was created; and, so death passed upon him, as the inevitable consequence of his sin.[3] As the children of fallen Adam, all mankind bear his image. They partake of his nature, and are involved in the consequences of his fall. To every member of every successive generation, the words of the Redeemer are alike applicable, "Ye must be born again."[4] But while we hold these views of the lost condition of man in the fall, we rejoice to believe that sin is not imputed to any, until they transgress the divine law, after sufficient capacity has been given to understand it; and that infants, though inheriting this fallen nature, are saved in the infinite mercy of God through the redemption which is in Christ Jesus.

[1] Gn 2.7, 1.26, 27; [2] Gn 3.1–7; [3] Rom 5.12; [4] Jn 3.7

6. JUSTIFICATION AND SANCTIFICATION

"God so loved the world that he gave his only-begotten Son, that whosoever believeth him should not perish, but have everlasting life."[1] We believe that justification is of God's free grace, through which, upon repentance and faith, he pardons our sins, and imparts to us a new life. It is received, not for any works of righteousness that we have done,[2] but in the unmerited mercy of God in Christ Jesus. Through faith in him, and the shedding of his precious blood, the guilt of sin is taken away, and we stand reconciled to God. The offering up of Christ as the propitiation for the sins of the whole world, is the appointed manifestation both of the righteousness and of the love of God. In this propitiation the pardon of sin involves no abrogation or relaxation of the law of holiness. It is the vindication and establishment of the law,[3] in virtue of the free and righteous submission of the Son of God himself to all its requirements. He, the unchangeably just, proclaims himself justifier of him that believeth in Jesus.[4] From age to age, the sufferings and death of Christ have been a hidden mystery, and a rock of offense to the unbelief and pride of man's fallen nature; yet, to the humble penitent whose heart is broken under the conviction power of the Spirit, life is revealed in that death. As he looks upon him who was wounded for our transgressions,[5] and upon whom the Lord was pleased to lay the iniquity of us all,[6] his eye is more and more opened to see, and his heart to understand, the exceeding sinfulness of sin for which the Savior died; whilst, in the sense of pardoning grace, he will joy in God through our Lord Jesus Christ, by whom we have now received the atonement.[7]

We believe that in connection with justification is regeneration: that they who come to this experience know that they are not their own,[8] that being reconciled to God by the death of his Son, we are saved by his life;[9] a new heart is given and new desires; old things are passed away, and we become new creatures,[10] through faith in Christ Jesus; our will being surrendered to his holy will, grace reigns through righteousness, unto eternal life, by Jesus Christ our Lord.[11]

Sanctification is experienced in the acceptance of Christ in living faith for justification, in so far as the pardoned sinner, through faith in Christ, is clothed with a measure of his righteousness and receives the Spirit of promise; for, as saith the apostle, "Ye are washed, ye are sanctified, ye are justified, in the name of the Lord Jesus, and by the Spirit of our God."[12] We rejoice to believe that the provisions of God's grace are sufficient to deliver from the power, as well as from the guilt, of sin, and to enable his believing children always to triumph in Christ.[13] How full of encouragement is the declaration, "According to your faith be it unto you."[14] Whatsoever submits himself wholly to God, believing and appropriating his promises, and exercising faith in Christ Jesus, will have his heart continually cleansed from all sin, by his precious blood, and, through the renewing, refining power of the Holy Spirit, be kept in conformity to the will of God, will love him with all his heart, mind, soul, and strength, and be able to say, with the apostle Paul, "The law of the Spirit of life in Christ Jesus hath made me free from the law of sin and death."[15] Thus, in its full experience, sanctification is deliverance from the pollution, nature, and love of sin. To this we are every one called, that we may serve the Lord without fear, in holiness and righteousness before him, all the days of our life.[16] It was the prayer of the apostle for the believers, "The very God of peace sanctify you wholly; and I pray God your whole spirit and soul and body be preserved blameless unto the coming of our Lord Jesus Christ. Faithful is he that calleth you who also will do it." [17] Yet the most holy Christian is still liable to temptation, is exposed to the subtle assaults of Satan, and can only continue to follow holiness as he humbly watches unto prayer, and is kept in constant dependence upon his Savior, walking in the light,[18] in the loving obedience of faith.

[1] Jn 3.16; [2] Ti 3.5; [3] Rom 3.31; [4] Rom 3.26; [5] Is 53.5; [6] Is 53.6; [7] Rom 5.11; [8] 1 Cor 6.19; [9] Rom 5.10; [10] 2 Cor 5.17; [11] Rom 5.21; [12] 1 Cor 6.11; [13] 2 Cor 2.14; [14] Mt 9.29; [15] Rom 8.2; [16] Lk 1.74, 75; [17] 1 Thes 5.23, 24; [18] 1 Jn 1.7

7. THE RESURRECTION AND FINAL JUDGMENT

We believe, according to the Scriptures, that there shall be a resurrection from the dead, both of the just and of the unjust,[1] and that God hath appointed a day in which he will judge the world in righteousness, by Jesus Christ whom he hath ordained.[2] For, as saith the apostle, "We must all appear before the judgment seat of Christ, that every one may receive the things done in his body, according to that he hath done, whether it be good or bad." [3]

We sincerely believe, not only a resurrection in Christ from the fallen and sinful state here, but a rising and ascending into glory with him hereafter; that when he at last appears we may appear with him in glory. But that all the wicked, who live in rebellion against the light of grace, and die finally impenitent, shall come forth to the resurrection of condemnation. And that the soul of every man and woman shall be reserved, in its own distinct and proper being, and shall have its proper body as God is pleased to give it. It is sown a natural body, it is raised a spiritual body;[4] that being first which is natural, and afterward that which is spiritual. And though it is said, "this corruptible shall put on incorruption, and this mortal shall put on immortality," [5] the change shall be such as will accord with the declaration, "Flesh and blood cannot inherit the kingdom of God, neither doth corruption inherit incorruption." [6] We shall be raised out of all corruption and corruptibility, out of all mortality, and shall be the children of God, being the children of resurrection.[7]

"Our citizenship is in heaven," [8] from whence also we look for the Savior the Lord Jesus Christ, who shall change our vile body that it may be fashioned like unto his glorious body, according to the working whereby he is able even to subdue all things unto himself.[9]

We believe that the punishment of the wicked and the blessedness of the righteous shall be everlasting; according to the declaration of our compassionate

Redeemer, to whom the judgment is committed, "These shall go away into eternal punishment, but the righteous into eternal life."[10]

[1]Acts 24.15; [2]Acts 27.31; [3]2 Cor 5.10; [4]1 Cor 15.44; [5]1 Cor 15.53; [6]1 Cor 15.50; [7]Lk 20.36; [8]Phil 3.20; [9]Phil 3.20, 21; [10]Mt 25.46

8. BAPTISM

We would express our continued conviction that our Lord appointed no outward rite or ceremony for observance in his church. We accept every command of our Lord in what we believe to be its genuine import, as absolutely conclusive. The question of the use of outward ordinances is with us question, not as to the authority of Christ, but as to his real meaning. We reverently believe that, as there is one Lord and one faith, so there is, under the Christian dispensation, but one baptism,[1] even that whereby all believers are baptized in the one Spirit into the one body.[2] This is not an outward baptism with water, but a spiritual experience; not the putting away of the filth of the flesh,[3] but that inward work which, by transforming the heart and settling the soul upon Christ, brings forth the answer of a good conscience towards God, by the resurrection of Jesus Christ, in the experience of his love and power, as the risen and ascended Savior. No baptism in outward water can satisfy the description of the apostle, of being buried with Christ by baptism unto death.[4] It is with the Spirit alone that any can thus be baptized. In this experience the announcement of the forerunner of our Lord is fulfilled, "He shall baptize you with the Holy Ghost and with fire."[5] In this view we accept the commission of our Blessed Lord as given in Matthew 28.18, 19, and 20th verses: "And Jesus came to them and spake unto them saying, All authority hath been given unto me in heaven and on earth. Go ye, therefore, and make disciples of all the nations, baptizing them into the name of the Father and of the Son and of the Holy Ghost; teaching them to observe all things whatsoever I commanded you, and, lo, I am with you always, even unto the end of the world." This commission, as we believe, was not designed to set up a new ritual under the new covenant, or to connect the initiation into a membership, in its nature essentially spiritual, with a mere ceremony of a typical character. Otherwise it was not possible for the apostle Paul, who was not a whit behind the very chieftest apostle,[6] to have disclaimed that which would, in that case, have been of the essence of his commission when he wrote, "Christ sent me not to baptize, but to preach the gospel."[7] Whenever an external ceremony is commanded, the particulars, the mode and incidents of that ceremony, become of its essence. There is an utter absence of these particulars, in the text before us, which confirms our persuasion that the commission must be construed in connection with the spiritual power which the risen Lord promised should attend the witness of his apostles and of the church to him, and which, after Pentecost, so mightily accompanied their ministry of the word and prayer, that those to whom they were sent were introduced into an experience wherein they had a saving knowledge of, and living fellowship with, the Father and the Son and the Holy Spirit.

[1]Eph 4.4, 5; [2]1 Cor 12.13; [3]1 Pt 3.21; [4]Rom 6.4; [5]Mt 3.11; [6]2 Cor 11.5; [7]1 Cor 1.77

9. THE SUPPER OF THE LORD

Intimately connected with the conviction already expressed is the view that we have ever maintained as to the true supper of the Lord. We are well aware that our Lord was pleased to make use of a variety of symbolical utterances, but he often gently up-braided his disciples for accepting literally what he had intended only in its spiritual meaning. His teaching, as in his parables or in the command to wash one another's feet, was often in symbols, and ought ever to be received in the light of his own emphatic declaration, "The words that I speak unto you they are spirit and they are life."[1] The old covenant was full of ceremonial symbols; the new covenant, to which our Savior alluded at the last supper, is expressly declared by the prophet to be "not according to the old."[2] We cannot believe that in setting up this new cove-nant the Lord Jesus intended an institution out of harmony with the spirit of this prophecy. The eating of his body and the drinking of his blood cannot be an out-ward act. They truly partake of them who habitually rest upon the sufferings and death of their Lord as their only hope, and to whom the indwelling Spirit gives to drink of the fullness that is in Christ. It is this inward and spiritual partaking that is the true supper of the Lord.

The presence of Christ with his church is not designed to be by symbol or representation, but in the real communication of his own Spirit. "I will pray the Father and he shall give you another Comforter, who shall abide with you forever,"[3] convincing of sin, testifying of Jesus, taking of the things of Christ, this blessed Comforter communicates to the believer and to the church, in a gracious, abiding manifestation, the real presence of the Lord. As the great remembrancer, through whom the promise is fulfilled, he needs no ritual or priestly intervention in bringing to the experience of the true commemoration and communion. "Behold," saith the risen Redeemer, "I stand at the door and knock. If any man hear my voice and open the door, I will come in and sup with him and he with me."[4] In an especial manner, when assembled for congregational worship, are believers invited to the festival of the Savior's peace, and, in a united act of faith and love, unfettered by any outward rite or ceremonial, to partake together of the body that was broken and of the blood that was shed for them, without the gates of Jerusalem. In such a worship they are enabled to understand the words of the apostle as expressive of a sweet and most real experience: "The cup of blessing which we bless, is it not the communion of the blood of Christ? The bread that we break, is it not the communion of the body of Christ? For we being many of one bread, and one body; for we are all partakers of that one bread."[5]

[1] Jn 6.63; [2] Jer 31.32, Heb 8.9; [3] Jn 14.16; [4] Rv 3.20; [5] 1 Cor 10.16–17

10. PUBLIC WORSHIP

Worship is the adoring response of the heart and mind to the influence of the Spirit of God. It stands neither in forms nor in the formal disuse of forms: it may be without words as well as with them, but it must be in spirit and in truth.[1] We recognize the value of silence, not as an end, but as a means toward the attainment of the end; a silence, not of listlessness or of vacant musing, but of holy expectation before the Lord. Having become his adopted children through faith in the Lord Jesus Christ, it is our privilege to meet together and unite in the worship of Almighty God, to wait upon him for the renewal of our strength, for communion one with another, for the edification of believers in the exercise of various spiritual gifts, and for the declaration of the glad tidings of salvation to the unconverted who may gather with us. This worship depends not upon numbers. Where two or three are gathered together in the name of Christ there is a church, and Christ, the living Head, in the midst of them. Through his mediation without the necessity for any inferior instrumentality, is the Father to be approached and reverently worshiped. The Lord Jesus has forever fulfilled and ended the typical and sacrificial worship under the law, by the offering up of himself upon the cross for us, once for all. He has opened the door of access into the inner sanctuary, and graciously provided spiritual offerings for the service of his temple, suited to the several conditions of all who worship in spirit and in truth. The broken and the contrite heart, the confession of the soul prostrate before God, the prayer of the afflicted when he is overwhelmed, the earnest wrestling of the spirit, the outpouring of humble thanksgiving, the spiritual song and melody of the heart,[2] the simple exercise of faith, the self-denying service of love, these are among the sacrifices which he, our merciful and faithful High Priest, is pleased to prepare, by his Spirit, in the hearts of them that receive him, and to present with acceptance unto God.

By the immediate operations of the Holy Spirit, he as the Head of the church, alone selects and qualifies those who are to present his messages or engage in other service for him; and, hence, we cannot commit any formal arrangement to any one in our regular meetings for worship. We are well aware that the Lord has provided a diversity of gifts[3] for the needs both of the church and of the world, and we desire that the church may feel her responsibility, under the government of her great Head, in doing her part to foster these gifts, and in making arrangements for their proper exercise.

It is not for individual exaltation, but for mutual profit, that the gifts are bestowed;[4] and every living church, abiding under the government of Christ is humbly and thankfully to receive and exercise them, in subjection to her holy Head. The church that quenches the Spirit and lives to itself alone must die.

We believe the preachings of the gospel to be one of the chief means, divinely appointed, for the spreading of the glad tidings of life and salvation through our crucified Redeemer, or the awakening and conversion of sinners, and for the comfort and edification of believers. As it is the prerogative of the great Head of the church alone to select and call the ministers of his gospel, so we believe that both the gift and the qualification to exercise it must be derived immediately from him; and that, as in the primitive church, so now also, he confers spiritual gifts upon women as well as upon men, agreeably to the prophecy recited by the apostle Peter, "It shall come to pass in the last days, saith God, I will pour out my Spirit upon all flesh; and your sons and your daughters shall prophesy."[5] Respecting which the apostle declares, "the promise is unto you, and to your children, and to all that are afar off, even as many as the Lord our God shall call."[6] As the gift is freely received so it is to be freely exercised,[7] in simple obedience to the will of God.

Spiritual gifts, precious as they are, must not be mistaken for grace; they add to our responsibility, but do not raise the minister above his brethren or sisters. They must be exercised in continued dependence upon our Lord, and blessed is that ministry in which man is humbled, and Christ and his grace exalted. "He that is greatest among you," said our Lord and Master, "let him be as the younger; and he that is chief as he that doth serve. I am among you as he that serveth."[8]

While the church cannot confer spiritual gifts, it is its duty to recognize and foster them, and to promote their efficiency by all the means in its power. And while, on the one hand, the gospel should never be preached for money,[9] on the other, it is the duty of the church to make such provision that it shall never be hindered for want of it.

The church, if true to her allegiance, cannot forget her part in the command, "Go ye into all the world, and preach the gospel to every creature."[10] Knowing that it is the Spirit of God that can alone prepare and qualify the instruments who fulfill this command, the true disciple will be found still sitting at the feet of Jesus, listening that he may learn, and learning that he may obey. He humbly places himself at his Lord's disposal, and, when he hears the call, "Whom shall I send, and who will go for us?" is prepared to respond, in childlike reverence and love, "Here am I, send me." [11]

[1] Jn 4.24; [2] Eph 5.19; [3] 1 Cor 12.4–6; [4] 1 Cor 12.7; [5] Acts 2.17; [6] Acts 2.39; [7] Mt 10.8. See also Acts 20.33–35; [8] Lk 22.26, 27; [9] Acts 8.20, 20.33–35; [10] Mk 16.15; [11] Is 6.8

11. PRAYER AND PRAISE

Prayer is the outcome of our sense of need, and of our continual dependence upon God. He who uttered the invitation, "Ask and it shall be given you," [1] is himself the Mediator and High Priest who, by his Spirit, prompts the petition, and who presents it with the acceptance before God. With such an invitation, prayer becomes the duty and the privilege of all who are called by his name. Prayer is, in the awakened soul, the utterance of the cry, "God be merciful to me a sinner," [2] and, at every stage of the believer's course, prayer is essential to his spiritual life. A life without prayer is a life practically without God. The Christian's life is a continual asking. The thirst that prompts the petition produces, as it is satisfied, still deeper longings, which prepare for yet more bounteous supplies, from him who delights to bless. Prayer is not confined to the closet. When uttered in response to the promptings of the Holy Spirit, it becomes an important part of public worship, and, whenever the Lord's people meet together in his name, it is their privilege to wait upon him for the spirit of grace and supplications. [3] A life of prayer cannot be other than a life of praise. As the peace of Christ reigns in the church, her living members accept all that they receive, as from his pure bounty, and each day brings them fresh pledges of their Father's love. Satisfied with the goodness of his house, whether as individuals, in families, or in congregations, they will be still praising him, [4] heart answering to heart, "Bless the Lord, O my soul: and all that is within me, bless his holy name." [5]

[1] Mt 7.7; [2] Lk 18.13; [3] Zec 12.10; [4] Ps 84.4; [5] Ps 103.1

12. LIBERTY OF CONSCIENCE IN ITS RELATION TO CIVIL GOVERNMENT

That conscience should be free, and that in matters of religious doctrine and worship man is accountable only to God, are truths which are plainly declared in the New Testament; and which are confirmed by the whole scope of the gospel, and by the example of our Lord and his disciples. To rule over the conscience, and to command the spiritual allegiance of his creature man, is the high and sacred prerogative of God alone. In religion every act ought to be free. A forced worship is plainly a contradiction in terms, under that dispensation in which the worship of the Father must be in spirit and in truth.[1]

We have ever maintained that it is the duty of Christians to obey the enactments of civil government, except those which interfere with our allegiance to God. We owe much to its blessings. Through it we enjoy liberty and protection, in connection with law and order. Civil government is a divine ordinance,[2] instituted to promote the best welfare of man, hence magistrates are to be regarded as God's ministers who should be a terror to evildoers and a praise to them that do well. Therefore, it is with us a matter of conscience to render them respect and obedience in the exercise of their proper functions.

[1] Jn 4.24; [2] Rom 13.1; 1 Pt 2.13–16

13. MARRIAGE

Marriage is an institution graciously ordained by the Creator himself, for the help and continuance of the human family. It is not a mere civil contract, and ought never to be entered upon without a reference to the sanction and blessing of him who ordained it. It is a solemn engagement for the term of life,[1] designed for the mutual assistance and comfort of both sexes, that they may be helpmeets to each other in things temporal and spiritual. To this end it should imply concurrence in spiritual as well as temporal concerns, and should be entered upon discreetly, soberly, and in the fear of the Lord.[2]

[1] Mt 19.5, 6; [2] *Book of Common Prayer:* "The Form of Solemnization of Matrimony"

14. PEACE

We feel bound explicitly to avow our unshaken persuasion that all war is utterly incompatible with the plain precepts of our divine Lord and Lawgiver, and the whole spirit of his gospel, and that no plea of necessity or policy, however urgent or peculair, can avail to release either individuals or nations from the paramount allegiance which they owe to him who hath said, "Love your enemies."[1] In enjoining this love, and the forgiveness of injuries, he who has bought us to himself has not prescribed for man precepts which are incapable of being carried into practice, or of which the practice is to be postponed until all shall be persuaded to act upon them. We cannot doubt that they are incumbent now, and that we have in the prophetic Scriptures the distinct intimation of their direct application not only to individuals, but to nations also.[2] When nations conform their laws to this divine teaching, wars must necessarily cease.

We would, in humility, but in faithfulness to our Lord, express our firm persuasion that all the exigencies of civil government and social order may be met under the banner of the Prince of Peace, in strict conformity with his commands.

[1]Mt 5.44, Lk 6.27; [2]Is 2.4, Mi 4.1

15. OATHS

We hold it to be the inalienable privilege of the disciple of the Lord Jesus that his statements concerning matters of fact within his knowledge should be accepted, under all circumstances, as expressing his belief as to the fact asserted. We rest upon the plain command of our Lord and Master, "Swear not at all";[1] and we believe any departure from this standard to be prejudicial to the cause of truth and to that confidence between man and man, the maintenance of which is indispensable to our mutual well-being. This command, in our persuasion, applies not to profane swearing only, but to judicial oaths also. It abrogates any previous permission to the contrary, and is, for the Christian, absolutely conclusive.

[1]Mt 5.34

16. THE FIRST DAY OF THE WEEK

Whilst the remembrance of our Creator ought to be at all times present with the Christian, we would express our thankfulness to our heavenly Father that he has been pleased to honor the setting apart of one day in seven for the purposes of holy rest, religious duties, and public worship; and we desire that all under our name may avail themselves of this great privilege as those who are called to be risen with Christ, and to seek those things that are above where he sitteth at the right hand of God.[1] May the release thus granted from other occupations be diligently improved. On this day of the week especially ought the households of Friends to be assembled for the reading of the Scriptures and for waiting upon the Lord; and we trust that, in a Christianly wise economy of our time and strength, the engagements of the day may be so ordered as not to frustrate the gracious provision thus made for us by our Heavenly Father, or to shut out the opportunity either for public worship or for private retirement and devotional reading.

In presenting this declaration of our Christian faith, we desire that all our members may be afresh encouraged, in humility and devotedness, to renewed faithfulness in fulfilling their part in the great mission of the church, and through the church to the world around us, in the name of our crucified Redeemer. Life *from* Christ, life *in* Christ, must ever be the basis of life for Christ. For this we have been created and redeemed, and, by this alone, can the longings of our immortal souls be satisfied.

[1] Col 3.1

Old Catholic Church, *The Declaration of Utrecht,* 1889

Having joined with spokesmen for Eastern Orthodoxy and Anglicanism in → *The Fourteen Theses of the First Reunion Conference at Bonn* of 1874, the Old Catholic Church in the German-speaking lands of Austria, Switzerland, and Germany did not have a confession of its own. But in 1889, under the new leadership of Archbishop Johannes Heykamp of the Old Catholic Church of the Netherlands (which had arisen already in the eighteenth century, thus long before the First Vatican Council), such a confession was produced. It had been from the Dutch Old Catholics that the German Old Catholics received episcopal consecration. Now, as Moss put it, "Utrecht had given the Old Catholics their episcopal succession and their jurisdiction: it remained for Utrecht to give them a firm dogmatic basis."[1]

A conference of five Old Catholic bishops and several theologians met at Utrecht on 24 September 1889 and adopted *The Declaration of Utrecht.*

Edition and translation: *Statut der Internationalen Altkatholischen Bischof-konferenz* 2001, 25–27, 40–42.

Literature: Arx 1989, 1994; Conzemius 1969; Küppers 1978; Küry 1982; Moss 1964, 278–82; *ODCC* 1673.

1. Moss 1964, 279.

Old Catholic Church, *The Declaration of Utrecht,* 1889

In nomine ss. Trinitatis

Johannes Heykamp, archbishop of Utrecht, Casparus Johannes Rinkel, bishop of Haarlem, Cornelius Diependaal, bishop of Deventer, Joseph Hubert Reinkens, bishop of the Old Catholic Church of Germany, Eduard Herzog, bishop of the Christian-Catholic Church of Switzerland, assembled in the archiepiscopal residence at Utrecht on the four and twentieth day of September, 1889, after invocation of the Holy Spirit, address the following declaration to the Catholic Church.

Being assembled for a conference in response to an invitation from the undersigned archbishop of Utrecht, we have resolved henceforth to meet from time to time for consultations on subjects of common interest, in conjunction with our assistants, councillors, and theologians.

We deem it appropriate at this our first meeting to summarize in a common declaration the ecclesiastical principles on which we have hitherto exercised and will continue to exercise our episcopal ministry, and which we have repeatedly had occasion to state in individual declarations.

1. We adhere to the principle of the ancient church laid down by St. Vincent of Lérins in these terms: "Id teneamus, quod ubique, quod semper, quod ab omnibus creditum est; hoc est etenim vere proprieque catholicum [We hold that which has been believed everywhere, always, and by all; that is truly and properly catholic]."[1]

Therefore we abide by the faith of the ancient church as it is formulated in the ecumenical symbols and in the universally accepted dogmatic decisions of the ecumenical synods held in the undivided church of the first millennium.

2. We therefore reject as contradicting the faith of the ancient church and destroying her constitution, the Vatican decrees, promulgated July 18, 1870, concerning the infallibility and the universal episcopate or ecclesiastical plenitude of power of the Roman pope. This, however, does not prevent us from acknowledging the historic primacy which several ecumenical councils and the fathers of the ancient church with the assent of the whole church have attributed to the bishop of Rome by recognizing him as the *primus inter pares* [first among equals].

3. We also reject the dogma of the immaculate conception promulgated by

---

1. Vincent of Lérins *Commonitorium* 2.6 (*NPNF*–II 11:132).

Pope Pius IX in 1854 as being without foundation in Holy Scriptures and the tradition of the first centuries.

4. As for the other dogmatic decrees issued by the bishops of Rome in the last centuries, the bulls *Unigenitus* and *Auctorem fidei,* the Syllabus of 1864, etc., we reject them on all such points as are in contradiction with the doctrine of the ancient church, and do not recognize them as binding. Moreover we renew all those protests which the ancient Catholic Church of Holland has made against Rome in the past.

5. We refuse to accept the decisions of the Council of Trent in matters of discipline, and we accept its dogmatic decisions only insofar as they agree with the teaching of the ancient church.

6. Considering that the holy eucharist has always been the true focal point of worship in the Catholic Church, we consider it our duty to declare that we maintain in all faithfulness and without deviation the ancient Catholic doctrine concerning the holy sacrament of the altar, by believing that we receive the body and the blood of our Savior Jesus Christ himself under the species of bread and wine.

The eucharistic celebration in the church is neither a continual repetition nor a renewal of the expiatory sacrifice which Christ offered once and for all on the cross; the sacrificial character of the eucharist, however, consists in its being the perpetual commemoration of that sacrifice and a real representation, being enacted on earth, of the one offering which Christ according to Heb 9.11–12 continuously makes in heaven for the salvation of redeemed humanity, by appearing now for us in the presence of God (Heb 9.24).

This being the character of the eucharist in relation to Christ's sacrifice, it is at the same time a sacrificial meal, by means of which the faithful, in receiving the body and blood of the Lord, have communion with one another (1 Cor 10.17).

7. We hope that the theologians, while maintaining the faith of the undivided church, will succeed in their efforts to establish an agreement on the differences that have arisen since the divisions of the church. We urge the priests under our jurisdiction in the first place to stress, both by preaching and by religious instruction, the essential Christian truths professed in common by all the divided confessions, carefully to avoid, in discussing still-existing differences, any violation of truth or charity, and, in word and deed, to set an example to the members of our parishes of how to act towards people of a different belief in a way that is in accordance with the spirit of Jesus Christ, who is the Savior of us all.

8. We believe that it is in faithfully maintaining the teaching of Jesus Christ, while rejecting all the errors that have been added to it through human sin, as well as rejecting all the abuses in ecclesiastical matters and hierarchical tendencies, that

we shall best counteract unbelief and that religious indifference which is the worst evil of our day.

Given at Utrecht, the 24th September, 1889.

Johannes Heykamp.
Casparus Johannes Rinkel.
Cornelis Diependaal.
Joseph Hubert Reinkens.
Eduard Herzog.

The Twentieth Century: Globalization of Churches and Confessions

"And in one holy, catholic, and apostolic church": this fourth-century creedal affirmation, which echoed earlier formulas and has in turn been echoed by later ones ever since, has repeatedly collided with what Karl Adam calls "the spotted actuality" of empirical Christendom. People, priests, and prelates were often anything but holy, and there were tares among the wheat; apostolic authority was regularly cited to justify flagrantly nonapostolic teachings and actions; parochialism (the term is, after all, a Christian invention) and denominationalism belied the claim of catholicity and universality; and Paul's rhetorical question to the Corinthians "Is Christ divided?" has seemed, especially in the modern period, to demand an embarrassed Yes as its answer.

The first of those issues as listed above (*holy*) had engaged the creeds and confessions of the early church, especially in response to the Donatist challenge; and the second (*apostolic* authority) became the first article in many Reformation confessions. But in the modern period, and above all in the twentieth century, "the great new fact" of church history and of its confessional expressions was the geographical spread of the gospel through the expansion of Christendom during the nineteenth century, "the great century" of missions, together with the closely related (though not identical) attention to the imperative in the high-priestly prayer of Christ "that they all may be one": therefore *catholic* and *one*.

The World Conference on Faith and Order at Lausanne in 1927, one of the pioneer gatherings of the ecumenical movement of the twentieth century, acknowledged this conjunction in its *Call to Unity:* "Our missions count that as a necessity which we are inclined to look on as a luxury. Already the mission field [soon to be called 'the younger churches'] is impatiently revolting from the divisions of the Western Church to make bold adventure for unity in its own right. We of the churches represented in this Conference cannot allow our spiritual children to outpace us." Among these "impatient revolts" and "bold adventures" all over Christendom and all over the globe, the new creeds and confessions of faith of the twentieth century were major experiments in globalization, indigenization, and ecumenical discovery, which also often, perhaps paradoxically, included the rediscovery of the creedal and confessional tradition, an "ecumenism in time" as well as in space.

397

Friends General Conference, *Belief*, 1900

In various earlier statements of faith, beginning already with → Robert Barclay's *Confession of Faith Containing XXIII Articles* of 1673 but then especially in → *The Richmond Declaration of Faith* of 1887, various communities and movements within the Society of Friends (Quakers) had been as specific as their principles permitted in articulating which beliefs they shared with other traditions and which they held in distinction from these.

As the closing paragraph of this statement of faith makes clear again, *The Richmond Declaration of Faith* continued to stand as the nearest to a conventional "creed" or "confession of faith" most Friends were willing to espouse. But the need to encapsulate the beliefs professed there in a more compact and thetical form was responsible in 1900 for the production of a text originally labeled simply *Belief* but eventually *Essential Truths*, issued by the Friends General Conference.

Edition: *Constitution and Discipline* 1925, 10–13.

Literature: R. Jones [1927] 2002; Minear 1987, 130–34; Steere 1955.

1. The vital principle of the Christian faith is the truth that man's salvation and higher life are personal matters between the individual soul and God.

2. Salvation is deliverance from sin and the possession of spiritual life. This comes through a personal faith in Jesus Christ as the Savior, who, through his love and sacrifice draws us to him.

3. Conviction for sin is awakened by the operation of the Holy Spirit causing the soul to feel its need of reconciliation with God. When Christ is seen as the only hope of salvation, and man yields to him, he is brought into newness of life, and realizes that his sonship to God has become an actual reality. This transformation is wrought without the necessary agency of any human priest, or ordinance, or ceremony whatsoever. A changed nature and life bear witness to this new relation to him.

4. The whole spiritual life grows out of the soul's relation to God and its cooperation with him, not from any outward or traditional observances.

5. Christ himself baptizes the surrendered soul with the Holy Spirit, enduing it with power, bestowing gifts for service. This is an efficient baptism, a direct incoming of divine power for the transformation and control of the whole man. Christ himself is the spiritual bread which nourishes the soul, and he thus enters into and becomes a part of the being of those who partake of him. This participation with Christ and apprehension of him become the goal of life for the Christian. Those who thus enter into oneness with him become also joined in living union with each other as members of one body.

6. Both worship and Christian fellowship spring out of this immediate relation of believing souls with their Lord.

7. The Holy Scriptures were given by inspiration of God and are the divinely authorized record of the doctrines which Christians are bound to accept, and of the moral principles which are to regulate their lives and actions. In them, as interpreted and unfolded by the Holy Spirit, is an ever-fresh and unfailing source of spiritual truth for the proper guidance of life and practice.

8. The doctrines of the apostolic days are held by the Friends as essentials of Christianity. The fatherhood of God, the deity and humanity of the Son; the gift of the Holy Spirit; the atonement through Jesus Christ by which men are reconciled to God; the resurrection; the high-priesthood of Christ, and the individual priest-

hood of believers, are most precious truths, to be held, not as traditional dogmas, but as vital, life-giving realities.

9. The sinful condition of man and his proneness to yield to temptation, the world's absolute need of a Savior, and the cleansing from sin in forgiveness and sanctification through the blood of Jesus Christ, are unceasing incentives to all who believe to become laborers together with God in extending his kingdom. By this high calling the Friends are pledged to the proclamation of the truth wherever the Spirit leads, both in home and foreign fields.

10. The indwelling Spirit guides and controls the surrendered life, and the Christian's constant and supreme business is obedience to him. But while the importance of individual guidance and obedience is thus emphasized, this fact gives no ground for license; the sanctified conclusions of the church are above the judgment of a single individual.

11. The Friends find no scriptural evidence or authority for any form or degree of sacerdotalism in the Christian Church, or for the establishment of any ordinance or ceremonial rite for perpetual observance. The teachings of Jesus Christ concerning the spiritual nature of religion, the impossibility of promoting the spiritual life by the ceremonial application of material things, the fact that faith in Jesus Christ himself is all-sufficient, the purpose of his life, death, resurrection, and ascension, and his presence in the believer's heart, virtually destroy every ceremonial system and point the soul to the only satisfying source of spiritual life and power.

12. With faith in the wisdom of Almighty God, the Father, the Son, and the Holy Spirit, and believing that it is his purpose to make his church on earth a power for righteousness and truth, the Friends labor for the alleviation of human suffering; for the intellectual, moral, and spiritual elevation of mankind; and for purified and exalted citizenship. The Friends believe war to be incompatible with Christianity, and seek to promote peaceful methods for the settlement of all the differences between nations and between men.

13. It is an essential part of the faith that a man should be in truth what he professes in word, and the underlying principle of life and action for individuals, and also for society, is transformation through the power of God and implicit obedience to his revealed will.

14. For more explicit and extended statements of belief, reference is made to those officially put forth at various times, especially to the letter of George Fox to the governor of Barbados in 1671, and to the Declaration of Faith issued by the Richmond Conference in 1887.

Pius X, *Lamentabili,* 1907

As had become evident from the issuance of → *The Syllabus of Errors* of 1864 and from some of the condemnatory clauses in the dogmatic legislation of the → First Vatican Council in 1870, the Roman Catholic Church in the nineteenth century had not been immune to the inroads of modern critical thought and its application both to the teachings of the church and to the Bible and other authoritative dogmatic texts, but was facing some of the same challenges that Protestantism did. Especially in France and Germany, some Roman Catholic scholars were subjecting these texts to critical-historical methods similar to those that their colleagues employed in studying secular sources, and were claiming for themselves the same academic freedom in the use of those methods even when the results of such study did not conform to Catholic dogma.

Thus was precipitated what several authors writing in different languages have labeled "the Modernist crisis." In his twenty-five-year reign from 1878 to 1903, Pope Leo XIII, whose endorsement of the Thomist revival did much to combat Modernism but who seems to have been reluctant to suppress scholarly and scientific inquiry outright, did not act openly against it. But his successor, Pope Pius X, did: first in *Lamentabili* issued by the Holy Office on 3 July 1907, and the accompanying encyclical *Pascendi dominici gregis* of 8 September; and then in *Sacrorum antistites* with the attached → *Antimodernist Oath* of 1910.

As in the condemnation of the "five propositions" of Jansenism and in the *Syllabus,* the false teachings are condemned without a corresponding affirmation of correct teaching.

Edition: Denzinger, 3401–66.

Translation: Based on Deferrari [1957] 2002, 508–13.

Literature: Heiner 1908; McCarthy 1998; Vidler 1976.

Pius X, *Lamentabili*, 1907

On the Emancipation of Exegesis from the Magisterium of the Church

1. The ecclesiastical law which prescribes that books dealing with the Divine Scriptures be submitted to a previous censorship does not extend to critical scholars, or to scholars of the scientific exegesis of books of the Old and New Testaments.

2. The church's interpretation of the Sacred Books is not indeed to be spurned, but it is subject to the more accurate judgment and the correction of exegetes.

3. From the ecclesiastical judgments and censures passed against free and more learned exegesis, it can be gathered that the faith proposed by the church contradicts history, and that Catholic teachings cannot in fact be reconciled with the truer origins of the Christian religion.

4. The *magisterium* of the church, even by dogmatic definitions, cannot determine the genuine sense of the Sacred Scriptures.

5. Since in the deposit of faith only revealed truths are contained, in no respect does it pertain to the church to pass judgment on the assertions of human disciplines.

6. In defining truths the learning church and the teaching church so collaborate that there is nothing left for the teaching church but to sanction the common opinions of the learning church.

7. When the church proscribes errors, she cannot exact any internal assent of the faithful, by which the judgments published by her are embraced.

8. Those who consider to be of no account the reprobations published by the Sacred Congregation of the Index, or by other sacred Roman congregations are to be regarded as free of all blame.

On the Inspiration and Inerrancy of Holy Scripture

9. They display excessive simplicity or ignorance, who believe that God is truly the author of Holy Scripture.

10. The inspiration of the books of the Old Testament consists in this: that the Israelite writers have handed down religious doctrines under a peculiar aspect which is little known, or not known at all to the Gentiles.

11. Divine inspiration does not so extend to all Sacred Scripture that it fortifies each and every part of it against all error.

12. The exegete, if he wishes to apply himself advantageously to biblical studies, should divest himself especially of any preconceived opinion about the supernatural origin of Holy Scripture, and should interpret it just as he would other, merely human documents.

13. The evangelists themselves and the Christians of the second and third generation have artificially distributed the parables of the Gospels, and thus have given a reason for the small fruit of the preaching of Christ among the Jews.

14. In many narratives the evangelists related not so much what is true, as what they thought to be more profitable for the reader, although false.

15. The Gospels up to the time of the defining and establishment of the canon have been augmented continually by additions and corrections; hence, there has remained in them only a slight and uncertain trace of the teaching of Christ.

16. The narrations of John are not properly history, but the mystical contemplation of the gospel; the discourses contained in his Gospel are theological meditations on the mystery of salvation, devoid of historical truth.

17. The Fourth Gospel exaggerated miracles, not only that the extraordinary might stand out more, but also that they might become more suitable for signifying the work and glory of the Word Incarnate.

18. John, indeed, claims for himself the character of a witness concerning Christ; but in reality he is nothing but a distinguished witness of the Christian life, or of the life of the Christian church at the end of the first century.

19. Heterodox exegetes have more faithfully expressed the true sense of Scripture than Catholic exegetes.

On the Concept of Revelation and of Dogma

20. Revelation could have been nothing other than the consciousness acquired by man of his relation to God.

21. Revelation, constituting the object of Catholic faith, was not completed with the apostles.

22. The dogmas which the church professes as revealed are not truths fallen from heaven, but they are a kind of interpretation of religious facts, which the human mind by a laborious effort prepared for itself.

23. Opposition can and actually does exist between facts which are narrated in Sacred Scripture, and the dogmas of the church based on these, so that a critic can reject as false, facts which the church believes to be most certain.

24. An exegete is not to be reproved who constructs premises from which it

follows that dogmas are historically false or dubious, provided he does not directly deny the dogmas themselves.

25. The assent of faith ultimately depends on an accumulation of probabilities.

26. The dogmas of faith are to be held only according to a practical sense, that is, as preceptive norms for acting, but not as norms for believing.

On Christ

27. The divinity of Jesus Christ is not proved from the Gospels, but is a dogma which the Christian conscience has deduced from the notion of the Messiah.

28. When Jesus was exercising his ministry, he did not speak with this purpose, to teach that he was the Messiah, nor did his miracles have as their purpose to demonstrate this.

29. It may be conceded that the Christ whom history presents is far inferior to the Christ who is the object of faith.

30. In all the Gospel texts the name *Son of God* is equivalent to the name of *Messiah,* but it does not at all signify that Christ is truly and by nature the Son of God.

31. The doctrine about Christ which Paul, John, and the Councils of Nicaea, Ephesus, and Chalcedon hand down, is not that which Jesus taught, but which the Christian conscience conceived about Jesus.

32. The natural sense of the Gospel texts cannot be reconciled with that which our theologians teach about the consciousness and the infallible knowledge of Jesus Christ.

33. It is evident to everyone who is not influenced by preconceived opinions that either Jesus professed an error concerning the immediate coming of the Messiah, or the greater part of the doctrine contained in the Synoptic Gospels is void of authenticity.

34. The critic cannot ascribe to Christ knowledge circumscribed by no limit, except on the supposition which can by no means be conceived historically, and which is repugnant to the moral sense, namely, that Christ as man had the knowledge of God, and nevertheless was unwilling to share the knowledge of so many things with his disciples and posterity.

35. Christ did not always have the consciousness of his messianic dignity.

36. The resurrection of the Savior is not properly a fact of the historical order, but a fact of the purely supernatural order, neither demonstrated nor demonstrable, and which the Christian conscience gradually derived from other sources.

37. Faith in the resurrection of Christ was from the beginning not so much of the fact of the resurrection itself, as of the immortal life of Christ with God.

38. The doctrine of the expiatory death of Christ is not from the Gospels but only from Paul.

On the Sacraments

39. The opinions about the origin of the sacraments with which the fathers of Trent were imbued and which certainly had an influence on their dogmatic canons are far different from those which now rightly obtain among historical investigators of Christianity.

40. The sacraments had their origin in this, that the apostles and their successors, swayed and moved by circumstances and events, interpreted some idea and intention of Christ.

41. The sacraments have this one end, to call to man's mind the ever-beneficent presence of the Creator.

42. The Christian community has introduced the necessity of baptism, adopting it as a necessary rite, and adding to it the obligation of professing Christianity.

43. The practice of conferring baptism on infants was a disciplinary evolution, which was one reason for resolving the sacrament into two, baptism and penance.

44. There is no proof that the rite of the sacrament of confirmation was practiced by the apostles; but the formal distinction between the two sacraments, namely, baptism and confirmation, by no means goes back to the history of primitive Christianity.

[1 Cor 11.23–25]   45. Not all that Paul says about the institution of the eucharist is to be taken historically.

46. There was no conception in the primitive church of the Christian sinner reconciled by the authority of the church, but the church only very gradually became accustomed to such a conception. Indeed, even after penance was recognized as an institution of the church, it was not called by the name "sacrament" for the reason that it would have been held as a shameful sacrament.

47. The words of the Lord, "Receive ye the Holy Ghost; whose sins ye shall
[Jn 20.22–23]   forgive they are forgiven them, and whose sins ye shall retain they are retained," do not refer at all to the sacrament of penance, whatever the fathers of Trent were pleased to say.

[Jas 5.14–15]   48. James in his epistle does not intend to promulgate some sacrament of

Christ, but to commend a certain pious custom, and if in this custom by chance he perceives some means of grace, he does not accept this with that strictness with which the theologians have accepted it, who have established the notion and the number of the sacraments.

49. As the Christian supper gradually assumed the nature of a liturgical action, those who were accustomed to preside at the supper acquired the sacerdotal character.

50. The elders who fulfilled the function of watching over gatherings of Christians were instituted by the apostles as presbyters or bishops to provide for the necessary arrangement of the increasing communities, not properly for perpetuating the apostolic mission and power.

51. Matrimony could not have emerged as a sacrament of the new law in the church, since in order that matrimony might be held to be a sacrament, it was necessary that a full theological development of the doctrine on grace and the sacraments take place first.

On the Constitution of the Church

52. It was foreign to the mind of Christ to establish a church as a society upon earth to endure for a long course of centuries; rather, in the mind of Christ the kingdom of heaven together with the end of the world was to come presently.

53. The organic constitution of the church is not immutable; but Christian society, just as human society, is subject to perpetual evolution.

54. The dogmas, the sacraments, the hierarchy, as far as pertains both to the notion and to the reality, are nothing but interpretations and the evolution of the Christian intelligence, which have increased and perfected the little germ latent in the gospel.

55. Simon Peter never even suspected that the primacy of the church was entrusted to him by Christ.

56. The Roman Church became the head of all the churches not by the ordinances of divine providence, but purely by political factors.

57. The church shows herself to be hostile to the advances of the natural and theological sciences.

On the Immutability of Religious Truths

58. Truth is no more immutable than man himself, inasmuch as it is evolved with him, in him, and through him.

59. Christ did not teach a defined body of doctrine applicable to all times and to all men, but rather began a religious movement adapted, or to be adapted to different times and places.

60. Christian doctrine in its beginnings was Judaic, but through successive evolutions it became first Pauline, then Johannine, and finally Hellenic and universal.

61. It can be said without paradox that no chapter of Scripture, from the first of Genesis to the last of the Apocalypse, contains doctrine entirely identical with that which the church hands down on the same subject; and so no chapter of Scripture has the same sense for the critic as for the theologian.

62. The principal articles of the Apostles' Creed did not have the same meaning for the Christians of the earliest times as they have for the Christians of our time.

63. The church shows herself unequal to the task of preserving the ethics of the gospel, because she clings obstinately to immutable doctrines which cannot be reconciled with present-day advances.

64. The progress of the sciences demands that the concepts of Christian doctrine about God, creation, revelation, the person of the Incarnate Word, the redemption, be recast.

65. Present-day Catholicism cannot be reconciled with true science, unless it be transformed into a kind of nondogmatic Christianity, that is, into a broad and liberal Protestantism.

Censure of the holy pontiff: "His Holiness has approved and confirmed the decree of the most eminent fathers, and has ordered that all and every proposition enumerated above be held as condemned and proscribed."

Church of the Nazarene, *Articles of Faith*, 1908

The addition of an article on "Entire Sanctification" to → *The Articles of Religion* of the Free Methodist Church of 1866 showed how central the issue of "holiness" had become in much of the Wesleyan tradition. As a result, any sense that the issue was no longer being taken with due seriousness by Methodists would produce protest — and could produce separation.

A combination of pastoral and personal experience was responsible for the commitment of the Reverend Phineas F. Bressee, a Methodist minister in Iowa and then in California, to the doctrine of entire sanctification and to the possibility of complete perfection. The consequent tensions with the Methodist Church led him in 1894 to withdraw from the ministry and in the following year to found the Church of the Nazarene, which soon became national.

A decade later, the drafting of a *Constitution of the Church of the Nazarene* became the occasion also for the formulation of *Articles of Faith* as part of the constitution.

Edition: *Manual of the Church of the Nazarene 1952, 25–32.*

Literature: C. E. Jones 1974; Lippy and Williams 1988, 2:822–24.

Church of the Nazarene, *Articles of Faith*, 1908

Preamble

In order that we may preserve our God-given heritage, the faith once delivered to the saints, especially the doctrine and experience of sanctification as a second work of grace, and also that we may cooperate effectually with other branches of the church of Jesus Christ in advancing God's kingdom among men, we, the ministers and lay members of the Church of the Nazarene, in accordance with the principles of constitutional legislation established among us, do hereby ordain, adopt, and set forth as the fundamental law or constitution of the Church of the Nazarene the Articles of Faith, the General Rules, and the Articles of Organization and Government here following, to wit:

1. Articles of Faith

1. THE TRIUNE GOD

1. We believe in one eternally existent, infinite God, Sovereign of the universe; that he only is God, creative and administrative, holy in nature, attributes, and purpose; that he, as God, is triune in essential being, revealed as Father, Son, and Holy Spirit.

2. JESUS CHRIST

2. We believe in Jesus Christ, the second person of the triune Godhead; that he was eternally one with the Father; that he became incarnate by the Holy Spirit and was born of the Virgin Mary, so that two whole and perfect natures, that is to say the Godhead and manhood, are thus united in one person very God and very man, the God-man.

We believe that Jesus Christ died for our sins, and that he truly arose from the dead and took again his body, together with all things appertaining to the perfection of man's nature, wherewith he ascended into heaven and is there engaged in intercession for us.

3. THE HOLY SPIRIT

3. We believe in the Holy Spirit, the third person of the triune Godhead, that he is ever present and efficiently active in and with the church of Christ, convincing the [Jn 16.8–9] world of sin, regenerating those who repent and believe, sanctifying believers, and [Jn 16.13] guiding into all truth as it is in Jesus.

4. THE HOLY SCRIPTURES

4. We believe in the plenary inspiration of the Holy Scriptures, by which we understand the sixty-six books of the Old and New Testaments given by divine inspiration, inerrantly revealing the will of God concerning us in all things necessary to our salvation, so that whatever is not contained therein is not to be enjoined as an article of faith.

5. ORIGINAL SIN, OR DEPRAVITY

5. We believe that original sin, or depravity, is that corruption of the nature of all the offspring of Adam by reason of which every one is very far gone from original righteousness or the pure state of our first parents at the time of their creation, is averse to God, is without spiritual life, and inclined to evil, and that continually. We further believe that original sin continues to exist with the new life of the regenerate, until eradicated by the baptism with the Holy Spirit.

6. ATONEMENT

6. We believe that Jesus Christ, by his sufferings, by the shedding of his own blood, and by his meritorious death on the cross, made a full atonement for all human sin, and that this atonement is the only ground of salvation, and that it is sufficient for every individual of Adam's race. The atonement is graciously efficacious for the salvation of the irresponsible and for the children in innocency, but is efficacious for the salvation of those who reach the age of responsibility only when they repent and believe.

7. FREE AGENCY

7. We believe that man's creation in God-likeness included ability to choose between right and wrong, and that thus he was made morally responsible; that through the fall of Adam he became depraved so that he cannot now turn and prepare himself by his own natural strength and works to faith and calling upon God. But we also believe that the grace of God through Jesus Christ is freely bestowed upon all men, enabling all who will to turn from sin to righteousness, believe on Jesus Christ for pardon and cleansing from sin, and follow good works pleasing and acceptable in his sight.

We believe that man, though in the possession of the experience of regeneration and entire sanctification, may fall from grace and apostatize and, unless he repent of his sin, be hopelessly and eternally lost.

8. REPENTANCE

8. We believe that repentance, which is a sincere and thorough change of the mind in regard to sin, involving a sense of personal guilt and a voluntary turning away from sin, is demanded of all who have by act or purpose become sinners against God. The Spirit of God gives to all who will repent the gracious help of penitence of heart and hope of mercy, that they may believe unto pardon and spiritual life.

9. JUSTIFICATION, REGENERATION, AND ADOPTION

9. We believe that justification is that gracious and judicial act of God, by which he grants full pardon of all guilt and complete release from the penalty of sins committed, and acceptance as righteous, to all who believe on Jesus Christ and receive him as Lord and Savior.

10. We believe that regeneration, or the new birth, is that gracious work of God whereby the moral nature of the repentant believer is spiritually quickened and given a distinctively spiritual life, capable of faith, love, and obedience.

11. We believe that adoption is that gracious act of God by which the justified and regenerated believer is constituted a son of God.

12. We believe that justification, regeneration, and adoption are simultaneous in the experience of seekers after God and are obtained upon the condition of faith, preceded by repentance; and that to this work and state of grace the Holy Spirit bears witness.

10. ENTIRE SANCTIFICATION

13. We believe that entire sanctification is that act of God, subsequent to regeneration, by which believers are made free from original sin, or depravity, and brought into a state of entire devotement to God, and the holy obedience of love made perfect.

It is wrought by the baptism with the Holy Spirit, and comprehends in one experience the cleansing of the heart from sin and the abiding indwelling presence of the Holy Spirit, empowering the believer for life and service.

Entire sanctification is provided by the blood of Jesus, is wrought instantaneously by faith, preceded by entire consecration; and to this work and state of grace the Holy Spirit bears witness.

This experience is also known by various terms representing its different phases, such as "Christian Perfection," "Perfect Love," "Heart Purity," "The Baptism with the Holy Spirit," "The Fullness of the Blessing," and "Christian Holiness."

11. SECOND COMING OF CHRIST

14. We believe that the Lord Jesus Christ will come again; that we who are alive at his coming shall not precede them that are asleep in Christ Jesus; but that, if we are abiding in him, we shall be caught up with the risen saints to meet the Lord in the air, so that we shall ever be with the Lord. [1 Thes 4.15–17]

12. RESURRECTION, JUDGMENT, AND DESTINY

15. We believe in the resurrection of the dead, that the bodies both of the just and of the unjust shall be raised to life and united with their spirits—"they that have done good, unto the resurrection of life; and they that have done evil, unto the resurrection of damnation." [Jn 5.29]

16. We believe in future judgment in which every man shall appear before God to be judged according to his deeds in this life.

17. We believe that glorious and everlasting life is assured to all who savingly believe in, and obediently follow, Jesus Christ our Lord; and that the finally impenitent shall suffer eternally in hell.

13. BAPTISM

18. We believe that Christian baptism is a sacrament signifying acceptance of the benefits of the atonement of Jesus Christ, to be administered to believers as declarative of their faith in Jesus Christ as their Savior, and full purpose of obedience in holiness and righteousness.

Baptism being the symbol of the New Testament, young children may be baptized, upon request of parents or guardians who shall give assurance for them of necessary Christian training.

Baptism may be administered by sprinkling, pouring, or immersion, according to the choice of the applicant.

14. THE LORD'S SUPPER

19. We believe that the memorial and communion supper instituted by our Lord and Savior Jesus Christ is essentially a New Testament sacrament, declarative of his sacrificial death, through the merits of which believers have life and salvation and promise of all spiritual blessings in Christ. It is distinctively for those who are prepared for reverent appreciation of its significance and by it they show forth the Lord's death till he come again. It being the communion feast, only those who have [1 Cor 11.26] faith in Christ and love for the saints should be called to participate therein.

15. DIVINE HEALING

20. We believe in the Bible doctrine of divine healing and urge our people to seek to offer the prayer of faith for the healing of the sick. Providential means and agencies when deemed necessary should not be refused.

The Methodist Episcopal Church,
The Social Creed of Methodism, 1908

Ever since the ministry of John Wesley to the British working class, Methodism had been characterized by a special sense of the social responsibility not only of the individual Christian believer but of the corporate church. In the United States, that social sense had been sorely tested but eventually vindicated in the struggle for the emancipation of the slaves: as Abraham Lincoln observed, both sides prayed to the same God and quoted the same Bible, but the abolition of slavery was a moral victory at least as much as a military victory.

Although slavery was no more, the social and economic conditions under which industrial laborers had to work and live during the decades following the Civil War often seemed to be not much better. Building on that tradition of social concern, the leading spokesman for a new Christian response to this crisis was Walter Rauschenbusch. His *Christianity and the Social Crisis* of 1907 "became one of the most influential religious books of the century."[1] Both explicitly and above all implicitly, this book and the Social Gospel of which it became the handbook represented a frontal attack on creeds and confessions of faith as one of the principal factors deflecting the churches from their social mission.

Nevertheless, the Methodist social thinker Harry F. Ward found it appropriate to resort to the modality of the creed and, with several associates from the Methodist Federation for Social Service, also founded in 1907, composed the document that eventually acquired the title *The Social Creed of Methodism,* which the Methodist Episcopal General Conference adopted on 30 May 1908. It became the basis for → *The Social Creed of the Churches* adopted by the Federal Council of the Churches of Christ in America later the same year.

Edition: Goodsell, Hingeley, and Buckley 1908, 480.

Literature: Gorrell 1988; Handy 1966; Hopkins 1940; Muelder 1961; Ward 1912.

1. *ODCC* 1368.

Methodist Episcopal Church,
The Social Creed of Methodism, 1908

The Methodist Episcopal Church stands—

1. For equal rights and complete justice for all men in all stations of life.

2. For the principle of conciliation and arbitration in industrial dissensions.

3. For the protection of the worker from dangerous machinery, occupational diseases, injuries, and mortality.

4. For the abolition of child labor.

5. For such regulation of the conditions of labor for women as shall safeguard the physical and moral health of the community.

6. For the suppression of the "sweating system."

7. For the gradual and reasonable reduction of the hours of labor to the lowest practical point, with work for all; and for the degree of leisure for all which is the condition of the highest human life.

8. For a release from employment one day in seven.

9. For a living wage in every industry.

10. For the highest wage that each industry can afford, and for the most equitable division of the products of industry that can ultimately be devised.

11. For the recognition of the Golden Rule and the mind of Christ as the supreme law of society and the sure remedy of all social ills.

The Federal Council of the Churches of Christ in America, *The Social Creed of the Churches*, 1908

The composition and adoption of → *The Social Creed of Methodism* in May 1908 had an immediate siginificance far beyond its original denominational boundaries, for it coincided with the founding of the Federal Council of the Churches of Christ in America in December of the same year.

On the basis of the Methodist document, therefore, Frank Mason North, who had collaborated with Harry F. Ward on the Methodist *Social Creed*, prepared the original text of *The Social Creed of the Churches*, which the Federal Council adopted on 4 December 1908. In spite of its great importance, the text of this creed has not been transmitted in anything approaching a fixed or stable form, but various bodies and even individuals seem to have felt free to make additions or substractions over the years. "Unlike the Apostles' or Nicene Creeds," Gorrell has explained, "whose strength lay in their unchanged wording, a Social Creed had to be changed periodically to keep it relevant to changing conditions."[1] With *The Social Creed of the Churches*, as with *The Social Creed of Methodism*, we reproduce here what is represented to be the *editio princeps* of 1908.

Edition: Ward 1912, 3–4.

Literature: Gorrell 1988; Handy 1966; Hopkins 1940; Muelder 1961; Ward 1912.

1. Gorrell 1988, 220.

The Federal Council of the Churches of Christ in America, *The Social Creed of the Churches*, 1908

The Federal Council of the Churches of Christ in America stands:

1. For equal rights and complete justice for all men in all stations of life.

2. For the abolition of child labor.

3. For such regulation of the conditions of toil for women as shall safeguard the physical and moral health of the community.

4. For the suppression of the "sweating system."

5. For the gradual and reasonable reduction of the hours of labor to the lowest practicable point, and for that degree of leisure for all which is the condition of the highest human life.

6. For a release from employment one day in seven.

7. For the right of all men to the opportunity for self-maintenance, a right ever to be wisely and strongly safeguarded against encroachments of every kind.

8. For the right of workers to some protection against the hardships often resulting from the swift crises of industrial change.

9. For a living wage as a minimum in every industry, and for the highest wage that each industry can afford.

10. For the protection of the worker from dangerous machinery, occupational disease, injuries, and mortality.

11. For suitable provision for the old age of the workers and for those incapacitated by injury.

12. For the principle of conciliation and arbitration in industrial dissensions.

13. For the abatement of poverty.

14. For the most equitable division of the products of industry that can ultimately be devised.

Pius X, *Sacrorum antistitum*
(Antimodernist Oath), 1910

After his condemnation of Modernism in → *Lamentabili* and *Pascendi* of 1907, Pope Pius X returned to the subject three years later, in *Sacrorum antistitum,* issued on 1 September 1910. What this *motu proprio* ("on his own initiative") added to the earlier actions was the requirement that professors of theology, in addition to their other affirmations of faith, take a special oath abjuring the errors of Modernism.

Patterned in some respects after → *The Tridentine Profession of Faith* of 1564, which had put the dogmatic decisions of the Council of Trent into the form of a personal creed in the first person singular, the *Antimodernist Oath,* which remained in effect until the time of the Second Vatican Council, concentrated on the questions of authority and orthodoxy as these had been formulated at the First Vatican Council of 1869–70 and in various papal definitions.

→ *Ad tuendam fidem,* the motu proprio of Pope John Paul II issued in 1998, was seen as an effort to reinstate the doctrinal discipline represented by these earlier regulations.

Edition: Denzinger, 3537–50.

Translation: Based on DeFerrari [1957] 2002, 549–51.

Literature: *DTC* 10:2009–47 (J. Rivière); Heiner 1908; McCarthy 1998; Vidler 1976.

Pius X, *Sacrorum antistitum* (*Antimodernist Oath*), 1910

The Oath Against the Errors of Modernism

1. I . . . firmly embrace and accept all and everything that has been defined, affirmed, and declared by the unerring *magisterium* of the church, especially those chief doctrines which are directly opposed to the errors of this time.

2. And first, I profess that God, the beginning and end of all things, can be certainly known and thus can also be demonstrated by the natural light of reason [Rom 1.20] "by the things that are made," that is, by the visible works of creation, as the cause by the effects.

3. Secondly, I admit and recognize the external arguments of revelation, that is, divine facts, and especially miracles and prophecies, as very certain signs of the divine origin of the Christian religion; and I hold that these same arguments have been especially accommodated to the intelligence of all ages and men, even of these times.

4. Thirdly, likewise, with a firm faith I believe that the church, guardian and mistress of the revealed word, was instituted proximately and directly by the true and historical Christ himself, while he sojourned among us, and that the same was built upon Peter, the chief of the apostolic hierarchy, and his successors until the end of time.

5. Fourthly, I accept sincerely the doctrine of faith transmitted from the apostles through the orthodox fathers, always in the same sense and interpretation, even to us; and so I reject the heretical invention of the evolution of dogmas, passing from one meaning to another, different from that which the church first had; and likewise I reject all error whereby a philosophic fiction is substituted for the divine deposit, given over to the spouse of Christ and to be guarded faithfully by her, or a creation of the human conscience formed gradually by the efforts of men and to be perfected by indefinite progress in the future.

6. Fifthly, I hold most certainly and profess sincerely that faith is not a blind religious feeling bursting forth from the recesses of the subconscious, unformed morally under the pressure of the heart and the impulse of the will, but the [Rom 10.17] true assent of the intellect to the truth received extrinsically "by hearing," whereby we believe that what has been said, attested, and revealed by the personal God, our Creator and Lord, to be true on account of the authority of God the highest truth.

7. I also subject myself with the reverence which is proper, and I adhere with my whole soul to all the condemnations, declarations, and prescriptions which are contained in the Encyclical letter, *Pascendi,* and in the Decree, *Lamentabili,* especially on that which is called the history of dogma.

8. In the same manner I disapprove the error of those who affirm that the faith proposed by the church can be in conflict with history, and that Catholic dogmas, in the sense in which they are now understood, cannot be reconciled with the more authentic origins of the Catholic religion.

9. I also condemn and reject the opinion of those who say that the more erudite Christian puts on a dual personality, one of the believer, the other of the historian, as if it were permitted the historian to hold what is in contradiction to the faith of the believer; or to establish premises from which it follows that dogmas are either false or doubtful, provided they are not directly denied.

10. I disapprove likewise that method of studying and interpreting Sacred Scripture, which disregards the tradition of the church, the analogy of faith, and the norms of the apostolic see, and adheres to the fictions of the rationalists, and no less freely than boldly adopts textual criticism as the only and supreme rule.

11. Besides I reject the opinion of those who hold that to present the historical and theological disciplines the teacher or the writer on these subjects must first divest himself of previously conceived opinion either on the supernatural origin of Catholic tradition, or on the aid promised by God for the perpetual preservation of every revealed truth; then that the writings of the individual fathers are to be interpreted only by the principles of science, setting aside all divine authority, and by that freedom of judgment with which any profane document is customarily investigated.

12. Finally, in short, I profess to be utterly free of the error according to which the modernists hold that there is nothing divine in the sacred tradition; or, what is far worse, admit this in the pantheistic sense, so that nothing remains but the bare and simple fact to be assimilated with the common facts of history, namely, of men by their industry, skill, and genius continuing through subsequent ages the school inaugurated by Christ and his disciples.

13. So I retain most firmly the faith of the fathers, and shall retain it until the final breath of life, regarding the certain gift of truth, which is, was, and will be always in the succession of the episcopacy from the apostles, not so that what may seem better and more fitting according to each one's period of culture may be held, but so that the absolute and immutable truth preached by the apostles from the beginning may never be believed otherwise, may never be understood otherwise.

14. All things I promise that I shall faithfully, completely, and sincerely keep and inviolably watch, never deviating from them in word and writing either while teaching or in any other pursuit. So I promise, so I swear, so may God, etc.

The Polish National Catholic Church,
Confession of Faith, 1912/1914

Caught between Orthodox Russia and the Protestant lands of Germany, and therefore repeatedly subjected to partitions from one or the other side or from both, Poland has for centuries found in the See of Rome an anchor, and in its Roman Catholicism the guarantee of its national and cultural identity.

But the *Los-von-Rom-Bewegung* of the late nineteenth century and the rise of the Old Catholic Church in the aftermath of the First Vatican Council (which expressed itself confessionally in → *The Fourteen Theses of the First Reunion Conference at Bonn* of 1874, and in → *The Declaration of Utrecht* of 1889), had an effect even in Roman Catholic Poland, as well as in the Polish émigré communities of North America. This led to the founding of the Polish National Catholic Church. The scholarly literature about it, both in Poland and in the United States, has rightly emphasized the social and political factors in its history.[1] But as this *Confession of Faith* makes clear, doctrinal concerns have always been prominent in its life and witness. The *Confession* was ratified by the Third General Synod, which met in 1914.

Accompanying the text of *The Confession of Faith* is the official explanation: "The doctrinal symbols of the Polish National Catholic Church are the Apostles and Nicene Creeds. As a member of the Old Catholic Union of Utrecht, we have also endorsed the Declaration of Utrecht."

Edition and translation: *The Confession of Faith and the Eleven Great Principles of the Polish National Catholic Church* 1975, 1–7.

Literature: Andrews 1953; Kubiak 1982; Wozniak 1997.

1. Kubiak 1982; Wozniak 1997.

The Polish National Catholic Church, *Confession of Faith*, 1912/1914

1. I believe in Almighty God, the cause of all existence, in a Being who permeates the universe and is the source of its life and development, both material (physical) as well as spiritual and moral. In relation to man, God reveals himself through his creative power, his inexpressible wisdom, his provident influence on the formation of the destiny of individual man, nations, states, and all of humanity. In a more particular way, God as the Spirit of life, light, and goodness, influences chosen spirits of nations, who in a given epoch of human development, are the creative agent in the building of God's kingdom on earth. This direct influence of God—is not limited to one nation, to one epoch, but is directed to all nations and times—for the purpose of stimulating life, progress, and the attainment of the highest degree of culture by individual nations, states, and all mankind; it is the outpouring of divine forces acting upon humanity and the benefiting from these forces by individuals, nations, states, and all mankind.

2. I believe in Jesus Christ, the Savior and spiritual Regenerator of the world.

3. I believe that Christ the Lord, was the Emissary of God, of one substance with him, and as to humanity born of the humble woman Mary. I believe that this Nazarene Master revealed his divine mission on earth through his life, an unsurpassed ideal of goodness, wisdom, and self-sacrifice for others, especially for sinful and disinherited people; that by his work, teaching, and sacrificial death, he became the glowing ember of a new life of mankind, taking its beginning and deriving its strength and fullness in knowing God, loving him, and fulfilling his holy will.

4. I believe that the Holy Spirit, the Spirit of God, rules the world in the natural as well as in the moral order; that all the laws of the universe, as well as those by which the soul of individual man and humanity as a whole are guided, are an emanation of the will, goodness, and righteousness of the Divine Being.

5. I believe that from the Holy Spirit flows grace, that is an invisible power which brings it to pass that, when a man cooperates and works in harmony with it, he becomes better, more perfect, better fitted for his tasks, a participant in the peace of heart and soul, until one day, through union with God in eternity, he finds infinite bliss and the fulfillment of his own being.

6. I believe in the need of uniting all followers of Christ's religion into the one body of God's church, and that the church of Christ, apostolic and univer-

sal, is the representation of this divine community of mankind, which the Savior proclaimed, for the realization of which all noble-minded people labored, are still laboring and for which the soul of man yearns, desiring truth, light, love, justice, and consolation in God.

7. I believe that the church of Christ is the true teacher of both individual man as well as of all human society, that it is a steward of divine graces, a guide and a light in man's temporal pilgrimage to God and salvation; in so far as the followers and members of this church, both lay and clerical, are united with the divine Founder through faith and life proceeding from this faith.

8. I believe that every true Christian should take an active and vital part in the spiritual life of the church; through the hearing of the word of God, through the receiving of the holy sacraments, through fulfilling the laws and regulations established by Christ and his apostles, as defined and given us by the church.

9. I believe that all people as children of one Father, God, are equal in themselves; that privileges arising from differences in rank, from possession of immense riches or from differences of faith, sex, and race, are a great wrong, for they are a violation of the rights of man which he possesses by his nature and the dignity of his divine origin, and are a barrier to the purposeful development of man.

10. I believe that all people have an equal right to life, happiness, and those ways and means which lead to the preservation of existence, to advancement and salvation, but I also believe, that all people have sacred obligations toward God, themselves, their nation, state, and all of human society.

11. I believe in the ultimate justice of God, in a future life beyond the grave, which will be a continuation of this temporal life and which, as to its condition and degree of perfection and happiness is dependent on our present life, but above all on the state of our soul in the final hour before death.

12. I believe in immortality and everlasting happiness in eternity, in the union with God of all people, races, and ages, because I believe in the divine power of love, mercy, and justice and for nothing else do I yearn, but that it may be to me according to my faith.

The Assemblies of God, *A Statement of Fundamental Truths*, 1916

The Assemblies of God came into being as a distinct church in the context of the international Pentecostal movement, which flourished especially in the United States. Because of its emphasis on the extraordinary operations of the Holy Spirit (including "the baptism of the Holy Spirit" and the gift of healing) in the individual heart and in the congregation, Pentecostalism laid little or no emphasis on the traditional creeds and confessions of faith, and did not resort to creed-making as a way of affirming its identity. But the creedal and confessional imperative asserted itself nevertheless in this *Statement of Fundamental Truths*, which was approved by the General Council of the Assemblies of God, meeting in Saint Louis, on 2–7 October 1916. As the preamble makes clear, "this Statement of Fundamental Truths is not intended as a creed for the church, nor as a basis of fellowship among Christians, but only as a basis of unity for the ministry alone."

Edition: *Minutes of the General Council of the Assemblies of God in the United States of America, Canada, and Foreign Lands* 1916, 10–13.

Literature: Blumhofer 1993; Burgess and McGee 1988; Lippy and Williams 1988, 2:933–45; Menzies 1971.

The Assemblies of God, *A Statement of Fundamental Truths,* 1916

This Statement of Fundamental Truths is not intended as a creed for the church, nor as a basis of fellowship among Christians, but only as a basis of unity for the ministry alone (i.e., that we all speak the same thing, 1 Cor 1.10; Acts 2.42). The human phraseology employed in such statement is not inspired nor contended for, but the truth set forth in such phraseology is held to be essential to a full gospel ministry. No claim is made that it contains all truth in the Bible, only that it covers our present needs as to these fundamental matters.

1. THE SCRIPTURES INSPIRED

The Bible is the inspired word of God, a revelation from God to man, the infallible rule of faith and conduct, and is superior to conscience and reason, but not contrary to reason. 2 Tm 3.15, 16; 1 Pt 2.2.

2. THE ONE TRUE GOD

The one true God has revealed himself as the eternally self-existent, self-revealed "I AM"; and has further revealed himself as embodying the principles of relationship and association, i.e., as Father, Son, and Holy Ghost. Dt 6.4; Mk 12.29; Is 43.10, 11; Mt 28.19.

3. MAN, HIS FALL AND REDEMPTION

Man was created good and upright; for God said, "Let us make man in our image and in our likeness." But man, by voluntary transgression, fell, and his only hope of redemption is in Jesus Christ the Son of God. Gn 1.26–31, 3.1–7; Rom 5.12–21.

4. THE SALVATION OF MAN

(a) *Conditions to salvation.* The grace of God that brings salvation to all men has appeared through the preaching of repentance toward God and faith toward the Lord Jesus Christ; whereupon man is saved by the washing of regeneration and renewing of the Holy Ghost which is shed upon him richly through Jesus Christ our Savior; and, having been justified by grace through faith, he becomes an heir of God according to the hope of eternal life. Ti 2.11; Rom 10.13–15; Lk 24.47; Ti 3.5–7.

(b) *The evidences of salvation.* The *inward* evidence to the believer of his salvation, is the direct witness of the Spirit. Rom 8.16. The *outward* evidence to all men is a life of righteousness and true holiness, Lk 1.73–75; Ti 2.12–14; the fruit of the Spirit, Gal 5.22, and brotherly love, Jn 13.35; Heb 13.1; 1 Jn 3.14.

5. THE PROMISE OF THE FATHER

All believers are entitled to, and should ardently expect, and earnestly seek the promise of the Father, the baptism in the Holy Ghost and fire, according to the command of our Lord Jesus Christ. This was the normal experience of all in the early Christian church. With it comes the enduement of power for life and service, the bestowment of the gifts and their uses in the work of the ministry. Lk 24.49; Acts 1.4, 1.8; 1 Cor 12.1–31.

6. THE FULL CONSUMMATION OF THE BAPTISM IN THE HOLY GHOST

The full consummation of the baptism of believers in the Holy Ghost and fire is indicated by the initial sign of speaking in tongues, as the Spirit of God gives utterance. Acts 2.4. This wonderful experience is distinct from and subsequent to the experience of the new birth. Acts 10.44–46, 11.14–16, 15.8, 9.

7. ENTIRE SANCTIFICATION, THE GOAL FOR ALL BELIEVERS

The Scriptures teach a life of holiness without which no man shall see the Lord. By the power of the Holy Ghost we are able to obey the command, "be ye holy for I am holy." Entire sanctification is the will of God for all believers, and should be earnestly pursued by walking in obedience to God's word. Heb 12.14; 1 Pt 1.15, 16; 1 Thes 5.23, 24; 1 Jn 2.6.

8. THE CHURCH A LIVING ORGANISM

The church is a living organism; a living body; yea the body of Christ; a habitation of God through the Spirit, with divine appointments for the fulfillment of her great commission. Every local assembly is an integral part of the general assembly and church of the Firstborn, written in heaven. Eph 1.22, 23, 2.22; Heb 12.23.

9. THE MINISTRY AND EVANGELISM

A divinely called and a scripturally ordained ministry for the evangelization of the world, is the command of the Lord, and the chief concern of the church. Mk 16.15–20; Eph 4.11–13.

10. THE LORD'S SUPPER

The Lord's supper, consisting of the elements, bread and the fruit of the vine, is the symbol expressing our sharing the divine nature of our Lord Jesus Christ, 2 Pt 1.4; a memorial of his suffering and death, 1 Cor 11.26; and a prophecy of his second coming, 1 Cor 11.26; and is enjoined on all believers "until he comes."

11. BAPTISM IN WATER

The ordinance of baptism by a burial with Christ should be observed as commanded in the Scriptures, by all who have really repented and in their hearts have truly believed on Christ as Savior and Lord. In so doing, they have the body washed in pure water as an outward symbol of cleansing while their heart has already been sprinkled with the blood of Christ as an inner cleansing. Thus they declare to the world that they have died with Jesus and that they have also been raised with him to walk in newness of life. Mt 28.19; Acts 10.47–48; Rom 6.4; Acts 20.21; Heb 10.22.

12. DIVINE HEALING

Deliverance from sickness is provided for in the atonement, and is the privilege of all believers. Is 53.4, 5; Mt 8.16, 17.

13. THE ESSENTIALS AS TO THE GODHEAD

(a) *Terms explained.* The terms "Trinity" and "persons," as related to the Godhead, while not found in the Scriptures, yet are words in harmony with Scripture, whereby we may convey to others our immediate understanding of the doctrine of Christ respecting the Being of God, as distinguished from "gods many and lords many." We, therefore, may speak with propriety of the Lord our God, who is one Lord, as a Trinity or as one Being of three persons, and still be absolutely scriptural. (Examples: Mt 2.6, 8.16, 17; Acts 15. 15–18.)

(b) *Distinction and relationship in the Godhead.* Christ taught a distinction of persons in the Godhead which he expressed in specific terms of relationship, as Father, Son, and Holy Ghost; and that this distinction and relationship, as to its existence, is an eternal fact, but as to its mode it is *inscrutable* and *incomprehensible*, because *unexplained.* (That is, it is not explained as to how there can be three persons in the Godhead.) (Lk 1.35; 1 Cor 1.24; Mt 11.25–27, 28.19; 2 Cor 13.14; 1 Jn 1.3, 4.)

(c) *Unity of the one being of Father, Son, and Holy Ghost.* Accordingly, therefore, there is *that* in the Father which constitutes him *the Father* and not the Son; there is *that* in the Son which constitutes him *the Son* and not the Father; and there is *that* in the Holy Ghost which constitutes him *the Holy Ghost* and not either the

Father or the Son. Wherefore, the Father is the Begetter; the Son is the Begotten; and the Holy Ghost is the one proceeding from the Father and the Son. Therefore, because these three eternally *distinct* and *related* persons in the Godhead are in a state of *unity*, there is but one Lord God Almighty and his name one. Jn 1.18, 15.26, 17.11, 21; Zec 14.9.

(*d*) *Identity and cooperation in the Godhead.* The Father, the Son, and the Holy Ghost are never *identical* as to *person;* nor *confused* as to *relation;* nor *divided* in respect of the Godhead; nor *opposed* as to *cooperation.* The Son is *in* the Father and the Father is *in* the Son as to relationship. The Son is *with* the Father and the Father is *with* the Son as to fellowship. The Father is not *from* the Son, but the Son is *from* the Father, as to authority. The Holy Ghost is *from* the Father and the Son proceeding, as to nature, relationship, cooperation, and authority. Hence, neither person in the Godhead either exists or works separately or independently of the others. Jn 5.17–30.

(*e*) *The title, Lord Jesus Christ.* The appellation "Lord Jesus Christ" is a proper name. It is never applied, in the New Testament, either to the Father or to the Holy Ghost. It therefore belongs exclusively to the *Son of God.* Rom 1.1–3, 7; 2 Jn 3.

(*f*) *The Lord Jesus Christ, God with us.* The Lord Jesus Christ, as to his divine and eternal nature, is the proper and only Begotten of the Father; but, as to his human nature, he is the proper Son of man. He is, therefore, acknowledged to be both God and man; who, because he is God and man, is "Immanuel," God with us. Mt 1.23; 1 Jn 4.2, 10, 14; Rv 1.13, 14–17.

(*g*) *The title, Son of God.* Since the name "Immanuel" embraces both God and man in the one person, our Lord Jesus Christ, it follows that the title, Son of God, describes his proper deity, and the title, Son of man, his proper humanity. Therefore, the title, Son of God, belongs to the *order of eternity,* and the title, Son of man, to the *order of time.* Mt 1.23, 21; 2 Jn 3; 1 Jn 3.8; Heb 7.3, 1.1–13.

(*h*) *Transgression of the doctrine of Christ.* Wherefore, it is a transgression of the doctrine of Christ to say that Jesus Christ derived the title, Son of God, either from the fact of the incarnation, or because of his relation to the economy of redemption. Therefore, to deny that the Father is a real and eternal Father, and that the Son is a real and eternal Son, is a denial of the distinction and relationship in the being of God; a denial of the Father and the Son; and a *displacement* of the truth that Jesus Christ is come in flesh. 2 Jn 9; Jn 1.1, 2, 14, 18, 29, 49, 8.57, 58; 1 Jn 2.22, 23, 4.1–5; Heb 12.3, 4.

(*i*) *Exaltation of Jesus Christ as Lord.* The Son of God, our Lord Jesus Christ, having by himself purged our sins, sat down on the right hand of the Majesty on high; angels and principalities and powers having been made subject unto him. And, having been made both Lord and Christ, he sent the Holy Ghost that we, in the name of Jesus, might bow our knees and confess that Jesus Christ is Lord to the glory of God the Father until the end, when the Son shall become subject to the Father that God may be all in all. Heb 1.3; 1 Pt 3.22; Acts 2.32–36; Rom 14.11; 1 Cor 15.24–28.

(*j*) *Equal honor to the Father and the Son.* Wherefore, since the Father has delivered all judgment unto the Son, it is not only the *express duty* of all things in heaven and in earth to bow the knee, but it is an *unspeakable* joy in the Holy Ghost to ascribe unto the Son all the attributes of Deity, and to give him all the honor and the glory contained in all the names and titles of the Godhead (except those which express relationship; see paragraphs *b, c,* and *d*), and thus honor the Son even as we honor the Father. Jn 5.22, 23; 1 Pt 1.8; Rv 5.6–14; Phil 2.9, 8; Rv 7.9, 10, 4.8–11.

14. THE BLESSED HOPE

The resurrection of those who have fallen asleep in Christ, the rapture of believers which are alive and remain, and the translation of the true church, this is the blessed hope set before all believers. 1 Thes 4.16, 17; Rom 8.23; Ti 2.13.

15. THE IMMINENT COMING AND MILLENNIAL REIGN OF JESUS

The premillennial and imminent coming of the Lord to gather his people unto himself, and to judge the world in righteousness while reigning on the earth for a thousand years is the expectation of the true church of Christ.

16. THE LAKE OF FIRE

The devil and his angels, the beast and false prophet, and whosoever is not found written in the Book of Life, the fearful and unbelieving, and abominable, and murderers and whoremongers, and sorcerers, and idolaters and all liars shall be consigned to everlasting punishment in the lake which burneth with fire and brimstone, which is the second death. [Rv 20.14]

17. THE NEW HEAVENS AND NEW EARTH

We look for new heavens and a new earth wherein dwelleth righteousness. 2 Pt 3.13; Rv 21 and 22.

Jehovah's Witnesses (International Bible Students), *Statement of Faith*, 1918

Under various denominational labels, including "Russellites" for its founder, C. T. Russell (1852–1916), and "International Bible Students," his preferred label, the group usually identified as "Jehovah's Witnesses" shared some of the outlook of the → Adventists, but its eventual system of doctrines diverged more radically from historic Christian teaching. They have received the greatest amount of public (and governmental) attention for their refusal to salute the flag and give other evidences of allegiance to the state. In the first issue of their *Herald of Christ's Kingdom*, dated 1 December 1918, they published this *Statement of Faith*, which has continued to appear in the literature of "the Watch Tower Bible and Tract Society," including the *Watchtower*.

Edition: *Herald of Christ's Kingdom*, 1 December 1918.

Literature: Bergman 1984; Bowman 1991; *ODCC* 865.

Jehovah's Witnesses (International Bible Students), *Statement of Faith*, 1918

To us the Scriptures clearly teach

1. That the church is "the temple of the living God"—peculiarly "his workmanship"; that its construction has been in progress throughout the gospel age—ever since Christ became the world's Redeemer and the chief cornerstone of his temple, through which, when finished, God's blessing shall come "to all people," and they find access to him. 1 Cor 3.16, 17; Eph 2.20–22; Gn 28.14; Gal 3.29.

2. That meantime the chiseling, shaping, and polishing of consecrated believers in Christ's atonement for sin, progresses; and when the last of these "living stones," "elect and precious," shall have been made ready, the great Master Workman will bring all together in the first resurrection; and the temple shall be filled with his glory, and be the meeting place between God and men throughout the millennium. Rv 15.5–8.

3. That the basis of hope, for the church and the world, lies in the fact that "Jesus Christ, by the grace of God, tasted death for every man," "a ransom for all," and will be "the true light which lighteth every man that cometh into the world," "in due time." Heb 2.9; Jn 1.9; 2 Tm 2.5, 6.

4. That the hope of the church is that she may be like her Lord, "see him as he is," be "partaker of the divine nature," and share his glory as his joint heir. 1 Jn 3.2; Jn 17.24; Rom 8.17; 2 Pt 1.4.

5. That the present mission of the church is the perfecting of the saints for the future work of service; to develop in herself every grace; to be God's witness to the world; and to prepare to be kings and priests in the next age. Eph 4.12; Mt 24.14; Rv 1.6, 20.6.

6. That the hope for the world lies in the blessings of knowledge and opportunity to be brought to all by Christ's millennial kingdom—the restitution of all that was lost in Adam, to all the willing and obedient, at the hands of their Redeemer and his glorified church—when all the willfully wicked will be destroyed. Acts 3.19–23; Is 35.

7. We affirm the pre-existence of Jesus as the mighty Word (Logos-spokesman), "the beginning of the creation of God," "the Firstborn of every creature," the active agent of the heavenly Father, Jehovah, in all the work of creation. "Without him was not anything made that was made." Rv 3.14; Col 1.15; Jn 1.3.

8. We affirm that the Word (Logos) was made flesh—became the babe of

433

Bethlehem—thus becoming the man Jesus, "holy, harmless, undefiled, separate from sinners." As we affirm the humanity of Jesus, we equally affirm the divinity of Christ —"God also hath highly exalted him, and given him a name which is above every name." Heb 7.26; Phil 2.9.

9. We acknowledge that the personality of the Holy Spirit is the Father and the Son; that the Holy Spirit proceeds from both, and is manifested in all who receive the begetting of the Holy Spirit and thereby become sons of God. Jn 1.13; 1 Pt 1.3.

10. We affirm the resurrection of Christ—that he was put to death in flesh, but quickened in Spirit. We deny that he was raised in the flesh, and challenge any statement to that effect as being unscriptural. 1 Pt 3.18; 2 Cor 3.17; 1 Cor 15.8; Acts 26.13–15.

The African Orthodox Church, *Doctrine*, 1921

The African Orthodox Church was organized on 2 September 1921, laying claim to "apostolic succession from Antioch, the first see of St. Peter, Apostle." In its constitution it affirmed itself open to "persons of all races," but stipulated that "it seeks particularly to reach out and enfold the millions of African descent in both hemispheres." To that end "the A. O. C. declares itself to be and is perpetually autonomous, autocephalous and controlled by Negroes . . . independent of every other Orthodox Eastern Church or Jurisdiction." It embraces an American Province and an African Province. This declaration of faith was adopted as being "in conformity with the Orthodox Churches of the East from which its Episcopate is derived."

Edition: Terry-Thompson 1956, 44.

Literature: M. R. Johnson 1999; Terry-Thompson 1956.

435

The African Orthodox Church, *Doctrine,* 1921

1. The doctrine of the African Orthodox Church, in common with all Orthodox, Eastern churches, accepts the Holy Scriptures as the word of God, the holy traditions and the dogmatic decisions of the seven ecumenical councils, the Holy Scriptures being interpreted in accordance with the teachings of the apostles, the holy fathers, and the decisions of the ecumenical councils.

2. We accept further, the Niceno-Constantinopolitan Creed, without the "Filioque" as our authoritative and binding symbol of faith. We also believe the other two symbols known as the Apostles' Creed and the Creed of St. Athanasius.

3. We believe, acknowledge, and recognize our Blessed Lord Jesus Christ at the sole head of the Christian and catholic church.

4. We believe in the infallibility of the ecclesia.

5. We believe that the third person of the Blessed Trinity, the Holy Spirit, proceeds from the Father alone.

6. We honor the Blessed Virgin Mary as "Theotokos" (Mother of God). Believe in the three hierarchies and nine choirs of angels and all the holy saints of God.

7. We reverence the relics of the holy saints of God, the icons or pictures of holy subjects.

8. We believe and accept seven sacraments, namely—baptism, confirmation, holy eucharist, holy orders, holy matrimony, penance, and holy unction.

9. We hold the true doctrine of transubstantiation to be the real presence.

10. We hold that belief in the "communion of saints" requires us to pray for the dead as well as for the living.

11. We reject the false doctrine of predestination and believe that for justification both faith and works are necessary.

12. The central act of worship is the celebration of the divine liturgy and it is obligatory.

13. We believe in both a particular and a general judgment.

Southern Baptist Convention, *Baptist Faith and Message*, 1925

As Baptist writers themselves have frequently observed, it is a remarkable historical paradox that an avowedly nonconfessional group like the Baptists should in fact have composed so many confessions. These included → *The [First] London Confession* of 1644, → *The Faith and Practice of Thirty Congregations Gathered According to the Primitive Pattern* of 1651, → *The Philadelphia Confession* of 1742, and → *The New Hampshire Confession* of 1833, together with many other statements of faith.

In 1858 the Southern Baptists in the United States had issued their → *Abstract of Principles for Southern Baptist Seminary,* which dealt, strictly speaking, only with the doctrinal responsibility of seminary professors but which spoke for the stance of the denomination as a whole. But the issues of biblical inspiration, inerrancy, and authority became increasingly urgent, also because of public controversy over the teaching of evolution in the public schools as it would be dramatized in the Scopes Trial of 1925. During the early 1920s, therefore, the agitation for a new statement of faith finally led to the composition and adoption of *Baptist Faith and Message* in 1925, which was based on *The New Hampshire Confession.* As the report of the Committee on Baptist Faith and Message explained, "The present occasion for a reaffirmation of Christian fundamentals is the prevalence of naturalism in the modern teaching and preaching of religion. . . . We repudiate every theory of religion which denies the supernatural elements in our faith."

The five prefatory explanations of Baptist attitudes toward confessions are included.

In 1963 the Southern Baptist Convention issued a revised form of the 1925 document; but, it explained, "in no case has it sought to delete from or to add to the basic contents of the 1925 Statement."

Edition: Lumpkin 1959, 392–98.

Literature: Hobbs 1979; Lumpkin 1959, 390–92.

Southern Baptist Convention, *Baptist Faith and Message*, 1925

Baptists approve and circulate confessions of faith with the following understanding, namely:

(1) That they constitute a consensus of opinion of some Baptist body, large or small, for the general instruction and guidance of our own people and others concerning those articles of the Christian faith which are most surely held among us. They are not intended to add anything to the simple conditions of salvation revealed in the New Testament, namely, repentance towards God and faith in Jesus Christ as Savior and Lord.

(2) That we do not regard them as complete statements of our faith, having any quality of finality or infallibility. As in the past so in the future Baptists should hold themselves free to revise their statements of faith as may seem to them wise and expedient at any time.

(3) That any group of Baptists, large or small, have the inherent right to draw up for themselves and publish to the world a confession of their faith whenever they may think it advisable to do so.

(4) That the sole authority for faith and practice among Baptists is the Scriptures of the Old and New Testaments. Confessions are only guides in interpretation, having no authority over the conscience.

(5) That they are statements of religious convictions, drawn from the Scriptures, and are not to be used to hamper freedom of thought or investigation in other realms of life.

THE SCRIPTURES

1. We believe that the Holy Bible was written by men divinely inspired and is a perfect treasure of heavenly instruction; that it has God for its author, salvation for its end, and truth, without any mixture of error, for its matter; that it reveals the principles by which God will judge us; and therefore is, and will remain to the end of the world, the true center of Christian union, and the supreme standard by which all human conduct, creeds, and religious opinions should be tried.

GOD

2. There is one and only one living and true God, an intelligent, spiritual, and personal Being, the Creator, Preserver, and Ruler of the universe, infinite in holiness

and all other perfections, to whom we owe the highest love, reverence, and obedience. He is revealed to us as Father, Son, and Holy Spirit, each with distinct personal attributes, but without division of nature, essence, or being.

THE FALL OF MAN

3. Man was created by the special act of God, as recorded in Genesis. Gn 1.27; Gn 2.7. He was created in a state of holiness under the law of his Maker, but, through the temptation of Satan he transgressed the command of God and fell from his original holiness and righteousness; whereby his posterity inherit a nature corrupt and in bondage to sin, are under condemnation, and as soon as they are capable of moral action, become actual transgressors.

THE WAY OF SALVATION

4. The salvation of sinners is wholly of grace, through the mediatorial office of the Son of God, who by the Holy Spirit was born of the Virgin Mary and took upon him our nature, yet without sin; honored the divine law by his personal obedience, and made atonement for our sins by his death. Being risen from the dead, he is now enthroned in heaven, and, uniting in his person the tenderest sympathies with divine perfections, he is in every way qualified to be a compassionate and all-sufficient Savior.

JUSTIFICATION

5. Justification is God's gracious and full acquittal upon principles of righteousness of all sinners who believe in Christ. This blessing is bestowed, not in consideration of any works of righteousness which we have done, but through the redemption which is in and through Jesus Christ. It brings us into a state of most blessed peace and favor with God, and secures every other needed blessing.

THE FREENESS OF SALVATION

6. The blessings of salvation are made free to all by the gospel. It is the duty of all to accept them by penitent and obedient faith. Nothing prevents the salvation of the greatest sinner except his own voluntary refusal to accept Jesus Christ as teacher, Savior, and Lord.

REGENERATION

7. Regeneration or the new birth is a change of heart wrought by the Holy Spirit, whereby we become partakers of the divine nature and a holy disposition is given, leading to the love and practice of righteousness. It is a work of God's free grace

conditioned upon faith in Christ and made manifest by the fruit which we bring forth to the glory of God.

REPENTANCE AND FAITH

8. We believe that repentance and faith are sacred duties, and also inseparable graces, wrought in our souls by the regenerating Spirit of God; whereby being deeply convinced of our guilt, danger, and helplessness, and of the way of salvation by Christ, we turn to God with unfeigned contrition, confession, and supplication for mercy; at the same time heartily receiving the Lord Jesus Christ as our Prophet, Priest, and King and relying on him alone as the only and all-sufficient Savior.

GOD'S PURPOSE OF GRACE

9. Election is the gracious purpose of God, according to which he regenerates, sanctifies, and saves sinners. It is perfectly consistent with the free agency of man, and comprehends all the means in connection with the end. It is a most gracious display of God's sovereign goodness, and is infinitely wise, holy, and unchangeable. It excludes boasting and promotes humility. It encourages the use of means in the highest degree.

SANCTIFICATION

10. Sanctification is the process by which the regenerate gradually attain to moral and spiritual perfection through the presence and power of the Holy Spirit dwelling in their hearts. It continues throughout the earthly life, and is accomplished by the use of all the ordinary means of grace, and particularly by the word of God.

PERSEVERANCE

11. All real believers endure to the end. Their continuance in well-doing is the mark which distinguishes them from mere professors. A special providence cares for them, and they are kept by the power of God by faith unto salvation.

A GOSPEL CHURCH

12. A church of Christ is a congregation of baptized believers, associated by covenant in the faith and fellowship of the gospel; observing the ordinances of Christ, governed by his law, and exercising the gifts, rights, and privileges invested in them by his word, and seeking to extend the gospel to the ends of the earth. Its scriptural officers are bishops or elders and deacons.

BAPTISM AND THE LORD'S SUPPER

13. Christian baptism is the immersion of a believer in water in the name of the Father, the Son and the Holy Spirit. The act is a symbol of our faith in a crucified, buried, and risen Savior. It is prerequisite to the privileges of a church relation and to the Lord's supper, in which the members of the church, by the use of bread and wine, commemorate the dying love of Christ.

THE LORD'S DAY

14. The first day of the week is the Lord's day. It is a Christian institution for regular observance. It commemorates the resurrection of Christ from the dead, and should be employed in exercises of worship and spiritual devotion, both public and private, and by refraining from worldly amusements, and resting from secular employments, works of necessity and mercy only excepted.

THE RIGHTEOUS AND THE WICKED

15. There is a radical and essential difference between the righteous and the wicked. Those only who are justified through the name of the Lord Jesus Christ and sanctified by the Holy Spirit are truly righteous in his sight. Those who continue in impenitence and unbelief are in his sight wicked and are under condemnation. This distinction between the wicked and the righteous holds in and after death, and will be made manifest at the judgment when final and everlasting awards are made to all men.

THE RESURRECTION

16. The Scriptures clearly teach that Jesus rose from the dead. His grave was emptied of its contents. He appeared to his disciples after his resurrection in many convincing manifestations. He now exists in his glorified body at God's right hand. There will be a resurrection of the righteous and the wicked. The bodies of the righteous will conform to the glorious spiritual body of Jesus.

THE RETURN OF THE LORD

17. The New Testament teaches in many places the visible and personal return of Jesus to this earth. "This same Jesus which is taken up from you into heaven, shall so come in like manner as ye have seen him go into heaven." The time of his coming [Acts 1.11] is not revealed (Mt 24.36). It is the duty of all believers to live in readiness for his coming and by diligence in good works to make manifest to all men the reality and power of their hope in Christ.

RELIGIOUS LIBERTY

18. God alone is Lord of the conscience, and he has left it free from the doctrines and commandments of men which are contrary to his word or not contained in it. Church and state should be separate. The state owes to the church protection and full freedom in the pursuit of its spiritual ends. In providing for such freedom no ecclesiastical group or denomination should be favored by the state more than others. Civil government being ordained of God, it is the duty of Christians to render loyal obedience thereto in all things not contrary to the revealed will of God. The church should not resort to the civil power to carry on its work. The gospel of Christ contemplates spiritual means alone for the pursuit of its ends. The state has no right to impose penalties for religious opinions of any kind. The state has no right to impose taxes for the support of any form of religion. A free church in a free state is the Christian ideal, and this implies the right of free and unhindered access to God on the part of all men, and the right to form and propagate opinions in the sphere of religion without interference by the civil power.

PEACE AND WAR

19. It is the duty of Christians to seek peace with all men on principles of righteousness. In accordance with the spirit and teachings of Christ they should do all in their power to put an end to war.

The true remedy for the war spirit is the pure gospel of our Lord. The supreme need of the world is the acceptance of his teachings in all the affairs of men and nations, and the practical application of his law of love.

We urge Christian people throughout the land to pray for the reign of the Prince of Peace, and to oppose everything likely to provoke war.

EDUCATION

20. Christianity is the religion of enlightenment and intelligence. In Jesus Christ [Col 2.3] are hidden all the treasures of wisdom and knowledge. All sound learning is therefore a part of our Christian heritage. The new birth opens all human faculties and creates a thirst for knowledge. An adequate system of schools is necessary to a complete spiritual program for Christ's people. The cause of education in the kingdom of Christ is coordinate with the causes of missions and general benevolence, and should receive along with these the liberal support of the churches.

SOCIAL SERVICE

21. Every Christian is under obligation to seek to make the will of Christ regnant in his own life and in human society; to oppose in the spirit of Christ every form

of greed, selfishness, and vice; to provide for the orphaned, the aged, the helpless, and the sick; to seek to bring industry, government, and society as a whole under the sway of the principles of righteousness, truth, and brotherly love; to provide these ends Christians should be ready to work with all men of goodwill in any good cause, always being careful to act in the spirit of love without compromising their loyalty to Christ and his truth. All means and methods used in social service for the amelioration of society and the establishment of righteousness among men must finally depend on the regeneration of the individual by the saving grace of God in Christ Jesus.

COOPERATION

22. Christ's people should, as occasion requires, organize such associations and conventions as may best secure cooperation for the great objects of the kingdom of God. Such organizations have no authority over each other or over the churches. They are voluntary and advisory bodies designed to elicit, combine, and direct the energies of our people in the most effective manner. Individual members of New Testament churches should cooperate with each other, and the churches themselves should cooperate with each other in carrying forward the missionary, educational, and benevolent program for the extension of Christ's kingdom. Christian unity in the New Testament sense is spiritual harmony and voluntary cooperation for common ends by various groups of Christ's people. It is permissible and desirable as between the various Christian denominations, when the end to be attained is self-justified, and when such cooperation involves no violation of conscience or compromise of loyalty to Christ and his word as revealed in the New Testament.

EVANGELISM AND MISSIONS

23. It is the duty of every Christian man and woman, and the duty of every church of Christ, to seek to extend the gospel to the ends of the earth. The new birth of man's spirit by God's Holy Spirit means the birth of love for others. Missionary effort upon the part of all rests thus upon a spiritual necessity of the regenerate life. It is also expressly and repeatedly commanded in the teachings of Christ. It is the duty of every child of God to seek constantly to win the lost to Christ by personal effort and by all other methods sanctioned by the gospel of Christ.

STEWARDSHIP

24. God is the source of all blessings, temporal and spiritual; all that we have and are we owe to him. We have a spiritual debtorship to the whole world, a holy trustee-ship in the gospel, and a binding stewardship in our possessions. We are therefore

under obligation to serve him with our time, talents, and material possessions; and should recognize all these as entrusted to us to use for the glory of God and helping others. Christians should cheerfully, regularly, systematically, proportionately, and liberally contribute of their means to advancing the Redeemer's cause on earth.

THE KINGDOM

25. The kingdom of God is the reign of God in the heart and life of the individual in every human relationship, and in every form and institution of organized society. The chief means for promoting the kingdom of God on earth are preaching the gospel of Christ, and teaching the principles of righteousness contained therein. The kingdom of God will be complete when every thought and will of man shall be brought into captivity to the will of Christ. And it is the duty of all Christ's people to pray and labor continually that his kingdom may come and his will be done on earth as it is in heaven.

The United Church of Canada, *The Basis of Union*, 1925

On 10 June 1925, The Congregational Churches of Canada, The Methodist Church, The Presbyterian Church in Canada, and the Local Union Churches in Western Canada came together to form a new church body, called "The United Church of Canada" and committed to "the hope that this settlement of unity may in due time, so far as Canada is concerned, take shape in a church which may fittingly be described as national." Absent from the United Church, in addition of course to the Roman Catholic, Orthodox, and other churches that had no part in the negotiations (and some parts of the Presbyterian Church), was the Anglican Church of Canada, which had participated but was finally unable to join on the prescribed terms. For an understanding of the the the role of confessions in fostering or inhibiting ecumenism, therefore, the Canadian experiment and the → South Indian experiment should be studied together.

Edition: *The United Church of Canada Year Book* 1928, 483–87.

Literature: Kilpatrick 1928; Lane 1974.

The United Church of Canada, *The Basis of Union*, 1925

General

1. The name of the church formed by the union of the Presbyterian, Methodist, and Congregational churches in Canada, shall be "The United Church of Canada."

2. It shall be the policy of the United Church to foster the spirit of unity in the hope that this settlement of unity may in due time, so far as Canada is concerned, take shape in a church which may fittingly be described as national.

Doctrine

We, the representatives of the Presbyterian, the Methodist, and the Congregational branches of the church of Christ in Canada, do hereby set forth the substance of the Christian faith, as commonly held among us. In doing so, we build upon the foundation laid by the apostles and prophets, Jesus Christ himself being the chief [Eph 2.20] cornerstone. We affirm our belief in the Scriptures of the Old and New Testaments as the primary source and ultimate standard of Christian faith and life. We acknowledge the teaching of the great creeds of the ancient church. We further maintain our allegiance to the evangelical doctrines of the Reformation, as set forth in common in the doctrinal standards adopted by the Presbyterian Church in Canada, by the Congregational Union of Ontario and Quebec, and by the Methodist Church. We present the accompanying statement as a brief summary of our common faith and commend it to the studious attention of the members and adherents of the negotiating churches, as in substance agreeable to the teaching of the Holy Scriptures.

ARTICLE 1. OF GOD

We believe in the one only living and true God, a Spirit, infinite, eternal, and unchangeable, in his being and perfections; the Lord Almighty, who is love, most just in all his ways, most glorious in holiness, unsearchable in wisdom, plenteous in mercy, full of compassion, and abundant in goodness and truth. We worship him in the unity of the Godhead and the mystery of the Holy Trinity, the Father, the Son, and the Holy Spirit, three persons of the same substance, equal in power and glory.

ARTICLE 2. OF REVELATION

We believe that God has revealed himself in nature, in history, and in the heart of man; that he has been graciously pleased to make clearer revelation of himself to

men of God who spoke as they were moved by the Holy Spirit; and that in the full-   [2 Pt 1.21]
ness of time^a he has perfectly revealed himself in Jesus Christ, the Word made flesh,^b
who is the brightness of the Father's glory and the express image of his person. We   [Heb 1.2]
receive the Holy Scriptures of the Old and New Testaments, given by inspiration
of God, as containing the only infallible rule of faith and life, a faithful record of
God's gracious revelations, and as the sure witness to Christ.

ARTICLE 3. OF THE DIVINE PURPOSE

We believe that the eternal, wise, holy, and loving purpose of God so embraces all
events that while the freedom of man is not taken away, nor is God the author of
sin, yet in his providence he makes all things work together in the fulfillment of his
sovereign design and the manifestation of his glory.

ARTICLE 4. OF CREATION AND PROVIDENCE

We believe that God is the creator, upholder, and governor of all things; that he
is above all his works and in them all; and that he made man in his own image,
meet for fellowship with him, free and able to choose between good and evil, and
responsible to his Maker and Lord.

ARTICLE 5. OF THE SIN OF MAN

We believe that our first parents, being tempted, chose evil, and so fell away from
God and came under the power of sin, the penalty of which is eternal death; and
that, by reason of this disobedience, all men are born with a sinful nature, that we
have broken God's law, and that no man can be saved but by his grace.

ARTICLE 6. OF THE GRACE OF GOD

We believe that God, out of his great love for the world, has given his only-begotten
Son to be the Savior of sinners, and in the gospel freely offers his all-sufficient salvation to all men. We believe also that God, in his own good pleasure, gave to his
Son a people, an innumerable multitude, chosen in Christ unto holiness, service,
and salvation.

a. [Gal 4.4]
b. [Jn 1.14]

ARTICLE 7. OF THE LORD JESUS CHRIST

We believe in and confess the Lord Jesus Christ, the only Mediator between God and man, who, being the eternal Son of God, for us men and for our salvation[1] became truly man, being conceived of the Holy Spirit and born of the Virgin Mary, yet without sin. Unto us he has revealed the Father, by his word and Spirit, making known the perfect will of God. For our redemption he fulfilled all righteousness, offered himself a perfect sacrifice on the cross, satisfied divine justice, and made propitation for the sins of the whole world. He rose from the dead and ascended into heaven, where he ever intercedes for us. In the hearts of believers he abides forever as the indwelling Christ; above us and over us all he rules; wherefore, unto him we render love, obedience, and adoration as our Prophet, Priest, and King.

[Mt 3.15]

ARTICLE 8. OF THE HOLY SPIRIT

We believe in the Holy Spirit, the Lord and giver of life, who proceeds from the Father and the Son,[2] who moves upon the hearts of men to restrain them from evil and to incite them unto good, and whom the Father is ever willing to give unto all who ask him. We believe that he has spoken by holy men of God in making known his truth to men for their salvation; that, through our exalted Savior, he was sent forth in power to convict the world of sin, to enlighten men's minds in the knowledge of Christ, and to persuade and enable them to obey the call of the gospel; and that he abides with the church, dwelling in every believer as the spirit of truth, of power, of holiness, of comfort, and of love.

[Jn 16.8]

ARTICLE 9. OF REGENERATION

We believe in the necessity of regeneration, whereby we are made new creatures in Christ Jesus by the Spirit of God, who imparts spiritual life by the gracious and mysterious operation of his power, using as the ordinary means the truths of his word and the ordinances of divine appointment in ways agreeable to the nature of man.

ARTICLE 10. OF FAITH AND REPENTANCE

We believe that faith in Christ is a saving grace whereby we receive him, trust in him, and rest upon him alone for salvation as he is offered to us in the gospel, and that this saving faith is always accompanied by repentance, wherein we confess and forsake our sins with full purpose of and endeavor after a new obedience to God.

1. N-CP 3.
2. N-CP Occ 8.

ARTICLE 11. OF JUSTIFICATION AND SONSHIP

We believe that God, on the sole ground of the perfect obedience and sacrifice of Christ, pardons those who by faith receive him as their Savior and Lord, accepts them as righteous, and bestows upon them the adoption of sons, with a right to all the privileges therein implied, including a conscious assurance of their sonship.

ARTICLE 12. OF SANCTIFICATION

We believe that those who are regenerated and justified grow in the likeness of Christ through fellowship with him, the indwelling of the Holy Spirit, and obedience to the truth; that a holy life is the fruit and evidence of saving faith; and that the believer's hope of continuance in such a life is in the preserving grace of God. And we believe that in this growth in grace Christians may attain that maturity and full assurance of faith whereby the love of God is made perfect in us.

ARTICLE 13. OF PRAYER

We believe that we are encouraged to draw near to God, our heavenly Father, in the name of his Son, Jesus Christ, and on our own behalf and that of others to pour out our hearts humbly yet freely before him, as becomes his beloved children, giving him the honor and praise due his holy name, asking him to glorify himself on earth as in heaven, confessing unto him our sins, and seeking of him every gift needful for this life and for our everlasting salvation. We believe also that, inasmuch as all true prayer is prompted by his Spirit, he will in response thereto grant us every blessing according to his unsearchable wisdom and the riches of his grace in Jesus Christ.

ARTICLE 14. OF THE LAW OF GOD

We believe that the moral law of God, summarized in the Ten Commandments, testified to by the prophets and unfolded in the life and teachings of Jesus Christ, stands forever in truth and equity, and is not made void by faith, but on the contrary is established thereby. We believe that God requires of every man to do justly, to love mercy, and to walk humbly with God; and that only through this harmony with the [Mi 6.8] will of God shall be fulfilled that brotherhood of man wherein the kingdom of God is to be made manifest.

ARTICLE 15. OF THE CHURCH

We acknowledge one holy catholic church, the innumerable company of saints of every age and nation, who being united by the Holy Spirit to Christ their Head are one body in him and have communion with their Lord and with one another. Further, we receive it as the will of Christ that his church on earth should exist as a

visible and sacred brotherhood, consisting of those who profess faith in Jesus Christ
and obedience to him, together with their children, and other baptized children,
and organized for the confession of his name, for the public worship of God, for
the administration of the sacraments, for the upbuilding of the saints, and for the
universal propagation of the gospel; and we acknowledge as a part, more or less
pure, of this universal brotherhood, every particular church throughout the world
which professes this faith in Jesus Christ and obedience to him as divine Lord and
Savior.

ARTICLE 16. OF THE SACRAMENTS

We acknowledge two sacraments, baptism and the Lord's supper, which were instituted by Christ, to be of perpetual obligation as signs and seals of the covenant
ratified in his precious blood, as means of grace, by which, working in us, he doth
not only quicken, but also strengthen and comfort our faith in him, and as ordinances through the observance of which his church is to confess her Lord and be
visibly distinguished from the rest of the world.

[Mt 28.19]

1. Baptism with water into the name of the Father and of the Son and of the
Holy Spirit is the sacrament by which are signified and sealed our union to Christ
and participation in the blessings of the new covenant. The proper subjects of baptism are believers, and infants presented by their parents or guardians in the Christian faith. In the latter case the parents or guardians should train up their children

[Eph 6.4]

in the nurture and admonition of the Lord, and should expect that their children
will, by the operation of the Holy Spirit, receive the benefits which the sacrament
is designed and fitted to convey. The church is under the most solemn obligation to
provide for their Christian instruction.

2. The Lord's supper is the sacrament of communion with Christ and with
his people, in which bread and wine are given and received in thankful remembrance
of him and his sacrifice on the cross; and they who in faith receive the same do,
after a spiritual manner, partake of the body and blood of the Lord Jesus Christ to
their comfort, nourishment, and growth in grace. All may be admitted to the Lord's
supper who make a credible profession of their faith in the Lord Jesus Christ and
of obedience to his law.

ARTICLE 17. OF THE MINISTRY

We believe that Jesus Christ, as the supreme Head of the church, has appointed
therein a ministry of the word and sacraments, and calls men to this ministry; that
the church, under the guidance of the Holy Spirit, recognizes and chooses those
whom he calls, and should thereupon duly ordain them to the work of the ministry.

ARTICLE 18. OF CHURCH ORDER AND FELLOWSHIP

We believe that the supreme and only Head of the Church is the Lord Jesus Christ; that its worship, teaching, discipline, and government should be administered according to his will by persons chosen for their fitness and duly set apart to their office; and that although the visible church may contain unworthy members and is liable to err, yet believers ought not lightly to separate themselves from its communion, but are to live in fellowship with their brethren, which fellowship is to be extended, as God gives opportunity, to all who in every place call upon the name of the Lord Jesus.

ARTICLE 19. OF THE RESURRECTION, THE LAST JUDGMENT, AND THE FUTURE LIFE

We believe that there shall be a resurrection of the dead, both of the just and of the unjust, through the power of the Son of God, who shall come to judge the living and the dead; that the finally impenitent shall go away into eternal punishment and the righteous into life eternal.

ARTICLE 20. OF CHRISTIAN SERVICE AND THE FINAL TRIUMPH

We believe that it is our duty as disciples and servants of Christ, to further the extension of his kingdom, to do good unto all men, to maintain the public and private worship of God, to hallow the Lord's day, to preserve the inviolability of marriage and the sanctity of the family, to uphold the just authority of the state, and so to live in all honesty, purity, and charity that our lives shall testify of Christ. We joyfully receive the word of Christ, bidding his people go into all the world and make disciples of all nations,[a] declaring unto them that God was in Christ reconciling the world unto himself, and that he will have all men to be saved, and come to the knowledge [2 Cor 5.19] of the truth. We confidently believe that by his power and grace all his enemies shall [1 Tm 2.4] finally be overcome, and the kingdoms of this world be made the kingdom of our [1 Cor 15.25] God and of his Christ. [Rv 11.15]

Polity

The Joint Committee, after an examination of the forms of church government of the negotiating churches and the practical working thereof, is greatly gratified to find:

---

a. [Mk 16.15; Mt 28.19]

1. That while the officers and courts of the negotiating churches may bear different names, there is a substantial degree of similarity in the duties and functions of these officers and courts.

2. That, engaged in the same work, with the same object in view, and earnestly endeavoring to meet the conditions confronting the churches in Canada, the negotiating churches have been steadily approximating more nearly to each other, both in forms of church government and methods of administration.

3. That there are distinctive elements in each which would add to the efficiency of a united church, and which can be preserved with great advantage in the form of polity to be adopted for the United Church.

4. That in this view it is possible to provide for substantial local freedom, and at the same time secure the benefits of a strong connectional tie and cooperative efficiency.

The United Presbyterian Church of North America,
The Confessional Statement, 1925

The nineteenth-century controversies and schisms over revivalism, over slavery, and even over biblical criticism having largely been resolved, American Presbyterianism in the twentieth century moved toward reconciliation, reunion, and confessional restatement.

The initial outcome of that process was the *Testimony* of 1858, and its eventual outcome was to be the → *Confession* of 1967. But the most important landmark after the nineteenth-century affirmations such as → *The Confession of Faith* of the Cumberland Presbyterian Church in the United States of 1814/1883 was *The Confessional Statement of the United Presbyterian Church of North America* of 1925.

As the preface to the 1956 official edition explains, "The General Assembly of 1919 appointed a Committee on Revision of Doctrinal Standards. In 1923 that Committee presented to the General Assembly the outcome of its work in what was entitled 'The Confessional Statement of the United Presbyterian Church of North America,' and this was sent the presbyteries in overture." Except for the Preamble and article 28, "Of Praise," *The Confessional Statement* was approved; after further discussion and revision, these two sections were also accepted, so that "the approval of the Church followed, and the enactment of the article as part of the Confessional Statement took place in 1925," although there was some further redrafting and amendment of the article in 1945.

The proof texts as they appear here are part of "the authoritative text as duly adopted by the United Presbyterian Church of North America" and therefore are reprinted in that format.

Edition: Board of Christian Education of the United Presbyterian Church of North America 1956, 7–31.

Literature: Dowey 1968; Jamison 1958; Lippy and Williams 1988, 1:499–510.

The United Presbyterian Church of North America, *The Confessional Statement*, 1925

Preamble

The United Presbyterian Church of North America declares afresh its adherence to the Westminster Confession of Faith and Catechisms, Larger and Shorter, as setting forth the system of doctrine taught in the Scriptures, which are the only infallible and final rule of faith and practice. Along with this it affirms the right and duty of a living church to restate its faith from time to time so as to display any additional attainments in truth it may have made under the guidance of the Holy Spirit. Accordingly, by constitutional action consummated June 2, 1925, it adopted the following Confessional Statement. This statement contains the substance of the Westminster symbols, together with certain present-day convictions of the United Presbyterian Church. It takes the place of the Testimony of 1858, and wherever it deviates from the Westminster Standards its declarations are to prevail.

Subscription to the foregoing subordinate standards is subject to the principle maintained by our fathers, that the forbearance in love which is required by the law of God is to be exercised toward any brethren who may not be able fully to subscribe to the standards of the church, while they do not determinedly oppose them, but follow the things which make for peace and things wherewith one may edify another.

In keeping with its creedal declaration of truth, the United Presbyterian Church believes that among the evangelical communions of the world there is "one Lord, one faith, one baptism," and therefore, shunning sectarian temper, it cherishes brotherly love toward all branches of the church universal and seeks to keep the unity of the Spirit in the bond of peace.

ARTICLE 1. OF GOD

We believe that there is one living and true God, a self-existent, personal Spirit, eternal and unchangeable, the Creator, Upholder, and Ruler of the universe, a God of infinite love, mercy, holiness, righteousness, justice, truth, wisdom, and might. We believe that the one God exists as the Father, the Son, and the Holy Spirit, and that these three persons are the same in substance, equal in power and glory.

Gn 1.1, 26, 27, 17.1; Ex 3.14, 34.6; Dt 6.4, 32.4, 33.27; Neh 9.6; Ps 9.8, 62.11, 90.2, 103.19, 108.4, 145.8, 9; Is 6.3, 40.26, 28, 45.21, 22, 57.15, 65.16; Jer 10.10, 31.3; Mal 3.6; Mt 28.19; Mk 12.29; Jn 4.24, 5.19, 26, 10.30, 38, 17.3, 5;

Acts 17.28; Rom 2.5, 5.8, 11.33; 2 Cor 13.14; Eph 1.11, 19, 2.4; Phil 2.6; 1 Thes 1.9; 1 Tm 1.17; Jas 1.17; 1 Pt 1.2; 1 Jn 4.8; Rv 4.11.

ARTICLE 2. OF DIVINE REVELATION

We believe that the works of nature, the mind and heart of man, and the history of nations are sources of knowledge concerning God and his will, though insufficient for human need; that a clearer revelation came through men who spake from God, being moved by the Holy Spirit; and that in the fullness of the time God perfectly revealed himself in Jesus Christ, the Word made flesh.

Gn 1.27; Dt 32.8; Ps 19.1–6, 119.105; Lk 1.70; Jn 1.1, 10, 14, 18, 5.39, 10.30, 14.9; Acts 3.21, 14.17, 17.26, 27, 30; Rom 1.18–21, 2.14, 15; 1 Cor 1.21; Gal 1.12; Heb 1.1–3; 2 Pt 1.21.

ARTICLE 3. OF HOLY SCRIPTURE

We believe that the Scriptures of the Old and New Testaments are the word of God and are inspired throughout, in language as well as thought; that their writers, though moved by the Holy Spirit, wrought in accordance with the laws of the human mind; that they faithfully record God's gracious revelation of himself and bear witness of Christ; and that they are infallible rule of faith and practice and the supreme source of authority in spiritual truth.

Dt 18.15; Ps 19.7-11, 119.160; Is 8.20, 11.1, 2; Mt 4.4; Lk 16.29, 24.27, 44; Jn 5.39, 10.35, 16.13; Acts 1.16, 3.18, 8.35, 10.43; Rom 1.1–4, 3.2; 1 Cor 2.13; Gal 3.16, 3.3–5; 2 Tm 3.16; Heb 3.7; 1 Pt 1.10, 11; 2 Pt. 1.21.

ARTICLE 4. OF THE DIVINE PURPOSE

We believe that all things which have come to pass, or are yet to come to pass, lie within the eternal and sovereign purpose of God, either positively or permissively, and are ordained for the manifestation of his glory; yet is God not the author of sin, nor is the free agency of moral beings taken away.

Gn 45.7, 8, 50.20; Job 1.12, 2.6; Ps 33.11; Prv 16.33; Is 46.9–11; Lk 22.22; Acts 2.23, 4.27, 28, 13.29; Rom 8.28, 11.36; Eph 1.4–6, 11, 12, 3.10, 11; Phil 2.12, 13; Jas 1.13, 14.

ARTICLE 5. OF CREATION

We believe that God, for his own wise ends, was pleased in the beginning to create by his infinite power the universe of worlds, and that all intelligent beings, human and superhuman, are the product of his will; that through progressive stages he fashioned and ordered this world in which we dwell, giving life to every creature; and that he created man with a material body and with an immortal spirit made in his own image, with intelligence, feeling, and will, possessed of holiness and happiness, capable of fellowship with him, free and able to choose between good and evil, and therefore morally responsible.

Gn 1.1–31, 2.7, 16, 17; Dt 30.19; Jos 24.15; Ps 33.6; Is 40.26; Jer 27.5; Acts 17.24, 25; 1 Cor 8.6; Eph 3.9; Col 3.10; Heb 11.3, 12.9; 1 Jn 1.3; Rv 4.11.

ARTICLE 6. OF PROVIDENCE

We believe that God is above all his works and in them all; that he upholds all things by his own supreme will and energy, providing for and preserving his creatures according to the laws of their being; and that he directs and governs all events to the praise of his glory. We believe that, while in relation to the eternal purpose of God, the First Cause, all things are fixed immutably, they are accomplished through the operation of second causes, although, as an extraordinary proof of his presence, God may dispense with natural means and instrumentalities.

Ex 15.18; Jos 24.17; Neh 9.6; Ps 22.28, 47.7, 77.13–15, 93.1, 103.19, 135.6, 145.9, 15; Is 40.26; Ez 21.27; Dn 4.25; Zec 14.9; Mt 5.45, 6.26; Acts 2.23, 17.25, 28, 27.24, 31; Rom 11.36; Jas 1.17; 1 Pt 5.7.

ARTICLE 7. OF ANGELS

We believe that God created a superhuman order of intelligent and immortal beings, mighty in strength, to be the servants of his will; that these are of various ranks; that, having been placed under probation, some kept their original holiness and were confirmed therein, while some fell into sin, and remain fallen; that holy angels are the ministers of God's providence in the interests of his kingdom and the human race; and that the apostate angels, led by Satan, their personal head, are seeking to establish a dominion of evil by the temptation and corruption of men.

Gn 19.1; Ps 91.11, 103.20, 21; Mt 4.3, 13.41, 24.31; Jn 8.44; Acts 7.53, 12.7–11; 2 Cor 4.4; Eph 1.21, 6.11, 12; 1 Tm 5.21; Heb 1.14; 1 Pt 3.22; 2 Pt 2.4; Jude 6; Rv 20.1–3.

ARTICLE 8. OF THE SIN OF MAN

We believe that our first father Adam was created sinless and that there was held out to him a promise of eternal life dependent on perfect obedience for a season, while the penalty of disobedience was to be death, bodily and spiritual; that Adam, as the common ancestor of the race, was constituted the representative head of the human family; that he broke the divine command through temptation of the devil, by which transgression he fell from his original state of holiness and communion with God and came into bondage to sin; that in consequence all men descending from him by ordinary generation have come under condemnation and are born with a sinful nature which is alienated from God and from which proceed all actual transgressions; and that out of this condition of guilt and depravity none are able to deliver themselves.

Gn 2.16, 17, 3.19; Hos 6.7; Jn 6.44, 8.34; Rom 3.19, 20, 5.12, 14, 17, 6.23; 1 Cor 2.14, 15.22; 2 Cor 11.3.

ARTICLE 9. OF SALVATION

We believe that God, who is rich in mercy, out of his infinite love for the world, entered from all eternity into a covenant of grace with his only-begotten Son, wherein the Son, standing as the representative of sinners and their Mediator with God, freely consented to secure for them a full salvation by taking their humanity and through a life of obedience and a vicarious death satisfying the divine law and providing a perfect righteousness for all who believe on him; that because of this covenant there was held forth from the first, immediately after the fall, a promise of redemption, in fulfillment of which, when the time of preparation was ended, Christ Jesus came into the world and wrought out a salvation sufficient for all and adapted to all; and that they who accept this salvation, being born anew, are restored to the fellowship of God, given a desire to forsake sin and live unto righteousness, and made heirs of eternal life.

Gn 3.15; Ps 40.7, 8; Is 42.21, 53.4–6, 55.1; Jer 31.3; Jn 1.12, 3.16, 5.24, 10.29, 17.1–26; Acts 5.81; Rom 3.22, 5.1–11, 8.5, 30, 10.4, 12.1; 1 Cor 1.30; Gal 4.4, 5; Eph 1.7, 2.4, 5, 4.20–24; 1 Tm 2.5; Ti 1.2, 3; Heb 7.22, 25, 8.6, 9.12, 15, 28, 12.24, 13.20; 1 Pt 2.24; 1 Jn 4.10, 5.11, 12; Rv 22.17.

ARTICLE 10. OF ELECTION

We believe that the eternal Father, before the foundation of the world, in his own good pleasure gave to his Son a people, an innumerable multitude, chosen in Christ unto salvation, holiness, and service; that all of these who come to years of discretion receive this salvation through faith and repentance; and that all who die in infancy, and all others who are given by the Father to the Son and are beyond the reach of the outward means of grace, are regenerated and saved by Christ through the Holy Spirit, who works when and where and how he pleases.

Mk 10.14, 15; Lk 18.16; Jn 6.37, 39, 17.6, 9; Acts 10.35, 13.48, 17.27; Rom 8.29, 30; Eph 1.4, 2.10; 2 Thes 2.13; 2 Tm 1.9; 1 Pt 1.1, 2; Rv 5.9, 7.9.

ARTICLE 11. OF GOD THE FATHER

We believe that within the Godhead the Father is the first person in the order of office and operation; that in some inconceivable manner, by eternal generation, he is the Father of the only-begotten Son; that from him and from the Son the Holy Spirit proceeds; that with the Son and the Holy Spirit he abides in mutual union and fellowship; and that he is the originating source in creation and redemption. We believe that he is the Father of all men as his rational and moral creatures, made after his likeness; that, beyond his universal benevolence, he so loved the world of humanity as to provide a common salvation at the cost of immeasurable self-sacrifice; and that, though men as sinners have lost the privileges of sonship and denied its obligations, they still retain traces of their heavenly Father's image and share in his providential care and bounty. We believe in the fatherhood of God in a preeminent sense with reference to those who become his children by regeneration and adoption, and who yield a filial response to his love; that in his parental relationship with these he attains to the satisfaction of his desires for men; that he welcomes them into communion with himself, makes them partakers of his holiness, and works out for them his gracious purpose in all that pertains to their present and eternal well-being.

Gn 1.26, 27, 6.2; Nm 16.22; Ps 2.7; Is 63.16; Mal 2.10; Mt 3.17, 5.45, 6.9, 17.5; Lk 3.38, 15.11–32; Jn 1.14, 18, 3.16, 5.20, 26, 10.29, 16.28; Acts 2.33, 17.26–29; Rom 8.11, 14, 15, 28; 1 Cor 8.6; Gal 3.26, 4.6; Eph 3.14, 15; Heb 1.2, 3, 5, 12.9, 10; Jas 3.9; 1 Pt 1.3, 11, 17; 2 Pt 1.4; 1 Jn 4.7, 9.

ARTICLE 12. OF THE LORD JESUS CHRIST

We believe that the Lord Jesus Christ is the eternal Son of God, having a sonship that is natural and necessary, inhering in the very constitution of the Godhead; that, freely laying aside his divine glory and majesty, he became man by taking to himself a true body and soul, yet without sin, being conceived by the power of the Holy Spirit and born of the Virgin Mary; that thus he is very God and very man, two whole and distinct natures, the divine and the human, being joined together in his one person, never to be divided; and that he, the God-man, is the sole Mediator between God and men, by whom alone we must be saved. We believe that the Lord Jesus Christ was anointed by the Holy Spirit to be our perfect and eternal Prophet, Priest, and King; that he has revealed the will and counsel of God; that for our redemption he fulfilled all righteousness by his holy obedience and his propitiatory sacrifice for the sin of the world; that, having died upon the cross and been buried, he rose from the dead by a physical resurrection and ascended into heaven, where as their advocate he makes continual intercession for his people; that he abides in believers as an indwelling presence, communicating newness of life and power, and making them sharers of what he has and is; that he sits at the right hand of God as the Head of his church and kingdom, with dominion over all created persons and things; and that he will come again in glory for the vanquishing of evil and the restoration of all things.

Mt 1.20, 3.15, 28.16–20; Lk 1.30–35, 3.21, 22, 4.18; Jn 1.1, 14, 18, 33, 3.13, 16, 10.36, 14.6, 15.5, 17.5, 20.19–29; Acts 1.9–11, 2.33, 3.21, 4.12, 10.38; Rom 3.24, 25, 8.3, 17, 32, 34, 9.5; 1 Cor 15.3, 4, 25; Gal 1.12, 4.4, 5; Eph 1.20–23, 3.17; Phil 2.6–11; 2 Thes 1.7–10; 1 Tm 1.15, 2.5; Heb 1.5, 8, 13, 2.14, 7.25, 26, 12.24; 1 Pt 1.7, 13, 3.22; 1 Jn 1.5, 2.1, 2, 4.2; Rv 1.5, 6.

ARTICLE 13. OF THE HOLY SPIRIT

We believe that the Holy Spirit is a real personality, the third person within the Divine Being, proceeding from the Father and the Son, and together with the Father and the Son is to be believed in, loved, obeyed, and worshiped; that he shared in the work of creation, and is the Lord and Giver of all life; that he is everywhere present with men, inclining them unto good and restraining them from evil; that he spoke by the prophets and apostles and inspired all writers of the Holy Scriptures to record infallibly the mind and will of God; that he had peculiar relations with the Lord Jesus Christ enabling the Son of God to assume our nature without being defiled by sin, and guiding, animating, and supporting the Savior in his mediatoral work; that the dispensation of the gospel is especially committed to him, in that he accompanies it with his persuasive power and urges its message upon the reason and conscience of men, so that they who refuse its merciful offer are without excuse. We believe that the Holy Spirit is the only efficient agent in the application of redemption, convicting men of sin, enlightening them in the knowledge of spiritual realities, moving them to heed the call of the gospel, uniting them to Christ, and dwelling in them as the source of faith, of power, of holiness, of comfort, and of love; that he abides in the church as a living presence, giving efficacy to its ordinances, imparting various gifts and graces to its members, calling and anointing its ministers for their holy service, and qualifying all other officers for their special work; and that by him the church will be preserved, edified, extended throughout the world, and at last be glorified in the heavenly places with Christ.

Gn 1.2; 2 Sm 23.2; Job 26.13; Ps 139.7; Zec 4.6; Mt 1.18–25, 4.1, 12.28, 28.19; Lk 1.35, 4.14; Jn 14.16, 26, 15.26, 16.7–14; Acts 1.2, 8, 2.1–4, 38, 7.51, 8.17, 10.38, 16.7; Rom 8.9, 11, 13, 16, 26; 1 Cor 2.4, 10–13, 12.4; 2 Cor 13.14; Gal 4.6, 5.16–23, 25; Eph 2.18, 3.16, 4.30; Phil 1.19; 1 Thes 1.5; Heb 9.14; 1 Pt 1.11; 2 Pt 1.21; 1 Jn 2.20.

ARTICLE 14. OF THE ATONEMENT

We believe that our Lord Jesus Christ, by the appointment of the Father, and by his own gracious and voluntary act, gave himself a ransom for all; that as a substitute for sinful man his death was a propitiatory sacrifice of infinite value, satisfying divine justice and holiness, and giving free access to God for pardon and restoration; and that this atonement, though made for the sin of the world, becomes efficacious to those only who are led by the Holy Spirit to believe in Christ as their Savior.

Ps 40.7, 8, 130.7; Mt 20.28; Jn 1.29, 3.16, 10.18; Rom 3.25, 8.3, 4; 1 Cor 15.3; Gal 2.20, 3.13; 1 Tm 2.4–6, 4.10; Heb 10.5–10, 14, 19; 1 Pt 1.19; 1 Jn 2.2, 4.10.

ARTICLE 15. OF THE GOSPEL CALL

We believe that the gospel is a revelation of grace to sinners as such, and that it contains a free and unconditional offer of salvation through Christ to all who hear it, whatever may be their character or condition; that the offer is in itself a proper motive to obedience; and that nothing but a sinful unwillingness prevents its acceptance.

Is 55.1; Mt 9.13, 11.28; Jn 3.16, 6.37; Rom 1.16, 17, 10.8–10; Eph 1.13, 14; Heb 4.7; Rv 22.17.

ARTICLE 16. OF REGENERATION

We believe in the necessity of regeneration, whereby we who by nature are spiritually dead are made new creatures, established union with Christ, released from bondage to sin, and made alive unto God; that this is the immediate act of the Holy Spirit, who changes the governing disposition of the soul by a secret and direct operation of his power; and that ordinarily, where years of understanding have been reached, regeneration is wrought in connection with the use of divine truth as a means.

Ez 11.19; Jn 3.3–6; 1 Cor 1.30; 2 Cor 5.17; Gal 4.5–7; Eph 2.1, 5, 5.26; Ti 3.5, 6; Jas 1.18; 1 Pt 1.23.

ARTICLE 17. OF SAVING FAITH

We believe that saving faith is the gift of God; that in it there is not merely an assent to the truth that the Lord Jesus Christ is the Savior of sinners, but also a cordial acceptance and appropriation of him, and a fixed reliance upon him, as our Savior; that this faith, which involves the conviction of the mind, the trust of the heart, and the obedience of the will, rests solely upon the free and unlimited offer of Christ made in the gospel to sinners of mankind; and that such faith is the necessary and all-sufficient condition and channel for the communication of every spiritual gift and the progressive realization of salvation.

Mk 1.15; Jn 1.12, 3.16, 20.27, 28; Acts 10.43, 15.9; Rom 10.17, 13.14; Gal 2.16, 5.6; Eph 2.8; Col 2.6; 2 Tm 1.12; Heb 3.15, 11.6; Jas 2.14–26; 1 Pt 1.21; 1 Jn 5.4, 10.

ARTICLE 18. OF REPENTANCE

We believe that saving faith issues in repentance, which is essentially a turning away from sin unto God, accompanied not only with sorrow over sin, but with hatred of sin and with an earnest desire and sincere purpose to obey God's righteous law; that, while repentance is produced in the believing sinner by the Holy Spirit, it springs from a sense of sin as involving guilt and defilement and from an apprehension of God's mercy in Christ; that it is not to be rested in as any satisfaction for sin, or any ground of the pardon thereof, and yet it is of such necessity that none are saved without it; and that it is evidenced by humble confession of sin before God and by reparation for wrongs done to men.

Is 6.5; Mt 3.2, 8; Lk 3.3, 8, 5.32, 13.5, 15.18, 24.47; Jn 16.8; Acts 2.38, 15.9, 20.21, 26.20; Rom 2.4, 7.24; 2 Cor 7.10, 11; 1 Thes 1.9; 2 Pt 3.9.

ARTICLE 19. OF JUSTIFICATION

We believe that justification is a judicial act of God by which in his free grace he places sinners in a new relation to himself and his law, so that henceforth they are forgiven and accepted as righteous in his sight; that the procuring cause or ground of this is not anything wrought in them, or done by them, but only the perfect righteousness of Christ, embracing all that he did in the way of obedience and all that he suffered in their stead while on earth, a righteousness imputed to them, and received by faith alone; and that the evidence of justification is holy living.

Is 53.11; Acts 13.39; Rom 3.22–26, 4.25, 5.1, 9, 16, 18; Rom 6.22, 8.1, 30, 33; 1 Cor 6.11; Gal 2.16, 3.24; Eph 1.7; Phil 3.9; Ti 3.7; Jas 2.18.

ARTICLE 20. OF ADOPTION

We believe that adoption is an act of the free grace of God whereby those that are justified are received into the number of his saved children, have his name put upon them, have the Spirit of his Son given them, are the objects of his fatherly care and discipline, are admitted to the liberties and privileges of the family of God, and are made heirs of all the promises and fellow heirs with Christ in glory.

Jn 1.12; Rom 8.15–17, 23; 2 Cor 6.18; Gal 3.26, 4.4–6; Eph 1.5; Ti 3.7; Heb 12.7, 8; 1 Jn 3.1; Rv 3.12.

ARTICLE 21. OF SANCTIFICATION

We believe that sanctification is the carrying on to completion of the great change effected in regeneration, being a progressive deliverance from the dominion and defilement of sin and a corresponding growth in holy character; that it is wrought by the power of the indwelling Spirit, whereby union with Christ is maintained and holy dispositions are fostered; that in sanctification believers are fellow-workers with the Holy Spirit, being called to faith and repentance, to true obedience in motive and act, to dedication of themselves to the will of God, and to a diligent use of the outward means of grace; and that, while, because of defective faith and human frailty, perfection never can be reached in the present life, it is nevertheless the duty of believers to aim at entire conformity to the will of God, to which, with advancing experience and fuller appropriation of Christ, they may increasingly approach.

Ps 19.12, 13; Ez 36.25–27; Mt 5.48; Jn 17.17; Acts 15.9, 20.32; Rom 6.1–6, 12, 14, 7.18, 23, 8.13, 13.14; 1 Cor 1.30, 6.11; 2 Cor 3.18, 7.1; Gal 2.20, 5.16, 17, 24; Eph 1.4, 3.16–19, 4.11, 12, 15, 16, 23, 24, 5.26, 6.10; Phil 2.12, 13, 3.12–14, 4.13; Col 1.10, 11; 1 Thes 5.23; 2 Thes 2.13; 2 Tm 2.21; Heb 12.1, 14; 1 Pt 1.2, 2.11; 2 Pt 3.18; 1 Jn 1.5–10, 3.6, 9, 5.4.

ARTICLE 22. OF UNION WITH CHRIST

We believe that all who receive Christ by saving faith are made one with him in a mystical union through the Holy Spirit; that thereby they become vitally related to him as the sin-bearer and the life-giver, insuring their acceptance with God, their renewal of nature, and their growth in holiness and fruitfulness; and that believers thus joined to Christ as their Head, and nourished by his life communicated to them, are bound together in one spiritual organism, which is called the body of Christ.

Jn 14.19, 15.1–5, 17.21–23; Rom 6.3–5, 8.1; 1 Cor 1.30, 12.12, 13, 27; 2 Cor 4.10, 11, 5.17; Eph 1.23, 5.30; Col 2.10, 19.

ARTICLE 23. OF THE SECURITY OF BELIEVERS

We believe that, because of the original purpose, the unchanging love, and the constant operation of God, all who are brought into vital union with Christ, and are members of his mystical body, abide permanently in a state of grace and finally are made perfect in glory; that, while such fall into sin, and come under God's fatherly displeasure, until they humble themselves and make confession, they never become utterly apostate; and that this continuance on the part of believers is accomplished by the Holy Spirit in harmony with their rational nature, the warnings, cautions, and exhortations of Scripture addressed to them being used to foster self-examination, watching, prayer, and the faithful observance of all sacred ordinances.

Ps 51.1–17, 73.23; Jer 31.3, 32.40; Mt 24.24, 26.69–74; Lk 22.31, 32; Jn 8.31, 10.28, 29, 17.2, 3, 11, 24; Rom 8.31–39; 1 Cor 1.8, 9, 9.27; Eph 4.30; Phil 1.6; 2 Thes 3.3; 2 Tm 2.19; Heb 3.12, 4.1, 7, 6.4–6, 9, 10, 7.25, 10.10, 14, 13.20, 21; 1 Pt 1.5, 8, 9; 2 Pt 1.10; 1 Jn 2.17, 19, 27, 3.9; Jude 20, 21, 24.

ARTICLE 24. OF ASSURANCE

We believe that from the first the believer has a persuasion, proportioned to the strength of his faith, that he is saved, this initial confidence resting on the promise and power and faithfulness of God; that, in addition, there is the assurance of sense or feeling, to which he attains through his conscious possession of the graces of the children of God and through the inner witness of the Holy Spirit; and that it is the privilege and duty of every believer to give diligence to attain this conscious assurance of salvation, whereby he may live in joy and peace, may be moved the more by love and thanksgiving to God, and may be led to a fuller obedience and service.

Ps 23.1–6, 73.23–26; Rom 5.2, 5, 8.16, 38, 39, 15.13; 2 Cor 1.21, 22; Eph 1.13, 14, 4.30; Col 2.2; 2 Tm 1.12; Ti 2.11–14; Heb 6.11, 17–19, 10.22; 1 Pt 1.3; 2 Pt 1.4, 10, 11; 1 Jn 2.3, 3.2, 3, 14, 19, 21, 24, 4.13, 16, 5.13.

ARTICLE 25. OF THE LAW OF GOD

We believe that the moral law of God summarized in the Ten Commandments, proclaimed by the prophets, and unfolded in the life and teachings of Jesus Christ, is of perpetual obligation; that it demands not only right acts and words, but also right dispositions and states of mind; that it is of use to all men in setting before them the inflexibly holy will of God, in discovering to them sin in its true light, and in preparing the way for the gospel of grace; and that although believers, because of their justification, are not subject to it as a condition of salvation, they are required to obey it as a rule of action and standard of character.

Ps 19.7, 8, 11, 119.4; Jer 31.33; Mt 5.17-19, 21-48, 6.1-34, 22.37-40; Acts 13.39; Rom 3.20, 31, 6.14, 7.4, 6, 7, 9, 12, 14, 22, 25, 8.4, 10.4, 13.8; 1 Cor 7.19, 9.20, 21; Gal 2.16, 3.13, 21, 24, 4.4, 5, 5.14; Eph 6.2; 1 Tm 1.8; Heb 8.10; Jas 1.25, 2.8, 9, 12; 1 Jn 2.3, 4, 7, 8.

ARTICLE 26. OF THE STUDY OF GOD'S WORD

We believe that Holy Scripture, as God's written word, is adapted to the spiritual needs of man, containing whatever doctrine is necessary to salvation and all things that pertain to life and godliness; that, therefore, it deserves and demands our reverent attention and our deepest thought; and that the reading and study of the word, when entered upon with a mind illumined by the Holy Spirit and with prayerful reflection, will always prove an efficacious means of grace, transforming life and character.

Ps 1.1-3, 19.7, 119.130; Mt 21.42, 22.29; Lk 24.27, 32; Jn 5.39; Acts 8.30-35, 17.11; Rom 15.4; Eph 6.17, 18; 1 Tm 4.6; 2 Tm 3.15-17; Heb 4.2; Jas 1.21, 25.

ARTICLE 27. OF PRAYER

We believe that prayer is an indispensable condition of fellowship with God and a vital requirement in spiritual growth and the obtaining of promised mercies; that it must be offered in the name of Christ, in reliance on his merits, and by the help of the Holy Spirit; that it includes adoration, thanksgiving, aspiration, the outpouring of the soul in converse with God, confession of sin and shortcomings, supplication for pardon and all blessings promised in the gospel, and petition for such temporal benefits as may be agreeable to the divine will; that remembrance of others at the throne of grace is an obligation without which the life of prayer cannot be fully realized; and that God has given the intercession of his children an essential place in bringing about the salvation of men and in promoting the advance of his kingdom and the doing of his will on earth.

Neh 1.4-11; Ps 17.1, 32.5, 62.8, 122.6; Ez 36.37; Dn 9.4; Mt 5.44, 6.9-15, 7.7, 8, 11; Mk 11.24; Lk 11.2-4, 18.9-14; Jn 14.13, 14, 16.23, 24; Acts 9.11; Rom 8.26, 27; 1 Cor 1.2; Eph 1.3, 15-23, 3.14-19, 6.18, 19; Phil 1.9, 4.6; Col 4.3, 12; 1 Thes 5.25; 1 Tm 2.1-4, 8; Heb 4.16; Jas 1.5-8, 5.16; 1 Pt 2.5; 1 Jn 1.9, 5.14, 15; Jude 20, 21, 25.

ARTICLE 28. OF PRAISE

We believe that God is worthy of all praise and adoration because of his glorious perfections as unfolded in creation, providence, and redemption; that praise as a definite ordinance of worship is expressed in words joined to music; and that in this ordinance the Psalms of the Bible, by reason of their divine inspiration, their excellence, and their evident design, are accredited for permanent use, together with meritorious evangelical hymns in which are expressed the experiences, privileges, and duties of the Christian life.

2 Sm 23.1, 2; 1 Chr 16.7–9, 23; 2 Chr 29.30; Ps 47.6, 7, 95.1, 2, 105.2, 137.3, 147.1, 150.1, 2; Mt 26.30; Lk 20.42, 24.44; Acts 1.20; Rom 15.9; Eph 1.6, 12, 14, 5.19; Col 3.16; 2 Tm 3.16; Rv 4.11, 5.9–14, 14.3, 15.3, 4.

ARTICLE 29. OF SABBATH OBSERVANCE

We believe that the holy Sabbath, originally a memorial of creation, is an institution which has its foundation in the revealed will of God, which was established for the physical, moral, and spiritual well-being of man, and which was designed for all ages and nations; that its transfer from the last day of the week to the first, commemorating the resurrection of the Redeemer of mankind, was effected by Christ's own example and by apostolic sanction; that, in the spirit of gratitude for the blessings it conveys, the Sabbath, or the Lord's day, should be hallowed by refraining from worldly employments and recreations and, aside from the duties of necessity and mercy, by devoting the day to public and private worship, spiritual culture, and Christian activities; and that the civil Sabbath of legally protected rest, because of its great and manifold benefits to human society, should be maintained and defended against desecration.

Gn 2.2, 3; Ex 20.8–11, 31.13; Lv 19.30; Neh 13.15–22; Is 56.2–7, 58.13, 14, 66.23; Jer 17.24–27; Mt 5.17, 18, 12.2–12; Mk 2.27, 28; Lk 4.16; Jn 20.19, 26; Acts 2.1, 20.7; 1 Cor 16.2; Rv 1.10.

ARTICLE 30. OF THE SACRAMENTS

We believe that the sacraments of baptism and the Lord's supper were instituted by Christ and are of perpetual validity and obligation; that they are signs and seals of the new covenant and channels of a real communication of grace to those receiving them in faith; and that through their observance the church of Christ confesses her Lord and is visibly distinguished from the world.

We believe that baptism with water into the name of the Father and of the Son and of the Holy Spirit is the sacrament that recognizes membership within the church, in which are set forth union to Christ, regeneration and cleansing by the Spirit, the remission of sins, and our engagement to be the Lord's; that it is rightly administered by the pouring or sprinkling of water upon the person, but the mode is not essential; that not only are adult believers to be baptized, but also the children of believers before reaching the age of accountability, on the faith of the parents, who appropriate for their children the benefits which the sacrament offers and promise to rear them in the nurture and admonition of the Lord.

We believe that the Lord's supper is the sacrament of communion with Christ, in which bread and wine are given and received in thankful remembrance of him and of his sacrifice on the cross, and they who in faith receive the same partake of the body and blood of the Lord Jesus Christ, after a spiritual manner, to their building up in grace; that it should never be engaged in without previous self-examination as to a sincere desire to be cleansed from all sin, a true and living faith in the Lord Christ, and brotherly love toward all; and that all are to be invited to the Lord's supper who have confessed their faith in Christ and are leading a Christian life.

Gn 17.7; Is 52.15; Ez 36.25; Mt 26.26–30, 28.19; Mk 10.13–16, 14.22–25; Lk 18.15–17, 22.17–20; Jn 3.5, 6.48–58; Acts 2.38–41, 8.12, 37, 38, 16.15, 33, 22.16; Rom 4.11, 6.3, 4; 1 Cor 7.14, 10.1–4, 16, 17, 21, 11.23–34, 12.13; Gal 3.27; Eph 5.25, 26; Col 2.12; Ti 3.5; 1 Pt 3.21.

ARTICLE 31. OF LAWFUL OATHS AND VOWS

We believe that an oath is an act of religious worship in which we solemnly call upon the only true and living God to witness the truth of what we affirm or our voluntary assumption of an obligation to do something in the future, with an implied imprecation of God's judgment if we lie or prove false to our engagements; that the proper circumstances under which an oath may be taken are those in which serious and perfectly lawful interests are involved, in which an appeal to God is necessary to secure confidence and end strife, and where the oath is imposed by the duly constituted authority of church or state.

We believe that a vow is a promise formally made to God, in way of thankfulness for mercy received, or for the obtaining of what we desire; that it is of like sacred nature with an oath, because it is God to whom the promise is made; that a vow cannot bind to do that which is unlawful or impossible, nor where its continued observance is inconsistent with our spiritual interests; and that to vow on a trifling occasion, or, having rightly vowed, to fail in performance, is to be guilty of profanity.

Gn 24.2–9, 28.20–22; Ex 20.7; Lv 19.12; Dt 6.13, 10.20, 23.21; Jgs 11.30, 36, 39; 2 Chr 6.22, 23; Neh 5.12, 13.25; Ps 15.4, 61.8, 66.13, 14, 76.11, 116.14; Prv 20.25; Eccl 5.5; Is 65.16; Jer 4.2; Mt 5.33–37; Mk 6.23, 26; Acts 18.18, 23.12–14; 2 Cor 1.23; Gal 1.20; Heb 6.16; Jas 5.12.

ARTICLE 32. OF THE CHURCH

We believe that there is one holy catholic or universal church, consisting of the whole number of those of every age and nation who have been chosen of God unto salvation and redeemed by the Lord Jesus, and who, being united by the Holy Spirit to Christ their living Head, are one spiritual body in him; that it is the will of Christ that his church on earth should exist as a visible brotherhood, composed of all those who profess faith in him and obedience to his laws, together with their children, organized for the confession of his name, the public worship of God, the preaching and teaching of the word, the administration of the sacraments, the nurture and fellowship of the children of God, the propagation of the gospel, and the promotion of social righteousness; and that all particular churches or ecclesiastical denominations throughout the world which hold the fundamental truths of evangelical religion and own allegiance to Jesus Christ as divine Lord and Savior are to be regarded as within the one visible church.

Ps 2.8, 22.27-31; Mt 16.18, 18.17, 28.18-20; Jn 10.16, 17.21, 24, 21.15-17; Acts 8.1, 13.1, 20.28; Rom 15.9-12, 16.1, 3-5, 16, 23; 1 Cor 1.2, 4.17, 10.32, 12.12, 13, 28, 15.9, 16.19; Gal 1.2, 13, 22; Eph 1.10, 22, 23, 2.19, 20, 3.10, 4.11-13, 5.23-32; Phil 3.6, 4.15; Col 1.18, 24; 1 Tm 3.15; Heb 12.23; Rv 7.9, 10, 22.16.

ARTICLE 33. OF CHURCH ORDER

We believe that the supreme and only Head of the church is the Lord Jesus Christ, under whose authority and according to whose will the worship, teaching, discipline, and government of the church are to be administered; that through those who serve lawfully in the offices of the church Christ exercises mediately his own power and enforces his own laws; and that the presbyterian form of church polity is in accordance with the Scriptures.

Mt 16.19, 18.17, 18, 28.18-20; Jn 20.23; Acts 14.23, 15.2-29, 16.4, 20.17, 28; 1 Cor 12.28; 2 Cor 2.6-8; Eph 4.11, 12, 5.24; Phil 1.1; Col 1.18; 1 Thes 5.12; 1 Tm 3.1-13, 4.14, 5.17; Ti 1.5-9, Heb 13.7, 17, 24; 1 Pt 5.1.

ARTICLE 34. OF THE MINISTRY

We believe that Jesus Christ as the Head of the church has appointed therein the official ministry of reconciliation; that he calls men to this ministry through the working of the Holy Spirit in their hearts and by the orderings of providence; and that those thus called are to be set apart by ordination, whereby they are solemnly invested with the authority, powers, and duties of their sacred office.

Mt 9.38; Acts 13.2, 3; 1 Cor 3.5, 4.1, 12.28; 2 Cor 5.18; Eph 4.11, 12, 6.21; Phil 1.1; Col 1.7, 4.7, 17; 1 Thes 3.2; 1 Tm 4.14, 5.22; 2 Tm 1.6, 4.5; Heb 13.7, 17; 1 Pt 5.1-4.

ARTICLE 35. OF CHURCH FELLOWSHIP

We believe that all who have accepted Christ as their Redeemer should unite themselves with some branch of the visible church, in order to share in the privileges and responsibilities of its members and confess Christ before men; that under Christ they should yield the church their supreme loyalty, honoring its ordinances and seeking its welfare in season and out of season; and that with this they should forsake all associations, whether secret or open, that they find prejudicial to their church allegiance and a hindrance to the fulfillment of Christian duties.

Mt 10.32; Acts 2.41, 42, 47, 11.26; 1 Cor 10.32, 12.13, 16.2; 2 Cor 6.14–18; Eph 4.11–13, 5.11; 1 Tm 3.15; Heb 10.25; 1 Jn 2.15, 16, 19; Rv 18.4.

ARTICLE 36. OF THE FAMILY

We believe that the family is the unit of society and is fundamental to human welfare; that marriage is ordained of God, and is therefore an institution which involves a religious as well as a civil contract; that the law of marriage, requiring monogamy, governing the prohibited degrees of consanguinity or affinity, and establishing the permanence of the tie, is laid down in the word of God, upon which the enactments of the state may not transgress rightfully; that the true Christian home is built on the divine ideal of marriage, is sanctified by the Holy Spirit, and is observant of family religion; and that it is the duty of parents to dedicate their children to God and give them a moral and spiritual training for the making of character. We believe that, since the standard of marriage is a lifelong union of one man and one woman, its dissolution is not to be lightly regarded; that, where warrantable, this can be effected only by competent civil authority; and that the remarriage of divorced persons is permissible, while both parties are living, only when the divorce has been obtained on the ground of adultery, and then for the innocent party alone.

Gn 1.27, 28, 2.24, 5.1; Lv 18.6–30; Dt 6.6, 7; 1 Sm 1.11, 28; Jer 1.5; Am 2.7; Mt 5.31, 32, 19.3–9; Mk 6.18, 10.2–12; Rom 7.2, 3; 1 Cor 5.1, 7.10–16, 39; Gal 1.15; Eph 5.22–33, 6.1–4; Col 3.18–21; 2 Tm 3.15; Heb 13.4.

ARTICLE 37. OF CIVIL GOVERNMENT

We believe that civil government is an ordinance of God, instituted for his glory and the welfare of society, and that the sovereign authority of the Lord Jesus Christ extends over this province of human life, so that states and their rulers are responsible to him and are bound to render him obedience and to seek the furtherance of his kingdom upon earth, not, however, in any way constraining religious belief, imposing religious disabilities, or invading the rights of conscience; that it is binding on all to yield willing submission to constituted authorities, except where this very clearly conflicts with the still higher duty of obedience to God; and that the due fulfillment of our duties as citizens includes a loyal consent to taxation for the necessities of the state and the lesser civic communities, the giving of aid to all worthy public causes, and faithful participation in the government of the country.

Ps 2.10–12, 22.28, 47.7–9, 82.1, 2; Prv 8.15, 16; Mt 22.21; Acts 4.19; Rom 13.1–7; Eph 1.20–22; 1 Tm 2.1, 2; Ti 3.1; 1 Pt 2.13, 14, 17; Rv 17.14, 19.16.

ARTICLE 38. OF THE SOCIAL ORDER

We believe that the divine plan for mankind includes a social order in harmony with the ideals and spirit of Jesus Christ; that the triumph of the kingdom of God in its present aspect would mean not only its establishment in the hearts of men individually, but a world in which righteousness and brotherhood should prevail; and that a primary duty of the church is to give positive witness that the Christian principles of justice and love should have full expression in all relationships whatsoever—personal, industrial, business, civic, national, and international.

Ex 20.1-17; Mi 6.8, Mk 12.30, 31; Acts 17.26; Rom 13.1-10; Eph 6.5-9; Phil 1.27; Col 3.22-4.1; Jas 5.1-6.

ARTICLE 39. OF THE INTERMEDIATE STATE

We believe that the souls of the righteous dead are immediately made perfect in holiness, and during the interval until the resurrection, though separated from the body, continue conscious, active, and at peace in the presence and fellowship of Christ, who, after his ascension, sat down on the right hand of God; that in the abode of woe the souls of the impenitent wicked also continue conscious and active, enduring punishment for their sins; and that this intermediate state is one of incompleteness, the supreme blessedness of the saints and the utter wretchedness of the lost beginning only with their resurrection and the judgment.

Lk 9.28-36, 16.19-31, 23.43; Jn 8.56, 14.3; Rom 8.23; 1 Cor 15.26; 2 Cor 5.8-10; Phil 1.6, 23; 1 Thes 1.10; Heb 11.39, 40, 12.23; 1 Pt 1.7, 3.19; 1 Jn 3.2; Jude 6; Rv 7.9, 19.1-5.

ARTICLE 40. OF THE SECOND ADVENT

We believe that the Lord Jesus Christ, who at his ascension was received up into heaven, will come again to earth in person, visibly, with power and great glory; that his coming marks the consummation of the kingdom of God; that the time thereof is reserved in the divine counsels; and that this blessed hope is to be cherished as an incentive to watchful living and faithful witness-bearing on the part of Christ's followers.

Mt 24.29-51, 25.1-13, 31-46; Mk 13.33-37; Lk 9.26; Acts 1.7, 11, 3.21; 1 Thes 1.10, 4.16, 17, 5.1-11; Heb 9.28; 1 Pt 5.4; 2 Pt 3.8-13; Rv 1.7.

ARTICLE 41. OF THE RESURRECTION

We believe that through the power of Almighty God there will be a bodily resurrection of all the dead, both of the just and of the unjust; that to the just it will be a resurrection unto life and to the unjust a resurrection unto condemnation; and that the mortal bodies of those who are fallen asleep in Jesus, as well as of the faithful who are alive at his coming, will be fashioned anew and conformed to the body of his glory.

Jb 19.26; Dn 12.2; Jn 5.25, 28, 29, 11.23–25; Acts 24.15; Rom 8.11, 23; 1 Cor 15.12–58; 2 Cor 4.14; Phil 3.11, 21; 1 Thes 4.15, 16; 2 Tm 2.18; Heb 11.35.

ARTICLE 42. OF THE JUDGMENT

We believe that, at the resurrection, he who alone can read the heart will judge the world in righteousness by Jesus Christ; that the wicked, being condemned for their inexcusable sin and depravity, will go away into eternal punishment; and that the righteous, although made manifest before the judgment-seat of Christ, will be acquitted and eternally accepted, and of God's grace rewarded according to their deeds.

Gn 18.25; Mt 10.15, 12.36, 25.31–46; Lk 12.47, 48, 16.26; Jn 5.22, 24, 27–29, 10.42, 17.31, 24.25; Rom 2.5–16, 8.33, 14.10; 1 Cor 4.4, 5, 6.2, 3, 11.32; 2 Cor 5.10; 2 Thes 1.8, 9; 1 Tm 5.24; 2 Tm 4.1; Heb 6.2, 9.27, 10.27, 12.23; Jas 1.12; 2 Pt 2.4, 3.7; 1 Jn 4.17; Jude 6, 14, 15; Rv 20.11–15.

ARTICLE 43. OF THE LIFE EVERLASTING

We believe in, and with glad and solemn hearts look for, the consummation and bliss of the life everlasting, wherein the people of God, freed from sin and sorrow, shall receive their inheritance of glory in the kingdom of their Father, and, with capacities and powers exalted and enlarged, shall be made fully blessed in the fellowship of Christ, in the perfected communion of saints, and in the service of God, whom they shall enjoy forever and ever.

Ps 16.9–11, 17.15, 23.6, 73.24–26; Mt 25.21, 23, 34, 46; Lk 23.43; Jn 3.15, 16, 14.3, 17.22–24; Rom 6.22, 8.18–25; 1 Cor 13.12; 2 Cor 4.17, 5.8; Phil 1.23; Col 3.4; 2 Tm 4.8; Heb 9.15, 12.22–24; Jas 1.12, 2.5; 1 Pt 1.3–5, 5.1, 10; 2 Pt 1.11; 1 Jn 3.2; Rv 3.4, 7.13–17, 14.13, 21.3, 4, 22.1–5.

ARTICLE 44. OF CHRISTIAN SERVICE AND THE FINAL TRIUMPH

We believe that, as disciples and servants of Christ, we are bound to further the extension of his kingdom by our prayers, gifts, and personal efforts, to defend the truth, to do good to all men, to maintain the public worship of God, to hallow the Sabbath, to preserve the inviolability of marriage and the sanctity of the family, to uphold the just authority of the state, and to live in all honesty, purity, and charity. We obediently receive the word of Christ bidding his people go into all the world and make disciples of the nations, declaring unto them that God is in Christ reconciling the world unto himself, and that he will have all men to be saved and come to the knowledge of the truth. We confidently believe in the ultimate and complete triumph of our Savior King, that by his grace and power all his enemies shall finally be overthrown, and the kingdom of the world shall become the kingdom of our Lord and of his Christ.

Ex 20.8; Ps 2.1–12, 22.27, 28, 72.8–17; Mt 6.10, 13.31, 32, 16.18, 19.3–9, 24.14, 28.19, 20; Rom 7.2, 3, 13.1–7; 1 Cor 15.24–28; 2 Cor 5.19, 9.7–15; Gal 6.10; Eph 4.1, 2; 2 Thes 1.7–10; 1 Tm 2.4; Ti 2.11–14; Heb 10.25, 13.4; 1 Pt 2.13, 14; Jude 3; Rv 5.12–14, 11.15, 19.11–16, 22.17.

Faith and Order Conference at Lausanne, *The Call to Unity*, 1927

The Conference on Faith and Order was the forum in which, during the twentieth century, the differences between Christian confessions were explored, to a considerable extent defined, and to some extent transcended. Working at first in parallel, and eventually in merger, with the Conference on Life and Work, Faith and Order held two world conferences, at Lausanne, Switzerland, in 1927, and at Edinburgh, Scotland, in 1938, before becoming part of the World Council of Churches, where it has continued to function as the principal ongoing venue for confessional discussion.

Attended by members of about ninety churches, Lausanne was in the nature of the case merely exploratory. In the reports of the discussions of its seven sections —and then in the responses from the churches to its final message and reports[1]— confessional disagreements inevitably figured more prominently than agreements. But viewed, as it must be, in the light of later developments, notably of → *Baptism, Eucharist, Ministry*, the "Lima Text" of Faith and Order from 1982, the identification of the divisive issues at Lausanne and its summons to address those issues candidly but constructively make its message an important chapter in the history of ecumenical statements of faith in the modern period.

Although *The Call to Unity* is, technically, the title only of the first of the several "Reports" adopted or received and then published by the Lausanne Conference, we have, for the sake of convenience, made it into the general title for all of them.

Edition: Bate 1928, 460–75.

Literature: Bate 1928; Hodgson 1934; Visser 't Hooft et al. 1977.

1. Hodgson 1934.

Faith and Order Conference at Lausanne,
The Call to Unity, 1927

1. THE CALL TO UNITY

God wills unity. Our presence in this conference bears testimony to our desire to bend our wills to his. However we may justify the beginnings of disunion, we lament its continuance and henceforth must labor, in penitence and faith, to build up our broken walls.

God's Spirit has been in the midst of us. It was he who called us hither. His presence has been manifest in our worship, our deliberations, and our whole fellowship. He has discovered us to one another. He has enlarged our horizons, quickened our understanding, and enlivened our hope. We have dared and God has justified our daring. We can never be the same again. Our deep thankfulness must find expression in sustained endeavor to share the visions vouchsafed us here with those smaller home groups where our lot is cast.

More than half the world is waiting for the gospel. At home and abroad sad multitudes are turning away in bewilderment from the church because of its corporate feebleness. Our missions count that as a necessity which we are inclined to look on as a luxury. Already the mission field is impatiently revolting from the divisions of the Western Church to make bold adventure for unity in its own right. We of the churches represented in this conference cannot allow our spiritual children to outpace us. We with them must gird ourselves to the task, the early beginnings of which God has so richly blessed, and labor side by side until our common goal is reached.

Some of us, pioneers in this undertaking, have grown old in our search for unity. It is to youth that we look to lift the torch on high. We men have carried it too much alone through many years. The women henceforth should be accorded their share of responsibility. And so the whole church will be enabled to do that which no section can hope to perform.

It was God's clear call that gathered us. With faith stimulated by his guidance to us here, we move forward.

2. THE CHURCH'S MESSAGE TO THE WORLD — THE GOSPEL

The message of the church to the world is and must always remain the gospel of Jesus Christ.

The gospel is the joyful message of redemption, both here and hereafter, the gift of God to sinful man in Jesus Christ.

The world was prepared for the coming of Christ through the activities of God's Spirit in all humanity, but especially in his revelation as given in the Old Testament; and in the fullness of time the eternal Word of God became incarnate, and was made man, Jesus Christ, the Son of God and the Son of man, full of grace and truth. [Gal 4.4] [Jn 1.14]

Through his life and teaching, his call to repentance, his proclamation of the coming of the kingdom of God and of judgment, his suffering and death, his resurrection and exaltation to the right hand of the Father, and by the mission of the Holy Spirit, he has brought to us forgiveness of sins, and has revealed the fullness of the living God, and his boundless love toward us. By the appeal of that love, shown in its completeness on the cross, he summons us to the new life of faith, self-sacrifice, and devotion to his service and the service of men.

Jesus Christ, as the crucified and the living one, as Savior and Lord, is also the center of the worldwide gospel of the apostles and the church. Because he himself is the gospel, the gospel is the message of the church to the world. It is more than a philosophical theory; more than a theological system; more than a program for material betterment. The gospel is rather the gift of a new world from God to this old world of sin and death; still more, it is the victory over sin and death, the revelation of eternal life in him who has knit together the whole family in heaven and on earth in the communion of saints, united in the fellowship of service, of prayer, and of praise.

The gospel is the prophetic call to sinful man to turn to God, the joyful tidings of justification and of sanctification to those who believe in Christ. It is the comfort of those who suffer; to those who are bound, it is the assurance of the glorious liberty of the sons of God. The gospel brings peace and joy to the heart, and produces in men self-denial, readiness for brotherly service, and compassionate love. It offers the supreme goal for the aspirations of youth, strength to the toiler, rest to the weary, and the crown of life to the martyr.

The gospel is the sure source of power for social regeneration. It proclaims the only way by which humanity can escape from those class and race hatreds which devastate society at present into the enjoyment of national well-being and international friendship and peace. It is also a gracious invitation to the non-Christian world, East and West, to enter into the joy of the living Lord.

Sympathizing with the anguish of our generation, with its longing for intellectual sincerity, social justice, and spiritual inspiration, the church in the eternal gospel meets the needs and fulfills the God-given aspirations of the modern world.

Consequently, as in the past so also in the present, the gospel is the only way of salvation. Thus, through his church, the living Christ still says to men, "Come unto me! . . . He that followeth me shall not walk in darkness, but shall have the light of [Jn 8.12]   life."

3. THE NATURE OF THE CHURCH

God who has given us the gospel for the salvation of the world has appointed his church to witness by life and word to its redeeming power. The church of the living God is constituted by his own will, not by the will or consent or beliefs of men whether as individuals or as societies, though he uses the will of men as his instrument. Of this church Jesus Christ is the Head, the Holy Spirit its continuing life.

The church as the communion of believers in Christ Jesus is, according to the New Testament, the people of the new covenant; the body of Christ; and the temple of God, built upon the foundation of the apostles and prophets, Jesus Christ [Eph 2.20]   himself being the chief cornerstone.

The church is God's chosen instrument by which Christ, through the Holy Spirit, reconciles men to God through faith, bringing their wills into subjection to his sovereignty, sanctifying them through the means of grace, and uniting them in love and service to be his witnesses and fellow workers in the extension of his rule on earth until his kingdom come in glory.

As there is but one Christ, and one life in him, and one Holy Spirit who [Jn 16.13]   guides into all truth, so there is and can be but one church, holy, catholic, and apostolic.[1]

The church on earth possesses certain characteristics whereby it can be known of men. These have been, since the days of the apostles, at least the following:

(1) The possession and acknowledgment of the word of God as given in Holy Scripture and interpreted by the Holy Spirit to the church and to the individual. (Note A.)

(2) The profession of faith in God as he is incarnate and revealed in Christ.

(3) The acceptance of Christ's commission to preach the gospel to every creature.

(4) The observance of the sacraments.

(5) A ministry for the pastoral office, the preaching of the word, and the administration of the sacraments.

(6) A fellowship in prayer, in worship, in all the means of grace, in the pursuit of holiness, and in the service of man.

1. N-CP 9.

As to the extent and manner in which the church thus described finds expression in the existing churches, we differ. Our differences chiefly concern:

(1) The nature of the church visible and the church invisible, their relation to each other, and the number of those who are included in each. (Note B.)

(2) The significance of our divisions past and present. (Note C.)

Whatever our views on these points, we are convinced that it is the will of Christ that the one life of the one body should be manifest to the world. To commend the gospel to doubting, sinful, and bewildered men, a united witness is necessary. We therefore urge most earnestly that all Christians, in fulfillment of our Savior's prayer that his disciples may be one, reconsecrate themselves to God, that by the [Jn 17.21] help of his Spirit the body of Christ may be built up, its members united in faith and love, and existing obstacles to the manifestation of their unity in Christ may be removed; that the world may believe that the Father has sent him.

We join in the prayer that the time may be hastened when in the name of Jesus every knee shall bow and every tongue confess that Jesus Christ is Lord to the glory of God the Father. [Phil 2.10–11]

Notes

(A) Some hold that this interpretation is given through the tradition of the church; others through the immediate witness of the Spirit to the heart and conscience of believers; others through both combined.

(B) For instance

(1) Some hold that the invisible church is wholly in heaven; others include in it all true believers on earth, whether contained in any organization or not.

(2) Some hold that the visible expression of the church was determined by Christ himself and is therefore unchangeable; others that the one church under the guidance of the Holy Spirit may express itself in varying forms.

(3) Some hold that one or other of the existing churches is the only true church; others that the church as we have described it is to be found in some or all of the existing communions taken together.

(4) Some, while recognizing other Christian bodies as churches, are persuaded that in the providence of God and by the teaching of history a particular form of ministry has been shown to be necessary to the best welfare of the church; others hold that no one form of organization is inherently preferable; still others, that no organization is necessary.

(C) One view is that no division of Christendom has ever come to pass without sin. Another view is that the divisions were the inevitable outcome of different gifts of the Spirit and different understandings of the truth. Between these, there is the view of those who look back on the divisions of the past with penitence and sorrow coupled with a lively sense of God's mercy, which in spite of and even through these divisions has advanced his cause in the world.

4. THE CHURCH'S COMMON CONFESSION OF FAITH

We members of the Conference on Faith and Order, coming from all parts of the world in the interest of Christian unity, have with deep gratitude to God found ourselves united in common prayer, in God our heavenly Father and his Son Jesus Christ, our Savior, in the fellowship of the Holy Spirit.

Notwithstanding the differences in doctrine among us, we are united in a common Christian faith which is proclaimed in the Holy Scriptures and is witnessed to and safeguarded in the Ecumenical Creed, commonly called the Nicene, and in the Apostles' Creed, which faith is continuously confirmed in the spiritual experience of the church of Christ.

We believe that the Holy Spirit in leading the church into all truth may enable it, while firmly adhering to the witness of these creeds (our common heritage from the ancient church), to express the truths of revelation in such other forms as new problems may from time to time demand.

Finally, we desire to leave on record our solemn and unanimous testimony that no external and written standards can suffice without an inward and personal experience of union with God in Christ.

Notes

1. It must be noted that the Orthodox Eastern Church can accept the Nicene Creed only in its uninterpolated form without the Filioque clause; and that although the Apostles' Creed has no place in the formularies of this church, it is in accordance with its teaching.

2. It must be noted also that some of the churches represented in this conference conjoin tradition with the Scriptures, some are explicit in subordinating creeds to the Scriptures, some attach a primary importance to their particular confessions, and some make no use of creeds.

3. It is understood that the use of these creeds will be determined by the competent authority in each church, and that the several churches will continue to make use of such special confessions as they possess.

5. THE MINISTRY OF THE CHURCH

We members of the Conference on Faith and Order are happy to report that we find ourselves in substantial accord in the following five propositions:

(1) The ministry is a gift of God through Christ to his church and is essential to the being and well-being of the church.

(2) The ministry is perpetually authorized and made effective through Christ and his Spirit.

(3) The purpose of the ministry is to impart to men the saving and sanctifying benefits of Christ through pastoral service, the preaching of the gospel, and the administration of the sacraments, to be made effective by faith.

(4) The ministry is entrusted with the government and discipline of the church, in whole or in part.

(5) Men gifted for the work of the ministry, called by the Spirit and accepted by the church, are commissioned through an act of ordination by prayer and the laying on of hands to exercise the function of this ministry.

Within the many Christian communions into which in the course of history Christendom has been divided, various forms of ministry have grown up according to the circumstances of the several communions and their beliefs as to the mind of Christ and the guidance of the New Testament. These communions have been, in God's providence, manifestly and abundantly used by the Holy Spirit in his work of enlightening the world, converting sinners, and perfecting saints. But the differences which have arisen in regard to the authority and functions of these various forms of ministry have been and are the occasion of manifold doubts, questions, and misunderstandings.

These differences concern the nature of the ministry (whether consisting of one or several orders), the nature of ordination and of the grace conferred thereby, the function and authority of bishops, and the nature of apostolic succession. We believe that the first step toward the overcoming of these difficulties is the frank recognition that they exist, and the clear definition of their nature. We therefore add as an appendix to our report such a statement, commending it to the thoughtful consideration of the churches we represent.

By these differences the difficulties of intercommunion have been accentuated to the distress and wounding of faithful souls, while in the mission field, where the church is fulfilling its primary object to preach the gospel to every creature, the [Mk 16.15] young churches find the lack of unity a very serious obstacle to the furtherance of the gospel. Consequently the provision of a ministry acknowledged in every part of the church as possessing the sanction of the whole church is an urgent need.

There has not been time in this conference to consider all the points of difference between us in the matter of the ministry with that care and patience which could alone lead to complete agreement. The same observation applies equally to proposals for the constitution of the united church. Certain suggestions as to possible church organization have been made, which we transmit to the churches with the earnest hope that common study of these questions will be continued by the members of the various churches represented in this conference.

In view of (1) the place which the episcopate, the councils of presbyters, and the congregation of the faithful, respectively, had in the constitution of the early church, and (2) the fact that episcopal, presbyteral, and congregational systems of government are each today, and have been for centuries, accepted by great communions in Christendom, and (3) the fact that episcopal, presbyteral, and congregational systems are each believed by many to be essential to the good order of the church, we therefore recognize that these several elements must all, under conditions which require further study, have an appropriate place in the order of life of a reunited church, and that each separate communion, recalling the abundant blessing of God vouchsafed to its ministry in the past, should gladly bring to the common life of the united church its own spiritual treasures.

If the foregoing suggestion be accepted and acted upon, it is essential that the acceptance of any special form of ordination as the regular and orderly method of introduction into the ministry of the church for the future should not be interpreted to imply the acceptance of any one particular theory of the origin, character, or function of any office in the church, or to involve the acceptance of any adverse judgment on the validity of ordination in those branches of the church universal that believe themselves to have retained valid and apostolic orders under other forms of ordination; or as disowning or discrediting a past or present ministry of the word and sacrament which has been used and blessed by the Spirit of God.

It is further recognized that inasmuch as the Holy Spirit is bestowed upon every believer, and each believer has an immediate access to God through Jesus Christ, and since special gifts of the Holy Spirit, such as teaching, preaching, and spiritual counsel, are the treasures of the church as well as of the individual, it is necessary and proper that the church should make fuller use of such gifts for the development of its corporate spiritual life and for the extension of the kingdom of Jesus Christ, our Lord.

In particular, we share in the conviction, repeatedly expressed in this conference, that pending the solution of the questions of faith and order in which agreements have not yet been reached, it is possible for us, not simply as individuals but as churches, to unite in the activities of brotherly service which Christ has committed to his disciples. We therefore commend to our churches the consideration of the steps which may be immediately practicable to bring our existing unity in service to more effective expression.

In conclusion, we express our thankfulness to Almighty God for the great progress which has been made in recent years in the mutual approach of the churches to one another, and our conviction that we must go forward with faith and courage, confident that with the blessing of God we shall be able to solve the problems that lie before us.

Notes

1. The following is the view of the Orthodox Church, as formulated for us by its representatives. "The Orthodox Church, regarding the ministry as instituted in the church by Christ himself, and as the body which by a special *charisma* is the organ through which the church spreads its means of grace such as the sacraments, and believing that the ministry in its threefold form of bishops, presbyters, and deacons can only be based on the unbroken apostolic succession, regrets that it is unable to come in regard to the ministry into some measure of agreement with many of the churches represented at this conference; but prays God that he, through his Holy Spirit, will guide to union even in regard to this difficult point of disagreement."

2. In Western Christendom also there are conspicuous differences.

One representative view includes the following points: (a) that there have always been various grades of the ministry, each with its own function; (b) that ordination is a sacramental act of divine institution, and therefore indispensable, conveying the special *charisma* for the particular ministry; (c) that bishops who have received their office by succession from the apostles are the necessary ministers of ordination; (d) that the apostolic succession so understood is necessary for the authority of the ministry, the visible unity of the church, and the validity of the sacraments.

On the other hand it is held by many churches represented in the conference (a) that essentially there is only one ministry, that of the word and sacraments; (b) that the existing ministries in these churches are agreeable to the New Testament, are proved by their fruits, and have due authority in the church, and the sacraments ministered by them are valid; (c) that no particular form of ministry is necessary to be received as a matter of faith; (d) that the grace which fits men for the ministry is immediately given by God, and is recognized, not conferred, in ordination.

Further we record that there are views concerning the ministry which are intermediate between the types just mentioned. For instance, some who adhere to an episcopal system of church government do not consider that the apostolic succession as described above is a vital element of episcopacy, or they reject it altogether. Others do not regard as essential the historic episcopate. Those who adhere to presbyteral systems of church government believe that the apostolic ministry is transmissible and has been transmitted through presbyters orderly associated for the purpose. Those who adhere to the congregational system of government define their ministry as having been and being transmitted according to the precedent and example of the New Testament.

6. THE SACRAMENTS

We are convinced that for the purpose in view in this conference we should not go into detail in considering sacraments—by some called "mysteries." The purpose therefore of this statement is to show that there may be a common approach to and appreciation of sacraments on the part of those who may otherwise differ in conception and interpretation.

We testify to the fact that the Christian world gives evidence of an increasing sense of the significance and value of sacraments, and would express our belief that this movement should be fostered and guided as a means of deepening the life and experience of the churches. In this connection we recognize that the sacraments have special reference to the corporate life and fellowship of the church and that the grace is conveyed by the Holy Spirit, taking of the things of Christ and applying them to the soul through faith.

We agree that sacraments are of divine appointment and that the church ought thankfully to observe them as divine gifts.

We hold that in the sacraments there is an outward sign and an inward grace, and that the sacraments are means of grace through which God works invisibly in us. We recognize also that in the gifts of his grace God is not limited by his own sacraments.

The Orthodox Church and others hold that there are seven sacraments and that for their valid administration there must be a proper form, a proper matter, and a proper ministry. Others can regard only baptism and the Lord's supper as sacraments. Others again, while attaching high value to the sacramental principle, do not make use of the outward signs of sacraments, but hold that all spiritual benefits are given through immediate contact with God through his Spirit. In this conference we lay stress on the two sacraments of baptism and the Lord's supper, because they are the sacraments which are generally acknowledged by the members of this conference.

We believe that in baptism administered with water in the name of the Father, the Son, and the Holy Spirit, for the remission of sins, we are baptized by one Spirit into one body. By this statement it is not meant to ignore the differences in conception, interpretation, and mode which exist among us.

We believe that in the holy communion our Lord is present, that we have fellowship with God our Father in Jesus Christ his Son, our living Lord, who is our one bread, given for the life of the world, sustaining the life of all his people, and that we are in fellowship with all others who are united to him. We agree that the sacrament of the Lord's supper is the church's most sacred act of worship, in which the Lord's atoning death is commemorated and proclaimed, and that it is a sacrifice of praise and thanksgiving and an act of solemn self-oblation.

There are among us divergent views, especially as to (1) the mode and manner of the presence of our Lord; (2) the conception of the commemoration and the sacrifice; (3) the relation of the elements to the grace conveyed; and (4) the relation between the minister of this sacrament and the validity and efficacy of the rite. We are aware that the reality of the divine presence and gift in this sacrament cannot be adequately apprehended by human thought or expressed in human language.

We close this statement with the prayer that the differences which prevent full communion at the present time may be removed.

CONCLUDING STATEMENT

We have finished our immediate task. From first to last we are able to express it in constructive terms written and received, whether they be statements of agreement or statements of difference, in brotherly love and mutual consideration. They are the product of the minds of men who earnestly desired and strove to place and keep themselves under the guidance of God's Holy Spirit. Human imperfections which mingle with them we pray God to pardon. In offering to him our handiwork, we are but returning to him that which he has given to us. We pray his acceptance of and blessing upon our offering.

However, we have not finished our whole task. We have but taken a step on a long journey. The conference was only a new starting point. What we did there will crumble into dust unless the representatives at Lausanne bring home to their several churches the duty and responsibility of studying the reports which they themselves received for this very purpose. The conference should be repeated in every main ecclesiastical assembly, as well as in each separate congregation, throughout our entire Christian constituency if we are to take full advantage of the progress registered. By our presence and activity at Lausanne we are solemnly pledged to reproduce, each in his own local circle, the spirit and method which made the World Conference on Faith and Order what it was. "I pray you to give me the utter joy of knowing you are living in harmony, with the same feelings of love, with one heart and soul, never acting for private ends or from vanity, but humbly considering each other the better man, and each with an eye to the interests of others as well as to [Phil 2.2–5] his own. Treat one another with the same spirit as you experience in Christ Jesus."

We who have been privileged to labor together have done so in the joyousness of unhampered freedom. We must not forget, in the liberty which is to us a commonplace, the sufferings which some of our Christian brethren are at this very moment undergoing. Deprived of liberty, in hostile surroundings, their cry goes up to God from the house of their martyrdom. Our prayers enfold them and our sympathy stretches out affectionate arms toward them.

Finally, we commend the Christian churches, whether represented in the conference or not, to our heavenly Father's guidance and safekeeping, looking earnestly toward the day when the full mind of God will control all the affairs of mankind.

The Church of Christ in China,
The Bond of Union, 1927

Among the "younger churches" struggling to find and to articulate their identity in the twentieth century, the churches in China that had come out of the China Inland Mission and other endeavors at evangelization have been, even more than those in other cultures, drawn in various directions by the intensifying self-assertions of their own land and the gospel as they had learned it from their Western teachers but were increasingly making their own.

As a confessional experiment growing out of that tension, this *Bond of Union* of 1927 opens, significantly, with the declaration of "the principle of the freedom of formulating *her own faith,*" but closes with the reaffirmation of → *The Apostles' Creed.*

It was approved as article 3 of the Constitution by the First General Assembly of the Churches of Christ in China in October 1927.

Edition: Chinese Christian Church, *Presbyterian Church Bulletin* 1/1 (1928): 12.

Translation: Anderson, 249.

Literature: Anderson, 249; Latourette 1967; Merwin 1974, 65–67, 214–16.

The Church of Christ in China, *The Bond of Union*, 1927

Based on the principle of the freedom of formulating her own faith, the bond of union shall consist:

1. In our faith in Jesus Christ as our Redeemer and Lord on whom the Christian church is founded; and in an earnest desire for the establishment of his kingdom throughout the whole earth.

2. In our acceptance of the Holy Scriptures of the Old and New Testaments as the divinely inspired word of God, and the supreme authority in matters of faith and duty.

3. In our acknowledgment of the Apostles' Creed as expressing the fundamental doctrines of our common evangelical faith.

The Korean Methodist Church, *Doctrinal Statement*, 1930

During the decade that Tongshik Ryu has labeled "the flowering stage of Korean theology (1928–1939)," the missionaries and native leaders of two Protestant dominations were the most influential, Presbyterians and Methodists. "The Methodists," he adds, "with an attitude of openness regarding the transition taking place in theology, made no issue of commitment to its past tradition."

That "attitude of openness" makes itself evident in this brief *Doctrinal Statement*, written in 1930 and published in 1931, which simultaneously pays tribute to → *The Methodist Articles of Religion* as "our heritage and our glorious possession" but declares that "we impose no doctrinal test" and that "we sanction the fullest liberty of belief for the individual Christian."

Edition: *Discipline of the Korean Methodist Church* 1931, sec. 35.

Translation: *Discipline of the Korean Methodist Church* 1932, 25–26.

Literature: Tongshik Ryu in Anderson, 161–77; *Discipline of the Korean Methodist Church* 1932, 1–8; Poitras 1997; Ryang 1934.

The Korean Methodist Church,
Doctrinal Statement, 1930

The fundamental principles of Christianity have been set forth at various times and in various forms in the historic creeds of the church, and have been interpreted by Mr. Wesley in the Articles of Religion and in his sermons and Notes on the New Testament. This evangelical faith is our heritage and our glorious possession.

Upon those persons who desire to unite with us as members, we impose no doctrinal test. Our main requirement is loyalty to Jesus Christ and a purpose to follow him. With us, as with Mr. Wesley in the earliest General Rules of the United Societies, the conditions of membership are moral and spiritual rather than theological. We sanction the fullest liberty of belief for the individual Christian, so long as his character and his works approve themselves as consistent with true godliness.

It is fitting, however, that we should state the chief doctrines which are most surely believed among us.

1. We believe in the one God, Maker and Ruler of all things, Father of all men; the source of all goodness and beauty, all truth and love.

2. We believe in Jesus Christ, God manifest in the flesh, our Teacher, Example, and Redeemer, the Savior of the world.

3. We believe in the Holy Spirit, God present with us for guidance, for comfort, and for strength.

4. We believe in the forgiveness of sins, in the life of love and prayer, and in grace equal to every need.

5. We believe in the word of God contained in the Old and New Testaments as the sufficient rule both of faith and of practice.

6. We believe in the church as the fellowship for worship and for service of all who are united to the living Lord.

7. We believe in the kingdom of God as the divine rule in human society; and in the brotherhood of man under the fatherhood of God.

8. We believe in the final triumph of righteousness, and in the life everlasting. Amen.

Evangelical Lutheran Synod of Missouri, Ohio, and Other States, *A Brief Statement*, 1932

As had become evident with the issuance of the → *Definite Platform* of the Lutheran General Synod in 1855, the asseveration of loyalty to → *The Augsburg Confession* of 1530 or even to the entire → *Book of Concord* of 1580 could no longer be relied upon as an adequate expression of authentic Lutheranism in a society that had no established church and was religiously pluralistic: necesssary, but no longer sufficient.

The principal defender of Lutheran confessionalism in the United States was the Evangelical Lutheran Synod of Missouri, Ohio, and Other States (Missouri Synod), which had been involved in doctrinal controversies, especially over the doctrine of the ministry and the doctrine of election, during the nineteenth century. The various mergers of Lutheran synods from 1917 onward were changing the denominational, and inevitably therefore also the confessional, landscape of American Lutheranism. At its convention of 1929, the Missouri Synod mandated the preparation of a document briefly setting forth its confessional position vis-à-vis those earlier controversies and this new situation.

The result was *A Brief Statement of the Doctrinal Position of the Evangelical Lutheran Synod of Missouri, Ohio, and Other States*. It was completed in 1931, and the draft was circulated within the synod for discussion and reaction. After a consideration of the document and of those reactions, it was voted on and accepted "as a brief Scriptural statement of the doctrinal position of the Missouri Synod" by the 1932 convention. This was reaffirmed at the centennial convention of the Lutheran Church–Missouri Synod in 1947.

Edition: *Doct Dec* 42–57.

Literature: Lueker 1954, 139–40.

Evangelical Lutheran Synod of Missouri, Ohio, and Other States, *A Brief Statement*, 1932

OF THE HOLY SCRIPTURES

1. We teach that the Holy Scriptures differ from all other books in the world in that they are the word of God. They are the word of God because the holy men of God who wrote the Scriptures wrote only that which the Holy Ghost communicated to them by inspiration, 2 Tm 3.16; 2 Pt 1.21. We teach also that the verbal inspiration of the Scriptures is not a so-called theological deduction, but that it is taught by direct statements of the Scriptures, 2 Tm 3.16; Jn 10.35; Rom 3.2; 1 Cor 2.13. Since the Holy Scriptures are the word of God, it goes without saying that they contain no errors or contradictions, but that they are in all their parts and words the infallible truth, also in those parts which treat of historical, geographical, and other secular matters, Jn 10.35.

2. We furthermore teach regarding the Holy Scriptures that they are given by God to the Christian Church for the foundation of faith, Eph 2.20. Hence the Holy Scriptures are the sole source from which all doctrines proclaimed in the Christian Church must be taken and therefore, too, the sole rule and norm by which all teachers and doctrines must be examined and judged. —With the confessions of our church we teach also that the "rule of faith" (*analogia fidei*) according to which the Holy Scriptures are to be understood are the clear passages of *the Scriptures themselves* which set forth the individual doctrines.[1] The rule of faith is not the man-made so-called totality of Scripture (*"Ganzes der Schrift"*).

3. We reject the doctrine which under the name of science has gained wide popularity in the church of our day that Holy Scripture is not in all its parts the word of God, but in part the word of God and in part the word of man and hence does, or at least might, contain error. We reject this erroneous doctrine as horrible and blasphemous, since it flatly contradicts Christ and his holy apostles, sets up men as judges over the word of God, and thus overthrows the foundation of the Christian Church and its faith.

OF GOD

4. On the basis of the Holy Scriptures we teach the sublime article of the Holy Trinity; that is, we teach that the one true God, Dt 6.4; 1 Cor 8.4, is the Father and

---

1. *Apol Aug* 27.60.

the Son and the Holy Ghost, three distinct *persons,* but of one and the same divine *essence,* equal in power, equal in eternity, equal in majesty, because each person possesses the one divine essence *entire,* Col 2.9; Mt 28.19. We hold that all teachers and communions that deny the doctrine of the Holy Trinity are outside the pale of the Christian Church. The triune God is the God who is *gracious* to man, Jn 3.16–18; 1 Cor 12.3. Since the fall no man can believe in the "fatherhood" of God except he believe in the eternal Son of God, who became man and reconciled us to God by his vicarious satisfaction, 1 Jn 2.23; Jn 14.6. Hence we warn against Unitarianism, which in our country has to a great extent impenetrated the sects and is being spread particularly also through the influence of the lodges.

OF CREATION

5. We teach that God has created heaven and earth, and that in the manner and in the space of time recorded in the Holy Scriptures, especially Genesis 1 and 2, namely, by his almighty creative word, and in six days. We reject every doctrine which denies or limits the work of creation as taught in Scripture. In our days it is denied or limited by those who assert, ostensibly in deference to science, that the world came into existence through a process of evolution; that is, that it has, in immense periods of time, developed more or less out of itself. Since no man was present when it pleased God to create the world, we must look for a reliable account of creation to God's own record, found in God's own book, the Bible. We accept God's own record with full confidence and confess with Luther's Catechism: "I believe that God has made me and all creatures."[2]

OF MAN AND OF SIN

6. We teach that the first man was not brutelike nor merely capable of intellectual development, but that God created man *in his own image,* Gn 1.26, 27; Eph 4.24; Col 3.10, that is, in true knowledge of God and in true righteousness and holiness and endowed with a truly scientific knowledge of nature, Gn 2.19–23.

7. We furthermore teach that sin came into the world by the fall of the first man, as described Genesis 3. By this fall not only he himself, but also all his natural offspring have lost the original knowledge, righteousness, and holiness, and thus all men are sinners already by birth, dead in sins, inclined to all evil, and subject to the wrath of God, Rom 5.12, 18; Eph 2.1–3. We teach also that men are unable, through any efforts of their own or by the aid of "culture and science," to reconcile themselves to God and thus to conquer death and damnation.

2. *Luth Sm Cat* 2.2.

OF REDEMPTION

8. We teach that in the fullness of time the eternal Son of God *was made man* by assuming, from the Virgin Mary through the operation of the Holy Ghost, a human nature like unto ours, yet without sin, and receiving it into his divine person. Jesus Christ is therefore "true God, begotten of the Father from eternity, and also true man, born of the Virgin Mary," true God and true man in *one* undivided and indivisible person. The purpose of this miraculous incarnation of the Son of God was that he might become the *Mediator* between God and men, both fulfilling the divine law and suffering and dying in the place of mankind. In this manner God has reconciled the whole sinful world unto himself, Gal 4.4, 5, 3.13; 2 Cor 5.18, 19.

OF FAITH IN CHRIST

9. Since God has reconciled the whole world unto himself through the vicarious life and death of his Son and has commanded that the reconciliation effected by Christ be proclaimed to men in the gospel, to the end that they may *believe* it, 2 Cor 5.18, 19; Rom 1.5, therefore faith in Christ is the only way for men to obtain personal reconciliation with God, that is, forgiveness of sins, as both the Old and the New Testament Scriptures testify, Acts 10.43; Jn 3.16–18, 36. By this faith in Christ, through which men obtain the forgiveness of sins, is not meant any human effort to fulfill the law of God after the example of Christ, but faith in the gospel, that is, in the forgiveness of sins, or justification, which was fully earned for us by Christ and is offered in the gospel. This faith justifies, not inasmuch as it is a work of man, but inasmuch as it lays hold of the grace offered, the forgiveness of sins, Rom 4.16.

OF CONVERSION

10. We teach that conversion consists in this, that a man, having learned from the law of God that he is a lost and condemned sinner, *is brought to faith in the gospel,* which offers him forgiveness of sins and eternal salvation for the sake of Christ's vicarious satisfaction, Acts 11.21; Lk 24.46, 47; Acts 26.18.

11. All men, since the fall, are dead in sins, Eph 2.1–3, and inclined only to evil, Gn 6.5, 8.21; Rom 8.7. For this reason, and particularly because men regard the gospel of Christ, crucified for the sins of the world, as foolishness, 1 Cor 2.14, faith in the gospel, or conversion to God, is neither wholly nor in the least part the work of man, but the work of God's grace and almighty power alone, Phil 1.29; Eph 2.8, 1.19; Jer 31.18. Hence Scripture calls the faith of man, or his conversion, a raising from the dead, Eph 1.20; Col 2.12, a being born of God, Jn 1.12, 13, a new

birth by the gospel, 1 Pt 1.23–25, a work of God like the creation of light at the creation of the world, 2 Cor 4.6.

12. On the basis of these clear statements of the Holy Scriptures we reject every kind of *synergism,* that is, the doctrine that conversion is wrought not by the grace and power of God alone, but in part also by the cooperation of man himself, by man's right conduct, his right attitude, his right self-determination, his lesser guilt or less evil conduct as compared with others, his refraining from willful resistance, or anything else whereby man's conversion and salvation is taken out of the gracious hands of God and made to depend on what man does or leaves undone. For this refraining from willful resistance or from any kind of resistance is also solely a work of grace, which "changes unwilling into willing men," Ez 36.26; Phil 2.13. We reject also the doctrine that man is able to decide for conversion through "powers imparted by grace," since this doctrine presupposes that *before* conversion man still possesses spiritual powers by which he can make the right use of such "powers imparted by grace."

13. On the other hand, we reject also the *Calvinistic* perversion of the doctrine of conversion, that is, the doctrine that God does not desire to convert and save all hearers of the word, but only a portion of them. Many hearers of the word indeed remain unconverted and are not saved, not because God does not earnestly desire their conversion and salvation, but solely because they stubbornly resist the gracious operation of the Holy Ghost, as Scripture teaches, Acts 7.51; Mt 23.37; Acts 13.46.

14. As to the question why not all men are converted and saved, seeing that God's grace is universal and all men are equally and utterly corrupt, we confess that we cannot answer it. From Scripture we know only this: A man owes his conversion and salvation, not to any lesser guilt or better conduct on his part, but solely to the grace of God. But any man's nonconversion is due to himself alone: it is the result of his obstinate resistance against the converting operation of the Holy Ghost, Hos 13.9.

15. Our refusal to go beyond what is revealed in these two scriptural truths is not "masked Calvinism" ("Crypto-calvinism"), but *precisely* the scriptural teaching of the Lutheran Church as it is presented in detail in the Formula of Concord: "That one is hardened, blinded, given over to a reprobate mind, while another, who is indeed in the same guilt, is converted again, etc.,—in these and similar questions Paul fixes a certain limit to us how far we should go, namely, that in the one part we should recognize God's *judgment.* For they are well-deserved penalties of sins when God so punished a land or nation for despising his word that the punishment

extends also to their posterity, as is to be seen in the Jews. And thereby God in some lands and persons exhibits his severity to those that are his in order to indicate what we all would have well deserved and would be worthy and worth, since we act wickedly in opposition to God's word and often grieve the Holy Ghost sorely; in order that we may live in the fear of God and acknowledge and praise God's *goodness,* to the exclusion of, and contrary to, our merit and with *us,* to whom he gives his word and with whom he leaves it and whom he does not harden and reject. . . . And this his righteous, well-deserved judgment he displays in some countries, nations, and persons in order that, when we are placed alongside of them and compared with them (*quam simillimi illis deprehensi,* i.e., and found to be most similar to them), we may learn the more diligently to recognize and praise God's pure, unmerited grace in the vessels of mercy. . . . When we proceed thus far in this article, we remain on the right way, as it is written, Hos 13.9: 'O Israel, thou hast destroyed thyself; but in me is thy help.' However, as regards these things in this disputation which would soar too high and beyond these limits, we should with Paul place the finger upon our lips and remember and say, Rom 9.20: 'O man, who art thou that repliest against God?'" The Formula of Concord describes the mystery which confronts us here not as a mystery in man's heart (a "psychological" mystery), but teaches that, when we try to understand why "one is hardened, blinded, given over to a reprobate mind, while another, who is indeed in the same guilt, is converted again," we enter the domain of the unsearchable judgments of God and ways past finding out, which are not revealed to us in his word, but which we shall know in eternal life, 1 Cor 13.12.[3]

16. Calvinists solve this mystery, which God has not revealed in his word, by denying the *universality* of grace; synergists, by denying that salvation is by grace *alone.* Both solutions are utterly vicious, since they contradict Scripture and since every poor sinner stands in need of, and must cling to, both the unrestricted *universal grace* and the unrestricted "by grace *alone,*" lest he despair and perish.

OF JUSTIFICATION

17. Holy Scripture sums up all its teachings regarding the love of God to the world of sinners, regarding the salvation wrought by Christ, and regarding faith in Christ as the only way to obtain salvation, in the article of *justification.* Scripture teaches that God has already declared the whole world to be righteous in Christ, Rom 7.19; 2 Cor 5.18–21; Rom 4.25; that therefore not for the sake of their good works, but without the works of the law, by grace, for Christ's sake, he *justifies,* that is, ac-

3. *Form Conc Sol Dec* 11.57–59, 60, 62–63.

counts as righteous, all those who believe in Christ, that is, believe, accept, and rely on, the fact that for Christ's sake their sins are forgiven. Thus the Holy Ghost testifies through St. Paul: "There is no difference; for all have sinned and come short of the glory of God, being justified freely by his grace, through the redemption that is in Christ Jesus," Rom 3.23, 24. And again: "Therefore we conclude that a man is justified by faith, without the deeds of the law," Rom 3.28.

18. Through this doctrine alone Christ is given the *honor* due him, namely, that through his holy life and innocent suffering and death he is our Savior. And through this doctrine alone can poor sinners have the abiding *comfort* that God is assuredly gracious to them. We reject *as apostasy from the Christian religion* all doctrines whereby man's own works and merit are mingled into the article of justification before God. For the Christian religion is the faith that we have forgiveness of sins and salvation through faith in Christ Jesus, Acts 10.43.

19. We reject as apostasy from the Christian religion not only the doctrine of the *Unitarians,* who promise the grace of God to men on the basis of their moral efforts; not only the gross work-doctrine of the papists, who expressly teach that good works are necessary to obtain justification; but also the doctrine of the *synergists,* who indeed use the terminology of the Christian Church and say that man is justified "by faith," "by faith alone," but again mix human works into the article of justification by ascribing to man a cooperation with God in the kindling of faith and thus stray into papistic territory.

OF GOOD WORKS

20. Before God only those works are good which are done for the glory of God and the good of man, according to the rule of the divine law. Such works, however, no man performs unless he first believes that God has forgiven him his sins and has given him eternal life by grace, for Christ's sake, without any works of his own, Jn 15.4, 5. We reject as a great folly the assertion, frequently made in our day, that works must be placed in the fore, and "faith in dogmas"—meaning the gospel of Christ crucified for the sins of the world—must be relegated to the rear. Since good works never precede faith, but are always and in every instance the *result* of faith in the gospel, it is evident that the only means by which we Christians can become rich in good works (and God would have us to be rich in good works, Ti 2.14) is unceasingly to remember the grace of God which we have received in Christ, Rom 12.1; 2 Cor 8.9. Hence we reject as unchristian and foolish any attempt to produce good works by the compulsion of the law or through carnal motives.

OF THE MEANS OF GRACE

21. Although God is present and operates everywhere throughout all creation and the whole earth is therefore full of the *temporal* bounties and blessings of God, Col 1.17; Acts 17.28, 14.17, still we hold with Scripture that God offers and communicates to men the *spiritual* blessings purchased by Christ, namely, the forgiveness of sins and the treasures and gifts connected therewith, only through the external means of grace ordained by him. These means of grace are the word of the gospel, in every form in which it is brought to man, and the sacraments of holy baptism and of the Lord's supper. The word of the gospel promises and applies the grace of God, works faith and thus regenerates man, and gives the Holy Ghost, Acts 20.24; Rom 10.17; 1 Pt 1.23; Gal 3.2. Baptism, too, is applied for the remission of sins and is therefore a washing of regeneration and renewing of the Holy Ghost, Acts 2.38, 22.16; Ti 3.5. Likewise the object of the Lord's supper, that is, of the ministration of the body and blood of Christ, is none other than the communication and sealing of the forgiveness of sins, as the words declare: "Given for you," and: "Shed for you for the remission of sins," Lk 22.19, 20; Mt 26.28, and: "This cup is the New Testament in my blood," 1 Cor 11.23; Jer 31.31–34 ("new covenant").

22. Since it is only through the external means ordained by him that God has promised to communicate the grace and salvation purchased by Christ, the Christian Church must not remain at home with the means of grace entrusted to it, but go into the whole world with the preaching of the gospel and the administration of the sacraments, Mt 28.19, 20; Mk 16.15, 16. For the same reason also the churches at home should never forget that there is no other way of winning souls for the church and keeping them with it than the faithful and diligent use of the divinely ordained means of grace. Whatever activities do not either directly apply the word of God or subserve such application we condemn as "new methods," unchurchly activities, which do not build, but harm, the church.

23. We reject as a dangerous error the doctrine, which disrupted the church of the Reformation, that the grace and the Spirit of God are communicated not through the external means ordained by him, but by an *immediate* operation of grace. This erroneous doctrine bases the forgiveness of sins, or justification, upon a fictitious "infused grace," that is, upon a quality of man, and thus again establishes the work-doctrine of the papists.

OF THE CHURCH

24. We believe that there is *one* holy Christian Church on earth, the Head of which is Christ and which is gathered, preserved, and governed by Christ through the gospel.

The members of the Christian Church are the *Christians*, that is, all those who have despaired of their own righteousness before God and believe that God forgives their sins for Christ's sake. The Christian Church, in the proper sense of the term, is composed of believers only, Acts 5.14, 26.18; which means that no person in whom the Holy Ghost has wrought faith in the gospel, or—which is the same thing—in the doctrine of justification, can be divested of his membership in the Christian Church; and, on the other hand, that no person in whose heart this faith does not dwell can be invested with such membership. All unbelievers, though they be in external communion with the church and even hold the office of teacher or any other office in the church, are not members of the church, but, on the contrary, dwelling-places and instruments of Satan, Eph 2.2. This is also the teaching of our Lutheran Confessions: "It is certain, however, that the wicked are in the power of the devil and members of the kingdom of the devil, as Paul teaches, Eph 2.2, when he says that 'the devil now worketh in the children of disobedience,'" etc.[4]

25. Since it is by faith in the gospel alone that men become members of the Christian Church, and since this faith cannot be seen by men, but is known to God alone, 1 Kgs 8.39; Acts 1.24; 2 Tm 2.19, therefore the Christian Church on earth is *invisible,* Lk 17.20, and will remain invisible till judgment day, Col 3.3, 4. In our day some Lutherans speak of two sides of the church, taking the means of grace to be its "visible side." It is true, the means of grace are necessarily related to the church, seeing that the church is created and preserved through them. But the means of grace are not for that reason a part of the church; for the church in the proper sense of the word consists only of *believers,* Eph 2.19, 20; Acts 5.14. Lest we abet the notion that the Christian Church in the proper sense of the term is an external institution, we shall continue to call the means of grace the "marks" of the church. Just as wheat is to be found only where it has been sown, so the church can be found only where the word of God is in use.

26. We teach that this church, which is the invisible communion of all believers, is to be found not only in those external church communions which teach the word of God purely in every part, but also where, along with error, so much of the word of God still remains that men may be brought to the knowledge of their sins and to faith in the forgiveness of sins, which Christ has gained for all men, Mk 16.16; Samaritans: Lk 17.16; Jn 4.25.

27. *Local Churches or Local Congregations.*—Holy Scripture, however, does not speak merely of the *one* church, which embraces the believers of all places, as in Mt 16.18; Jn 10.16, but also of churches in the *plural,* that is, of *local churches,* as in 1 Cor 16.19, 1.2; Acts 8.1: the churches of Asia, the church of God in Corinth, the

---

4. *Apol Aug* 7.16.

church in Jerusalem. But this does not mean that there are *two kinds* of churches, for the local churches also, in as far as they are churches, consist solely of believers, as we see clearly from the addresses of the epistles to local churches; for example, "Unto the church which is at Corinth, to *them that are sanctified* in Christ Jesus, called to be *saints*," 1 Cor 1.2; Rom 1.7, etc. The visible society, containing hypocrites as well as believers, is called a church only in an improper sense, Mt 13.47–50, 24–30, 38–43.

28. *On Church-Fellowship.* — Since God ordained that his word *only*, without the admixture of human doctrine, be taught and believed in the Christian Church, 1 Pt 4.11; Jn 8.31, 32; 1 Tm 6.3, 4, all Christians are required by God to discriminate between orthodox and heterodox church-bodies, Mt 7.15, to have church-fellowship only with orthodox church-bodies, and, in case they have strayed into heterodox church-bodies, to leave them, Rom 16.17. We repudiate *unionism*, that is, church-fellowship with the adherents of false doctrine, as disobedience to God's command, as causing divisions in the church, Rom 16.17; 2 Jn 9.10, and as involving the constant danger of losing the word of God entirely, 2 Tm 2.17–21.

29. The orthodox character of a church is established not by its mere name nor by its outward acceptance of, and subscription to, an orthodox creed, but by the doctrine which is *actually* taught in its pulpits, in its theological seminaries, and in its publications. On the other hand, a church does not forfeit its orthodox character through the casual intrusion of errors, provided these are combated and eventually removed by means of doctrinal discipline, Acts 20.30; 1 Tm 1.3.

30. *The Original and True Possessors of All Christian Rights and Privileges.* — Since the Christians are the church, it is self-evident that they alone *originally* possess the spiritual gifts and rights which Christ has gained for, and given to, his church. Thus St. Paul reminds all believers: "All things are yours," 1 Cor 3.21, 22, and Christ himself commits to all believers the keys of the kingdom of heaven, Mt 16.13–19, 18.17–20; Jn 20.22, 23, and commissions all believers to preach the gospel and to administer the sacraments, Mt 28.19, 20; 1 Cor 11.23–25. Accordingly, we reject all doctrines by which this spiritual power or any part thereof is adjudged as *originally* vested in certain individuals or bodies, such as the pope, or the bishops, or the order of the ministry, or the secular lords, or councils, or synods, etc. The officers of the church publicly administer their offices only by virtue of delegated powers, conferred on them by the original possessors of such powers, and such administration remains under the supervision of the latter, Col 4.17. Naturally all Christians have also the right and the duty to judge and decide matters of doctrine, not according to their own notions, of course, but according to the word of God, 1 Jn 4.1; 1 Pt 4.11.

OF THE PUBLIC MINISTRY

31. By the public ministry we mean the office by which the word of God is preached and the sacraments are administered *by order and in the name* of a Christian congregation. Concerning this office we teach that it is a *divine ordinance;* that is, the Christians of a certain locality must apply the means of grace not only privately and within the circle of their families nor merely in their common intercourse with fellow Christians, Jn 5.39; Eph 6.4; Col 3.16, but they are also required, by the divine order, to make provision that the word of God be publicly preached in their midst, and the sacraments administered according to the institution of Christ, by persons qualified for such work, whose qualifications and official functions are exactly defined in Scripture, Ti 1.5; Acts 14.23, 20.28; 2 Tm 2.2.

32. Although the office of the ministry is a divine ordinance, it possesses no other power than the power of the word of God, 1 Pt 4.11; that is to say, it is the duty of Christians to yield unconditional obedience to the office of the ministry whenever, and as long as, the minister proclaims to them the word of God, Heb 13.17; Lk 10.16. If, however, the minister, in his teachings and injunctions, were to go beyond the word of God, it would be the duty of Christians not to obey, but to disobey him, so as to remain faithful to Christ, Mt 23.8. Accordingly, we reject the false doctrine ascribing to the office of the ministry the right to demand obedience and submission in matters which Christ has not commanded.

33. Regarding *ordination* we teach that it is not a divine, but a commendable ecclesiastical ordinance.[5]

OF CHURCH AND STATE

34. Although both church and state are ordinances of God, yet they must not be commingled. Church and state have entirely different aims. By the church, God would save men, for which reason the church is called the "mother" of believers, Gal 4.26. By the state, God would maintain external order among men, "that we may lead a quiet and peaceable life in all godliness and honesty," 1 Tm 2.2. It follows that the means which church and state employ to gain their ends are entirely different. The church may not employ any other means than the preaching of the word of God, Jn 18.11, 36; 2 Cor 10.4. The state, on the other hand, makes laws bearing on civil matters and is empowered to employ for their execution also the sword and other corporal punishments, Rom 13.4.

Accordingly we condemn the policy of those who would have the power of the state employed "in the interest of the church" and who thus turn the church into

---

5. *Smal Art* tr 70.

a secular dominion; as also of those who, aiming to govern the state by the word of God, seek to turn the state into a church.

OF THE ELECTION OF GRACE

35. By election of grace we mean this truth, that all those who by the grace of God alone, for Christ's sake, through the means of grace, are brought to faith, are justified, sanctified, and preserved in faith *here in time,* that all these have already from eternity been endowed by God with faith, justification, sanctification, and preservation in faith, and this *for the same reason,* namely, by grace alone, for Christ's sake, and by way of the means of grace. That this is the doctrine of Holy Scripture is evident from Eph 1.3–7; 2 Thes 2.13, 14; Acts 13.48; Rom 8.28–30; 2 Tm 1.9; Mt 24.22–24.[6]

36. Accordingly we reject as an anti-scriptural error the doctrine that not alone the grace of God and the merit of Christ are the cause of the election of grace, but that God has, in addition, found or regarded something good *in us* which prompted or caused him to elect us, this being variously designated as "good works," "right conduct," "proper self-determination," "refraining from willful resistance," etc. Nor does Holy Scripture know of an election "by foreseen faith," "in view of faith," as though the faith of the elect were to be placed before their election; but according to Scripture the faith which the elect have in time belongs to the spiritual blessings with which God has endowed them by his eternal election. For Scripture teaches, Acts 13.48: "And as many as were ordained unto eternal life believed." Our Lutheran Confession also testifies: "The eternal election of God, however, not only foresees and foreknows the salvation of the elect, but is also, from the gracious will and pleasure of God in Christ Jesus, a cause which procures, works, helps, and promotes our salvation and what pertains thereto; and upon this our salvation is so founded that the gates of hell cannot prevail against it, Mt 16.18, as is written Jn 10.28: 'Neither shall any man pluck my sheep out of my hand'; and again, Acts 13.48: 'And as many as were ordained to eternal life believed.'"[7]

37. But as earnestly as we maintain that there is an election of *grace,* or a predestination to salvation, so decidedly do we teach, on the other hand, that there is no election of wrath, or predestination to *damnation.* Scripture plainly reveals the truth that the love of God for the world of lost sinners is universal, that is, that it embraces all men without exception, that Christ has fully reconciled all men unto God,

6. *Form Conc Sol Dec* 11.5, 8, 23.
7. *Form Conc Sol Dec* 11.8.

and that God earnestly desires to bring all men to faith, to preserve them therein, and thus to save them, as Scripture testifies, 1 Tm 2.4: "God will have all men to be saved and to come to the knowledge of the truth." No man is lost because God has predestinated him to eternal damnation.—Eternal election is a cause why the elect are brought to faith in time, Acts 13.48; but election is *not* a cause why men remain unbelievers when they hear the word of God. The reason assigned by Scripture for this sad fact is that these men judge *themselves* unworthy of everlasting life, putting the word of God from them and obstinately resisting the Holy Ghost, whose earnest will it is to bring also them to repentance and faith by means of the word, Acts 13.46, 7.51; Mt 23.37.

38. To be sure, it is necessary to observe the scriptural distinction between the election of grace and the universal will of grace. This universal gracious will of God embraces all men; the election of grace, however, does not embrace all, but only a definite number, whom "God hath from the beginning chosen to salvation," 2 Thes 2.13, the "remnant," the "seed" which "the Lord left," Rom 9.27-29, the "election," Rom 11.7; and while the universal will of grace is frustrated in the case of most men, Mt 22.14; Lk 7.30, the election of grace attains its end with all whom it embraces, Rom 8.28-30. Scripture, however, while distinguishing between the universal will of grace and the election of grace, does not place the two in opposition to each other. On the contrary, it teaches that the grace dealing with those who are lost is altogether earnest and fully efficacious for conversion. Blind reason indeed declares these two truths to be contradictory; but we impose silence on our reason. The seeming disharmony will disappear in the light of heaven, 1 Cor 13.12.

39. Furthermore, by election of grace, Scripture does not mean that *one* part of God's counsel of salvation according to which he will receive into heaven those who persevere in faith unto the end, but, on the contrary, Scripture means this, that God, before the foundation of the world, from pure grace, because of the redemption of Christ, has chosen for his own a definite number of persons out of the corrupt mass and has determined to bring them, through word and sacrament, to faith and salvation.

40. Christians can and should be assured of their eternal election. This is evident from the fact that Scripture addresses them as the chosen ones and comforts them with their election, Eph 1.4; 2 Thes 2.13. This assurance of one's personal election, however, springs only from faith in the gospel, from the assurance that God so loved the world that he gave his only-begotten Son, that whosoever believeth in him should not perish, but have everlasting life. For God sent not his Son into the world to *condemn* the world; on the contrary, through the life, suffering, and death of his

Son he fully *reconciled* the whole world of sinners unto himself. Faith in this truth leaves no room for the fear that God might still harbor thoughts of wrath and damnation concerning us. Scripture inculcates that in Rom 8.32, 33: "He that spared not his own Son, but delivered him up for us all, how shall he not with him also freely give us all things? Who shall lay anything to the charge of God's elect? It is God that justifieth." Luther's pastoral advice is therefore in accord with Scripture: "Gaze upon the wounds of Christ and the blood shed for you; there predestination will shine forth."[8] That the Christian obtains the personal assurance of his eternal election in this way is taught also by our Lutheran Confessions.[9] "Of this we should not judge according to our reason nor according to the law or from any external appearance. Neither should we attempt to investigate the secret, concealed abyss of divine predestination, but should give heed to the revealed will of God. For he has made known unto us the mystery of his will and made it manifest through *Christ* that it might be preached, Eph 1.9ff.; 2 Tm 1.9f."—In order to ensure the proper method of viewing eternal election and the Christian's assurance of it, the Lutheran Confessions set forth at length the principle that election is not to be considered "in a bare manner (*nude*), as though God only held a muster, thus: 'This one shall be saved, that one shall be damned'";[10] but "the Scriptures teach this doctrine in no other way than to direct us thereby to the *word*, Eph 1.13; 1 Cor 1.7; exhort to repentance, 2 Tm 3.16; urge to godliness, Eph 1.14; Jn 15.3; strengthen faith and assure us of our salvation, Eph 1.13; Jn 10.27 f.; 2 Thes 2.13 f."[11] To sum up, just as God in time draws the Christians unto himself through the gospel, so he has already in his eternal election endowed them with "sanctification of the Spirit and belief of the truth," 2 Thes 2.13. Therefore: If, by the grace of God, you believe in the gospel of the forgiveness of your sins for Christ's sake, you are to be certain that you also belong to the number of God's elect, even as Scripture, 2 Thes 2.13, addresses the believing Thessalonians as the chosen of God and gives thanks to God for their election.

OF SUNDAY

41. We teach that in the New Testament God has abrogated the Sabbath and all the holy days prescribed for the church of the old covenant, so that neither "the keeping of the Sabbath nor of any other day" nor the observance of at least one specific day

8. *Luther's Works* 5.47.
9. *Form Conc Sol Dec* 11.26.
10. *Form Conc Sol Dec* 11.9.
11. *Form Conc Sol Dec* 11.12.

of the seven days of the week is ordained or commanded by God, Col 2.16; Rom 14.5.[12]

The observance of Sunday and other church festivals is an ordinance of the church, made by virtue of Christian liberty.[13] Hence Christians should not regard such ordinances as ordained by God and binding upon the conscience, Col 2.16; Gal 4.10. However, for the sake of Christian love and peace they should willingly observe them, Rom 14.13; 1 Cor 14.40.[14]

OF THE MILLENNIUM

42. With the Augsburg Confession[15] we reject every type of millennialism, or chiliasm, the opinions that Christ will return visibly to this earth a thousand years before the end of the world and establish a dominion of the church over the world; or that before the end of the world the church is to enjoy a season of special prosperity; or that before the general resurrection on judgment day a number of departed Christians or martyrs are to be raised again to reign in glory in this world; or that before the end of the world a universal conversion of the Jewish nation (of Israel according to the flesh) will take place.

Over against this, Scripture clearly teaches, and we teach accordingly, that the kingdom of Christ on earth will remain under the cross until the end of the world, Acts 14.22; Jn 16.33, 18.36; Lk 9.23, 14.27, 17.20–37; 2 Tm 4.18; Heb 12.28; Lk 18.8; that the second visible coming of the Lord will be his final advent, his coming to judge the quick and the dead, Mt 24.29, 30, 25.31; 2 Tm 4.1; 2 Thes 2.8; Heb 9.26–28; that there will be but one resurrection of the dead, Jn 5.28, 6.39, 40; that the time of the last day is, and will remain, unknown, Mt 24.42, 25.13; Mk 13.32, 37; Acts 1.7, which would not be the case if the last day were to come a thousand years after the beginning of a millennium; and that there will be no general conversion, a conversion *en masse*, of the Jewish nation, Rom 11.7; 2 Cor 3.14; Rom 11.25; 1 Thes 2.16.

According to these clear passages of Scripture we reject the whole of millennialism, since it not only contradicts Scripture, but also engenders a false conception of the kingdom of Christ, turns the hope of Christians upon earthly goals, 1 Cor 15.19; Col 3.2, and leads them to look upon the Bible as an obscure book.

12. *Aug* 28.51–60.
13. *Aug* 28.51–53, 60.
14. *Aug* 28.53–56.
15. *Aug* 17.5.

OF THE ANTICHRIST

43. As to the Antichrist we teach that the prophecies of the Holy Scriptures concerning the Antichrist, 2 Thes 2.3–12; 1 Jn 2.18, have been fulfilled in the pope of Rome and his dominion. All the features of the Antichrist as drawn in these prophecies, including the most abominable and horrible ones, for example, that the Antichrist "as God sitteth in the temple of God," 2 Thes 2.4; that he anathematizes the very heart of the gospel of Christ, that is, the doctrine of the forgiveness of sins by grace alone, for Christ's sake alone, through faith alone, without any merit or worthiness in man (Rom 3.20–28; Gal 2.16); that he recognizes only those as members of the Christian Church who bow to his authority; and that, like a deluge, he had inundated the whole church with his antichristian doctrines till God revealed him through the Reformation,—these very features are the outstanding characteristics of the papacy.[16] Hence we subscribe to the statement of our confessions that the pope is "the very Antichrist."[17]

OF OPEN QUESTIONS

44. Those questions in the domain of Christian doctrine may be termed open questions which Scripture answers either not at all or not clearly. Since neither an individual nor the church as a whole is permitted to develop or augment the Christian doctrine, but are rather ordered and commanded by God to continue in the doctrine of the apostles, 2 Thes 2.15; Acts 2.42, open questions must remain open questions.—Not to be included in the number of open questions are the following: the doctrine of the church and the ministry, of Sunday, of chiliasm, and of Antichrist, these doctrines being clearly defined in Scripture.

OF THE SYMBOLS OF THE LUTHERAN CHURCH

45. We accept as our confessions all the symbols contained in the Book of Concord of the year 1580. —The symbols of the Lutheran Church are not a rule of faith beyond, and supplementary to, Scripture, but a confession of the doctrines of Scripture over against those who deny these doctrines.

46. Since the Christian Church cannot make doctrines, but can and should simply profess the doctrine revealed in Holy Scripture, the doctrinal decisions of the symbols are binding upon the conscience not because our church has made them nor because they are the outcome of doctrinal controversies, but only because they are the doctrinal decisions of Holy Scripture itself.

16. *Smal Art* tr 39–41, 45.
17. *Smal Art* 2.4.10.

47. Those desiring to be admitted into the public ministry of the Lutheran Church pledge themselves to teach according to the symbols not "insofar as," but "because," the symbols agree with Scripture. He who is unable to accept as scriptural the doctrine set forth in the Lutheran symbols and their rejection of the corresponding errors must not be admitted into the ministry of the Lutheran Church.

48. The confessional obligation covers all doctrines, not only those that are treated *ex professo*, but also those that are merely introduced in support of other doctrines.

The obligation does not extend to historical statements, "purely exegetical questions," and other matters not belonging to the doctrinal content of the symbols. All *doctrines* of the symbols are based on clear statements of Scripture.

German Evangelical Church, *Barmen Declaration*, 1934

"The Barmen Declaration," as Hans-Georg Link has pointed out, "is the first confessional document within German Protestantism since the time of the Reformation."[1] All three of the major confessional branches of German Protestantism—the Lutheran, the Reformed, and the *uniert* adherents of the Prussian Union—were among the 138 delegates who met on 31 May 1934 in Wuppertal-Barmen to declare a confession of faith.

The provocation for this unprecedented action was the perceived threat to authentic Christian belief and confession that was coming from the "German Christians" and from their compromises with the ideology of National Socialism. On the basis of an earlier draft that had been prepared by Karl Barth, a three-member interconfessional commission, which included Barth, Hans Asmussen, and Thomas Breit, prepared and submitted the text at Barmen.

Since its adoption, the *Barmen Declaration* [*Theologische Erklärung zur gegenwärtigen Lage der Deutschen Evangelischen Kirche*] has acquired confessional or at least quasi-confessional status in most of the Protestant churches of Germany, in some Protestant churches of the United States, and in the "postcolonial" churches of several developing countries. Because of the statement in its introduction, "We commit to God what this may mean for the relationship of the confessional churches with each other," it has also figured prominently in ecumenical debates, and has produced a substantial scholarly literature, especially in German.

Edition: Niemöller 1959, 2:196–202.

Translation: Cochrane, 332–36.

Literature: Ahlers 1986; Burgsmüller and Weth 1983; Cochrane 1962; Link 1985.

1. Link 1985, 147.

German Evangelical Church, *Barmen Declaration*, 1934

1. An Appeal to the Evangelical Congregations and Christians in Germany

The Confessional Synod of the German Evangelical Church met in Barmen, May 29–31, 1934. Here representatives from all the German Confessional Churches met with one accord in a confession of the one Lord of the one, holy, apostolic church. In fidelity to their confession of faith, members of Lutheran, Reformed, and United Churches sought a common message for the need and temptation of the church in our day. With gratitude to God they are convinced that they have been given a common word to utter. It was not their intention to found a new church or to form a union. For nothing was farther from their minds than the abolition of the confessional status of our churches. Their intention was, rather, to withstand in faith and unanimity the destruction of the confession of faith, and thus of the Evangelical Church in Germany. In opposition to attempts to establish the unity of the German Evangelical Church by means of false doctrine, by the use of force and insincere practices, the Confessional Synod insists that the unity of the Evangelical churches in Germany can come only from the word of God in faith through the Holy Spirit. Thus alone is the church renewed.

Therefore the Confessional Synod calls upon the congregations to range themselves behind it in prayer, and steadfastly to gather around those pastors and teachers who are loyal to the confessions.

Be not deceived by loose talk, as if we meant to oppose the unity of the German nation! Do not listen to the seducers who pervert our intentions, as if we wanted to break up the unity of the German Evangelical Church or to forsake the confessions of the fathers!

Try the spirits whether they are of God! Prove also the words of the Confessional Synod of the German Evangelical Church to see whether they agree with Holy Scripture and with the confessions of the fathers. If you find that we are speaking contrary to Scripture, then do not listen to us! But if you find that we are taking our stand upon Scripture, then let no fear or temptation keep you from treading with us the path of faith and obedience to the word of God, in order that God's people be of one mind upon earth and that we in faith experience what he himself has said: "I will never leave you, nor forsake you." Therefore, "Fear not, little flock, for it is your Father's good pleasure to give you the kingdom." [1 Jn 4.1]

[Heb 13.5]

[Lk 12.32]

2. Theological Declaration Concerning the Present Situation
of the German Evangelical Church

According to the opening words of its constitution of July 11, 1933, the German Evangelical Church is a federation of confessional churches that grew out of the Reformation and that enjoy equal rights. The theological basis for the unification of these churches is laid down in article 1 and article 2 (1) of the constitution of the German Evangelical Church that was recognized by the Reich government on July 14, 1933:

> Article 1. The inviolable foundation of the German Evangelical Church is the gospel of Jesus Christ as it is attested for us in Holy Scripture and brought to light again in the confessions of the Reformation. The full powers that the church needs for its mission are hereby determined and limited.
>
> Article 2 (1). The German Evangelical Church is divided into member churches (*Landeskirchen*).

We, the representatives of Lutheran, Reformed, and United Churches, of free synods, church assemblies, and parish organizations united in the Confessional Synod of the German Evangelical Church, declare that we stand together on the ground of the German Evangelical Church as a federation of German confessional churches. We are bound together by the confession of the one Lord of the one, holy, catholic, and apostolic church.

We publicly declare before all evangelical churches in Germany that what they hold in common in this confession is grievously imperiled, and with it the unity of the German Evangelical Church. It is threatened by the teaching methods and actions of the ruling church party of the "German Christians" and of the church administration carried on by them. These have become more and more apparent during the first year of the existence of the German Evangelical Church. This threat consists in the fact that the theological basis, in which the German Evangelical Church is united, has been continually and systematically thwarted and rendered ineffective by alien principles, on the part of the leaders and spokesmen of the "German Christians" as well as on the part of the church administration. When these principles are held to be valid, then, according to all the confessions in force among us, the church ceases to be the church and the German Evangelical Church, as a federation of confessional churches, becomes intrinsically impossible.

As members of Lutheran, Reformed, and United Churches we may and must speak with one voice in this matter today. Precisely because we want to be and to remain faithful to our various confessions, we may not keep silent, since we believe that we have been given a common message to utter in a time of common need and temptation. We commend to God what this may mean for the interrelations of the confessional churches.

In view of the errors of the "German Christians" of the present Reich Church government which are devastating the church and are also thereby breaking up the unity of the German Evangelical Church, we confess the following evangelical truths:

1. "I am the way, and the truth, and the life; no one comes to the Father, but by me" (Jn 14.6). "Truly, truly, I say to you, he who does not enter the sheepfold by the door but climbs in by another way, that man is a thief and a robber. . . . I am the door; if anyone enters by me, he will be saved" (Jn 10.1, 9).

Jesus Christ, as he is attested for us in Holy Scripture, is the one Word of God which we have to hear and which we have to trust and obey in life and in death.

We reject the false doctrine, as though the church could and would have to acknowledge as a source of its proclamation, apart from and besides this one Word of God, still other events and powers, figures and truths, as God's revelation.

2. "Christ Jesus, whom God made our wisdom, our righteousness and sanctification and redemption" (1 Cor 1.30).

As Jesus Christ is God's assurance of the forgiveness of all our sins, so in the same way and with the same seriousness he is also God's mighty claim upon our whole life. Through him befalls us a joyful deliverance from the godless fetters of this world for a free, grateful service to his creatures.

We reject the false doctrine, as though there were areas of our life in which we would not belong to Jesus Christ, but to other lords—areas in which we would not need justification and sanctification through him.

3. "Rather, speaking the truth in love, we are to grow up in every way into him who is the head, into Christ, from whom the whole body [is] joined and knit together" (Eph 4.15, 16).

The Christian Church is the congregation of the brethren in which Jesus Christ acts presently as the Lord in word and sacrament through the Holy Spirit. As the church of pardoned sinners, it has to testify in the midst of a sinful world, with its faith as with its obedience, with its message as with its order, that it is solely his property, and that it lives and wants to live solely from his comfort and from his direction in the expectation of his appearance.

We reject the false doctrine, as though the church were permitted to abandon the form of its message and order to its own pleasure or to changes in prevailing ideological and political convictions.

4. "You know that the rulers of the Gentiles lord it over them, and their

great men exercise authority over them. It shall not be so among you; but whoever would be great among you must be your servant" (Mt 20.25, 26).

The various offices in the church do not establish a dominion of some over the others; on the contrary, they are for the exercise of the ministry entrusted to and enjoined upon the whole congregation.

We reject the false doctrine, as though the church, apart from this ministry, could and were permitted to give to itself, or allow to be given to it, special leaders vested with ruling powers.

5. "Fear God. Honor the emperor" (1 Pt 2.17).

Scripture tells us that, in the as yet unredeemed world in which the church also exists, the state has by divine appointment the task of providing for justice and peace. [It fulfills this task] by means of the threat and exercise of force, according to the measure of human judgment and human ability. The church acknowledges the benefit of this divine appointment in gratitude and reverence before him. It calls to mind the kingdom of God, God's commandment and righteousness, and thereby the responsibility both of rulers and of the ruled. It trusts and obeys the power of the word by which God upholds all things.

We reject the false doctrine, as though the state, over and beyond its special commission, should and could become the single and totalitarian order of human life, thus fulfilling the church's vocation as well.

We reject the false doctrine, as though the church, over and beyond its special commission, should and could appropriate the characteristics, the tasks, and the dignity of the state, thus itself becoming an organ of the state.

6. "Lo, I am with you always, to the close of the age" (Mt 28.20). "The word of God is not fettered" (2 Tm 2.9).

The church's commission, upon which its freedom is founded, consists in delivering the message of the free grace of God to all people in Christ's stead, and therefore in the ministry of his own word and work through sermon and sacrament.

We reject the false doctrine, as though the church in human arrogance could place the word and work of the Lord in the service of any arbitrarily chosen desires, purposes, and plans.

The Confessional Synod of the German Evangelical Church declares that it sees in the acknowledgment of these truths and in the rejection of these errors the indispensable theological basis of the German Evangelical Church as a federation of confessional churches. It invites all who are able to accept its declaration to be mindful of these theological principles in their decisions in church politics. It entreats all whom it concerns to return to the unity of faith, love, and hope.

The word of God remains eternal.

Unitarian General Convention,
The Washington Profession, 1935

The merger of the Universalist Church of America with the American Unitarian Association in 1961, creating "the Unitarian Universalist Association," was not "confessional" in the sense that the mergers of other, more traditional churches were: → *The Winchester Profession* of 1803 did not have to be abrogated or even revised, although many had grown restive with its formulations.

But in each of the two bodies, and then in the merged association, many of these vestigial remnants of biblical and creedal belief that had still been visible in the statement of 1803 no longer represented the convictions of clergy and people. The result of this change was the adoption of *The Washington Profession*, which, according to a standard history of Universalism, "supplemented rather than replaced" *The Winchester Profession* and its successors.[1]

The evident contradiction in the final sentence, "Neither this nor any other statement shall be imposed as a creedal text, *provided that the faith thus indicated be professed*," was resolved in 1953 by deleting the closing words.

Edition: Robinson 1970, 160.

Literature: Lippy and Williams 1988, 1:579–93; R. E. Miller 1979–85; Robinson 1970.

---

1. Robinson 1970, 160.

Unitarian General Convention,
The Washington Profession, 1935

The bond of fellowship in this convention shall be a common purpose to do the will of God as Jesus revealed it and to cooperate in establishing the kingdom for which he lived and died.

　　To that end we avow our faith in God as Eternal and All-Conquering Love, in the spiritual leadership of Jesus, in the supreme worth of every human personality, in the authority of truth known or to be known, and in the power of men of goodwill and sacrificial spirit to overcome all evil and progressively establish the kingdom of God. Neither this nor any other statement shall be imposed as a creedal test, provided that the faith thus indicated be professed.

Faith and Order Conference at Edinburgh, *The Grace of Our Lord Jesus Christ* and *Affirmation of Union*, 1937

The → Faith and Order Conference at Lausanne in 1927 was largely an experiment in confessional cartography, bringing together, in many cases for the first time, churches that had experienced separate histories and had developed distinct vocabularies but that still shared, in the Scriptures but also in the creeds and traditions of the church, a more or less common heritage. The response to its *Call to Unity* was a growth in the number of bilateral and multilateral exchanges at various levels. When Faith and Order met again ten years later, in August 1937 in Edinburgh, therefore, the 414 delegates representing 122 churches from 43 countries felt able to report with gratification that "during recent years we have been drawn together; prejudices have been overcome, misunderstandings removed, and real, if limited, progress has been made towards our goal of a common mind" (2.5). At the same time, the process of getting to know one another better had likewise disclosed new and unexpected areas of difference, in which the use of the same biblical or creedal words (for example, "communion of saints" in → *The Apostles' Creed*) masked some fundamental, often seemingly irreconcilable, confessional disagreements.

Traveling on a parallel track, the World Conference on Life and Work, in which such confessional disagreements took second place to the urgency of joint Christian service, especially in the aftermath of the First World War, had met in Stockholm in 1925. In 1937, the same year as the Edinburgh Conference on Faith and Order, Life and Work met in Oxford. The outcome of the two world conferences held in the British Isles was the move to bring them together into a single body, which was to be the World Council of Churches, formed in the aftermath of yet another world war, in 1948 at Amsterdam. Because it had become evident that the confessional questions with which Faith and Order was concerned demanded attention also from those for whom the service orientation of Life and Work took priority, the formulation of → *The Doctrinal Basis of the World Council of Churches* in 1948 would become what has to be called an "interconfessional confessional question."

Edition: Hodgson 1938, 224–27, 275–76.

Literature: Hodgson 1938; *ODCC* 531.

Faith and Order Conference at Edinburgh, *The Grace of Our Lord Jesus Christ* and *Affirmation of Union*, 1937

1. The Grace of Our Lord Jesus Christ

With deep thankfulness to God for the spirit of unity, which by his gracious blessing upon us has guided and controlled all our discussions on this subject, we agree on the following statement and recognize that there is in connection with this subject no ground for maintaining division between churches.

1. THE MEANING OF GRACE

When we speak of God's grace, we think of God himself as revealed in his Son Jesus Christ. The meaning of divine grace is truly known only to those who know that God is love, and that all that he does is done in love in fulfillment of his righteous purposes. His grace is manifested in our creation, preservation, and all the blessings of this life, but above all in our redemption through the life, death, and resurrection of Jesus Christ, in the sending of the holy and life-giving Spirit, in the fellowship of the church and in the gift of the word and sacraments.

Man's salvation and welfare have their source in God alone, who is moved to his gracious activity towards man not by any merit on man's part, but solely by his free, outgoing love.

2. JUSTIFICATION AND SANCTIFICATION

God in his free outgoing love justifies and sanctifies us through Christ, and his grace thus manifested is appropriated by faith, which itself is the gift of God.

Justification and sanctification are two inseparable aspects of God's gracious action in dealing with sinful man.

Justification is the act of God, whereby he forgives our sins and brings us into fellowship with himself, who in Jesus Christ, and by his death upon the cross, has condemned sin and manifested his love to sinners, reconciling the world to himself.

Sanctification is the work of God, whereby through the Holy Spirit he continually renews us and the whole church, delivering us from the power of sin, giving us increase in holiness, and transforming us into the likeness of his Son through participation in his death and in his risen life. This renewal, inspiring us to continual spiritual activity and conflict with evil, remains throughout the gift of God. Whatever our growth in holiness may be, our fellowship with God is always based upon God's forgiving grace.

Faith is more than intellectual acceptance of the revelation in Jesus Christ; it is whole-hearted trust in God and his promises, and committal of ourselves to Jesus Christ as Savior and Lord.

3. THE SOVEREIGNTY OF GOD AND MAN'S RESPONSE

In regard to the relation of God's grace and man's freedom, we all agree simply upon the basis of Holy Scripture and Christian experience that the sovereignty of God is supreme. By the sovereignty of God we mean his all-controlling, all-embracing will and purpose revealed in Jesus Christ for each man and for all mankind. And we wish further to insist that this eternal purpose is the expression of God's own loving and holy nature. Thus we men owe our whole salvation to his gracious will. But, on the other hand, it is the will of God that his grace should be actively appropriated by man's own will and that for such decision man should remain responsible.

Many theologians have made attempts on philosophical lines to reconcile the apparent antithesis of God's sovereignty and man's responsibility, but such theories are not part of the Christian faith.

We are glad to report that in this difficult matter we have been able to speak with a united voice, so that we have found that here there ought to be no ground for maintaining any division between churches.

4. THE CHURCH AND GRACE

We agree that the church is the body of Christ and the blessed company of all faithful people, whether in heaven or on earth, the communion of saints. It is at once the realization of God's gracious purposes in creation and redemption, and the continuous organ of God's grace in Christ by the Holy Spirit, who is its pervading life, and who is constantly hallowing all its parts.

It is the function of the church to glorify God in its life and worship, to proclaim the gospel to every creature, and to build up in the fellowship and life of the Spirit all believing people, of every race and nation. To this end God bestows his grace in the church on its members through his word and sacraments, and in the abiding presence of the Holy Spirit.

5. GRACE, THE WORD, AND THE SACRAMENTS

We agree that the word and the sacraments are gifts of God to the church through Jesus Christ for the salvation of mankind. In both the grace of God in Christ is shown forth, given, and through faith received; and this grace is one and indivisible.

The word is the appointed means by which God's grace is made known to men, calling them to repentance, assuring them of forgiveness, drawing them to obedience, and building them up in the fellowship of faith and love.

The sacraments are not to be considered merely in themselves, but always as sacraments of the church, which is the body of Christ. They have their significance in the continual working of the Holy Spirit, who is the life of the church. Through the sacraments God develops in all its members a life of perpetual communion lived within its fellowship, and thus enables them to embody his will in the life of the world; but the loving-kindness of God is not to be conceived as limited by his sacraments.

Among or within the churches represented by us there is a certain difference of emphasis placed upon the word and the sacraments, but we agree that such a difference need not be a barrier to union.

6. *SOLA GRATIA*

Some churches set great value on the expression *sola gratia,* while others avoid it. The phrase has been the subject of much controversy, but we can all join in the following statement: Our salvation is the gift of God and the fruit of his grace. It is not based on the merit of man, but has its root and foundation in the forgiveness which God in his grace grants to the sinner whom he receives to sanctify him. We do not, however, hold that the action of the divine grace overrides human freedom and responsibility; rather, it is only as response is made by faith to divine grace that true freedom is achieved. Resistance to the appeal of God's outgoing love spells, not freedom, but bondage, and perfect freedom is found only in complete conformity with the good and acceptable and perfect will of God.

2. Affirmation of Union

In allegiance to our Lord Jesus Christ, adopted by the conference [at Edinburgh] by a standing vote on 18th August 1937, nemine contradicente

The Second World Conference on Faith and Order, held in Edinburgh in August 1937, brought together four hundred and fourteen delegates from one hundred and twenty-two Christian communions in forty-three different countries. The delegates assembled to discuss together the causes that keep Christian communions apart, and the things that unite them in Christian fellowship. The conference approved the following statement *nemine contradicente:*

1. We are one in faith in our Lord Jesus Christ, the incarnate Word of God.

We are one in allegiance to him as Head of the church, and as King of kings and Lord of lords. We are one in acknowledging that this allegiance takes precedence of any other allegiance that may make claims upon us.

2. This unity does not consist in the agreement of our minds or the consent of our wills. It is founded in Jesus Christ himself, who lived, died, and rose again to bring us to the Father, and who through the Holy Spirit dwells in his church. We are one because we are all the objects of the love and grace of God, and called by him to witness in all the world to his glorious gospel.

3. Our unity is of heart and spirit. We are divided in the outward forms of our life in Christ, because we understand differently his will for his church. We believe, however, that a deeper understanding will lead us towards a united apprehension of the truth as it is in Jesus.

4. We humbly acknowledge that our divisions are contrary to the will of Christ, and we pray God in his mercy to shorten the days of our separation and to guide us by his Spirit into fullness of unity.

5. We are thankful that during recent years we have been drawn together; prejudices have been overcome, misunderstandings removed, and real, if limited, progress has been made towards our goal of a common mind.

6. In this conference we may gratefully claim that the Spirit of God has made us willing to learn from one another, and has given us a fuller vision of the truth and enriched our spiritual experience.

7. We have lifted up our hearts together in prayer; we have sung the same hymns; together we have read the same Holy Scriptures. We recognize in one another, across the barriers of our separation, a common Christian outlook and a common standard of values. We are therefore assured of a unity deeper than our divisions.

8. We are convinced that our unity of spirit and aim must be embodied in a way that will make it manifest to the world, though we do not yet clearly see what outward form it should take.

9. We believe that every sincere attempt to cooperate in the concerns of the kingdom of God draws the severed communions together in increased mutual understanding and goodwill. We call upon our fellow Christians of all communions to practice such cooperation; to consider patiently occasions of disunion that they may be overcome; to be ready to learn from those who differ from them; to seek to remove those obstacles to the furtherance of the gospel in the non-Christian world which arise from our divisions; and constantly to pray for that unity which we believe to be our Lord's will for his church.

10. We desire also to declare to all men everywhere our assurance that

Christ is the one hope of unity for the world in face of the distractions and dissensions of this present time. We know that our witness is weakened by our divisions. Yet we are one in Christ and in the fellowship of his Spirit. We pray that everywhere, in a world divided and perplexed, men may turn to Jesus Christ our Lord, who makes us one in spite of our divisions; that he may bind in one those who by many worldly claims are set at variance; and that the world may at last find peace and unity in him; to whom be glory forever.

The Church of South India, *Constitution,* "Governing Principles," 1947

Although Indian Christianity traces its origins back to the early centuries of the church, traditionally to the apostle Thomas, its modern history began with the missions that were made possible by the European voyages of exploration, trade, and colonization. Eventually there were in India daughter churches of many of the major confessions and denominations. Because of the place of India in the British empire, the Protestant churches of Great Britain—Anglican, Presbyterian, Congregationalist, Methodist—were especially prominent.

As each of these daughter churches came of age during the nineteenth century, the question of the relations among them acquired increasing urgency. At a conference in Bangalore in 1879 there was serious discussion of the possibility of a specifically Indian reunion. That discussion made possible in 1908 what *The Oxford Dictionary of the Christian Church* calls "the first trans-confessional union of modern times,"[1] the South India United Church, bringing together Congregationalists and Presbyterians.

But this was seen as only the first important step toward a more comprehensive body, the Church of South India. *The Scheme of Church Union* of 1929 articulated the ecumenical imperative, but at the same time identified the sticking points, chief of which was polity or church order: episcopal, presbyterian, and congregational (upper- and lowercase). For almost two decades, the constituting churches, as well as their mother churches in Great Britain, debated the issues, above all what → *The Chicago/Lambeth Quadrilateral* of 1886/1888 had called "the historic episcopate, locally adapted in the methods of its administration to the various needs of the nations and peoples."

This statement of "Governing Principles" in the *Constitution* of 1947 was the confessional outcome of those debates; it has since also been taken as a model for other ecumenical experiments.

Edition: Anderson, 228–34.

Literature: Hollis 1966; Newbigin [1948] 1960; *ODCC* 1522–23; Sundkler 1954.

1. *ODCC* 828.

The Church of South India, *Constitution,* "Governing Principles," 1947

1. THE FAITH OF THE CHURCH

The Church of South India accepts the Holy Scriptures of the Old and New Testaments as containing all things necessary to salvation and as the supreme and decisive standard of faith; and acknowledges that the church must always be ready to correct and reform itself in accordance with the teaching of those Scriptures as the Holy Spirit shall reveal it.

It also accepts the Apostles' Creed and the creed commonly called the Nicene, as witnessing to and safeguarding that faith; and it thankfully acknowledges that same faith to be continuously confirmed by the Holy Spirit in the experience of the church of Christ.

Thus it believes in God, the Father, the Creator of all things, by whose love we are preserved;

It believes in Jesus Christ, the incarnate Son of God and Redeemer of the world, in whom alone we are saved by grace, being justified from our sins by faith in him;

It believes in the Holy Spirit, by whom we are sanctified and built up in Christ and in the fellowship of his body;

And in this faith it worships the Father, Son, and Holy Spirit, one God in Trinity and Trinity in unity.

The Church of South India is competent to issue supplementary statements concerning the faith for the guidance of its teachers and the edification of the faithful, provided that such statements are not contrary to the truths of our religion revealed in the Holy Scriptures.

2. THE SACRAMENTS IN THE CHURCH

The Church of South India believes that the sacraments of baptism and the supper of the Lord are means of grace through which God works in us, and that while the mercy of God to all mankind cannot be limited there is in the teaching of Christ the plain command that men should follow his appointed way of salvation by a definite act of reception into the family of God and by continued acts of fellowship with him in that family, and that this teaching is made explicit in the two sacraments which he has given us. In every communion the true celebrant is Christ alone, who continues in the church today that which he began in the upper room. In the visible

518

church, the celebration of the Lord's supper is an act of the church, the company of believers redeemed by Christ, who act as the local manifestation of the whole church of Christ in heaven and on earth. It has in experience been found best that one minister should lead the worship of the church, and pronounce the words of consecration in the service of holy communion. From very early times it has been the custom of the church that those only should exercise this function who have received full and solemn commission from the church to do so; this commission has ordinarily been given by the laying on of hands in ordination.

The only indispensable conditions for the ministration of the grace of God in the church are the unchangeable promise of God himself and the gathering together of God's elect people in the power of the Holy Ghost. God is a God of order; it has been his good pleasure to use the visible church and its regularly constituted ministries as the normal means of the operation of his Spirit. But it is not open to any to limit the operation of the grace of God to any particular channel, or to deny the reality of his grace when it is visibly manifest in the lives of churches and individuals.

In the Church of South India the sacraments will be observed with unfailing use of Christ's words of institution and of the elements ordained by him.

3. THE MINISTRY IN THE CHURCH

The Church of South India believes that the ministry is a gift of God through Christ to his church, which he has given for the perfecting of the life and service of all its members. All members of the church have equally access to God. All, according to their measure, share in the heavenly high priesthood of the risen and ascended Christ from which alone the church derives its character as a royal priesthood. All alike are called to continue upon earth the priestly work of Christ by showing forth in life and word the glory of the redeeming power of God in him. No individual and no one order in the church can claim exclusive possession of this heavenly priesthood.

But in the church there has at all times been a special ministry, to which men have been called by God and set apart in the church. Those who are ordained to the ministry of the word and sacraments can exercise their offices only in and for the church, through the power of Christ the one High Priest.

The vocation of the ordained ministry is to bring sinners to repentance, and to lead God's people in worship, prayer, and praise, and through pastoral ministrations, the preaching of the gospel, and the administration of the sacraments (all these being made effective through faith) to assist men to receive the saving and sanctifying benefits of Christ and to fit them for service. The Church of South India believes that in ordination, God, in answer to the prayers of his church, bestows on and assures to those whom he has called and his church has accepted for any particular form of the ministry a commission for it and the grace appropriate to it.

4. NECESSARY ELEMENTS IN THE LIFE OF THE CHURCH OF SOUTH INDIA

The Church of South India recognizes that episcopal, presbyteral, and congregational elements must all have their place in its order of life, and that the episcopate, the presbyterate, and the congregation of the faithful should all in their several spheres have responsibility and exercise authority in the life and work of the church, in its governance and administration, in its evangelical and pastoral work, in its discipline, and in its worship.

The Congregation in the Church of South India. The Church of South India accepts the principle that as the church of a whole region, being in fellowship with other regional churches, is ideally the embodiment of the church universal in that region, and as similarly the church of a diocese as a living part of a regional church is the church universal expressing its one life in that diocese, so also in the purpose of God every local group of the faithful, organized for Christian life and worship as a congregation or pastorate within the fellowship of the diocese, represents in that place the same one, holy, catholic, and apostolic church.

Subject to the provisions of this constitution, and to such general regulations thereunder as may be issued in any matter by the synod of the church or by a diocesan council, every congregation of the church shall, with its pastor, be responsible for watching over its members, for keeping its life and doctrine pure, for ordering its worship, and for the proclaiming of the gospel to those outside the church; and every pastorate shall have general administrative authority within its area, shall have certain responsibilities in church discipline, and shall have an opportunity of expressing its judgment both as to the appointment of its pastor and the selection of candidates for ordination from that pastorate.

The Presbyterate in the Church of South India. The Church of South India believes that presbyters are specially called and commissioned by God to be dispensers of his word and sacraments, to declare his message of pardon to penitent sinners, to build up the members of the church in their most holy faith, and, through the councils of the church and otherwise, to share with the bishops and lay members in its government and in the administration of its discipline.

It is a rule of order in the Church of South India that the celebration of the holy communion shall be entrusted only to those who have by ordination received authority thereto. But it is desired that, with the ordained presbyter, there be present to assist him in the administration of the Lord's supper others appointed by the church for this purpose.

The Episcopate in the Church of South India. The Church of South India accepts and will maintain the historic episcopate in a constitutional form. But this acceptance does not commit it to any particular interpretation of episcopacy or to any particular view or belief concerning orders of the ministry, and it will not require the acceptance of any such particular interpretation or view as a necessary qualification for its ministry.

Whatever differing interpretations there may be, however, the Church of South India agrees that, as episcopacy has been accepted in the church from early times, it may in this sense fitly be called historic, and that it is needed for the shepherding and extension of the church in South India. Any additional interpretations, though held by individuals, are not binding on the Church of South India.

The meaning in which the Church of South India thus officially accepts a historic and constitutional episcopacy is that in it: (i) the bishops shall perform their functions in accordance with the customs of the church, those functions being named and defined in the later chapters of this constitution; (ii) the bishops shall be elected, both the diocese concerned in each particular case and the authorities of the Church of South India as a whole having an effective voice in their appointment; (iii) continuity with the historic episcopate will be effectively maintained, it being understood that, as stated above, no particular interpretation of the historic episcopate as that is accepted in the Church of South India is thereby implied or shall be demanded from any minister or member of the church; and (iv) every ordination of presbyters shall be performed by the laying on of hands by the bishops and presbyters, and all consecrations of bishops shall be performed by the laying on of hands at least of three bishops.

The Church of South India believes that in all ordinations and consecrations the true ordainer and consecrator is God, who in response to the prayers of his church, and through the words and acts of its representatives, commissions and empowers for the office and work to which they are called the persons whom it has selected.

In the service of consecration of a bishop in the Church of South India, the person to be consecrated shall be solemnly presented to the bishop presiding at the consecration by three presbyters of the diocese to which he is to be appointed, and these three presbyters shall join with the bishops in the laying on of hands. If, however, the diocesan council concerned specially so determine, hands shall be laid on by the bishops only.

In making the provision for episcopal ordination and consecration, the

Church of South India declares that it is its intention and determination in this manner to secure the unification of the ministry, but that this does not involve any judgment upon the validity or regularity of any other form of the ministry, and the fact
that other churches do not follow the rule of episcopal ordination will not in itself
preclude it from holding relations of communion and fellowship with them.

5. THE WORSHIP OF THE CHURCH OF SOUTH INDIA

The Church of South India will aim at conserving for the common benefit whatever of good has been gained in the separate history of those churches from which
it has been formed, and therefore in its public worship will retain for its congregations freedom either to use historic forms or not to do so as may best conduce to
edification and to the worship of God in spirit and in truth.

No forms of worship which before the union have been in use in any of
the uniting churches shall be forbidden in the Church of South India, nor shall any
wonted forms be changed or new forms introduced into the worship of any congregation without the agreement of the pastor and the congregation arrived at in
accordance with the conditions laid down in chapter 10 of this constitution.

Subject to these conditions, and to the provisions of this constitution and
any special regulations which may hereafter be issued by the synod under the constitution with regard to the services of ordination and consecration and the essential
elements or central parts of other services, especially those of baptism, holy communion, and marriage, every pastor and congregation shall have freedom to determine
the forms of their public worship.

6. UNITY IN MINISTRY AND LIFE WITHIN
THE CHURCH OF SOUTH INDIA

Every presbyter of the Church of South India may minister and celebrate the holy
communion in any church of the united church, and is eligible to be appointed to
any charge therein, subject only to the subsequent provisions of this section.

The Church of South India recognizes that the act of union has initiated a
process of growing together into one life and of advance towards complete spiritual
unity. One essential condition of the attainment of such complete unity is that all
the members of the church should be willing and able to receive communion equally
in all of its churches, and it is the resolve of the Church of South India to do all in
its power to that end.

But it is convinced that this can only take place on the basis of freedom of
opinion on debatable matters and respect for even large differences of opinion and
practice, and it believes that this freedom and mutual respect can be safeguarded

not by the framing of detailed regulations but by assurances given and received in a spirit of confidence and love.

The Church of South India therefore pledges itself that it will at all times be careful not to allow any overriding of conscience either by church authorities or by majorities, and will not in any of its administrative acts knowingly transgress the long-established traditions of any of the churches from which it has been formed. Neither forms of worship or ritual, nor a ministry, to which they have not been accustomed, or to which they conscientiously object, will be imposed upon any congregation; and no arrangements with regard to these matters will knowingly be made, either generally or in particular cases, which would either offend the conscientious convictions of persons directly concerned, or which would hinder the development of complete unity within the church or imperil its progress towards union with other churches.

7. THE RELATIONS OF THE CHURCH OF SOUTH INDIA WITH OTHER CHURCHES

The Church of South India desires to be permanently in full communion and fellowship with all the churches with which its constituent groups have had such communion and fellowship.

Any communicant member of any church with which the Church of South India has relations of fellowship shall be at liberty to partake of the holy communion in any church of the Church of South India, and any minister of such a church shall be free as a visitor to minister or celebrate the holy communion in any church of the Church of South India, if he is invited to do so.

The Church of South India will also gladly accept invitations to send delegates as visitors to the assemblies or other representative bodies of the churches through whose labors its constituent groups have come into being, and will seek, by interchange of visiting delegates or such other means as may be available, to promote and maintain brotherly relations with other churches in India, Burma, and Ceylon and to work towards a wider union of churches in those countries.

8. THE RELATIONS OF THE MINISTERS AND MEMBERS OF THE CHURCH OF SOUTH INDIA WITH OTHER CHURCHES

None of the ministers or members of the Church of South India shall because of the union forgo any rights with regard to intercommunion and intercelebration which they possessed before the union.

Every minister of the Church of South India who was ordained outside its area shall be at liberty to retain the ecclesiastical status (e.g., connection with a home presbytery or conference) which he had before the union in the church in which he was ordained, subject to such arrangements between the Church of South India and any of the churches concerned as may be found necessary, and provided that he shall not by any such arrangement be released from the obligations of his position as minister of the Church of South India.

Every minister of the Church of South India shall be at liberty to exercise any ministry in a church outside its area which he was entitled to exercise before the union, provided that that church permit him to do so.

Every minister of the Church of South India shall be at liberty to minister and to celebrate the holy communion in any church of a church with which any of the uniting churches have enjoyed relations of fellowship, if he is invited to do so.

In all these, as in other matters, the Church of South India desires to avoid on the one hand any encouragement of license or condonation of breaches of church comity and fellowship, and on the other hand any unchristian rigidity in its regulations or in their application; and in all its actions it will seek the preservation of unity within, the attainment of wider union, and the avoidance of immediate contests on particular cases.

Philippine Independent Church, *Declaration of the Faith and Articles of Religion,* 1947

In some respects, the founding of the Philippine Independent Church [*Iglesia Filipina Independiente*] may be seen as part of the international *Los-von-Rom-Bewegung* of the late nineteenth and the twentieth centuries, in reaction against papal expressions of the centralization of authority, including → the decree of the First Vatican Council on infallibility. Out of this movement came various "Old Catholic" churches, as well as several confessions, among them → *The Declaration of Utrecht* and → *The Confession of the Polish National Catholic Church.*

But as is evident from this *Declaration of the Faith and Articles of Religion* and as the researches of Filipino scholars such as Emerito P. Nacpil confirm, what was at work in the rise of this church and the production of this confession is an indigenous effort to transcend the categories imported by the missions, Roman Catholic but also Protestant, and to examine afresh the traditional issues of Christian dogma as well as the special issues of a radically new cultural and social context. Alongside the polemics against Roman Catholicism, therefore, the confession makes audible a Christian response to these new challenges.

It was adopted by the General Assembly of the Philippine Independent Church, meeting in Manila on 5 August 1947.

Edition: Anderson, 255–60.

Literature: Nacpil 1976.

Philippine Independent Church, *Declaration of the Faith and Articles of Religion*, 1947

We, the bishops, priests, and lay members, delegates to the General Assembly of the Philippine Independent Church (Iglesia Filipina Independiente), held in the city of Manila on the 5th day of August, A.D. 1947, do reiterate our faith and publicly declare that

1. We Believe In

1. THE HOLY TRINITY

One God, true and living, of infinite power, wisdom, and goodness; the Maker and Preserver of all things visible and invisible. And that in the unity of this Godhead there be three persons, of one substance, power, and eternity—the Father who is made of none, neither created nor begotten; the Son who is of the Father alone, not made nor created, but begotten; the Holy Ghost who is of the Father and the Son, neither made, nor created, nor begotten, but proceeding.[1]

2. JESUS CHRIST, THE ONLY-BEGOTTEN SON OF GOD

Jesus Christ, the only-begotten Son of God, the second person of the Trinity, very and eternal God, of one substance with the Father, took man's nature in the womb of the Blessed Virgin, after she had conceived by the Holy Ghost. He suffered under Pontius Pilate, was crucified, died, and was buried. He descended into hell. The third day he rose again from the dead, he ascended into heaven, and sitteth at the right hand of God the Father Almighty: from thence he shall come to judge the living and the dead.[2]

3. THE HOLY GHOST

The Holy Ghost, the Lord, and the Giver of life, who proceedeth from the Father and the Son: whom with the Father and the Son together we worship and glorify.[3]

1. *Ath* 21-23.
2. *Ap* 3-7.
3. N-CP 8.

4. ONE CATHOLIC AND APOSTOLIC CHURCH

The church, holy, catholic, and apostolic,[4] which is the body of Christ, founded by Christ for the redemption and sanctification of mankind, and to which church he gave power and authority to preach his gospel to the whole world under the guidance of his Holy Spirit.

2. We Hold to the Following Articles of Religion Taught by This Church

1. SALVATION

Salvation is obtained only through a vital faith in Jesus Christ, the Son of God, as Lord and Savior. This faith should manifest itself in good works.

2. HOLY SCRIPTURES

The Holy Scriptures contain all things necessary to salvation and nothing which cannot be proved thereby should be required to be believed.

3. THE CREEDS

The articles of the Christian faith as contained in the ancient creeds known as the Apostles' and Nicene Creeds are to be taught by this church and accepted by the faithful.

4. THE SACRAMENTS

1. The sacraments are outward and visible signs of our faith and a means whereby God manifests his goodwill towards us and confers grace upon us. Two sacraments, baptism and holy communion commonly called the mass, ordained by Christ himself, are held to be generally necessary to salvation.

2. *Baptism* is necessary for salvation. It signifies and confers grace, cleansing from original sin, as well as actual sin previously committed; makes us children of God and heirs of everlasting life. It effects our entrance into the church of God. It is administered with water in the name of the Father, the Son, and the Holy Ghost.

3. *Confirmation,* whereby, through the imposition of the bishop's hands, anointing, and prayer, baptized Christians are strengthened by the gifts of the Holy Spirit and confirmed in the faith.

4. *Penance,* the confession of sins as commanded by Jesus Christ.

5. *The holy eucharist,* the sacrament of the body and blood of Christ, taken

4. N-CP 9.

and received by the faithful for the strengthening and refreshing of their bodies and souls.

6. *Holy unction,* whereby the sick, especially one in danger of death, is anointed with oil with prayer. He receives, if necessary, remission of sins, the strengthening of his soul, and, if it be God's will, restoration to health.

7. *Holy orders,* a sacrament by which bishops, priests, and deacons are ordained and receive power and authority to perform their sacred duties.

8. *Holy matrimony,* a sacrament in which a man and a woman are joined together in the holy estate of matrimony.

5. THE HOLY EUCHARIST

The holy eucharist, commonly called the mass, is the central act of Christian worship. It is the sacrament of our redemption by Christ's death. Those who partake of it receive the body and blood of Christ. All who purpose to make their communion should diligently try and examine themselves before they presume to eat of that bread and drink of that cup. For as the benefit is great, if with a true penitent heart and lively faith a man receive that holy sacrament, so is the danger great if he receive the same unworthily.

The mass is to be said in the official language of the church in such a way that it can be heard by the worshipers.

The authorized order for the celebration of the mass is that set forth in the Filipino Missal or Book of Divine Office adopted by this church.

6. SACRED MINISTRY

From apostolic times there have been three orders of ministers in the church of God: bishops, priests, and deacons. These orders are to be reverently esteemed and continued in this church. And no man is to be accepted as a lawful bishop, priest, or deacon in this church, or permitted to execute any functions pertaining to these orders, except he be called, tried, examined, and admitted thereunto according to the canons of this church, and in accordance with the order prescribed by this church for making, ordaining, and consecrating bishops, priests, and deacons, or has had episcopal consecration or ordination.

7. CELIBACY OF THE CLERGY

Bishops, priests, and deacons are not commanded by God's law to marry or to abstain from marriage, therefore they are permitted to marry at their own discretion, as they shall judge the same to serve better to godliness.

8. CHURCH BUILDINGS

Churches for the worship of God are to be erected and separated from all unhallowed, worldly, and common uses, that men may reverence the majesty of God and show forth greater devotion and humility in his service.

9. THE ALTAR

The altar is the most sacred part of the church because there Jesus is sacramentally present. It symbolizes Mount Calvary, and, therefore, if images of saints are used for adornment, care is to be exercised that such ornaments may not distract the minds of the worshipers from the person of Jesus Christ.

10. WORSHIP, RITES, AND CEREMONIES

Only such orders of service as have been authorized by this church shall be used in public worship; provided, however, that the diocesan bishop or the supreme council of bishops may authorize orders of service for special occasions.

11. LANGUAGE OF PUBLIC SERVICE

All public services shall be conducted in the official language of the church, or in any other language the supreme council of bishops may prescribe.

12. PURITY OF LIFE

Holiness, altruism, obedience to God's commandments, and a zeal for his honor and glory are incumbent upon the clergy and laity alike, therefore all should be trained in a clean and disciplined life, not neglecting prayer, study, and the exercise of moral discipline.

13. KNOWLEDGE

All truth is of God, therefore, the church should promote sound knowledge and good learning. No books except those detrimental to good morals are to be prohibited.

14. THE BLESSED VIRGIN

The Virgin Mary was chosen by God to be the Mother of Jesus Christ. As Jesus Christ is truly God and Mary is the Mother of Jesus Christ, she is the Mother of God in his human generation. She whom God honored is to be honored above all.

15. THE SAINTS

Persons universally recognized for their holiness of life, loyalty, and courage, especially the Blessed Virgin and the New Testament saints, are to be held in reverent remembrance. Veneration of saints is not contrary to God's commandments as revealed in the Scriptures; but their deification is condemned by the church as a monstrous blasphemy. Veneration of the saints must not obscure the duty of the faithful to direct approach to God through Jesus Christ. Honor rendered the saints must in no wise detract from the honor due the three persons of the Holy Trinity.

16. MIRACLES

Holy Scriptures teach us that events take place in the natural world, but out of its established order, which are possible only through the intervention of divine power, like the incarnation of Jesus Christ. So-called miracles, based not on well-authenticated facts but on merely fantastic rumors, are repudiated. Belief in unsubstantial miracles leads to pagan fanaticism and is to be condemned as destructive to the true faith.

17. ATTITUDE TOWARDS THE ROMAN CHURCH

When this church withdrew from the Roman Catholic Church, it repudiated the authority of the pope and such doctrines, customs, and practices as were inconsistent with the word of God, sound learning, and a good conscience. It had no intention of departing from Catholic doctrine, practice, and discipline as set forth by the councils of the undivided church. Such departures as occurred were due to the exigencies of the times, and are to be corrected by official action as opportunity affords, so that this church may be brought into the stream of historic Christianity and be universally acknowledged as a true branch of the Catholic Church.

18. ATTITUDE TOWARDS OTHER CHURCHES

Opportunity is to be sought for closer cooperation with other branches of the catholic church, and cordial relations maintained with all who acknowledge Jesus Christ as Lord and Savior.

19. CHURCH AND STATE

This church is politically independent of the state, and the state of the church. The church does not ally itself with any particular school of political thought or with any political party. Its members are politically free and are urged to be exemplary citizens and to use their influence for the prosperity and welfare of the state.

20. DOCTRINE AND CONSTITUTIONAL RULES OF THE CHURCH AND THE FUNDAMENTAL EPISTLES

The Doctrine and Constitutional Rules of the Philippine Independent Church, adopted on October 28th, 1903, and subsequently amended, and the Fundamental Epistles of the Philippine Independent Church, are henceforth not to be held as binding either upon the clergy or laity of this church in matters of doctrine, discipline, or order, wherein they differ in substance from the Declaration of Faith or the Articles of Religion contained herein. They are to be valued as historical documents promulgated by the founders of this church when they were seeking to interpret the catholic faith in a manner understood by the people. Under the inspiration of the Holy Spirit the church has sought to eradicate such errors of judgment and doctrine as crept into its life and official documents in times past.

21. ADDITIONS, AMENDMENTS, REPEAL

The Declaration of Faith shall not be altered, amended, or repealed. However, the Articles of Religion may be amended, repealed, or added to by an absolute majority of the delegates to the General Assembly having the right to vote. Such action before it becomes binding upon the church must be ratified by the supreme council of bishops and approved by the supreme bishop.

The World Council of Churches, *Doctrinal Basis*, 1948/1961

Bringing together the emphasis on Christian service of the World Conference on Life and Work and the emphasis on Christian doctrine of the World Conference on Faith and Order, the World Council of Churches, which came into being with its first assembly at Amsterdam in 1948, could not evade the creedal and confessional imperative even in its response to the urgent moral imperatives of the conditions in the world after the Second World War. Nor could it, however, permit the doctrinal controversies of the history of Christian theology to paralyze that response.

The resolution of that dilemma was a one-sentence *Doctrinal Basis*. Each of the principal grammatical components of the sentence reflected past controversies and sparked future ones: Did "fellowship of churches" obligate all members of the World Council to acknowledge all other members as "churches" in the complete and normative sense of that word, and to extend "fellowship" to them in sacrament and ministry? Did "accept our Lord Jesus Christ" carry with it the entire dogmatic deposit of the creeds, councils, and confessions — and of which of these? Did "Jesus Christ as God and Savior" perpetuate the underemphasis on the humanity of Jesus of which those creeds, councils, and confessions had allegedly been guilty? Or did it, on the contrary, ignore the trinitarian witness that had been so central for them?

Although it was thus too much for some and too little for others, this *Doctrinal Basis* did nevertheless prove to be adequate for the founding of the new council. But the discussion continued, until finally, at the New Delhi Assembly in 1961, the World Council adopted an amended and expanded doctrinal statement: the added words appear here in brackets.

Edition: Visser 't Hooft 1949, 197.

Literature: *DEM* 1096–98 (T. K. Thomas); *ODCC* 1765–66; Rouse and Neill 1986; Theurer 1967.

The World Council of Churches, *Doctrinal Basis,* 1948/1961

The World Council of Churches is a fellowship of churches which accept our [confess the] Lord Jesus Christ as God and Savior [according to the Scriptures and therefore seek to fulfill together their common calling to the glory of the one God, Father, Son, and Holy Spirit].

Pius XII, *Munificentissimus Deus,* 1950

Already at the time of the promulgation of the dogma of the immaculate conception of Mary by → *Ineffabilis Deus* of Pope Pius IX in 1854, there was a widespread expectation that a similar definition of the doctrine of her bodily assumption into heaven could not be far behind. It had, in fact, engendered far less controversy among Roman Catholic theologians than the immaculate conception had, especially in the later Middle Ages. Petitions for such a definition came to Rome in large volume, some of them no doubt stimulated from above, others spontaneous. And in the encyclical *Deiparae Virginis Mariae* of 1 May 1946, Pope Pius XII solicited the hierarchy of the Roman Catholic Church for their opinion "whether it would be lawful, convenient, and useful" to issue a formal official definition of the dogma at this time.

Encouraged by their "almost unanimous affirmative response" (12), he issued the apostolic constitution *Munificentissimus Deus* on 1 November 1950, All Saints' Day. Its method of argumentation is designed to deal with the difficult question of the silence of the New Testament on the subject. Therefore he insists, quoting the First Vatican Council, that he had no authority to "manifest new doctrine" (12). Various Christian writers, he acknowledges, had been "rather free in their use of events and expressions taken from Sacred Scripture to explain their belief in the assumption," employing proofs for it that "are based upon the Sacred Writings as their *ultimate foundation*," by the use of "various images and analogies of Sacred Scripture" (26, 38, 29). Celebrated as the "dormition [*koimēsis*] of the Theotokos," the assumption had a long tradition in Eastern and Western liturgy and iconography as well as theology, but its promulgation "by the authority of our Lord Jesus Christ, of the blessed apostles Peter and Paul, *and by our own authority*" (44) summoned up the controversies of the preceding century over papal infallibility. As with *Ineffabilis,* we have presented only the doctrinal definition; but we have retained the numbering of the complete text.

Edition: Denzinger, 3900–3904.

Translation: *Our Lady* 1961, 299–320.

Literature: Balić 1948; Cicognani 1951; Daley 1998; Duggan 1989; Heinrich and Moos 1942.

Pius XII, *Munificentissimus Deus*, 1950

Definition of the Assumption of the Blessed Virgin Mary

38. All these proofs and considerations of the holy fathers and the theologians are based upon the Sacred Writings as their ultimate foundation. These set the loving Mother of God as it were before our very eyes as most intimately joined to her divine Son and as always sharing his lot. Consequently it seems impossible to think of her, the one who conceived Christ, brought him forth, nursed him with her milk, held him in her arms, and clasped him to her breast, as being apart from him in body, even though not in soul, after this earthly life. Since our Redeemer is the Son of Mary, he could not do otherwise, as the perfect observer of God's law, than to honor, not only his eternal Father, but also his most beloved Mother. And, since it was within his power to grant her this great honor, to preserve her from the corruption of the tomb, we must believe that he really acted in this way.

39. We must remember especially that, since the second century, the Virgin Mary has been designated by the holy fathers as the new Eve, who, although subject to the new Adam, is most intimately associated with him in that struggle against the infernal foe which, as foretold in the protoevangelium, would finally result in that [Gn 3.15] most complete victory over the sin and death which are always mentioned together in the writings of the Apostle of the Gentiles.[a] Consequently, just as the glorious resurrection of Christ was an essential part and the final sign of this victory, so that struggle which was common to the Blessed Virgin and her divine Son should be brought to a close by the glorification of her virginal body, for the same apostle says: "When this mortal thing hath put on immortality, then shall come to pass the saying that is written: Death is swallowed up in victory." [1 Cor 15.54]

40. Hence the revered Mother of God, from all eternity joined in a hidden way with Jesus Christ in one and the same decree of predestination, immaculate in her conception, a most perfect virgin in her divine motherhood, the noble associate of the divine Redeemer who has won a complete triumph over sin and its consequences, finally obtained, as the supreme culmination of her privileges, that she should be preserved free from the corruption of the tomb and that, like her own Son, having overcome death, she might be taken up body and soul to the glory of heaven where, as queen, she sits in splendor at the right hand of her Son, the immortal King of the ages. [1 Tm 1.17]

a. [1 Cor 15.21–26, 54–57]

535

[Jn 14.17]   41. Since the universal church, within which dwells the Spirit of truth, who infallibly directs it toward an ever more perfect knowledge of the revealed truths, has expressed its own belief many times over the course of the centuries, and since the bishops of the entire world are almost unanimously petitioning that the truth of the bodily assumption of the Blessed Virgin Mary into heaven should be defined as a dogma of divine and Catholic faith—this truth which is based on the Sacred Writings, which is thoroughly rooted in the minds of the faithful, which has been approved in ecclesiastical worship from the most remote times, which is completely in harmony with the other revealed truths, and which has been expounded and explained magnificently in the work, the science, and the wisdom of the theologians—we believe that the moment appointed in the plan of divine providence for the solemn proclamation of this outstanding privilege of the Virgin Mary has already arrived. . . .

[Jn 14.17]   44. For which reason, after we have poured forth prayers of supplication again and again to God, and have invoked the light of the Spirit of truth, for the glory of Almighty God who has lavished his special affection upon the Virgin Mary, for the honor of her Son, the immortal King of the ages and the victor over sin and death, for the increase of the glory of that same august Mother, and for the joy and exultation of the entire church; by the authority of our Lord Jesus Christ, of the blessed apostles Peter and Paul, and by our own authority, we pronounce, declare, and define it to be a divinely revealed dogma: that the Immaculate Mother of God, the Ever-Virgin Mary, having completed the course of her earthly life, was assumed body and soul into heavenly glory.

45. Hence if anyone, which God forbid, should dare willfully to deny or to call into doubt that which we have defined, let him know that he has fallen away completely from the divine and Catholic faith.

The China Christian Three-Self Patriotic Movement, *Christian Manifesto,* "Direction of Endeavor for Chinese Christianity in the Construction of New China," 1950

In → *The Bond of Union* of 1927, the Church of Christ in China had attempted to articulate its own statement of faith, but in continuity with → *The Apostles' Creed* and the church as a whole. But the victory of the Chinese Communist Party over the Nationalist Party in 1949 was a crisis for all the churches of China: for Roman Catholics, because their central authority was in Rome, not in China, a situation that the authorities found intolerable; for Protestants, because the missionary societies and churches to which they owed their origin were identified with Western imperialism and colonialism, so that most of the Protestant missionaries eventually had to return home.

One response to this crisis was the "Three-Self Patriotic Movement": a church that was self-supporting, self-governing, self-propagating. The documents coming out of the movement, as these have been collected and published by the National Council of the Churches of Christ in the United States of America,[1] show that it involved a variety of experiments at accommodating to the regime while maintaining some freedom of self-determination. Confessionally, it produced this *Christian Manifesto* of May 1950. As Jones explains, "Forty outstanding Christian leaders were the charter signers of this blast against missionary imperialism. Many of the more moderate leaders were aghast at the severity of the language in the Manifesto, and at first refused to sign. But the campaign for signatures continued with increasing intensity for several years, and the total claimed finally reached 400,000."[2]

Edition: *Tianfeng* nos. 233–34 (30 September 1950): 2 (reprinted in Chao 1983, 271–72).

Translation: F. P. Jones 1963, 19–20.

Literature: F. P. Jones 1963; Latourette 1967.

1. F. P. Jones 1963.
2. F. P. Jones 1963, iii.

The China Christian Three-Self Patriotic Movement, *Christian Manifesto,* "Direction of Endeavor for Chinese Christianity in the Construction of New China," 1950

Protestant Christianity has been introduced to China for more than a hundred and forty years. During this period it has made a not unworthy contribution to Chinese society. Nevertheless, and this was most unfortunate, not long after Christianity's coming to China, imperialism started its activities here; and since the principal groups of missionaries who brought Christianity to China all came themselves from these imperialistic countries, Christianity consciously or unconsciously, directly or indirectly, became related with imperialism. Now that the Chinese revolution has achieved victory, these imperialistic countries will not rest passively content in face of this unprecedented historical fact in China. They will certainly seek to contrive by every means the destruction of what has actually been achieved; they may also make use of Christianity to forward their plot of stirring up internal dissension, and creating reactionary forces in this country. It is our purpose in publishing the following statement to heighten our vigilance against imperialism, to make known the clear political stand of Christians in New China, to hasten the building of a Chinese church whose affairs are managed by the Chinese themselves, and to indicate the responsibilities that should be taken up by Christians throughout the whole country in national reconstruction in New China. We desire to call upon all Christians in the country to exert their best efforts in putting into effect the principles herein presented.

The Task in General

Christian Churches and organizations give thoroughgoing support to the "Common Political Platform," and under the leadership of the government oppose imperialism, feudalism, and bureaucratic capitalism, and take part in the effort to build an independent, democratic, peaceable, unified, prosperous, and powerful New China.

Fundamental Aims

1. Christian churches and organizations in China should exert their utmost efforts, and employ effective methods, to make people in the churches everywhere recognize clearly the evils that have been wrought in China by imperialism; recognize the

fact that in the past imperialism has made use of Christianity; purge imperialistic influences from within Christianity itself; and be vigilant against imperialism, and especially American imperialism, in its plot to use religion in fostering the growth of reactionary forces. At the same time, the churches and organizations should call upon Christians to participate in the movement opposing war and upholding peace, and teach them thoroughly to understand and support the government's policy of agrarian reform.

2. Christian churches and organizations in China should take effective measures to cultivate a patriotic and democratic spirit among their adherents in general, as well as a psychology of self-respect and self-reliance. The movement for autonomy, self-support, and self-propagation hitherto promoted in the Chinese church has already attained a measure of success. This movement from now onwards should complete its tasks within the shortest possible period. At the same time, self-criticism should be advocated, all forms of Christian activity re-examined and readjusted, and thoroughgoing austerity measures adopted, so as to achieve the goals of a reformation in the church.

Concrete Methods

1. All Christian churches and organizations in China that are still relying upon foreign personnel and financial aid should work out concrete plans to realize within the shortest possible time their objective of self-reliance and rejuvenation.

2. From now onwards, as regards their religious work, Christian churches and organizations should lay emphasis upon a deeper understanding of the nature of Christianity itself, closer fellowship and unity among the various denominations, the cultivation of better leadership personnel, and reform in systems of church organization. As regards their more general work, they should emphasize anti-imperialistic, anti-feudalistic and anti-bureaucratic-capitalistic education, together with such forms of service to the people as productive labor, teaching them to understand the New Era, cultural and recreational activities, literacy education, medical and public health work, and care of children.

Anglican Church in China, *Sheng Kung Hui* *Pastoral Letter,* 1950

The issuance of → the *Christian Manifesto* by the China Christian Three-Self Patriotic Movement in May 1950 elicited reactions both in the Western churches and in China itself. Among these, the *Pastoral Letter* signed by "The Standing Committee of the General Synod and The House of Bishops" of the Anglican Church in China on 5 July 1950 was intended, Jones says, "as an alternative statement," even though, as it turned out, "they all" ended up accepting the *Christian Manifesto*.

English Edition: F. P. Jones 1963, 21–22.

Literature: Gray 1996; F. P. Jones 1963.

Anglican Church in China, *Sheng Kung Hui* *Pastoral Letter,* 1950

We, the members of the Standing Committee and the House of Bishops at the joint meeting in Shanghai on July 5, 1950, send to you, our fellow members in the Lord in the whole nation, our greetings and respects!

At this joint meeting we have discussed in detail the problems of the church in relation to this new era. Herewith are the important results of our discussions.

1. We consider that the church not only cannot compromise with imperialism, feudalism, or bureaucratic capitalism, but also that these are fundamentally against the faith of the church. Therefore we oppose them. Christianity has always recognized that to welcome and cooperate with the powerful and the rich and to oppress the masses is against the spirit of Christ. Christ himself never compromised with the powerful and the rich; records of such lessons by the apostles are numerous in the Bible.

2. Christianity believes that God is Lord of all the universe. The purpose of God's love of the world in sending his Son to be born as man is to give freedom to the oppressed. Therefore we feel deeply fortunate to have the national liberation and heartily support the Common Platform (provisional national constitution) with its guarantee of freedom of religious belief.

3. In self-government, self-support, and self-propagation our church has made some achievements. Hereafter we determine to cooperate with all the members of the church to reach the goal of self-reliance in the shortest possible time.

4. In the midst of the church there are indeed a few corrupt members not following the purpose of the church and against the Christ. Their personal and individual behavior cannot represent the whole church and their sins are condemned by the church. Therefore we should hereafter endeavor to inoculate the spirit of holiness and universality into the church.

5. Hereafter our church should on the one hand positively promote spiritual life and religious education, so as to enable us all to have the Christlike personality and family, and on the other hand pay attention to productive labor and social service.

6. Christ is the King of Peace! Our church has been promoting peace and we oppose all the cruel and human killing weapons.

Finally we must strengthen our church; we must prepare ourselves to overcome difficulties. We have recommended that all the members of our church in

China during the coming year have a few minutes' intercession before our noonday meal. Thus we shall be reminded of our united mission and burden at mealtimes. For the concrete work of our church and the deeper understanding of our faith by our church members, we are preparing a number of church handbooks to be distributed later.

Protestant Christian Batak Church (Huria Kristen Batak Protestant), *Confession of Faith*, 1951

The Protestant Christian Batak Church (Huria Kristen Batak Protestant) brought together Indonesian Christians from several missions. Among these, the Lutheran group was sufficiently important to make membership in the Lutheran World Federation a serious possibility for the Batak Church. But such membership had, as a precondition of eligibility, the acceptance of → *The Augsburg Confession*. To meet that requirement when it applied for membership, the Batak Church in 1951 composed this *Confession of Faith*, setting it forth as documentation of its confessional stance and of its loyalty to the *Confessio Augustana*.

The nature and content of the confession has been examined by Schreiner 1966. In the introduction to it that he cowrote with Edward Nyhus, the confessional (and interconfessional) stance of the document is characterized this way: "Influence of the Augsburg Confession is traceable in its ethics, and in the polemical passages. . . . The teaching on the sacraments, modeled after Luther's Small Catechism, has been agreed to by Reformed churchmen in Indonesia. The confession of faith does not hinder intercommunion, because it transcends the confessional positions of Western Protestantism. Significantly, the East Asia Christian Conference pointed out that 'the Batak Church could equally well belong to the Presbyterian World Alliance as to the Lutheran World Federation.'" That Reformed background is evident, for example, in the statement at the conclusion of article 8, "The Church," that one of the marks of the true church, in addition to the preaching of the gospel and the administration of the sacraments, is "the exercise of church discipline in order to prevent sin."

Edition: *Panindangion Haporseaon (Confessie) ni Huria Kristen Batak Protestant* 1966, 3–24.

Translation: Anderson, 214–26.

Literature: Oosthuizen 1958; Schreiner 1966; T. B. Simatupang in Anderson, 87–116; Vajta and Weissgerber 1963.

Protestant Christian Batak Church (Huria Kristen Batak Protestant), *Confession of Faith,* 1951

Preface

A "Confession of Faith" is of the utmost necessity for establishing our faith and opposing heresy. In the early church there were ecumenical confessions of faith which opposed heresy. At the time of the Reformation there were creeds which opposed the doctrine of the Roman Catholic Church. So it has been that new creeds have arisen whenever heresy has appeared to trouble the church. However, in opposing new heresies, the new confessions did not forget the first confession. Thus the church, in opposing heresies which arise, continuously requires new confessions. The Reformers, for example, did not only use previous confessions, because a different form was required for their situation. Therefore the church may not just doze, content with the former confessions, but rather in every age must renew and reform them.

In Germany new heresies appeared after 1933. The churches there were aroused at that time because they realized that the previous confessions were no longer adequate to oppose these heresies. Therefore they formulated a new confession called "The Barmen Declaration" (May 31, 1934). They emphasized the sovereignty of Christ alone, opposing such sovereignty of men in the matter of religion as was claimed by Hitler and his cohorts.

In Holland too an effort was made to draw up a new confession. This new confession was also based on the previous confessions but spoke with a new voice to the modern world.

Because of the pressures upon our church, our thinking must be aroused at the present time to confront the doctrines and religions around us. Until recently there were actually only two religions surrounding us, namely animism and Islam. However there are now many more which have come from without as well as grown up from within. We will name them individually:

1. *Roman Catholics.* Now they come again to spread their wings. Our doctrine stands in opposition to their teaching.

2. *Adventists.* They have established their seminary in Pematang Siantar. They spread their doctrine by distributing their books and by propagating their views for several evenings in a given area.

3. *Pentecostals.* Their doctrine has spread to nearly every part of our area.

They stress the spirit and speaking in tongues. They pray at great length and sing "hallelujah." Their newspaper, published in Jakarta, is entitled "Penjuluh."

4. *Enthusiasts.* There are many varieties of enthusiasts in our midst. Some call themselves "The Holiness Church," others "the Church of the Atonement." Some refrain from eating blood, as in Pagar Sinondi and Pematang Siantar, while others at Sionomhudon and Laeparira are followers of Sibindanamora. They say that their doctrine has a biblical basis, but their interpretation is absolutely wrong because they only follow their own notions.

5. *Siradjabatak.* This group has also spread widely in many areas. They claim to be only a [secular] party or group, but it is clearly evident in their constitution that they preserve the precepts of the old animism.

6. *The Bible-Circle Group.* This group came from Balata and has spread to Siantar. It is like a woodworm in the church bringing ruin to the souls of our fellow Christians. They stress that there are many errors in the work of our church which are not in accordance with the Bible. They have also moved into Tapanuli.

7. *Nationalistic Christianity.* This [movement] developed during World War II. They falsify Christian doctrine by making it conform to nationalistic aspirations.

8. *Syncretism.* Its adherents say: "All religions are good with only slight differences in value." A religion has grown up in Djakarta called "Islam–Isa," a combination of Islam, Christianity, and Judaism. They also send information about their doctrines to us. Their estimate of various religions is as follows: Their religion is the highest, like 24-carat pure gold; Christianity is 22 carats, a high religion; Judaism is 20 carats, a medium-high religion; Islam is 18 carats, medium; all other religions are 16 carats, inferior.

9. Doctrines which come from *Theosophy, Communism,* and *Capitalism.* There are indeed many teachings which come from them that can confuse faith.

10. Besides these there have arisen *groups which have separated themselves from our church,* such as Mission Batak, H.Ch.B., P.K.B. and H.K.I. We know that there will be others which will arise in the future, and it is to be expected that their teachings will differ from the teachings of our church.

11. *Animism* and *Islam* which surround us. Their doctrines deviate sharply from the Bible. Making the matter worse is the fact that they come to our church in another form. Remnants of animism are still deeply rooted in many members of our church, like the roots of a great tree which have penetrated into the soil where it grows.

12. One other thing is very important. Our confession must be well defined over against the *customs and culture of our people.* We must direct more attention, especially toward these two matters, so that they do not destroy our faith. At the

present time our people urge that our customs and culture must be preserved. This is good, but although we consider it good, not all of it is in harmony with our faith; there are inherent dangers. These various religions and doctrines constitute a real danger for our church.

Because of these things which have been enumerated above, the present time requires of us: there must be in our church a "Confession of Faith" containing pure doctrine in accordance with what we have confessed from the beginning. This will be a symbol and foundation for us.

Moreover, it is necessary that there be a "Confession of Faith" in our church which includes the entire basis of what we believe so that it will not be vague to others, for this is required of a Christian group which calls itself a "church." A Christian group cannot be called a "church" if it has no confession. It is therefore urgent that this confession be recorded in order that the understanding of all our church members will become clearer, thereby establishing their faith.

The necessity [for this confession] may be summarized as follows:

1. Because faith results in confession, as the apostle Paul said to the Corinthians (2 Cor 4.13), "I believed, and so I spoke."

2. Because the church must witness against the world, as the apostle Peter said (1 Pt 3.15), "Always be prepared to make a defense to anyone who calls you to account for the hope that is in you." 1 Tm 4.6, "If you put these instructions before the brethren, you will be a good minister of Christ Jesus, nourished on the words of the faith and of the good doctrine which you have followed."

3. Because it is an illuminator which makes known what is true and what is false doctrine. 1 Jn 4.2, 4.

4. Because unity in the life of the church requires unity in the confession of faith. Eph 4.5; Jn 17.21.

5. Because it is a valuable inheritance for future generations of the church in order that they may follow in the faith of their fathers. Dt 6.7.

The Authority of the Confession

Only Holy Scripture has ultimate authority, for God devised or created it. But a confession of faith also has authority. To be sure, it has been formulated by men but it is firmly based on the word of God. 2 Cor 1.21; 2 Tm 3.16–17.

It is proper that the members of the church be subject to this authority, but it should not be a forced subjection and it should not stifle conscience. One must be free to examine the confession. If anyone finds something which is not in accordance with the holy word he may convey his objections to the church leadership.

The confession of faith herein recorded is that approved by the General Synod at Sipoholon on November 28–30, 1951.

Confession of Faith of the H.K.B.P.

INTRODUCTION

1. This confession of faith of the H.K.B.P. is a continuation of the previously existing creeds, namely the *three* creeds which were confessed by the church fathers, which are called: (1) The Apostles' Creed; (2) The Nicene Creed; (3) The Athanasian Creed.

2. This confession of faith is the summary of what we believe and hope for in this life and in the life to come.

3. This confession of faith is the basis of the H.K.B.P. for what is to be preached, taught, and lived. Mt 16.16.

4. This confession of faith is the basis in the H.K.B.P. for rejecting and opposing all false doctrine and heresy which is not in accordance with the word of God.

ARTICLE 1. CONCERNING GOD

We believe and confess:

God is one, without beginning and end, almighty, unchangeable, faithful, omniscient, inscrutable, a righteous judge, of great mercy, gracious. He fills heaven and earth and is true, holy, and loving. Dt 6.4; Ex 3.14; Gn 17.1; Ps 105.8; 1 Cor 1.9; 2 Thes 3.3; Lk 1.37; Rom 11.33; Dt 10.17; Rom 2.11; 1 Cor 1.30; Ps 103.8; Ps 24.1; Is 6.3; Jn 3.16; 1 Tm 6.15–16.

By means of this doctrine we reject and oppose the custom of calling God "Grandfather," and the view which regards God as only gracious, as well as the conviction that blessing can come from the spirits of the ancestors, as is usual with the animist. Likewise [we reject] the choosing of fortunate days, fortune-telling, and palm-reading.

By means of this doctrine we also reject the teaching which considers God's power to be greater than his holiness and love.

ARTICLE 2. THE TRIUNE NATURE OF GOD

We believe and confess:

Our God is one, and also triune, namely, God the Father, God the Son, and God the Holy Spirit. Jn 5.19, 14.11, 1.1, 15.26; 2 Cor 13.13; Mt 28.19.

The Father has eternally begotten his Son of his own being, that is, just as the Father has no beginning and no end, so also the Son. Likewise the Holy Spirit, who proceeds from the Father and the Son, has no beginning and no end. Jn 15.26.

By means of this doctrine we oppose and reject the conception which states that God is only one (Maha Esa), with understanding that the Son and the Spirit are considered subordinate to the Father.

We also oppose the doctrine which states that the persons of the Trinity are God the Father; his Son, the Lord Jesus Christ; and the *Mother*, the Holy Spirit.

ARTICLE 3. THE SPECIAL ACTS OF THE TRIUNE GOD
We believe and confess:

A. God the Father creates, preserves, and rules all things visible and invisible.

By means of this doctrine we reject and oppose the doctrine of fatalism (predestination, fate, allotted destiny).

B. God the Son, who became man, was born of the Virgin Mary, conceived by the Holy Spirit, and is called Lord Jesus. Two natures are found in him, namely, the divine and human, inseparable in one person. Jesus Christ is true God but also true man. He suffered in agony at the time of the rule of Pilate, was crucified and died in order to deliver us from sin, from death, and from the power of the devil. He became the perfect sacrifice to make reconciliation with God because of all the sins of mankind. He was buried, descended into hell, rose again on the third day, ascended into heaven to sit at the right hand of God Jehovah, his Father, who has glory forever. He is in heaven interceding for us, ruling everything, until he will come again to the earth to judge the quick and the dead. Mt 28.18; Eph 1.20-22, 1.7; Jn 3.16; Heb 9.14; Phil 2.9-11.

By means of this doctrine we reject and oppose:

1. The Roman Catholic doctrine which teaches that Mary, the mother of the Lord Jesus or, as they call her, "saint," can pray for us to God.

2. The Roman Catholic doctrine which teaches that "a priest can sacrifice Christ in the mass."

3. The false Roman Catholic doctrine that the pope in Rome is the vicar of Christ on earth. Mt 23.8-10.

4. The human view which equates the Lord Jesus with the prophets who are in this world.

C. God the Holy Spirit calls and teaches the church and preserves it in faith and holiness in the gospel for the glory of God. Rom 8.14-17; 1 Cor 3.16. (Compare the explanation of the third article.)

By means of this doctrine we oppose and reject the doctrine which states that the Holy Spirit can descend on man through his own efforts, not necessarily through the gospel.

Likewise we oppose and reject the doctrine which states that the Holy Spirit can descend only through ecstasy and speaking in tongues.

Likewise we reject and oppose the doctrine which states that it is not necessary to be treated medically but that it is enough only to pray to the Holy Spirit; as well as the false prophecies in the name of the Holy Spirit; and the dissolute and immoderate fellowship which they claim has been filled by the Holy Spirit.

We oppose and reject all these doctrines because they *falsely rely on the name of the Holy Spirit*.

ARTICLE 4. THE WORD OF GOD

We believe and confess:

The words written in the Bible, namely, in the Old and New Testaments, are truly the words of God. "For prophecy came not in old times by the will of man, but men moved by the Holy Spirit spoke from God" (2 Pt 1.21). "All scripture is inspired by God and profitable for teaching, for reproof, for correction, and for training in righteousness, that the man of God may be complete, equipped for every good work" (2 Tm 3.16–17).

By means of this doctrine we emphasize that the Holy Scripture is completely sufficient to reveal God's being and his will, and it is sufficiently taught in the Holy Scripture what man is to believe as a means to eternal life. Rv 22.18–19.

The Holy Scripture alone is the beginning and the conclusion of all thought, knowledge, and work in the church and in the person of the believers.

By means of this doctrine we oppose and reject any learning and wisdom of man that diverges from the word of God. Prv 3.5; Ps 111.10.

ARTICLE 5. THE ORIGIN OF SIN

The devil is the source of sin and he desires that all men become sinners who turn away from God. Jn 8.44; Gn 3.1–7; Rv 20.10.

Thus, although the first persons (Adam and Eve) were good and able to act according to God's will, they nevertheless, because of the seduction of the devil, transgressed the commandment which God had given them and turned away from God. "Sin is transgression." 1 Jn 3.4; Jas 1.15.

ARTICLE 6. ORIGINAL SIN

We believe and confess:

Since Adam and Eve fell into sin, sin has passed on to all their descendants.

Therefore all men are born in sin and sin enslaves them so that they transgress God's commandments. Sin brings judgment and eternal death. Ps 51.7, 58.4; Gn 8.21; Rom 5.12, 3.12, 23; Ti 3.5; Jn 3.5, 6.63.

By means of this doctrine we oppose and reject the view that children born into this world have not yet sinned. Likewise the view diverging from the word of God which says that man is led to commit sin only because he is urged on by poverty, penury, or misery, and that such [transgressions] need not be considered sin.

Likewise we reject the doctrine which states that the heart of man is like blank paper on which nothing has yet been written.

ARTICLE 7. SALVATION FROM SIN

We believe and confess:

"Salvation from sin cannot be gained by means of good works," or through one's own strength, but only by the grace of God through the redemption of Jesus Christ. It is received by faith which is wrought by the Holy Spirit, so that one appropriates the forgiveness of sin which Jesus Christ has provided through his death. Such faith is reckoned by God as righteousness before him. Jn 3.16; 2 Cor 8.9; Acts 4.12.

ARTICLE 8. THE CHURCH

A. We believe and confess:

The church is the gathering of those who believe in Jesus Christ, who are called, gathered, sanctified, and preserved by God through the Holy Spirit. 1 Cor 1.2; 1 Pt 2.9; Eph 1.22; 1 Cor 3.

By means of this doctrine we oppose and reject: (1) A church (a certain group) established by men *of their own will*, which for this reason separates itself from our church and not because there has been any doctrine in our church contrary to the word of God; (2) The conception which states that only the authority of the leaders, the assemblies, and the rights of the members govern the church: for only Christ has authority in the church and only that order which is according to his word is to be followed. It is not *Democracy* which rules the church, but "*Christocracy*"; (3) The conception which states that our church should be a "*state-church*," for the duty of the state is different from the ministry of the church; (4) The conception which states that the church is a gathering based upon and bound to *custom;* as well as the false opinion that the life of the church depends only upon organization.

B. We believe and confess:

The church is holy. The church is called holy, not because of the holiness of its members but because of the *holiness of Christ*, its Head. Thus the church becomes holy because Christ has sanctified it and God reckons them as saints. Because of the holiness of the church it is called a holy people, a temple of the Holy Spirit, a habitation of God. 1 Pt 2.9; Eph 2.22; Rv 1.6; Eph 3.21; 1 Cor 3.16.

By means of this doctrine we oppose and reject the doctrine which states that holiness can be gained through one's own efforts; likewise [we reject] the despair and separatism caused by the continuing presence of church members who are seen to commit sin.

C. We believe and confess:

The church is universal. The universal church is the gathering of all saints who are partakers in the Lord Jesus Christ and his gifts—the gospel, the Holy Spirit, faith, love, and hope. They are from every country, people, tribe, race, and language, although their ceremonies and forms differ. Rv 7.9.

By means of this doctrine we oppose and reject the interpretation which considers the church to be a religion of one people, and those who think that churches have no relationship with one another.

D. We believe and confess:

There is *one* church. This is based on Ephesians 4.4; 1 Corinthians 12.20. "For there is *one* body, that is the church, and even though there are many members there is but one body." Because it is spiritual unity, the unity of the church which is expressed here is different from secular unity, usually asserted by men. Jn 17.20–21.

By means of this doctrine we oppose and reject any separations that are based only on external forms and not on the doctrine of faith.

E. Signs of the true church.

We believe and confess that the signs of the true church are: (a) the pure preaching of the gospel; (b) the proper administration of the two sacraments as instituted by the Lord Jesus; (c) the exercise of church discipline in order to prevent sin.

ARTICLE 9. THOSE WHO MINISTER IN THE CHURCH

We believe and confess:

All Christians are called to be Christ's witnesses. In order to carry out the work in the church, God has called through the church those who minister according to the threefold office of Christ—Prophet, Priest, and King. These ought to be observed in the church. 1 Cor 12.28.

The offices of the ministry are: (1) Preaching of the gospel to the members of the church and those who are not yet members; (2) Administering of the two sacraments, namely, holy baptism and holy communion; (3) Pastoral care of the members of the church; (4) Preserving pure doctrine through the exercise of spiritual discipline, together with opposition to false doctrine; (5) Doing works of mercy (diakonia).

For this work there are appointed in the church apostles, prophets, evangelists, pastors, and teachers, Eph 4.11, and deacons, Acts 6.

By means of this doctrine we oppose and reject the conception of those who, on the basis of their own opinion and not because of anything done contrary to the office, reject and deny the office of the ministry.

By means of this doctrine we also oppose and reject anyone in the church who arises to preach, teach, and administer the sacraments without being installed by the church to the office of ministering in the church.

ARTICLE 10. THE SACRAMENTS

We believe and confess:

There are only two sacraments commanded by the Lord Jesus which we should administer, holy baptism and holy communion. The Lord Jesus has instituted them for his church in order to grant through visible signs his invisible grace, namely, forgiveness of sins, salvation, life, and bliss, which are to be appropriated by faith. Mt 28.19; Mk 16.15-16; Mt 26; Mk 14; Lk 22; 2 Cor 11.

By means of this doctrine we oppose and reject the Roman Catholic doctrine which states that there are seven sacraments.

A. Holy Baptism

We believe and confess:

Holy baptism is a means of God's grace toward men, for through baptism the believer obtains forgiveness of sin, second birth, deliverance from death and the devil, and everlasting bliss.

By means of this doctrine we confess that children also should be baptized, since by this means they will be brought into the company of those for whom Christ has given himself. This is also in accordance with Jesus' acceptance of children. Mk 10.14; Lk 18.16.

When baptizing it is not necessary to immerse into water. Acts 2.41, 10.48, 16.33; Rom 6.4; 1 Cor 10.1-4; Ti 3.5; Heb 11.29; 1 Pt 3.21.

B. Holy Communion

We believe and confess:

Holy communion is the eating of the bread as a means of mediating the body of our Lord Jesus Christ, and the drinking of the wine as a means of mediating the blood of our Lord Jesus Christ, whereby we obtain forgiveness of sins, life, and bliss. 1 Cor 11.17-34; Mt 26; Mk 14; Lk 22.

By means of this doctrine we oppose and reject the doctrine which states that only the bread without the wine should be given to the members of the church, for the Lord Jesus himself, when he instituted the Lord's supper, spoke the words, "Drink of it, all of you." The early church also acted in accordance with this, 1 Cor 11.24–25. The mass is not based on the word of God (that is, when it says that our Lord is sacrificed each time in the mass). Therefore we definitely reject it.

ARTICLE 11. CHURCH ORDER

We confess:

There must be a church order which is based upon the word of God, for it is an instrument which regulates the life of the church and gives it peace. 1 Cor 14.33. Likewise the church festivals are to be celebrated, namely, the festivals of the birth, death, resurrection, and ascension of the Lord Jesus, and the feast of Pentecost. But it must be distinctly remembered that the faithful observance of all these cannot bring us the benefit of the forgiveness of sin.

ARTICLE 12. CONCERNING GOVERNMENT

We confess:

The government which has authority comes from God; that is, a government which opposes evil and administers justice, which helps the believers to live in peace and tranquillity, according to what is written in Romans 13 and 1 Timothy 2.2. Nevertheless one should also remember what is written in Acts 5.29: "We ought to obey God rather than man."

By means of this doctrine we confess that the church ought to pray for the government that it may walk in righteousness. However, the church should also let its voice be heard by the government.

By means of this doctrine we oppose and reject the conception that *"the state is a religious state,"* for the state remains the state and the church remains the church. Mt 22.21.

When it is necessary to go to court in order to seek justice, a Christian is permitted to take an oath. The same may be done at the time of induction into an office or position.

ARTICLE 13. SUNDAY

We keep Sunday holy:

It is *"the Lord's day"* (the first day of creation by God), the day of the resurrection of the Lord Jesus, and the day of the outpouring of the Holy Spirit, which has been celebrated by Christians from the beginning of the church. Because we are Christians we do not return to the Jewish Sabbath.

By means of this doctrine we oppose and reject the doctrine of the Sabbatarians who say that Saturday is the Sabbath to be kept holy.

ARTICLE 14. CONCERNING FOOD

We believe and confess:

Everything created by God is good, and nothing is prohibited which is received with thanksgiving, for it is sanctified by the word of God and by prayer.

Man does not become holy by observing prohibitions concerning foods, for faith receives holiness from God. Man does not become holy by observing food regulations. This is the reason the apostle Paul opposed the Jewish laws concerning food. The gospel must not be pushed into the background by prohibitions resulting from Moslem laws or other traditions. Mt 15; Rom 14; Col 2; Acts 15; 1 Tm 4.4–5.

By means of this doctrine we oppose and reject the doctrine of those who teach these things.

ARTICLE 15. FAITH AND GOOD WORKS

We believe and confess:

Good works must be the fruit of faith. He errs who hopes to obtain righteousness, life, comfort, and bliss by doing good works. The Lord Jesus alone can forgive sins and reconcile man with God.

We must keep the Ten Commandments. However, man lives by faith and not only by doing good works. The Holy Spirit moves men to do good works. (If not moved by the Spirit, good works become sin.) Jn 5.15–16; Eph 2.8; Rom 5.1.

ARTICLE 16. REMEMBRANCE OF THE DEAD

We believe and confess:

"It is appointed for men to die once, and after that comes judgment." Heb 9.27. They will rest from their labors. Rv 14.13. Jesus Christ is the Lord of the quick and the dead. So in remembering the dead we remember our own passing and strengthen our hope in the fellowship of those who believe in God, thereby establishing our hearts in this life of struggle.

By means of this doctrine we oppose and reject the teaching of animism which states that the souls of the dead have a relationship with the living, as well as the doctrine which teaches that the souls of the deceased remain in the grave. We also oppose and reject the Roman Catholic doctrine which teaches that there is a purgatory through which the dead must pass for the purification of their souls before they can enter into life; furthermore, that a mass may be said for the dead and that the dead may be prayed for in order that they may more quickly be released from purgatory. We also reject prayers to the souls of the deceased saints, and the expectation that the power and holiness of the dead may pass over from their tombs, clothes, belongings, or bones (mementos, relics).

ARTICLE 17. CONCERNING THE ANGELS
We believe and confess:

The angels were created by God to serve him; they are ministering spirits "sent forth to serve, for the sake of those who are to obtain salvation." Heb 1.14.

ARTICLE 18. THE LAST JUDGMENT
We believe and confess:

The Lord Jesus Christ will come on the last day to awaken the dead. Jn 5.28; 1 Thes 4.16; Mt 24.3; Lk 21.28; Rv 20.11–15. He will judge all men. Mt 25; 1 Cor 15.52; 2 Cor 5.10. Then he will call the believers to inherit everlasting life. Mt 25.34. But the unbelievers will go into everlasting torment. Mt 25. The portion of the believers with God is sure throughout eternity.

By means of this doctrine we oppose and reject the doctrine which states: (a) the time of Christ's second coming may be calculated by men; (b) after death there is still a period of grace.

We strongly emphasize that his coming will be unexpected. Thes 5.2; Mt 24.42, 44, 50; Lk 12.35–36. Therefore we should always be ready, as he reminded us. Lk 12.35–36.

The United Church of Christ in Japan, *Confession of Faith*, 1954

The United Church of Christ in Japan (Nihon Kirisuto Kyodan) came into being in 1941, as the result of what Yoshinobu Kumazawa has described as "a combination of the ecumenical motive of unity for mission (part of the tradition of Japanese Protestantism) and the nationalistic motive for unity of the nation (a response to the request for government)."

In this *Confession of Faith* of 1954, a group of theologians representing various denominational backgrounds that had been brought together into the Kyodan sought, under the leadership of Kazo Kitamori, to address what he called "the Kyodan's most important and difficult task," which was "to declare her special nature as one Church, and this lay in her work of declaring her Confession of Faith."

For that task, as the closing article of the *Confession of Faith* makes clear, a reaffirmation of → *The Apostles' Creed* was the essential element.

Edition: *Nihon Kirisuto Kyodan Kyouken Kyouki oyobi syokisoku* 2001, 3–4.

Translation: Anderson, 253–54.

Literature: Kitamari 1968; Yoshinobu Kumazawa in Anderson, 179–208 (with bibliographic endnotes).

The United Church of Christ in Japan, *Confession of Faith*, 1954

We believe and confess that:

1. The Old and New Testaments, inspired of God, testify to Christ, reveal the truth of the gospel, and are the sole canon upon which the church should depend. By the Holy Spirit the Holy Bible is the word of God which gives us full knowledge of God and salvation, and is the unerring standard of faith and life.

2. The one God, revealed by the Lord Jesus Christ, and testified to in the Holy Scriptures, being Father, Son, and Holy Spirit, is the triune God. The Son, for the salvation of us sinners, became man, was crucified, offered himself to God as the perfect sacrifice once for all, and became our redemption.

3. God chooses us by his grace, and by faith in Christ alone he forgives our sins and justifies us. In this unchangeable grace the Holy Spirit accomplishes his work by sanctifying us and causing us to bear fruits of righteousness.

4. The church is the body of Christ the Lord, and is the congregation of those who are called by grace. The church observes public worship, preaches the gospel aright, administers the sacraments of baptism and the Lord's supper, and being diligent in works of love, waits in hope for the coming again of the Lord.

5. Thus we believe, and with the saints in all ages we confess the Apostles' Creed:

6. I believe in God the Father Almighty, Maker of heaven and earth; and in Jesus Christ his only Son our Lord; who was conceived by the Holy Spirit, born of the Virgin Mary, suffered under Pontius Pilate, was crucified, dead, and buried; he descended into hell; the third day he arose again from the dead; he ascended into heaven, and sitteth on the right hand of God the Father Almighty; from thence he shall come to judge the quick and the dead. I believe in the Holy Spirit; the holy catholic church; the communion of saints; the forgiveness of sins; the resurrection of the body; and the life everlasting. Amen.

Evangelical Church of Germany, *Arnoldshain Theses,* 1957

Ever since → *The Marburg Articles* of 1529 and → *The Wittenberg Concord* of 1536, Reformed and Lutheran theologians, especially in Germany and Switzerland, had been looking for a formula to transcend their differences on the most divisive doctrine of all, the presence of the body and blood of Christ in the Lord's supper. During the nineteenth century, the Prussian Union of Lutheran and Reformed Churches and, in the United States, → *The Definite Platform, Doctrinal and Disciplinarian* of the Lutheran General Synod in 1855, had striven to mitigate the differences, but neither succeeded in winning over the churches, particularly the Lutheran.

Having found a deeper unity in their common opposition to National Socialism, as that unity was expressed in → *The Barmen Declaration* of 1934, German Protestants in the twentieth century, working within the Evangelical Church of Germany, continued the effort. They came to a new measure of consensus also as a result of the recent work of biblical scholarship, which suggested to them interpretations of the key texts of the New Testament that went beyond the usual polemical alternatives as the Reformation confessions had formulated them.

The fruits of that consensus were, above all, two documents: these *Arnoldshain Theses* [*Arnoldshainer Abendmahlsthesen*] of 1957; and → the *Leuenberg Concord* [*Konkordie reformatorischer Kirchen in Europa*] of 1973. The *Arnoldshain Theses,* its authors emphasized, came from theologians, not from churches, and therefore were not intended as a confession in the precise sense; but the *Leuenberg Concord,* as its title indicates, did speak for the churches.

Edition: *Evangelisch-Lutherische Kirchenzeitung* 12 (1958): 302–3.

Translation: Bretscher 1959, 85–91.

Literature: Boelens 1964; Kandler 1970; Kruse 1975; Schulz 1966.

Evangelical Church of Germany, *Arnoldshain Theses*, 1957

What do we who are members of the one apostolic church believe to be the decisive content in the biblical record of the Lord's supper?

THESIS 1

a. The Lord's supper which we celebrate has its origin in the institution and command of Jesus Christ. He is the Lord, who gave himself for us into death and rose again.

b. In the Lord's supper the exalted Lord invites his own to his table and has them participate even now in that fellowship in the kingdom of God which lies in the future.

THESIS 2

a. In the celebration of the Lord's supper Jesus Christ himself is active. He acts in and through the activity of the church. He acts as the Lord, who is present by means of his word in the Holy Spirit.

b. The Lord's supper, like the sermon, baptism, and private absolution, is one of those means through which Christ appropriates to us the gifts of the saving gospel.

THESIS 3

a. The Lord's supper is an act of divine worship. This act takes place when the congregation is assembled in the name of Jesus.

b. In the Lord's supper the meal is inseparably connected with the proclamation of the saving benefit of the death of Jesus. This proclamation is made in the preached word.

c. Accompanied by prayer, thanksgiving, and the glorification of God, bread and wine are taken, the words of institution spoken, and bread and wine offered to the congregation to eat and to drink.

d. In the Lord's supper we remember the death of Christ, through whom God has once and for all times reconciled the world. In the Lord's supper we confess the presence among us of the resurrected Lord and, as those called to the glory which will be ours at the consummation of all things, we joyfully await his return.

THESIS 4

The words which our Lord Jesus Christ speaks in the course of the distribution of bread and wine tell us what he himself gives in this meal to all who approach his altar. What does he give? He, the crucified and risen Lord, allows himself to be taken by us in his body given into death for all and in his blood shed for all. He allows himself to be taken by us with bread and wine through his word of promise. In this way he receives us, by virtue of the Holy Spirit, into his triumphant rulership in order that we, by believing in his promise, might have forgiveness of sins, life, and salvation.

THESIS 5

Accordingly the event which takes place in the Lord's supper is not adequately described

a. if one teaches that through the Lord's words of institution bread and wine are changed into a supernatural substance so that bread and wine cease to be bread and wine;

b. if one teaches that a reenactment of the soteriological event takes place in the Lord's supper;

c. if one teaches that in the Lord's supper a naturelike or supernatural substance is offered to the communicants;

d. if one teaches that there is involved in the Lord's supper a parallel eating: a bodily eating and a spiritual eating, and that these two kinds of eating take place independently of each other;

e. if one teaches that bodily eating in itself has a saving effect, or that participation in the body and blood of Christ is a mere spiritual process.

THESIS 6

a. Jesus Christ, who has delivered us from God's wrathful judgment which results in death, is at the same time the first member and Head of a new creation;

b. Through him we who receive his body and his blood are united in his body, the church, and share in the promised new covenant which God instituted through the blood of Jesus.

c. The Lord's supper places us into the fellowship of the brethren and thus certifies that whatever enslaves and separates us in this life is overcome in Christ and that the Lord establishes in the midst of pardoned sinners the beginning of a new humanity.

THESIS 7

a. The Lord's supper enables us to walk the path of the cross of Christ. It directs our path into the stark realities of this world. But when we are weak, the grace of God is powerful. When we die, we live with him. His victory is still hidden behind temptation and suffering. Therefore the Lord supplies us with nourishment through his meal in order to strengthen us for the battle into which he sends his own, and in order to arm us against every kind of enthusiasm and every degree of lassitude. For he does not want that we, by indulging in false dreams, proleptically wrest to ourselves what is reserved for us in the future. On the other hand, he does not want that we, in a spirit of dejection, give up hope.

b. In the congregation to which he gives himself in the Lord's supper we are brethren. This fellowship lives only in that love with which he first loved us. Even as he had pity on us—the Righteous One among those who are unrighteous, the Liberated One among those who are not free, the Exalted One among those of low degree—so also we should share with those who are in need of our help all that we are and possess.

THESIS 8

a. Faith receives what has been promised it and builds on this promise and not on its own unworthiness;

b. The word of God warns us against every manner of disregard and misuse of holy communion in order that we might not sin against the majesty of this gift and thus invite upon us God's judgment;

c. Because the Lord is rich in mercy toward all who call upon him, all members of his congregation are invited to his meal, and forgiveness of sins is promised to all who hunger after the righteousness of God.

The Church of Jesus Christ in Madagascar, Statement of Faith, 1958/1968

Like other confessions in what had once been mission fields and colonies of the West, this *Statement of Faith* became necessary when, in the middle of the twentieth century, churches that had come out of Western missions instituted discussions and negotiations for unity among themselves. More than had been the case in the negotiations leading to the creation of → the Church of South India, however, this confession acknowledges, on one hand, "that it is the child of the Reformation carried out in the sixteenth century" (pr 2), and, on the other hand, that, surrounded as it is by a paganism that is far from extinct, it is doing its duty only when it "rejects and abominates the worship of false gods, ancestors, and idolatry (e.g., superstition, the observance of any kind of taboo, spells, divination, astrological predictions, spirit possession and trances, and the like)" (1). This latter abjuration is one of the most detailed and pronounced in any twentieth-century confession from the "Third World."

As its editor explains, "it was approved in 1958 and officially received in 1968."

Edition: *Fiangonan' i Jesoa Kristy eto Madagasikara 1968.*

Translation: Link, 2:6-7.

Literature: *EKL* 3:244-47 (Aidan W. Southall).

The Church of Jesus Christ in Madagascar
Statement of Faith, 1958/1968

Preamble

1. As it seeks to declare its faith, the church is deeply aware that its central emphasis throughout must be: "JESUS CHRIST, THE SON OF GOD, IS LORD AND SAVIOR." It confesses this faith in communion with the Christian Church throughout the world.

2. It acknowledges the Holy Scriptures (i.e., the Old Testament and the New Testament) to be the only source and standard of its faith and life. It also holds the Apostles' Creed. And it is conscious that it is the child of the Reformation carried out in the sixteenth century.

3. At the same time, in all humility it remembers that human speech is unable to express the revelation received from God adequately.

Therefore, the church confesses and proclaims:

1. Its faith in one God, Father of Jesus Christ, and Father of all men in Jesus Christ. He is the Creator and Ruler of the universe, who sustains and provides for our life in his everlasting love (Mt 6.32). He is a holy God, who does not give his glory to others (Is 42.8), and so he rejects and abominates the worship of false gods, ancestors, and idolatry (e.g., superstition, the observance of any kind of taboo, spells, divination, astrological predictions, spirit possession and trances, and the like).

2. Its faith in Jesus Christ, the Lord, the only-begotten Son of God (Jn 1.18); "for there is one Mediator between God and man, the man Christ Jesus, who gave himself a ransom for all" (1 Tm 2.5–6). "Wherefore God also hath highly exalted him, and given him a name which is above every name . . . for Jesus Christ is Lord, to the glory of God the Father" (Phil 2.9–11). Jesus Christ alone is our hope and through him we await the final victory.

3. Its faith in the Holy Spirit, who is the Spirit of the Father and the Son, bringing about faith unto the new birth through which salvation is received. He is the teacher, who explains God's word to us (Jn 14.26), and he enables us to bring forth good works to the glory of God (Gal 5.22–23).

He is the earnest of our inheritance hereafter (Eph 1.14).

In this faith the church worships the Father, and the Son, and the Holy Spirit, one God in Trinity.

The church further accepts and proclaims:

4. The word of God, as it manifests itself in the Holy Scripture, and according to the illumination by the Holy Spirit contains the full revelation by God to us of himself and the work accomplished through his Son for the salvation of the world. Because of that the church is prepared to correct and reform itself in accordance with the teaching of the Holy Scripture. Therefore, the church rejects every doctrine which opposes it.

5. That sin separates man from God, and that man's reconciliation with God was accomplished in Jesus Christ as the Scriptures proclaim: "God was in Christ reconciling the world unto himself, not reckoning unto them their trespasses" (2 Cor 5.19). "For God so loved the world that he gave his only-begotten Son, that whosoever believeth in him should not perish, but have everlasting life" (Jn 3.16), and again, "for by grace are ye saved through faith, and that not of yourselves; it is the gift of God" (Eph 2.8).

6. Within the church through the preaching of the gospel, all generations receive the fruits of the saving work of Christ. For one is the Head, namely Christ, and one is the body, namely the church. "For by one Spirit are we all baptized into one body, whether we be Jews or Gentiles, whether we be bond or free" (1 Cor 12.13). In Christ, men of different nations and castes are all one, so there should be no divisions within the church. For this reason we are conscious of our communion with the church universal. "But ye are a chosen generation, a royal priesthood, a holy nation, a peculiar people; that ye should shew forth the praises of him who has called you out of darkness into his marvelous light" (1 Pt 2.9). We realize that it is the church's duty to preach the gospel of Christ to all men without exception, by word, the sacraments, by works, and example. Every Christian ought to work according to the spiritual gifts he has received (1 Cor 12). Faithful is the Lord and he will fulfill this in us.

7. Jesus Christ is "the resurrection and the life" (Jn 11.25). He has been raised from the dead, "the first fruits of them that are asleep" (1 Cor 15.20). When a believer dies he is "in Christ" (Phil 1.22) because "neither death nor life . . . shall be able to separate us from the love of God, which is in Christ Jesus, our Lord" (Rom 8.38–39). Christ will come again to judge the living and the dead, and then will be fulfilled the promise to the faithful, "shall fashion anew the body of our humiliation, that it may be conformed to the body of his glory, according to the working of his power" (Phil 3.21).

Doxology

"Now unto him that is able to do exceeding abundantly above all that we ask or think, according to the power that worketh in us, unto him be glory in the church by Christ Jesus throughout all ages, world without end. Amen" (Eph 3.20–21).

The United Church of Christ, *Statement of Faith*, 1959/1981

As the product of the merger in 1957 between the Evangelical and Reformed Church of German Reformed background and the Congregational Christian Churches of British and American background—both of these being themselves the results of earlier mergers—the United Church of Christ was one of the first union churches in the United States to bring together churches that traced their origins to both sides of the English Channel.

Confessionally, too, these churches represented quite divergent traditions, all the way from → *The Heidelberg Catechism* to → *The Commission Creed*. At the time of the merger, no new confession was adopted by the newly constituted church body as the doctrinal basis of the union; nor were the older confessions of each group either superseded or made binding on the other. But two years later, in 1959, the Second General Synod of the United Church of Christ approved this *Statement of Faith*, drafted principally by Roger Shinn. A revised version, with more "inclusive language" and other changes, was approved by the United Church Executive Council in 1981. It is that revised version (with versification added, for ease in reference) that we present here.

Edition: *Book of Worship* 1986, 514.

Literature: Horton 1962; *ODCC* 1660; Shinn 1990.

The United Church of Christ,
Statement of Faith, 1959/1981

1. We believe in you, O God, Eternal Spirit, God of our Savior Jesus Christ and our God, and to your deeds we testify:

2. You call the worlds into being, create persons in your own image, and set before each one the ways of life and death.

3. You seek in holy love to save all people from aimlessness and sin.

4. You judge people and nations by your righteous will declared through prophets and apostles.

5. In Jesus Christ, the man of Nazareth, our crucified and risen Savior, you have come to us and shared our common lot, conquering sin and death and reconciling the world to yourself.

6. You bestow upon us your Holy Spirit, creating and renewing the church of Jesus Christ, binding in covenant faithful people of all ages, tongues, and races.

7. You call us into your church to accept the cost and joy of discipleship, to be your servants in the service of others, to proclaim the gospel to all the world and resist the powers of evil, to share in Christ's baptism and eat at his table, to join him in his passion and victory.

8. You promise to all who trust you forgiveness of sins and fullness of grace, courage in the struggle for justice and peace, your presence in trial and rejoicing, and eternal life in your realm which has no end.

9. Blessing and honor, glory and power be unto you. Amen.

Congregation of the Holy Ghost in East Nigeria,
The Masai Creed, c. 1960

The Congregation of the Holy Ghost, also sometimes called "Spiritans," were founded at the beginning of the nineteenth century with the establishment of a seminary. Practically from the beginning, and particularly after their merger with the Congregation of the Holy Heart of Mary, the Spiritans manifested a zeal for the foreign missions.

One of the most noteworthy of their mission fields was East Africa, present-day Nigeria, beginning in the second half of the nineteenth century.[1] And it was there, through their evangelization of the Masai people, that they engaged in some of the earliest and most successful experiments in "enculturation."

The results of that enculturation are visible in their homegrown adaptations of the liturgy of the mass and other Roman Catholic services.[2] Although it was composed primarily by Western missionaries, *The Masai Creed*, drafted in about 1960, consciously strove to incorporate elements of the native culture—"always on safari," "but the hyenas did not touch him"—into the fundamental trinitarian structure of primitive creeds.

Edition: Donovan, 200.

Literature: Donovan; Hillman 1993; Koren 1958; Ogudo 1988.

1. Koren 1958, 196.
2. Ogudo 1988.

Congregation of the Holy Ghost in East Nigeria,
The Masai Creed, c. 1960

1. We believe in the one High God, who out of love created the beautiful world and everything good in it. He created man and wanted man to be happy in the world. God loves the world and every nation and tribe on the earth. We have known this High God in the darkness, and now we know him in the light. God promised in the book of his word, the Bible, that he would save the world and all the nations and tribes.

    2. We believe that God made good his promise by sending his Son, Jesus Christ, a man in the flesh, a Jew by tribe, born poor in a little village, who left his home and was always on safari doing good, curing people by the power of God, teaching about God and man, showing that the meaning of religion is love. He was rejected by his people, tortured and nailed hands and feet to a cross, and died. He lay buried in the grave, but the hyenas did not touch him, and on the third day, he rose from the grave. He ascended to the skies. He is the Lord.

    3. We believe that all our sins are forgiven through him. All who have faith in him must be sorry for their sins, be baptized in the Holy Spirit of God, live the rules of love, and share the bread together in love, to announce the good news to others until Jesus comes again. We are waiting for him. He is alive. He lives. This we believe. Amen.

Roman Catholic Church, *Doctrinal Decrees of the Second Vatican Council, 1962–65*

5.1. *Lumen gentium; 5.3. Unitatis redintegratio; 8. Dei verbum; 9. Dignitatis humanae*

Widely regarded as the most important event in the modern history of the Roman Catholic Church, at least since → the Council of Trent of 1545–63, the Second Vatican Council also represented the restoration of the church council to the decisive position it had held in earlier centuries. The promulgation of the dogma of papal infallibility by → the First Vatican Council, the definition of the dogma of the immaculate conception of the Virgin Mary by → Pius IX in 1854, and the definition of the dogma of her bodily assumption by → *Munificentissimus Deus* of Pius XII in 1950 might have seemed to make councils obsolete as the legislative instrumentality for dealing with unresolved questions of doctrine, in favor of the seemingly quicker, neater, and more efficient papal fiat.

But when, responding to an inspiration that he ascribed directly to the Holy Spirit, John XXIII convoked a council, it took up the assignment of reviewing and reforming the entire life of the church. Therefore in one sense, of course, most of the decrees of the Second Vatican Council, as of most other councils, could carry the label "doctrinal" or even "dogmatic" and "creedal and confessional," based as they were on the doctrine of the authority of Scripture, church, and tradition. But within the body of this council's legislation, the four affirmations presented here do hold a special position as "confessions" in the sense in which we have been using the title in these volumes:

Lumen gentium, the Dogmatic Constitution on the Church of 21 November 1964 as the first decree of the fifth session, has been called "perhaps the greatest achievement of the Council."[1] It is a confession about the nature of the church as indeed a juridical and hierarchical institution, in keeping with definitions by previous councils and popes, but first and foremost as "the people of God," in whose total corporate life, expressed above all through the liturgy, even institution and hierarchy take their proper place. *Lumen gentium* is in many respects foundational for all the other actions of the council, not only for its legislation about bishops and about religious orders but for these three other decrees.

Unitatis redintegratio, the Decree on Ecumenism, the third decree of the

---

1. John Linnan in O'Connell 1986, 43.

fifth session, makes official and universal the new commitment of the Roman Catholic Church to the quest for Christian unity and reunion. Together with the immediately preceding decree on the Eastern churches, it identifies, as its opening words declare, "the restoration of unity among all Christians [as] one of the principal concerns of the Second Vatican Synod" (5.3.1). This it does without acknowledging in so many words that the church as such has ever been divided; for each of the four attributes of the "one holy, catholic, and apostolic church" is, technically, inviolable, and "this unity . . . subsists in the Catholic Church as something she can never lose" (5.3.4). But "Christendom" undeniably had been divided, and several times, and was therefore in need of *unitatis redintegratio*.

In *Dei verbum,* the eighth session of the council reexamined and restated Roman Catholic teaching about Scripture, which had been the central problem at the fourth session of → the Council of Trent. Reaffirming with Trent the inseparability of Scripture and tradition, Vatican II went beyond Trent in several important ways. It not only approved, but encouraged, the study of the Bible by the laity, albeit with appropriate interpretive aids. To that end, while repeating the earlier tributes to the Septuagint and especially to the Vulgate, it urged translation "especially from the original texts of the Sacred Books" (8.22), rather than only from the Vulgate, and continued the commitment of the encyclical *Divino afflante Spiritu* of Pius XII (1943) to promoting sound and critical biblical scholarship.

Dignitatis humanae on religious liberty is in many respects the most innovative of its declarations. Therefore it takes pains, already in its first paragraph, to explain that "this Vatican synod examines the sacred tradition and teaching of the church from which it continually draws new insights in harmony with the old" (9.1), even as it goes on in a later paragraph to acknowledge that "at times in the life of the people of God, as it has pursued its pilgrimage through the twists and turns of human history, there have been ways of acting hardly in tune with the spirit of the gospel, indeed contrary to it" (9.12).

Like the source notes in → *The Syllabus of Errors,* the footnotes—and in this form—are an integral and official part of the conciliar decrees and therefore are included here.

Edition and translation: *DEC* 2:849–*1011 .

Literature: Alberigo 1995; *LTK* Supplement 1–3; O'Connell 1986; *ODCC* 1682–83.

Roman Catholic Church, *Doctrinal Decrees of the Second Vatican Council, 1962–65*

5.1. Lumen gentium: Dogmatic Constitution on the Church

CHAPTER 1. THE MYSTERY OF THE CHURCH

1. Since Christ is the light of the nations, this holy synod, called together in the Holy Spirit, strongly desires to enlighten all people with his brightness, which gleams over the face of the church, by preaching the gospel to every creature (see Mk 16.15). And since the church is in Christ as a sacrament or instrumental sign of intimate union with God and of the unity of all humanity, the council, continuing the teaching of previous councils, intends to declare with greater clarity to the faithful and the entire human race the nature of the church and its universal mission. This duty of the church is made more urgent by the particular circumstances of our day so that all people, more closely bound together as they are by social, technological, and cultural bonds, may also attain full unity in Christ.

2. The eternal Father, by a completely free and mysterious design of his wisdom, created the whole world. He decided to raise human beings to share in the divine life; and when in Adam they fell, he did not abandon them but provided them always with the means of salvation, having in view Christ the Redeemer, "who is the image of the invisible God, the first-born of all creation" (Col 1.15). All those chosen before time began the Father "foreknew and predestined to be conformed to the image of his Son, in order that he might be the first-born among many brethren" (Rom 8.29). All those who believe in Christ he decided to call together within holy church, which right from the beginning of the world had been foreshadowed, wonderfully prepared in the history of the people of Israel and in the ancient covenant,[1] established in these last times and made manifest through the outpouring of the Spirit; it will reach its glorious completion at the end of time. Then, as we read in the holy fathers, all the just from Adam onward, "from Abel the just right to the last of the elect,"[2] will be gathered together in the universal church in the Father's presence.

---

1. See Cyprian, *Epist. (Letters)*, 64, 4: PL 3, 1017; CSEL (Hartel), III B, p. 720. Hilary of Poitiers, *In Mt. (On Matthew)*, 23, 6: PL 9, 1047. Augustine, *passim.* Cyril of Alexandria, *Glaph. in Gen. (Explanations of Genesis)*, 2, 10: PG 69, 110 A.

2. Gregory the Great, *Hom. in Evang. (Homilies on the Gospels)*, 19, 1: PL 76, 1154 B. See Au-

3. The Son came, therefore, sent by the Father, who chose us in him before the foundation of the world and predestined our adoption as sons and daughters, because he had decided to restore all things in him (see Eph 1.4-5, 10). Consequently, Christ, to carry out the will of the Father, has inaugurated the kingdom of heaven on earth and has revealed the mystery to us, and through his obedience has brought about the redemption. The church, as the kingdom of Christ already present in mystery, grows visibly in the world through the power of God. This beginning and this growth were symbolized by the blood and water that issued from the open side of Jesus crucified (see Jn 19.34), and were predicted by the words of the Lord concerning his death on the cross: "And I, when I am lifted up from the earth, will draw all people to myself" (Jn 12.32 Greek text). As often as the sacrifice of the cross, by which "Christ our paschal lamb has been sacrificed" (1 Cor 5.7), is celebrated on the altar, there is effected the work of our redemption. At the same time, through the sacrament of the eucharistic bread, there is represented and produced the unity of the faithful, who make up one body in Christ (see 1 Cor 10.17). All people are called to this union with Christ, who is the light of the world; from him we come, through him we live, and towards him we direct our lives.

4. When the task that the Father had entrusted to the Son on earth had been completed (see Jn 17.4), on the day of Pentecost the Holy Spirit was sent to sanctify the church continually and so that believers would have through Christ access to the Father in one Spirit (see Eph 2.18). This is the Spirit of life or the fountain of water bubbling up for eternal life (see Jn 4.14, 7.38-39), through whom the Father restores life to human beings who were dead through sin, until he raises up their mortal bodies in Christ (see Rom 8, 10-11). The Spirit dwells in the church and in the hearts of the faithful as in a temple (see 1 Cor 3.16, 6.19), and he prays in them and bears witness to their adoption as children (see Gal 4.6; Rom 8.15-16, 26). He leads the church into all truth (see Jn 16.13), and he makes it one in fellowship and ministry, instructing and directing it through a diversity of gifts both hierarchical and charismatic, and he adorns it with his fruits (see Eph 4.11-12; 1 Cor 12.4; Gal 5.22). Through the power of the gospel he rejuvenates the church, continually renewing it and leading it to perfect union with its spouse.[3] For the Spirit and the bride say to the Lord Jesus: Come! (see Rv 22.17). In this way the universal church

gustine, *Serm. (Sermons)*, 341, 9, 11: PL 39 1499 f. John Damascene, *Adv. Iconcl. (Against the Iconoclasts)*, 11: PG 96, 1357.

3. See Irenaeus, *Adv. Haer. (Against Heresies)*, III, 24, 1: PG 7, 966 B; Harvey 2, 131, ed. Sagnard, SC, p. 398.

appears as "a people made one by the unity of the Father and the Son and the Holy Spirit."[4]

5. The mystery of holy church is clearly visible in its foundation. For the Lord Jesus inaugurated the church when he preached the happy news of the coming of the kingdom of God that had been promised in the Scriptures for centuries: "The time is fulfilled and the kingdom of God is at hand" (Mk 1.15; see Mt 4.17). And this kingdom shines forth for humanity in the words, works, and presence of Christ. The word of the Lord is compared to seed sown in a field (see Mk 4.14): those who hear this word with faith and belong to the little flock of Christ (see Lk 12.32) have accepted the kingdom itself; the seed then through its own power germinates and grows until the harvest time (see Mk 4.26-29). The miracles of Jesus provide further evidence that the kingdom has come on earth: "If it is by the finger of God that I cast out demons, then the kingdom of God has come upon you" (Lk 11.20; see Mt 12.28). Above all, however, the kingdom is made manifest in the very person of Christ, Son of God and Son of man, who came "to serve and to give his life as a ransom for many" (Mk 10.45).

Then when Christ, having undergone the death of the cross for humanity rose from the dead, he appeared as Lord and Christ and Priest set up forever (see Acts 2.36; Heb 5.6, 7.17-21), and poured on his disciples the Spirit that had been promised by the Father (Acts 2.33). When, therefore, the church, equipped with the gifts of its founder and faithfully keeping his precepts of love, humility, and penance, receives the mission of announcing the kingdom of Christ and of God and of inaugurating it among all peoples, it has formed the seed and the beginning of the kingdom on earth. Meanwhile as it gradually grows, it aspires after the completion of the kingdom, and hopes and desires with all its strength to be joined with its King in glory.

6. As in the Old Testament the revelation of the kingdom is often proposed figuratively, so also now the inner nature of the church is revealed to us through a variety of images. These have been taken from the life of a shepherd, from agriculture, from the construction of buildings, and even from the family and betrothal; all of which are prepared in the books of the prophets. So the church is the *sheepfold*, whose single necessary door is Christ (see Jn 10.1-10). It is also the flock, of which God himself foretold that he would be the shepherd (see Is 40.11; Ez 34.11ff.), and whose sheep, even though governed by human shepherds, are continuously led

---

4. Cyprian, *De Orat. Dom. (The Lord's Prayer)*, 23: PL 4, 553; Hartel, III A, p. 285; CChr 3 A, 105. Augustine, *Serm. (Sermons)*, 71, 20, 33: PL 38, 463 f. John Damascene, *Adv. Iconocl. (Against the Iconoclasts)*, 12: PG 96, 1358 D.

and nourished by Christ himself, the good shepherd and prince of shepherds (see Jn 10.11; 1 Pt 5.4), who laid down his life for the sheep (see Jn 10.11–15).

The church is the *estate* or field of God (see 1 Cor 3.9). In this field the ancient olive grows whose holy root was constituted by the patriarchs, and in which was and will be effected the reconciliation of Jews and Gentiles (see Rom 11.13–16). The church has been planted by the heavenly vinedresser as a chosen vineyard (see Mt 21.33–43 and parallels; Is 5.1ff.). Christ is the true vine who gives life and fruitfulness to us the branches; through the church we abide in him, and without him we can do nothing (see Jn 15.1–5).

More often the church is called God's *building* (see 1 Cor 3.9). The Lord compared himself to the stone which the builders rejected but which was made the cornerstone (see Mt 21.42 and parallels; Acts 4.11; 1 Pt 2.7; Ps 117.22). On this foundation the church is built by the apostles (see 1 Cor 3.11), and from this it receives cohesion and stability. This building is called various names: God's household (see 1 Tm 3.15), in which his *family* lives, the dwelling-place of God in the Spirit (see Eph 2.19–22), "God's dwelling with human beings" (Rv 21.3), and above all the church is the holy *temple* which is praised by the fathers of the church when they find it represented in sanctuaries made of stone, and in the liturgy it is rightly likened to the holy city, the new Jerusalem.[5] For in it we are built up as living stones here on earth (see 1 Pt 2.5). John contemplates this holy city coming down out of heaven from God at the renewal of the world, "prepared as a bride adorned for her husband" (Rv 21.1f.).

Moreover the church, "which is the Jerusalem above" and is called "our mother" (Gal 4.26; see Rv 12.17), is described as the immaculate *spouse* of the immaculate lamb (see Rv 19.7, 21.2, 9, 22.17), whom Christ "loved . . . and for whom he delivered himself up that he might make her holy" (Eph 5.25–26). He has bound the church to himself by an indissoluble covenant and continuously "nourishes and cherishes" it (Eph 5.29), wanting it cleansed and joined to himself and subject to himself in love and fidelity (see Eph 5.24); which finally he has enriched with heavenly goods forever, so that we may understand the love of God and of Christ towards us which surpasses all knowledge (see Eph 3.19). While, however, here on earth the

5. See Origen, *In Mt. (On Matthew)*, 16, 21: PG 13, 1443 C; Tertullian, *Adv. Marc. (Against Marcion)*, 3, 7: PL 2, 357 C; CSEL 47, 3, p. 386; CChr 1, 516. For the liturgical documents, see *Gregorian Sacramentary*: PL 78, 160 B; or C. Mohlberg, *Liber Sacramentorum Romanae Ecclesiae*, Rome, 1960, p. 111, XC: "God, who from the entire joining together of the saints make for yourself an eternal dwelling . . . ." Hymn *Urbs Jerusalem beata* in the monastic breviary, and *Coelestis urbs Jerusalem* in the Roman breviary.

church is on pilgrimage from the Lord (see 2 Cor 5.6), it is like an exile who seeks and savors the things that are above, where Christ is seated at the right hand of God, where the life of the church is hidden with Christ in God until it appears in glory with its spouse (see Col 3.1–4).

7. The Son of God, in the human nature he had united to himself, overcame death by his own death and resurrection and in this way redeemed humanity and made it into a new creation (see Gal 6.15; 2 Cor 5.17). And by the communication of his Spirit he constituted his sisters and brothers, gathered from all nations, as his own mystical body.

In this body the life of Christ is communicated to believers, who by means of the sacraments in a mysterious but real way are united to Christ who suffered and has been glorified.[6] By baptism we are made into the likeness of Christ: "For by one Spirit we were all baptized into one body" (1 Cor 12.13). Through this sacred rite the union with the death and resurrection of Christ is both symbolized and effected: "We were buried with him by baptism into death," but if "we have been united with him in a death like his, we shall certainly be united with him in a resurrection like his" (Rom 6.4–5). When we really participate in the body of the Lord through the breaking of the eucharistic bread, we are raised up to communion with him and among ourselves. "Because there is one bread, we who are many are one body, for we all partake of the one bread" (1 Cor 10.17). In this way all of us are made members of this body (see 1 Cor 12.27), "individually members one of another" (Rom 12.5).

Just as all the members of the human body, although they are many, nevertheless make up one body, in the same way the faithful are one in Christ (see 1 Cor 12.12). In the structure of the body of Christ, too, there is a diversity of members and of functions. There is one Spirit who distributes his various gifts for the good of the church according to his own riches and the needs of the ministries (see 1 Cor 12.1–11). Among these gifts the grace of the apostles holds first place, and the Spirit himself makes even the charismatics subject to their authority (see 1 Cor 14). The same Spirit makes the body one through himself and by his power and by the inner cohesion of the members, and he produces and urges charity among the faithful. Therefore, if one member suffers in any way, all the members suffer along with that member, and if one member is honored then all the members rejoice together (see 1 Cor 12.26).

Christ is the Head of this body. He is the image of the invisible God and in him all things have their foundation. He is before all things and all things are

---

6. See Thomas Aquinas, *Summa Theologiae* III, quest. 62, art. 5, to 1.

held together in him. He is the Head of the body which is the church. He is the beginning, the first-born from the dead, so that he may hold the primacy among all things (see Col 1.15–18). By the might of his power he dominates all creatures both in heaven and on earth, and through his supereminent perfection and activity he fills the whole body with the riches of his glory (see Eph 1.18–23).[7]

All the members must be made into his likeness until Christ is formed in them (see Gal 4.19). Therefore we are taken up into the mysteries of his life, we are made like to him, we die and are raised to life with him, until we reign together with him (see Phil 3.21; 2 Tm 2.11; Eph 2.6; Col 2.12; etc.). While we are still making our pilgrimage on earth and follow in his footsteps in tribulation and persecution, we are associated with his sufferings as a body with its head, sharing his suffering that we may also share his glory (see Rom 8.17).

From him "the whole body, nourished and knit together through its joints and ligaments, grows with a growth that is from God" (Col 2.19). He perpetually distributes the gift of ministries in his body which is the church; and with these gifts, through his power, we provide each other with helps towards salvation, so that doing the truth in love, we grow up in all things into him who is our Head (see Eph 4.11–16 Greek text).

In order that we may be continually renewed in him (see Eph 4.23), he gave us a share in his Spirit, who is one and the same in head and members. This Spirit gives life, unity, and movement to the whole body, so that the fathers of the church could compare his task to that which is exercised by the life-principle, the soul, in the human body.[8]

Christ loves the church as his bride and has made himself the model of the husband loving his wife as his own body (see Eph 5.25–28); and the church is submissive to its head (ibid. 23–24). "For in him the whole fullness of deity dwells bodily" (Col 2.9); and he fills with his divine gifts the church, which is his body and his fullness (see Eph 1.22–23), so that it may aspire towards and arrive at the whole fullness of God (see Eph 3.19).

8. Christ, the one Mediator, set up his holy church here on earth as a visible

---

7. See Pius XII, Encyclical *Mystici Corporis,* 29 June 1943: AAS 35 (1943), p. 208.

8. See Leo XIII, Encyclical *Divinum illud,* 9 May 1897: ASS 29 (1896–97), p. 650. Pius XII, Encyclical *Mystici Corporis,* loc. cit., pp. 219–220: D 2288 (3808). Augustine, *Serm. (Sermons),* 268, 2: PL 38, 1232, and elsewhere. John Chrysostom, *In Eph. (On Ephesians),* homily 9, 3: PG 62, 72. Didymus of Alexandria, *Trin. (The Trinity),* 2, 1: PG 39, 449 f. Thomas Aquinas, *In Col. (On Colossians),* 1, 18, lection 5: ed. Marietti, II, no. 46: "As one body is constituted by the unity of the soul, so is the church by the unity of the Spirit . . . ."

structure, a community of faith, hope, and love; and he sustains it unceasingly[9] and through it he pours out grace and truth on everyone. This society, however, equipped with hierarchical structures, and the mystical body of Christ, a visible assembly and a spiritual community, an earthly church and a church enriched with heavenly gifts, must not be considered as two things, but as forming one complex reality comprising a human and a divine element.[10] It is therefore by no mean analogy that it is likened to the mystery of the incarnate Word. For just as the assumed nature serves the divine Word as a living instrument of salvation inseparably joined with him, in a similar way the social structure of the church serves the Spirit of Christ who vivifies the church towards the growth of the body (see Eph 4.16).[11]

This is the unique church of Christ, which in the creed we profess to be one, holy, catholic, and apostolic.[12] After his resurrection our Savior gave the church to Peter to feed (see Jn 21.17), and to him and the other apostles he committed the church to be governed and spread (see Mt 28.18ff.); and he set it up for all time as the pillar and foundation of the truth (1 Tm 3.15). This church, set up and organized in this world as a society, subsists in the catholic church, governed by the successor of Peter and the bishops in communion with him,[13] although outside its structure many elements of sanctification and of truth are to be found which, as proper gifts to the church of Christ, impel towards catholic unity.

Just as Christ carried out the work of redemption in poverty and persecution, so the church is called to follow along the same way in order that it may communicate to humanity the fruits of salvation. "Though he was in the form of God," Christ Jesus "emptied himself, taking the form of a servant" (Phil 2.6–7); and for our sake "though he was rich, he became poor" (2 Cor 8.9). So also the church, though it needs human resources to carry out its mission, is not set up to seek earthly glory, but to spread humility and self-denial also through its own ex-

9. See Leo XIII, Encyclical *Sapientiae christianae,* 10 Jan. 1890: ASS 22 (1889–90), p. 392. Id., Encyclical *Satis cognitum,* 29 June 1896: ASS 28 (1895–96), pp. 710 and 724 ff. Pius XII, Encyclical *Mystici Corporis,* loc. cit. pp. 199–200.

10. See Pius XII, Encyclical *Mystici Corporis,* loc. cit., p. 221 ff. Id., Encyclical *Humani generis,* 12 Aug. 1950: AAS 42 (1950), p. 571.

11. See Leo XIII, Encyclical *Satis cognitum,* loc. cit., p. 713.

12. See *Apostles' creed:* D 6–9 (10–30); *Nicene-Constantinopolitan creed:* D86 (150); compare *Tridentine profession of faith:* D 994 and 999 (1862 and 1868).

13. It is called "holy (catholic apostolic) Roman church" in *Tridentine profession of faith,* loc. cit., and in Vatican council I, dogmatic constitution on the catholic faith, *Dei Filius:* D 1782 (3001).

ample. Christ was sent by the Father "to preach good news to the poor . . . to restore the broken-hearted" (Lk 4.18), "to seek and to save the lost" (Lk 19.10): in the same way the church surrounds with love all who are afflicted with human infirmity, indeed in the poor and the suffering it recognizes the face of its poor and suffering founder, it endeavors to relieve their need, and in them it strives to serve Christ. While Christ "holy, blameless, unstained" (Heb 7.26) knew no sin (see 2 Cor 5.21), and came only to expiate the sins of the people (see Heb 2.17), the church, containing sinners in its own bosom, is at one and the same time holy and always in need of purification and it pursues unceasingly penance and renewal.

The church "proceeds on its pilgrim way amidst the persecutions of the world and the consolations of God,"[14] proclaiming the cross and the death of the Lord until he comes (see 1 Cor 11.26). But it draws strength from the power of the risen Lord, to overcome with patience and charity its afflictions and difficulties, from within and from without; and reveals his mystery faithfully in the world—albeit amid shadows—until in the end it will be made manifest in the fullness of light.

CHAPTER 2. THE PEOPLE OF GOD

9. At all times and in every nation whoever fears God and does what is right is acceptable to God (see Acts 10.35). It has pleased God, however, to sanctify and save men and women not individually and without regard for what binds them together, but to set them up as a people who would acknowledge him in truth and serve him in holiness. Therefore he chose the people of Israel as a people for himself, and he made a covenant with them and instructed them step by step, making himself and his intention known to them in their history and sanctifying them for himself. All this took place, however, as a preparation and a figure of that new and perfect covenant which was to be struck with Christ, and of the more complete revelation that was to be made through the Word of God himself made flesh. "Behold, the days are coming, says the Lord, when I will make a new covenant with the house of Israel and the house of Juda . . . I will put my law within them, and I will write it in their hearts; and I will be their God, and they shall be my people . . . for they shall all know me, from the least of them to the greatest, says the Lord" (Jer 31.31–34). This is the new covenant that Christ instituted, the new testament in his blood (see 1 Cor 11.25), calling together from Jews and Gentiles a people which would be bound together in unity not according to the flesh but in the Spirit, and which would be the new people of God. Believers in Christ have been born again not from a per-

---

14. Augustine, *De civ. Dei (The city of God)*, XVIII, 51, 2: PL 41, 614; CChr 48, 650.

ishable but from an imperishable seed through the word of the living God (see 1 Pt 1.23), not of flesh but of water and the Holy Spirit (see Jn 3.5–6); and they have been finally set up as "a chosen race, a royal priesthood, a holy nation, God's own people . . . once no people but now God's people" (1 Pt 2.9–10).

This messianic people has for its Head Christ, "who was put to death for our trespasses and raised for our justification" (Rom 4.25); and now having gained possession of that name which is above all names, he reigns gloriously in heaven. This people has been given the dignity and the freedom of sons and daughters of God, in whose hearts the Holy Spirit dwells as in a temple. For its law it has the new commandment of love just as Christ has loved us (see Jn 13.34). And finally for its goal it has the kingdom of God: inaugurated on earth by God himself and to be further extended until, at the end of time, it will be brought to its completion by the Lord when Christ will appear, our life (see Col 3.4), and "creation itself will be set free from its bondage to decay and obtain the glorious liberty of the children of God" (Rom 8.21). Consequently this messianic people, although in fact it does not include everybody, and more than once may appear as a tiny flock, nevertheless it constitutes for the whole human race a most firm seed of unity, hope, and salvation. It has been set up by Christ as a communion of life, love, and truth; by him too it is taken up as the instrument of salvation for all, and sent as a mission to the whole world as the light of the world and the salt of the earth (see Mt 5.13–16).

Just as Israel according to the flesh, who wandered in the desert, is already called the church of God (see 2 Est 13.1; Nm 20.4; Dt 23.1ff.), so the new Israel, while journeying through this present world in search of a permanent city which lies in the future (see Heb 13.14), is also called the church of Christ (see Mt 16.18), since he has acquired it by his own blood (see Acts 20.28), has filled it with his Spirit and set it up with means suitable for visible and social unity. God has called together the assembly of those who look to Jesus in faith as the author of salvation and the principle of unity and peace, and he has constituted the church that it may be for one and all the visible sacrament of this saving unity.[1] In order to spread to all regions, it enters into the history of humanity while at the same time transcending both times and the boundaries of nations. As the church journeys through temptations and tribulations, it is strengthened by the power of the grace of God that was promised it by the Lord, so that it does not fall away from perfect fidelity through the weakness of the flesh, but remains the worthy spouse of its Lord, and

---

1. See Cyprian, *Epist. (Letters)*, 69, 6: PL 3, 1142 B; Hartel 3 B, p. 754: "inseparable sacrament of unity."

so that, under the action of the Holy Spirit, it does not cease from renewing itself until, through the cross, it arrives at the light which knows no setting.

10. Christ the Lord, the High Priest chosen from among human beings (see Heb 5.1–5), has made the new people "a kingdom, priests to his God and Father" (Rv 1.6; see 5.9–10). For by the regeneration and anointing of the Holy Spirit the baptized are consecrated as a spiritual dwelling and a holy priesthood, so that through all the activity of Christian living they may offer spiritual sacrifices, and declare the powers of him who called them out of darkness into his marvelous light (see 1 Pt 2.4–10). Therefore, all the disciples of Christ, persevering in prayer and praising God together (see Acts 2.42–47), are to present themselves as a living sacrifice, holy and pleasing to God (see Rom 12.1), witnessing to Christ throughout the world, and explaining to those who ask the hope they possess of eternal life (see 1 Pt 3.15).

The common priesthood of the faithful and the ministerial or hierarchical priesthood, though they differ in essence and not simply in degree, are nevertheless interrelated: each in its own particular way shares in the one priesthood of Christ.[2] On the one hand, the ministerial priest, through the sacred power that he enjoys, forms and governs the priestly people; in the person of Christ he brings about the eucharistic sacrifice and offers this to God in the name of the whole people. The faithful, on the other hand, by virtue of their royal priesthood, join in the offering of the eucharist,[3] and they exercise their priesthood in receiving the sacraments, in prayer and thanksgiving, through the witness of a holy life, by self-denial, and by active charity.

11. The sacred character and the organic structure of the priestly community are brought into effect by means of the sacraments and the virtues. Incorporated into the church through baptism, the faithful are by the baptismal character given a place in the worship of the Christian religion; and reborn as children of God, they have an obligation to profess publicly the faith they have received from God through the church.[4] With the sacrament of confirmation they are bound more completely to the church; they are enriched by a special strength of the Holy Spirit, and in this way are under more pressing obligation to spread the faith by word and deed as true

2. See Pius XII, Allocution *Magnificate Dominum,* 2 Nov. 1954: AAS 46 (1954), p. 669. Encyclical *Mediator Dei,* 20 Nov. 1947: AAS 39 (1947), p. 555.

3. See Pius XI, Encyclical *Miserentissimus Redemptor,* 8 May 1928: AAS 20 (1928), p. 171 f. Pius XII, Allocution *Vous nous avez,* 22 Sept. 1956: AAS 48 (1956), p. 714.

4. See Thomas Aquinas, *Summa Theologiae,* III, quest. 63, art. 2.

witnesses of Christ.[5] When they take part in the eucharistic sacrifice, the source and the culmination of all Christian life, they offer to God the divine victim and themselves along with him;[6] and so both in this offering and in holy communion all fulfill their own part in the liturgical action, not in a confused manner but one in one way and one in another. Indeed, refreshed as they are by the body of Christ in the sacred gathering, they show forth in a concrete way the unity of the people of God, which in this most noble sacrament is both suitably symbolized and wonderfully brought about.

Those who approach the sacrament of penance, through the mercy of God obtain pardon for an offense committed against him, and at the same time are reconciled with the church which they wounded by their sin and which strives for their conversion through charity, example, and prayers. Through the sacred anointing of the sick and the prayer of the priests, the whole church commends the sick to the suffering and glorified Lord that he might relieve them and restore them to health (see Jas 5.14–16), and indeed it exhorts them freely to associate themselves with the passion and death of Christ (see Rom 8.17; Col 1.24; 2 Tm 2.11–12; 1 Pt 4.13), and so contribute to the good of the people of God. Those of the faithful who are marked by holy order are appointed in the name of Christ to feed the church with the word and the grace of God. Finally, by virtue of the sacrament of matrimony, by which they both share in and symbolize the unity and the fertile love between Christ and the church (see Eph 5.32), married Christians help each other towards holiness in their married life and in the acceptance and education of children. And so in their state and way of life, they have their own particular gift within the people of God.[7] From this married life comes the family, in which are born new citizens of human society who, by the grace of the Holy Spirit, are raised by baptism to the status of heirs of God to carry on his people through the centuries. This is, as it were, the domestic church in which the parents must be for their children, by word and by example, the first preachers of the faith, encouraging each in her or his vocation and paying special attention to a sacred vocation.

5. See Cyril of Jerusalem, *Catech. (Catecheses)*, 17, de Spiritu sancto, II, 35–37: PG 33, 1009–1012. Nicholas Cabasilas, *De vita in Christo (Life in Christ)*, book 3, de utilitate chrismatis: PG 150, 569–580. Thomas Aquinas, *Summa Theologiae*, III, quest. 65, art. 3 and quest. 72, art. 1 and 5.
6. See Pius XII, Encyclical *Mediator Dei*, 20 Nov. 1947: AAS 39 (1947), especially p. 552 f.
7. 1 Cor 7.7: "Each has his or her own special gift from God, one of one kind and one of another." See Augustine, *De Dono Persev. (The Gift of Perseverance)*, 14, 37: PL 45, 1015 f.: "Not only is continence a gift of God, but so also is the chastity of married people."

Protected by such great and wonderful means of salvation, all the faithful of every state and condition are called by the Lord, each in their own way, to that perfect holiness whereby the Father is perfect.

12. The holy people of God has a share, too, in the prophetic role of Christ, when it renders him a living witness, especially through a life of faith and charity, and when it offers to God a sacrifice of praise, the tribute of lips that honor his name (see Heb 13.15). The universal body of the faithful who have received the anointing of the holy one (see 1 Jn 2.20, 27), cannot be mistaken in belief. It displays this particular quality through a supernatural sense of the faith in the whole people when "from the bishops to the last of the faithful laity,"[8] it expresses the consent of all in matters of faith and morals. Through this sense of faith which is aroused and sustained by the Spirit of truth, the people of God, under the guidance of the sacred magisterium to which it is faithfully obedient, receives no longer the words of human beings but truly the word of God (see 1 Thes 2.13); it adheres indefectibly to "the faith which was once for all delivered to the saints" (Jude 3); it penetrates more deeply into that same faith through right judgment and applies it more fully to life.

Moreover, the same Holy Spirit not only sanctifies and guides the people of God by means of the sacraments and the ministries and adorns it with virtues, he also apportions his gifts "to each individually as he wills" (1 Cor 12.11), and among the faithful of every rank he distributes special graces by which he renders them fit and ready to undertake the various tasks and offices which help the renewal and the building up of the church, according to that word: "To each is given the manifestation of the Spirit for the common good" (1 Cor 12.7). These charismatic gifts, whether they be very outstanding or simpler and more widely diffused, are to be accepted with thanksgiving and consolation, since they are primarily suited to and useful for the needs of the church. Extraordinary gifts should not, however, be sought rashly nor should the fruits of apostolic works be presumptuously expected from them. The judgment about their genuineness and their ordered use belongs to those who preside over the church, to whom it belongs especially not to extinguish the Spirit but to test everything and hold fast to what is good (see 1 Thes 5.12, 19–21).

13. All human beings are called to the new people of God. Therefore this people, while remaining one and unique, is to be spread throughout the whole world and through every age to fulfill the design of the will of God, who in the beginning made one human nature and decreed that his children who had been scattered

8. Augustine, *De Praed. Sanct. (Predestination of Saints),* 14, 27: PL 44, 980.

should at last be gathered together into one (see Jn 11.52). For this God sent his Son, whom he appointed heir of all things (see Heb 1.2), that he might be Master, King, and Priest of all, Head of the new and universal people of the children of God. For this finally God sent the Spirit of his Son, the Lord and Giver of life, who is for the whole church and for each and every one of the faithful the principle of union and of unity in the teaching of the apostles, in communion, in the breaking of bread, and in prayers (see Acts 2.42 Greek text).

For all the nations of the earth, therefore, there is one people of God since it draws its citizens from all nations, but the kingdom is not earthly in character, but heavenly. For all the faithful scattered throughout the world are in communion with the rest in the Holy Spirit, and so "the person who lives in Rome knows that Indians are his members."[9] Since, however, the reign of Christ is not of this world (see Jn 18.36), therefore the church as the people of God, in bringing this kingdom into being, takes nothing away from the temporal well-being of any people. On the contrary, it takes up and encourages the riches, resources, and customs of peoples in so far as they are good; and in taking them up it purifies, strengthens, and raises them up. The church is mindful of the fact that it must gather in along with that King to whom the nations have been given for an inheritance (see Ps 2.8), and into whose city they bring gifts and offerings (see Ps 71[72].10; Is 60.4-7; Rv 21.24). This note of universality, which adorns the people of God, is a gift of the Lord himself by which the catholic church effectively and continually tries to recapitulate the whole of humanity, with all its riches, under Christ the head in the unity of his Spirit.[10] By virtue of this catholicity, the individual parts bring their own gifts to the other parts and to the whole church, in such a way that the whole and individual parts grow greater through the mutual communication of all and their united efforts towards fullness in unity. It follows from this that the people of God is not only gathered together from diverse peoples, but within itself is made up out of the union of different orders. In fact among its members there is a diversity either because of duties, since some are engaged in the sacred ministry for the good of their sisters and brothers, or because of the conditions and arrangements of their lives, since many in the religious state, striving towards holiness by a stricter path, are a stimulus to their fellow Christians by their example. So also, within the ecclesiastical communion, there are lawfully particular churches which enjoy their own proper traditions, while the primacy of the See of Peter remains intact, which presides over the uni-

---

9. John Chrysostom, *In Io. (On John)*, Homily 65, 1: PG 59, 361.

10. See Irenaeus, *Adv. Haer. (Against Heresies)*, III, 16, 6; III, 22, 1–3: PG 7, 925C–926A and 955C–958A; Harvey 2, 87 f. and 120–123; Sagnard, ed. *SC*, pp. 290–292 and 372 ff.

versal communion of charity[11] and safeguards legitimate differences while taking care that what is particular not only does no harm to unity but rather is conducive to it. Finally, between the different parts of the church there are bonds of intimate communion with regard to spiritual riches, apostolic workers, and temporal assistance. For the members of the people of God are called to share their goods, and the words of the apostle are applicable also to the individual churches: "As each has received a gift, employ it for one another, as good stewards of God's varied grace" (1 Pt 4.10).

Therefore to this catholic unity of the people of God, which prefigures and promotes universal peace, all are called, and they belong to it or are ordered to it in various ways, whether they be Catholic faithful or others who believe in Christ or finally all people everywhere who by the grace of God are called to salvation.

14. The holy synod turns its attention first of all to the Catholic faithful. Relying on Sacred Scripture and tradition, it teaches that this pilgrim church is necessary for salvation. For Christ alone, who is present to us in his body, which is the church, is the Mediator and the way of salvation; and he, while expressly insisting on the need for faith and baptism (see Mk 16.16; Jn 3.5), at the same time confirmed the need for the church, into which people enter through baptism as through a door. Therefore, those cannot be saved who refuse to enter the church or to remain in it, if they are aware that the Catholic Church was founded by God through Jesus Christ as a necessity for salvation.

They are fully incorporated into the society of the church who, possessing the Spirit of Christ, accept its whole structure and all the means of salvation that have been established within it, and within its visible framework are united with Christ, who governs it through the supreme pontiff and the bishops, by the bonds of profession of faith, the sacraments, ecclesiastical government, and communion. That person is not saved, however, even though he might be incorporated into the church, who does not persevere in charity; he does indeed remain in the bosom of the church "bodily," but not "in his heart."[12] But all sons and daughters of the church must be mindful that they owe their distinguished status not to their own merits but to Christ's special grace; and if they fail to respond to this grace in

---

11. See Ignatius of Antioch, *Ad Rom. (To the Romans)*, preface: ed. Funk, I, 252.

12. See Augustine, *Bapt. c. Donat. (On Baptism against the Donatists)*, V, 28, 39: PL 43, 197: "It is certainly clear that when we speak of 'within' and 'without' with regard to the church, our consideration should be directed to what is in the heart, not to what is in the body." See *ibid.*, III, 19, 26: col. 152; V, 18, 24: col. 189; *In Io. (On John)*, Treatise 61, 2: CChr 36, 481; PL 35, 1800, and frequently elsewhere.

thought, word, and deed, not only will they not be saved, they will be judged more severely.[13]

Catechumens who, under the impulse of the Holy Spirit, expressly ask to be incorporated into the church are by this very desire joined to it, and Mother Church already embraces them with love and care as its own.

15. For several reasons the church recognizes that it is joined to those who, though baptized and so honored with the Christian name, do not profess the faith in its entirety or do not preserve the unity of communion under the successor of Peter.[14] For there are many who hold the Sacred Scripture in honor as the norm for believing and living, and display a sincere religious zeal. They lovingly believe in God the Almighty Father and in Christ, the Son of God and Savior.[15] They are marked by baptism, by which they are joined to Christ; and indeed there are other sacraments that they recognize and accept in their own churches or ecclesiastical communities. Several among them possess the episcopate, celebrate the sacred eucharist, and foster devotion to the Virgin Mother of God.[16] In addition to this, there is a communion in prayers and other spiritual benefits. Indeed there is a true bond in the Holy Spirit, since it is he who is also at work in these persons with his sanctifying power through gifts and graces, and he has strengthened some of them to the point of the shedding of their blood. In this way the Spirit arouses in all of Christ's disciples desire and action so that all may be peacefully united, in the way established by Christ, in one flock under one shepherd.[17] To obtain this the church does not cease to pray, to hope, and to work, and it exhorts its children to purification and renewal so that the sign of Christ may shine more clearly over the face of the church.

16. Finally, those who have not yet accepted the gospel are related to the people of God in various ways.[18] In the first place, there is that people to whom the

---

13. Lk 12.48: "Every one to whom much is given, of him much will be required." See Mt 5.19-20, 7.21-22, 25.41-46; Jas 2.14.

14. See Leo XIII, Apostolic letter *Praeclara gratulationis,* 20 June 1894: ASS 26 (1893-94), p. 707.

15. See Leo XIII, Encyclical *Satis cognitum,* 29 June 1896; ASS 28 (1895-96), p. 738. Encyclical *Caritatis studium,* 25 July 1898: ASS 31 (1898-99), p. 11. Pius XII, Radio message *Nell'alba,* 24 Dec. 1941: AAS 34 (1942), p. 21.

16. See Pius XI, Encyclical *Rerum Orientalium,* 8 Sept. 1928: AAS 20 (1928), p. 287. Pius XII, Encyclical *Orientalis Ecclesiae,* 9 April 1944: AAS 36 (1944), p. 137.

17. See instruction of the Holy Office, 20 Dec. 1949: AAS 42 (1950), p. 142.

18. See Thomas Aquinas, *Summa Theologiae,* III, quest. 8, art. 3, to 1.

testaments and promises were given and from whom Christ was born according to the flesh (see Rom 9.4–5), a people according to their election most dear because of their ancestors: for God never goes back on his gifts and his calling (see Rom 11.28–29). But the plan of salvation also embraces those who acknowledge the Creator, and among these the Moslems are first; they profess to hold the faith of Abraham and along with us they worship the one merciful God who will judge humanity on the last day. There are others who search for the unknown God in shadows and images; God is not far from people of this kind since he gives to all life and breath and everything (see Acts 17.25–28), and the Savior wishes all to be saved (see 1 Tm 2.4). There are those who without any fault do not know anything about Christ or his church, yet who search for God with a sincere heart and, under the influence of grace, try to put into effect the will of God as known to them through the dictate of conscience: these too can obtain eternal salvation.[19] Nor does divine Providence deny the helps that are necessary for salvation to those who, through no fault of their own, have not yet attained to the express recognition of God yet who strive, not without divine grace, to lead an upright life. For whatever goodness and truth is found in them is considered by the church as a preparation for the gospel[20] and bestowed by him who enlightens everyone that they may in the end have life. More often, however, deceived by the evil one, people have gone astray in their thinking and exchanged the truth about God for a lie and served the creature rather than the Creator (see Rom 1.21, 25), or living and dying in this world without God they are exposed to the extreme of despair. For this reason, to promote the glory of God and the salvation of all these people, the church is mindful of the Lord's command when he said: "Preach the gospel to the whole creation" (Mk 16.15), and so it sedulously encourages the missions.

17. Just as the Son was sent by the Father, he too sent the apostles (see Jn 20.21), saying: "Go therefore and make disciples of all nations, baptizing them in the name of the Father and of the Son and of the Holy Spirit, teaching them to observe all that I have commanded you; and look, I am with you always, to the close of the age" (Mt 28.19–20). This solemn command of Christ, to announce the saving truth, the church has received from the apostles to fulfill right to the ends of the earth (see Acts 1.8). Therefore it makes its own the words of the apostle: "Woe . . . to me if I do not preach the gospel" (1 Cor 9, 16), and so it continues without ceasing to send out preachers until new churches are fully established and they themselves

19. See *Letter* of the Holy Office to the archbishop of Boston: D 3869–72.
20. See Eusebius of Caesarea, *Praeparatio Evangelica (Preparation for the Gospel)*, 1, 1: PG 21, 28AB; GCS VIII/1, 8.

continue the work of evangelizing. For it is compelled by the Holy Spirit to cooperate in bringing to actual completion the design of God, who constituted Christ as the principle of salvation for the whole world. By preaching the gospel the church draws its hearers to faith and the profession of faith; it disposes them for baptism, draws them out of servitude to error, and incorporates them into Christ, so that through charity they may grow to fullness in him. The result of its activity is that the good seed that is found in people's hearts and minds, or in their particular rites and cultures, is not only saved from destruction but is made whole, raised up, and brought to completion to the glory of God, the confusion of the devil, and the happiness of humanity. The duty of spreading the faith is incumbent on every disciple of Christ in so far as he or she can.[21] However, though anyone can baptize those who believe, it is the task of the priest to complete the building up of the body through the eucharistic sacrifice, fulfilling the words of God spoken through the prophets: "From the rising of the sun to its setting my name is great among the nations, and in every place sacrifice is offered to my name, and a pure offering" (Mal 1.11).[22] So the church prays and works at the same time so that the fullness of the whole world may move into the people of God, the body of the Lord and the temple of the Holy Spirit, and that all honor and glory be rendered in Christ, the Head of all, to the Creator and Father of all.

CHAPTER 3. THE HIERARCHICAL CONSTITUTION OF THE CHURCH AND IN PARTICULAR THE EPISCOPATE

18. For the nourishment and continual growth of the people of God, Christ the Lord instituted a variety of ministries which are directed towards the good of the whole body. Ministers who are endowed with sacred power are at the service of their brothers and sisters, so that all who belong to the people of God, and therefore enjoy real Christian dignity, by cooperating with each other freely and in an orderly manner in pursuit of the same goal, may attain salvation.

This holy synod, following in the footsteps of the First Vatican Council, teaches along with that council and declares that Jesus Christ, the eternal shepherd, built holy church by sending apostles just as he himself had been sent by the Father

21. See Benedict XV, Apostolic letter *Maximum illud*: AAS 11 (1919), p. 440, especially p. 451 ff. Pius XI, Encyclical *Rerum Ecclesiae*: AAS 18 (1926), pp. 68–69. Pius XII, Encyclical *Fidei Donum*, 21 April 1957: AAS 49 (1957), pp. 236–237.
22. See *Didache*, 14: ed. Funk, I, p. 32. Justin, *Dial. (Dialogue)*, 41: PG 6, 564. Irenaeus, *Adv. Haer. (Against Heresies)*, IV, 17, 5: PG 7, 1023; Harvey, 2, p. 199 f. Council of Trent, session 22, ch. 1: D 939 (1742).

(see Jn 20.21); it was his will that their successors, namely the bishops, should be shepherds in his church right to the end of the world. So that the episcopate itself, however, should be one and undivided, he placed blessed Peter over the rest of the apostles, and in him he instituted a perpetual and visible principle and foundation for the unity of faith and communion.[1] This doctrine of the institution, the perpetuity, the force, and the nature of the sacred primacy of the Roman pontiff and of his infallible magisterium, the synod once more sets out to be firmly believed by all the faithful. Continuing this same undertaking, it has decided to profess before all and to declare the teaching concerning the bishops, the successors of the apostles, who along with the successors of Peter, the vicar of Christ[2] and visible head of the whole church, govern the house of the living God.

19. The Lord Jesus, after he had poured forth prayers to the Father, called to himself those whom he wished, and he appointed twelve to be with him whom he would send out to preach the kingdom of God (see Mk 3.13–19; Mt 10.1–42). These apostles (see Lk 6.13) he established as a college or a permanent group over which he placed Peter, chosen from among them (see Jn 21.15–17). He sent them first to the children of Israel and then to all nations (see Rom 1.16), so that, sharing in his power, they might make all peoples his disciples, sanctify and govern them (see Mt 28.16–20; Mk 16.15; Lk 24.45–48; Jn 20.21–23), and in this way spread the church, and by their ministry, under the guidance of the Lord, they would nourish it all days to the end of the world (see Mt 28.20). In this mission they were fully confirmed on the day of Pentecost (see Acts 2.1–36), in accordance with the Lord's promise: "You shall receive power when the Holy Spirit has come upon you; and you shall be my witnesses in Jerusalem and in all Judaea and in Samaria and to the end of the earth" (Acts 1.8). By preaching the gospel everywhere (see Mk 16.20), which was accepted by their hearers through the work of the Holy Spirit, the apostles gather together the universal church which the Lord founded on the apostles and built over their leader, blessed Peter, while the chief cornerstone is Christ Jesus himself (see Rv 21.14; Mt 16.18; Eph 2.20).[3]

---

1. See Vatican council I, Dogmatic constitution on the church of Christ, *Pastor aeternus:* D 1821 (3050 f.).

2. See council of Florence, *Decree* for the Greeks: D 694 (1307), and Vatican council I, *ibid.*: D 1826 (3059).

3. See *Gregorian Sacramentary,* prefaces of the birthdays of Matthias and Thomas: PL 78, 51 and 152; see codex Vatican lat. 3548, f. 18. Hilary, *In Ps. (On the Psalms),* 67, 10: PL 9, 450; CSEL 22, p. 286. Jerome, *Adv. Iovin. (Against Jovinian),* 1, 26; PL 23, 247A. Augustine, *In Ps. (On the Psalms),* 86, 4: PL 37, 1103; CChr 39, 1201. Gregory the Great, *Mor. in Iob (Morals*

20. This divine mission, entrusted by Christ to the apostles, will continue to the end of the world (see Mt 28.20), since the gospel which is to be handed on by them is for all time the principle of all life for the church. For this reason the apostles, within this hierarchically structured society, took care to arrange for the appointment of successors. For not only did they have various helpers in the ministry,[4] but also, so that the mission entrusted to them might go on after their death, they handed on to their immediate fellow workers, as a kind of testament, the task of perfecting and consolidating the work that had been begun by themselves,[5] commending to their attention the whole flock in which the Holy Spirit had placed them to nourish the church of God (see Acts 20.28). They therefore appointed such men and then ordered them that when they died other approved men would take on their ministry.[6] Among the different ministries that have been carried on in the church right from the earliest times, as tradition witnesses, the chief place belongs to the task of those who, having been appointed to the episcopate through a succession that goes back to the beginning,[7] possess the shoots that have grown from the apostolic seed.[8] So, as St. Irenaeus testifies, through those who were appointed bishops by the apostles and through their successors right down to us, the apostolic tradition is manifested[9] and safeguarded[10] all over the world.

The bishops, therefore, have undertaken along with their fellow workers, the priests and deacons, the service of the community,[11] presiding in the place of

on Job), XXVIII, V: PL 76, 455–456; CChr 143 B, 1405–6. Primasius, *Comm. in Apoc. (Commentary on Apocalypse)*, V: PL 68, 924 BC; CChr 92, 290. Paschasius Radbertus, *In Mt. (On Matthew)*, book 8, ch. 16: PL 120, 561 C. See Leo XIII, Letter *Et sane*, 17 Dec. 1888: ASS 21 (1888), p. 321.

4. See Acts 6.2–6, 11.30, 13.1, 14.23, 20.17; 1 Thes 5.12–13; Phil 1.1; Col 4.11 and *passim*.

5. See Acts 20.25–27; 2 Tm 4.6 f.; compare 1 Tm 5.22; 2 Tm 2.2; Ti 1.5; Clement of Rome, *Ad Cor. (To the Corinthians)*, 44, 3: ed. Funk, I, p. 156.

6. See Clement of Rome, *Ad Cor. (To the Corinthians)*, 44, 2: ed. Funk, I, p. 154 f.

7. See Tertullian, *Praescr. Haer. (Prescription against Heretics)*, 32: PL 2, 52 f.; CChr 1, 212 f. Ignatius of Antioch, *passim*.

8. See Tertullian, *Praescr. Haer. (Prescription against Heretics)*, 32: PL 2, 53; CChr 1, 212.

9. See Irenaeus, *Adv. Haer. (Against Heresies)*, III, 3, 1: PG 7, 848A; Harvey 2, 8; Sagnard, p. 100 f.: "manifested."

10. See Irenaeus, *Adv. Haer. (Against Heresies)*, III, 2, 2: PG 7, 847; Harvey 2, 7; Sagnard, p. 100: "is safeguarded," see *ibid*. IV, 26, 2: col. 1053; Harvey 2, 236; also IV, 33, 8: col. 1077; Harvey 2, 262.

11. See Ignatius of Antioch, *Philad. (To the Philadelphians)*, Preface: ed. Funk, I, p. 264.

God over the flock,[12] whose shepherds they are, as teachers of doctrine, priests of sacred worship, and ministers of government.[13] Just as the office that was given individually by the Lord to Peter, the first of the apostles, is permanent and meant to be handed on to his successors, so also the office of the apostles of nourishing the church is a permanent one that is to be carried out without interruption by the sacred order of bishops.[14] Therefore the synod teaches that by divine institution the bishops have succeeded to the place of the apostles[15] as shepherds of the church: and the one who hears them hears Christ but whoever rejects them rejects Christ and him who sent Christ (see Lk 10.16).[16]

21. In the bishops, therefore, assisted by the priests, there is present in the midst of believers the Lord Jesus Christ, the supreme High Priest. Seated at the right hand of God the Father, he is not absent from the community of his pontiffs,[17] but primarily through their distinguished ministry he preaches the word of God to all nations and administers without ceasing the sacraments of faith to believers; by their fatherly office (see 1 Cor 4.15) he incorporates new members into his body by a regeneration from above; and finally it is by their wisdom and prudence that he directs and governs the people of the new testament in its pilgrimage towards eternal happiness. These shepherds, chosen to nourish the Lord's flock, are the ministers of Christ and the dispensers of the mysteries of God (see 1 Cor 4.1), to whom has been entrusted the bearing of witness to the gospel of God's grace (see Rom 15.16; Acts 20.24), and the service of the Spirit and of justice in glory (see 2 Cor 3.8–9).

For the fulfillment of such great duties, the apostles were enriched by Christ with a special outpouring of the Holy Spirit who came down upon them (see Acts 1.8, 2.4; Jn 20.22–23), and they by the imposition of hands handed on the spiri-

---

12. See Ignatius of Antioch, *Philad. (To the Philadelphians)*, 1, 1; *Magn. (To the Magnesians)*, 6, 1: ed. Funk, I, 264 and 234.

13. Clement of Rome, loc. cit., 42, 3–4; 44, 3–4; 57, 1–2: ed. Funk, I, 152, 156, 171 f.; Ignatius of Antioch, *Philad. (To the Philadelphians)*, 2; *Smyrn. (To the Smyrnaeans)*, 8; *Magn. (To the Magnesians)*, 3; *Trall. (To the Trallians)*, 7: ed. Funk, I, p. 265 f., 282, 232, 246 f. etc.; Justin, *Apol. (Apologies)*, 1, 65: PG 6, 428; Cyprian, *Epist. (Letters)*, passim.

14. See Leo XIII, Encyclical *Satis cognitum*, 29 June 1896: ASS 28 (1895–96), p. 732.

15. See council of Trent, Decree *On the sacrament of order*, ch. 4: D 960 (1768); Vatican council I, Dogmatic constitution on the church of Christ, *Pastor Aeternus*, ch. 3: D 1828 (3061). Pius XII, Encyclical *Mystici Corporis*, 29 June 1943: AAS 35 (1943), pp. 209 and 212. CIC, canon 329 §1.

16. See Leo XIII, Letter *Et sane*, 17 Dec. 1888: ASS 21 (1888), p. 321 f.

17. See Leo the Great, *Serm. (Sermons)*, 5, 3: PL 54, 154.

tual gift to their helpers (see 1 Tm 4.14; 2 Tm 1.6-7); and this has been handed down to us in episcopal consecration.[18] The synod teaches that the fullness of the sacrament of order is conferred by episcopal consecration; and this, both by the liturgical custom of the church and the voice of the holy fathers, is undoubtedly called the supreme priesthood, the highest point of the ministry.[19] Episcopal consecration, along with the office of sanctifying, confers also the offices of teaching and governing; these however by their very nature can only be exercised in hierarchical communion with the head of the college and its members. For it is clear from tradition—a tradition expressed especially in the liturgical rites and in the usage of the church both Eastern and Western—that through the imposition of hands and the words of consecration the grace of the Holy Spirit is so conferred,[20] and the sacred character so imprinted,[21] that bishops in an eminent and visible way take on the functions of Christ the teacher, shepherd, and pontiff and act in his person.[22] It is the task of bishops, by means of the sacrament of order, to admit those who have been newly elected into the episcopal order.

22. Just as, by the Lord's decree, St. Peter and the other apostles constitute one apostolic college, so in a similar way the Roman pontiff, Peter's successor, and the bishops, successors of the apostles, are joined together. The collegial character

---

18. Council of Trent, session 23, ch. 3, quotes the words of 2 Tm 1.6-7, to show that Order is a true sacrament: D 959 (1766).

19. In *Apostolic Tradition*, 3: ed. Botte, SC, pp. 27-30, the "primacy of priesthood" is attributed to the bishop. See *Sacramentarium Leonianum,* ed. C. Mohlberg, *Sacramentarium Veronese,* Rome 1955, p. 119: "to the ministry of the high priesthood . . . Complete in your priests the highest point of your mystery." Idem, *Liber Sacramentorum Romanae ecclesiae,* Rome 1960, pp. 121-122: "Give them, Lord, the episcopal throne to rule your church and the whole people." See PL 78, 224.

20. See *Apostolic Tradition,* 2: ed. Botte, p. 27.

21. See council of Trent, session 23, ch. 4, which teaches that the sacrament of Order imprints an indelible character, D 960 (1767). See John XXIII, Allocution *Iubilate Deo,* 8 May 1960: AAS 52 (1960), p. 466. Paul VI, Homily in the Vatican basilica, 20 Oct. 1963: AAS 55 (1963), p. 1014.

22. Cyprian, *Epist. (Letters),* 63, 14: PL 4, 386; Hartel, III B, p. 713: "The priest truly acts in the place of Christ." John Chrysostom, *In 2 Tm. (On 2 Timothy),* homily 2, 4: PG 62, 612: The priest is the "symbol" of Christ. Ambrose, *In Ps. (On the Psalms),* 38, 25-26: PL 14, 1051-52; CSEL 64, 203-204. Ambrosiaster, *In 1 Tm. (On 1 Timothy),* 5, 19: PL 17, 479 C; CSEL 81, 3, p. 284; and *In Eph. (On Ephesians),* 4, 11-12: PL 17, 387 C; CSEL 81, 3, pp. 98-101. Theodore of Mopsuestia, *Hom. Catech. (Catechetical Homilies),* XV, 21 and 24; ed. Tonneau, pp. 497 and 503. Hesychius of Jerusalem, *In Lev. (On Leviticus),* book 2, 9, 23: PG 93, 894B.

and nature of the episcopal order is shown in the very ancient practice by which bishops appointed throughout the world maintained communion with each other and with the bishop of Rome in the bonds of unity, charity, and peace;[23] this is also shown in the councils that were convened,[24] by which all the most important matters were settled in common[25] and a decision carefully arrived at through the counsel of many.[26] This is clearly confirmed by the ecumenical councils that have been celebrated down the centuries. The same thing is already to be seen in that custom, going back to antiquity, of calling together several bishops to take part in raising a newly elected person to the ministry of the high priesthood. A person is constituted a member of the episcopal body by virtue of sacramental consecration and by hierarchical communion with the head and members of the college.

However, the college or body of bishops does not have authority unless this is understood in terms of union with the Roman pontiff, Peter's successor, as its head, and the power of this primacy is maintained intact over all, whether they be shepherds or faithful. For the Roman pontiff has, by virtue of his office as vicar of Christ and shepherd of the whole church, full, supreme, and universal power over the church, a power he is always able to exercise freely. However, the order of bishops, which succeeds the college of apostles in teaching authority and pastoral government, and indeed in which the apostolic body continues to exist without interruption, is also the subject of supreme and full power over the universal church, provided it remains united with its head, the Roman pontiff, and never without its head;[27] and this power can be exercised only with the consent of the Roman pontiff. The Lord made Simon alone the rock and key-bearer of the church (see Mt 16.18–19), and constituted him shepherd of his whole flock (see Jn 21.15ff.). It is clear, however, that this office of binding and loosing which was given to Peter (see Mt 16.19), was also granted to the college of apostles in union with its head (see Mt 18.18, 28.16–20).[28] This college, in so far as it is composed of many, expresses

23. See Eusebius, *Hist. Eccl. (Ecclesiastical History)*, V, 24, 10: GCS II, 1, p. 495; ed. Bardy, SC, II, p. 69. Denis, in Eusebius, *ibid.*, VII, 5, 2: GCS II, 2, p. 638 f.; Bardy, II, p. 168 f.

24. See for the early councils, Eusebius, *Hist. Eccl. (Ecclesiastical History)*, V, 23–24: GCS II, 1, p. 488 ff.; Bardy, II, p. 66 ff. and *passim.* Council of Nicaea I, canon 5.

25. See Tertullian, *De Ieiunio (On Fasting)*, 13: PL 2, 972B; CSEL 20, p. 292, lines 13–16.

26. See Cyprian, *Epist. (Letters)*, 56, 3; Hartel, III B, p. 650; Bayard, p. 154.

27. See the official report of Zinelli at Vatican council I: Msi 52, 1109C.

28. See Vatican council I, Schema of dogmatic constitution 2, *De Ecclesia Christi*, ch. 4: Msi 53, 310. See the report of Kleutgen on the revised schema: Msi 53, 321 B-322 B; and the statement of Zinelli: Msi 52, 1110A. See also Leo the Great, *Serm. (Sermons)*, 4, 3: PL 54, 151A.

the variety and the universality of the people of God, but in so far as it is gathered under one head it expresses the unity of the flock of Christ. In it the bishops, while faithfully maintaining the primacy and preeminence of its head, exercise their own proper power for the good of their faithful and indeed of the whole church, while the Holy Spirit is constantly strengthening its organic structure and its harmony. The supreme power over the whole church which this college enjoys is solemnly exercised in an ecumenical council. There is never an ecumenical council which is not confirmed as such or at least accepted as such by the successor of Peter. It is the prerogative of the Roman pontiff to convoke these councils, to preside over them, and to confirm them.[29] The same collegial power can be exercised by the bishops throughout the world in conjunction with the pope, provided that the head of the college calls them to collegial action or at least approves of, or willingly accepts, the united action of the dispersed bishops in such a way that the result is a truly collegial act.

23. Collegial unity can be seen also in the mutual relations of individual bishops with particular churches and with the universal church. The Roman pontiff, as the successor of Peter, is the perpetual and visible principle and foundation of unity both of the bishops and of the multitude of the faithful.[30] The individual bishops, however, are the visible principle and foundation of unity in their own particular churches,[31] formed in the likeness of the universal church; in and from these particular churches there exists the one unique catholic church.[32] For this reason individual bishops represent their own church, while all of them together with the pope represent the whole church in the bond of peace, love, and unity. The individual bishops who are placed over particular churches exercise their pastoral government over the portion of the people of God that has been entrusted to their care, but not over other churches nor over the universal church. But as members of the episcopal college and legitimate successors of the apostles, the individual bishops, through the institution and command of Christ, are bound to be concerned about the whole church,[33] and even though this solicitude is not exercised by any act of

---

29. See CIC, canons 222 and 227.

30. See Vatican council I, Dogmatic constitution *Pastor Aeternus:* D 1821 (3050 f.).

31. See Cyprian, *Epist. (Letters)*, 66, 8: Hartel, III, 2, p. 733: "The bishop in the church and the church in the bishop."

32. See Cyprian, *Epist. (Letters)*, 55, 24: Hartel, p. 624, line 13: "One church throughout the whole world divided into many members"; *Epist. (Letters)*, 36, 4: Hartel, p. 575, lines 20–21.

33. See Pius XII, Encyclical *Fidei Donum*, 21 April 1957: AAS 49 (1957), p. 237.

jurisdiction, nevertheless it makes a very great contribution to the well-being of the universal church. All the bishops, in fact, have a duty to promote and defend the unity of faith and discipline common to the whole church, to instruct the faithful in the love of the whole mystical body of Christ—especially those members who are poor and suffering and those who are undergoing persecution for righteousness' sake (see Mt 5.10)—and finally, to promote every activity that is common to the whole church, especially that which is aimed at the spread of the faith and the rising of the light of full truth over all people. For the rest, it is a holy reality that by governing well their own church as a portion of the universal church, they themselves make an effective contribution to the whole mystical body, which is also a body of churches.[34]

The charge of announcing the gospel throughout the world belongs to the body of shepherds, to all of whom in common Christ gave the command and imposed a common office, as Pope Celestine once commended to the fathers of the Council of Ephesus.[35] Therefore the individual bishops, as far as the carrying out of their own particular task allows, are bound to collaborate among themselves and along with the successor of Peter, to whom the exalted task of spreading the Christian name has been entrusted in a special way.[36] With all their strength, therefore, they ought to supply the missions not only with laborers for the harvest, but also with the spiritual and material helps both directly by themselves and also by arousing the ardent cooperation of the faithful. Finally, in the universal communion of charity, let the bishops willingly offer paternal aid to other churches, especially to neighboring churches and to those that are in greater need, following the venerable example of antiquity. By divine providence it has come about that various churches, founded in various places by the apostles and by their successors, have in the course of time become joined together into several groups, organically united, which, while maintaining the unity of faith and the unique divine constitution of the universal

---

34. See Hilary of Poitiers, *In Ps. (On the Psalms)*, 14, 3: PL 9, 206; CSEL 22, p. 86. Gregory the Great, *Moral. (Morals)*, IV, 7, 12: PL 75, 643C; CChr 143, 170–171. Pseudo-Basil, *In Is. (On Isaiah)*, 15, 296: PG 30, 637C.

35. See Celestine, *Epist. (Letters)*, 18, 1–2, to the council of Ephesus: PL 50, 505AB; Schwarz, *Acta Conc. Oec.* I, 1, 1, p. 22. See Benedict XV, Apostolic letter *Maximum illud*: AAS 11 (1919), p. 440. Pius XI, Encyclical *Rerum Ecclesiae*, 28 Feb. 1926: AAS 18 (1926), p. 69. Pius XII, Encyclical *Fidei Donum*, loc. cit.

36. See Leo XIII, Encyclical *Grande munus*, 30 Sept. 1880: ASS 13 (1880), p. 145. See CIC, canon 1327, canon 1350 §2.

church, enjoy their own discipline, their own liturgical usage, and their own theological and spiritual patrimony. Among these there are some, especially the ancient patriarchal churches, like matrices of the faith, which have given birth to others as daughters; and right down to our own times they are more closely bound to these churches by the bond of charity in sacramental life and in mutual respect for rights and duties.[37] This variety of local churches, in harmony among themselves, demonstrates with greater clarity the catholicity of the undivided church. In a similar way episcopal conferences can today make a manifold and fruitful contribution to the concrete application of the spirit of collegiality.

24. The bishops, as successors of the apostles, receive from the Lord, to whom all power in heaven and on earth has been given, the mission to teach all nations and to preach the gospel to every creature, so that all may gain salvation through faith, baptism, and the keeping of the commandments (see Mt 28.18, 20; Mk 16.15–16; Acts 26.17f.). To carry out this mission Christ the Lord promised the apostles the Holy Spirit and on the day of Pentecost he sent him from heaven, that by his strength they might be witnesses to him to the ends of the earth before nations and peoples and kings (see Acts 1.8, 2.1ff., 9.15). This office which the Lord entrusted to the shepherds of his people is a true service, and in Holy Scripture it is significantly called "diaconia" or ministry (see Acts 1.17, 25, 21.19; Rom 11.13; 1 Tm 1.12).

The canonical mission of bishops can come into being by means of lawful customs which have not been revoked by the supreme and universal power of the church, or by means of laws made by that same authority or recognized by it, or directly by the successor of Peter himself; and if the latter opposes the appointment or refuses apostolic communion, the bishop cannot be admitted to office.[38]

25. Among the principal tasks of bishops the preaching of the gospel is preeminent.[39] For the bishops are the heralds of the faith who bring new disciples to Christ. They are the authentic teachers, that is, teachers endowed with the authority of Christ, who preach to the people entrusted to them the faith to be believed and put into practice; they illustrate this faith in the light of the Holy Spirit, drawing out

---

37. For the rights of the patriarchal sees, see council of Nicaea I, canon 6 for Alexandria and Antioch, and canon 7 for Jerusalem. Lateran council IV, in 1215, constitution 5, *On the dignity of patriarchs.* Council of Ferrara-Florence.

38. See *Codex Iuris Canonici, pro Ecclesiis Orientalibus,* canons 216–314 on patriarchs, canons 324–339 on archbishops, canons 326–391 on other dignitaries, in particular canons 238 §3, 216, 240, 251 and 255 on the nomination of bishops by the patriarch.

39. See council of Trent, Decree *On reform,* session 5, ch. 2, no. 9, and session 24, canon 4.

of the treasury of revelation things new and old (see Mt 13.52), they make it bear fruit, and they vigilantly ward off errors that are threatening their flock (see 2 Tm 4.1–4). The bishops, when they are teaching in communion with the Roman pontiff, are to be respected by all as witnesses to the divine and catholic truth; and the faithful ought to concur with their bishop's judgment concerning faith and morals which he delivers in the name of Christ, and they are to adhere to this with a religious assent of the mind. The religious assent of will and intellect is to be given in a special way to the authentic teaching authority of the Roman pontiff even when he is not speaking *ex cathedra*; in such a way, that is, that his supreme teaching authority is respectfully acknowledged, and sincere adherence given to decisions he has delivered, in accordance with his manifest mind and will which is communicated chiefly by the nature of the documents, by the frequent repetition of the same doctrine, or by the style of verbal expression.

Although individual bishops do not enjoy the prerogative of infallibility, nevertheless, even though dispersed throughout the world, but maintaining the bond of communion among themselves and with the successor of Peter, when in teaching authentically matters concerning faith and morals they agree about a judgment as one that has to be definitively held, they infallibly proclaim the teaching of Christ.[40] This takes place even more clearly when they are gathered together in an ecumenical council and are the teachers and judges of faith and morals for the whole church. Their definitions must be adhered to with the obedience of faith.[41]

This infallibility, however, with which the divine Redeemer willed his church to be endowed in defining doctrine concerning faith or morals, extends just as far as the deposit of divine revelation that is to be guarded as sacred and faithfully expounded. The Roman pontiff, head of the college of bishops, by virtue of his office, enjoys this infallibility when, as supreme shepherd and teacher of all Christ's faithful, who confirms his brethren in the faith (see Lk 22.32), he proclaims in a definitive act a doctrine on faith or morals.[42] Therefore his definitions are rightly said to be irreformable of themselves, and not from the consent of the church, for they are delivered with the assistance of the Holy Spirit which was promised to him in blessed Peter; and therefore they have no need of approval from others nor do

---

40. See Vatican council I, Dogmatic constitution *Dei Filius*, 3: D 1792 (3011). See the note added to schema 1 *De Ecclesia* (taken from St. Robert Bellarmine): Msi 51, 579C; also the revised schema of constitution 2 *De Ecclesia Christi*, together with the commentary of Kleutgen: Msi 53, 313AB. Pius IX, Letter *Tuas libenter*: D 1683 (2879).

41. See CIC, canons 1322–1323.

42. See Vatican council I, Dogmatic constitution *Pastor Aeternus*, 4: D 1839 (3074).

they admit any appeal to any other judgment. For then the Roman pontiff is not delivering a judgment as a private person, but as the supreme teacher of the universal church, in whom the church's own charism of infallibility individually exists, he expounds or defends a doctrine of the catholic faith.[43] The infallibility promised to the church exists also in the body of bishops when, along with the successor of Peter, it exercises the supreme teaching office. The assent of the church, however, can never fail to be given to these definitions on account of the activity of the same Holy Spirit, by which the whole flock of Christ is preserved in the unity of faith and makes progress.[44]

But when the Roman pontiff or the body of bishops together with him define a decision, they do so in accordance with revelation itself, by which all are obliged to abide and to which all must conform. This revelation, as written or as handed down in tradition, is transmitted in its entirety through the lawful succession of the bishops and in the first place through the care of the Roman pontiff himself; and in the light of the Spirit of truth, this revelation is sacredly preserved in the church and faithfully expounded.[45] The Roman pontiff and the bishops, in virtue of their office and the seriousness of the matter, work sedulously through the appropriate means duly to investigate this revelation and give it suitable expression.[46] However, they do not accept any new public revelation as belonging to the divine deposit of faith.[47]

26. The bishop, marked with the fullness of the sacrament of order, is "the steward of the grace of the supreme priesthood,"[48] especially in the eucharist which he offers or which he ensures is offered,[49] and by which the church continuously lives and grows. This church of Christ is truly present in all the lawful local congregations of the faithful which, united to their shepherds, are themselves called churches in the New Testament.[50] For in their own locality, these are the new people called by God in the Holy Spirit and with full conviction (see 1 Thes 1.5). In these the faithful are gathered together by the preaching of the gospel of Christ and the

---

43. See the explanation of Gasser at Vatican council I: Msi 52, 1213 AC.

44. See Gasser, *ibid.*: Msi 1214A.

45. See Gasser, *ibid.*: Msi 1215CD, 1216–1217A.

46. See Gasser, *ibid.*: Msi 1213.

47. See Vatican council I, Dogmatic constitution *Pastor Aeternus*, 4: D 1836 (3070).

48. Prayer of episcopal consecration in the Byzantine rite: *Euchologion to mega*, Rome 1873, p. 139.

49. See Ignatius of Antioch, *Smyrn. (To the Smyrnaeans)*, 8, 1: ed. Funk, I, p. 282.

50. See Acts 8.1; 14.22–23; 20.17, and *passim*.

mystery of the Lord's supper is celebrated, "so that the whole fellowship is joined together through the flesh and blood of the Lord's body."[51] In any community of the altar, under the sacred ministry of the bishop,[52] there is made manifest the symbol of that charity and "unity of the mystical body without which there can be no salvation."[53] In these communities, although frequently small and poor, or dispersed, Christ is present by whose power the one, holy, catholic, and apostolic church is gathered together.[54] For "participation in the body and blood of Christ has no other effect than to make us pass over into what we are consuming."[55]

Every lawful celebration of the eucharist is directed by the bishop, to whom has been entrusted the duty of presenting the worship of the Christian religion to the Divine Majesty, and of regulating it according to the commands of the Lord and the church's laws, which are further determined for the diocese by his particular judgment.

In this way the bishops, in their prayer and work for the people, pour forth abundantly and in many ways from the fullness of the holiness of Christ. By the ministry of the word they communicate to the faithful the power of God for their salvation (see Rom 1.16), and through the sacraments, the regular and fruitful distribution of which they direct by their authority,[56] they sanctify the faithful. They direct the conferring of baptism, through which participation in the royal priesthood of Christ is granted. They are the original ministers of confirmation, the dispensers of sacred orders, and the directors of penitential discipline. With solicitude they exhort and instruct their people so that in the liturgy, especially in the holy sacrifice of the mass, they fulfill their part with faith and devotion. Finally, they have a duty to help those over whom they are placed by the example of their manner of life, keeping their behavior free from all evil and, as far as they can with the help of God, turning evil to good, so that, together with the flock entrusted to them, they may attain eternal life.[57]

27. The bishops govern the churches entrusted to them as vicars and legates

---

51. Mozarabic prayer: PL 96, 759B.

52. See Ignatius of Antioch, *Smyrn. (To the Smyrnaeans)*, 8, 1: ed. Funk, I, p. 282.

53. Thomas Aquinas, *Summa Theologiae*, III, quest. 73, art. 3.

54. See Augustine, *C. Faustum (Against Faustus)*, 12, 20: PL 42, 265; *Serm. (Sermons)*, 57, 7: PL 38, 389, etc.

55. Leo the Great, *Serm. (Sermons)*, 63, 7: PL 54, 357C.

56. See *Apostolic Tradition* of Hippolytus, 2–3: ed. Botte, pp. 26–30.

57. See the text of the *Examination* at the beginning of the consecration of a bishop, and the *Prayer* at the end of the mass of the same consecration, after the *Te Deum*.

of Christ,[58] by counsel, persuasion, and example and indeed also by authority and sacred power which they make use of only to build up their flock in truth and holiness, remembering that the greater must become as the younger and the leader as one who serves (see Lk 22.26–27). This power which they exercise personally in the name of Christ is proper, ordinary, and immediate, although its exercise is ultimately controlled by the supreme authority of the church and can be circumscribed within certain limits for the good of the church or the faithful. By virtue of this power, bishops have the sacred right and duty before the Lord of making laws for their subjects, of passing judgment on them, and of directing everything that concerns the ordering of worship and the apostolate. The pastoral office, that is to say the habitual and daily care of their sheep, is completely entrusted to the bishops and they are not to be considered vicars of the Roman pontiffs, because they exercise a power that is proper to themselves and most truly are said to be presidents of the peoples they govern.[59] Therefore their power is not destroyed by the supreme and universal power, but on the contrary it is affirmed, strengthened, and vindicated by it,[60] since the Holy Spirit unfailingly preserves the form of government established in his church by Christ the Lord.

Sent by the head of the household to govern his family, the bishop must keep before his eyes the example of the good Shepherd, who came not to be served but to serve (Mt 20.28; Mk 10.45) and to lay down his life for his sheep (see Jn 10.11). Taken from among human beings and subject to weakness himself, the bishop can sympathize with those who are ignorant and who go astray (see Heb 5.1–2). Let him not refuse to listen to his subjects whom he looks after as truly his daughters and sons and whom he exhorts cheerfully to cooperate with him. As one who will have to give an account to God for their souls (see Heb 13.7), by prayer, preaching, and every work of charity let him look after both them and also those who are not yet members of the one flock but whom he must consider as com-

---

58. Benedict XIV, Brief *Romana Ecclesia*, 5 Oct. 1752, §1: *Bullarium Benedicti XIV,* tome IV, Rome 1758, 21: "A bishop bears the likeness of Christ and carries out his work." Pius XII, Encyclical *Mystici Corporis,* loc. cit., p. 211: "Each of them takes care of and rules in the name of Christ the flock assigned to him."

59. See Leo XIII, Encyclical *Satis cognitum,* 29 June 1896: ASS 28 (1895–96), p. 732. Idem, Letter *Officio sanctissimo,* 22 Dec. 1887: ASS 20 (1887), p. 264. Pius IX, Apostolic letter to the bishops of Germany, 12 March 1875, and Consistorial allocution, 15 March 1875: D 3112–3117, only in recent editions.

60. See Vatican council I, Dogmatic constitution *Pastor Aeternus,* 3: D 1828 (3061). See the report of Zinelli: Msi 52, 1114D.

mended to him in the Lord. Since like the apostle Paul he is debtor to all, let him be ready to preach the gospel to all (see Rom 1.14–15), and exhort his faithful to apostolic and missionary activity. The faithful must adhere to the bishop as the church does to Jesus Christ, and as Jesus Christ does to the Father, so that all things may agree together through unity[61] and abound to the glory of God (see 2 Cor 4.15).

28. Christ, whom the Father sanctified and sent into the world (see Jn 10.36), has through his apostles made their successors, the bishops, share in his consecration and his mission;[62] and these have legitimately handed on the office of their ministry in varying degrees to various subjects in the church. In this way the divinely instituted ecclesiastical ministry is exercised in different orders by those who right from ancient times are called bishops, priests, and deacons.[63] Although they do not possess the highest honor of the pontificate and depend on the bishops for the exercise of their power, priests nevertheless are united with them in priestly honor,[64] and by virtue of the sacrament of order[65] they are consecrated in the image of Christ, the high and eternal Priest (see Heb 5.1–10, 7.24, 9.11–28), as true priests of the new testament,[66] to preach the gospel and nourish the faithful and celebrate divine worship. In their own degree of ministry they share in the office of Christ the one Mediator (see 1 Tm 2.5), and proclaim the divine word to all people. But it is above all in the eucharistic worship or synaxis that they exercise their sacred function, when, acting in the person of Christ[67] and proclaiming his mystery, they unite the prayers of the faithful to the sacrifice of their Head, and in the sacrifice of the mass make present and apply, until the coming of the Lord (see 1 Cor 11.26), the one

61. See Ignatius of Antioch, *Ad Ephes. (To the Ephesians)*, 5, 1: ed. Funk, I, p. 216.

62. See Ignatius of Antioch, *Ad Ephes. (To the Ephesians)*, 6, 1: ed Funk, I, p. 218.

63. See council of Trent, *On the sacrament of Order*, ch. 2: D 958 (1765), and canon 6: D 966 (1776).

64. See Innocent I, Letter to Decentius: PL 20, 554A; Msi 3, 1029; D 98 (215): "Presbyters, although they are *priests* of the second rank, do not possess the *summit* of the pontificate." Cyprian, *Epist. (Letters)*, 61, 3: ed. Hartel, p. 696.

65. See council of Trent, *On the sacrament of Order*: D 956a–968 (1763–1778), especially canon 7: D 967 (1777). Pius XII, Apostolic constitution *Sacramentum Ordinis*: D 2301 (3857–61).

66. See Innocent I, loc. cit. Gregory of Nazianzen, *Apol. (Apology)*, II, 22: PG 35, 432B. Pseudo-Denis, *Eccl. Hier. (Ecclesiastical Hierarchy)*, 1, 2: PG 3, 372D.

67. See council of Trent, session 22: D 940 (1743). Pius XII, Encyclical *Mediator Dei*, 20 Nov. 1947: AAS 39 (1947), p. 553; D 2300 (3850).

sacrifice of the new testament, that is, the sacrifice of Christ who once and for all offers himself as an unblemished victim to the Father (see Heb 9.11–28).[68] For the faithful who are penitent or who are sick they exercise fully the ministry of reconciliation and comfort, and they convey to God the Father the needs and prayers of the faithful (see Heb 5.1–3). According to their share of authority they exercise the office of Christ the Shepherd and Head,[69] they gather together the family of God as a fellowship inspired by the spirit of unity[70] and lead them through Christ in the Spirit to God the Father. In the midst of the flock they adore him in spirit and in truth (see Jn 4.24). Finally, they labor in preaching and teaching (see 1 Tm 5.17), believing what they have read and meditated in the law of the Lord, teaching what they have believed, and putting into practice what they have taught.[71]

As prudent cooperators of the episcopal order[72] and its instrument and help, priests are called to the service of the people of God and constitute along with their bishop one presbyterium[73] though destined to different duties. In the individual local congregations of the faithful in a certain sense they make the bishop present and they are united with him in a spirit of trust and generosity; and in accordance with their position they undertake his duties and his concern and carry these out with daily dedication. Under the authority of the bishop, priests sanctify and govern the portion of the Lord's flock entrusted to them, in their own locality they make visible the universal church and they provide powerful help towards the building up of the whole body of Christ (see Eph 4.12). However, attentive always to the welfare of the children of God, they are to take pains that their work contributes to the pastoral work of the whole diocese, and indeed of the whole church. Because of this sharing in the priesthood and mission, priests are to recognize the bishop as truly their father and reverently obey him. The bishop, for his part, is to consider the priests his cooperators as sons and friends, just as Christ calls his disciples no longer servants but friends (see Jn 15.15). By reason, therefore, of order and ministry, all priests both diocesan and religious, are associated with the body

68. See council of Trent, session 22: D 938 (1739–40). Vatican council II, Constitution on the sacred liturgy, *Sacrosanctum Concilium,* no. 7 and no. 47: AAS 56 (1964), pp. 100 and 113.
69. See Pius XII, Encyclical *Mediator Dei,* loc. cit., under no. 67.
70. See Cyprian, *Epist. (Letters),* 11, 3: PL 4, 242B; Hartel, II, 2, p. 497.
71. See *Roman pontifical,* Ordination of priests, at the clothing with vestments.
72. See *Roman pontifical,* Ordination of priests, Preface.
73. See Ignatius of Antioch, *Philad. (To the Philadelphians),* 4: ed. Funk, I, p. 266. Cornelius I, in Cyprian, *Epist. (Letters),* 48, 2: Hartel, III, 2, p. 610.

of bishops and according to their grace and vocation they work for the good of the whole church.

In virtue of sacred ordination and the mission they have in common, all priests are bound together in a close fraternity, which should be seen spontaneously and freely in mutual help both spiritual and material, both pastoral and personal, in reunions and in the fellowship of life, work, and charity.

Like fathers in Christ, they are to look after the faithful whom they have spiritually brought to birth by baptism and by their teaching (see 1 Cor 4.15; 1 Pt 1.23). Having become examples to the flock (see 1 Pt 5.3), they are to preside over their local community and serve it in such a way that it may deserve to be called by that name by which the one and entire people of God is distinguished, namely the church of God (see 1 Cor 1.2; 2 Cor 1.1; and passim). In their daily conduct and care they are to remember to present to the faithful and to unbelievers, to Catholics and non-Catholics, the face of a ministry that is truly priestly and pastoral, and that to all people they have a duty to bear witness to truth and life; and that, as good shepherds, they are to go in search of those (see Lk 15.4–7) who, although baptized in the Catholic Church, have fallen away from the practice of the sacraments or even from the faith.

Since today the human race is moving together more and more towards civil, economic, and social unity, it is that much more necessary that priests by their united care and resources, under the leadership of the bishops and the supreme pontiff, wipe out every cause of division so that the whole human race may be brought into the unity of God's family.

29. At a lower degree of the hierarchy stand the deacons, on whom hands are imposed "not for the priesthood, but for the ministry."[74] For strengthened by sacramental grace, they are at the service of the people of God in the ministry of the liturgy, the word, and charity, in communion with the bishop and his presbyterium. To the extent that he has been authorized by competent authority, he is to administer baptism solemnly, to reserve and distribute the eucharist, to assist at and bless marriages in the name of the church, to take viaticum to the dying, to read Sacred Scripture to the faithful, to instruct and exhort the people, to preside at the worship and prayer of the faithful, to administer sacramentals, and to preside at funeral services and burials. Dedicated to duties of charity and administration, deacons should bear in mind the admonition given by blessed Polycarp: "Merciful,

---

74. *Constitutiones Ecclesiae Aegyptiacae*, III, 2: ed. Funk, *Didascalia*, II, p. 103. *Statuta Ecclesiae Antiqua*, 37–41: Msi 3, 954.

sedulous, and walking in accordance with the truth of the Lord, who became the servant of all."[75]

Since these tasks, which are supremely necessary for the life of the church, can only with difficulty be carried out in many regions, according to the current discipline of the Latin church, the diaconate can for the future be restored as a proper and permanent grade of the hierarchy. It is, however, the responsibility of the competent territorial conferences of bishops, which are of different kinds, to decide with the approval of the supreme pontiff himself whether and where it is opportune for such deacons to be appointed for the care of souls. With the consent of the Roman pontiff it will be possible to confer this diaconate on men of more mature age, even upon those living in the married state, and also on suitable young men for whom, however, the law of celibacy must remain in force.

CHAPTER 4. THE LAITY

30. Having set forth the functions of the hierarchy, the synod gladly turns its attention to the status of those members of the faithful who are called the laity. Although everything that was said about the people of God applies equally to the laity, religious, and clerics, nevertheless there are certain points which have special reference to the laity because of their situation and their mission. Because of the special circumstances of our time, these points call for a deeper examination. The sacred pastors are well aware of how much the laity contribute to the well-being of the whole church. They know that they were not instituted by Christ to undertake by themselves alone the church's whole mission of salvation to the world; but that it is their noble task to tend the faithful in such a way, and to acknowledge their ministries and their charisms, so that all may cooperate unanimously, each in her or his own way, in the common task. For it is necessary that all of us "doing . . . the truth in love, are to grow up in every way in him who is the head, Christ, from whom the whole body, joined and knit together by every joint with which it is supplied, when each part is working properly, makes bodily growth and upbuilds itself in love" (Eph 4.15–16).

31. Under the title of laity are here understood all Christ's faithful, except those who are in sacred orders or are members of a religious state that is recognized by the church; that is to say, the faithful who, since they have been incorporated into Christ by baptism, constitute the people of God and, in their own way made

---

75. Polycarp, *Ad Phil. (To the Philippians)*, 5, 2: ed. Funk, I, p. 300: It is said that Christ "became the servant of all." See *Didache*, 15, 1: ibid., p. 32. Ignatius of Antioch, *Trall. (To the Trallians)*, 2, 3: ibid., p. 242. *Apostolic Constitutions*, 8, 28, 4: ed. Funk, *Didascalia*, I, p. 530.

sharers in Christ's priestly, prophetic, and royal office, play their own part in the mission of the whole Christian people in the church and in the world.

The laity have their own special character which is secular. For, although those in sacred orders can be engaged in secular activities, even practicing a secular profession, they are by reason of their particular vocation principally and professedly ordained for the sacred ministry, while religious by their state give noble and outstanding witness to the fact that the world cannot be transformed and offered to God without the spirit of the Beatitudes. It is the special vocation of the laity to seek the kingdom of God by engaging in temporal affairs and ordering these in accordance with the will of God. They live in the world, that is to say, in each and all of the world's occupations and affairs, and in the ordinary circumstances of family and social life; these are the things that form the context of their life. And it is here that God calls them to work for the sanctification of the world as it were from the inside, like leaven, through carrying out their own task in the spirit of the gospel, and in this way revealing Christ to others principally through the witness of their lives, resplendent in faith, hope, and charity. It is, therefore, their special task to shed light upon and order all temporal matters, in which they are closely involved, in such a way that these are always carried out and developed in Christ's way and to the praise of the Creator and Redeemer.

32. Holy church, by divine institution, is ordered and directed with wonderful variety. "As in one body we have many members, and all the members do not have the same function, so we, though many, are one body in Christ, and individually members one of another" (Rom 12.4–5).

Therefore the chosen people of God is one: "one Lord, one faith, one baptism" (Eph 4.5). There is the common dignity of the members from their regeneration in Christ; they share in common the grace of being heirs, the call to perfection, one salvation, one hope, and one undivided charity. There is, therefore, no inequality in Christ and in the church, with regard to race or nation, social condition or sex, because "there is neither Jew nor Greek, there is neither slave nor free, there is neither male nor female; for you are all *one* in Christ Jesus" (Gal 3.28 Greek text; see Col 3.11).

If, therefore, in the church all do not walk along the same path, nevertheless all are called to holiness and have received an equal faith in the righteousness of God (see 2 Pt 1.1). And if some are appointed, by the will of Christ, as teachers, dispensers of the mysteries, and pastors for the others, yet there is a true equality of all with regard to the dignity and action common to all the faithful concerning the building up of the body of Christ. For the distinction which the Lord made between sacred ministers and the rest of the people of God brings with it a connection between them, since pastors and the other faithful are bound together by a common bond. The church's pastors, following the Lord's example, are to minister to each other and to the rest of the faithful, and the faithful are to cooperate gladly with the pastors and teachers. So, in their variety, all bear witness to the wonderful unity in the body of Christ: for this very diversity of graces, ministries, and works gathers the children of God into one, because "all are inspired by one and the same Spirit" (1 Cor 12.11).

The laity, therefore, just as they have by divine condescension Christ as their brother who, although Lord of all, came not to be served but to serve (see Mt 20.28), so also they have as brothers those who have been appointed to the sacred ministry and who by Christ's authority—through teaching, sanctifying, and governing—so look after the family of God that the new commandment of love is fulfilled by all. Concerning which St. Augustine has this very fine statement: "When what I am for you frightens me, what I am with you consoles me. For you I am a bishop, with you I am a Christian. The former is a title of duty, the latter is one of grace. The former is a danger, the latter is a title to salvation."[1]

33. The laity, gathered together in the people of God and established in the one body of Christ under a single head, whoever they are, are called as living members to work with all the strength they have received from the goodness of the Creator and the grace of the Redeemer for the growth of the church and its continual sanctification.

The apostolate of the laity is a sharing in the church's mission of salvation, and everyone is commissioned to this apostolate by the Lord himself through baptism and confirmation. By the sacraments, especially by the sacred eucharist, there is communicated and nourished that love for God and for people which is the soul of the entire apostolate. The laity, however, have the specific vocation to make the church present and active in those places and circumstances where only through them can it become the salt of the earth.[2] In this way every lay person, because of the gifts received, is at the same time a witness and a living instrument of the church's mission "according to the measure of Christ's gift" (Eph 4.7).

This apostolate concerns every one of Christ's faithful, but in addition the laity can also be called in various ways to a more immediate cooperation in the apostolate of the hierarchy,[3] like those men and women who assisted the apostle Paul in

---

1. Augustine, *Serm. (Sermons)*, 340, 1: PL 38, 1483.
2. See Pius XI, Encyclical *Quadragesimo anno*, 15 May 1931: AAS 23 (1931), p. 221 f. Pius XII, Allocution *De quelle consolation*, 14 Oct. 1951: AAS 43 (1951), p. 790 f.
3. See Pius XII, Allocution *Six ans se sont écoulés*, 5 Oct. 1957: AAS 49 (1957), p. 927.

the gospel, working hard in the Lord (see Phil 4.3; Rom 16.3ff.). They may also be appointed by the hierarchy to carry out certain ecclesiastical offices which have a spiritual aim in view.

It is, therefore, the glorious task of all the faithful to work for the ever greater extension of the divine plan of salvation to all people everywhere and of every period. So then let every opportunity be given them to share zealously in the saving work of the church in accordance with their ability and the needs of the times.

34. Jesus Christ, the supreme and eternal Priest, wants to continue his witness and service also through the laity. So he gives them life through his Spirit and unceasingly urges them on to every good and perfect work.

He associates them intimately with his life and mission and has also given them a share in his priestly office of offering spiritual worship, so that God may be glorified and human beings be saved. The laity, therefore, dedicated as they are to Christ and anointed by the Holy Spirit, are wonderfully called and instructed so that ever more abundant fruits of the Spirit may be produced in them. For all their works, if done in the Spirit, become spiritual sacrifices acceptable to God through Jesus Christ: their prayers and apostolic works, their married and family life, their daily work, their mental and physical recreation, and even life's troubles if they are patiently borne (see 1 Pt 2.5). In the eucharistic celebration these are offered with very great piety to the Father along with the offering of the body of the Lord. In this way the laity too, as worshipers carrying out their holy activity everywhere, consecrate the world itself to God.

35. Christ, the great Prophet, who by the witness of his life and the power of his word, proclaimed the Father's kingdom, continues to carry out his prophetic task, until the full manifestation of his glory, not only through the hierarchy who teach in his name and by his power, but also through the laity whom he constitutes his witnesses and equips with an understanding of the faith and a grace of speech (see Acts 2.17–18; Rv 19.10) precisely so that the power of the gospel may shine forth in the daily life of family and society. The laity show that they are children of the promise, if strong in faith and hope they make full use of the present moment (see Eph 5.16; Col 4.5) and await with patience the glory that is to come (see Rom 8.25). This hope, however, is not to be hidden in the depths of their hearts. It has also to be expressed through the structures of secular life, through their continual conversion and their struggle "against the world rulers of the present darkness, against the spiritual hosts of wickedness" (Eph 6.12).

Just as the sacraments of the new law, by which the life and apostolate of the faithful are nourished, foreshadow the new heaven and the new earth (see Rv 21.1), so the laity become effective heralds of faith in the things we hope for (see

Heb 11.1) if they firmly combine the profession of faith to a life of faith. This evangelization—that is, the message of Christ proclaimed by word and the witness of life—takes on a special quality and a particular effectiveness from the fact that it is carried out in ordinary worldly situations.

In this task, that state of life is of great value which is sanctified by a special sacrament, namely married and family life. Here, where the Christian religion pervades the whole structure of life and increasingly transforms it day by day, there is both the practice and the outstanding school of the lay apostolate. Here husband and wife have their particular vocation to be witnesses to each other and to their children of their faith and love of Christ. The Christian family proclaims aloud both the virtues of the kingdom of God here and now and the hope of a blessed life to come. In this way, by example and by witness, it accuses the world of sin and enlightens those who seek the truth.

Therefore, even when occupied with temporal cares, the laity can and must perform the valuable task of evangelizing the world. Some lay people, when there is a shortage of sacred ministers or when these are impeded by a persecuting government, supply some of the sacred offices in so far as they can; a greater number are engaged totally in apostolic work. It is, however, the duty of all to work together for the extension and growth of the kingdom of Christ on earth. Consequently the laity have a duty to try diligently to deepen their knowledge of revealed truth and earnestly to pray to God for the gift of wisdom.

36. Christ, obedient unto death and for this reason exalted by the Father (see Phil 2.8–9), has now entered into the glory of his kingdom. To him all things are made subject until he subjects himself and all created things to the Father, so that God may be all in all (see 1 Cor 15.27–28). This power he has communicated to his disciples so that they too may be constituted in a royal freedom, and through self-denial and a holy life may overcome the reign of sin within themselves (see Rom 6.12), and indeed that serving Christ also in others, they may through humility and patience lead their sisters and brothers to the King to serve whom is to reign. For the Lord desires that the faithful laity also should extend his kingdom, the kingdom of "truth and life, the kingdom of holiness and grace, the kingdom of justice, love, and peace,"[4] in which creation itself will be set free from its bondage to decay and obtain the glorious liberty of the children of God (see Rom 8.21). It is certainly a great promise that is given to the disciples, a great commandment: "All things are yours; and you are Christ's; and Christ is God's" (1 Cor 3.23).

The faithful have, therefore, a duty to acknowledge the inner nature and

---

4. *Roman Missal,* preface of the feast of Christ the King.

the value of the whole of creation and its orientation to the praise of God; they must help each other towards greater holiness of life even through their secular activity, so that the world may be penetrated with the spirit of Christ and more effectively attain its purpose in justice, in love, and in peace. In the universal fulfillment of this task the laity have the principal role. So through their competence in secular disciplines and their activity, interiorly raised up by the grace of Christ, they are to work effectively so that the goods of creation, in accordance with the plan of the Creator and the light of his word, through human work, technical skill, and civilization, may be developed for the good of everyone without exception, that there be a more equitable distribution of these goods, and that they may lead in their own way to universal progress in human and Christian freedom. In this way, through the members of the church, Christ will increasingly enlighten the whole of human society with his saving light.

Moreover, the laity should even band together to improve those secular structures and conditions which constitute an inducement to sin, in such a way that all these things are brought into harmony with the rules of justice and become an encouragement to the practice of virtue rather than an obstacle. By acting in this way they will imbue human work and culture with a moral value. In this way too the field of the world is better prepared for the seed of the divine word, and the doors of the church are opened more widely for the entry into the world of the proclamation of peace.

Because of the economy of salvation itself, the faithful must learn carefully to distinguish between the rights and duties which are theirs in so far as they are members of the church, and those which belong to them as members of human society. They are to labor carefully that both of these work harmoniously together, remembering that temporal matters are to be guided by their Christian conscience, since there is no human activity—not even in temporal matters—that can be withdrawn from God's dominion. However, it is particularly important in this our time that this distinction and at the same time this harmony should be very clearly evident in the conduct of the faithful, so that the mission of the church may be more able to meet the particular needs of the modern world. And just as one must recognize that the earthly city, rightly taken up with secular cares, is governed by its own principles, so also must that misguided teaching be rightly rejected which claims to construct society without any reference to religion, and which attacks and undermines the religious freedom of the citizens.[5]

5. See Leo XIII, Encyclical *Immortale Dei*, 1 Nov. 1885: ASS 18 (1885), p. 166 ff. Idem, Encyclical *Sapientiae christianae*, 10 Jan. 1890: ASS 22 (1889–90), p. 397 ff. Pius XII, Allocution

37. The laity have the right, as do all the faithful, to receive abundant help from the sacred pastors out of the spiritual goods of the church, especially the help provided by the word of God and the sacraments;[6] and they should make known to these pastors their needs and desires with that freedom and confidence which befits children of God and sisters and brothers in Christ. In accordance with the knowledge, competence, or authority that they possess, they have the right and indeed sometimes the duty to make known their opinion on matters which concern the good of the church.[7] If possible this should be done through the institutions set up for this purpose by the church; and it should always be done with respect for the truth, with courage, and with prudence, and in a spirit of reverence and love towards those who by reason of their sacred office represent Christ. The laity, like all the faithful, should be prompt to accept in a spirit of Christian obedience those decisions that the sacred pastors make as teachers and governors of the church and as representatives of Christ; in doing so they follow the example of Christ, who by his obedience unto death opened to all people the blessed way of the freedom of the children of God. Nor should they neglect to commend to God in their prayers those who have been placed over them, that they may do their work with joy and not sadly (see Heb 15.17); they are after all keeping watch as persons who will have to give an account for our souls.

However, the sacred pastors are to acknowledge and promote the dignity and the responsibility of the laity in the church; they should willingly make use of their prudent counsel; they should confidently entrust to them offices in the service of the church and leave them freedom and space to act. Indeed they should encourage them to take up work on their own initiative. With a father's love they should pay careful attention in Christ to the projects, the requests, and the desires put forward by the laity.[8] The pastors must, moreover, carefully acknowledge that just freedom which belongs to all in the earthly city.

From this familiar relationship between laity and pastors many advantages for the church can be expected: for in this way there is strengthened in the laity a sense of their own responsibility, their enthusiasm is fired, and the strengths of the

---

Alla vostra filiale, 23 March 1958: AAS 50 (1958), p. 220: "the legitimate and healthy lay nature of the state."

6. See CIC, canon 682.

7. See Pius XII, Allocution *De quelle consolation,* loc. cit., p. 789: "In decisive battles it happens at times that the best initiatives come from the frontline . . . ." Idem, Allocution *L'importance de la presse catholique,* 17 Feb. 1950: AAS 42 (1950), p. 256.

8. See 1 Thes 5.19, and 1 Jn 4.1.

laity are more easily joined to the work of the pastors. The pastors, for their part, helped by the experience of the laity, are able to make clearer and more suitable decisions both in spiritual and in temporal affairs. In this way the whole church, strengthened by all its members, is able more effectively to carry out its mission for the life of the world.

38. Every individual lay person ought to be a witness to the world of the resurrection and life of the Lord Jesus and a sign of the living God. All of them together, and each for her or his own part, should nourish the world with the fruits of the Spirit (see Gal 5.22), and spread throughout the world that spirit which is the life of the poor, the meek, and the peacemakers, whom the Lord proclaimed blessed in the Gospel (see Mt 5.3–9). In a word, "Christians should be in the world what the soul is in the body."[9]

CHAPTER 5. THE UNIVERSAL CALL
TO HOLINESS IN THE CHURCH

39. The church, whose mystery is being set forth by this synod, is held to be indefectibly holy as a matter of faith. For Christ, the Son of God, who with the Father and the Spirit "alone is holy,"[1] loved the church as his bride and delivered himself up for it that he might sanctify it (see Eph 5.25–26), and he joined it to himself as his body and bestowed on it the gift of the Holy Spirit to the glory of God. For this reason everyone in the church is called to holiness, whether he belongs to the hierarchy or is cared for by the hierarchy, according to the saying of the apostle: "This is the will of God, your sanctification" (1 Thes 4.3; see Eph 1.4). This holiness of the church is shown continuously, and it should be shown, in those fruits of grace which the Spirit produces in the faithful; it is expressed in many different ways in the lives of those individuals who in their manner of life tend towards the perfection of charity and in so doing are a source of edification for others. In a particularly appropriate way it can be seen in the practice of those counsels which are customarily called evangelical. Through the inspiration of the Holy Spirit the practice of the counsels has been undertaken by many Christians, either privately or in some condition or state authorized by the church, and provides in the world, as it should, an outstanding witness and example of this holiness.

40. The Lord Jesus, the divine master and model of all perfection, preached

---

9. *Letter to Diognetus,* 6: ed. Funk, I, p. 400. See John Chrysostom, *In Mt. (On Matthew),* Homily 46 (47), 2: PG 58, 478, on the leaven in the dough.

1. *Roman Missal,* The Gloria. See Lk 1.35; Mk 1.24; Lk 4.34; Jn 6.69 (the Holy One of God); Acts 3.14, 4.27, 30; Heb 7.26; 1 Jn 2.20; Rv 3.7.

holiness of life, which he himself both initiates and perfects, to each and every one of his disciples no matter what their condition of life: "You, therefore, must be perfect, as your heavenly Father is perfect" (Mt 5.4–8).[2] To all of them he sent the Holy Spirit to inspire them from within to love God with all their heart, all their soul, all their mind, and with all their strength (see Mk 12.30) and to love one another even as Christ has loved them (see Jn 13.34, 15.12). The followers of Christ, called by God not for their achievements but in accordance with his plan and his grace, and justified in the Lord Jesus, by their baptism in faith have been truly made children of God and sharers in the divine nature (2 Pt 1.4), and are therefore really made holy. This holiness, therefore, which they have received by the gifts of God, they must maintain and perfect by their way of life. They are warned by the apostle to live "as is fitting among saints" (Eph 5.3), "as God's chosen ones, holy and beloved," to put on "compassion, kindness, lowliness, meekness, and patience" (Col 3.12); to possess the fruits of the Spirit for sanctification (see Gal 5.22; Rom 6.22). And since all of us commit many faults (see Jas 3.2), we are in continuous need of the mercy of God and our daily prayer has to be: "And forgive us our trespasses" (Mt 6.12).[3]

It is therefore evident to everyone that all the faithful, whatever their condition or rank, are called to the fullness of the Christian life and the perfection of charity.[4] And this sanctity is conducive to a more human way of living even in society here on earth. To attain this perfection the faithful should exert their strength in the measure in which they have received this as Christ's gift, so that following in his footsteps and forming themselves in his likeness, obedient in all things to the Father's will, they may be wholeheartedly devoted to the glory of God and the service of their neighbor. In this way the holiness of the people of God will produce fruit in abundance, as is clearly shown in the history of the church by the lives of so many saints.

41. In the different kinds of life and its different duties, there is one holiness

---

2. See Origen, *Comm. Rom. (Commentary on Romans)*, 7, 7: PG 14, 1122B. Pseudo-Macarius, *De Oratione (On Prayer)*, 11: PG 34, 861AB. Thomas Aquinas, *Summa Theologiae*, II–II, quest. 184, art. 3.

3. See Augustine, *Retract. (Retractations)*, II, 18: PL 32, 637 f. Pius XII, Encyclical *Mystici Corporis*, 29 June 1943: AAS 35 (1943), p. 225.

4. See Pius XI, Encyclical *Rerum omnium*, 26 June 1923: AAS 15 (1923), pp. 50 and 59–60. Idem, Encyclical *Casti Connubii*, 31 Dec. 1930: AAS 22 (1930), p. 548. Pius XII, Apostolic constitution *Provida Mater*, 2 Feb. 1947: AAS 39 (1947), p. 117. Idem, Allocution *Annus sacer*, 8 Dec. 1950: AAS 43 (1951), pp. 27–28. Idem, Allocution *Nel darvi*, 1 July 1956: AAS 48 (1956), pp. 574 f.

cultivated by all who are led by the Spirit of God; obeying the voice of the Father and worshiping God the Father in spirit and in truth, they follow Christ poor and humble in carrying his cross so that they may deserve to be sharers in his glory. All, however, according to their own gifts and duties and without hesitation, must commit themselves to that pathway of living faith which stirs up hope and works through love.

In the first place the pastors of Christ's flock, in accordance with the pattern set by the eternal High Priest, must carry out their ministry with holiness and zeal, with humility and courage. Fulfilled in this way their ministry will be also for themselves an excellent means of sanctification. Called to the fullness of the priesthood, they receive a sacramental grace which enables them perfectly to fulfill their duty of pastoral love through prayer, the offering of the holy sacrifice and preaching, and through everything that calls for episcopal care and service.[5] Nor need they be afraid to give their lives for their sheep and, making themselves an example for their flock (see 1 Pt 5.3), they should lead the church, also by their own example, to a daily higher level of holiness.

Priests form the spiritual crown of the bishop;[6] and like the order of bishops they share in their grace of office through Christ the unique and eternal Mediator. Through the daily performance of their office they should grow in the love of God and of their neighbor, safeguard the bond of priestly communion, abound in every spiritual good, and give to all a living witness to God,[7] rivaling those priests who down the centuries have left a glorious pattern of holiness, often in a form of service that was humble and hidden. Their praise lives on in the church. For their own people and for the whole people of God they have a duty to pray and offer sacrifice, realizing what they are doing and imitating what they are handling;[8] and far from being held back by their apostolic cares, dangers, and tribulations, by these very means they should rise to greater heights of sanctity, nourishing and fostering their action from the rich source of meditation, to the delight of the whole of God's church. All priests, especially those who because of their particular title of ordination are called diocesan priests, should bear in mind how much loyal union

5. See Thomas Aquinas, *Summa Theologiae,* II–II, quest. 184, art. 5 and 6. Idem, *De perf. vitae spir. (Perfection of the Spiritual Life),* ch. 18. Origen, *In Is. (On Isaiah),* homily 6, 1: PG 13, 239.

6. See Ignatius of Antioch, *Magn. (To the Magnesians),* 13, 1: ed. Funk, I, p. 241.

7. See Pius X, Exhortation *Haerent animo,* 4 Aug. 1908: ASS 41 (1908), p. 560 f. CIC, canon 124. Pius XI, Encyclical *Ad catholici sacerdotii,* 20 Dec. 1935: AAS 28 (1936), p. 22.

8. See *Roman Pontifical,* Ordination of priests, the initial exhortation.

and generous cooperation with their bishop contributes to their sanctification. In the mission and grace of the supreme Priest, those persons also participate in a particular way who belong to a lower order of the ministry, in the first place deacons. Since they are servants of the mysteries of Christ and of the church,[9] they must keep themselves from all vice, be pleasing to God, and be a source of all good in the sight of people (see 1 Tm 3.8–10, 12–13). Clerics, who have been called by the Lord and set apart for his service, should prepare themselves for the duties of the ministry under the pastors' watchful care; they are bound to keep their hearts and minds in harmony with such a glorious vocation by being assiduous in prayer, fervent in love, and with their mind intent on all that is true, just, and of good repute, and doing everything for the glory and honor of God. There are in addition those chosen lay people who are called by the bishop to dedicate themselves completely to apostolic works; these persons work very fruitfully in the Lord's field.[10]

Christian married couples and parents should follow their own way, supporting one another in grace all through life with faithful love. They should imbue their children, lovingly welcomed from God, with Christian truths and gospel virtues. Thus they offer to all an example of untiring and generous love, they build up the community of love, and they bear witness to and cooperate in the fruitfulness of Mother Church. They are a sign of and share in the love with which Christ loved his bride and gave himself to her.[11] A similar example is given, in a different way, by widows and single people, who can make a great contribution towards holiness and activity in the church. Those who engage in work, which is often toilsome, can through their labors perfect themselves, help their fellow citizens, and raise up all of society and creation itself to a better state. Indeed by their active charity, rejoicing in hope and bearing one another's burdens, they imitate Christ who worked as a carpenter and is always working with the Father for the salvation of all; by their daily work they may rise to a higher and truly apostolic holiness.

As for those also who are crushed by poverty, weakness, disease, or various other hardships, or who suffer persecution for the sake of justice, they should realize that they are united in a special way with Christ in his suffering for the world's salvation. In the Gospel the Lord called these people blessed, and after they "have suffered a little while, the God of all grace, who has called us to his eternal glory in Christ Jesus, will himself restore, establish, and strengthen" them (1 Pt 5.10).

---

9. See Ignatius of Antioch, *Trall. (To the Trallians)*, 2, 3: ed. Funk, I, p. 244.
10. See Pius XII, Allocution *Sous la maternelle protection*, 9 Dec. 1957, AAS 50 (1958), p. 36.
11. See Pius XI, Encyclical *Casti Connubii*, 31 Dec. 1930: AAS 22 (1930), p. 548 f. John Chrysostom, *In Ephes. (On Ephesians)*, homily 20, 2: PG 62, 136 ff.

All the faithful, therefore, whatever their condition of life, their duties, or their circumstances, and through all of them, will grow daily in holiness if they accept all these things in faith from the hand of their heavenly Father and if they cooperate with the divine will by making manifest to all, even as they carry out their work here on earth, that love with which God has loved the world.

42. "God is love, and whoever abides in love abides in God, and God abides in him" (1 Jn 4.16). God has poured out his love in our hearts by the Holy Spirit who has been given to us (see Rom 5.5). Therefore the first and most necessary gift is that charity by which we love God above all things and our neighbor for God's sake. However if charity is to grow in the soul like good seed and bear fruit, each individual believer must give the word of God a willing hearing and with the help of his grace do God's will, take part often in the sacraments, especially the eucharist, and in the sacred liturgy. He should apply himself constantly to prayer, self-denial, active fraternal service, and the practice of all the virtues. For charity, as the bond of perfection and fullness of the law (see Col 3.14; Rom 13.10), directs all the means of sanctification, gives them their form, and brings them to their goal.[12] The true disciple of Christ is, therefore, characterized by his love for God and for his neighbor. Since Jesus, the Son of God, has shown his love by laying down his life for us, no one has greater love than he who lays down his life for Christ and for his sisters and brothers (see 1 Jn 3.16; Jn 15.13). Right from the beginning, therefore, some Christians have been called to bear this highest witness of love in the sight of all and especially of persecutors; and some Christians will always be called to do this. Through martyrdom the disciple is made like his Master in willing acceptance of death for the salvation of the world and resembles him by the shedding of his blood. For this reason, therefore, martyrdom is held by the church to be the highest gift and the supreme proof of love. This is given to few, yet all must be prepared to confess Christ before people and to follow him along the ways of the cross amid the persecutions which the church never lacks.

The holiness of the church is also nourished in a special way by the manifold counsels the observance of which the Lord in the Gospel commends to his disciples.[13] Outstanding among these is that precious gift of divine grace which is

---

12. See Augustine, *Enchir. (Enchiridion)*, 121, 32: PL 40, 288. Thomas Aquinas, *Summa Theologiae*, II–II, quest. 184, art. 1. Pius XII, Apostolic exhortation *Menti nostrae*, 23 Sept. 1950: AAS 42 (1950), p. 660.

13. On the counsels in general, see Origen, *Comm. Rom. (Commentary on Romans)*, 10, 14: PG 14, 1275B. Augustine, *De S. Virginitate (Holy Virginity)*, 15, 15: PL 40, 403. Thomas Aquinas, *Summa Theologiae*, I–II, quest. 100, art. 2 C (at end); II–II, quest. 44, art. 4, to 3.

granted to some by the Father (see Mt 19.11; 1 Cor 7.7), that in the state of virginity or celibacy they may more easily devote themselves to God alone with an undivided heart (see 1 Cor 7.32–34).[14] This perfect continence for the sake of the kingdom of heaven has always been held in particular esteem by the church as a sign and a stimulus of charity and as a singular source of spiritual fruitfulness in the world. The church reflects too on the advice of the apostle who, in urging the faithful to charity, exhorted them to have the same sentiments as Christ Jesus who "emptied himself, taking the form of a servant . . . and became obedient unto death" (Phil 2.7–8), and for our sake "though he was rich, he became poor" (2 Cor 8.9). The disciples must always imitate this charity and humility of Christ and bear witness to it. Therefore Mother Church rejoices that it has within itself many men and women who follow more closely this self-emptying of the Savior and show it forth more clearly by undertaking poverty with the freedom of God's children and by renouncing their own will; that is to say, they make themselves subject to another person for the love of God, going beyond what is of precept in the matter of perfection so that they may resemble more closely the obedient Christ.[15]

All the faithful are, therefore, invited and bound to strive towards holiness and the perfection of their particular state of life. Consequently all must be careful to keep due control over their emotions, so as not to be held back from the pursuit of perfect charity by using this world's goods and being attached to riches in a way that is against the spirit of evangelical poverty; as the apostle warns us: "Those who deal with the world must not be attached to it, for the form of this world is passing away" (see 1 Cor 7.31 Greek text).[16]

CHAPTER 6. RELIGIOUS

43. The evangelical counsels of chastity consecrated to God, poverty, and obedience constitute a divine gift which the church has received from its Lord and maintains

---

14. On the excellence of holy virginity, see Tertullian, *Exhort. Cast. (Exhortation to Chastity)*, 10: PL 2, 925C; CChr 2, 1029. Cyprian, *Hab. Virg. (Dress of Virgins)*, 3 and 22: PL 4, 443B and 461A f. Athanasius (?), *De Virg. (On Virginity)*: PG 28, 252 ff. John Chrysostom, *De Virg. (On Virginity)*: PG 48, 533 ff.

15. On spiritual poverty, see Mt 5.3, 19.21; Mk 10.21; Lk 18.22. With regard to obedience, the example of Christ is given: Jn 4.34, 6.38; Phil 2.8–10; Heb 10.5–7. The fathers and the founders of religious orders have written much on these matters.

16. On the effective practice of the counsels which is not imposed on all, see John Chrysostom, *In Mt. (On Matthew)*, homily 7, 7: PG 57, 81 f. Ambrose, *De Viduis (On Widows)*, 4, 23: PL 16, 241 f.

always with the help of his grace. For they have their foundation in the words and example of the Lord and are recommended by the apostles and fathers, by the doctors of the church and its pastors. The authority of the church, under the guidance of the Holy Spirit, has taken on the task of interpreting these counsels and regulating their practice as well as establishing stable forms of living according to them. And so it has come about that, like a tree growing from a seed planted by God and spreading out its branches in a wonderful and varied way in the field of the Lord, there has grown up a variety of forms of solitary or community life and different families which increase their resources both for the progress of their members and the good of the whole body of Christ.[1] These families provide their members with the support of greater stability in their way of life, a proven doctrine that is able to lead to perfection, a fellowship in the army of Christ, and a freedom strengthened by obedience. And so they are able to live up to their religious profession without anxiety, maintain fidelity to it, and, rejoicing in spirit, make progress along the way of charity.[2]

If one considers the divine and hierarchical constitution of the church, the religious state is not an intermediate condition between the clerical and the lay. But some faithful, from each of these two conditions (clerical and lay), are called by God to enjoy a particular gift in the life of the church and, each in their own way, to help the church in its mission of salvation.[3]

44. By the vows, or other sacred bonds which of their nature resemble vows, by which some of the faithful bind themselves to these three evangelical counsels that have just been mentioned, they consecrate themselves totally to God whom they love above all things, in such a way that by a new and particular title they are committed to the service and honor of God. Certainly by baptism they have died to sin and have been dedicated to God; however, in order to draw more abundant fruit from that baptismal grace, by profession in the church of the evangelical counsels they aim to free themselves from obstacles which could hinder the fervor of love and the pursuit of perfection in divine worship, and they consecrate themselves more

---

1. See Rosweydus, *Vitae Patrum*, Antwerp 1628. *Apophtegmata Patrum*: PG 65. Palladius, *Historia Lausiaca*: PG 34, 995 ff.; ed. C. Butler, Cambridge 1898 (1904). Pius XI, Apostolic constitution *Umbratilem*, 8 July 1924: AAS 16 (1924), pp. 386–387. Pius XII, Allocution *Nous sommes heureux*, 11 April 1958: AAS 50 (1958), p. 283.

2. See Paul VI, Allocution *Magno gaudio*, 23 May 1964: AAS 56 (1964), p. 566.

3. See CIC, canons 487 and 488, 4°. Pius XII, Allocution *Annus sacer*, 8 Dec. 1950: AAS 43 (1951), p. 27 f. Pius XII, Apostolic constitution *Provida Mater*, 2 Feb. 1947: AAS 39 (1947), p. 120 ff.

closely to the service of God.[4] And this consecration will be the more perfect in as much as by firmer and more stable bonds Christ is more clearly seen to be united to his bride the church by an indissoluble bond.

By the charity to which they lead,[5] the evangelical counsels in a special way unite those who make profession of them with the church and its mystery. Consequently, the spiritual life of these persons must be dedicated to the good of the whole church. This is the source of their duty to strive, so far as they can and according to their own particular vocation, through prayer or active works, to implant and strengthen the reign of Christ in souls and to extend it everywhere. Therefore the church both protects and encourages the particular character of the different religious institutes.

The profession of the evangelical counsels is seen, therefore, as a sign which can and should effectively draw all the members of the church to carry out zealously the duties of the Christian vocation. The people of God have here no abiding city; they seek rather one that is to come. Therefore the religious state, while giving its followers greater freedom from earthly cares, also makes clearer to all believers the heavenly goods that are already present in this world. It both bears witness to the new and eternal life won through Christ's redemption and foretells the resurrection that is to come and the glory of the heavenly kingdom. Moreover, the religious state imitates more closely and shows forth in the church unceasingly the form of life that the Son of God took on when he came into the world to do the will of the Father and which he proposed to the disciples who followed him. And it makes clear in a particular way how the kingdom of God surpasses all earthly things and how high are its requirements. It demonstrates to all people the incomparable grandeur of the power of Christ the King and the infinite power of his Spirit which is wonderfully active in the church.

This state, therefore, which is constituted by the profession of the evangelical counsels, although it does not belong to the hierarchical structure of the church, does, however, belong unquestionably to its life and holiness.

45. Since it is the duty of the ecclesiastical hierarchy to feed the people of God and lead them to the richest of pastures (see Ez 34.14), it is the task of the same hierarchy wisely to regulate by law the practice of the evangelical counsels by

---

4. See Paul VI, loc. cit., p. 567.
5. See Thomas Aquinas, *Summa Theologiae*, II–II, quest. 184, art. 3, and quest. 188, art. 2. Bonaventure, Opusc. XI, *Apologia Pauperum*, ch. 3, 3: ed. Opera, Quaracchi, tome 8, 1898, p. 245 a.

which perfect charity towards God and one's neighbor is encouraged in a special way.[6] Moreover, in docile submission to the inspiration of the Holy Spirit, the hierarchy accepts rules put forward by outstanding men and women and, once these have been further revised, gives them official approval. It also provides vigilant and protective authority to see that institutes that have been set up here and there for the building up of the body of Christ develop and flourish in accordance with the spirit of their founders.

To meet the needs of the whole of the Lord's flock more effectively, any institute of perfection and its individual members can, for the general good of the church, be exempted by the supreme pontiff from the jurisdiction of local ordinaries and subjected to him alone; this is possible by reason of his primacy over the universal church.[7] Similarly they can be left or committed to their own patriarchal authorities. The members themselves, in carrying out their duty towards the church which arises from their particular form of life, have a duty of reverence and obedience, in accordance with the canon laws, towards the bishops, because of their authority in the particular churches and because of the need for unity and harmony in apostolic work.[8]

However, not only does the church by its authority raise religious profession to the dignity of a canonical state, it also shows through its liturgical action that it is a state consecrated to God. For it is the church, through the authority committed to it by God, which receives the vows of persons making profession, by its public prayer asks of God help and grace for them, commends them to God, imparts to them its spiritual blessings, and links their self-oblation to the eucharistic sacrifice.

46. Religious should try hard to ensure that through them the church more effectively shows forth the real Christ—to believers and unbelievers—in prayer on the mountain, or announcing the kingdom of God to the crowds, or healing the sick and the wounded and turning sinners to a better life, or blessing children and doing

6. See Vatican council I, Schema *De Ecclesia Christi,* ch. 15, and annotation 48: Msi 51, 549 f. and 619 f. Leo XIII, Letter *Au milieu des consolations,* 23 Dec. 1900: ASS 33 (1900–01), p. 361. Pius XII, Apostolic constitution *Provida Mater,* loc. cit., p. 114 f.

7. See Leo XIII, Constitution *Romanos Pontifices,* 8 May 1881: ASS 13 (1880–81), p. 483. Pius XII, Allocution *Annus sacer,* 8 Dec. 1950: AAS 43 (1951), p. 28 f.

8. See Pius XII, Allocution, loc. cit., p. 28. Pius XII, Apostolic constitution *Sedes Sapientiae,* 31 May 1956: AAS 48 (1956), p. 355. Paul VI, Allocution *Magno gaudio,* 23 May 1964: AAS 56 (1964), pp. 570–571.

good to everybody, always, however, in obedience to the will of the Father who sent him.[9]

Finally, all should realize clearly that although profession of the evangelical counsels entails the renunciation of goods which are without doubt to be held in high esteem, nevertheless it is not an obstacle to the development of the human person but by its very nature is highly conducive to this development. For the counsels, willingly undertaken in accordance with the personal vocation of each individual, contribute not a little to the purification of the heart and to spiritual freedom; they keep ablaze continuously the fervor of charity, and, as is confirmed by the example of so many holy founders, are able to bring the Christian into greater conformity with that kind of virginal and poor life which Christ the Lord chose for himself and which his Virgin Mother embraced. Nor should anyone think that religious by their consecration become either alienated from humanity or useless in the earthly city. For even if at times they do not assist directly their contemporaries, yet in a deeper way they hold them present in the bowels of Christ and cooperate spiritually with them, so that the building up of the earthly city may be always founded in the Lord and directed towards him, lest those who are constructing it may have labored in vain.[10]

Therefore the holy synod confirms and praises the men and women, the brothers and sisters, who in monasteries or in schools and hospitals, or in the missions, by their persevering and humble fidelity in the above-mentioned consecration honor the spouse of Christ and provide all humankind with generous and very diverse forms of service.

47. Let all, then, who have been called to the profession of the counsels make every effort to persevere and make greater progress in the vocation to which God has called them, for the richer holiness of the church and the greater glory of the one and undivided Trinity, which in Christ and through Christ is the source and origin of all holiness.

CHAPTER 7. THE ESCHATOLOGICAL CHARACTER OF THE PILGRIM CHURCH AND ITS UNION WITH THE HEAVENLY CHURCH

48. The church, to which we are all called in Christ Jesus and in which through the grace of God we attain sanctity, will reach its completion only in the glory of

---

9. See Pius XII, Encyclical *Mystici Corporis,* 29 June 1943: AAS 35 (1943), p. 214 f.

10. See Pius XII, Allocution *Annus sacer,* loc. cit., p. 30. Idem, Allocution *Sous la maternelle protection,* 9 Dec. 1957: AAS 50 (1958), p. 39 f.

heaven, when the time for the restoration of all things will come (see Acts 3.21) and along with the human race the whole universe, which is intimately united to humanity and through it attains its goal, will be established perfectly in Christ (see Eph 1.10; Col 1.20; 2 Pt 3.10–13).

Christ, when he was lifted up from the earth, drew all people to himself (see Jn 12.32 Greek text); rising from the dead (see Rom 6.9), he sent his lifegiving Spirit down on his disciples and through him he constituted his body which is the church as the universal sacrament of salvation; sitting at the right hand of the Father he is continuously at work in the world to lead people to the church and through it to join them more closely to himself; and he nourishes them with his own body and blood to make them sharers in his glorious life. The promised restoration, therefore, which we await, has already begun in Christ, is advanced through the mission of the Holy Spirit and by means of the Spirit continues in the church in which, through faith, we are instructed concerning the meaning of our temporal life, while we, as we hope for the benefits that are to come, bring to its conclusion the work entrusted to us in the world by the Father and work out our salvation (see Phil 2.12).

Already, therefore, the end of the ages has reached us (see 1 Cor 10.11) and the renewal of the world has been irrevocably constituted and is being anticipated in this world in a real sense: for already on earth the church is adorned with true though imperfect holiness. However, until the arrival of the new heavens and the new earth in which justice dwells (see 2 Pt 3.13), the pilgrim church in its sacraments and institutions, which belong to this age, carries the figure of this world which is passing and it dwells among creatures who groan and till now are in the pains of childbirth and await the revelation of the children of God (see Rom 8.19–22). Joined, therefore, to Christ in the church and sealed by the Holy Spirit "who is the guarantee of our inheritance" (Eph 1.14), we are called and really are children of God (see 1 Jn 3.1), but we have not yet appeared with Christ in glory (see Col 3.4), in which we will be like God, for we shall see him as he is (see 1 Jn 3.2). So, while we are at home in the body, we are away from the Lord (2 Cor 5.6); and possessing the first fruits of the Spirit we groan within ourselves (see Rom 8.23) and desire to be with Christ (see Phil 1.23). But we are urged on by this same love to live more for him who died for us and rose again (see 2 Cor 5.15). We try therefore in all things to please God (2 Cor 5.9), and we put on the armor of God, so that we can stand up against the snares of the devil and resist in the evil day (see Eph 6.11–13). Since, however, we know neither the day nor the hour, at the Lord's warning we must be constantly on the watch so that, at the end of our single course of life on earth (see Heb 9.27), we may deserve to enter the nuptial celebration with him and be counted among the blessed (see Mt 25.31–46), and not be ordered, like the evil and lazy servants (see Mt 25.26), to go down into the eternal fire (see Mt 25.41), into the exterior darkness where "there will be weeping and gnashing of teeth" (Mt 22.13, 25.30). For before we reign with Christ in glory we must all appear "before the judgment seat of Christ, so that each one may receive good or evil, according to what he has done in the body" (2 Cor 5.10); and at the end of the world "they will come forth, those who have done good to the resurrection of life, and those who have done evil to the resurrection of judgment" (Jn 5.29; see Mt 25.46). Considering, therefore, that "the sufferings of this time are not worth comparing with the glory that is to be revealed in us" (Rom 8.18; see 2 Tm 2.11–12), strong in faith we await "our blessed hope, the appearing of the glory of our great God and Savior Jesus Christ" (Ti 2.13), "who will change our lowly body to be like his glorious body" (Phil 3.21); and he will come "to be glorified in his saints and to be marveled at in all who have believed" (2 Thes 1.10).

49. Until, therefore, the Lord comes in his majesty and all his angels with him (see Mt 25.31) and, when death has been destroyed, all things will have been made subject to him (see 1 Cor 15.26–27), some of his disciples are pilgrims on earth, others who have departed this life are being purified, while others are in glory gazing "clearsighted on God himself as he is, three in one";[1] all of us, however, though in a different degree and manner, communicate in the same love of God and our neighbor and sing the same hymn of glory to our God. For all who are in Christ, possessing his Spirit, are joined together into one church and united with each other in him (see Eph 4, 16). The union, therefore, of those who are still pilgrims with their sisters and brothers who have gone to sleep in the peace of Christ, is by no means broken, indeed according to the perennial faith of the church it is strengthened through participation in spiritual benefits.[2] Because those who are in heaven are more intimately united with Christ, they bring greater consolation to the holiness of the whole church, they ennoble the worship offered to God by the church here on earth and in a variety of ways contribute to the greater building-up of the church (see 1 Cor 12.12–27).[3] For, since they have been admitted into their homeland and are present before the Lord (see 2 Cor 5.8), through him and with him and

---

1. Council of Florence, *Decree for the Greeks:* D 693 (1305).

2. Besides earlier documents against any kind of evocation of spirits, from the time of Alexander IV (27 Sept. 1258), see the encyclical of the Holy Office, *De magnetismi abusu,* 4 August 1856: ASS (1865), pp. 177–178; D 1653–1654 (2823–2825); the reply of the Holy Office, 24 April 1917: AAS 9 (1917), p. 268; D 2182 (3642).

3. For a synthetic exposition of this Pauline teaching, see Pius XII, Encyclical *Mystici Corporis:* AAS 35 (1943), p. 200 and *passim.*

in him they do not cease to intercede for us to the Father,[4] displaying the merits they gained on earth through the one Mediator between God and humanity, Christ Jesus (see 1 Tm 2.5), in all things serving the Lord and fulfilling in their flesh all that is lacking in the sufferings of Christ for the sake of his body which is the church (see Col 1.24).[5] Therefore by their fraternal solicitude our weakness is helped in many ways.

50. Fully acknowledging this communion of the whole mystical body of Jesus Christ, right from the very early period of the Christian religion the pilgrim church has with great respect honored the memory of the dead[6] and, since "it is a holy and wholesome thought to pray for the dead that they may be loosed from their sins" (2 Mc 12.46), it has also offered prayers for them. The church has, however, always believed that the apostles and martyrs of Christ, who have given the supreme witness to their faith and charity by the shedding of their blood, are more closely united to us in Christ, has honored them as well as the Blessed Virgin Mary and the holy angels with a special affection,[7] and has piously implored the help of their intercession. To these there were soon added those others who had imitated more closely the virginity and the poverty of Christ,[8] and finally there were added others whom the outstanding practice of the Christian virtues[9] and the divine charismata recommended to the pious devotion and imitation of the faithful.[10]

For when we look at the lives of those men and women who have faithfully followed Christ, we are spurred on by a new reason to seek after the city that is to come (see Heb 13.14, 11.10), and at the same time we are educated in the safest way by which, through the world's changing patterns, in accordance with the state and condition of each individual, we will be able to attain perfect union with Christ and

---

4. See, for example, Augustine, *Enarr. in Ps. (Exposition of the Psalms)*, 85, 24: PL 37, 1099; CChr 39, 1196: Jerome, *Liber contra Vigilantium (Against Vigilantius)*, 6: PL 23, 344. Thomas Aquinas, *In 4m Sentent.*, dist. 45, quest. 3, art. 2. Bonaventure, *In 4m Sentent.*, dist. 45, art. 3, quest. 2; etc.

5. See Pius XII, Encyclical *Mystici Corporis*: AAS 35 (1943), p. 245.

6. See many inscriptions in the Roman catachombs.

7. See Gelasius I, Decretal *De libris recipiendis*, 3: PL 59, 160; D 165 (353).

8. See Methodius, *Symposion (Symposium)*, 7, 3: GCS (Bonwetsch), p. 74.

9. See Benedict XV, *Decretum approbationis virtutum in Causa beatificationis et canonizationis Servi Dei Ioannis Nepomuceni Neumann*: AAS 14 (1922), p. 23. Many allocutions of Pius XI on the saints: *Inviti all'eroismo*, in *Discorsi e Radiomessaggi*, tomes I–III, 1941–1942, *passim*. Pius XII, *Discorsi e Radiomessaggi*, tome X, 1949, 37–43.

10. See Pius XII, Encyclical *Mediator Dei*: AAS 39 (1947), p. 581.

holiness.[11] In the lives of those who, while sharing our humanity, are nevertheless more perfectly transformed into the image of Christ (see 2 Cor 3.18), God makes vividly manifest to humanity his presence and his face. He himself speaks to us in them and provides us with a sign of his kingdom[12] towards which we are powerfully drawn, having before us so great a cloud of witnesses (see Heb 12.1) and such an affirmation of the truth of the gospel. However, we cultivate the memory of the saints in heaven not by reason of their example only, but still more so that through the practice of fraternal charity the union of the whole church in the Spirit may be strengthened (see Eph 4.1–6). For just as Christian communion among pilgrims brings us closer to Christ, so our communion with the saints joins us to Christ, from whom as from the source and the head flows all grace and life of the people of God itself.[13] It is therefore most fitting that we love these friends and coheirs of Jesus Christ who are also our sisters and brothers and outstanding benefactors, that we give due thanks to God for them,[14] "that we invoke them and that we have recourse to their prayers and helpful assistance to obtain blessings from God through his Son our Lord Jesus Christ, who is our sole Redeemer and Savior."[15] For every authentic testimony of love that we offer to the saints, by its nature tends towards Christ and finds its goal in him who is "the crown of all the saints,"[16] and through him to God, who is wonderful in his saints and in them is glorified.[17]

Our union with the church in heaven is realized in a most noble way when, especially in the sacred liturgy, in which the power of the Holy Spirit acts on us by means of the sacramental signs, we celebrate together in common exultation the praise of the divine majesty,[18] and all who have been redeemed in the blood of Christ from every tribe and tongue and people and nation (see Rv 5.9) and gathered

---

11. See Heb 13.7; Ecli chs. 44–50; Heb 11.3–40. See also Pius XII, Encyclical *Mediator Dei*: AAS 39 (1947), pp. 582–583.

12. See Vatican council I, Dogmatic constitution on the catholic faith, *Dei Filius,* ch. 3: D 1794 (3013).

13. See Pius XII, Encyclical *Mystici Corporis*: AAS 35 (1943), p. 216.

14. With regard to gratitude to the saints, see E. Diehl, *Inscriptiones latinae christianae veteres,* I, Berlin 1925, nos. 2008, 2382 and *passim.*

15. See council of Trent, Decree *On invocation . . . of the saints:* D 984 (1821).

16. *Roman Breviary,* Invitatory of the feast of all Saints.

17. See for example, 2 Thes 1.10.

18. Vatican council II, Constitution on the sacred liturgy, *Sacrosanctum Concilium,* ch. 5, no. 104: AAS 56 (1964), pp. 125-126.

together into one church, in one canticle of praise glorify God who is one and three. When we celebrate, therefore, the eucharistic sacrifice we join very closely the worship of the heavenly church, communicating and celebrating the memory in the first place of the glorious and Ever-Virgin Mary, and also of blessed Joseph and blessed apostles and martyrs and all the saints.[19]

51. This venerable faith of our forefathers concerning the living communion with our brothers and sisters who are in heavenly glory or still being purified after death, this holy synod accepts with great respect, and it reiterates the decrees of the sacred councils of Nicaea II,[20] Florence,[21] and Trent.[22] At the same time, however, in its pastoral solicitude it exhorts all whom it concerns to do their best to get rid of or to correct any abuses, excesses, or deficiencies that may have crept in here and there and to restore all to the fuller praise of Christ and of God. Let them, therefore, teach the faithful that the genuine cult of the saints does not so much consist in a multiplicity of external acts but rather in the intensity of our active love by which, for the greater good of ourselves and of the church, we ask of the saints "example from their way of life, a sharing in their communion and help from their intercession."[23] On the other hand, let them instruct the faithful that our relationship with the saints in heaven, provided this is conceived in the fuller light of faith, in no way weakens the latreutic cult given to the Father through Christ in the Spirit, but on the contrary it greatly enriches it.[24]

For, all of us who are children of God and constitute one family in Christ (see Heb 3.6), while we communicate with each other in mutual love and in the one praise of the most Holy Trinity, are responding to the intimate vocation of the church and getting a foretaste of the liturgy of consummated glory.[25] For when Christ appears and the glorious resurrection of the dead takes place, the brightness of God will illuminate the heavenly city and the Lamb will be its lamp (see Rv

---

19. See *Roman Missal*, canon of the mass.

20. See council of Nicaea II, session 7: D 302 (600).

21. See council of Florence, *Decree for the Greeks:* D 693 (1304).

22. See council of Trent, Decree *On invocation, veneration and relics of saints and on sacred images:* D 984–988 (1821–1824); Decree *On purgatory:* D 983 (1820); Decree *On justification,* canon 30: D 840 (1580).

23. *Roman Missal*, Preface of saints, granted to dioceses in France.

24. See Peter Canisius, *Catechismus Maior seu Summa Doctrinae christianae*, ch. 3 (critical edn. by F. Streicher), Part 1, pp. 15–16, no. 44 and pp. 100–101, no. 49.

25. See Vatican council II, Constitution on the sacred liturgy, *Sacrosanctum Concilium*, ch. 1, no. 8: AAS 56 (1964), p. 401.

21.23). Then the whole church of the saints in the supreme happiness of love will adore God and "the Lamb who was slain" (Rv 5.12), with one voice proclaiming: "To him who sits upon the throne and to the Lamb be blessing and honor and glory and might for ever and ever" (Rv 5.13).

CHAPTER 8. THE BLESSED VIRGIN MARY, MOTHER OF GOD, IN THE MYSTERY OF CHRIST AND THE CHURCH
1. Introduction

52. God in his very great goodness and supreme wisdom wishing to bring about the redemption of the world, "when the time had fully come, sent forth his Son, born of a woman . . . so that we might receive adoption as children (Gal 4.4–5). He was the Son "who for us human beings and for our salvation came down from the heavens and was made incarnate by the Holy Spirit of the Virgin Mary."[1] This divine mystery of salvation is revealed to us and continues in the church, which the Lord constituted as his body and in which the faithful, adhering to Christ their Head and in communion with all his saints, must venerate also the memory "first of all, of the glorious Mary Ever-Virgin, Mother of Jesus Christ, our Lord and God."[2]

53. For the Virgin Mary, who at the message of an angel received the word of God in her heart and her body and brought forth life for the world, is recognized and honored as the true Mother of God and of the Redeemer. In view of the merits of her Son, redeemed in a more sublime manner and united to her Son by a tight and indissoluble bond, she is enriched by this supreme office and dignity of being the Mother of God the Son, and therefore she is the specially loved daughter of the Father and the shrine of the Holy Spirit; and by this gift of preeminent grace she surpasses by far all other creatures in heaven and on earth. At the same time, however, she is united in Adam's race with all human beings who are to be saved, indeed she is "clearly mother of the members (of Christ) . . . for she has cooperated with love in the birth of the faithful in the church, who are members of its head."[3] Therefore she is also acknowledged as the supereminent and uniquely special member of the church as well as its model in faith and love and its most outstanding exemplar; and the Catholic Church, instructed by the Holy Spirit, with the affection of filial piety, treats her as its most loving mother.

1. Constantinopolitan creed: Msi 3, 566. See council of Ephesus: Msi 4, 1130 (also Msi 2, 665 and 4, 1071); council of Chalcedon: Msi 7, 111–116; council of Constantinople II: Msi 9, 375–396; *Roman Missal*, creed.
2. *Roman Missal*, canon.
3. Augustine, *De S. Virginitate (Holy Virginity)*, 6: PL 40, 399.

54. Therefore the holy synod, while it expounds the doctrine of the church in which the divine Redeemer effects salvation, intends to illustrate carefully both the role of the Blessed Virgin Mary in the mystery of the incarnate Word and of the mystical body, and the duties of redeemed humanity towards the Mother of God, mother of Christ, and mother of humankind, especially of the faithful, without however intending to put forward a complete doctrine concerning Mary or of settling questions which have not yet been brought fully to light through the work of theologians. The right remains therefore to discuss those opinions, which are freely put forward in Catholic schools, concerning her who in holy church occupies the place that is highest after Christ and nearest to us.[4]

2. The Role of the Blessed Virgin in the Economy of Salvation

55. The sacred books of the Old and the New Testament and venerable tradition show ever more clearly the role of the mother of the Savior in the economy of salvation and, in a manner of speaking, put it forward for our consideration. The books of the Old Testament describe the history of salvation in which the coming of Christ into the world is slowly prepared. These ancient documents, as they are read in the church and understood in the light of the later and full revelation, gradually put forward ever more clearly the figure of the woman, the mother of the Redeemer. In this light she is already prophetically adumbrated in the promise, made to the first parents when they had fallen into sin, concerning the victory over the serpent (see Gn 3.15). Similarly, she is the Virgin who will conceive and bring forth a Son whose name will be Emmanuel (see Is 7.14; compare Mi 5.2–3; Mt 1.22–23). She is outstanding among the humble and the poor of the Lord, who await with confidence and receive salvation from him. With her, finally, the exalted daughter of Zion, after the long wait for the fulfillment of the promise, the ages come to fulfillment and the new economy is begun, when the Son of God took from her his human nature so that through the mysteries of his flesh he might free humanity from sin.

56. The Father of mercies willed that the acceptance of her, who was predestined to be the mother, should precede the incarnation so that just as a woman contributed to the coming of death so also a woman should contribute to the coming of life. This is preeminently true of the mother of Jesus who brought into the world life itself that renewed all things, and was enriched by God with gifts worthy of such a role. Consequently it is no surprise to find that the custom grew up among the fathers by which they called the Mother of God allholy and free from all stain

4. See Paul VI, Allocution at the council, 4 Dec. 1963: AAS 56 (1964), p. 37.

of sin, as though fashioned by the Holy Spirit and made a new creature.[5] Enriched from the first instant of her conception by the splendor of a most singular holiness, the Virgin from Nazareth is greeted by the angel of the annunciation, at God's command, as "full of grace" (see Lk 1.28), and she replies to the messenger from heaven: "Behold I am the handmaid of the Lord; let it be to me according to your word" (Lk 1.38). And so Mary, the daughter of Adam, by consenting to the divine word, became the mother of Jesus, and embracing the salvific will of God wholeheartedly and without being held back by any sin, dedicated herself totally as the handmaid of the Lord to the person and work of her Son, putting herself under him and with him, by the grace of Almighty God, at the service of the mystery of redemption. Rightly, therefore, the holy fathers maintain that Mary was not simply a passive instrument in the hands of God, but that she cooperated in the salvation of the human race with free faith and obedience. In fact, as St. Irenaeus says, "by her obedience she became the cause of salvation for herself and for the whole human race."[6] Consequently not a few of the ancient fathers in their preaching willingly join him in asserting: "The knot of Eve's disobedience was untied through the obedience of Mary; what the virgin Eve had bound up through her lack of faith, the Virgin Mary untied by her faith";[7] and taking over this comparison with Eve, they call Mary "the mother of the living"[8] and frequently assert that "death came through Eve, but life through Mary."[9]

57. This union of the mother with the Son in the work of redemption is manifest from the instant of the virginal conception of Christ right on to his death. First of all when Mary, rising up in haste to visit Elizabeth, was proclaimed blessed

---

5. See Germanus of Constantinople, *Hom. in Annunt. Deiparae (Homily on the Annunciation)*: PG 98, 328A; *In Dorm. (On the Dormition)*, 2: PG 98, 357. Anastasius of Antioch, *Serm. 2 de Annunt. (Sermon 2 on the Annunciation)*, 2: PG 89, 1377AB; *Serm. (Sermons)*, 3, 2: PG 89, 1388C. Andrew of Crete, *Can. in B.V. Nat. (Canon for the blessed Virgin's Birthday)*, 4: PG 97, 1321B; *In B.V. Nat. (The blessed Virgin's Birthday)*, 1: PG 97, 812A; *Hom. in dorm. (Homily on the Dormition)*, 1: PG 97, 1068C. Sophronius, *Or. 2 in Annunt. (Oration 2 on the Annunciation)*, 18: PG 87 (3), 3237BD.

6. Irenaeus, *Adv. Haer. (Against Heresies)*, III, 22, 4: PG 7, 959A; Harvey 2, 123.

7. Irenaeus, *ibid.*: Harvey 2, 124.

8. Epiphanius, *Haer. (Heresies)*, 78, 18: PG 42, 728CD–729AB.

9. Jerome, *Epist. (Letters)*, 22, 21: PL 22, 408. See Augustine, *Serm. (Sermons)*, 51, 2, 3, and 232, 2: PL 38, 335, and 1108. Cyril of Jerusalem, *Catech. (Catecheses)*, 12, 15: PG 33, 741AB. John Chrysostom, *In Ps. (On the Psalms)*, 44, 7: PG 55, 193. John Damascene, *Hom. 2 in dorm. B. M. V. (Homily 2 on the Dormition)*, 3: PG 96, 728.

by her because of her faith in the salvation that had been promised, and the precursor leapt in his mother's womb (see Lk 1.41–45); at the nativity, when the Mother of God was happy to show to the shepherds and the magi the Son, her first-born, who did not diminish her virginal integrity but consecrated it.[10] And when she presented him to the Lord in the temple with the offering of the poor, she heard Simeon foretell at one and the same time that the Son would become a sign of contradiction and that a sword would pierce the soul of his mother, so that the intimate thoughts of many hearts would be revealed (see Lk 2.34–35). And after having lost the child Jesus and searched for him anxiously, his parents found him in the temple occupied in his Father's business, and they did not understand the words of the Son. His mother kept all these things in her heart to meditate on (see Lk 2.41–51).

58. In the public life of Jesus his mother appears in a significant role: at first when she was moved by compassion at the wedding feast at Cana in Galilee, and by her intercession caused the first of the signs of Jesus the Messiah (see Jn 2.1–11). During his preaching she accepted the words by which the Son exalted the kingdom above the reasons and ties of flesh and blood and called those people blessed who hear and guard the word of God (see Mk 3.35; Lk 11.27–28), just as she herself was doing faithfully (see Lk 2.19, 51). In this way even the Blessed Virgin made progress in her pilgrimage of faith, and maintained faithfully her union with the Son right up to the cross where, in keeping with the divine plan, she stood (see Jn 19.25), suffering very profoundly with her only-begotten Son, and associated herself with a mother's heart with his sacrifice, lovingly consenting to the immolation of the victim that had been born from her; and finally by the same Christ Jesus, when he was dying on the cross, was given to the disciple as his mother in these words: "Woman, behold your son" (see Jn 19.26–27).[11]

59. Since it pleased God not to make a solemn manifestation of the mystery of the human race's salvation before he had poured forth the Spirit that had been promised by Christ, before the days of Pentecost we see the apostles "with one accord devoting themselves to prayer, together with the women and Mary the mother of Jesus, and with his brethren" (Acts 1.14), and Mary also imploring by her prayers the gift of the Spirit who had already overshadowed her at the annunciation. And finally the Immaculate Virgin, preserved free from every stain of original sin,[12]

---

10. See Lateran council in 649, canon 3: Msi 10, 1151. Leo I, *Epist. ad Flav. (Letter to Flavian)*: PL 54, 759. Council of Chalcedon: Msi 7, 462. Ambrose, *De instit. virg. (Consecration of a Virgin)*: PL 16, 320.

11. See Pius XII, Encyclical *Mystici Corporis*, 29 June 1943: AAS 35 (1943), pp. 247–248.

12. See Pius IX, Bull *Ineffabilis*, 8 Dec. 1954: *Acta* of Pius IX, 1, I, p. 616; D 1641 (2803).

when the course of her earthly life was completed, was taken up body and soul to heavenly glory,[13] and exalted by the Lord as queen of all so that she might be more fully conformed to her Son, the Lord of lords (see Rv 19.16) and Victor over sin and death.[14]

3. The Blessed Virgin and the Church

60. According to the words of the apostle, our Mediator is unique: "There is one God, and there is one mediator between God and human beings, the man Christ Jesus who gave himself as a ransom for them all" (1 Tm 2.5–6). Now the maternal role of Mary towards humanity in no way obscures or diminishes this unique mediation of Christ; rather it shows forth its power. For every saving influence that the Blessed Virgin has on humanity arises not from any natural necessity but from the divine good pleasure; it flows forth from the superabundance of Christ's merits, is founded on his mediation, completely depends on this, and from this draws all its power; it in no way hinders the direct union of believers with Christ, rather it fosters this union.

61. The Blessed Virgin, predestined from eternity as the Mother of God along with the incarnation of the divine Word, by the design of divine providence was the loving mother of the divine Redeemer here on earth, a singularly generous companion beyond others, and the humble handmaid of the Lord. She conceived Christ, gave birth to him and nourished him, presented him to the Father in the temple, and suffered with her Son as he was dying on the cross; in doing all this she cooperated in a very special way in the work of the Savior—through her obedience, faith, hope, and burning charity—towards the restoration of the supernatural life of souls. For this reason she has become our mother in the order of grace.

62. This motherhood of Mary in the economy of grace goes on without interruption from the consent she faithfully gave at the annunciation, which she

---

13. See Pius XII, Apostolic constitution *Munificentissimus,* 1 Nov. 1950: AAS 42 (1950); D 2333 (3903). See John Damascene, *Enc. in dorm. Dei genitricis (Encomium on the Dormition),* homilies 2 and 3: PG 96, 721–761, especially 728B. Germanus of Constantinople, *In S. Dei gen. dorm. (On the Dormition),* sermons 1 and 3: PG 98 (6), 340–348 and 361. Modestus of Jerusalem, *In dorm. SS. Deiparae (On the Dormition):* PG 86 (2), 3277–3312.

14. See Pius XII, Encyclical *Ad coeli Reginam,* 11 Oct. 1954: AAS 46 (1954), pp. 633–636; D 3913 ff. See Andrew of Crete, *Hom. 3 in dorm. SS. Deiparae (Homily 3 on the Dormition):* PG 97, 1089–1109. John Damascene, *De fide orth. (The orthodox Faith),* 4, 14: PG 94, 1153–1161.

upheld without wavering at the foot of the cross, right on to the perpetual consummation of all the elect. For assumed into heaven she has not put aside this saving role, rather she continues by her many prayers of intercession to obtain for us gifts of eternal salvation.[15] In her motherly love she looks after the sisters and brothers of her Son who are still on their pilgrimage and placed amidst dangers and difficulties, until they are led to their happy homeland. Therefore in the church the Blessed Virgin is invoked by the titles of advocate, benefactress, helper, and mediatrix.[16] This, however, must be understood in such a way that it takes away nothing from the dignity and power of Christ the one Mediator, and adds nothing on to this.[17] For no creature can ever be counted along with the incarnate Word and Redeemer; but just as the priesthood of Christ is shared in a variety of ways both by ministers and by the faithful people, and just as the one goodness of God is really poured out on creatures in diverse ways, so also the one mediation of the Redeemer does not rule out, but rouses up among creatures, participated cooperation from the one unique source.

This subordinate task of Mary the church does not hesitate to profess. The church experiences it continually and commends it to the heart of the faithful, so that supported by this motherly protection they may be more closely united to their Mediator and Savior.

63. The Blessed Virgin, through the gift and office of the divine motherhood which unites her with the Son the Redeemer, and by reason of her singular graces and gifts, is also intimately united to the church: the Mother of God is the type of the church, as already St. Ambrose used to teach, that is to say, in the order of faith, charity, and perfect union with Christ.[18] For in the mystery of the church, which is also rightly called mother and virgin, the Blessed Virgin Mary has taken

---

15. See Kleutgen, revised text *De mysterio Verbi incarnati*, ch. 4: Msi 53, 290. See Andrew of Crete, *In nat. Mariae (On Mary's Birthday)*, sermon 4: PG 97, 865A. Germanus of Constantinople, *In annunt. Deiparae (On the Annunciation)*: PG 98, 321BC; *In dorm. Deiparae (On the Dormition)*, 3: PG 98, 361D. John Damascene, *In dorm. B. V. Mariae (On the Dormition)*, homily 1, 8: PG 96, 712BC–713A.

16. See Leo XIII, Encyclical *Adiutricem populi*, 5 Sept. 1895: ASS 15 (1895–96), p. 303. Pius X, Encyclical *Ad diem illum*, 2 Feb. 1904: *Acta* of Pius X, I, p. 154: D 1978 a (3370). Pius XI, Encyclical *Miserentissimus*, 8 May 1928: AAS 20 (1928), p. 178. Pius XII, Radio message of 13 May 1946: AAS 38 (1946), p. 266.

17. See Ambrose, *Epist. (Letters)*, 63: PL 16, 1218.

18. See Ambrose, *Expos. Lc. (Commentary on Luke)*, 2, 7: PL 15, 1555; CChr 14, 33.

precedence, providing in a preeminent and singular manner the exemplar both as virgin and as mother.[19] For by her faith and obedience she brought forth on earth the very Son of the Father, and this without sexual intercourse but under the shadow of the Holy Spirit, believing like a new Eve not the ancient serpent but the messenger of God with a faith that was not adulterated by any doubt. She brought forth the Son whom God placed as the first-born among many brothers and sisters (see Rom 8.29), that is to say, of the faithful in whose birth and education she cooperates with motherly love.

64. The church, contemplating her hidden holiness and imitating her love, and faithfully carrying out the will of the Father, by faithfully accepting the word of God also becomes a mother: for by preaching and baptism it brings forth to new and immortal life children conceived of the Holy Spirit and born of God. The church is also a virgin who keeps integral and pure the faith she has given to her spouse; and in imitation of the mother of its Lord, by the power of the Holy Spirit, it preserves virginally intact its faith, solid its hope, and sincere its love.[20]

65. While in the Most Blessed Virgin the church has already attained the perfection by which it is without stain or wrinkle (see Eph 5.27), the faithful continue to strive by overcoming sin to grow in holiness; therefore they lift up their eyes to Mary who shines out to the whole community of the elect as the model of virtues. The church, when it thinks of her piously and contemplates her in the light of the Word made man, enters with reverence more deeply into the inmost mystery of the incarnation and becomes more and more like its spouse. For Mary, who has entered deeply into the history of salvation, in a certain way unites within herself the greatest truths of the faith and echoes them; and when she is preached about and honored she calls believers to her Son, to his sacrifice, and to the love of the Father. And the church in giving glory to Christ is made more like its exalted model, making continuous progress in faith, hope, and love and seeking and obeying the divine will in all things. Even in its apostolic work, therefore, the church rightly looks to her

---

19. See Pseudo-Peter Damian, *Serm. (Sermons)*, 63: PL 144, 861AB. Godfrey of Saint-Victor, *In nat. B. M. (The birth of blessed Mary)*, Ms. Paris, Mazarin 1002, fol. 109r. Gerhoh of Reichersberg, *De gloria et honore Filii hominis*, 10: PL 194, 1105AB.

20. See Ambrose, *Expos. in Lc. (Commentary on Luke)*, 2, 7, and 10, 24–25: PL 15, 1555 and 1810; CChr 14, 33 and 353. Augustine, *In Io. (On John)*, Treatise 13, 12: PL 35, 1499; CChr 36, 137; see *Serm. (Sermons)*, 191, 2, 3: PL 38, 1010; etc. See also Bede, *In Lc. Expos. (Commentary on Luke)*, 1, ch. 2: PL 92, 330; CChr 120, 47–48. Isaac of Stella, *Serm. (Sermons)*, 51: PL 194, 1863A.

who brought forth Christ so conceived by the Holy Spirit and born of the Virgin, that through the church he may also be born and grow in the hearts of the faithful. For this virgin in her life was the model of that motherly love which should inspire all who work together in the church's apostolic mission for the regeneration of humanity.

4. The Cult of the Blessed Virgin in the Church

66. Mary, exalted by the grace of God, after the Son, above all angels and human beings because she is the most Holy Mother of God who took part in the mysteries of Christ, is rightly honored by the church with a special cult. Clearly from the most ancient times the Blessed Virgin has been honored with the title of "Mother of God," to whose protection the faithful run in all their dangers and needs.[21] Especially from the Council of Ephesus the cult of the people of God for Mary has grown wonderfully in love and veneration, in invocation, and in imitation, in accordance with her own prophetic words: "All generations will call me blessed; for he who is mighty has done great things for me" (Lk 1.48–49). This cult, as it has always existed in the church, although it is a very special cult, differs essentially from the cult of adoration which is given to the incarnate Word and equally to the Father and the Holy Spirit, and it very greatly fosters this cult of adoration. The church has approved a variety of forms of devotion to the Mother of God within the limits of sound and orthodox doctrine and according to circumstances of time and place and the temperament and character of the faithful; but these devotions are such that, while the mother is honored, the Son for whom all things exist (see Col 1.15–16), and in whom it was the eternal Father's "good pleasure to let all fullness dwell" (Col 1.19), should be duly known, loved, and glorified and his commandments observed.

67. The holy synod expressly teaches this catholic doctrine and at the same time exhorts all the members of the church generously to foster the cult, especially the liturgical cult, of the Blessed Virgin, to hold in high esteem those pious practices recommended down the centuries by the magisterium, and carefully to observe what has been laid down in the past concerning the cult of images of Christ, of the Blessed Virgin, and of the saints.[22] It earnestly exhorts theologians and preachers

---

21. See *Roman Breviary*, antiphon "We fly to your protection" at 1st vespers of the little office of the Blessed Virgin Mary.

22. See council of Nicaea II, in 787: Msi 13, 378–379; D 302 (600–601); Council of Trent, session 25: Msi 33, 171–172.

of the divine word carefully to avoid all false exaggeration and equally a too narrow mentality in considering the special dignity of the Mother of God.[23] Through
the study of Holy Scripture, of the holy fathers and doctors, and of the liturgies of
the church, under the guidance of the magisterium, they should explain correctly the
gifts and privileges of the Blessed Virgin, which always have Christ in view, who
is the origin of all truth, holiness, and piety. They should sedulously avoid, both in
what they say and in what they do, anything that might lead our separated brothers
and sisters or any other people into error concerning the true teaching of the church.
Let the faithful also bear in mind that true devotion consists neither in sterile and
passing feelings nor in an empty credulity, but that it arises out of that true faith
by which we are brought to acknowledge the excellence of the Mother of God and
urged on towards filial love for our mother and imitation of her virtues.

5. Mary, the Sign of Sure Hope and Comfort
for the Pilgrim People of God

68. Meanwhile, however, the Mother of Jesus, as already glorified in body and soul
in heaven she is the image and the beginning of the church which will receive fulfillment in the age that is to come, so here on earth until the day of the Lord arrives
(see 2 Pt 3.10) she shines forth as a sign of sure hope and comfort for the pilgrim
people of God.

69. It brings great joy and consolation to this holy synod that people are not
lacking among our separated sisters and brothers who duly honor the mother of our
Lord and Savior, especially among Eastern Christians who honor the Ever-Virgin
Mother of God with fervor and devotion.[24] Let all Christians pour forth insistent
prayers to the Mother of God and mother of the human race that she who stood
by the primitive church with her prayers, now also, exalted in heaven above all the
blessed and the angels, in communion with all the saints may intercede with her
Son so that all the families of peoples, both those that are honored by the Christian name and those who do not yet know their Savior, may be happily gathered
together in peace and harmony into one people of God to the glory of the most holy
and undivided Trinity.

23. See Pius XII, Radio message of 24 Oct. 1954: AAS 46 (1954), p. 679. Encyclical *Ad caeli
Reginam*, 11 Oct. 1954: AAS 46 (1954), p. 637.
24. See Pius XI, Encyclical *Ecclesiam Dei*, 12 Nov. 1923: AAS 15 (1923), p. 581. Pius XII,
Encyclical *Fulgens corona*, 8 Sept. 1953: AAS 45 (1953), pp. 590–591.

5.3. Unitatis redintegratio: Decree on Ecumenism
Introduction

1. The restoration of unity among all Christians is one of the principal concerns of the Second Vatican Synod. Christ the Lord founded one church and one church only. Nevertheless, many Christian communions claim to be the true inheritance of Jesus Christ. All, indeed, avow that they are followers of the Lord, but they are divided in their convictions and go their different ways, as if Christ himself were divided.[1] Such division is clearly contrary to Christ's will. It is a scandal to the world and damages the sacred cause of preaching the gospel to every creature.

But the Lord of the ages works out with patience and wisdom the plan of his grace on our behalf, sinners though we are. In recent times more than ever before he has been rousing divided Christians to repentance over their divisions and to a longing for unity. Everywhere large numbers have felt the impulse of his grace; and among our separated brothers and sisters likewise, through the inspiration of the Holy Spirit, a movement has grown and developed, whose aim is the restoration of the unity of all Christians. Participation in this movement, called "ecumenical," entails invoking the triune God and confessing Jesus Christ as Lord and Savior, not merely as individuals, but also as members of the corporate bodies in which they have heard the gospel, and which each regards as his or her church and as God's church. Yet almost all, though in different ways, long for the one visible church of God, that truly universal church whose mission is to convert the whole world to the gospel, so that the world may be saved, to the glory of God. It is with joy that this holy synod has given its attention to all these aspirations. It has already declared its teaching about the church, and now, moved by desire for the restoration of unity among all the followers of Christ, it wishes to set before all Catholics the resources, the ways, and the means by which they can respond to the grace of his divine call.

CHAPTER 1. CATHOLIC PRINCIPLES OF ECUMENISM

2. In this the love of God was made manifest among us, that the Father sent his only-begotten Son into the world so that, becoming human, he might by his redemption give new life and unity to the entire human race.[2] Before offering himself up as a spotless victim upon the altar of the cross, Christ prayed to his Father for all who believe in him: "that they may all be one, even as you, Father, are in me, and I in you, that they also may be one in us; so that the world may believe that you have sent

1. See 1 Cor 1.13.
2. See 1 Jn 4.9; Col 1.18–20; Jn 11.52.

me" (Jn 17.21). In his church he instituted the wonderful sacrament of the eucharist, by which the unity of the church is both signified and made a reality. He gave his followers a new commandment to love one another,[3] and promised the Spirit, their advocate[4] who, as Lord and life-giver, should remain with them forever.

After being lifted up on the cross and glorified, the Lord Jesus poured forth his Spirit as he had promised, and through the Spirit he has called and gathered together the people of the new covenant, which is the church, into a unity of faith, hope, and charity, as the apostle teaches us: "There is one body and one Spirit, just as you were called to the one hope of your calling; one Lord, one faith, one baptism" (Eph 4.4–5). For "all you who have been baptized into Christ have put on Christ . . . for you are all one in Christ Jesus" (Gal 3.27–28 Greek text). It is the Holy Spirit, dwelling in those who believe and filling and ruling over the church as a whole, who brings about that wonderful communion of the faithful. He brings them all into intimate union with Christ, so that he is the principle of the church's unity. The distribution of graces and offices is his work too,[5] enriching the church of Jesus Christ with different functions "in order to equip the saints for the work of service, so as to build up the body of Christ" (Eph 4.12).

In order to establish this his holy church everywhere in the world till the end of time, Christ entrusted to the college of the twelve the task of teaching, ruling, and sanctifying.[6] Among their number he selected Peter, and after his confession of faith determined that on him he would build his church. To Peter also he promised the keys of the kingdom of heaven,[7] and after his profession of love, entrusted all his sheep to him to be confirmed in faith[8] and shepherded in perfect unity.[9] Christ Jesus himself was forever to remain the chief cornerstone[10] and shepherd of our souls.[11]

Through the faithful preaching of the gospel by the apostles and their successors—the bishops with Peter's successor at their head—through their administration of the sacraments, and through their governing of the church in love, Jesus

3. See Jn 13.34.

4. See Jn 16.7.

5. See 1 Cor 12.4–11.

6. See Mt 28.18–20, compare Jn 20.21–23.

7. See Mt 16.19, compare Mt 18.18.

8. See Lk 22.32.

9. See Jn 21.15–17.

10. See Eph 2.20.

11. See 1 Pt 2.25; Vatican council I, constitution *Pastor Aeternus:* Coll. Lac. 7, 482 a.

Christ wills his people to increase under the action of the Holy Spirit, and he perfects his people's fellowship in unity: in their confessing one faith, celebrating divine worship in common, and keeping the harmony of God's family.

The church, then, is God's only flock; it is like a standard lifted high for the nations to see it.[12] For it serves all humanity through the gospel of peace[13] as it makes its pilgrim way in hope towards the homeland in heaven which is its goal.[14]

This is the sacred mystery of the unity of the church, in Christ and through Christ, while the action of the Holy Spirit produces a variety of gifts. It is a mystery that finds its highest model and source in the unity of the persons of the Trinity: the unity of the one God, the Father and the Son in the Holy Spirit.

3. Even in the beginnings of this one and only church of God there arose certain rifts,[15] which the apostle strongly condemned.[16] But in subsequent centuries much more extensive dissensions made their appearance and large communities came to be separated from the full communion of the Catholic Church—for which, often enough, people of both sides were to blame. Those who are now born into these communities and who are brought up in the faith of Christ cannot be accused of the sin involved in the separation, and the Catholic Church looks upon them as sisters and brothers, with respect and love. For those who believe in Christ and have been truly baptized are in some kind of communion with the Catholic Church, even though this communion is imperfect. The differences that exist in varying degrees between them and the Catholic Church—whether in doctrine and sometimes in discipline, or concerning the structure of the church—do indeed create many obstacles, sometimes serious ones, to full ecclesiastical communion. The ecumenical movement is striving to overcome these obstacles. But even in spite of them it remains true that all who have been justified by faith in baptism are members of Christ's body,[17] and have a right to be called Christians, and so are deservedly recognized as sisters and brothers in the Lord by the children of the Catholic Church.[18]

Moreover some, and even most, of the significant elements and endowments which together go to build up and give life to the church itself, can exist outside the visible boundaries of the Catholic Church: the written word of God;

---

12. See Is 11.10–12.
13. See Eph 2.17–18, compare Mk 16.15.
14. See 1 Pt 1.3–9.
15. 1 Cor 11.18–19; Gal 1.6–9; 1 Jn 2.18–19.
16. See 1 Cor 1.11 ff, 11.22.
17. See council of Florence, session 8, decree *Exultate Deo:* Msi 31, 1055A.
18. See Augustine, *In Ps. 32, Enarr. II,* 29: PL 36, 299; CChr 38, 272.

the life of grace; faith, hope, and charity, with the other interior gifts of the Holy Spirit, and visible elements too. All of these, coming from Christ and leading back to Christ, properly belong to the one church of Christ.

Our separated brothers and sisters also celebrate many sacred actions of the Christian religion. These most certainly can truly engender a life of grace in ways that vary according to the condition of each church or community, and must be held capable of giving access to that communion in which is salvation.

It follows that the separated churches[19] and communities as such, though we believe them to be deficient in some respects, have by no means been deprived of significance and importance in the mystery of salvation. For the Spirit of Christ has not refrained from using them as means of salvation whose efficacy comes from that fullness of grace and truth which has been entrusted to the Catholic Church.

Nevertheless, our separated fellow Christians, whether considered as individuals or as communities and churches, are not blessed with that unity which Jesus Christ wished to bestow on all those who through him were born again into one body, and with him quickened to newness of life—that unity which the Holy Scriptures and the ancient tradition of the church proclaim. For it is only through Christ's Catholic Church, which is the all-embracing means of salvation, that the fullness of the means of salvation can be attained. We believe that our Lord entrusted all the blessings of the new covenant to the one apostolic college of which Peter is the head, in order to establish the one body of Christ on earth into which all should be fully incorporated who belong in any way to the people of God. This people of God, though still in its members liable to sin, is growing in Christ during its pilgrimage on earth, and is guided by God's gentle wisdom, according to his hidden designs, until it shall happily arrive at the fullness of eternal glory in the heavenly Jerusalem.

4. Today, in many parts of the world, under the inspiring grace of the Holy Spirit, many efforts are being made in prayer, word, and action to attain that fullness of unity which Jesus Christ desires. This synod, therefore, exhorts all the Catholic faithful to recognize the signs of the times and to take an intelligent part in the work of ecumenism.

The term "ecumenical movement" indicates the measures and activities planned and undertaken, according to the various needs of the church and as opportunities offer, to promote Christian unity. These are: first, every effort to avoid expressions, judgments, and actions which do not represent the condition of our

19. See Lateran council IV, constitution 4: Msi 22, 990; council of Lyons II, Profession of faith of Michael Palaeologus: Msi 24, 71E; council of Florence, session 6, definition *Laetentur caeli:* Msi 31, 1026E.

separated sisters and brothers with truth and fairness and so make mutual relations with them more difficult; then, "dialogue" between competent experts at meetings of Christians from different churches and communities. At these meetings, which are organized in a religious spirit, each explains the teaching of their communion in greater depth and brings out clearly its distinctive features. In such dialogue, everyone gains a truer knowledge and more just appreciation of the teaching and the life of each communion. In addition, the way is prepared for fuller cooperation between them in the duties for the common good of humanity which are demanded by every Christian conscience; and, wherever this is allowed, there is prayer in common. Finally, all are led to examine their own faithfulness to Christ's will for the church and accordingly to undertake with vigor the task of renewal and reform.

When such actions are undertaken prudently and patiently by the Catholic faithful, with the attentive guidance of their bishops, they promote justice and truth, concord and collaboration, as well as the spirit of love and unity. This is the way that, when the obstacles to perfect ecclesiastical communion have been gradually overcome, all Christians will at last, in a common celebration of the eucharist, be gathered into the unity of the one and only church. Christ bestowed this unity on his church from the beginning. We believe that it subsists in the Catholic Church as something she can never lose; and we cherish the hope that it will go on increasing until the end of time. However, it should be evident that, when individuals wish for full Catholic communion, their preparation and reconciliation is an undertaking which of its nature is distinct from ecumenical action. But there is no opposition between the two, since each proceeds from the marvelous providence of God. Catholics, in their ecumenical work, must assuredly be concerned for other Christians, praying for them, keeping them informed about the church, making the first approaches towards them. But their especial duty is to make a careful and honest appraisal of whatever needs to be renewed in the Catholic household itself, in order that its life may bear witness more faithfully and clearly to the teachings and ordinances which have come to it from Christ through the hands of the apostles.

For although the Catholic Church has been endowed with all divinely revealed truth and with all means of grace, yet its members fail to live by them with all the fervor that they should, so that the radiance of the church's image is less in the eyes of our separated fellow Christians and of the world at large, and the growth of God's kingdom is delayed. All Catholics must therefore aim at Christian perfection[20] and, each according to their situation, play their part that the church, bearing

20. See Jas 1.4; Rom 12.1-2.

in her own body the lowly and dying state of Jesus,[21] may be daily more purified and renewed, against the day when Christ will present her to himself in all her glory without spot or wrinkle.[22]

All in the church must preserve unity in essentials. But let all, according to the gifts they have received, maintain a proper freedom in their various forms of spiritual life and discipline, in their different liturgical rites, and even in their theological elaborations of revealed truth. In all things let charity prevail. If they are true to this course of action, they will be giving ever better expression to the authentic catholicity and apostolicity of the church.

On the other hand, Catholics must gladly acknowledge and esteem the truly Christian endowments which derive from our common heritage and which are to be found among our separated brothers and sisters. It is right and salutary to recognize the riches of Christ and the virtuous deeds in the lives of others who bear witness to Christ, even at times to the shedding of their blood. For God is always wonderful and his works too deserve our wonder.

Nor should we forget that anything wrought by the grace of the Holy Spirit in the hearts of our separated fellow Christians can be a help to our own edification. Whatever is truly Christian is never contrary to what genuinely belongs to the faith; indeed, it can always bring a deeper realization of the mystery of Christ and the church.

Nevertheless, the divisions among Christians prevent the church from realizing in practice the fullness of catholicity proper to her, in those of her sons and daughters who, though attached to her by baptism, are yet separated from full communion with her. Furthermore, the church herself finds it more difficult to express in actual life her full catholicity in all its bearings. This synod is gratified to note that the participation by the Catholic faithful in ecumenical work is growing daily. It recommends bishops everywhere in the world to stimulate this work intelligently and to guide it with prudence.

CHAPTER 2. THE PRACTICE OF ECUMENISM

5. The restoration of unity is the concern of the whole church, faithful and clergy alike. This concern extends to everyone according to their talents, whether it be exercised in ordinary Christian life or in theological and historical research. This very concern itself reveals to some extent the bond of fellowship between all Christians and it helps towards that full and perfect unity which God in his kindness wills.

21. See 2 Cor 4.10; Phil 2.5–8.
22. See Eph 5.27.

6. Every renewal of the church[1] essentially consists in an increase of fidelity to the church's own calling. Undoubtedly this is the reason for the movement towards unity. In its pilgrimage on earth Christ summons the church to continual reformation, of which it is always in need, in so far as it is an institution of human beings here on earth. Thus if, in various times and circumstances, there have been deficiencies in moral conduct or in church discipline, or even in the way that church teaching has been formulated—to be carefully distinguished from the deposit of faith itself—these should be set right in the proper way at the opportune moment.

Such renewal has therefore notable ecumenical importance. In various spheres of the church's life, this renewal is already taking place. The biblical and liturgical movements, the preaching of the word of God and catechetics, the apostolate of the laity, new forms of religious life, the spirituality of married life, and the church's social teaching and activity—all these should be considered as promises and guarantees for the future progress of ecumenism.

7. There can be no ecumenism worthy of the name without a change of heart. For it is from the renewal of our minds,[2] from self-denial and an unstinted love that desires of unity take their rise and develop. We should therefore pray to the Holy Spirit for the grace to be genuinely self-denying, humble, gentle in the service of others, and to have an attitude of generosity towards them. Saint Paul says: "I, therefore, a prisoner for the Lord, beg you to lead a life worthy of the calling to which you have been called, with all lowliness and meekness, with patience, forbearing one another in love, eager to maintain the unity of the Spirit in the bond of peace" (Eph 4.1–3). This exhortation is directed especially to those raised to sacred orders precisely so that the work of Christ may be continued, for he came among us "not to be served but to serve" (Mt 20.28).

The words of St. John hold good about sins against unity: "If we say we have not sinned, we make him a liar, and his word is not in us" (1 Jn 1.10). So we humbly beg pardon of God and of our separated sisters and brothers, just as we forgive them that trespass against us.

All the faithful should remember that the more effort they make to live holier lives according to the gospel, the better will they further Christian unity and put it into practice. For the closer their union with the Father, the Word, and the Spirit, the more deeply and easily will they be able to grow in mutual love.

8. This change of heart and holiness of life, along with public and private

1. See Lateran council V, session 12, constitution *Constituti*: Msi 32, 988 B-C.
2. See Eph 4.23.

prayer for the unity of Christians, should be regarded as the soul of the whole ecumenical movement, and merits the name "spiritual ecumenism."

It is a recognized custom for Catholics to have frequent recourse to that prayer for the unity of the church in which the Savior himself on the eve of his death so fervently appealed to his Father, "that they may all be one" (Jn 17.21). In certain special circumstances, such as the prescribed prayers "for unity," and during ecumenical gatherings, it is allowable and indeed desirable that Catholics should join in prayer with other Christians. Such prayers in common are certainly an effective means of obtaining the grace of unity, and they are a true expression of the ties which still bind Catholics to their separated fellow Christians: "for where two or three are gathered together in my name, there am I in the midst of them" (Mt 18.20).

Yet worship in common is not to be considered as a means to be used indiscriminately for the restoration of Christian unity. There are two main principles governing the practice of such common worship: first, the bearing witness to the unity of the church, and second, the sharing in the means of grace. Witness to the unity of the church generally forbids common worship, but the grace to be had from it sometimes commends this practice. The course to be adopted, with due regard to all the circumstances of time, place, and persons, is to be decided by local episcopal authority, unless it is otherwise determined by the bishops' conference according to its own statutes, or by the Holy See.

9. We must get to know the outlook of our separated fellow Christians. To achieve this purpose, study is of necessity required, and this must be pursued in fidelity to the truth and with goodwill. Catholics, if they are properly equipped for the task, need to acquire a more adequate understanding of the respective doctrines of other Christians, their history, their spiritual and liturgical life, their religious psychology and culture.

Most valuable for this purpose are meetings of the two sides—especially for discussion of theological problems—where each side can treat with the other on an equal footing, provided that those who take part in them under the guidance of their authorities are truly competent. From such dialogue will emerge still more clearly what the position of the Catholic Church really is. In this way too the outlook of our separated brothers and sisters will be better understood, and our own beliefs more aptly explained.

10. Theology and other branches of knowledge, especially of an historical nature, must be taught with a due regard for the ecumenical point of view, so that at every point they may correspond more exactly with the facts.

It is most important that future pastors and priests should have mastered a theology that has been carefully worked out in this way and not controversially, especially with regard to those aspects which concern the relations of separated Christians with the Catholic Church. For the instruction and spiritual formation of the faithful and of religious depends very largely on the formation which their priests have received.

Moreover, Catholics engaged in missionary work in the same territories as other Christians ought, particularly in these times, to know the problems and the benefits in their apostolate which derive from the ecumenical movement.

11. The way in which the Catholic faith is expressed should never become an obstacle to dialogue with other Christians. It is, of course, essential that the doctrine should be clearly presented in its entirety. Nothing is so alien to the spirit of ecumenism as a false irenicism, in which the purity of Catholic doctrine suffers loss and its assured and genuine meaning is clouded.

At the same time, the Catholic faith must be explained more profoundly and precisely, in such a way and in such terms as our separated fellow Christians also can really understand.

Furthermore, in ecumenical dialogue, when Catholic theologians join with other Christians in common study of the divine mysteries, while standing fast by the teaching of the church, they should pursue the work with love for the truth, with charity, and with humility. When comparing doctrines with one another, they should remember that in Catholic doctrine there exists an order or "hierarchy" of truths, since they vary in their connection with the foundation of the Christian faith. Thus the way will be opened for this kind of friendly emulation to incite all to a deeper awareness and a clearer manifestation of the unfathomable riches of Christ.[3]

12. Before the whole world let all Christians confess their faith in God, one and three, in the incarnate Son of God, our Redeemer and Lord. United in their efforts, and with mutual respect, let them bear witness to our hope which does not disappoint us. In these days when cooperation in social matters is so widespread, all people without exception are called to work together. This applies with much greater reason to all those who believe in God, and most of all, to Christians in that they bear the name of Christ. Cooperation among all Christians vividly expresses the relationship which in fact already unites them, and it sets in a clearer light the features of Christ the servant. Such cooperation, which has already begun in many countries, should be developed more and more, particularly in regions where a social and technical evolution is taking place. It should contribute to a just evaluation of the dignity of the human person, to the establishment of the blessings of peace,

3. See Eph 3.8.

the application of gospel principles to social life, and the advancement of the arts and sciences in a truly Christian spirit. It should employ every possible means to relieve the afflictions of our times such as famine and natural disasters, illiteracy and poverty, lack of housing, and the unequal distribution of wealth. All believers in Christ can, through such cooperation, easily learn to acquire a better knowledge and appreciation of one another, so as to make the road which leads to Christian unity more smooth.

CHAPTER 3. CHURCHES AND ECCLESIAL COMMUNITIES
SEPARATED FROM THE ROMAN APOSTOLIC SEE

13. We now turn our attention to the two chief types of division as they affect the seamless robe of Christ.

The first division occurred in the East, when the dogmatic formulas of the councils of Ephesus and Chalcedon were challenged, and later when ecclesiastical communion between the Eastern patriarchates and the Roman See was dissolved.

Other divisions arose more than four centuries later in the West, stemming from the events which are usually referred to as "the Reformation." As a result, many communions, national or confessional, were separated from the Roman See. Among those in which catholic traditions and institutions in part continue to subsist, the Anglican communion occupies a special place.

These various divisions differ greatly from one another not only by reason of their origins, place, and time, but still more in serious matters concerning belief and the structure of the church. Therefore, without minimizing the differences between the various Christian bodies, and without overlooking the bonds between them which exist in spite of these differences, this synod has decided to propose the following considerations for prudent ecumenical action.

1. The Special Position of the Eastern Churches

14. For many centuries the churches of the East and the West followed their separate ways though linked in a union of faith and sacramental life; the Roman See by common consent acted as guide when disagreements arose between them over matters of faith and discipline. Among other matters of moment, it is a pleasure for this synod to remind everyone that there exist in the East many particular or local churches, among which the patriarchal churches hold first place, and many of which are proud to trace their origins back to the apostles themselves. Hence a matter of primary concern and care among the Easterns has been, and still is, to

preserve the family ties of common faith and charity which ought to exist between local churches, as between sisters.

Similarly it must not be forgotten that from the beginning the churches of the East have had a treasury from which the Western church has drawn extensively — in liturgical practice, spiritual tradition, and canon law. Nor must we undervalue the fact that it was the ecumenical councils held in the East that defined the basic dogmas of the Christian faith, on the Trinity and on the Word of God, who took flesh of the Virgin Mary. To preserve this faith these churches have suffered and still suffer much.

However, the inheritance handed on by the apostles was received with differences of form and manner, and from the earliest times of the church it was explained variously in different places, owing to diversities of character and condition of life. All this, quite apart from external causes, prepared the way for divisions arising also from a lack of mutual understanding and charity.

For this reason this synod urges all, but especially those who intend to devote themselves to the restoration of full communion which is desired between the churches of the East and the Catholic Church, to give due consideration to this special feature of the origin and growth of the Eastern churches, and to the character of the relations which obtained between them and the Roman See before separation, and to learn to give due weight to all these factors. Where this is done, it will greatly contribute to the dialogue in view.

15. Everyone knows with what great love the Christians of the East celebrate the sacred liturgy, especially the eucharistic mystery, which is the source of the church's life and the pledge of future glory. In this celebration the faithful, united with their bishop, have access to God the Father through the Son, the Word made flesh, suffering, and glorified, and so, in the outpouring of the Holy Spirit, they enter into communion with the most Holy Trinity, being made "partakers of the divine nature" (2 Pt 1.4). Hence, through the celebration of the holy eucharist in each of these churches, the church of God is built up and grows,[1] and through concelebration their communion with one another is made manifest. In their liturgical worship, the Christians of the East pay high tribute, in beautiful hymns, to Mary Ever-Virgin, whom the ecumenical Synod of Ephesus solemnly proclaimed to be the Holy Mother of God, so that Christ might be acknowledged as being truly and properly Son of God and Son of man, according to the Scriptures. Many also are the saints whose praise they sing, among them the fathers of the universal church.

These churches, though separated from us, yet possess true sacraments,

---

1. See John Chrysostom, *In Ioannem Homelia (Homilies on John)*, 46: PG 59, 260–262.

above all, by apostolic succession, the priesthood, and the eucharist, whereby they are still linked with us in closest intimacy. Therefore some worship in common, given suitable circumstances and the approval of church authority, is not merely possible but to be encouraged.

Moreover, in the East are to be found the riches of those spiritual traditions which are given expression especially in monastic life. From the glorious times of the holy fathers, monastic spirituality flourished in the East, then later flowed over into the Western world, and there provided the source from which Latin monastic life took its rise and has drawn fresh vigor ever since. Catholics therefore are earnestly recommended to avail themselves still more of these spiritual riches of the Eastern fathers which lift up the whole person to the contemplation of the divine.

All should recognize that to know, venerate, preserve, and cherish the rich liturgical and spiritual heritage of the Eastern churches is of supreme importance for the faithful preservation of the fullness of Christian tradition, and for bringing about reconciliation between Eastern and Western Christians.

16. Moreover from the earliest times the Eastern churches followed their own disciplines, which were sanctioned by the approval of the fathers of the church and of synods, even of ecumenical synods. Far from being an obstacle to the church's unity, a certain diversity of customs and observances only adds to her beauty and is of great help in carrying out her mission, as has been stated. To remove all shadow of doubt, then, this synod solemnly declares that the churches of the East, while mindful of the necessary unity of the whole church, have the right to govern themselves according to the disciplines proper to themselves, since these are better suited to the character of their faithful, and more for the good of their souls. The perfect observance of this principle which is sanctioned by long-standing tradition, but in fact has not always been followed, is one of the essential prerequisities for the restoration of unity.

17. What has just been said about legitimate variety must also be taken to apply to the differences in theological expression of doctrine. In the study of revelation East and West have followed different methods, and taken different steps, towards their understanding and confession of God's truth. It is hardly surprising, then, if from time to time one tradition has come nearer to a full appreciation of some aspects of a mystery of revelation than the other, or has expressed it to better advantage. In such cases, these various theological expressions are often to be considered as mutually complementary rather than conflicting. Where the authentic theological traditions of the Eastern church are concerned, we must recognize the admirable way in which they have their roots in Holy Scripture, how they are nurtured and given expression in liturgical life, how they derive their strength from the

living tradition of the apostles and from the works of the fathers and the spiritual writers of the Eastern churches, and how they promote the right ordering of life and, indeed, pave the way to the full contemplation of Christian truth.

This synod thanks God that many Eastern daughters and sons of the Catholic Church, who preserve this heritage and wish to express it more faithfully and completely in their lives, are already living in full communion with their brothers and sisters who follow the tradition of the West. It declares that all this heritage of spirituality and liturgy, of discipline and theology, in its various traditions, belongs to the full catholic and apostolic character of the church.

18. After taking all these factors into consideration, this holy synod solemnly repeats the declaration of previous councils and Roman pontiffs, that for the restoration or the maintenance of unity and communion it is necessary "to impose no burden beyond what is essential" (Acts 15.28). It is the synod's urgent desire that, in the various organizations and forms of church life, every effort should be made towards the gradual realization of this unity, especially by prayer and by amicable discussions on points of doctrine and on the more pressing pastoral problems of our time. Similarly, the synod commends to the pastors and faithful of the Catholic Church the development of close relations with those who are no longer living in the East but are far from home, so that friendly collaboration with them may increase, in the spirit of love, to the exclusion of all feeling of rivalry or strife. If this cause is wholeheartedly promoted, the synod hopes that the barrier dividing the church between East and West will be removed, and that at last there may be but the one dwelling, firmly established on Christ Jesus, the cornerstone, who will make both one.[2]

2. Separated Churches and Ecclesial Communities in the West

19. The churches and ecclesial communities which came to be separated from the apostolic see of Rome in the great upheaval which began in the West at the end of the Middle Ages and in later times too, have retained a special affinity and close relationship with the Catholic Church as a result of the long centuries in which all Christendom lived together in ecclesiastical communion.

However, since these churches and ecclesial communities, on account of their differences of origin, doctrine, and spirituality, differ considerably not only from us but also among themselves, the task of describing them adequately is extremely difficult; and we have no intention of making such an attempt here.

---

2. See council of Florence, session 6, definition *Laetentur caeli:* Msi 31, 1026 E.

Although the ecumenical movement and the desire for peace with the Catholic Church have not yet taken hold everywhere, it is our hope that among all Christians ecumenical feeling and mutual esteem may gradually increase. It must however be admitted that in these churches and ecclesial communities there exist important differences from the Catholic Church, not only of an historical, sociological, psychological, and cultural character, but especially in the interpretation of revealed truth. To make easier the establishment of ecumenical dialogue in spite of these differences, we wish to set down some considerations which can, and indeed should, serve as a basis and encouragement for such dialogue.

20. Our thoughts turn first to those Christians who make open confession to Jesus Christ as God and Lord and as the one Mediator between God and human beings, to the glory of the one God, Father, Son, and Holy Spirit. We are aware indeed that there exist considerable divergences from the doctrine of the Catholic Church even concerning Christ himself, the Word of God made flesh, the work of redemption, and, consequently, concerning the mystery and ministry of the church, and the role of Mary in the work of salvation. But we rejoice to see that our separated fellow Christians look to Christ as the source and center of ecclesiastical communion. Their longing for union with Christ inspires them to seek an ever closer unity, and also to bear witness to their faith among all nations everywhere.

21. Love and reverence, almost a cult, for Holy Scripture leads our brothers and sisters to a constant and expert study of the Sacred Text. For the gospel "is the power of God for salvation to every one who has faith, to the Jew first and then to the Greek" (Rom 1.16).

Calling upon the Holy Spirit, they seek God in the Scriptures as speaking to them in Christ, the Word of God made flesh for us, whom the prophets foretold. They contemplate in the Scriptures the life of Christ and what the divine Master taught and did for our salvation, especially the mysteries of his death and resurrection.

But while our separated fellow Christians hold strongly to the divine authority of the Sacred Books, they differ from us—some in one way, some in another—regarding the relationship between Scripture and the church. For, according to catholic belief, the authentic teaching office has a special place in the interpretation and preaching of the written word of God.

But the sacred utterances provide for the work of dialogue an instrument of the highest value in the mighty hand of God for the attainment of that unity which the Savior holds out to all.

22. Whenever the sacrament of baptism is duly administered as our Lord instituted it, and is received with the right dispositions, a person is truly incorpo-

rated into the crucified and glorified Christ, and reborn to a sharing of the divine life, as the apostle says: "you were buried together with him in baptism, in which you were also raised with him through faith in the working of God, who raised him from the dead" (Col 2.12).[3]

Thus baptism establishes a sacramental bond of unity existing among all who have been reborn by it. But of itself baptism is only a beginning, an inauguration wholly directed towards the acquisition of the fullness of life in Christ. Baptism, therefore, is oriented towards the complete profession of faith, complete incorporation into the institution of salvation such as Christ willed it to be, and finally the completeness of unity which eucharistic communion gives.

Though the ecclesial communities which are separated from us lack the fullness of unity with us which flows from baptism, and though we believe they have not retained the authentic and full reality of the eucharistic mystery, especially because the sacrament of orders is lacking, nevertheless when they commemorate his death and resurrection in the Lord's supper, they profess that it signifies life in communion with Christ and look forward to his coming in glory. For these reasons dialogue should include among its subjects the Lord's supper and other sacraments, worship, and the church's ministry.

23. The daily Christian lives of these our sisters and brothers are nourished by their faith in Christ and strengthened by the grace of baptism and by hearing the word of God. This shows itself in their private prayer, their meditation on the Bible, in their Christian family life, and in the worship of a community gathered together to praise God. Moreover, their form of worship not seldom displays notable features of the ancient common liturgy. Their faith in Christ bears fruit in praise and thanksgiving for the good things received from the hands of God. Among them, too, is a strong sense of justice and a true charity towards others. This active faith has been responsible for many organizations for the relief of spiritual and material distress, the advancement of the education of youth, the establishment of more humane social conditions of life, and the promotion of peace throughout the world.

While it is true that some Christians do not always understand the moral teaching of the gospel in the same way as Catholics, and do not accept the same solutions to the more difficult problems of modern society, nevertheless they share our desire to stand by the word of Christ as the source of Christian virtue, and to obey the command of the apostle: "Whatever you do, in word or in work, do all in the name of the Lord Jesus Christ, giving thanks to God the Father through him"

3. See Rom 6.4.

(Col 3.17). For that reason an ecumenical dialogue might start with discussion of the application of the gospel to moral questions.

24. Now that we have briefly set out the conditions for ecumenical action and the principles by which it is to be directed, we look with confidence to the future. This holy synod exhorts the faithful to avoid not only all superficiality but also any importunate zeal, either of which would only hinder real progress towards unity. Their ecumenical action must be fully and sincerely catholic, that is to say, faithful to the truth which we have received from the apostles and fathers, in harmony with the faith which the Catholic Church has always professed, and at the same time directed towards that fullness to which our Lord wills his body to grow in the course of time.

It is the urgent wish of this holy synod that the measures undertaken by the sons and daughters of the Catholic Church should in practice develop in conjunction with those of our separated sisters and brothers, so as to place no obstacle to the ways of divine providence and to avoid prejudging the future inspirations of the Holy Spirit. The synod moreover professes its awareness that human powers and capacities cannot achieve this holy objective—the reconciling of all Christians in the unity of the one and only church of Christ. It is because of this that the synod grounds its hope deeply on Christ's prayer for the church, on the Father's love for us, and on the power of the Holy Spirit. "And hope does not disappoint us, because God's love has been poured into our hearts through the Holy Spirit, who has been given to us" (Rom 5.5).

8. Die verbum: Dogmatic Constitution on Divine Revelation
Introduction

1. The word of God calls for reverent attention and confident proclamation. In response this council does as St. John says: "We proclaim to you the eternal life which was with the Father and was made manifest to us—that which we have seen and heard we proclaim also to you, so that you may have fellowship with us, and that our fellowship may be with the Father and with his Son Jesus Christ" (1 Jn 1.2–3). This council aims, then, following in the steps of the councils of Trent and Vatican I, to set forth authentic teaching on God's revelation and how it is communicated, desiring that the whole world may hear the message of salvation, and thus grow from hearing to faith, from faith to hope, and from hope to love.[1]

1. See Augustine, *De catechizandis rudibus (On catechizing the uninstructed)*, 4, 8: PL 40, 316; CChr 46, 128.

CHAPTER I. REVELATION IN ITSELF

2. It has pleased God, in his goodness and wisdom, to reveal himself and to make known the secret purpose of his will (see Eph 1.9). This brings it about that through Christ, God's Word made flesh, and in his Holy Spirit, human beings can draw near to the Father and become sharers in the divine nature (see Eph 2.18; 2 Pt 1.4). By thus revealing himself God, who is invisible (see Col 1.15; 1 Tm 1.17), in his great love speaks to humankind as friends (see Ex 33.11; Jn 15.14–15) and enters into their life (see Bar 3.38), so as to invite and receive them into relationship with himself. The pattern of this revelation unfolds through deeds and words bound together by an inner dynamism, in such a way that God's works, effected during the course of the history of salvation, show forth and confirm the doctrine and the realities signified by the words, while the words in turn proclaim the works and throw light on the meaning hidden in them. By this revelation the truth, both about God and about the salvation of humankind, inwardly dawns on us in Christ, who is in himself both the Mediator and the fullness of all revelation.[2]

3. God creates and conserves all things through his Word (see Jn 1.3). In the created order he offers to humankind a lasting testimony to himself (see Rom 1.19–20). Further, in his plan to open up the way of heavenly salvation, he made himself known to our first parents from the beginning. After their fall he aroused them to hope for salvation by the promise of redemption (see Gn 3.15), and he has constantly kept the human race in his care, so as to grant eternal life to all those who persevere in doing good in search of salvation (see Rom 2.6–7). In his good time he called Abraham, in order to make of him a great nation (see Gn 12.2–3). After the era of the patriarchs, he taught this nation, through Moses and the prophets, to acknowledge himself as the only living and true God, the all-caring Father and just judge, and to wait for the promised Savior. In this way, down the centuries, he prepared the way for the gospel.

4. After God had spoken in many and various ways by the prophets, "in these last days he has spoken to us by a Son" (Heb 1.1–2). He sent his Son, the eternal Word who enlightens all humankind, to live among them and to tell them about the inner life of God (see Jn 1.1–18). Thus it is that Jesus Christ, the Word made flesh, sent as a human being among humans,[3] "speaks the words of God" (Jn 3.34) and accomplishes the work of salvation which the Father gave him to do (see Jn 5.36, 17.4). To see Jesus is to see his Father also (see Jn 14.9). This is why Jesus completes the work of revelation and confirms it by divine testimony. He did this

---

2. See Mt 11.27; Jn 1.14, 17, 14.6, 17.1–3; 2 Cor 3.16, 4.6; Eph 1.3–14.
3. *Letter to Diognetus*, 7, 4: ed. F. X. Funk, *Patres Apostolici*, Tübingen 1901, I, p. 403.

by the total reality of his presence and self-manifestation—by his words and works, his symbolic acts and miracles, but above all by his death and his glorious resurrection from the dead, crowned by his sending the Spirit of truth. His message is that God is with us, to deliver us from the darkness of sin and death, and to raise us up to eternal life.

The Christian dispensation is the new and definitive covenant. It follows that it will never pass away, and that no new public revelation is to be expected before the glorious manifestation of our Lord Jesus Christ (see 1 Tm 6.14 and Ti 2.13).

5. In response to God's revelation our duty is "the obedience of faith" (see Rom 16.26; compare Rom 1.5; 2 Cor 10.5–6). By this, a human being makes a total and free self-commitment to God, offering "the full submission of intellect and will to God as he reveals,"[4] and willingly assenting to the revelation he gives. For this faith to be accorded we have need of God's grace, both anticipating and then accompanying our act, together with the inward assistance of the Holy Spirit, who works to stir the heart and turn it towards God, to open the eyes of the mind, and to give "to all facility in accepting and believing the truth."[5] The same Holy Spirit constantly perfects faith by his gifts, to bring about an ever deeper understanding of revelation.

6. By divine revelation God has chosen to manifest and communicate both himself and the eternal decrees of his will for the salvation of humankind, "so as to share those divine treasures which totally surpass human understanding."[6]

This council reaffirms that "God, the first principle and last end of all things, can be known with certainty from the created order by the natural light of human reason" (see Rom 1.20). Further, this teaching is to be held about revelation: "In the present condition of the human race, even those truths about God which are not beyond the reach of human reason, require revelation for them to be known by all without great effort, with firm certainty, and without error entering in."[7]

---

4. Vatican council I, Dogmatic constitution on the Catholic faith, *Dei Filius*, ch. 3: D 1789 (3008).

5. Council of Orange II (529), canon 7: D 180 (377); Vatican council I, loc. cit.: D 1791 93010).

6. Vatican council I, Dogmatic constitution on the Catholic faith, *Dei Filius*, ch. 2: D 1786 (3005).

7. Ibid.: D 1785 and 1786 (3004 and 3005).

CHAPTER 2. THE TRANSMISSION OF DIVINE REVELATION

7. God in his goodness arranged that whatever he had revealed for the salvation of all nations should last forever in its integrity and be handed on to all generations. Accordingly Christ our Lord, in whom the whole revelation of God is summed up (see 2 Cor 1.20, 3.16–4.6), entrusted the apostles with his gospel. This had been promised through the prophets; he revealed its fullness and published it by his own lips, to be a universal source of saving truth and moral teaching.[1] This gospel the apostles were to preach to all peoples, sharing God's gifts with them. This has in fact been faithfully carried out. The apostles handed on, by their own preaching and examples and by their dispositions, whatever they had received from Christ's lips, his way of life, or his works, or had learned by the prompting of the Holy Spirit; secondly, some apostles, with others of the apostolic age, under the interior guidance of the same Spirit, committed the message of salvation to writing.[2]

In order that the gospel should be preserved in the church forever living and integral, the apostles left as their successors the bishops, "handing on their own teaching function" to them.[3] By this link, this sacred tradition and the Sacred Scripture of the two Testaments are like a mirror in which the church, during its pilgrimage of earth, contemplates God, the source of all that it has received, until it is brought home to see him face to face as he is (see 1 Jn 3.2).

8. Thus the apostolic preaching, which is expressed in a special way in the inspired books, was to be preserved by a continuous succession until the end of time. This is why the apostles, handing on what they had received, warn the faithful to hold fast the traditions which they had learned, either by word of mouth or by letter (see 2 Thes 2.15), and to fight for the faith that had been delivered to them once for all (see Jude 3).[4] The expression "what has been handed down from the apostles" includes everything that helps the people of God to live a holy life and to grow in faith. In this way the church, in its teaching, life, and worship, perpetuates and hands on to every generation all that it is and all that it believes.

This tradition which comes from the apostles progresses in the church un-

1. See Mt 28.19–20 and Mk 16.15. Council of Trent, Decree *On the canonical Scriptures*: D 783 (1501).

2. See council of Trent, loc. cit.; Vatican council I, Dogmatic constitution on the Catholic faith, *Dei Filius*, ch. 2: D 1787 (3006).

3. Irenaeus, *Adv. Haer. (Against Heresies)*, III, 3, 1: PG 7, 848; Harvey, 2, p. 9.

4. See council of Nicaea II: D 303 (602). Council of Constantinople IV, session 10, canon 1: D 336 (650–652).

der the assistance of the Holy Spirit.[5] There is growth in understanding of what is handed on, both the words and the realities they signify. This comes about through contemplation and study by believers, who "ponder these things in their hearts" (see Lk 2.19, 51); through the intimate understanding of spiritual things which they experience; and through the preaching of those who, on succeeding to the office of bishop, receive the sure charism of truth. Thus, as the centuries advance, the church constantly holds its course towards the fullness of God's truth, until the day when the words of God reach their fulfillment in the church.

The fathers of the church bear witness to the enlivening presence of this tradition, and show how its riches flow into the practice and life of the believing and praying church. By this tradition comes the church's knowledge of the full canon of biblical books; by this too, the Scripture itself comes to be more profoundly understood and to realize its power in the church. In this way the God who spoke of old still maintains an uninterrupted conversation with the bride of his beloved Son. The Holy Spirit, too, is active, making the living voice of the gospel ring out in the church, and through it in the world, leading those who believe into the whole truth, and making the message of Christ dwell in them in all its richness (see Col 3.16).

9. Hence sacred tradition and Scripture are bound together in a close and reciprocal relationship. They both flow from the same divine wellspring, merge together to some extent, and are on course towards the same end. Scripture is the utterance of God as it is set down in writing under the guidance of God's Spirit; tradition preserves the word of God as it was entrusted to the apostles by Christ our Lord and the Holy Spirit, and transmits it to their successors, so that these in turn, enlightened by the Spirit of truth, may faithfully preserve, expound, and disseminate the word by their preaching. Consequently, the church's certainty about all that is revealed is not drawn from Holy Scripture alone; both Scripture and tradition are to be accepted and honored with like devotion and reverence.[6]

10. Tradition and Scripture together form a single sacred deposit of the word of God, entrusted to the church. Holding fast to this, the entire holy people, united with its pastors, perseveres always faithful to the apostles' teaching and shared life, to the breaking of bread and prayer (see Acts 2.42 Greek text). Thus, as they hold, practice, and witness to the heritage of the faith, bishops and faithful display a unique harmony.[7]

---

5. See Vatican council I, Dogmatic constitution on the Catholic faith, *Dei Filius,* ch. 4: D 1800 (3020).

6. See council of Trent, Decree *On the canonical Scriptures:* D 783 (1501).

7. See Pius XII, Apostolic constitution *Munificentissimus Deus,* 1 Nov. 1950: AAS 42 (1950),

The task of authentically interpreting the word of God, whether in its written form or in that of tradition,[8] has been entrusted only to those charged with the church's ongoing teaching function,[9] whose authority is exercised in the name of Jesus Christ. This teaching function is not above the word of God but stands at its service, teaching nothing but what is handed down, according as it devotedly listens, reverently preserves, and faithfully transmits the word of God, by divine command and with the help of the Holy Spirit. All that it proposes for belief, as being divinely revealed, is drawn from the one deposit of faith.

Thus it is clear that, by God's wise design, tradition, Scripture, and the church's teaching function are so connected and associated that one does not stand without the others, but all together, and each in its own way, subject to the action of the one Holy Spirit, contribute effectively to the salvation of souls.

CHAPTER 3. THE DIVINE INSPIRATION OF HOLY SCRIPTURE AND ITS INTERPRETATION

11. Those things revealed by God which are contained and presented in the text of Holy Scripture were written under the influence of the Holy Spirit. By the faith handed down from the apostles, Holy Mother Church accepts as sacred and canonical all the books of both the Old Testament and the New, in their entirety and with all their parts, in the conviction that they were written under the inspiration of the Holy Spirit (see Jn 20.31; 2 Tm 3.16; 2 Pt 1.19-21, 3.15-16) and therefore have God as their originator: on this basis they were handed on to the church.[1] In the process of composition of the Sacred Books God chose and employed human agents, using their own powers and faculties,[2] in such a way that they wrote as authors in the true sense, and yet God acted in and through them,[3] directing the content entirely and

p. 756. Compare the words of Cyprian, *Epist. (Letters)*, 66, 8: CSEL 3, 2, 733: "The church [is] the people united with the priest, the flock adhering to its shepherd."

8. See Vatican council I, Dogmatic constitution on the Catholic faith, *Dei Filius*, ch. 3: D 1792 (3011).

9. See Pius XII, Encyclical *Humani Generis*, 12 Aug. 1950: AAS 42 (1950), pp. 568–569: D 2314 (3886).

1. See Vatican council I, Dogmatic constitution on the Catholic faith, *Dei Filius*, ch. 2: D 1787 (3006). Pontifical biblical commission, Decree of 18 June 1915: D 2180 (3629); EB 420. Holy Office, Letter of 22 Dec. 1923: EB 499.

2. See Pius XII, Encyclical *Divino afflante*, 30 Sept. 1943: AAS 35 (1943), p. 314; EB 556.

3. *In* and *through* human beings: see Heb 1.1, 4.7 (*in*): 2 Kg 23.2; Mt 1.22 and passim (*through*); Vatican council I, Schema on Catholic doctrine, note 9: Collectio Lacensis, VII, 522.

solely as he willed.[4] It follows that we should hold that whatever the inspired authors or "sacred writers" affirm, is affirmed by the Holy Spirit; we must acknowledge that the books of Scripture teach firmly, faithfully, and without error such truth as God, for the sake of our salvation, wished the biblical text to contain.[5] Therefore "all Scripture is inspired by God and profitable for teaching, for reproof, for correction, and for training in righteousness, that the man of God may be complete, equipped for every good work" (2 Tm 3.16–17 Greek text).

12. Now since in the Bible God has spoken through human agents to humans,[6] if the interpreter of Holy Scripture is to understand what God has wished to communicate to us, he must carefully investigate what meaning the biblical writers actually had in mind; that will also be what God chose to manifest through their words.

In order to get at what the biblical writers intended, attention should be paid (among other things) to *literary genres.*

This is because truth is presented and expressed differently in historical, prophetic, or poetic texts, or in other styles of speech. The interpreter has to look for that meaning which a biblical writer intended and expressed in his particular circumstances, and in his historical and cultural context, by means of such literary genres as were in use at his time.[7] To understand correctly what a biblical writer intended to assert, due attention is needed both to the customary and characteristic ways of feeling, speaking, and storytelling which were current in his time, and to the social conventions of the period.[8]

Further, Holy Scripture requires to be read and interpreted in the light of the same Spirit through whom it was written.[9] Consequently a right understand-

4. Leo XIII, Encyclical *Providentissimus Deus*, 18 Nov. 1893: D 1952 (3293); EB 125.

5. See Augustine, *De Gen. ad litt. (On the words of Genesis)*, 2, 9, 20: PL 34, 270–271; CSEL 28, 1, 46–47; and *Epist. (Letters)*, 82, 3: PL 33, 277; CSEL 34, 2, 354. Thomas Aquinas, *De Veritate*, quest. 12, art. 2, C. Council of Trent, Decree *On the canonical Scriptures:* D 783 (1501). Leo XIII, Encyclical *Providentissimus Deus:* EB 121, 124, 126–127. Pius XII, Encyclical *Divino afflante:* EB 539.

6. See Augustine, *De Civ. Dei (City of God)*, XVII, 6, 2: PL 41, 537; CSEL 40, 2, 228; CChr 48, 567.

7. See Augustine, *De Doctr. Christ. (On Christian Doctrine)*, III, 18, 26: PL 34, 75–76; CSEL 80, 95; CChr 32, 93.

8. See Pius XII, loc. cit.: D 2294 (3829–3830); EB 557–562.

9. See Benedict XV, Encyclical *Spiritus Paraclitus*, 15 Sept. 1920: EB 469. Jerome, *In Gal. (On Galatians)*, 5, 19–21: PL 26, 417 A.

ing of the Sacred Texts demands attention, no less than that mentioned above, to the content and coherence of Scripture as a whole, taking into account the whole church's living tradition and the sense of perspective given by faith. It is the function of exegetes to work, in accord with these rules, towards a more perceptive understanding and exposition of the meaning of Holy Scripture, so that through their study the church's judgment may mature. All that concerns the way to interpret Scripture is ultimately subject to the judgment of the church, to which God has entrusted the commission and ministry of preserving and interpreting the word of God.[10]

13. In Holy Scripture, together with the manifestation of God's truth and holiness, we see the eternal wisdom stoop down, as it were, "to teach us God's inexpressible kindness, and how thoughtfully he has accommodated his way of speaking to our nature."[11] Indeed, God's words, expressed through human language, have taken on the likeness of human speech, just as the Word of the eternal Father, when he assumed the flesh of human weakness, took on the likeness of human beings.

CHAPTER 4. THE OLD TESTAMENT

14. God in his supreme love and concern intended the salvation of the entire human race. In preparation for this, by a special plan, he chose a people for himself, to entrust with his promises. By making his covenant with Abraham (see Gn 15.18) and with the people of Israel through Moses (see Ex 24.8) he "acquired" a people for himself, and by words and acts revealed himself to it as the only God, true and living. His purpose was that Israel might learn by experience how God acts towards human beings; that, as he spoke through the prophets, his people might understand his ways ever more deeply and clearly, and demonstrate them more widely to the nations (see Ps 22.27-28, 96.1-3; Is 2.1-4; Jer 3.17). This plan and pattern of salvation—foretold, recounted, and explained by the biblical writers—is there to read, as the true word of God, in the books of the Old Testament. These books, therefore, written as they are under divine inspiration, retain lasting value: "Whatever was written in former days was written for our instruction, that by steadfastness and by the encouragement of the Scriptures we might have hope" (Rom 15.4).

15. The plan and pattern of the Old Testament was directed above all towards the coming of Christ, the universal Redeemer, and of the messianic kingdom:

---

10. See Vatican council I, Dogmatic constitution on the Catholic faith, *Dei Filius,* ch. 2: D 1788 (3007).

11. John Chrysostom, *In Gen. (On Genesis),* 3, 8 (homily 17, 1): PG 53, 134. "Accommodated," Greek συγκατάβασις.

to prepare for this, to announce it prophetically (see Lk 24.44; Jn 5.39; 1 Pt 1.10) and to point towards it by various foreshadowing symbols (see 1 Cor 10.11). The Old Testament books manifest to all readers the knowledge of God and of humankind, and how God in his justice and mercy acts towards them, in the context of human history before the era of salvation brought by Christ. These books, though they also contain things that are imperfect and of merely temporary value, still demonstrate God's ways of teaching.[1] They ought therefore to be accepted by Christians, because they express a vivid sense of God, because they enshrine sublime teaching about God, salutary wisdom for human life, and wonderful treasures of prayer, and finally because in the Old Testament books our salvation in Christ is hinted at under signs and symbols.

16. Thus God, the inspirer and originator of the books of both Testaments, has brought it about in his wisdom that the New Testament should be hidden in the Old, and the Old Testament should be made manifest in the New.[2] Though Christ established the new covenant in his blood (see Lk 22.20; 1 Cor 11.25), nevertheless the Old Testament books, all and entire, were retained in the preaching of the gospel;[3] in the New Testament they acquire and display their full meaning (see Mt 5.17; Lk 24.27; Rom 16.25–26; 2 Cor 3.14–16), and in their turn they shed light on it and explain it.

CHAPTER 5. THE NEW TESTAMENT

17. The word of God, which is the power of God for salvation to everyone who has faith (see Rom 1.16), is presented and shows its force supremely in the writings of the New Testament. When the fullness of time came (see Gal 4.4), the Word became flesh and dwelt among us, full of grace and truth (see Jn 1.14). Christ inaugurated the reign of God on earth, manifested his Father and himself by deeds and words, and completed his work by his death, resurrection, and glorious ascension, and by sending the Holy Spirit. Lifted up from the earth, he draws all to himself (see Jn 12.32 Greek text)—he who alone has the words of eternal life (see Jn 6.68). This is a mystery which was not made known to other generations as it has now been revealed to his holy apostles and prophets through the Holy Spirit (see Eph 3.4–6

1. See Pius XI, Encyclical *Mit brennender Sorge*, 14 March 1937: AAS 29 (1937), p. 151.
2. See Augustine, *Quaest. in Hept. (Questions on the Heptateuch)*, 2, 73: PL 34, 623; CChr 33, 106.
3. See Irenaeus, *Adv. Haer. (Against Heresies)*, III, 21, 3: PG 7, 950; (= 25, 1) Harvey, 2, p. 115. Cyril of Jerusalem, *Catech. (Catecheses)*, 4, 35: PG 33, 497. Theodore of Mopsuestia, *In Soph. (On Zephaniah)*, 1, 4–6: PG 66, 452D–453A.

Greek text), so that they might preach the gospel, stir up faith in Jesus as Christ and Lord, and bring together the church. The writings of the New Testament stand as a perpetual and divine testimony to all this.

18. It is evident that among all the inspired writings, even those of the New Testament, the Gospels rightly have the supreme place, because they form the primary testimony to the life and teaching of the incarnate Word, our Savior.

The four Gospels originate from the apostles, as the church has held always and everywhere and still holds. The apostles preached as Christ had charged them to do. Then, under the guidance of the Spirit of God, they and others of the apostolic age delivered to us the same preaching in writing, as the foundation of our faith, the fourfold Gospel, according to Matthew, Mark, Luke, and John.[1]

19. Holy Mother Church has firmly and constantly held, and continues to hold and unhesitatingly assert, that the four Gospels just named are historical documents and faithfully communicate what Jesus, the Son of God, during his life among men and women, actually did and taught for their eternal salvation, until the day when he was taken up (see Acts 1.1–2). First the apostles, after the Lord's ascension, passed on to their hearers what he had said and done, but—having learned by experiencing the glorious events of Christ and by enlightenment from the Spirit of truth[2]—with the fuller insight which they now possessed.[3] Next, inspired writers composed the four Gospels, by various processes. They selected some things from the abundant material already handed down, orally or in writing. Other things they synthesized, or explained with a view to the needs of the churches. They preserved the preaching style, but worked throughout so as to communicate to us a true and sincere account of Jesus;[4] for whether they wrote from their own memory and recollections, or from the evidence of "those who from the beginning were eyewitnesses and ministers of the word," their intention was that we might know "the truth" concerning the things of which we have been informed (see Lk 1.2–4).

20. Besides the four Gospels, the New Testament canon also contains the letters of St. Paul and other apostolic writings, which were also composed under the inspiration of the Holy Spirit. By God's wise plan, these writings contain confirmation of what is told about Christ, give further explanation of his authentic teaching, preach about how Christ's divine work has power to save, tell the story of the

1. See Irenaeus, *Adv. Haer. (Against Heresies)*, III, 11, 8: PG 7, 885; ed. Sagnard, p. 194.

2. See Jn 14.26, 16.13.

3. See Jn 2.22, 12.16; compare 14.26, 16.12–13, 7.39.

4. See the instruction *Sancta Mater Ecclesia* of the Pontifical Biblical Commission: AAS 56 (1964), p. 715.

church's beginnings and wonderful expansion, and foretell its glorious consummation.

For the Lord Jesus was with the apostles as he had promised (see Mt 28.20), and he sent them the Spirit, the counselor, to lead them into the fullness of truth (see Jn 16.13).

CHAPTER 6. HOLY SCRIPTURE IN THE LIFE OF THE CHURCH

21. The church has always held the Divine Scriptures in reverence no less than it accords to the Lord's body itself, never ceasing—especially in the sacred liturgy—to receive the bread of life from the one table of God's word and Christ's body, and to offer it to the faithful. The church has kept and keeps the Scriptures, together with tradition, as the supreme rule of its faith, since the Bible, being inspired by God and committed to writing once for all, communicates the word of God in an unalterable form, makes the voice of the Holy Spirit sound through the words of the prophets and the apostles. Accordingly all the church's preaching, no less than the whole Christian religion, ought to be nourished and ruled by Holy Scripture. In the Sacred Books the Father who is in heaven comes lovingly to meet his children and talks with them. There is such force and power in the word of God that it stands as the church's support and strength, affording her children sturdiness in faith, food for the soul, and a pure and unfailing fount of spiritual life. It is supremely true of Holy Scripture that "the word of God is living and active" (Heb 4.12), "which is able to build you up and to give you the inheritance among all those who are sanctified" (Acts 20.32; see 1 Thes 2.13).

22. Easy access to Holy Scripture should be available to all the Christian faithful. This is why, from the very beginning, the church took as its own the ancient translation of the Old Testament called the Septuagint; it also keeps in honor the other versions, in Oriental languages and in Latin, especially that known as the Vulgate. Further, since the word of God ought to be available at all times, the church, with motherly care, sees to it that appropriate and correct translations are made into different languages, especially from the original texts of the Sacred Books. If the opportunity arises, and church authority approves, such versions may be prepared in collaboration with Christians of other denominations; all Christians will then be able to use them.

23. The church, the "spouse of the incarnate Word," taught by the Holy Spirit, strives to attain, day by day, to an ever deeper understanding of Holy Scripture, so that she may never fail to nourish her children with God's utterances. With this in view the church appropriately encourages the study also of the fathers of the church, both Eastern and Western, and of the sacred liturgies. Catholic exegetes and

other theologians should work together, under the eye of the church's teaching authority, taking all suitable means to study and expound the Bible, so that ministers of the word may be able, as widely as possible, to nourish God's people with the food of the Scriptures, and so produce the effect of enlightening minds, strengthening wills, and firing hearts with the love of God.[1] The synod encourages those members of the church who are engaged in biblical studies to renew their efforts and forge ahead, thinking with the church, in the work they have so happily undertaken.[2]

24. Sacred theology takes its stand on the written word of God, together with tradition, as its permanent foundation. By this word it is made firm and strong, and constantly renews its youth, as it investigates, by the light of faith, all the truth that is stored up in the mystery of Christ. The Holy Scriptures contain the word of God and, since they are inspired, really *are* the word of God; therefore the study of the "sacred page" ought to be the very soul of theology.[3] The same word of Scripture is the source of healthy nourishment and holy vitality for the ministry of the word— pastoral preaching, catechetics, and all forms of Christian instruction, among which the liturgical homily should have the highest place.

25. For these reasons it is essential that all the clergy, especially priests of Christ and others who as deacons or catechists are officially engaged in the ministry of the word, should stick at their spiritual reading and at serious Bible study. It must not happen that any of them becomes "an empty preacher of the word of God outwardly, who is not a listener inwardly,"[4] when it is their duty to be sharing the abundant riches of the divine word with the faithful entrusted to their care, especially in the sacred liturgy. Likewise the synod strongly and specially urges all the faithful, particularly religious, to learn by frequent study of the Scriptures "the surpassing worth of knowing Jesus Christ" (Phil 3.8), for "ignorance of the Scriptures is ignorance of Christ."[5] They should approach the Sacred Text with joy—when it is expounded during the liturgy, or in private spiritual reading, or by means of

---

1. See Pius XII, Encyclical *Divino afflante,* 30 Sept. 1943: EB 551, 553, 567. Pontifical Biblical Commission, *Instructio de S. Scriptura in Clericorum Seminariis et Religiosorum Collegiis recte docenda,* 13 May 1950: AAS 42 (1950), pp. 495-505.

2. See Pius XII, ibid.: EB 569.

3. See Leo XIII, Encyclical *Providentissimus Deus:* EB 114; Benedict XV, Encyclical *Spiritus Paraclitus,* 15 Sept. 1920: EB 483.

4. Augustine, *Serm. (Sermons),* 179, 1: PL 38, 966.

5. Jerome, *Comm. in Is. (Commentary on Isaiah),* Prologue: PL 24, 17; CChr 73, 1. See Benedict XV, Encyclical *Spiritus Paraclitus:* EB 475-480. Pius XII, Encyclical *Divino afflante:* EB 544.

Bible courses or other aids to study, such as, with the approval and involvement of the church's pastors, we are glad to see are widely available today. Let it never be forgotten that prayer should accompany the reading of Holy Scripture, so that it becomes a dialogue between God and the human reader; for "when we pray, we talk to him: when we read the divine word, we listen to him."[6]

It is the duty of bishops, "who have the apostolic ministry of teaching,"[7] duly to instruct the faithful entrusted to them in the right use of the biblical books, especially of the New Testament and above all of the Gospels. Biblical translations should be published, equipped with such explanatory notes as are necessary and really meet all needs, so that members of the church can become familiar with Holy Scripture to their profit and without danger of misunderstanding, and can become soaked in its spirit.

Further, editions of Holy Scripture should be prepared with suitable notes which are adapted to the conditions of non-Christians also, and both pastors and Christians of whatever walk of life should take all means to distribute these imaginatively.

26. Thus, in conclusion, by reading and study of the Sacred Books "may the word of the Lord speed on and triumph" (2 Thes 3.1), and the treasure of revelation, entrusted to the church, fill human hearts ever more and more. Just as faithful and frequent reception of the eucharistic mystery makes the church's life grow, so we may hope that its spiritual life will receive a new impulse from increased devotion to the word of God, which "abides forever" (Is 40.8; 1 Pt 1.23–25).

9. Dignitatis humanae: Declaration on Religious Freedom
On the Right of Persons and Communities to Social and
Civil Liberty in Religious Matters

1. The dignity of the human person is a concern of which people of our time are becoming increasingly more aware.[1] In growing numbers they demand that they should enjoy the use of their own responsible judgment and freedom, and decide on their actions on grounds of duty and conscience, without external pressure or coercion. They also urge that bounds be set to government by law, so that the limits of reasonable freedom should not be too tightly drawn for persons or for social

6. Ambrose, *De officiis ministrorum (Duties of Ministers)*, I, 20, 88: PL 16, 50.
7. Irenaeus, *Adv. Haer. (Against Heresies)*, IV, 32, 1: PG 7, 1071; (= 49, 2) Harvey, 2, p. 255.
1. See John XXIII, Encyclical *Pacem in terris*, 11 April 1963: AAS 55 (1963), p. 279; *ibid.*, p. 265; Pius XII, Radio message, 24 Dec. 1944: AAS 37 (1945), p. 14.

groups. This demand in human society for freedom is chiefly concerned with the values of the human spirit, above all with the free and public practice of religion. Keenly aware of these aspirations, and wishing to assert their consonance with truth and justice, this Vatican Synod examines the sacred tradition and teaching of the church from which it continually draws new insights in harmony with the old.

First, then, this holy synod proclaims that God has himself made known to the human race the way by which, in obedience to him, human beings may reach salvation and blessedness in Christ. We believe that this one and only true religion subsists in the Catholic and apostolic church, to which the Lord Jesus entrusted the task of spreading it to all people, when he said to the apostles: "Go therefore and make disciples of all nations, baptizing them in the name of the Father and of the Son and of the Holy Spirit, teaching them to observe all that I have commanded you" (Mt 28.19–20). But all people are bound to seek for the truth, especially about God and his church, and when they have found it to embrace and keep it.

The synod further proclaims that these obligations touch and bind the human conscience, and that truth imposes itself solely by the force of its own truth, as it enters the mind at once gently and with power. Indeed, since people's demand for religious liberty in carrying out their duty to worship God concerns freedom from compulsion in civil society, it leaves intact the traditional Catholic teaching on the moral obligation of individuals and societies towards the true religion and the one church of Christ. Furthermore, in treating of this religious freedom the synod intends to develop the teaching of more recent popes on the inviolable rights of the human person and on the regulating of society by law.

1. The General Principle of Religious Freedom

2. This Vatican Synod declares that the human person has a right to religious freedom. Such freedom consists in this, that all should have such immunity from coercion by individuals, or by groups, or by any human power, that no one should be forced to act against his conscience in religious matters, nor prevented from acting according to his conscience, whether in private or in public, whether alone or in association with others, within due limits. The synod further declares that the right to religious freedom is firmly based on the dignity of the human person as this is known from the revealed word of God and from reason itself.[2] This right of the

---

2. See John XXIII, Encyclical *Pacem in terris*, 11 April 1963: AAS 55 (1963), pp. 260–261; Pius XII, Radio message, 24 Dec. 1942: AAS 35 (1943), p. 19; Pius XI, Encyclical *Mit bren-*

human person to religious freedom should have such recognition in the regulation of society by law as to become a civil right.

In accordance with their dignity as persons, equipped with reason and free will and endowed with personal responsibility, all are impelled by their own nature and are bound by a moral obligation to seek truth, above all religious truth. They are further bound to hold to the truth once it is known, and to regulate their whole lives by its demands. But people are only able to meet this obligation in ways that accord with their own nature, if they enjoy both psychological freedom and freedom from external coercion. Thus the right to religious freedom is based on human nature itself, not on any merely personal attitude of mind. Therefore this right to non-interference persists even in those who do not carry out their obligation of seeking the truth and standing by it; and the exercise of the right should not be curtailed as long as due public order is preserved.

3. These truths become even plainer when one reflects that the supreme rule of life is the divine law itself, the eternal, objective, and universal law by which God out of his wisdom and love arranges, directs, and governs the whole world and the paths of the human community. God has enabled people to share in this divine law, and hence they are able under the gentle guidance of God's providence increasingly to recognize the unchanging truth.[3] Therefore all have both the right and the duty to search for religious truth, so that they may by the prudent use of appropriate means form for themselves right and true moral judgments.

Truth, however, is to be sought in a manner befitting the dignity and social nature of the human person, namely by free inquiry assisted by teaching and instruction, and by exchange and discussion in which people explain to each other the truth as they have discovered it or as they see it, so as to assist each other in their search. Once the truth is known, it should be embraced by a personal act of assent.

People grasp and acknowledge the precepts of the divine law by means of their own consciences, which they are bound to follow faithfully in all their activity, so as to come to God, their end. They must therefore not be forced to act against their conscience. Nor must they be prevented from acting according to it, especially in religious matters. The practice of religion of its very nature consists principally in internal acts that are voluntary and free, in which one relates oneself to God directly; and these can neither be commanded nor prevented by any merely human

---

nender Sorge, 14 March 1937: AAS 29 (1937), p. 160; Leo XIII, Encyclical *Libertas praestantissimum,* 20 June 1888: *Acta* of Leo XIII, 8 (1888), pp. 237–238.

3. See Thomas Aquinas, *Summa Theologiae,* I–II, quest. 91, art. 1; quest. 93, art. 1–2.

power.[4] The social nature of human beings, however, requires that they should express these interior religious acts externally, share their religion with others, and witness to it communally.

Hence wrong is done to the human person and to the order established for people by God, if they are denied the free and corporate practice of their religion within the limits set by due public order.

Furthermore, those private and public acts of religion by which people relate themselves to God from the sincerity of their hearts, of their nature transcend the earthly and temporal levels of reality. So the state, whose proper purpose it is to provide for the temporal common good, should certainly recognize and promote the religious life of its citizens. With equal certainty it exceeds the limits of its authority, if it takes upon itself to direct or to prevent religious activity.

4. The liberty or freedom from coercion in religion which is proper to all as persons must also be allowed them when they act together. For religious community is required by the social nature both of human beings and of religion itself.

Hence such communities, as long as they do not disturb the proper requirements of public order, are entitled to due freedom in conducting their affairs in their own way, in honoring the Deity in public worship, in assisting their members to practice their religion, in nourishing them with instruction, and in developing institutions in which their members can cooperate in ordering their lives according to their own religious tenets.

Religious communities also have the right not to be prevented by the state by legal or administrative measures from choosing, training, appointing, and transferring their own ministers, from communicating with religious authorities and communities in other parts of the world, from constructing buildings for religious purposes, or from acquiring and using appropriate property.

In addition, religious communities are entitled to teach and give witness to their faith publicly in speech and writing without hindrance. But in propagating their religious belief they must always abstain from any kind of action that savors of undue pressure or improper enticement, particularly in regard to the poor or uneducated. Any such course of action must be held an abuse of their own rights and an infringement of the rights of others.

It is a further component of religious liberty that religious communities should not be prevented from freely expounding the special value of their teach-

4. See John XXIII, Encyclical *Pacem in terris*, 11 April 1963: AAS 55 (1963), p. 270; Paul VI, Radio message, 22 Dec. 1964: AAS 57 (1965), pp. 181–182; Thomas Aquinas, *Summa Theologiae*, I–II, quest. 91, art. 4 c.

ing for the right ordering of society and for the revitalizing of all human activity. Finally, the right of those who are stirred by religious ideals freely to hold meetings and to form associations for educative, cultural, charitable, and social purposes, is grounded both in the social nature of human beings and in the very character of religion.

5. Any family, since it is a society enjoying its own basic rights, has the right to organize its own religious life at home under the supervision of the parents. These have the right to decide on the kind of religious education to be given to their children, according to the religious convictions of the parents. Hence the state must recognize the right of parents to have a truly free choice of schools or other means of education, and no unjust burdens should be laid on them directly or indirectly as a result of this freedom of choice. The rights of parents are infringed if their children are forced to attend classes which conflict with the religious convictions of the parents, or if a single pattern of education is imposed from which all religious training is excluded.

6. The common good of society is made up of those conditions of social living which enable people to develop their own qualities most fully and easily. It consists chiefly in the safeguarding of the rights and duties of the human person.[5] Hence protection of the right to religious freedom lies with individual citizens and with social groups, with the civil authorities, with the church and other religious communities, each in their own way in view of their obligation towards the common good.

It is an integral part of the duty of every civil authority to safeguard and promote inviolable human rights.[6] The state is therefore obliged to give effective protection to the religious liberty of all citizens by just laws and other suitable means, and to ensure favorable conditions for fostering religious life. By these means citizens will have the real opportunity to exercise their religious rights and fulfill their duties, and society will itself benefit from the fruits of justice and peace which result from people's fidelity to God and his holy will.[7]

If in view of particular demographic conditions special recognition is given in the constitution to one religious community, the right of all citizens and religious communities to religious freedom must at the same time be recognized and upheld.

---

5. See John XXIII, Encyclical *Mater et Magistra*, 15 May 1961: AAS 53 (1961), p. 417; Idem, Encyclical *Pacem in terris*, 11 April 1963: AAS 55 (1963), p. 273.
6. See John XXIII, Encyclical *Pacem in terris*, 11 April 1963: AAS 55 (1963), pp. 273–274; Pius XII, Radio message, 1 June 1942: AAS 33 (1941), p. 200.
7. See Leo XIII, Encyclical *Immortale Dei*, 1 Nov. 1885: AAS 18 (1885), p. 161.

Finally, the state must ensure that the equality of citizens before the law, which is itself part of the common good of society, should never be impaired either openly or covertly for religious reasons, and that there should be no discrimination against any of them.

It follows from this that it is wrong for a civil power to use force or fear or other means to impose the acceptance or rejection of any religion, or to prevent anyone from entering or leaving a religious body. It is even more against the will of God and contrary to the sacred rights of the human person and of the family of nations, when force of any kind is used to destroy or to repress religion either in the whole human race or in any region or in any particular group.

7. The exercise of the right to religious freedom takes place in human society and is therefore subject to certain modifying principles.

The moral maxim of personal and social responsibility must be followed in the exercise of all liberties: in the use of their rights individuals and social groups are bound by the moral law to have regard to the rights of others, to their own duties towards others, and to the common good of all. All should be treated with justice and humanity.

Further, as society has the right to protect itself against the abuses that can occur under the guise of religious liberty, it is chiefly for the state to provide the relevant safeguards. This should be done neither arbitrarily nor with inequitable discrimination, but by legal rules in accord with the objective moral order. Such rules are required for the effective protection and peaceful harmonizing of the rights of all citizens. They are required to make adequate provision for that general peace and good order in which people live together in true justice. They are required for the due protection of public morality. These factors together constitute a fundamental part of the common good, and are included in the idea of public order. Nevertheless, that principle of full freedom is to be preserved in society according to which people are given the maximum of liberty, and only restrained when and in so far as is necessary.

8. People today are restricted in various ways and are in danger of being robbed of their power of free decision. At the same time many appear so assertive that in the name of freedom they reject all control and discount every duty of obedience.

Hence this Vatican Synod exhorts all, and particularly those who have the charge of educating others, to apply themselves to bringing up people who will respect the moral law, obey legitimate authority, and have a love for genuine freedom; that is, people who will use their own judgment to make decisions in the light of truth, plan their activities with a sense of responsibility, and freely combine their efforts with others to achieve all that is just and true. Therefore religious freedom should serve this further purpose, that people should act with greater responsibility in fulfilling their social functions in life.

2. Religious Freedom in the Light of Revelation

9. The statements made by this Vatican Synod on the right of people to religious freedom have their basis in the dignity of the person, the demands of which have come to be more fully known to human reason from the experience of centuries. But this teaching on freedom also has roots in divine revelation, and is for that reason to be held all the more sacred by Christians. For although revelation does not affirm the right of immunity from external coercion in religious affairs in so many words, it nevertheless makes plain the whole scope of the dignity of the human person; it manifests the respect Christ showed for the freedom of people in fulfilling their duty in believing in the word of God; and it instills in us the spirit that the followers of such a Master should always have as their ideal and model. In all these ways light is thrown on the general principles on which the teaching of this declaration on religious freedom is based. And first and foremost religious freedom in the social order fully corresponds with the freedom of the act of Christian faith.

10. One of the chief catholic teachings, found in the word of God and repeatedly preached by the fathers of the church,[8] is that the response of people to God in faith should be voluntary; so no one must be forced to embrace the faith against her or his will.[9] Indeed, the act of faith is by its very nature voluntary. Human

8. See Lactantius, *Divinarum Institutionum (The Divine Institutes)*, book 5, 19: CSEL 19, pp. 463–465; PL 6, 614 and 616 (chapter 20); Ambrose, *Epistola ad Valentinianum Imp. (Letter to Emperor Valentinian)*, Letter 21: PL 16, 1005; Augustine, *Contra litteras Petiliani (Against the letter of Petilian)*, book 2, ch. 83: CSEL 52, p. 112; PL 43, 315; see C. 23, quest. 5, canon 33 (ed. Friedberg, 1, 939); Idem, Letter 23: PL 33, 98; Idem, Letter 34: PL 33, 132; Idem, Letter 35: PL 33, 135; Gregory the Great, *Epistola ad Virgilium et Theodorum Episcopos Massiliae Galliarum (Letter to Bishops Virgilius and Theodore)*, Registrum epistolarum, I, 45: MGH Ep. 1, p. 72; PL 77, 510–511 (book 1, letter 47); CChr 140, 59; Idem, *Epistola ad Iohannem Episcopum Constantinopolitanum (Letter to John, bishop of Constantinople)*, Registrum epistolarum, III, 52: MGH Ep. I, p. 210; PL 77, 649 (book 3, letter 53); CChr 140, 199; see D. 45, canon 1 (ed. Friedberg, 1, 160); council of Toledo IV (633), canon 57: Msi 10, 633; see D. 45, canon 5 (ed. Friedberg, 1, 161–162); Clement III: *Decretals*, V, 6, 9 (ed. Friedberg, 2, 774); Innocent III, *Epistola ad Arelatensem Archiepiscopum (Letter to the archbishop of Arles)*: Decretals, III, 42, 3 (ed. Friedberg, 2, 646).
9. See CIC, canon 1351; Pius XII, Allocution to the prelate auditors and other officials and

beings, redeemed by Christ their Savior and called to adoptive sonship through Jesus Christ,[10] can only respond to God as he reveals himself if, with the Father drawing them,[11] they give to God a free and rational allegiance of faith. It is therefore entirely in accord with the nature of faith that every kind of human coercion should be excluded from religion. And so the ideal of religious freedom greatly helps to produce the conditions in which people can be openly invited to Christian faith, and can embrace it of their own accord and witness to it in action in their whole manner of life.

11. God calls people to serve him in spirit and in truth, so that they are bound to him by personal decision and not by external force. For he looks to the dignity of the human person, whom he has created and who needs to be guided by his own judgment and enjoy his freedom. This shone out most clearly in Christ Jesus, in whom God fully revealed himself and his ways. For Christ, who is our Master and Lord,[12] but is also gentle and humble of heart,[13] patiently attracted and invited his disciples.[14] Certainly he illuminated and confirmed his teaching with miracles, to stir up and strengthen the faith of his hearers, though not to exert pressure on them.[15] Certainly, too, he reproved the disbelief of his hearers, but he left the verdict of God to the day of judgment.[16] When he sent his apostles out to the world, he told them: "Whoever believes and is baptized will be saved; whoever does not believe will be condemned" (Mt 16.16). But, knowing that wheat and cockle were sown together, he ordered that both be allowed to grow till the harvest at the end of time.[17] Refusing to be a political messiah who prevailed by force,[18] he preferred to call himself the Son of man who came "to serve and to give his life as a ransom for many" (Mk 10.45). He showed himself the perfect servant of God,[19] who "will not break a bruised reed or quench a smoldering wick" (Mt 12.20). He recognized the

---

administrators of the Roman Rota, 6 Oct. 1946: AAS 38 (1946), p. 394; Idem, Encyclical *Mystici Corporis*, 29 June 1943: AAS (1943), p. 243.

10. See Eph 1.5.

11. See Jn 6.44.

12. See Jn 13.13.

13. See Mt 11.29.

14. See Mt 11.28–30; Jn 6.67–68.

15. See Mt 9.28–29; Mk 9.23–24, 6.5–6; Paul VI, Encyclical *Ecclesiam suam*, 6 Aug. 1964: AAS 56 (1964), pp. 642–643.

16. See Mt 11.20–24; Rom 12.19–20; 2 Thes 1.8.

17. See Mt 13.30, 40–42.

18. See Mt 4.8–10; Jn 6.15.

19. See Is 42.1–4.

civil power and its laws, and ordered that tax be paid to Caesar, but clearly warned that the higher laws of God should be kept: "Render therefore to Caesar the things that are Caesar's, and to God the things that are God's" (Mt 22.21). Finally, when completing on the cross his work of redemption by which he won salvation and true freedom for humanity, he brought his revelation to perfection. He bore witness to the truth,[20] and would not let force be used on those who opposed it. For his kingdom is not upheld by the sword,[21] but is founded on hearing and witnessing to the truth, and grows by the love whereby Christ raised on the cross draws people to himself.[22]

The apostles, taught by Christ's word and example, followed the same course. From the very beginnings of the church the followers of Christ strove to convert people to the confession of Christ as Lord, not by any coercive measures or by devices unworthy of the gospel, but chiefly by the power of God's message.[23] They vigorously proclaimed to all the design of God the Savior, "who desires all to be saved and to come to the knowledge of the truth" (1 Tim 2.4); but at the same time they respected the weak even though they were caught up in error, thus making plain how "each of us shall give an account of himself to God" (Rom 14.12)[24] and in the end is bound to obey his own conscience. Like Christ himself, the apostles always strove to give public testimony to God's truth and to speak "the word of God with boldness" (Acts 4.31)[25] with the greatest daring before people and princes. For they firmly believed that the gospel was in very truth the power of God for salvation to everyone who has faith.[26] So, scorning every kind of "worldly weapon"[27] and following the example of Christ's meekness and moderation, they preached the word of God with full reliance on the divine power of this word to destroy forces hostile to God[28] and to bring people to faith in Christ and allegiance to him.[29] As had the Master, so too the apostles acknowledged legitimate civil authority: "For there is no authority except from God," the apostle teaches, and so adds this instruction: "Let every person be subject to the governing authorities . . . anyone who resists the

---

20. See Jn 18.37.
21. See Mt 26.51–53; Jn 18.36.
22. See Jn 12.32.
23. See 1 Cor 2.3–5; 1 Thes 2.3–5.
24. See Rom 14.1–23; 1 Cor 8.9–13, 10.23–33.
25. See Eph 6.19–20.
26. See Rom 1.16.
27. See 2 Cor 10.4; 1 Thes 5.8–9.
28. See Eph 6.11–17.
29. See 2 Cor 10.3–5.

authorities resists what God has appointed" (Rom 13.1–2).[30] At the same time they were not afraid to confront those in public office when they opposed the holy will of God: "We must obey God rather than men" (Acts 5.29).[31] Martyrs and faithful without number have trodden this path throughout the ages and throughout the world.

12. Hence the church is being faithful to the truth of the gospel and is following the way of Christ and the apostles, when it sees the principle of religious freedom as in accord with human dignity and the revelation of God, and when it promotes it. Throughout the centuries it has guarded and handed on the teaching received from the Master and from the apostles. Although at times in the life of the people of God, as it has pursued its pilgrimage through the twists and turns of human history, there have been ways of acting hardly in tune with the spirit of the gospel, indeed contrary to it, nevertheless the church's teaching that no one's faith should be coerced has held firm.

Thus the leaven of the gospel has long been at work in the minds of people and has played a great part in the course of time in the growing recognition of the dignity of the human person, and in the maturing of the conviction that in religious matters this dignity must be preserved intact in society from any kind of human coercion.

13. Among the values which contribute most to the well-being of the church, as of civil society itself, and which are always to be upheld and safeguarded from all damage, the chief is unquestionably that the church should enjoy all the freedom of action it needs to care for the salvation of humanity.[32] For this is a sacred liberty with which the only-begotten Son of God endowed the church he obtained with his own blood. It is so integral to the church that any who attack it are acting against the will of God. This freedom of the church is a fundamental principle in all relations between the church and both the state and the whole social order.

In human society and in the presence of any civil power the church claims freedom for itself as a spiritual authority, established by Christ the Lord, on whom lies the duty by divine command of going into the whole world and preaching the gospel to the whole creation.[33] The church further claims freedom in that it is a

30. See 1 Pt 2.13–17.

31. See Acts 4.19–20.

32. See Leo XIII, Letter *Officio sanctissimo*, 22 Dec. 1887: ASS 20 (1887), p. 269; Idem, Letter *Ex litteris*, 7 April 1887: ASS 19 (1886), p. 465.

33. See Mk 16.15; Mt 28.18–20; Pius XII, Encyclical *Summi Pontificatus*, 20 Oct. 1939: AAS 31 (1939), pp. 445–446.

human association enjoying the right to live in civil society according to the requirements of Christian faith.[34]

Indeed, if the principle of religious freedom prevails, as one not merely set
forth in words nor just sanctioned by law, but genuinely put into practice, then the
church truly has the solid basis in law and in fact for that independence which is necessary for the fulfillment of its divine mission, and which church authorities more
and more insistently claim in today's world.[35] At the same time the faithful, like
other people, have the civil right not to be prevented from living their lives as conscience directs. There is therefore a harmony between the freedom of the church
and that religious liberty which should be accorded as a right to all individuals and
communities, and should be sanctioned by legal enactment.

14. To obey the divine command, "teach all nations" (Mt 28.19), the Catholic Church must work unremittingly "that the word of God may speed on and triumph" (2 Thes 3.1).

So the church earnestly begs its children that as a matter of the greatest
moment there be made "supplications, prayers, intercessions, and thanksgivings for
everyone. . . . For this is good, and it is acceptable in the sight of God our Savior,
who desires everyone to be saved and to come to the knowledge of the truth" (1 Tm
2.1–4).

In forming their consciences the Christian faithful should give careful attention to the sacred and certain teaching of the church.[36] For the Catholic Church
is by the will of Christ the teacher of truth. Its charge is to announce and authentically teach that truth which is Christ, and at the same time to give authoritative
statement and confirmation of the principles of the moral order which derive from
human nature itself. In addition, all Christians should find prudent ways in which
to spread the light of life to those outside their fold, "by the Holy Spirit, genuine
love, truthful speech" (2 Cor 6.6–7), with the confidence[37] and boldness of apostles,
even to the shedding of their blood.

For the disciple of Christ owes to his Master the serious obligation of ab-
sorbing ever more deeply the truth learnt from him, of announcing it loyally and
defending it vigorously, but always without recourse to means that go against the
spirit of the gospel. At the same time the love of Christ presses the disciple to deal
lovingly, prudently, and patiently with those who are ignorant or mistaken about

34. See Pius XI, Letter *Firmissimam constantiam,* 28 March 1937: AAS 29 (1937), p. 196.
35. See Pius XII, Allocution *Ci riesce,* 6 Dec. 1953: AAS 45 (1953), p. 802.
36. See Pius XII, Radio message, 23 March 1952: AAS 44 (1952), pp. 270–278.
37. See Acts 4.29.

the faith.[38] So account must be taken of one's obligations to the proclamation of Christ the life-giving Word, of the rights of the human person, and of the measure of the grace of Christ given to each by God to summon him to the free acceptance and profession of the faith.

15. There is general recognition that people today want to be able to give free expression to their religion in public and in private, and that religious freedom is stated as a civil right in many constitutions and given solemn recognition in international documents.[39]

But there are some regimes in which, though freedom of religious worship has constitutional recognition, the state nonetheless tries to deter its citizens from any religious allegiance and to make life arduous and even dangerous for religious communities.

This holy synod warmly greets the former more positive signs of our times, while it sadly exposes the latter facts and condemns them. It urges Catholics and begs all people to reflect deeply on the degree to which religious freedom is a paramount necessity in the present situation of the human family.

For quite clearly all nations are daily becoming more united, people of different culture and religious belief are bound together by closer ties, and there is a growing awareness of the responsibility of each. To the end, therefore, that relations of peace and harmony may be established and deepened in the human race, it is essential that religious freedom be given adequate legal protection throughout the world, and that the supreme duties and rights of people in regard to the freedom of their religious life in society should be upheld.

May the God and Father of all bring it to pass that the human family, by carefully tending the principle of religious freedom in society, may be led through the grace of Christ and the power of the Holy Spirit to the enduring heights of "the glorious liberty of the children of God" (Rom 8.21).

38. See John XXIII, Encyclical *Pacem in terris*, 11 April 1963: AAS 55 (1963), pp. 299–300.
39. See John XXIII, Encyclical *Pacem in terris*, 11 April 1963: AAS 55 (1963), pp. 295–296.

The Mennonite Church in America (Old Mennonites), *Mennonite Confession of Faith*, 1963

Ever since the sixteenth century, the Mennonites have been the most assiduous among the adherents of the Radical Reformation in preparing confessional statements. → *The Schleitheim Confession of Faith* of 1527 took its place among the classic statements of Reformation teaching alongside → *The Augsburg Confession*, → *The Tetrapolitan Confession*, and other formularies. Again, in the post-Reformation period, → *The Mennonite Confession of Dordrecht* of 1632 served to express and to help achieve concord among sometimes fractious Mennonite groups. Other confessions, too, such as → the *Mennonite Articles of Faith* by Cornelis Ris, were issued in response to the changing situations of a church whose cultivation of fraternal community within the church and whose opposition to war and violence set them apart from most other churches.

In the New World, especially Canada and the United States, religious liberty and an open society faced the Mennonite Church with new opportunities—and with new temptations. While reaffirming their historic affirmations of faith and doctrine, especially *Dordrecht,* the Mennonite General Conference became convinced "that it is imperative to draw up a new confession of faith, not to repudiate any earlier confession, but to restate the doctrinal position of the church in terms relevant to today's issues, and especially to incorporate the insights of the various doctrinal pronouncements of the Mennonite General Conference."[1]

The result was this *Mennonite Confession of Faith* of 1963. It was commissioned by the biennial session of the church in 1957, submitted six years later, and, after further revision, approved in this final form by the Mennonite General Conference on 22 August 1963. In that final form, as an official note explains, the supplied proof texts are "representative, but not exhaustive"; they are reproduced here as they stand there.

Edition: Wenger 1966, 332–42.

Literature: Loewen, 27; Wenger 1966.

---

1. Wenger 1966, 332.

The Mennonite Church in America (Old Mennonites), *Mennonite Confession of Faith*, 1963

Preamble

The Mennonite Church, begun in Switzerland in 1525, was a part of the Reformation which attempted to restore the New Testament church. We conceive the church to be a body of regenerated believers, a fellowship of holy pilgrims baptized upon confession of faith in Christ. As committed believers we seek to follow the way of Christian love and nonresistance, and to live separate from the evil of the world. We earnestly endeavor to make Christian disciples of all the nations.

In its beliefs the Mennonite Church is bound ultimately to the Holy Scriptures, not to any human formulation of doctrine. We regard this present confession as a restatement of the Eighteen Articles adopted at Dordrecht in the Netherlands in 1632 and of the other statements adopted by our church. In this expression of our faith we sincerely accept the lordship of Jesus Christ and the full authority of the written word of God, the Bible, and seek to promote the unity of the brotherhood, to safeguard sound doctrine and life, and to serve as a testimony to others.

ARTICLE 1. GOD AND HIS ATTRIBUTES

1. We believe in Almighty God, the eternal Spirit who is infinite in his attributes of holiness, love, righteousness, truth, power, goodness, and mercy. This one and only God has revealed himself as existing eternally as Father, Son, and Holy Spirit.

2. *The Father.* We believe that God is the Creator of all things, a God of providence, and the author of our salvation through Christ. Although he is too great to be comprehended by the human mind, through Christ we can truly know him. In redeeming love he entered into a covenant relationship with Abraham, later with the people of Israel, and has now made through Christ an eternal covenant in which he offers to the human race the forgiveness of sins and the blessings of divine sonship to those who will repent and believe.

3. *The Son.* We believe in Jesus Christ the divine Son of God, who was with the Father from all eternity, who for our salvation took upon himself human nature, and who by his redemptive death and resurrection conquered the forces of sin and Satan and atoned for the sins of mankind. He was conceived by the Holy Spirit, born of the Virgin Mary, lived a sinless life, and in God's redemptive purpose was crucified. He rose from the dead, ascended into heaven, and now as Lord and Christ at the right hand of the Father intercedes for the saints. He is the Lord and Savior of

all Christian believers, and the coming judge of the living and the dead. We believe in his full deity and full humanity according to the Scriptures.

4. *The Holy Spirit.* We believe in the Holy Spirit, who was sent by the Father and the Son to bring to individuals the redemption of Christ. We believe in his personality as set forth in the Scriptures: that he loves, searches, testifies, guides, empowers, and intercedes for the saints.

Dt 6.4, 5; Mt 22.37; Jn 1.18, 3.16; Rom 8.1-17; 2 Cor 13.14; 1 Tm 3.16; Heb 11.6.

ARTICLE 2. DIVINE REVELATION

1. We believe that the God of creation and redemption has revealed himself and his will for men in the Holy Scriptures, and supremely and finally in his incarnate Son, the Lord Jesus Christ. God's purpose in this revelation is the salvation of all men. Although God's power and deity are revealed in his creation, so that the nations are without excuse, this knowledge of him cannot save men, for it cannot make Christ known. God revealed himself in saving word and deed to Israel as recorded in the Old Testament; he fulfilled this revelation of himself in the word and deed of Christ as recorded in the New Testament. We believe that all Scripture is given by the inspiration of God, that men moved by the Holy Spirit spoke from God. We accept the Scriptures as the authoritative word of God, and through the Holy Spirit as the infallible guide to lead men to faith in Christ and to guide them in the life of Christian discipleship.

2. We believe that the Old Testament and the New Testament together constitute the word of God, that the old covenant was preparatory, that its institutions were temporary in character, and that the new covenant in Christ is the fulfillment of the old. We believe that the Old Testament writings are inspired and profitable, and as the divine word of promise are to be interpreted in conjunction with the divine act of fulfillment recorded in the New. Christian doctrine and practice are based upon the whole word of God, the word of promise of the Old Covenant as fulfilled in the New.

3. The message of the Bible points to the Lord Jesus Christ. It is to him that the Scriptures of the Old Testament bear witness, and he is the one whom the Scriptures of the New Testament proclaim. He is the key to the proper understanding of the entire Bible.

Ps 19; Lk 24.27, 44; Jn 1.1-16, 20.31; Rom 1.19, 20; 2 Tm 3.15, 16; Heb 1.1, 2, 8.6, 7; 1 Jn 1.1-5.

ARTICLE 3. GOD'S CREATION AND PROVIDENCE

1. We believe that in the beginning God created all things by his Son, and that all existence is therefore finite and dependent upon God, the Source and End of all things visible and invisible. He created man in his own image, which set man apart from the animal creation. In free will, moral character, superior intellect, and spiritual nature, man bore the image of his Creator.

2. In his providence God is concerned with the lives of his children, and in everything works for their eternal good. He hears and answers their prayers. By Jesus Christ he upholds the entire creation. He is sovereign over all things, but he is not the author of sin. He has endowed man with the power of self-determination, and he holds him responsible for his moral choices.

Gn 1.1, 26, 27; Ps 139.7–12; Mt 10.29; Jn 1.3; Rom 8.28; Col 1.16, 17; Jas 5.16.

ARTICLE 4. MAN AND HIS SIN

1. We believe that God created man sinless and holy, and subjected man to a moral test as a means of bringing him to full spiritual maturity. Man yielded, however, to the temptation of Satan and by willful disobedience to God failed to maintain that holy condition in which he had been created. This sin brought depravity and death to the race. Although men are sinners by nature because of Adam's fall, they are not guilty of his sin. Those who perish eternally do so only because of their own sin. The most grievous sin is the stubborn refusal to acknowledge Jesus Christ as Savior and Lord. As a fallen creature man is self-centered, self-willed, rebellious toward God, unwilling to yield to Christ, unable to break with sin, and under divine judgment.

2. We believe that children are born with a nature which will manifest itself as sinful as they mature. When they come to know themselves to be responsible to God, they must repent and believe in Christ in order to be saved. Before the age when children are accountable to God, their sins are atoned for through the sacrifice of Christ. Jesus himself assured us that children are in the kingdom of God.

Gn 1.27, 31, 3.1–19; Mt 18.1–14; Lk 18.16; Rom 5.12–21; Eph 2.1–3; 1 Tm 4.10.

ARTICLE 5. CHRIST, THE SAVIOR FROM SIN

1. We believe that there is one Mediator between God and men, the man Christ Jesus. The purpose of the incarnation of God's eternal Son was to redeem men from sin and death, to destroy the power and works of the devil, and to reconcile men to God. As a Prophet, the Lord Jesus not only proclaimed God's word; he was in his very person the Word of God. As a Priest, he himself was the sacrifice for sin, and

now makes intercession with the Father for the saints. As our risen Lord and King, he is vested with all authority in heaven and on earth.

2. In his life the Lord Jesus demonstrated perfectly the will of God. Although tempted in all points as we are, yet he never sinned. Through the shedding of his blood he inaugurated the new covenant, broke the power of sin for those who exercise faith in him, and triumphed over Satan. By his resurrection from the dead, Christ accomplished the full justification of those who believe in him. By faith each believer is united with the risen and glorified Christ, the Lord of glory.

Lk 19.10; Jn 1.1; Acts 2.33; Rom 5.11; 2 Cor 5.21; Col 2.15; 1 Tm 2.5; Heb 2.14, 15, 4.15, 7.11.

ARTICLE 6. SALVATION BY GRACE THROUGH FAITH

We believe that men are saved, not by character, law, good works, or ceremonies, but by the grace of God. The merits of the death and resurrection of Christ are adequate for the salvation of all men, are offered to all, and are intended for all. Salvation is appropriated by faith in Christ. From all eternity God knew who would be believers in Christ, and these persons foreknown as believers are elect according to the foreknowledge of God. Those who repent and believe in Christ as Savior and Lord receive the gift of righteousness, are born again, and are adopted into the family of God. Saving faith involves the giving of the self to Christ, a full surrender of the will, a confident trust in him, a joyful obedience to his word as a faithful disciple, and an attitude of love to all men. It is the privilege of every believer to have the assurance of salvation. The God who saves is also able to keep each believer unto a happy end in Christ. As long as the believer lives, he stands in need of the forgiveness, cleansing, and grace of Christ.

Jn 3.16, 10.27-29; Rom 4; Eph 2.8-10; 1 Pt 1.2; 1 Jn 1.8-10, 5.13; Jude 24.

ARTICLE 7. THE HOLY SPIRIT AND THE CHRISTIAN LIFE

We believe that Christ as Lord and Savior does his work through the Holy Spirit. The Holy Spirit convicts of sin. Through the Holy Spirit those who believe are born again. The supreme ministry of the Spirit is to lead men to Christ and his salvation. As Christians yield to Christ and obey his word, the Holy Spirit transforms them into the spiritual image of Jesus Christ, and enables perseverance in faith and holiness. He empowers them as effective witnesses to Christ and his salvation, fills their hearts with love for all men, and moves them to practice Christian discipleship. The Holy Spirit bestows upon each believer such gifts as he wills for the building up of the body of Christ. The indwelling of the Holy Spirit is God's seal of ownership of the Christian believer. He is God's guarantee that he will also redeem the bodies of believers on the day of Christ.

Jn 16.7–15; Acts 1.8, 2.1–21; 1 Cor 3.16, 17, 6.19, 12.11–13, chs 12–14; Gal 5.22–24; Eph 1.13, 14, 5.30.

ARTICLE 8. THE CHURCH OF CHRIST

1. *Nature.* We believe that God's redemptive work in history has led to the establishment of the Christian Church. Christ established his church when he poured out his Spirit on the day of Pentecost. In preparation for this church he entered into covenant relationships with Abraham and his seed. Today the spiritual "seed of Abraham" are those who have faith in Christ, the people of God, the body of Christ, composed of believers from all races and nations. The church is the fellowship of those who are in the kingdom of Christ, the assembly of those who believe in him, the brotherhood of the saints. The church is corporately the dwelling place of God in the Spirit, his holy temple. It is the visible body of those who are Christian disciples. Membership in the church is dependent upon a voluntary response to God's offer of salvation in Christ.

The primary unit of the church is the local assembly of believers. It is in the congregation that the work of teaching, witnessing, and disciplining is carried on. In order to maintain the unity of the church it is scriptural and profitable for congregational representatives to meet together in conferences. The concern for the welfare of the whole church calls for Spirit-led conferences to assist local congregations in maintaining biblical standards of faith, conduct, stewardship, and missions. The decisions of such conferences should be respected by the individual congregations and members.

2. *Function.* It is the function of the church to demonstrate to the world the will of God, to witness to all men of the saving power and intention of God in Christ, and to make disciples of all the nations. The church seeks to lead all men to the obedience of faith. Believers unite in the church for instruction and nurture, for worship, for inclusion in the witnessing and evangelizing body of Christ, for the observance of the ordinances, for Christian fellowship, and for the discipline of the word and the Spirit of God. The Spirit leads the church to discover the gifts which he has bestowed upon the members for the building up of the body. The church has the obligation to speak authoritatively on God's will. It shall listen to the word of God and obey it in the moral and spiritual conflicts of each era of history.

The church is called to be a brotherhood under the lordship of Jesus Christ, a loving fellowship of brethren and sisters who are concerned for the total welfare, both spiritual and material, of one another. This concern results in the attempt to help the erring brother find the right path; it includes sharing generously both financial aid and the word of encouragement, and a willingness to give and receive counsel.

3. *Discipline*. We believe that the Lord Jesus has given authority to his church to exercise discipline. The purposes of discipline are to lead each member to full stature in Christ, to restore to full fellowship the members who fall into sin, to clarify for all members the meaning of Christian discipleship, to promote the purity of the church, to warn the weak and immature of the serious character of sin and disobedience to God's word, and to maintain the good name and witness of the church before the world. In this work the church employs public teaching, private counseling, intercessory prayer, earnest warning and rebuke, and sympathetic encouragement. If disobedience persists, the church may withhold the right to commune until the individual repents. And the church must, with a deep sense of loss, recognize that the one who goes on to full apostasy and spiritual ruin has severed his relation with Christ and his body. The standard in church discipline is the word of God as interpreted by the brotherhood. The entire congregation should share in the work of discipline and seek earnestly to win the fallen member.

4. *Ceremonies and Practices*. The Lord Jesus and his apostles instituted ordinances for the church to observe permanently as symbols of Christian truths. The apostolic church literally observed them. Among these are baptism with water, the communion of the Lord's supper, the washing of the saints' feet, the holy kiss, the laying on of hands in ordination, the veiling of Christian women, the anointing of the sick with oil, and the institution of Christian marriage. When the church observes ordinances as expressions of a heart of faith, divine blessings are received, and a Christian witness is given.

Since the Lord Jesus arose from the dead on the first day of the week, the Christian church, following apostolic precedent, observes the first day of each week in memory of the Lord's resurrection.

5. *The Church and Healing*. We believe that the church should exercise a ministry of prayer for those who are in need. Prayer for the sick may be accompanied by a symbolic anointing with oil by the elders of the church. In response to the prayer of faith, and in accordance with his will, God heals in various ways, through the use of the healing arts, or by direct intervention. When healing does not occur, we believe that God's grace is sufficient. The full redemption of the body will come only at the return of Christ.

Ex 2.24, 24.8; Mt 5.13, 14, 23, 24, 18.15–18, 28.19, 20; Acts 15; 1 Cor 3.16, 17, 5.11–13; 2 Cor 2.6–11, 3.2, 12.9; Gal 3.6–9, 6.1; Eph 2.11–22, 4.13; 1 Tm 5.20; Jas 2.14–17, 5.14–16; 1 Pt 2.9.

ARTICLE 9. THE MISSION OF THE CHURCH TO SOCIETY

We believe that Christ has commissioned the church to go into all the world and make disciples of all the nations, baptizing them, and teaching them to observe his commandments. Jesus entrusted to the church the stewardship of the gospel, and promised the power of the Holy Spirit for the work of evangelism and missions. This ministry of reconciliation is inherent in the very nature of the church. The church is interested not only in the spiritual welfare of men but in their total well-being. Jesus himself fed the hungry, healed the sick, and had compassion on the poor. The church should likewise minister to those who are in physical or social need and to those who are physically or emotionally ill. The church should witness against racial discrimination, economic injustice, and all forms of human slavery and moral degradation.

Am 5.21–24; Mt 28.18–20; Mk 6.56; Rom 1.16, 8.23.

ARTICLE 10. THE MINISTERS OF THE CHURCH

We believe that it is the intention of Christ that there should be shepherds in his congregations to feed the flock, to serve as leaders, to expound the word of God, to administer the ordinances, to exercise, in cooperation with the congregation, a scriptural church discipline, and in general to function as servants of the church. Ordination is accompanied by a laying on of hands, symbolic of the church assigning responsibility and of God imparting strength for the assignment. In addition to the primary office of apostle, in the New Testament church there were such gifts as prophets, evangelists, pastors, and teachers. The early church had regional overseers such as Timothy, and bishops (pastors) and deacons in the local congregations. Upon the pastors lay the responsibility for the leadership and pastoral care of the congregations, and the deacons served as their helpers. In each era of the life of the church, Christ through his Spirit seeks to lead the church to adapt its organization to the needs of time and place. The church is a brotherhood, and its organizational structure should insure the full participation of the members with their spiritual gifts in its life and discipline. It is the duty of the church to give financial support to those whom it asks to serve as evangelists, pastors, and teachers.

Mt 23.8, 28.19; Acts 15.6, 20.28; 1 Cor 5.4, 5, 9.14; Eph 4.11, 12; Phil 1.1; 1 Tm 3.1–13, 4.14; 2 Tm 4.12; Ti 1.5–9; Heb 13.17; 1 Pt 5.2, 3.

ARTICLE 11. CHRISTIAN BAPTISM

We believe in obeying the instruction of the Lord Jesus to baptize believers with water in the name of the Father and of the Son and of the Holy Spirit. In order to qualify for baptism one must repent, turn to Christ in sincere faith, and accept him as Lord. We regard water baptism as an ordinance of Christ which symbolizes the baptism of the Holy Spirit, divine cleansing from sin and its guilt, identification with Christ in his death and resurrection, and the commitment to follow him in a life of faithful discipleship. Since baptism with the Holy Spirit is a pouring out, we generally practice pouring as our mode of water baptism.

Mt 28.18–20; Acts 2.16–21, 22.16; Rom 6.4–6; 1 Cor 12.13; 1 Pt 3.21.

ARTICLE 12. THE LORD'S SUPPER

We believe in observing the communion of the Lord's supper as an ordinance instituted by Jesus Christ to symbolize the new covenant. We recognize the bread and the cup as symbols commemorating Christ's broken body and shed blood, of our spiritual life in him, and of the spiritual unity and fellowship of the body of Christ. Each believer shall examine himself so as not to partake of the sacred emblems carelessly or while living in sin. The church shall invite to the Lord's table only those who have peace with God and with their fellowmen, and who share the faith of the church. The Lord's supper shall be observed faithfully until the Lord comes.

Lk 22.19, 20; 1 Cor 5.13, 10.16, 17, 11.24, 26.

ARTICLE 13. SYMBOLS OF CHRISTIAN BROTHERHOOD

We believe in the observance of the washing of the saints' feet as an ordinance instituted by the Lord Jesus. By his example Christ rebuked the pride and rivalry of the apostles and showed them that Christian discipleship involves obedience to his lordship and loving service. This ordinance reminds us of the brotherhood character of the church, of our mutual duty to serve and admonish one another, and of our need for continuous cleansing in our daily walk. In the New Testament the holy kiss and the right hand of fellowship are also symbols of Christian love in the church of Christ.

Lk 22.24; Jn 13.1–17; Rom 16.16; Gal 2.9; 1 Tm 5.10.

ARTICLE 14. SYMBOLS OF CHRISTIAN ORDER

We believe that in their relation to the Lord men and women are equal, for in Christ there is neither male nor female. But in the order of creation God has fitted man and woman for differing functions; man has been given a primary leadership role, while the woman is especially fitted for nurture and service. Being in Christ does not nullify these natural endowments, either in the home or in the church. The New Testament symbols of man's headship are to be his short hair and uncovered head while praying or prophesying, and the symbols of woman's role are her long hair and her veiled head. The acceptance by both men and women of the order of creation in no way limits their rightful freedom, but rather insures their finding the respective roles in which they can most fruitfully and happily serve.

Gn 2.18–25; 1 Cor 11.2–16; Gal 3.28.

ARTICLE 15. MARRIAGE AND THE HOME

We believe that at the beginning of human history God instituted marriage. He ordained that a man shall leave his father and mother and cleave to his wife, and that the two shall become one in love and mutual submission. It is God's will that marriage be a holy state, monogamous, and for life. It is also fully acceptable to God to serve Christ unmarried. Marriage was instituted for the happiness of the husband and wife and for the procreation and Christian nurture of children. Christians shall marry only in the Lord, and for the sake of spiritual unity in the home they should become members of the same congregation. The Christian home ought regularly to have family worship, to seek faithfully to live according to the word of God, and to support loyally the church in its mission. We believe it is appropriate for parents to pledge themselves to the faithful Christian nurture of their children.

Gn 1.27, 28, 2.24; Mt 19.3–9; Mk 10.2–12; Eph 6.1–4.

ARTICLE 16. DISCIPLESHIP AND NONCONFORMITY

We believe that there are two opposing kingdoms to which men give their spiritual allegiance, that of Christ and that of Satan. Those who belong to Satan's kingdom live for sin and self, and refuse the obedience of faith. The kingdom of Christ is composed of those who have been born again and have entered into a faith union with the Lord Jesus Christ. In them the fruit of the Spirit is in evidence. They recognize the lordship of Christ, and perform all manner of good works. They seek for holiness of heart, life, and speech, and refuse any unequal yoke with unbelievers. They manifest only love toward those of other races, cultures, and economic levels. They regard their bodies as temples of the Holy Spirit and crucify their flesh with its affections and lusts. They therefore avoid such things as harmful drugs, beverage alcohol, and tobacco. We believe that their adornment should be a beauty of spirit, expressed in attire that is modest, economical, simple, and becoming to those professing Christian faith. They should seek to be Christian in their stewardship of money and possessions. Their recreational life should be consistent with the Christian walk. Through the Spirit they should put off the old man and put on the new.

Mt 7.13, 14; Lk 9.23–26; Rom 12.1, 2; 1 Cor 6.12, 19; 2 Cor 6.14–18; Gal 5.22–24; Eph 4.20–32; Col 1.13; 1 Tm 2.9, 10; 1 Pt 3.3, 4.

ARTICLE 17. CHRISTIAN INTEGRITY

We believe that it is a major Christian obligation to be strictly truthful and transparent in life and doctrine, with no secrecy or hypocrisy. The Lord Jesus Christ has forbidden to his followers the use of any and all oaths, because of the finite limitations of human beings, and the obligation always to speak the truth. In legal matters we therefore simply affirm the truth. We are opposed to membership in secret societies or lodges, because such membership would involve an unequal yoke with unbelievers, and because these organizations employ hierarchical titles, require oaths, stand for organized secrecy, and may offer salvation on grounds other than faith in the Lord Jesus Christ. We believe that it is in the church that we should find love, fellowship, and security.

Mt 5.33–37, 23.7–10, 16.22; Jn 18.20; Acts 4.12; 2 Cor 6.14–7.1; Jas 5.12.

ARTICLE 18. LOVE AND NONRESISTANCE

We believe that it is the will of God for his children to follow Christian love in all human relationships. Such a life of love excludes retaliation and revenge. God pours his love into the hearts of Christians so that they desire the welfare of all men. The supreme example of nonresistance is the Lord Jesus himself. The teaching of Jesus not to resist him who is evil requires the renunciation by his disciples of all violence in human relations. Only love must be shown to all men. We believe that this applies to every area of life: to personal injustice, to situations in which people commonly resort to litigation, to industrial strife, and to international tensions and wars. As nonresistant Christians we cannot serve in any office which employs the use of force. Nor can we participate in military service, or in military training, or in the voluntary financial support of war. But we must aggressively, at the risk of life itself, do whatever we can for the alleviation of human distress and suffering.

Mt 5.38–48; Jn 18.36; Rom 5.5, 12. 18–21; 1 Cor 6.1–8; 2 Cor 10.3, 4; Jas 2.8; 1 Pt 2.23, 4.1.

ARTICLE 19. THE CHRISTIAN AND THE STATE

We believe that the state is ordained of God to maintain law and order. We seek to obey the New Testament commands to render honor to the authorities, to pay our taxes, to obey all laws which do not conflict with the higher law of God, and to pray for our rulers. The church should also witness to the authorities of God's redeeming love in Christ, and of his sovereignty over all men. In law enforcement the state does not and cannot operate on the nonresistant principles of Christ's kingdom. Therefore, nonresistant Christians cannot undertake any service in the state or in society which would violate the principles of love and holiness as taught by Christ and his inspired apostles.

Acts 4.19, 5.29; Rom 13.1–7; Eph 1.20–22, 5.23; 1 Tm 2.1, 2.

ARTICLE 20. THE FINAL CONSUMMATION

We believe that in addition to the physical order with which our senses are related, there also exists an eternal spiritual order, the realm of God, of Christ, of the Holy Spirit, of the angels, and of the church triumphant. We believe that at death the righteous enter at once into conscious joy and fellowship with Christ, while the wicked are in a state of conscious suffering. The church militant lives and witnesses in this present evil world, a world in which apostasy from God is to become even more pronounced. The church also looks forward with hope to the day of the Lord, to the personal return of Christ, and the glorious future of the kingdom of God. In his triumphant second coming Christ will judge Satan, and usher in the consummation of all things. His coming will introduce the resurrection, the transformation of the living saints, the judgment of the just and the unjust, and the fulfillment of his glorious reign. He will deliver the kingdom to God the Father, cleanse the world by fire, create new heavens and a new earth, consign unbelievers to eternal punishment, and usher his children into the eternal bliss of the world to come.

Dn 12.2; Mt 25.34, 41; Mk 9.43–48; Lk 16.22, 23; Jn 5.22; 1 Cor 15.24, 35–58; 2 Cor 5.1–4; Phil 1.23; 1 Thes 4.13–5.4; 1 Pt 1.4; 2 Pt 3.3–13; Rv 15.3; 21.4, 22.3.

May God enable us all to attain his eternal kingdom prepared for us from the foundation of the world, that with his blessed Son we may enjoy fullness of life forever and ever.

The Church of Lanka, *Scheme of Church Union in Ceylon: Faith and Order*, 1963

The movement for church union in Ceylon (Sri Lanka) was closely related to the discussions and negotiations that created → the Church of South India and, as the secretary of the commission acknowledged, "made the South India Scheme the basis of its discussions." The churches that participated were: the [Anglican] Church of India, Pakistan, Burma, and Ceylon; the Methodist Church in Ceylon; the Baptist Churches in Ceylon; the Presbyterian Churches in Ceylon; and the Jaffna Diocese of the Church of South India.

In Ceylon as in South India, the doctrine of the ministry—congregational, presbyteral, episcopal—was the main point of disagreement. Therefore the declaration that "the uniting churches recognize that episcopal, presbyteral, and congregational elements all have their place in the order of life of the Church of Lanka" (7) is not only an administrative compromise but a doctrinal consensus. But in words of the Indian ecumenical leader D. T. Niles that are applicable well beyond Ceylon, "the problem simply is that, in seeking union, we face the consequence of the paradox that the Church is indivisible and that yet it is divided."[1] Within the total *Scheme of Church Union in Ceylon,* as a dissertation on the subject puts it, "Section II on Faith and Order contains what might be called the 'Creed' of the Church of Lanka, divided into twelve headings."[2] The Negotiating Committee, made up of six members from each of the five churches named above, presented several drafts of *The Scheme* from 1941 to 1953. They formally proposed it to the governing bodies of churches in Ceylon in 1955, and the entire document was officially accepted at the Union in 1963. As we have with other constitutional confessions, we reproduce here the doctrinal articles, but not the purely administrative ones.

Edition: *Proposed Scheme of Church Union in Ceylon* 1955, 9–30.

Literature: Boisvert 1964; Niles 1962; Soysa 1962.

1. Niles 1962, 307.
2. Boisvert 1964, 56

The Church of Lanka, *Scheme of Church Union in Ceylon: Faith and Order,* 1963

The governing principles with respect to the Faith and Order of the Church of Lanka are here set forth in a series of agreed resolutions by the uniting churches. These resolutions not only reflect the intentions of the uniting churches for the United Church as they enter into union; but also form a part of the Constitution of the United Church, by which it is governed.

1. The Nature of the Union

The uniting churches agree that it is the will of Christ that his church should be one. To the church which is his body he promised the manifold gifts of his grace. It is also his will that there should be a ministry accepted and fully effective throughout the worldwide church. But, in the present divided state of Christendom, since the ministries of all separated communions are by the fact of separation imperfect and limited in authority, the ministry can recover fullness only by the union of all the parts of the one body.

The uniting churches recognize, however, that their ministries have all been blessed by God who is Sovereign over his church, and owned by the Holy Spirit as effective means of grace. They acknowledge one another's ministries to be real ministries of the word and sacraments, and confidently expect that these ministries hitherto separate will, when united, be used for a yet fuller manifestation of God's power and glory.

The Church of Lanka will be formed by a combination of different elements, each bringing its contribution to the whole, and not by the absorption of any one by any other. It will, therefore, be an integral church in which its members, firmly holding the fundamentals of the faith and order of the church universal, will have freedom of opinion in all other matters, and freedom of action in such differences of practice as are consistent with the general framework of the church as one organic body.

In laying down laws and principles for the life of the Church of Lanka, the uniting churches do not seek thereby to express a judgment upon the teaching or practice of the uniting churches hitherto.

2. The Church and Its Membership

The uniting churches acknowledge that the church is the body of Christ, and that its members are the members of his body knit together in the fellowship of the Holy Spirit. They agree that only those shall be members of the Church of Lanka who have been baptized with water into the name of the Father and of the Son and of the Holy Spirit and, who, receiving the calling and grace of God with faith, remain therein. Members of the church maintain their vital union with the Head of the body, Jesus Christ, by the same faith through the various means of grace which he has provided in his church, and glorify his name by such good works as he has prepared for them to walk in.

3. The Faith of the Church

The uniting churches hold the faith which the church has ever held in Jesus Christ, the Redeemer of the world, in whom men are saved by grace through faith; and in accordance with the revelation of God which he made, being himself God incarnate, they worship one God in three persons, unity in Trinity and Trinity in unity.

Under the guidance of the Holy Spirit, the church has handed down the Holy Scriptures of the Old and New Testaments. The uniting churches receive and accept these Scriptures as containing all things necessary to salvation,[1] and as the standard of faith.

They accept the creeds commonly called Apostles' and Nicene, as witnessing to and safeguarding that faith which is continuously confirmed in the spiritual experience of the church of Christ; and as containing a sufficient statement thereof for a basis of union. The use of the creeds in worship is an act of adoration and thanksgiving towards Almighty God for his nature and for his acts of love and mercy, as well as a joyful remembrance of the faith which binds together the worshipers. In the preparation of candidates for baptism and for confirmation the Apostles' Creed or, if so desired, the Nicene Creed shall be used as a necessary part of the specified instruction.

Note:

(i) It is understood that it will be competent for the Church of Lanka to issue supplementary statements concerning the faith, for the guidance of its teachers and the edification of the faithful, provided that such statements are agreeable to the truths of our religion revealed in the Holy Scriptures.

(ii) Any traditional declaration of faith, used for instruction of the faithful

1. *39 Art* 6.

in any of the uniting churches, may continue to be so used after the act of union, so long as it is consistent with the doctrinal standards officially set forth by the Church of Lanka.

(iii) In the reading of Holy Scripture in the public service of the church, the use of the books known as the Apocrypha shall be permitted, it being understood that they are read for profit and instruction and not for the establishment of doctrine.

4. The Worship of the Church

In the worship of Almighty God, the Church of Lanka will aim at conserving for the common benefit whatever spiritual riches have been gained by the uniting churches in their separate experience.

Forms of worship which before the union were generally accepted and used in any of the uniting churches shall not be forbidden in the Church of Lanka, nor shall any wonted form be changed or new form introduced into the worship of any congregation without the agreement of the presbyter and the congregation. Subject to these provisions, and to any special regulations which may be made by the Synod of the Church of Lanka with regard to the essential elements or central parts of the services of baptism, holy communion, and marriage, every presbyter and congregation shall have freedom to choose the forms of their public worship.

5. The Sacraments of the Church

The uniting churches believe that, while the operations of divine grace cannot be limited, the two sacraments of baptism and the supper of the Lord were ordained by Christ himself as means of grace by which we are united to God and through which God works in us.

a. Baptism

1. Baptism is a sign and seal of engrafting into Christ and entrance into the covenant of grace. In him we receive the new birth, the forgiveness of sins, and the gift of the Holy Spirit. Those who are baptized are by this sacrament solemnly admitted into the fellowship of the church and engaged to be the Lord's.

2. The grace of Christ conferred in baptism is appropriated unto salvation by repentance and faith.

In sponsored baptism in infancy, the sponsors, whether parents or godparents, together with the congregation, undertake in the name of the church to bring up the child in the fear and nurture of the Lord; the child himself being baptized into the repenting and believing life of the church.

In believer's baptism, the candidate himself, led by God's grace to repentance and faith, bears witness to these and, in the sacrament, responds to the action of God. So he enters consciously into the repenting and believing life of the church in which the event of baptism takes place.

3. Full Christian initiation is a process which is concluded only when the initiate participates for the first time in holy communion. By coming to the holy communion the initiate declares his resolve, sustained by his union with Christ, to persevere within this realm of life which is pledged to him from his baptism, and in which the benefits of the divine forgiveness and the powers of the age to come are at work.

[Mt 28.19]   4. Baptism shall be administered with water by immersion or affusion or sprinkling in the name of the Father and of the Son and of the Holy Spirit.

5. A person may receive either sponsored baptism in infancy or believer's baptism. Where parents do not wish their children to receive sponsored baptism they shall bring them to a service of dedication. By such a service the church recognizes the place of the child within the Christian fellowship and emphasizes the duty of the parents and of the church to bring up children so dedicated in the fear and nurture of the Lord.

6. The full Service of Initiation of Believers shall include the following elements:

(i) Declaration of Christ's commission to the church to baptize.

(ii) Confession to God by the candidate of his sin.

(iii) Witness before the congregation by the candidate of his belief in Jesus Christ as Lord and Savior.

(iv) Assent by the candidate to the Apostles' Creed.

(v) Baptism of the candidate with water in the name of the Father and of the Son and of the Holy Spirit.

(vi) Presentation of the candidate to the bishop by the presbyter, the bishop thereupon laying his hands upon the candidate's head with the prayer that he receive power by the gift of the Holy Spirit.

(vii) Welcoming of the candidate into the fellowship of the congregation by the presbyter who will give him the right hand of fellowship.

But (vi) and (vii) can also constitute a separate Service of Confirmation to be held in the case of those who are admitted to communicant membership of the church sometime after they have received believer's baptism.

7. A person who has received sponsored baptism in infancy shall be admitted to communicant membership of the church in a Service of Confirmation, such service to provide for a candidate to accept and ratify the vows made on his behalf when he was baptized. The other elements which shall be provided for in this Service of Confirmation will be those numbered (ii), (iii), (iv), (vi), and (vii) in the full Service of Initiation of Believers.

8. The Service of Holy Communion will usually follow the Service of Confirmation and the full Service of Believer's Baptism.

Note:

(i) Where a minister has scruples in regard to the administration of baptism to infants, he shall invite some other minister of the Church of Lanka to perform the rite.

(ii) The service of baptism shall usually be held in the course of a service of public worship.

(iii) It is recognized that there will be in the Church of Lanka those who do not accept the practice of sponsored baptism, but their requirement that it is on a profession of faith that a person becomes a full member of the church is adequately met by provisions (ii), (iii), and (iv) in the Service of Confirmation.

(iv) In immersion, the candidate is dipped completely under the water. In affusion, water is poured on to the head of the candidate. In sprinkling, the minister dips his hand in the water and places it on the head of the candidate.

b. The Supper of the Lord

1. The Lord's supper was instituted by Christ himself who in the same night in which he was betrayed took bread, blessed, broke, and gave it to his disciples and in like manner blessed and gave the cup as the new covenant in his blood.

In doing this in obedience to our Lord's command with the unfailing use of his words of institution we shew forth the Lord's death until he come and receive [1 Cor 11.23–26] him in holy communion by faith with thanksgiving.

2. The uniting churches agree that any new form of the service of holy communion drawn up by the Church of Lanka shall include the following elements of worship:

(i) Thanksgiving for God's glory and goodness, with the expression of penitence, and prayer that all may communicate worthily.

(ii) Commemoration of Christ's life and work through the ministry of the word, and through the recitation of the creed.

(iii) Showing forth, and pleading before the Father, Christ's sacrifice once for all offered; invoking Christ's merits for the whole church; remembering his resurrection and ascension, his session at the right hand of God; and looking for his coming again, in glory.

(iv) Presenting ourselves—our souls and bodies—as a living sacrifice unto God.

(v) Acknowledging Christ who is present in his church, which is his mystical body, as the true celebrant and the bread of life in the Communion Service.

(vi) Communion and fellowship with God, with one another, with the people of God on earth, and with all the company of heaven.

(vii) Offering to God praise and thanksgiving for the grace received in holy communion.

3. Any form of the service of holy communion which before the union was in use in any of the uniting churches may be used in the Church of Lanka; and every presbyter and congregation shall have freedom to choose the form of service which they will use, provided that it shall include those elements which the Synod of the Church of Lanka shall declare to be essential. In the service of holy communion, bread and wine shall be set apart with the unfailing use of Christ's words of institution.

Note:

(i) It shall be a rule of order that the Church of Lanka will entrust the celebration of the holy communion only to its bishops and presbyters.

(ii) Visiting ministers from other churches may be invited to celebrate the holy communion in the Church of Lanka.

6. The Ministry of the Church

The uniting churches believe that, because the church is the body of Christ, it is [1 Pt 2.9] therefore a royal priesthood through which Christ the risen and ascended High-Priest continues his priestly work. All its members are called, in virtue of their union with Christ, to a priestly ministry; both Godward, in the offering of spiritual sacrifices, gifts, and prayers for mankind; and manward, in the showing forth by life and word of the glory of the redeeming power of God. No individual and no one order in the church can claim exclusive possession of this priesthood.

The uniting churches believe that the ordained ministry is a gift of God to his church through Christ, who gave to his apostles a commission which he perpetuates in the church. They believe that God himself calls men into the ministry through his Holy Spirit, and that their vocation as ministers is to bring sinners to repentance, to lead God's people in worship, prayer and praise, and, through pastoral ministrations, the preaching of the gospel and the administration of the sacraments, to assist men by faith to receive the saving and sanctifying benefits of Christ and to fit them for service. They believe that in ordination God, in answer to the prayers of his church, sets apart for the ministry those whom he has called and whom his church has accepted, and bestows on and assures to them a commission for it and the grace appropriate to it.

A minister, who for any cause has ceased to exercise his ministry, shall not be reordained on beginning again to exercise that ministry.

7. The Order of Life of the Church

The uniting churches recognize that episcopal, presbyteral, and congregational elements all have their place in the order of life of the Church of Lanka, and that the episcopate, the presbyterate, the diaconate, and the congregation of the faithful should all, in accordance with their several functions, have responsibility and exercise authority in the life and work of the church, in its governance and administration, in its evangelistic and pastoral work, in its discipline and in its worship.

1. THE FUNCTIONS OF THE CONGREGATION
IN THE CHURCH OF LANKA

The uniting churches believe that every member of the church is bound, in virtue of his living membership of the body of Christ, to take his share in the life of the worshiping church by participating in the worship of the church on the Lord's day after the manner of the apostolic church, by giving of his substance for the support of the church and ministry, by witnessing to his faith in his life and daily conduct, and by seeking to bring others into discipleship to Jesus Christ.

The uniting churches believe also that as the church of a whole region (being in fellowship with other regional churches) is ideally the embodiment of the church universal in that region, and as similarly the church of a diocese (as a living part of a regional church) is the church universal expressing its one life in that diocese; so also in the purpose of God every local group of the faithful, organized for Christian life and worship as a congregation or pastorate within the fellowship of the diocese, represents in that place the same one, holy, catholic, and apostolic church.[2]

Subject, therefore, to such general regulations as may be issued by the Synod of the Church of Lanka or by a diocesan council, every congregation of the

2. N-CP 9.

Church of Lanka shall, with its pastor, have responsibility in the admission and nurture of its members, in maintaining the purity of its life and doctrine, in ordering its corporate worship, and in the proclamation of the gospel to those outside the church. Every pastorate will have general administrative authority within its area, its pastorate session, representation on the diocesan council, certain responsibilities in church discipline, and opportunity for expressing its judgment both as to the appointment of its pastor and the selection of candidates for ordination from that pastorate.

There will be a church meeting in each pastorate where the communicant members in that pastorate will meet together to discharge the responsible tasks committed to them. There will also be provision in the Church of Lanka for the order of deaconnesses and for the exercise by lay men and women of functions such as those of evangelists, lay elders, class leaders, and lay preachers.

2. THE FUNCTIONS OF THE MINISTRY IN THE CHURCH OF LANKA

The uniting churches agree that the ministry is the organ and instrument of the church which is the body of Christ and the royal priesthood. Consequently, the functions of the ministerial priesthood are in direct relation to these purposes of the church, viz., to worship God; to evangelize the nations; to teach the faith; to preach the word; and to administer the means of grace to its children.

The office of the ministry, therefore, is liturgical, missionary, teaching, prophetic, and pastoral, and in each of these activities its priesthood is representative and organic, not substitutionary. "Organic" means acting as an organ or limb, such as the eye or hand, which cannot act apart from the living body but must act organi-
[1 Cor 12.21]   cally to the whole body. The difference, therefore, between the ministry and laity is not a difference in kind but in function.

The functions of the ministry are to feed the flock of God, to deliver the whole counsel of God by the ministry of the word, to care for the church committed to its charge, to baptize, to confirm, to ordain, and to fulfill the ministry of reconciliation by declaring to penitent sinners God's forgiveness both in the public and the private exercise of that ministry, to administer Christ's sacraments, and to pronounce God's blessing in the name of the church. These functions will be performed by bishops, presbyters, and deacons, as set forth below. Bishop, presbyter, and deacon shall be the terms used by the Church of Lanka to designate its threefold ministry.

a. The Episcopate in the Church of Lanka

The uniting churches accept the historic episcopate, in a constitutional form, as part of their basis of union. By "historic episcopate" is meant the episcopate which has historic continuity with that of the undivided church. No one particular theological interpretation of episcopacy shall be demanded from any minister or member of the Church of Lanka.

(i) Every bishop in the Church of Lanka shall perform the functions of the historic episcopate in accordance with the Constitution of the Church of Lanka. These include all the functions of the ministry as set out above.

(ii) Bishops of dioceses shall be elected; both the diocese concerned in each particular case, and the authorities of the Church of Lanka as a whole, sharing responsibility in their appointment.

(iii) Continuity with the historic episcopate shall be maintained.

b. The Presbyterate in the Church of Lanka

A presbyter, as priest and prophet, shall perform all the functions of the ministry as set out above, except those reserved to the bishop.

c. The Diaconate in the Church of Lanka

The functions of a deacon are to assist the bishop or presbyter in the administration of holy communion, to preach and to teach the word, and in all respects to help the presbyter to whom he shall be licensed in the fulfillment of his responsibilities.

3. ORDINATION IN THE CHURCH OF LANKA

1. All consecrations of bishops shall be performed by the laying on of hands of at least three bishops.

2. Every ordination of presbyters shall be performed by the laying on of hands by a bishop and presbyters together.

3. The ordination of a deacon shall be performed by the laying on of hands of a bishop.

8. The Church's Initial Membership and Ministry
a. Membership

The uniting churches agree that all baptized persons who at the time of the union are communicant members of any of the uniting churches in the area of the union shall have the privileges and responsibilities of communicant members of the Church of Lanka, and, as such, shall be at liberty to receive communion in any of its churches unless they express dissent from its doctrine and discipline. Similarly all baptized members and catechumens belonging to any of the uniting churches shall be acknowledged as baptized members and catechumens respectively of the Church of Lanka.

b. Ministry

With respect to the initial ministry of the Church of Lanka, the uniting churches desire the unification of the ministries of the several uniting churches at the inauguration of union. For this purpose the uniting churches adopt the following proposals:

(i) At the inauguration of union all those duly elected to be bishops of the Church of Lanka who have not already received episcopal consecration shall be consecrated by three duly authorized bishops, if possible from outside Ceylon, representing differing church traditions and acceptable to all the uniting churches. Immediately thereafter, all those who have been elected to be bishops of the Church of Lanka and have been duly consecrated shall receive, by prayer and the laying on of hands by ministers of all the uniting churches duly appointed for this purpose, a commission to exercise their ministry in the Church of Lanka.

The specific preface and formula to be used in this service will be:

Preface: The good hand of God being upon us, these several churches, called together into visible unity as part of the universal church with an agreed basis of faith and order, desire, at the inauguration of union, by the use of the liturgical forms herein set forth, to bring about by God's grace and mercy such a unification of the sacred ministry in this church as shall join together in one all the several inheritances of grace and authority which have hitherto been the possession of each church in separation. In so doing, it is the intention of this church to continue and reverently to use and esteem the threefold ministry of bishop, presbyter, and deacon which existed in the undivided church.

Since the uniting churches, while assured that each of them has received from Christ a real ministry of the word and sacraments, have been accustomed in diverse manners to seek authority from God for their ministries, which have been exercised in diverse ways, this United Church humbly trusts that in this service God by the operation of the Holy Spirit will bestow on each of the persons elected and consecrated bishops such grace, gifts, character, and authority as they severally may now need to fulfill the charge to be committed to them in the United Church.

Formula: "Forasmuch as you have been consecrated to the office and order of bishop in the church of God and have been elected to be a bishop of the Church of Lanka, we, on behalf of the uniting churches, commission you as a bishop of the Church of Lanka and acknowledge you to be now possessed of the fullness of the ministry of this church in which are joined together our diverse ministries. The grace of the Holy Spirit be with you, enlightening, strengthening, and endowing you with wisdom all the days of your life, in the name of the Father and of the Son and of the Holy Spirit. Amen."

(ii) After the bishops of the Church of Lanka have been elected, consecrated, and commissioned, each bishop shall, with prayer and the laying on of hands, receive into the presbyterate of the Church of Lanka all the ministers of the uniting churches in his diocese who desire to be presbyters in the Church of Lanka, and are eligible to be so by their standing in their own church. In the formula used at this service acknowledgment will be made of their ordination already received, then will follow prayer that God bestow upon them the power and grace of the Holy Spirit to exercise a wider ministry in the church of God as presbyter within the Church of Lanka and authorization will be given to them in the name of the newly United Church to exercise their ministry within it. . . .

9. Marriage in the Church

1. Marriage is a holy estate, instituted by God[3] and so existing in the natural order. The Church of Lanka declares its belief that our Lord's principle and standard of marriage is that it is a divine institution, involving a lifelong union for better or for worse of one man with one woman to the exclusion of all others on either side; and that the marriage relation signifies the mystical union that is between Christ and his church.

2. The Church of Lanka acknowledges its responsibility for doing all that lies in its power both to provide proper instruction in the meaning, privileges and duties of Christian marriage, and to insure, when it solemnizes a marriage, that the contracting parties have not only received and understood such instruction but also intend that their married life shall conform to the Christian standard.

3. Where it appears that a marriage of its members is in danger of being broken, the Church of Lanka will seek to effect a reconciliation; but if the attempt at reconciliation shall fail, or if a marriage is already broken, the Church of Lanka will seek so to order all its actions towards the parties involved as both to unfold

3. *BCP.*

the standard of Christian marriage and the church's witness to it, and also minister Christ's mercy and his gift of renewal.

10. Legislation in the Church

1. In the sphere of legislation the ultimate authority of the Church of Lanka resides in the harmony of bishops, presbyters and laity. Thus, except where by constitution any administrative function is reserved for any person or body of persons, all matters concerning the Church of Lanka shall be decided in synod by the vote of bishops, presbyters, and laity sitting together.

But where any proposition concerns (*a*) the faith and doctrine of the church, (*b*) the conditions of membership in the church, and the rules which govern excommunication from the church, (*c*) the functions of the ordained ministry of the church, (*d*) the worship of the church, and any forms of worship proposed for general use in the church, (*e*) relations with other churches, (*f*) negotiation for union with any other church or churches, it shall be considered to be passed only if accepted by a majority of the bishops, presbyters, and laity voting separately, and a majority consisting of two-thirds of those present of the whole synod voting together.

2. There shall also be a permanent theological commission in the Church of Lanka, ordinarily composed of bishops, presbyters, and laity, who shall act as an advisory body to the church and its bishops on all questions of faith and order.

3. The Church of Lanka affirms its intention to remain at one in faith with the church universal and to maintain the fundamental principles of the same.

11. Relations with Other Churches

The relations of the Church of Lanka to other churches are determined by the nature of the union whereby the Church of Lanka is formed, and are as follows:

1. The fact that other churches do not follow the rule of episcopal ordination will not preclude the Church of Lanka from holding relations of communion and fellowship with them.

2. Any communicant member of any church which is, at the time of union, in full communion with any of the uniting churches will be at liberty to communicate in any place of worship of the Church of Lanka.

3. Any ordained minister of any church which is, at the time of union, in full communion with any of the uniting churches will be free as a visitor to min-

ister in any congregation of the Church of Lanka if he is invited to do so by the presbyter-in-charge.

Any such visiting minister may celebrate the holy communion if invited to do so by the presbyter-in-charge under the regulation of the bishop.

It shall be the duty of the Synod in framing these rules, and of the bishop in administering them, to safeguard the faith and order of the Church of Lanka, and in the application of these provisions to take care that no arrangement will knowingly be made in worship or practice which would either offend the conscience of the congregation, or imperil the progress of the Church of Lanka towards union with other churches.

4. An ordained minister of any church which is in full communion, at the time of union, with any of the uniting churches shall, if he is accepted for service in the Church of Lanka as one of its ministers, be received by the Church of Lanka.

5. Any baptized person who is of communicant status in any church which is in full communion, at the time of union, with any of the uniting churches, who desires to become a member of the Church of Lanka, shall be accepted as a communicant member of the Church of Lanka.

12. The Autonomy of the Church

The uniting churches agree that the Church of Lanka should of right be free in all spiritual matters from the direction or interposition of any civil government.

They further agree that the Church of Lanka must possess complete autonomy and be free from any control, legal or otherwise, of any church or society, external to itself, even of the churches from which it has been formed.

At the same time, they remember that the Church of Lanka, on account of its origin and history, must have special relations with the churches in the West and they are confident that the Church of Lanka will seek so to regulate its acts as to secure a complete recognition of its ministry and membership by those churches of which the uniting churches now form a part: and also a full recognition of and communion with those churches and with other branches of the catholic church with which the uniting churches are now in communion.

They also recognize that the Church of Lanka, as a part of the church universal, must give full weight to the pronouncements of bodies representative of the whole church, and in particular would desire to take part in the deliberations and decisions of any future ecumenical council.

The Church of North India and the Church of Pakistan, *Plan of Church Union: The Doctrines of the Church,* 1965

Following upon the negotiations leading to the founding of → the Church of South India and those leading to the founding of → the Church of Lanka, the no less difficult and protracted consideration of church union in North India and in neighboring Pakistan learned from those negotiations and borrowed from their results, but also followed a distinct course.

The differences were due in part to the division between Pakistan and India that came out of the achievement of independence from the British empire, and in part to the different configuration of the constituting churches, which included the Council of the Baptist Churches in Northern India, the Church of the Brethren in India, the Disciples of Christ, the Church of India, Pakistan, Burma, and Ceylon, the Methodist Church (British and Australasian Conferences), the Methodist Church in Southern Asia, and the United Church of Northern India. As a result, a major scholarly study of the historical process reports that "in reading the minutes of these committees, one gets a first impression of a long drawn-out debate whereby one paragraph was eventually written and then changed over and over again."[1]

Confessionally, the outcome of those debates was this creedal formulation of "The Doctrines of the Church," which constitutes part 4 of the *Plan of Union* and then the *Constitution.*

Edition: *Plan of Church Union in North India and Pakistan* 1965, 4–6.

Literature: Bayne 1960; Kellock 1965; Sahu 1994; Vischer, 350–51.

---

1. Sahu 1994, 106.

The Church of North India and the Church of Pakistan, *Plan of Church Union: The Doctrines of the Church*, 1965

1. The Church of North India/Pakistan holds the faith which the church has ever held in Jesus Christ, the Redeemer of the world, in whom alone men are saved by grace through faith, and in accordance with the revelation of God which he made, being himself God incarnate, it worships one God, Father, Son, and Holy Spirit.

2. It accepts the Holy Scriptures of the Old Testament and the New Testament as the inspired word of God, as containing all things necessary to salvation, and as the supreme and decisive standard of faith, and acknowledges that the church must always be ready to correct and reform itself in accordance with the teaching of those Scriptures as the Holy Spirit shall reveal it.

3. It accepts the creeds commonly called the Apostles' and Nicene as witnessing to and guarding that faith, which is continuously confirmed by the Holy Spirit in the experience of the church of Christ.

The use of the creeds in worship is an act of adoration and thanksgiving toward Almighty God for his nature and for his acts of love and mercy, as well as a joyful affirmation of the faith which binds together the worshipers.

4. The Church of North India/Pakistan is keenly aware of the fact that divergence of conviction on certain other matters of faith and practice is something which can only be borne within one fellowship by the exercise of much mutual forbearance and charity. Nevertheless, it believes that it is called to make this act of faith in the conviction that it is not the will of the Lord of the church that they who are one in him should be divided even for such causes as these. It further believes itself to be called to this venture in the confidence that in brotherly converse within one church those of diverse convictions will be led together in the unity of the Spirit to learn what is his will in these matters of difference.

5. For the confession of its faith before the world and for the guidance of its teachers and the edification of the faithful, it shall be competent for the Church of North India/Pakistan to issue its own statements, provided always that such statements are agreeable to the Holy Scriptures.

The Church of North India/Pakistan furthermore acknowledges the witness to the catholic faith contained in the confessions of faith adopted both at the time of the Reformation and subsequently, and formulated by the uniting churches or their parent churches. In particular, the Church of North India/Pakistan accepts the following statements as consistent with the doctrinal standards of this church: (a) Declaration 1 of the Constitution of the Church of India, Pakistan, Burma, and Ceylon; (b) The Confession of Faith of the United Church of Northern India; (c) The General Rules as contained in the Discipline of the Methodist Church in Southern Asia; (d) The doctrinal standards of the Methodist Church (British Conference); (e) The Baptist Church Covenant. (C.B.C.N.I.)

Any other traditional declarations of faith, generally used for the instruction of the faithful in any of the uniting churches, may continue to be so used after the union, so long as they are consistent with the doctrinal standards officially set forth by the Church of North India/Pakistan.

Ghana Church Union Committee,
The Faith of the Church, 1965

Beginning in 1957, the Ghana Church Union Committee brought together representatives of the following churches: the Diocese of Accra, the [Anglican] Church of the Province of West Africa; the Evangelical Presbyterian Church; the Methodist Church, Ghana; the Presbyterian Church of Ghana.

Several years of discussion led to the publication of the first edition of *The Proposed Basis of Union* in 1963. It acknowledged a "considerable" debt to "material from Church Union Schemes in other countries, particularly the Nigeria Scheme, which itself depends heavily on the Basis of Union of the Church of South India." After further discussion and revision, the Ghana Church Union Committee submitted this revised version of the document to the constituting churches in 1965.

As the reference to being heavily dependent on the development of → the Church of South India suggests, the main point of division here, as there, was the doctrine of the ministry. The multilayered resolution of this issue, as set forth in this document as a whole, is partly doctrinal or confessional and partly administrative or constitutional. Although *The Faith of the Church* is, strictly speaking, the title only of article 3 of the *Proposed Basis,* we have extended it to the entire dogmatic and creedal portion of the document, which embraces articles 1–5 and article 11 on worship. For consistency in reference, we have, however, retained the original numbering of the articles.

Edition: *Proposed Basis of Union* 1965, 9–13, 25.

Literature: *DEM* 4–10 (John S. Pobee); Vischer, 272–87.

Ghana Church Union Committee,
The Faith of the Church, 1965

1. OUR APPROACH TO CHURCH UNITY

1. What we are trying to do:

a. We are seeking the true and visible unity of the church in Ghana.

b. Believing that God created one church, a spiritual union and fellowship of those who are in Christ through the indwelling power of the Holy Spirit, we pray and seek for a visible expression of this *oneness* in the worship, life, and witness of the church here and now.

c. We intend that the united church shall maintain fellowship with all those parts of the church of Christ with which we separately enjoy fellowship now.

d. We also desire, as opportunity offers, to seek an ever-widening union with other parts of the universal church.

e. With full trust in the Holy Spirit, we are looking towards a united church which, as its members learn together in a wider fellowship, will maintain in reverent humility a readiness to correct and reform itself as God's will becomes more clearly known.

f. Though we were established as separate churches in Ghana through the missionary zeal of Christians in other lands, we desire to heal these historic separations without the surrender of any principle of faith or order which, through mutual prayer and deliberation, we believe to be within the will of God for the one holy, catholic, and apostolic church of which our Lord Jesus Christ is the Founder and Head.

g. We are agreed in seeking a united church which will be an integral part of the universal church, and yet develop the special and distinctive gifts which God has given to the people of Ghana in the expression of its worship, its faith, and its common life.

2. Why we are trying to do it:

a. We are seeking union because we believe that the restoration of the visible unity of the church on earth is the will of God, and we believe that the Holy Spirit is leading us to resolve the differences which at present separate us. Our Lord Jesus Christ prayed: "that they all may be one; as thou, Father, art in me, and I in thee, that they also may be one in us: that the world may believe that thou hast sent me"

(Jn 17.21). We believe that here, as elsewhere in the New Testament, there is no thought of a spiritual unity as distinct from a visible unity. The unity which the one Spirit creates is realized in the visible life of the one body.

b. We believe that the unity to which God is leading us will make the church in Ghana a more effective instrument for his work, more eager and powerful to proclaim by word and deed the gospel of Christ, filled with greater charity and peace, and enriched in worship and fellowship.

3. How we are trying to do it:

c. The negotiating churches humbly and thankfully recognize one another as parts of the one church of Jesus Christ. God in his mercy has blessed them and used them for his redemptive work in Ghana. Each church in separation has received gifts from God and has borne special witness to certain elements of the truth; yet all believe that the perfecting of the whole body requires the heritage of each, as also of every part of the universal church.

d. They also acknowledge one another's ministries to be real ministries of the word and sacraments and recognize the spiritual efficacy of sacraments and ministrations which God has clearly blessed. Yet they believe that God, in willing his church to be one, wills that its ministry should be one ministry, acknowledged by every part of the universal church. So long as the churches are in separation, there can be no ministry which fully corresponds with the purpose of God, namely, that the body of Christ be built up until it "attain to the unity of the faith and of the knowledge of the Son of God, to mature manhood, to the measure of the stature of the fullness of Christ" (Eph 4.13).

e. In the light of these convictions we do not desire that any one church shall absorb other churches, nor that one tradition shall be imposed upon all; but rather that each church shall bring the true riches of its inheritance into the united church to which we look forward. We intend that it shall be a church which, while holding to the fundamental faith and order of the universal church, shall assure to its members such freedom of opinion and action as is consistent with the life of the church as one organic body.

2. THE CHURCH AND ITS MEMBERSHIP

The negotiating churches acknowledge that the church is the body of Christ in which members are knit together in the fellowship of the Holy Spirit. They agree that those are members according to the will and purpose of God who have been baptized with water into the name of the Father and of the Son and of the Holy

Spirit, and who are born again by the grace of God through faith. They agree that members of the church in fellowship with one another, maintain their vital union with the head of the body by faith through the various means of grace which he has provided in his church, and glorify his name by such good works as he has prepared for them to walk in.

3. THE FAITH OF THE CHURCH

1. The negotiating churches are united in their faith in Jesus Christ, the Redeemer of the world, in whom alone is salvation by grace through faith, and they worship one God, Father, Son, and Holy Spirit, as revealed by God in Jesus Christ, who is God incarnate.

2. They accept the Holy Scriptures of the Old and New Testaments as the word of God, as containing all things necessary to salvation, and as the supreme and decisive standard of faith. They acknowledge that the church must always be ready to correct and reform itself in accordance with the teaching of those Scriptures as the Holy Spirit continues to reveal it.

3. They accept the creeds commonly called the Apostles' and Nicene as witnessing to and safeguarding that faith which is continuously confirmed by the Holy Spirit in the experience of the church. They believe that these creeds are a sufficient statement of that faith to be a basis of union.

4. Note: While the negotiating churches have taken traditional statements of the faith (The Apostles' and Nicene Creeds) as sufficient to serve as a basis of union, they are agreed that the church has a continuing responsibility to make its faith clear both to itself and to those outside, restating that faith in relation to the contemporary situation in which the church stands and in relation to the beliefs, hopes and fears of the world around it. They believe that it should be an early task of the united church to take up this responsibility.

4. THE SACRAMENTS OF THE CHURCH

The negotiating churches believe that the sacraments of baptism and the supper of the Lord are means of grace through which God works in us and by which we are united to God. They also believe that while the mercy of God to all mankind cannot be limited, there is in the teaching of Christ the plain command that men should follow his appointed way of salvation by a definite act of reception into the family of God and by continued acts of fellowship with him in that family, and that this teaching is made explicit in the two sacraments which he has given us. The negotiating churches agree that the sacraments should be ministered in the united church with unfailing use of Christ's words of institution and with the elements ordained by him.

5. THE MINISTRY OF THE WHOLE CHURCH

1. The negotiating churches believe that the risen and ascended Christ continues his ministry to the world in and through the church. All the members of the church are called, in virtue of their union with Christ, to participate in this ministry. Among its aspects are the prophetic ministry in which God's word is made known to men; the priestly ministry in which worship and intercession are offered on behalf of mankind; the pastoral ministry in which God's concern for the life of men is expressed. All this is *ministry* or service, and the church is sent among men as a servant in the spirit and power of Christ who himself was sent into the world as the Servant. No individual and no one order in the church can claim exclusive possession of this ministry.

2. The whole church is thus apostolic: as the Father sent the Son into the world, so the Son sends those who believe that God sent him. The whole company of those who are baptized into his name have a mission to the world, which is continued down the ages in spite of all defects in individuals and in order. Inspired by the same Holy Spirit, witnessing to and obeying the same gospel, living by the same Scriptures, and receiving the tradition and doctrine of the apostles, the whole church continues their mission and ministry.

3. The negotiating churches believe that within this ministry of the whole church Christ has given a special ministry of the word and sacraments. To this special ministry some members of the church are called by God and set apart by ordination, receiving authority in and through the church from Christ its head. The ordained ministry is an organ of the body through which Christ the head acts by the Holy Spirit to build up the body and to equip its members for their part in the ministry of the whole church.

11. THE WORSHIP OF THE UNITED CHURCH

1. In the worship of Almighty God the united church will aim at conserving for the common benefit whatever spiritual riches have been gained by the uniting churches in their separate experience. Forms of worship that were authorized in any of the uniting churches at the time of union shall be permitted in the united church. No such form of worship, rite, or ceremony to which a congregation conscientiously objects shall be imposed upon it in the united church. In course of time, as a common mind develops, the General Conference of the united church may make regulations in respect of public worship.

2. The united church will, however, seek to develop forms of worship in which the distinctive gifts which God has given to the people of Ghana may be reverently used and offered. It is also expected that in due time the united church will produce a common service book, which will arise naturally from the process of growing together and itself strengthen that process.

The United Church of Zambia, *Doctrinal Statement*, 1965/1994

The United Church of Zambia brought together missionary churches that had been the products of three "sending churches": Congregational, Presbyterian, and Methodist. The union was consummated on 16 January 1965 and celebrated at Mindolo Church. This *Doctrinal Statement* is incorporated into the *Constitution of the United Church of Zambia*. The statement is revised every ten years, and it appears here in its most recent revision.

Edition: *Constitution, Rules and Regulations of the United Church of Zambia* 1994, 1-3.

Literature: Bolink 1967; Bwalya 2000, 5-7.

The United Church of Zambia, *Doctrinal Statement,* 1965/1994

1. The United Church holds the faith which the church has ever held in Jesus Christ, the Redeemer of the world, in whom we are saved by grace through faith, and in accordance with the revelation of God which he made, being himself God incarnate, it worships one God, Father, Son, and Holy Spirit.

2. The United Church accepts the Holy Scriptures of the Old and New Testaments, and the creeds commonly called "Apostles'" and "Nicene" as witnessing to and guarding that faith which is continuously confirmed in the spiritual experience of the church of Christ and adopts the following brief summary of our common faith, agreeable in substance with the teaching of Holy Scripture.

3. The word of God, which is contained in the Scriptures of the Old and New Testaments, is the supreme rule of faith and conduct.

4. There is one God: the Father, the Son, and the Holy Spirit. These three are one God, equal in power and glory, and he alone is to be worshiped.

5. All men are sinners and are therefore in need of salvation, and can be saved only by the grace of God through the redeeming work of Christ and the regenerating and sanctifying work of the Holy Spirit.

6. The salvation gained for us by Christ is applied to us by the Holy Spirit, who works through faith in us and thus unites us to Christ, enabling us to receive him as he is freely offered to us in the gospel, and so bring forth the fruits of righteousness. This salvation is for the whole man—body, mind, and spirit. In his gracious work the Spirit uses all means of grace, especially the word, the sacraments, and prayer.

7. The church is the family of all those who respond to God's calling by repenting their sins and believing in Christ as Lord and Savior and by worshiping him. Of this community the Lord Jesus Christ alone is King and Head. The church is commissioned to bring the gospel to the whole world.

8. The United Church believes that, while the divine grace cannot be limited, there are two sacraments ordained by Christ and of perpetual obligation— *baptism* whereby believers and their children enter into a covenant relationship with God and the *Lord's supper* whereby the family of God is continually strengthened and sustained.

9. The church has authority to interpret its doctrine but always in agree-

ment with the word of God. Of this agreement the United Church itself through its synod will be sole judge with due regard to liberty of opinion on matters which do not affect the fundamentals of the faith.

The North American Area Council of the World Alliance of Reformed Churches, *Statement of Faith,* 1965

Because of the characteristic Reformed emphasis on individual confessions by individual churches, each in its own national context, which had produced, for example in the period of the Reformation, such individual formularies as → *The French Confession,* → *The Belgic Confession,* → *The Scots Confession,* → *The First Helvetic Confession* and → *The Second Helvetic Confession,* and → *The Westminster Confession of Faith,* Reformed churches were at a disadvantage when engaging in ecumenical discussions with other communions, and they felt the need for a succinct statement of the faith that united them.

With the founding of the World Alliance of Reformed Churches, and of a North American Area Council within the alliance, there was an agency for promulgating such a statement of faith, which was produced and submitted to the constituent churches of the alliance in 1965.

Edition: Link, 2:94.

The North American Area Council of the World Alliance of Reformed Churches, *Statement of Faith*, 1965

1. We believe in God the Father Almighty, Creator, Sustainer, and Sovereign Lord of all, who rules over all for the fulfillment of his holy, wise, and loving purposes in the world.

2. And in Jesus Christ, his Son our Savior and Lord, through whose perfect sacrificial life and death, and triumphant resurrection and exaltation, we have forgiveness and are reconciled to God and to one another.

3. And in the Holy Spirit, the Spirit of the Father and of the Son, through whose indwelling working we are brought into the fellowship of the church, the body of Christ. In this fellowship we become partakers of his mighty power to renew life in all its relationships, persuaded that, for life here and hereafter, he is able to do for us and in us and through us exceeding abundantly above all that we ask or think.

4. In this faith we worship the one God—Father, Son, and Holy Spirit—and commit ourselves in humble penitence and grateful trust to his service in the world.

The United Presbyterian Church in the United States of America, *Confession,* 1967

The many confessions bearing the name "Presbyterian," many but not all of which appear here as units of "Statements of Faith in Modern Christianity," seemed by their very number and frequency to give the impression of less agreement among the believers and churches bearing that name than was in fact the case. Therefore the movement toward Presbyterian reunification, which marked the twentieth century after the divisions and schisms of the nineteenth, needed to express itself confessionally.

The response to that need was the *Confession* of 1967 adopted by the United Presbyterian Church in the United States of America, as well as its incorporation into an entire *Book of Confessions* of that same year, which includes in addition the following eight statements of faith: → *The Niceno-Constantinopolitan Creed;* → *The Apostles' Creed;* → *The Scots Confession;* → *The Heidelberg Catechism;* → *The Second Helvetic Confession;* → *The Westminster Confession;* → *The Westminster Shorter Catechism;* → *The Barmen Declaration.* (In citing it, we follow the standard system of numbering employed for the *Confession* of 1967 as the ninth component of the *Book of Confessions,* which therefore includes the digit "9." followed by the paragraph number.)

Its acceptance of those earlier creeds and confessions enables this *Confession* to declare in one sentence that "the Trinity and the person of Christ are not redefined but are recognized and reaffirmed as forming the basis and determining the structure of the Christian faith" (9.05).

In 1983, the United Presbyterian Church in the United States of America and the Presbyterian Church in the United States came together again, after a separation of 124 years, to form the Presbyterian Church (USA). To mark this occasion, a committee drafted "A Brief Statement of Faith," which was issued in 1989 to "affirm the traditions of Reformed doctrines while addressing certain pressing [social] issues."[1]

Edition: *Book of Confessions* 1996, 321–30.

Literature: Balcomb 1967; Dowey 1968; Rogers 1985.

1. *The Book of Confessions* 1996, 338; the text of the Confession appears on 341–42.

The United Presbyterian Church in the United States of America, *Confession*, 1967

Preface

9.01. The church confesses its faith when it bears a present witness to God's grace in Jesus Christ.

9.02. In every age the church has expressed its witness in words and deeds as the need of the time required. The earliest examples of confession are found within the Scriptures. Confessional statements have taken such varied forms as hymns, liturgical formulas, doctrinal definitions, catechisms, theological systems in summary, and declarations of purpose against threatening evil.

9.03. Confessions and declarations are subordinate standards in the church, subject to the authority of Jesus Christ, the Word of God, as the Scriptures bear witness to him. No one type of confession is exclusively valid, no one statement is irreformable. Obedience to Jesus Christ alone identifies the one universal church and supplies the continuity of its tradition. This obedience is the ground of the church's duty and freedom to reform itself in life and doctrine as new occasions, in God's providence, may demand.

9.04. The United Presbyterian Church in the United States of America acknowledges itself aided in understanding the gospel by the testimony of the church from earlier ages and from many lands. More especially it is guided by the Nicene and Apostles' Creeds from the time of the early church; the Scots Confession, the Heidelberg Catechism, and the Second Helvetic Confession from the era of the Reformation; the Westminster Confession and Shorter Catechism from the seventeenth century; and the Theological Declaration of Barmen from the twentieth century.

9.05. The purpose of the Confession of 1967 is to call the church to that unity in confession and mission which is required of disciples today. This Confession is not a "system of doctrine," nor does it include all the traditional topics of theology. For example, the Trinity and the person of Christ are not redefined but are recognized and reaffirmed as forming the basis and determining the structure of the Christian faith.

9.06. God's reconciling work in Jesus Christ and the mission of reconciliation to which he has called his church are the heart of the gospel in any age. Our generation stands in peculiar need of reconciliation in Christ. Accordingly this Confession of 1967 is built upon that theme.

The Confession

9.07. In Jesus Christ God was reconciling the world to himself. Jesus Christ is God with man. He is the eternal Son of the Father, who became man and lived among us to fulfill the work of reconciliation. He is present in the church by the power of the Holy Spirit to continue and complete his mission. This work of God, the Father, Son, and Holy Spirit, is the foundation of all confessional statements about God, man, and the world. Therefore the church calls men to be reconciled to God and to one another.

Part 1. God's Work of Reconciliation
SECTION A. THE GRACE OF OUR LORD JESUS CHRIST
1. Jesus Christ

9.08. In Jesus of Nazareth true humanity was realized once for all. Jesus, a Palestinian Jew, lived among his own people and shared their needs, temptations, joys, and sorrows. He expressed the love of God in word and deed and became a brother to all kinds of sinful men. But his complete obedience led him into conflict with his people. His life and teaching judged their goodness, religious aspirations, and national hopes. Many rejected him and demanded his death. In giving himself freely for them he took upon himself the judgment under which all men stand convicted. God raised him from the dead, vindicating him as Messiah and Lord. The victim of sin became victor, and won the victory over sin and death for all men.

9.09. God's reconciling act in Jesus Christ is a mystery which the Scriptures describe in various ways. It is called the sacrifice of a lamb, a shepherd's life given for his sheep, atonement by a priest; again it is ransom of a slave, payment of debt, vicarious satisfaction of a legal penalty, and victory over the powers of evil. These are expressions of a truth which remains beyond the reach of all theory in the depths of God's love for man. They reveal the gravity, cost, and sure achievement of God's reconciling work.

9.10. The risen Christ is the Savior for all men. Those joined to him by faith are set right with God and commissioned to serve as his reconciling community. Christ is Head of this community, the church, which began with the apostles and continues through all generations.

9.11. The same Jesus Christ is the Judge of all men. His judgment discloses the ultimate seriousness of life and gives promise of God's final victory over the power of sin and death. To receive life from the risen Lord is to have life eternal; to refuse life from him is to choose the death which is separation from God. All who put their trust in Christ face divine judgment without fear, for the Judge is their Redeemer.

2. The Sin of Man

9.12. The reconciling act of God in Jesus Christ exposes the evil in men as sin in the sight of God. In sin men claim mastery of their own lives, turn against God and their fellow men, and become exploiters and despoilers of the world. They lose their humanity in futile striving and are left in rebellion, despair, and isolation.

9.13. Wise and virtuous men through the ages have sought the highest good in devotion to freedom, justice, peace, truth, and beauty. Yet all human virtue, when seen in the light of God's love in Jesus Christ, is found to be infected by self-interest and hostility. All men, good and bad alike, are in the wrong before God and helpless without his forgiveness. Thus all men fall under God's judgment. No one is more subject to that judgment than the man who assumes that he is guiltless before God or morally superior to others.

9.14. God's love never changes. Against all who oppose him, God expresses his love in wrath. In the same love God took on himself judgment and shameful death in Jesus Christ, to bring men to repentance and new life.

SECTION B. THE LOVE OF GOD

9.15. God's sovereign love is a mystery beyond the reach of man's mind. Human thought ascribes to God superlatives of power, wisdom, and goodness. But God reveals his love in Jesus Christ by showing power in the form of a servant, wisdom in the folly of the cross, and goodness in receiving sinful men. The power of God's love in Christ to transform the world discloses that the Redeemer is the Lord and Creator who made all things to serve the purpose of his love.

9.16. God has created the world of space and time to be the sphere of his dealings with men. In its beauty and vastness, sublimity and awfulness, order and disorder, the world reflects to the eye of faith the majesty and mystery of its Creator.

9.17. God has created man in a personal relation with himself that man may respond to the love of the Creator. He has created male and female and given them a life which proceeds from birth to death in a succession of generations and in a wide complex of social relations. He has endowed man with capacities to make the world serve his needs and to enjoy its good things. Life is a gift to be received with gratitude and a task to be pursued with courage. Man is free to seek his life within the purpose of God: to develop and protect the resources of nature for the common welfare, to work for justice and peace in society, and in other ways to use his creative powers for the fulfillment of human life.

9.18. God expressed his love for all mankind through Israel, whom he chose to be his covenant people to serve him in love and faithfulness. When Israel was unfaithful, he disciplined the nation with his judgments and maintained his cause through prophets, priests, teachers, and true believers. These witnesses called all Israelites to a destiny in which they would serve God faithfully and become a light to the nations. The same witnesses proclaimed the coming of a new age, and a true servant of God in whom God's purpose for Israel and for mankind would be realized.

9.19. Out of Israel God in due time raised up Jesus. His faith and obedience were the response of the perfect child of God. He was the fulfillment of God's promise to Israel, the beginning of the new creation, and the pioneer of the new humanity. He gave history its meaning and direction and called the church to be his servant for the reconciliation of the world.

SECTION C. THE COMMUNION OF THE HOLY SPIRIT

9.20. God the Holy Spirit fulfills the work of reconciliation in man. The Holy Spirit creates and renews the church as the community in which men are reconciled to God and to one another. He enables them to receive forgiveness as they forgive one another and to enjoy the peace of God as they make peace among themselves. In spite of their sin, he gives them power to become representatives of Jesus Christ and his gospel of reconciliation to all men.

1. The New Life

9.21. The reconciling work of Jesus was the supreme crisis in the life of mankind. His cross and resurrection become personal crisis and present hope for men when the gospel is proclaimed and believed. In this experience the Spirit brings God's forgiveness to men, moves them to respond in faith, repentance, and obedience, and initiates the new life in Christ.

9.22. The new life takes shape in a community in which men know that God loves and accepts them in spite of what they are. They therefore accept themselves and love others, knowing that no man has any ground on which to stand except God's grace.

9.23. The new life does not release a man from conflict with unbelief, pride, lust, fear. He still has to struggle with disheartening difficulties and problems. Nevertheless, as he matures in love and faithfulness in his life with Christ, he lives in freedom and good cheer, bearing witness on good days and evil days, confident that the new life is pleasing to God and helpful to others.

9.24. The new life finds its direction in the life of Jesus, his deeds and words, his struggles against temptation, his compassion, his anger, and his willingness to suffer death. The teaching of apostles and prophets guides men in living this life, and the Christian community nurtures and equips them for their ministries.

9.25. The members of the church are emissaries of peace and seek the good of man in cooperation with powers and authorities in politics, culture, and economics. But they have to fight against pretensions and injustices when these same powers endanger human welfare. Their strength is in their confidence that God's purpose rather than man's schemes will finally prevail.

9.26. Life in Christ is life eternal. The resurrection of Jesus is God's sign that he will consummate his work of creation and reconciliation beyond death and bring to fulfillment the new life begun in Christ.

2. The Bible

9.27. The one sufficient revelation of God is Jesus Christ, the Word of God incarnate, to whom the Holy Spirit bears unique and authoritative witness through the Holy Scriptures, which are received and obeyed as the word of God written. The Scriptures are not a witness among others, but the witness without parallel. The church has received the books of the Old and New Testaments as prophetic and apostolic testimony in which it hears the word of God and by which its faith and obedience are nourished and regulated.

9.28. The New Testament is the recorded testimony of apostles to the coming of the Messiah, Jesus of Nazareth, and the sending of the Holy Spirit to the Church. The Old Testament bears witness to God's faithfulness in his covenant with Israel and points the way to the fulfillment of his purpose in Christ. The Old Testament is indispensable to understanding the New, and is not itself fully understood without the New.

9.29. The Bible is to be interpreted in the light of its witness to God's work of reconciliation in Christ. The Scriptures, given under the guidance of the Holy Spirit, are nevertheless the words of men, conditioned by the language, thought forms, and literary fashions of the places and times at which they were written. They reflect views of life, history, and the cosmos which were then current. The church, therefore, has an obligation to approach the Scriptures with literary and historical understanding. As God has spoken his word in diverse cultural situations, the church is confident that he will continue to speak through the Scriptures in a changing world and in every form of human culture.

9.30. God's word is spoken to his church today where the Scriptures are faithfully preached and attentively read in dependence on the illumination of the Holy Spirit and with readiness to receive their truth and direction.

Part 2. The Ministry of Reconciliation
SECTION A. THE MISSION OF THE CHURCH
1. Direction

9.31. To be reconciled to God is to be sent into the world as his reconciling community. This community, the church universal, is entrusted with God's message of reconciliation and shares his labor of healing the enmities which separate men from God and from each other. Christ has called the church to this mission and given it the gift of the Holy Spirit. The church maintains continuity with the apostles and with Israel by faithful obedience to his call.

9.32. The life, death, resurrection, and promised coming of Jesus Christ has set the pattern for the church's mission. His life as man involves the church in the common life of men. His service to men commits the church to work for every form of human well-being. His suffering makes the church sensitive to all the sufferings of mankind so that it sees the face of Christ in the faces of men in every kind of need. His crucifixion discloses to the church God's judgment on man's inhumanity to man and the awful consequences of its own complicity in injustice. In the power of the risen Christ and the hope of his coming the church sees the promise of God's renewal of man's life in society and of God's victory over all wrong.

9.33. The church follows this pattern in the form of its life and in the method of its action. So to live and serve is to confess Christ as Lord.

2. Forms and Order

9.34. The institutions of the people of God change and vary as their mission requires in different times and places. The unity of the church is compatible with a wide variety of forms, but it is hidden and distorted when variant forms are allowed to harden into sectarian divisions, exclusive denominations, and rival factions.

9.35. Wherever the church exists, its members are both gathered in corporate life and dispersed in society for the sake of mission in the world.

9.36. The church gathers to praise God, to hear his word for mankind, to baptize and to join in the Lord's supper, to pray for and present the world to him in worship, to enjoy fellowship, to receive instruction, strength, and comfort, to order and organize its own corporate life, to be tested, renewed, and reformed, and to speak and act in the world's affairs as may be appropriate to the needs of the time.

9.37. The church disperses to serve God wherever its members are, at work or play, in private or in the life of society. Their prayer and Bible study are part of the church's worship and theological reflection. Their witness is the church's evangelism. Their daily action in the world is the church in mission to the world. The quality of their relation with other persons is the measure of the church's fidelity.

9.38. Each member is the church in the world, endowed by the Spirit with some gift of ministry and is responsible for the integrity of his witness in his own particular situation. He is entitled to the guidance and support of the Christian community and is subject to its advice and correction. He in turn, in his own competence, helps to guide the church.

9.39. In recognition of special gifts of the Spirit and for the ordering of its life as a community, the church calls, trains, and authorizes certain members for leadership and oversight. The persons qualified for these duties in accordance with the polity of the church are set apart by ordination or other appropriate act and thus made responsible for their special ministries.

9.40. The church thus orders its life as an institution with a constitution, government, officers, finances, and administrative rules. These are instruments of mission, not ends in themselves. Different orders have served the gospel, and none can claim exclusive validity. A presbyterian polity recognizes the responsibility of all members for ministry and maintains the organic relation of all congregations in the church. It seeks to protect the church from exploitation by ecclesiastical or secular power and ambition. Every church order must be open to such reformation as may be required to make it a more effective instrument of the mission of reconciliation.

3. Revelation and Religion

9.41. The church in its mission encounters the religions of men and in that encounter becomes conscious of its own human character as a religion. God's revelation to Israel, expressed within Semitic culture, gave rise to the religion of the Hebrew people. God's revelation in Jesus Christ called forth the response of Jews and Greeks and came to expression within Judaism and Hellenism as the Christian religion. The Christian religion, as distinct from God's revelation of himself, has been shaped throughout its history by the cultural forms of its environment.

9.42. The Christian finds parallels between other religions and his own and must approach all religions with openness and respect. Repeatedly God has used the insight of non-Christians to challenge the church to renewal. But the reconciling word of the gospel is God's judgment upon all forms of religion, including the Christian. The gift of God in Christ is for all men. The church, therefore, is commissioned to carry the gospel to all men whatever their religion may be and even when they profess none.

4. Reconciliation in Society

9.43. In each time and place there are particular problems and crises through which God calls the church to act. The church, guided by the Spirit, humbled by its own complicity and instructed by all attainable knowledge, seeks to discern the will of God and learn how to obey in these concrete situations. The following are particularly urgent at the present time.

9.44. a. God has created the peoples of the earth to be one universal family. In his reconciling love he overcomes the barriers between brothers and breaks down every form of discrimination based on racial or ethnic difference, real or imaginary. The church is called to bring all men to receive and uphold one another as persons in all relationships of life: in employment, housing, education, leisure, marriage, family, church, and the exercise of political rights. Therefore the church labors for the abolition of all racial discrimination and ministers to those injured by it. Congregations, individuals or groups of Christians who exclude, dominate, or patronize their fellowmen, however subtly, resist the Spirit of God and bring contempt on the faith which they profess.

9.45. b. God's reconciliation in Jesus Christ is the ground of the peace, justice, and freedom among nations which all powers of government are called to serve and defend. The church, in its own life, is called to practice the forgiveness of enemies and to commend to the nations as practical politics the search for cooperation and peace. This search requires that the nations pursue fresh and responsible relations across every line of conflict, even at risk to national security, to reduce areas of strife and to broaden international understanding. Reconciliation among nations becomes peculiarly urgent as countries develop nuclear, chemical, and biological weapons, diverting their manpower and resources from constructive uses and risking the annihilation of mankind. Although nations may serve God's purposes in history, the church which identifies the sovereignty of any one nation or any one way of life with the cause of God denies the Lordship of Christ and betrays its calling.

9.46. c. The reconciliation of man through Jesus Christ makes it plain that enslaving poverty in a world of abundance is an intolerable violation of God's good creation. Because Jesus identified himself with the needy and exploited, the cause of the world's poor is the cause of his disciples. The church cannot condone poverty, whether it is the product of unjust social structures, exploitation of the defenseless, lack of national resources, absence of technological understanding, or rapid expansion of populations. The church calls every man to use his abilities, his possessions, and the fruits of technology as gifts entrusted to him by God for the maintenance of his family and the advancement of the common welfare. It encourages those forces in human society that raise men's hopes for better conditions and provide them with opportunity for a decent living. A church that is indifferent to poverty, or evades responsibility in economic affairs, or is open to one social class only, or expects gratitude for its beneficence makes a mockery of reconciliation and offers no acceptable worship to God.

9.47. d. The relationship between man and woman exemplifies in a basic way God's ordering of the interpersonal life for which he created mankind. Anarchy in sexual relationships is a symptom of man's alienation from God, his neighbor, and himself. Man's perennial confusion about the meaning of sex has been aggravated in our day by the availability of new means for birth control and the treatment of infection, by the pressures of urbanization, by the exploitation of sexual symbols in mass communication, and by world overpopulation. The church, as the household of God, is called to lead men out of this alienation into the responsible freedom of the new life in Christ. Reconciled to God, each person has joy in and respect for his own humanity and that of other persons; a man and woman are enabled to marry, to commit themselves to a mutually shared life, and to respond to each other in sensitive and lifelong concern; parents receive the grace to care for children in love and to nurture their individuality. The church comes under the judgment of God and invites rejection by man when it fails to lead men and women into the full meaning of life together, or withholds the compassion of Christ from those caught in the moral confusion of our time.

SECTION B. THE EQUIPMENT OF THE CHURCH

9.48. Jesus Christ has given the church preaching and teaching, praise and prayer, and baptism and the Lord's supper as means of fulfilling its service of God among men. These gifts remain, but the church is obliged to change the forms of its service in ways appropriate to different generations and cultures.

1. Preaching and Teaching

9.49. God instructs his church and equips it for mission through preaching and teaching. By these, when they are carried on in fidelity to the Scriptures and dependence upon the Holy Spirit, the people hear the word of God and accept and follow Christ. The message is addressed to men in particular situations. Therefore effective preaching, teaching, and personal witness require disciplined study of both the Bible and the contemporary world. All acts of public worship should be conducive to men's hearing of the gospel in a particular time and place and responding with fitting obedience.

2. Praise and Prayer

9.50. The church responds to the message of reconciliation in praise and prayer. In that response it commits itself afresh to its mission, experiences a deepening of faith and obedience, and bears open testimony to the gospel. Adoration of God is acknowledgment of the Creator by the creation. Confession of sin is admission of all men's guilt before God and of their need for his forgiveness. Thanksgiving is rejoicing in God's goodness to all men and in giving for the needs of others. Petitions and intercessions are addressed to God for the continuation of his goodness, the healing of men's ills, and their deliverance from every form of oppression. The arts, especially music and architecture, contribute to the praise and prayer of a Christian congregation when they help men to look beyond themselves to God and to the world which is the object of his love.

3. Baptism

9.51. By humble submission to John's baptism Christ joined himself to men in their need and entered upon his ministry of reconciliation in the power of the Spirit. Christian baptism marks the receiving of the same Spirit by all his people. Baptism with water represents not only cleansing from sin but a dying with Christ and a joyful rising with him to new life. It commits all Christians to die each day to sin and to live for righteousness. In baptism the church celebrates the renewal of the covenant with which God has bound his people to himself. By baptism individuals are publicly received into the church to share in its life and ministry, and the church becomes responsible for their training and support in Christian discipleship. When those baptized are infants the congregation, as well as the parents, has a special obligation to nurture them in the Christian life, leading them to make, by a public profession, a personal response to the love of God shown forth in their baptism.

4. The Lord's Supper

9.52. The Lord's supper is a celebration of the reconciliation of men with God and with one another, in which they joyfully eat and drink together at the table of their Savior. Jesus Christ gave his church this remembrance of his dying for sinful men so that by participation in it they have communion with him and with all who shall be gathered to him. Partaking in him as they eat the bread and drink the wine in accordance with Christ's appointment, they receive from the risen and living Lord the benefits of his death and resurrection. They rejoice in the foretaste of the kingdom which he will bring to consummation at his promised coming, and go out from the Lord's table with courage and hope for the service to which he has called them.

Part 3. The Fulfillment of Reconciliation

9.53. God's redeeming work in Jesus Christ embraces the whole of man's life: social and cultural, economic and political, scientific and technological, individual and corporate. It includes man's natural environment as exploited and despoiled by sin. It is the will of God that his purpose for human life shall be fulfilled under the rule of Christ and all evil be banished from his creation.

9.54. Biblical visions and images of the rule of Christ such as a heavenly city, a father's house, a new heaven and earth, a marriage feast, and an unending day culminate in the image of the kingdom. The kingdom represents the triumph of God over all that resists his will and disrupts his creation. Already God's reign is present as a ferment in the world, stirring hope in men and preparing the world to receive its ultimate judgment and redemption.

9.55. With an urgency born of this hope the church applies itself to present tasks and strives for a better world. It does not identify limited progress with the kingdom of God on earth, nor does it despair in the face of disappointment and defeat. In steadfast hope the church looks beyond all partial achievement to the final triumph of God.

9.56. "Now to him who by the power at work within us is able to do far more abundantly than all we ask or think, to him be glory in the church and in Christ Jesus to all generations, forever and ever. Amen."

Christian Church (Disciples of Christ), *The Design for the Christian Church*, 1968

Thomas Campbell's *Propositions* from his → *Declaration and Address* of 1809 made clear that those whom he inspired to found the Christian Church (Disciples of Christ) wanted nothing to do with denominational labels—or with creeds and confessions of faith. Various "denominational statements" or explanations of the Disciples that occasionally came from one or another individual or group within what was called simply "the Brotherhood" did not, and by definition could not, carry the force and authority of a creed or confession. Yet something more was needed.

As Richard L. Hamm, general minister and president, has explained, "Our communion was founded in large measure in *reaction* to the use of creeds and confessions in the 19th century as 'tests of fellowship.' Believing as we do in the essential unity of all Christians, we have therefore historically rejected creeds and confessions. We do, however, have an 'affirmation of faith' that appears as the Preamble to our General Design (which constitutes our life together as a communion)."[1]

It was submitted to the assembly of 1967, and took effect the following year.

Edition: Provided by the Christian Church (Disciples of Christ).

Literature: Garrison and De Groot 1958; J. Jones 1980; Lippy and Williams 1988, 2:845–58; Osborn 1979.

1. Richard L. Hamm, letter of 13 May 1998.

Christian Church (Disciples of Christ), *The Design for the Christian Church*, 1968

Preamble

I.

1. As members of the Christian Church,
   We confess that Jesus is the Christ,
      the Son of the living God,
      and proclaim him Lord and Savior of the world.

2. In Christ's name and by his grace
      we accept our mission of witness
      and service to all people.

3. We rejoice in God,
      Maker of heaven and earth,
      and in the covenant of love
      which binds us to God and one another.

4. Through baptism into Christ
      we enter into newness of life
      and are made one with the whole people of God.

5. In the communion of the Holy Spirit
      we are joined together in discipleship
      and in obedience to Christ.

6. At the table of the Lord
      we celebrate with thanksgiving
      the saving acts and presence of Christ.

7. Within the universal church
      we receive the gift of ministry
      and the light of Scripture.

8. In the bonds of Christian faith
      we yield ourselves to God
      that we may serve the one
      whose kingdom has no end.

9. Blessing, glory, and honor
      be to God forever. Amen.

2.

Within the whole family of God on earth, the church appears wherever believers in Jesus Christ are gathered in his name. Transcending all barriers within the human family such as race and culture, the church manifests itself in ordered communities of disciples bound together for worship, for fellowship, and for service, and in varied structures for mission, witness, and mutual discipline, and for the nurture and renewal of its members. The nature of the church, given by Christ, remains constant through the generations: yet in faithfulness to its mission it continues to adapt its structures to the needs and patterns of a changing world. All dominion in the church belongs to Jesus Christ, its Lord and Head, and any exercise of authority in the church on earth stands under his judgment.

3.

Within the universal body of Christ, the Christian Church (Disciples of Christ) in the United States of America and in Canada is identifiable by its tradition, name, institutions, and relationships. Across national boundaries this church expresses itself in free and voluntary relationships in congregational, regional, and general manifestations. Each manifestation, with reference to the function for which it is uniquely responsible, is characterized by its integrity, self-government, authority, rights, and responsibilities. The Christian Church (Disciples of Christ) confesses Jesus Christ as Lord and constantly seeks in all its actions to be obedient to his authority.

4.

In order that the Christian Church (Disciples of Christ) through free and voluntary relationships may faithfully express the ministry of Christ made known through Scripture, may provide comprehensiveness in witness, mission, and service, may furnish means by which congregations may fulfill their ministries with faithfulness in Christian stewardship, may assure both unity and diversity, and may advance responsible ecumenical relationships, as a response to God's covenant, we commit ourselves to one another in adopting this design for the Christian Church (Disciples of Christ).

5.

In keeping with this design the Christian Church (Disciples of Christ) shall: establish a General Assembly, a General Board, and an Administrative Committee of the General Board; provide for general administrative units and such other organizations as may be required, provide for and act in and through related regional manifestations (hereinafter referred to as "regions"), establish, receive, and nurture congregations; define procedures for the ordering of its ministry; develop or recognize new forms of ministries for mission, education, and service; provide for appropriate consultation and procedures whereby existing organizations may make any necessary transition within the provisions of this design; and seek to provide for continuing renewal and reformation.

United Church of Canada, *A New Creed*, 1968/1980/1994

Having come into being with the adoption of its → *Basis of Union* of 1925, the United Church of Canada had continued to use → *The Apostles' Creed* in its liturgy and baptismal ritual. But in 1965 its Committee on Christian Faith was charged by the Committee on Church Worship and Ritual with producing "a new creed." Three years later, the Twenty-third General Council of the United Church of Canada accepted it, and it was circulated for use by the churches. As a spokesman for the United Church has explained, "'A New Creed' has twice been revised—once in 1980 to make the language inclusive, and once in 1994 to add the line 'to live with respect to Creation.'"[1] As is appropriate for a bilingual church in a bilingual nation, *A New Creed* is used in both French and English.

Edition: *Voices United* 1996, 918–19.

Note: The French version of this bilingual creed appears on the accompanying CD-ROM.

Literature: Wells 1992.

1. Peter Wyatt, letter of 8 October 1998.

United Church of Canada, *A New Creed*, 1968/1980/1994

We are not alone, we live in God's world.

We believe in God: who has created and is creating, who has come in Jesus, the Word made flesh, to reconcile and make new, who works in us and others by the Spirit.

We trust in God.

We are called to be the church: to celebrate God's presence, to live with respect in creation, to love and serve others, to seek justice and resist evil, to proclaim Jesus, crucified and risen, our judge and our hope.

In life, in death, in life beyond death, God is with us.

We are not alone.

Thanks be to God.

The Methodist Church of Brazil, *Social Creed,* 1971

Although it has obviously been influenced by → *The Social Creed* of the Methodist Episcopal Church in the United States of 1908 and → *The Social Creed of the
Churches* that came out of that affirmation, also in 1908 with the founding of the
Federal Council of Churches, which it acknowledges in its first chapter as its "Inheritance," the version produced by the Methodist Church of Brazil in 1971 as its
Social Creed is an independent document. Among other distinctive features is its
more explicit biblical and confessional basis.

As it stands here, this text is the first three chapters of that *Social Creed*
(which is the portion that the church itself continues to publish and affirm, omit-
ting what it calls "those chapters dealing with 'civil responsibility' and 'social problems,'" presumably because these were more topical and specific and therefore
changeable). It was voted on and accepted in Rio de Janeiro on 5 February 1971 by
the Tenth General Council of the Methodist Church. In its present form, this *Social Creed* is attached to a more comprehensive *Plan for the Life and the Mission of
the Methodist Church in Brazil,* which the church adopted at its Thirteenth General
Council in July 1982.

Edition: *Vida é Missão* 1982, 55–62.

Translation: Link, 4:60–63.

Literature: *EC* 1:293–97; *ODCC* 233.

The Methodist Church of Brazil, *Social Creed*, 1971

1. OUR INHERITANCE

1. The Methodist Church affirms its Christian responsibility for man's integral well-being as flowing from its fidelity to the word of God expressed in the Scriptures of the Old and New Testaments.

2. This awareness of social responsibility is part of the precious inheritance entrusted to Methodists by the historical witness of John Wesley.

3. The accomplishment of this mission is inseparable from the worldwide Methodism with which the Methodist Church is linked by unity of faith and relations of a structural kind established in the canons.

4. The Methodist Church shares the aims of Christian unity and world service of the World Council of Churches.

5. In the present age of gigantic scientific and technological progress, the Methodist Church reaffirms the truth proclaimed by John Wesley in eighteenth-century England: "We shall unite science and vital piety which have been separated for so long."

2. BIBLICAL BASES

1. We believe in God, the Creator of all things and Father of the whole human family, source of all love, justice, and peace, sovereign, ever-present authority.

2. We believe in Jesus Christ, God the Son who became man like each one of us, friend and redeemer of sinners, Lord and Servant of all men, in whom all things were created.

3. We believe in the Holy Spirit, God the Advocate, who leads men freely to truth, convincing the world concerning sin, righteousness, and judgment. [Jn 16.8]

4. We believe that the one God was in Christ, reconciling the world to himself and creating a new order of things in history by forgiving the sins of men and entrusting us with the ministry of reconciliation. [1 Cor 5.19]

5. We believe in the kingdom of God and his justice which comprises the whole creation, calling all men to receive one another as brothers by sharing in Christ in a new fullness of life. [Mt 6.33]

6. We believe that the gospel, taking human form in Jesus of Nazareth, Son of Mary and Joseph, the carpenter, is the power of God which frees man completely, by proclaiming that no value is higher than the human person created to the image and likeness of God. [Rom 1.16]

[Gn 1.27]

7. We believe that the universal Christian community is the servant of the Lord; its mission always emerges within the mission of the one Lord who is Jesus Christ. Christian unity is the gift of sacrifice of the Lamb of God: to live divided is to deny the gospel.

[Jn 1.29]

8. We believe that blessed are the poor in spirit, those who suffer, the meek, those who hunger and thirst for righteousness, those who show mercy, the pure in heart, those who work for peace, those who are persecuted for righteousness' sake and for the name of the Lord.

[Mt 5.3-10]

9. We believe that the law and the prophets are fulfilled by loving God with all our vital powers and by loving our neighbor as ourselves. For no one can love God and despise his brother.

[Mk 12.29-33]

10. We believe that the earth is the Lord's and the fullness thereof, the world and all who live in it; consequently we proclaim that full human development, true social security, and order, are only achieved to the extent that all technological and economic resources and institutional values are at the service of human dignity in effectual social justice.

[Ps 24.1]

11. We believe that the true worship which God accepts from men is that which includes the demonstration of a loving way of life, the practice of justice and the way of humility with the Lord.

[Mi 6.8]

3. THE POLITICO-SOCIAL AND ECONOMIC ORDER

1. The social nature of man issues from the order of creation and means that his full realization is only achieved in life in community.

2. The family community, resulting from the nature of man, the economic order, resulting from the complex of human activities of production, consumption and trade in goods, and the political order, express necessary requirements of the right order of God's creation.

3. The state is a basic necessity, not only for the defense of the life and liberty of the human person but for furthering the common good by promoting justice and peace in the social order.

4. At all times and places, problems, crises and challenges emerge through which God calls the church to serve. The church guided by the Holy Spirit, conscious of its own guilt and instructed by appropriate knowledge, seeks to discern and obey God's will in these particular situations.

5. The Methodist Church in the present situation of the country and the world, considers clear perception of the following realities to be particularly important for its social responsibility:

a. God created the nations to form a universal family. His reconciling love in Jesus Christ overcomes barriers between brothers and destroys every form of discrimination between human beings. The church is called to lead all to welcome and affirm one another as persons in all their relationships: in the family, neighborhood, work, education, leisure, religion, and the exercise of political rights.

b. The reconciliation of the world in Jesus Christ is the source of justice, peace, and freedom among nations; all the structures and authorities of society are called to participate in this new order. The church is the community that exemplifies these new relations of forgiveness, justice, and freedom, commending them to governments and nations as a way towards a responsible policy of cooperation and peace.

c. Reconciliation between nations becomes particularly urgent at a time when countries are developing nuclear, chemical, and biological weapons, diverting vast resources from constructive purposes and putting mankind at risk.

d. The reconciliation of man in Jesus Christ makes it clear that enslaving poverty in a world of plenty is a grave violation of God's order; the identification of Jesus Christ with the needy and the oppressed, and the priority of justice in the Scriptures, proclaim that the cause of the poor in the world is that of his disciples.

e. The poverty of an enormous part of the human family, a result of economic imbalances, unjust social structures, exploitation of the defenseless, lack of knowledge, is a grave negation of God's justice.

f. The extreme cultural, social, and economic inequalities are a denial of justice and put peace at risk, and urgently require appropriate intervention with effective planning to overcome them.

g. It is unjust to increase the wealth of the rich and the power of the strong by increasing the distress of the poor and oppressed. Programs to increase the national income should provide for an equitable distribution of resources, combat discrimination, overcome economic injustices, and free man from want.

h. In individualism and in collectivism, and in programs for economic growth and social progress, we encounter the risks of partial humanisms. It is urgent to promote an integral humanism. The full human measure is found only in the new relationships created by God in Jesus Christ.

6. The Methodist Church recognizes the relevant services of the United Nations Organization in the promotion and defense of human rights, as well as its efforts on behalf of justice and peace between nations. It commends as most opportune the Universal Declaration of Human Rights and that on Development and Social Progress adopted by the Assembly in December 1969.

The Evangelical Church of Togo, *Our Faith*, 1971

From the prominent place of → the Church of South India in the secondary literature on the subject it would be easy, but mistaken, to conclude that the impulse
toward acculturation and creedal indigenization was confined to the mission fields
and former colonies of the English-speaking world, because of the unique complexity of Protestant denominationalism there. But the → *Confession of Faith* issued
by the Protestant Christian Batak Church of Indonesia in 1951 is only one example
among many of how ecumenical this impulse has in fact been, across not only ecclesiastical but cultural, political, and linguistic boundaries.

Another example is this modest statement of *Our Faith* adopted by the
Agou-Agbetiku Synod of the Evangelical Church of Togo in late 1970 and issued
in January 1971. It was originally written in French and Ewe.

English Edition: Link, 2:5.

Literature: Trimua 1984.

The Evangelical Church of Togo, *Our Faith*, 1971

With the universal church of which it is part and in accordance with the Apostles' Creed, the Evangelical Church of Togo acknowledges Jesus Christ as attested in Holy Scripture as the source of its faith.

1. We believe that God has a plan for the world in general and for humanity in particular.

2. We believe that human sin is an impediment to this plan and made the coming of a Savior necessary. This Savior, the one and only, is Jesus Christ our Lord.

3. We believe that the plan of God was accomplished in Jesus Christ and we await its full manifestation.

4. We proclaim that the church is the community of all those who in the power of the Holy Spirit glorify God in Jesus Christ. In this way we become his witnesses and coworkers in the world. It is this which constitutes our joy.

The United Reformed Church, *The Faith of the United Reformed Church*, 1972/1981/1997/2000

Under the title *A Statement of Convictions on Which a United Church, Both Catholic and Reformed, Might Be Built,* the Joint Committee for Conversations between the Congregational Church in England and Wales, which historically affirmed → *The Savoy Declaration,* and the Presbyterian Church of England, standing in the tradition of → *The Westminster Confession of Faith,* laid out basic principles of doctrine and polity in 1965. After several years of discussions and revisions, the two churches elected to form "The United Reformed Church" and to adopt *The Basis of Union* of 1972, which included the original version of this statement of faith.

When the Reformed Association of Churches of Christ, which drew its inspiration from → Thomas Campbell's *Declaration and Address,* joined this union church in 1981, further changes were made. A version in free verse was issued in 1997.[1] The text presented here includes amendments adopted in 2000. Not only on the continuing problems of polity and ministry, whether congregational or presbyteral, but on the tension between infant baptism and believers' baptism, the signatories to this union document agreed to disagree without sacrificing the unity of the church; and the united church "recognizes as its own particular heritage the formulations and declarations of faith which have been valued by Congregationalists, Presbyterians, and members of the Churches of Christ as stating the gospel and seeking to make its implications clear" (14, 18), referring thereby to all of these historic confessions.

Because it is part of a larger text, *The Basis of Union,* whose paragraphs are individually numbered, we have retained those numbers, for clarity of citation.

Edition: *Manual* 2000, A2–A3.

Literature: Moss, 281–82; D. M. Thompson 1990.

---

1. See *Manual* 2000, A5–A6.

The United Reformed Church, *The Faith of the United Reformed Church*, 1972/1981/1997/2000

12. The United Reformed Church confesses the faith of the church catholic in one God, Father, Son, and Holy Spirit. It acknowledges that the life of faith to which it is called is a gift of the Holy Spirit continually received in word and sacrament and in the common life of God's people. It acknowledges the word of God in the Old and New Testaments, discerned under the guidance of the Holy Spirit, as the supreme authority for the faith and conduct of all God's people.

13. The United Reformed Church believes that, in the ministry of the word, through preaching and the study of the Scriptures, God makes known in each age his saving love, his will for his people, and his purpose for the world.

14. The United Reformed Church observes the gospel sacrament of baptism into Christ as a gift of God to his church, and as an appointed means of grace. Baptism is administered with water in the name of the Father and of the Son and of the Holy Spirit. It is the sacrament of entry into the church and is therefore administered once only to any person.

When the church observes this sacrament it makes explicit at a particular time and place and for a particular person what God has accomplished in Christ for the whole creation and for all humankind—the forgiveness of sins, the sanctifying power of the Holy Spirit, and newness of life in the family of God. In this sacrament the church affirms its faith in the action of God in Jesus Christ; and takes corporate responsibility for those receiving baptism, promising to support and nourish them as it receives them into its fellowship. Baptism may be administered in infancy or at an age of responsibility. Both forms of baptism shall be made available in the life of every worshiping congregation. In either case the sacrament of baptism is a unique part of the total process of Christian initiation. When baptism is administered at an age of responsibility, upon profession of faith, those baptized enter at once upon the full privileges and responsibilities of membership. When baptism is administered to infants, upon profession of faith by their parent(s), they are placed under the nurture of the church that they may be led by the Holy Spirit in due time to make their own profession of faith in Christ as their Savior and Lord, and enter upon the full privileges and responsibilities of membership. These two patterns of Christian initiation are recognized by the United Reformed Church.

The profession of faith to be made prior to baptism by a believer or at an age of responsibility by one baptized in infancy is indicated in Schedule A. This profession, and its acceptance by the church which shares in it, is a necessary part of the process of initiation and whenever possible it should be made at a celebration of the Lord's supper.

The United Reformed Church includes within its membership both persons whose conviction it is that baptism can only be appropriately administered to a believer and those whose conviction it is that infant baptism also is in harmony with the mind of Christ. Both convictions are honored by the church and both forms of baptism are understood to be used by God in the upbuilding of faith. Should these differences of conviction within the one church result in personal conflict of conscience it will require to be pastorally reconciled in mutual understanding and charity, and in accordance with the Basis of Union, in the first instance by the elders' meeting of the local congregation, and if necessary by the wider councils of the church. Whether the baptism is of an infant or a believer, whether it is by pouring or immersion, it shall not be such to which a conscientious objection is taken either by the person administering baptism, or by the person seeking it, or by the parent(s) requesting it for an infant.

15. The United Reformed Church celebrates the gospel sacrament of the Lord's supper. When in obedience to the Lord's command his people show forth his sacrifice on the cross by the bread broken and the wine outpoured for them to eat and drink, he himself, risen and ascended, is present and gives himself to them for their spiritual nourishment and growth in grace. United with him and with the whole church on earth and in heaven, his people gathered at his table present their sacrifice of thanksgiving and renew the offering of themselves, and rejoice in the promise of his coming in glory.

16. The United Reformed Church gives thanks for the common life of the church, wherein the people of God, being made members one of another, are called to love and serve one another and all people everywhere and to grow together in grace and in the knowledge of the Lord Jesus Christ. Participating in the common life of the church within the local church, they enter into the life of the church throughout the world. With that whole church they also share in the life of the church in all ages and in the communion of saints have fellowship with the church triumphant.

17. The United Reformed Church at the date of formation confesses its faith in the words of this statement:

1. We believe in the one living and true God, Creator, Preserver, and Ruler of all things in heaven and earth, Father, Son, and Holy Spirit. Him alone we worship, and in him we put our trust.

2. We believe that God, in his infinite love for men, gave his eternal Son, Jesus Christ our Lord, who became man, lived on earth in perfect love and obedience, died upon the cross for our sins, rose again from the dead, and lives for evermore, Savior, Judge, and King.

3. We believe that, by the Holy Spirit, this glorious Gospel is made effective so that through faith we receive the forgiveness of sins, newness of life as children of God and strength in this present world to do his will.

4. We believe in the one, holy, catholic, apostolic church, in heaven and on earth, wherein by the same Spirit, the whole company of believers is made one body of Christ, to worship God and serve him and all men in his kingdom of righteousness and love.

5. We rejoice in the gift of eternal life, and believe that, in the fullness of time, God will renew and gather in one all things in Christ, to whom, with the Father and the Holy Spirit, be glory and majesty, dominion and power, both now and ever.

18. The United Reformed Church, under the authority of Holy Scripture and in corporate responsibility to Jesus Christ its everliving head, acknowledges its duty to be open at all times to the leading of the Holy Spirit and therefore affirms its right to make such new declarations of its faith and for such purposes as may from time to time be required by obedience to the same Spirit.

At the same time the United Reformed Church accepts with thanksgiving the witness borne to the catholic faith by the Apostles' and Nicene Creeds. It recognizes as its own particular heritage the formulations and declarations of faith which have been valued by Congregationalists, Presbyterians, and members of Churches of Christ as stating the gospel and seeking to make its implications clear.

Korean Christians, *Theological Declaration*, 1973

Among the calls for social and political reform in the Korea of the 1970s were Christian voices as well. Although some of these Christian calls were indistinguishable from secular statements of political opposition to the authoritarian regime, *The Theological Declaration of Korean Christians* of 1973 embedded its expression of such opposition in a trinitarian and christological context. Therefore it is on the basis of a doctrine of God and of the kingdom of God that it calls for "the radical reform of the structures of power and . . . the creation of a new society and history" (3).

English Edition: Link, 2:13 (for full text, see Anderson, 241–45).

Korean Christians, *Theological Declaration,* 1973

Faith in God, Lord of history, in Jesus, Proclaimer of the kingdom of God, and in the Spirit, who is mightily at work in the course of history, this is the firm foundation of our words and deeds. We believe that God is finally the Liberator of the oppressed, the weak, and the poor. He will judge the evil powers. We believe that Jesus Christ proclaimed the coming of the kingdom of God to cast down the evil powers and that he will establish justice and peace for the oppressed, the outcasts, and the downtrodden. We also believe that the Spirit not only renews and sanctifies individual human beings but also re-creates the cosmos and history.

The following therefore is the confession of our faith as Christians:

1. We believe that we are destined by God the Judge and Lord of history to be representatives of the whole people and to pray for the deliverance of the oppressed and those who suffer wrong.

2. We believe that our Lord Jesus Christ calls us to live with the oppressed, the poor, and the outcast and to share their lot, just as he did in Judaea; as Jesus witnessed to the truth before Pontius Pilate, the representative of the Roman empire, so we are called today to speak the truth to the rulers.

3. We believe that the Spirit constrains us to play our part not only in the transformation of our own character but also in the radical reform of the structures of power and in the creation of a new society and history. This Spirit is the Spirit of the kingdom of God who summons us to the struggle for social and political reconstruction.

Reformation Churches in Europe,
The Leuenberg Agreement, 1973

The achievement of a considerable measure of common understanding between Lutheran and Reformed on the eucharist that was expressed in → *The Arnoldshain Theses* of 1957, together with their shared experience and confession articulated in → *The Barmen Declaration* of 1934, provided the context for a series of consultations that led to *The Leuenberg Agreement*. Participants in those consultations included, as the introduction explains, "Lutheran and Reformed churches in Europe along with the Union churches which grew out of them, and the related pre-Reformation churches, the Waldensian Church and the Church of the Czech Brethren," each of which had issued confessions of faith of its own.

Historically, *The Leuenberg Agreement* is the outcome of several generations of new research into the Protestant Reformation and into the New Testament. Modern Reformation research, which originally concentrated on Luther but then extended itself to the other Reformers, had led to a renewed awareness of how much the confessions of the Protestant Reformation had in common in their doctrines of Scripture and of justification by faith. The issues that separated them—the presence in the eucharist, the relation of the divine and human in Christ, and predestination—all came to be seen as shaped by the thought-patterns and "style of theological thinking" (3) of the time. At the same time, the achievements of biblical study, when applied to these very issues, became a means of transcending the historic differences among the sixteenth-century confessions.

The agreement explicitly states that "it leaves intact the binding force of the confessions within the participating churches. It is not to be regarded as a new confession of faith" (37). As the concluding paragraphs make clear, therefore, the agreement left it up to the churches—in Europe, but also on other continents—to devise the practical implementation of its consensus.

Edition: Hüffmeier and Müller 1995, 274–82.

Translation: Rusch and Martensen 1989, 144–54.

Literature: Rusch and Martensen 1989 (with chapters by theologians of several denominations).

744

Reformation Churches in Europe,
The Leuenberg Agreement, 1973

1. On the basis of their doctrinal discussions, the churches assenting to this Agreement—namely, Lutheran and Reformed churches in Europe along with the Union churches which grew out of them, and the related pre-Reformation churches, the Waldensian Church and the Church of the Czech Brethren—affirm together the common understanding of the gospel elaborated below. This common understanding of the gospel enables them to declare and to realize church fellowship. Thankful that they have been led closer together, they confess at the same time that guilt and suffering have also accompanied and still accompany the struggle for truth and unity in the church.

2. The church is founded upon Jesus Christ alone. It is he who gathers the church and sends it forth, by the bestowal of his salvation in preaching and the sacraments. In the view of the Reformation, it follows that agreement in the right teaching of the gospel, and in the right administration of the sacraments, is the necessary and sufficient prerequisite for the true unity of the church. It is from these Reformation criteria that the participating churches derive their view of church fellowship as set out below.

I. The Road to Fellowship

3. Faced with real differences in style of theological thinking and church practice, the fathers of the Reformation, despite much that they had in common, did not see themselves in a position, on grounds of faith and conscience, to avoid divisions. In this agreement the participating churches acknowledge that their relationship to one another has changed since the time of the Reformation.

1. COMMON ASPECTS AT THE OUTSET
OF THE REFORMATION

4. With the advantage of historical distance, it is easier today to discern the common elements in the witness of the churches of the Reformation, in spite of the differences between them: Their starting point was a new experience of the power of the gospel to liberate and assure. In standing up for the truth which they saw, the Reformers found themselves drawn together in opposition to the church traditions of that time. They were, therefore, at one in confessing that the church's life and

doctrine are to be gauged by the original and pure testimony to the gospel in Scripture. They were at one in bearing witness to God's free and unconditional grace in the life, death, and resurrection of Jesus Christ for all those who believe this promise. They were at one in confessing that the practice and form of the church should be determined only by the commission to deliver this testimony to the world, and that the word of God remains sovereign over every human ordering of the Christian community. In so doing, they were at one with the whole of Christendom in receiving and renewing the confession of the triune God and the God-manhood of Jesus Christ as expressed in the ancient creeds of the church.

2. CHANGED ELEMENTS IN THE CONTEMPORARY SITUATION

5. In the course of four hundred years of history, the churches of the Reformation have been led to new and similar ways of thinking and living: by theological wrestling with the questions of modern times, by advances in biblical research, by the movements of church renewal, and by the rediscovery of the ecumenical horizon. These developments certainly have also brought with them new differences cutting right across the confessions. But, time and again, there has also been an experience of brotherly fellowship, particularly in times of common suffering. The result of all these factors was a new concern on the part of the churches, especially since the revival movement, to achieve a contemporary expression both of the biblical witness and of the Reformation confessions of faith. In the process they have learned to distinguish between the fundamental witness of the Reformation confessions of faith and their historically conditioned thought forms. Because these confessions of faith bear witness to the gospel as the living word of God in Jesus Christ, far from barring the way to continued responsible testimony to the word, they open up this way with a summons to follow it in the freedom of faith.

2. The Common Understanding of the Gospel

6. In what follows, the participating churches describe their common understanding of the gospel insofar as this is required for establishing church fellowship between them.

1. THE MESSAGE OF JUSTIFICATION AS THE MESSAGE OF THE FREE GRACE OF GOD

7. The gospel is the message of Jesus Christ, the salvation of the world, in fulfillment of the promise given to the people of the old covenant.

8. a. The true understanding of the gospel was expressed by fathers of the Reformation in the doctrine of justification.

9. b. In this message, Jesus Christ is acknowledged as the one in whom God became man and bound himself to man; as the crucified and risen one who took God's judgment upon himself and, in so doing, demonstrated God's love to sinners; and as the coming one who, as Judge and Savior, leads the world to its consummation.

10. c. Through his word, God by his Holy Spirit calls all men to repent and believe, and assures the believing sinner of his righteousness in Jesus Christ. Whoever puts his trust in the gospel is justified in God's sight for the sake of Jesus Christ, and set free from the accusation of the law. In daily repentance and renewal, he lives within the fellowship in praise of God and in service to others, in the assurance that God will bring his kingdom in all its fullness. In this way, God creates new life, and plants in the midst of the world the seed of a new humanity.

11. d. This message sets Christians free for responsible service in the world and makes them ready to suffer in this service. They know that God's will, as demand and succor, embraces the whole world. They stand up for temporal justice and peace between individuals and nations. To do this they have to join with others in seeking rational and appropriate criteria, and play their part in applying these criteria. They do so in the confidence that God sustains the world and as those who are accountable to him.

12. e. In this understanding of the gospel, we take our stand on the basis of the ancient creeds of the church, and reaffirm the common conviction of the Reformation confessions that the unique mediation of Jesus Christ in salvation is the heart of the Scriptures, and the message of justification as the message of God's free grace is the measure of all the church's preaching.

2. PREACHING, BAPTISM, AND THE LORD'S SUPPER

13. The fundamental witness to the gospel is the testimony of the apostles and prophets in the Holy Scriptures of the Old and New Testaments. It is the task of the church to spread this gospel by the spoken word in preaching, by individual counseling, and by baptism and the Lord's supper. In preaching, baptism, and the Lord's supper, Jesus Christ is present through the Holy Spirit. Justification in Christ is thus imparted to men, and in this way the Lord gathers his people. In doing so he employs various forms of ministry and service, as well as the witness of all those belonging to his people.

a. Baptism

14. Baptism is administered in the name of the Father and of the Son and of the Holy Spirit with water. In baptism, Jesus Christ irrevocably receives man, fallen prey to sin and death, into his fellowship of salvation so that he may become a new creature. In the power of his Holy Spirit, he calls him into his community and to a new life of faith, to daily repentance, and to discipleship.

b. The Lord's Supper

15. In the Lord's supper the risen Christ imparts himself in his body and blood, given up for all, through his word of promise with bread and wine. He thereby grants us forgiveness of sins, and sets us free for a new life of faith. He enables us to experience anew that we are members of his body. He strengthens us for service to all men.

16. When we celebrate the Lord's supper we proclaim the death of Christ through which God has reconciled the world with himself. We proclaim the presence of the risen Lord in our midst. Rejoicing that the Lord has come to us, we await his future coming in glory.

3. Accord in Respect of the Doctrinal Condemnations of the Reformation Era

17. The differences which from the time of the Reformation onwards have made church fellowship between Lutheran and Reformed churches impossible, and have led them to pronounce mutual condemnations, relate to the doctrine of the Lord's supper, Christology, and the doctrine of predestination. We take the decisions of the Reformation fathers seriously, but are today able to agree on the following statements in respect of these condemnations:

1. THE LORD'S SUPPER

18. In the Lord's supper the risen Jesus Christ imparts himself in his body and blood, given up for all, through his word of promise with bread and wine. He thus gives himself unreservedly to all who receive the bread and wine; faith receives the Lord's supper for salvation, unfaith for judgment.

19. We cannot separate communion with Jesus Christ in his body and blood from the act of eating and drinking. To be concerned about the manner of Christ's presence in the Lord's supper in abstraction from this act is to run the risk of obscuring the meaning of the Lord's supper.

20. Where such a consensus exists between the churches, the condemnations pronounced by the Reformation confessions are inapplicable to the doctrinal position of these churches.

2. CHRISTOLOGY

21. In the true man Jesus Christ, the eternal Son, and so God himself, has bestowed himself upon lost mankind for its salvation. In the word of the promise and in the sacraments, the Holy Spirit, and so God himself, makes the crucified and risen Jesus present to us.

22. Believing in this self-bestowal of God in his Son, the task facing us, in view of the historically conditioned character of traditional thought forms, is to give renewed and effective expression to the special insights of the Reformed tradition, with its concern to maintain unimpaired the divinity and humanity of Jesus, and to those of the Lutheran tradition, with its concern to maintain the unity of Jesus as a person.

23. In these circumstances, it is impossible for us to reaffirm the former condemnations today.

3. PREDESTINATION

24. In the gospel we have the promise of God's unconditional acceptance of sinful man. Whoever puts his trust in the gospel can know that he is saved, and praise God for his election. For this reason we can speak of election only with respect to the call to salvation in Christ.

25. Faith knows by experience that the message of salvation is not accepted by all; yet it respects the mystery of God's dealings with men. It bears witness to the seriousness of human decisions, and at the same time to the reality of God's universal purpose of salvation. The witness of the Scriptures to Christ forbids us to suppose that God has uttered an eternal decree for the final condemnation of specific individuals or of a particular people.

26. When such a consensus exists between churches, the condemnations pronounced by the Reformation confessions of faith are inapplicable to the doctrinal position of these churches.

4. CONCLUSIONS

27. Wherever these statements are accepted, the condemnations of the Reformation confessions in respect of the Lord's supper, Christology, and predestination are inapplicable to the doctrinal position. This does not mean that the condemnations

pronounced by the Reformation fathers are irrelevant; but they are no longer an obstacle to church fellowship.

28. There remain considerable differences between our churches in forms of worship, types of spirituality, and church order. These differences are often more deeply felt in the congregations than the traditional doctrinal differences. Nevertheless, in fidelity to the New Testament and Reformation criteria for church fellowship, we cannot discern in these differences any factors which should divide the church.

4. The Declaration and Realization of Church Fellowship

29. In the sense intended in this agreement, church fellowship means that, on the basis of the consensus they have reached in their understanding of the gospel, churches with different confessional positions accord each other fellowship in word and sacrament, and strive for the fullest possible cooperation in witness and service to the world.

1. DECLARATION OF CHURCH FELLOWSHIP

30. In assenting to this agreement the churches, in loyalty to the confessions of faith which bind them, or with due respect for their traditions, declare:

31. a. that they are one in understanding the gospel as set out in parts 2 and 3;

32. b. that, in accordance with what is said in part 3, the doctrinal condemnations expressed in the confessional documents no longer apply to the contemporary doctrinal position of the assenting churches;

33. c. that they accord each other table and pulpit fellowship; this includes the mutual recognition of ordination and the freedom to provide for intercelebration.

34. With these statements, church fellowship is declared. The divisions which have barred the way to this fellowship since the sixteenth century are removed. The participating churches are convinced that they have been put together in the one church of Jesus Christ, and that the Lord liberates them for, and lays upon them the obligation of, common service.

2. REALIZING CHURCH FELLOWSHIP

35. It is in the life of the churches and congregations that church fellowship becomes a reality. Believing in the unifying power of the Holy Spirit, they bear their

witness and perform their service together, and strive to deepen and strengthen the fellowship they have found together.

a. Witness and Service

36. The preaching of the churches gains credibility in the world when they are at one in their witness to the gospel. The gospel liberates and binds together the churches to render common service. Being the service of love, it turns to man in his distress and seeks to remove the causes of that distress. The struggle for justice and peace in the world increasingly demands of the churches the acceptance of a common responsibility.

b. The Continuing Theological Task

37. The agreement leaves intact the binding force of the confessions within the participating churches. It is not to be regarded as a new confession of faith. It sets forth a consensus reached about central matters, one which makes church fellowship possible between churches of different confessional positions. In accordance with this consensus, the participating churches will seek to establish a common witness and service, and pledge themselves to their common doctrinal discussions.

38. The common understanding of the gospel on which church fellowship is based must be further deepened, tested in the light of the witness of Holy Scripture, and continually made relevant in the contemporary scene.

39. The churches have the task of studying further these differences of doctrine which, while they do not have divisive force, still persist within and between the participating churches. These include: hermeneutical questions concerning the understanding of Scripture, confession of faith, and church; the relation between law and gospel; baptismal practice; ministry and ordination; the "two kingdom" doctrine, and the doctrine of the sovereignty of Christ; and church and society. At the same time newly emerging problems relating to witness and service, order and practice, have to be considered.

40. On the basis of their common heritage, the churches of the Reformation must determine their attitude to trends toward the theological polarization increasingly in evidence today. To some extent the problems here go beyond the doctrinal differences which were once at the basis of the Lutheran-Reformed controversy.

41. It will be the task of common theological study to testify to the truth of the gospel and to distinguish it from all distortions.

c. Organizational Consequences

42. This declaration of church fellowship does not anticipate provisions of church law on particular matters of interchurch relations, or within the churches. The churches will, however, take the agreement into account considering such provisions.

43. As a general rule, the affirmation of pulpit and table fellowship and the mutual recognition of ordination do not affect the rules in force in the participating churches for induction to a pastoral charge, the exercise of the pastoral ministry, or the ordering of congregational life.

44. The question of organic union between particular participating churches can only be decided in the situation in which these churches live. In examining this question the following points should be kept in mind:

45. Any union detrimental to the lively plurality in styles of preaching, ways of worship, church order, and in diaconal and social action, would contradict the very nature of the church fellowship inaugurated by this declaration. On the other hand, in certain situations, because of the intimate connection between witness and order, the church's service may call for formal legal unification. Where organizational consequences are drawn from this declaration, it should not be at the expense of freedom of decision in minority churches.

d. Ecumenical Aspects

46. In establishing and realizing church fellowship among themselves, the participating churches do so as part of their responsibility to promote the ecumenical fellowship of all Christian churches.

47. They regard such a fellowship of churches in the European area as a contribution to this end. They hope that the ending of their previous separation will influence churches in Europe and elsewhere who are related to them confessionally. They are ready to examine with them the possibilities of wider church fellowship.

48. This hope applies equally to the relationship between the Lutheran World Federation and the World Alliance of Reformed Churches.

49. They also hope that the achievement of church fellowship with each other will provide a fresh stimulus to conference and cooperation with churches of other confessions. They affirm their readiness to set their doctrinal discussions within this wider context.

International Congress on World Evangelization, *The Lausanne Covenant*, 1974

The International Congress on World Evangelization, meeting in Lausanne, Switzerland, on 16–25 July 1974, brought together, on an individual basis, 2,700 participants from 150 nations and 135 denominations, with half the participants coming from developing countries of "the Third World." The dominant theological position at the congress was Evangelical, "our common submission to the supreme authority of Scripture."[1]

The Lausanne Covenant was accepted by most of the participants. Its principal author was the Evangelical Anglican John Stott, who saw "perhaps the first major achievement of the Congress . . . in our clarified understanding of the mission of the people of God"; this mission, he continued, "includes social as well as evangelistic activity," neither without the other. It was, therefore, a conscious critique of the social-political orientation of → *The Social Creed of the Churches* of 1908 as well as more recent ecumenical statements, while at the same time it sought to transcend the individualistic understanding of salvation characteristic of most Evangelical theologies. In opposition to what it took to be a widespread relativization of the historic Christian claim about Jesus Christ that "there is salvation in no one else, for there is no other name under heaven given among men by which we must be saved,"[2] it affirmed "the uniqueness and universality of Christ" (3).

Edition: *International Review of Mission* 63 (1974): 570–74.

Literature: Jong 1975; Stott 1975.

1. Stott 1975, 288.
2. Acts 4.12.

International Congress on World Evangelization, *The Lausanne Covenant,* 1974

INTRODUCTION

We, members of the Church of Jesus Christ, from more than 150 nations, participants in the International Congress on World Evangelization at Lausanne, praise God for his great salvation and rejoice in the fellowship he has given us with himself and with each other. We are deeply stirred by what God is doing in our day, moved to penitence by our failures, and challenged by the unfinished task of evangelization. We believe the gospel is God's good news for the whole world, and we are determined by his grace to obey Christ's commission to proclaim it to all mankind and to make disciples of every nation. We desire, therefore, to affirm our faith and our resolve, and to make public our covenant.

1. THE PURPOSE OF GOD

We affirm our belief in the one eternal God, Creator and Lord of the world, Father, Son, and Holy Spirit, who governs all things according to the purpose of his will. He has been calling out from the world a people for himself, and sending his people back into the world to be his servants and his witnesses, for the extension of his kingdom, the building up of Christ's body, and the glory of his name. We confess with shame that we have often denied our calling and failed in our mission, by becoming conformed to the world or by withdrawing from it. Yet we rejoice that even when borne by earthen vessels the gospel is still a precious treasure. To the task of making that treasure known in the power of the Holy Spirit we desire to dedicate ourselves anew. (Is 40.28; Mt 28.19; Eph 1.11; Acts 15.14; Jn 17.6, 18; Eph 4.12; 1 Cor 5.10; Rom 12.2; 2 Cor 4.7.)

2. THE AUTHORITY AND POWER OF THE BIBLE

We affirm the divine inspiration, truthfulness, and authority of both Old and New Testament Scriptures in their entirety as the only written word of God, without error in all that it affirms, and the only infallible rule of faith and practice. We also affirm the power of God's word to accomplish his purpose of salvation. The message of the Bible is addressed to all mankind. For God's revelation in Christ and in Scripture is unchangeable. Through it the Holy Spirit still speaks today. He illumines the minds of God's people in every culture to perceive its truth freshly through their own eyes and thus discloses to the whole church ever more of the many-colored wisdom of

God. (2 Tm 3.16; 2 Pt 1.21; Jn 10.35; Is 55.11; 1 Cor 1.21; Rom 1.16; Mt 5.17, 18; Jude 3; Eph 1.17, 18, 3.10, 18.)

3. THE UNIQUENESS AND UNIVERSALITY OF CHRIST

We affirm that there is only one Savior and only one gospel, although there is a wide diversity of evangelistic approaches. We recognize that all men have some knowledge of God through his general revelation in nature. But we deny that this can save, for men suppress the truth by their unrighteousness. We also reject as derogatory to Christ and the gospel every kind of syncretism and dialogue which implies that Christ speaks equally through all religions and ideologies. Jesus Christ, being himself the only God-man, who gave himself as the only ransom for sinners, is the only Mediator between God and man. There is no other name by which we must be saved. All men are perishing because of sin, but God loves all men not wishing that any should perish but that all should repent. Yet those who reject Christ repudiate the joy of salvation and condemn themselves to eternal separation from God. To proclaim Jesus as "the Savior of the world" is not to affirm that all men are either automatically or ultimately saved, still less to affirm that all religions offer salvation in Christ. Rather it is to proclaim God's love for a world of sinners and to invite all men to respond to him as Savior and Lord in the wholehearted personal commitment of repentance and faith. Jesus Christ has been exalted above every other name; we long for the day when every knee shall bow to him and every tongue shall confess him Lord. (Gal 1.6–9; Rom 1.18–32; 1 Tm 2.5, 6; Acts 4.12; Jn 3.16–19; 2 Pt 3.9; 2 Thes 1.7–9; Jn 4.42; Mt 11.28; Eph 1.20, 21; Phil 2.9–11.)

4. THE NATURE OF EVANGELISM

To evangelize is to spread the good news that Jesus Christ died for our sins and was raised from the dead according to the Scriptures, and that as the reigning Lord he now offers the forgiveness of sins and the liberating gift of the Spirit to all who repent and believe. Our Christian presence in the world is indispensable to evangelism, and so is that kind of dialogue whose purpose is to listen sensitively in order to understand. But evangelism itself is the proclamation of the historical, biblical Christ as Savior and Lord, with a view to persuading people to come to him personally and so be reconciled to God. In issuing the gospel invitation we have no liberty to conceal the cost of discipleship. Jesus still calls all who would follow him to deny themselves, take up their cross, and identify themselves with his new community. The results of evangelism include obedience to Christ, incorporation into his church and responsible service in the world. (1 Cor 15.3, 4; Acts 2.32–39; Jn 20.21; 1 Cor 1.23; 2 Cor 4.5, 5.11, 20; Lk 14.25–33; Mk 8.34; Acts 2.40, 47; Mk 10.43–45.)

5. CHRISTIAN SOCIAL RESPONSIBILITY

We affirm that God is both the Creator and the Judge of all men. We therefore should share his concern for justice and reconciliation throughout human society and for the liberation of men from every kind of oppression. Because mankind is made in the image of God, every person, regardless of race, religion, color, culture, class, sex, or age, has an intrinsic dignity because of which he should be respected and served, not exploited. Here too we express penitence both for our neglect and for having sometimes regarded evangelism and social concern as mutually exclusive. Although reconciliation with man is not reconciliation with God, nor is social action evangelism, nor is political liberation salvation, nevertheless we affirm that evangelism and sociopolitical involvement are both part of our Christian duty. For both are necessary expressions of our doctrines of God and man, our love for our neighbor and our obedience to Jesus Christ. The message of salvation implies also a message of judgment upon every form of alienation, oppression, and discrimination, and we should not be afraid to denounce evil and injustice wherever they exist. When people receive Christ they are born again into his kingdom and must seek not only to exhibit but also to spread its righteousness in the midst of an unrighteous world. The salvation we claim should be transforming us in the totality of our personal and social responsibilities. Faith without works is dead. (Acts 17.26, 31; Gn 18.25; Is 1.17; Ps 45.7; Gn 1.26, 27; Jas 3.9; Lv 19.18; Lk 6.27, 35; Jas 2.14–26; Jn 3.3, 5; Mt 5.20, 6.33; 2 Cor 3.18; Jas 2.20.)

6. THE CHURCH AND EVANGELISM

We affirm that Christ sends his redeemed people into the world as the Father sent him, and that this calls for a similar deep and costly penetration of the world. We need to break out of our ecclesiastical ghettos and permeate non-Christian society. In the church's mission of sacrificial service evangelism is primary. World evangelization requires the whole church to take the whole gospel to the whole world. The church is at the very center of God's cosmic purpose and is his appointed means of spreading the gospel. But a church which preaches the cross must itself be marked by the cross. It becomes a stumbling block to evangelism when it betrays the gospel or lacks a living faith in God, a genuine love for people, or scrupulous honesty in all things including promotion and finance. The church is the community of God's people rather than an institution, and must not be identified with any particular culture, social or political system, or human ideology. (Jn 17.18, 20.21; Mt 28.19, 20; Acts 1.8, 20.27; Eph 1.9, 10, 3.9–11; Gal 6.14, 17; 2 Cor 6.3, 4; 2 Tm 2.19–21; Phil 1.27.)

7. COOPERATION IN EVANGELISM

We affirm that the church's visible unity in truth is God's purpose. Evangelism also summons us to unity, because our oneness strengthens our witness, just as our disunity undermines our gospel of reconciliation. We recognize, however, that organizational unity may take many forms and does not necessarily forward evangelism. Yet we who share the same biblical faith should be closely united in fellowship, work, and witness. We confess that our testimony has sometimes been marred by sinful individualism and needless duplication. We pledge ourselves to seek a deeper unity in truth, worship, holiness, and mission. We urge the development of regional and functional cooperation for the furtherance of the church's mission, for strategic planning, for mutual encouragement, and for the sharing of resources and experience. (Jn 17.21, 23; Eph 4.3, 4; Jn 13.35; Phil 1.27; Jn 17.11–23.)

8. CHURCHES IN EVANGELISTIC PARTNERSHIP

We rejoice that a new missionary era has dawned. The dominant role of Western missions is fast disappearing. God is raising up from the younger churches a great new resource for world evangelization, and is thus demonstrating that the responsibility to evangelize belongs to the whole body of Christ. All churches should therefore be asking God and themselves what they should be doing both to reach their own area and to send missionaries to other parts of the world. A reevaluation of our missionary responsibility and role should be continuous. Thus a growing partnership of churches will develop and the universal character of Christ's church will be more clearly exhibited. We also thank God for agencies which labor in Bible translation, theological education, the mass media, Christian literature, evangelism, missions, church renewal, and other specialist fields. They too should engage in constant self-examination to evaluate their effectiveness as part of the church's mission. (Rom 1.8; Phil 1.5, 4.15; Acts 13.1–3; 1 Thes 1.6–8.)

9. THE URGENCY OF THE EVANGELISTIC TASK

More than 2,700 million people, which is more than two-thirds of mankind, have yet to be evangelized. We are ashamed that so many have been neglected; it is a standing rebuke to us and to the whole church. There is now, however, in many parts of the world an unprecedented receptivity to the Lord Jesus Christ. We are convinced that this is the time for churches and para-church agencies to pray earnestly for the salvation of the unreached and to launch new efforts to achieve world evangelization. A reduction of foreign missionaries and money in an evangelized country may sometimes be necessary to facilitate the national church's growth in self-reliance and to release resources for unevangelized areas. Missionaries should flow ever more freely from and to all six continents in a spirit of humble service. The goal should be, by all available means and at the earliest possible time, that every person will have the opportunity to hear, understand, and receive the good news. We cannot hope to attain this goal without sacrifice. All of us are shocked by the poverty of millions and disturbed by the injustices which cause it. Those of us who live in affluent circumstances accept our duty to develop a simple lifestyle in order to contribute more generously to both relief and evangelism. (Jn 9.4; Mt 9.35–38; Rom 9.1–3; 1 Cor 9.19–23; Mk 16.15; Is 58.6, 7; Jas 1.27, 2.1–9; Mt 25.31–46; Acts 2.44, 45, 4.34, 35.)

10. EVANGELISM AND CULTURE

The development of strategies for world evangelization calls for imaginative pioneering methods. Under God, the result will be the rise of churches deeply rooted in Christ and closely related to their culture. Culture must always be tested and judged by Scripture. Because man is God's creature, some of his culture is rich in beauty and goodness. Because he has fallen, all of it is tainted with sin and some of it is demonic. The gospel does not presuppose the superiority of any culture to another, but evaluates all cultures according to its own criteria of truth and righteousness and insists on moral absolutes in every culture. Missions have all too frequently exported with the gospel an alien culture, and churches have sometimes been in bondage to culture rather than to the Scripture. Christ's evangelists must humbly seek to empty themselves of all but their personal authenticity in order to become the servants of others, and churches must seek to transform and enrich culture, all for the glory of God. (Mk 7.8, 9, 13; Gn 4.21, 22; 1 Cor 9.19–23; Phil 2.5–7; 2 Cor 4.5.)

11. EDUCATION AND LEADERSHIP

We confess that we have sometimes pursued church growth at the expense of church depth, and divorced evangelism from Christian nurture. We also acknowledge that some of our missions have been too slow to equip and encourage national leaders to assume their rightful responsibilities. Yet we are committed to indigenous principles, and long that every church will have national leaders who manifest a Christian style of leadership in terms not of domination but of service. We recognize that there is a great need to improve theological education, especially for church leaders. In every nation and culture there should be an effective training program for pastors and laymen in doctrine, discipleship, evangelism, nurture, and service. Such training programs should not rely on any stereotyped methodology but should be developed by creative local initiatives according to biblical standards. (Col 1.27, 28; Acts 14.23; Ti 1.5, 9; Mk 10.42–45; Eph 4.11, 12.)

12. SPIRITUAL CONFLICT

We believe that we are engaged in constant spiritual warfare with the principalities and powers of evil, who are seeking to overthrow the church and frustrate its task of world evangelization. We know our need to equip ourselves with God's armor and to fight this battle with the spiritual weapons of truth and prayer. For we detect the activity of our enemy, not only in false ideologies outside the church, but also inside it in false gospels which twist Scripture and put man in the place of God. We need both watchfulness and discernment to safeguard the biblical gospel. We acknowledge that we ourselves are not immune to worldliness of thought and action, that is, to a surrender to secularism. For example, although careful studies of church growth, both numerical and spiritual, are right and valuable, we have sometimes neglected them. At other times, desirous to ensure a response to the gospel, we have compromised our message, manipulated our hearers through pressure techniques, and become unduly preoccupied with statistics or even dishonest in our use of them. All this is worldly. The church must be in the world; the world must not be in the church. (Eph 6.12; 2 Cor 4.3, 4; Eph 6.11, 13–18; 2 Cor 10.3–5; 1 Jn 2.18–26, 4.1–3; Gal 1.6–9; 2 Cor 2.17, 4.2; Jn 17.15.)

13. FREEDOM AND PERSECUTION

It is the God-appointed duty of every government to secure conditions of peace, justice, and liberty in which the church may obey God, serve the Lord Christ, and preach the gospel without interference. We therefore pray for the leaders of the nations and call upon them to guarantee freedom of thought and conscience, and freedom to practice and propagate religion in accordance with the will of God and set forth in the Universal Declaration of Human Rights. We also express our deep concern for all who have been unjustly imprisoned, and especially for our brethren who are suffering for their testimony to the Lord Jesus. We promise to pray and work for their freedom. At the same time we refuse to be intimidated by their fate. God helping us, we too will seek to stand against injustice and to remain faithful to the gospel, whatever the cost. We do not forget the warnings of Jesus that persecution is inevitable. (1 Tm 1.1–4; Acts 4.19, 5.29; Col 3.24; Heb 13.1–3; Lk 4.18; Gal 5.11, 6.12; Mt 5.10–12; Jn 15.18–21.)

14. THE POWER OF THE HOLY SPIRIT

We believe in the power of the Holy Spirit. The Father sent his Spirit to bear witness to his Son; without his witness ours is futile. Conviction of sin, faith in Christ, new birth and Christian growth are all his work. Further, the Holy Spirit is a missionary spirit; thus evangelism should arise spontaneously from a Spirit-filled church. A church that is not a missionary church is contradicting itself and quenching the Spirit. Worldwide evangelization will become a realistic possibility only when the Spirit renews the church in truth and wisdom, faith, holiness, love, and power. We therefore call upon all Christians to pray for such a visitation of the sovereign Spirit of God that all his fruit may appear in all his people and that all his gifts may enrich the body of Christ. Only then will the whole church become a fit instrument in his hands, that the whole earth may hear his voice. (1 Cor 2.4; Jn 15.26, 27, 16.8-11; 1 Cor 12.3; Jn 3.6-8; 2 Cor 3.18; Jn 7.37-39; 1 Thes 5.19; Acts 1.8; Ps 85.4-7, 67.1-3; Gal 5.22, 23; 1 Cor 12.4-31; Rom 12.3-8.)

15. THE RETURN OF CHRIST

We believe that Jesus Christ will return personally and visibly in power and glory, to consummate his salvation and his judgment. This promise of his coming is a further spur to our evangelism, for we remember his words that the gospel must first be preached to all nations. We believe that the interim period between Christ's ascension and return is to be filled with the mission of the people of God, who have no liberty to stop before the end. We also remember his warning that false Christs and false prophets will arise as precursors of the final Antichrist. We therefore reject as a proud, self-confident dream the notion that man can ever build a utopia on earth. Our Christian confidence is that God will perfect his kingdom, and we look forward with eager anticipation to that day, and to the new heaven and earth in which righteousness will dwell and God will reign forever. Meanwhile, we rededicate ourselves to the service of Christ and of men in joyful submission to his authority over the whole of our lives. (Mk 14.62; Heb 9.28; Mk 13.10; Acts 1.8-11; Mt 28.20; Mk 13.21-23; Jn 2.18, 4.1-3; Lk 12.32; Rv 21.1-5; 2 Pt 3.13; Mt 28.18.)

CONCLUSION

Therefore, in the light of this our faith and our resolve, we enter into a solemn covenant with God and with each other, to pray, to plan, and to work together for the evangelization of the whole world. We call upon others to join us. May God help us by his grace and for his glory to be faithful to this our covenant! Amen, Alleluia!

The Presbyterian-Reformed Church in Cuba, *Confession of Faith*, 1977

The Presbyterian-Reformed Church in Cuba (PRCC) was founded by mission congregations belonging to the United Presbyterian Church in the USA. After peaceful dismissal in 1964, these congregations formed themselves into an autonomous church body in 1967.

This *Confession of Faith* was the result of the action of the General Assembly of the PRCC in 1973, calling for a new constitution and for a new confession of faith appropriate to its position in the People's Republic of Cuba. The drafting committee incorporated into the book of confessions → the *Confession* of 1967 of the United Presbyterian Church in the United States of America, together with the earlier confessions that this *Confession* affirmed. It also enunciated the criteria that a new confession was to meet: "1. The 'anthropocentripetal' criterion declares that the human being is the center of all interest and the standard for everything; 2. The criterion of historical impetus defines history as the history of liberation and salvation of humankind; 3. The 'ecclesiocentrifugal' criterion understands the church not as an end in itself, but as an instrument of liberation in history."

Those three criteria enabled the PRCC to voice here its approval of the Cuban revolution and of the socialist society that came out of the revolution. The *Confession of Faith* was approved on 28–30 January 1977 at Matanzas by the Eleventh General Assembly of the church.

Edition: *Confesión de fé* 1978, 11–40.

Translation: Vischer, 168–90.

Literature: Stock 1980; Vischer, 166–67.

The Presbyterian-Reformed Church in Cuba, *Confession of Faith*, 1977

Preface

The Presbyterian-Reformed Church in Cuba confesses its faith as it offers this testimony to the significance that the gospel of Jesus Christ has today for the church in Cuba.

The mere fact that this is done at this time and place is already an essential part of the proclamation of its faith in God the Father Creator; of the reason for its hope in the Incarnate Son Reconciler; and of the action of its love in the Holy Spirit Redeemer.

This testimony constitutes the affirmation of the joy which the church of Jesus Christ experiences in the gospel as it lives this historic moment of humanity and especially as it proclaims the meaning faith has for us in the midst of the Cuban revolutionary process.

God's incarnation in Jesus of Nazareth and the liberating vocation this fact implies for the church constitute the spiritual foundation for the historical commitment to which the church feels it is called.

It is necessary for the church to clarify the meaning of this commitment. As it does this, the church gives the reason for its hope and lives its love confessing in this way its faith.

Obligated to carry out this commitment, the church, by the Spirit and through its own action, is nourished by the knowledge it needs to have about God's redeeming purpose in Jesus Christ as it is revealed in the Scriptures, norm of its faith, paradigm for its action.

The Presbyterian-Reformed Church in Cuba, with a profound sense of its apostolicity and catholicity, calls all human beings to join in the task of realizing fully the new humanity on the earth, which would mean the installation of a fraternal and solidary community which, including all alike, achieves love as its supreme law. This fact constitutes the only evangelical way of being able to know God, and thus the only way of proclaiming him to all human beings.

We, the members of this church, join all believers in Jesus Christ—praying for the coming of the kingdom of God—in the hope of its realization, and, strengthened in fraternal love, we confess our faith as the church of Jesus Christ in Cuba.

Section 1. The Centrality of the Human Being Given in Jesus Christ

The church believes in God because it believes in the human being, and it believes in the human being because it believes in Jesus Christ, the "Son of God," our Older Brother.

This centrality of the human being in the faith of the church is presented within the framework of those two references which are very explicit and very clear: one, God, the Father Creator of every human being; and the other, Jesus Christ, the Older Brother Reconciler of every human being. As we present it in this way, we do not deny, but rather just the opposite, we reaffirm both as essentials of the faith.

Faith in Jesus Christ obligates the church to place the human being in the center of its interest and concern, and to consider him as a parameter to judge all things, especially to evaluate its own doctrinal teaching, its specific ecclesiastical structures and its particular mission as the church.

The church considers that God in Jesus Christ reveals to us that the center of his interest, concern, and value judgment of all things is in his human "creature," to the point of "stripping himself bare"[a] and becoming "sinful flesh"[b] for his redemption.

A. JESUS CHRIST: THE CENTER OF OUR INTEREST

The church affirms that the center of its interest is Jesus Christ.

The church believes in Jesus Christ. In Jesus Christ, in the human event of Jesus Christ, God reveals to us his redeeming purpose.

In the historic realization of the revelation in Jesus Christ, God does not graze in a tangential way the concrete reality of the human being, but rather, on the contrary, he inserts himself in history, taking it on as his own. In that way he calls us all to fulfill ourselves as human beings through concrete historical projects of redemption.

The insertion of God in history requires of him that "he strip himself bare" and take on the form of the oppressed one, the form "of a slave." This speaks, on the one hand, of love's sacrificial magnitude and on the other, of its solidary magnitude. [Phil 2.7]

When the church proclaims that it believes in Jesus Christ, it is affirming that to know God is to know Jesus Christ, and that to know God in Jesus Christ is to know truly the human being; because within the concrete and historic reality of

a. [Phil 2.7]
b. [Jn 1.14; 2 Cor 5.21]

the life of the Oppressed One, the Divine is realized in its greatest possible human magnitude, showing in turn the human meaning of life lived unconditionally in, by, and for other human beings.

[Rom 8.29]   When the church teaches that Jesus Christ is the Son of God, our Older Brother, incarnate and resurrected, "first-born among many brothers," it is giving the reason for its hope in the possibility of historically realizing justice and peace in the world, since in his death he overcomes the sin of injustice and hatreds and also overcomes the death of radical and incontrovertible frustrations.

[1 Cor 2.2]   When the church lives its love for "Jesus Christ and him crucified," it takes on in full responsibility the solution presented by God to the human problem through sacrificial and solidary love which works justice and establishes peace.

B. THE HUMAN BEING: THE CENTER OF GOD'S INTEREST

The Scriptures witness to the fact that the human being is the center of all God's interest. All through the pages of the Bible, God's love for the creature is not only made evident, but it is also presented as a divine necessity. God's loving interest in [1 Jn 4.8] the human creature is identified in the Scriptures with God's very essence.

      The church finds in this love, and only in it, all the theological material with which to formulate its doctrinal truth. The doctrinal development of the church and all the doctrines it has elaborated in its theological undertakings through the centuries, are valid to the extent that they explain in a better way God's loving purpose for the human being.

      When the church emphasizes the doctrines of incarnation and atonement, it witnesses to God's love for the human being, since it proclaims the magnitude of his sacrificial and solidary nature.

      In this way, the church raises God's interest and concern and his valuation of all things centered in the human being, to the level of a divine necessity, interpreting correctly what the Scriptures teach us about his "nature" and "attributes."

C. THE HUMAN BEING: THE CENTER OF THE CHURCH'S INTEREST IN JESUS CHRIST

The church on being interested in Jesus Christ and only in Jesus Christ and him crucified and risen from the dead, centers its interest in the human being.

      The church's faithfulness to Jesus Christ ties it to its Lord's historic commitment, a commitment of human redemption through sacrificial, solidary, and unconditional love for the human being.

      When the church proclaims that Jesus Christ is the "Incarnate Son of God," and our "Risen Older Brother," it witnesses to the fact that sacrificial and solidary love is not only a divine necessity, but also a human necessity, "signs" of the "mystery of God" and of the "mystery of man."

When the church teaches that the Scriptures witness to the supreme value God places on the human creature, becoming his Creator, Reconciler, and Redeemer, it recognizes the fact that sacrificial, and solidary and unconditional love for the human being constitutes its one and only necessity.

The church recognizes that sacrificial, solidary, and unconditional love is necessary for it to be the church of Jesus Christ; and, espousing the cause of human dignity and decorum in every moment and in whatever place, as its only reason for being—without placing any condition on its commitment, and without having it matter what the circumstances are in which it lives or the risk it runs—it participates fully in human redemption.

When the church lives this way, it is living in God, by God, and for God. To serve and love God in Jesus Christ is for the church to center its interest, its concern, and its valuation of all things in the human being, appropriating the christological form of being as the only way for God to make himself accessible to the creature and the only way for the church to make itself acceptable to God and to other human beings.

If the church should cease existing for, by, and in the human being, it would cease being the church of Jesus Christ, the Son of God, and our Older Brother.

When the church lives its historical reality placing the human being in the very center of its interest in Jesus Christ, it does not lose its identity as the "body of Christ" or as "Christ's bride," but all the contrary; even in its greatest degree of secularization, the church achieves the realization of its irrenunciable commitment of serving and loving Jesus Christ, since in him, at his own expense, God is secularized radically and unconditionally in his redemptive task of working for the fullness of the decorum and dignity of all human beings.

Section 2. The Human Being: An "Econome"

The Scriptures teach us that the human being is characterized by being an "econome" of all things, God's "steward." All goods, material and spiritual, that we [Lk 12.42–44] obtain as persons or as nations, cannot be considered in the final analysis as "individual" or "national" property in an exclusive way, be it individualistic, classist, elitist, or nationalistic. Much less can they have a transcendent value which, by reason of the "natural law" or "divine law," has been given goods as private ownership of the means of production.

To make human spiritual essentiality depend on the exercising of the so-called "right to private property," constitutes one of the most tragic aberrations—because of its consequences—that human spirituality has suffered to this day.

[1 Pt 4.10]
[1 Cor 4.1–2]
The Scriptures teach us that the human being will be whatever he is able to do and become as an "econome." The word "econome" (*oikōnomos*) is the one most used in the New Testament when it is a matter of judging the achievements of human life. In the Old Testament the term "econome" (*menshala*) is given equal importance.

When the Marxists insist on the "economical" as the basic element, fundamental for interpreting the significance of human life as it is developed in history, they make the church—one of those ironies of history—reconsider the biblical criterion of the human being as an "econome."

The church proclaims that the human vocation is that of being a "good econome." The "house" that the human creature administers is the whole world of creation; and each person is responsible for it to his fellow creatures and to God.

The responsibility of creating goods and administrating them is the first right of every human being, the essential principle of his spirituality. The church teaches that each and every human being should share responsibly in the mutual exercise of that right. To violate that right is the first criminal act against human dignity and decorum.

The most perfect social system will be the one that guarantees the responsible participation of all citizens in the matters of "public administration." The effective respect for that right is necessary in order for the society to be made up of persons and not infrahuman individuals. Such is the real principle of true "democracy."

The church teaches that the committed participation of its members in public life, in the administration of its economy, is not something one can choose to add or not to add to his condition of believer; on the contrary, the responsible exercise of this right is an integral and inseparable part of the loving practice of the Christian faith.

Therefore the church teaches that it is an integral part of the life of the Christian believer to exercise his rights and to fulfill his duties as a citizen, especially in our case, where democracy is made effective through the constitution of the Popular Power and the participation in labor unions in the different places of work.

The aberrations of a "faith" which calls itself "a-political," are of such consequence for the falsification of human spirituality and the meaning of the social nature of life, that the church, indignant, rejects them and combats them as "heretical." Only an interested distortion of the faith—against all argumentation grounded on scriptural truth—can make the simple Christian believer renounce the struggle and effort to find, together with his fellow countrymen, the most adequate solutions to the problems patent in the neighborhood, in the city, or in the nation, and keep him from enriching the life of all and making it more decorously human through a better "economy" of his time, his abilities, his knowledge, and the goods he produces.

A. WORK: A PRINCIPLE OF HUMAN SPIRITUALITY

The Scripture teaches us that work is the means through which we exercise our vocation as "economes," both in the creation of material and spiritual goods, and also in their "good" administration.

The Scriptures teach us also that when we affirm that the human being is primarily a worker, we are proclaiming that he is created "in the image and likeness of God." In the Old Testament he is ordered "in the image and likeness of God" [Gn 1.27] to "work six days" so that he can "rest the seventh." In the New Testament we are [Ex 34.21] called to be workers "in the image and likeness of Christ." God and Christ are "one and the same thing," the content of which is defined by Jesus Christ himself: "My Father works and I work." In the New Testament they go so far as to deny the right [Jn 5.17] to eat—which is like denying the right to live—to anyone "who will not work." [2 Thes 3.10] Idleness is the sacrilegious vice of the "old man." [Eph 4.22]

In the Old Testament we are also ordered to exercise dominion and control over all things so that we be the "image and likeness of God." In the New Testament [Gn 1.28] we are called to be no longer "slaves" that carry out the "order" to work, but rather "friends" of Jesus Christ working freely God's will. [Jn 15.15]

The church is faithful to the Scriptures and to the gospel when it invites all human beings, and especially the Christian believers, to enter into the historical project of "dominating" nature through creative work and administration of goods produced. These human activities are to be exercised in such a way that justice and peace are established in the world as the only manifestation of God's redeeming, sacrificial, and solidary love for all human beings.

B. THE COMMUNITARIAN BEING: THE SPECIFICITY OF THAT WHICH IS HUMAN

The human being is a social being. The Scriptures teach that the social nature of the human being is an essential part of his existence "in the image and likeness of God."

The human being is a "political" being. The Scriptures teach that to be human is to live in community and in a community structured in some form. The fact of the life and death of Jesus Christ exemplifies for the church how decisive the specific social-political nature of the human being is for God.

The "secret" of the full social-political life—which makes possible the fulfillment of the vocation of the human being "econome"—is revealed in Jesus Christ, who "came, not to be served, but to serve and give his life as a ransom for his
[Mt 20.28]   people."

Therefore the church proclaims that wherever there is a genuine and effective service of human recuperation, living sacrificial and solidary love, unconditioned and unrestricted, for others, there Jesus Christ is present. His presence has
[Lk 22.27]   only one identification: "I am among you as one who serves."

The church teaches that creative work and the administrative task accompanying it, must be presided over by the fraternal community spirit, making all human beings brothers in the political activity that makes all better "economes" every day.

The church, in its members, lives the community action KOINONIA of the
[2 Cor 13.14]   Holy Spirit that makes us "companions" KOINONOS of our fellowmen and God's
[1 Cor 3.9]   "Coadjutors" in the task of human redemption, when said members are realized as faithful "economes" before God and before their neighbors.

C. FREEDOM: A HUMAN RESPONSIBILITY

The Scriptures teach that the human being, different from any other creature, is a "free" being. Human freedom is, however, a "responsible freedom." According to the Scriptures, human freedom is not doing what one wishes "out of whim or conceit." Neither is it the "free will" of the philosophers. The Bible teaches that human freedom is responsible, voluntary, and conscious obedience of the divine will.

The will of God—as it is described in the Bible—is a will of loving grace for the creature. God's loving grace for the human being is revealed concretely in the realization of justice and peace in the world, in the establishment of his kingdom of freedom and love.

Therefore, the church proclaims that the human being is "predestined to be free."

The church teaches that we will be free to the extent which we obey the loving will of God, serving effectively the cause of justice and peace among all human beings.

The church lives in a real and concrete practice of human freedom on the part of the members as they become committed participants in the quantitative growth and the qualitative development of "love-justice" in the social-political economical structures of human society, including the very structure of the church as a social-juridical institution.

D. THE HUMAN BEING—"ECONOME": THE CENTER OF THE INTEREST OF THE CHURCH

The human being, according to the Scriptures, is the "econome" which serves God in service to his neighbors in all tasks of human redemption. All the parables Jesus uses to judge our human situation and condition take as an evaluative norm the fidelity of the human being to his vocation of "econome."

Therefore the church does not support nor serve the interests of the oppressing classes that rob the human being of his vocation to be responsible free "economes," exploiting the work of many to increase the riches of few at the expense of the generalized increase of human misery, a "sign" of the frustration of God's love.

The church proclaims that human beings, as persons and as nations, "are to work with their own hands in order to have something to give to those in need," [Eph 4.28] fulfilling thus their vocation as "economes."

The church teaches the seriousness of what is involved in the human historical process, both in that which has to do with personal particularity and with general universality. For the church, what is involved is precisely the full realization of God's redeeming purpose in nature, history, and human conscience; that is, the coming of the kingdom of God.

The church lives its love centered in the human being, in the measure in which its members really become a community of "economes" who feel responsible before God to try to live their condition of human beings genuinely in complete fulfillment of their responsibilities in the redemption of nature, history, and human conscience.

Section 3. History: Integrating Reconstruction of the Human Being

The Scriptures teach us that the human being has been converted into an explicit contender against the redeeming purpose of God. "Sin" disfigures the "image and likeness of God" in the creature. The Bible also tells us that in Jesus Christ, God reconciles the human being with his redeeming purpose.

All human history is illuminated in this way as a process of integrating reconstruction of the human being. This process, for the Scriptures, does not march forward in a straight lineal form, but presents its great ups and downs. Biblical history continually shows us the ascendent and descendent direction that this process takes on.

In the Scriptures, what is called "sin" is the historical and concrete forms adopted by those "inferior moments" within the process of human redemption. [Gn 3.16–19] "Sin" imposes "pain" and "sweat" on the human being in the process of his history, under the sign of "death."

The church proclaims the fidelity of God to his creature, fidelity which is manifested in the continuous call of God to all human beings to overcome their "disintegration" of sin and death. God, "with strands of love," binds all those who hear his call and follow him, to his creating, reconciling, and redeeming work.

The church teaches that in life and death, resurrection and ascension of Jesus Christ, God himself puts an end to the disintegrating power of sin and death, and opens the possibility of salvation for all humankind.

The church lives in the militant and committed participation of each one of its members in the task of the integrating reconstruction of the human being. This reconstruction touches man in his spiritual, social, economical, and ecological totality.

A. THE HUMAN BEING: A BEING DISINTEGRATED BY SIN

The Bible teaches us that in "sin" there is a disintegrating distortion that acts on human life, tragically frustrating it both in its universal and its personal aspects.

"Sin" is the aberrant disintegrating distortion that transforms human work —the very principle of human spirituality—into an accursed task imposed on us for subsistence characterized by competition and discrimination.

"Sin" is the aberrant disintegrating distortion that transforms social-political life—the very specificity of the human being in community—into a battleground where hatred and jealousy, envy and selfishness produce fratricidal struggle, crime and the "exploitation of man by man."

"Sin" is the aberrant disintegrating distortion that transforms freedom— the responsibility of obeying the absolute demands of love-justice—into the slavery which affirms exclusively the particularized interests of our "individuality," "race," or "nationality" in detriment of the dignity and decorum of others, and therefore, to our own detriment as persons, races, or nations.

"Sin" is the aberrant disintegrating distortion that transforms material and spiritual goods, gifts of God and human achievements—for the usufruct of all alike —into factors of contradictions and discriminations among human beings through class-divided social structures. These factors reach the very altar of the church, the altar of a Father of all human beings.

Therefore the church knows that because of "sin," work has been converted into frustrated and frustrating activity which "separates" us fundamentally from our own vocation as "economes" and therefore makes us enemies of God, Father and Creator. Because of "sin," life in community has been converted into a dehumanized and dehumanizing jungle which "separates" us fundamentally from our fellowmen, our "brothers," and therefore makes us enemies of Jesus Christ, Reconciler. And because of "sin," freedom has been converted into an anarchy which, trying to pillage nature and exploit our neighbor, "separates" us fundamentally from the work of our hands, and therefore makes us enemies of the Holy Spirit, the redeeming presence of God Creator and Jesus Christ Reconciler.

The church proclaims the human possibility of reconstruction beyond "sin" because of the faithfulness of God, who, in his sacrificial and solidary love, unconditional and unrestricted, offers us "forgiveness" in Jesus Christ.

The church teaches that the written word reveals to us that social-political-economical liberation of the Hebrew people, exploited and oppressed under the domination of Egypt, resulted in being the explicit, concrete, and valid expression of their salvation, which constituted them as God's people. In that very same way the "living and active" word reveals to us that the victorious struggle for the social-political-economical liberation from the exploitation with which capitalistic, monopolistic, and imperialistic interests oppress the underdeveloped peoples of today, is the explicit, concrete, and valid expression of their salvation, which constitute them as God's new humanity. This teaching of the church does not contradict, but on the contrary, reaffirms and gives meaning to the gospel proclaimed by Jesus Christ as it is revealed in the Scriptures.

The church lives in its members when they contribute in a real way and with concrete historic actions to the disappearance of the "old man," disintegrated by "sin" and "death." The church realizes thus—and not in any other way—its true catholicity and apostolicity as the "body of Christ," "the bride of Lamb," the "people of God," according to the evangelical teaching.

B. SALVATION: THE HISTORY OF THE SPIRITUAL RECONSTRUCTION OF THE HUMAN BEING

Salvation as the history of the spiritual reconstruction of the human being is a required theme of Christian preaching, a specific expression of Christian faith, hope, and love.

Jesus Christ describes this spiritual reconstruction as the "birth of a new man." The assured possibility—that the "old man" disintegrated by "sin," will "die" to give way to a "new man," who will have eternal life—is affirmed in the New Tes- [Eph 4.21–24] tament in terms of a "new creation," a "new creature" when it is said that the "old

[2 Cor 5.17]   things have all passed away and everything is made new."

The "new man" does not cease being "human," but just the opposite. He is

[1 Pt 1.23]   a human being, who, having been "born again," can then realize his full humanity,
liberated from the chains that bound him irremissibly to the anti-human, sinful past.
His condition of "econome" does not change; it is just that before him there opens

[Mt 7.14]   up a "narrow way" which leads to his being one fully, "an open door that one can
close."

Creative work which makes it possible for the human being to be like God,
the principle of genuine spirituality, transforms him in a true and faithful "lieu-
tenant of God" like his Older Brother. The pedagogical nature of work, a theme
so highly esteemed by our reformed fathers, is affirmed when work is given, in the
reconstruction of the human being, its fundamental spiritual value.

The church proclaims the urgency for all human beings, and especially
Christian believers, to "discern the time in which they live, a time to rise up from
sleep" and wake up to the reality that "we are now closer to the day of our salvation

[Rom 13.11]   than when we believed."

The church teaches that the present "time" is the time of judgment of
"death" over the sins of an unjust and cruel structural order that has exploited, for
the benefit of only a few, the "vices of the old man" on which it has sustained itself.
The working class, precisely because it is the "working" class, has been constituted
in this "time," "time to rise up from sleep," in the legitimate standard bearers of
the construction of the new order which is more human and just for all. If Jesus
of Nazareth, the Son of God and our Older Brother, was a manual worker, and if
the ethics of the "new man" in the teaching of the New Testament states that work
is an essential element of the "holiness and righteousness according to God," then
the church can proclaim with all certainty and assurance, if it wants to be faithful
to the gospel, that "we are nearer today to the day of our salvation than when we
believed."

The church teaches—to be faithful to the gospel—that Jesus Christ took
the side of the oppressed and exploited class of his time and that "social-political
option" took him, objectively speaking, to the cross.

The church lives in its members when they, faithful to the gospel and to

[Mt 6.24]   their Lord and knowing that it is not possible to serve two masters, repudiate service to God-Money. The church is thus freed from the oppressive power with which
the ideologies of domination and exploitation to this day have kept it captive, especially when under the imperialistic political-cultural power it (the church) is aware

of how the greatest enemies of the human being today, and therefore, the greatest enemies of God, try to use it to defend their anti-Christian interests.

C. SALVATION: THE HISTORY OF THE SOCIAL-ECONOMICAL RECONSTRUCTION OF THE HUMAN BEING

Salvation for Scriptures means the reconstruction of the human being as "co-heir of all things"; that is, of those goods which, in faithfulness to his vocation as "eco-nome," he has, with his work, co-created or re-created. Salvation is also, thus, the history of the reconstruction of his being in community. [Rom 8.17]

The "creation" of a "new man" means the establishment of a new community life in the new society, where there is no place for the exploitation of the work of another, nor for racial discrimination, nor the subjection of women as objects of mercantile, commercial, or sexual consumption; nor will there be tolerance for the self-interested use of the legitimate values of family life in benefit of the false interests of the classist and discriminatory society.

The Scriptures teach us that salvation necessarily includes the emerging of a new fraternal solidarity that is made concrete in a "community of goods" where "private property" is abolished in order for all of us to be able to enjoy the goods produced.

The Bible teaches us, in the Old Testament, that a liberating process involves "as is written, that he who gathers much has nothing left over nor he who gathers little has lack." In the New Testament we are shown in a reliable way that [Prv 13.11] the liberating fact of the gospel, accepted fully, has as an inevitable consequence that, "uniting us all" ideologically, we "have all things in common," receiving "each [Acts 2.44–45] one according to his need."

The church proclaims, following the biblical-prophetic line carried to its final expression in Jesus Christ, that the entrance to the kingdom is closed to the "rich," to the extent that their riches are the products of violence and injustice; and, [Mt 19.23] in a specific way, it points out to all and especially to the Christian believers, the fact that the capitalistic system of social organization, in order to endure, has to maintain a manipulated and enslaving education that produces egoists who distort the meaning of human life and see as the supreme ideals of human life, unending consumption, insatiable satisfaction of getting rich, materialistic fetishism, and the drive for luxury and ostentation. As a result, this brings about a dehumanized society where most ferocious competition is of utmost importance and in which its victims are inculcated [with] social evasions by means of drugs, sexual excesses, gambling, and alienating religiosity.

The church teaches, according to its best reformed tradition, that "God desires that there be such identification and equality among us that each help . . . according to his capacities, so that some do not have things left over while others are in need . . . that possessions and other goods be distributed according to the needs of each one."

The church teaches that in the stability of the government—in spite of its necessary ambiguities—we can find a guarantee for the administration of justice and the maintenance of peace when it is a case of "non-classist" societies, where the power of the state is not in the hands of exploiting and oppressing classes, but in the hands of the workers.

The church lives in the same measure in which each one of its members works for the social-economical reconstruction of the human being within the so-cialist state; because, of all the historical forms of state known and experienced to this day, it is the society organized with such (socialist) structures which offers the most concrete possibilities for making workable a more and more fairly distributive justice, which progressively reaches all citizens with greater efficiency.

D. SALVATION: THE HISTORY OF THE ECOLOGICAL RECONSTRUCTION OF THE HUMAN BEING

"Sin," according to the Bible, distorts the human being's relationship with nature. The human being converted into an unscrupulous pillager of natural resources, not only has abused them, but also has made a diabolic use of them, making them a part of exploitation, oppression, and domination of his fellow creatures.

The human being has pathologically altered the development of nature and has become, not its guardian, but its perverter. Doing this, he has upset and dam-aged his own human nature from a biological point of view. As a psycho-social-somatic unit, given the complexity of his nature, the human being has found him-self affected in biological development as well as in his psychic health and social promotion.

Nevertheless the church affirms that the technical-scientific activities of the human being, in his eagerness to dominate and control nature, do not work against God's redeeming purpose which proposes—according to the Scriptures—"to put [Ps 8.6] all things under his feet." The "way" of salvation that God works in Jesus Christ, includes the full realization of that domination and control. The Bible uses the same [2 Cor 6.2] word "health" (*salud*) for "salvation" and for "liberation." We can not overlook the fact that in order to achieve a better human "health," both in the biological and in the psychic and social sense, it is necessary to control nature more perfectly and dominate its "mysteries" more completely.

The church proclaims that although it is an extremely secularizing society we are dealing with, this does not mean that God would be absent from it; rather it would mean the opposite. To believe in the doctrine of incarnation means we believe in a God radically secularized in Jesus of Nazareth as the only way to the possibility of human redemption.

The church teaches that the human technological undertaking serves to help create a new humanity to the extent it makes achievable a greater deepening of human spirituality with the disappearance of work as "exploitation."

The church teaches that modern technology, when it is at the service of the interests of exploiting classes, has produced a series of false idols, such as utilitarian logic, the *cosificación* of human beings (*cosa* = thing, *cosificación* = making into a thing) and technocratic nihilism. All Christian believers should fight committedly — together with those who strive to eradicate such idols — for the disappearance of their "creators."

The church teaches that, when our people chose the Marxist-Leninist way of development through a social-political revolution, a more human relationship with nature has been brought about as well as a primary concern for the health of the people. The Marxist-Leninist Revolution has proved to be the only way which makes the technological and ecological development possible and which successfully puts an end to underdevelopment. This phenomenon of underdevelopment has produced infrahuman beings, victims of exploitation and oppression with the world capitalistic and imperialistic system.

The church joyfully lives in the midst of the socialist revolution, since the revolution has concrete and historically inaugurated a series of values in human relations that make it possible for the whole technical-scientific development to be at the service of the full dignity of human beings.

E. THE INTEGRAL HUMAN BEING: THE CENTER OF THE CHURCH'S INTEREST IN HISTORY

The church is interested specifically in human history not only because, for almost two thousand years, it has been an important part of its development, but, principally because it is precisely within the process of human history where God in Jesus Christ has proposed to reconstruct the human being integrally. To cut up that reconstruction into sections has been the temptation the church has fallen into as a consequence of the ideological captivity in which it has been engulfed for centuries, putting itself at the service of the exploiting classes, especially in the period of monopolistic capitalism.

The church proclaims that there is only one history, and that it is not so much concerned about guaranteeing its own interests in the institutional-ecclesiasti-

[Rom 8.21]

cal order, inherited from the past, as about assuring the readiness and willingness of its members to respond freely "with the glorious freedom of the children of God" to the historical demands that God makes of them in the conquest of a society in which the integrally reconstructed human being—which is the purpose of the gospel—can emerge little by little.

[Mt 16.3]

The church teaches that the "atheism" of the ideology sustained by the social revolution, makes more clearly evident the atheism of the "believers" who are not capable of "discerning the signs of the times" in the midst of the new society being constructed, in which the radical transformations of the unjust structures make possible the creation of a more integrally reconstructed human being. The most important thing, in this case, is that the atheist-communists serve as an inspiration to us because of their readiness and willingness to live sacrificial, solidary, and effective love.

The church should be juridically separated from the state. This does not mean however that the church relinquishes its historical-political responsibility nor that the Christian believers should withhold their most decided contribution to the construction of the new socialist society.

The church lives this new situation without fears, proclaiming the truth of the gospel, confiding only in its Lord and captive only of Jesus Christ. In that way it finds its place in the human-historical process of integral recuperation. To do this the church does not begrudge any sacrifices that may be necessary to fulfill its mission, the special characteristics of which vary in accordance with the moment and the place it has to live in.

The church lives through the concrete love practiced by its members when they serve the socialist society without hostility, trusting the divine-human sense of history and trusting the future which envisions a more effective peace among nations and a more real justice among human beings.

Section 4. The Kingdom of God and the Fullness of History

The Scriptures teach that the kingdom of God is inaugurated in history in Jesus Christ in an inescapable and indefectible way. His birth as one of the poor of the kingdom, his class option as a worker for the kingdom, his evangelizing, preaching as a prophet of the kingdom, his life as a neighbor of the kingdom, his death as a Reconciler for the kingdom, his resurrection as the Older Brother in the kingdom, and his ascension as heir of the kingdom, constitute him in the kingdom itself. Today the kingdom is present among human beings through the action of his Spirit, his Holy Spirit.

These realities of faith constitute the foundation of the hope of the church and the reason for its commitment of unlimited and unconditional love, to which it is bound in the search for justice and peace in the world.

The church—which has elaborated doctrines such as the doctrines of incarnation, atonement, resurrection—rejects all dualism that leads to understanding human history divided into two sections, one profane and another religious.

The church proclaims its faith in the final coming of the kingdom grounded on the "mystery of the will" of God, who "according to his purpose set forth in Jesus Christ, at the fullness of time, to unite all things in Christ." [Eph 1.10]

A. THE DYNAMIC FORCE OF HISTORY

The Scriptures teach, typifying in the history of "God's people," the way in which human history is constituted as "history of salvation" through a series of experiences in which people grow in their awareness of the universal and totalizing nature of human redemption.

The biblical stories of salvation—from Noah to Jesus Christ, passing through Abraham, Moses, David, and all the prophets and leaders of the Hebrew people before and after the Babylonian exile—show that the church can teach, without fear of going wrong, that characteristic conflictivity of the economical-social-political process of liberation energizes (*dinamiza*) human history.

The class struggle that is manifested in the Bible in the contradiction evidenced between oppressors and oppressed, between "just" and "unjust," between rich that exploit and the exploited poor, together with the proclamation of God as the "realizer of justice" obligate the church to accept the close relationship between the kingdom of God for which we pray and the realization of justice, and therefore of peace, in the world.

The church proclaims that God "realizer of justice" "abides in us in love," [1 Jn 4.16] in the "effective love" that contributes to making God's redeeming purpose for human beings a reality shared by all, starting in the "here" and "now."

B. THE KINGDOM THAT ADVANCES

The Scriptures illustrate the kingdom of God in various ways. Sometimes, it is like a small seed that, once sown, grows to be a leafy tree. On other occasions, it is [Mt 13.31–32] like a field of wheat in which the enemy sows tares. These evangelical images teach [Mt 13.24–30] us that behind the incessant and constant process of struggles and contradictions which energize (*dinamiza*) history, a development of irrecusable permanent value is realized.

The church proclaims that the kingdom of God grows constantly and that the achievements of justice and peace in the world are achievements that enter to form part of the kingdom as fullness of history. The church is the place where the hope of a full realization of human life is cultivated in all its creativity and solidarity, as an expression of the "glorious freedom of the children of God" who are "loaded with fruits of justice."

[Rom 8.21]

The church joyfully teaches that the New Socialist Constitution of our country gives shape to the establishment of a more just society when it affirms that "the first law of our Republic is the cult of the Cubans to the full dignity of man." [1]

The church teaches that the new meaning which family relations have acquired—as expressed in the New Family Code—reflects a step forward in the reconstruction of the family life so necessary in today's world.

The church lives in the responsible participation of its members in the construction of the New Society through all its activities: in the committees of defense of the revolution, in the labor unions, in the Federation of Cuban Women, in the organizations of pioneers, students, peasants; in every effort and work carried out to create a new society of producers and not just consumers, where there is a place therefore for the creation of a new kind of human being, for whom love is no longer a Sunday commandment but rather the law which governs all his daily actions.

The church proclaims that peace is possible in the world. The Scriptures teach us that peace (*Shalom*) is not, in its essence, the absence of war, but the presence of justice. The church prays for peace and works for peace, and doing so, fulfills its mission as the church of Jesus Christ, the "Prince of Peace."

[Is 9.6]

The church joyfully teaches that the consolidation and development of the "socialist camp" in the world today and the policy of peace that its peoples and governments set forth as an essential part of socialism, as well as the extension and depth which the liberating anti-imperialist struggles have acquired in the exploited peoples of the so-called "Third World" all constitute "signs of the times" which point toward a real possibility of achieving a world of greater justice in relations among nations.

[Mt 16.3]

The church lives in the responsible and committed work of its members who join in the struggle to halt the present arms race, to achieve the total disappearance of all testing of weapons of mass destruction and the establishment of a complete disarmament in the world. In a world where there exist a United Nations Organization and a Helsinki Agreement of Pacific and Cooperative Relations Among Nations, it becomes necessary for all government and non-government organizations to make a special effort to guarantee all peoples the achievement of their

1. A quotation from José Martí.

full and responsible participation in the creation of a world which is more just and more nobly human. The church is called to take part in this effort because of its very nature and mission.

The church lives concretely in the intimate relations which exist between the coming of Jesus Christ the Savior and the definitive achievement of "peace on earth among men of good will," the announcement of his coming. Thus the church [Lk 2.14] is committed to the ecumenical struggle for the unity and peace of the whole catholic church, with the understanding that such efforts, in order to be genuine, must be realized as "signs" of our commitment to the struggle for the unity and peace of all of humanity. In this sense we live our ecumenical task within the different organizations and movements to which we belong up until now (Cuban Ecumenical Council, World Alliance of Reformed Churches, Christian Peace Conference, World Council of Churches) and we support every effort for the achievement of such unity and peace in the "body of Christ."

C. THE KINGDOM: THE CENTER OF
THE CHURCH'S INTEREST IN GOD

The Scriptures urge us to pray for the kingdom, to preach its imminence, to teach its hope, to live its norms. The church speaks of God by proclaiming his reality, teaching his truth, living his will.

The ultimate interest of the church in God is not the interest in maintaining a particular type of worship, in propagating a precise "idea," in defending a specific "religion." The ultimate interest of the church in God is the interest in his kingdom.

The church that is identified as the church of Jesus Christ is constituted as the advance guard of the kingdom, because in him, and for him "the kingdom is among us" and it is not just a case of "it will come." [Lk 17.21]

The Scriptures teach us that the "kingdom is peace, justice, and joy in the [Rom 14.17] Holy Spirit," the "convincer of all sin, of all justice, and of all judgment." The Scrip- [Jn 16.8] tures teach us that "to speak by the Spirit" is "to prophesy." [Lk 1.67]

The Scriptures teach us that "prophetism" is essential to the life of the church. The church "prophesies" when it proclaims that the construction of the socialist society—which brings us closer to the reconstruction of the human being as a worker and "econome" and as a free and communitarian being—is a most essential part of the march of the human historical process, a march in which the achievements of the human spirit remain as concrete signs of the historic action of the Spirit in bringing about the kingdom.

The church "prophesies" when it lives, in each one of its faithful, the triumph of love over un-love, justice over exploitation, truth over injustice, peace over competition, decorum over human indignity. The church lives "prophetically" in its members when they become committed participants in the death of the capitalist society and the dehumanizing and decrepit values it represents. Otherwise the church would be converted into a "scandal" for God and a "reproach" for men,

[Dt 13.1–5]   and its "destruction will not be long in coming" like that of all "false prophets."

The church "prophesies" when its members joyfully live the feelings and actions of growing solidarity of our socialist people for all the peoples of the world. The church "prophesies" when it expresses its joy for the evident fact that this deep feeling of solidarity is becoming a generalized characteristic of the common citizen.

Conclusion

As we finish this Declaration of Faith, the Presbyterian-Reformed Church in Cuba recognizes that its declared faith can only be certain when we confidently live the truths implicit in it: That this world is "God's world"; that nature is the "theater" where God and his creature meet to be mutually realized in a concrete and eternal alliance through the implanting of peace by the establishment of structures of love-justice which normalize human relations; that history is the "plot" of the development and strengthening of that alliance or "covenant"; that the kingdom is the "unraveling of the plot"—slowly at times and suddenly other times—with realizations and achievements that the "plot" from time to time has, since in the kingdom, God, and his creature are identified with each other, because the kingdom, Jesus Christ himself, is the Son of God and our Older Brother.

The Presbyterian-Reformed Church in Cuba is aware that, as it lives these truths, it comes dangerously close to the radical secularization taken on by God in Jesus Christ, and runs the same risks that he did of misunderstandings, sufferings, and crucifixion.

Nevertheless, the Presbyterian-Reformed Church in Cuba hopes confidently and joyfully that, as it does this, it may become more fully a part of the glorious freedom of the Risen One, a freedom which will free it from the alienating ideologizations that in the past and still in the present have kept and keep the church of Jesus Christ, in many aspects and in many places, captive of unjust and oppres-

[Eph 6.12]   sive structures, of "principalities and powers." These structures and "powers" have made the human being an exploiter of his neighbor. The church that is not ashamed of this, has distorted and distorts the gospel of Jesus Christ.

The Presbyterian-Reformed Church in Cuba hopes confidently and humbly that this liberation will capacitate it to respond with greater effectiveness to the primary inevitable question with which God confronts all human beings without exception: "Where is your brother?"   [Gn 4.9]

The Presbyterian-Reformed Church in Cuba, with the confidence and assurance that spring from the gospel, and only from the gospel, looks for the concrete answer to the divine questions in "love that faith sets in motion," knowing in "hope against hope," that is the only way given to the human being by God in Jesus Christ   [Rom 4.18] to find the divine answer to his crucially final question as a creature: "Tell me your name"; "Tell me who I am."

The Presbyterian-Reformed Church in Cuba, in all humility before its Lord and before all the people, finally questions itself: Will we definitively come to know "Who he is" and "Who we are" in order to be able to communicate this with redeeming effectiveness, the sign of our evangelizing mission, the identity of the church? Only in the measure in which we fulfill the concrete loving demands of justice and peace which the divine requirement imposes on us, will we be able to satisfy the hope of really being the church of Jesus Christ in this world, because then "we will be like him," for "as he is, so are we in this world" in the fullness of love.   [1 Jn 3.2, 4.17]

Commission on Faith and Order of the World Council of Churches at Bangalore, *A Common Statement of Our Faith*, 1978

It is a measure of the achievements of three decades of ecumenical theological discussion that → *The Doctrinal Basis* of the World Council of Churches adopted in 1948, which even in its minimalist form had evoked vigorous debate, should have led in August 1978 at Bangalore, India, to the possibility of issuing a document from the Faith and Order Commission that speaks of "*our* faith" as something that could be held and affirmed in "common."

The drafting committee explained: "We have not been working on a better edition of the creeds nor on a comprehensive statement of the gospel, but rather we have tried to express what binds our churches together in the present situation. What we have produced is an expression of our common faith and is not meant to replace the ancient creeds; indeed, we are offering a description of where we are as regards our common faith—we have not written a statement that is full and adequate in the mind of everyone."

A Common Statement of Our Faith is, therefore, interesting at least as much for what it omits as for what it affirms. But many of the issues that it omits were already under intense discussion in the three commissions that produced the constituent parts of → *Baptism, Eucharist, Ministry,* to be issued by Faith and Order at Lima in 1982. It is, however, a widely held view among ecumenists that Lima would probably not have come without Bangalore.

Edition: *Sharing in One Hope* 1979, 244–46.

Literature: Beaupère 1979; *Giving Account of the Hope Together* 1978; Pamenberg 1979.

Commission on Faith and Order of the World Council of Churches at Bangalore, *A Common Statement of Our Faith*, 1978

Preamble

As we seek to give a common statement of our faith, we are mindful of the existing fellowship of churches which is marked by a common confession of "the Lord Jesus Christ as God and Savior according to the Scriptures." Already we have joined hands seeking to fulfill together our "common calling to the glory of the one God, Father, Son, and Holy Spirit."

Because we have traveled together on the road of faith, experiencing, in spite of our historical divisions, the unifying power of Jesus Christ and his salvation and growing together in his service, we desire to express more fully our common faith in the triune God who has called us to himself and wants us to share in his mission for the salvation of all humankind.

As we seek to confess our faith together, we want to be faithful to the apostolic faith according to the Scriptures, handed down to us through the centuries. At the same time we want to face the new situation and the challenge for mission today. Furthermore, we are aware that a common confession of faith should be the sign of our reconciliation.

Part 1

As Christians we confess Jesus Christ, the only source of salvation for humankind and for each individual human person. He is the one Lord of his church, the cornerstone of its unity. The church is based on his ministry, remembers in her worship his incarnation, his suffering, crucifixion, and death, proclaims with joy his resurrection and eagerly awaits his second coming. As our Savior he is truly God and truly man. He has authority to grant us communion with God in the presence of his reign, which overcomes the power of death and sin and every misery, division, and separation among us; but he also shares in our sufferings and temptations so that in spite of them we may have confidence in him and in the promise of his kingdom. He is the new Adam, in whom we recognize the destiny of human beings and into whose image our lives shall be transformed.

In Jesus' ministry we encounter the one God and Creator of all things, whose eternal love is concerned for every single human person and thus constitutes the dignity of each human being. God, the Holy Spirit, is the eternal link of love, between God the Father, and God the Son, and spreads abroad God's love to all his creatures to overcome their miseries and separations. In the ministry of the Spirit we receive life and are transfigured, inspired, and liberated by the divine presence among his creatures and are sealed in hope. God, the Father, Son, and Holy Spirit extends love and judgment to all creation to overcome its separations and calls the church into the unity of one body, in order to be more fully the sign of a new humanity.

The one faith is confessed and lived in the community of the faithful who have been called through the preaching of the gospel and gather around the Lord in the Spirit. We enter into this community through baptism which is our participation in the death and resurrection of Jesus Christ. We are incorporated into the eucharistic community in which the word is proclaimed and the sacrament duly celebrated.

The one faith is the full responsibility of each member of the community, not, however, separately one from the other, but in communion. The presence of the Lord in the midst of his people expresses itself in a variety of charisms and services, which equip them for their mission among men. Such charisms and services are the instruments of the Holy Spirit in the building up of the church, enabling its community to persevere in the apostolic teaching, in fraternal communion, in the breaking of bread, and in prayer (Acts 2.42). The one(s) who presides over the community has the particular responsibility of being, in the Holy Spirit, the servant of the unity of the church by the proclamation of the word in the eucharistic community. His (their) service aims at reinforcing the communication in the community, with a vision of fuller communion.

The confession of the one faith is not a question of majority, but rather, it is a confession in one Spirit. Such a confession naturally implies a total commitment of life on the part of all members of the community.

The community experiences a communion in one Spirit which is not limited to one period in time or to one given place (*hic et nunc*); it is the communion with all witnesses to the apostolic faith in all places and at all times. It is a confession in the communion of saints.

Part 2

Growing together in one faith, the divided Christian communities are prepared to share already now a doxology, taken from our common heritage, the Scriptures.

One passage which condenses many aspects of our common confession is to be found in Ephesians 1.3–15.

Together with this doxology:

We confess God's involvement in the history of humankind, revealed through Israel, fulfilled in Jesus Christ, communicated to us by the Holy Spirit, into which fulfillment all humanity is called;

we confess the destiny and dignity of all *human beings,* rooted in God's initiative and design;

we confess our dependence upon *God's redeeming and liberating grace,* because we are caught up in the ambiguities of our history and because we live in sin;

we confess the reality of the *event of Jesus Christ*—his life, his death, his resurrection—and the reality of our answer of faith, given to that event, that brings us, through the Spirit, to the incorporation into Christ, which means our salvation;

we confess the reality of *the church,* being the body of Christ, called to be the nucleus and servant of the unity of humankind and of the universe. We confess our responsibility as Christians to have the mind of Christ and to live and act accordingly in the community of humankind; faith without work is dead;

we confess the presence and the working of *the Spirit,* the pledge and seal of the kingdom, into which we are confirmed.

Reformed Church in America, *Our Song of Hope*, 1978

As the heir of the classic Reformed confessions, especially of → *The Heidelberg Catechism,* which had circulated widely in the Netherlands, and of the confessions that came out of the Low Countries, including → *The Belgic Confession* and → *The Canons of the Synod of Dort,* the [Dutch] Reformed Church in America strove in *Our Song of Hope* of 1978 to go beyond the abstract dogmatic terminology of those formularies and, heeding John Calvin's reminder that → *The Niceno-Constantinopolitan Creed* was better sung than spoken, to articulate its faith, which it shared with other Reformed churches, in an innovative literary form that could speak to and for the entire Christian church at the end of the twentieth century. *Our Song of Hope* went through many drafts before being approved for study in 1974, and then adopted officially in 1978 "as a statement of the church's faith for use in its ministry of witness, teaching, and worship," but not on the same level with those earlier Reformed confessions.

Edition: *Liturgy and Confessions* 1990.

Literature: Heideman 1975.

Reformed Church in America, *Our Song of Hope*, 1978

We sing to our Lord a new song;   [Ps 96.1]
We sing in our world a sure hope:
    Our God loves this world,
        God called it into being,
        God renews it through Jesus Christ,
        God governs it by the Spirit.
God is the world's true hope.

1. OUR HOPE IN THE COMING OF THE LORD

1. We are a people of hope
        waiting for the return of our Lord.
    God has come to us
        through the ancient people of Israel,
        as the true Son of God, Jesus of Nazareth,
        as the Holy Spirit at work in our world.
    Our Lord speaks to us now through the inspired
        Scriptures.
        Christ is with us day by day.

2. OUR SONG IN A HOPELESS WORLD

2. We know Christ to be our only hope.
    We have enmeshed our world in a realm of sin,
        rebelled against God,
        accepted inhuman oppression of humanity,
        and even crucified God's Son.
    God's world has been trapped by our fall,
        governments entangled by human pride,
        and nature polluted by human greed.

3. JESUS CHRIST OUR ONLY HOPE

3. Our only hope is Jesus Christ.
    After we refused to live in the image of God,
    He was born of the Virgin Mary,
        sharing our genes and our instincts,

entering our culture, speaking our language,
    fulfilling the law of our God.
Being united to Christ's humanity,
    we know ourselves when we rest in him.

4. Jesus Christ is the hope of God's world.
    In his death,
        the justice of God is established;
        forgiveness of sin is proclaimed.
    On the day of the resurrection,
        the tomb was empty; his disciples saw him;
        death was defeated; new life had come.
        God's purpose for the world was sealed.

5. Our ascended Lord gives hope for two ages.
    In the age to come, Christ is the Judge,
        rejecting unrighteousness,
        isolating God's enemies to hell,
        blessing the new creation in Christ.
    In this age, the Holy Spirit is with us,
        calling nations to follow God's path,
        uniting people through Christ in love.

4. OUR HOPE IN GOD'S WORDS

6. The Holy Spirit speaks through the Scriptures.
    The Spirit has inspired Hebrew and Greek words,
        setting God's truth in human language,
        placing God's teaching in ancient cultures,
        proclaiming the gospel in the history of the world.
    The Spirit speaks truly what the nations must know,
        translating God's word into modern languages,
        impressing it on human hearts and cultures.

7. The Holy Spirit speaks through the church,
        measuring its words by the canonical Scriptures.
    The Spirit has spoken in the ancient creeds,
        and in the confessions of the Reformation.
    The world is called to bear witness to Christ

in faithfulness to the Scriptures,
in harmony with the church of the ages,
and in unity with all Christ's people.

8. God's Spirit speaks in the world
according to God's ultimate word in Christ.
In every time and place,
in ancient cities and distant lands,
in technology and business,
in art and education,
God has not been left without a witness.
The word has entered where we have failed to go.

9. In each year and in every place
we expect the coming of Christ's Spirit.
As we listen to the world's concerns,
hear the cry of the oppressed,
and learn of new discoveries,
God will give us knowledge,
teach us to respond with maturity,
and give us courage to act with integrity.

5. OUR HOPE IN DAILY LIFE

10. As citizens we acknowledge the Spirit's work in human
government
for the welfare of the people,
for justice among the poor,
for mercy towards the prisoner,
against inhuman oppression of humanity.
We must obey God above all rulers,
waiting upon the Spirit,
filled with the patience of Christ.

11. We pray for the fruits of the Spirit of Christ
who works for peace on earth,
commands us to love our enemies,
and calls for patience among the nations.
We give thanks for God's work among governments,

seeking to resolve disputes by means other than war,
placing human kindness above national pride,
replacing the curse of war with international
self-control.

12. We hear the Spirit's call to love one another
opposing discrimination of race or sex,
inviting us to accept one another,
and to share at every level
in work and play,
in church and state,
in marriage and family,
and so fulfill the love of Christ.

13. As male and female we look to the Spirit
Who makes us the stewards of life
to plan its beginning,
to love in its living,
and to care in its dying.
God makes us the stewards of marriage
with its lifelong commitment to love;
yet God knows our frailty of heart.

[Jn 16.13]   14. The Spirit leads us into truth
the truth of Christ's salvation,
into increasing knowledge of all existence.
He rejoices in human awareness of God's creation
and gives freedom to those on the frontiers of
research.
We are overwhelmed by the growth in our knowledge.
While our truths come in broken fragments,
we expect the Spirit to unite these in Christ.

6. OUR HOPE IN THE CHURCH
15. Christ elects the church
to proclaim the word and celebrate the sacraments,
to worship God's name,
and to live as true disciples.

He creates a community
    to be a place of prayer,
    to provide rest for the weary,
    and to lead people to share in service.

16. The Holy Spirit sends the church
    to call sinners to repentance,
    to proclaim the good news
        that Jesus is personal Savior and Lord.
    The Spirit sends it out in ministry
        to preach good news to the poor,   [Is 61.1; Lk 4.18]
        righteousness to the nations,
        and peace among all people.

17. The Holy Spirit builds one church,
        united in one Lord and one hope,   [Eph 4.4–5]
        with one ministry around one table.
    The Spirit calls all believers in Jesus
        to respond in worship together,
        to accept all the gifts from the Spirit,
        to learn from each other's traditions,
        to make unity visible on earth.

18. Christ places baptism in the world
    as a seal of God's covenant people,
        placing them in ministry,
        assuring them of the forgiveness of sins.
    God knows those who are baptized in Jesus' name,
        guiding the church gently to lead us,
        calling us back when we go astray,
        promising life amid trials and death.

19. Christ places the Lord's table in this world.
    Jesus takes up our bread and wine
        to represent his sacrifice,
    to bind his ministry to our daily work,
        to unite us in his righteousness.
    Here Christ is present in his world

[1 Cor 11.26]   proclaiming salvation until he comes,
                                 a symbol of hope for a troubled age.

                    7. OUR HOPE IN THE AGE TO COME
               20. God saves the world through Jesus.
                         Those who call on that name will have life.
                    Christ's hand reaches out beyond those who say "Lord"
                         to the infants who live in the atmosphere of faith,
                         even to the farthest stars and planets, all creation.
                    The boundaries of God's love are not known,
                         the Spirit works at the ends of the world
                         before the church has there spoken a word.

               21. God will renew the world through Jesus,
                         who will put all unrighteousness out,
                              purify the works of human hands,
                              and perfect their fellowship in divine love.
                         Christ will wipe away every tear;
                              death shall be no more.
[Rv 21.1–4]   There will be a new heaven and a new earth,
                              and all creation will be filled with God's glory.

                              Our Prayer

[Rv 22.20]   Come, Lord Jesus:
                         We are open to your Spirit.
                         We await your full presence.
                         Our world finds rest in you alone.

The Presbyterian Church in South Africa, *Declaration of Faith,* 1979/1981

In the 1970s, as the struggle over apartheid was tearing apart the social and political life of the Union of South Africa, the churches, too, were riven by the tension between two New Testament imperatives, to "be subject to the governing authorities" and "to set at liberty those who are oppressed."[1] Of the many unofficial manifestos and broadsides generated by the struggle, most of them coming from individuals or groups rather than from churches as such (including the strong *Theological Declaration* by the "Broederkring" of the Dutch Reformed Church of the Union of South Africa in 1979), this *Declaration of Faith* by the Presbyterian Church in South Africa, also from 1979, is sufficiently "creedal" in its provenance, structure, and message to warrant its inclusion in this collection of *Creeds and Confessions of Faith.* It was composed by the Life and Work Committee of the Presbyterian Church in South Africa amid the conflicts of 1973, and in September 1979 the General Assembly of the Presbyterian Church adopted it for liturgical use. With some minor changes, it was issued in this definitive form in 1981.

Edition: Vischer, 27–28.

Literature: Link, 2:1; Vischer, 24–27.

1. Rom 13.1; Lk 4.18.

The Presbyterian Church in South Africa, *Declaration of Faith*, 1979/1981

1. We believe in God the Father
   who created all the world,
   who will unite all things in Christ
   and who wants all people to live together
   as brothers and sisters in one family.

2. We believe in God the Son
   who became man, died, and rose in triumph,
   to reconcile all the world to God,
   to break down every separating barrier
   of race, culture, or class,
   and to unite all people into one body.

   He is exalted as Lord over all,
   the only Lord over every area of man's life.
   He summons both the individual and society,
   both the church and the state,
   to seek reconciliation and unity between all
   and justice and freedom for all.

3. We believe in God the Spirit,
   the pledge of God's coming reign,
   who gives the church power to proclaim the good news to all
      the world,
   to love and serve all people,
   to strive for justice and peace,
   to warn that God judges both the individual and the nation,
   and to summon all the world to accept God's reign here and
      now.

The Credo from *The Mass of the Marginalized People*, Honduras, 1980

The definition of salvation as "liberation," as this was voiced in the context of a Marxist-Leninist society by → the *Confession* of the Presbyterian-Reformed Church of Cuba in 1977, is part of a larger and far more complex phenomenon, which is often (and not always accurately) labeled "liberation theology." It is by no means an exclusively Protestant movement; in fact, its most articulate (and often its most radical) voices have been Roman Catholic, particularly in the new ecclesiological atmosphere stimulated by → *Lumen gentium* of the Second Vatican Council. After the centuries in which the institutional church had appeared to be the bulwark of imperial, colonial, and feudal power structures, the official Vatican doctrine of "a preferential option for the poor" has become the basis for clergy and laity of the Roman Catholic Church, above all in Latin America, to go far beyond that doctrine in aligning the church with the downtrodden and "marginalized." Although its primary expression has been a call to concrete social and political action, this realignment has also occasionally taken liturgical and even creedal form, as in this *Credo,* which is part of *The Mass of the Marginalized People* of 1980, as in Carlos Mejía Godoy's *Misa campesina* from Nicaragua (1975), in Guillermo Cuéllar's *Misa popular salvadoreña,* written at the request of Archbishop Oscar Romero in the late 1970s,[1] and in this Credo from the Honduran *Mass of the Marginalized People,* which, though not quite possessing similar status, has become known outside Latin America through its inclusion in Hans-Georg Link's collection, *Confessing Our Faith Around the World.*

Edition: *Misa del pueblo marginado*. World Council of Churches Archives, Faith and Order, Latin American Confessions of Faith, box 23.7.060.

Translation: Link, 3:45.

Literature: Gibellini 1979.

---

1. See Vigil and Torellas 1988 for the Credo texts in Carlos Mejía Godoy's *Misa campesina* and Guillermo Cuéllar's *Misa popular salvadoreña.*

The Credo from *The Mass of the Marginalized People*, Honduras, 1980

Refrain: I believe, God, that you made
the earth, the sky, the sea.
Everything that is in them,
it all belongs to you.
Father and Lord of humankind,
before you we are all equal.
You are father to the poor,
because all are of value in your eyes.
Father and Lord of humankind,
before you we are all equal.
You are father to the poor,
because all are of value in your eyes.

1.   I believe that you became human
in the womb of Mary,
a village woman, a poor woman,
a virgin dedicated to God.
You give people
new dignity and value,
restoring in us the image
in which we were made by God.

2.   I believe you are life and light,
truly God and truly human.
You reveal the Father
who loves and cares for us.
When the powerful killed you,
you remained with us,
and you live now for ever
bearing oppression's weight.

3.   I believe you are transforming
     this death-dealing world
     through the Holy Spirit,
     who is God's love and power.
     You live raised from death,
     and are present in the fight
     in which we build your kingdom
     of justice, peace, and love.

Church of Toraja, Indonesia, *Confession,* 1981

Because the Protestant Christian Batak Church (Huria Kristen Batak Protestant) of Indonesia issued its → *Confession of Faith* of 1951 partly as a means of explaining and justifying its existence to the West, including the Lutheran World Federation to which it was applying for membership, that has been the one Indonesian confession with which a broader ecumenical audience has been the best acquainted. But Indonesian Christians in the twentieth century have produced several other confessions, including some that do not appear in this set, such as the *Common Comprehension of Faith* issued by the Protestant Church in Indonesia in 1967 and the *Basic Confession of the Kero-Batak Church* of 1979.

Coming after all three of those confessional statements is this *Confession* of the Church of Toraja. Toraja has been taken as an interesting case history of "the encounter between the Christian message and culture," as the subtitle of a monograph on that church has called it.[1] That encounter is especially noticeable in several of the paragraphs of the seventh chapter of the *Confession,* entitled "The World," especially in the references to "the various structures of society, both *traditional* and modern" (7.4) and to "customary laws [*adat*]" (7.8).

Edition: *Pengakuan Gereja Toraja* 1994, 3–28.

Translation: Vischer, 48–58.

Literature: Kobong 1992.

---

1. Kobong 1992.

Church of Toraja, Indonesia, *Confession,* 1981

Under the leadership of the Holy Spirit and on the basis of the word of God, we believe that the Lord God was pleased to reveal himself, that is his will, his love and his power to us in Jesus Christ, so that we reach the confession: "Jesus Christ is Lord and Savior."

He redeems and saves us from destruction, so that we become his possession and receive eternal life.

Under the leadership of the Holy Spirit we bring the sovereignty of Jesus Christ to bear upon our lives.

In connection with the Ecumenical and Reformed Confessions, we, together with all the saints of all ages and in all places, confess that:

Notes:

Ecumenical Confessions: The Apostles' Creed, the Nicene Creed, and the Athanasian Creed; Reformed Confessions: The Three Documents of Unity, the Geneva Confession, the Westminster Confession, etc.

CHAPTER 1. THE LORD GOD

1. God is one. [Dt 6.4]

The essence of the one and only God is love, which has been revealed by [1 Jn 4.8] him in the history of his work of salvation in three persons, that is: God the Father, God the Son, and God the Holy Spirit.

2. God is the one and only source of life, blessing, and goodness. It is only he who may be worshiped.

3. The eternal God the Father created everything, both that which is visible and that which is invisible.

The eternal God cares for and saves his creation in justice and truth, because of his goodness and love.

4. The eternal God the Son was born and became man so as to carry out the salvation of the world.

5. The eternal God the Spirit bears witness to the salvation of the world. He convinces us and seals this salvation in the hearts and lives of mankind.

6. The Trinity cannot be understood by the mind of mankind, but the word of God declares him to mankind so that thus he can be accepted and trusted in, on the basis of the faithful love of the eternal God towards his creation.

CHAPTER 2. THE WORD OF GOD

1. Jesus Christ is the Word of God who calls us to believe in him. In him the promise of salvation has been fulfilled and because of that takes effect for us.

2. Through his creation and his acts in nature and history God continually reveals himself.

The response of mankind to the general revelation of God cannot bring him to a true knowledge of God. The Bible as the particular revelation of God bears witness that only in Jesus Christ can God be known as the Father who saves.

3. The Bible is the word of God, which has been communicated to mankind through the prophets and apostles, and which consists of the canonical books of the Old Testament and the New Testament, in which God has revealed his will so as to save mankind.

The Old Testament and the New Testament as the promises of salvation and new life are a unity, which complete each other and which cannot be separated the one from the other.

4. The Bible as a book does not have any power in itself. The Holy Spirit bears witness to us that the Bible is the word of God, and he convinces us so that we accept it as renewing and saving power.

5. Strengthened by the power of the Holy Spirit, the word of God brings mankind to salvation in Jesus Christ in the midst of the struggles of life through its proclamation and reading.

Exegesis is the attempt of believers to understand the word of God, so that it can be applied in their situation here and now.

6. The word of God, that is the Old Testament and the New Testament, is the only normative rule of conduct for the life of believers, both in private and as a community.

7. The Bible is a book of the history of God's saving activity, which calls mankind to believe. The Bible is not a handbook of knowledge, and therefore it may not be contrasted with scientific principles.

CHAPTER 3. MANKIND

[Gn 1.27]   1. Mankind was created by God in accordance with his image.

The image of God is the relationship of responsibility with God, with his fellow men and with the whole of the natural world, in true knowledge and in holiness, truth, and love.

2. The image of God, as the relationship of responsibility, places the whole of mankind in the same position and ties the whole of mankind in a unity to a life of mutual love.

3. The image of God, as the relationship of responsibility, differentiates mankind from the other creatures, and gives him the position to govern, subdue, and care for the natural world as the mandatory of God.

4. Mankind was created in a unity of body and soul. The soul is not divine and is not more important than the body, and so too vice versa; therefore, spirit and body, and spiritual and physical things, are of equal importance.

Mankind is called to care for his body as a temple of God in holiness. [1 Cor 6.19]

5. Mankind as the good creation of God fell into sin, because of mankind's desire to become like God. [Gn 3.5]

6. Sin is the breaking of the true relationship with God and rebellion against God in daily life.

The breaking of the relationship with God means mankind's death completely.

7. The breaking of the true relationship with God resulted in mankind no longer being able to live in truth and holiness and in obedience to the law of God, in his relations with his fellow men and with the world of nature, so that mankind was under the condemnation of the anger of God.

8. We know of our sin from the Bible and not from various disasters, illnesses, and sufferings which come as a result of it.

It is the Holy Spirit who makes us aware of our sins.

9. The faithful love of God was so great that he restored the true relationship with his mankind again in Jesus Christ, the true and genuine man.

CHAPTER 4. REDEMPTION

1. Jesus Christ, God the Son, left his glory and emptied himself by becoming genuine man. [Phil 2.7–8]

2. Genuine man is man who is the same as us, except in the matter of sin. He was not sinful, but he bore the curse of our sin, so that in him we might be justified before God. [Gal 3.13]

3. In the life and work of Jesus Christ the kingdom of God became present among mankind. Its signs were, among other things, the healing of the sick, the raising of the dead, the driving out of devils, and the proclamation of the good news.

4. In his work of salvation Jesus Christ experienced the life of mankind with all its humiliations, weaknesses, and sorrows, and moreover he was tempted in all things, but he did not commit sin. [Heb 4.15]

5. Jesus Christ bore the curse of the anger of God towards our sin through his sufferings even as far as death on the cross, and moreover he descended to the kingdom of death.

All of this was done by him so as to be a substitute for us, and thus he redeemed us from the power of death to become his possession.

6. Jesus Christ rose from among the dead. His victory and resurrection are the guarantee of our being justified before God and the guarantee of our resurrection at the end of time. Thus we participate in the victory and resurrection together with Christ, leading to new life now and in the future.

7. Our salvation and security now and in the future do not depend upon offerings, like: the sacrifice of animals, charitable works, and our virtue and piety.

Sinners are justified before God only through the sacrifice of Jesus Christ.

8. Jesus Christ, who rose, ascended to heaven to become the Intermediary, and he has been installed as King. To him has been granted all power, both in heaven
[Mt 28.18]   and on earth.

As Intermediary he has become our Intercessor, he has prepared a place for us, and he is the guarantee of the resurrection of mankind completely.

From there he shall come back as Judge.

9. Through the mediation of the Holy Spirit, Jesus Christ is continually
[Mt 28.20]   with us, until the end of time.

CHAPTER 5. SANCTIFICATION

1. God the Holy Spirit has been sent by God the Father and God the Son to apply God's work of salvation in Jesus Christ in our lives.

2. In the Holy Spirit God is present and works in the midst of the world. He cares for, frees, and governs this world in the framework of the realization of the kingdom of God.

This presence of God is the power which reorganizes, renews, and sanctifies us, so that we leave behind the old life and live in a new life.

3. The Holy Spirit convinces us through the word of God that we have been
[2 Cor 5.17]   justified in Jesus Christ, so that we are a new creation.

4. In faith, as a close relationship between us and God, we assent to our justification in Jesus Christ, and we entrust our whole life into the hands of God as our genuine service.

Through prayer we declare and experience our close relationship with God.

5. From the time that we believe in Jesus Christ, we are in a new life; however, sin still constantly is a reality in our life. The life of faith places us in a struggle between sin and grace, between the old and the new. The Holy Spirit makes us aware of sin and truth, and brings us to repentance from day to day. He convinces and comforts us regarding the certainty of our victory.

6. The man of faith as a new creation cannot any more live in sin; on the

contrary, his life forms a living offering. To be charitable and to carry out deeds of virtue are not obligations, but rather are the norms of our life and culture as the fruits of faith for the glory of God.

Notes:

Section 6: "living in sin" = permanently resident in sin; "obligations" are used to oppose moralism; to carry out that which is good is the essence of new life.

CHAPTER 6. THE PEOPLE OF GOD

1. God has called and chosen one people and has built his church as a fellowship of believers and his possession, so as to be a blessing to all nations.

He has made a covenant with his people on the basis of his faithful love in the realization of his plan of salvation in Jesus Christ. God calls this people through the mediation of his Spirit and word to come out of darkness and to enter God's marvelous light, to come out from not being his people and to become the holy people of God. [1 Pt 2.9]

2. This people of God is a new fellowship, the possession of Jesus Christ, which administers its own life on the basis of the word of God, and not according to the norms of the old life, nor according to any other power.

On the basis of the word of God and under the leadership of the Holy Spirit, the people of God carry out their prophetic task so as to convince the world of sin and truth.

3. The people of God is sent out into the world for the world; it is in the world, but not of the world. In its existence the church is like a lodger and a traveler. [Jn 15.19]

The church has to be willing to suffer as a sign of her faithfulness whenever the world hates and persecutes her. Her strength lies in the victory of the Lord.

4. This new fellowship is the body of Christ and the family of God, with Christ as Head. Therefore, this fellowship lives within one brotherhood, with equal status for all, without differentiation of race, nation, tribe, or social class. The Holy Spirit, who lives in it, distributes gifts from the variety of gifts to each member, for the building up of the body of Christ. [Eph 4.12]

5. This new fellowship, as the first-fruits of the kingdom of God, makes itself visible by redeeming all the walls of partition in the structures and norms of the old life, with all its expressions. Each of its activities is a sign of the new life, both whenever the congregation gathers together and whenever it spreads out, to serve and bear witness in the midst of the world.

6. The people of God as the body of Christ is not a static fellowship and does not live for itself, but rather the congregation is a dynamic and open procession and invites all, through the witness of its life, through service and through its

proclamation, to partake in that procession pointing to the fullness of life in the kingdom of God.

7. This procession is continually being built up and cared for by the Holy Spirit and the word of God in the whole of its life and in all its activities in the midst of the world.

Sunday is the day of the Lord, which has been given to us for special fellowship with God and with our fellow brethren. On these days the fellowship is visible in praise, prayer, the reading and proclamation of the word, confession, offering, baptism, and the Lord's supper.

8. Jesus Christ has graciously given to his church the sacraments of baptism and the Lord's supper as means of grace and signs of his covenant, that is the visible word.

These two sacraments are signs and seals of the grace of salvation based upon the death and resurrection of Jesus Christ.

Sacraments are guarantees of our salvation, to comfort us and to strengthen our faith.

Water, bread, and wine in the sacraments do not have power in themselves. The grace which is signified and sealed by them only has effect for us when we receive it with true faith.

9. Sacraments are the visible word, and therefore cannot be separated from the proclamation of the word.

Sacraments are signs of fellowship. Baptism signifies that we belong to the members of the body of Christ, and the Lord's supper signifies that we have fellowship with Christ and with our fellow members. Baptism and the Lord's supper, as signs of God's covenant and of fellowship, cannot be isolated the one from the other.

[Rom 6.3] 10. In baptism we are baptized into the death of Christ, and thus we are sanctified from all our sins, and are raised up together with Christ into a new life. Baptism is administered only once to each member of the congregation, both of those who are adults and of those who are children. On the basis of God's covenant children of members of the congregation should be baptized.

Parents are responsible for leading their children to a knowledge of Jesus Christ so that they themselves may profess their faith.

11. The Lord's supper is a guarantee to us that our sin has been forgiven in Jesus Christ and that we have been raised to new life in fellowship with him.

In the Lord's supper Jesus Christ is present in his Spirit, and we celebrate it as the feast of the first-fruits of eternal joy.

12. Jesus Christ governs his congregation by appointing special officials to

minister, to govern, and to equip the saints, so that they may be able to carry out their function in the general task of believers in the midst of this world.

The status of a minister lies in his appointment by Jesus Christ himself, and in his obedience, service, and faithfulness to him.

13. Every local church where the word of God is proclaimed in an orderly manner, where the two sacraments are administered, where the apostolic function is carried out and where discipline is exercised is a full manifestation of the catholic church, that is of the one people.

Thus, every church or congregation is in an ecumenical relationship with other churches or congregations. The people of God as the body of Christ is one, and Christ is its Head.

Notes:

The word "congregation" is used in the meaning of "the local church"; section 13: the "apostolic function" is explained in sections 5 and 6.

CHAPTER 7. THE WORLD

1. This world and everything that is in it is the good creation of God. That which has been created is not divine and therefore may not be worshiped or feared.

2. The transient corruptibility of the world and of all of nature was caused by sin, which damaged the relationship between God and mankind and between fellow men, one with another. Because of this, the world and all of nature again need liberation and renewal.

3. This world, which has been damaged by sin, is full of the powers of darkness, so that mankind lives in fear and in beliefs in various superstitions and charms, and also makes use of all kinds of ways so as to safeguard his livelihood. However, Jesus Christ, the light of the world, has brought all the powers of darkness into subjection.

4. Religions and religious institutions are the manifestations of the consciousness of man about the existence of God or some power outside his life whom he fears and worships. Religion which is true and which brings one to salvation is that which is based upon the particular revelation of God in Jesus Christ.

5. The life of mankind is out of balance, and this is especially clear in the distinction and difference of socioeconomic position, which has been legalized in the various structures of society, both traditional and modern.

The socioeconomic structures which cause injustice need to be taken down and renewed by the power of the Holy Spirit so that they may be in accordance with the will of God.

6. The government and its institutions are instruments in the hand of the

Lord for taking care of well-being, justice, and truth and for shedding light upon evil, in responsibility to the Lord and to the people. It has continually to be under the critical review of the word of God. Therefore, we should pray for and assist the government so that it can carry out its task in accordance with the will of God for the well-being of mankind.

7. To cultivate is a task from God.

Culture is the activity of the intellect and feeling of mankind in fashioning and controlling nature for the material and spiritual needs of life. Therefore, culture must be dynamic and must continually be developed in a double wrestle, that is in a wrestling of man in his relationships with God and with the world.

8. Customary laws (*adat*) are the traditions which regulate the life of society on the basis of the standards and convictions of each society or group and party. Therefore, customary law (*adat*) cannot be separated from conviction and religion, so that we should test each customary law (*adat*) to see whether it is in accordance with the will of God or not.

9. Marriage as a partnership of love is a gracious gift and task from God, which has to be built up and to be treated with responsibility for the glory of God. Happy marriages and families form the basis of a thriving society and nation. Therefore, we should protect them in holiness of life in accordance with the will of God.

10. Knowledge is a gracious gift of God, which can lead man to efforts of upbuilding for the improvement and development of his livelihood to the glory of God. That gracious gift of God demands a great responsibility, because of the inclination of man to misuse knowledge and technology for his own interests, or the interests of each group and party to damage nature, mutually to destroy, and indeed to deny God.

11. This world, with all the institutions in it, which has been put into disorder by sin, is constantly loved, cared for, and governed by God in his faithfulness. God has liberated and renewed, and is liberating and renewing, this world in Jesus Christ, towards its fullness in the new heaven and earth.

CHAPTER 8. THE END OF TIME

1. The end of time has begun with the coming of Jesus Christ.

In his resurrection we are raised to a new life which is full of hope.

2. Jesus Christ, who has ascended to heaven, shall come back again in his glory, as Judge and Savior, to make salvation real in the perfection of the kingdom of God. Therefore, with great longing we await that moment of time.

3. At the time of his return, which no one at all knows, he shall judge all

people who are alive and dead according to their faith and actions. The world shall be purified, restored, and renewed to become an incorruptible world.

4. The resurrection is the resurrection of mankind totally. Every believer shall be raised up to new life in the new world, while every unbeliever shall be raised up to circumstances outside fellowship with God in an everlasting punishment.

5. The wages of sin are death. Death is the death of mankind completely. To [Rom 6.23] seek relationships with departed souls, to worship them, and to hope for blessing from them is a fruitless exercise, and moreover one which damages the relationship with God, and it is sin.

6. Life in relationship with God is eternal life, which cannot be canceled out by any power at all. God in his power and faithful love continues that relationship so that every believer, after he dies, is together with Christ. Every unbeliever then is outside any fellowship with Christ.

7. Everlasting life is life in relationships which have been restored between God and man, between fellow men, one with another, and between man and nature, and this shall be perfected in a new heaven and earth, where God shall be [Rv 21.1] worshiped and glorified forever and ever.

8. This everlasting life gives meaning to our life, here and now, so that everything which we carry out in fellowship with Jesus Christ is not in vain. For everything is from him, by him, and to him. To him be glory forever and ever. [Rom 11.36]

Note:

"Incorruptible" means—in harmony, completely pristine, not yet touched by human hand, secure, everlasting.

North American Baptist Conference, *Statement of Beliefs,* 1982

Unlike most of the Baptist bodies in the English-speaking world, from whom there have come the several Baptist confessions that appear earlier in this set, the North American Baptist Conference was originally the product of German immigrants who came to the United States and Canada in the nineteenth century. As its official description of itself explains, "the first church was organized by Rev. Konrad Fleischmann in Philadelphia in 1843. In 1865, delegates of the churches met in Wilmot, Ontario, and organized the North American Baptist Conference."

This *Statement of Beliefs* was adopted on 10–15 August 1982 by the delegates of the North American Baptist Conference, assembled in Niagara Falls, New York.

Edition: Provided by the North American Baptist Conference.

North American Baptist Conference, *Statement of Beliefs,* 1982

Preface

Baptists, since their beginnings, repeatedly have composed confessions which expressed the doctrinal consensus among related churches. In principle, however, Baptists always have insisted that no statement of faith can be considered creedally binding even upon concurring congregations. The purpose of their doctrinal summaries was to explain to other Christians and to the larger society what Baptists believed and practiced. Within and among Baptist churches, statements of faith also provided a standard for instruction, counsel, and fellowship.

We, as the North American Baptist Conference, presently feel the need to state more fully our Baptist understanding of the Christian faith. The purpose that guided us in writing and the use that we intend for this declaration are: (1) to further the sense of identity and the spirit of unity within our North American Baptist Conference by declaring our common doctrinal understandings; (2) to provide a basis for doctrinal instruction within our conference; (3) to provide a basis for doctrinal discussions in the hiring of conference personnel; (4) to serve as a reference point when opinions differ; (5) to provide a basis for doctrinal discussion in admitting new churches and new pastors into our various associations; (6) to provide a doctrinal guide for new churches; and (7) to give a doctrinal witness beyond our conference.

In continuity with our immediate forefathers and the larger fellowship of Baptists throughout history, we seek to practice and propagate by God's grace the following convictions:

I

We believe the Bible is God's word given by divine inspiration, the record of God's revelation of himself to humanity (2 Tm 3.16). It is trustworthy, sufficient, without error—the supreme authority and guide for all doctrine and conduct (1 Pt 1.23–25; Jn 17.17; 2 Tm 3.16–17.) It is the truth by which God brings people into a saving relationship with himself and leads them to Christian maturity (Jn 20.31; 1 Jn 5.9–12; Mt 4.4; 1 Pt 2.2).

2

We believe in the one living and true God, perfect in wisdom, sovereignty, holiness, justice, mercy, and love (1 Tm 1.17; Ps 86.15; Dt 32.3–4). He exists eternally in three coequal persons who act together in creation, providence, and redemption (Gn 1.26; 1 Pt 1.2; Heb 1.1–3).

a. The Father reigns with providential care over all life and history in the created universe; he hears and answers prayer (1 Chr 29.11–13; Mt 7.11). He initiated salvation by sending his Son, and he is Father to those who by faith accept his Son as Lord and Savior (1 Jn 4.9–10; Jn 3.16, 1.12; Acts 16.31).

b. The Son became man, Jesus Christ, who was conceived of the Holy Spirit and born of the Virgin Mary (Jn 1.14; Mt 1.18). Being fully God and fully man, he revealed God through his sinless life, miracles, and teaching (Jn 14.9; Heb 4.15; Mt 4.23–24). He provided salvation through his atoning death in our place and by his bodily resurrection (1 Cor 15.3–4; 2 Cor 5.21; Rom 4.23–25). He ascended into heaven where he rules over all creation (Phil 2.5–11). He intercedes for all believers and dwells in them as their ever-present Lord (Rom 8.34; Jn 14.23).

c. The Holy Spirit inspired men to write the Scriptures (2 Pt 1.21). Through this word, he convicts individuals of their sinfulness and of the righteousness of Christ, draws them to the Savior, and bears witness to their new birth (Jas 1.18; Jn 16.7–11; 1 Thes 1.5–6; Rom 8.16). At regeneration and conversion, the believer is baptized in the Holy Spirit (1 Cor 12.13). The Spirit indwells, seals, and gives spiritual gifts to all believers for ministry in the church and society (Rom 8.9–11; Eph 1.13–14; Rom 12.5–8; 1 Pt 4.10). He empowers, guides, teaches, fills, sanctifies, and produces the fruit of Christ-likeness in all who yield to him (Acts 4.31; Rom 8.14; 1 Cor 2.10–13; Eph 5.18; 2 Thes 2.13; Gal 5.16, 22–23).

3

We believe God created an order of spiritual beings called angels to serve him and do his will (Ps 148.1–5; Col 1.16). The holy angels are obedient spirits ministering to the heirs of salvation and glorifying God (Heb 1.6–7, 13–14). Certain angels, called demons, Satan being their chief, through deliberate choice revolted and fell from their exalted position (Rv 12.7–9). They now tempt individuals to rebel against God (1 Tm 4.1; 1 Pt 5.8). Their destiny in hell has been sealed by Christ's victory over sin and death (Heb 2.14; Rv 20.10).

4

We believe God created man in his own image to have fellowship with himself and to be steward over his creation (Gn 1.26–28). As a result, each person is unique, possesses dignity, and is worthy of respect (Ps 139.13–17). Through the temptation of Satan, Adam chose to disobey God; this brought sin and death to the human race and suffering to all creation (Gn 3; Rom 5.12–21, 8.22). Therefore, everyone is born with a sinful nature and needs to be reconciled to God (Rom 3.9–18, 23). Satan tempts people to rebel against God, even those who love him (Eph 4.27; 2 Cor 2.11; Mt 16.23). Nonetheless, everyone is personally responsible to God for thoughts, actions, and beliefs and has the right to approach him directly through Jesus Christ, the only Mediator (Rom 14.12; 1 Tm 2.5).

5

We believe salvation is redemption by Christ of the whole person from sin and death (2 Tm 1.9–10; 1 Thes 5.23). It is offered as a free gift by God to all and must be received personally through repentance and faith in Jesus Christ (1 Tm 2.4; Eph 2.8–9; Acts 20.21). An individual is united to Christ by the regeneration of the Holy Spirit (Gal 2.20; Col 1.27). As a child of God, the believer is acquitted of all guilt and brought into a new relationship of peace (Rom 5.1). Christians grow as the Holy Spirit enables them to understand and obey the word of God (2 Pt 3.18; Eph 4.15; 1 Thes 3.12).

6

We believe the church is the body of which Christ is the Head and all who believe in him are members (Eph 1.22–23; Rom 12.4–5). Christians are commanded to be baptized upon profession of faith and to unite with a local church for mutual encouragement and growth in discipleship through worship, nurture, service, and the proclamation of the gospel of Jesus Christ to the world (Acts 2.41–42, 47; Lk 24.45–48). Each church is a self-governing body under the lordship of Christ with all members sharing responsibility (Acts 13.1–3, 14.26–28). The form of government is understood to be congregational (Mt 18.17; Acts 6.3–6, 15.22–23).

The ordinances of the church are baptism and the Lord's supper. Baptism is the immersion of a believer in water in the name of the Father, and of the Son, and of the Holy Spirit (Mt 28.18–20). It is an act of obedience symbolizing the believer's identification with the death, burial, and resurrection of the Savior Jesus Christ (Rom 6.3–5). The Lord's supper is the partaking of the bread and of the cup by believers together as a continuing memorial of the broken body and shed blood of Christ. It is an act of thankful dedication to him and serves to unite his people until he returns (1 Cor 11.23–26).

To express unity in Christ, local churches form associations and a conference for mutual counsel, fellowship, and a more effective fulfillment of Christ's commission (Acts 15; 1 Cor 6.1–3).

7

We believe religious liberty, rooted in Scripture, is the inalienable right of all individuals to freedom of conscience with ultimate accountability to God (Gn 1.27; Jn 8.32; 2 Cor 3.17; Rom 8.21; Acts 5.29). Church and state exist by the will of God. Each has distinctive concerns and responsibilities, free from control by the other (Mt 22.21). Christians should pray for civil leaders, and obey and support government in matters not contrary to Scripture (1 Tm 2.1–4; Rom 13.1–7; 1 Pt 2.13–16). The state should guarantee religious liberty to all persons and groups regardless of their religious preferences, consistent with the common good.

8

We believe Christians, individually and collectively, are salt and light in society (Mt 5.13–16). In a Christlike spirit, they oppose greed, selfishness, and vice; they promote truth, justice, and peace; they aid the needy and preserve the dignity of people of all races and conditions (Heb 13.5; Lk 9.23; Ti 2.12; Phil 4.8–9; 1 Jn 3.16–17; Jas 2.1–4).

We affirm the family as the basic unit of society and seek to preserve its integrity and stability (Gn 2.21–25; Eph 6.1–4).

9

We believe God, in his own time and in his own way, will bring all things to their appropriate end and establish the new heaven and the new earth (Eph 1.9–10; Rv 21.1). The certain hope of the Christian is that Jesus Christ will return to the earth suddenly, personally, and visibly in glory according to his promise (Ti 2.13; Rv 1.7, 3.11; Jn 14.1–3). The dead will be raised, and Christ will judge mankind in righteousness (Jn 5.28–29). The unrighteous will be consigned to the everlasting punishment prepared for the devil and his angels (Mt 25–41, 46; Rv 20.10). The righteous, in their resurrected and glorified bodies, will receive their reward and dwell forever with the Lord (Phil 3.20–21; 2 Cor 5.10; 1 Thes 4.13–18).

Commission on Faith and Order, Lima, Peru,
Baptism, Eucharist, Ministry, 1982

As became clear in the negotiations leading up to the founding of → the Church of South India, → the Church of Sri Lanka, and → the Ghana Church Union, as well as in the discussions and debates at successive gatherings of → the World Council of Churches and its → Faith and Order Commission, most of the obstacles to further church fellowship and reunion are connected in one way or another with the doctrine of the church—authority, ministry, sacraments.

Charged with the responsibility of addressing the theological issues of greatest concern to the churches, the Faith and Order Commission of the World Council of Churches undertook to examine, in initially separate study groups, the three central questions of baptism (including especially infant baptism and believers' baptism), eucharist (including preconditions for eucharistic fellowship and differing understandings of the eucharistic presence), and ministry (including the relation of episcopal, presbyteral, and congregational doctrines of polity and authority). The document on the eucharist came first (1967), followed by the one on baptism (1968), then by the one on ministry (1972), under the theological and editorial leadership of Max Thurian.

The three documents were then brought together in a single text, which was distributed, discussed, and revised, before final acceptance at Lima, Peru, in 1982. As the accompanying message from Faith and Order notes, "Those who know how widely the churches have differed in doctrine and practice on baptism, eucharist, and ministry will appreciate the importance of the large measure of agreement registered here. . . . That theologians of such widely different traditions should be able to speak so harmoniously about baptism, eucharist, and ministry is unprecedented in the modern ecumenical movement."

Edition: *Baptism, Eucharist, and Ministry* 1982, 2–32.

Literature: *DEM* 80–83 (Max Thurian); Thurian 1983; Thurian and Wainwright 1984; Wainwright 1986.

Commission on Faith and Order, Lima, Peru, *Baptism, Eucharist, Ministry,* 1982

1. Baptism

1. THE INSTITUTION OF BAPTISM

1. Christian baptism is rooted in the ministry of Jesus of Nazareth, in his death, and in his resurrection. It is incorporation into Christ, who is the crucified and risen Lord; it is entry into the new covenant between God and God's people. Baptism is a gift of God, and is administered in the name of the Father, the Son, and the Holy Spirit. Saint Matthew records that the risen Lord, when sending his disciples into the world, commanded them to baptize (Mt 28.18-20). The universal practice of baptism by the apostolic church from its earliest days is attested in letters of the New Testament, the Acts of the Apostles, and the writings of the fathers. The churches today continue this practice as a rite of commitment to the Lord who bestows his grace upon his people.

2. THE MEANING OF BAPTISM

2. Baptism is the sign of new life through Jesus Christ. It unites the one baptized with Christ and with his people. The New Testament Scriptures and the liturgy of the church unfold the meaning of baptism in various images which express the riches of Christ and the gifts of his salvation. These images are sometimes linked with the symbolic uses of water in the Old Testament. Baptism is participation in Christ's death and resurrection (Rom 6.3-5; Col 2.12); a washing away of sin (1 Cor 6.11); a new birth (Jn 3.5); an enlightenment by Christ (Eph 5.14); a reclothing in Christ (Gal 3.27); a renewal by the Spirit (Ti 3.5); the experience of salvation from the flood (1 Pt 3.20-21); an exodus from bondage (1 Cor 10.1-2) and a liberation into a new humanity in which barriers of division whether of sex or race or social status are transcended (Gal 3.27-28; 1 Cor 12.13). The images are many but the reality is one.

A. Participation in Christ's Death and Resurrection

3. Baptism means participating in the life, death, and resurrection of Jesus Christ. Jesus went down into the River Jordan and was baptized in solidarity with sinners in order to fulfill all righteousness (Mt 3.15). This baptism led Jesus along the way of the Suffering Servant, made manifest in his sufferings, death, and resurrection

(Mk 10.38–40, 45). By baptism, Christians are immersed in the liberating death of Christ where their sins are buried, where the "old Adam" is crucified with Christ, and where the power of sin is broken. Thus those baptized are no longer slaves to sin, but free. Fully identified with the death of Christ, they are buried with him and are raised here and now to a new life in the power of the resurrection of Jesus Christ, confident that they will also ultimately be one with him in a resurrection like his (Rom 6.3–11; Col 2.13, 3.1; Eph 2.5–6).

B. Conversion, Pardoning, and Cleansing

4. The baptism which makes Christians partakers of the mystery of Christ's death and resurrection implies confession of sin and conversion of heart. The baptism administered by John was itself a baptism of repentance for the forgiveness of sins (Mk 1.4). The New Testament underlines the ethical implications of baptism by representing it as an ablution which washes the body with pure water, a cleansing of the heart of all sin, and an act of justification (Heb 10.22; 1 Pt 3.21; Acts 22.16; 1 Cor 6.11). Thus those baptized are pardoned, cleansed, and sanctified by Christ, and are given as part of their baptismal experience a new ethical orientation under the guidance of the Holy Spirit.

C. The Gift of the Spirit

5. The Holy Spirit is at work in the lives of people before, in and after their baptism. It is the same Spirit who revealed Jesus as the Son (Mk 1.10–11) and who empowered and united the disciples at Pentecost (Acts 2). God bestows upon all baptized persons the anointing and the promise of the Holy Spirit, marks them with a seal, and implants in their hearts the first installment of their inheritance as sons and daughters of God. The Holy Spirit nurtures the life of faith in their hearts until the final deliverance when they will enter into its full possession, to the praise of the glory of God (2 Cor 1.21–22; Eph 1.13–14).

D. Incorporation into the Body of Christ

6. Administered in obedience to our Lord, baptism is a sign and seal of our common discipleship. Through baptism, Christians are brought into union with Christ, with each other, and with the church of every time and place. Our common baptism, which unites us to Christ in faith, is thus a basic bond of unity. We are one people and are called to confess and serve one Lord in each place and in all the world. The

union with Christ which we share through baptism has important implications for Christian unity. "There is . . . one baptism, one God and Father of us all . . ." (Eph 4.4–6). When baptismal unity is realized in one holy, catholic, apostolic church, a genuine Christian witness can be made to the healing and reconciling love of God. Therefore, our one baptism into Christ constitutes a call to the churches to overcome their divisions and visibly manifest their fellowship.

E. The Sign of the Kingdom

7. Baptism initiates the reality of the new life given in the midst of the present world. It gives participation in the community of the Holy Spirit. It is a sign of the kingdom of God and of the life of the world to come. Through the gifts of faith, hope, and love, baptism has a dynamic which embraces the whole of life, extends to all nations, and anticipates the day when every tongue will confess that Jesus Christ is Lord to the glory of God the Father.

3. BAPTISM AND FAITH

8. Baptism is both God's gift and our human response to that gift. It looks towards a growth into the measure of the stature of the fullness of Christ (Eph 4.13). The necessity of faith for the reception of the salvation embodied and set forth in baptism is acknowledged by all churches. Personal commitment is necessary for responsible membership in the body of Christ.

9. Baptism is related not only to momentary experience, but to lifelong growth into Christ. Those baptized are called upon to reflect the glory of the Lord as they are transformed by the power of the Holy Spirit, into his likeness, with ever increasing splendor (2 Cor 3.18). The life of the Christian is necessarily one of continuing struggle yet also of continuing experience of grace. In this new relationship, the baptized live for the sake of Christ, of his church, and of the world which he loves, while they wait in hope for the manifestation of God's new creation and for the time when God will be all in all (Rom 8.18–24; 1 Cor 15.22–28, 49–57).

10. As they grow in the Christian life of faith, baptized believers demonstrate that humanity can be regenerated and liberated. They have a common responsibility, here and now, to bear witness together to the gospel of Christ, the Liberator of all human beings. The context of this common witness is the church and the world. Within a fellowship of witness and service, Christians discover the full significance of the one baptism as the gift of God to all God's people. Likewise, they acknowledge that baptism, as a baptism into Christ's death, has ethical implica-

tions which not only call for personal sanctification, but also motivate Christians to strive for the realization of the will of God in all realms of life (Rom 6.9ff.; Gal 3.27–28; 1 Pt 2.21–4.6).

4. BAPTISMAL PRACTICE
A. Baptism of Believers and Infants

11. While the possibility that infant baptism was also practiced in the apostolic age cannot be excluded, baptism upon personal profession of faith is the most clearly attested pattern in the New Testament documents.

In the course of history, the practice of baptism has developed in a variety of forms. Some churches baptize infants brought by parents or guardians who are ready, in and with the church, to bring up the children in the Christian faith. Other churches practice exclusively the baptism of believers who are able to make a personal confession of faith. Some of these churches encourage infants or children to be presented and blessed in a service which usually involves thanksgiving for the gift of the child and also the commitment of the mother and father to Christian parenthood.

All churches baptize believers coming from other religions or from unbelief who accept the Christian faith and participate in catechetical instruction.

12. Both the baptism of believers and the baptism of infants take place in the church as the community of faith. When one who can answer for himself or herself is baptized, a personal confession of faith will be an integral part of the baptismal service. When an infant is baptized, the personal response will be offered at a later moment in life. In both cases, the baptized person will have to grow in the understanding of faith. For those baptized upon their own confession of faith, there is always the constant requirement of a continuing growth of personal response in faith. In the case of infants, personal confession is expected later, and Christian nurture is directed to the eliciting of this confession. All baptism is rooted in and declares Christ's faithfulness unto death. It has its setting within the life and faith of the church and, through the witness of the whole church, points to the faithfulness of God, the ground of all life in faith. At every baptism the whole congregation reaffirms its faith in God and pledges itself to provide an environment of witness and service. Baptism should, therefore, always be celebrated and developed in the setting of the Christian community.

13. Baptism is an unrepeatable act. Any practice which might be interpreted as "re-baptism" must be avoided.

B. Baptism—Chrismation—Confirmation

14. In God's work of salvation, the paschal mystery of Christ's death and resurrection is inseparably linked with the pentecostal gift of the Holy Spirit. Similarly, participation in Christ's death and resurrection is inseparably linked with the receiving of the Spirit. Baptism in its full meaning signifies and effects both.

Christians differ in their understanding as to where the sign of the gift of the Spirit is to be found. Different actions have become associated with the giving of the Spirit. For some it is the water rite itself. For others, it is the anointing with chrism and/or the imposition of hands, which many churches call confirmation. For still others it is all three, as they see the Spirit operative throughout the rite. All agree that Christian baptism is in water and the Holy Spirit.

C. Towards Mutual Recognition of Baptism

15. Churches are increasingly recognizing one another's baptism as the one baptism into Christ when Jesus Christ has been confessed as Lord by the candidate or, in the case of infant baptism, when confession has been made by the church (parents, guardians, godparents and congregation) and affirmed later by personal faith and commitment. Mutual recognition of baptism is acknowledged as an important sign and means of expressing the baptismal unity given in Christ. Wherever possible, mutual recognition should be expressed explicitly by the churches.

16. In order to overcome their differences, believer baptists and those who practice infant baptism should reconsider certain aspects of their practices. The first may seek to express more visibly the fact that children are placed under the protection of God's grace. The latter must guard themselves against the practice of apparently indiscriminate baptism and take more seriously their responsibility for the nurture of baptized children to mature commitment to Christ.

5. THE CELEBRATION OF BAPTISM

17. Baptism is administered with water in the name of the Father, the Son, and the Holy Spirit.

18. In the celebration of baptism the symbolic dimension of water should be taken seriously and not minimalized. The act of immersion can vividly express the reality that in baptism the Christian participates in the death, burial, and resurrection of Christ.

19. As was the case in the early centuries, the gift of the Spirit in baptism may be signified in additional ways; for example, by the sign of the laying on of

hands, and by anointing or chrismation. The very sign of the cross recalls the promised gift of the Holy Spirit who is the installment and pledge of what is yet to come when God has fully redeemed those whom he has made his own (Eph 1.13–14). The recovery of such vivid signs may be expected to enrich the liturgy.

20. Within any comprehensive order of baptism at least the following elements should find a place: the proclamation of the Scriptures referring to baptism; an invocation of the Holy Spirit; a renunciation of evil; a profession of faith in Christ and the Holy Trinity; the use of water; a declaration that the persons baptized have acquired a new identity as sons and daughters of God, and as members of the church, called to be witnesses of the gospel. Some churches consider that Christian initiation is not complete without the sealing of the baptized with the gift of the Holy Spirit and participation in holy communion.

21. It is appropriate to explain in the context of the baptismal service the meaning of baptism as it appears from Scriptures (i.e., the participation in Christ's death and resurrection, conversion, pardoning and cleansing, gift of the Spirit, incorporation into the body of Christ, and sign of the kingdom).

22. Baptism is normally administered by an ordained minister, though in certain circumstances others are allowed to baptize.

23. Since baptism is intimately connected with the corporate life and worship of the church, it should normally be administered during public worship, so that the members of the congregation may be reminded of their own baptism and may welcome into their fellowship those who are baptized and whom they are committed to nurture in the Christian faith. The sacrament is appropriate to great festival occasions such as Easter, Pentecost, and Epiphany, as was the practice in the early church.

2. Eucharist

1. THE INSTITUTION OF THE EUCHARIST

1. The church receives the eucharist as a gift from the Lord. Saint Paul wrote: "I have received from the Lord what I also delivered to you, that the Lord Jesus on the night when he was betrayed took bread, and when he had given thanks, he broke it, and said: 'This is my body, which is for you. Do this in remembrance (*anamnesis*) of me.' In the same way also the cup, after supper, saying: 'This cup is the new covenant in my blood. Do this, as often as you drink it, in remembrance of me'" (1 Cor 11.23–25; see Mt 26.26–29; Mk 14.22–25; Lk 22.14–20).

The meals which Jesus is recorded as sharing during his earthly ministry proclaim and enact the nearness of the kingdom, of which the feeding of the multi-

tudes is a sign. In his last meal, the fellowship of the kingdom was connected with
the imminence of Jesus' suffering. After his resurrection, the Lord made his presence
known to his disciples in the breaking of the bread. Thus the eucharist continues
these meals of Jesus during his earthly life and after his resurrection, always as a sign
of the kingdom. Christians see the eucharist prefigured in the Passover memorial
of Israel's deliverance from the land of bondage and in the meal of the covenant on
Mount Sinai (Ex 24). It is the new paschal meal of the church, the meal of the new
covenant, which Christ gave to his disciples as the anamnesis of his death and resurrection, as the anticipation of the supper of the Lamb (Rv 19.9). Christ commanded
his disciples thus to remember and encounter him in this sacramental meal, as the
continuing people of God, until his return. The last meal celebrated by Jesus was a
liturgical meal employing symbolic words and actions. Consequently the eucharist
is a sacramental meal which by visible signs communicates to us God's love in Jesus
Christ, the love by which Jesus loved his own "to the end" (Jn 13.1). It has acquired
many names: for example, the Lord's supper, the breaking of bread, the holy communion, the divine liturgy, the mass. Its celebration continues as the central act of
the church's worship.

2. THE MEANING OF THE EUCHARIST

2. The eucharist is essentially the sacrament of the gift which God makes to us in
Christ through the power of the Holy Spirit. Every Christian receives this gift of
salvation through communion in the body and blood of Christ. In the eucharistic
meal, in the eating and drinking of the bread and wine, Christ grants communion
with himself. God himself acts, giving life to the body of Christ and renewing each
member. In accordance with Christ's promise, each baptized member of the body of
Christ receives in the eucharist the assurance of the forgiveness of sins (Mt 26.28)
and the pledge of eternal life (Jn 6.51-58). Although the eucharist is essentially one
complete act, it will be considered here under the following aspects: thanksgiving to
the Father, memorial of Christ, invocation of the Spirit, communion of the faithful,
meal of the kingdom.

A. The Eucharist as Thanksgiving to the Father

3. The eucharist, which always includes both word and sacrament, is a proclamation and a celebration of the work of God. It is the great thanksgiving to the Father
for everything accomplished in creation, redemption, and sanctification, for everything accomplished by God now in the church and in the world in spite of the sins
of human beings, for everything that God will accomplish in bringing the kingdom

to fulfillment. Thus the eucharist is the benediction (*berakah*) by which the church expresses its thankfulness for all God's benefits.

4. The eucharist is the great sacrifice of praise by which the church speaks on behalf of the whole creation. For the world which God has reconciled is present at every eucharist: in the bread and wine, in the persons of the faithful, and in the prayers they offer for themselves and for all people. Christ unites the faithful with himself and includes their prayers within his own intercession so that the faithful are transfigured and their prayers accepted. This sacrifice of praise is possible only through Christ, with him and in him. The bread and wine, fruits of the earth and of human labor, are presented to the Father in faith and thanksgiving. The eucharist thus signifies what the world is to become: an offering and hymn of praise to the Creator, a universal communion in the body of Christ, a kingdom of justice, love, and peace in the Holy Spirit.

B. The Eucharist as Anamnesis or Memorial of Christ

5. The eucharist is the memorial of the crucified and risen Christ, i.e., the living and effective sign of his sacrifice, accomplished once and for all on the cross and still operative on behalf of all humankind. The biblical idea of memorial as applied to the eucharist refers to this present efficacy of God's work when it is celebrated by God's people in a liturgy.

6. Christ himself with all that he has accomplished for us and for all creation (in his incarnation, servanthood, ministry, teaching, suffering, sacrifice, resurrection, ascension, and sending of the Spirit) is present in this anamnesis, granting us communion with himself. The eucharist is also the foretaste of his *parousia* and of the final kingdom.

7. The anamnesis in which Christ acts through the joyful celebration of his church is thus both representation and anticipation. It is not only a calling to mind of what is past and of its significance. It is the church's effective proclamation of God's mighty acts and promises.

8. Representation and anticipation are expressed in thanksgiving and intercession. The church, gratefully recalling God's mighty acts of redemption, beseeches God to give the benefits of these acts to every human being. In thanksgiving and intercession, the church is united with the Son, its great High Priest and Intercessor (Rom 8.34; Heb 7.25). The eucharist is the sacrament of the unique sacrifice of Christ, who ever lives to make intercession for us. It is the memorial of all that God has done for the salvation of the world. What it was God's will to accomplish in the incarnation, life, death, resurrection, and ascension of Christ, God does not repeat.

These events are unique and can neither be repeated nor prolonged. In the memorial of the eucharist, however, the church offers its intercession in communion with Christ, our great High Priest.

9. The anamnesis of Christ is the basis and source of all Christian prayer. So our prayer relies upon and is united with the continual intercession of the risen Lord. In the eucharist, Christ empowers us to live with him, to suffer with him, and to pray through him as justified sinners, joyfully and freely fulfilling his will.

10. In Christ we offer ourselves as a living and holy sacrifice in our daily lives (Rom 12.1; 1 Pt 2.5); this spiritual worship, acceptable to God, is nourished in the eucharist, in which we are sanctified and reconciled in love, in order to be servants of reconciliation in the world.

11. United to our Lord and in communion with all saints and martyrs, we are renewed in the covenant sealed by the blood of Christ.

12. Since the anamnesis of Christ is the very content of the preached word as it is of the eucharistic meal, each reinforces the other. The celebration of the eucharist properly includes the proclamation of the word.

13. The words and acts of Christ at the institution of the eucharist stand at the heart of the celebration; the eucharistic meal is the sacrament of the body and blood of Christ, the sacrament of his real presence. Christ fulfills in a variety of ways his promise to be always with his own even to the end of the world. But Christ's mode of presence in the eucharist is unique. Jesus said over the bread and wine of the eucharist: "This is my body . . . this is my blood . . ." What Christ declared is true, and this truth is fulfilled every time the eucharist is celebrated. The church confesses Christ's real, living, and active presence in the eucharist. While Christ's real presence in the eucharist does not depend on the faith of the individual, all agree that to discern the body and blood of Christ, faith is required.

C. The Eucharist as Invocation of the Spirit

14. The Spirit makes the crucified and risen Christ really present to us in the eucharistic meal, fulfilling the promise contained in the words of institution. The presence of Christ is clearly the center of the eucharist, and the promise contained in the words of institution is therefore fundamental to the celebration. Yet it is the Father who is the primary origin and final fulfillment of the eucharistic event. The incarnate Son of God by and in whom it is accomplished is its living center. The Holy Spirit is the immeasurable strength of love which makes it possible and continues to make it effective. The bond between the eucharistic celebration and the mystery of the Triune God reveals the role of the Holy Spirit as that of the one who makes

the historical words of Jesus present and alive. Being assured by Jesus' promise in the words of institution that it will be answered, the church prays to the Father for the gift of the Holy Spirit in order that the eucharistic event may be a reality: the real presence of the crucified and risen Christ giving his life for all humanity.

15. It is in virtue of the living word of Christ and by the power of the Holy Spirit that the bread and wine become the sacramental signs for Christ's body and blood. They remain so for the purpose of communion.

16. The whole action of the eucharist has an "epikletic" character because it depends upon the work of the Holy Spirit. In the words of the liturgy, this aspect of the eucharist finds varied expression.

17. The church, as the community of the new covenant, confidently invokes the Spirit, in order that it may be sanctified and renewed, led into all justice, truth, and unity, and empowered to fulfill its mission in the world.

18. The Holy Spirit through the eucharist gives a foretaste of the kingdom of God: the church receives the life of the new creation and the assurance of the Lord's return.

D. The Eucharist as Communion of the Faithful

19. The eucharistic communion with Christ who nourishes the life of the church is at the same time communion within the body of Christ which is the church. The sharing in one bread and the common cup in a given place demonstrates and effects the oneness of the sharers with Christ and with their fellow sharers in all times and places. It is in the eucharist that the community of God's people is fully manifested. Eucharistic celebrations always have to do with the whole church, and the whole church is involved in each local eucharistic celebration. In so far as a church claims to be a manifestation of the whole church, it will take care to order its own life in ways which take seriously the interests and concerns of other churches.

20. The eucharist embraces all aspects of life. It is a representative act of thanksgiving and offering on behalf of the whole world. The eucharistic celebration demands reconciliation and sharing among all those regarded as brothers and sisters in the one family of God and is a constant challenge in the search for appropriate relationships in social, economic, and political life (Mt 5.23f.; 1 Cor 10.16f., 11.20–22; Gal 3.28). All kinds of injustice, racism, separation, and lack of freedom are radically challenged when we share in the body and blood of Christ. Through the eucharist the all-renewing grace of God penetrates and restores human personality and dignity. The eucharist involves the believer in the central event of the world's history. As participants in the eucharist, therefore, we prove inconsistent if we are

not actively participating in this ongoing restoration of the world's situation and the human condition. The eucharist shows us that our behavior is inconsistent in face of the reconciling presence of God in human history: we are placed under continual judgment by the persistence of unjust relationships of all kinds in our society, the manifold divisions on account of human pride, material interest, and power politics and, above all, the obstinacy of unjustifiable confessional oppositions within the body of Christ.

21. Solidarity in the eucharistic communion of the body of Christ and responsible care of Christians for one another and the world find specific expression in the liturgies: in the mutual forgiveness of sins; the sign of peace; intercession for all; the eating and drinking together; the taking of the elements to the sick and those in prison or the celebration of the eucharist with them. All these manifestations of love in the eucharist are directly related to Christ's own testimony as a servant, in whose servanthood Christians themselves participate. As God in Christ has entered into the human situation, so eucharistic liturgy is near to the concrete and particular situations of men and women. In the early church the ministry of deacons and deaconesses gave expression in a special way to this aspect of the eucharist. The place of such ministry between the table and the needy properly testifies to the redeeming presence of Christ in the world.

E. The Eucharist as Meal of the Kingdom

22. The eucharist opens up the vision of the divine rule which has been promised as the final renewal of creation, and is a foretaste of it. Signs of this renewal are present in the world wherever the grace of God is manifest and human beings work for justice, love, and peace. The eucharist is the feast at which the church gives thanks to God for these signs and joyfully celebrates and anticipates the coming of the kingdom in Christ (1 Cor 11.26; Mt 26.29).

23. The world, to which renewal is promised, is present in the whole eucharistic celebration. The world is present in the thanksgiving to the Father, where the church speaks on behalf of the whole creation; in the memorial of Christ, where the church, united with its great High Priest and Intercessor, prays for the world; in the prayer for the gift of the Holy Spirit, where the church asks for sanctification and new creation.

24. Reconciled in the eucharist, the members of the body of Christ are called to be servants of reconciliation among men and women and witnesses of the joy of resurrection. As Jesus went out to publicans and sinners and had table-fellowship with them during his earthly ministry, so Christians are called in the eu-

charist to be in solidarity with the outcast and to become signs of the love of Christ who lived and sacrificed himself for all and now gives himself in the eucharist.

25. The very celebration of the eucharist is an instance of the church's participation in God's mission to the world. This participation takes everyday form in the proclamation of the gospel, service of the neighbor, and faithful presence in the world.

26. As it is entirely the gift of God, the eucharist brings into the present age a new reality which transforms Christians into the image of Christ and therefore makes them his effective witnesses. The eucharist is precious food for missionaries, bread and wine for pilgrims on their apostolic journey. The eucharistic community is nourished and strengthened for confessing by word and action the Lord Jesus Christ who gave his life for the salvation of the world. As it becomes one people, sharing the meal of the one Lord, the eucharistic assembly must be concerned for gathering also those who are at present beyond its visible limits, because Christ invited to his feast all for whom he died. Insofar as Christians cannot unite in full fellowship around the same table to eat the same loaf and drink from the same cup, their missionary witness is weakened at both the individual and the corporate levels.

3. THE CELEBRATION OF THE EUCHARIST

27. The eucharistic liturgy is essentially a single whole, consisting historically of the following elements in varying sequence and of diverse importance:

- hymns of praise;
- act of repentance;
- declaration of pardon;
- proclamation of the word of God, in various forms;
- confession of faith (creed);
- intercession for the whole church and for the world;
- preparation of the bread and wine;
- thanksgiving to the Father for the marvels of creation, redemption, and sanctification (deriving from the Jewish tradition of the berakah);
- the words of Christ's institution of the sacrament according to the New Testament tradition;
- the anamnesis or memorial of the great acts of redemption, passion, death, resurrection, ascension, and Pentecost, which brought the church into being;
- the invocation of the Holy Spirit (*epiklesis*) on the community, and

the elements of bread and wine (either before the words of institution or after the memorial, or both; or some other reference to the
Holy Spirit which adequately expresses the "epikletic" character
of the eucharist);
- consecration of the faithful to God;
- reference to the communion of saints;
- prayer for the return of the Lord and the definitive manifestation
of his kingdom;
- the Amen of the whole community;
- the Lord's Prayer;
- sign of reconciliation and peace;
- the breaking of the bread;
- eating and drinking in communion with Christ and with each
member of the church;
- final act of praise;
- blessing and sending.

28. The best way towards unity in eucharistic celebration and communion is the renewal of the eucharist itself in the different churches in regard to teaching and liturgy. The churches should test their liturgies in the light of the eucharistic agreement now in the process of attainment.

The liturgical reform movement has brought the churches closer together in the manner of celebrating the Lord's supper. However, a certain liturgical diversity compatible with our common eucharistic faith is recognized as a healthy and enriching fact. The affirmation of a common eucharistic faith does not imply uniformity in either liturgy or practice.

29. In the celebration of the eucharist, Christ gathers, teaches, and nourishes the church. It is Christ who invites to the meal and who presides at it. He is the Shepherd who leads the people of God, the Prophet who announces the word of God, the Priest who celebrates the mystery of God. In most churches, this presidency is signified by an ordained minister. The one who presides at the eucharistic celebration in the name of Christ makes clear that the rite is not the assemblies' own creation or possession; the eucharist is received as a gift from Christ living in his church. The minister of the eucharist is the ambassador who represents the divine initiative and expresses the connection of the local community with other local communities in the universal church.

30. Christian faith is deepened by the celebration of the Lord's supper. Hence the eucharist should be celebrated frequently. Many differences of theology,

liturgy, and practice are connected with the varying frequency with which the holy communion is celebrated.

31. As the eucharist celebrates the resurrection of Christ, it is appropriate that it should take place at least every Sunday. As it is the new sacramental meal of the people of God, every Christian should be encouraged to receive communion frequently.

32. Some churches stress that Christ's presence in the consecrated elements continues after the celebration. Others place the main emphasis on the act of celebration itself and on the consumption of the elements in the act of communion. The way in which the elements are treated requires special attention. Regarding the practice of reserving the elements, each church should respect the practices and piety of the others. Given the diversity in practice among the churches and at the same time taking note of the present situation in the convergence process, it is worthwhile to suggest: that, on the one hand, it be remembered, especially in sermons and instruction, that the primary intention of reserving the elements is their distribution among the sick and those who are absent, and on the other hand, it be recognized that the best way of showing respect for the elements served in the eucharistic celebration is by their consumption, without excluding their use for communion of the sick.

33. The increased mutual understanding expressed in the present statement may allow some churches to attain a greater measure of eucharistic communion among themselves and so bring closer the day when Christ's divided people will be visibly reunited around the Lord's table.

3. Ministry

I. THE CALLING OF THE WHOLE PEOPLE OF GOD

1. In a broken world God calls the whole of humanity to become God's people. For this purpose God chose Israel and then spoke in a unique and decisive way in Jesus Christ, God's Son. Jesus made his own the nature, condition, and cause of the whole human race, giving himself as a sacrifice for all. Jesus' life of service, his death and resurrection, are the foundation of a new community which is built up continually by the good news of the gospel and the gifts of the sacraments. The Holy Spirit unites in a single body those who follow Jesus Christ and sends them as witnesses into the world. Belonging to the church means living in communion with God through Jesus Christ in the Holy Spirit.

2. The life of the church is based on Christ's victory over the powers of evil and death, accomplished once for all. Christ offers forgiveness, invites to repentance and delivers from destruction. Through Christ, people are enabled to turn in praise

to God and in service to their neighbors. In Christ they find the source of new life in freedom, mutual forgiveness, and love. Through Christ their hearts and minds are directed to the consummation of the kingdom where Christ's victory will become manifest and all things made new. God's purpose is that, in Jesus Christ, all people should share in this fellowship.

3. The church lives through the liberating and renewing power of the Holy Spirit. That the Holy Spirit was upon Jesus is evidenced in his baptism, and after the resurrection that same Spirit was given to those who believed in the risen Lord in order to recreate them as the body of Christ. The Spirit calls people to faith, sanctifies them through many gifts, gives them strength to witness to the gospel, and empowers them to serve in hope and love. The Spirit keeps the church in the truth and guides it despite the frailty of its members.

4. The church is called to proclaim and prefigure the kingdom of God. It accomplishes this by announcing the gospel to the world and by its very existence as the body of Christ. In Jesus the kingdom of God came among us. He offered salvation to sinners. He preached good news to the poor, release to the captives, recovery of sight to the blind, liberation to the oppressed (Lk 4.18). Christ established a new access to the Father. Living in this communion with God, all members of the church are called to confess their faith and to give account of their hope. They are to identify with the joys and sufferings of all people as they seek to witness in caring love. The members of Christ's body are to struggle with the oppressed towards that freedom and dignity promised with the coming of the kingdom. This mission needs to be carried out in varying political, social, and cultural contexts. In order to fulfill this mission faithfully, they will seek relevant forms of witness and service in each situation. In so doing they bring to the world a foretaste of the joy and glory of God's kingdom.

5. The Holy Spirit bestows on the community diverse and complementary gifts. These are for the common good of the whole people and are manifested in acts of service within the community and to the world. They may be gifts of communicating the gospel in word and deed, gifts of healing, gifts of praying, gifts of teaching and learning, gifts of serving, gifts of guiding and following, gifts of inspiration and vision. All members are called to discover, with the help of the community, the gifts they have received and to use them for the building up of the church and for the service of the world to which the church is sent.

6. Though the churches are agreed in their general understanding of the calling of the people of God, they differ in their understanding of how the life of the church is to be ordered. In particular, there are differences concerning the place and forms of the ordained ministry. As they engage in the effort to overcome these

differences, the churches need to work from the perspective of the calling of the whole people of God. A common answer needs to be found to the following question: How, according to the will of God and under the guidance of the Holy Spirit, is the life of the church to be understood and ordered, so that the gospel may be spread and the community built up in love?

2. THE CHURCH AND THE ORDAINED MINISTRY

7. Differences in terminology are part of the matter under debate. In order to avoid confusion in the discussions on the ordained ministry in the church, it is necessary to delineate clearly how various terms are used in the following paragraphs.

a. The word *charism* denotes the gifts bestowed by the Holy Spirit on any member of the body of Christ for the building up of the community and the fulfillment of its calling.

b. The word *ministry* in its broadest sense denotes the service to which the whole people of God is called, whether as individuals, as a local community, or as the universal church. Ministry or ministries can also denote the particular institutional forms which this service may take.

c. The term *ordained ministry* refers to persons who have received a charism and whom the church appoints for service by ordination through the invocation of the Spirit and the laying on of hands.

d. Many churches use the word *priest* to denote certain ordained ministers. Because this usage is not universal, this document will discuss the substantive questions in paragraph 17.

A. The Ordained Ministry

8. In order to fulfill its mission, the church needs persons who are publicly and continually responsible for pointing to its fundamental dependence on Jesus Christ, and thereby provide, within a multiplicity of gifts, a focus of its unity. The ministry of such persons, who since very early times have been ordained, is constitutive for the life and witness of the church.

9. The church has never been without persons holding specific authority and responsibility. Jesus chose and sent the disciples to be witnesses to the kingdom (Mt 10.1–8). The twelve were promised that they would "sit on thrones judging the tribes of Israel" (Lk 22.30). A particular role is attributed to the twelve within the communities of the first generation. They are witnesses of the Lord's life and resurrection (Acts 1.21–26). They lead the community in prayer, teaching, the breaking of bread, proclamation, and service (Acts 2.42–47, 6.2–6, etc.). The very existence

of the twelve and other apostles shows that, from the beginning, there were differentiated roles in the community.

10. Jesus called the twelve to be representatives of the renewed Israel. At that moment they represent the whole people of God and at the same time exercise a special role in the midst of that community. After the resurrection they are among the leaders of the community. It can be said that the apostles prefigure both the church as a whole and the persons within it who are entrusted with the specific authority and responsibility. The role of the apostles as witnesses to the resurrection of Christ is unique and unrepeatable. There is therefore a difference between the apostles and the ordained ministers whose ministries are founded on theirs.

11. As Christ chose and sent the apostles, Christ continues through the Holy Spirit to choose and call persons into the ordained ministry. As heralds and ambassadors, ordained ministers are representatives of Jesus Christ to the community, and proclaim his message of reconciliation. As leaders and teachers they call the community to submit to the authority of Jesus Christ, the Teacher and Prophet, in whom law and prophets were fulfilled. As pastors, under Jesus Christ the chief Shepherd, they assemble and guide the dispersed people of God, in anticipation of the coming kingdom.

12. All members of the believing community, ordained and lay, are interrelated. On the one hand, the community needs ordained ministers. Their presence reminds the community of the divine initiative, and of the dependence of the church on Jesus Christ, who is the source of its mission and the foundation of its unity. They serve to build up the community in Christ and to strengthen its witness. In them the church seeks an example of holiness and loving concern. On the other hand, the ordained ministry has no existence apart from the community. Ordained ministers can fulfill their calling only in and for the community. They cannot dispense with the recognition, the support, and the encouragement of the community.

13. The chief responsibility of the ordained ministry is to assemble and build up the body of Christ by proclaiming and teaching the word of God, by celebrating the sacraments, and by guiding the life of the community in its worship, its mission, and its caring ministry.

14. It is especially in the eucharistic celebration that the ordained ministry is the visible focus of the deep and all-embracing communion between Christ and the members of his body. In the celebration of the eucharist, Christ gathers, teaches and nourishes the church. It is Christ who invites to the meal and who presides at it. In most churches this presidency is signified and represented by an ordained minister.

B. Ordained Ministry and Authority

15. The authority of the ordained minister is rooted in Jesus Christ, who has received it from the Father (Mt 28.18), and who confers it by the Holy Spirit through the act of ordination. This act takes place within a community which accords public recognition to a particular person. Because Jesus came as one who serves (Mk 10.45; Lk 22.27), to be set apart means to be consecrated to service. Since ordination is essentially a setting apart with prayer for the gift of the Holy Spirit, the authority of the ordained ministry is not to be understood as the possession of the ordained person but as a gift for the continuing edification of the body in and for which the minister has been ordained. Authority has the character of responsibility before God and is exercised with the cooperation of the whole community.

16. Therefore, ordained ministers must not be autocrats or impersonal functionaries. Although called to exercise wise and loving leadership on the basis of the word of God, they are bound to the faithful in interdependence and reciprocity. Only when they seek the response and acknowledgment of the community can their authority be protected from the distortions of isolation and domination. They manifest and exercise the authority of Christ in the way Christ himself revealed God's authority to the world, by committing their life to the community. Christ's authority is unique. "He spoke as one who has authority (*exousia*), not as the scribes" (Mt 7.29). This authority is an authority governed by love for the "sheep who have no shepherd" (Mt 9.36). It is confirmed by his life of service and, supremely, by his death and resurrection. Authority in the church can only be authentic as it seeks to conform to this model.

C. Ordained Ministry and Priesthood

17. Jesus Christ is the unique Priest of the new covenant. Christ's life was given as a sacrifice for all. Derivatively, the church as a whole can be described as a priesthood. All members are called to offer their being "as a living sacrifice" and to intercede for the church and the salvation of the world. Ordained ministers are related, as are all Christians, both to the priesthood of Christ, and to the priesthood of the church. But they may appropriately be called priests because they fulfill a particular priestly service by strengthening and building up the royal and prophetic priesthood of the faithful through word and sacraments, through their prayers of intercession, and through their pastoral guidance of the community.

D. The Ministry of Men and Women in the Church

18. Where Christ is present, human barriers are being broken. The church is called to convey to the world the image of a new humanity. There is in Christ no male or female (Gal 3.28). Both women and men must discover together their contributions to the service of Christ in the church. The church must discover the ministry which can be provided by women as well as that which can be provided by men. A deeper understanding of the comprehensiveness of ministry which reflects the interdependence of men and women needs to be more widely manifested in the life of the church.

Though they agree on this need, the churches draw different conclusions as to the admission of women to the ordained ministry. An increasing number of churches have decided that there is no biblical or theological reason against ordaining women, and many of them have subsequently proceeded to do so. Yet many churches hold that the tradition of the church in this regard must not be changed.

3. THE FORMS OF THE ORDAINED MINISTRY
A. Bishops, Presbyters, and Deacons

19. The New Testament does not describe a single pattern of ministry which might serve as a blueprint or continuing norm for all future ministry in the church. In the New Testament there appears rather a variety of forms which existed at different places and times. As the Holy Spirit continued to lead the church in life, worship, and mission, certain elements from this early variety were further developed and became settled into a more universal pattern of ministry. During the second and third centuries, a threefold pattern of bishop, presbyter, and deacon became established as the pattern of ordained ministry throughout the church. In succeeding centuries, the ministry by bishop, presbyter, and deacon underwent considerable changes in its practical exercise. At some points of crisis in the history of the church, the continuing functions of ministry were in some places and communities distributed according to structures other than the predominant threefold pattern. Sometimes appeal was made to the New Testament in justification of these other patterns. In other cases, the restructuring of ministry was held to lie within the competence of the church as it adapted to changed circumstances.

20. It is important to be aware of the changes the threefold ministry has undergone in the history of the church. In the earliest instances, where threefold ministry is mentioned, the reference is to the local eucharistic community. The bishop was the leader of the community. He was ordained and installed to proclaim the word and preside over the celebration of the eucharist. He was surrounded by

a college of presbyters and by deacons who assisted in his tasks. In this context the bishop's ministry was a focus of unity within the whole community.

21. Soon, however, the functions were modified. Bishops began increasingly to exercise *episkopē* over several local communities at the same time. In the first generation, apostles had exercised episkopē in the wider church. Later Timothy and Titus are recorded to have fulfilled a function of episkopē in a given area. Later again this apostolic task is carried out in a new way by the bishops. They provide a focus for unity in life and witness within areas comprising several eucharistic communities. As a consequence, presbyters and deacons are assigned new roles. The presbyters become the leaders of the local eucharistic community, and as assistants of the bishops, deacons receive responsibilities in the larger area.

22. Although there is no single New Testament pattern, although the Spirit has many times led the church to adapt its ministries to contextual needs, and although other forms of the ordained ministry have been blessed with the gifts of the Holy Spirit, nevertheless the threefold ministry of bishop, presbyter, and deacon may serve today as an expression of the unity we seek and also as a means for achieving it. Historically, it is true to say, the threefold ministry became the generally accepted pattern in the church of the early centuries and is still retained today by many churches. In the fulfillment of their mission and service the churches need people who in different ways express and perform the tasks of the ordained ministry in its diaconal, presbyteral, and episcopal aspects and functions.

23. The church as the body of Christ and the eschatological people of God is constituted by the Holy Spirit through a diversity of gifts or ministries. Among these gifts a ministry of episkopē is necessary to express and safeguard the unity of the body. Every church needs this ministry of unity in some form in order to be the church of God, the one body of Christ, a sign of the unity of all in the kingdom.

24. The threefold pattern stands evidently in need of reform. In some churches the collegial dimension of leadership in the eucharistic community has suffered diminution. In others, the function of deacons has been reduced to an assistant role in the celebration of the liturgy: they have ceased to fulfill any function with regard to the diaconal witness of the church. In general, the relation of the presbyterate to the episcopal ministry has been discussed throughout the centuries, and the degree of the presbyter's participation in the episcopal ministry is still for many an unresolved question of far-reaching ecumenical importance. In some cases, churches which have not formally kept the threefold form have, in fact, maintained certain of its original patterns.

25. The traditional threefold pattern thus raises questions for all the churches. Churches maintaining the threefold pattern will need to ask how its poten-

tial can be fully developed for the most effective witness of the church in this world. In this task churches not having the threefold pattern should also participate. They will further need to ask themselves whether the threefold pattern as developed does not have a powerful claim to be accepted by them.

B. Guiding Principles for the Exercise of the Ordained Ministry in the Church

26. Three considerations are important in this respect. The ordained ministry should be exercised in a personal, collegial, and communal way. It should be *personal* because the presence of Christ among his people can most effectively be pointed to by the person ordained to proclaim the gospel and to call the community to serve the Lord in unity of life and witness. It should also be *collegial,* for there is need for a college of ordained ministers sharing in the common task of representing the concerns of the community. Finally, the intimate relationship between the ordained ministry and the community should find expression in a *communal* dimension where the exercise of the ordained ministry is rooted in the life of the community and requires the community's effective participation in the discovery of God's will and the guidance of the Spirit.

27. The ordained ministry needs to be constitutionally or canonically ordered and exercised in the church in such a way that each of these three dimensions can find adequate expression. At the level of the local eucharistic community there is need for an ordained minister acting within a collegial body. Strong emphasis should be placed on the active participation of all members in the life and the decision-making of the community. At the regional level there is again need for an ordained minister exercising a service of unity. The collegial and communal dimensions will find expression in regular representative synodal gatherings.

C. Functions of Bishops, Presbyters, and Deacons

28. What can then be said about the functions and even the titles of bishops, presbyters, and deacons? A uniform answer to this question is not required for the mutual recognition of the ordained ministry. The following considerations on functions are, however, offered in a tentative way.

29. *Bishops* preach the word, preside at the sacraments, and administer discipline in such a way as to be representative pastoral ministers of oversight, continuity, and unity in the church. They have pastoral oversight of the area to which they are called. They serve the apostolicity and unity of the church's teaching, wor-

ship, and sacramental life. They have responsibility for leadership in the church's mission. They relate the Christian community in their area to the wider church, and the universal church to their community. They, in communion with the presbyters and deacons and the whole community, are responsible for the orderly transfer of ministerial authority in the church.

30. *Presbyters* serve as pastoral ministers of word and sacraments in a local eucharistic community. They are preachers and teachers of the faith, exercise pastoral care, and bear responsibility for the discipline of the congregation to the end that the world may believe and that the entire membership of the church may be renewed, strengthened, and equipped in ministry. Presbyters have particular responsibility for the preparation of members for Christian life and ministry.

31. *Deacons* represent to the church its calling as servant in the world. By struggling in Christ's name with the myriad needs of societies and persons, deacons exemplify the interdependence of worship and service in the church's life. They exercise responsibility in the worship of the congregation: for example by reading the Scriptures, preaching, and leading the people in prayer. They help in the teaching of the congregation. They exercise a ministry of love within the community. They fulfill certain administrative tasks and may be elected to responsibilities for governance.

D. Variety of Charisms

32. The community which lives in the power of the Spirit will be characterized by a variety of charisms. The Spirit is the giver of diverse gifts which enrich the life of the community. In order to enhance their effectiveness, the community will recognize publicly certain of these charisms. While some serve permanent needs in the life of the community, others will be temporary. Men and women in the communities of religious orders fulfill a service which is of particular importance for the life of the church. The ordained ministry, which is itself a charism, must not become a hindrance for the variety of these charisms. On the contrary, it will help the community to discover the gifts bestowed on it by the Holy Spirit and will equip members of the body to serve in a variety of ways.

33. In the history of the church there have been times when the truth of the gospel could only be preserved through prophetic and charismatic leaders. Often new impulses could find their way into the life of the church only in unusual ways. At times reforms required a special ministry. The ordained ministers and the whole community will need to be attentive to the challenge of such special ministries.

4. SUCCESSION IN THE APOSTOLIC TRADITION
A. Apostolic Tradition in the Church

34. In the Creed, the church confesses itself to be apostolic. The church lives in continuity with the apostles and their proclamation. The same Lord who sent the apostles continues to be present in the church. The Spirit keeps the church in the apostolic tradition until the fulfillment of history in the kingdom of God. Apostolic tradition in the church means continuity in the permanent characteristics of the church of the apostles: witness to the apostolic faith, proclamation and fresh interpretation of the gospel, celebration of baptism and the eucharist, the transmission of ministerial responsibilities, communion in prayer, love, joy, and suffering, service to the sick and the needy, unity among the local churches, and sharing the gifts which the Lord has given to each.

B. Succession of the Apostolic Ministry

35. The primary manifestation of apostolic succession is to be found in the apostolic tradition of the church as a whole. The succession is an expression of the permanence and, therefore, of the continuity of Christ's own mission in which the church participates. Within the church the ordained ministry has a particular task of preserving and actualizing the apostolic faith. The orderly transmission of the ordained ministry is therefore a powerful expression of the continuity of the church throughout history; it also underlines the calling of the ordained minister as guardian of the faith. Where churches see little importance in orderly transmission, they should ask themselves whether they have not to change their conception of continuity in the apostolic tradition. On the other hand, where the ordained ministry does not adequately serve the proclamation of the apostolic faith, churches must ask themselves whether their ministerial structures are not in need of reform.

36. Under the particular historical circumstances of the growing church in the early centuries, the succession of bishops became one of the ways, together with the transmission of the gospel and the life of the community, in which the apostolic tradition of the church was expressed. This succession was understood as serving, symbolizing, and guarding the continuity of the apostolic faith and communion.

37. In churches which practice the succession through the episcopate, it is increasingly recognized that a continuity in apostolic faith, worship, and mission has been preserved in churches which have not retained the form of historic episcopate. This recognition finds additional support in the fact that the reality and function of the episcopal ministry have been preserved in many of these churches, with or without the title "bishop." Ordination, for example, is always done in them

by persons in whom the church recognizes the authority to transmit the ministerial commission.

38. These considerations do not diminish the importance of the episcopal ministry. On the contrary, they enable churches which have not retained the episcopate to appreciate the episcopal succession as a sign, though not a guarantee, of the continuity and unity of the church. Today churches, including those engaged in union negotiations, are expressing willingness to accept episcopal succession as a sign of the apostolicity of the life of the whole church. Yet, at the same time, they cannot accept any suggestion that the ministry exercised in their own tradition should be invalid until the moment that it enters into an existing line of episcopal succession. Their acceptance of the episcopal succession will best further the unity of the whole church if it is part of a wider process by which the episcopal churches themselves also regain their lost unity.

5. ORDINATION
A. The Meaning of Ordination

39. The church ordains certain of its members for the ministry in the name of Christ by the invocation of the Spirit and the laying on of hands (1 Tm 4.14; 2 Tm 1.6); in so doing it seeks to continue the mission of the apostles and to remain faithful to their teaching. The act of ordination by those who are appointed for this ministry attests the bond of the church with Jesus Christ and the apostolic witness, recalling that it is the risen Lord who is the true ordainer and bestows the gift. In ordaining, the church, under the inspiration of the Holy Spirit, provides for the faithful proclamation of the gospel and humble service in the name of Christ. The laying on of hands is the sign of the gift of the Spirit, rendering visible the fact that the ministry was instituted in the revelation accomplished in Christ, and reminding the church to look to him as the source of its commission. This ordination, however, can have different intentions according to the specific tasks of bishops, presbyters, and deacons as indicated in the liturgies of ordination.

40. Properly speaking, then, ordination denotes an action by God and the community by which the ordained are strengthened by the Spirit for their task and are upheld by the acknowledgment and prayers of the congregation.

B. The Act of Ordination

41. A long and early Christian tradition places ordination in the context of worship and especially of the eucharist. Such a place for the service of ordination preserves the understanding of ordination as an act of the whole community, and not of a

certain order within it or of the individual ordained. The act of ordination by the laying on of hands of those appointed to do so is at one and the same time invocation of the Holy Spirit (*epiklesis*); sacramental sign; acknowledgment of gifts and commitment.

42. a. Ordination is an invocation to God that the new minister be given the power of the Holy Spirit in the new relation which is established between this minister and the local Christian community and, by intention, the church universal. The otherness of God's initiative, of which the ordained ministry is a sign, is here acknowledged in the act of ordination itself. "The Spirit blows where it wills" (Jn 3.3): the invocation of the Spirit implies the absolute dependence on God for the outcome of the church's prayer. This means that the Spirit may set new forces in motion and open new possibilities "far more abundantly than all that we ask or think" (Eph 3.20).

43. b. Ordination is a sign of the granting of this prayer by the Lord who gives the gift of the ordained ministry. Although the outcome of the church's epiklesis depends on the freedom of God, the church ordains in confidence that God, being faithful to his promise in Christ, enters sacramentally into contingent, historical forms of human relationship and uses them for his purpose. Ordination is a sign performed in faith that the spiritual relationship signified is present in, with, and through the words spoken, the gestures made, and the forms employed.

44. c. Ordination is an acknowledgment by the church of the gifts of the Spirit in the one ordained, and a commitment by both the church and the ordained to the new relationship. By receiving the new minister in the act of ordination, the congregation acknowledges the minister's gifts and commits itself to be open towards these gifts. Likewise those ordained offer their gifts to the church and commit themselves to the burden and opportunity of new authority and responsibility. At the same time, they enter into a collegial relationship with other ordained ministers.

C. The Conditions for Ordination

45. People are called in differing ways to the ordained ministry. There is a personal awareness of a call from the Lord to dedicate oneself to the ordained ministry. This call may be discerned through personal prayer and reflection, as well as through suggestion, example, encouragement, guidance coming from family, friends, the congregation, teachers, and other church authorities. This call must be authenticated by the church's recognition of the gifts and graces of the particular person, both

natural and spiritually given, needed for the ministry to be performed. God can use people both celibate and married for the ordained ministry.

46. Ordained persons may be professional ministers in the sense that they receive their salaries from the church. The church may also ordain people who remain in other occupations or employment.

47. Candidates for the ordained ministry need appropriate preparation through study of Scripture and theology, prayer and spirituality, and through acquaintance with the social and human realities of the contemporary world. In some situations, this preparation may take a form other than that of prolonged academic study. The period of training will be one in which the candidate's call is tested, fostered, and confirmed, or its understanding modified.

48. Initial commitment to ordained ministry ought normally to be made without reserve or time limit. Yet leave of absence from service is not incompatible with ordination. Resumption of ordained ministry requires the assent of the church, but no re-ordination. In recognition of the God-given charism of ministry, ordination to any one of the particular ordained ministries is never repeated.

49. The discipline with regard to the conditions for ordination in one church need not be seen as universally applicable and used as grounds for not recognizing ministry in others.

50. Churches which refuse to consider candidates for the ordained ministry on the ground of handicap or because they belong, for example, to one particular race or sociological group should reevaluate their practices. This reevaluation is particularly important today in view of the multitude of experiments in new forms of ministry with which the churches are approaching the modern world.

C. TOWARDS THE MUTUAL RECOGNITION
OF THE ORDAINED MINISTRIES

51. In order to advance towards the mutual recognition of ministries, deliberate efforts are required. All churches need to examine the forms of ordained ministry and the degree to which the churches are faithful to its original intentions. Churches must be prepared to renew their understanding and their practice of the ordained ministry.

52. Among the issues that need to be worked on as churches move towards mutual recognition of ministries, that of apostolic succession is of particular importance. Churches in ecumenical conversations can recognize their respective ordained ministries if they are mutually assured of their intention to transmit the ministry of word and sacrament in continuity with apostolic times. The act of transmis-

sion should be performed in accordance with the apostolic tradition, which includes the invocation of the Spirit and the laying on of hands.

53. In order to achieve mutual recognition, different steps are required of different churches. For example:

a. Churches which have preserved the episcopal succession are asked to recognize both the apostolic content of the ordained ministry which exists in churches which have not maintained such succession and also the existence in these churches of a ministry of episkopē in various forms.

b. Churches without the episcopal succession, and living in faithful continuity with the apostolic faith and mission, have a ministry of word and sacrament, as is evident from the belief, practice, and life of those churches. These churches are asked to realize that the continuity with the church of the apostles finds profound expression in the successive laying on of hands by bishops and that, though they may not lack the continuity of the apostolic tradition, this sign will strengthen and deepen that continuity. They may need to recover the sign of the episcopal succession.

54. Some churches ordain both men and women, others ordain only men. Differences on this issue raise obstacles to the mutual recognition of ministries. But those obstacles must not be regarded as substantive hindrance for further efforts towards mutual recognition. Openness to each other holds the possibility that the Spirit may well speak to one church through the insights of another. Ecumenical consideration, therefore, should encourage, not restrain, the facing of this question.

55. The mutual recognition of churches and their ministries implies decision by the appropriate authorities and a liturgical act from which point unity would be publicly manifest. Several forms of such public act have been proposed: mutual laying on of hands, eucharistic concelebration, solemn worship without a particular rite of recognition, the reading of a text of union during the course of a celebration. No one liturgical form would be absolutely required, but in any case it would be necessary to proclaim the accomplishment of mutual recognition publicly. The common celebration of the eucharist would certainly be the place for such an act.

The Evangelical Presbyterian Church of Chile, *Creed*, 1983

Although "liberation theology," as it speaks for example in the creed of 1980 produced by Roman Catholics in Honduras, → *The Credo* from *The Mass of the Marginalized People,* has been more visibly associated with confessions of Latin American Roman Catholicism, Protestant confessions, too, show its influence. That influence is evident in a special manner and degree in → the *Confession of Faith* of the Presbyterian-Reformed Church in Cuba from 1977, with its declarations concerning the Marxism-Leninism of the Cuban revolution. But in a less overtly political voice, it can be heard also in this *Creed* of the Evangelical Presbyterian Church of Chile. This church was the product of the efforts of Presbyterian missionaries beginning in 1845. It adopted its own *Creed* in 1983.

Edition: Provided by the Evangelical Presbyterian Church of Chile.

Translation: Link, 4:66–68.

The Evangelical Presbyterian Church of Chile, *Creed*, 1983

1. I believe in one God, Father, Son, and Holy Spirit, the fount and future of life for the whole creation.

2. I believe in God the Father, Creator and Master of all, provider and sustainer of life; he created us of one blood in his own image, expressed in creativity, solidarity, and responsibility; he gave us the riches of nature to care for and to use for the benefit of all; he calls us to respect each individual's dignity, which requires a society which is just, sharing, and human towards all.

3. I believe that sin is a real force which radically disrupts our relationship with God; it manifests itself personally and socially; it turns both our desires and our deeds towards egoism, destruction, and death.

4. I believe in God the Son, who was incarnate in Jesus Christ, and became one with the human race to set us free from the sin and evil that oppress us; he proclaimed and inaugurated the kingdom of God; he condemned injustice and offered us reconciling and liberating grace, thus giving us hope of the kingdom's fullness; he bore the human lot of suffering, and pledged himself even to death under the Roman power; he rose from the dead, triumphantly asserting the power of the God of life over life-negating forces of oppression and injustice both personal and corporate; he ascended and assumed his kingly reign, whereby he will judge and transform the world until God's justice and peace prevail; he will come again to reunite all his own, and to establish the kingdom of God in all its fullness.

5. I believe in the Holy Spirit, the permanent presence and power of God, who makes the Lordship of Jesus Christ real in the world; he unites, empowers, and guides the church; he inspired and interprets the Holy Scriptures, and works through the sacraments and ministries of the church to create faith and to guide our life.

6. I believe that the church, the people of God, is one and universal, directed by Christ himself; it comes to life in local communities where fellowship is rooted in the love of Jesus Christ spread abroad and making us brothers and sisters in him, creating a spirit of unity and sharing amongst us; we all receive both the call and the gifts necessary to fulfill various ministries of equal value to build up the church and to carry out its task in the world; as the church, our mission is to share our faith with all humankind; to denounce the divisive power of evil and pro-

claim reconciling grace; in this way to be the instrument for making the universal Lordship of Christ present every day, everywhere.

To this end, it is our responsibility to identify ourselves with all people and to serve them; to fight against those forces which oppress human beings and bar the way to their full realization as children of God.

Salvadoran Basic Ecclesial Communities, *Profession of Faith*, 1984

One of the most important phenomena in the Roman Catholic Church of Latin America in the wake of the Second Vatican Council was the rise of *comunidades eclesiales de base,* "basic ecclesial communities" (often abbreviated as CEB in Spanish and Portuguese, BEC in English). They differ from the many other forms of social-political agitation and popular fronts in Latin America by virtue of their being *ecclesial.* As one theological interpreter has put it, speaking specifically about Brazil but in terms that are more broadly applicable, "The catalysts of this ecclesiality in the Brazilian BECs have been the unity in and of faith and the linkage to the institutional Church. Even when BECs are ecumenically oriented, experience has proven that the sharing of a specific, common faith was a crucial element for fostering the internal growth of the community."[1] Therefore the Third General Assembly of Latin American Bishops, held in 1979, affirmed: "As an ecclesial reality, it is a community of faith, hope, and charity. It celebrates the Word of God and takes its nourishment from the eucharist, the culmination of all the sacraments." For the basic ecclesial communities of El Salvador, the assassination of Archbishop Oscar Romero at mass the following year, on 24 March 1980, became a rallying point. They expressed their basic ecclesial character as well as their solidarity with the poor by issuing this *Profession of Faith* on 12 February 1984.

Edition: *Noticias Aliadas,* 5 April 1984, 3.

Translation: *Latinamerica Press,* 5 April 1984, 3.

Literature: Azevedo 1985; Berryman 1986.

1. Azevedo 1985, 602.

Salvadoran Basic Ecclesial Communities,
Profession of Faith, 1984

We believe in God our Father, who has made us free and who accompanies our people in the struggle for liberation.

We believe in Christ, crucified again and again in the suffering of the poor —a suffering that is capable of awakening people's consciences—and a suffering that necessarily leads to resurrection.

We believe in that power of the Spirit, capable of provoking a generosity that has led our dearest brothers and sisters to martyrdom.

We believe in the church, because it has been convoked by Jesus and the Spirit, and because, in coming together, Jesus is with us, as is our mother Mary, that woman so faithful to God.

We believe in the Christian base community as the place where we can realize the Christian ideal and from which we can proclaim that ideal with all its power and truth.

We believe in and are building a church where together we reflect over our situation, share our lives and our earthly goods with each other, lead a life enriched by prayer and the sacraments, and are inspired by the prophetic mission of Jesus. As such, we make present the reign of God on earth.

We believe we must love one another but must also fraternally correct one another, accepting each other's errors and weaknesses in our efforts to make our conversion process a reality.

We believe that the marginalized, the persecuted, the victims of torture, the illiterate, and the sick among us are those poor of whom the Gospel speaks as the preferred of Jesus. It is with their eyes that Jesus challenges us to work for justice and peace.

We also believe that the face of Christ is present in our brothers and sisters enslaved by their passions. We pray for their conversion and to love them even though they calumniate, persecute, and kill us. We commit ourselves to look for ways of helping them so that one day they too will be included among God's humble people.

The United Church of Christ in the Philippines, *Statement of Faith*, 1986/1992

The United Church of Christ in the Philippines is the outcome of a series of mergers during the twentieth century, culminating in 1948, which eventually brought together Presbyterian and Congregationalist churches forming the United Evangelical Church (1929), Disciples of Christ and United Brethren forming the Evangelical Church of the Philippines (1943), and the Philippine Methodist Church.

Although the merged church was still able to say in its *Handbook of Member Churches* for 1985 that "there is no common credal formula," its Faith and Order Committee drew up this *Statement of Faith*, which was approved by the General Assembly in 1986 and revised in 1992. M. R. Spindler has called attention to "the very classical construction of the Statement and its affirmation of the Trinitarian dimension of the Christian faith."[1]

Edition: *Constitution and Bylaws* 1996 (for 1986 text, see Cariño 1987, v–vi).

Literature: Aoanan 1996; Cariño 1987; Spindler 1990.

---

1. Spindler 1990, 154.

The United Church of Christ in the Philippines,
Statement of Faith, 1986/1992

[1.] We believe

In one God: Creator, Redeemer, and Sustainer, who provides order, purpose, meaning, and fulfillment to all creation.

That in Jesus Christ, who was born of Mary, God became man and is sovereign Lord of life and history.

That in the Holy Spirit God is present in the world, empowering and guiding believers to understand and live out their faith in Jesus Christ.

[2.] We believe

That persons are created in the image of God and destined to live in community with God, and with other persons and with all creation.

That, by disobedience, they have become sinful, but by grace through faith, they are redeemed in Jesus Christ.

That being entrusted with God's creation, they are called to participate in the establishment of a just and compassionate social order.

[3.] We believe

That the church is the one body of Christ, the whole community of persons reconciled to God through Jesus Christ and entrusted with God's ministry.

[4.] We believe

That the Holy Bible is a faithful and inspired witness to God's self-revelation in Jesus Christ and in history to illumine, guide, correct, and edify believers in their faith and witness.

[5.] We believe

God is at work, to make each person a new being in Christ, and the whole world God's kingdom—in which love, justice, and peace prevail.

The kingdom of God is present where faith in Jesus Christ is shared, where healing is given to the sick, where food is given to the hungry, where light is given to the blind, and where liberty is given to the captive and oppressed.

[6.] We believe

The resurrection of Jesus Christ has overcome the power of death and gives assurance of life after death.

And we look forward to his coming again in all fullness and glory to make all creation new and to gather all the faithful under God's kingdom. Amen.

Joint International Commission for Theological Dialogue Between the Roman Catholic Church and the Orthodox Church, Balamand, Lebanon, *Uniatism, Method of Union of the Past, and the Present Search for Full Communion: Ecclesiological Principles,* 1993

Ever since the consummation of the schism between East and West—as articulated at → Constantinople in 1054, addressed at → Lyons in 1274, and resolved (but unsuccessfully) at → Florence in 1439—the effort to achieve reconciliation has taken various paths. One of these paths was to found, within the lands that were historically Eastern Orthodox, Eastern Rite Catholic (or "Uniate") churches, that is, churches in communion with the See of Rome that retain Eastern, non-Latin liturgies and canon law, which includes such Eastern practices as baptism by immersion, communion under both kinds, and the ordination of married men. The most ambitious such attempt was the Union of Brest-Litovsk of 1595, but there are Uniate churches in many other countries.

Two events of the twentieth century have chiefly been responsible for a fundamental reconsideration of this attempted resolution of the schism: the Second Vatican Council, whose → *Unitatis redintegratio* and *Orientalium Ecclesiarum* not only committed the Roman Catholic Church to ecumenism but articulated and fostered a new appreciation of the distinctive liturgy, spirituality, and theology of Eastern Orthodoxy; and the fall of Communism, which set the (largely Orthodox) churches of Eastern Europe free, but also, above all in Ukraine, brought into the open the tensions between the suppressed Eastern Catholics and the Orthodox.

It was in that charged atmosphere that the Joint International Commission for Theological Dialogue Between the Roman Catholic Church and the Orthodox Church held its seventh plenary session at Balamand in Lebanon and, on 23 June 1993, produced this confessional statement to address the tensions. The second part of the document promulgates "Practical Rules," but we are presenting only the first part, entitled "Ecclesiological Principles," retaining the original numbering for ease in reference.

Edition: *Gr Agr II* 680–85.

Literature: Attwater 1935; Hajjar 1995; Pallath 1994; Pelikan 1990c.

Joint International Commission for Theological Dialogue Between the Roman Catholic Church and the Orthodox Church, Balamand, Lebanon, *Uniatism, Method of Union of the Past, and the Present Search for Full Communion: Ecclesiological Principles,* 1993

6. The division between the churches of the East and of the West has never quelled the desire for unity wished by Christ. Rather this situation, which is contrary to the nature of the church, has often been for many the occasion to become more deeply conscious of the need to achieve this unity, so as to be faithful to the Lord's commandment.

7. In the course of the centuries various attempts were made to reestablish unity. They sought to achieve this end through different ways, at times conciliar, according to the political, historical, theological and spiritual situation of each period. Unfortunately, none of these efforts succeeded in reestablishing full communion between the church of the West and the church of the East, and at times even made oppositions more acute.

8. In the course of the last four centuries, in various parts of the East, initiatives were taken within certain churches and impelled by outside elements, to restore communion between the church of the East and the church of the West. These initiatives led to the union of certain communities with the See of Rome and brought with them, as a consequence, the breaking of communion with their mother churches of the East. This took place not without the interference of extra-ecclesial interests. In this way Oriental Catholic Churches came into being. And so a situation was created which has become a source of conflicts and of suffering in the first instance for the Orthodox but also for Catholics.

9. Whatever may have been the intention and the authenticity of the desire to be faithful to the commandment of Christ: "that all may be one" expressed in [Jn 17.21] these partial unions with the See of Rome, it must be recognized that the reestablishment of unity between the church of the East and the church of the West was not achieved and that the division remains, embittered by these attempts.

10. The situation thus created resulted in fact in tensions and oppositions. Progressively, in the decades which followed these unions, missionary activity tended to include among its priorities the effort to convert other Christians, individually or in groups, so as "to bring them back" to one's own church. In order

849

to legitimize this tendency, a source of proselytism, the Catholic Church developed the theological vision according to which she presented herself as the only one to whom salvation was entrusted. As a reaction, the Orthodox Church, in turn, came to accept the same vision according to which only in her could salvation be found. To assure the salvation of "the separated brethren" it even happened that Christians were rebaptized and that certain requirements of the religious freedom of persons and of their act of faith were forgotten. This perspective was one to which that period showed little sensitivity.

11. On the other hand, certain civil authorities made attempts to bring back Oriental Catholics to the church of their fathers. To achieve this end they did not hesitate, when the occasion was given, to use unacceptable means.

12. Because of the way in which Catholics and Orthodox once again consider each other in their relationship to the mystery of the church and discover each other once again as sister churches, this form of "missionary apostolate" described above, and which has been called "uniatism," can no longer be accepted either as a method to be followed nor as a model of the unity our churches are seeking.

13. In fact, especially since the Pan-Orthodox Conferences and the Second Vatican Council, the rediscovery and the giving again of proper value to the church as communion, both on the part of Orthodox and of Catholics, has radically altered perspectives and thus attitudes. On each side it is recognized that what Christ has entrusted to his church—profession of apostolic faith, participation in the same sacraments, above all the one priesthood celebrating the one sacrifice of Christ, the apostolic succession of bishops—cannot be considered the exclusive property of one of our churches.

14. It is in this perspective that the Catholic Churches and the Orthodox Churches recognize each other as sister churches, responsible together for maintaining the church of God in fidelity to the divine purpose, most especially in what concerns unity. According to the words of Pope John Paul II, the ecumenical endeavor of the sister churches of East and West, grounded in dialogue and prayer, is the search for perfect and total communion, which is neither absorption nor fusion, but a meeting in truth and love.[1]

15. While the inviolable freedom of persons and their obligation to follow the requirements of their conscience remain secure, in the search for reestablishing unity there is no question of conversion of people from one church to the other in order to ensure their salvation. There is a question of achieving together the will of Christ for his own and the design of God for his church by means of a common

1. John Paul II *Slavorum Apostoli* 27.

quest by the churches for a full accord on the content of the faith and its implications. This effort is being carried on in the current theological dialogue. The present document is a necessary stage in this dialogue.

16. The Oriental Catholic Churches who have desired to reestablish full communion with the See of Rome and have remained faithful to it, have the rights and obligations which are connected with this communion. The principles determining their attitude towards Orthodox Churches are those which have been stated by the Second Vatican Council and have been put into practice by the popes who have clarified the practical consequences flowing from these principles in various documents published since then. These churches, then, should be inserted, on both local and universal levels, into the dialogue of love, in mutual respect and reciprocal trust found once again, and enter into the theological dialogue, with all its practical implications.

17. In this atmosphere, the considerations already presented and the practical guidelines which follow, insofar as they will be effectively received and faithfully observed, are such as to lead to a just and definitive solution to the difficulties which these Oriental Catholic Churches present to the Orthodox Church.

18. Towards this end, Pope Paul VI affirmed in his address at the Phanar in July 1967: "It is on the heads of the churches, of their hierarchy, that the obligation rests to guide the churches along the way that leads to finding full communion again. They ought to do this by recognizing and respecting each other as pastors of that part of the flock of Christ entrusted to them, by taking care for the cohesion and growth of the people of God, and avoiding everything that could scatter it or cause confusion in its ranks."[2] In this spirit Pope John Paul II and Ecumenical Patriarch Dimitrios I together stated clearly: "We reject every form of proselytism, every attitude which would be or could be perceived to be a lack of respect."[3]

2. Paul VI *Tomos Agapis* 172.
3. Joint statement of 7 December 1987.

The Roman Catholic Church and the Assyrian Church of the East, *Common Christological Declaration*, 1994

At the same time as the efforts to transcend the historic differences between episcopal, presbyteral, and congregational polities in the creation of → the Church of South India, and, in → *The Leuenberg Agreement* as well as in → *Baptist, Eucharist, Ministry,* to reconsider the controversies of the sixteenth century over the eucharist and then, in → the *Lutheran-Catholic Joint Declaration on the Doctrine of Justification,* to redefine the doctrine that underlay the division of the Western Church at the Reformation—a division more than three times as old was also receiving ecumenical attention, not from individual theologians but from the supreme hierarchical authorities: the division over the relation of the divine and human in Christ. The third and the fourth ecumenical councils, → Ephesus in 431 and → Chalcedon in 451, had formulated the orthodox doctrine of that relation and had condemned both the "Nestorianism" that was accused of separating the divine and the human natures and the "Monophysitism" that was rejected for blurring the distinction between them. The careful historical work of several generations of scholars had shown, as this *Declaration* puts it, that "the controversies of the past [which] led to anathemas . . . . [and] the divisions brought about in this way were due in large part to misunderstandings"; and it had made it possible to employ the formula of *The Definition of Chalcedon:* "without confusion or change, without division or separation."[1] A similar conciliatory tone in the other direction, toward those who had historically been labeled "Monophysite," is audible in → the *Common Declaration* of Pope John Paul II of the Roman Catholic Church and Catholicos Karekin I of the Armenian Apostolic Church of 1996.

English Edition: *Gr Agr II* 711-12.

Literature: Dinkha 1994; Hennessey 1998.

1. *Chr Dec* 4, 2; *Chal* 17-18.

The Roman Catholic Church and the Assyrian Church of the East, *Common Christological Declaration*, 1994

His Holiness John Paul II, bishop of Rome and pope of the Catholic Church, and His Holiness Mar Dinkha IV, catholicos-patriarch of the Assyrian Church of the East, give thanks to God who has prompted them to this new brotherly meeting.

Both of them consider this meeting as a basic step on the way towards the full communion to be restored between their churches. They can indeed, from now on, proclaim together before the world their common faith in the mystery of the incarnation.

1. As heirs and guardians of the faith received from the apostles as formulated by our common fathers in the Nicene Creed, we confess one Lord Jesus Christ, the only Son of God, begotten of the Father from all eternity, who in the fullness of time, came down from heaven and became man for our salvation. The Word of God, second person of the Holy Trinity, became incarnate by the power of the Holy Spirit in assuming from the Holy Virgin Mary a body animated by a rational soul, with which he was indissolubly united from the moment of his conception.

2. Therefore our Lord Jesus Christ is true God and true man, perfect in his divinity and perfect in his humanity, consubstantial with the Father and consubstantial with us in all things but sin. His divinity and his humanity are united in one person, without confusion or change, without division or separation. In him has been preserved the difference of the natures of divinity and humanity, with all their properties, faculties, and operations. But far from constituting "one and another," the divinity and humanity are united in the person of the same and unique Son of God and Lord Jesus Christ, who is the object of a single adoration.

3. Christ therefore is not an "ordinary man" whom God adopted in order to reside in him and inspire him, as in the righteous ones and the prophets. But the same God the Word, begotten of his Father before all worlds without beginning according to his divinity, was born of a mother without a father in the last times according to his humanity. The humanity to which the Blessed Virgin Mary gave birth always was that of the Son of God himself. That is why the Assyrian Church of the East is praying to the Virgin Mary as "the Mother of Christ our God and Savior." In the light of this same faith the Catholic tradition addresses the Virgin Mary as "the Mother of God" and also as "the Mother of Christ." We both recognize the

legitimacy and rightness of these expressions of the same faith and we both respect the preference of each church in her liturgical life and piety.

4. This is the unique faith that we profess in the mystery of Christ. The controversies of the past led to anathemas, bearing on persons and on formulas. The Lord's Spirit permits us to understand better today that the divisions brought about in this way were due in large part to misunderstandings.

5. Whatever our Christological divergences have been, we experience ourselves united today in the confession of the same faith in the Son of God who became man so that we might become children of God by his grace. We wish from now on to witness together to this faith in the one who is the way, the truth, and the life, proclaiming it in appropriate ways to our contemporaries, so that the world may believe in the gospel of salvation.

6. The mystery of the incarnation which we profess in common is not an abstract and isolated truth. It refers to the Son of God sent to save us. The economy of salvation, which has its origin in the mystery of communion of the Holy Trinity — Father, Son, and Holy Spirit — is brought to its fulfillment through the sharing in this communion, by grace, within the one, holy, catholic, and apostolic church, which is the people of God, the body of Christ, and the temple of the Spirit.

7. Believers become members of this body through the sacrament of baptism, through which, by water and the working of the Holy Spirit, they are born again as new creatures. They are confirmed by the seal of the Holy Spirit who bestows the sacrament of anointing. Their communion with God and among themselves is brought to full realization by the celebration of the unique offering of Christ in the sacrament of the eucharist. This communion is restored for the sinful members of the church when they are reconciled with God and with one another through the sacrament of forgiveness. The sacrament of ordination to the ministerial priesthood in the apostolic succession assures the authenticity of the faith, the sacraments, and the communion in each local church.

8. Living by this faith and these sacraments, it follows as a consequence that the particular Catholic churches and the particular Assyrian churches can recognize each other as sister churches. To be full and entire, communion presupposes the unanimity concerning the content of the faith, the sacraments and the constitution of the church. Since this unanimity for which we aim has not yet been attained, we cannot unfortunately celebrate together the eucharist which is the sign of the ecclesial communion already fully restored.

9. Nevertheless, the deep spiritual communion in the faith and the mutual trust already existing between our churches entitle us from now on to consider wit-

nessing together to the gospel message and cooperating in particular pastoral situations, including especially the areas of catechesis and the formation of future priests.

10. In thanking God for having made us rediscover what already unites us in the faith and the sacraments, we pledge ourselves to do everything possible to dispel the obstacles of the past which still prevent the attainment of full communion between our churches, so that we can better respond to the Lord's call for the unity of his own, a unity which has of course to be expressed visibly. To overcome these obstacles, we now establish a Mixed Committee for theological dialogue between the Catholic Church and the Assyrian Church of the East.

Unitas Fratrum (Moravian Church in America), *The Ground of the Unity,* 1995

Best known confessionally for its → *Easter Litany* of 1749, the Unitas Fratrum or Moravian Church has supplemented that statement of faith with more recent confessions, most notably in the United States with *The Ground of the Unity* of 1995.

This document originated in 1957 with the celebration of the five-hundredth anniversary of the founding of the original Hussite Unitas Fratrum in 1457, which the modern Unitas Fratrum commemorated by drawing up a new doctrinal statement. In the decades that followed, it was discussed and reviewed at the so-called Unity Synods of the church. The present form bears the subtitle: "A doctrinal statement adopted by the Unity Synod of the Unitas Fratrum, or Moravian Church, held at Dar es Salaam, Tanzania, August 13 to 25, 1995."

Edition: Provided by the Moravian Church in America Provincial Elders' Conference, Southern Province.

Literature: Hamilton 1900; Langton 1956; J. T. Müller 1922–31; Schweinitz 1901.

Unitas Fratrum (Moravian Church in America), *The Ground of the Unity*, 1995

The Lord Jesus Christ calls his church into being so that it may serve him on earth until he comes. The Unitas Fratrum is, therefore, aware of its being called in faith to serve humanity by proclaiming the gospel of Jesus Christ. It recognizes this call to be the source of its being and the inspiration of its service. As is the source, so is the aim and end of its being based upon the will of its Lord. [1 Cor 11.26]

1. THE BELIEF OF THE CHURCH

With the whole of Christendom we share faith in God the Father, the Son, and the Holy Spirit. We believe and confess that God has revealed himself once and for all in his Son Jesus Christ; that our Lord has redeemed us with the whole of humanity by his death and his resurrection; and that there is no salvation apart from him. We believe that he is present with us in the word and the sacrament; that he directs and unites us through his Spirit and thus forms us into a church. We hear him summoning us to follow him, and pray him to use us in his service. He joins us together mutually, so that knowing ourselves to be members of his body we become willing to serve each other.

In the light of divine grace, we recognize ourselves to be a church of sinners. We require forgiveness daily, and live only through the mercy of God in Christ Jesus our Lord. He redeems us from our isolation and unites us into a living church of Jesus Christ.

2. PERSONAL BELIEF

The belief of the church is effected and preserved through the testimony of Jesus Christ and through the work of the Holy Spirit. This testimony calls each individual personally, and leads each one to the recognition of sin and to the acceptance of the redemption achieved by Christ. In fellowship with him the love of Christ becomes more and more the power of the new life, power which penetrates and shapes the entire person. As God's Spirit so effects living belief in the hearts of individuals, he grants them the privilege to share in the fruits of Christ's salvation and membership in his body.

3. GOD'S WORD AND DOCTRINE

The Triune God as revealed in the Holy Scripture of the Old and New Testaments is the only source of our life and salvation; and this Scripture is the sole standard of the doctrine and faith of the Unitas Fratrum and therefore shapes our life.

The Unitas Fratrum recognizes the word of the cross as the center of Holy Scripture and of all preaching of the gospel, and it sees its primary mission, and its reason for being, to consist in bearing witness to this joyful message. We ask our Lord for power never to stray from this.

The Unitas Fratrum takes part in the continual search for sound doctrine. In interpreting Scripture and in the communication of doctrine in the church, we look to two millennia of ecumenical Christian tradition and the wisdom of our Moravian forebears in the faith to guide us as we pray for fuller understanding and ever clearer proclamation of the gospel of Jesus Christ. But just as the Holy Scripture does not contain any doctrinal system, so the Unitas Fratrum also has not developed any of its own because it knows that the mystery of Jesus Christ, which is attested to in the Bible, cannot be comprehended completely by any human mind or expressed completely in any human statement. Also it is true that through the Holy Spirit the recognition of God's will for salvation in the Bible is revealed completely and clearly.

4. CREEDS AND CONFESSIONS

The Unitas Fratrum recognizes in the creeds of the church the thankful acclaim of the body of Christ. These creeds aid the church in formulating a scriptural confession, in marking the boundary of heresies, and in exhorting believers to an obedient and fearless testimony in every age. The Unitas Fratrum maintains that all creeds formulated by the Christian church stand in need of constant testing in the light of the Holy Scriptures. It acknowledges as such true professions of faith the early
[Phil 2.11] Christian witness: "Jesus Christ is Lord!" and also especially the ancient Christian creeds and the fundamental creeds of the Reformation.*

---

* Note: In the various Provinces of the Renewed Unitas Fratrum the following creeds in particular gained special importance, because in them the main doctrines of the Christian faith find clear and simple expression: The Apostles' Creed; The Athanasian Creed; The Nicene Creed; The Confession of the Unity of the Bohemian Brethren of 1535; The Twenty-One Articles of the unaltered Augsburg Confession; The Shorter Catechism of Martin Luther; The Synod of Berne of 1532; The Thirty-Nine Articles of the Church of England; The Theological Declaration of Barmen of 1934; The Heidelberg Catechism.

5. THE UNITAS FRATRUM AS A UNITY

We believe in and confess the unity of the church given in the one Lord Jesus Christ as God and Savior. He died that he might unite the scattered children of God. As the living Lord and Shepherd, he is leading his flock toward such unity.

The Unitas Fratrum espoused such unity when it took over the name of the Old Bohemian Brethren's Church, "Unitas Fratrum" (Unity of Brethren). Nor can we ever forget the powerful unifying experience granted by the crucified and risen Lord to our ancestors in Herrnhut on the occasion of the Holy Communion of August 13, 1727, in Bethelsdorf.

It is the Lord's will that Christendom should give evidence of and seek unity in him with zeal and love. In our own midst we see how such unity has been promised us and laid upon us as a charge. We recognize that through the grace of Christ the different churches have received many gifts. It is our desire that we may learn from each other and rejoice together in the riches of the love of Christ and the manifold wisdom of God.

We confess our share in the guilt which is manifest in the severed and divided state of Christendom. By means of such divisions we ourselves hinder the message and power of the gospel. We recognize the danger of self-righteousness and judging others without love.

Since we together with all Christendom are pilgrims on the way to meet our coming Lord, we welcome every step that brings us nearer the goal of unity in him. He himself invites us to communion in his supper. Through it he leads the church toward that union which he has promised. By means of his presence in the holy communion he makes our unity in him evident and certain even today.

6. THE CHURCH AS A BROTHERHOOD

The church of Jesus Christ, despite all the distinctions between male and female, Jew and non-Jew, white and colored, poor and rich, is one in its Lord. The Unitas Fratrum recognizes no distinction between those who are one in the Lord Jesus Christ. We are called to testify that God in Jesus Christ brings his people out of "every race, kindred, and tongue" into one body, pardons sinners beneath the cross, [Rv 7.9] and brings them together. We oppose any discrimination in our midst because of race or standing, and we regard it as a commandment of the Lord to bear public witness to this and to demonstrate by word and deed that we are brothers and sisters in Christ.

7. THE CHURCH AS A COMMUNITY OF SERVICE

[Mt 20.28]   Jesus Christ came not to be served but to serve. From this, his church receives its mission and its power for its service, to which each of its members is called. We believe that the Lord has called us particularly to mission service among the peoples of the world. In this, and in all other forms of service both at home and abroad, to which the Lord commits us, he expects us to confess him and witness to his love in unselfish service.

8. SERVING OUR NEIGHBOR

Our Lord Jesus entered into this world's misery to bear it and to overcome it. We seek to follow him in serving his people. Like the love of Jesus, this service knows no bounds. Therefore we pray the Lord ever anew to point out to us the way to reach our neighbors, opening our heart and hand to them in their need.

9. SERVING THE WORLD

Jesus Christ maintains in love and faithfulness his commitment to this fallen world. Therefore we must remain concerned for this world. We may not withdraw from it through indifference, pride or fear. Together with the universal Christian Church, the Unitas Fratrum challenges all with the message of the love of God, striving to promote the peace of the world and seeking to attain what is best for all people. For the sake of this world, the Unitas Fratrum hopes for and looks to the day when the victory of Christ will be manifest over sin and death and the new world will appear.

CONCLUSION

Jesus Christ is the one Lord and Head of his body, the church. Because of this, the church owes no allegiance to any authority whatsoever which opposes his dominion. The Unitas Fratrum treasures in its history the vital experience of the headship of Christ of September 16 and November 13, 1741.

The Unitas Fratrum recognizes that it is called into being and has been sustained hitherto only by the incomprehensible grace of God. Thanksgiving and praise for this grace remain the keynote of its life and ministry.

In this spirit it awaits the appearing of Jesus Christ, goes forward to meet its Lord with joy, and prays to be found ready when he comes.

The Alliance of Confessing Evangelicals,
Cambridge Declaration, 1996

Alongside the ecumenism represented by the World Council of Churches and its Commission on Faith and Order, and often in reaction against it, twentieth-century Evangelicalism developed its own interconfessional movement, as Evangelicals discovered that they had more in common with Evangelicals adhering to other confessions than they did with some members of their own confessional tradition.

The Alliance of Confessing Evangelicals arose out of this discovery. Its charter statement explains that, "drawing on the consensus of apostolic Christianity, summarized in the ecumenical creeds and in the sixteenth century Reformation," it "exists to promote biblical and Reformation Christianity." Evangelicalism, therefore, is intended to be, not a new denomination with a new confession, but a movement "to understand the challenges and opportunities of our time and place, and to articulate constructive responses in a challenging ecclesiastical context."

Yet because it is an alliance of *confessing* Evangelicals, those "constructive responses" have naturally taken on a confessional character. Of the various calls to action and other documents that have issued from the Alliance of Confessing Evangelicals, *The Cambridge Declaration* of 1996 is a defining affirmation. Meeting in Cambridge, Massachusetts, in April 1996, theologians from several confessional traditions—Lutheran, Reformed, and Free Church—met to discuss the doctrinal condition of Protestant denominations and theological seminaries, and, in *The Cambridge Declaration*, to summon them back to the fundamentals of the Reformation confessions.

Edition: Alliance of Confessing Evangelicals 1996, 3–11.

Literature: Boice 1996.

The Alliance of Confessing Evangelicals, *The Cambridge Declaration*, 1996

Evangelical churches today are increasingly dominated by the spirit of this age rather than by the Spirit of Christ. As evangelicals, we call ourselves to repent of this sin and to recover the historic Christian faith.

In the course of history words change. In our day this has happened to the word "evangelical." In the past it served as a bond of unity between Christians from a wide diversity of church traditions. Historic evangelicalism was confessional. It embraced the essential truths of Christianity as those were defined by the great ecumenical councils of the church. In addition, evangelicals also shared a common heritage in the "solas" of the sixteenth-century Protestant Reformation.

Today the light of the Reformation has been significantly dimmed. The consequence is that the word "evangelical" has become so inclusive as to have lost its meaning. We face the peril of losing the unity it has taken centuries to achieve. Because of this crisis and because of our love of Christ, his gospel, and his church, we endeavor to assert anew our commitment to the central truths of the Reformation and of historic evangelicalism. These truths we affirm not because of their role in our traditions, but because we believe that they are central to the Bible.

1. Sola Scriptura: The Erosion of Authority

Scripture alone is the inerrant rule of the church's life, but the evangelical church today has separated Scripture from its authoritative function. In practice, the church is guided, far too often, by the culture. Therapeutic technique, marketing strategies, and the beat of the entertainment world often have far more to say about what the church wants, how it functions, and what it offers, than does the word of God. Pastors have neglected their rightful oversight of worship, including the doctrinal content of the music. As biblical authority has been abandoned in practice, as its truths have faded from Christian consciousness, and as its doctrines have lost their saliency, the church has been increasingly emptied of its integrity, moral authority, and direction.

Rather than adapting Christian faith to satisfy the felt needs of consumers, we must proclaim the law as the only measure of true righteousness and the gospel as the only announcement of saving truth. Biblical truth is indispensable to the church's understanding, nurture, and discipline.

Scripture must take us beyond our perceived needs to our real needs and liberate us from seeing ourselves through the seductive images, clichés, promises, and priorities of mass culture. It is only in the light of God's truth that we understand ourselves aright and see God's provision for our need. The Bible, therefore, must be taught and preached in the church. Sermons must be expositions of the Bible and its teachings, not expressions of the preacher's opinions or the ideas of the age. We must settle for nothing less than what God has given.

The work of the Holy Spirit in personal experience cannot be disengaged from Scripture. The Spirit does not speak in ways that are independent of Scripture. Apart from Scripture we would never have known of God's grace in Christ. The biblical word, rather than spiritual experience, is the test of truth.

THESIS 1. SOLA SCRIPTURA

We reaffirm the inerrant Scripture to be the sole source of written divine revelation, which alone can bind the conscience. The Bible alone teaches all that is necessary for our salvation from sin and is the standard by which all Christian behavior must be measured.

We deny that any creed, council, or individual may bind a Christian's conscience, that the Holy Spirit speaks independently of or contrary to what is set forth in the Bible, or that personal spiritual experience can ever be a vehicle of revelation.

2. Solus Christus: The Erosion of Christ-Centered Faith

As evangelical faith becomes secularized, its interests have been blurred with those of the culture. The result is a loss of absolute values, permissive individualism, and a substitution of wholeness for holiness, recovery for repentance, intuition for truth, feeling for belief, chance for providence, and immediate gratification for enduring hope. Christ and his cross have moved from the center of our vision.

THESIS 2. SOLUS CHRISTUS

We reaffirm that our salvation is accomplished by the mediatorial work of the historical Christ alone. His sinless life and substitutionary atonement alone are sufficient for our justification and reconciliation to the Father.

We deny that the gospel is preached if Christ's substitutionary work is not declared and faith in Christ and his work is not solicited.

3. Sola Gratia: The Erosion of the Gospel

Unwarranted confidence in human ability is a product of fallen human nature. This false confidence now fills the evangelical world; from the self-esteem gospel, to the health and wealth gospel, from those who have transformed the gospel into a product to be sold and sinners into consumers who want to buy, to others who treat Christian faith as being true simply because it works. This silences the doctrine of justification regardless of the official commitments of our churches.

God's grace in Christ is not merely necessary but is the sole efficient cause of salvation. We confess that human beings are born spiritually dead and are incapable even of cooperating with regenerating grace.

THESIS 3. SOLA GRATIA

We reaffirm that in salvation we are rescued from God's wrath by his grace alone. It is the supernatural work of the Holy Spirit that brings us to Christ by releasing us from our bondage to sin and raising us from spiritual death to spiritual life.

We deny that salvation is in any sense a human work. Human methods, techniques, or strategies by themselves cannot accomplish this transformation. Faith is not produced by our unregenerated human nature.

4. Sola Fide: The Erosion of the Chief Article

Justification is by grace alone through faith alone because of Christ alone. This is the article by which the church stands or falls. Today this article is often ignored, distorted, or sometimes even denied by leaders, scholars, and pastors who claim to be evangelical. Although fallen human nature has always recoiled from recognizing its need for Christ's imputed righteousness, modernity greatly fuels the fires of this discontent with the biblical gospel. We have allowed this discontent to dictate the nature of our ministry and what it is we are preaching.

Many in the church growth movement believe that sociological understanding of those in the pew is as important to the success of the gospel as is the biblical truth which is proclaimed. As a result, theological convictions are frequently divorced from the work of the ministry. The marketing orientation in many churches takes this even further, erasing the distinction between the biblical word and the world, robbing Christ's cross of its offense, and reducing Christian faith to the principles and methods which bring success to secular corporations.

While the theology of the cross may be believed, these movements are actually emptying it of its meaning. There is no gospel except that of Christ's substitution in our place whereby God imputed to him our sin and imputed to us his righteousness. Because he bore our judgment, we now walk in his grace as those who are forever pardoned, accepted, and adopted as God's children. There is no basis for our acceptance before God except in Christ's saving work, not in our patriotism, churchly devotion, or moral decency. The gospel declares what God has done for us in Christ. It is not about what we can do to reach him.

THESIS 4. SOLA FIDE

We reaffirm that justification is by grace alone through faith alone because of Christ alone. In justification Christ's righteousness is imputed to us as the only possible satisfaction of God's perfect justice.

We deny that justification rests on any merit to be found in us, or upon the grounds of an infusion of Christ's righteousness in us, or that an institution claiming to be a church that denies or condemns sola fide can be recognized as a legitimate church.

5. Soli Deo Gloria: The Erosion of God-Centered Worship

Wherever in the church biblical authority has been lost, Christ has been displaced, the gospel has been distorted, or faith has been perverted, it has always been for one reason: our interests have displaced God's and we are doing his work in our way. The loss of God's centrality in the life of today's church is common and lamentable. It is this loss that allows us to transform worship into entertainment, gospel preaching into marketing, believing into technique, being good into feeling good about ourselves, and faithfulness into being successful. As a result, God, Christ, and the Bible have come to mean too little to us and rest too inconsequentially upon us.

God does not exist to satisfy human ambitions, cravings, the appetite for consumption, or our own private spiritual interests. We must focus on God in our worship, rather than the satisfaction of our personal needs. God is sovereign in worship; we are not. Our concern must be for God's kingdom, not our own empires, popularity, or success.

THESIS 5. SOLI DEO GLORIA

We reaffirm that because salvation is of God and has been accomplished by God, it is for God's glory that we must glorify him always. We must live our entire lives before the face of God, under the authority of God, and for his glory alone.

We deny that we can properly glorify God if our worship is confused with entertainment, if we neglect either law or gospel in our preaching, or if self-improvement, self-esteem, or self-fulfillment are allowed to become alternatives to the gospel.

6. A Call to Repentance and Reformation

The faithfulness of the evangelical church in the past contrasts sharply with its unfaithfulness in the present. Earlier in this century, evangelical churches sustained a remarkable missionary endeavor, and built many religious institutions to serve the cause of biblical truth and Christ's kingdom. That was a time when Christian behavior and expectations were markedly different from those in the culture. Today they often are not. The evangelical world today is losing its biblical fidelity, moral compass, and missionary zeal.

We repent of our worldliness. We have been influenced by the "gospels" of our secular culture, which are no gospels. We have weakened the church by our own lack of serious repentance, our blindness to the sins in ourselves which we see so clearly in others, and our inexcusable failure to adequately tell others about God's saving work in Jesus Christ.

We also earnestly call back erring professing evangelicals who have deviated from God's word in the matters discussed in this declaration. This includes those who declare that there is hope of eternal life apart from explicit faith in Jesus Christ, who claim that those who reject Christ in this life will be annihilated rather than endure the just judgment of God through eternal suffering, or who claim that Evangelicals and Roman Catholics are one in Jesus Christ even where the biblical doctrine of justification is not believed.

The Alliance of Confessing Evangelicals asks all Christians to give consideration to implementing this declaration in the church's worship, ministry, policies, life, and evangelism.

For Christ's sake. Amen.

John Paul II and Armenian Catholicos Karekin I, *Common Declaration*, 1996

The same historical reconsideration and ecumenical impulse that two years earlier had led the Roman Catholic Church and the Assyrian Church of the East to issue their → *Common Christological Declaration* were also at work in this conciliatory move toward the Armenian Apostolic Church, which had long been labeled "Monophysite" because, while accepting the decisions of → the Council of Ephesus of 431, it had not gone on to affirm the subsequent christological decisions of → the Council of Chalcedon of 451, much less those of → the Second and Third Councils of Constantinople.

Not only lamenting the division but acknowledging publicly that "linguistic, cultural, and political factors have immensely contributed towards the theological divergences that have found expression in their terminology of formulating their doctrines" (4), the two prelates, speaking for their churches, employ the very words of the Council of Chalcedon, "without confusion, without alteration, without division, without any form of separation" to declare their common faith and "unity in Christ, the Word of God made flesh" (3). And they join in sharing "the hope for and commitment to the recovery of full communion between them" (6).

English Edition: *Gr Agr II* 707–8.

Literature: *ODCC* 106, 1104–5; Sarkissian 1965.

John Paul II and Armenian Catholicos Karekin I,
Common Declaration, 1996

1. As they bring to a close their solemn meeting which they are deeply convinced has been of particular significance for the ongoing relations between the Catholic Church and the Armenian Apostolic Church, His Holiness John Paul II, bishop of Rome and pope of the Catholic Church, and His Holiness Karekin I, supreme patriarch and catholicos of all Armenians, give humble thanks to the Lord and Savior Jesus Christ who has enabled them to meet in his love for prayer together, for a fruitful discussion of their common desire to search out a more perfect unity in the Holy Spirit, and for an exchange of views about how their churches may give a more effective witness to the gospel in a world approaching a new millennium in the history of salvation.

2. Pope John Paul II and Catholicos Karekin I recognize the deep spiritual communion which already unites them and the bishops, clergy, and lay faithful of their churches. It is a communion which finds its roots in the common faith in the holy and life-giving Trinity proclaimed by the apostles and transmitted down the centuries by the many church fathers, church doctors, bishops, priests, and martyrs who have followed them. They rejoice in the fact that recent developments of ecumenical relationships and theological discussions carried out in the spirit of Christian love and fellowship have dispelled many misunderstandings inherited from the controversies and dissensions of the past. Such dialogues and encounters have prepared a healthy situation of mutual understanding and recovery of the deeper spiritual communion based on the common faith in the Holy Trinity that they have been given through the gospel of Christ and in the holy tradition of the church.

3. They particularly welcome the great advance that their churches have registered in their common search for their unity in Christ, the Word of God made flesh. Perfect God as to his divinity, perfect man as to his humanity, his divinity is united in him to his humanity in the person of the only-begotten Son of God, in a union which is real, perfect, without confusion, without alteration, without division, without any form of separation.

4. The reality of this common faith in Jesus Christ and in the same succession of apostolic ministry has at times been obscured or ignored. Linguistic, cultural, and political factors have immensely contributed towards the theological divergences that have found expression in their terminology of formulating their doctrines. His Holiness John Paul II and His Holiness Karekin I have expressed

their determined conviction that because of the fundamental common faith in God and in Jesus Christ, the controversies and unhappy divisions which sometimes have followed upon the divergent ways in expressing it, as a result of the present declaration, should not continue to influence the life and witness of the church today.

5. They humbly declare before God their sorrow for these controversies and dissensions and their determination to remove from the mind and memory of their churches the bitterness, mutual recriminations and even hatred which have sometimes manifested themselves in the past, and may even today cast a shadow over the truly fraternal and genuinely Christian relations between leaders and the faithful of both churches, especially as these have developed in recent times.

6. The communion already existing between the two churches and the hope for and commitment to the recovery of full communion between them should become factors of motivation for further contact, more regular and substantial dialogue, leading to a greater degree of mutual understanding and recovery of the communality of their faith and service.

7. Pope John Paul II and Catholicos Karekin I give their blessing and pastoral support to the further development of existing contacts and to new manifestations of that dialogue of charity between their respective pastors and faithful which will bear fruit in the fields of common action on the pastoral, catechetical, social, and intellectual levels.

8. Such a dialogue is particularly imperative in these present times when the churches are faced with new challenges to their witness to the gospel of Jesus Christ arising out of the rapidly changing situations in the modern world so deeply affected by an extreme secularistic and secularizing pace of life and culture. It requires closer collaboration, mutual confidence, and a greater degree of concern for common action. It presumes and requires an attitude of service which is not self-seeking and which is characterized by a mutual respect for the fidelity of the faithful to their own churches and Christian traditions.

9. They appeal to their clergy and laity to carry out more actively and effectively their full cooperation in all fields of diakonia, and to become agents of reconciliation, peace, and justice, struggling for the true recognition of human rights and dedicating themselves to the support of all those who are suffering and are in spiritual and material need throughout the world.

10. John Paul II and Karekin I express a particular pastoral concern for the Armenian people, both those living in their historic motherland where freedom and independence were once more recovered and reestablished recently through the creation of the new independent state of Armenia, those living in Nagorno Karabagh in need of permanent peace, and those who live in a state of worldwide diaspora.

Amid upheavals and tragedies, especially during this century, these people have remained faithful to the apostolic faith, the faith of martyrs and confessors, the faith
of millions of unnamed believers for whom Jesus Christ, the Son of God incarnate
and Savior of the world, has been the foundation of their hope, and whose Spirit
has guided them across the centuries. As they approach the seventeenth centenary
of the official establishment of the church in Armenia, may they receive the special
blessings of the Triune God for peace with justice and for a renewed dedication to
witnessing faithfully to the Lord Jesus Christ.

John Paul II, Apostolic Letter Motu Proprio
Ad tuendam fidem, 1998

The creeds and dogmatic decrees of the ecumenical councils not only anathematized heresies as false doctrine but enforced these anathemas with threats of punishment, up to and including excommunication. That pattern was continued after the schism between East and West and the Protestant Reformation: from → *The Profession of the Tridentine Faith* of 1564 to → *Sacrorum antistitum (Antimodernist Oath)* of 1910, the magisterium of the Roman Catholic Church defined creedal orthodoxy as a matter both of doctrine and of canon law, stipulating, as authoritative and enforceable, not only *The Niceno-Constantinopolitan Creed* and the ecumenical dogmas but the later definitions by the magisterium.

But when the revised text of he Code of Canon Law was promulgated on 25 January 1983, it did not make that stipulation explicit. Reacting to ongoing controversies within Roman Catholic theology after the Second Vatican Council over questions of bioethics, women's ordination, and papal infallibility itself, Pope John Paul II on 18 May 1998 issued an apostolic letter *motu proprio* ("on his own initiative") entitled *Ad tuendam fidem* ("to protect the faith"), following up on the admonition of the Second Vatican Council that "the religious assent of will and intellect is to be given in a special way to the authentic teaching authority of the Roman pontiff even when he is not speaking *ex cathedra.*"[1] In its form it is, technically, a codicil to the canon law, repairing certain lacunae; but in its substance it amounts to a profession of faith in its own right. It reaffirms the threefold categorization of Catholic teaching by the pope or the college of bishops—(1) infallible; (2) defined but not declared infallible; (3) certain but not (or not yet) defined—and extends the oath at least to the second and perhaps even to the third, "even if they do not intend to proclaim these teachings by a definitive act." Immediately upon its issuance it evoked controversy.

The notes are as provided in the original document.

Edition: *L'Osservatore Romano,* 30 June 1998, 1–2.

Translation: *L'Osservatore Romano* (English edition), 15 July 1998, 1–2.

Literature: Provost 1998; Ratzinger and Bertone; Sullivan 1998.

1. Vat II 5.1.25.

John Paul II, Apostolic Letter Motu Proprio
Ad tuendam fidem, 1998

To protect the faith of the Catholic Church against errors arising from certain members of the Christian faithful, especially from among those dedicated to the various disciplines of sacred theology, we, whose principal duty is to confirm the brethren in the faith (Lk 22.32), consider it absolutely necessary to add to the existing texts of the Code of Canon Law and the Code of Canons of the Eastern Churches, new norms which expressly impose the obligation of upholding truths proposed in a definitive way by the magisterium of the church, and which also establish related canonical sanctions.

1. From the first centuries to the present day, the church has professed the truths of her faith in Christ and the mystery of his redemption. These truths were subsequently gathered into the symbols of the faith, today known and proclaimed in common by the faithful in the solemn and festive celebration of mass as the Apostles' Creed or the Nicene-Constantinopolitan Creed.

This same Nicene-Constantinopolitan Creed is contained in the profession of faith developed by the Congregation for the Doctrine of the Faith,[1] which must be made by specific members of the faithful when they receive an office, that is directly or indirectly related to deeper investigation into the truths of faith and morals, or is united to a particular power in the governance of the church.[2]

2. The profession of faith, which appropriately begins with the Nicene-Constantinopolitan Creed, contains three propositions or paragraphs intended to describe the truths of the Catholic faith, which the church, in the course of time and under the guidance of the Holy Spirit "who will teach the whole truth" (Jn 16.13), has ever more deeply explored and will continue to explore.[3]

The first paragraph states: "With firm faith, I also believe everything contained in the word of God, whether written or handed down in tradition, which the church either by a solemn judgment or by the ordinary and universal magisterium

---

1. Congregation for the Doctrine of the Faith, "Profession of Faith and Oath of Fidelity" (9 January 1989): *AAS* 81 (1989), 105.

2. Cf. Code of Canon Law, Canon 833.

3. Cf. Code of Canon Law, Canon 747 § 1; Code of Canons of the Eastern Churches, Canon 595 § 1.

sets forth to be believed as divinely revealed."[4] This paragraph appropriately confirms and is provided for in the church's universal legislation, in canon 750 of the Code of Canon Law[5] and canon 598 of the Code of the Canons of the Eastern Churches.[6]

The third paragraph states: "Moreover I adhere with submission of will and intellect to the teachings which either the Roman pontiff or the College of Bishops enunciate when they exercise their authentic magisterium, even if they do not intend to proclaim these teachings by a definitive act."[7] This paragraph has its corresponding legislative expression in canon 752 of the Code of Canon Law[8] and canon 599 of the Code of Canons of the Eastern Churches.[9]

4. Cf. Second Vatican Ecumenical Council, *Dogmatic Constitution on the Church Lumen Gentium,* 25; *Dogmatic Constitution on Divine Revelation Dei Verbum,* 5; Congregation for the Doctrine of the Faith, "Instruction on the Ecclesial Vocation of the Theologian *Donum veritatis*" (24 May 1990), 15: *AAS* 82 (1990), 1556.

5. Code of Canon Law, Canon 750: Those things are to be believed by divine and catholic faith which are contained in the word of God as it has been written or handed down by tradition, that is, in the single deposit of faith entrusted to the church, and which are at the same time proposed as divinely revealed either by the solemn magisterium of the church, or by its ordinary and universal magisterium, which in fact is manifested by the common adherence of Christ's faithful under the guidance of the sacred magisterium. All are therefore bound to avoid any contrary doctrines.

6. Code of Canons of the Eastern Churches, Canon 598: Those things are to be believed by divine and catholic faith which are contained in the word of God as it has been written or handed down by tradition, that is, in the single deposit of faith entrusted to the church, and which are at the same time proposed as divinely revealed either by the solemn magisterium of the church, or by its ordinary and universal magisterium, which in fact is manifested by the common adherence of Christ's faithful under the guidance of the sacred magisterium. All Christian faithful are therefore bound to avoid any contrary doctrines.

7. Cf. Congregation for the Doctrine of the Faith, "Instruction on the Ecclesial Vocation of the Theologian *Donum veritatis* (24 May 1990)," 17: *AAS* 82 (1990), 1557.

8. Code of Canon Law, Canon 752: While the assent of faith is not required, a religious submission of intellect and will is to be given to any doctrine which either the supreme pontiff or the College of Bishops, exercising their authentic magisterium, declare upon a matter of faith and morals, even though they do not intend to proclaim that doctrine by definitive act. Christ's faithful are therefore to ensure that they avoid whatever does not accord with that doctrine.

9. Code of Canons of the Eastern Churches, Canon 599: While the assent of faith is not required, a religious submission of intellect and will is to be given to any doctrine which either

3. The second paragraph, however, which states "I also firmly accept and hold each and everything definitively proposed by the Church regarding teaching on faith and morals,"[10] has no corresponding canon in the codes of the Catholic Church. This second paragraph of the profession of faith is of utmost importance since it refers to truths that are necessarily connected to divine revelation. These truths, in the investigation of Catholic doctrine, illustrate the Divine Spirit's particular inspiration for the church's deeper understanding of a truth concerning faith and morals, with which they are connected either for historical reasons or by a logical relationship.

4. Moved therefore by this need, and after careful deliberation, we have decided to overcome this lacuna in the universal law in the following way:

A. Canon 750 of the Code of Canon Law will now consist of two paragraphs; the first will present the text of the existing canon; the second will contain a new text. Thus, canon 750, in its complete form, will read:

> Canon 750. § 1. Those things are to be believed by divine and catholic faith which are contained in the word of God as it has been written or handed down by tradition, that is, in the single deposit of faith entrusted to the church, and which are at the same time proposed as divinely revealed either by the solemn magisterium of the church, or by its ordinary and universal magisterium, which in fact is manifested by the common adherence of Christ's faithful under the guidance of the sacred magisterium. All are therefore bound to avoid any contrary doctrines.
>
> § 2. Furthermore, each and everything set forth definitively by the magisterium of the church regarding teaching on faith and morals must be firmly accepted and held; namely, those things required for the holy keeping and faithful exposition of the deposit of faith; therefore, anyone who rejects propositions which are to be held definitively sets himself against the teaching of the Catholic Church.

the supreme pontiff or the College of Bishops, exercising their authentic magisterium, declare upon a matter of faith and morals, even though they do not intend to proclaim that doctrine by definitive act. Christ's faithful are therefore to ensure that they avoid whatever does not accord with that doctrine.

10. Cf. Congregation for the Doctrine of the Faith, "Instruction on the Ecclesial Vocation of the Theologian *Donum veritatis*" (24 May 1990), 16: *AAS* 82 (1990), 1557.

Canon 1371, n. 1 of the Code of Canon Law, consequently, will receive an appropriate reference to canon 750 § 2, so that it will now read:

> Canon 1371. The following are to be punished with a just penalty:
>
> 1° a person who, apart from the case mentioned in canon 1364 § 1, teaches a doctrine condemned by the Roman pontiff, or by an ecumenical council, or obstinately rejects the teachings mentioned in canon 750 § 2 or in canon 752 and, when warned by the apostolic see or by the ordinary, does not retract;
>
> 2° a person who in any other way does not obey the lawful command or prohibition of the apostolic see or the ordinary or superior and, after being warned, persists in disobedience.

B. Canon 598 of the Code of Canons of the Eastern Churches will now have two paragraphs: the first will present the text of the existing canon and the second will contain a new text. Thus canon 598, in its complete form, will read as follows:

> Canon 598. § 1. Those things are to be believed by divine and catholic faith which are contained in the word of God as it has been written or handed down by tradition, that is, in the single deposit of faith entrusted to the church, and which are at the same time proposed as divinely revealed either by the solemn magisterium of the church, or by its ordinary and universal magisterium, which in fact is manifested by the common adherence of Christ's faithful under the guidance of the sacred magisterium. All Christian faithful are therefore bound to avoid any contrary doctrines.
>
> § 2. Furthermore, each and everything set forth definitively by the magisterium of the church regarding teaching on faith and morals must be firmly accepted and held; namely, those things required for the holy keeping and faithful exposition of the deposit of faith; therefore, anyone who rejects propositions which are to be held definitively sets himself against the teaching of the Catholic Church.

Canon 1436 § 2 of the Code of Canons of the Eastern Churches, consequently, will receive an appropriate reference to canon 598 § 2, so that it will now read:

Canon 1436. § 1. Whoever denies a truth which must be believed with divine and catholic faith, or who calls into doubt, or who totally repudiates the Christian faith, and does not retract after having been legitimately warned, is to be punished as a heretic or an apostate with a major excommunication; a cleric moreover can be punished with other penalties, not excluding deposition.

§ 2. In addition to these cases, whoever obstinately rejects a teaching that the Roman pontiff or the College of Bishops, exercising the authentic magisterium, have set forth to be held definitively, or who affirms what they have condemned as erroneous, and does not retract after having been legitimately warned, is to be punished with an appropriate penalty.

5. We order that everything decreed by us in this apostolic letter, given motu proprio, be established and ratified, and we prescribe that the insertions listed above be introduced into the universal legislation of the Catholic Church, that is, into the Code of Canon Law and into the Code of Canons of the Eastern Churches, all things to the contrary notwithstanding.

Given in Rome, at St. Peter's, on 18 May, in the year 1998, the twentieth of our pontificate.

Lutheran–Roman Catholic Dialogue, *Joint Declaration on the Doctrine of Justification*, 1999

The centrality of the doctrine of justification by faith (*sola fide*) in the confessions of the Reformation, both Lutheran and Reformed (see Part Four above), and of the doctrine of justification by faith *and* works in → the decrees of the Council of Trent, had made it, throughout the centuries following the Reformation, a principal obstacle to ecumenical relations between the Roman Catholic Church and the Lutheran Church.

At the same time that the *sola Scriptura* of the Reformation controversies was being reconsidered by both sides, with a new emphasis on the authority of Scripture and on the study of it by the Second Vatican Council in → *Dei verbum* and a new appreciation of tradition by many Protestants, Lutherans and Roman Catholics undertook a reconsideration of the positions they had taken in the sixteenth century on the doctrine of justification. They were, as this *Joint Declaration on the Doctrine of Justification* makes clear, coming out of a shared "way of listening to the word of God in Scripture" (8), which had corrected and amplified the understanding by both sides of the vocabulary of the New Testament.

Appended to the *Joint Declaration* when it was issued on Reformation Day, 31 October 1999, at Augsburg, the site of → *The Augsburg Confession* of 1530, were: "Resources," an "Official Common Statement by the Lutheran World Federation and the Catholic Church," and an "Annex" with further clarifications.

Edition: *Gr Agr II* 566–73.

Literature: Donfried 1999; Dulles 1999; Kasper 1999; Noko 1999.

Lutheran–Roman Catholic Dialogue, *Joint Declaration on the Doctrine of Justification*, 1999

PREAMBLE

1. The doctrine of justification was of central importance for the Lutheran Reformation of the sixteenth century. It was held to be the "first and chief article"[1] and at the same time the "ruler and judge over all other Christian doctrines."[2] The doctrine of justification was particularly asserted and defended in its Reformation shape and special valuation over against the Roman Catholic Church and theology of that time, which in turn asserted and defended a doctrine of justification of a different character. From the Reformation perspective, justification was the crux of all the disputes. Doctrinal condemnations were put forward both in the Lutheran confessions[3] and by the Roman Catholic Church's Council of Trent.[4] These condemnations are still valid today and thus have a church-dividing effect.

2. For the Lutheran tradition, the doctrine of justification has retained its special status. Consequently it has also from the beginning occupied an important place in the official Lutheran-Roman Catholic dialogue.

3. Special attention should be drawn to the following reports: "The Gospel and the Church" (1972) and "Church and Justification" (1994) by the Lutheran-Roman Catholic joint commission, "Justification by Faith" (1983) of the Lutheran-Roman Catholic dialogue in the USA and "The Condemnations of the Reformation Era: Do They Still Divide?" (1986) by the ecumenical working group of Protestant and Catholic theologians in Germany. Some of these dialogue reports have been officially received by the churches. An important example of such reception is the binding response of the United Evangelical Lutheran Church of Germany to the "condemnations" study, made in 1994 at the highest possible level of ecclesiastical recognition together with the other churches of the Evangelical Church in Germany.

4. In their discussion of the doctrine of justification, all the dialogue reports as well as the responses show a high degree of agreement in their approaches and conclusions. The time has therefore come to take stock and to summarize the results of the dialogues on justification so that our churches may be informed about the

1. *Smal Art* 2.1.
2. Luther WA 39/1:205.
3. *Apol Aug* 4.
4. *Trent* 6.

overall results of this dialogue with the necessary accuracy and brevity, and thereby be enabled to make binding decisions.

5. The present joint declaration has this intention: namely, to show that on the basis of their dialogue the subscribing Lutheran churches and the Roman Catholic Church are now able to articulate a common understanding of our justification by God's grace through faith in Christ. It does not cover all that either church teaches about justification; it does encompass a consensus on basic truths of the doctrine of justification and shows that the remaining differences in its explication are no longer the occasion for doctrinal condemnations.

6. Our declaration is not a new, independent presentation alongside the dialogue reports and documents to date, let alone a replacement of them. Rather, as the appendix of sources shows, it makes repeated reference to them and their arguments.

7. Like the dialogues themselves, this joint declaration rests on the conviction that in overcoming the earlier controversial questions and doctrinal condemnations, the churches neither take the condemnations lightly nor do they disavow their own past. On the contrary, this declaration is shaped by the conviction that in their respective histories our churches have come to new insights. Developments have taken place which not only make possible, but also require the churches to examine the divisive questions and condemnations and see them in a new light.

1. BIBLICAL MESSAGE OF JUSTIFICATION

8. Our common way of listening to the word of God in Scripture has led to such new insights. Together we hear the gospel that "God so loved the world that he gave his only Son, so that everyone who believes in him may not perish but may have eternal life" (Jn 3.16). This good news is set forth in Holy Scripture in various ways. In the Old Testament we listen to God's word about human sinfulness (Ps 51.1-5; Dn 9.5f.; Ecc 8.9f.; Ezr 9.6f.) and human disobedience (Gn 3.1-19; Neh 9.16f., 26) as well as of God's "righteousness" (Is 46.13, 51.5-8, 56.1 [see 53.11]; Jer 9.24) and "judgment" (Ecc 12.14; Ps 9.5f., 76.7-9).

9. In the New Testament diverse treatments of "righteousness" and "justification" are found in the writings of Matthew (5.10, 6.33, 21.32), John (16.8-11), Hebrews (5.3, 10.37f.), and James (2.14-26). In Paul's letters also, the gift of salvation is described in various ways, among others: "for freedom Christ has set us free" (Gal 5.1-13; see Rom 6.7), "reconciled to God" (2 Cor 5.18-21; see Rom 5.11), "peace with God" (Rom 5.1), "new creation" (2 Cor 5.17), "alive to God in Christ Jesus" (Rom 6.11, 23), or "sanctified in Christ Jesus" (see 1 Cor 1.2, 1.30; 2 Cor 1.1). Chief among these is the "justification" of sinful human beings by God's

grace through faith (Rom 3.23–25), which came into particular prominence in the Reformation period.

    10. Paul sets forth the gospel as the power of God for salvation of the person who has fallen under the power of sin, as the message that proclaims that "the righteousness of God is revealed through faith for faith" (Rom 1.16f.) and that grants "justification" (Rom 3.21–31). He proclaims Christ as "our righteousness" (1 Cor 1.30), applying to the risen Lord what Jeremiah proclaimed about God himself (Jer 23.6). In Christ's death and resurrection all dimensions of his saving work have their roots, for he is "our Lord, who was put to death for our trespasses and raised for our justification" (Rom 4.25). All human beings are in need of God's righteousness, "since all have sinned and fall short of the glory of God" (Rom 3.23; see Rom 1.18–3.20, 11.32; Gal 3.22). In Galatians (3.6) and Romans (4.3–9), Paul understands Abraham's faith (Gn 15.6) as faith in the God who justifies the sinner (Rom 4.5) and calls upon the testimony of the Old Testament to undergird his gospel that this righteousness will be reckoned to all who, like Abraham, trust in God's promise. "For the righteous will live by faith (Hab 2.4; see Gal 3.11; Rom 1.17). In Paul's letters, God's righteousness is also God's power for those who have faith (Rom 1.16f.; 2 Cor 5.21). In Christ he makes it our righteousness (2 Cor 5.21). Justification becomes ours through Christ Jesus "whom God put forward as a sacrifice of atonement by his blood, effective through faith" (Rom 3.25; see 3.21–28). "For by grace you have been saved through faith, and this is not your own doing; it is the gift of God—not the result of works" (Eph 2.8f.).

    11. Justification is the forgiveness of sins (see Rom 3.23–25; Acts 13.39; Lk 18.14), liberation from the dominating power of sin and death (Rom 5.12–21) and from the curse of the law (Gal 3.10–14). It is acceptance into communion with God: already now, but then fully in God's coming kingdom (Rom 5.1f.). It unites with Christ and with his death and resurrection (Rom 6.5). It occurs in the reception of the Holy Spirit in baptism and incorporation into the one body (Rom 8.1f., 9f.; 1 Cor 12.12f.). All this is from God alone, for Christ's sake, by grace, through faith in "the gospel of God's Son" (Rom 1.1–3).

    12. The justified live by faith that comes from the word of Christ (Rom 10.17) and is active through love (Gal 5.6), the fruit of the Spirit (Gal 5.22f.). But since the justified are assailed from within and without by powers and desires (Rom 8.35–39; Gal 5.16–21) and fall into sin (1 Jn 1.8, 10), they must constantly hear God's promises anew, confess their sins (1 Jn 1.9), participate in Christ's body and blood, and be exhorted to live righteously in accord with the will of God. That is why the apostle says to the justified: "Work out your own salvation with fear and trembling; for it is God who is at work in you, enabling you both to will and to work

for his good pleasure" (Phil 2.12f.). But the good news remains: "there is now no condemnation for those who are in Christ Jesus" (Rom 8.1), and in whom Christ lives (Gal 2.20). Christ's "act of righteousness leads to justification and life for all" (Rom 5.18).

2. THE DOCTRINE OF JUSTIFICATION AS ECUMENICAL PROBLEM

13. Opposing interpretations and applications of the biblical message of justification were in the sixteenth century a principal cause of the division of the Western church and led as well to doctrinal condemnations. A common understanding of justification is therefore fundamental and indispensable to overcoming that division. By appropriating insights of recent biblical studies and drawing on modern investigations of the history of theology and dogma, the post–Vatican II ecumenical dialogue has led to a notable convergence concerning justification, with the result that this joint declaration is able to formulate a consensus on basic truths concerning the doctrine of justification. In light of this consensus, the corresponding doctrinal condemnations of the sixteenth-century do not apply to today's partner.

3. THE COMMON UNDERSTANDING OF JUSTIFICATION

14. The Lutheran churches and the Roman Catholic Church have together listened to the good news proclaimed in Holy Scripture. This common listening, together with the theological conversations of recent years, has led to a shared understanding of justification. This encompasses a consensus in the basic truths; the differing explications in particular statements are compatible with it.

15. In faith we together hold the conviction that justification is the work of the Triune God. The Father sent his Son into the world to save sinners. The foundation and presupposition of justification is the incarnation, death, and resurrection of Christ. Justification thus means that Christ himself is our righteousness, in which we share through the Holy Spirit in accord with the will of the Father. Together we confess: By grace alone, in faith in Christ's saving work and not because of any merit on our part, we are accepted by God and receive the Holy Spirit, who renews our hearts while equipping and calling us to good works.

16. All people are called by God to salvation in Christ. Through Christ alone are we justified, when we receive this salvation in faith. Faith is itself God's gift through the Holy Spirit who works through word and sacrament in the community of believers and who, at the same time, leads believers into that renewal of life which God will bring to completion in eternal life.

17. We also share the conviction that the message of justification directs us

in a special way towards the heart of the New Testament witness to God's saving action in Christ: it tells us that as sinners our new life is solely due to the forgiving and renewing mercy that God imparts as a gift and we receive in faith, and never can merit in any way.

18. Therefore the doctrine of justification, which takes up this message and explicates it, is more than just one part of Christian doctrine. It stands in an essential relation to all truths of faith, which are to be seen as internally related to each other. It is an indispensable criterion which constantly serves to orient all the teaching and practice of our churches to Christ. When Lutherans emphasize the unique significance of this criterion, they do not deny the inter-relation and significance of all truths of faith. When Catholics see themselves as bound by several criteria, they do not deny the special function of the message of justification. Lutherans and Catholics share the goal of confessing Christ in all things, who alone is to be trusted above all things as the one Mediator (1 Tm 2.5f.) through whom God in the Holy Spirit gives himself and pours out his renewing gifts.

4. EXPLICATING THE COMMON UNDERSTANDING OF JUSTIFICATION

4.1. Human Powerlessness and Sin in Relation to Justification

19. We confess together that all persons depend completely on the saving grace of God for their salvation. The freedom they possess in relation to persons and the things of this world is no freedom in relation to salvation, for as sinners they stand under God's judgment and are incapable of turning by themselves to God to seek deliverance, of meriting their justification before God, or of attaining salvation by their own abilities. Justification takes place solely by God's grace. Because Catholics and Lutherans confess this together, it is true to say:

20. When Catholics say that persons "cooperate" in preparing for and accepting justification by consenting to God's justifying action, they see such personal consent as itself an effect of grace, not as an action arising from innate human abilities.

21. According to Lutheran teaching, human beings are incapable of cooperating in their salvation, because as sinners they actively oppose God and his saving action. Lutherans do not deny that a person can reject the working of grace. When they emphasize that a person can only receive (mere passive) justification, they mean thereby to exclude any possibility of contributing to one's own justification, but do not deny that believers are fully involved personally in their faith, which is effected by God's word.

4.2. Justification as Forgiveness of Sins and Making Righteous

22. We confess together that God forgives sin by grace and at the same time frees human beings from sin's enslaving power and imparts the gift of new life in Christ. When persons come by faith to share in Christ, God no longer imputes to them their sin and through the Holy Spirit effects in them an active love. These two aspects of God's gracious action are not to be separated, for persons are by faith united with Christ, who in his person is our righteousness (1 Cor 1.30): both the forgiveness of sin and the saving presence of God himself. Because Catholics and Lutherans confess this together, it is true to say that:

23. When Lutherans emphasize that the righteousness of Christ is our righteousness, their intention is above all to insist that the sinner is granted righteousness before God in Christ through the declaration of forgiveness and that only in union with Christ is one's life renewed. When they stress that God's grace is forgiving love ("the favor of God"), they do not thereby deny the renewal of the Christian's life. They intend rather to express that justification remains free from human cooperation and is not dependent on the life-renewing effects of grace in human beings.

24. When Catholics emphasize the renewal of the interior person through the reception of grace imparted as a gift to the believer, they wish to insist that God's forgiving grace always brings with it a gift of new life, which in the Holy Spirit becomes effective in active love. They do not thereby deny that God's gift of grace in justification remains independent of human cooperation.

4.3. Justification by Faith and Through Grace

25. We confess together that sinners are justified by faith in the saving action of God in Christ. By the action of the Holy Spirit in baptism, they are granted the gift of salvation, which lays the basis for the whole Christian life. They place their trust in God's gracious promise by justifying faith, which includes hope in God and love for him. Such a faith is active in love and thus the Christian cannot and should not remain without works. But whatever in the justified precedes or follows the free gift of faith is neither the basis of justification nor merits it.

26. According to Lutheran understanding, God justifies sinners in faith alone (*sola fide*). In faith they place their trust wholly in their Creator and Redeemer and thus live in communion with him. God himself effects faith as he brings forth such trust by his creative word. Because God's act is a new creation, it affects all dimensions of the person and leads to a life in hope and love. In the doctrine of "justification by faith alone," a distinction but not a separation is made between

justification itself and the renewal of one's way of life that necessarily follows from justification and without which faith does not exist. Thereby the basis is indicated from which the renewal of life proceeds, for it comes forth from the love of God imparted to the person in justification. Justification and renewal are joined in Christ, who is present in faith.

27. The Catholic understanding also sees faith as fundamental in justification. For without faith, no justification can take place. Persons are justified through baptism as hearers of the word and believers in it. The justification of sinners is forgiveness of sins and being made righteous by justifying grace, which makes us children of God. In justification the righteous receive from Christ faith, hope and love and are thereby taken into communion with him. This new personal relation to God is grounded totally on God's graciousness and remains constantly dependent on the salvific and creative working of this gracious God, who remains true to himself, so that one can rely upon him. Thus justifying grace never becomes a human possession to which one could appeal over against God. While Catholic teaching emphasizes the renewal of life by justifying grace, this renewal in faith, hope, and love is always dependent on God's unfathomable grace and contributes nothing to justification about which one could boast before God (Rom 3.27).

4.4. The Justified as Sinner

28. We confess together that in baptism the Holy Spirit unites one with Christ, justifies and truly renews the person. But the justified must all through life constantly look to God's unconditional justifying grace. They also are continuously exposed to the power of sin still pressing its attacks (see Rom 6.12–14) and are not exempt from a life-long struggle against the contradiction to God within the selfish desires of the old Adam (see Gal 5.16; Rom 7.7–10). The justified also must ask God daily for forgiveness as in the Lord's Prayer (Mt 6.12; 1 Jn 1.9), are ever again called to conversion and penance, and are ever again granted forgiveness.

29. Lutherans understand this condition of the Christian as a being "at the same time righteous and sinner." Believers are totally righteous, in that God forgives their sins through word and sacrament and grants the righteousness of Christ which they appropriate in faith. In Christ, they are made just before God. Looking at themselves through the law, however, they recognize that they remain also totally sinners. Sin still lives in them (1 Jn 1.8; Rom 7.17, 20), for they repeatedly turn to false gods and do not love God with that undivided love which God requires as their Creator (Dt 6.5; Mt 22.36–40 pr.). This contradiction to God is as such truly sin. Nevertheless, the enslaving power of sin is broken on the basis of the merit of Christ.

It no longer is a sin that "rules" the Christian for it is itself "ruled" by Christ with whom the justified are bound in faith. In this life, then, Christians can in part lead a just life. Despite sin, the Christian is no longer separated from God, because in the daily return to baptism, the person who has been born anew by baptism and the Holy Spirit has this sin forgiven. Thus this sin no longer brings damnation and eternal death. Thus, when Lutherans say that justified persons are also sinners and that their opposition to God is truly sin, they do not deny that, despite this sin, they are not separated from God and that this sin is a "ruled" sin. In these affirmations, they are in agreement with Roman Catholics, despite the difference in understanding sin in the justified.

30. Catholics hold that the grace of Jesus Christ imparted in baptism takes away all that is sin "in the proper sense" and that is "worthy of damnation" (Rom 8.1). There does, however, remain in the person an inclination (concupiscence) which comes from sin and presses towards sin. Since, according to Catholic conviction, human sins always involve a personal element and since this element is lacking in this inclination, Catholics do not see this inclination as sin in an authentic sense. They do not thereby deny that this inclination does not correspond to God's original design for humanity and that it is objectively in contradiction to God and remains one's enemy in lifelong struggle. Grateful for deliverance by Christ, they underscore that this inclination in contradiction to God does not merit the punishment of eternal death and does not separate the justified person from God. But when individuals voluntarily separate themselves from God, it is not enough to return to observing the commandments, for they must receive pardon and peace in the sacrament of reconciliation through the word of forgiveness imparted to them in virtue of God's reconciling work in Christ.

4.5. Law and Gospel

31. We confess together that persons are justified by faith in the gospel "apart from works prescribed by the law" (Rom 3.28). Christ has fulfilled the law and by his death and resurrection has overcome it as a way to salvation. We also confess that God's commandments retain their validity for the justified and that Christ has by his teaching and example expressed God's will which is a standard for the conduct of the justified also.

32. Lutherans state that the distinction and right ordering of law and gospel is essential for the understanding of justification. In its theological use, the law is demand and accusation. Throughout their lives, all persons, Christians also, in that they are sinners, stand under this accusation which uncovers their sin so that,

in faith in the gospel, they will turn unreservedly to the mercy of God in Christ, which alone justifies them.

33. Because the law as a way to salvation has been fulfilled and overcome through the gospel, Catholics can say that Christ is not a lawgiver in the manner of Moses. When Catholics emphasize that the righteous are bound to observe God's commandments, they do not thereby deny that through Jesus Christ God has mercifully promised to his children the grace of eternal life.

4.6. Assurance of Salvation

34. We confess together that the faithful can rely on the mercy and promises of God. In spite of their own weakness and the manifold threats to their faith, on the strength of Christ's death and resurrection they can build on the effective promise of God's grace in word and sacrament and so be sure of this grace.

35. This was emphasized in a particular way by the Reformers: in the midst of temptation, believers should not look to themselves but look solely to Christ and trust only him. In trust in God's promise they are assured of their salvation, but are never secure looking at themselves.

36. Catholics can share the concern of the Reformers to ground faith in the objective reality of Christ's promise, to look away from one's own experience, and to trust in Christ's forgiving word alone (see Mt 16.19, 18.18). With the Second Vatican Council, Catholics state: to have faith is to entrust oneself totally to God, who liberates us from the darkness of sin and death and awakens us to eternal life. In this sense, one cannot believe in God and at the same time consider the divine promise untrustworthy. No one may doubt God's mercy and Christ's merit. Every person, however, may be concerned about his salvation when he looks upon his own weaknesses and shortcomings. Recognizing his own failures, however, the believer may yet be certain that God intends his salvation.

4.7. The Good Works of the Justified

37. We confess together that good works—a Christian life lived in faith, hope, and love—follow justification and are its fruits. When the justified live in Christ and act in the grace they receive, they bring forth, in biblical terms, good fruit. Since Christians struggle against sin their entire lives, this consequence of justification is also for them an obligation they must fulfill. Thus both Jesus and the apostolic Scriptures admonish Christians to bring forth the works of love.

38. According to Catholic understanding, good works, made possible by

grace and the working of the Holy Spirit, contribute to growth in grace, so that the righteousness that comes from God is preserved and communion with Christ is deepened. When Catholics affirm the "meritorious" character of good works, they wish to say that, according to the biblical witness, a reward in heaven is promised to these works. Their intention is to emphasize the responsibility of persons for their actions, not to contest the character of those works as gifts, or far less to deny that justification always remains the unmerited gift of grace.

39. The concept of a preservation of grace and a growth in grace and faith is also held by Lutherans. They do emphasize that righteousness as acceptance by God and sharing in the righteousness of Christ is always complete. At the same time, they state that there can be growth in its effects in Christian living. When they view the good works of Christians as the fruits and signs of justification and not as one's own "merits," they nevertheless also understand eternal life in accord with the New Testament as unmerited "reward" in the sense of the fulfillment of God's promise to the believer.

5. THE SIGNIFICANCE AND SCOPE OF THE CONSENSUS REACHED

40. The understanding of the doctrine of justification set forth in this declaration shows that a consensus in basic truths of the doctrine of justification exists between Lutherans and Catholics. In light of this consensus the remaining differences of language, theological elaboration and emphasis in the understanding of justification described in paragraphs 18 to 39 are acceptable. Therefore the Lutheran and the Catholic explications of justification are in their difference open to one another and do not destroy the consensus regarding the basic truths.

41. Thus the doctrinal condemnations of the sixteenth century, in so far as they relate to the doctrine of justification, appear in a new light. The teaching of the Lutheran churches presented in this declaration does not fall under the condemnations from the Council of Trent. The condemnations in the Lutheran confessions do not apply to the teaching of the Roman Catholic Church presented in this declaration.

42. Nothing is thereby taken away from the seriousness of the condemnations related to the doctrine of justification. Some were not simply pointless. They remain for us "salutary warnings" to which we must attend in our teaching and practice.

43. Our consensus in basic truths of the doctrine of justification must come to influence the life and teachings of our churches. Here it must prove itself. In this respect, there are still questions of varying importance which need further clarification. These include, among other topics, the relationship between the word of God

and church doctrine, as well as ecclesiology, ecclesial authority, church unity, ministry, the sacraments, and the relation between justification and social ethics. We are convinced that the consensus we have reached offers a solid basis for this clarification. The Lutheran churches and the Roman Catholic Church will continue to strive together to deepen this common understanding of justification and to make it bear fruit in the life and teaching of the churches.

44. We give thanks to the Lord for this decisive step forward on the way to overcoming the division of the church. We ask the Holy Spirit to lead us further towards that visible unity which is Christ's will.

Bibliography

Aalen, Leiv. 1981. "Confessio Augustana, 1530–1980: Jubilaeum oder Mausoleum? Zur Bedeutung des Schrifttheolgen Luther für die Augsburgische Konfession und das lutherische Bekenntnis." In *Luther und die Bekenntnisschriften* 1981, 20–45.

Abate, Eshetu. 1989. "Confessing Christ in the Apostles' Creed." *East Africa Journal of Evangelical Theology* 8/1:29–40.

Abramowski, Luise. 1975. "Die Synode von Antiochien 324/25 und ihr Symbol." *ZKG* 86/3: 356–66.

———. 1976. "Das Bekenntnis des Gregor Thaumaturgus bei Gregor von Nyssa und das Problem seiner Echtheit." *ZKG* 87/2–3:145–66.

Acta et scripta theologorum Wirtembergensium et Patriarchae Constantinopolitani D. Hieremiae quae utrique ab anno M.D.LXXVI. usque ad annum M.D. LXXXI. 1584. Wittenberg: Johannes Crato.

Afanas'ev, Nikolaj. 1931. *Provincialnija sobranija rimskoj imperii i vselenskie sobory* [Provincial gatherings of the Roman Empire and the ecumenical councils]. Belgrade: Zapiski Russkago Otdělný ottisk.

Ahlers, Rolf. 1986. *The Barmen Theological Declaration of 1934: The Archeology of a Confessional Text.* Lewiston, N.Y.: Edwin Mellen Press.

Ahlstrom, Sydney E. 1972. *A Religious History of the American People.* New Haven and London: Yale University Press.

Aktensammlung zur Geschichte der Berner-Reformation, 1521–1532. 1918–23. 2 vols. Edited by R. Steck and G. Tobler. Bern: K. J. Wyss Erben.

Alberigo, G. 1959. *I vescovi italiani al concilio di Trento (1545–47).* Florence: G. C. Sansoni.

———. 1988. "The Council of Trent." In *Catholicism in Early Modern History,* 211–26. Edited by John W. O'Malley. Saint Louis, Mo.: Center for Reformation Research.

———, ed. 1991. *Christian Unity: The Council of Ferrara-Florence, 1438/39–1989.* Bibliotheca Ephemeridum Theologicarum Lovaniensium, 97. Louvain: Peeters.

———. 1995. *Announcing and Preparing Vatican Council II: Toward a New Era in Catholicism.* English version edited by Joseph A. Komonchak. Maryknoll, N.Y.: Orbis.

Aldama, J. A. de. 1934. *El Simbolo Toledano I.* Analecta Gregoriana, 8. Rome: Pontificia Universitas Gregoriana.

Alexakis, Alexander. 1997. "Before the Lateran Council of 649: The Last Days of Herakleios the Emperor and Monotheletism." In *Synodus,* 93–101. Edited by Remigius Bäumer, Evangelos Chrysos, et al. Paderborn, Germany: Ferdinand Schöningh.

Alliance of Confessing Evangelicals. 1996. *The Cambridge Declaration.* [Anaheim, Calif.: Alliance of Confessing Evangelicals.]

Altaner, B., and A. Stuiber. 1978. *Patrologie: Leben Schriften und Lehre der Kirchenväter.* 8th ed. Freiburg: Herder.

Amato, Angelo. 1983. "La dimension 'thérapeutique' du sacrement de la pénitence dans la théologie et la praxis de l'Eglise greco-orthodoxe." *Revue des sciences philosophiques et théologiques* 67:233–54.

Anabaptism Revisited: Essays on Anabaptist/Mennonite Studies in Honor of C. J. Dyck. 1992. Edited by Walter Klaassen. Scottdale, Pa.: Herald Press.

Anderson, David, tr. 1980. *On the Holy Spirit by Basil of Caesarea.* Crestwood, N.Y.: Saint Vladimir's Seminary Press.

Andrews, Theodore. 1953. *The Polish National Catholic Church in America and Poland.* London: S.P.C.K.

Androutsos, Chrēstos. 1930. *Symbolikē ex epopseōs Orthodoxou.* [Symbolics from an Orthodox perspective]. 2d ed. Athens: Typois I. A. Aleuropoulou.

———. 1956. *Dogmatikē tēs Orthodoxou Anatolikēs Ekklēsias.* Athens: Aster.

Aoanan, Melanio La Guardia. 1996. *Pagkakaisa at Pagbabago: Ang Patotoo ng United Church of Christ in the Philippines.* Quezon City, Philippines: New Day Publishers.

The Apocryphal New Testament. 1993. Edited and translated by J. K. Elliott. Oxford: Oxford University Press.

The Apostolic Fathers. 1999. 3d ed. Edited and translated by J. B. Lightfoot and J. R. Harmer; updated and revised by Michael W. Holmes. Grand Rapids, Mich.: Baker Book House.

Applegate, Stephen H. 1981. "The Rise and Fall of the Thirty-Nine Articles: An Inquiry into the Identity of the Protestant Episcopal Church in the United States." *Historical Magazine of the Protestant Episcopal Church* 50/4:409–21.

Arens, Heribert. 1982. *Die christologische Sprache Leos des Grossen: Analyse des Tomus an den Patriarchen Flavian.* Freiburg: Herder.

Armand-Hugon, A., and G. Gonnet. 1953. *Bibliografia Valdese.* Torre Pellice, Italy: Tipografia Subalpina.

Armstrong, Maurice W., Lefferts A. Loetscher, and Charles A. Anderson, eds. 1956. *The Presbyterian Enterprise: Sources of American Presbyterian History.* Philadelphia: Westminster.

Arpee, Leon. 1909. *The Armenian Awakening: A History of the Armenian Church, 1820–1860.* Chicago: University of Chicago Press.

———. 1946. *A History of Armenian Christianity from the Beginning to Our Own Time.* New York: Armenian Missionary Association of America.

Arquillière, Henri Xavier. 1926. *Le plus ancien traite de l'Eglise: Jacques de Viterbe "De regimine christiano" (1301–1302). Etude des sources et edition critique.* Paris: Beauchesne.

Arx, Urs von. 1989. *Koinonia auf altkirchlicher Basis: Deutsche Gesamtausgabe der gemeinsamen Texte des orthodox-altkatholischen Dialogs 1975–1987 mit französischer und englischer Übersetzung.* Bern: n.p.

———. 1994. "Der ekklesiologische Charakter der Utrechter Union." *Internationale Kirchliche Zeitschrift* 84:20–61.

Ascough, Richard S. 1994. "An Analysis of the Baptismal Ritual of the Didache." *Studia Liturgica* 24/2:201–13.

Aston, Margaret. 1984. *Lollards and Reformers: Images and Literacy in Late Medieval England.* London: Hambledon Press.

———. 1987. "Wyclif and the Vernacular." In *From Ockham to Wyclif,* 281–330. Edited by Anne Hudson and Michael Wilks. Oxford: Basil Blackwell.

———, and Colin Richmond, eds. 1997. *Lollardy and the Gentry in the Later Middle Ages.* New York: St. Martin's Press.

Atkinson, James. 1983. "Luthers Beziehungen zu England." In Junghans 1983, 1:677–87.

Attwater, Donald. 1935. *The Catholic Eastern Churches*. Milwaukee, Wis.: Bruce Publishing.

Aturan ni Huria Kristen Batak Protestan (H.K.B.P.). 1962. Pearadja, Tarutung, Indonesia: H.K.B.P.

Audisio, Gabriel. 1989. *Les "Vaudois": Naissance, vie et mort d'une dissidence (XIIme–XVIme siècles)*. Turin: Albert Meynier.

Ayer, Joseph C. [1913] 1970. *A Source Book for Ancient Church History from theApostolic Age to the Close of the Conciliar Period*. Reprint, New York: AMS Press.

Azevedo, Marcello de C. 1985. "Basic Ecclesial Communities: A Meeting Point of Ecclesiologies." *Theological Studies* 46:601–20.

Backus, Irena. 1990. "Polemic, Exegetical Tradition, and Ontology: Bucer's Interpretation of John 6:52, 53, and 64 Before and After the Wittenberg Concord." In *The Bible in the Sixteenth Century*, 167–80. Edited by David C. Steinmetz. Durham, N.C.: Duke University Press.

———, and Claire Chimelli, eds. 1986. *"La vraie piété": Divers traités de Jean Calvin et Confession de foi de Guillaume Farel*. Geneva: Labor et Fides.

Bainton, Roland H. 1949. "Luther and the *via media* at the Marburg Colloquy." *Lutheran Quarterly* 1:394–98.

Baker, J. Wayne. 1988. "Church, State and Dissent: The Crisis of the Swiss Reformation, 1531–1536." *Church History* 57:135–52.

Bakhuizen van den Brink, J. N., ed. 1974. *Ratramnus, De corpore et sanguine Domini*. Amsterdam: North-Holland Publishing.

Balcomb, Raymond E. 1967. "United Presbyterian General Assembly." *Christian Century* 84:788–90.

Balić, Carolus. 1948. *Tractatus de immortalitate beatae virginis Mariae*. Rome: Academia Mariana.

Balmas, Enea, and Menascé, Esther. 1981. "L'opinione pubblica inglese e le 'Pasque Piemontesi': Nuovi documenti." *Bollettino della Società di Studi Valdesi* 150:3–26.

Balthasar, Hans Urs von, ed. 1984. *Sedet ad dexteram Patris*. Special issue of *Internationale Katholische Zeitschrift "Communio"* 13:1–34.

———. 1990. *Credo: Meditations on the Apostles' Creed*. Introduction by Medard Kehl; translated by David Kipp. New York: Crossroad.

Bangs, Carl. 1985. *Arminius: A Study in the Dutch Reformation*. 2d ed. Grand Rapids, Mich.: Asbury Press.

Baptism, Eucharist, and Ministry. 1982. Faith and Order Paper 111. 35th printing. Geneva: World Council of Churches Publications.

Barbour, Hugh Christopher. 1993. *The Byzantine Thomism of Gennadios Scholarios*. Vatican City: Libreria Editrice Vaticana.

Barclay, Robert. [1673]. *A Catechism and Confession of Faith*. Urie, Scotland: n.p.

———. 1857. *A Catechism and Confession of Faith*. Philadelphia: n.p.

Bardy, Gustave. 1926. "Saint Alexandre d'Alexandrie a-t-il connu la *Thalie* d'Arius?" *Revue des sciences religieuses* 6:527–32.

Baring, Georg. 1959. "Hans Denck und Thomas Müntzer in Nürnberg 1524." *ARG* 50:145–81.

Barker, William S. 1984. "Subscription to the Westminster Confession of Faith and Catechisms." *Presbyterion* 10/1-2:1-19.

———. 1994. "The Men and Parties of the Assembly." In Carson and Hall 1994, 47-61.

Bârlea, Octavian. 1948. *De Confessione Orthodoxa Petri Mohilae*. Frankfurt: Josef Knecht.

———. 1989. *Die Konzile des 13.-15. Jahrhunderts und die ökumenische Frage*. Wiesbaden: Harrassowitz.

Barnard, Leslie William. 1962. "The Problem of Saint Polycarp's Epistle to the Philippians." *Church Quarterly Review* 163:421-30.

———. 1967. *Justin Martyr: His Life and Thought*. Cambridge: Cambridge University Press.

———. 1974. *The Graeco-Roman and Oriental Background of the Iconoclastic Controversy*. Leiden: Brill.

———. 1980. "Marcellus of Ancyra and the Eusebians." *GOTR* 25:63-76.

———. 1983. *The Council of Serdica, 343 A.D.* Sofia: Synodal Publishing House.

———, tr. 1997. *St. Justin Martyr: The First and Second Apologia*. New York: Paulist Press.

Barnes, Michel R., and Daniel H. Williams, eds. 1993. *Arianism After Arius: Essays on the Development of the Fourth-Century Trinitarian Conflicts*. Edinburgh: T. and T. Clark.

Barnes, T. D. 1990. "The Consecration of Ulfila." *JTS* 41:541-45.

Barr, O. Sydney. 1964. *From the Apostles' Faith to the Apostles' Creed*. New York: Oxford University Press.

Barrus, Ben M., Milton L. Baughn, and Thomas H. Campbell. 1972. *A People Called Cumberland Presbyterians*. Memphis, Tenn.: Frontier Press.

Barth, Karl. 1948a. *Die christliche Lehre nach dem Heidelberger Katechismus*. Zurich: Evangelischer Verlag. [Translated, together with *Einführung in den Heidelberger Katechismus* (1960) in *The Heidelberg Catechism for Today*. London: Epworth Press, 1964.]

———. 1948b. *Credo: Die Hauptprobleme der Dogmatik dargestellt im Anschluss an das Apostolische Glaubensbekenntnis; 16 Vorlesungen, gehalten an der Universität Utrecht im Februar und März 1935*. Zöllikon, Switzerland: Evangelischer Verlag. [English translation by J. Strathearn McNab. New York: C. Scribner's Sons, 1936.]

———. 1953. *Dogmatique: La doctrine de la parole de Dieu*. Geneva: Labor et Fides.

———. 1959. *Protestant Thought from Rousseau to Ritschl*. Translated by Brian Cozens. Introduction by Jaroslav Pelikan. New York: Harper and Brothers.

Bate, Herbert Newell. 1928. *Faith and Order: Proceedings of the World Conference Lausanne, August 3-21, 1927*. Garden City, N.Y.: Doubleday.

Batiffol, P. 1925/1927. "Les sources de l'histoire du Concile de Nicée." *Echos d'Orient* 24:385-402, 26:5-17.

Bauer, Johannes B. 1995. *Die Polykarpbriefe*. Göttingen: Vandenhoeck und Ruprecht.

Bauman, Clarence, ed. and trans. 1991. *The Spiritual Legacy of Hans Denck*. Leiden: E. J. Brill.

Baumer, Franklin Le Van. 1960. *Religion and the Rise of Scepticism*. New York: Harcourt, Brace and World.

Bäumer, Remigius, ed. 1979. *Concilium Tridentinum*. Darmstadt: Wissenschaftliche Buchgesellschaft.

Baur, August. 1883. *Die erste Zürcher Disputation*. Halle: Niemeyer.

Bavaud, Georges. 1956. *La Dispute de Lausanne (1536): Une étape de l'évolution doctrinale de réformateurs romands*. Fribourg, Switzerland: Editions Universitaires.

Baxter, Anthony. 1989. "Chalcedon and the Subject of Christ." *Downside Review* 107:1-21.

Bayne, Stephen Fielding. 1960. *Ceylon, North India, Pakistan: A Study in Ecumenical Decision.* London: S.P.C.K., 1960.

Bays, Daniel H., ed. 1996. *Christianity in China: From the Eighteenth Century to the Present.* Stanford, Calif.: Stanford University Press.

Bazaar of Heraclides. 1925. Edited and translated by Godfrey Rolles Driver and Leonard Hodgson. Oxford: Clarendon Press.

Beaupère, René. 1979. "La réunion piénière de Foi et Constitution à Bangalore." *Istina* 24: 352-65, 391-412.

Beck, Hildebrand. 1937. *Vorsehung und Vorherbestimmung in der theologischen Literatur der Byzantiner.* Rome: Pontificale Institutum Orientalium Studiorum.

Becker, Karl Josef. 1967. *Die Rechtfertigungslehre nach Domingo de Soto: Das Denken eines Konzilstellnehmers vor, in und nach Trient.* Rome: Gregorian University.

Bedouelle, Guy. 1989. "L'eglise du Concile de Trente." In *Visages de l'eglise: Cours d'ecclésiologie,* 9-23. Edited by Patrick de Laubier. Fribourg, Switzerland: Editions Universitaires.

Beggiato, Fabrizio, ed. 1977. *Le lettere di Abelardo ed Eloisa nella traduzione di Jean de Meun.* Modena: S.T.E.M. Mucchi.

Békés, Gerard J., and Harding Meyer, eds. 1982. *Confessio fidei: International Ecumenical Colloquium, Rome, 3-8 November 1980.* Rome: Pontificio Ateneo S. Anselmo.

Benrath, Gustav Adolf. 1963. "Die Eigenart der Pfälzischen Reformation und die Vorgeschichte des Heidelberger Katechismus." *Heidelberger Jahrbuch* 7:13-32.

———. 1965. "Wyclif und Hus." *Zeitschrift für Theologie und Kirche* 62/2:196-216.

Bente, F. [1921] 1965. *Historical Introductions to the Symbolical Books of the Evangelical Lutheran Church.* Reprint, Saint Louis, Mo.: Concordia Publishing House.

Benz, Ernst. 1949. *Wittenberg und Byzanz: Zur Begegnung und Auseinandersetzung der Reformation und der Östlich-orthodoxen Kirche.* Marburg: L. Elwert-Gräfe und Unzer.

Berkhof, Hendrikus. 1963. "The Catechism in Historical Context" and "The Catechism as an Expression of Our Faith." In *Essays on the Heidelberg Catechism,* 76-92, 93-123. A collection of essays by Bard Thompson, Hendrikus Berkhof, Eduard Schweizer, and Howard Hageman. Philadelphia: United Church Press.

Bergman, Jerry. 1984. *Jehovah's Witnesses and Kindred Groups: A Historical Compendium and Bibliography.* New York: Garland.

Berryman, Phillip. 1986. "El Salvador: From Evangelization to Insurrection." In *Religion and Political Conflict in Latin America,* 58-78. Edited by Daniel H. Levine. Chapel Hill: University of North Carolina Press.

Bettenson, Henry Scowcroft, ed. 1963. *Documents of the Christian Church.* 2d ed. London; New York: Oxford University Press.

Bettenson, Henry Scowcroft, and Chris Maunder. 1999. *Documents of the Christian Church.* 3d ed. Edited by Chris Maunder. Oxford: Oxford University Press.

Beveridge, William. [1904] 1993. *A Short History of the Westminster Assembly.* Reprint, Greenville, S.C.: A Press.

Bicknell, E. J. 1955. *A Theological Introduction to the Thirty-Nine Articles of the Church of England.* 3d ed. revised by H. J. Carpenter. London: Longmans.

Biel, Pamela. 1991. *Doorkeepers at the House of Righteousness: Heinrich Bullinger and the Zurich Clergy, 1535-1575*. Bern: Peter Lang.

Bieler, Ludwig. 1986. *Studies on the Life and Legend of St. Patrick*. Edited by Richard Sharpe. London: Variorum Reprints.

Bienert, Wolfgang A. 1981. "The Significance of Athanasius of Alexandria for Nicene Orthodoxy." *Irish Theological Quarterly* 48:181-95.

Bierma, Lyle D. 1982. "Olevianus and the Authorship of the Heidelberg Catechism: Another Look." *Sixteenth Century Journal* 13:17-28.

Bindley, T. Herbert. 1950. *The Oecumenical Documents of the Faith*. 4th ed., revised by F. W. Green. London: Methuen.

Birnbaum, Philip, tr. 1977. *Daily Prayer Book*. New York: Hebrew Publishing.

Bitterman, M. G. F. 1973. "The Early Quaker Literature of Defense." *Church History* 42:203-28.

Bizer, Ernest. 1955-56. "Zum geschichtlichen Verständnis von Luthers Schmalkaldischen Artikeln." *ZKG* 67/1-2:61-92.

———. 1957. "Noch einmal: Die Schmalkaldischen Artikel." *ZKG* 68:287-94.

———. 1962. *Studien zur Geschichte des Abendmahlsstreits im 16. Jahrhundert*. Darmstadt: Wissenschaftliche Buchgesellschaft.

Blanke, Fritz. 1966. "Zwingli's 'Fidei Ratio' (1530)." *ARG* 57:96-102. Abbreviated form of introduction in *CR* 93/2:754-89.

———, and Immanuel Leuschner. 1990. *Heinrich Bullinger: Vater der reformierten Kirche*. Zurich: Theologischer Verlag.

Blankenship, Paul F. 1964. "The Significance of John Wesley's Abridgement of the Thirty-Nine Articles as Seen from His Deletions." *Methodist History* 3:34-47.

Blumhofer, Edith Waldvogel. 1993. *Restoring the Faith: The Assemblies of God, Pentecostalism, and American Culture*. Urbana: University of Illinois Press.

Board of Christian Education of the United Presbyterian Church of America. 1956. *The Confessional Statement and the Book of Government and Worship of the United Presbyterian Church of North America*. Pittsburgh, Pa.: Board of Christian Education of the United Presbyterian Church of North America.

Boase, T. S. R. 1933. *Boniface VIII*. London: Constable.

Boccassini, Daniela. 1984. "Il massacro dei Valdesi di Provenza per una rilettura." *Bollettino della Societa di Studi Valdesi* 154:59-73.

Boelens, Wim L. 1964. *Die Arnoldshainer Abendmahlsthesen: Die Suche nach einem Abendmahlskonsens in der Evangelischen Kirche in Deutschland, 1947-1957, und eine Würdigung aus katholischer Sicht*. Assen, Netherlands: Van Gorcum.

Boespflug, François, and Nicolas Lossky, eds. 1987. *Nicée II, 787-1987: Douze siècles d'images religieuses*. Paris: Editions du Cerf.

Boettner, Loraine. 1983. *The Reformed Faith*. Phillipsburg, Pa.: Presbyterian and Reformed Publishing.

Bogolepov, Aleksandr Aleksandrovich. 1963. "Which Councils Are Recognized as Ecumenical?" *Saint Vladimir's Seminary Quarterly* 7/2:54-72.

Boice, James Montgomery. 1996. *Here We Stand: A Call from Confessing Evangelicals*. Grand Rapids, Mich.: Baker Book House.

Boisvert, Robert G. 1964. *The Scheme of Church Union in Ceylon and the Problems It Presents to the Anglican Community*. Rome: Catholic Book Agency.

Bolink, Peter. 1967. *Towards Church Union in Zambia*. Franeker, Netherlands: T. Wever.

The Book of Confessions. Part I: The Constitution of the Presbyterian Church (U.S.A.). 1996. Louisville, Ky.: Office of the General Assembly.

Book of Worship: United Church of Christ. 1986. New York: United Church of Christ Office for Church Life and Leadership.

Bornkamm, Heinrich. 1952. *Martin Bucers Bedeutung für die europäische Reformationsgeschichte*. Schriften des Vereins für Reformationsgeschichte, 169. Gütersloh, Germany: C. Bertelsmann.

Botte, Bernard. 1984. *La tradition apostolique*. 2d ed. Paris: Editions du Cerf.

Bouman, Walter R. 1969. "The Gospel and the Smalcald Articles." *Concordia Theological Monthly* 40:407–18.

Bouwsma, William James. 1989. *John Calvin: A Sixteenth-Century Portrait*. New York: Oxford University Press.

Bovon-Thurneysen, Annegreth. 1973. "Ethik und Eschatologie im Philipperbrief des Polycarp von Smyrna." *Theologische Zeitschrift* 29:241–56.

Bowman, Robert M. 1991. *Understanding Jehovah's Witnesses: Why They Read the Bible the Way They Do*. Grand Rapids, Mich.: Baker Book House.

Bradow, Charles King. 1960. "The Career and Confession of Cyril Loukaris: The Greek Orthodox Church and Its Relations with Western Christians (1543–1638)." Ph.D. diss., Ohio State University.

Brady, Thomas A. 1973. "Jacob Sturm of Strasbourg and the Lutherans at the Diet of Augsburg, 1530." *Church History* 42/2:183–202.

Braekman, Emile-Michel. 1988. "Les interventions de Calvin." In *La Dispute de Lausanne* 1988, 170–77.

———, and J. F. Gilmont. 1971. "Les écrits de Guy de Brès: Editions des XVe et XVIIe siècles. *Annales. Société d'Histoire du Protestantisme Belge*, 5th ser., 8:265–75.

Braght, Thieleman J. van, comp. 1985. *The Bloody Theater or Martyrs Mirror*. Translated from the 1660 edition by Joseph F. Sohm. Scottdale, Pa.: Herald Press.

Brandi, Karl. 1965. *The Emperor Charles V*. London: J. Cape.

Brändle, Werner. 1989. "Hinabgestiegen in das Reich des Todes." *Kerygma und Dogma* 35:54–68.

Brandt, Caspar. 1908. *Life of James Arminius*. Translated by John Guthrie. Nashville, Tenn.: Publishing House of the Methodist Episcopal Church South.

Bray, Gerald. 1983. "The *filioque* Clause in History and Theology." *Tyndale Bulletin* 34:91–144.

Brecht, Martin. 1983. "Luthers Beziehungen zu den Oberdeutschen und Schweizern von 1530–1531 bis 1546." In Junghans 1983, 1:497–517.

———. 1985–93. *Martin Luther*. 3 vols. Translated by James L. Schaaf. Minneapolis, Minn.: Fortress Press.

———, and Reinhard Schwarz, eds. 1980. *Bekenntnis und Einheit der Kirche: Studien zum Konkordienbuch*. Stuttgart: Calwer Verlag.

———. 1990. *Martin Luther: Shaping and Defining the Reformation, 1521-1532*. Translated by James L. Schaaf. Minneapolis, Minn.: Fortress Press.

Bréhier, Louis. [1904] 1969. *La querelle des images (VIIIe-IXe siècles)*. Reprint, New York: Burt Franklin.

Brennecke, Hanns Christof. 1988. *Studien zur Geschichte der Homöer*. Tübingen: Mohr.

———. 1993. "Lukian von Antiochien in der Geschichte der arianischen Streites." In *Logos: Festschrift für Luise Abramowski*, 170-92. Edited by Hanns Christof Brennecke, Ernst Ludwig Grasmück, and Christoph Markschies. Beihefte zur Zeitschrift für die neutestamentliche Wissenschaft und die Kunde der älteren Kirche, 67. Berlin: W. de Gruyter.

Brent, Allen. 1992. "The Ignatian Epistles and the Threefold Ecclesiastical Order." *Journal of Religious History* 17:18-32.

———. 1995. *Hippolytus and the Roman Church in the Third Century: Communities in Tension Before the Emergence of a Monarch Bishop*. Leiden: E. J. Brill.

Bretscher, Paul M. 1959. "The Arnoldshain Theses on the Lord's Supper." *Concordia Theological Monthly* 30:83-91.

Brewer, Priscilla J. 1986. *Shaker Communities, Shaker Lives*. Hanover, N.H.: University Press of New England.

Brightman, F. E. 1896. *Liturgies, Eastern and Western, Being the Texts, Original or Translated, of the Principal Liturgies of the Church*. Edited with introductions and appendices on the basis of former work by C. E. Hammond. Oxford: Clarendon Press.

Brinton, Howard H. 1973. *The Religious Philosophy of Quakerism: The Beliefs of Fox, Barclay, and Penn as Based on the Gospel of John*. Wallingford, Pa.: Pendle Hill Publications.

Brost, Eberhard. 1979. *Abaelard: Die Leidensgeschichte und der Briefwechsel mit Heloisa*. Heidelberg: Lambert Scheider.

Brouwer, Christian. 1996. "Les condamnations de Bérenger de Tours (XIe siècle)." In *Le penseur, la violence, la religion*, 9-23. Edited by Alain Dierkens. Brussels: Editions de l'Université de Bruxelles.

Brown, G. Thompson. 1986. *Christianity in the People's Republic of China*. Atlanta, Ga.: John Knox Press.

Brown, Peter. 1973. "A Dark Age Crisis: Aspects of the Iconoclastic Controversy." *English Historical Review* 88:1-34.

Brown, Robert McAfee. 1979. "Confession of Faith of the Presbyterian-Reformed Church in Cuba, 1977." *Religion in Life* 48:268-82.

Brown, Thomas. [1812] 1977. *An Account of the People Called Shakers: Their Faith, Doctrines, and Practice*. Reprint, New York: AMS Press.

Bruckner, Aleksander. 1979. "The Polish Reformation in the Sixteenth Century." In *Polish Civilization*, 68-87. Edited by Mieczyslaw Giergielewicz and Ludwik Krzyzanowski. New York: New York University Press.

Brunner, Peter. 1963. "Die Rechtfertigungslehre des Konzils von Trient." In *Pro veritate: Ein theologischer Dialog*, 59-96. Edited by Edmund Schlink and Hermann Volk. Münster: Aschendorffsche Verlagsbuchhandlung.

Brüsewitz, J., and M. A. Krebber, eds. 1982. *Confessie van Dordrecht, 1632*. Introduction by Irvin B. Horst. Amsterdam: Doopgezinde Historische Kring.

Bucer, Martin. 1969. *Martin Bucers Deutsche Schriften*. Vol. 3. Edited by Bernd Moeller. Series editor, Robert Stupperich. Gütersloh, Germany: Gerd Mohn.

Bucke, Emory Stevens, ed. 1964. *History of American Methodism*. 3 vols. Nashville, Tenn.: Abingdon Press.

Buehrens, John A., ed. 1999. *The Unitarian Universalist Pocket Guide*. 3d ed. Boston: Skinner House Books.

Bunting, Ian D. 1966. "The *Consensus Tigurinus*." *Journal of Presbyterian History* 44:45–61.

Burchill, Christopher J. 1986. "On the Consolation of a Christian Scholar: Zacharias Ursinus (1534–1583) and the Reformation of Heidelberg." *Journal of Ecclesiastical History* 37/ 4:568–83.

Burckhardt, Paul. 1946. *Basel in den ersten Jahren nach der Reformation*. Basler Neujahrsblatt, 124. Basel: R. Reich.

Burckhardt-Biedermann, Thomas. 1896. "Zur Publikation des ersten Basler Glaubensbekenntnisses." *Anzeiger für schweizerische Geschichte, 359*.

Burg, B. R. 1974. "The Cambridge Platform: A Reassertion of Ecclesiastical Authority." *Church History* 43:470–87.

Burgess, Joseph A., ed. 1980. *The Role of the Augsburg Confession: Catholic and Lutheran Views*. Philadelphia: Fortress Press.

Burgess, Stanley M., and Gary B. McGee, eds. 1988. *Dictionary of Pentecostal and Charismatic Movements*. Grand Rapids, Mich.: Regency Reference Library.

Burgsmüller, Alfred, and Rudolf Weth, eds. 1983. *Die Barmer Theologische Erklärung: Einführung und Dokumentation*. Foreword by Eduard Lohse. Neukirchen-Vluyn, Germany: Neukirchener Verlag des Erziehungsvereins.

Burkhardt, C. A. H. 1879. *Geschichte der sächsischen Kirchen- und Schulvisitationen von 1524– 45*. Leipzig: F. W. Grunow.

Burn, Andrew Ewbank. 1906. *The Apostles' Creed*. New York: E. S. Gorham.

———. 1909. *Facsimiles of the Creeds from Early Manuscripts*. Paleographic notes by Ludwig Traube. London: Harrison and Sons.

———. 1925–26. "The Authorship of the *Quicumque Vult*." *JTS* 27:19–28.

———. 1930. *The Athanasian Creed*. London: Rivingtons.

———. [1896] 1967. *The Athanasian Creed and Its Early Commentaries*. Texts and Studies: Contributions to Biblical and Patristic Literature, 4/1. Reprint, Nendeln, Liechtenstein: Kraus Reprint.

Burnett, Charles S. F. 1986. "Confessio fidei ad Heloisam." *Mittellateinisches Jahrbuch* 21: 147–55.

Burrage, Champlin. 1906. *The True Story of Robert Browne (1550?-1633), Father of Congregationalism*. Oxford: Oxford University Press.

Bury, J. B. 1964. *History of the Papacy in the Nineteenth Century: Liberty and Authority in the Roman Catholic Church*. Augmented ed. New York: Schocken Books.

Büsser, Fritz. 1985. *Wurzeln der Reformation in Zürich: Zum 500ten Geburtstag des Reformators Huldrych Zwingli*. Leiden: E. J. Brill.

Butterworth, G. W., tr. 1966. *On First Principle, Being Koetschau's Text of the De principiis of Origen*. New York: Harper and Row.

Butterworth, Robert, ed. and tr. 1977. *Contra Noetum*. London: Heythrop College, University of London.

Bwalya, Musonda. 2000. "The Present State of Theological Education in Zambia: With a Focus on the United Church of Zambia." Presented at the United Church of Zambia Theological College Golden Jubilee Celebrations. Kitwe, Zambia, August 2000. Supplied by the author.

Calvin, John. 1926–59. *Opera Selecta*. 5 vols. Edited by Petrus Barth, Wilhelm Niesel, and Dora Scheuner. Munich: Kaiser.

Camelot, P.-Th. 1962. *Ephèse et Chalcédoine*. Mainz: Matthias-Grünewald-Verlag.

Camenisch, Emil. 1920. *Bündnerische Reformationsgeschichte*. Chur, Switzerland: Bischofberger und Hotzenköcherle.

Capelle, B. 1922. "La lettre d'Auxence sur Ulfila." *Revue Bénédictine* 34:224–33.

Capern, Amanda. 1991. "'Slipperye times and dangerous dayes': James Ussher and the Calvinist Reformation of Britain, 1560–1660." Ph.D. diss., University of New South Wales, 1991.

Cappuyns, M. 1934. "L'origine des 'Capitula' d'Orange 529." *Recherches de théologie ancienne et médiévale* 6:121–42.

Carcione, Filippo. 1985. "Enérgheia, Thélema, e Theokínetos nella lettera Sergio, Patriarca di Constantinopolim a Papa Onorio Primo." *Orientalia Christiana perodica* 51/2:263–76.

Cariño, Feliciano V., ed. 1987. *Like a Mustard Seed: Commentaries on the Statement of Faith of the United Church of Christ in the Philippines*. Quezon City, Philippines: United Church of Christ in the Philippines.

Carrington, Philip. 1940. *The Primitive Christian Catechism: A Study in the Epistles*. Cambridge: Cambridge University Press.

Carruthers, Samuel William. 1897. *The Shorter Catechism of the Westminster Assembly of Divines*. London: Publication Office of the Presbyterian Church of England.

———. 1957. *Three Centuries of the Westminster Shorter Catechism*. Fredericton: University of New Brunswick.

———. [1937] 1995. *The Westminster Confession of Faith*. Reprint, Greenville, S.C.: Reformed Academic Press.

Carson, John L., and David W. Hall, ed. 1994. *To Glorify and Enjoy God: A Commemoration of the 350th Anniversary of the Westminster Assembly*. Carlisle, Pa.: Banner of Truth Trust.

Cartellieri, A., and W. Stechele, eds. 1909. *Chronicon universale anonymi Laudunensis*. Leipzig: Dyksche Buchhandlung.

Carton, Raoul. 1930. "Le christianisme et l'Augustinisme de Boéce." *Revue de philosophie*, n.s., 1:573–659.

Caspar, E. 1932. "Die Lateransynod von 649." *ZKG* 51:75–137.

Caspari, C. P. [1866] 1964. *Ungedruckte, unbeachtete und wenig beachtete Quellen zur Geschichte des Taufsymbols und der Glaubensregel*. 3 vols. Reprint, Brussels: Culture et Civilisation.

Cather, Willa, and Georgine Milmine. 1993. *The Life of Mary Baker G. Eddy and the History of Christian Science*. Introduction and afterword by David Stouck. Lincoln: University of Nebraska Press.

Catto, Jeremy. 1987. "Some English Manuscripts of Wyclif's Latin Works." In *From Ockham to Wyclif,* 353–59. Edited by Anne Hudson and Michael Wilks. Studies in Church History, Subsidia, 5. Oxford: Basil Blackwell.

———. 1992. "Theology After Wycliffism." In *The History of the University of Oxford.* Volume 2 of *Late Medieval Oxford,* 263–80. Edited by J. I. Catto and T. A. R. Evans. Oxford: Clarendon Press.

Cavadini, John. 1993. *The Last Christology of the West: Adoptionism in Spain and Gaul, 785–820.* Philadelphia: University of Pennsylvania Press.

Cazacu, M. 1984. "Pierre Mohyla (Petru Movil) et la Roumanie: Essai historique et bibliographique." *Harvard Ukrainian Studies* 8:188–221.

Cegna, Romolo. 1982. *Fede ed etica Valdese nel Quattrocento.* Turin: Editrice Claudiana.

Chadwick, Henry. 1955. "Exile and Death of Flavian of Constantinople: A Prologue to the Council of Chalcedon." *JTS* 6:17–34.

———. 1958. "Ossius of Cordova and the Presidency of the Council of Antioch, 325." *JTS* 9:292–304.

———. 1965. "Justin Martyr's Defence of Christianity." *Bulletin of the John Rylands Library* 47:275–97.

———. 1966. *Early Christian Thought and the Classical Tradition: Studies in Justin, Clement, and Origen.* New York: Oxford University Press.

———. 1980. "The Authenticity of Boethius' Fourth Tractate *De fide catholica.*" *JTS,* n.s., 31:551–56.

———. 1981. *Boethius: The Consolations of Music, Logic, Theology, and Philosophy.* Oxford: Clarendon Press.

———. 1990. "Symbol and Reality: Berengar and the Appeal to the Fathers." In Ganz, Huygens, and Niewöhner 1990, 29–46.

Chao, Jonathan, ed. 1983. *Zhonggong yu Jidujiao de Zhengce* [Chinese Communist policy toward Christianity]. Hong Kong: Chinese Church Research Center.

———, and Richard Van Houten, interviewers. 1988. *Wise as Serpents, Harmless as Doves: Christians in China Tell Their Story.* Pasadena, Calif.: Chinese Church Research Center.

Chatzēantōniou, Georgios A. 1954. *Kyrillos Loukaris.* Athens: n.p.

Chenu, Marie-Dominique. 1964. *Toward Understanding Saint Thomas.* Translated by A.-M. Landry and D. Hughes. Chicago: Henry Regnery.

Chrestou, Panagiotes. 1982. "The Ecumenical Character of the First Synod of Constantinople, 381." *GOTR* 27:359–74.

Christensen, Carl C. 1984. "John of Saxony's Diplomacy, 1529–1530: Reformation or Realpolitik?" *Sixteenth Century Journal* 15/4:419–30.

Cicognani, A. G. 1951. "The Assumption—and Devotion to Mary in America." *Thomist* 14:22–30.

Clapsis, Emmanuel. 1982. "The *filioque* Question." *Patristic and Byzantine Review* 1/2:127–36.

Clark, Donald N. 1986. *Christianity in Modern Korea.* New York: University Press of North America.

Clark, E. A. 1992. *The Origenist Controversy.* Princeton, N.J.: Princeton University Press.

Cochrane, Arthur C. 1962. *The Church's Confession Under Hitler.* Philadelphia: Westminster Press.

Cochrane, Charles Norris. 1944. *Christianity and Classical Culture: A Study of Thought and Action from Augustus to Augustine.* London: Oxford University Press.

Codrington, H. W. 1952. *Studies of the Syrian Liturgies.* London: Coldwell.

Coggins, James R. 1986. "A Short Confession of Hans de Ries: Union and Separation in Early Seventeenth-Century Holland." *MQR* 60:128–38.

———. 1991. *John Smyth's Congregation: English Separatism, Mennonite Influence and the Elect Nation.* Scottdale, Pa.: Herald Press.

Colish, Marcia L. 1994. *Peter Lombard.* 2 vols. Leiden: E. J. Brill.

Comba, Emilio. 1889. *History of the Waldenses of Italy.* London: Truslove and Shirley.

Confesión de fe 1977 de la Iglesia Presbiteriana Reformada en Cuba. 1978. Havana: Editorial Orbe.

The Confession of Faith and the Eleven Great Principles of the Polish National Catholic Church. 1975. [Scranton, Pa.]: [Polish National Catholic Church].

Congar, Yves. 1972. "Reception as an Ecclesiological Reality." In *Election and Consensus in the Church,* 43–68. Edited by Giuseppe Alberigo and Anton Weiler. New York: Herder and Herder.

———. 1985. "De Marburg (1529) à Leuenberg (1971): Lutheriens et Reformes au temps de l'opposition et sur la voie d'une union." *Istina* 30:47–65.

Constantelos, Demetrios J. 1962–63. "Justinian and the Three Chapters Controversy." *GOTR* 8/1–2:71–94.

———. 1982. "Toward the Convocation of the Second Ecumenical Synod." *GOTR* 27:395–405.

Constitution and Bylaws of the United Church of Christ in the Philippines. 1996. [Quezon City], Phillipines: United Church of Christ in the Philippines.

Constitution and Discipline for the American Yearly Meetings of Friends. 1925. Boston: Permanent Board of the Yearly Meeting of the Friends for New England.

Constitution and Laws of the Polish National Church. 1991. Scranton, Pa.: Polish National Catholic Church.

Constitution, Rules and Regulations of the United Church of Zambia. 1994. Kitwe, Zambia: United Church Publications.

Conzemius, Victor. 1969. *Katholizismus ohne Rom: Die altkatholische Kirchengemeinschaft.* Zurich: Benziger.

Cook, William R. 1973. "John Wyclif and Hussite Theology, 1415–1436." *Church History* 42:335–49.

———. 1975. "The Eucharist in Hussite Theology." *ARG* 66:23–35.

Corpus juris canonici. [1879] 1959. 2 vols. Edited by E. Friedberg. Reprint, Graz: Akademische Druck- u. Verlagsanstalt.

Corwin, Virginia. 1960. *St. Ignatius and Christianity in Antioch.* New Haven: Yale University Press.

Countryman, L. William. 1974. "Monothelite Kontakion of the Seventh Century." *GOTR* 19:23–36.

———. 1982. "Tertullian and the Regula Fidei." *Second Century* 2/4:208–27.

Courvoisier, Jaques. 1944. *La confession helvétique postérieure: Texte français de 1566.* Neuchâtel: Editions Delachaux et Niestlé.

Cowan, Ian Borthwick. 1982. *The Scottish Reformation: Church and Society in Sixteenth-Century Scotland.* New York: St. Martin's Press.

Crabbe, Anna M. 1981. "The Invitation List to the Council of Ephesus and Metropolitan Hierarchy in the Fifth Century." *JTS* 32:369-400.

Creed and Constitution of the Cumberland Presbyterian Church. 1892. Nashville, Tenn.: Cumberland Presbyterian Publishing House.

Creighton, Mandell. 1901-2. "Introductory Note." *The Cambridge Modern History,* 1:1-6. Cambridge: Cambridge University Press.

Cross, Frank Leslie. 1939. "The Council of Antioch, AD 325." *Church Quarterly Review* 128: 49ff.

———, ed. [1960] 1986. *St. Cyril of Jerusalem's Lectures on the Christian Sacraments: The Procatechesis and the Five Mystagogical Catecheses.* Translated by R. W. Church. Reprint, Crestwood, N.Y.: Saint Vladimir's Seminary Press.

Crouzel, Henri. 1971. *Bibliographie critique d'Origèneis. Instrumenta Patristica,* 8 and 8A. Supplement published in 1982. Steenbrugge, Netherlands: Abbey of St. Peter, and The Hague: Nijhoff.

———. 1980. "La cristologia in Gregorio Taumaturgo." *Gregorianum* 61/4:745-55.

———. 1989. *Origen.* Translated by A. S. Worrall. San Francisco: Harper and Row.

Cullmann, Oscar. 1949. *The Earliest Christian Creeds.* Translated by J. K. S. Reid. London: Lutterworth.

Curtius, Ernst Robert. 1953. *European Literature and the Latin Middle Ages.* Translated from the German by Willard R. Trask. New York: Pantheon Books.

Daily Prayer Book [Ha-Siddur Ha-Shalem]. 1977. Translated by Philip Birnbaum. New York: Hebrew Publishing.

Daley, Brian E. 1998. *On the Dormition of Mary: Early Patristic Homilies.* Crestwood, N.Y.: Saint Vladimir's Seminary Press.

Davey, Colin. 1987. *Pioneer for Unity: Metrophanes Kritopoulos (1589-1639) and Relations Between the Orthodox, Roman Catholic and Reformed Churches.* London: British Council of Churches.

Davies, Andrew A. 1979. "The Marburg Colloquy." In *Union and Communion,* 92-101. Edited by Philip H. Eveson et al. London: Westminster Conference.

Davis, J. F. 1982. "Lollardy and the Reformation in England." *ARG* 73:217-36.

Davis, Leo Donald. 1987. *The First Seven Ecumenical Councils (325-787).* Wilmington, Del.: Michael Glazer.

Dawley, Powel Mills. 1954. *John Whitgift and the English Reformation.* New York: Scribner.

DeClercq, V. C. 1954. *Ossius of Cordova: A Contribution to the History of the Constantinian Period.* Washington, D.C.: Catholic University of America Press.

DeFerrari, Roy J, tr. [1957] 2002. *The Sources of Catholic Dogma: From the Thirtieth Edition of Henry Denzinger's Enchiridion Symbolorum.* Reprint, Fitzwilliam, N.H.: Loreto Publications.

Definite Platform, Doctrinal and Disciplinarian, for Evangelical Lutheran District Synods: Construed in Accordance with the Principles of the General Synod. 1856. 2d ed. Philadelphia: Miller and Burlock.

Dehandschutter, Boudewijn. 1989. "Polycarp's Epistle to the Philippians: An Early Example of 'Reception.'" In *The New Testament in Early Christianity*, 275–91. Edited by J. M. Sevrin. Leuven: Leuven University Press.

De Jong, Peter Y., ed. 1968. *Crisis in the Reformed Churches: Essays in Commemoration of the Great Synod of Dort, 1618–19*. Grand Rapids, Mich.: Reformed Fellowship.

Delagneau, G. 1931. "Le Concil de Sens de 1140: Abélard et Saint Bernard." *Revue apologétique* 52:385–408.

Delius, Hans Ulrich. 1983. "Die Marburger Artikel, 1529." In *Martin Luther Studienausgabe*, 3:463–76. Berlin: Evangelische Verlagsanstalt.

Deluz, René, and Henri Meylan. 1936. *La Dispute de Lausanne (Octobre 1536)*. Lausanne: Bibliothèque de la Faculté de Théologie.

DeSimone, Russell J. 1970. *The Treatise of Novatian the Roman Presbyter on the Trinity*. Studia Ephemeridis Augustinianum, 4. Rome: Institutum Patristicum Augustinianum.

Dewar, Michael Willoughby. 1992. "The British Delegation at the Synod of Dort: Assembling and Assembled, Returning and Returned." *Churchman* 106/2:130–46.

Dewart, Leslie. 1966. *The Future of Belief: Theism in a World Come of Age*. New York: Herder and Herder.

de Zwaan, J. 1933. "Date and Origin of the Epistle of the Eleven Apostles." In *Amicitiae Corolla*, 344–55. Edited by H. G. Wood. London: University of London Press.

Diekamp, Franz. 1899. *Die Origenistischen Streitigkeiten im sechsten Jahrhundert und das fünfte allgemeine Concil*. Münster: Aschendorff.

Dieter, Hans Jörg. 1991. *Leben wie es Gott gefällt: Confessio Taboritarum von 1434*. Berlin: Alektor Verlag.

Dinkha, K. Mar. 1994. "A Common Christological Declaration Between the Roman Catholic Church and the Assyrian Church of the East." *Ecumenical Trends* 23:173–74.

Discipline of the Korean Methodist Church [Korean]. 1931. Seoul: General Board of the Korean Methodist Church.

Discipline of the Korean Methodist Church. 1932. Translated by E. M. Cable. Seoul: General Board of the Korean Methodist Church.

La Dispute de Lausanne, 1536: La théologie réformée après Zwingli et avant Calvin. 1988. Edited by Eric Junod. Bibliothèque historique vaudoise, 90. [Proceedings of the Colloque international sur la Dispute de Lausanne, 1986.] Lausanne: Presses Centrales Lausanne.

Dix, Gregory, ed. and tr. 1992. *The Treatise on the Apostolic Tradition of St. Hippolytus of Rome*. Reissued with corrections, preface, and bibliography by Henry Chadwick. London: S.P.C.K.

Doctrines and Discipline of the Free Methodist Church. 1866. Rochester, N.Y.: General Conference.

Dods, Marcus. 1883. *The Works of Aurelius Augustine*. Volume 9: *On Christian Doctrine; The Enchiridion; On Catechising and On Faith and The Creed*. Edinburgh: T. and T. Clark.

Donaldson, Gordon. 1960. *The Scottish Reformation*. Cambridge: Cambridge University Press.

Dondaine, A. 1946. "Aux orignines du valdéisme: Une profession de foi de Valdès." *Archivum Fratrum Praedicatorum* 16:191–235.

Donfried, Karl P. 2000. "Augsburg, 1999: By Grace Alone, Some Reflections by a Participant." *Pro Ecclesia* 9/1:5–7.

Dowey, Edward A. 1966. "Der theologische Aufbau des Zweiten Helvetischen Bekennt- nisses." In *Glauben und Bekennen: Vierhundert Jahre Confessio Helvetica Posterior*, 205-34. Edited by Joachim Staedtke. Zurich: Zwingli Verlag.

———. 1968. *A Commentary on the Confession of 1967 and an Introduction to the Book of Confessions.* Philadelphia: Westminster Press.

Drickamer, John M. 1982. "The Religion of 'The Large Catechism.'" *Concordia Journal* 8:139-42.

Duensing, Hugo. 1925. *Epistula Apostolorum.* Kleine Texte für Vorlesungen und Übungen, 152. Bonn: Marcus and Weber.

Duggan, Paul E. 1989. *The Assumption Dogma: Some Reactions and Ecumenical Implications in the Thought of English-Speaking Theologians.* [Cleveland, Ohio: Emerson Press].

Dugmore, C. W. 1980. "Foundation Documents of the Faith, VI: The Thirty-Nine Articles." *Expository Times* 91:164-67.

Duke, Alastair. 1990. *Reformation and Revolt in the Low Countries.* London: Hambledon Press.

Dulles, Avery. 1980. "The Augsburg Confession and Contemporary Catholicism." In Burgess 1980, 131-38.

———. 1998. "Two Languages of Salvation: The Lutheran-Catholic Joint Declaration." *First Things* 98:25-30.

Dummville, David N., ed. 1993. *Saint Patrick, A.D. 493-1993.* Rochester, N.Y.: Boydell Press.

Duval, André. 1985. *Des Sacrements au Concile de Trente.* Paris: Editions du Cerf.

Dvornik, Francis. 1948. *The Photian Schism, History and Legend.* Cambridge: Cambridge University Press.

———. 1958. *The Idea of Apostolicity in Byzantium and the Legend of the Apostle Andrew.* Cambridge, Mass.: Harvard University Press.

———. 1970. *Byzantine Missions Among the Slavs: SS. Constantine-Cyril and Methodius.* New Brunswick, N.J.: Rutgers University Press.

Dwight, H. G. O. 1854. *Christianity in Turkey: A Narrative of the Protestant Reformation in the Armenian Church.* London: J. Nesbit.

Dyck, C. J. 1964. "A Short Confession of Faith by Hans de Ries." *MQR* 38:5-19.

———, ed. 1993. *An Introduction to Mennonite History: A Popular History of the Anabaptists and the Mennonites.* Scottdale, Pa.: Herald Press.

Ebel, Jobst Christian. 1978. "Jacob Andreae (1528-1590) als Verfasser der Konkordienfor- mel." *ZKG* 89/1-2:78-119.

———. 1980. "Die Herkunft des Konzeptes der Konkordienformel: Die Funktionen der 5 Verfasser neben Andreae beim Zustandekommen der Formel." *ZKG* 91/2-3:237-82.

———. 1981. *Wort und Geist bei den Verfassern der Konkordienformel.* Munich: Kaiser.

Eberhard, Winifried. 1981. *Konfessionsbildung und Stände in Böhmen, 1478-1530.* Munich: R. Oldenbourg.

Eck, Johannes. 1530. *Repulsio articulorum Zwinglii Ceas. Maiestati oblatorum.* [Augsburg: Alexander Weissenhorn].

Ecumenical Creeds and Reformed Confessions. 1988. Grand Rapids, Mich.: CRC Publications.

Eddy, Mary Baker. 1906. *Manual of the Mother Church, The First Church of Christ, Scientist in Boston, Massachusetts.* Boston: J. Armstrong.

————. 1906. *Science and Health, with Key to the Scriptures.* Boston: Joseph Armstrong.

Eeg-Olofsson, Ansgar. 1954. *The Conception of the Inner Light in Robert Barclay's Theology.* Lund, Sweden: C. W. K. Gleerup.

Eells, Hastings. 1931. *Martin Bucer.* New Haven: Yale University Press.

Ehrenström, Nils, and Günther Gassmann. 1979. *Confessions in Dialogue: Survey of Bilateral Conversations Among World Confessional Families.* 4th ed. Geneva: World Council of Churches.

Ehrhardt, A. A. T. 1964. "Judaeo-Christians in Egypt: The *Epistula Apostolorum* and the Gospel to the Hebrews." *Studia Evangelica* 3, 360–82. Edited by F. L. Cross. [2d International Conference on New Testament Studies, Oxford.] Berlin: Akademie-Verlag.

Eichenseer, Caelestis. 1960. *Das Symbolum apostolicum beim heiligen Augustinus: Mit Berücksichtigung des dogmengeschichtlichen Zusammenhangs.* Kirchengeschichtliche Quellen und Studien, 4. St. Ottilien, Germany: EOS.

Eire, Carlos M. N. 1986. *War Against the Idols: The Reformation of Worship from Erasmus to Calvin.* Cambridge: Cambridge University Press.

Elbogen, Ismar. [1931] 1962. *Der jüdische Gottesdienst in seiner geschichtlichen Entwicklung.* 3d ed. Reprint, Hildesheim: Georg Olms.

Elliger, Walter. 1931. "Zur bilderfeindlichen Bewegung des achten Jahrhunderts." In *Forschungen zur Kirchengeschichte und zur christlichen Kunst,* 40–60. Festschrift für Johannes Ficker. Edited by Walter Elliger. Leipzig: Dieterich.

Elliott, J. K. 1993. *The Apocryphal New Testament.* Oxford: Clarendon Press.

Encyclical Epistle of the One Holy Catholic and Apostolic Church, to the Faithful Everywhere: Being a Reply to the Epistle of Pius IX to the Easterns, Dated January 6, 1848. 1867. Papers of the Russo-Greek Committee of the Orthodox Eastern Church, 2d ser., no. 1. New York: John F. Trow.

Endriss, J. 1931. *Das Ulmer Reformationsjahr 1531 in seinem entscheidenen Vorgängen.* Ulm: K. Höhn.

Erickson, Scott E., ed. 1996. *American Religious Influences in Sweden.* Uppsala: Svenska kyrkans forskningsråd och fösfattarna.

Esbroeck, Michel van. 1989. "The Credo of Gregory the Wonderworker and Its Influence Through Three Centuries." In *Studia Patristica,* 19: *Historica, Theologica, Gnostica, Biblica et Apocrypha* [Tenth International Conference on Patristic Studies, Oxford, 1987], 255–66. Edited by Elizabeth A. Livingstone. Louvain: Peeters.

Esser, Helmut Hans. 1992. "Die Stellung des 'Summaire' von Guillaume Farel innerhalb der frühen reformierten Bekenntnisschriften." In *Reformiertes Erbe: Festschrift für Gottfried W. Locher zu seinem 80. Geburtstag,* 92–114. Edited by Heiko A. Oberman, Ernst Saxer, et al. Zurich: Theologischer Verlag Zurich.

Essig, K.-G. 1986. "Erwägungen zum geschichtlichen Ort der Apologie des Aristides." *ZKG* 97:163–88.

Ettlinger, Gerard H. 1982. "The Holy Spirit in the Theology of the Second Ecumenical Synod and in the Undivided Church." *GOTR* 27:431–40.

Eutudjian, Stepan. 1914. *Dzakoumn yev Entazn Avedaranagan Ee Hais.* Constantinople: Arax Press.

Evans, G. R., and J. Robert Wright, eds. 1991. *The Anglican Tradition: A Handbook of Sources.* London: S.P.C.K.; Minneapolis, Minn.: Fortress Press.

Ewing, John W. 1946. *Goodly Fellowship: A Centenary Tribute to the Life and Work of the World's Evangelical Alliance, 1846-1946.* London: Marshall, Morgan, and Scott.

Eynde, Damien van den. 1933. *Les normes de l'enseignement chrétien dans la littérature patristique des trois premiers siècles.* Gembloux, Belgium: J. Duculot; Paris: Gabalda et Fils.

Fagley, Frederick L., and Henry Wilder Foote. 1948. *The Cambridge "Platform of Church Discipline," 1648.* Boston: Joint Commission of the Congregational Christian Churches of the United States and the American Unitarian Association.

Farel, Guillaume. 1980. *Sommaire et brève déclaration, 1525.* Edited by Arthur L. Hofer. Neuchâtel: Editions Belle Rivière.

Fasciculi Zizaniorum magistri Johannis Wyclif cum tritico [1858] 1965. Attributed to Thomas Netter. Edited by Walter Waddington Shirley. Reprint, Wiesbaden: Kraus.

Fatio, Olivier, ed. 1986. *Confessions et Catechismes de la foi Reformée.* Paris: Labor et Fides.

Fenlon, Dermot. 1980. "Foundation Documents of the Faith, V: The Tridentine Profession of Faith [1564]." *Expository Times* 91:133-37.

Ferm, Vergilius Ture Anselm, ed. 1945. *An Encyclopedia of Religion.* New York: Philosophical Library.

Festugière, André J., ed. 1982. *Ephèse et Chalcédoine: Actes des conciles.* Paris: Beauchesne.

Fiangonan' i Jesoa Kristy eto Madagasikara. 1968. Antananarivo, Madagascar: F.J.K.M. Imarivolanitra.

Flavian. 1903. *Appellatio Flaviani: The Letters of Appeal from the Council of Ephesus, 449, Addressed by Flavian and Eusebius to St. Leo of Rome.* Edited by T. A. Lacey. London: S.P.C.K.

Florovsky, Georges. 1972-89. *Collected Works of Georges Florovsky.* 14 vols. Belmont, Mass.: Nordland Publishing.

Ford, Alan. 1996. "The Origins of Irish Dissent." In *The Politics of Irish Dissent, 1650-1800,* 9-30. Edited by Kevin Herlihy. Dublin: Four Courts Press.

————. 1997. *The Protestant Reformation in Ireland, 1590-1641.* 2d ed. Dublin: Four Courts Press.

Förstmann, Karl Eduard, ed. [1833] 1966. *Urkundenbuch zu der Geschichte des Reichstages zu Augsburg im Jahre 1530.* Reprint, Osnabrück, Germany: Biblio Verlag.

Frank, Franz Hermann Reinhold. 1858-65. *Die Theologie der Concordienformel historischdogmatisch entwickelt und beleuchtet.* 4 vols. Erlangen, Germany: T. Blaesing.

Frank, G. L. C. 1991. "The Council of Constantinople II as a Model Reconciliation Council." *Theological Studies* 52:636-50.

Freeman, Ann. 1957. "Theodulf of Orleans and the *Libri Carolini.*" *Speculum* 32:663-70.

————. 1965. "Further Studies in the *Libri Carolini:* I. Palaeographical Problems in Vaticanus Latinus 7207, II." *Speculum* 40:203-89.

————. 1994. "Scripture and Images in the Libri Carolini." In *Testo e immagine nell'altomedioevo,* 1:163-95. Edited by Giovanni Tabacco et al. Spoleto: Centro Italiano di Studi sull'Alto Medioevo.

Frei, Hans W. 1974. *The Eclipse of Biblical Narrative: A Study in Eighteenth- and Nineteenth-Century Hermeneutics.* New Haven and London: Yale University Press.

Frend, W. H. C. 1972. *The Rise of the Monophysite Movement*. Cambridge: Cambridge University Press.

———. 1991. *The Early Church: From the Beginnings to 461*. 3d ed. London: SCM Press.

Friedmann, Robert. 1931-32. "Eine dogmatische Hauptschrift der hutterischen Täufergemeinschaften in Mähren." *ARG* 28:80-111, 207-41, 29:1-17.

———. 1942. "The Schleitheim Confession (1527) and Other Doctrinal Writings of the Swiss Brethren in a Hitherto Unknown Edition." *MQR* 16/2:82-87.

Fries, Paul R., and Tiran Nersoyan, eds. 1987. *Christ in East and West*. Macon, Ga.: Mercer University Press.

Froehlich, Karlfried. 1992. "The Libri Carolini and the Lessons of the Iconoclastic Controversy." In *The One Mediator, the Saints, and Mary*, 193-208. Edited by H. George Anderson, J. Francis Stafford, and Joseph A. Burgess. Lutherans and Catholics in Dialogue, 8. Minneapolis, Minn.: Augsburg Publishing House.

Froidevaux, L. 1929. "Le Symbole de Saint Grégoire le Thaumaturge." *Recherches de science religieuse* 19:193-247.

Froom, LeRoy Edwin. 1946-54. *The Prophetic Faith of Our Fathers: The Historical Development of Prophetic Interpretation*. 4 vols. Washington, D.C.: Review and Herald.

Frost, Francis. 1975. "Le Concile de Trente et la doctrine protestante." In *Culpabilité fondamentale: Péché originel et anthropologie moderne*, 80-105. Edited by Paul Guilluy. Gembloux, Belgium: J. Duculot; Lille: Centre des Facultés Catholiques.

Fudge, Thomas A. 1998. *The Magnificent Ride: The First Reformation in Hussite Bohemia*. St. Andrews Studies in Reformation History. Aldershot, England: Ashgate.

Funk, F. X. 1901. *Das Testament unseres Herrn und die verwandten Schriften*. Mainz: Kirchheim.

Furcha, E. J., trans. 1984. *The Defense of the Reformed Faith*. Volume 1 of *Huldrych Zwingli: Writings*. Allison Park, Pa.: Pickwick Publications.

Gäbler, Ulrich. 1979. "Das Zustandekommen des Consensus Tigurinus im Jahre 1549." *Theologische Literatur-Zeitung* 104:321-32.

———. 1983a. *Huldrych Zwingli: Eine Einführung in sein Leben und sein Werk*. Munich: Beck.

———. 1983b. "Luthers Beziehungen zu den Schweizern und Oberdeutschen von 1526 bis 1530-31." In Junghans 1983, 1:481-96.

Gaffney, Declan. 1989. "The Practice of Religious Controversy in Dublin, 1600-1641." In *The Churches, Ireland and the Irish*, 145-58. Edited by William J. Sheils and Diana Wood. Studies in Church History, 25. Oxford: Blackwell.

Galbreath, Paul. 1996. "The Apostles' Creed in Liturgy." *Reformed Liturgy and Music* 30/4:189-92.

Galot, Jean. 1989. "Une seule personne, une seule hypostase: Origine et sens de la formule de Chalcédoine." *Gregorianum* 70:251-76.

Gams, Pius Bonifatius. [1862-79] 1956. *Die Kirchengeschichte von Spanien*. Reprint, Graz: Akademische Druck- u. Verlagsanstalt.

Ganz, Peter, R.B. C. Huygens, and Friedrich Niewöhner, eds. *Auctoritas und Ratio: Studien zu Berengar von Tours*. Wiesbaden: Harrassowitz.

Ganzer, Klaus. 1985. "Das Konzil von Trient und die theologische Dimension der katholischen Konfessionalisierung." In *Die katholische Konfessionalisierung: Wissenschaftliche*

Symposion der Gesellschaft zur Herausgabe des Corpus Catholicorum und des Vereins für Reformationsgeschichte, 50–69. Edited by Wolfgang Reinhard and Heinz Schilling. Münster: Aschendorff.

Garegin II, Catholicos of Cilicia. 1965. *The Council of Chalcedon and the Armenian Church.* London: S.P.C.K.

Garfiel, Evelyn. 1989. *Service of the Heart: A Guide to the Jewish Prayer Book.* Northvale, N.J.: Jason Aronson.

Garrison, Winfred Ernest, and Alfred T. DeGroot. 1958. *The Disciples of Christ: A History.* Saint Louis, Mo.: Bethany Press.

Gassmann, Günther. 1985. "Towards Common Confession of Apostolic Faith: Ecumenical Investigation into Fundamentals of Faith." *Centro Pro Unione Bulletin* 28:38–44.

———. 1988. "100 Jahre Lambeth-Quadrilateral: Die anglikanische Einheitscharta und ihre ökumenische Wirkung." *Ökumenische Rundschau* 37:301–11.

Gaudemet, Jean, and Brigitte Basdevant-Gaudemet. 1989. *Les Canons des Conciles Mérovingiens (VIe–VIIe siècles).* Paris: Editions du Cerf.

Gauss, J. 1940. "Die Dictatusthesen Gregors VII. als Unionsforderungen: Ein historischer Erklärungsversuch." *Zeitschrift der Savigny-Stiftung für Rechtsgeschichte.* Kanonistische Abteilung, 29:1–115.

Geanakoplos, Deno J. 1966. "The Council of Florence (1438–39) and the Problem of Union Between the Byzantine and Latin Churches." In *Byzantine East and Latin West: Two Worlds of Christendom in Middle Ages and Renaissance; Studies in Ecclesiastical and Cultural History,* 84–109. New York: Harper Torchbooks.

———. 1982. "The Second Ecumenical Synod of Constantinople (381): Proceedings and Theology of the Holy Spirit." *GOTR* 27:407–29.

Gee, Henry, and William John Hardy. 1896. *Documents Illustrative of English Church History.* London: Macmillan.

Geisberg, Max. 1923. "Cranach's Illustrations to the Lord's Prayer and the Editions of Luther's Catechism." *Burlington Magazine* 43:84–87.

George, Timothy. 1988. "John Calvin and the Agreement of Zurich (1549)." In *Calvin Studies* 4, 25–40. Edited by W. Stacy Johnson and John H. Leith. Davidson, N.C.: Davidson College.

———, and Denise George, eds. 1996. *Baptist Confessions, Covenants, and Catechisms.* Nashville, Tenn.: Broadman and Holman.

Georgi, Curt Robert Armin. 1940. *Die Confessio Dosithei (Jerusalem 1672): Geschichte, Inhalt und Bedeutung.* Munich: Ernst Reinhardt.

Gerhardsson, Birger. 1992. "The Shema in Early Christianity." In *The Four Gospels,* 1:275–93. Festschrift for Frans Neirynck. Edited by Frans van Segbroeck, Christopher M. Tuckett, et al. Bibliotheca Ephemeridum Theologicarum Lovaniensium, 100. Louvain: Peeters.

Gero, Stephen. 1973a. *Byzantine Iconoclasm During the Reign of Leo III, with Particular Attention to the Oriental Sources.* Louvain: Corpus Scriptorum Christianorum Orientalium.

———. 1973b. "Libri Carolini and the Image Controversy." *GOTR* 18:7–34.

———. 1977. *Byzantine Iconoclasm During the Reign of Constantine V, with Particular Attention to the Oriental Sources.* Louvain: Corpus Scriptorum Christianorum Orientalium.

Ghellinck, Joseph de. 1946. *Les recherches sur les origines du symbole des apôtres.* Volume 1 of *Patristique et moyen âge: Etudes d'histoire littéraire et doctrinale.* Museum Lessianum. Section historique, 6. Gembloux, Belgium: J. Duculot.

Giakalis, Ambrosios. 1994. *Images of the Divine: The Theology of Icons at the Seventh Ecumenical Council.* Leiden: E. J. Brill.

Gibbon [1776-88] 1896-1900. *The History of the Decline and Fall of the Roman Empire.* Edited by J. B. Bury. 7 vols. London: Methuen.

Gibellini, Rosino, ed. 1979. *Frontiers of Theology in Latin America.* Translated by J. Drury. Maryknoll, N.Y.: Orbis Books.

Gibson, Margaret T., ed. 1981. *Boethius: His Life, Thought and Influence.* Oxford: Blackwell.

Giet, Stanislas. 1955. "Saint Basile et le Concile de Constantinople de 360." *JTS* 6:94-99.

Gil, Juan. 1973. *Corpus Scriptorum Muzarabicorum.* 2 vols. Madrid: Instituto Antonio de Nebrija.

Gill, Joseph. 1964. *Personalities of the Council of Florence.* Oxford: Oxford University Press.

———. [1959] 1982. *The Council of Florence.* Reprint, New York: AMS Press.

Gillespie, George. [1846] 1991. *Notes of Debates and Proceedings of the Assembly of Divines at Westminster, February 1644 to January 1645.* Reprint, Edmonton: Still Waters Revival Books.

Gillet, Lev. 1987. *The Jesus Prayer.* 2d ed. Foreword by Kallistos Ware. Crestwood, N.Y.: Saint Vladimir's Seminary Press.

Gillett, Ezra Hall. 1863. *The Life and Times of John Huss: or, The Bohemian Reformation of the Fifteenth Century.* 2 vols. New York: AMS Press.

Gilliam, Elizabeth, and W. J. Tighe. 1992. "To 'Run with the Time': Archbishop Whitgift, the Lambeth Articles, and the Politics of Theological Ambiguity in Late Elizabethan England." *Sixteenth Century Journal* 23:325-40.

Gilmont, Jean-François. 1990. *La Réforme et le livre: L'Europe de l'imprimé (1517-v. 1570).* Paris: Editions du Cerf.

Gilson, Etienne. 1953. *Heloise and Abelard.* Translated by L. K. Shook. London: Hollis and Carter.

———. [1951] 1957. "Historical Research and the Future of Scholasticism." In *A Gilson Reader,* 156-67. Edited with an introduction by Anton C. Pegis. Garden City, N.Y.: Hanover House.

Gindely, Antonin. 1857-58. *Geschichte der Böhmischen Brüder.* Prague: C. Bellmann.

Girod, Gordon H. 1978. *The Deeper Faith: An Exposition of the Canons of the Synod of Dort.* Grand Rapids, Mich.: Baker Book House.

Giving Account of the Hope Together. 1978. Compiled by the World Council of Churches, Commission on Faith and Order. Geneva: World Council of Churches.

Gloer, W. Hulitt. 1984. "Homologies and Hymns in the New Testament: Form, Content and Criteria for Identification." *Perspectives in Religious Studies* 11:115-32.

Godfrey, W. Robert. 1982. "Calvin and Calvinism in the Netherlands." In *John Calvin: His Influence in the Western World,* 95-120. Edited by W. Stanford Reid. Grand Rapids, Mich.: Zondervan.

Golubev, Stefan Timofeevich. 1883-98. *Kievskii mitropolit Petr Mogila i ego spodvizhniki: Opyt istoricheskago izsliedovaniia.* 2 vols. Kiev: Tip. G. T. Korchak-Hovitskago.

González, Justo L. 1987. *A History of Christian Thought.* Revised ed. 3 vols. Nashville, Tenn.: Abingdon Press.

Goodenough, E. R. 1923. *The Theology of Justin Martyr.* Jena, Germany: Frommann.

Goodsell, Daniel A., Joseph B. Hingeley, and James M. Buckley, eds. 1908. *The Doctrines and Discipline of the Methodist Episcopal Church.* New York: Eaton and Mains.

Gorrell, Donald K. 1988. "The Social Creed and Methodism Through Eighty Years." *Methodist History* 26:213–28.

Göszwein, G. 1886. *Eine Union in der Wahrheit.* Saint Louis, Mo.: Concordia Publishing House.

Gould, Graham. 1988. "Cyril of Alexandria and the Formula of Reunion." *Downside Review* 106:235–52.

Grabmann, Martin. [1909] 1957. *Die Geschichte der scholastischen Methode: Nach den gedruckten und ungedruckten Quellen.* 2 vols. Graz: Akademische Druck- und Verlagsanstalt.

Grant, Robert M. 1966. *Ignatius of Antioch.* Camden, N.J.: Nelson.

———. 1988. *Greek Apologists of the Second Century.* Philadelphia: Westminster Press.

Gray, G. F. S. 1996. *Anglicans in China: A History of the Zhonghua Shenggong Hui.* New Haven: Episcopal China Mission History Project.

Gray, Patrick T. R. 1979. *The Defense of Chalcedon in the East (451–553).* Leiden: Brill.

———. 1987. "Ecumenical Dialogue, Ecumenical Council, and Constantinople II." *Toronto Journal of Theology* 3:50–59.

———, and Michael W. Herren. 1994. "Columbanus and the Three Chapters Controversy: A New Approach." *JTS* 45:160–70.

Green, Lowell C. 1976. "What Was the True Issue at Marburg in 1529?" *Springfielder* 40:102–6.

———. 1977. *The Formula of Concord: An Historical and Bibliographical Guide.* Saint Louis, Mo.: Center for Reformation Research.

Gregg, Robert C., ed. 1985. *Arianism: Historical and Theological Reassessments.* [Ninth International Conference on Patristic Studies, Oxford, 1983.] Patristic Monograph Series, 11. Philadelphia: Philadelphia Patristic Foundation.

Gregory of Nyssa. 1960. *Contra Eunomium.* Edited by Werner Jaeger. Leiden: Brill.

Greschat, Martin. 1985. "Martin Bucers Anteil am Bericht der oberländischen Prediger über den Abschluß der Wittenberger Konkordie (1536)." *ARG* 76:296–98.

Grillmeier, Aloys. 1964. *Christ in Christian Tradition.* Volume 1 of *From the Apostolic Age to Chalcedon.* Translated by J. S. Bowden. London: A. R. Mowbray.

———. 1975. *Christ in Christian Tradition.* Volume 1 of *From the Apostolic Age to Chalcedon (451).* 2d revised ed. Translated by John Bowden. London: Mowbrays.

———. 1980. *Nicaea (325) und Chalcedon (451): Um das christliche Gottes- und Menschenbild.* Donauwörth, Germany: Ludwig Auer.

———. 1987. *Christ in Christian Tradition.* Vol. 2/1: *Reception and Contradiction from Chalcedon to Justinian I.* Translated by Pauline Allen and John Cawte. Atlanta, Ga.: John Knox Press.

———, and Heinrich Bacht. 1951–54. *Das Konzil von Chalcedon: Geschichte und Gegenwart.* 4th ed. 3 vols. Würzburg: Echter-Verlag.

Gritsch, Eric W., and Robert Jenson. 1976. *Lutheranism: The Theological Movement and Its Confessional Writings*. Philadelphia: Fortress Press.

Grumel, A. A. 1928-30. "Recherches sur l'histoire du monothélisme." *Echos d'Orient* 27:6-16, 257-77, 28:19-34, 272-82, 29:16-28.

Grüneisen, Ernst. 1938. "Grundlegendes für die Bilder in Luthers Katechismen." *Luther-Jahrbuch* 20:1-44.

Guerra, A. J. 1992. "The Conversion of Marcus Aurelius and Justin Martyr: The Purpose, Genre, and Context of the First Apology." *Second Century* 9:129-87.

Guerrier, Louis, and L. Grébaut, eds. and trans. 1913. *Le Testament en Galilée de Notre-Seigneur Jesus-Christ*. Paris: Firmin-Didot.

Guggisberg, Hans. 1982. *Basel in the Sixteenth Century: Aspects of the City Republic Before, During, and After the Reformation*. Saint Louis, Mo.: Center for Reformation Research.

Guggisberg, Kurt. 1958. *Bernische Kirchengeschichte*. Bern: P. Haupt.

Guillaume Farel, 1489-1565: Biographie nouvelle écrite d'après les documents originaux. 1930. Edited by the Comité Farel. Neuchâtel: Delachaux et Niestlé.

Gussmann, Wilhelm, ed. 1911. *Quellen und Forschungen zur Geschichte des Augsburgischen Glaubensbekenntnisses*. Volume 1 of *Die Ratschläge der evangelischen Reichstände zum Reichstag von Augsburg 1530*. Leipzig: Teubner.

Haas, Martin. 1969. *Huldrych Zwingli und seine Zeit: Leben und Werk des Züricher Reformators*. Zurich: Zwingli Verlag.

———. 1982. "Michael Sattler: On the Way to Anabaptist Separation." In *Profiles of Radical Reformers: Biographical Sketches from Thomas Müntzer to Paracelsus*, 132-43. Edited by Hans J. Goertz. Scottdale, Pa.: Herald Press.

Hadjiantoniou, Georgios A. 1961. *Protestant Patriarch: The Life of Cyril Lucaris, 1572-1638, Patriarch of Constantinople*. Richmond, Va.: John Knox Press.

Haelst, J. van. 1970. "Le Papyrus der Balizeh: Une nouvelle interprétation." In *Ecclesia a spiritu sancto edocta*, 201-12. Edited by Joseph C. Coppens et al. Bibliotheca Ephemeridum Theologicarum Lovaniensium, 27. Gembloux, Belgium: J. Duculot.

Hagen, Kenneth. 1987. "The Historical Context of the Smalcald Articles." *Concordia Theological Quarterly* 51:245-53.

Hagenbach, K. R. 1827. *Kritische Geschichte der Entstehung und der Schicksale der ersten Basler Confession und der auf sie gegründeten Kirchenlehre*. Basel: Neukirch.

Hägglund, Bengt. 1958. "Die Bedeutung der *Regula fidei* als Grundlage theologischer Aussagen." *Studia Theologica* 12:1-44.

———. 1980. "Melanchthon versus Luther: The Contemporary Struggle." *Concordia Theological Quarterly* 44:123-33.

———. 1981. "Die Rezeption Luthers in der Konkoridenformel." In *Luther und die Bekenntnisschriften*, 107-20. Edited by Joachim Heubach, Maurice Schild, Leiv Aalen, et al. Erlangen, Germany: Martin Luther-Verlag.

Haidostian, Paul. 1996. "Armenian Evangelical Vision and Revision." *Near East School of Theology Theological Review* 17:52-60.

Hajjar, Joseph. 1962. *Le synode permanent dans l'Eglise byzantine des origines au 11e siècle*. Rome: Pontificium Institutum Orientalium Studiorum.

———. 1995. *Les Chrétiens uniates du Proche-Orient*. Damascus: Dar Tlass.

Halecki, Oskar. 1958. *From Florence to Brest (1439-1596)*. New York: Fordham University Press.

Hall, Stuart G. 1965. *Christ in the Christian Tradition: From the Apostolic Age to Chalcedon (451)*. Translated by J. S. Bowden. New York: Sheed and Ward.

———. 1980. "Nicaea (325) und Chalcedon (451): Um das christliche Gottes- und Menschenbild." In *Wegmarken der Christologie*, 43-80. Edited by Anton Ziegenaus. Donauwörth, Germany: Verlag Ludwig Auer.

———. 1987. "The Understanding of the Christological Definitions of Both (Oriental Orthodox and Roman Catholic) Traditions in the Light of the Post-Chalcedonian Theology." In Fries and Nersoyan 1987, 65-82.

———. 1989. "The Creed of Sardica." In *Studia Patristica*, 19: *Historica, Theologica, Gnostica, Biblica et Apocrypha* [Tenth International Conference on Patristic Studies, Oxford, 1987], 173-84. Edited by Elizabeth A. Livingstone. Louvain: Peeters.

———. 1991. *Doctrine and Practice in the Early Church*. London: S.P.C.K.

Hall, Thor. 1961. "Possibilities of Erasmian Influence on Denck and Hubmaier and Their Views on the Freedom of the Will." *MQR* 35:149-70.

Halleux, André de. 1985. "La réception du symbole oecuménique, de Nicée à Chalcédoine." *Ephemerides Theologicae Lovanienses* 61/1:5-47.

———. 1993. "La première session du Concile d'Ephèse." *Ephemerides Theologicae Lovanienses* 69:48-87.

Hamann, Henry P. 1988. "The Smalcald Articles as a Systematic Theology: A Comparison with the Augsburg Confession." *Concordia Theological Quarterly* 52:29-40.

Hamilton, John Taylor. 1900. *A History of the Church Known as the Moravian Church, or, The Unitas Fratrum, or, The Unity of the Brethren, During the Eighteenth and Nineteenth Centuries*. Bethlehem, Pa.: Times Publishing.

Handlingar vid de Svenska Baptistförsamlingarnas: Tredje allmäna Konferens. [1861?]. [Stockholm]: n.p.

Handy, Robert T., ed. 1966. *The Social Gospel in America, 1870-1920*. New York: Oxford University Press.

Hanson, Richard P. C. 1954. *Origen's Doctrine of Tradition*. London: S.P.C.K.

———. 1983. "The Doctrine of the Trinity Achieved in 381." *Scottish Journal of Theology* 36:41-57.

———. 1985. *Studies in Christian Antiquity*. Edinburgh: T. and T. Clark.

———. 1988. *The Search for the Christian Doctrine of God: The Arian Controversy, 318-381*. Edinburgh: T. and T. Clark.

Harder, Leland. 1980. "Zwingli's Reaction to the Schleitheim Confession of Faith of the Anabaptists." *Sixteenth Century Journal* 11/4:51-66.

Hardon, John A. 1968. *The Spirit and Origins of American Protestantism: A Source Book in Its Creeds*. Dayton, Ohio: Pflaum Press.

Hardwick, Charles. 1876. *A History of the Articles of Religion*. 3d ed. London: George Bell and Sons.

Harman, Allan M. 1973. "Speech About the Trinity: With Special Reference to Novatian, Hilary and Calvin." *Scottish Journal of Theology* 26:385-400.

Harmon, Nolan B., and John W. Bardsley. 1953. "John Wesley and the Articles of Religion." *Religion in Life* 22:280–91.

Harnack, Adolf von. 1897. *Die Chronologie der altchristlichen Litteratur bis Eusebius.* 2 vols. Leipzig: J. C. Hinrichs.

———. 1901. *The Apostles' Creed.* Translated by Stewart Means from article in Herzog's *Real-Encyclopädie,* 3d ed. London: A. and C. Black.

———. 1931–32. *Lehrbuch der Dogmengeschichte.* 3 vols. Tübingen: J. C. B. Mohr (Paul Siebeck).

———. [1900] 1957. *What Is Christianity?* Translated by Thomas Bailey Saunders. Introduction by Rudolf Bultmann. Reprint, New York: Harper Torchbooks.

———. [1898] 1958. *History of Dogma.* Translated by J. Millar, Neil Buchanan, E. B. Speirs, and W. M. Gilchrist from the 3d ed. 7 vols. Reprint, New York: Russell and Russell.

———. [1908] 1961a. *The Mission and Expansion of Christianity in the First Three Centuries.* Translated by James Moffatt. Reprint ed. Introduction by Jaroslav Pelikan. New York: Harper Torchbooks.

———. [1893] 1961b. *History of Dogma.* Translated from the third German edition by Neil Buchanan. 7 vols. Reprint, New York: Dover.

Harnack, Theodosius. 1856. *Der Kleine Katechismus Dr. Martin Luthers in seiner Urgestalt.* Stuttgart: S. G. Liesching.

Harris, James Rendel, ed. 1887. *The Teaching of the Apostles (Didache ton Apostolon).* Baltimore: C. J. Clay and Sons.

———, ed. and tr. [1893] 1967. *The Apology of Aristides on Behalf of the Christians, from a Syriac Ms. Preserved on Mount Sinai.* Greek text edited by J. Armitage Robinson. 2d ed. Reprint, Nendeln, Liechtenstein: Kraus.

Harrison, A. W. 1926. *The Beginnings of Arminianism to the Synod of Dort.* London: University of London Press.

———. 1937. *Arminianism.* London: Duckworth.

Hartfelder, Karl. [1889] 1964. *Philipp Melanchthon als Praeceptor Germaniae.* Reprint, Nieuwkoop, Netherlands: B. de Graaf.

Hartman, Lars. 1994. "Obligatory Baptism—But Why? On Baptism in the *Didache* and in the *Shepherd of Hermas.*" *Svensk Exegetisk Årsbok* 59:127–43. Uppsala: Uppsala Exegetiska Sällskap.

Hasler, August. 1981. *How the Pope Became Infallible: Pius IX and the Politics of Persuasion.* Translated by Peter Heinegg. Garden City, N.Y.: Doubleday.

Haugaard, William P. 1968. *Elizabeth and the English Reformation: The Struggle for a Stable Settlement of Religion.* London: Cambridge University Press.

Haugh, Richard. 1975. *Photius and the Carolingians: The Trinitarian Controversy.* Belmont, Mass.: Nordland Publishers.

Hausammann, Susi. 1966. "Die Marburger Artikel: Eine echte Konkordie." *ZKG* 77/3–4: 288–321.

Hausherr, Irénée. 1966. *Hésychasme et prière.* Rome: Pontificale Institutum Orientalium Studiorum.

Hauzenberger, Hans. 1985. *Einheit auf evangelischer Grundlage: Von Werden und Wesen der Evangelischen Allianz.* Giessen, Germany: Brunnen Verlag.

Hazlett, W. Ian P. 1987. "The Scots Confession 1560: Context, Complexion and Critique." *ARG* 78:287–320.

———. 1994. "Eucharistic Communion: Impulses and Directions in Martin Bucer's Thought." In *Martin Bucer: Reforming Church and Community*, 72–82. Edited by D. F. Wright. Cambridge: Cambridge University Press.

Heather, P. J., and John Matthews. 1991. *The Goths in the Fourth Century.* Liverpool: Liverpool University Press.

Hebart, Friedemann, ed. and tr. 1983. *Luther's Large Catechism: Anniversary Translation.* Adelaide, Australia: Lutheran Publishing House.

Hefele, Karl Joseph von. 1869–90. *Conciliengeschichte. Nach den Quellen bearbeitet.* 9 vols. Vols. 1–6 in 2d ed.; vols. 5–6 edited by Alois Knöpfler; vols. 8–9 edited by Cardinal Hergenröther. Freiburg: Herder.

Hefner, Philip J. 1963. "Saint Irenaeus and the Hypothesis of Faith." *Dialog* 2:300–306.

Hege, Christian. 1908. *Die Täufer in der Kurpfalz.* Frankfurt: Hermann Minjon.

The Heidelberg Catechism: Four Hundredth Anniversary Edition, 1563–1963. 1963. Philadelphia: United Church Press.

Heideman, Eugene P. 1975. *Our Song of Hope: A Provisional Confession of Faith of the Reformed Church in America.* Grand Rapids, Mich.: Eerdmans.

Heijting, Willem. 1989. *De catechismi en confessies in de Nederlandse reformatie tot 1585.* 2 vols. Nieuwkoop: De Graaf.

Heil, Gunther, ed. 1990– . *Gregorii Nysseni Opera. Sermones.* Leiden: E. J. Brill.

Heiner, Franz Xavier. 1908. *Der neue Syllabus Pius' X. oder Dekret des Heiligen Offiziums "Lamentabili" vom 3. Juli 1907, dargestellt und kommentiert.* 2d ed. Mainz: Verlag von Kirchheim.

Heinrich, Wilhelm, and Rudolf Walter de Moos. 1942. *Petitiones de assumptione corporea B.V. Mariae in caelum definienda ad Sanctam Sedem delatae: Propositae secundum ordinem hierarchicum dogmaticum, geographicum, chronologicum ad consensum ecclesiae manifestandum.* 2 vols. Rome: Typis Polyglottis Vaticanis.

Henderson, George D., ed. 1937. *The Scots Confession, 1560 (Confessio Scoticana), and Negative Confession, 1581 (Confessio Negativa).* Edinburgh: Church of Scotland, Committee on Publications.

———, ed. [1960]. *The Scots Confession.* Rendering into modern English by James Bulloch. Edinburgh: Saint Andrew Press.

Hendricks, Dan L. 1978. "The Bern Disputation: Some Observations." *Zwingliana* 14:565–75.

Hennecke, Edgar. [1896] 1990. *Altchristliche Malerei und altkirchliche Literatur: Eine Untersuchung über den biblischen Cyklus der Gemälde in den römischen Katakomben.* Reprint, Leipzig: Veit.

Hennessey, Lawrence R. 1998. "A Moment of Grace: Some Reflections on the Common Christological Declaration Between the Assyrian Church of the East and the Roman Catholic Church." *Ecumenical Trends* 27:26–29.

Henry, Patrick. 1974. "The Formulators of Icon Doctrine." In *Schools of Thought in the Christian Tradition*, 75–89. Edited by Patrick Henry. Philadelphia: Fortress Press.

———. 1977. "Images of the Church in the Second Nicene Council and the Libri Carolini."

In *Law, Church, and Society: Essays in Honor of Stephan Kuttner*, 237–52. Edited by Kenneth Pennington and Robert Somerville. Philadelphia: University of Pennsylvania Press.

Heppe, Heinrich. 1885. *Die Bekenntnisschriften der altprotestantischen Kirche Deutschlands.* Kassel: T. Fischer.

Hergenröther, Joseph Adam Gustav. 1867–69. *Photius, Patriarch von Konstantinopel.* 3 vols. Regensburg: G. J. Manz.

Herrin, Judith. 1987. *The Formation of Christendom.* Oxford: Basil Blackwell.

Hertz, Joseph H. 1948. *The Authorized Daily Prayer Book.* Revised ed. New York: Bloch.

Hess, H. 1958. *The Canons of the Council of Sardica, A.D. 343: A Landmark in the Early Development of Canon Law.* Oxford: Clarendon Press.

Heymann, Frederick Gotthold. 1955. *John Zizka and the Hussite Revolution.* Princeton, N.J.: Princeton University Press.

————. 1961. "The Hussite-Utraquist Church in the Fifteenth and Sixteenth Centuries." *ARG* 52/1:1–16.

Hicks, Eric. 1991. *La vie et les epistres: Pierres Abaelart et Heloys sa fame.* Paris: Champion.

Higman, Francis. 1988. "La Dispute de Lausanne, carrefour de la Réformation française." In *La Dispute de Lausanne 1988,* 23–35.

Hildebrandt, Walter, and Rudolf Zimmermann. 1938. *Bedeutung und Geschichte des zweiten Helvetischen Bekenntnisses.* Zurich: Zwingli-Verlag.

————. 1966. *Das Zweite Helvetische Bekenntnis.* Zurich: Zwingli-Verlag.

Hillman, Eugene. 1993. *Toward an African Christianity: Inculturation Applied.* New York: Paulist Press.

Hinson, E. Glenn. 1979. "Confessions or Creeds in Early Christian Tradition." *Review and Expositor* 76:5–16.

Hirsch, Emanuel. 1960. *Geschichte der neuern evangelischen Theologie im Zusammenhang mit den allgemeinen Bewegungen des europäischen Denkens.* 5 vols. Gütersloh, Germany: C. Bertelsmann Verlag.

Hitchcock, F. R. Montgomery. 1932. "The Creeds of SS. Irenaeus and Patrick." *Hermathena* 48:232–37.

Hobbs, Herschel H. 1979. "Southern Baptists and Confessionalism: A Comparison of the Origins and Contents of the 1925 and 1963 Confessions." *Review and Expositor* 76/1:55–68.

Hodgson, Leonard G., ed. 1934. *Convictions: A Selection from the Responses of the Churches to the Report of the World Conference on Faith and Order, Held at Lausanne in 1927.* London: SCM Press.

————, ed. 1938. *The Second World Conference on Faith and Order Held at Edinburgh, August 3–18, 1937.* New York: Macmillan.

Hoekema, Anthony A. 1968a. "Needed: A New Translation of the Canons of Dort." *Calvin Theological Journal* 3:41–47.

————. 1968b. "New English Translation of the Canons of Dort." *Calvin Theological Journal* 3:133–61.

————. 1972. "Missionary Focus of the Canons of Dort." *Calvin Theological Journal* 7:209–20.

Hoenderdaal, J. 1969. "De Kerkorderlijke Kant van de Dortse Synode." *Nederlands Theologisch Tijdschrift* 23:349–63.

———. 1970–71. "Remonstrantie en Contraremonstrantie." *Nederlands Archief voor Kerkgeschiedenis,* n.s., 51:49–92.

———. 1975. "The Debate About Arminius Outside the Netherlands." In *Leiden University in the Seventeenth Century: An Exchange of Learning,* 137–59. Edited by Th. H. Lunsingh Scheurleer and G. H. M. Posthumus Meyjes. Leiden: Brill.

Hofmann, Georg, ed. 1935–51. *Documenta Concilii Florentini de unione Orientalium.* 3 vols. Rome: Pontificia Università Gregoriana.

Hofmann, Johann Christian Konrad von. 1857. *Das Bekenntniss der lutherischen Kirche von der Versöhnung und die Versöhnungslehre.* Erlangen, Germany: T. Bläsing.

Hofmann, Karl. 1933. *Der "Dictatus papae" Gregors VII: Eine Rechtsgeschichtliche Erklärung.* Paderborn, Germany: Ferdinand Schöningh.

Hofmann, Rudolph. 1857. *Symbolik oder systematische Darstellung des symbolischen Lehrbegriffs der verschiedenen christlichen Kirchen und namhaften Sekten.* Leipzig: Friedrich Voigt.

Holl, Karl. 1898. *Enthusiasmus und Bussgewalt beim griechischen Mönchtum: Eine Studie zu Symeon dem neuen Theologen.* Leipzig: J. C. Hinrichs.

———. [1919] 1928. "Zur Auslegung des 2. Artikels des sog. Apostolischen Glaubensbekenntinisses." In *Gesammelte Aufsätze zur Kirchengeschichte,* 2:115–28. Tübingen: J. C. B. Mohr (Paul Siebeck).

Holland, David Larrimore. 1965. "The Earliest Text of the Old Roman Symbol: A Debate with Hans Lietzmann and J. N. D. Kelly." *Church History* 34:262–81.

———. 1969. "Creeds of Nicaea and Constantinople Reexamined." *Church History* 38:248–61.

———. 1970. "Die Synode von Antiochien (324/25) und ihre Bedeutung für Eusebius von Caesarea und das Konzil von Nizäa." *ZKG* 81/2:163–81.

Hollis, Michael. 1966. *The Significance of South India.* London: Lutterworth.

Hollweg, Walter. 1968. *Neue Untersuchungen zur Geschichte und Lehre des Heidelberger Katechismus.* Neukirchen, Germany: Verlag des Erziehungsverein.

Holstein, Henri. 1976. "Cène et la messe dans la doctrine du sacrifice eucharistique du Concile de Trente." In *Humanisme et foi chrétienne,* 649–62. Edited by Charles Kannengiesser and Yves Marchasson. Paris: Beauchesne.

Hopkins, C. H. 1940. *The Rise of the Social Gospel in American Protestantism.* New Haven: Yale University Press.

Hörcsik, Richard. 1994. "John Calvin in Geneva, 1536–38: Some Questions About Calvin's First Stay at Geneva." In *Calvinus Sacrae Scripturae professor: Calvin as Confessor of Holy Scriptures,* 155–65. Edited by Wilhelm H. Neuser. Grand Rapids, Mich.: W. B. Eerdmans.

Hornschuh, M. 1965. *Studien zur Epistula Apostolorum.* Patristische Texte und Studien, 5. Berlin: De Gruyter.

Horst, Irvin B. 1982. "The Dordrecht Confession of Faith: 350 Years." *Pennsylvania Mennonite Heritage* 5:2–8.

———, tr. and ed. 1988. *Mennonite Confession of Faith.* Mennonite Sources and Documents, 2. Lancaster, Pa.: Lancaster Mennonite Historical Society.

Horton, Douglas. 1962. *The United Church of Christ: Its Origins, Organization, and Role in the World Today.* New York: T. Nelson.

Houssiau, A. 1955. *La Christologie de saint Irénée.* Gembloux, Belgium: J. Duculot.

Howlett, D. R. 1994. *Liber epistolarum sancti Patricii episcopi. The Book of Letters of Saint Patrick the Bishop.* Dublin: Four Courts Press.

Hrejsa, Ferdinand. 1912. *Česká konfesse, její vznik, podstata a dějiny.* Prague: Česká Akademie Císaře Františka Josefa.

Hudson, Anne. 1978. *Selections from English Wycliffite Writings.* Cambridge: Cambridge University Press.

Hüffmeier, Wilhelm, and Christine-Ruther Müller, eds. 1995. *Wachsende Gemeinschaft in Zeugnis und Dienst: Reformatorische Kirchen in Europa.* Frankfurt: Otto Lembeck.

Huhn, Joseph. 1954. *Das Geheimnis der Jungfrau-Mutter Maria nach dem Kirchenvater Ambrosius.* Würzburg: Echter-Verlag.

Huizing, Petrus, and Knut Walf. 1983. *The Ecumenical Council: Its Significance in the Constitution of the Church.* Edinburgh: T. and T. Clark.

Hulme, Edward M. [1931] 1968. "Lelio Sozzini's Confession of Faith." In *Persecution and Liberty: Essays in Honor of George Lincoln Burr.* Reprint, Freeport, N.Y.: Books for Libraries Press.

Hunt, E. 1957. *St. Leo the Great: Letters.* Fathers of the Church, 34. New York: Fathers of the Church.

Hunter, Alan, and Kim-Kwong Chan. 1993. *Protestantism in Contemporary China.* Cambridge: Cambridge University Press.

Hussey, Joan Mervyn. 1986. *The Orthodox Church in the Byzantine Empire.* Oxford: Clarendon Press.

Idelsohn, A. Z. 1932. *Jewish Liturgy and Its Development.* New York: Henry Holt.

Ihm, Claudia Carlen. 1981. *The Papal Encyclicals, 1939–1958.* Raleigh, N.C.: McGrath Publishing.

Immenkötter, Herbert, ed. 1979. *Die Confutatio der Confessio Augustana von 3. August 1530.* Münster: Aschendorff.

Ionesco, Teofil. 1944. *La vie et l'oeuvre de Pierre Movila, Métropolite de Kiev.* Paris: Nidot.

Jackson, Samuel Macauley. [1901] 1972. *Huldreich Zwingli: The Reformer of German Switzerland, 1484–1531.* 2d ed. Reprint, New York: AMS Press.

Jacobs, Henry E., ed. and trans. 1893. *The Book of Concord; or, The Symbolic Books of the Evangelical Lutheran Church.* Philadelphia: G. W. Frederick.

Jacobs, Paul. 1959. *Theologie reformierter Bekenntnisschriften in Grundzügen.* Neukirchen, Germany: Neukirchener Verlag.

Jahr, Hannelore. 1964. *Studien zur Überlieferungsgeschichte der Confession de foi von 1559.* Neukirchen, Germany: Verlag des Erziehungsverein.

James, M. R. 1900–1904. *Western Manuscripts in the Library of Trinity College, Cambridge: A Descriptive Catalogue.* 4 vols. Cambridge: Cambridge University Press.

Jamison, Wallace N. 1958. *The United Presbyterian Story: A Centennial Study, 1858–1958.* Pittsburgh, Pa.: Geneva Press.

Janetzki, Elvin W. 1980. "Teaching Luther's *Small Catechism* as Law and Gospel." *Lutheran Theological Journal* 14:73–79.

Jecker, G. 1927. *Die Heimat des heiligen Pirmin: Des Apostels der Alamannen.* Münster: Aschendorff.

Jedin, Hubert. 1941. *Krisis und Wendpunkt des Trienter Konzils, 1562–1563.* Würzburg: Rita-Verlag und -Druckerei der Augustiner.

———. 1946. *Katholische Reformation oder Gegenreformation? Ein Versuch zur Klärung der Begriffe nebst einer Jubiläumsbetrachtung über das Trienter Konzil.* Lucerne: Josef Stocker.

———. 1948. *Das Konzil von Trient: Eine Überblick über die Erforschung seiner Geschichte.* Rome: Edizioni di Storia e letteratura.

———. 1948–75. *Geschichte des Konzils von Trient.* 4 vols. Freiburg: Herder.

———. 1957–61. *A History of the Council of Trent.* Translated by Ernest Graf. Saint Louis, Mo.: Herder.

———, and John Dolan, eds. 1980. *History of the Church.* 10 vols. New York: Seabury Press.

Jefford, Clayton N., ed. 1995. *The Didache in Context: Essays on Its Text, History, and Transmission.* Supplements to *Novum Testamentum,* 77. Leiden: Brill.

———. 1996. *Reading the Apostolic Fathers: An Introduction.* With Kenneth J. Harder and Louis D. Amezaga. Peabody, Mass.: Hendrickson.

Jenny, Beatrice. 1951. *Das Schleitheimer Täuferbekenntnis, 1527.* Thayngen, Switzerland: Karl Augustin.

Jobert, Ambroise. 1974. *De Luther à Mohila: La Pologne dans la crise de la chretienté, 1517–1648.* Collection historique de l'Institut d'études slaves, 21. Paris: Institut d'Etudes Slaves.

Joest, Wilfried. 1962. "The Doctrine of Justification of the Council of Trent." *Lutheran World* 9:204–18.

John Paul II, Pope. 1992. "Déclaration du pape Jean-Paul II sur la Procession du Saint-Esprit." [Reprint from *L'Osservatore Romano,* French ed. 13 November 1990] *Istina* 37:78–83.

———. 1998. "Ad Tuendam Fidem." *L'Osservatore Romano* 28 (1550), 15 July 1998.

John, Jeffrey, ed. 1994. *Living the Mystery: Affirming Catholicism and the Future of Anglicanism.* London: Darton, Longman and Todd.

Johnson, John F. 1989. "Polemicism or Ecumenism: Another Look at the Smalcald Articles." In *Promoting Unity: Themes in Lutheran-Catholic Dialogue,* 39–49. Edited by H. George Anderson and James R. Crumley, Jr. Minneapolis, Minn.: Augsburg Publishing House.

Johnson, Morris R. 1999. *Archbishop Daniel William Alexander and the African Orthodox Church.* San Francisco: International Scholars.

Johnston, Paul. 1993. "Reu's Understanding of *The Small Catechism.*" *Lutheran Quarterly,* n.s., 7:425–50.

Jones, Charles Edwin. 1974. *A Guide to the Study of the Holiness Movement.* Metuchen, N.J.: Scarecrow Press.

Jones, Francis Price. 1962. *The Church in Communist China: A Protestant Appraisal.* New York: Friendship Press.

———, consultant and ed. 1963. *Documents of the Three-Self Movement: Source Materials for the Study of the Protestant Church in Communist China.* New York, N.Y.: Far Eastern Office, Division of Foreign Missions, National Council of the Churches of Christ in the U.S.A.

Jones, Joe R. 1980. "A Theological Analysis of the Design." *Mid-Stream* 19/3:309–21.

Jones, Rufus M. [1927] 2002. *The Faith and Practice of the Quakers.* Reprint, Richmond, Ind.: Friends United Press.

Jordan, H. William. 1977. "A Model for the Church in Conflict: The Smalcald Articles and the Treatise on the Power and Primacy of the Pope." *Currents in Theology and Mission* 4/1:22–27.

Junghans, Helmar, ed. 1983. *Leben und Werk Martin Luthers von 1526 bis 1546. Festgabe zu seinem 500. Geburtstag.* 2 vols. Göttingen: Vandenhoeck und Ruprecht.

Jungkuntz, Theodore R. 1977a. *Formulators of the Formula of Concord: Four Architects of Lutheran Unity.* Saint Louis, Mo.: Concordia Publishing House.

———. 1977b. "Sectarian Consequences of Mistranslation in Luther's Smalcald Articles." *Currents in Theology and Mission* 4/3:166–67.

Kahle, Paul Eric, ed. 1954. *Bala'izah: Coptic Texts from Deir el Bala'izah in Upper Egypt.* London: Griffith Institute; Oxford: Oxford University Press.

Kaminsky, Howard. 1967. *A History of the Hussite Revolution.* Berkeley: University of California Press.

Kandler, Karl-Hermann. 1970. *Luther, Arnoldshain, und das Abendmahl: Die Herausforderung der lutherischen Abendmahlslehre durch die Arnoldshainer Abendmahlsthesen.* Berlin: Evangelische Verlagsanstalt.

Kannengiesser, Charles. 1970. *Traité sur l'incarnation du Verbe et sur sa manifestation corporelle en notre faveur.* Paris: Institut Catholique.

———. 1981. "Athanasius of Alexandria and the Holy Spirit Between Nicaea I and Constantinople I." *Irish Theological Quarterly* 48:166–80.

Karmirēs, Ioannēs, ed. 1937. *Mētrophanēs ho Kritopoulos kai hē anekdotos allēgographia autou.* Athens: Paraskeua Lēonē.

———. 1949. *Heterodoxoi epidraseis epi tas homologias tou IZ' Aiōnos.* Jerusalem: Typois Hierou Koinou P. Taphou.

Kartašev, Anton Vladimirovič. 1932. *Na put'ach k vselenskomu soboru* [On the way to an ecumenical council]. Paris: YMCA Press.

Kasper, Walter. 2000. "The Joint Declaration on the Doctrine of Justification: Cause for Hope." *Centro Pro Unione Bulletin* 57:3–6.

Keller, Ludwig. 1882. *Ein Apostel der Wiedertäufer.* Leipzig: Hirzel.

Keller-Hüschemenger, Max. 1967. "Die Wittenberger Artikel von 1536." *Kergyma und Dogma* 22/2:149–61.

Kellock, James. 1965. *Breakthrough for Church Union in North India and Pakistan.* Madras: Christian Literature Society.

Kelly, Douglas F. 1994. "The Westminster Shorter Catechism." In Carson and Hall 1994, 101–26.

Kelly, J. N. D., tr. 1955. *A Commentary on the Apostles' Creed* by Rufinus. Westminster, Md.: Newman Press.

———. 1958. *Early Christian Doctrine.* New York: Harper and Brothers.

———. 1964. *The Athanasian Creed.* The Paddock Lectures for 1962–3. New York: Harper and Row.

———. 1983. "The Nicene Creed: A Turning Point." *Scottish Journal of Theology* 36/1:29–39.

———. 1986. *The Oxford Dictionary of the Popes.* Oxford: Oxford University Press.

Kendall, R. T. 1981. *Calvin and English Calvinism to 1649.* New York: Oxford University Press.

Kessler, Juan B. A. 2001. *Limits of Spiritual Unity: A History of the Evangelical Alliance in Great Britain from Origins to 1960s.* Denver, Colo.: Academic Books.

Kidd, B. J. 1911. *The Thirty-Nine Articles: Their History and Explanation.* 5th ed. 2 vols. London: Rivingtons.

Kilpatrick, Thomas B. 1928. *Our Common Faith, with a Brief History of the Church Union Movement in Canada.* Toronto: Ryerson Press.

King, N. G. 1957. "The 150 Holy Fathers of the Council of Constantinople 381." *Studia Patristica* 1:635–41.

Kingdon, Robert M. 1974. "Was the Protestant Reformation a Revolution? The Case of Geneva." In *Transition and Revolution: Problems and Issues of European Renaissance and Reformation History,* 53–76. Edited by Robert M. Kingdon. Minneapolis, Minn.: Burgess Publishing.

———, ed. 1977. *Formula of Concord: Quadricentennial Essays.* Special issue of *Sixteenth Century Journal* 8/4:9–123.

———. 1985. *Church and Society in Reformation Europe.* London: Variorum Reprints.

Kinzig, Wolfram, Christoph Markschies, and Markus Vinzent. 1999. *Tauffragen und Bekenntnis: Studien zur sogenannten "Traditio apostolica," zu den "Interrogationes de fide" und zum "Römischen Glaubensbekenntnis."* Berlin: W. de Gruyter.

Kirchner, Hubert. 1983. "Luther und das Papsttum." In Junghans 1983, 1:441–56.

Kistemaker, Simon. 1968. "Leading Figures at the Synod of Dort." In *Crisis in the Reformed Churches: Essays in Commemoration of the Great Synod of Dort, 1618-1619,* 39–51. Edited by Peter Y. De Jong. Grand Rapids, Mich.: Reformed Fellowship.

Kitamori, Kazo. 1968. *Nihon Kirisuto Kyodan Shinko Kokuhaku.* Tokyo: Nihon Kirisuto Kyodan Shuppan Kyoku.

Kittelson, James M. 1973. "Martin Bucer and the Sacramentarian Controversy: The Origins of His Policy of Concord." *ARG* 64:166–83.

———. 1975. *Wolfgang Capito: From Humanist to Reformer.* Leiden: Brill.

———. 1993. "Martin Bucer: Forgotten Man in the Late Sixteenth Century?" In *Martin Bucer and Sixteenth-Century Europe: Actes du colloque de Strasbourg,* 2:705–14. Edited by Christian Krieger and Marc Lienhard. Leiden: Brill.

———, and Ken Schurb. 1986. "The Curious Histories of the Wittenberg Concord." *Concordia Theological Quarterly* 50/2:119–37.

Kiwiet, Jan J. 1957. "The Life of Hans Denck." *MQR* 31:227–59.

———. 1958. "The Theology of Hans Denck." *MQR* 32:3–27.

Klooster, Fred H. 1986. "The Priority of Ursinus in the Compostion of the Heidelberg Catechism." In Visser 't Hooft 1986, 73–100.

———. 1994. "Calvin's Attitude to the Heidelberg Catechism." In *Later Calvinism: International Perspectives,* 311–31. Edited by W. Fred Graham. Sixteenth Century Essays and Studies, 22. Kirksville, Mo.: Sixteenth Century Journal Publishers.

Klug, Eugene F. 1980. "Luther's Contribution to the Augsburg Confession." *Concordia Theological Quarterly* 44:155–72.

Knight, George W. 1984. "A Response to Dr. William Barker's Article 'Subscription to the Westminster Confession of Faith and Catechisms.'" *Presbyterion* 10/1-2:56–63.

Knoch, Otto. 1981. "Petrus und Paulus in den Schriften der Apostolischen Väter." In *Kon-*

tinuität und Einheit: Für Franz Mussner, 240-60. Edited by Paul G. Mueller. Freiburg: Herder.

Knox, John. 1949. *John Knox's History of the Reformation in Scotland*. Edited by William Croft Dickinson. 2 vols. London: Thomas Nelson and Sons.

Knox, R. Buick. 1967. *James Ussher, Archbishop of Armagh*. Cardiff: University of Wales Press.

Knox, Ronald A. 2000. *Enthusiasm: A Chapter in the History of Religion, with Special Reference to the Seventeenth and Eighteenth Centuries*. Oxford: Clarendon Press.

Kobong, Theodorus. 1992. *Aluk, adat, dan kebudayaan Toraja dalam perjumpaannya dengan Injil*. [Rantepao, Indonesia]: Pusbang, Badan Pekerja Sinode, Gereja Toraja.

Koch, Ernst. 1966. "Die Textüberlieferung der Confessio Helvetica Posterior und ihre Vorgeschichte." In *Glauben und Bekennen: Vierhundert Jahre Confessio Helvetica Posterior*, 13–40. Edited by Joachim Staedtke. Zurich: Zwingli Verlag.

———. 1968. *Die Theologie der Confessio Helvetica Posterior*. Neukirchen, Germany: Neukirchener Verlag des Erziehungsvereins.

———. 1992. "Beobachtungen zur Vorgeschichte der Confessio Helvetica Posterior." In *Reformiertes Erbe*, 223–32. Edited by Heiko Oberman, Ernst Saxer, Alfred Schindler, et al. Special issue of *Zwingliana* (19/1). Zurich: Theologischer Verlag.

———. 1995. "Zwingli und die Berner Reformation." *Theologische Rundschau* 60/2:131-51.

Koelpin, Arnold J., ed. 1980. *No Other Gospel: Essays in Commemoration of the Four Hundredth Anniversary of the Formula of Concord, 1580-1980*. Milwaukee, Wis.: Northwestern Publishing House.

Koestlin, Julius. 1875. *Martin Luther: Sein Leben und Seine Schriften*. Elberfeld, Germany: R. L. Friedrichs.

Köhler, Walther, ed. 1908. *Brüderlich Vereinigung etzlicher Kinder Gottes Sieben Artikel betreffend: Item ein Sendbrief Michael Sattlers an eine gemeine Gottes samt seinem Martyrium (1527)*. Halle: R. Haupt.

———. 1953. *Zwingli und Luther: Ihr Streit über das Abendmahl nach seinen politischen und religiösen Beziehungen*. Vol. 2. Vol. 7 of *Quellen und Forschungen zur Reformationsgeschichte*. Edited by Ernst Kohlmeyer and Heinrich Bornkamm. Gütersloh, Germany: C. Bertelsmann.

Kolb, Robert. 1977. *Andreae and the Formula of Concord: Six Sermons on the Way to Lutheran Unity*. Saint Louis, Mo.: Concordia Publishing House.

———. 1979. "The Layman's Bible: The Use of Luther's Catechisms in the German Late Reformation." In Scaer and Preus 1979, 16–26.

———. 1980. "Augsburg 1530: German Lutheran Interpretations of the Diet of Augsburg to 1577." *Sixteenth Century Journal* 11/3:47-61.

———. 1984. "The German Lutheran Reaction to the Third Period of the Council of Trent." *Lutherjahrbuch* 1984:63-95.

———. 1988. "Luther's Smalcald Articles: Agenda for Testimony and Confession." *Concordia Journal* 14:115-37.

———. 1995. "'That I May Be His Own': The Anthropology of Luther's Explanation of the Creed." *Concordia Journal* 21:28-41.

———, and James A. Nestingen, eds. 2001. *Sources and Contexts of the Book of Concord*. Minneapolis, Minn.: Fortress Press.

Kolfhaus, W. 1909. "Der Verkehr Calvins mit Bullinger." In *Calvinstudien: Festschrift zum 400. Geburtstage Johann Calvins*, 27-125. Edited by J. Bohatec. Leipzig: Rudolf Haupt.

Konidaris, G. 1971. "The Christological Decisions of Chalcedon: Their History down to the Sixth Ecumenical Synod (451-680/1)." *GOTR* 16:63-78.

Koop, Karl Peter. 1999. "Early Seventeenth Century Mennonite Confessions of Faith: The Development of an Anabaptist Tradition." Ph.D. diss., University of St. Michael's College, Toronto.

Kopecek, Thomas A. 1979. *A History of the Neo-Arianism.* 2 vols. Patristic Monograph Series, 8. Philadelphia: Philadelphia Patristic Foundation.

Koren, Henry J. 1958. *The Spiritans: A History of the Congregation of the Holy Ghost.* Pittsburgh, Pa.: Duquesne University.

Kraft, Heinrich. 1980. "Das Apostolicum—Das apostolische Symbol." In *Studien zur Bekenntnisbildung*, 16-29. Edited by Peter Meinhold. Wiesbaden: Steiner.

Krauth, Charles Porterfield. [1899] 1963. *The Conservative Reformation and Its Theology.* Reprint, Minneapolis, Minn.: Augsburg.

Krummel, Leopold. 1871. *Ultraquisten und Taboriten.* Gotha: Friedrich Andreas Perthes.

Kruse, Martin. 1975. "Abendmahl im Wandel." *Evangelische Theologie* 35:481-96.

Kubiak, Hieronim. 1982. *The Polish National Catholic Church in the United States of America from 1897 to 1980.* Kraków: Jagiellonian University.

Kucharek, Casimir A. 1971. *The Byzantine-Slav Liturgy of St. John Chrysostom: Its Origin and Evolution.* Allendale, N.J.: Alleluia Press.

Küng, Hans, and Jürgen Moltmann, eds. 1979. *An Ecumenical Confession of Faith?* New York: Seabury Press.

———. 1992. *Credo: Das Apostolische Glaubensbekenntnis-Zeitgenossen erklärt.* Munich: Piper. [English translation: *Credo: The Apostles' Creed Explained for Today.* Translated by John Bowden. London: SCM Press, 1993.]

Künstle, Karl. 1900. *Eine Bibliothek der Symbole und theologischer Tractate zur Bekämpfung des Priscillianismus und westgothischen Arianismus aus dem 6. Jahrhundert: Ein Beitrag zur Geschichte der theologischen Litteratur in Spanien.* Mainz: F. Kirchheim.

Küppers, Werner. 1978. "Verbindliches Lehren im Lichte des Verständnisses und der Ausübung von Autorität in der alten Kirche." In *Verbindliches Lehren der Kirche Heute*, 79-93. Frankfurt: Otto Lembeck.

———, Peter Hauptmann, and Friedrich Baser. 1964. *Symbolik der kleineren Kirchen, Freikirchen und Sekten des Westens.* Stuttgart: A. Hiersemann.

Küry, Urs, and Christian Oeyen. 1982. *Die altkatholische Kirche: Ihre Geschichte, Ihre Lehre, Ihr Anliegen.* Frankfurt: Evangelisches Verlagswerk.

Kuttner, Stephen Georg. 1947. "Liber canonicus: A Note on the 'Dictatus Pape' c. 17." In *Studi Gregoriani: Per la storia di Gregorio VII e della Riforma Gregoriana*, 2:387-401. Edited by G. B. Borino. Rome: Abbazia di San Paolo di Roma.

Kydd, Ronald. 1977. "Novatian's *De trinitate*, 29: Evidence of the Charismatic?" *Scottish Journal of Theology* 30/4:313-18.

Labunka, Miroslav. 1990. *Mitropolit Ilarion I joho pisannja* [Metropolitan Ilarion and his writings]. Rome: Ukrainian Catholic University.

Lacko, Michael. 1966. *The Union of Užhorod.* Cleveland, Ohio: Slovak Institute.

Lagorio, Valerie. M. 1974. "The Text of the *Quicunque vult* in Codex Ottob. Lat. 663." *JTS* 25:127–28.

Lake, Kirsopp, tr. 1959. *The Apostolic Fathers*. 2 vols. Cambridge, Mass.: Harvard University Press.

Lake, Peter. 1982. *Moderate Puritans and the Elizabethan Church*. Cambridge: Cambridge University Press.

————. 1987. "Calvinism and the English Church, 1570–1635." *Past and Present* 114:22–76.

Lambert, Malcolm. 1977. *Medieval Heresy: Popular Movements from Bogomil to Hus*. New York: Holmes and Meier.

The Lambeth Conference 1930: Encyclical Letter from the Bishops with Resolutions and Reports. 1930. London: S.P.C.K; New York: Macmillan.

Lamm, Norman. 1998. *The Shema: Spirituality and Law in Judaism*. Philadelphia: Jewish Publication Society.

Lamont, William. 1985. "The Rise of Arminianism Reconsidered." *Past and Present* 107:227–31.

Lampe, Geoffrey William Hugo. 1960. "The Evidence in the New Testament for Early Creeds, Catechisms and Liturgy." *Expository Times* 71:359–63.

Land, Gary, ed. 1998. *Adventism in America: A History*. Revised ed. Barren Springs, Mich.: Andrews University Press.

Landgraf, Artur Michael. 1952–56. *Dogmengeschichte der Frühscholastik*. 4 vols. Regensburg: Verlag Friedrich Pustet.

Lane, Grace. 1974. *Brief Halt at Mile "50": A Half Century of Church Union*. [N.p.:United Church Publishing House].

Lange, Albert de, ed. 1990. *Dall'Europa alle Valli Valdesi*. Turin: Editrice Claudiana.

Langton, Edward. 1956. *History of the Moravian Church: The Story of the First International Protestant Church*. London: Allen and Unwin.

Lankshear, David W., and Leslie J. Francis. 1991. "The Use of the Revised Catechism in Anglican Churches." *British Journal of Religious Education* 13:95–100.

Lanne, Emmanuel. 1977. "Eglise une." *Irénikon* 50:46–58.

————. 1984. "The Apostolic Faith as Expressed in the Apostles' Creed, Especially Compared with the Nicene Creed." In *The Roots of Our Common Faith: Faith in the Scriptures and in the Early Church*, 95–105. Edited by Hans-Georg Link. Faith and Order Paper, 119. Geneva: World Council of Churches.

Latourette, Kenneth Scott. 1937–45. *A History of the Expansion of Christianity*. 7 vols. New York: Harper and Brothers.

————. 1967. *A History of Christian Missions in China*. New York: Russell and Russell.

Lavater, Hans Rudolf. 1980. "Zwingli und Bern." In *450 Jahre Berner Reformation: Beiträge zur Geschichte der Berner Reformation und zu Niklaus Manuel*, 60–103. Edited by Hans A. Michel, Rudolf Dellsperger, Hans Rudolf Lavater, et al. Bern: Historische Verein des Kantons Bern.

Lawson, John. 1974. "Articles of Religion." *The Encyclopedia of World Methodism*, 1:146–58, s.v. "American Methodism." Edited by Nolan B. Harmon. Nashville, Tenn.: United Methodist Publishing House.

Lecoy de la Marche, A., ed. 1877. *Anecdotes historiques légendes et apologues tirés du recueil inédit d'Etienne de Bourbon, dominicain du XIIIe siècle.* Paris: Société de l'Histoire de France.

Leduc-Fayette, Denise. 1996. *Fénelon et l'amour de Dieu.* Paris: Presses Universitaires de France.

Leff, Gordon. 1967. *Heresy in the Later Middle Ages.* 2 vols. Manchester: Manchester University Press; New York: Barnes and Noble.

———. 1986. *Wyclif in His Times.* Oxford: Clarendon Press.

Leger, Jean. 1669. *Histoire generale des Eglises evangeliques des vallees de Piemont; ou Vaudoises.* 2 vols. Leyde: Le Carpentier.

Leith, John H. 1973. *Assembly at Westminster.* Richmond, Va.: John Knox Press.

———. 1982. *Creeds of the Churches.* 3d ed. Atlanta, Ga.: John Knox Press.

Lennerz, H. 1924. "Wurde die 11. Synode von Toledo (675) von Innozenz III als 'authentisch' erklärt?" *ZfkT* 48:322–23.

Leonard, Emile G. 1959. "Légende et histoire du synode de 1559." *Etudes évangéliques de la Faculté de théologie d'Aix* 1959:12–27.

Lewis, Jack P. 1983. "Baptismal Practices of the Second- and Third-Century Church." *Restoration Quarterly* 26/1:1–17.

Lewis, Keith D. 1985. "Johann Faber and the First Zürich Disputation,1523: A Pre-Tridentine Catholic Response to Ulrich Zwingli and His Sixty-Seven Articles." Ph.D. diss., Catholic University of America.

L'Huillier, Peter. 1982. "Faits et fiction à propos du deuxième concile oecuménique." *Eglise et théologie* 13:135–56.

———. 1996. *The Church of the Ancient Councils: The Disciplinary Work of the First Four Ecumenical Councils.* Crestwood, N.Y.: Saint Vladimir's Seminary Press.

Lietzmann, Hans. 1921. "Die Anfänge des Glaubensbekenntnisses." In *Festgabe für D. Dr. A. von Harnack . . . zum siebzigsten Geburtstag dargebracht von Fachgenossen und Freunden,* 226–42. Tübingen: J. C. B. Mohr (Paul Siebeck).

———. [1925] 1963. *Die Entstehung der christlichen Liturgie nach den ältesten Quellen.* Reprint, Darmstadt: Wissenschaftliche Buchgesellschaft.

———. 1966. *Symbolstudien I–XIV.* Sonderausgabe. Darmstadt: Wissenschaftliche Buchgesellschaft.

———, and Martin Dibelius. [1910] 1921. *Die Briefe des Apostels Paulus.* Tübingen: J. C. B. Mohr (P. Siebeck).

Lightfoot, J. B., ed. and tr. [1889–90] 1981. *The Apostolic Fathers: Clement, Ignatius, and Polycarp.* 2d ed. Reprint, Grand Rapids, Mich.: Baker Book House.

Limberis, Vasiliki. 1995. "The Council of Ephesos: The Demise of the See of Ephesos and the Rise of the Cult of the Theotokos." In *Ephesos: Metropolis of Asia: An Interdisciplinary Approach to Its Archaeology, Religion, and Culture,* 321–40. Edited by Helmut Koester. Harvard Theological Studies, 41. Valley Forge, Pa.: Trinity Press International.

Linde, Simon van der. 1966. "Die Lehre von der Kirche in der *Confessio Helvetica Posterior.*" In *Glauben und Bekennen: Vierhundert Jahre Confessio Helvetica Posterior,* 337–67. Edited by Joachim Staedtke. Zurich: Zwingli Verlag.

Link, Hans-Georg. 1985. *Apostolic Faith Today: A Handbook for Study.* Geneva: World Council of Churches.

Lippy, Charles H., and Peter Williams, eds. 1988. *Encyclopedia of the American Religious Experience: Studies of Traditions and Movements*. 3 vols. New York: Charles Scribner's Sons.

Littell, Franklin Hamlin. 1958. *The Anabaptist View of the Church: A Study in the Origins of Sectarian Protestantism*. Boston: Starr King Press.

Little, Edward. 1973. "Bernard and Abelard at the Council of Sens, 1140." In *Bernard of Clairvaux: Studies Presented to Dom Jean Leclerq*, 67–71. Edited by Henri Rochais. Spencer, Mass.: Cistercian Publications.

———. 1977. "Relations Between St. Bernard and Abelard Before 1139." In *Saint Bernard of Clairvaux: Studies Commemorating the Eighth Centenary of His Canonization*, 155–68. Edited by M. Basil Pennington. Kalamazoo, Mich.: Cistercian Publications.

Liturgienbuch der evangelischen Brüdergemeine. 1873. Gnadau: C. H. Pemsel.

Liturgy and Confessions. 1990– . Looseleaf collection issued by the Reformed Church in America. [New York]: Reformed Church Press.

Locher, Gottfried W. 1978. "Die deutsche Reformation aus Schweizer Sicht." *ZKG* 89/1–2:31–35.

———. 1980a. "Von der Standhaftigkeit: Zwinglis Schlusspredigt an der Berner Disputation als Beitrag zu seiner Ethik." In *Humanität und Glaube: Gedenkschrift für Kurt Guggisberg*, 29–41. Edited by Ulrich Neuenschwander and Rudolf Dellsperger. Bern: Paul Haput.

———. 1980b. "Die Berner Disputation 1528." In *450 Jahre Berner Reformation: Beiträge zur Geschichte der Berner Reformation und zu Niklaus Manuel*, 138–55. Edited by Hans A. Michel, Rudolf Dellsperger, Hans Rudolf Lavater, et al. Bern: Historische Verein des Kantons Bern.

———. 1988. "Die Lausanne Disputationsthesen als Dokument Zwinglischer Theologie." In *La Dispute de Lausanne 1988*, 91–103.

———. 1990. "Huldrych Zwingli an Karl V: Das Vorwort zur *Fidei Ratio* 1530." *Theologische Zeitschrift* 46/3:205–18.

Lochman, Jan M. 1975. "Not Just One Reformation: The Waldensian and Hussite Heritage." *Reformed World* 33:218–24.

Logan, Samuel T. 1994. "The Context and Work of the Assembly." In Carson and Hall 1994, 27–46.

Lo Grasso, Giovanni B. 1939. *Ecclesia et status: De mutuis officiis et iuribus, fontes selecti*. Rome: Apud Aedes Universitatis Gregorianae.

Lohse, Bernhard. 1968. "Hans Denck und der 'linke Flügel' der Reformation." In *Humanitas-Christianitas*, 74–83. Edited by G. M. Beyschlag and E. Wölfel. Festschrift for Walther von Loewenich. Witten, Germany: Luther Verlag.

———. 1979. "Augsburger Bekenntnis I." In *TRE* 4:616–27.

———. 1980a. "Luther und das Augsburger Bekenntnis." In *Das Augsburger Bekenntnis von 1530: Damals und Heute*, 144–63. Edited by Bernhard Lohse and Otto Hermann Pesch. Munich: Kaiser, and Mainz: Grünewald.

———. 1980b. "Lehrentscheidungen ohne Lehramt: Die Konkordienformel als Modell theologischer Konfliktbewältigung." *Kerygma und Dogma* 26:174–87.

———. 1983. "Philipp Melanchthon in seinen Beziehungen zu Luther." In Junghans 1983, 1:403–18.

———. 1986. "Die ökumenische Bedeutung von Luthers Schmalkaldischen Artikeln." In

Kirchengemeinschaft: Anspruch und Wirklichkeit, 165–75. [Festschrift für Georg Kretschmar zum 60. Geburtstag.] Edited by Wolf-Dieter Hauschild et al. Stuttgart: Calwer Verlag.

Loofs, F. 1909. "Das Glaubensbekenntnis der Homousianer von Sardica." *Abhandlungen der königlichen preußischen Akademie der Wissenschaften,* Phil.-hist. Klaße 1:3–39.

———. 1914. *Nestorius and His Place in the History of Christian Doctrine.* Cambridge: Cambridge University Press.

Lossky, Vladimir. 1976. *The Mystical Theology of the Eastern Church.* Translated by members of the Fellowship of Saint Alban and Saint Sergius. Crestwood, N.Y.: Saint Vladimir's Seminary Press.

Lovisa, Barbro. 1994. *Italienische Waldenser und das protestantische Deutschland, 1655–1989.* Göttingen: Vandenhoeck und Ruprecht.

Lubac, Henri de. 1950. *Histoire et esprit: L'intelligence de l'Ecriture d'après Origène.* Paris: Aubier.

———. 1959. *Exégèse médiéval: Les quatres sens de l'ecriture.* 2 vols. [Paris]: Aubier. [English: *Medieval Exegesis.* Translated by Mark Sebanc. Grand Rapids, Mich.: Eerdmans, 1998– 2000.]

———. 1969. *L'Eglise dans la crise actuelle.* Paris: Editions du Cerf.

———. 1970. *La foi chrétienne: Essai sur la structure de symbole des apôtres.* Paris: Aubier-Montaigne. [English: *The Christian Faith: An Essay on the Structure of the Apostles' Creed.* Translated by Richard Arnandez. San Francisco: Ignatius Press, 1986.]

———. 1975. "Das apostolische Glaubensbekenntnis." *Internationale Katholische Zeitschrift "Communio"* 4:1–9.

Lubieniecki, Stanislas. 1994. *History of the Polish Reformation.* Translated and interpreted by George Hunston Williams. Minneapolis, Minn.: Fortress Press.

Lueker, Erwin L., ed. 1954. *Lutheran Cyclopedia.* Saint Louis, Mo.: Concordia Publishing House.

Luibhéid, Colm. 1981. *Eusebius of Caesarea and the Arian Crisis.* Dublin: Irish Academic Press.

———. 1982. *The Council of Nicaea.* Galway: Galway University Press.

———. 1983. "The Alleged Second Session of the Council of Nicaea." *Journal of Ecclesiastical History* 34:165–74.

Lumpkin, William Latane, ed. 1959. *Baptist Confessions of Faith.* Chicago: Judson Press.

Luther und die Bekenntnisschriften. 1981. Edited by R. Heinrich Foerster. Erlangen, Germany: Martin Luther-Verlag.

McBeth, H. Leon. 1990. *A Sourcebook for Baptist Heritage.* Nashville, Tenn.: Broadman Press.

McCallum, James Ramsay. 1948. *Abelard's Christian Theology.* Oxford: Basil Blackwell.

Maccarrone, Michele. 1961. *Papato e Impero dalla elezione di Federico I alla morte di Adriano IV, 1152–1159.* Rome: Pontificia Universitas Lateranensis, Facultas Theologica.

McCarthy, Timothy. 1998. *The Catholic Church: The Church in the Twentieth Century.* 2d ed. Chicago: Loyola University Press.

McComish, William. 1981. "Reazioni inglesi alla 'primavera di sangue' valdese del 1655." Translated by Giorgio Vola. *Bollettino della Società di Studi Valdesi* 149:3–10.

McCulloh, Gerald O., ed. 1962. *Man's Faith and Freedom: The Theological Influences of Jacobus Arminius.* Nashville, Tenn.: Abingdon Press.

McElrath, Damian. 1964. *The Syllabus of Pius IX: Some Reactions in England.* Louvain: Bibliothèque de l'université.

McGrath, Alister E. 1990. *Life of John Calvin: A Study in the Shaping of Western Culture.* Grand Rapids, Mich.: Baker Book House.

McHardy, A. K. 1987. "The Dissemination of Wyclif's Ideas." In *From Ockham to Wyclif,* 361–68. Edited by Anne Hudson and Michael Wilks. Studies in Church History, Subsidia, 5. Oxford: Basil Blackwell.

Macholz, Waldemar Karl Ludwig. 1902. *Spuren binitarischern Denkweise im Abendlande seit Tertullian.* Jena: A. Kämpfe.

McHugh, J. F. 1995. "The Sacrifice of the Mass at the Council of Trent." In *Sacrifice and Redemption,* 157–81. Edited by Stephen W. Sykes. Cambridge: Cambridge University Press.

McNeill, John Thomas. 1964. *Unitive Protestantism: The Ecumenical Spirit and Its Persistent Expression.* Revised ed. Richmond, Va.: John Knox Press.

McShane, Philip. 1983. "Leo the Great, Guardian of Doctrine and Discipline." *Eglise et théologie* 14:9–24.

Macy, Gary. 1984. *The Theologies of the Eucharist in the Early Scholastic Period: A Study of the Salvific Function of the Sacrament According to the Theologians, c. 1080–c. 1220.* New York: Oxford University Press.

———. 1990. "Berengar's Legacy as Heresiarch." In *Auctoritas und Ratio,* 47–68. Edited by Peter Ganz, R. B. C. Huygens, and Friedrich Niewöhner. Wiesbaden: Harrassowitz.

Madoz, Joseph. 1938. *Le Symbole du XIe Concile de Tolèdo, ses sources, sa date, sa valeur.* Louvain: Spicilegium Sacrum Lovaniense.

Magee, John. 1988. "Note on Boethius, Consolatio I, 1:5, 3:7: A New Biblical Parallel." *Vigiliae Christianae* 42/1:79–82.

Maichle, Albert. 1929. *Der Kanon der biblischen Bücher und das Konzil von Trient.* Freiburg: Herder.

Maloney, George A. 1976. *A History of Orthodox Theology Since 1453.* Belmont, Mass.: Nordland.

Malvy, Antoine, and Marcel Viller. 1927. *La confession orthodoxe de Pierre Moghila, métropolite de Kiev (1633-1646), approuvée par les patriarches grecs du XVIIe siècle.* Rome: Pontificale Institutum Orientalium Studiorum.

Manns, Peter. 1981. "Luther auf der Koburg das Reichstagsgeschehen von Augsburg und die Entstehung der *Confessio Augustana.*" In *Luther und die Bekenntnisschriften* 1981, 121–30.

Manschreck, Clyde L. 1957. "The Role of Melanchthon in the Adiaphora Controversy." *ARG* 48:165–82.

Mantzaridēs, Gēorgios I. 1984. *The Deification of Man: St. Gregory Palamas and the Orthodox Tradition.* Translated by Liadain Sherrard. Foreword by Bishop Kallistos of Diokleia. Crestwood, N.Y.: Saint Vladimir's Seminary Press.

The Manual. 2000. London: United Reformed Church.

Manual of the Church of the Nazarene: History, Constitution, Government, Ritual. 1952. Kansas City, Mo.: Nazarene Publishing House.

Marcel, Pierre, ed. 1952. *La confession de foi des Eglises réformés en France dite Confession de La Rochelle.* [St.-Germain-en-Laye (Seine-et-Oise)]: La Revue Réformée.

Marcovich, Miroslav, ed. 1994. Justin Martyr. *Apologiae pro Christianis*. Patristische Texte und Studien, 38. Berlin: W. De Gruyter.

Marsden, George M. 1970. *The Evangelical Mind and the New School Presbyterian Experience: A Case Study of Thought and Theology in Nineteenth-Century America*. New Haven and London: Yale University Press.

Marshall, Paul V. 1989. *Prayer Book Parallels*. 2 vols. New York: Church Hymnal Corp.

Mastrantonis, George. 1982. *Augsburg and Constantinople: The Correspondence Between the Tübingen Theologians and Patriarch Jeremiah II of Constantinople on the Augsburg Confession*. Brookline, Mass.: Holy Cross Orthodox Press.

Mathisen, Ralph W. 1989. *Ecclesiastical Factionalism and Religious Controversy in Fifth-Century Gaul*. Washington, D.C.: Catholic University of America.

Matthews, A. G., ed. 1959. *The Savoy Declaration of Faith and Order, 1658*. With an additional notice by Daniel T. Jenkins. London: Independent Press.

Maurer, Wilhelm. 1962. "Confessio Augustan Variata." *ARG* 53:97–151.

———. 1986. *Historical Commentary on the Augsburg Confession*. Translated by H. George Anderson. Philadelphia: Fortress Press.

Mehl, Roger. 1959. *Explication de la confession de foi de La Rochelle*. Paris: Les Bergers et les Mages.

———. 1977. "Strasbourg et Luther: La Tétrapolitaine." In *Strasbourg au coeur religieux du XVIe siècle: Actes du colloque international de Strasbourg, 1975*, 145–52. Edited by Georges Livet and Francis Rapp. Strasbourg: Librairie Istra.

Mehlhausen, Joachim. 1980. "Der Streit um die Adiaphora." In *Bekenntnis und Einheit der Kirche: Studien zum Konkordienbuch*, 105–28. Edited by Martin Brecht and Reinhard Schwarz. Stuttgart: Calwer Verlag.

Meigs, Samantha A. 1997. *The Reformations in Ireland: Tradition and Confessionalism, 1400–1690*. New York: St. Martin's Press.

Meihuizen, Hendrick W. 1967a. "Who Were the False Brethren Mentioned in the Schleitheim Articles?" *MQR* 41:200–222.

———, ed. 1967b. Menno Simons. *Dat Fundament des Christelycken leers*. The Hague: Martin Nijhoff.

Meijering, E. P. 1987. *Augustine: De Fide et Symbolo*. Amsterdam: J. C. Gieben.

Meinhold, Peter. 1971. "Christologie und Jungfrauengeburt bei Ignatius von Antiochien." In *Studia mediaevalia et mariologica*, 465–76. Edited by Pedro Capkun-Delic. Rome: Edizione Antonianum.

———. 1979. *Studien zu Ignatius von Antiochien*. Veröffentlichungen des Institus für Europäische Geschichte, Mainz. Wiesbaden: Steiner.

Melia, Pius. 1870. *The Origin, Persecutions, and Doctrine of the Waldenses*. London: James Toovey.

Mentz, Georg, ed. [1905] 1968. *Die Wittenberger Artikel von 1536*. Darmstadt: Wissenschaftliche Buchgesellschaft.

Menzies, William W. 1971. *Anointed to Serve: The Story of the Assemblies of God*. Springfield, Mo.: Gospel Publishing House.

Merdinger, J. E. 1997. *Rome and the African Church in the Time of Augustine*. New Haven and London: Yale University Press.

Meridith, Anthony. 1981. "The Pneumatology of the Cappadocian Fathers and the Creed of Constantinople." *Irish Theological Quarterly* 48:197–211.

Merwin, Wallace C. 1974. *Adventure in Unity: The Church of Christ in China*. Grand Rapids, Mich.: Eerdmans.

Mews, Constant J. 2002. *Reason and Belief in the Age of Roscelin and Abelard*. Aldershot, England: Ashgate.

Meyendorff, John. 1964–65. "Chalcedonians and Monophysites After Chalcedon." *GOTR* 10/2:16–36.

———. 1966. *Orthodoxy and Catholicity*. New York: Sheed and Ward.

———. 1969. *Christ in Eastern Thought*. Washington, D.C.: Corpus Books.

———. 1974. *Byzantine Hesychasm: Historical, Theological, and Social Problems*. London: Variorum Reprints.

———. 1982. *The Byzantine Legacy in the Orthodox Church*. Crestwood, N.Y.: Saint Vladimir's Seminary Press.

———. 1989. *Imperial Unity and Christian Divisions: The Church, 450–680 A.D.* Crestwood, N.Y.: Saint Vladimir's Seminary.

———. 1996. *Rome, Constantinople, Moscow: Historical and Theological Studies*. Crestwood, N.Y.: Saint Vladimir's Seminary Press.

———. 1998. *Saint Gregory Palamas and Orthodox Spirituality*. Translated by Adele Fiske. Crestwood, N.Y.: Saint Vladimir's Seminary Press.

———, ed. 1983. Gregory Palamas. *The Triads*. Translated by Nicholas Gendle. Preface by Jaroslav Pelikan. New York: Paulist Press.

Meyendorff, Paul, ed. and tr. 1984. *Saint Germanus of Constantinople on the Divine Liturgy*. Crestwood, N.Y.: Saint Vladimir's Seminary Press.

———. 1989. "Reflections on Russian Liturgy: A Retrospective on the Occasion of the Millennium." In *Saint Vladimir's Theological Quarterly* 33/1:21–34.

Meyer, Carl S. 1972. "Melanchthon's Visitation Articles of 1528." *Journal of Ecclesiastical History* 23:309–22.

Michel, Anton. 1924–30. *Humbert und Kerullarios*. 2 vols. Paderborn, Germany: F. Schöningh.

Miller, Allen O., and M. Eugene Osterhaven. 1963. *The Heidelberg Catechism: Four Hundredth Anniversary Edition, 1563–1963*. Philadelphia: United Church Press.

Miller, Ed L. 1982. "Oecolampadius: The Unsung Hero of the Basel Reformation." *Iliff Review* 39:5–25.

Miller, Russell E. 1979–85. *The Larger Hope*. 2 vols. Boston: Unitarian Universalist Association.

Miller, Victoria C. 1994. *The Lambeth Articles: Doctrinal Development and Conflict in Sixteenth-Century England*. Oxford: Latimer House.

Millet, Robert L., ed. 1989. *Joseph Smith: Selected Sermons and Writings*. New York: Paulist Press.

Minear, Mark. 1987. *Richmond, 1987: A Quaker Drama Unfolds*. Richmond, Ind.: Friends United Press.

Minutes of the Auburn Convention, Held August 17, 1837, to Deliberate upon the Doings of the Last General Assembly in Relation to the Synods of Western Reserve, Utica, Geneva and Genesee, and the Third Presbytery of Philadelphia. 1837. Auburn, N.Y.: Auburn Convention.

Mirbt, Carl. 1924. *Quellen zur Geschichte des Papsttums und des römischen Katholizismus.* 4th ed. Tübingen: J. C. B. Mohr [Paul Siebeck].

Mitchell, Alexander F. 1884. *The Westminster Assembly: Its History and Its Standards.* Philadelphia: Board of Publications.

———, and John Struthers, eds. 1874. *Minutes of the Sessions of the Westminster Assembly of Divines.* Edinburgh: William Blackwood and Sons.

Moberly, R. 1990. "Yahweh Is One: The Translation of the Shema." In *Studies in the Pentateuch,* 209–15. Edited by J. A. Emerton. Supplements to Vetus Testamentum, 41. Leiden: E. J. Brill.

Möhler, Johann Adam. [1832] 1958–61. *Symbolik: Oder Darstellung der dogmatischen Gegensätze der Katholiken und Protestanten nach ihren öffentlichen Bekenntnisschriften.* Reprint, Cologne: Jakob Hegner.

Molnar, Amedeo. 1973. "Czech Confession of 1575." *Communio-Viatorum* 16/4:241–47.

———. 1983. "Luthers Beziehungen zu den Böhmischen Brüdern." In Junghans 1983, 1:627–39.

Montclos, Jean de. 1993. "Lanfranc et Bérenger: Les origines de la doctrine de la transsubstantiation." In *Lanfranco di Pavia e l'Europa del secolo XI nel IX centenario della morte (1089-1989),* 297–326. Rome: Herder.

Montgomery, John W. 1976. "Chemnitz on the Council of Trent." In *Soli Deo Gloria: Essays in Reformed Theology,* 73–94. Edited by Robert C. Sproul. Nutley, N.J.: Presbyterian and Reformed Publishing.

Moreton, M. 1989. "Commandment and Remembrance in the Shema and in the Eucharistic Prayer." In *Studia Patristica,* 20: *Critica, Classica, Orientalia, Ascetica, Liturgica* [Tenth International Conference on Patristic Studies, Oxford, 1987], 384–88. Edited by Elizabeth A. Livingstone. Louvain: Peeters.

Morin, G. 1901. "Le Symbole d'Athanase et son premier témoin, S. Césaire d'Arles." *Revue Bénédictine* 18:337–62.

———. 1932. "L'Origine du symbole d'Athanase: témoignage inédit de S. Césaire d'Arles." *Revue Bénédictine* 44:207–19.

Morris, Kenneth R. 1994. "'Pure Wheat of God' or Neurotic Deathwish? A Historical and Theological Analysis of Ignatius of Antioch's Zeal for Martyrdom." *Fides et Historia* 26: 24–41.

Morrow, Hubert W. 1970. "Cumberland Presbyterian Theology: A Nineteenth-Century Development in American Presbyterianism." *Journal of Presbyterian History* 48:203–20.

Moss, C. B. 1964. *The Old Catholic Movement: Its Origins and History.* 2d ed. London: S.P.C.K.

Muelder, Walter G. 1961. *Methodism and Society in the Twentieth Century.* New York: Abingdon Press.

Mueller, John T. 1949. "Notes on the Consensus Tigurinus of 1549." *Concordia Theological Monthly* 20:894–909.

Mueller, William A. 1959. *A History of Southern Baptist Theological Seminary.* Nashville, Tenn.: Broadman Press.

Müller, Ewald. 1934. *Das Konzil von Vienne, 1311–1312: Seine Quellen und seine Geschichte.* Münster: Aschendorff.

Müller, Gerhard. 1968. "Pius IX. und die Entwicklung der römisch-katholischen Mariologie." *Neue Zeitschrift für systematische Theologie und Religionsphilosophie* 10:111–30.

Müller, Joseph Theodor. 1922–31. *Geschichte der Böhmischen Brüder.* 3 vols. Herrnhut, Germany: Missionsbuchhandlung.

Muller, Richard A. 1991. *God, Creation, and Providence in the Thought of Jacob Arminius: Sources and Directions of Scholastic Protestantism.* Grand Rapids, Mich.: Baker Book House.

Muralt, Leonhard von. 1930. "Stadtgemeinde und Reformation in der Schweiz." *Zeitschrift für schweizerische Geschichte* 10:349–84.

———. 1969. "Der Anfang der Reformation in Zurich." *Reformatio* 18:3–9.

Murphy, Francis X., and P. Sherwood. 1974. *Constantinople II et Constantinople III.* Vol. 3 of *Histoire des conciles oecuméniques.* Paris: Orante.

Müsing, Hans-Werner. 1977. "The Anabaptist Movement in Strasbourg from Early 1526 to July 1577." *MQR* 51:91–126.

My People's Prayer Book: Traditional Prayers, Modern Commentaries. 1997. Edited by Lawrence A. Hoffman. Woodstock, Vt.: Jewish Lights Publishing.

Nacpil, Emerito P. 1976. "A Gospel for the New Filipino." In Anderson, 117–45.

Navè, Pnina. 1974. "Höre Israel: Talmudische und liturgische Traditionen über Dt 6, 4–9, 11, 13–21; Nm 15, 37–41." In *Das Vaterunser: Gemeinsames im Beten von Juden und Christen,* 56–76. Edited by Michael Brocke, Jakob J. Petuchowski, and Walter Strolz. Frieburg: Herder.

Nelson, E. Clifford, ed. 1980. *The Lutherans in North America.* 2d ed. Philadelphia: Fortress Press.

Nelson, Stanley A. 1994. "Reflecting on Baptist Origins: The London Confession of Faith of 1644." *Baptist History and Heritage* 29:33–46.

Nestorius. 1925. *The Bazaar of Heraclides.* Edited and translated by G. R. Driver and L. Hodgson. Oxford: Clarendon Press.

Netter, Thomas. 1858. *Fasciculi Zizaniorum magistri Johannis Wyclif cum tritico.* London: Longman, Brown, Green, Longmans, and Roberts.

Neuner, J., and J. Dupuis. 2001. *The Christian Faith in the Doctrinal Documents of the Catholic Church.* New York: Alba House.

Newbigin, Lesslie, J. E. [1948] 1960. *The Reunion of the Church: A Defence of the South India Scheme.* 2d ed. Reprint, London: SCM Press.

Newman, John Henry. 1841. *Tract Ninety* [Remarks on Certain Passages in the Thirty-Nine Articles]. London: J. G. F. and J. Rivington.

Nichols, Robert L., and Theofanis George Stavrou. 1978. *Russian Orthodoxy Under the Old Regime.* Minneapolis: University of Minnesota Press.

Niederwimmer, Kurt, ed. 1993. *Die Didache.* 2d ed. Göttingen: Vandenhoeck und Ruprecht. Also published with English translation of commentary, Minneapolis, Minn.: Fortress Press, 1998.

Niemöller, Gerhard, ed. 1959. *Die erste Bekenntnissynode der Deutschen Evangelischen Kirche zu Barmen.* Göttingen: Vandenhoeck und Ruprecht.

Nienkirchen, Charles. 1982. "Reviewing the Case for a Non-Separatist Ecclesiology in Early Swiss Anabaptism." *MQR* 56:227–41.

Nihon Kirisuto Kyodan Kyouken Kyouki oyobi syokisoku. 2001. Tokyo: Nihon Kirisuto Kyodan Shyuppankyoku.

Niles, D. T. 1962. "Church Union in North India, Pakistan, and Ceylon." *Ecumenical Review* 14: 305–22.

Noko, Ishmael. 2000. "The Joint Declaration on the Doctrine of Justification: Some Observations." *Centro Pro Unione Bulletin* 57:7–9.

Nordström, N. J. 1928. *Svenska Baptistsamfundets Historia.* Stockholm: Baptistmissionens Bokförlags.

Norris, Frederick W. 1978. "Apostolic, Catholic, and Sensible: The *Consensus Fidelium.*" In *Essays on New Testament Christianity,* 15–29. Edited by C. Robert Wetzel. Cincinnati, Ohio: Standard Publishing.

Norris, R. A. 1990. "Irenaeus' Use of Paul in His Polemic Against the Gnostics." In *Paul and the Legacies of Paul,* 79–98, 337–40. Edited by William S. Babcock. Dallas: SMU Press.

Nulman, Macy. 1993. "Shema." In *The Encyclopedia of Jewish Prayer: Ashkenazic and Sephardic Rites,* 294–98. Northvale, N.J.: Jason Aronson.

Oberdorfer, Bernd. 2001. *Filioque: Geschichte und Theologie eines ökumenischen Problems.* Göttingen: Vandenhoeck und Ruprecht.

Oberman, Heiko A. 1981. *Masters of the Reformation.* Cambridge: Cambridge University Press.

———. 1994. "Initia Calvini: The Matrix of Calvin's Reformation." In *Calvinus Sacrae Scripturae professor: Calvin as Confessor of Holy Scripture,* 113–54. Edited by Wilhelm H. Neuser. Grand Rapids, Mich.: W. B. Eerdmans.

O'Connell, Timothy E., ed. 1986. *Vatican II and Its Documents: An American Reappraisal.* Wilmington, Del.: Michael Glazier.

O'Connor, Edward D. 1958. *The Dogma of the Immaculate Conception: History and Significance.* Notre Dame, Ind.: University of Notre Dame Press.

O'Dea, Thomas F. 1957. *The Mormons.* Chicago: University of Chicago Press.

Odložilik, Otakar. 1940. "Two Reformation Leaders of the Unitas Fratrum." *Church History* 9:253–63.

O'Donnell, James J. 1985. *Augustine.* Boston: Twayne.

O'Donovan, Oliver. 1986. *On the Thirty Nine Articles: A Conversation with Tudor Christianity.* Exeter, England: Paternoster Press for Latimer House, Oxford.

Ogudo, Donatus Emeka Onyemaobi. 1988. *The Catholic Missionaries and the Liturgical Movement in Nigeria: An Historical Overview.* Paderborn, Germany: Verlag Bonifatius-Druckerei.

Olbricht, Thomas H., and Hans Rollmann, eds. 2000. *The Quest for Christian Unity, Peace, and Purity in Thomas Campbell's "Declaration and Address": Text and Studies.* Lanham, Md.: Scarecrow Press.

Olmsted, Wendy Raudenbush. 1989. "Philosophical Inquiry and Religious Transformation in Boethius's *The Consolation of Philosophy* and Augustine's *Confessions.*" *Journal of Religion* 69:14–35.

Onasch, Konrad, and Annemarie Schnieper. 1997. *Icons: The Fascination and the Reality.* New York: Riverside Book.

Oosthuizen, Gerhard Cornelis. 1958. *Theological Discussions and Confessional Developments in the Churches of Asia and Africa.* Franeker, Netherlands: T. Wever.

Opitz, Hans-Georg, ed. 1934–41. *Athanasius. Werke.* 3 vols. Berlin: Walter de Gruyter.

Opitz, Peter, trans. 1995. *Rechenschaft über den Glauben* [translation of Zwingli's "Fidei ratio"]. Vol. 4 of *Huldrych Zwingli Schriften.* Edited by Thomas Brunnschweiler and Samuel Lutz. Zurich: Theologischer Verlag Zurich.

Ordo Missae Cum Populo / The Ordinary of the Mass in Eight Languages. 1992. Collegeville, Minn.: Liturgical Press.

Orthodox Church in America. 1967. *The Divine Liturgy, According to St. John Chrysostom, with Appendices.* New York: Orthodox Eastern Church.

Ortiz de Urbina, Ignacio. 1963. *Nicée et Constantinople.* Paris: Editions de l'Orante.

Osborn, Eric F. 1989. "Reason and the Rule of Faith in the Second Century A.D." In *The Making of Orthodoxy: Essays in Honour of Henry Chadwick,* 40–61. Edited by Rowan Williams. Cambridge: Cambridge University Press.

Osborn, Ronald E. 1979. *The Faith We Affirm: Basic Beliefs of Disciples of Christ.* St. Louis, Mo.: Bethany Press.

Oulton, John Ernest Leonard. 1940. *The Credal Statements of St. Patrick.* Dublin: Hodges, Figgis.

Our Lady. 1961. Selected and arranged by the Benedictine monks of Solesmes. Translated by the Daughters of St. Paul. Boston: St. Paul Editions.

Outler, Albert C. 1991. *The Wesleyan Theological Heritage.* Edited by Thomas C. Oden and Leicester R. Longden. Grand Rapids, Mich.: Zondervan.

Overduin, Daniel C. 1980. *Reflections on Luther's Small Catechism.* Saint Louis, Mo.: Concordia Press.

Ozment, Steven. 1973. *Mysticism and Dissent.* New Haven and London: Yale University Press.

Packull, Werner O. 1982. "Hans Denck: Fugitive from Dogmatism." In *Profiles of Radical Reformers: Biographical Sketches from Thomas Müntzer to Paracelsus,* 62–71. Edited by Hans Goertz. Scottdale, Pa.: Herald Press.

Palacký, František, ed. 1829. *Staří letopisové čeští, 1378–1527. Scriptorum rerum bohemicarum,* vol. 3. Prague: J. H. Pospissila.

———. 1844–67. *Geschichte von Böhmen.* 5 vols. Prague: Kronberger und Weber.

Pallath, Paul, ed. 1994. *Catholic Eastern Churches: Heritage and Identity.* Rome: Mar Thoma Yogam (The St. Thomas Christian Fellowship in Rome).

Palmer, Paul F., ed. 1952. *Mary in the Documents of the Church.* Westminster, Md.: Newman Press.

Palmieri, Aurelio. 1909. *Dositeo, patriarca greco di Gerusalemme (1641–1707): Contributo alla storia della teologia greco-ortodossa nel secolo XVII.* Florence: Libreria Editrice Fiorentina.

Panindangion Haporseaon (Confessie) ni Huria Kristen Batak Protestant (H.K.B.P.). 1966. Pearadja Tarutung, Indonesia: H.K.B.P. Pusat.

Pannenberg, Walter. 1979. "Faith and Disorder in Bangalore." *Worldview* 22:37–40.

Pannier, Jacques. 1936. *Les origines de la confession de foi et la discipline des Eglises réformées de France.* Paris: F. Alcan.

Papademetriou, George C., ed. 1989. *Photian Studies.* Brookline, Mass.: Holy Cross Orthodox Press.

Papadopoulos, Chrysostomos. 1939. *Kyrillos Loukaris.* Edited by Grēgorios Papamichaēl. 2nd ed. Athens: Phoinikos.

Paret, Friedrich. 1891. *Priscillianus, ein Reformator des vierten Jahrhunderts: Eine Kirchengeschichtlich Studie, zugleich ein Kommentar zu den erhaltenen Schriften Priscillians.* Würzburg: A. Stuber.

Parker, G. Keith. 1982. *Baptists in Europe: History and Confessions of Faith.* Nashville, Tenn.: Broadman Press.

Pas, P. 1954. "La doctrine de la double justice au Concile de Trent." *Ephemerides Theologicae Lovanienses* 30:5–53.

Patch, Howard Rollin. 1935. *The Tradition of Boethius: A Study of His Importance in Medieval Culture.* New York: Oxford University Press.

Patschovsky, Alexander, and Kurt-Victor Selge. 1973. *Quellen zur Geschichte der Waldenser.* Gütersloh, Germany: Gerd Mohn.

Patterson, Lloyd G. 1982. "Nikaia to Constantinople: The Theological Issues." *GOTR* 27: 375–93.

Pauck, Wilhelm. 1950. *The Heritage of the Reformation.* Glencoe, Ill.: Free Press.

Paul, Robert S. 1985. *The Assembly of the Lord: Politics and Religion in the Westminster Assembly and the "Grand Debate."* Edinburgh: T. and T. Clark.

Paulsen, Henning. 1985. *Die Briefe des Ignatius von Antiochia und der Brief des Polykarp von Smyrna.* 2d ed. Tübingen: Mohr.

Payne, Ernest A. 1952. "Michael Sattler and the Schleitheim Confession, 1527." *Baptist Quarterly* 14:337–44.

Peel, Robert. 1958. *Christian Science: Its Encounter with American Culture.* New York: Henry Holt.

Peitz, W. M. 1917. "Martin I und Maximus Confessor: Beiträge zur Geschichte des Monotheletenstreits in den Jahren 642–68." *Historisches Jahrbuch* 38:213–36, 429–58.

Pelikan, Jaroslav. 1948. "Luther's Attitude Toward John Hus." *Concordia Theological Monthly* 19:747–63.

———. 1949a. "Luther's Endorsement of the *Confessio Bohemica.*" *Concordia Theological Monthly* 20:829–43.

———. 1949b. "Luther's Negotiations with the Hussites." *Concordia Theological Monthly* 20:496–517.

———. 1951a. "Chalcedon After Fifteen Centuries." *Concordia Theological Monthly* 22:926–36.

———. 1951b. "Church and Church History in the Confessions." *Concordia Theological Monthly* 22:305–20.

———. 1967. "Verius Servamus Canones: Church Law and Divine Law in the Apology of the Augsburg Confession." In *Studia Gratiana* 11, special issue, *Collectanea Stephan Kuttner,* 1:367–88. Edited by Alphons M. Stickler.

———. 1971. *Historical Theology: Continuity and Change in Christian Doctrine.* New York: Corpus.

———. 1974. "The Doctrine of *filioque* in Thomas Aquinas and Its Patristic Antecedents:

An Analysis of *Summa theologiae*, Part I, Question 36." In *St. Thomas Aquinas, 1274-1974*, 1:315-36. Edited by Etienne Gilson et al. Toronto: Pontifical Institute of Mediaeval Studies.

———. 1985. *Jesus Through the Centuries: His Place in the History of Culture*. New Haven and London: Yale University Press.

———. 1990a. *Imago Dei: The Byzantine Apologia for Icons*. The A. W. Mellon Lectures in the Fine Arts, 1987. Princeton, N.J.: Princeton University Press.

———. 1990b. *Eternal Feminines: Three Theological Allegories in Dante's "Paradiso."* New Brunswick, N.J.: Rutgers University Press.

———. 1990c. *Confessor Between East and West*. Grand Rapids, Mich.: Eerdmans.

———. 1993. *Christianity and Classical Culture: The Metamorphosis of Natural Theology in the Christian Encounter with Hellenism*. New Haven and London: Yale University Press.

———. 1996. *Mary Through the Centuries: Her Place in the History of Culture*. New Haven and London: Yale University Press.

———. 1997. *The Reformation of the Bible/The Bible of the Reformation*. Catalogue of the exhibition by David Price and Valerie R. Hotchkiss. New Haven and London: Yale University Press.

Pengakuan Gereja Toraja dalam bahasa Toraja. 1994. 2d ed. Rantepao, Indonesia: Pusbang-Badan Pekerja Sinode Gereja Toraja.

Perkins, Carl M. 1994. "The Evening Shema: A Study in Rabbinic Consolation." *Judaism* 43:26-36.

Peronnet, Michel. 1988. "Guillaume Farel à Lausanne en 1536." In *La Dispute de Lausanne* 1988, 133-41.

Perosanz, J. M. 1976. *El simbolo atanasiano*. Madrid: Palabra.

Péry, Andé. 1959. *Le Catéchisme de Heidelberg*. Geneva: Labor et Fides.

Peter, Carl J. 1985. "The Decree on Justification in the Council of Trent." In *Justification by Faith*, 218-29. Edited by H. George Anderson, T. Austin Murphy, and Joseph A. Burgess. Minneapolis, Minn.: Augsburg Publishing House.

Peters, Albrecht. 1981. "Die Bedeutung der Katechismen Luthers innerhalb der Bekenntnisschriften." In *Luther und die Bekenntnisschriften* 1981, 46-89.

Petersen, Peter. [1921] 1964. *Geschichte der aristotelischen Philosophie im protestantischen Deutschland*. Reprint, Stuttgart: Frommann.

Petit, Louis, Xénophon Sidéridès, and Martin Jugie, eds. 1928-36. *Georgiou tou Skolariou Apanta ta euriskomena = Oeuvres complètes de Georges Scholarios*. Paris: Maison de la Bonne Presse.

Pfister, Rudolf. 1966. "Die Zweite Helvetische Bekenntnis in der Schweiz." In *Glauben und Bekennen: Vierhundert Jahre Confessio Helvetica Posterior*, 54-80. Edited by Joachim Staedtke. Zurich: Zwingli Verlag.

Pfnür, Vinzenz. 1970. *Einig in der Rechtfertigungslehre? Die Rechtfertigungslehre der "Confessio Augustana" (1530) und die Stellungnahme der katholischen Kontroverstheologie zwischen 1530 und 1533*. Wiesbaden: Franz Steiner.

Pharantos, Mega L. 1969. *Hē theologia Gennadiou tou Scholariou* [The theology of Gennadius Scholarius]. Athens: University of Athens.

Phougias, Methodios G. 1990. *Hē ekklēsiastikē antiparathesis Hellēnōn kai Latinōn: Apo tēs epochēs tou Megalou Phōtiou mechri tēs Synodou tēs Phlōrentias, 853-1439.* Athens: Heptalophos.

Piaget, Arthur, ed. 1928. *Les actes de la Dispute de Lausanne, 1536.* Neuchâtel: Secrétariat de l'Université.

Piepkorn, Arthur Carl. 1993. *The Church: Selected Writings of Arthur Carl Piepkorn.* Edited by Michael P. Plekon and William S. Wiecher. Afterword by Richard John Neuhaus. Delhi, N.Y.: ALPB Books.

Pii IX Pontificis Maximi Acta. 1854-78. 9 vols. [Rome]: Ex Typographia Bonarum Artium.

Pillinger, Renate. 1975. "Die Taufe nach der Didache: Philologisch-archäologische Untersuchung der Kapitel 7, 9, 10 und 14." *Wiener Studien; Zeitschrift für Klassische Philologie und Patristik* 88:152-60.

Pin, Jean-Pierre. 1979. "Pour une analyse textuelle du catechisme (1542) de Jean Calvin." In *Calvinus ecclesiae doctor,* 159-70. Edited by W. H. Neuser. Kampen, Netherlands: J. H. Kok.

Pinnock, Clark H., ed. 1989. *The Grace of God, the Will of Man: A Case for Arminianism.* Grand Rapids, Mich.: Zondervan.

Pipkin, H. Wayne, and John H. Yoder, trans. and eds. 1989. *Balthasar Hubmaier, Theologian of Anabaptism.* Scottdale, Pa.: Herald Press.

Plan of Church Union in North India and Pakistan. 1965. 4th ed. Madras: Christian Literature Society for the Negotiating Committee.

Plantinga, Cornelius, Jr. 1979. *A Place to Stand: A Reformed Study of Creeds and Confessions.* Board of Publications of the Christian Reformed Church.

Podskalsky, Gerhard. 1988. *Griechische Theologie in der Zeit der Türkenherrschaft (1453-1821): Die Orthodoxie im Spannungsfeld der nachreformatorischen Konfessionen des Westens.* Munich: C. H. Beck.

Poitras, Edward. 1997. "How Korean Is the Methodist 'Korean Creed'?" *Methodist History* 36:3-16.

Polish National Catholic Church of America. 1975. *The Confession of Faith and the Eleven Great Principles of the Polish National Catholic Church.* [Scranton, Pa.]: [Polish National Catholic Church].

Poll, G. J. van de. 1954. *Martin Bucer's Liturgical Ideas.* Assen: Van Gorcum.

Pollard, John E. 1995. "Patristic Sources of the Catechism of the Catholic Church." *Josephinum Journal of Theology,* n.s., 2:18-42.

Pollet, Jacques V. 1963. *Huldrych Zwingli et la Réforme en Suisse.* Paris: Presses Universitaires de France.

Pont, A. D. 1991. "Confession of Faith in Calvin's Geneva." In *Calvin: Erbe und Auftrag,* 106-16. Edited by Willem van 't Spijker. Kampen, Netherlands: Kok Pharos.

Pontal, Odette. 1986. *Die Synoden im Merowingerreich.* Paderborn, Germany: Ferdinand Schöningh.

Popescu, T., ed. 1935. *Enciclica Patriarhilor Ortodocsi dela 1848: Studiu introductive, text si traducere.* Bucharest: n.p.

Popivchak, Ronald Peter. 1975. "Peter Mohila, Metropolitan of Kiev (1633-47): Translation and Evaluation of His 'Orthodox Confession of Faith' (1640)." Ph.D. diss., Catholic University of America.

Porter, Harry Culverwell. 1958. *Reformation and Reaction in Tudor Cambridge.* Cambridge: Cambridge University Press.

Potter, G. R. 1976. *Zwingli.* Cambridge: Cambridge University Press.

Pottmeyer, Hermann Joseph. 1968. *Der Glaube vor dem Anspruch der Wissenschaft: Die Konstitution über den katholischen Glauben, Dei Filius des 1. Vatikanischen Konzils.* Freiburg: Herder.

———. 1975. *Unfehlbarkeit und Souveränität: Die päpstliche Unfehlbarkeit im System der ultramontanischen Ekklesiologie des 19. Jahrhunderts.* Mainz: Matthias-Grünewald-Verlag.

Potz, Richard. 1971. *Patriarch und Synode in Konstantinopel: Das Verfassungrecht des ökumenischen Patriarchates.* Vienna: Herder.

Poythress, Vern S. 1976. "Is Romans 1:3–4 a Pauline Confession After All?" *Expository Times* 87:180–83.

Praamsma, Louis. 1968. "Background of the Arminian Controversy (1586–1618)." In *Crisis in the Reformed Churches: Essays in Commemoration of the Great Synod of Dort, 1618–1619,* 22–38. Edited by Peter Y. De Jong. Grand Rapids, Mich.: Reformed Fellowship.

The Prayer Book Dictionary. [1918]. Edited by George Harford, Morley Stevenson, and J. W. Tyrer. London: Waverly Book.

Praying Together. 1988. Prepared by the English Language Liturgical Consultation. Revised ed. Nashville, Tenn.: Abingdon Press.

Prestige, George Leonard. 1956. *St. Basil the Great and Apollinaris of Laodicea.* Edited by Henry Chadwick. London: S.P.C.K.

Principe, Walter Henry. 1963–75. *The Theology of the Hypostatic Union in the Early Thirteenth Century.* 4 vols. Toronto: Pontifical Institute of Mediaeval Studies.

Pritsak, Omeljan, et al. 1984. *The Kiev Mohyla Academy: Commemorating the 350th Anniversary of Its Founding (1632).* Cambridge, Mass.: Ukrainian Research Institute, Harvard University.

Prokurat, Michael, Alexander Golitzin, and Michael D. Peterson. 1996. *Historical Dictionary of the Orthodox Church.* Lanham, Md.: Scarecrow Press.

Proposed Basis of Union. 1965. [Accra]: Ghana Church Union Committee.

Proposed Scheme of Church Union in Ceylon. 1955. 3d revised ed. Madras: Christian Literature Society.

Provost, James H. 1998. "Safeguarding the Faith." *America* 179/3:8.

Pruett, Gordon E. 1975. "A Protestant Doctrine of the Eucharistic Presence." *Calvin Theological Journal* 10:142–74.

Psalter Hymnal: Including the Psalms, Bible Songs, Hymns, Ecumenical Creeds, Doctrinal Standards, and Liturgical Forms of the Christian Reformed Church in North America. 1988. Grand Rapids, Mich.: CRC Publications.

Quellen zur Geschichte der Täufer in der Schweiz. 1973. Edited by Heinold Fast. 4 vols. Zurich: Theologischer Verlag.

Raabe, Paul R. 1989. "Children's Sermons and Luther's *Small Catechism.*" *Concordia Journal* 15:100–102.

Radice, Betty, tr. 1974. *The Letters of Abelard and Heloise.* Baltimore: Penguin.

Railton, Nicholas. 2000. *No North Sea: The Anglo-German Evangelical Network in the Middle of the Nineteenth Century.* Leiden: Brill.

Rand, E. K. 1928. *Founders of the Middle Ages*. Cambridge, Mass.: Harvard University Press.

Rankin, D. 1995. *Tertullian and the Church*. Cambridge: Cambridge University Press.

Ratzinger, Joseph, Cardinal, and Tarcisio Bertone. 1998. "Commentary on the Profession of Faith." *L'Osservatore Romano*, 15 July 1998, 3-4.

Rauschenbusch, Walter. 1907. *Christianity and the Social Crisis*. Reprint, New York: Macmillan.

Reardon, Bernard M. G. 1989. "The Thirty-Nine Articles and the Augsburg Confession." *Lutheran Quarterly* 3/1:91-106.

Reed, Stephen D. 1983. "The Decalogue in Luther's *Large Catechism*." *Dialog* 22:264-69.

Rees, Thomas. [1818] 1962. *The Racovian Catechism*. Reprint, Lexington, Ky.: American Theological Library Association.

Reinhard, Wolfgang. 1977. "Gegenreformation als Modernisierung? Prolegomena zu einer Theorie des konfessionellen Zeitalters." *ARG* 68:226-52.

———, and Heinz Schilling, eds. 1995. *Die katholische Konfessionalisierung*. Gütersloh, Germany: Gütersloher Verlagshaus.

Rembert, Karl. 1899. *Die "Wiedertäufer" im Herzogtum Jülich*. Berlin: R. Gaertners Verlagsbuchhandlung.

Renihan, James M. 1996. "An Examination of the Possible Influence of Menno Simons' *Foundation Book* upon the Particular Baptist Confession of 1644." *American Baptist Quarterly* 15:190-207.

Resolutions of the First Synod of Old Catholics of the German Empire: Articles Adopted by the Conference Held at Bonn, 14-16 Sept. 1874. 1874. Cambridge: J. Palmer.

Reu, Johann Michael. [1904] 1976. *Quellen zur Geschichte des kirchlichen Unterrichts in der evangelischen Kirche Deutschlands zwischen 1530 und 1600*. Reprint, Hildesheim: Olms.

———. 1929. *Dr. Martin Luther's Small Catechism: A History of Its Origin, Its Distribution, and Its Use*. Chicago: Wartburg.

Rhee, Jong Sung. "The Significance of the Lausanne Covenant." *Northeast Asia Journal of Theology* 15:26-37.

Řičan, Rudolf. 1992. *The History of the Unity of Brethren: A Protestant Hussite Church in Bohemia and Moravia*. Translated by C. Daniel Crews. Bethlehem, Pa.: Moravian Church in America.

Richmond, Mary L. Hurt. 1977. *Shaker Literature: A Bibliography*. Hancock, Mass.: Shaker Community; distributed by the University Press of New England.

Ridley, Jasper. 1962. *Thomas Cranmer*. Oxford: Oxford University Press.

Riedinger, Rudolf. 1976. "Aus den Akten der Lateran-Synode von 649." *Byzantinische Zeitschrift* 69:17-29.

———. 1981. "Das Bekenntnis des Gregor Thaumaturgus bei Sophronius von Jerusalem und Macarius von Antiocheia." *ZKG* 92/2-3:311-14.

———. 1982. "Die Lateransynode von 649 und Maximos der Bekenner." In *Maximus Confessor*, 111-21. Edited by Felix Heinzer and Christoph Schönborn. Fribourg, Switzerland: Editions Universitaires.

Ries, Hans de. 1686. *Corte belijdenisse des geloofs*. Edited by Pieter Jansz. Amsterdam: Joannes van Veen.

Ris, Cornelis. 1766. *De geloofsleere der waare Mennoniten of Doopsgezinden.* Hoorn: T. Tjallingius.

———. 1904. *Mennonite Articles of Faith as Set Forth in Public Confession of the Church: A Translation.* Berne, Iowa: Mennonite Book Concern.

Ritschl, Dietrich. 1979. "The History of the *filioque* Controversy." Translated by R. Nowell. In *Conflicts About the Holy Spirit,* 3–14. Edited by Hans Küng and Jürgen Moltmann. New York: Seabury Press.

———. 1981. "Historical Development and Implications of the *filioque* Controversy." In *Spirit of God, Spirit of Christ: Ecumenical Reflections on the filioque Controversy,* 46–65. Edited by Lukas Vischer. Geneva: World Council of Churches.

———. 1982. "Warum wir Konzilien feiern: Konstantinopel 381." *Theologische Zeitschrift* 38:213–25.

Ritter, Adolf Martin. 1965. *Das Konzil von Konstantinopel und sein Symbol: Studien zur Geschichte und Theologie des II. Ökumenischen Konzils.* Göttingen: Vandenhoeck und Ruprecht.

———. 1981. "The Dogma of Constantinople (381) and Its Reception Within the Churches of the Reformation." *Irish Theological Quarterly* 48:228–32 [Special issue commemorating 1600th anniversary of the first council of Constantinople].

Rivera, Juan Francisco. 1940. *Elipando de Toledo: Nueva aportación a los estudios Mozárabes.* Toledo: Editorial Católica Toledana.

Rivière, Jean. 1926. *Le problème de l'Eglise et de l'Etat au temps de Philippe le Bel: Etude de théologie positive.* Louvain: Spicilegium Sacrum Lovaniense.

Roberg, Burkhard. 1990. *Das Zweite Konzil von Lyon [1274].* Paderborn, Germany: Ferdinand Schöningh.

Roberts, Benjamin Titus. 1984. *Why Another Sect?* New York: Garland.

Roberts, C. H., and Dom B. Capelle, eds. 1949. *An Early Euchologium: The Dêr-Balizeh Papyrus Enlarged and Reedited.* Louvain: Bureaux du Muséon.

Robertson, J. N. W. B. 1899. *The Acts and Decrees of the Synod of Jerusalem in 1672.* London: Baker.

Robinson, Elmo Arnold. 1970. *American Universalism: Its Origins, Organization, and Heritage.* New York: Exposition Press.

Robinson, J. Armitage, ed. 1920. *The Demonstration of the Apostolic Preaching of St. Irenaeus.* London: S.P.C.K.

Robson, J. A. 1961. *Wyclif and the Oxford Schools.* Cambridge: Cambridge University Press.

Rogers, Jack Bartelett. 1967. *Scripture in the Westminster Confession: A Problem of Historical Interpretation for American Presbyterianism.* Grand Rapids, Mich.: W. B. Eerdmans.

———. 1985. *Presbyterian Creeds: A Guide to the Book of Confessions.* Philadelphia: Westminster Press.

Rohls, Jan. 1987. *Theologie reformierter Bekenntnisschriften: Von Zürich bis Barmen.* Göttingen: Vandenhoeck und Ruprecht.

Roloff, Hans-Gert. 1988 "Die Funktion von Hus-Texten in der Reformations-Polemik." In *De captu lectoris: Wirkungen des Buches im 15. und 16. Jahrhundert,* 219–56. Edited by Wolfgang Milde and Werner Schuder. Berlin: de Gruyter.

Romanides, John S. 1987. "St. Cyril's 'One Physis or Hypostasis of God the Logos Incarnate' and Chalcedon." In Fries and Nersoyan 1987, 15–34.

The Roman Missal, Revised by Decree of the Second Vatican Ecumenical Council. The Sacramentary. 1995. Collegeville, Minn.: Liturgical Press.

Rordorf, Willy. 1972. "Le baptême selon la Didaché." In *Mélanges liturgiques offerts à Bernard Botte de l'Abbaye du Mont César*, 499–509. Edited by Jean J. von Allmen et al. Louvain: Abbaye du Mont César.

————, and André Tuilier, eds. and trans. 1998. *La doctrine des douze apôtres (Didachè).* Source chrétiennes, 248. Paris: Editions du Cerf.

Rorem, Paul. 1988. "Calvin and Bullinger on the Lord's Supper: The Agreement." *Lutheran Quarterly*, n.s., 2:357–89.

————. 1994. "The Consensus Tigurinus (1549): Did Calvin Compromise?" In *Calvinus Sacrae Scripturae professor: Calvin as Confessor of Holy Scripture*, 72–90. Edited by Wilhelm H. Neuser. Grand Rapids, Mich.: W. B. Eerdmans.

Rothschild, Fritz 1964. *The Shema.* New York: Burning Bush Press.

Rotondò, Antonio, ed. 1986. *Lelio Sozzini: Opere.* Florence: L. S. Olschki.

Rouse, Ruth, and Stephen C. Neill, eds. 1986. *A History of the Ecumenical Movement, 1517–1948.* 3d ed. Geneva: World Council of Churches.

Rousseau, Adelin, and Louis Doutreleau, eds. and trans. 1952–82. *Contre les hérésies.* 5 vols. in 11. Paris: Editions du Cerf.

Routley, Erik. 1963. *Creeds and Confessions: From the Reformation to the Modern Church.* Philadelphia: Westminster Press.

Rückert, Hanns. 1925. *Die Rechtfertigungslehre auf dem Tridentinischen Konzil.* Bonn: A. Marcus und E. Weber.

Rusch, William G., and Daniel F. Martensen, eds. 1989. *The Leuenberg Agreement and Lutheran-Reformed Relationships: Evaluations by North American and European Theologians.* Minneapolis, Minn.: Augsburg Publishing House.

Russell, William. 1991a. "A Theological Guide to the Smalcald Articles." *Lutheran Quarterly*, n.s., 5:469–92.

————. 1991b. "The Smalcald Articles, Luther's Theological Testament." *Lutheran Quarterly*, n.s., 5:277–96.

————. 1994. "Martin Luther's Understanding of the Pope as the Antichrist." *ARG* 85:32–44.

————. 1995. *Luther's Theological Testament: The Schmalkald Articles.* Minneapolis, Minn.: Fortress Press.

Ryang, J. S. 1934. *Fiftieth Anniversary of Korean Methodism.* [Seoul?]: Korean Methodist Church.

Sahas, Daniel J. 1986. *Icon and Logos: Sources in Eighth-Century Iconoclasm.* Toronto: University of Toronto Press.

Sahu, Dhirendra Kumar. 1994. *The Church of North India: A Historical and Systematic Theological Inquiry into an Ecumenical Ecclesiology.* Frankfurt: P. Lang.

Samuel, Vinay C. 1984. "The Nicene Creed: Compared to the Apostles' Creed, the Quicunque Vult and the New Testament." In *The Roots of Our Common Faith: Faith in the*

Scriptures and in the Early Church, 81–93. Edited by Hans-Georg Link. Faith and Order Paper, 119. Geneva: World Council of Churches.

Sandall, Robert. [1947–73] 1979. *The History of the Salvation Army.* 6 vols. Vols. 4–5 by Arch R. Wiggins; vol. 6 by Frederick Coutts. Reprint, New York: Salvation Army.

Sanders, Paul. 1992. "Heinrich Bullinger et le Zwinglianisme tardif aux lendemains du 'Consensus Tigurinus.'" In *Reformiertes Erbe,* 307–23. Festschrift für Gottfried W. Locher zu seinem 80. Geburtstag. Edited by Heiko Oberman, Ernst Saxer, Alfred Schindler, et al. Special issue of *Zwingliana* (19/1). Zurich: Theologischer Verlag.

Sansbury, Christopher J. 1985. "Athanasius, Marcellus, and Eusebius of Caesarea: Some Thoughts on Their Resemblances and Disagreements." In Gregg 1985, 281–86.

Sarkissian, Karekin. 1965. *The Council of Chalcedon and the Armenian Church.* London: S.P.C.K.

Sasse, Herman. 1959. *This Is My Body: Luther's Contention for the Real Presence.* Minneapolis, Minn.: Augsburg Publishing House.

The Savoy Declaration of Faith and Order, 1658. 1971. With an extract from the original preface by John Owen, and a foreword by Derek Swann. London: Evangelical Press.

Scaer, David P., and Robert D. Preus, eds. 1979. *Luther's Catechisms—450 Years: Essays Commemorating the Small and Large Catechisms of Dr. Martin Luther.* Fort Wayne, Ind.: Concordia Theological Seminary Press.

Schaaf, James L. 1969. "The Smalcald Articles and Their Significance: Luther's Own Confession." In *Interpreting Luther's Legacy: Essays in Honor of Edward C. Fendt,* 68–82. Edited by Fred W. Meuser and Stanley D. Schneider. Minneapolis, Minn.: Augsburg Publishing House.

———. 1979. "*The Large Catechism:* A Pastoral Tool." In Scaer and Preus 1979, 41–46.

Schäferdiek, Knut. 1967. *Die Kirche in den Reichen der Westgoten und Suewen bis zur Errichtung der westgotischen katholischen Staatskirche.* Berlin: de Gruyter.

———. 1979. "Wulfila: Vom Bischof von Gotien zum Gotenbischof." *ZKG* 90/1:107–46.

Scheele, Paul W. 1981. "1600 Jahre Konzil von Konstantinopel: Ein ökumenisches Signal." *Catholica* 35/4:249–64.

Scheible, Heinz. 1997. *Melanchthon: Eine Biographie.* Munich: C. H. Beck.

Schermann, Theodor. 1910. *Der liturgische Papyrus von Dêr-Balyzeh eine Abendmahlsliturgie des Ostermorgens.* Leipzig: J. C. Hinrichs.

Schiess, Traugott, ed. 1908–12. *Briefwechsel der Brüder Ambrosius und Thomas Blaurer, 1509–1548.* 3 vols. Freiburg: F. E. Fehsenfeld.

Schindler, Alfred. 1965. *Wort und Analogie in Augustins Trinitätslehre.* Tübingen: J. C. B. Mohr.

Schmaus, Michael. 1927. *Die psychologische Trinitätslehre des heiligen Augustinus.* Münster: Aschendorff.

Schmidt, Carl. [1919] 1967. *Gespräche Jesu mit seinen Jüngern nach der Auferstehung.* Reprint, Hildesheim: Georg Olms.

Schmidt, Kurt Dietrich, 1939–41. *Die Bekehrung der Germanen zum Christentum.* 2 vols. Göttingen: Vandenhoeck und Ruprecht.

Schneemelcher, Wilhelm, ed. 1991. *New Testament Apocrypha.* English translation edited by R. McL. Wilson. Revised ed. 2 vols. Cambridge: James Clark; Louisville, Ky.: Westminster.

Schoedel, William R. 1985. *Ignatius of Antioch: A Commentary on the Letters of Ignatius of Antioch.* Edited by Helmut Koester. Hermeneia. Philadelphia: Fortress Press.

Schomann, Georg. 1574. *Catechesis et confessio fidei coetus per Poloniam congregati in nomine Iesu Christi, domini nostri crucifixi et resuscitati.* Kraków: Typis Alexandri Turobini.

Schönborn, Christoph von. 1982. "681-1981: Ein vergessenes Konzilsjubiläum, eine versäumte ökumenische Chance." *Freiburger Zeitschrift für Philosophie und Theologie* 29:157-74.

Schrader, Clemens. 1865. *Pius IX. als Papst und als Koenig, dargestellt aus den Acten seines Pontificates von den Verfasser der Broschüre: Der Papst und die modernen Ideen, mit einem Päpstlichen Belobungschreiben.* Vienna: C. Sartori.

Schreiner, Lothar. 1966. *Das Bekenntnis der Batak Kirche: Entstehung, Gestalt, Bedeutung und eine revidierte Übersetzung.* Munich: Chr. Kaiser Verlag.

Schroeder, Gustavus W. 1898. *History of the Swedish Baptists in Sweden and America.* New York: Schroeder.

Schulz, Frieder. 1966. "Communio Sanctorum: Apostolisches Symbol und Arnoldshainer Thesen." *Kerygma und Dogma* 12/2:154-79.

Schummer, Leopold. 1982. "La Communio Sanctorum dans les confessions de foi et les Catechismes reformes du XVIme siècle." In *Communio Sanctorum: Mélanges offerts à Jean-Jacques von Allmen,* 114-27. Edited by Boris Bobrinskoy et al. Geneva: Labor et Fides.

Schwartz, Eduard. 1905/1908. "Zur Geschichte des Athanasius, VI and VII." In *Nachrichten von der (königlichen) Gesellschaft (Akademie) der Wissenschaften zu Göttingen* 1905:271ff., 1908:305ff.

Schwarzlose, Karl. [1890] 1970. *Der Bilderstreit: Ein Kampf der griechischen Kirche um ihre Eigenart und um ihre Freiheit.* Reprint, Amsterdam: Rodopi.

Schwarzwäller, Klaus. 1989. "Rechtfertigung und Ekklesiologie in den Schmalkaldischen Artikeln: Eine dogmatische Studie." *Kergyma und Dogma* 35:84-105.

Schweinitz, Edmund de. 1901. *The History of the Church Known as the Unitas Fratrum or the Unity of the Brethren.* Bethlehem, Pa.: Moravian Publication Concern.

Schweitzer, Albert. [1906] 1961. *The Quest of the Historical Jesus: A Critical Study of Its Progress from Reimarus to Wrede.* Translated by W. Montgomery. Reprint, New York: Macmillan.

Schwöbel, Heide. 1982. *Synode und König im Westgotenreich: Grundlagen und Formen ihrer Beziehung.* Cologne: Böhlau.

Scott, S. Herbert. 1928. *The Eastern Churches and the Papacy.* London: Sheed and Ward.

Seebass, Gottfried. 1976. "Hans Denck." *Frankische Lebensbilder* 6:107-29.

———. 1984. "The Importance of Luther's Writings in the Formation of Protestant Confessions of Faith in the Sixteenth Century." In *Luther's Ecumenical Significance: An Interconfessional Consultation,* 71-80. Edited by Peter Manns and Harding Meyer. Philadelphia: Fortress Press; New York: Paulist Press.

———. 1993. "Martin Bucer und die Reichsstadt Augsburg." In *Martin Bucer and Sixteenth-Century Europe: Actes du colloque de Strasbourg,* 2:478-91. Edited by Christian Krieger and Marc Lienhard. Leiden: E. J. Brill.

Seeberg, Alfred. [1903] 1966. *Der Katechismus der Urchristenheit.* Reprint, Munich: Kaiser.

Seguenny, André. 1979. "Hans Denck et ses disciples." In *L'humanisme allemand (1480-1540),*

441–54. Edited by Georges Livet, William Melczer, Pierre Aquilon, et al. Munich: Fink Verlag; Paris: J. Vrin.

Sehling, Emil. 1902– . *Die evangelischen Kirchenordnungen des XVI Jahrhunderts*. Leipzig: O. R. Reisland.

Selge, Kurt-Victor. 1967. *Die ersten Waldenser*. Berlin: Walter de Gruyter.

Sellers, R. V. 1961. *The Council of Chalcedon: A Historical and Doctrinal Survey*. London: S.P.C.K.

Selwyn, D. G. 1964. "Neglected Edition of Cranmer's Catechism." *JTS* 15:76–91.

Ševčenko, Ihor. [1984] 1992. "The Many Worlds of Peter Mohyla." In *Byzantium and the Slavs in Letters and Culture*, 651–87. Cambridge, Mass.: Harvard Ukrainian Research Institute.

Sha'are tefilah [Siddur]. 1975. *The Gates of Prayer: The New Union Prayerbook*. New York: Central Conference of American Rabbis.

Sharing in One Hope: Bangalore 1978. Reports and Documents from the Meeting of the Faith and Order Commission, 15–30 August, 1978, Ecumenical Christian Centre, Bangalore, India. 1979. Geneva: World Council of Churches.

Shinn, Roger L. 1990. *Confessing Our Faith: An Interpretation of the Statement of Faith of the United Church of Christ*. New York: Pilgrim Press.

Sider, Robert D. 1982. "Approaches to Tertullian: A Study of Recent Scholarship." *Second Century* 2:228–60.

Sieben, Hermann J. 1979. "Die früh- und hochmittelalterliche Konzilsidee im Kontext der *Filioque*-Kontroverse." *Traditio* 35:173–207.

Simpson, Robert. 1965. *The Interpretation of Prayer in the Early Church*. Philadelphia: Westminster Press.

Sitompul, A. A., and Arne Sovik, eds. 1986. *Horas HKBP! Essays for a 125-Year-Old Church*. Pematangsiantar, North Sumatra: Sekolah Tinggi Teologia HKBP.

Skarsaune, O. 1976. "The Conversion of Justin Martyr." *Studia theologica* 30:53–73.

Sladeczek, Franz Josef. 1988. "'Die götze in miner herren chilchen sind gerumpt." *Theologische Zeitschrift* 44/4:289–311.

Slusser, Michael. 1990. "The Issues in the Definition of the Council of Chalcedon." *Toronto Journal of Theology* 6:63–69.

Smend, Julius. 1898. *Kelchversagung und Kelchspendung im Abendland: Ein Beitrag zur Kultusgeschichte*. Göttingen: Vandenhoeck und Ruprecht.

Smith, Mahlon H. 1978. *And Taking Bread: Cerularius and the Azyme Controversy of 1054*. Paris: Editions Beauchesne.

Smith, Page. 1964. *The Historian and History*. New York: Alfred A. Knopf.

Smith, Wanda Willard. 1997. *Selina Hastings: The Countess of Huntingdon*. Dallas: Bridwell Library.

Smolík, Josef. 1981. "*Filioque* in the Reformed Tradition." *Communio Viatorum* 24/4:219–22.

Smulders, Pieter. 1975. "The Sitz im Leben of the Old Roman Creed: New Conclusions from Neglected Data." *Studia Patristica* 13/2:409–21.

Snavely, Iren. 1994. "'The Evidence of Things Unseen': Zwingli's Sermon on Providence and the Colloquy of Marburg [1529]." *Westminster Theological Journal* 56:399–407.

Snyder, Arnold. 1984. *The Life and Thought of Michael Sattler*. Studies in Anabaptist and Mennonite History, 27. Scottdale, Pa.: Herald Press.

———. 1985. "The Schleitheim Articles in Light of the Revolution of the Common Man: Continuation or Departure?" *Sixteenth Century Journal* 16/4:419–30.

———. 1989. "The Influence of the Schleitheim Articles on the Anabaptist Movement: An Historical Evaluation." *MQR* 63:323–44.

Somerset, Fiona. "Answering the Twelve Conclusions: Dymmok's Halfhearted Gestures Towards Publication." In Aston and Richmond 1997, 52–76.

Soysa, Harold de. 1962. *Suggested Amendments to Scheme of Church Union in Ceylon.* N.p.

Spear, Wayne R. 1994. "The Westminster Confession of Faith and Holy Scripture." In Carson and Hall 1994, 85–100.

Spijker, W. van 't, et al. 1987. *De Synode van Dordrecht in 1618 en 1619.* Houten, Netherlands: Hertog.

Spindler, Marc Robert. 1990. "Creeds and Credibility in the Philippines: Introductory Notes to the Statement of Faith and Other Statements of the UCC in the Philippines." *Exchange* 19:152–71.

Spinka, Matthew. 1956. "Paul Krava and the Lollard-Hussite Relations." *Church History* 25: 16–26.

———. 1966. *John Hus' Concept of the Church.* Princeton, N.J.: Princeton University Press.

Spitz, Lewis W. 1954. "The Schism of the Eastern and Western Churches." *Concordia Theological Monthly* 25:881–91.

———, and Wenzel Lohff, eds. 1977. *Discord, Dialogue, and Concord: Studies in the Lutheran Reformation's Formula of Concord.* Philadelphia: Fortress Press.

Staats, Reinhart. 1981. "The Nicene-Constantinopolitan Creed as a Foundation for Church Unity? Protestant Thoughts on Its Centenary, 1981." *Irish Theological Quarterly* 48:212–27.

Stacy, Kevin M. 1993. "Augustine on Language and the Nature of Belief." In *Augustine: Presbyter Factus Sum*, 305–16. Edited by Joseph T. Lienhard, Earl C. Muller, and Roland J. Teske. New York: P. Lang.

Staedtke, Joachim. 1963. "Gibt es einen offiziellen Text der Confessio Helvetica Posterior?" *Theologische Zeitschrift* 19:29–41.

———. 1965. "Entstehung und Bedeutung des Heidelberger Katechismus." In *Warum Wirst Du Ein Christ Genannt*, 11–23. Edited by Walter Herrenbruck and Udo Smidt. Neukirchen, Germany: Neukirchener Verlag des Erziehungsvereins.

———. 1966. "Bibliographie des Zweiten Helvetischen Bekenntnisses." In *Glauben und Bekennen: Vierhundert Jahre Confessio Helvetica Posterior*, 41–53. Edited by Joachim Staedtke. Zurich: Zwingli Verlag.

———, and Gottfried W. Locher. 1967. *Vierhundert Jahre Confessio Helvetica Posterior; Akademische Feier.* Bern: P. Haupt.

Staehlin, Ernst, ed. 1929. *Das Buch der Basler Reformation.* Basel: Helbing and Lichtenhahn.

Starke, Elfriede. 1983. "Luthers Beziehungen zu Kunst und Künstlern." In Junghans 1983, 1:531–48.

Starowieyski, Marek. 1990. "La plus ancienne description d'une mariophanie par Grégoire de Nysse [Vita Gregorii Thaumaturgi]." In *Studien zu Gregor von Nyssa und der christlichen Spätantike*, 245–53. Festschrift for Andreas Spira. Edited by Hubertus R. Drobner and Christoph Klock. Vigiliae Christianae, Supplements, 12. Leiden: E. J. Brill.

Stassen, Glen H. 1962. "Anabaptist Influence in the Origin of the Particular Baptists." *MQR* 36:322–48.

Statut der Internationalen Altkatholischen Bischofkonferenz: Offizielle Ausgabe in fünf Sprachen. 2001. Edited and translated by Urs von Arx and Maja Weyermann. Bern: Stampfli.

Stauffer, Richard. 1977. "Zwingli et Calvin: Critiques de la confession de Schleitheim." In *Origins and Characteristics of Anabaptism / Les débuts et les caracteristiques de l'Anabaptisme,* 126–47. Edited by Marc Lienhard. The Hague: Martinus Nijhoff.

———. 1983. "Farel à la Dispute de Lausanne: Sa défense de la doctrine de la justification par la foi." *Cahiers de la Revue de théologie et de philosophie* 9/1:107–23.

Stead, George Christopher. 1973. "Eusebius and the Council of Nicaea." *JTS* 24:85–100.

Steck, Rudolf, and G. Tobler. 1923. *Aktensammlung zur Geschichte der Berner-reformation, 1521–1532.* Bern: K. J. Wyss Erben.

Steere, Douglas V. 1955. *Where Words Come From: An Interpretation of the Ground and Practice of Quaker Worship and Ministry.* London: Allen and Unwin.

Stegmüller, Friedrich, ed. 1947. *Repertorium commentariorum in sententias Petri Lombardi.* 2 vols. Würzburg: Schöningh.

Steinen, W. von den. 1929–30. "Entstehungsgeschichte der Libri Carolini." *Quellen und Forschungen aus italienischen Archiven und Bibliotheken* 21:1–93.

Stephens, John Vant. 1941. *The Genesis of the Cumberland Presbyterian Church.* Cincinnati, Ohio: n.p.

Stephens, Prescott. 1998. *The Waldensian Story: A Study in Faith, Intolerance, and Survival.* Lewes, Sussex: Book Guild.

Stephens, W. P. 1970. *The Holy Spirit in the Theology of Martin Bucer.* London: Cambridge University Press.

———. 1986. *Theology of Huldrych Zwingli.* Oxford: Oxford University Press.

———. 1992. *Zwingli: An Introduction to His Thought.* Oxford: Clarendon Press.

Stephenson, A. A. 1961. "The Text of the Jerusalem Creed." In *Studia Patristica* 3:303–13. Edited by F. L. Cross [Papers presented at the Third International Conference on Patristic Studies, Oxford 1959]. Berlin: Akademie Verlag.

Stevenson, J. [1966] 1989. *Creeds, Councils and Controversies: Documents Illustrating the History of the Church, AD 337–461.* Revised and enlarged by W. H. C. Frend. London: S.P.C.K.

Stewart, H. F., E. K. Rand, and S. J. Tester, trans. 1973. *The Theological Tractates of Boethius.* Cambridge, Mass.: Harvard University Press.

Stiglmayr, J. 1925. "Das 'Quicunque' und Fulgentius von Ruspe." *ZfKT* 49:341–57.

Stock, Konrad. 1980. *Cubanisches Glaubensbekenntnis: Einführung Text, Interpretation.* Munich: Kaiser; Mainz: Grünewald.

Stocking, Rachel L. 2000. *Bishops, Councils, and Consensus in the Visigothic Kingdom, 589–633.* Ann Arbor, Mich.: University of Michigan Press.

Stockmeier, Peter. 1972. "Zum Verhaltnis von Glaube und Religion bei Tertullian." *Studia Patristica* 11:242–46.

———. 1981. "Bemerkungen zur Christianisierung der Goten im 4. Jahrhundert." *ZKG* 92/1:315–24.

———. 1982. "Das Konzil von Chalkedon: Probleme der Forschung." *Freiburger Zeitschrift für Philosophie und Theologie* 29:140–56.

————. 1985. "Anmerkungen zum 'in' bzw. 'ex duabus naturis' in der Formel von Chalkedon." In *Studia Patristica* 18/1: 213-20.

————. 1986. "Universalis ecclesia: Papst Leo der Grosse und der Osten." *Kirchengemeinschaft—Anspruch und Wirklichkeit: Festschrift für Georg Kretschmar zum 60. Geburtstag,* 83-91. Edited by Wolf Dieter Hauschild, Carsten Nicolaisen, and Dorothea Wendebourg. Stuttgart: Calwer Verlag.

————. 1987. "Glaubenssymbol, Lehrschreiben und Dogma im Umfeld von Chalkedon." In *Weisheit Gottes—Weisheit der Welt: Festschrift für Joseph Kardinal Ratzinger zum 60. Geburtstag,* 689-96. Edited by Walter Baier, Stephan Otto Horn, Vinzenz Pfnür, et al. St. Ottilien, Germany: EOS Verlag.

Stoevesandt, Hinrich. 1970. *Die Bedeutung des Symbolums in Theologie und Kirche: Versuch einer dogmatisch-kritischen Ortsbestimmung aus evangelischer Sicht.* Munich: Christian Kaiser Verlag.

Stott, John R. W. 1975. "The Significance of Lausanne." *International Review of Missions* 64:288-94.

Strasser, Otto Erich. 1949. "Der Consensus Tigurinus." *Zwingliana* 9/1:1-16.

Strauss, Gerald. 1978. *Luther's House of Learning: Indoctrination of the Young in the German Reformation.* Baltimore: Johns Hopkins University Press.

Strehle, Stephen. 1989. "The Extent of the Atonement and the Synod of Dort." *Westminster Theological Journal* 51:1-23.

Strothmann, Jürgen. 1995. "Das Konzil von Sens 1138 und die Folgeereignisse 1140." *Theologie und Glaube* 85:238ff., 396ff.

Strupl, Milos. 1964. "Confessional Theology of the Unitas Fratrum." *Church History* 33:279-93.

Strype, John, ed. 1842-54. *Memorials of the Most Reverend Father in God Thomas Cranmer, Sometime Lord Archbishop of Cantebury.* Oxford: Ecclesiastical History Society.

Studer, Basil. 1990. "La recezione del concilio di Efeso del 431." *Studia Ephemeridis Augustinianum* 31:427-42.

Studer, Gerald C. 1984. "The Dordrecht Confession of Faith, 1632-1982." *MQR* 58:503-19.

Studien zur Bekenntnisbildung. 1980. Edited by Peter Meinhold. Wiesbaden: Steiner.

Stupperich, Robert. 1938. "Die Kirche in Martin Bucers theologischer Entwicklung." *ARG* 35:81-101.

Sullivan, Francis. 1998. "A New Obstacle to Anglican–Roman Catholic Dialogue." *America* 179/3:6.

Sundkler, Bengt. 1954. *Church of South India: The Movement Towards Union, 1900-1947.* London: Lutterworth Press.

Supplementa Melanchthoniana. 1915. Vol. 1. Edited by D. Ferdinand Cohrs. Leipzig: Rudolf Haupt.

Sysyn, F. E. 1984. "Peter Mohyla and the Kiev Academy in Recent Western Works: Divergent Views on Seventeenth-Century Ukrainian Culture." *Harvard Ukrainian Studies* 8:155-87.

Szczucki, Lech. 1982. "Polish and Transylvanian Unitarians." In *Antitrinitarianism in the Second Half of the Sixteenth Century,* 238-41. Edited by Róbert Dán and Antal Pirnát. Budapest: Akadémiai Kiadó; Leiden: E. J. Brill.

————, ed. 1983. *Socinianism and Its Role in the Culture of XVI-th to XVIII-th Centuries.*

Edited by Lech Szczucki in cooperation with Zbigniew Ogonowski and Janusz Tazbir. Warsaw: Polish Academy of Sciences, Institute of Philosophy and Sociology.

Szilágyi, Sandor, ed. 1875-99. *Monumenta Hungariae Historica*. 22 vols. Budapest: A.M.T. Akadémia Könyvkiadó-Hivatala.

Taft, Robert F. 1991. *The Diptychs*. Volume 4 of *A History of the Liturgy of St. John Chrysostom*. Rome: Pontificium Institutum Studiorum Orientalium.

Tangl, Georgine. 1992. *Die Teilnehmer an den allgemeinen Konzilien des Mittelalters*. Weimar: H. Böhlaus Nachfolger.

Tavard, George H. 1959. *Holy Writ or Holy Church: The Crisis of the Protestant Reformation*. New York: Harper and Brothers.

Terry-Thompson, Arthur Cornelius. 1956. *The History of the African Orthodox Church*. New York: Beacon Press.

Tetz, Martin. 1973. "Markellianer und Athanasios von Alexandrien: Die markellianische *Expositio fidei ad Athanasium* des Diakons Eugenios von Ankyra." *Zeitschrift für die Neutestamentliche Wissenschaft und die Kunde der Älteren Kirche* 64/1-2:75-112.

———. 1985. "Ante omnia de sancta fide et de integritate veritatis: Glaubensfragen auf der Synode von Serdika (342)." *Zeitschrift für die neutestamentliche Wissenschaft* 76:243-69.

Themel, Karl. 1973. "Dokumente von der Entstehung der Konkordienformel." *ARG* 64:287-313.

Theurer, Wolfdieter. 1967. *Die trinitarische Basis des Ökumenischen Rates der Kirchen*. Bergen-Enkheim: G. Kaffke.

Thomas Aquinas. 1954. *Opuscula theologica*. 2 vols. Turin: Marietti.

Thompson, Bard. 1963. "Historical Background of the Catechism" and "The Reformed Chruch in the Palatinate." In *Essays on the Heidelberg Catechism*, 8-30, 31-52. A Collection of Essays by Bard Thompson, Hendrikus Berkhof, Eduard Schweizer, and Howard Hageman. Philadelphia: United Church Press.

Thompson, David M., ed. 1990. *Stating the Gospel: Formulations and Declarations of Faith from the Heritage of the United Reformed Church*. Edinburgh: T. and T. Clark.

Thompson, E. A. 1960. "The Conversion of the Visigoths to Catholicism." *Nottingham Mediaeval Studies* 4:4-35.

———. 1966. *The Visigoths in the Time of Ulfila*. Oxford: Clarendon Press.

———. 1985. *Who Was Saint Patrick?* New York: St. Martin's Press.

Thomson, R. M. 1980. "The Satirical Works of Berengar of Poitiers." *Mediaeval Studies* 42:89-138.

Thomson, S. Harrison. 1932. "John Wyclif's 'Lost' *De fide sacramentorum*." *JTS* 33:359-65.

———. 1953. "Luther and Bohemia." *ARG* 44/2:160-81.

Thurian, Max. 1983. *Ecumenical Perspectives on Baptism, Eucharist, and Ministry*. Geneva: World Council of Churches.

———, and Geoffrey Wainwright. 1984. *Baptism and Eucharist: Ecumenical Convergence in Celebration*. Grand Rapids, Mich.: Eerdmans.

Tideman, J. 1851. *De remonstrantie en het remonstrantisme: Historisch onderzoek*. Te Haarlem: Bij de Erven F. Bohn.

Tidner, E. 1963. *Didascalia Apostolorum, Canonum Ecclesiasticorum, Traditionis Apostolicae Versiones Latinae*. Berlin: Akademie-Verlag.

Tierney, Brian. 1972. *Origins of Papal Infallibility, 1150-1350: A Study on the Concepts of Infallibility, Sovereignty, and Tradition in the Middle Ages.* Leiden: E. J. Brill.

———. 1988. *Origins of Papal Infallibility, 1150-1350: A Study on the Concepts of Infallibility, Sovereignty, and Tradition in the Middle Ages.* 2d ed. Leiden: E. J. Brill.

———. 1998. *Foundations of the Conciliar Theory: The Contribution of the Medieval Canonists from Gratian to the Great Schism.* Enlarged new ed. Leiden: Brill.

Tjernagel, N. S. 1965. *Henry VIII and the Lutherans: A Study in Anglo-Lutheran Relations from 1521 to 1547.* Saint Louis, Mo.: Concordia Publishing House.

Tokuzen, Yoshikazu. 1983. "Pädagogik bei Luther." In Junghans 1983, 1:323-30.

Tootikian, Vahan H. 1982. *The Armenian Evangelical Church.* Detroit, Mich.: Armenian Heritage Committee.

Torrance, Thomas Forsyth. 1983. "The Deposit of Faith." *Scottish Journal of Theology* 36/1:1-28.

———. 1985. "The Trinitarian Foundation and Character of Faith and of Authority in the Church." In *Theological Dialogue Between Orthodox and Reformed Churches,* 1:79-120. Edited by T. F. Torrance. Edinburgh: Scottish Academic Press.

———. 1988. *The Trinitarian Faith: The Evangelical Theology of the Ancient Catholic Church.* Edinburgh: T. and T. Clark.

Tourn, Giorgio. 1980. *The Waldensians: The First Eight Hundred Years.* Translated by Camillio P. Merlino. Turin: Editrice Claudiana.

———. 1989. *You Are My Witnesses: The Waldensians Across Eight Hundred Years.* Turin: Editrice Claudiana.

Trakatellis, Demetrios. 1991. "God Language in Ignatius of Antioch." In *The Future of Early Christianity: Essays in Honor of Helmut Koester,* 422-30. Edited by Birger A. Pearson et al. Minneapolis, Minn.: Fortress Press.

Trevett, Christine. 1992. *A Study of Ignatius of Antioch in Syria and Asia.* Lewiston, N.Y.: E. Mellen.

Trilling, Lionel. [1950] 2000. "Wordsworth and the Rabbis." In Leon Wieseltier, ed., *The Moral Obligation to Be Intelligent: Selected Essays,* 188-202. New York: Farrar, Straus, Giroux.

Trimua, Ekom Dake. 1984. "Naissance et développement de l'Eglise Evangélique au Togo, de 1847 à 1980." Ph.D. diss., University of Strasbourg.

Troeltsch, Ernst. 1891. *Vernunft und Offenbarung bei Johann Gerhard und Melanchthon: Untersuchung zur Geschichte der altprotestantischen Theologie.* Göttingen: Vandenhoeck und Ruprecht.

Tschackert, Paul. 1910. *Die Entstehung der lutherischen und der reformierten Kirchenlehre: Samt ihren innerprotestantischen Gegensätzen.* Göttingen: Vandenhoeck und Ruprecht.

Turner, C. H. 1910. "A Critical Text of the *Quicunque vult.*" *JTS* 11:401-11.

———. 1921-22. "The 'Blessed Presbyters' Who Condemned Noetus." *JTS* 23:28-35.

Tyacke, Nicholas. 1986. *Anti-Calvinists: The Rise of English Arminianism, c. 1590-1640.* Oxford: Clarendon Press.

Uhlirz, Mathilde. 1914. *Die Genesis der vier Prager Artikel.* Sitzungsberichte der Kaiserlichen Akademie der Wissenschaften, 175/3. Vienna: Kaiserliche Akademie der Wissenschaften.

Ullrich, Lothar. 1985. "Die Bedeutung des Symbolum Chalcedonense für die Christologie:

Eine dogmengeschichtliche Übersicht zu den trinitarischen und christologischen Entscheidungen der Alten Kirche in systematischer Absicht." *Theologische Versuche* 15:135–49. Edited by Joachim Rogge and Gottfried Schille. Berlin: Evangelische Verlagsanstalt.

Ulrich, Jörg. 1994. *Die Anfänge der abendländischen Rezeption des Nizänums.* Berlin: W. de Gruyter.

The United Church of Canada Yearbook 1928, Including Record of Proceedings of Third General Council, Winnipeg, September, 1928, Statistics of the Church, April 1st–December 31st, 1927, Pastoral Charges and the Ministers at June 30th, 1927. 1928. Toronto: United Church of Canada General Offices.

Urban, Hans Jörg. 1972. *Bekenntnis, Dogma, kirchliches Lehramt: Die Lehrautorität der Kirche in heutiger evangelischer Theologie.* Wiesbaden: F. Steiner.

Vaggione, Richard Paul, ed. and tr. 1987. *Eunomius, the Extant Works.* Oxford: Clarendon Press.

Vajta, Vilmos. 1983. "Luther als Beter." In Junghans 1983, 1:279–95.

———, and Hans Weissgerber. 1963. *The Church and the Confessions: The Role of the Confessions in the Life and Doctrine of the Lutheran Churches.* Philadelphia, Pa.: Fortress Press.

Van Dam, Raymond. 1982. "History and Hagiography: The Life of Gregory Thaumaturgus." *Classical Antiquity* 1:272–308.

Van Engen, John. 1993. "Anticlericalism Among the Lollards." In *Anticlericalism in Late Medieval and Early Modern Europe,* 53–63. Edited by Peter A. Dykema and Heiko A. Oberman. Leiden: E. J. Brill.

Van Halsema, Thea Bouma. 1961. *Glorious Heretic: The Story of Guido de Brès.* Grand Rapids, Mich.: Eerdmans.

van Unnik, W. C. 1961. "Die Gotteslehre bei Aristides und in gnostischen Schriften." *Theologische Zeitschrift* 17:166–74.

Vasileiadēs, Nikolaos P. 1983. *Markos ho Eugenikos kai hē henōsis tōn ekklēsiōn* [Markos Eugenikos and the union of the churches]. 3d ed. Athens: Adelphotēs Theologōn "Ho Sōtēr."

Vasiliev, A. A. 1964. *History of the Byzantine Empire, 324–1453.* 2 vols. Madison: University of Wisconsin Press.

Veijola, Timo. 1992. "Das Bekenntnis Israels: Beobachtungen zur Geschichte und Theologie von Dtn 6,4–9." *Theologische Zeitschrift* 48/3–4:369–81.

Venard, Marc, ed. 1992. *Histoire du christianisme des origines à nos jours.* Vol. 8 of *Le temps des confessions (1530–1620/30).* Paris: Desclée.

Vercruysse, Jos E. 1983. "Schlüsselgewalt und Beichte bei Luther." In Junghans 1983, 153–69.

Verghese, Paul. 1968. "The Monothelete Controversy: A Historical Survey." *GOTR* 13/2:196–211.

———. 1971. "Ecclesiological Issues Concerning the Relation of Eastern Orthodox and Oriental Orthodox Churches." *GOTR* 16/1–2:133–43.

Vida è Missâo: Decisoes do XIII Concílio Geral da Igreja Metodista e Credo social da Igreja Metodista. 1982. Piracicaba, Brazil: Editora Unimep.

Vidler, Alexander R. 1976. *The Modernist Movement in the Roman Church, Its Origins and Outcome.* New York: Gordon Press.

450 Jahre Zürcher Reformation. 1969. Sonderdruck aus *Zwingliana* 13/1. Zurich: Buchdrückerei Berichthaus.

Vigil, J. M., and A. Torrellas. 1988. *Misas Centroamericanas*. Managua: CAV-CEBES.

Vinay, Valdo. 1975. *Le Confessione di Fede dei Valdesi riformati*. Turin: Editrice Claudiana.

——. 1983. "Waldes." In *Gestalten der Kirchengeschichte*, 3:238–48. Edited by Martin Greschat. Stuttgart: Kohlhammer.

Vinogradský, Nicolaj Fedorovič. 1899. *Cerkovný sobor v Moskvě 1682 goda* [The ecclesiastical synod in Moscow of the year 1682]. Smolensk: Ja. N. Podzemský.

Vischer, Lukas, ed. 1981. *Spirit of God, Spirit of Christ: Ecumenical Reflections on the filioque Controversy*. Faith and Order Paper, 103. Geneva: World Council of Churches.

——, ed. 1987. *Was bekennen die evangelischen Kirchen in der Schweiz?* Bern: Evangelische Arbeitsstelle Oekumene Schweiz.

Visser, Derk. 1983. *Zacharias Ursinus: The Reluctant Reformer, His Life and Times*. New York: United Church Press.

——, ed. 1986. *Controversy and Conciliation: The Reformation and the Palatinate, 1559–1583*. Allison Park, Pa.: Pickwick Publications.

Visser, Dirk, comp. 1975. *A Checklist of Dutch Mennonite Confessions of Faith to 1800*. Amsterdam: Commissie tot de uitgave van Documenta Anabaptistica Neerlandica.

Visser 't Hooft, W. A. 1949. *The First Assembly of the World Council of Churches, Held at Amsterdam, August 22nd to September 4th, 1948*. Volume 5 of *Man's Disorder and God's Design*. New York: Harper.

——, et al. 1977. *Lausanne 77, Fifty Years of Faith and Order (1927–1977)*. Geneva: World Council of Churches.

Voelz, James W. 1979. "Luther's Use of Scripture in the *Small Catechism*." In Scaer and Preus 1979, 55–64.

Vogel, Cornelia J. de. 1973. "The Problem of Philosophy and Christian Faith in Boethius' Consolatio." In *Romanitas et Christianitas*, 357–70. Edited by W. den Boer. Amsterdam: North-Holland Publishing.

Vogt, Hermann Josef. 1968. *Coetus Sanctorum: Der Kirchenbegriff des Novatian und die Geschichte seiner Sonderkirche*. Bonn: Peter Hanstein.

——. 1993. "Unterschiedliches Konzilsverständnis der Cyrillianer und der Orientalen beim Konzil von Ephesus 431." In *Logos: Festschrift für Luise Abramowski*, 429–51. Edited by Hanns Christof Brennecke, Ernst Ludwig Grasmück, and Christoph Markschies. Beihefte zur Zeitschrift für die neutestamentliche Wissenschaft und die Kunde der älteren Kirche, 67. Berlin: W. de Gruyter.

Voices United: The Hymn and Worship Book of the United Church of Canada. 1996. Ontario: United Church Publishing House.

Vola, Giorgio. 1984. "Mais où sont les neiges d'antan: La colletta inglese del 1655 per i Valdesi." *Bollettino della Società di studi valdesi* 155:3–20.

Volz, Hans. 1957. "Luthers Schmalkaldische Artikel." *ZKG* 68:259–86.

——. 1963. "Zur Entstehungsgeschichte von Luthers Schmalkaldischen Artikeln." *ZKG* 74/3–4:316–20.

Vries, Wilhelm de. 1987. "The Reasons for the Rejection of the Council of Chalcedon by the Oriental Orthodox Churches." In Fries and Nersoyan 1987, 3–13.

Wagner, Georg. 1973. *Der Ursprung der Chrysostomusliturgie*. Münster: Aschendorff.

Wainwright, Geoffrey, ed. 1986. *Baptism, Eucharist, and Ministry: A Liturgical Appraisal of the Lima Text*. Rotterdam: Liturgical Ecumenical Center Trust.

Wakefield, Walter L., and Austin P. Evans. 1969. *Heresies of the High Middle Ages*. New York: Columbia University Press.

Walker, Peter W. L. 1990. *Holy City, Holy Places: Christian Attitudes to Jerusalem and the Holy Land in the Fourth Century*. Oxford: Clarendon Press.

Wallace, R. S. 1988. *Calvin, Geneva and the Reformation*. Grand Rapids, Mich.: Baker Book House.

Wallace, Robert. 1850. *Antitrinitarian Biography*. 3 vols. London: E. T. Whitfield.

Wallace-Hadrill, D. S. 1961. *Eusebius of Caesarea*. Westminster, Md.: Canterbury Press.

Wandel, Lee Palmer. 1995. *Voracious Idols and Violent Hands: Iconoclasm in Reformation Zurich, Strasbourg, and Basel*. Cambridge: Cambridge University Press.

Ward, Harry Frederick, ed. 1912. *The Social Creed of the Churches*. New York: Eaton and Maine; Cincinnati, Ohio: Jennings and Graham.

Warfield, Benjamin Breckinridge. 1901-2. "The Printing of the Westminster Confession." Extract from *The Presbyterian and Reformed Review* (October 1901, January 1902, April 1902). Philadelphia: MacCalla.

———. 1931. *The Westminster Assembly and Its Work*. New York: Oxford University Press.

———. 1956. *Calvin and Augustine*. Edited by Samuel G. Craig. Philadelphia: Presbyterian and Reformed Publishing.

Wartenberg, Günther. 1983a. "Unterricht der Visitatoren an die Pfarrherrn im Kurfürstentum Sachsen, 1528 und spätere Ausgaben." In *Martin Luther Studienausgabe*, 3:402-62. Edited by Hans Ulrich Delius. Berlin: Evangelische Verlagsanstalt.

———. 1983b. "Luthers Beziehungen zu den sächsischen Fürsten." In Junghans 1983, 1:549-71.

Waterland, Daniel. 1724. *A Critical History of the Athanasian Creed*. Cambridge: Cambridge University Press.

Webb, Henry E. 1990. *In Search of Christian Unity: A History of the Restoration Movement*. Cincinnati, Ohio: Standard Publishing.

Weber, Georg Gottlieb. 1783-84. *Kritische Geschichte der Augspurgischen Confession aus archivalischen Nachrichten nebst einigen diplomatischen Zeichnungen*. 2 vols. Frankfurt: Varrentrapp Sohn und Wenner.

Weingart, Richard E. 1970. *The Logic of Divine Love: A Criticial Analysis of the Soteriology of Peter Abailard*. London: Clarendon Press.

Weischer, Bernd M. 1977. "Die Glaubenssymbole des Epiphanios von Salamis und des Gregorios Thaumaturgos im Qerello." In *Oriens Christianus*, 61:20-40. Edited by Joseph Molitor. Wiesbaden: Otto Harrassowitz.

Weismann, Christoph, ed. 1995. *Eine Kleine Biblia: Die Katechismen von Luther und Brenz*. Stuttgart: Calwer Verlag.

Welch, Claude. 1972-85. *Protestant Thought in the Nineteenth Century*. 2 vols. New Haven and London: Yale University Press.

Welch, Herbert. [1946]. *The Story of a Creed*. Reprinted with slight changes from the *Nashville Christian Advocate*, 1 August 1946, 937-44.

Wells, Patricia. 1992. *Welcome to the United Church of Canada*. [Toronto]: Division of Mission in Canada, United Church of Canada.

Wendenbourg, Dorothea. 1986. *Reformation und Orthodoxie (Der ökumenische Briefwechsel zwischen der Leitung der Würtembergischen Kirche und Patriarch Jeremias II von Konstantinopel, 1573-1581)*. Göttingen: Vandenhoeck und Ruprecht.

Wenger, John Christian. 1952. *The Doctrines of the Mennonites*. Scottdale, Pa.: Mennonite Publishing House.

———. 1966. *The Mennonite Church in America*. Scottdale, Pa.: Herald Press.

———, and Leonard Verduin, eds. and trans. 1978. *The Complete Writings of Menno Simons, c. 1496-1561*. Corrected ed. Scottdale, Pa.: Herald Press.

Wenz, Gunther. 1996. *Theologie der Bekenntnisschriften der evangelisch-lutherischen Kirche: Eine historische und systematische Einführung in das Konkordienbuch*. Berlin: Walter de Gruyter.

Westin, Gunnar, and Torsten Bergsten. 1962. *Balthasar Hubmaier: Schriften*. Gütersloh, Germany: Gerd Mohn.

White, B. R. 1968. "The Doctrine of the Church in the Particular Baptist Confession of 1644." *JTS*, n.s., 19:570-90.

———. 1996. *The English Baptists of the Seventeenth Century*. Oxford: Baptist Historical Society.

Whitehead, Alfred North. [1925] 1952. *Science and the Modern World*. Lowell Lectures for 1925. Reprint, New York: New American Library.

Whitley, W. T. 1923. *A History of British Baptists*. London: Charles Griffin.

Whitson, Robley Edward, ed. 1983. *The Shakers: Two Centuries of Spiritual Reflection*. New York: Paulist Press.

Wilbur, Earl Morse. 1942. *A History of Unitarianism in Transylvania, England, and America*. Cambridge, Mass.: Harvard University Press.

Wilckens, Ulrich. 1961. *Die Missionsreden der Apostelgeschichte; Form- und traditionsgeschichtliche Untersuchungen*. Neukirchen, Germany: Neukirchener Verlag.

Wiles, Maurice. 1989. "Eunomius: Hair-Splitting Dialectician or Defender of the Accessibility of Salvation?" *The Making of Orthodoxy: Essays in Honour of Henry Chadwick*, 157-72. Edited by Rowan Williams. Cambridge: Cambridge University Press.

———. 1996. *Archetypal Heresy: Arianism Through the Centuries*. Oxford: Clarendon Press.

Wilken, Robert L. 1979. "Introducing the Athanasian Creed." *Currents in Theology and Mission* 6:4-10.

Wilks, M. J. 1969. "The Early Oxford Wyclif: Papalist or Nominalist?" In *Studies in Church History*, 5:69-98. Edited by G. J. Cuming. Leiden: E. J. Brill.

Will, Cornelius. 1861. *Acta et scripta quae de controversies ecclesiae Graecae et Latinae saeculo undecimo composita extant*. Paris: n.p.

Williams, Daniel H. 1996. "Another Exception to Later Fourth-Century 'Arian' Typologies: The Case of Germinius of Sirmium." *Journal of Early Christian Studies* 4:335-57.

Williams, George Hunston. 1951. "Christology and Church-State Relations in the Fourth Century." *Church History* 20/3:3-33, 20/4:3-26.

———. 1960. *Anselm: Communion and Atonement*. Saint Louis, Mo.: Concordia.

————. 1990. "Radicalization of the Reformed Church in Poland, 1547–1574: A Regional Variant of Sixteenth-Century Anabaptism." *MQR* 65:54–68.

Williams, Rowan. 2002. *Arius: Heresy and Tradition.* Revised ed. Grand Rapids, Mich.: Eerdmans.

Willis-Watkins, David. 1994. "The Third Part of Christian Freedom Misplaced, Being an Inquiry into the Lectures of the Late Rev. Samuel Willard on the Assembly's Shorter Catechism." In *Later Calvinism: International Perspectives,* 471–88. Edited by W. Fred Graham. Kirksville, Mo.: Sixteenth Century Journal Publishing.

Wilson, N. G., ed. 1994. *The "Bibliotheca" of Photius: A Selection.* London: Duckworth.

The Winchester Centennial, 1803–1903: Historical Sketch of the Universalist Profession of Belief: Adopted at Winchester, N.H., September 22, 1803, with the Address and Sermons at the Commemorative Services Held in Winchester, Rome City, Ind., and Washington, D.C., September and October, 1903. 1903. Boston: Universalist Publishing House.

Windhorst, Christof. 1978. "Balthasar Hubmaier: Professor, Prediger, Politiker." In *Radikale Reformatoren.* Edited by Hans-Jürgen Goertz, 125–36. Munich: Beck.

Winter, Sean F. 1991. "Michael Sattler and the Schleitheim Articles: A Study in the Background to the First Anabaptist Confession of Faith." *Baptist Quarterly* 34:52–66.

Witte, John. 1997. *From Sacrament to Contract: Marriage, Religion, and Law in the Western Tradition.* Louisville, Ky.: Westminster John Knox Press.

Wolf, Ernst, ed. 1959. *Christusbekenntnis im Atomzeitalter?* Munich: Christian Kaiser Verlag.

————. 1962. "Die Schmalkaldischen Artikel und die Gegenwart." *Communio Viatorum* 5:88–102.

Wolfson, Harry Austryn. 1947. *Philo: Foundations of Religious Philosophy in Judaism, Christianity, and Islam.* 2 vols. Cambridge, Mass.: Harvard University Press.

Wolter, H., and H. Holstein. 1967. *Lyon I et Lyon II.* Histoire des conciles oecuméniques, 7. Paris: Editions de l'Orante.

Wood, Edward. 1961. *Whosoever Will; Quicunque vult.* London: Faith Press.

World Council of Churches, Commission on Faith and Order. 1984. "The Apostolic Faith in the Scriptures and in the Early Church: Report of the Faith and Order Consultation Held in Rome, 1–8 October 1983." *Ecumenical Review* 36:329–37.

————. 1986. "Nous croyons en Dieu, le Père, le Fils et l'Esprit Saint: Une explication oecuménique de la foi apostolique exprimée dans le Symbole de Nicée-Constantinople (381)." *Istina* 31/1:63–129.

Wouk, Herman. 1978. *War and Remembrance.* Boston: Little, Brown.

Wozniak, Casimir J. 1997. *Hyphenated Catholicism: A Study of the Polish-American Model of Church, 1890–1908.* San Francisco: International Scholars Publications.

Wright, A. D. 1975. "The Significance of the Council of Trent." *Journal of Ecclesiastical History* 26:353–62.

Wright, David F. 1982. "Christian Faith in the Greek World: Justin Martyr's Testimony." *Evangelical Quarterly* 54:77–87.

Wright, J. Robert, ed. 1988. *Quadrilateral at One Hundred: Essays on the Centenary of the Chicago-Lambeth Quadrilateral, 1886/88–1986/88.* Cincinnati, Ohio: Forward Movement Publications.

Wright, Susan J. 1988. "Catechism, Confirmation and Communion: The Role of the Young in the Post-Reformation Church." In *Parish Church and People: Local Studies in Lay Religion, 1350-1750*, 203-27. Edited by Susan J. Wright. London: Hutchinson.

Wright, William. 1985. "Philip of Hesse's Vision of Protestant Unity and the Marburg Colloquy." In *Pietas et Societas: New Trends in Reformation Social History*, 163-79. Edited by Kyle C. Sessions and Phillip N. Bebb. Kirksville, Mo.: Sixteenth Century Journal Publishers.

Wyschogrod, Michael. 1984. "The 'Shema Israel' in Judaism and the New Testament." In *The Roots of Our Common Faith: Faith in the Scriptures and in the Early Church*, 23-32. Edited by Hans-Georg Link. Faith and Order Paper, 119. Geneva: World Council of Churches.

Wyznanie wiary Kościoła Polskiego Narodowego Katolickiego w Ameryce. 1936. Scranton, Pa.: Drukiem "Strączy."

Yoder, John H. 1959. "Balthasar Hubmaier and the Beginnings of Swiss Anabaptism." *MQR* 33:5-17.

———, tr. and ed. 1973. *The Legacy of Michael Sattler*. Scottdale, Pa.: Herald Press.

Young, Frances M. 1983. *From Nicaea to Chalcedon: A Guide to the Literature and Its Background*. Philadelphia: Fortress Press.

Zahn-Harnack, Agnes von. 1951. *Adolf von Harnack*. 2d ed. Berlin: Walter de Gruyter.

Zdenek, David V. 1999. "Utraquists, Lutherans, and the Bohemian Confession of 1575." *Church History* 68/2:294-336.

Zerbi, Piero. 1975. "San Bernardo e il Concilio di Sens." In *Studi su S Bernardo di Chiaravalle nell'ottavo centenario della canonizzazione*, 49-73. Rome: Editiones Cistercienses.

Zēsēs, Theodōros. 1980. *Gennadios B' Scholarios—Bios, syngrammata, didaskalia* [Gennadius II Scholarius—life, writings, doctrine]. Thessalonica: Patriarchikon Idryma Paterikōn Meletōn.

Ziegenaus, Anton. 1989. "Die Jungfrauengeburt im Apostolischen Glaubensbekenntnis: Ihre Interpretation bei Adolf von Harnack." In *Divergenzen in der Mariologie: Zur ökumenischen Diskussion um die Mutter Jesu*, 35-55. Edited by Heinrich Petri. Regensburg, Germany: Friedrich Pustet.

Ziegler, Aloysius K. 1930. *Church and State in Visigothic Spain*. Washington, D.C.: Catholic University of America.

Zimmermann, Gunter. 1989. "Die pneumatologische Tradition in der reformierten Bekenntnisbildung." *Theologische Zeitschrift* 45:352-74.

Zimmermann, Rudolf, and Walter Hildebrandt, trans. 1967. *Das Zweite Helvetische Bekenntnis*. Zurich: Zwingli Verlag.

Zovatto, Pietro. 1968. *La polemica Bossuet-Fénelon: Introduzione critico-bibliografica*. Padua: Gregoriana.

Žukovský, Arkadij. 1997. *Petro Mohyla j pytannja ednosty cerkov* [Petro Mohyla and the problem of the unity of the churches]. Kiev: Mystectvo.

Zwingli, Ulrich. 1994. *Huldrych Zwingli: Schriften*. Edited by Thomas Brunnschweiler, Samuel Lutz, et al. 4 vols. Zurich: Theologischer Verlag.

A Comparative Creedal Syndogmaticon,
with Alphabetical Index

Although it is, lamentably, still true, as Robert L. Collison observed in his hand-book of 1962, *Indexing Books: A Manual of Basic Principles,* that "few indexes make a conscientious attempt to index ideas," precisely that must be the chief business of an index to *Creeds and Confessions of Faith in the Christian Tradition.* The title "Syndogmaticon" is adapted from "Syntopicon," which was coined to identify the comprehensive index of "102 Great Ideas," constructed for *Great Books of the West-ern World* under the editorship of Mortimer J. Adler and published in 1952 by *Encyclopaedia Britannica.* But here it is "Syn*dogmati*con," because the "topics" with which this index deals are in fact the *dogmata* and doctrines of the Christian tradi-tion as these appear in the various creeds and confessions of faith. The problem is that not every dogma appears in every creed or confession, and that even when they do appear, the doctrines do not always employ the same terminology or follow in the same sequence. Instead of a conventional index, therefore, what is needed here is a doctrinal roadmap, a Syndogmaticon, to serve not as a substitute for, but as a guide to, the close reading of the creedal and confessional texts themselves. This Comparative Creedal Syndogmaticon does not pretend to be a comprehensive concordance to all the topics and theological opinions that happen to have been touched on somewhere in the thousands of pages of creeds and confessions, espe-cially in texts as bulky and discursive as *The Westminster Confession of Faith* or *The Solid Declaration* of *The Formula of Concord* or *The Doctrinal Decrees of the Second Vatican Council.* Nor does it aspire to be used as a miniature *summa theologica,* as may be possible for indexes that confine themselves to the more or less homogene-ous confessions coming out of a single tradition, the most notable of these being the "Index Systematicus Rerum" to the Denzinger *Enchiridion.* The Syndogmaticon is "comparative": it does not itself work out a point-by-point comparison, as a textbook or course in Comparative Symbolics might; but, by locating where a par-ticular doctrine is treated in a particular confession, it does make such comparison and contrast possible across the boundaries of confessions, denominations, and historical periods, documenting the sometimes surprising convergences as well as the striking divergences among them. And it is "creedal," both because the texts it indexes are all creeds and confessions of faith and because it is organized on the basis of the text of *The Niceno-Constantinopolitan Creed* of 381 (more commonly, though less precisely, known as *The Nicene Creed*). The Alphabetical Index serves, in turn, as an "index to the index."

In the roster of all the hundreds and even thousands of creeds and confessions of faith that have been composed over a span of two millennia, *The Niceno-Constanti-nopolitan Creed* must hold pride of place. It has a special standing *among* all the creeds and confessions of faith of Christian history as the only truly ecumenical creed, one that is shared by West and East: including under "West" not only Western Catholicism but much (though by no means all) of Western Protestantism; and including under "East" not only the Eastern Orthodox Church but the Oriental Orthodox Churches and the Assyrian Church of the East. Though often linked with *The Apostles' Creed* and *The Athanasian Creed* as one of "the three ecumenical creeds," particularly in the West, this creed also occupies an authoritative place that is distinctive *within* many of the subsequent confessions of those several traditions (see Ecclesiastical Index, s.v. *Niceno-Constantinopolitan Creed*). Thus it represents an outstanding instance of what indexers refer to as a "controlled vocabulary": all, or virtually all, the authors of subsequent creeds and confessions for over sixteen centuries have known its text; most of them have ascribed greater or lesser authority to it; and many of them have prayed its words in their liturgies. Therefore it is uniquely suited to provide, phrase by phrase, the outline for this Comparative Creedal Syndogmaticon. Even what later generations have sometimes perceived to be its lacunae—its silence on the doctrines of election (3.2), justification (3.5), and atonement (4.1); its evident indifference to particular questions of ethics and society (7.3; 8.4); its failure to affirm the inspiration and inerrancy of Holy Scripture (8.14); its lack of specific prescriptions about polity, ministry, and church order (9.8); its reference only to baptism among the sacraments (10.2)—may serve to emphasize this unparalleled position of *The Niceno-Constantinopolitan Creed*. Explicating the text of an ancient creed phrase by phrase to present a summary of Christian doctrine follows ecumenical precedent across the confessions and across the centuries, for example: *The Catechetical Lectures* by Cyril of Jerusalem for the Greek church fathers; *A Commentary on the Apostles' Creed* by Rufinus of Aquileia for the Latin fathers; *The Heidelberg Catechism* for the Protestant Reformation; *The Orthodox Confession of the Catholic and Apostolic Eastern Church* by Peter Mogila for Eastern Orthodoxy; and the *Catechism of the Catholic Church* for Roman Catholicism.

Basically, the Syndogmaticon reproduces and follows the text of *The Niceno-Constantinopolitan Creed* just as Part One of *Creeds and Confessions of Faith in the Christian Tradition* has presented it, dividing it into the traditional twelve articles. But on account of their historical importance, the two most significant of the later divergences from that original text of the First Council of Constantinople in 381 have been added, in brackets: the substitution—or, if it was originally a baptismal creed, actually the restoration—in both Eastern and Western Christendom, of the singular "I believe" in place of the council's original plural "We believe" as the opening of article 1 (which carries through to the other plural verbs, in articles 11 and 12 of the creed); and, in article 8, the addition, by Western Christendom, of "and from the Son [*Filioque*]" to the original phrase about the Holy Spirit, "proceeding forth from the Father," as this *Western Recension* appears at the beginning of Part Three.

Because *The Niceno-Constantinopolitan Creed* serves as the outline of the Syndogmaticon, it would have been redundant to include its individual articles among the references; the same applies to the "creeds" in the Bible, which go on to serve as proof texts for other creeds. Certain other brief creedal formulas, too, especially from the early period and then the modern period, are indexed sometimes according to the individual doctrines in them when these are distinctive or unusually emphatic or prominent (which in the early period is usually the Trinity or the incarnation, and in the modern period often the church and the ministry) or sometimes (as in the case of most early creeds, or of the one-sentence *Doctrinal Basis* of the World Council of Churches of 1948 and other ecumenical affirmations) simply under "1.1. The Faith and Creed of the Church." This heading is therefore also the place to look for early references to such teachings as "6.1. The Ascension of Christ" and others that did not become controversial questions and therefore creedal and confessional issues until later. For similar reasons, as the cross-references and the Alphabetical Index indicate but cannot of course indicate exhaustively, it is always necessary to look up not only a specific doctrinal subject but others that are adjacent or closely related to it (for instance, not only 8.1 on the person of the Holy Spirit, but 1.8 on the Trinity); otherwise, it would be easy to miss what a particular creed or confession teaches on that subject, or even to draw the mistaken conclusion that it says nothing about it.

1. WE BELIEVE [I BELIEVE] IN ONE GOD THE FATHER ALL-POWERFUL, MAKER OF HEAVEN AND EARTH, AND OF ALL THINGS BOTH SEEN AND UNSEEN.

2. AND IN ONE LORD JESUS CHRIST, THE ONLY-BEGOTTEN SON OF GOD, BEGOTTEN FROM THE FATHER BEFORE ALL THE AGES, LIGHT FROM LIGHT, TRUE GOD FROM TRUE GOD, BEGOTTEN NOT MADE, CONSUBSTANTIAL WITH THE FATHER; THROUGH WHOM ALL THINGS CAME TO BE,

3. WHO FOR US HUMANS AND FOR OUR SALVATION CAME DOWN FROM THE HEAVENS AND BECAME INCARNATE FROM THE HOLY SPIRIT AND THE VIRGIN MARY, BECAME HUMAN

4. AND WAS CRUCIFIED ON OUR BEHALF UNDER PONTIUS PILATE; HE SUFFERED AND WAS BURIED

5. AND ROSE UP ON THE THIRD DAY IN ACCORDANCE WITH THE SCRIPTURES.

6. AND HE WENT UP INTO THE HEAVENS AND IS SEATED AT THE FATHER'S RIGHT HAND;

7. HE IS COMING AGAIN WITH GLORY TO JUDGE THE LIVING AND THE DEAD; HIS KINGDOM WILL HAVE NO END.

8. AND IN THE SPIRIT, THE HOLY, THE LORDLY AND LIFE-GIVING ONE, PROCEEDING FORTH FROM THE FATHER [AND THE SON], CO-WORSHIPED AND CO-GLORIFIED WITH FATHER AND SON, THE ONE WHO SPOKE THROUGH THE PROPHETS;

9. IN ONE, HOLY, CATHOLIC, AND APOSTOLIC CHURCH.

10. WE CONFESS [I CONFESS] ONE BAPTISM FOR THE FORGIVING OF SINS.

11. WE LOOK FORWARD [I LOOK FORWARD] TO A RESURRECTION OF THE DEAD

12. AND LIFE IN THE AGE TO COME.

1. WE BELIEVE

1.1 . The Faith and Creed of the Church: Believing "that"
[*fides quae creditur*]

I: *Ign; Just; Tert; Hipp; Orig; Dêr Bal; Novat; Greg Thaum; Cyr Jer; Ant 325; Ant 341; N*

II: *Jer II* 1.2; *Metr Crit* 1; *Mogila* 1.4–5; *Dosith* decr 9; *Vald*

III: *Ap* 1; *Ath* 1–2, 42; *No Afr; Patr; Fid cath; Lat 1215*

IV: 17 *Art* 1; *Luth Sm Cat* 3.5; *Apol Aug* 4.337–38, 4.383; *Form Conc Epit* 3.6; *Heid* 22–24; *Denck* 1; *Ries* 19; *Witt Art* 4; *Trid Prof* 9

V: *Geloof* 20.5; *Dec Addr* 6–7; *Vat I* 3.3, can 3.2; *Sacr ant* 6; *Br St Luth* 20; *WCC; Un Ch Japan* 5; *Sri Lanka* 3; *Zambia* 1; *Un Ref Ch* 12; *Laus Cov* 1; *F&O Ban; Un Ch Can: Crd; Chile; BEC*

1.2. Knowledge of God and of the Will of God Through Creation, History, Conscience, and Reason

II: *Gennad* 12.2, 4; *Metr Crit* 4.2–6; *Dosith* decr 14

III: *Tol XI* 9; *Petr Ab* 1

IV: 17 *Art* 12; *Apol Aug* 18.9; *Form Conc Epit* 1.9; *Form Conc Sol Dec* 2.9; *Genv Cat* 113; *Helv II* 9.6, 12.1, 16.9; *Dort* 3/4.4; *West* 1.1, 16.7

V: *Gen Bap* 4–10, 28; *Sav* 1.1, 16.7; *Geloof* 1, 11.1; *Cumb Pres* 38, 67; *Syl* 3–6, 8–9, 15–16, 56; *Vat I* 3.2, 3.4, 3 can 2.1, can 3.1–3; *Com Cr* 4; *Richmond* 3; *Sacr ant* 2; *Pol Nat* 1; *Un Ch Can: Union* 2; *Un Pres* 2; *Barm* 1; *Munif* 12; *Vat II* 8.6, 9.3; *Menn Con* 2.1; *Pres USA* 9.13, 9.41–42; *Laus Cov* 9–10; *Toraja* 2.2, 7.4

1.3. The Revelation of Divine Mystery, Its Scope and Language
(*see also 8.11–15*)

I: *Alex; Eph 431 Form Un*

II: *CP 1351* 15; *Metr Crit* 1.3; *Mogila* 1.8–10

IV: *Gall* 2; *Scot I* 4; *Belg* 2; *West* 1.1

V: *London I* 1; *Sav* 1.1; *Friends I* 11; *Geloof* 2.1–2, 9.4, 17.5; *Aub* 1; *Syl* 5; *Vat I* 3.2, 3.4, 3 can 2.2–3, 3 can 4.1; *Com Cr* 4; *Lam* 20–26, 58–65; *Pol Nat* 1; *Assem* 13b; *Un Ch Can: Union* 2; *Un Pres* 2, 15; *Br St Luth* 14–16; *Madag* pr 3; *Vat II* 8.2–6; *Menn Con* 1.2, 2.1; *PRCC* 1a; *Toraja* pr, 1.1, 2.2, 7.4; *Bap Conf* 1; *Morav Am* 1, 3

1.4. The Rule of Faith; Authority of Creeds and Confessions
(*see also* 8.11–12, 9.6, 9.8, Ecclesiastical Index)

I: *Iren; Tert; Tome* 1–2

II: *Phot* 8; *Dosith* decr 9; *Jer II* 1.1

III: *Boh I* 2

IV: *Apol Aug* 27.60; *Form Conc Epit* int; *Form Conc Sol Dec* int; *Irish* 1; *Witt Art* 1; *Trid Prof* 1

V: *Dec Addr* 3; *Def Plat* 1.1, 2 pr; *Adv* pr; *Lamb Quad* 2; *Utrecht* 1; *Lam* 62; *Assem* pr; *Afr Orth* 2; *So Bap* pr; *Un Ch Can: Union* pr; *Un Pres* pr; *F&O Laus* 4; *Chin Un* 3; *Ess* 14; *Meth Kor* pr; *Br St Luth* 29, 45–48; *Wash*; *CSI 1947* 1; *Philip Ind* 2.3, 2.21; *Bat* pr; *Un Ch Japan* 5; *Madag* pr 2; *Sri Lanka* 3; *CNI* 3; *Ghana* 3.3–4; *Zambia* 2; *Pres USA* 9.01–05; *Togo* pr; *Un Ref Ch* 18; *Leuen* 4, 12, 37; *RCA* 7; *Toraja* pr; *Bap Conf* pr; *Morav Am* 4; *Camb Dec* 1; *Ad tuendam* 1

1.5. The One Faith: Confession of Orthodox Doctrine and Anathema
Against Heresy (*see also* Ecclesiastical Index)

I: *Iren; Tome* 14; *Edict* 2, 56, 62–63, 77–78, anath 1–13; *Chal* ecth; *CP II* 1, 7, 12, anath 11; *CP III* 10

II: *Phot* 1; *CP 1351* 7, 51; *Mark Eph* 5; *Mogila* 1.91

III: *Lat 649* 18–20; *Sens* 1–19

IV: *Aug* 21 con; *Smal Art* 3.3.40; *Form Conc Epit* 12; *Form Conc Sol Dec* int 14–20, 12; *67 Art* 5; *10 Art* 1; *Ries* 29; *Trent* 3

V: *Sav* pr; *Cum occas; Dec Addr* 7; *Ev All* con; *Resp Pius IX* 1–3, 21; *Syl* 15–18; *Vat I* 3.pr; *Lam* 7–8, 22–24, 26; *Naz* pr; *Sacr ant* 1, 5, 7; *Br St Luth* 28–29, 44; *Barm* pr; *Munif* 12, 36; *Bap Assoc* 20; *Bat* pr 4, 9.4; *Madag* 1, 4; *Vat II* 5.3.11, 5.3.24; *CNI* 4–5; *Leuen* 2, 20, 23, 26, 27; *PRCC* pr, 1b; *Chr Dec* 4–5; *Morav Am* 3–4; *Camb Dec* pr; *Ad tuendam; LuRC Just* 7, 42

[I BELIEVE]

1.6. Saving Faith: Believing "in" [*fides qua creditur*] (*see also* 3.5)

II: *Jer II* 1.4, 6; *Lucar* 9, 13; *Mogila* 1.1–3; *Dosith* decr 9

III: *Ap* 1; *Ath* 1–2, 42; *R* 1; *Orange* 5–6; *Lat 1215*

IV: *17 Art* 2; *Luth Sm Cat* 1.1; *Luth Lg Cat* 1.1–29; *Aug* 20.8–26; *Apol Aug* 4.48–121, 4.153, 12.45; *Form Conc Epit* 3.5–6; *Form Conc Sol Dec* 3.11–14, 4.35; *Tetrapol* 3; *Bas Bek* 9; *Helv I* 13; *Genv Con* 11; *Genv Cat* 111–14; *Belg* 23; *Heid* 21; *Helv II* 16.1–4; *Irish* 37; *Dort* 3/4.14; *West* 11.2, 14.1–3, 18.2–4; *West Sh Cat* 86; *18 Diss* 1–3, 8; *Denck* 1; *Ries* 19, 20; *Marburg* 5; *Witt Art* 4; *Trent* 6 can 12–14

V: *London I* 22–24; *Camb Plat* 12.2–3; *Sav* 11.2, 14.1–3, 18.2–4; *Friends I* 12; *Morav* 1; *Geloof* 18, 20.3; *Meth Art* 9, 12; *Dec Addr* 8–9; *Cumb Pres* 45–47, 62–65; *New Hamp* 6, 8; *Aub* 11; *LDS* 4; *Abst Prin* 10; *Swed Bap* 6; *Vat I* 3.3, 3.4; *Bonn I* 5; *Salv Arm* 8–9; *Richmond* 6; *Sacr ant* 6; *So Bap* 8; *Un Ch Can: Union* 10; *Un Pres* 17, 19, 24; *Ess* 1–2; *Br St Luth* 9; *F&O Edin* 1.2; *Philip Ind* 2.1; *Bat* 7, 15; *Arn* 8a; *UCC* 1; *Vat II* 8.5, 9.9–10; *Menn Con* 6; *Un Ref Ch* 3; *PRCC* 1; *Toraja* 5.4; *BEM* 1.8–10; *Morav Am* 2; *Camb Dec* 4; *LuRC Just* 25–27

IN ONE GOD

1.7. The Monotheistic Faith and Its Confession (*see also* 1.8)

I: *Tert; Smyr*
II: *Gennad* 1
III: *Ath* 3, 6, 16; *Tol I* 1; *Tol XI* 7
IV: *Genv Con* 2; *Helv II* 3.1–2; *West* 2.1; *West Sh Cat* 5, 46–47; *Ries* 1; *Dordrecht* 1
V: *True Con* 1; *Sav* 2.1; *Friends I* 1; *Morav* 1; *Geloof* 4.1,5; *New Hamp* 2; *Winch* 2; *Arm Ev* 1; *Ev All* 3; *Abst Prin* 2; *Swed Bap* 2; *Free Meth* 1; *Vat I* 3.1, 3 can 1.1; *Adv* 1; *Salv Arm* 2; *Chr Sci* 2; *Com Cr* 1; *Richmond* 1; *Naz* 1; *Assem* 2; *So Bap* 2; *Un Ch Can: Union* 1; *Un Pres* 1; *Meth Kor* 1; *Br St Luth* 4; *Philip Ind* 1.1; *Madag* 1, 4; *Menn Con* 1.1; *Zambia* 1; *Un Ref Ch* 17.1; *Laus Cov* 1; *Toraja* 1.1; *Bap Conf* 2; *Philip UCC* 1

THE FATHER

1.8. The Trinity of Father, Son, and Holy Spirit (*see also* 1.9, 2.1, 8.1)

I: *Iren; Orig* 4; *Greg Thaum; Ar; Alex; Eus; Ant 341; Sard; Sirm; CP 360; Ulph; Epiph; Eun; Aug; Edict* 3, anath 1; *Ecth* 1; *N; CP I; CP II* anath 1, 10
II: *Lit Chrys; Phot* 8–23; *CP 1351* 9, 44; *Greg Palam* 1; *Gennad* 2–3; *Jer II* 1.1; *Metr Crit* 1; *Lucar* 1; *Mogila* 1.7–11; *Dosith* decr 1
III: *Ap; Ath; R; Tol I* 1–11, anath 2–4; *Fid cath; Tol III; Lat 649* 1; *Tol XI; Rom Syn* 1; *Fréjus* 1–5; *Sens* 1–2, 4, 14, 17; *Petr Ab* 2; *Lat 1215* 1; *Lyons; Flor Un; Flor Arm; Vald Boh I* 3
IV: *Aug* 1; *Apol Aug* 1; *Smal Art* 1.1–2; *Tetrapol* 2; *Fid rat* 1; *Bas Bek* 1; *Helv I* 6; *Genv Cat* 19–20; *Gall* 6; *Scot I* 1; *Belg* 8–9; *Heid* 25; *Helv II* 3.3–4; *39 Art* 1; *Irish* 8–10; *West* 2.3; *West Sh Cat* 6; *Cologne* 1; *Ries* 2–3; *Dordrecht* 1; *Marburg* 1
V: *True Con* 2; *London I* 2, 27; *Sav* 2.3; *Friends I* 1; *Morav* 1; *Geloof* 4; *Meth Art* 1; *Winch* 2; *Cumb Pres* 7; *New Hamp* 2; *LDS* 1; *Arm Ev* 2; *Ev All* 3; *Resp Pius IX* 5; *Abst Prin* 3; *Swed Bap* 2; *Free Meth* 1, 4; *Salv Arm* 3; *Chr Sci* 2; *Com Cr* 1; *Richmond* 1; *Am Bap* 2; *Naz* 1–2; *Assem* 2, 13; *So Bap* 2; *Un Ch Can: Union* 1; *Un Pres* 1, 11–13; *Meth Kor* 1–3; *Br St Luth* 4; *CSI 1947* 1; *Philip Ind* 1.1; *Bap Assoc* 1; *Bat* 2; *Un Ch Japan* 2;

Madag 1–3; *Menn Con* 1; *CNI* 1; *Ghana* 3.1; *Zambia* 1, 4; *Pres USA* 9.07; *Meth Braz* 2.1–3; *Un Ref Ch* 12, 17.1; *Laus Cov* 1; *RCA* pr; *Toraja* 1.1–6; *Bap Conf* 2; *Philip UCC* 1; *Morav Am* 1; *Com Dec* 2

ALL-POWERFUL

1.9. The Attributes, Hypostases, and "Energies" of God (*see also* 3.9–10)

I: *Edict* 33–41

II: *CP 1341* 8–46; *CP 1351* 9–11, 17–22, 27, 29–30, 32–35, 38, 40; *Greg Palam* 7; *Mogila* 1.11–17

III: *Tol I* 10; *Lat 649* 1; *Boh I* 3

IV: *Aug* 1.2; *Form Conc Epit* 2.8, 8.7, 11.2–4; *Form Conc Sol Dec* 4.16, 11.4–7; *Fid rat* 2; *Genv Cat* 9, 23–24, 271–74; *Gall* 1; *Scot I* 1; *Belg* 1; *Heid* 11; *Irish* 8; *Dort* 1.11; *West* 2.1–2; *West Sh Cat* 4; *Ries* 3

V: *True Con* 2; *London I* 2; *Gen Bap* 1; *Sav* 2.1–2; *Geloof* 1.1, 3.1; *Winch* 2; *Cumb Pres* 5–6; *Arm Ev* 1; *Resp Pius IX* 5; *Abst Prin* 3; *Syl* 1–2; *Free Meth* 1; *Vat I* 3.1, 3 can 1.3–5; *Adv* 1; *Richmond* 1; *Naz* 1; *Pol Nat* 1; *So Bap* 2; *Un Ch Can: Union* 1; *Un Pres* 1, 11; *Wash*; *Philip Ind* 1.1; *Bat* 1; *Madag* 1; *Menn Con* 1.1; *Pres USA* 9.15; *Meth Braz* 2.1; *Bap Conf* 2

MAKER OF HEAVEN AND EARTH AND OF ALL THINGS BOTH SEEN

1.10. God the Creator: Creation, Preservation, and Providence

I: *Ep Ap*; *Tert*; *Orig* 7; *Novat*

II: *CP 1351* 26; *Metr Crit* 2; *Lucar* 4–5; *Mogila* 1.18, 1.29–31; *Dosith* decr 5

III: *Ap* 1; *Tol I* 1, anath 1, 9, 14; *Lat 1215* 1

IV: *Luth Sm Cat* 2.2; *Luth Lg Cat* 2.9–24; *Bas Bek* 1, 3; *Genv Cat* 25–27; *Gall* 7–8; *Belg* 12; *Heid* 26–28; *Helv II* 6, 7.1–2; *Irish* 18; *West* 4–5; *West Sh Cat* 9, 11–12; *Dordrecht* 1

V: *Gen Bap* 2–3; *Sav* 4–5; *Geloof* 6.1; *Cumb Pres* 8–9, 10, 12–16; *Abst Prin* 4; *Syl* 1–2; *Vat I* 3.1, 3 can 1.1–5; *Salv Arm* 2; *Com Cr* 2; *Am Bap* pr, 3; *Sacr ant* 3; *So Bap* 11; *Un Ch Can: Union* 3–4; *Un Pres* 4–6; *Br St Luth* 5; *CSI 1947* 1; *Sheng Kung* 2; *Bap Assoc* 3; *Bat* 3A; *Madag* 1; *UCC* 2; *Masai* 1; *Menn Con* 1.2, 3.1–2; *Ref All* 1; *Pres USA* 9.16; *Design* 1.3; *Meth Braz* 2.1, 2.10; *Togo* 1; *PRCC* 1; *Hond* pr; *Pres So Afr* 1; *Toraja* 1.2–3, 7.1, 7.11; *Bap Conf* 2a; *Philip UCC* 1

1.11. God and the Powers of Evil (*see also* 1.14, 3.4, 4.1)

I: *Orig* 6; *CP III* 4

II: *Phot* 1; *CP 1054* 3; *CP 1351* 1; *Greg Palam* 5; *Jer II* 1.19; *Metr Crit* 2.4–5, 2.10; *Lucar* 4; *Mogila* 1.21; *Dosith* decr 3, 4, 5

III: *Sens* 7, 16; *Lat 1215* 1

IV: *Aug* 19; *Apol Aug* 19; *Form Conc Epit* 11.4; *Form Conc Sol Dec* 11.7; *Genv Cat* 28–29; *Gall* 8; *Belg* 13; *Helv II* 8.8–10; *Irish* 28; *Ries* 6; *Trent* 6 can 6

V: *True Con* 4; *Geloof* 36.4; *Cumb Pres* 14–15; *Chr Sci* 3; *Un Pres* 4, 7; *Wash*; *Bap Assoc* 4; *Bat* 5; *Menn Con* 3.2; *Laus Cov* 12; *Toraja* 7.3; *Bap Conf* 3

1.12. Creation of the Human Race in the Image of God (*see also* 3.4)

II: *Metr Crit* 2.6–8; *Mogila* 1.22–23

III: *Orange* 8; *Lat 1215* 1; *Vienne* 2

IV: *17 Art* 12; *Aug* 18; *Apol Aug* 2.18–22, 4.27, 18.4–8; *Form Conc Epit* 6.2; *Form Conc Sol Dec* 1.34–42, 2.1–90; *Bas Bek* 2; *Helv I* 7, 9; *Gall* 9; *Scot I* 2; *Belg* 14; *Heid* 6; *Helv II* 7.5–7, 9.1; *Irish* 21; *Dort* 3/4.1; *West* 4.2; *West Sh Cat* 10; *Ries* 4; *Dordrecht* 1

V: *True Con* 4; *London I* 4; *Gen Bap* 11–13; *Sav* 4.2; *Geloof* 5.1–3, 7.1; *Cumb Pres* 11; *Aub* 4; *Abst Prin* 6; *Swed Bap* 3; *Vat I* 3.1; *Chr Sci* 2; *Com Cr* 3; *Richmond* 5; *So Bap* 3; *Un Pres* 4, 11; *Br St Luth* 6; *UCC* 2; *Masai* 1; *Vat II* 9.2–3; *Menn Con* 3.1–2; *Pres USA* 9.17; *Meth Braz* 2.6, 3.1; *PRCC* 2a; *Hond* 1; *Toraja* 3.1–4; *Bap Conf* 3; *Philip UCC* 2

1.13. Freedom of the Will and the Sovereignty of God (*see also* 3.2, 8.5)

I: *Orig*

II: *Jer II* 1.18; *Lucar* 14; *Mogila* 1.27; *Dosith* decr 3

III: *Orange*; *Sens* 5

IV: *Aug* 18; *Apol Aug* 18; *West* 9; *Ries* 5; *Trent* 6 can 2, 4, 5

V: *Cum occas* 3; *Sav* 9; *Geloof* 11; *Meth Art* 8; *Cumb Pres* 34–37; *Aub* 14, 16; *Free Meth* 8; *Naz* 7; *So Bap* 9; *F&O Edin* 1.3; *Bat* 3A; *Menn Con* 3.2, 4.1

AND UNSEEN

1.14. The Doctrine of Angels (*see also* 1.11)

II: *CP 1341* 20–21; *Metr Crit* 2.2; *Lucar* 4; *Mogila* 1.19–20; *Dosith* decr 4

III: *Tol I* 11

IV: *Apol Aug* 21.8; *Gall* 7; *Helv II* 7.3–4; *Irish* 20; *Menn Con* 20

V: *Geloof* 5.1; *Vat I* 3.1; *Afr Orth* 6; *Un Pres* 7; *Bat* 17; *Bap Conf* 3

2. AND IN ONE LORD JESUS CHRIST, THE ONLY-BEGOTTEN SON OF GOD, BEGOTTEN FROM THE FATHER BEFORE ALL THE AGES, LIGHT FROM LIGHT, TRUE GOD FROM TRUE GOD, BEGOTTEN NOT MADE, CONSUBSTANTIAL WITH THE FATHER; THROUGH WHOM ALL THINGS CAME TO BE

2.1. Jesus Christ as Lord: Titles, Offices, States, Deeds, and Teachings

I: *Arist; Ep Ap; Tert; Smyr; N; Chal* 9

II: *Greg Palam* 2; *Mogila* 1.34–36

III: *Ap* 2; *Ath* 22, 29–41; *R* 2; *Tol I* 12–13, anath 3; *Lat* 649 2; *Tol XI* 2; *Boh I* 6

IV: *Luth Lg Cat* 3.27–31; *Apol Aug* 4.69, 21.17–20; *Laus Art* 2; *Genv Cat* 30–47, 54; *Gall* 13; *Scot I* 7–8; *Belg* 10, 26; *Heid* 29–31, 33–34; *Helv II* 5, 11, 18.4; *39 Art* 18; *Irish* 31; *West* 8; *West Sh Cat* 21, 23–26; *Cologne* 2; *Ries* 9, 11, 12, 17; *Tig* 4

V: *True Con* 9–15; *London I* 9–20; *Gen Bap* 20–23; *Friends I* 4; *Sav* 8; *Morav* 2; *Geloof* 4.3, 12–16; *Meth Art* 2; *Shkr* 3; *Cumb Pres* 27; *Abst Prin* 7; *Syl* 7; *Free Meth* 2; *Vat I* 3.3, 3 can 3.4; *Richmond* 2; *Am Bap* 5; *Lam* 13–18, 27–38; *Naz* 2; *Pol Nat* 2–3; *Assem* 13e-j; *Witness* 7; *Afr Orth* 3; *So Bap* 8; *Un Ch Can: Union* 2, 7; *Un Pres* 12; *Chin Un* 1; *Meth Kor* 2; *Barm* 2; *F&O Edin* 2.1–2; *Wash; CSI 1947* 1; *Philip Ind* 1.2, 2.16; *Bap Assoc* 6; *Bat* 9; *Madag* 2; *Masai* 2; *Menn Con* 5; *CNI* 1; *Ghana* 3.1; *Zambia* 5; *Ref All* 2; *Pres USA* 9.08–11, 9.19; *Design* 1.1–2; *Meth Braz* 2.2; *Togo* 2; *Leuen* 21; *Laus Cov* 3; *PRCC* 1a; *Pres So Afr* 2; *Toraja* pr, 1.4, 2.1, 4.3; *Philip UCC* 1

3. WHO FOR US HUMANS AND FOR OUR SALVATION

3.1. The Divine Economy of Salvation

I: *Iren; Tert; Orig* 4; *Tome* 6

II: *Metr Crit* 3; *Lucar* 7

III: *Ath* 38; *Sens* 3; *Lat* 1215 2; *Unam* 8

IV: *Form Conc Epit* 11.17–19; *Form Conc Sol Dec* 11.28; *Sax Vis* 1.4.2; *Belg* 17; *West* 7; *Cologne* 4; *Dordrecht* 3; *Trent* 6.2

V: *True Con* 5–6; *London I* 5–6; *Sav* 7; *Friends I* 10; *Geloof* 10; *Shkr* 1; *Dec Addr* 8; *Cumb Pres* 22–25; *New Hamp* 4; *Assem* 4; *So Bap* 4; *Un Ch Can: Union* 3, 6; *Philip Ind* 2.1; *UCC* 3; *Masai* 1; *Vat II* 8.2–4, 8.14–16; *Menn Con* 1.2; *Pres USA* 9.18; *PRCC* 3b; *Chr Dec* 6

3.2. Election, Predestination, and Divine Foreknowledge

II: *Metr Crit* 4; *Lucar* 3; *Mogila* 1.25–26, 1.30; *Dosith* decr 3

IV: *Form Conc Epit* 11; *Form Conc Sol Dec* 11; *Sax Vis* 1.4, 2.4; *Fid rat* 3; *Bas Bek* 1; *Helv I* 10; *Gall* 12; *Scot I* 8; *Belg* 16; *Lamb Art* 1–4; *Helv II* 10; *39 Art* 17; *Remon* 1; *Irish* 11–17; *Dort* 1; *West* 3.1–8, 17.2; *West Sh Cat* 7; *Ries* 7; *Trent* 6.12, 6 can 15, 17

V: *True Con* 3; *London I* 3, 21; *Sav* 3.1–8, 17.2; *Morav* 1; *Geloof* 9; *New Hamp* 9; *Aub* 2; *Abst Prin* 5; *Swed Bap* 6; *So Bap* 9; *Un Pres* 10; *Afr Orth* 11; *Br St Luth* 35–40; *Munif* 40; *Un Ch Japan* 3; *Vat II* 5.1.2–3; *Menn Con* 6; *Leuen* 24–26

3.3. Plan of Salvation; Gospel and Law; Preaching and Evangelization
(*see also* 8.5, 10.1)

II: *Metr Crit* 3.3–4

III: *Prague* 1; *Boh I* 10

IV: *Apol Aug* 4.5–6, 36–39, 43, 12.53–58; *Smal Art* 3.2, 3.4; *Form Conc Epit* 5; *Form Conc Sol Dec* 4.17, 5.3, 5.20; *67 Art* 1–2; *Helv I* 12; *Genv Con* 6; *Heid* 19, 65; *Helv II* 13; *Dort* 3/4.6–8; *West* 7.5–6; *18 Diss* 12; *Ries* 10; *Dordrecht* 5; *Marburg* 8; *Tig* 1

V: *London I* 24–25; *Sav* 7.5, 20.1–4; *Shkr* 2; *Cumb Pres* 69; *New Hamp* 12; *Arm Ev* 12; *Swed Bap* 7; *Richmond* 5; *So Bap* 23; *Un Ch Can: Union* 14; *Un Pres* 9, 15, 25; *F&O Laus* 2; *Barm* 6; *Bat* 9.1; *UCC* 7; *Vat II* 5.1.16–17, 5.1.25, 5.1.35, 8.18–19; *Menn Con* 8.2, 9; *CNI* 1; *Pres USA* 9.06, 9.49; *Meth Braz* 6; *Leuen* 13; *Laus Cov* pr, 1, 4, 6–10; *Pres So Afr* 3; *Toraja* 1.1, 2.1, 6.3; *Bap Conf* 5; *Morav Am* pr, 7; *LuRC Just* 31–33

3.4. The Need for Salvation: Sin and the Fall (*see also* 1.11, 1.13)

II: *Jer II* 1.3; *Metr Crit* 2.9–12; *Lucar* 6; *Mogila* 1.24–25; *Dosith* decr 6, 14

III: *Orange* 1–2, 8, 15, 21–22, con; *Sens* 8–10, 19; *Boh I* 4

IV: *Luth Lg Cat* 2.28; *Aug* 2; *Apol Aug* 2.3–6, 4.169–71; *Smal Art* 3.1; *Form Conc Epit* 1; *Form Conc Sol Dec* 1; *Fid rat* 2, 4–5; *Bas Bek* 2; *Helv I* 7–8; *Genv Con* 4–5; *Genv Cat* 197, 214–16; *Gall* 9–11; *Scot I* 3; *Belg* 15; *Heid* 3–10; *Helv II* 8.1–5, 9.2–12; *39 Art* 9–10, 15–16; *Remon* 3; *Irish* 22–24, 27, 43–44; *Dort* 3/4; *West* 6; *West Sh Cat* 13–19, 82–84; *Ries* 4; *Dordrecht* 2; *Marburg* 4; *Witt Art* 2; *Trent* 5, 6.1, 6 can 27–29; *Trid Prof* 4

V: *True Con* 4–5; *London I* 4–5; *Gen Bap* 14–16; *Cum occas* 2; *Sav* 6; *Geloof* 8; *Meth Art* 7; *Dec Addr* 8; *Cumb Pres* 17–21, 36; *New Hamp* 3; *Aub* 1, 3–7, 9; *LDS* 2; *Ev All* 4; *Abst Prin* 6; *Swed Bap* 3; *Free Meth* 7; *Salv Arm* 5; *Com Cr* 3; *Richmond* 5; *Naz* 5; *Assem* 3; *Arm Ev* 4; *So Bap* 3; *Un Ch Can: Union* 5; *Un Pres* 8; *Ess* 3, 9; *Br St Luth* 7; *Bap Assoc* 5; *Bat* 5–6; *Madag* 5; *Menn Con* 4.1–2; *Zambia* 5; *Pres USA* 9.12–14; *Togo* 2; *PRCC* 3a; *RCA* 2; *Toraja* 3.5–8, 7.2–3; *Bap Conf* 4; *Morav Am* 1

3.5. Salvation as Forgiveness, Adoption, Justification
(*see also* 1.6, 4.1, 8.2–3)

II: *Jer II* 1.4; *Metr Crit* 6.5; *Lucar* 9, 13; *Dosith* decr 13
III: *Ap* 10; *R* 10; *Boh I* 6
IV: *Luth Sm Cat* 3.16; *Luth Lg Cat* 3.85–98; *Aug* 4; *Apol Aug* 4; *Smal Art* 2.1.4, 3.13; *Form Conc Epit* 3; *Form Conc Sol Dec* 3; *Tetrapol* 3; *Genv Con* 7, 9; *Genv Cat* 101–5, 114–20, 280–86; *Gall* 18–20; *Belg* 22, 23; *Heid* 56, 59–64; *Lamb Art* 5–6; *Helv II* 15; *39 Art* 13; *Irish* 34–35; *West* 11; *West Sh Cat* 32–33; *Ries* 21; *Marburg* 7; *Witt Art* 4; *Tig* 3; *Trent* 6; *Trid Prof* 4
V: *London I* 28; *Sav* 11–12; *Friends I* 12; *Geloof* 20; *Meth Art* 9; *Shkr* 5; *Cumb Pres* 48–50; *New Hamp* 5; *Aub* 15; *Arm Ev* 7; *Ev All* 6; *Abst Prin* 11; *Free Meth* 9; *Vat I* 3.3; *Adv* 15; *Bonn I* 5; *Salv Arm* 8; *Chr Sci* 3; *Richmond* 6; *Naz* 9.9; *Assem* 4a; *Afr Orth* 11; *So Bap* 5; *Un Ch Can: Union* 11; *Un Pres* 19–20; *Ess* 2; *Meth Kor* 4; *Br St Luth* 9, 17–19; *F&O Edin* 1.2; *CSI 1947* 1; *Bap Assoc* 10; *Bat* 7; *UCC* 8; *Masai* 3; *Leuen* 6–8, 10, 12; *PRCC* 3c; *Toraja* 4.7, 5.3–4; *Bap Conf* 5; *Camb Dec* 4; *LuRC Just*

CAME DOWN FROM THE HEAVENS AND BECAME INCARNATE

3.6. The Incarnation of the Son of God

I: *Tert*; *Tome* 7–10; *Edict* 4, anath 2; *Ecth* 2; *Eph 431* ecth; *Chal* 13–15; *CP II* anath 2
II: *Greg Palam* 2; *Gennad* 4–5; *Metr Crit* 3.4–5; *Mogila* 1.38
III: *Ap* 3; *Ath* 29–37; *R* 3; *Tol I* 12–19, anath 5; *Lat 649* 2; *Tol XI* 9–15; *Rom Syn* 2; *Fréjus* 6–8; *Sens* 3; *Petr Ab* 3; *Lat 1215* 2; *Vienne* 1; *Vald*
IV: *Aug* 3; *Apol Aug* 3; *Smal Art* 1.3–4; *Form Conc Epit* 8; *Form Conc Sol Dec* 8.6; *Tetrapol* 2; *Fid rat* 1; *Bas Bek* 4; *Helv I* 11; *Genv Cat* 50–53; *Gall* 14; *Scot I* 6; *Belg* 18; *Heid* 35; *Helv II* 11; *39 Art* 2; *Irish* 29; *West* 8.2–3; *Ries* 8; *Dordrecht* 4; *Marburg* 2
V: *Sav* 8.2–3; *Friends I* 5; *Morav* 2; *Geloof* 12; *Meth Art* 2; *Cumb Pres* 28; *Ev All* 5; *Free Meth* 2; *Adv* 2; *Richmond* 2; *Naz* 2; *Witness* 8; *So Bap* 4; *Un Pres* 12; *Br St Luth* 8; *CSI 1947* 1; *Philip Ind* 2.16; *Bat* 3B; *Masai* 2; *Vat II* 8.4; *Menn Con* 1.3, 5.1; *Meth Braz* 2.3; *Leuen* 9; *PRCC* 1b; *RCA* 3; *Hond* 1; *Toraja* 1.4, 4.1; *Bap Conf* 2b; *Chr Dec* 1

FROM THE HOLY SPIRIT AND
THE VIRGIN MARY

3.7. Mary Virgin Mother and Theotokos;
Other Titles and Privileges of Mary

I: *Ign; Ep Ap; Tert; Tome* 4; *Edict* anath 5; *Ecth* 3; *Eph 431; Chal; CP II* 11, anath 6; *Nic II*

II: *Lit Chrys* I.A.2, II.F.5; *Greg Palam* 6; *Metr Crit* 9.5, 17.7–9; *Mogila* 1.39–42; *Dosith* decr 1.6, 8, q 4; *Rom Syn* 2

III: *Ap* 3; *R* 3; *Tol I* 12; *Lat 649* 3; *Tol XI* 9, 13; *Boh I* 17

IV: *Apol Aug* 21.27–28; *Smal Art* 1.4; *Trent* 5.6, 6 can 23; *Form Conc Epit* 8.12; *Form Conc Sol Dec* 8.24; *Genv Cat* 49

V: *Ineff; Bonn I* 10; *Utrecht* 3; *Am Bap* 4; *Afr Orth* 6; *Philip Ind* 2.14; *Munif; Bap Assoc* 6; *Bat* 3B1; *Vat II* 5.1.52–69, 5.3.15; *Hond* 1; *Chr Dec* 3

3.8. The Saints: Veneration and Invocation

II: *Jer II* 1.15, 1.21; *Metr Crit* 17; *Dosith* decr 8

III: *Ap* 9; *Boh I* 17

IV: *Aug* 21; *Apol Aug* 21; *Smal Art* 2.2; *67 Art* 19–21; *Bern* 6; *Tetrapol* 11; *10 Art* 7–8; *Genv Con* 12; *Genv Cat* 238–39; *Gall* 24; *Belg* 26; *Helv II* 5.4–6; *West* 21.2, 26.1–3; *Witt Art* 16; *Trent* 25.2

V: *Sav* 22.2; *Meth Art* 14; *Arm Ev* 9; *Bonn I* 7; *Afr Orth* 6–7; *Philip Ind* 2.15; *Vat II* 5.1.50–51, 5.1.66–69, 5.3.15

BECAME HUMAN

3.9. Fully Divine Nature and Fully Human Nature (*see also* 1.8–9, 3.10)

I: *Ign; Tome* 5; *Edict* 5–7, 13–18, 23–32, anath 8; *Ecth* 3–4; *Eph 431* ecth; *Chal* 5–12, 16–20; *Nic II*

II: *CP 1351* 13; *Greg Palam* 2; *Gennad* 6–7; *Metr Crit* 3.6–7

III: *Ath* 30–37; *Tol I* 13–15; *Lat 649* 4–5; *Rom Syn* 3; *Sens* 4; *Lat 1215* 2

IV: *Form Conc Epit* 8.8; *Form Conc Sol Dec* 1.43–44; *Sax Vis* 1.2, 2.2; *Fid rat* 1; *Gall* 15; *Belg* 19; *Helv II* 11.6–10

V: *Meth Art* 2; *Cumb Pres* 29; *Arm Ev* 5; *Swed Bap* 4; *Free Meth* 2; *Com Cr* 6; *Naz* 2; *Assem* 13f–g; *Witness* 8; *Un Pres* 12; *Ess* 8; *Bat* 3B; *Menn Con* 1.3; *Leuen* 22; *Hond* 2; *Toraja* 4.2; *Bap Conf* 2b; *Chr Dec* 2–3; *Com Dec* 3

3.10. Hypostatic Union of Two Natures, with Two Wills
and Two "Energies" (*see also* 1.9, 3.9)

I: *Edict 8–12, 19–22*, anath 4, 9; *Ecth 4–6*; *Eph 431* ecth; *Chal 19–24*; *CP II* anath 3–5, 7–9; *CP III 7–9*; *Nic II*
II: *CP 1351 14*
III: *Tol I* anath 13; *Lat 649 6–16*; *Rom Syn 3*; *Flor Arm 7–9*
IV: *Form Conc Epit 3.3, 3.12–13, 8.1–18*; *Form Conc Sol Dec 8.31–87*; *Sax Vis 1.2, 2.2*; *Fid rat 1*; *Gall 15*; *Belg 19*; *Helv II 11.6–10*
V: *Def Plat 2.7*; *Free Meth 2*; *Salv Arm 4*; *Naz 2*; *Un Pres 12*; *Leuen 22*

4. AND WAS CRUCIFIED ON OUR BEHALF UNDER PONTIUS PILATE

4.1. Reconciliation, Redemption, and Atonement

II: *Gennad 9*; *Mogila 1.50–51*
III: *Ath 38*; *Vienne 1*; *Boh I 6*
IV: *17 Art 9*; *Luth Sm Cat 2.4*; *Luth Lg Cat 2.31*; *Aug 3.3*; *Apol Aug 4.179, 24.22–24, 58–59*; *Smal Art 2.1*; *Form Conc Sol Dec 5.20–22*; *67 Art 54*; *Bern 3*; *Fid rat 3 Helv I 11*; *Genv Cat 56–61, 71*; *Gall 17*; *Scot I 9*; *Heid 12–18, 37–39*; *Helv II 11.15*; *39 Art 31*; *Remon 2*; *Irish 30*; *Dort 2*; *West 8.4–7*; *West Sh Cat 25*; *18 Diss 9*; *Ries 13*; *Dordrecht 4*; *Marburg 3*; *Trent 22.2*
V: *True Con 14*; *London I 17–18*; *Gen Bap 17–19*; *Cum occas 5*; *Sav 8.4–7*; *Friends I 6, 10*; *Geloof 13, 15.2*; *Meth Art 2, 20*; *Cumb Pres 31–33*; *Aub 8, 10*; *LDS 3*; *Arm Ev 5*; *Swed Bap 4*; *Free Meth 2, 20*; *Adv 2*; *Salv Arm 6*; *Chr Sci 4*; *Com Cr 6*; *Richmond 2, 6*; *Utrecht 6*; *Am Bap 6*; *Lam 38*; *Naz 2, 6*; *Pol Nat 3*; *Assem 12*; *Un Ch Can: Union 7*; *Un Pres 9, 12, 14*; *F&O Laus 2*; *Ess 8–9*; *Br St Luth 4, 8, 18*; *F&O Edin 1.1*; *Bap Assoc 7*; *Bat 3B*; *Un Ch Japan 2*; *Arn 3d*; *Madag 5*; *UCC 5*; *Menn Con 5.2*; *Ref All 2*; *Pres USA 9.09*; *Meth Braz 2.4*; *Un Ref Ch 17.2*; *Leuen 9*; *PRCC 1b*; *RCA 4*; *Toraja 4.4–5*; *Bap Conf 2b*; *Camb Dec 2*

HE SUFFERED AND WAS BURIED

4.2. Events of the Passion: Transfiguration, Crucifixion, Death, and Descent into Hades

I: *Ign*; *Tert*; *Tome 12–13*
II: *CP 1341*; *CP 1351 46*; *Metr Crit 3.8–11*; *Mogila 1.43–49*
III: *Ap 4*; *Ath 38*; *R 4*; *Tol I 16*, anath 6–7; *Sens 18*; *Lat 1215 2*

IV: *Form Conc Epit* 9; *Form Conc Sol Dec* 9; *Genv Cat* 55, 65–70; *Heid* 40–44; *Helv II* 11.10; *39 Art* 3; *West Sh Cat* 2

V: *Geloof* 15.2; *Cumb Pres* 30; *Free Meth* 2; *Chr Sci* 5; *Com Cr* 6; *Richmond* 2; *Naz* 2; *Un Pres* 12; *Masai* 2; *Hond* 2; *Toraja* 4.5

5. AND ROSE UP ON THE THIRD DAY IN ACCORDANCE WITH THE SCRIPTURES

5.1. The Resurrection of Christ (*see also* 11.4)

I: *Polyc; Tert; Tome* 11; *CP II* anath 12
II: *Metr Crit* 3.12; *Mogila* 1.52–53
III: *Ap* 5; *Ath* 38; *R* 5; *Tol I* 16–17
IV: *Aug* 3.4; *Lu Sm Cat* 2.4; *Lu Lg Cat* 2.31; *Tetrapol* 2; *Bas Bek* 4; *Helv I* 11; *Genv Cat* 73–74; *Scot I* 10; *Heid* 45; *Helv II* 11.11; *39 Art* 4; *West Sh Cat* 28; *Ries* 15
V: *Geloof* 15.3; *Meth Art* 3; *Free Meth* 3; *Chr Sci* 5; *Com Cr* 7; *Richmond* 2; *Am Bap* 7; *Lam* 36–37; *Naz* 2; *Witness* 10; *So Bap* 16; *Un Pres* 12; *Ess* 8; *Bap Assoc* 8; *Bat* 3B; *Madag* 7; *Masai* 2; *Pres USA* 9.26; *RCA* 4; *Hond* 3; *Toraja* 4.6; *Bap Conf* 2b; *Philip UCC* 6

6. AND HE WENT UP INTO THE HEAVENS AND IS SEATED AT THE FATHER'S RIGHT HAND

6.1. The Ascension of Christ into Heaven

II: *Gennad* 10; *Metr Crit* 3.13; *Lucar* 8; *Mogila* 1.55–56
III: *Ap* 6; *Ath* 39; *R* 6; *Tol I* 18; *Tol XI* 17
IV: *Form Conc Sol Dec* 7.93–103; *Genv Cat* 75–82; *Scot I* 11; *Heid* 46–51; *Helv II* 11.12; *39 Art* 4; *Ries* 16; *Tig* 25
V: *Meth Art* 3; *Com Cr* 7; *Richmond* 2; *Am Bap* 7; *Un Pres* 12; *Bap Assoc* 8; *Bat* 3B; *Masai* 2; *RCA* 5; *Toraja* 4.8–9; *Bap Conf* 2b

7. HE IS COMING AGAIN WITH GLORY TO JUDGE THE LIVING AND THE DEAD

7.1. The Second Coming of Christ to Judgment (*see also* 11–12)

I: *Tert*
II: *Gennad* 10; *Jer II* 1.17; *Mogila* 1.57–68

III: *Ap* 7; *Ath* 39–41; *R* 7; *Tol XI* 17; *Sens* 17; *Lat 1215* 2

IV: *Aug* 17; *Apol Aug* 17; *Bas Bek* 10; *Helv I* 11.5; *Genv Cat* 83–87; *Scot I* 11; *Heid* 52; *Helv II* 11.13; *Irish* 104; *West* 33.1; *Ries* 40

V: *Sav* 32.1; *Geloof* 33.3–4, 34.4; *Shkr* 3–4; *Cumb Pres* 114–15; *New Hamp* 18; *Ev All* 8; *Abst Prin* 20; *Swed Bap* 12; *Free Meth* 14; *Adv* 17–18; *Com Cr* 12; *Richmond* 2; *Am Bap* 8; *Naz* 11.14; *Assem* 15; *Witness* 2; *Afr Orth* 13; *So Bap* 17; *Un Ch Can: Union* 19; *Un Pres* 12, 40; *Br St Luth* 42; *Bap Assoc* 22; *Bat* 3B, 18; *Madag* 7; *Masai* 2; *Menn Con* 20; *Leuen* 9; *Laus Cov* 15; *RCA* con; *Toraja* 4.8, 8.2–3; *Bap Conf* 9; *Philip UCC* 6

HIS KINGDOM WILL HAVE NO END

7.2. The Kingdom of Christ and of God

II: *Jer II* 1.5

III: *Tol XI* 18

IV: *Luth Sm Cat* 3.7–8; *Luth Lg Cat* 3.51–58; *Aug* 17.5; *Genv Cat* 37, 42, 268–70; *Heid* 123; *Helv II* 11.14; *Irish* 104; *West Sh Cat* 26, 102; *Ries* 14, 18; *Tig* 4

V: *True Con* 15–16; *London I* 19–20; *Geloof* 16; *Com Cr* 9, 12; *Lam* 52; *Assem* 15; *So Bap* 25; *Un Ch Can: Union* 20; *Un Pres* 12, 37–38, 40, 43–44; *Chin Un* 1; *Meth Kor* 7; *Br St Luth* 42; *Barm* 5; *F&O Edin* 9; *Vat II* 5.1.3–5, 5.1.9–10, 5.1.36; *Pres USA* 9.53–55; *Design* 1.8; *Meth Braz* 2.5; *Korea* pr; *Laus Cov* 15; *PRCC* 4; *Hond* 3; *Pres So Afr* 3; *Toraja* 4.3, 5.2, 6.6; *BEM* 1.7, 2.22; *Philip UCC* 5

7.3. The Kingdoms of This World: Civil Government and Civil Society; Church and State

I: *Edict* 1; *Ecth* con; *CP II* 2; *CP III* 1, 5

II: *CP 1351* con; *Jer II* 1.14, 1.16

III: *Dict Pap* 9, 12, 19, 27; *Unam* 4–6; *Loll* 6, 10; *Prague* 3; *Boh I* 16

IV: *17 Art* 3, 4, 14; *Luth Sm Cat* pr 13, 21–22; *Aug* 16, 28; *Apol Aug* 16; *67 Art* 35–43; *Tetrapol* 23; *Fid rat* 11; *Bas Bek* 8; *Helv I* 26; *Laus Art* 8; *10 Art* pr 1; *Genv Con* 20; *Gall* 39–40; *Scot I* 24; *Belg* 36; *Helv II* 30; *39 Art* 37; *Irish* 57–62; *West* 22–23; *Schleit* 4, 6, 7; *Cologne* 12; *Ries* 37–38; *Dordrecht* 13–15; *Marburg* 12; *Witt Art* 11

V: *True Con* 39–44; *London I* 48–53; *Camb Plat* 17; *Sav* 23–24; *Friends I* 21–22; *Geloof* 28–30; *Meth Art* 23–25; *Cumb Pres* 81–88; *New Hamp* 16; *Swed Bap* 11; *Free Meth* 23; *LDS* 10, 12; *Syl* 20, 23–32, 39–55, 75–77; *Richmond* 12, 14, 15; *Soc Meth*; *Soc Ch*; *So Bap* 18–19; *Un Pres* 31, 37–38; *Ess* 12–13; *Br St Luth* 34; *Barm* pr, 4–5; *Philip Ind* 2.19; *Chin Man*; *Sheng Kung* 2, 6; *Bat* 8.3, 12; *Vat II* 5.3.12, 9.3, 9.6–7, 9.11–15; *Menn Con* 9, 17–19; *Pres USA* 9.43–47; *Meth Braz* 3; *Korea* 2–3; *Laus Cov* 5, 13; *PRCC* 2b, 3e; *RCA* 10–12; *Pres So Afr* 2; *Toraja* 7.5–8; *Bap Conf* 7; *Morav Am* con

8. AND IN THE SPIRIT, THE HOLY, THE LORDLY

8.1. The Divine Person of the Holy Spirit (*see also* 1.8)

I: *Tert; CP I*
II: *CP 1341* 30–31; *Greg Palam* 3; *Mogila* 1.69–70
III: *Ap* 8; *Ath* 23; *R* 8; *Tol I* anath 4; *Tol XI* 3; *Sens* 1–2
IV: *Belg* 11; *Heid* 53; *39 Art* 5; *Cologne* 3
  V: *Morav* 3; *Geloof* 4.4, 14.4; *Meth Art* 4; *Free Meth* 4; *Richmond* 3; *Naz* 3; *Pol Nat* 4; *Witness* 9; *Un Ch Can: Union* 8; *Un Pres* 13; *F&O Laus* 1; *Meth Kor* 3; *CSI 1947* 1; *Philip Ind* 1.3; *Bap Assoc* 9; *Madag* 3; *Menn Con* 1.4; *Meth Braz* 2.3; *Laus Cov* 14; *Toraja* 1.5, 4.9, 5.1–3; *Philip UCC* 1

AND LIFE-GIVING ONE

8.2. Life in the Spirit: Conversion, Regeneration, Sanctification, Restoration of the Divine Image, Participation in the Divine Nature

II: *CP 1341* 19, 35–38; *CP 1351* 36–37
III: *Orange* 4, 6
IV: *Luth Sm Cat* 2.6; *Luth Lg Cat* 2.35–45; *Apol Aug* 4.126; *Form Conc Sol Dec* 2.25–27, 3.19–23, 8.34; *Helv I* 11; *Genv Con* 8; *Genv Cat* 88–91; *Gall* 21; *Scot I* 12; *Belg* 24; *Dort* 3/4.11–13; *West* 10, 12–13, 26.3; *West Sh Cat* 29–39; *Denck* 3; *Ries* 19; *Marburg* 6
  V: *Sav* 10, 13, 27.1; *Friends I* 1–2, 7–8; *Geloof* 19; *Cumb Pres* 51–54; *New Hamp* 7, 10; *Aub* 12; *Arm Ev* 6; *Ev All* 7; *Abst Prin* 8, 12; *Adv* 5, 14; *Salv Arm* 7, 10; *Richmond* 3, 6; *Naz* 9.10, 10.13; *Assem* 4b, 19; *So Bap* 7, 10; *Un Ch Can: Union* 8–9, 12; *Un Pres* 11, 13, 16, 21; *Br St Luth* 10–16; *F&O Edin* 1.2; *Bap Assoc* 11; *Bat* 3C; *Madag* 3; *UCC* 6; *Masai* 3; *Vat II* 5.1.4; *Menn Con* 6–7; *Zambia* 6; *Ref All* 3; *Pres USA* 9.20; *Design* 1.5; *Meth Braz* 2.3; *Leuen* 10; *RCA* 6–9; *Hond* 3; *Toraja* 5.1–3

8.3. The Gifts of the Holy Spirit; Divine Grace and Human Merit

II: *Metr Crit* 3.14; *Mogila* 1.73–81; *Dosith* decr 3
III: *Orange* 3, 5–7, 12, 18–21, con; *Sens* 5
IV: *Apol Aug* 4.17, 4.19–20, 4.288, 4.316, 4.356–77; *Form Conc Sol Dec* 2.25–27; *Genv Cat* 115; *Lamb Art* 7; *Helv II* 16.11; *Remon* 4; *Irish* 26; *West* 7.3–6; *West Sh Cat* 20; *18 Diss* 16; *Witt Art* 5; *Trent* 6.15–16
  V: *Gen Bap* 25–26, 29–33; *Cum occas* 1–4; *Sav* 7.3–5; *Geloof* 17; *Cumb Pres* 39–40; *Aub* 13; *LDS* 4, 7; *Adv* 15–16; *Bonn I* 6; *Naz* 7; *Pol Nat* 5; *Assem* 6; *Un Pres* 13; *Meth Kor* 4; *F&O Edin* 1.1, 1.6; *Bat* 7; *Un Ch Japan* 3; *Vat II* 8.8; *Menn Con* 6–7; *Pres So Afr* 3; *BEM* 1.5; *Camb Dec* 3; *LuRC Just* 19–21, 25–27

8.4. Sanctification as a Life of Love, Christian Service, Virtue, and Good Works

II: *Jer II* 1.2, 1.5, 1.6, 1.20; *Lucar* 13; *Mogila* 1.3; *Dosith* decr 13

III: *Orange* 17; *Sens* 13; *Boh I* 7

IV: *Luth Sm Cat* 1, 9; *Luth Lg Cat* 1; *Aug* 20; *Apol Aug* 4.111–16, 4.122–58, 4.189–94, 20; *Form Conc Epit* 4; *Form Conc Sol Dec* 4; *67 Art* 22; *Tetrapol* 4–6; *10 Art* 3.8–10; *Genv Con* 10; *Genv Cat* 121–27; *Gall* 22; *Scot I* 13–14; *Belg* 24; *Heid* 86–91; *Helv II* 16; *Remon* 5; *Irish* 39–45, 63–67; *West* 16.1–6; *West Sh Cat* 39–84; *18 Diss* 4, 18; *Cologne* 13, 14, 16; *Ries* 22–23; *Dordrecht* 14; *Marburg* 10; *Witt Art* 4, 5; *Trent* 6.11, 6 can 18–21, 24–26, 31–32

V: *Gen Bap* 33–42; *Sav* 16; *Friends I* 13–14, 21; *Geloof* 20.6, 21.1–5, 22.4; *Meth Art* 10–11; *Winch* 3; *Cumb Pres* 55–59; *LDS* 13; *Arm Ev* 8; *Syl* 56–64; *Free Meth* 10–11, 13; *Chr Sci* 6; *Com Cr* 8; *Naz* 10.13; *Assem* 7; *So Bap* 21, 24; *Un Ch Can: Union* 12; *Un Pres* 44; *Br St Luth* 20; *F&O Edin* 2.8–10; *Philip Ind* 2.12; *Sheng Kung* 5; *Bat* 15; *Un Ch Japan* 3; *Masai* 3; *Vat II* 5.1.39–42; *Pres USA* 9.22–25; *Meth Braz* 9; *Leuen* 11; *PRCC* 1c; *RCA* 10–14; *Toraja* 5.5–6; *Bap Conf* 2c, 8; *Morav Am* 7–9; *LuRC Just* 37–39

8.5. Sanctification as Free Obedience to the Law of God
(*see also* 1.13, 3.3, 8.4)

II: *Metr Crit* 6; *Mogila* 1.86–95

III: *Orange* 13

IV: *17 Art* 2; *Luth Sm Cat* pr 17–18, 1; *Luth Lg Cat* 1; *Aug* 6; *Form Conc Epit* 6; *Form Conc Sol Dec* 6; *Genv Con* 3; *Genv Cat* 131–232; *Gall* 23; *Scot I* 15; *Heid* 92–115; *Helv II* 12; *Irish* 84; *West* 19–20; *Witt Art* 5

V: *London I* 29; *Gen Bap* 28; *Cum occas* 1; *Sav* 19, 21; *Meth Art* 6; *Cumb Pres* 37, 66–74; *New Hamp* 12; *Abst Prin* 18; *Adv* 11; *Un Ch Can: Union* 14; *Un Pres* 25; *Bat* 15

PROCEEDING FORTH FROM THE FATHER [AND THE SON]

8.6. The Procession of the Holy Spirit

I: *Tert*

II: *Phot* 8–23; *CP 1054* 3, 4; *Greg Palam* 3; *Mark Eph* 1–2, 6; *Metr Crit* 1.5–31; *Mogila* 1.71

III: *Ath* 23; *Tol XI* 3; *Fréjus* 4; *Lyons*; *Flor Un* 5–9; *Flor Arm* 6

IV: *Smal Art* 1.2; *Form Conc Sol Dec* 8.73; *Gall* 6; *Belg* 9, 11; *39 Art* 5; *Helv II* 3.3; *Irish* 10; *West* 2.3; *West Lg Cat* 10; *Cologne* 3; *Ries* 3

V: *True Con* 2; *Morav* 3; *Geloof* 4.4; *Meth Art* 4; *Free Meth* 4; *Resp Pius IX* 5–7;

Bonn I pr; *Bonn II*; *Richmond* 1; *Witness* 9; *Afr Orth* 2, 5; *Un Ch Can: Union* 8; *Un Pres* 11, 13; *F&O Laus* 4.1; *Philip Ind* 1.3

CO-WORSHIPED AND CO-GLORIFIED WITH FATHER AND SON

8.7. Worship

II: *Lit Chrys*; *Phot* 5, 29–30; *Jer II* 1.13, 1.24, 1.26; *Metr Crit* 9.2–6, 14–16, 18, 22.1–2, 23.9; *Mogila* 1.87–88, 1.93; *Dosith* q 4

III: *Ath* 27; *Tol I* anath 17; *Flor Arm* 27; *Loll* 5; *Boh I* 18

IV: *Luth Lg Cat* 1.79–102; *Aug* 15, 21, 24, 26; *Apol Aug* 4.10–11, 4.155, 15, 24.27–33, 24.81–83, 27.55–56; *Form Conc Epit* 10, *Form Conc Sol Dec* 10; *67 Art* 24–26; *Fid rat* 9; *Tetrapol* 7–10, 21; *Bas Bek* 11; *Helv I* 23–24; *Laus Art* 10; *10 Art* 9; *Genv Con* 13, 17; *Gall* 33; *Genv Cat* 141–42, 163–65, 183; *Helv II* 17, 22, 24.1–7, 27.1–3; *Irish* 49–56, 77; *West* 21; *18 Diss* 4–7, 10; *Denck* 3; *Cologne* 9; *Dordrecht* 11; *Marburg* 13; *Witt Art* 10, 12; *Tig* 26; *Trent* 13.5

V: *True Con* 30–31, 33; *Camb Plat* 1.3; *Gen Bap* 21, 35, 46; *Sav* 22; *Friends I* 17, 20; *Geloof* 23.7; *Meth Art* 15, 22; *Dec Addr* 5, 12–13; *Cumb Pres* 72, 75–80; *New Hamp* 15; *LDS* 11; *Arm Ev* 1, 9; *Resp Pius IX* 5.12; *Def Plat* 1.1, 1.3, 2.1, 2.2, 2.4; *Abst Prin* 17; *Swed Bap* 9–10; *Syl* 78–79; *Free Meth* 15, 19, 21; *Adv* 12–13; *Bonn I* 4; *Com Cr* 11; *Richmond* 10, 16; *Assem* 13j; *Afr Orth* 12; *So Bap* 14; *Un Ch Can: Union* 15, 20; *Un Pres* 28–29; *Ess* 3–6, 11; *Br St Luth* 41; *F&O Edin* 7; *CSI 1947* 1, 5; *Philip Ind* 2.5, 2.8–11; *Munif* 15–20, 23; *Bat* 11, 13, 14, 16; *Arn* 3; *Vat II* 5.3.8, 5.3.23, 5.3.66–67; *Menn Con* 8.4–5, 13–14; *Sri Lanka* 4–5; *CNI* 3; *Ghana* 11; *Ref All* 4; *Pres USA* 9.50; *Meth Braz* 2.11; *Un Ref Ch* 17.1, 17.4; *RCA* 17; *Toraja* 1.2, 6.7; *Camb Dec* 5

8.8. Prayer

II: *CP 1341* 13; *Jer II* 1.13, 1.15; *Metr Crit* 21; *Mogila* 1.92

III: *Orange* 3, 11; *Loll* 7; *Boh I* 2

IV: *17 Art* 3; *Luth Sm Cat* 3, 7–8; *Luth Lg Cat* 3; *67 Art* 44–46; *Tetrapol* 7; *Genv Cat* 233–95; *Heid* 116–29; *Helv II* 23; *Irish* 47–48; *West* 21.3–6; *West Sh Cat* 98–107; *Witt Art* 5

V: *True Con* 45; *Sav* 22.3–6; *Cumb Pres* 76; *Richmond* 11; *Un Ch Can: Union* 13; *Un Pres* 27; *Meth Kor* 4; *Sheng Kung* con; *Vat II* 5.1.15, 5.3.8; *Zambia* 6; *Toraja* 5.4; *Bap Conf* 2a

8.9. Prayer for the Departed (*see also* 12.1)

II: *Lit Chrys* I.D.1; *Jer II* 1.15; *Metr Crit* 20
III: *Loll* 7
IV: *Apol Aug* 24.89-98
V: *Cumb Pres* 76; *Arm Ev* 9; *Bonn I* 13; *Afr Orth* 10; *Vat II* 5.1.50; *Toraja* 8.5

8.10. Images in the Church

I: *Nic II* ecth, anath 1-3
II: *Phot* 43; *Greg Palam* 4; *Metr Crit* 15; *Lucar* q 4; *Dosith* q 4
III: *Loll* 8, 12; *Boh I* 17
IV: *Bern* 8; *Tetrapol* 22; *Laus Art* 7; *10 Art* 6; *Genv Cat* 143-49; *Heid* 96-98; *Helv II* 4; *Irish* 53; *West Sh Cat* 49-52; *18 Diss* 7; *Witt Art* 17; *Trent* 25.2; *Trid Prof* 6
V: *Meth Art* 14; *Arm Ev* 9; *Afr Orth* 7; *Madag* 1

THE ONE WHO SPOKE THROUGH THE PROPHETS

8.11. The Authority of Scripture as the Word of God
(*see also* 1.4, 8.12, 9.6, 9.8)

I: *Chal* 25
II: *Gennad* 12.1; *Jer II* 1 int; *Metr Crit* 7.6, 7.9; *Lucar* 2, q 1-2; *Mogila* 1.54, 1.72; *Dosith* decr 2, q 1-2
III: *Tol I* anath 8; *Prague* 1; *Boh I* 1
IV: *Form Conc Epit* int 3; *Form Conc Sol Dec* int 1-8; *Tetrapol* 1; *Helv I* 1, 5; *Genv Con* 1; *Genv Cat* 300-306; *Scot I* 5, 19; *Belg* 5; *Helv II* 1, 13.2; *39 Art* 6; *West* 1.4-6; *West Sh Cat* 3; *18 Diss* 8, 11-12
V: *True Con* 7-8; *London I* 7-8; *Gen Bap* 46; *Sav* 1.4-6; *Friends I* 3; *Geloof* 2, 14.3; *Meth Art* 5-6; *Winch* 1; *Dec Addr* 4; *Cumb Pres* 2, 68; *LDS* 8-9; *Arm Ev* 3; *Abst Prin* 1; *Swed Bap* 1; *Free Meth* 5-6; *Vat I* 3.pr; *Adv* 3, 6-7; *Bonn I* 2-3; *Salv Arm* 1; *Chr Sci* 1; *Com Cr* 5; *Lamb Quad* 1; *Richmond* 4; *Naz* 4; *Sacr ant* 3; *Afr Orth* 1; *So Bap* pr 4, 1; *Un Ch Can: Union* pr, 2; *Un Pres* 3, 26; *Chin Un* 2; *Meth Kor* 5; *Br St Luth* 2; *CSI 1947* 1; *Philip Ind* 2.2; *Munif* 12; *Bat* 4; *Un Ch Japan* 1; *Arn* 4; *Madag* pr 2, art 4; *Vat II* 8.7-10, 8.21-26; *Menn Con* pr, 2.1; *Sri Lanka* 3; *CNI* 2; *Ghana* 3.2; *Zambia* 2-3; *Pres USA* 9.27-28; *Design* 1.7; *Meth Braz* 1.1; *Un Ref Ch* 12; *Leuen* 4; *Laus Cov* 2; *RCA* 1; *Toraja* 2.3, 2.6; *Bap Conf* 1; *Philip UCC* 4; *Morav Am* 3; *Camb Dec* 1

8.12. The Authority of Church and Tradition (*see also* 1.4, 8.11, 9.6, 9.8)

I: *Iren; CP II* 7; *Nic II*

II: *Phot* 5; *Jer II* 1.26; *Metr Crit* 7.5, 7.10, 14.1–4; *Dosith* decr 2, 12

III: *Rom Syn* 4; *Boh I* 15

IV: *Aug* 26, *Apol Aug* pr 11, 4.393, 15.1–4; *Smal Art* 3.15; *Form Conc Sol Dec* 2.52; 67 *Art* 11, 16; *Bern* 2; *Tetrapol* 14; *Helv I* 3–4; *Gall* 5; *Belg* 7; *Helv II* 2.2, 2.5; 39 *Art* 34; *Scot II*; *Irish* 6; *Trent* 4.1; *Trid Prof* 2

V: *Dec Addr* 11; *Resp Pius IX* 17; *Vat I* 3.2, 4.4; *Bonn I* 9.1; *Utrecht* 1; *Lam* 1–8; *Sacr ant* 10–11; *Afr Orth* 1; *F&O Laus* 3A; *Ess* 10; *CSI* 1947 1; *Munif* 12; *Vat II* 5.1.20–21, 8.7–10, 8.24, 9.1, 9.14; *Com Dec* 2; *Ad tuendam* 4

8.13. The Canon of Scripture

II: *Metr Crit* 7.6–8; *Lucar* q 3; *Dosith* q 3

III: *Tol I* anath 12

IV: *Gall* 3–4; *Belg* 4, 6; *Helv II* 1.9; 39 *Art* 6; *Irish* 2–3; *West* 1.2–3; *Trent* 4.1

V: *Sav* 1.2–3; *Geloof* 2.3; *Meth Art* 5; *Cumb Pres* 1; *Free Meth* 5; *Vat I* 3.2, 3 can 2.4; *Bonn I* 1; *Vat II* 8.8; *Sri Lanka* 3.3; *RCA* 7; *Toraja* 2.3

8.14. The Inspiration and Inerrancy of Scripture

II: *Gennad* 12.2

IV: *Belg* 3; *West* 1.8

V: *Gen Bap* 46; *Sav* 1.8; *Geloof* 2.3–4; *Cumb Pres* 1; *New Hamp* 1; *Arm Ev* 3; *Ev All* 1; *Abst Prin* 1; *Syl* 7; *Vat I* 3.2; *Salv Arm* 1; *Am Bap* 1, 3; *Lam* 9–19; *Naz* 4; *Assem* 1; *So Bap* 1; *Un Pres* 3, 13; *Ess* 7; *Br St Luth* 1, 3; *Bap Assoc* 2–3; *Un Ch Japan* 1; *Vat II* 5.3.21, 8.7–8, 8.11, 8.14, 8.20; *Menn Con* 2.1; *Pres USA* 9.29; *Laus Cov* 2; *RCA* 6; *Toraja* 2.7; *Bap Conf* 1, 2c; *Philip UCC* 4; *Camb Dec* 1

8.15. Criteria of Scriptural Interpretation

I: *Orig* 8; *Tome* 1–2

II: *Dosith* decr 2

IV: *Apol Aug* 24.35; *Helv I* 2; *Scot I* 18; *Helv II* 2; *Irish* 5; *West* 1.7–10; 18 *Diss* 8, 10; *Denck* 1; *Trent* 4.2; *Trid Prof* 2

V: *True Con* 34; *Sav* 1.7–10; *Cumb Pres* 3–4; *Ev All* 2; *Syl* 22; *Vat I* 3.2; *Richmond* 4; *Lam* 1–8; *Sacr ant* 10; *Munif* 26; *Vat II* 8.10, 8.12; *Zambia* 9; *Pres USA* 9.29–30; *Leuen* 39; *Toraja* 2.5

9. IN ONE

9.1. Unity, Union, and Reunion with the Church of Christ

II: *Metr Crit* 7.2; *Mogila* 1.82–83

III: *Unam* 2–3; *Flor Un; Flor Arm; Boh I* 8

IV: *Aug* 7.2–4; *Apol Aug* 7/8.30–46; *Bas Bek* 5; *Helv II* 17.2–4; *Dordrecht* int

V: *Friends I* 9; *Geloof* 23.2; *Dec Addr* 1; *Vat I* 4 pr; *Lamb Quad* 4; *Pol Nat* 6, 9; *So Bap* 22; *Un Pres* 22, 32, 35; *F&O Laus* 1; *Br St Luth* 29; *Barm* pr; *F&O Edin* 1 pr, 2.1–10; *CSI 1947* 7–8; *Philip Ind* 2.18; *Bat* 8D; *Madag* 6; *Sri Lanka* 1, 11; *CNI* 4; *Ghana* 1; *Meth Braz* 1.4, 2.7; *Leuen* 1, 29–49; *Laus Cov* 7; *Balamand* 6–18; *Chr Dec* 8–10; *BEM* 1.15–16; *Morav Am* 5; *Com Dec* 5–6

9.2. Schism, Separation, and Division

II: *Phot; CP 1054*

III: *Flor Un*

IV: *Apol Aug* 23.59; *Helv I* 25; *Helv II* 17.10; *Schleit* 4

V: *True Con* 36; *London I* 46; *Camb Plat* 13.5, 14.9; *Dec Addr* 2, 10–11; *Resp Pius IX* 9; *Syl* 18, 38; *F&O Laus* 1; *Br St Luth* 28; *F&O Edin* 2.3–5; *Bat* 8.1; *Vat II* 5.1.15, 5.3.1, 5.3.3; *Pres USA* 9.34; *Morav Am* 5–6

HOLY

9.3. The Holiness of the Church and of the Means of Grace

II: *Jer II* 1.8

III: *Ap* 9; *R* 9; *Loll* 1; *Prague* 4; *Boh I* 11

IV: *Luth Lg Cat* 5.15–19; *Aug* 8; *Apol Aug* 7/8.47–50; *Genv Cat* 96, 99; *Gall* 28; *Helv II* 1.4, 18.21, 19.12; *39 Art* 26; *Irish* 70; *West* 27.3; *Witt Conc* 3; *Trent* 7 can 1.12

V: *Geloof* 23.3, 8; *Un Ch Can: Union* 18; *Sheng Kung* 4; *Bat* 8B; *Vat II* 5.1.8, 5.1.39–42

9.4. Church Discipline (*see also* 10.10)

III: *Boh I* 14

IV: *17 Art* 16; *Aug* 26.33–39; *Apol Aug* 15.45–48; *Smal Art* 3.7, 3.9; *Form Conc Epit* 4.17–18; *67 Art* 31–32; *Bas Bek* 7; *Genv Con* 19; *Belg* 29, 32; *Heid* 83–85; *Helv II* 18.15, 20; *39 Art* 33; *Irish* 73; *West* 30; *Schleit* 2; *Cologne* 7; *Ries* 35–36; *Dordrecht* 16–17

V: *True Con* 23–25; *London I* 42–43; *Camb Plat* 14; *Gen Bap* 55–56, 67–72; *Geloof* 27; *Bat* 8D, 9.4; *Vat II* 5.3.6; *Menn Con* 8.3

CATHOLIC

9.5. Catholicity of the Church

I: *Iren*
II: *Mogila* 1.84; *Dosith* decr 10
III: *Ap* 9
IV: *Genv Cat* 97; *Belg* 27; *Helv II* 17.2; *West* 25.1
V: *Camb Plat* 2.1; *Sav* 26.1–2; *Geloof* 23.4; *Un Pres* 32; *Sheng Kung* 4; *Madag* 6;
Vat II 5.1.13; *Toraja* 6.13

AND APOSTOLIC

9.6. Apostolic Authority in the Church (*see also* 1.4, 8.11–12, 9.8)

II: *Jer II* 1.int
III: *Dict Pap; Sens* 12; *Unam* 3, 7–8; *Flor Un* 14–15
IV: *Helv I* 16; *Helv II* 17.6–8; *39 Art* 20; *Scot II; Irish* 79–80
V: *Gen Bap* 51; *Cumb Pres* 108–11; *LDS* 5; *Resp Pius IX* 11–14; *Ineff; Syl* 21–23, 33;
Vat I 4.4; *Utrecht* 1–2, 4; *Lam* 55–56; *Sacr ant* 1; *Afr Orth* 3; *Br St Luth* 30; *Barm* 4;
Munif 12; *Bat* 3B3, 8.2; *Vat II* 5.1.12, 5.1.25; *Pres USA* 9.10

9.7. Apostolic Church Order and Polity; Hierarchy (*see also* 10.12)

II: *Jer II* 1.14, 1.28; *Metr Crit* 11.5–7, 11.9, 23.7–8; *Mogila* 1.84–85; *Dosith* decr 10
III: *Dict Pap; Boh I* 9
IV: *17 Art* pr; *Aug* 5, 14, 28; *Apol Aug* 14, 28; *Helv I* 15, 17, 19; *Laus Art* 5; *Genv
Cat* 307–8; *Gall* 25–26, 29–32; *Belg* 30–32; *Helv II* 18; *39 Art* 23; *Irish* 71; *Schleit* 5;
Cologne 10–11; *Ries* 25–28; *Dordrecht* 9; *Witt Art* 9; *Trent* 23 can 7
V: *True Con* 19–27; *London I* 44–45; *Camb Plat* 1, 4, 6, 7, 8; *Sav* con 1–30; *Dec Addr*
3; *Cumb Pres* 108–9; *LDS* 6; *Resp Pius IX* 6; *Vat I* 4.1–3; *Bonn I* 9.2; *Lamb Quad* 4;
Un Ch Can: Union 17–18, con; *Un Pres* 33; *F&O Laus* 5; *CSI* 1947 3–4, 6; *Philip Ind*
2.6; *Bat* 11; *Vat II* 5.1.10, 5.1.18–29; *Sri Lanka* 7; *Ghana* 5.2; *Pres USA* 9.38–40; *BEM*
3.34–38

9.8. Authority of Church Councils and Synods
(*see also* 1.4, 8.11–12, 9.7, Index B)

I: *Eph* 431 can 7; *CP II* 4, 5, con; *Nic II*
II: *Phot* 40–44; *Greg Palam* 6–7; *Mark Eph* 4; *Jer II* 1.int, 1.29; *Metr Crit* 15.4;
Mogila 1.4–5; *Dosith* decr 12

III: *Lat 649* 17, 20; *Dict Pap* 4, 16, 25

IV: *Smal Art* pr 1, 10–13; *Scot I* 20; *Helv II* 2.4; *39 Art* 21; *Irish* 76; *West* 31; *18 Diss* pr; *Trid Prof* 8

V: *Camb Plat* 16; *Resp Pius IX* 3, 5; *Syl* 23, 35–36; *Vat I* 3 pr, 4.4; *Utrecht* 1, 5; *Lam* 31; *Afr Orth* 1; *Philip Ind* 2.17; *Vat II* 5.1.22, 5.1.25; *Camb Dec* pr, 1

CHURCH

9.9. Definition of the True Church

II: *Jer II* 1.7, 1.8; *Metr Crit* 7; *Lucar* 10–12; *Mogila* 1.82–96; *Dosith* decr 10–12

III: *Ap* 9; *Tol XI* 18; *Unam* 1; *Boh I* 8

IV: *Luth Sm Cat* 2.6; *Luth Lg Cat* 2.47–56; *Aug* 7; *Apol Aug* 7/8.5–29; *Smal Art* 3.12; *67 Art* 8; *Tetrapol* 15; *Fid rat* 6; *Bas Bek* 5; *Helv I* 14; *Laus Art* 3; *Genv Con* 18; *Genv Cat* 93–95; *Gall* 27; *Scot I* 5, 16, 18; *Belg* 27, 29; *Heid* 54–55; *Helv II* 17; *39 Art* 19; *Irish* 68–69; *West* 25–26; *Ries* 24; *Dordrecht* 8; *Trid Prof* 7

V: *True Con* 17–18; *Camb Plat* 2–3; *Sav* 26–27; *Friends I* 16; *Morav* 3–4; *Meth Art* 13; *Shkr* 3; *Dec Addr* 1; *Cumb Pres* 93–97; *New Hamp* 13; *Arm Ev* 11; *Abst Prin* 14; *Swed Bap* 9; *Syl* 19; *Free Meth* 16; *Vat I* 3.3; *Com Cr* 10; *Richmond* 2; *Am Bap* 10–12; *Lam* 52–57; *Pol Nat* 6–8; *Assem* 8; *Witness* 1; *So Bap* 12; *Un Ch Can: Union* 15; *Un Pres* 32; *F&O Laus* 3; *Meth Kor* 6; *Br St Luth* 24–30; *Barm* 3; *F&O Edin* 1.4; *CSI 1947* 4; *Philip Ind* 1.4; *Chin Man*; *Bap Assoc* 15–19; *Bat* 8D; *Un Ch Japan* 4; *Arn* 6–7; *UCC* 7; *Vat II* 5.1; *Menn Con* pr, 8.1; *Sri Lanka* 2; *Ghana* 2; *Zambia* 7; *Pres USA* 9.31–33; *Design* 2; *Togo* 4; *Un Ref Ch* 17.4; *Laus Cov* 6; *PRCC* 1c; *RCA* 15–19; *Toraja* 6; *Bap Conf* 6; *Philip UCC* 3

10. WE CONFESS ONE BAPTISM FOR THE FORGIVING OF SINS

10.1. Word, Sacraments, and Means of Grace

II: *Jer II* 1.7, 1.13; *Metr Crit* 5; *Lucar* 15; *Mogila* 1.97–101; *Dosith* decr 10, 15

III: *Flor Arm* 10–20; *Boh I* 11

IV: *Luth Sm Cat* 4.10; *Luth Lg Cat* 4.21–22, 5.10–14; *Aug* 7.2, 13.1–3; *Apol Aug* 13, 24.69; *67 Art* 14; *Tetrapol* 16; *Fid rat* 7, 10; *Helv I* 16, 19–20; *Laus Art* 4; *Genv Con* 14; *Genv Cat* 309–20; *Gall* 34; *Scot I* 21–22; *Belg* 33; *Heid* 65–68; *Helv II* 17.7, 19, 25; *39 Art* 25; *Irish* 85–88; *West* 21.5, 27; *West Sh Cat* 88–93; *Ries* 17, 30; *Witt Art* 8; *Tig* 2, 6–20; *Trent* 5.2.9–10, 7, 13.3; *Trid Prof* 3

V: *True Con* 35; *Gen Bap* 47–52; *Sav* 28; *Meth Art* 16; *Cumb Pres* 25, 40–41, 98; *Arm Ev* 11; *Syl* 65–66; *Free Meth* 17; *Bonn I* 8; *Com Cr* 11; *Lamb Quad* 3; *Richmond* 10; *Lam* 39–51; *Afr Orth* 8; *Un Ch Can: Union* 16; *Un Pres* 16, 26, 30; *F&O Laus* 6; *Br St*

Luth 21–23; *F&O Edin* 1.5; *CSI* 1947 2; *Philip Ind* 2.4; *Bat* 8D, 9.2, 10; *Un Ch Japan* 4; *Arn* 2b; *UCC* 7; *Masai* 3; *Vat II* 5.1.11; *Sri Lanka* 5; *Ghana* 4; *Zambia* 6, 8; *Pres USA* 9.48–52; *Leuen* 13; *RCA* 15–16; *Toraja* 2.4–5, 6.8–11; *Morav Am* 1

10.2 Baptism

I: *Did; Just; Hipp*

II: *Jer II* 1.3, 1.7, 1.9; *Metr Crit* 5.2–3, 7.10, 8.2; *Lucar* 16; *Mogila* 1.102–4; *Dosith* decr 16

III: *Tol I* anath 18; *Orange* 8, 13; *Tol XI* 18; *Petr Ab* 3; *Lat 1215* 3; *Vienne* 3; *Flor Arm* 14; *Boh I* 12

IV: *17 Art* 5; *Luth Sm Cat* 4; *Luth Lg Cat* 4; *Aug* 9; *Apol Aug* 2.35–45, 9.1–3; *Smal Art* 3.5; *Sax Vis* 1.3, 2.3; *Tetrapol* 17; *Bas Bek* 5; *Helv I* 21; *10 Art* 2; *Genv Con* 15; *Genv Cat* 323–39; *Gall* 28, 35, 38; *Scot I* 21; *Belg* 34; *Heid* 69–74; *Helv II* 20; *39 Art* 27; *Irish* 89–91; *West* 28; *West Sh Cat* 94; *18 Diss* 8–9; *Denck* 2; *Schleit* 1; *Cologne* 5; *Ries* 31–32; *Dordrecht* 7; *Marburg* 9; *Witt Art* 3; *Trent* 7 can 1.9, 7 can 2.1–14

V: *London I* 39–41; *Camb Plat* 12.7; *Sav* 29; *Friends I* 18; *Morav* 4; *Geloof* 25; *Meth Art* 17; *Cumb Pres* 99–103; *New Hamp* 14; *LDS* 4; *Arm Ev* 11; *Ev All* 9; *Def Plat* 1.4, 2.5; *Abst Prin* 15; *Free Meth* 18; *Adv* 4; *Com Cr* 11; *Lamb Quad* 3; *Richmond* 8; *Lam* 42–43; *Naz* 13.18; *Assem* 11; *So Bap* 13; *Un Ch Can: Union* 16.1; *Un Pres* 30; *F&O Laus* 6; *Ess; Br St Luth* 21; *CSI* 1947 2; *Philip Ind* 2.4.2; *Bap Assoc* 12, 21; *Bat* 10A; *Masai* 3; *Vat II* 5.1.7, 5.1.40, 5.3.22; *Menn Con* 11; *Sri Lanka* 2, 5.1; *Pres USA* 9.36, 9.51; *Design* 1.4; *Un Ref Ch* 14; *Leuen* 14; *RCA* 18; *Toraja* 6.8–10; *Bap Conf* 6; *BEM* 1.1–23; *Chr Dec* 7; *LuRC Just* 28

10.3. The Mode and the Subject of Baptism

I: *Did; Hipp*

II: *Mogila* 1.103; *Dosith* decr 16

III: *Vienne* 3; *Boh I* 12

IV: *Luth Lg Cat* 4.47–86; *Apol Aug* 9.2–3; *Smal Art* 3.5.4; *Form Conc Epit* 11.6–8; *Form Conc Sol Dec* 12.11–13; *Sax Vis* 2.3.6; *Tetrapol* 17; *Fid rat* 7; *Bas Bek* 12; *10 Art* 2.2–4; *Genv Con* 15; *Genv Cat* 333–39; *Gall* 35; *Scot I* 23; *Belg* 34; *Heid* 74; *Helv II* 20.6; *39 Art* 27.2; *Irish* 90; *West* 28.3–4; *West Sh Cat* 95; *18 Diss* 8; *Ries* 31; *Marburg* 14; *Witt Conc* 4; *Witt Art* 3; *Trent* 5.4, 7 can 2.13–14

V: *True Con* 35; *London I* 39–41; *Sav* 29.3–4; *Gen Bap* 48; *Geloof* 25.2, 5–6; *Meth Art* 17; *Cumb Pres* 26, 102–3; *New Hamp* 14; *LDS* 4; *Resp Pius IX* 5.11; *Def Plat* 2.5–6; *Abst Prin* 15; *Swed Bap* 8; *Free Meth* 18; *Adv* 4; *Com Cr* 11; *Lam* 43; *Naz* 13.18; *Un Ch Can: Union* 16.1; *Un Pres* 30; *Bap Assoc* 12; *Bat* 10A; *Menn Con* 11; *Pres USA* 9.51; *Un Ref Ch* 14; *Leuen* 15–16, 18–20; *Toraja* 6.10; *Bap Conf* 6; *BEM* 1.11–12

10.4. Confirmation/Chrismation

II: *Phot 6–7, 32; Jer II 1.3, 1.7; Metr Crit 8; Mogila 1.104–5*
III: *Flor Arm 15*
IV: *Apol Aug 13.6; Genv Cat pr; Trent 7 can 1.9, 7 can 3.1–3*
V: *Lam 44; Philip Ind 2.4.3; Sri Lanka 5.1; BEM 1.14; Chr Dec 7*

10.5. The Eucharist/Lord's Supper

II: *Jer II 1.7, 1.10, 1.13; Metr Crit 5.2–3, 9.1–13; Lucar 17; Mogila 1.106–7; Dosith*
decr 17
   III: *Brngr 1059; Brngr 1079; Lat 1215 3; Flor Arm 16; Wyclif; Boh I 13*
   IV: *Luth Sm Cat 6; Luth Lg Cat 5; Aug 10; Apol Aug 10; Smal Art 3.6; Form Conc Epit 7; Form Conc Sol Dec 7; Sax Vis 1.1; Tetrapol 18; Fid rat 8; Bas Bek 6; Helv I 22; 10 Art 4; Genv Con 16; Genv Cat 340–73; Gall 36; Belg 35; Heid 75–82; Helv II 21; 39 Art 28; Irish 92–100; West 29; West Sh Cat 96–97; Denck 3; Schleit 3; Cologne 6; Ries 33–34; Dordrecht 10; Marburg 15; Trent 13*
   V: *True Con 35; Camb Plat 12.7; Sav 30; Friends I 19; Morav 4; Geloof 26; Meth Art 18; Cumb Pres 104–7; New Hamp 14; Arm Ev 11; Ev All 9; Abst Prin 16; Free Meth 19; Com Cr 11; Lamb Quad 3; Richmond 9; Lam 45, 49; Naz 14.19; Assem 10; So Bap 13; Un Ch Can: Union 16.2; Un Pres 30; F&O Laus 6; Br St Luth 21; CSI 1947 2; Philip Ind 2.4.5, 2.5; Bap Assoc 13; Bat 10B; Arn 1–8; Masai 3; Menn Con 12; Sri Lanka 5.2; Pres USA 9.36; Design 1.6; Un Ref Ch 15; RCA 19; Toraja 6.9,11; Bap Conf 6; BEM 2.1–33*

10.6. The Real Presence of the Body and Blood of Christ

   II: *Dosith decr 17*
   III: *Brngr 1059; Brngr 1079; Lat 1215 3; Boh I 13*
   IV: *17 Art 6; Luth Sm Cat 6.2; Luth Lg Cat 5.8–14; Aug 10; Apol Aug 10; Form Conc Epit 7.6–20; Form Conc Sol Dec 7.45–58; Sax Vis 1.1.1–6, 2.1.6; Bern 4; Fid rat 8; Genv Cat 354–55; Gall 37; Belg 35; Helv II 21.4, 10; Irish 94–96; Marburg 15; Witt Conc 1; Witt Art 6; Tig 21–22; Trent 13.1, 13 can 1, 3–4; Trid Prof 5*
   V: *Cumb Pres 105; Def Plat 1.5, 2.9; Utrecht 6; Afr Orth 9; F&O Laus 6; Bat 10B; Arn 4; Leuen 19; BEM 2.14–15, 2.32*

10.7. Change of the Eucharistic Elements into the Body and Blood of Christ

   II: *Lit Chrys II.F.5; Jer II 1.10; Metr Crit 9.11; Mogila 1.107; Dosith decr 17*
   III: *Brngr 1059; Brngr 1079; Lat 1215 3; Flor Un 10; Flor Arm 16; Loll 4*

IV: *Smal Art* 3.6.5; *Form Conc Epit* 7.22; *Form Conc Sol Dec* 7.108; *Scot I* 21; *Helv II* 19.9–10; *39 Art* 28.2; *Irish* 93; *West* 29.6; *Marburg*; *Witt Conc* 2; *Tig* 24; *Trent* 13.4, 13 can 2; *Trid Prof* 5

V: *Sav* 30.6; *Meth Art* 18; *Cumb Pres* 105; *Free Meth* 19; *Afr Orth* 9; *Arn* 5a

10.8. The Lord's Supper as Memorial and Communion

II: *Jer II* 1.22; *Metr Crit* 9.9–10; *Mogila* 1.107; *Dosith* decr 17
III: *Prague* 2

IV: *Aug* 22; *Apol Aug* 22; *Smal Art* 3.6.2–4; *Form Conc Epit* 7.24; *Form Conc Sol Dec* 7.110; *Genv Cat* 351–52; *Helv II* 21.2, 12; *39 Art* 30; *Irish* 97; *West* 29.2, 4; *18 Diss* 6–7; *Denck* 3; *Marburg* 15; *Witt Art* 12–13; *Trent* 21.1–3, 21 can 1–3; *Trid Prof* 5

V: *Gen Bap* 53; *Sav* 30.2, 4; *Meth Art* 19; *Cumb Pres* 104–5; *Resp Pius IX* 5.12; *Def Plat* 2.8; *Abst Prin* 16; *Utrecht* 6; *Naz* 14.19; *So Bap* 13; *Un Ch Can: Union* 16.2; *Un Pres* 30; *Vat II* 5.1.26, 5.3.2; *Pres USA* 9.52; *Bap Conf* 6; *Chr Dec* 8; *BEM* 2.5–13, 2.19–22

10.9. The Sacrifice of the Mass

II: *Mogila* 1.107; *Dosith* decr 17
III: *Flor Un* 11

IV: *Aug* 24; *Apol Aug* 24.9–77; *Smal Art* 2.2; *Form Conc Epit* 7.23; *67 Art* 18; *Bern* 5; *Tetrapol* 19; *Genv Con* 16; *Genv Cat* 350; *Scot I* 22; *Heid* 80; *Helv II* 21.13; *Irish* 99–100; *West* 30.2; *18 Diss* 5; *Witt Art* 12; *Trent* 22.1–9, 22 can 1–9; *Trid Prof* 5

V: *Sav* 30.2; *Meth Art* 20; *Free Meth* 20; *Bonn I* 14; *Utrecht* 6; *Bat* 3B2, 10B; *Arn* 5b; *Vat II* 5.1.3; *Chr Dec* 7; *BEM* 2.8

10.10. Penance/Repentance: Contrition, Confession, Absolution, Satisfaction

II: *Jer II* 1.4, 5, 7, 11–12, 25; *Metr Crit* 5.2–3, 10.1–4; *Mogila* 1.90, 1.112–14
III: *Flor Arm* 17; *Loll* 9; *Boh I* 5, 14
IV: *17 Art* 2, 7–9; *Luth Sm Cat* 5; *Luth Lg Cat* 6; *Aug* 11, 12, 25; *Apol Aug* 4.258–68, 4.272–74, 11, 12.11–12, 12.13–17, 35–38, 41, 98–177; *Smal Art* 3.3.1–8, 3.3.15–18, 3.3.39–45; *Form Conc Sol Dec* 5.7; *10 Art* 3; *Tetrapol* 20; *Laus Art* 6; *Genv Cat* 128; *Helv II* 14; *Irish* 74; *West* 15; *West Sh Cat* 87; *Dordrecht* 6; *Marburg* 11; *Witt Conc* 4; *Witt Art* 4, 7; *Trent* 14.1.1–9, 14 can 1.1–15
V: *Camb Plat* 12.5–7; *Gen Bap* 44–45; *Sav* 15; *Geloof* 19.3, 27.2–10; *Meth Art* 12; *Cumb Pres* 42–44; *New Hamp* 8; *LDS* 4; *Def Plat* 1.2, 2.3; *Abst Prin* 9; *Swed Bap* 5; *Bonn I* 11–12; *Salv Arm* 7; *Lam* 43, 46–47; *Naz* 8; *So Bap* 8; *Un Ch Can: Union* 10; *Un Pres* 18; *Philip Ind* 2.4.4; *Camb Dec* 6

10.11. The Anointing of the Sick/Extreme Unction

II: *Jer II* 1.7; *Metr Crit* 13; *Mogila* 1.117–19
III: *Flor Arm* 18
IV: *Apol Aug* 13.6; *Trent* 14.2, 14 can 2.1–4
V: *Lam* 48; *Friends I* 19; *Philip Ind* 2.4.6

10.12. Holy Orders/Ordination; Ordained Ministry and Priesthood (*see also* 9.7)

II: *Jer II* 1.7, 1.14; *Metr Crit* 11; *Mogila* 1.89, 1.108–11
III: *Flor Arm* 19; *Loll* 2; *Boh I* 9
IV: *Apol Aug* 13.12, 24.52–55; *Smal Art* 3.10; *67 Art* 61–63; *Tetrapol* 13; *Genv Con* 20; *Helv II* 18.8, 18.10–11; *39 Art* 36; *18 Diss* 12; *Trent* 7 can 1.9, 23.1–4, 23 can 1–8
V: *True Con* 19–27; *London I* 44–45; *Camb Plat* 9; *Gen Bap* 58–67, 73; *Sav* con 15; *Friends I* 16; *Geloof* 24; *Ev All* 9; *Syl* 30–32; *Lam* 50; *Assem* 9; *So Bap* 12; *Un Ch Can: Union* 17; *Un Pres* 34; *F&O Laus* 5; *Ess* 11; *Br St Luth* 31–33; *CSI 1947* 3–4, 6; *Philip Ind* 2.4.7, 2.6; *Bat* 9; *Vat II* 5.1.18–29; *Menn Con* 10; *Sri Lanka* 1, 6–8; *Ghana* 5; *Pres USA* 9.38–40; *Design* 1.7; *Toraja* 6.12; *BEM* 3.7–25, 3.39–50

10.13. Clerical Celibacy

II: *Phot* 5, 31; *CP 1054* 3; *Jer II* 1.23; *Metr Crit* 11.6
III: *Loll* 3; *Prague* 4; *Boh I* 9, 19
IV: *Aug* 23; *Apol Aug* 23; *Smal Art* 3.11; *67 Art* 28–30; *Bern* 9–10; *Helv I* 27; *Helv II* 29; *39 Art* 32; *Irish* 64; *Witt Art* 14; *Trent* 24.9
V: *Meth Art* 21; *Philip Ind* 2.7; *Vat II* 5.1.29, 5.1.42

10.14. Asceticism and Monasticism

II: *Jer II* 1.16, 1.20, 1.27; *Metr Crit* 19
III: *Loll* 11
IV: *Aug* 27; *Apol Aug* 27; *Smal Art* 3.14; *Tetrapol* 12; *Helv II* 18.7; *Witt Art* 15
V: *Sav* 23.6; *Vat II* 5.1.43–47, 5.3.15

10.15. Matrimony; Christian Marriage and the Family

II: *Jer II* 1.7; *Metr Crit* 12; *Mogila* 1.115–16
III: *Tol I* 16; *Flor Arm* 20

IV: *Luth Lg Cat* 1.200-221; *Apol Aug* 13.14-15; *Helv I* 27; *Laus Art* 9; *Helv II* 29.2-4; *Irish* 64; *West* 24; *Cologne* 8; *Ries* 39; *Dordrecht* 12; *Trent* 7.1.1-2, 24 decr

V: *Sav* 25; *Geloof* 31; *Cumb Pres* 89-92; *Syl* 65-74; *Richmond* 13; *Lam* 51; *Un Pres* 36; *Philip Ind* 2.4.8; *Vat II* 5.1.35, 9.5; *Menn Con* 16; *Sri Lanka* 9; *Pres USA* 9.47; *RCA* 13; *Toraja* 7.9

11. WE LOOK FORWARD TO A RESURRECTION OF THE DEAD

11.1. The Eschatological Hope (*see also* 7.1)

II: *Mogila* 1.120-24
III: *R* 11
IV: *Ries* 40; *Dordrecht* 18; *Trent* 6 can 26
V: *Morav* 5-6; *LDS* 10; *Syl* 17; *Adv* 8-10; *Pol Nat* 11-12; *Assem* 14; *Witness* 4, 6; *Meth Kor* 8; *UCC* 8; *Masai* 3; *Vat II* 5.1.48-51, 5.1.68; *Menn Con* 20; *Un Ref Ch* 17.5; *RCA* 21; *Bap Conf* 9

11.2. Final Preservation and Perseverance

III: *Boh I* 20
IV: *Remon* 5; *Dort* 5; *West* 17, 18.2-3; *Trent* 6.13, 6 can 16, 22-23
V: *London I* 23, 26; *Gen Bap* 43; *Sav* 17; *Friends I* 15; *Geloof* 22; *Cumb Pres* 60-61; *New Hamp* 11; *Abst Prin* 13; *So Bap* 11; *Un Pres* 23-24; *Bap Assoc* 15; *LuRC Just* 34-36

11.3. Antichrist

II: *Metr Crit* pr 3, 10.4, 23.2-4
III: *Boh I* 8
IV: *Apol Aug* 7/8.4, 15.18-19, 23.25; *Smal Art* 2.4.10-11; *Irish* 80; *West* 25.6
V: *True Con* 28; *Sav* 26.4-5; *Shkr* 3-4; *Adv* 13; *Br St Luth* 43; *Laus Cov* 15

11.4. The General Resurrection (*see also* 5.1)

II: *Gennad* 11
III: *Ap* 11; *Tol I* 20, anath 10; *Tol XI* 17; *Petr Ab* 4; *Lat 1215* 2
IV: *Luth Lg Cat* 2.60; *Form Conc Sol Dec* 1.46-47; *Genv Cat* 106-10; *Belg* 37; *Heid* 57; *Helv II* 11.14; *West* 32.2-3; *Cologne* 15
V: *Sav* 31.2-3; *Friends I* 23; *Morav* 5-6; *Geloof* 33; *Cumb Pres* 112-13; *New Hamp*

18; *Arm Ev* 10; *Ev All* 8; *Abst Prin* 19; *Swed Bap* 12; *Adv* 21–22; *Salv Arm* 11; *Com Cr* 12; *Richmond* 7; *Am Bap* 7; *Naz* 12.15; *Assem* 14; *So Bap* 16; *Un Ch Can: Union* 19; *Un Pres* 41; *Bap Assoc* 23; *Madag* 7; *Menn Con* 20; *Toraja* 4.6, 8.4; *Bap Conf* 9

11.5. Immortality of the Soul

II: *Gennad* 11; *Mogila* 1.28
III: *Tol I* 21, anath 11
IV: *Scot I* 17; *West* 32.1
    V: *Sav* 31.1; *Geloof* 5.1, 32.3; *Cumb Pres* 112; *Ev All* 8; *Adv* 19–20; *Salv Arm* 11; *Un Pres* 5; *Bat* 16; *Toraja* 3.4

12. AND LIFE IN THE AGE TO COME

12.1. Life Everlasting; Heaven, Hell, and Purgatory

I: *Orig* 5
II: *Jer II* 1.17; *Metr Crit* 20.4; *Lucar* 18; *Mogila* 1.60–68, 1.124–26; *Dosith* decr 18
III: *Ap* 12; *Ath* 41; *Sens* 15; *Lat 1215* 2; *Flor Un* 11–13
IV: *Smal Art* 2.2.12–15; *67 Art* 57–60; *Bern* 7; *Fid rat* 12; *10 Art* 10; *Genv Cat* 110; *Gall* 24; *Scot I* 17, 25; *Heid* 58; *Helv II* 26.4; *39 Art* 22; *Irish* 101–2; *West* 33.1–2; *18 Diss* 14; *Trent* 6 can 30, 25; *Trid Prof* 6
    V: *Sav* 32.1–2; *Geloof* 35–36; *Meth Art* 14; *Winch* 2; *Cumb Pres* 113–15; *New Hamp* 17–18; *Arm Ev* 10; *Ev All* 8; *Abst Prin* 20; *Swed Bap* 12; *Syl* 17; *Free Meth* 14; *Adv* 23–25; *Salv Arm* 11; *Com Cr* 12; *Richmond* 7; *Am Bap* 9; *Naz* 12.16–17; *Pol Nat* 11–12; *Assem* 16–17; *So Bap* 15; *Un Ch Can: Union* 19; *Un Pres* 39, 42–43; *Meth Kor* 8; *Bap Assoc* 24–25; *Bat* 16, 18; *Menn Con* 20; *RCA* 20–21; *Toraja* 8.6–8; *Bap Conf* 9; *Philip UCC* 6; *Camb Dec* 6

Alphabetical Index to the Comparative Creedal Syndogmaticon

Ecclesiastical Index: Churches, Heresies, Creeds, Confessions, Councils

What is a "church" (or even "*the* church") in one creed or confession is, of course, often a "heresy" for another. "Heresies" here are only those that are explicitly named as such (under one or another label) in a confession. Likewise, "creeds," "confessions," and "councils" are those that are expressly cited or quoted by another creed, confession, or council. Confessional references that speak in the name of a separate church, rather than about it (or against it), appear here in *italicized ALL CAPS*.

Adoptionism (Artemon)
    IV: *Helv II* 1.8
Aetianism
    IV: *Helv II* 3.5
Agnoetes
    IV: *Form Conc Sol Dec* 8.75
Anabaptism. *See* Baptists / Anabaptists
Anglicanism
    IV: *LAMB ART; 39 ART; WITT ART*
    V: *BONN* 9b; *LAMB QUAD; Vat II* 5.3.13
Anthropomorphism
    IV: *Helv II* 3.5
Apollinarianism
    I: *Edict* anath 9, 10; *Ecth* 7, *CP II* anath 4, 11, 14; *CP III* 1
    IV: *Helv II* 11.5
Apology of the Augsburg Confession (1531)
    IV: *Form Conc Epit* int 4; *Form Conc Sol Dec* int 6, 1.8–14, 2.25, 2.31–32, 3.6, 3.42–43, 4.14, 4.21, 4.33, 5.15, 5.27, 7.11, 7.55, 11.38
    V: *Def Plat*
Apostles' Creed
    IV: *Luth Sm Cat* 2; *Luth Lg Cat* 2; *Aug* 3.6; *Apol Aug* 3.1; *Smal Art* 1.4; *Form Conc Epit* int 3; *Form Conc Sol Dec* int 4; *Tetrapol* 15; *Genv Cat* 15–130; *Gall* 5; *Heid* 22–59; *Helv II* 17.17; *39 Art* 8; *Irish* 7; *West Sh Cat* con; *Witt Art* 1
    V: *Def Plat; Lamb Quad* 2; *Lam* 62; *Afr Orth* 2; *F&O Laus* 4; *Chin Un* 3; *Sri Lanka* 3; *CNI* 3; *Togo* pr; *Un Ref Ch* 18; *Toraja* pr; *Morav Am* 4; *Ad tuendam* 1
Arianism
    I: *AR; Sard; ULPH; EUN; Edict* 53, 59, anath 10; *Ecth* 1, 7; *N* anath; *CP II* anath 11; *CP III* 1; *Nic II*
    II: *Phot* 1; *CP 1054* 6; *CP 1351* 1, 38; *Greg Palam* 6
    III: *Lat 649* 18
    IV: *Aug* 1.5; *Form Conc Epit* 8.22; *Form Conc Sol Dec* 7.126; *Scot I* 6; *Belg* 9; *Helv II* 3.5, 11.3

Macedonianism
I: *Edict* 59, anath 10; *Ecth* 7; *CP II* anath 11; *CP III* 1; *Nic II*
II: *Phot* 1; *CP 1054* 4; *Greg Palam* 6
III: *Lat 649* 18;
IV: *Helv II* 3.5
V: *Resp Pius IX* 5.4, 11
Manichaeism
I: *Ar*
II: *Phot* 1, 5; *CP 1054* 6
III: *Fid cath; Unam* 7
IV: *Aug* 1.5; *Apol Aug* 18.1; *Form Conc Epit* 1.17, 1.19, 1.22, 2.8; *Form Conc Sol Dec*
1.3, 1.26–30, 2.74; *Belg* 9, 12; *Helv II* 1.8, 9.8, 9.12
Marcellianism
II: *CP 1351* 47–48
Marcionism
II: *Phot* 1
IV: *Form Conc Epit* 8.23; *Scot I* 6; *Belg* 9; *Helv II* 1.8, 11.4
Messalianism
IV: *Helv II* 19.11
Methodism
V: *METH ART; FREE METH; SOC METH; METH KOR; METH BRAZ*
Modernism
V: *Lam; Sacr ant*
Monarchianism
IV: *Helv II* 3.5
Monenergism
I: *CP III* 8–9
II: *Greg Palam* 6
Monophysitism
I: *Ecth* 7; *Chal* 5–12, 16–20; *Nic II*
II: *Phot* 2; *Greg Palam* 6
IV: *Helv II* 11.7
V: *Com Dec*
Monothelitism
I: *CP III* 4, 8–9
II: *CP 1351* 31
IV: *Helv II* 11.7
V: *Resp Pius IX* 11
Montanism
II: *Phot* 1
Moravian Church (Unitas Fratrum)
IV: *BOH I; BOH II*
V: *MORAV; MORAV AM*

Mormons (Church of Jesus Christ of Latter Day Saints)
V: *LSD*
Munificentissimus Deus (1950)
V: *Vat II* 5.1.59

Naturalism
V: *Syl* 1-7
Nazarene, Church of
V: *NAZ*
Nestorianism
I: *Edict* 47-49, 51, anath 7, 10; *Ecth* 6, 7; *Eph 431*; *Chal*; *CP II* 8, 10, anath 4, 11, 13, 14; *CP III* 1
II: *Phot* 1; *Greg Palam* 6; *Metr Crit* 9.5
III: *Lat 649* 18
IV: *Form Conc Epit* 8.18, 20; *Form Conc Sol Dec* 8.15; *Scot I* 6; *Helv II* 11.7
V: *Resp Pius IX* 11; *Chr Dec*
Nicaea, First Council of (325)
I: *Edict* 59, 65; *Ecth* 7; *Eph 431*; *Chal*; *CP II* 5, 11; *CP III* 1-2; *Nic II*
II: *Greg Palam* 6; *Jer II* 1.1, 1.14; *Metr Crit* 1.10; *Mogila* 1.5; *Dosith* decr 9
IV: *Apol Aug* 7/8.42; *Helv II* 11.18; *Marburg* 1; *Trent* 13.6
V: *Resp Pius IX* 5.4; *Lam* 31
Nicaea, Second Council of (787)
II: *Phot* 40-44; *Greg Palam* 6; *Metr Crit* 15.4
V: *Resp Pius IX* 5.5; *Vat II* 5.1.51
Niceno-Constantinopolitan Creed (381): aka *Nicene Creed*
I: *Edict* 55; *Eph 431*; *Chal* 27; *CP III* 1-4; *Nic II*
II: *Phot* 8-23; *CP 1054* 4; *Mark Eph* 3-8; *Jer II* 1.1-2; *Metr Crit* 7.2; *Mogila* 1.5-126; *Dosith* decr 9
III: *Flor Arm* 6
IV: *Aug* 1.1; *Apol Aug* 3.1; *Form Conc Epit* int 3; *Form Conc Sol Dec* int 4, 12.37; *Gall* 5; *39 Art* 8; *Irish* 7; *Marburg* 1; *Witt Art* 1; *Trid Prof* 1
V: *Resp Pius IX* 5; *Lamb Quad* 2; *Afr Orth* 2; *F&O Laus* 4; *Sri Lanka* 3; *CNI* 3; *Un Ref Ch* 18; *Toraja* pr; *Chr Dec* 1; *Morav Am* 5; *Ad tuendam* 1
Noetianism
IV: *Helv II* 3.5
Novatianism
II: *Metr Crit* 11.8
IV: *Aug* 12.9; *Helv II* 14.12; *Trent* 14.2

Old Catholic Church
V: *BONN I; BONN II; UTRECHT*
Origenism
I: *Ecth* 7; *CP II* anath 11; *CP III* 1; *Nic II*

V: *Resp Pius IX; INEFF; Def Plat* 1.1-2, 5, 2.1-3, 7; *VAT I; Bonn I* 8b, 10; *Utrecht*
2-5; *LAM; SACR ANT; MUNIF; Bat* pr, 3.Bst; *Masai; VAT II; HOND; BEC;*
BALAMAND; CHR DEC; COM DEC; AD TUENDAM; LURC JUST
Rus, Church of
   II: *Phot* 35

Sabellianism
   I: *Ar; Ecth* 1
   II: *CP 1351* 1
   III: *Lat 649* 18; *Petr Ab* 2
   IV: *Belg* 9; *Helv II* 3.5
Sacramentarianism
   IV: *Form Conc Epit* 7.2-5, 25-42; *Form Conc Sol Dec* 7; *Gall* 38
Salvation Army
   V: *SALV ARM*
Samosatenism
   II: *CP 1351* 47
   III: *Lat 649* 18
   IV: *Aug* 1.5; *Form Conc Sol Dec* 8.15-16; *Belg* 9; *Helv II* 3.5
Savoy Declaration (1658)
   V: *Un Ref Ch* 18
Schwenkfeldianism
   IV: *Form Conc Epit* 12.20-27; *Form Conc Sol Dec* 12.28-35; *Helv II* 11.9
Semipelagianism (*see also* Pelagianism)
   IV: *Form Conc Epit* 2.10
   V: *Cum occas* 4-5
Seventh-Day Adventist Church
   V: *ADV; Bat* pr
Shaker Church
   V: *SHKR*
Smalcald Articles (1537)
   IV: *Form Conc Epit* int 4; *Form Conc Sol Dec* int 7, 1.8, 1.52, 2.33-35, 5.14, 7.17-19,
10.18-23
Synergism
   IV: *Form Conc Sol Dec* 2.77-78

Tatianism
   IV: *Helv II* 24.8
Tetrapolitan Confession (1530)
   IV: *Form Conc Sol Dec* 7.1
Thirty-Nine Articles of the Church of England (1571)
   V: *Lamb Quad* 1; *Morav Am* 5
Three Chapters (Theodore of Mopsuestia, Theodoret, Ibas)

Index of References to Scripture

Mt 25.32–46	IV 767	Mt 26.64	I 54
Mt 25.33	IV 285	Mt 26.69–72	IV 628
Mt 25.34	II 402, 425, 587, III 810, IV 438, V 33, 34, 162, 196, 197, 469, 555, 685	Mt 26.69–74	V 462
		Mt 26.70	IV 627
		Mt 26.72	IV 627
Mt 25.34–36	IV 692, 731	Mt 26.74	IV 627, V 274
Mt 25.34–46	V 192	Mt 26.75	IV 621
Mt 25.35	II 469	Mt 27	IV 617
Mt 25.35–40	II 423	Mt 27.3–5	V 199
Mt 25.35–41	V 249	Mt 27.3–51	IV 136
Mt 25.40	II 469, IV 731	Mt 27.24	IV 326
Mt 25.41	II 305, 572, 591, III 833, IV 269, 610, 614, 733, V 34, 162, 196, 199, 622, 685, 812	Mt 27.33	II 633
		Mt 27.35	V 229
		Mt 27.46	IV 327, 416, 437, 617
		Mt 27.50	V 229
Mt 25.41–43	IV 438, 626	Mt 27.52	V 151
Mt 25.45	IV 626	Mt 27.52–53	IV 393
Mt 25.45–46	IV 431	Mt 27.57–60	II 282
Mt 25.46	III 804, IV 332, 478, V 161, 163, 192, 199, 235, 241, 364, 385, 469, 622, 812	Mt 27.59–60	IV 437
		Mt 27.64–66	II 583
		Mt 28.2–11	II 583
Mt 26	III 793, IV 275, 617, 736, V 552	Mt 28.4	IV 393
		Mt 28.5–6	IV 393
Mt 26.6–13	IV 267	Mt 28.16–19	V 59
Mt 26.11	IV 263	Mt 28.16–20	V 458, 589, 593
Mt 26.24	IV 733	Mt 28.17	II 503, IV 845
Mt 26.25	IV 780	Mt 28.18	II 488, IV 192, 194, 286, 288, 329, 418, 435, 438, 501, 617, 716, 719, V 36, 70, 76, 167, 380, 385, 548, 578, 596, 760, 802, 831
Mt 26.25–26	III 818		
Mt 26.26	II 420, 516, 625, 628, IV 264, 265, 289, 360, 385, 402, V 59		
Mt 26.26–27	II 604, IV 384, 643, V 43		
Mt 26.26–28	II 286, 414, III 793, 820, 822, IV 43, 444, 643, V 182, 183	Mt 28.18–20	IV 433, 644, 680, 737, V 45, 55, 58, 61, 94, 466, 636, 671, 681, 682, 811, 812, 814
Mt 26.26–29	I 23, II 555, IV 275, 385, 444, V 43, 247, 819	Mt 28.19	I 9, 11, 17, 27, 32, 33, 42, 45, 78, 83, 89, II 292, 388, 414, 514, 554, 565, 607, 625, III 667, 793, IV 40, 155, 275, 283, 286, 288, 362, 376, 383, 410, 422, 433, 439, 442, 446, 464, 509, 609, 616, 633, 640, 641, 642, 648, 697, 736, 777, 794, V 33, 158, 168, 180, 226, 236, 239, 243, 247, 263, 378, 381, 385, 427, 429, 450, 451, 454, 459, 465, 470, 489, 494, 496, 547, 552, 578, 672, 680, 681, 690, 754, 756
Mt 26.26–30	V 465		
Mt 26.27	IV 77, 78, 289, 514, 777		
Mt 26.27–28	IV 511, 640, 641		
Mt 26–28	I 23		
Mt 26.28	II 420, 628, IV 289, 441, V 494, 820		
Mt 26.29	IV 643, 741, V 824		
Mt 26.30	V 464		
Mt 26.33	V 274		
Mt 26.34	IV 275		
Mt 26.37–38	IV 617		
Mt 26.38	IV 476		
Mt 26.39	IV 736, V 46, 193		
Mt 26.41	IV 457, 592, V 176, 246, 274	Mt 28.19–20	II 376, III 817, IV 441, 616, 639, 641, 765, 778, 829, V 38, 59, 70, 239, 247, 587, 653, 663
Mt 26.42	V 46		
Mt 26.49	II 292		
Mt 26.51–53	V 670		
Mt 26.52	III 790, IV 214, 451		

Lk 2.52	IV 192
Lk 3.2–3	IV 737
Lk 3.3	IV 384, 737, V 460
Lk 3.6	II 488
Lk 3.8	III 806, IV 737, 834, 856
Lk 3.9	IV 737
Lk 3.10–14	IV 737
Lk 3.14	IV 453, 636, V 237
Lk 3.21	V 458
Lk 3.21–22	IV 435
Lk 3.22	V 458
Lk 3.23	V 52, 165
Lk 3.26	V 52
Lk 3.38	V 458
Lk 4.1–13	V 165
Lk 4.14	V 459
Lk 4.14–19	IV 435
Lk 4.16	IV 633, V 177, 248, 464
Lk 4.17	V 52
Lk 4.18	IV 715, V 458, 579, 759, 791, 793, 828
Lk 4.19	V 151
Lk 4.21	II 577
Lk 4.22	V 52
Lk 4.34	V 611
Lk 5.24	II 589, IV 213
Lk 5.32	V 460
Lk 6.12–13	IV 779
Lk 6.13	V 589
Lk 6.20	I 44
Lk 6.21	II 537
Lk 6.25	II 537
Lk 6.27	V 391, 756
Lk 6.27–28	IV 727
Lk 6.28	IV 726
Lk 6.29	II 539
Lk 6.30	IV 731
Lk 6.31	V 100
Lk 6.32	V 174, 187
Lk 6.33	V 187
Lk 6.35	IV 453, V 756
Lk 6.35–36	IV 731
Lk 6.36	III 810, IV 452, 772
Lk 6.37	IV 453
Lk 6.38	IV 731
Lk 6.46	II 453
Lk 6.48	V 354
Lk 7.6	V 170
Lk 7.16	V 165
Lk 7.29–30	IV 737
Lk 7.30	IV 642, V 97, 499
Lk 7.30–34	V 172
Lk 7.38	IV 483
Lk 7.47	II 588, V 174
Lk 7.48	IV 277
Lk 7.50	IV 43, 277
Lk 8.10	V 161, 169
Lk 8.13	IV 597
Lk 8.14	IV 597
Lk 8.15	IV 597
Lk 8.18	V 172
Lk 8.48	IV 43
Lk 9.1	V 178
Lk 9.1–6	III 814, V 165
Lk 9.2	V 178
Lk 9.23	V 180, 246, 501, 812
Lk 9.23–26	V 248, 683
Lk 9.26	IV 682, V 468
Lk 9.28–36	V 468
Lk 9.35	IV 278
Lk 9.55	II 363
Lk 9.62	II 403, 461
Lk 10.1	IV 282, 779
Lk 10.1–7	V 165
Lk 10.1–16	III 814
Lk 10.2	IV 282
Lk 10.3	IV 282, V 147, 188
Lk 10.7	IV 46
Lk 10.8	IV 227
Lk 10.10–16	V 243
Lk 10.16	II 444, 468, III 816, 823, IV 107, 108, 303, 355, 382, 460, V 36, 497, 591
Lk 10.20	IV 578, 611
Lk 10.22	V 137
Lk 10.24	V 163
Lk 10.27	IV 560
Lk 10.30	II 554
Lk 10.34	II 529
Lk 10.42	II 454
Lk 11	IV 677
Lk 11.1–4	IV 348, 369
Lk 11.2	II 441, IV 381, V 46
Lk 11.2–4	IV 455, 677, V 463
Lk 11.3	IV 381
Lk 11.4	IV 381
Lk 11.9	IV 475
Lk 11.9–13	IV 454
Lk 11.10	IV 475
Lk 11.11–13	IV 455
Lk 11.13	IV 723
Lk 11.20	IV 722, V 574
Lk 11.27–28	V 629
Lk 11.35	V 246
Lk 11.38	V 239, 312
Lk 11.39	V 174
Lk 11.46	III 825
Lk 11.47–52	IV 199
Lk 11.52	IV 485
Lk 12.1–5	V 175
Lk 12.4	II 594
Lk 12.4–5	V 248

Index of Names of Persons

Abelard, Peter (1079-1142/43), **III** 647, 655, 679, 733, 734, 735-36, 737-38

Adam, Karl (1876-1966), **V** 397

Agatho (c. 577-681), Pope, **I** 216, 223; **III** 722

Akindynos († c. 1349), **II** 334, 335, 336, 337, 338, 339, 345, 368

Alexander, St. († 328), Bp. of Alexandria, **I** 75, 79, 80-81

Alexander I (early 2d c.), Pope, **III** 760

Alexander III († 1181), Pope, **III** 769

Alexander VIII (1610-91), Pope, **V** 101

Ambrose, Pseudo. *See* Prosper of Aquitaine

Ambrose, St. (c. 339-97), Bp. of Milan, **I** 13, 102; **II** 260; **III** 667; **IV** 72, 74, 86, 266

Anastasius, St. († c. 700), **II** 357

Anastasius Bibliothecarius (9th c.), **V** 268

Anastasius I († 598), Patr. of Antioch, **II** 351

Anderson, David, **I** 13

Andreae, Jakob (1528-86), **IV** 166, *168-203*

Andrew of Crete, St. (c. 660-740), **II** 324-25

Androutsos, Chrestos, **II** 250

Anselm, St. (c. 1033-1109), Abp. of Canterbury, **III** 639, 654-55, 658

Anselm of Laon († 1117), **III** 735

Antoninus Pius, Roman Emperor 138-61, **I** 19, 22, 45

Antony of Egypt, St. (251?-356), **I** 23

Apollinaris. *See* Apollinarius, "the Younger"

Apollinarius, "the Younger" (c. 310-c. 390), **I** 146, 203, 219

Aquinas, Thomas. *See* Thomas Aquinas, St.

Argyrus, military governor of Byzantine Italy, **II** 313, 316

Aristides of Athens (2d c.), **I** 51, 52

Aristotle (384-322 B.C.), **II** 353, 505; **IV** 23

Arius († 336), **I** 75, 77-78, 87, 134, 136, 156, 219, 235; **II** 334, 353, 368; **III** 701, 737

Arminius, Jacob (1560-1609), **IV** 547

Arsenios, Metropolitan of Cyzicus, **II** 373

Asbury, Francis (1745-1816), **V** 201

Asmussen, Hans, **V** 504, *505-8*

Athanasius, St. (c. 296-373), Bp. of Alexandria, **I** 11, 18, 20, 23, 41, 87, 142, 145, 225; **II** 302, 327, 351, 352, 357, 360, 365-66, 369, 482-83, 491, 566, 592; **III** 646, 665, 673, 762, 765; **IV** 241, 300

Augusta, Jan († 1572), **III** 797

Augustine, Pseudo-, **V** 301-2, 303

Augustine of Hippo, St. (354-430), **I** 6, 21, 110-11, *112*, 192; **II** 260-61, 491, 627; **III** 643-46, 647-48, 670, 683, 728, 767, 802, 807; **IV** 15-16, 17, 68, 69, 72, 73, 92, 100, 108, 128, 142, 224-25, 234, 266-67, 461, 465, 466, 467, 468, 470, 472, 474, 504, 512; **V** 26-27, 101, 289, 304, 606

Barclay, Robert (1648-90), **V** 136, *137-48*, 377, 399

Barlaam of Calabria († 1350), **II** 318, 320, 322, 329, 332, 334, 336, 337, 338, 339, 345

Barrett, William, **IV** 545

Barth, Karl (1886-1968), **V** 18-19, 504, *505-8*

Basil, St., "the Great" (c. 330-79), **I** 6, 9, 13, 105, 132; **II** 302, 326-27, 327, 338, 341, 344, 349-50, 351, 352-53, 354-55, 357, 358, 359-60, 362, 365, 381, 384, 401, 402, 419, 431, 434, 443, 452, 460, 462-63, 464, 465-68, 469, 470-72, 532, 543, 575; **V** 273

Báthory, Stephen (1533-86), King of Transylvania, **IV** 745

Beck, Hans-Georg, **II** 379

Becket, St. Thomas (?1120-70), Abp. of Canterbury, **III** 789

Beham, Hans Sebald (1500-1550), **IV** 665

Benedict, St. (c. 480-c. 550), of Nursia, **I** 4

Benedict VIII, Pope 1012-24, **III** 645, 671

Berengar of Tours (c. 1010-88), **III** 650, 728, 729

Credits

We are grateful to the publishers, individuals, church bodies, religious organizations, and ecumenical agencies listed below for allowing us to reproduce texts and translations that appear in this work. The particular editions and translations we have used are acknowledged in the introductory note for each text. All possible care has been taken to trace ownership of every work. If any errors or omissions have accidentally occurred, they will be corrected in subsequent editions provided notification is sent to the publisher.

Abingdon Press; Academie Verlag; Akademische Druck- u. Verlagsanstalt; Alba House, a division of the Society of St. Paul; The Alliance of Confessing Evangelicals; American Bible Society; Andrews University Press; Arbeitsstelle Mittellateinisches Jahrbuch; *Archivum Fratrum Praedicatorum;* Urs von Arx; Augsburg/ Fortress Publishers; Baker Book House; Bayerische Akademie der Wissenschaften; Beacon Press; Verlag Hermann Böhlaus Nachfolger; Ton Bolland; Charles King Bradow; Brepols Editions; Brill Academic Publishers; Broadman and Holman Publishers; Cambridge University Press; Catholic University of America Press; Les Editions du Cerf; The Christian Church (Disciples of Christ); The Church of Jesus Christ in Madagascar; The Church of North India; The Church of Scotland; The Church of South India; The Church of Toraja, Indonesia; Clarendon Press; Columbia University Press; Concordia Publishing House; Continuum International Publishing Group; CRC Publications; Deutsche Bibelstiftung; Doopsgezinde Historische Kring; Eerdmans Publishing Company; The Evangelical Church of Togo; The Evangelical Presbyterian Church in South Africa; The Evangelical Presbyterian Church of Chile; Forward Movement Publications; Friends United Meeting; Friendship Press; General Secretariat of the Nihon Kirisuto Kyodan (United Church of Christ in Japan), Tokyo; Georgetown University Press; Verlagshaus Gerd Mohn; HarperCollins Publishers; *Harvard Theological Review;* Harvard University Press; Herald Press; Herder Verlag; Historical Committee of the Mennonite Church; Holy Cross Orthodox Press; Huria Kristen Batak Protestant Church; Ignatius Press; Jewish Lights Publishing; J. C. Gieben, Publisher; *Journal of Presbyterian History;* Judson Press; K. G. Saur Verlag; The Korean Methodist Church; Labor et Fides; Lancaster Mennonite Historical Society; Liverpool University Press; Longman Group, Ltd.; Loreto Publications; *L'Osservatore Romano;* L. S. Olschki; Mennonite Publishing House, Inc.; The Methodist Church of Brazil; Moravian Church in America; National Christian Council, Sri Lanka; Nazarene Publishing House; The North American Baptist Conference; *Noticias Aliadas;* Office of the General Assembly of the Presbyterian Church (USA); The Old Catholic Church–Utrecht Union; Openbook Publishers; Orbis Books; The Orthodox Church in America; Oxford University Press; Paulist Press; Pearson Education, Ltd.; Peeters Publishers and Booksellers; Penguin Group (U.K.); The Philippine Independent Church; The Polish National Catholic Church; Pontificia Università Gregoriana; The Presbyterian Church (USA); Presbyterian Publishing Corporation; The Presbyterian-Reformed Church in Cuba; The Reformed Church in America; Routledge; Rowman and Littlefield Publishers, Inc.; Saint Andrew Press; Saint Paul Editions; Saint Vladimir's Seminary Press; The Salvation Army; SCM-Canterbury Press, Ltd.; Scarecrow Press, Inc.; Sixteenth Century Journal Publishers; The Society for Promoting Christian Knowledge; *Spicilegium Sacrum Lovaniense;* Theologischer Verlag Zürich; Thomas Nelson Publishers; The Unitarian Universalist Association; The United Church of Canada; The United Church of Christ; The United Church of Christ in Japan; The United Church of Christ in the Philippines; The United Church of Zambia; The United Reformed Church; University Press Fribourg; Vandenhoeck und Ruprecht; Walter de Gruyter and Company; Westminster/John Knox Press; Rowan Williams, Archbishop of Canterbury; The World Council of Churches; *Zeitzeichen;* Zondervan Publishing House.